ORGANIZATIONAL BEHAVIOR AND MANAGEMENT

Organizational Behavior and Management

Third Edition

John M. Ivancevich
*Cullen Professor of Organizational
Behavior and Management*

Michael T. Matteson
*Professor of Organizational
Behavior and Management
Both of University of Houston*

IRWIN
Burr Ridge, Illinois
Boston, Massachusetts
Sydney, Australia

Sponsoring editor: Kurt L. Strand
Developmental editor: Laura Hurst Spell
Marketing manager: Kurt Messersmith
Project editor: Rita McMullen
Production manager: Bob Lange
Designer: Becky Lemna
Art coordinator: Mark Malloy
Photo research coordinator: Patricia A. Seefelt
Compositor: J. M. Post Graphics, Corp.
Typeface: 10/12 Sabon
Printer: R. R. Donnelley & Sons Company

Library of Congress Cataloging-in-Publication Data

Ivancevich, John M.
    Organizational behavior and management / John M. Ivancevich,
  Michael T. Matteson.—3rd ed.
       p.   cm.
    Includes indexes.
    ISBN 0-256-10725-4.—ISBN 0-256-11032-8 (instructor's ed.)
    ISBN 0-256-10812-9 (International ed.)
    1. Organizational behavior. I. Matteson, Michael T. II. Title.
HD58.7.I89   1993   92-17938
658.4--dc20   CIP

Printed in the United States of America

  2 3 4 5 6 7 8 9 0 DOC 9 8 7 6 5 4 3

Dedicated to our families:
Pegi and Dana Ivancevich
Danny and Susan Ivancevich
Jill and Paul Bradshaw
and
Celie Matteson
Marie and James Bayles
Kelly and Richard Martinez

Preface

Organizational Behavior and Management was a market success from the beginning. As experienced authors, we knew that continued success would come not from resting on the previous edition's success, but from forging ahead. The third edition of *Organizational Behavior and Management* is the result of listening to reviewers, teaching from the book ourselves, observing the dramatic changes occurring around the world, reviewing competitor's products, and striving to provide a comprehensive, accurate, and up-to-date picture of organizational behavior and management knowledge, applications, controversy, and concerns. Because we teach the book, we are able to keep in touch with students' understanding, needs, and values.

Thus we have done more than tinker with each new edition. The basic structure has been kept much as it was originally, but we have significantly expanded content of the chapters. We have added more text, resulting in a more comprehensive treatment of the content base. And, of course, we have updated all the information. Our intention in making these substantive changes has been to offer an intensive treatment of organizational behavior and management that helps instructors to teach easily and effectively. As dedicated teachers, we revise with our fellow teachers and the student population in mind. This book was not written as a research message or as a new theoretical model. The third edition of *Organizational Behavior and Management* contains knowledge that applies both inside and outside of the classroom.

Can the serious theory and research basis of organization behavior and management be presented to students in an exciting and challenging way? We believe that it can. Thus we expanded the theory, research, and applications in the revision of the book. The third edition also differs from the first edition in these ways:

1. Additional text makes it more comprehensive.
2. The application of theory and research in actual organizations is further emphasized.

3. More international examples showing applications of principles and models are provided. International issues, debates, and concepts, and examples are interspersed throughout the book and its elements.

4. Fundamental themes covering cultural diversity, total quality, ethics, and globalization are woven throughout the book.

5. The end-of-chapter elements—readings, exercises, and cases—have been redone. We have retained, deleted, and increased slightly the number of elements to be available to students and instructors. The elements included in our final array are insightful, up-to-date, teachable, and complete.

6. The materials—text, readings, exercises, and cases—stimulate students to think about how they would respond if they were in the situation being discussed or displayed.

7. A major section on performance evaluation in the revised chapter entitled, "Evaluating and Rewarding Individual Behavior," was added.

8. A major section on negotiations in the revised chapter entitled. "Organizational Power, Politics, and Negotiations," was added.

9. A major section on organizational culture in a revised chapter entitled, "Organizational Culture, Socialization, and Career Development," was added.

With *Organizational Behavior and Management* (*OBM*), students become involved participants in learning about behavior and management within work settings. We have designed the book with instructional flexibility in mind. *OBM* combines text, readings, self-learning exercises, group participation exercises, and cases. These elements are aimed at students interested in understanding interpreting, and attempting to predict the behavior of people working in organizations.

Organizational functioning is complex. No single theory or model of organizational behavior has emerged as the best or most practical. Thus, managers must be able to probe and diagnose organizational situations when they attempt to understand, interpret, and predict behavior. *OBM* devotes considerable attention to encouraging the development of these probing and diagnostic skills. The first step in this development is for each reader to increase his or her own self-awareness. Before a person can diagnose why another person (a friend, subordinate, or competitor) is behaving in a particular way, he or she must conduct a self-analysis. This introspective first step is built into each chapter's content and into the learning elements found at the end of *OBM's* chapters. The content and these elements encourage the students to relate their own knowledge and experience to the text, readings, exercises, and cases in the book.

FRAMEWORK OF THE BOOK

The book is organized into five parts containing a total of 16 chapters and an appendix. This framework highlights behavior, structure, and processes that are part of organizational life. The five parts are as follows:

Part One

The Field of Organizational Behavior. The first two chapters of *OBM* introduce the field of organizational behavior. They explore the how, what, why, and when of organizational behavior as viewed and practiced by managers.

Part Two

The Individual in the Organization. These four chapters focus on the individual, including topics such as "Individual Differences and Work Behavior" (Chapter 3), "Motivation" (Chapter 4), and "Evaluating and Rewarding Individual Behavior" (Chapter 5) and "Occupational Stress: An Individual View" (Chapter 6).

Part Three

Interpersonal Influence and Group Behavior. These two topics are explored in a four-chapter sequence: Chapter 7, "Group Behavior," Chapter 8, "Intergroup Behavior and Conflict," Chapter 9, "Organizational Power, Politics, and Negotiations," and Chapter 10, "Leadership."

Part Four

Organizational Structure and Job Design. The two chapters in this section are: "Organizational Structure and Design" (Chapter 11) and "Job Design" (Chapter 12).

Part Five

Organizational Process. Four chapters examine this aspect of organizational behavior. These include: Chapter 13, "Decision Making," Chapter 14, "Communication," and Chapter 15, "Organizational Culture, Socialization, and Career Development," and Chapter 16, "Organizational Change and Development." The tools for conducting research are spelled out in Appendix 2-A "Quantitative and Qualitative Research Techniques for Studying Organizational Behavior and Management Practice" which is found at the end of Chapter 2.

SPECIAL FEATURES OF THE THIRD EDITION

A total of 125 learning and knowledge enrichment elements are provided in the form of encounters, readings, exercises, and cases. These can be used by instructors in any combination that fits course objectives, teaching style, and classroom situation.

Encounters

There are 47 chapter encounters interspersed throughout the text. They focus on ethical issues, global examples, and general organizational behavior and management activities. The encounters bring the concepts to life by presenting a meaningful example or activity that ties in with the chapter content.

Readings

The book contains 23 carefully selected classic or contemporary readings from a variety of sources (e.g., *Academy of Management Executive, Harvard Business Review, Issues and Observations, Organizational Dynamics*). Ten of the readings are new to the third edition. Each of the readings is tied to a chapter's content.

Exercises

OBM also includes 32 self-learning and group exercises (6 new). Some of the exercises allow the individual student to participate in a way that enhances self-knowledge. These self-learning exercises illustrate how to gather and use feedback properly and emphasize the uniqueness of perception, values, personality, and communication abilities. In addition, a number of exercises apply theories and principles from the text in group activities. Working in groups is a part of organizational life, so these exercises introduce a touch of reality. Group interaction can generate debates, lively discussions, the testing of personal ideas, and the sharing of information.

Furthermore, the exercises are designed to involve the instructor in the learning process. Your participation allows you to try out techniques and patterns of behavior and to integrate exercise materials with the text. None of the exercises requires advance preparation for the instructor, although some require returning to a particular section or model in the chapters for information. The main objective is to get the reader involved. We want an involved, thinking, and questioning reader.

Cases

OBM contains 23 full-length cases. These realistic, dynamic cases link theory, research, and practice. They provide an inside view of various organizational settings and dynamics. The cases, like the real world, do not have one "right" solution. Instead, each case challenges students to experience the complexity of the work environment as if they were managers. The cases also are an invaluable teaching tool. They encourage the individual student to probe, diagnose, and creatively solve real problems. Group participation and learning are encouraged meanwhile through in-class discussion and debate. The questions at the end of each case are used to guide the discussion. A case analysis should follow the following format:

1. Read the case quickly.
2. Reread the case using the following model:
   a. Define the major problem in organizational behavior and management terms.

    b. If information is incomplete—which it is likely to be—make realistic assumptions.

    c. Outline the probable causes of the problem.

    d. Consider the costs and benefits of each possible solution.

    e. Choose a solution and describe how you would implement it.

    f. Go over the case again. Make sure the questions at the end are answered and make sure your solution is efficient, feasible, ethical, legally defensible, and can be defended in classroom debate.

INTEGRATING FRAMEWORK

Other books present text, readings, exercises, and cases. However, in most of these, there is no attempt to integrate, to tie together, to blend the content of the text with other elements. In *Organizational Behavior and Management*, a framework (Exhibit 1-3) is used to integrate the individual, group, and organizational level of analysis. The framework illustrates how the important pieces (the individual chapters) fit together. The dynamic perspective of the field of organizational behavior is captured as students become actively involved in the learning process through such elements as the readings, diagnostic exercises, group exercises, and cases.

NEW AND IMPROVED FEATURES

As is the tradition in revising *Organizational Behavior and Management*, a number of new and improved features are incorporated in the book. First, this edition includes 10 new articles, 7 new exercises, and 8 new cases. These new end-of-chapter elements were selected because of their relevance to the chapter content. Second, weaving global events, situations, and examples throughout the content, elements, and end-of-chapter material was purposefully directed. Globalization is such a vital area that it must be presented and covered throughout the book. Third, cultural diversity in the workplace is presented and discussed. Fourth, total quality management (TQM) is a major philosophy and practice that influences a firm's culture and competitiveness. Thus, TQM is introduced and reviewed. Fifth, ethics and ethical behavior are topics of major concern throughout the world. Examples, incidents, and debates that present ethical dilemmas are integrated in the book. Sixth, there is much more in-depth coverage of performance appraisal (Chapter 5) and negotiations (Chapter 9) in various chapters. These topics are meaningful and needed to be well covered in the book.

Seventh, the text introduces realism and relevancy. Examples of real world situations, problem solving, success, and failure are presented. Fortune 1000 companies do not dominate this book. Smaller and medium size firms that students may not be familiar with are used to illustrate organizational behavior and management activities. Finally, we have taken the time and space to explain the concepts, frameworks, and studies presented in the text. It was our intention to not be an encyclopedia of terms and references to colleagues. Instead, we used the ideas, work, and concepts of colleagues only when they added learning value to the chapter content. The goal of each presentation is to present something of value. A "cookbook" list of terms, names, historical points of reference, or empirical studies often becomes pedantic and boring. Comments on previous editions of this text suggest that the book is readable and teachable. These are attributes that are important to the success of the book.

Marginal Notations

Marginal notations are also used to highlight main points and to encourage the reader to think of how the ideas and concepts fit together. These marginal notations connect the text with the end-of-chapter readings, exercises, and cases. Every reading, exercise, and case elaborates some point made in the chapter that precedes it; the marginal notation draws attention to these discussions by indicating the number of the relevant reading, exercise, or case. The following symbols were chosen for easy reference:

Marginal Symbol:	*Refers to*:
● R1-1	Reading 1-1
■ E3-1	Exercise 3-1
▲ C7-2	Case 7-2

So, when the first reading for Chapter 2 is mentioned in the chapter text, the marginal notation ● R2-1 appears next to that paragraph to remind you that Reading 2-1 could be assigned or discussed at this point. Thus, the instructor can use the symbol to determine the best point in a lecture to incorporate each of the readings, exercises, and cases. The symbol also helps students, when they're reading and reviewing the chapter, to understand how each reading, exercise, and case fits into the overall framework of ideas in that chapter.

The marginal notations serve to tie together, to integrate, and to stimulate organized thinking. It is important that text content be lively, realistic, and stimulating to a reader. Thus, the marginal notations help to put the reader in the position of fitting the parts, pieces, and ideas together to improve learning.

Other Learning Devices

Learning objectives open each chapter to start the reader thinking about concepts, practices, and concerns. Each chapter also includes two or three Encounters and an end-of-chapter summary, which is a brief review of main points brought out in the chapter. In addition, a review and discussion section containing 10 questions is presented at the end of each chapter to test the students' understanding.

An important part of any course is vocabulary building. Thus we provide a thorough *Glossary* at the end of the book. Before a quiz or test, students should go through the glossary and pick out words that they will be expected to know and use.

Although it is difficult to paint a world-renowned portrait of organizational behavior and management, we were determined to help the reader paint his or her own picture. We hope the text, readings, exercises, cases, and learning and knowledge enrichment helps you become an adventurous explorer of how organizational behavior and management occur within organizations.

SUPPLEMENTARY MATERIALS

OBM includes a variety of supplementary materials, all designed to provide additional classroom support for instructors. These materials are as follows:

Instructor's Edition

The Instructor's edition is prepared by Jeanne Buckeye of the University of St. Thomas. Instructor's materials are conveniently bound together with the student text to help instructors streamline their lecture presentations. The instructor's edition is organized to follow each chapter in the text. It includes: chapter objectives, chapter synopses, chapter outlines with tips and ideas, and suggested films to supplement class discussion. For the first time, Encounter discussion questions and suggested answers have been added to help you incorporate these dynamic features into your lecture presentations. Suggested transparencies, term paper topics, and practical end-of-chapter exercises also are included. Transparency masters are provided to highlight illustrations from the text.

Color Acetates

These include key illustrations from the text, which can be used to visually enhance classroom presentations.

Test Bank

The Test Bank is prepared by Jean M. Hanebury of Salisbury State University. Completely updated to complement the third edition of the text, this testing resource contains a wide variety of questions, such as true/false, multiple choice, and essay questions. These items are categorized by type of question. Each question is classified according to level of difficulty and contains a page reference to the text. Additionally, the test bank includes questions that test students on concepts presented in the readings to enhance the integrative nature of the text.

Computest 3

Irwin's test-generation software allows instructors to add and edit questions online and select questions based on type, level of difficulty or key word. In addition those without access to a micro computer, or who prefer not to create tests, can use Irwin's Teletest service. The complete package we provide in the form of OBM and supplements is designed to encourage greater efficiency in learning, studying, retention, and applications. Let us know at Richard D. Irwin whether we are doing a good job and what we can do to improve.

CONTRIBUTORS

The authors wish to acknowledge the many scholars, managers, and researchers who contributed to *OBM*. We are indebted to all those individuals who granted permission for the use of readings, exercises, and cases. There were also adopters who made many useful suggestions, offered materials to incorporate, and let us know what worked well. These adopters are too numerous to list, but we appreciate your votes of confidence, your willingness to help us improve the book, and the obvious dedication each of you has to teaching.

In addition, the book was shaped significantly by two colleagues, James Donnelly, Jr., and James Gibson at the University of Kentucky. These two colleagues have shared and put into practice a common belief that teaching and learning about organizational behavior and management can be an exhilarating and worthwhile experience. Roger Blakeney, Sara Freedman, Dick DeFrank, Art Jago, Bob Keller, Tim McMahon, Jim Phillips, and John Zuckerman, all at the University of Houston, and Dave Schweiger at the University of South Carolina have exchanged materials, ideas, and opinions with the authors over the years, and these are reflected in *OBM*.

We are indebted to our panel of reviewers, who provided detailed and incisive feedback for the preparation of various editions of the book. These reviewers included John Cotton, Marquette University; Richard B. Simpson, University of Utah; Robert A. Reber, Western Kentucky University; Vickie Kaman, Colorado State University; Michael Frew, Oklahoma City University; Linda L. Neider, University of Miami; James L. Bowditch, Boston College; Bruce H. Johnson, Gustavus Adolphus College; and Pete Yeger, Virginia Commonwealth University. We would also like to acknowledge our testbank review panel: Robert Noe, East Texas State University; Patricia Fandt, University of Central Florida; and Connie Caruana, St. John's University. These three individuals' careful scrutiny of the testbank contributed to a top-notch teaching resource.

The detailed review work in the new edition of *OBM* was done by Jeanne Buckeye, University of St. Thomas; Cynthia Fukami, University of Denver; Denise Hoyer, Eastern Michigan University; Robert Lorenz, University of Vermont; and George M. Puia, University of Kansas.

There were also graduate students (some are now faculty members) who—in classes or discussion—shared ideas and suggestions about teaching organizational behavior and management. We personally thank the following individuals for their suggestions which have been merged into this integrated text: Kim Stewart, David Dean, Ki Baik, Chris Betts, Carrie Leana, Dennis Duchon, Jim Ragan, Jennifer Ettling, Shel Vernon, Wayne Smeltz, Dave Hunt, Terry Mullins, and Phyllis Finger.

The typing support and efforts of Jacque Franco are certainly appreciated. She has become an accomplished organizer and director of book preparation. Finally, the book is dedicated to our former "Organizational Behavior and Management" students at the University of Maryland, the University of Kentucky, and the University of Houston. We also dedicate this textbook to the students who are and will be the managers so vital to the improvement of the overall quality of life in society.

John M. Ivancevich
Michael T. Matteson

Contents in Brief

Contents

6   Occupational Stress:
An Individual View *242*

PART III

INTERPERSONAL INFLUENCE AND
GROUP BEHAVIOR *283*

7   **Group Behavior** *284*

PART V

ORGANIZATIONAL PROCESSES   581

THE FIELD OF ORGANIZATIONAL BEHAVIOR

What is a corporation?
Plants? Product lines?
Assembly lines? Bottom
lines? Distribution lines?
Not really. A corporation
is people. People
organized and working
and producing to serve
people. That's what it's
all about in the end.

**—Donald E. Peterson
past chairman and CEO,
Ford**

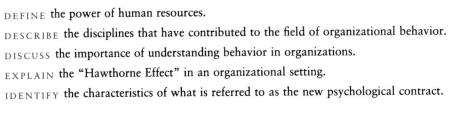

C H A P T E R

1

Introduction to Organizational Behavior

LEARNING OBJECTIVES

DEFINE the power of human resources.

DESCRIBE the disciplines that have contributed to the field of organizational behavior.

DISCUSS the importance of understanding behavior in organizations.

EXPLAIN the "Hawthorne Effect" in an organizational setting.

IDENTIFY the characteristics of what is referred to as the new psychological contract.

Imagine going to work in an office, plant, or store and finding co-workers who are excited about their jobs, managers who listen carefully to worker comments about the job, and a general atmosphere that is vibrant. What a pleasant setting where people want to work hard, have pride in the job they are doing, trust each other, and share ideas on how to improve performance. A setting in which groups work together, solve problems, set high quality standards, and enjoy the diversity of each co-worker's family, ethnic, and religious background.

Is this just an illusion or a dream of an ideal work setting? This is a sketch of a work setting that any manager would cherish, enjoy, and strive to maintain. It is a picture of the kind of workplace that managers should use as a target to achieve. This is the kind of workplace that will have to be created if a firm, entrepreneur, or institution is to survive in the coming years.

There are a number of forces that are reshaping the nature of managing within organizations. A limited number of companies have recognized these forces and are working to channel their managerial talents to accomplish goals by using their knowledge about each of four major forces.[1]

[1]Robert H. Rosen, *The Healthy Company,* (Los Angeles: Tarcher, Inc., 1991), pp. 2–7.

TALKING AND LISTENING TO EMPLOYEES

More than ever before chief executive officers (CEOs) appear to be devoting time and energy to staying in touch with their employees. Meetings, surveys, and informational videos are being used to keep in close contact with employees. Talking and listening to employees is becoming a requirement of holding a top-level management position. The emphasis is now on talking *with* people, not *at* people.

A pool of 212 chief executives of America's largest companies indicated that keeping in touch with people is a top priority. The survey results indicate that firms are doing a lot more today to communicate and to improve productivity. It was found that 41 percent of the CEOs hold regular meetings with employees.

Human resources are being treated as valuable assets that can't be ignored. Each person has a unique set of needs that CEOs are finally recognizing are different in many respects from their own needs. The regularly-held meeting helps individuals exchange ideas, express needs, and debate goals. The CEOs benefit from meetings because they learn what others feel are important. The employees learn from meetings how the CEO views them, the organization, and the progress of the firm.

As organizations become more competitive, as the psychological contract between workers and management changes, and as downsizing becomes a common practice, it is now a necessity for managers to observe, study, and interpret employee behavior. Managers must take control of communications, must listen to employees, and must take a hard look about how to efficiently manage people.

Source: Adapted from Anne B. Fisher, "CEOs Think That Morale Is Dandy," *Fortune,* November 18, 1991, pp. 83–84, and Kenneth Lavich, "Take Control of Your Career," *Fortune,* November 18, 1991, pp. 87–96.

The forces at work are the *power* of human resources. The way people (managers, technicians, and staff specialists) work, think, and behave dictates the direction and success of a firm. Unfortunately, there is a shrinking work force and a shortage of technically skilled workers. Managing the human resource as valuable assets to be maintained and improved is now more important than ever. The encounter above points out some areas that chief executive officers are working on to emphasize the importance of human resources.

The *culturally diverse* work force is becoming a reality in the United States. As the complexion of America's work force changes, managers and co-workers need to learn more about each other so that a receptive work culture is created.

The *rapidity* of change is another crucial force to recognize. The fax machine, genetic engineering, microchips, crumbling socialist empires, and a reconfigured Commonwealth of Independent States (e.g., Russia, Ukraine, Georgia) are some of the changes sweeping the world. Understanding, accommodating, and using change is now a part of a manager's job requirement.

The new worker-employer *psychological contract* is another force. From the employer's view, employees do not have lifetime jobs, guaranteed advancement or raises, and assurance that their job roles will be fixed. Employees believe that employers must be honest, open, and fair and also be willing to give workers a larger say in their jobs. Employees also want organizations to pay more attention

EXHIBIT 1-1

Organizations and Management in Society

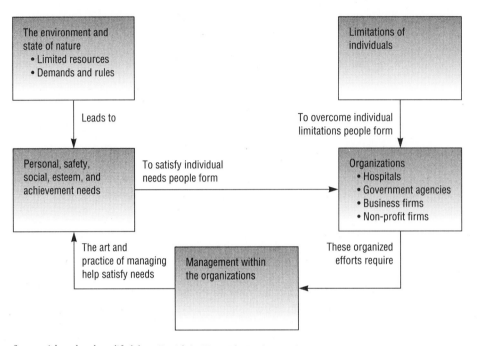

Source: Adapted and modified from Daniel A. Wren, *The Evolution of Management Thought* (New York: John Wiley & Sons, 1979, p. 10.

to their family situations and physical and mental health. Employees wants employers to appreciate the humanness of workers.

The four forces—power of human resources, cultural diversity, the rapidity of change, and a new worker-employer psychological contract—are inevitable. Resisting the reality of these forces will likely lead to unnecessary conflict, reduced managerial and nonmanagerial performance, and lost opportunities. In managerial terms, failing to cope and deal with these forces will likely result in job dissatisfaction, poor morale, reduced commitment, lower work quality, burnout, poor judgement, and a host of unhealthy consequences.

The purpose of this book is to help you learn how to manage individuals and groups as resources of organizations. These resources are operating in a world surrounded by change. Organizations are essential to the way our society operates in the world. In industry, education, health care, and defense, organizations have created impressive gains for our standard of living and our worldwide image. The size of the organizations with which you deal daily should illustrate the tremendous political, economic, and social powers they separately possess. For example, your college has much economic, political, and social power in its community. If a large firm announced that it was closing its plant in your community, the resulting impact might be devastating economically. On the other hand, if General Motors announced it was opening an automobile assembly plant in your community, the impact probably would be very positive. Exhibit 1-1 illustrates the role that organizations play in our changing world.

Organizations are, however, much more than means for providing goods and services.[2] They create the settings in which most of us spend our lives. In this respect, they have profound influence on our behavior. However, because large-scale organizations have developed only in recent times, we are just now beginning to recognize the necessity for studying them. Researchers have just begun the process of developing ways to study the behavior of people in organizations.

THE ORIGINS OF ORGANIZATIONAL BEHAVIOR

The modern study of what people do within organizations was developed in the mid- to late 1940s. The behavioral sciences—psychology, sociology, and cultural anthropology—have provided the principles, scientific rigor, and models for what we refer to today as organizational behavior. Exhibit 1-2 shows the different disciplinary views of what constitutes organizational behavior. Therefore, it is important to note that organizational behavior provides a multidisciplinary view of what people do in organizational settings.

Each of the disciplines that constitute organizational behavior provides a slightly different focus, analytical framework, and theme for helping managers answer questions about themselves, nonmanagers, and environmental forces (e.g., competition, legal requirements, and social-political changes).

The Hawthorne Studies

A team of Harvard University researchers were asked to study the activities of work groups at Western Electric's Hawthorne plant outside of Chicago (Cicero, Illinois).[3] Before the team arrived, an initial study at the plant studied the effects of illumination on worker output. It was proposed that "illumination" would affect the work group's output. One group of female workers completed its job tasks in a test room where the illumination level remained constant. The other study group was placed in a test room where the amount of illumination was changed (increased and decreased).

In the test room where illumination was varied, worker output increased when illumination increased. This, of course, was an expected result. However, output also increased when illumination was decreased. In addition, productivity increased in the control group test room, even though illumination remained constant throughout the study.

The Harvard team was called in to solve the mystery. The team concluded that something more than an economic approach to improve worker output was occurring within the work groups. The researchers conducted additional studies on the impact of rest pauses, shorter working days, incentives, and type

[2]See L. F. Urwick, "That Word *Organization*," *Academy of Management Review,* January 1976, pp. 89–91.

[3]E. Mayo, *The Social Problems of Industrial Civilization,* (Boston: Harvard University Press, 1945).

EXHIBIT 1-2

Major Disciplinary Approaches Contributing to Organizational Behavior

	Industrial Organizational	Human Factor	Social Psychological	Sociological
Unit of analysis	Individuals	Tasks	Groups and individuals in groups	Groups and organizations
Independent variables	Personal characteristics such as sex, age, and personality; perceptions of work environment; behaviors such as absenteeism and performance; attitudes such as satisfaction and involvement	Operator skills, physical states, and mental conditions; equipment complexity; characteristics of information received by operator; attributes of work setting	Individual attitudes, perceptions, attributes, and behaviors; group morale, composition, and roles	Group variables such as sex ratio, roles, and structure; organizational variables such as size, structure, technology, and environmental factors
Dependent variables	Attitudes such as satisfaction, behavior such as absenteeism, turnover, and performance, and self-reported psychological states such as motivation	Performance efficiency averaged across individuals	Individual attitudes, perceptions, and behaviors	Individual variables aggregated to group and organization levels such as quit or accident rates; group- and organization-level variables such as effectiveness, profitability, and structure
Focus of measurement	Attitudes, attributes, and perceptions generally assessed at individual level; individual behaviors measured through observation and company records	Task characteristics assessed through observation individual skill measured through task performance; performance measured by averaging across individuals performing the same task	Behavior, perceptions, and attitudes analyzed at individual level and aggregated to describe group responses and characteristics	Organizational and group variables derived from archival data, interviews with managers, and aggregation of individual variables
Boundaries between areas studied and areas omitted	Study of individual responses and perceptions of the work setting separated from objective characteristics of the organization	Study of task characteristics and individual skills separated from individual differences in motivation and perceptions and from organizational characteristics	Study of individual and group variables separated from task and organizational characteristics	Study of organizational and group variables separated from individual responses except when individual variables are aggregated
Role of individual	Individual-level variables are used to predict and explain individual responses	An individual's skills are considered relevant to task performance, but psychological factors such as motivation are not	Individual characteristics are combined to describe group processes; individual behaviors and attitudes result from group processes	No individual differences in responses are considered, although individual characteristics may be combined to describe group or organizational composition

EXHIBIT   1-2

Concluded

	Industrial Organizational	Human Factor	Social Psychological	Sociological
Role of task	Individual perceptions of tasks assessed	Task characteristics studied as important determinants of performance efficiency	Not specifically studied	Studied only as related to the technology of work groups or organizations
Role of group	Perceptions of group characteristics assessed	Studied only when interdependent tasks performed by a group of people are examined	Groups studied as important determinants of individual behaviors and attitudes and group morale and performance	Group processes studied as basis of organizational structure
Role of organization	Organizational charcteristics as perceived by individuals, such as climate, and objective charcteristics, such as size or level, are studied	Only features directly related to the production process, such as technology, are studied	Organizations are not specifically studied, since no reference is made to organizational context of groups	Organizations are viewed as entities, composed of groups, that respond to internal and external processes in ways predicted by organizational characteristics

Source: Karlene H. Roberts, Charles L. Hulin, and Denise M. Rousseau, *Developing and Interdisciplinary Science of Organizations* (San Francisco: Jossey-Bass, 1978), pp. 30–31.

of supervision on output. They also uncovered what is referred to as the "Hawthorne Effect" operating within the study groups.[4] That is, the workers felt important because someone was observing and studying them at work. Thus, they produced more because of being observed and studied.

Elton Mayo, Fritz Roethlisberger, and William Dickson were the leaders of the Harvard study team. They continued their work at the Hawthorne plant from 1924 to 1932. Eight years of study included over 20,000 Western Electric employees. The Harvard researchers found that individual behaviors were modified within and by work groups. In a study referred to as the "bank wiring room," the Harvard researchers were again faced with some perplexing results. The study group only completed two terminals per worker daily. This was considered to be a low level of output.

The bank wiring room workers appeared to be restricting output. The work group was being friendly, got along well on and off the job, and helped each other. There appeared to be a practice of protecting the slower workers. The fast producers did not want to outperform the slowest producers. The slow producers

[4]F. J. Roethlisberger and W. J. Dickson, *Management and the Worker* (Cambridge, Mass.: Harvard University Press, 1939).

were part of the team and fast workers were instructed to "slow it down." The group formed an informal production norm of only two completed boards per day.

The Harvard researchers learned that economic rewards did not totally explain worker behavior. Workers were observant, complied with norms, and respected the informal social structure of their group. It was also learned that social pressures could restrict output.

The Hawthorne studies are perhaps the most cited research in the applied behavioral science area. They are not referred to as the most rigorous series of studies. For example, it was determined that workers were replaced in the experimental groups when they did not produce adequately. Nonetheless, the Hawthorne studies did point out that workers are more complex than economic theories of the time proposed. Workers respond to group norms, social pressures, and observation. In 1924 to 1932 these were important revelations that changed the way management viewed workers.

THE IMPORTANCE OF STUDYING ORGANIZATIONAL BEHAVIOR

Why do employees behave as they do in organizations? Why is one individual or group more productive than another? Why do managers continually seek ways to design jobs and delegate authority? These and similar questions are important to the relatively new field of study known as **organizational behavior.** Understanding the behavior of people in organizations has become increasingly important as management concerns—such as employee productivity, the quality of work life, job stress, and career progression—continue to make front-page news.

Clearly understanding that organizational behavior (OB) has evolved from multiple disciplines, we will use the following definition of OB throughout this book:

> *The study of human behavior, attitudes, and performance within an organizational setting; drawing on theory, methods, and principles from such disciplines as psychology, sociology, and cultural anthropology to learn about* individual *perceptions, values, learning capacities, and actions while working in* groups *and within the total* organization; *analyzing the external environment's effect on the organization and its human resources, missions, objectives, and strategies.*

This multidisciplinary anchored view of organizational behavior illustrates a number of points. First, OB is a *way of thinking.* Behavior is viewed as operating at individual, group, and organizational levels. This approach suggests that when studying OB, we must identify clearly the level of analysis being used—individual, group, and/or organizational. Second, OB is **multidisciplinary.** This means that it utilizes principles, models, theories, and methods from other disciplines. The study of OB is not a discipline or a generally accepted science with an established theoretical foundation. It is a field that only now is beginning to grow and develop in stature and impact. Third, there is a distinctly **humanistic orientation** within organizational behavior. People and their attitudes, perceptions, learning capacities, feelings, and goals are of major importance to the organization. Fourth, the field of OB is **performance-oriented**. Why is performance low or high? How can performance be improved? Can training enhance on-the-job performance? These are important issues facing practicing managers. Fifth, the **external environment** is seen as having significant impact on organizational behavior. Sixth, since the field of OB relies heavily on recognized disciplines, the role of the **scientific method** is deemed important in studying variables and relationships. As the scientific method has been used in conducting research on organizational behavior, a set of principles and guidelines on what constitutes good research has emerged.[5] Finally, the field has a distinctive **applications orientation**; it is concerned with providing useful answers to questions which arise in the context of managing organizations.

To help you learn how to manage individuals and groups as resources of organizations, this book focuses on the behavior of *individuals, groups,* and *organizations.* Developing the model presented in this book required the use of several assumptions. These assumptions are explained briefly in the following paragraphs, which precede the model.[6]

Organizational Behavior Follows Principles of Human Behavior

The effectiveness of any organization is influenced greatly by human behavior. People are a resource common to all organizations. There is no such thing as a peopleless organization.

One important principle of psychology is that each person is different. Each person has unique perceptions, personalities, and life experiences; different capabilities for learning and stress; and different attitudes, beliefs, and aspiration levels. To be effective, managers of organizations must view each employee or member as a unique embodiment of all these behavioral factors.

Organizations as Social Systems

The relationships among individuals and groups in organizations create expectations for the behavior of individuals. These expectations result in certain roles that must be performed. Some people must perform the role of leader, while others must play the role of follower. Middle managers must perform both roles because they have both a superior and subordinates. Organizations have systems of authority, status, and power, and people in organizations have varying needs

---

[5]Edward E. Lawler III, "Challenging Traditional Research Assumptions," in *Doing Business That Is Useful for Theory and Practice,* ed. Edward E. Lawler III, Alan M. Mohrman, Jr., Susan A. Mohrman, Gerald E. Ledford, Jr., and Thomas G. Cummings (San Francisco: Jossey-Bass, 1985).

[6]Alan Berkeley Thomas, "Does Leadership Make a Difference to Organizational Performance?" *Administrative Science Quarterly,* September 1988, pp. 388–400; and Tom Peters, *Thriving on Chaos* (New York: Alfred A. Knopf, 1987)?

from each system. Groups in organizations also have a powerful impact on individual behavior and on organizational performance.

Many Factors Shape Organizational Behavior

Our behavior in any situation involves the interaction of our personal characteristics and the characteristics of the situation. Thus, identifying all of the factors is time-consuming and difficult; frequently, the task is impossible.

To help us identify the important managerial factors in organizational behavior, however, we use the **contingency** (or situational) **approach**. The basic idea of the contingency approach is that there is no one best way to manage. A method that is very effective in one situation may not even work in others. The contingency approach has grown in popularity over the last two decades because research has shown that, given certain characteristics of a job and certain characteristics of the people doing the job, some management practices work better than others. Thus, when facing a problem, a manager using the contingency approach does not assume that a particular approach will work. Instead, he or she diagnoses the characteristics of the individuals and groups involved, the organizational structure, and his or her own leadership style before deciding on a solution.

How Structure and Process Affect Organizational Behavior

An organization's **structure** is the formal pattern of how its people and jobs are grouped. Structure often is illustrated by an organization chart. **Process** refers to activities that give life to the organization chart. Communication, decision making, and organization development are examples of processes in organizations. Sometimes understanding process problems such as breakdowns in communication and decision making will result in a more accurate understanding of organizational behavior than if you simply examine structural arrangements.

Effective managers know what to look for in a work situation and how to understand what they find. Therefore, managers must develop diagnostic and action abilities. Managers must be trained to identify conditions symptomatic of a problem requiring further attention. A manager's problem indicators include declining profits, declining quantity or quality of work, increases in absenteeism or tardiness, and negative employee attitudes. Each of these problems is an issue of organizational behavior.

A MODEL FOR MANAGING ORGANIZATIONS: BEHAVIOR, STRUCTURE, PROCESSES

A model for understanding organizational behavior is presented in Exhibit 1-3. The model shows how the many topics covered in this book can be combined into a meaningful study of organizational behavior.

EXHIBIT 1-3

A Framework for the Study of Organizational Behavior and Management

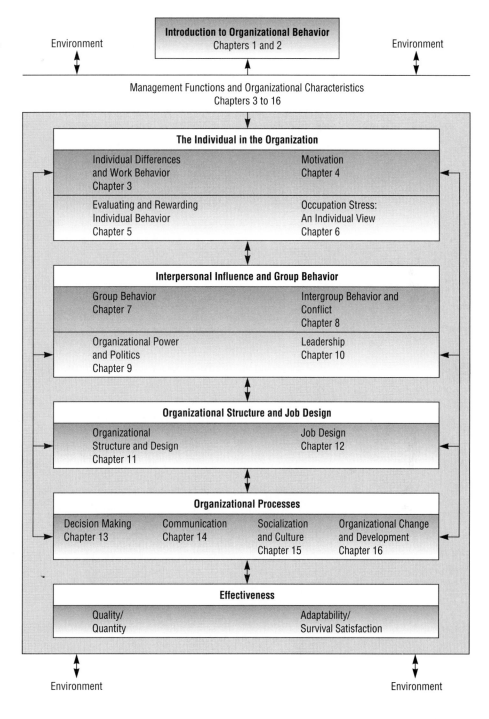

The Organization's Environment

Organizations exist in societies and are created by societies. Exhibit 1-3 draws attention to the relationships between organizations and the society that creates and sustains them. Within a society many factors impinge upon the effectiveness of an organization, and management must be responsive to them. Every organization must respond to the needs of its customers or clients, to legal and political constraints, and to economic and technological changes and developments. The model reflects environmental forces interacting within the organization, and throughout our discussion of each aspect of the model, the relevant environmental factors will be identified and examined.

The importance of environmental forces is pointed out in International Encounter 1-2, involving Procter & Gamble (P&G), on page 13. In the disposable diaper market in Japan, P&G failed to consider some important environmental forces, and this cost the firm valuable business. Significant market share was lost and has never been recovered.

The Individual in the Organization

Individual performance is the foundation of organizational performance. Understanding individual behavior therefore is critical for effective management, as illustrated in this account:

> *Ted Johnson has been a field representative for a major drug manufacturer since he graduated from college seven years ago. He makes daily calls on physicians, hospitals, clinics, and pharmacies as a representative of the many drugs his firm manufactures. During his time in the field, prescription rates and sales for all of his firm's major drugs have increased, and he has won three national sales awards given by the firm. Yesterday Ted was promoted to sales manager for a seven-state region. He no longer will be selling but instead will be managing 15 other representatives. Ted accepted the promotion because he believes he knows how to motivate and lead salespeople. He commented: "I know the personality of the salesperson. They are special people. I know what it takes to get them to perform. Remember, I am one. I know their values and attitudes and what it takes to motivate them. I know I can motivate a sales force."*

In his new job, Ted Johnson will be trying to maximize the individual performance of 15 sales representatives. In doing so he will be dealing with several facets of individual behavior. Our model includes four important influences on individual behavior and motivation in organizations: individual characteristics, individual motivation, rewards, and stress.

Individual Characteristics

Because organizational performance depends on individual performance, managers such as Ted Johnson must have more than a passing knowledge of the determinants of individual performance. Psychology and social psychology contribute a great deal of relevant knowledge about the relationships among attitudes, perceptions, personality, values, and individual performance. Understanding in-

LEARNING HOW TO DO BUSINESS OUTSIDE THE UNITED STATES: AN ENVIRONMENTAL LESSON

In the 1960s Procter & Gamble (P&G) introduced disposable diapers in the United States under the brand name Pampers. Within ten years P&G captured export markets in Canada and Europe. In 1978 P&G began exporting Pampers to Japan, where it gained almost 90 percent of the market niche immediately. In 1978 prestige-conscious Japanese consumers were willing to pay a premium for products made in the United States.

By 1979 P&G's original success turned to failure. Japanese competitors came up with a better and cheaper product. Japanese customers began reacting negatively to P&G's advertising campaigns and distribution policies. Unfortunately, P&G refused to adapt its product to the culture and environment of the Japanese.

The Japanese environment possessed a number of differences from the American environment. First, P&G advertised the product using a blond, blue-eyed baby, which was out of place among black-haired, dark-eyed Japanese. The ads also emphasized that mothers need not bother changing their babies' diapers. In Japan, mothers change their babies twice as often as do American mothers.

Second, Pampers were too bulky for Japanese babies and thus tended to leak in Japan, which was not the case in the U.S. Competitors such as Unicharm and Kao marketed disposable diapers to suit the size of Japanese babies.

Third, when things began to go wrong, P&G attempted to keep market share by cutting its price and reducing margins to its distributors. In Japan, discounted goods do not generate enough profits for the vast number of retailers who have very limited shelf space. When P&G introduced price-cutting, it devalued the Pampers brand name in the minds of Japanese consumers.

The differences in the environment and attempting to cope with them has made P&G a more competitive force around the world. P&G learned the hard way: that it is necessary to consider environmental forces and not assume that what works in the U.S. will work in other nations. P&G lost about $200 million in the disposable diaper market in Japan, but it learned that consumer needs must be met and that competition can come in quickly.

Source: Adapted from Douglas Lamont, *Winning Worldwide,* (Homewood, Ill.: Business One Irwin, 1991), pp. 43–49.

dividual capacity for learning and for coping with stress has become more and more important in recent years. Managers cannot ignore the necessity for acquiring and acting on knowledge of the individual characteristics of both their subordinates and themselves.

Individual Motivation

Motivation and ability to work interact to determine performance. Motivation theory attempts to explain and predict how the behavior of individuals is aroused, started, sustained, and stopped. Unlike Ted Johnson, not all managers and behavioral scientists agree on what is the "best" theory of motivation. In fact, motivation is so complex that it may be impossible to have an all-encompassing theory of how it occurs. However, managers must still try to understand it. They must be concerned with motivation because they must be concerned with performance.

Rewards

One of the most powerful influences on individual performance is an organization's reward system. Management can use rewards (or punishment) to increase performance by present employees. Management also can use rewards to attract skilled employees to join the organization. Pay checks, raises, and bonuses are important aspects of the reward system, but they are not the only aspects. Ted Johnson makes this point very clear in the account when he states, "I know what it takes to get them to perform." Performance of the work itself can provide employees with rewards, particularly if job performance leads to a sense of personal responsibility, autonomy, and meaningfulness.

Stress

Stress is an important result of the interaction between the job and the individual. Stress in this context is a state of imbalance within an individual that often manifests itself in such symptoms as insomnia, excessive perspiration, nervousness, and irritability. Whether stress is positive or negative depends on the individual's tolerance level. People react differently to situations that outwardly would seem to induce the same physical and psychological demands. Some individuals respond positively through increased motivation and commitment to finish the job. Other individuals respond less desirably by turning to such outlets as alcoholism and drug abuse. Hopefully, Ted Johnson will respond positively to the stresses of his new job.

Management's responsibility in managing stress has not been clearly defined, but there is growing evidence that organizations are devising programs to deal with work-induced stress.

Interpersonal Influence and Group Behavior

Interpersonal influence and group behavior are also powerful forces affecting organizational performance. The effects of these forces are illustrated in the following account:

Kelly McCaul spent 2¹/₂ years as a teller in the busiest branch of First National Bank. During that time she developed close personal friendships with her co-workers. These friendships extended off the job as well. Kelly and her friends formed a wine-and-cheese club and were the top team in the bankwide bowling league. In addition, several of the friends took ski trips together each winter.

Two months ago Kelly was promoted to branch manager. She was excited about the new challenge but was a little surprised that she got the promotion since some other likely candidates in the branch has been with the bank longer. She began the job with a great deal of optimism and believed her friends would be genuinely happy for her and supportive of her efforts. However, since she became branch manager, things haven't seemed quite the same. Kelly can't spend nearly as much time with her friends because she is often away from the branch attending management meetings at the main office. A training course she must attend two evenings a week has caused her to miss the last two wine-and-cheese club meetings, and she senses that some of her friends have been acting a little differently toward her lately.

Recently, Kelly said, "I didn't know that being part of the management team could make that much difference. Frankly, I never really thought about it. I guess I was naive. I'm seeing a totally different perspective of the business and have to deal with problems I never knew about."

Kelly McCaul's promotion has made her a member of more than one group. In addition to being a member of her old group of friends at the branch, she also is a member of the management team. She is finding out that group behavior and expectations have a strong impact on individual behavior and interpersonal influence. Our model includes four important aspects of group and interpersonal influence on organization behavior: leadership, group behavior, intergroup behavior and conflict, and organizational power and politics.

Leadership

Leaders exist within all organizations. Like the bank's Kelly McCaul, they may be found in formal groups, but they also may be found in informal groups. Leaders may be managers or nonmanagers. The importance of effective leadership for obtaining individual, group, and organizational performance is so critical that it has stimulated a great deal of effort to determine the causes of such leadership. Some people believe that effective leadership depends on traits and certain behaviors—separately and in combination. Other people believe that one leadership style is effective in all situations. Still others believe that each situation requires a specific leadership style.

Group Behavior

Groups form because of managerial action, and also because of individual efforts. Managers create work groups to carry out assigned jobs and tasks. Such groups, created by managerial decisions, are termed **formal groups**. The group that Kelly McCaul manages at her branch is a formal group.

Groups also form as a consequence of employees' actions. Such groups, termed **informal groups**, develop around common interests and friendships. The wine-and-cheese club at Kelly McCaul's branch is an informal group. Though not sanctioned by management, groups of this kind can affect organizational and individual performance. The effect can be positive or negative, depending on the intention of the group's members. If the group at Kelly's branch decided informally to slow the work pace, this norm would exert pressure on individuals who wanted to remain a part of the group. Effective managers recognize the consequences of individuals' need for affiliation.

Intergroup Behavior and Conflict

As groups function and interact with other groups, they develop their own unique set of characteristics, including structure, cohesiveness, roles, norms, and processes. As a result, groups may cooperate or compete with other groups, and intergroup competition can lead to conflict. If the management of Kelly's bank instituted an incentive program with cash bonuses to the branch bringing in the most new customers, this might lead to competition and conflict among the branches. While conflict among groups can have beneficial results for an organization, too much or the wrong kinds of intergroup conflict can have very negative results. Thus, managing intergroup conflict is an important aspect of managing organizational behavior.

Power and Politics

Power is the ability to get someone to do something you want done or to make things happen in the way you want them to happen. Many people in our society are very uncomfortable with the concept of power, and some are very offended by it. This is because the essence of power is control over others. To many Americans, control over others is an offensive thought. However, power is a reality in organizations. Managers derive power from both organizational and individual sources. Kelly McCaul has power by virtue of her position in the formal hierarchy of the bank. She controls performance evaluations and salary increases. However, she also may have power because her co-workers respect and admire the abilities and expertise she possesses. Managers therefore must become comfortable with the concept of power as a reality in organizations and managerial roles.

Organizational Structure and Design

To work effectively in organizations managers must have a clear understanding of the organizational structure. Viewing an organization chart on a piece of paper or framed on a wall, one sees only a configuration of positions, job duties, and lines of authority among the parts of an organization. However, organizational structures can be far more complex than that, as illustrated in the following account:

> *Dr. John Rice recently was appointed dean of the business school at a major university. Prior to arriving on campus, Rice spent several weeks studying the funding, programs, faculty, students, and organizational structure of the business school. He was trying to develop a list of priorities for things he believed would require immediate attention during his first year as dean. The president of the university had requested that he have such a list of priorities available when he arrived on campus.*
>
> *During his first official meeting with the president, Rice was asked the question he fully expected to be asked: "What will be your number one priority?" Rice replied: "Although money is always a problem, I believe the most urgent need is to reorganize the business school. At present, students can major in only one of two departments— accounting and business administration. The accounting department has 20 faculty*

members. The business administration department has 43 faculty members, including 15 in marketing, 16 in management, and 12 in finance. I foresee a college with four departments—accounting, management, marketing, and finance—each with its own chairperson. First, I believe such a structure will enable us to better meet the needs of our students. Specifically, it will facilitate the development of programs of majors in each of the four areas. Students must be able to major in one of the four functional areas if they are going to be prepared adequately for the job market. Finally, I believe such an organizational structure will enable us to more easily recruit faculty since they will be joining a group with interests similar to their own."

As this account indicates, an organization's structure is the formal pattern of activities and interrelationships among the various subunits of the organization. Our model includes two important aspects of organizational structure: the actual structure of the organization itself and job design.

Structure of the Organization

The **structure** of the organization refers to the components of the organization and how these components fit together. Dr. Rice plans to alter the basic structure of the business school. The result of his efforts will be a new structure of tasks and authority relationships that he believes will channel the behavior of individuals and groups toward higher levels of performance in the business school.

Job Design

This aspect of structure refers to the processes by which managers specify the contents, methods, and relationships of jobs and specific task assignments to satisfy both organizational and individual needs and requirements. Dr. Rice will have to define the content and duties of the newly created chairperson position and the relationship of that person to the dean's office and to the individual faculty members in each department.

Organizational Processes

Certain behavioral processes give life to an organization. When these processes do not function well, unfortunate problems can arise, as illustrated in this account:

When she began to major in marketing as a junior in college, Debra Washney knew that someday she would work in that field. Once she completed her MBA, she was more positive than ever that marketing would be her life's work. Because of her excellent academic record, she received several outstanding job offers. She decided to accept the job offer she received from one of the nation's largest consulting firms. She believed this job would allow her to gain experience in several areas of marketing and to engage in a variety of exciting work. On her last day on campus, she told her favorite professor; "This has got to be one of the happiest days of my life, getting such a great career opportunity."

Recently, while visiting the college placement office, the professor was surprised to hear that Debra had told the placement director that she was looking for another job.

Since she had been with the consulting company less than a year, the professor was somewhat surprised. He decided to call Debra and find out why she wanted to change jobs. This is what she told him: "I guess you can say my first experience with the real world was a 'reality shock.' Since being with this company, I have done nothing but gather data on phone surveys. All day long I sit and talk on the phone, asking questions and checking off the answers. In graduate school I was trained to be a manager, but here I am doing what any high school graduate can do. I talked to my boss, and he said that all employees have to pay their dues. Well, why didn't they tell me this while they were recruiting me? To say there was a conflict between the recruiting information and the real world would be a gross understatement. I'm an adult—why didn't they provide me with realistic job information then let me decide if I wanted it? A little bit of accurate communication would have gone a long way."

Our model includes four behavioral processes that contribute to effective organizational performance: communication, decision making, career and socialization, and organizational change and development.

Communication Process

Organizational survival is related to the ability of management to receive, transmit, and act on information. The communication process links the organization to its environment as well as to its parts. Information flows to and from the organization and within the organization. Information integrates the activities of the organization with the demands of the environment. But information also integrates the internal activities of the organization. Debra Washney's problem arose because the information that flowed *from* the organization was different from the information that flowed *within* the organization.

Decision-Making Process

The quality of decision making in an organization depends on selecting proper goals and identifying means for achieving them. With good integration of behavioral and structural factors, management can increase the probability that high-quality decisions will be made. Debra Washney's experience illustrates inconsistent decision making by different organizational units (personnel and marketing) in the hiring of new employees. Organizations rely on individual decisions as well as group decisions, and effective management requires knowledge of both types of decisions.

These days it is common to read about managerial decisions that are considered unethical. It is now accepted that most decisions made in an organization are permeated by ethics.[7] Managers are powerful, and, where power exists, there is potential for good and evil. Recent headlines emphasize the ethical nature of decision making: "Large Brokerage House Pays Large Bonuses to Top Managers

---

[7]W. F. Edmonson, "A Code of Ethics: Do Corporate Executives and Employees Need It?" (Fulton, Miss.: Itawamba Community College Press, 1990).

for Months before Declaring Bankruptcy;" "Lawyers and Arbitrators Trade Inside Information;" and "How Companies Spy on Employees."[8]

The power of managers is clearly portrayed in making decisions about employees' well-being, distributing organizational resources, and designing and implementing rules and policies. In Debra Washney's case, she claims that the consulting firm didn't provide a realistic job preview. She is making a statement that suggests unethical behavior on the part of the individuals who interviewed her for the consulting firm job. Was this the right thing for the company to do? Debra suggests that it was not the right thing or the ethical way to conduct an interview. Ethical dilemmas will be discussed throughout the book because managers and workers must make decisions every day that have an ethical component.

Career and Socialization Processes

A person's career involves a perceived sequence of attitudes and behaviors associated with job-related experiences and activities. One job experience doesn't mean the same thing as a career or a series of experiences. Debra Washney's first career opportunity didn't work out well. Her next experience may be more satisfactory and add to her pursuit of a marketing career.

Organizational Change and Development Processes

Managers sometimes must consider the possibility that effective organizational functioning can be improved by making significant changes in the total organization. Organizational change and development represent planned attempts to improve overall individual, group, and organizational performance. Debra Washney might well have been spared the disappointment she experienced had an organizational development effort uncovered and corrected the inconsistent communication and decision making that brought about Debra's unhappiness. Concerted, planned, and evaluative efforts to improve organizational functioning have great potential for success.

Performance Outcomes: Individual, Group, and Organizational

Individual performance contributes to group performance, which, in turn, contributes to organizational performance. In truly effective organizations, however, management helps create a positive synergy: that is, a whole that is greater than the sum of its parts.

No one measure, or criterion, adequately reflects effectiveness at any level. The next chapter introduces the idea that organizational effectiveness must be considered in terms of multiple measures within a time frame. But ineffective performance at any level is a signal to management to take corrective actions. All of management's corrective actions will focus on elements of organizational behavior, structure, or processes.

[8]Gene Bylinsky, "How Companies Spy on Employees," *Fortune,* November 4, 1991, pp. 131–40.

SUMMARY OF KEY POINTS

- The key to an organization's success is the institution's human resources. Organizations need human resources that work hard, think creatively, and perform excellently. Rewarding, encouraging, and nurturing the human resources in a timely and meaningful manner is what is required. Thus, the power of human resources refers to their importance.

- A number of contributing disciplines stand out such as psychology, sociology, and cultural anthropology. Psychology has contributed information and data about motivation, personality, perception, job satisfaction, and work stress. Sociology has offered information about group dynamics, communication problems, organizational change, and formal organization structure. Cultural anthropology has contributed information about culture, comparative attitudes, and cross-cultural studies.

- The behavior of employees is the key to achieving effectiveness. People behave in many predictable and unpre-

dictable ways. Each person has a unique behavioral pattern. Managers must observe, respond to, and cope with the array of behavior patterns displayed by employees.

- The "effect" is the behavior or reaction of a person who is being observed. Individuals who are being observed are likely to react in a nonroutine way because they are being watched or are a part of an experiment.

- Employers and employees enter into a psychological contract. The employer believes that no worker is guaranteed a lifelong job or pay raise. If the worker's performance is good and profit is earned, then employment continues and pay raises are provided. Employees today believe that employers should be honest, concerned about their families, and interested in their overall health. These assumptions are the basis of what is called the *new* psychological agreement.

REVIEW AND DISCUSSION QUESTIONS

1. Why is management so necessary in any organization—hospital, bank, or school?

2. Why is it useful to distinguish three levels of behavior—individual, group, and organizational—when discussing behavior in organizations?

3. "As organizations increase in size and complexity, managing the behavior of organizational members becomes more difficult." Do you agree or disagree with this statement? Why?

4. What knowledge about human behavior in the workplace was uncovered by the Hawthorne studies?

5. Organizations are characterized by their goal-directed behavior. So are people. How is the study of organizations similar to the study of people? How is it different?

6. What is *new* about how employees view management responsibilities in the 1990s?

7. Frequently, organizations are described in terms used to refer to personality characteristics—dynamic, greedy, creative, conservative, and so on. Is this a valid way to describe organizations? Does this mean that the people in the organization possess the same characteristics?

8. Organizations are influenced by the environment in which they operate; in turn, organizations influence their environments. List examples of both types of influence that you can recall from personal experience.

9. What are the characteristics of what we refer to as a "healthy" organization?

10. What behavioral sciences have contributed to the field of study that is called organizational behavior? Explain.

C H A P T E R

2

Managing Behavior in Organizations

LEARNING OBJECTIVES

DEFINE quality and explain its relationship to organizational effectiveness criteria.

DESCRIBE the goal approach to defining and measuring effectiveness.

EXPLAIN how managers attempt to measure what is called satisfaction.

DISCUSS how an organization's mission is used to determine whether it is effective.

EXPLAIN the interrelationships between planning and organizing as viewed by managers.

COMPARE an intuitive approach to studying the behavior of employees to a more systematic approach.

Over the past two decades, the public has shown increased interest in learning about what constitutes effective management, total quality improvement, and healthy organizations. *Theory Z,*[1] *In Search of Excellence,*[2] *Made in America,*[3] *Quality or Else,*[4] and *World Class Quality,*[5] are some of the popular and practitioner-oriented "how to be effective" books. The concern with such topics as

---

[1]William G. Ouchi, *Theory Z* (Reading, Mass.: Addison-Wesley Publishing, 1981).

[2]Thomas J. Peters and Robert H. Waterman, Jr., *In Search of Excellence* (New York: Harper & Row, 1982).

[3]Michael L. Dertouzos, *Made in America,* Cambridge, Mass.: The MIT Press, 1989.

[4]Lloyd Dobyns and Clare Crawford-Mason, *Quality or Else* (Boston, Mass.: Houghton-Mifflin, 1991).

[5]Keki R. Bhote, *World Class Quality* (New York: AMACOM, 1991).

effectiveness, quality, and excellence, however, is not a new phenomenon.[6] For centuries economists, philosophers, engineers, military generals, government leaders, and managers have attempted to define, measure, analyze, and capture the essence of effectiveness. Adam Smith wrote in the *Wealth of Nations* over two centuries ago that efficiency of operations can be achieved most easily through high degrees of specialization.

Whether—and how—managers can influence effectiveness are difficult to determine. There is still confusion about how to manage within organizations so that organizational effectiveness is the final result. Problems of definition, criteria identification, and finding the best model to guide research and practice continue to hinder, block, and discourage practitioners and researchers. Instead of simply ignoring effectiveness because of underlying confusion, we believe important insights can be found by attempting to clarify various perspectives.

As noted in the previous chapter, the field of organizational behavior identified three **levels of analysis** (1) individual, (2) group, and (3) organizational. Theorists and researchers in organizational behavior have accumulated a vast amount of information about each of these levels. These three levels of analysis also coincide with the three levels of managerial responsibility. That is, managers are responsible for the effectiveness of individuals, groups of individuals, and organizations themselves.

Harley-Davidson chairperson Vaughn Beals is an example of a leader who concluded that managers are responsible for the effectiveness of an organization. In the early 1980s he visited a Marysville, Ohio, plant of Harley's strongest competitor, Honda Motor.[7] Honda had seized a 44 percent share of the American heavy motorcycle market. Bikers found Honda's cheaper machines more reliable than Harley's. What was Honda's secret management plan?

Beals found no plan, no fancy or sophisticated robots, and no high technology. He found a staff of only 30 people besides the 470 production workers and highly satisfied employees. Honda seemed to pay attention to quality details, listened to employee suggestions on improving the production process, and had employees involved in all phases of decision making.

Five years after the disheartening visit to Honda, Beals had helped turn Harley around. Its share of U.S. heavy motorcycle sales increased from 23 to 46 percent. Harley learned from Honda that common sense and being concerned about the individual employee and work groups resulted in improved performance. Harley learned that quality is a key factor in consumer decisions. Prior to the Marysville, Ohio, visit, Harley's acceptance rate for motorcycles coming off the assembly line was about 60 percent. At Honda, the acceptance rate was over 95 percent.

[6]Arie Y. Lewin and Jon W. Minton, "Determining Organizational Effectiveness: Another Look and an Agenda for Research," *Management Science,* May 1986, pp. 514–35.

[7]Richard C. Whiteley, *The Customer Driven Company* (Reading, Mass.: Addison-Wesley Publishing, 1991), pp. 69–71.

ENCOUNTER • 2-1

FORTUNE'S SURVEY OF THE MOST ADMIRED COMPANIES

In 1991 *Fortune* magazine reported the results of a poll of 8,000 corporate executives, directors, and financial analysts to determine which companies they held in highest esteem. Half of these officials responded to *Fortune*'s request to rate 10 companies in their respective industries on eight "attributes of reputation" using a 10-point scale ranging from poor (1) to excellent (10) on each attribute. The eight attributes, the highest rated company on each attribute, and the companies' scores are listed in the actual article.

The champion, Merck, beat the competition by taking first place in six of the eight categories. For the sixth straight year, this pharmaceutical giant has earned the highest rating among 307 major companies.

Attributes Rated

Quality of management
Quality of products or service
Innovativeness
Long-term investment value

Attributes Rated

Financial soundness
Ability to attract, develop, and keep talented people
Community and environmental responsibility
Use of corporate assets

Company	Average Score on Attributes
Merck	9.02
Rubbermaid	8.66
Wal-Mart Stores	8.58
Liz Claiborne	8.43
Levi Strauss Associates	8.26
Johnson & Johnson	8.22
Coca-Cola	8.13
3M	8.12
Pepsico	8.00
Procter & Gamble	8.00

Source: Kate Ballen, "America's Most Admired Corporations," *Fortune,* February 10, 1992, pp. 40–72.

Vaughn Beals is an example of a leader who wanted to improve, who honestly appraised the effectiveness of his firm, and who accepted the fact that a competitor was doing a much better job. He also had some humility and was willing to learn from others.

Was Vaughn Beals any less of a person because he observed, listened, diagnosed, strategized, and admitted limitations of what was occurring at Harley-Davidson? We do not think so and, in fact, Vaughn Beals is an excellent example of how one man can make a difference in turning ineffective practices into an effective, competitive, healthy organization. He considered the individual employee, the customers, the competitors, the groups of Harley workers, and the organization's demise. He viewed the world at each of the three levels of analysis that predominate the view of the organizational behavior approach.

From the standpoint of society, the effectiveness of business organizations is critical. Publications that report business and economic events occasionally survey opinions about business performance. One such survey is reported in the Encounter on America's most admired companies. These companies apparently have managers who have learned and practiced these skills which Drucker discusses in Reading 2–1, "Teaching the Work of Management."

● R2–1

A BRIEF HISTORY OF EFFECTIVENESS RESEARCH

Perhaps the modern-era starting point of understanding effectiveness was the scientific management views proposed by Frederick Taylor. Taylor's work used motion and time studies to find the "one best way" to do an effective (efficient) job. In Taylor's viewpoint, the principle of specialization was causally linked to effectiveness. A more contemporary view of linking management action with effectiveness was advanced by Tom Peters in his book *Thriving on Chaos*.[8] He proposed that effective firms need to have fewer layers of organizational structure, be populated by more autonomous units, be quality and service conscious, and be much faster at innovation. Two concepts that are today more at center stage in managerial thinking are quality and innovation.

The historical search for organizational effectiveness is briefly traced in Exhibit 2-1. In this presentation, the word *attributes* is used to encompass both predictor variables (that predict) and indicator variables (that are of interest and indicate).[9]

As Exhibit 2-1 indicates, numerous perspectives, philosophies, and issues surround organizational effectiveness. Each has contributed to the notion that a universal, overarching view of effectiveness is not likely to be found. Instead, viewpoints that are insightful, practical, and relevant seem to offer the manager within organizations the most hope in managing organizational behavior.

TWO PERSPECTIVES ON EFFECTIVENESS

Since no viewpoint of effectiveness is universally accepted, we have decided to use multiple perspectives. Two of the most popular perspectives are the goal approach and the systems theory approach. Both of these views have guided researchers and intrigued practitioners.

---

[8]Tom Peters, *Thriving on Chaos* (New York: Alfred A. Knopf, 1987).

[9]This terminology is taken from Lewin and Minton, "Determining Organizational Effectiveness," and Kim S. Cameron, "Effectiveness as Paradox: Consensus and Conflict in Conceptions of Organizational Effectiveness," *Management Science*, May 1986, pp. 539–53.

EXHIBIT 2-1

Tracing the History of Organizational Research

Management Concept	Pioneers	Philosophical Position	Attributes
Scientific management	Frederick Taylor (1911)	Motion and time studies; finding most efficient way	Minimize cost, task specialization, maximize quantity (output)
Principles of management	Henri Fayol (1916–1925)	Management principles; training in use of principles	Order, equity, scalar chairs, division of work, discipline
Human relations	Elton Mayo (1933)	Psychological factors, job satisfaction, team work	Paying attention to workers' needs and satisfaction
Decision making	Herbert Simon (1947)	Bounded rationality, optimization of goals	Hierarchy of goals, effective use of resources
Socio-technical	E. L. Trist and K. W. Bamforth (1951)	Social systems view means that organization is an open system	Fit between social/technological factors
Behavioral	Douglas McGregor (1961) Rensis Likert (1967)	Individual needs and the importance of participative management	Cohesiveness, loyalty, commitment, and employee satisfaction
Strategic management	Alfred Chandler (1962)	Establish strategy, then structure is established	Strategy/structure fit needed to adapt to environmental changes
Contingency theory	P. R. Lawrence and J. W. Lorsch (1967)	Structure firm to meet environmental demands	Integration fit and differentiation fit
*Quality	Deming (1951 in Japan) and Juran (1954 in Japan)	Train and educate people how to detect and eliminate defects. Quality principles must be applied to everything done in and by a company	Instill pride in quality in employees and focus on customer satisfaction
Empowerment	No specific person (highlighted in report in 1984)	Giving workers a say and power in what they do will increase their ownership in the job	Employees feel more responsible, show more initiative, and are more satisfied
Proactive performance	Peters (1987)	Responsiveness to change, customers, and the need for social support	Integrate people, leaders that are change-oriented, autonomous units, focus on new market creation, flat structure

*Quality started to be much more recognized in the United States across industries and companies around 1980. Source: Portions of Exhibit 2-1 are modified from Mary Wilson, *Deming Management at Work* (New York: Putnam, 1990), pp. 11–13; Arie Y. Lewin and John W. Minton, "Determining Organizational Effectiveness: Another Look and an Agenda for Research," *Management Science*, May 1986, pp. 516–17; L. D. Ketchum, "How Redesigned Plants Really Work," *National Productivity Review*, 1984, pp. 246–54.

The Goal Approach

The goal approach to defining and measuring effectiveness is the oldest and most widely used evaluation technique.[10] In the view of this approach, an organization exists to accomplish goals. An early but influential practitioner and writer on management and organizational behavior stated: "What we mean by effectiveness . . . is the accomplishment of recognized objectives of cooperative effort. The degree of accomplishment indicates the degree of effectiveness."[11] The idea that organizations, as well as individuals and groups, should be evaluated in terms of goal accomplishment has widespread appeal. The goal approach reflects purposefulness, rationality, and achievement—the fundamental tenets of contemporary Western societies.

Many management practices are based on the goal approach. One widely used practice is management by objectives. Using this practice, managers specify in advance the goals they expect their subordinates to accomplish and periodically evaluate the degree to which the subordinates have accomplished these goals. The actual specifics of management by objectives vary from case to case. In some instances, the manager and subordinate discuss the objectives and attempt to reach mutual agreement. In other instances, the manager simply assigns the goals. The idea of management by objectives is to specify in advance the goals to be sought.

Yet the goal approach, for all of its appeal and apparent simplicity, has problems.[12] These are some of its more widely recognized difficulties:

1. Goal achievement is not readily measurable for organizations that do not produce tangible outputs. For example, the stated goal of a college may be "to provide a liberal education at a fair price." The question is: How would one know whether the college achieves that goal? What is a liberal education? What is a fair price? For that matter, what is education?
2. Organizations attempt to achieve more than one goal, and achievement of one goal often precludes or diminishes their ability to achieve other goals. A business firm may state that its goal is to attain a maximum profit and to provide absolutely safe working conditions. These two goals are in conflict because each of these goals is achieved at the expense of the other.
3. The very existence of a common set of official goals to which all members are committed is questionable. Various researchers have noted the difficulty

[10]Stephen Strasser, J. D. Eveland, Gaylord Cummins, O. Lynn Deniston, and John H. Romani, "Conceptualizing the Goal and System Models of Organizational Effectiveness," *Journal of Management Studies,* July 1981, p. 323.

[11]Chester I. Barnard, *The Functions of the Executive* (Cambridge, Mass.: Harvard University Press, 1938), p. 55.

[12]E. Frank Harrison, *Management and Organization* (Boston: Houghton Mifflin, 1978), pp. 404–14. This is an excellent survey of limitations of the goal approach.

of obtaining consensus among managers as to the specific goals of their organization.[13]

4. Sometimes, even if stated goals are achieved, the organization is considered to be ineffective.

Despite the problems of the goal approach, it continues to exert a powerful influence on the development of management and organizational behavior theory and practice. Saying that managers should achieve the goals of the organization is easy. Knowing how to do this is more difficult. The alternative to the goal approach is the systems theory approach. Through systems theory, the concept of effectiveness can be defined in terms that enable managers to take a broader view of the organization and to understand the causes of individual, group, and organizational effectiveness.

The Systems Theory Approach

Systems theory enables you to describe the behavior of organizations both internally and externally. Internally, you can see how and why people within organizations perform their individual and group tasks. Externally, you can relate the transactions of organizations with other organizations and institutions. All organizations acquire resources from the outside environment of which they are a part and, in turn, provide goods and services demanded by the larger environment. Managers must deal simultaneously with the internal and external aspects of organizational behavior. This essentially complex process can be simplified, for analytical purposes, by employing the basic concepts of systems theory.

In systems theory, the organization is seen as one element of a number of elements that act interdependently. The flow of inputs and outputs is the basic starting point in describing the organization. In the simplest terms, the organization takes resources (inputs) from the larger system (environment), processes these resources and returns them in changed form (output). Exhibit 2-2 displays the fundamental elements of the organization as a system.

An example of a systems explanation of organizational behavior is found in companies doing business in Germany. In April 1991 Germany's federal government passed a new packaging law that is the toughest in the world.[14] Starting in December 1991 companies must take back and recycle packaging used during transport or arrange for someone else to do so. By July 1, 1995, 80 percent of the packaging must be collected. Germany's law applies to everyone. The environmental cleanup will influence how business is done in every firm doing business in Germany.

[13]G. H. Gaertner and S. Ramnarayan, "Organizational Effectiveness: An Alternative Perspective," *Academy of Management Review*, January 1983, pp. 97–107.

[14]"Recycling in Germany: A Wall of Waste," *The Economist*, November 30, 1991, p. 73.

EXHIBIT 2-2

**The Basic Elements
of a System**

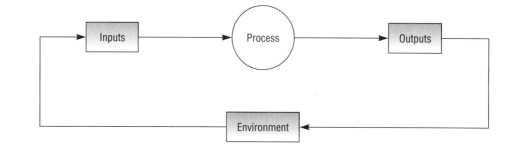

Hewlett-Packard, an American computer company, has redesigned its packaging worldwide to make it easier to recycle in Germany. Where possible, it has switched to cardboard, hired designers to alter products, and conducted marketing research surveys to determine if German consumers would accept products in reused boxes (they would). The inputs, processes, and outputs of Hewlett-Packard are influenced by the external environmental requirement.

Germany plans to extend recycling to manufacturers of cars and of electronic goods such as computers and televisions. Volkswagen has already practiced to the point of stripping down an automobile in 20 minutes.

Systems theory can also describe the behavior of individuals and groups. The "inputs" of individual behavior are "causes" that arise from the workplace. For example, the cause could be the directives of a manager to perform a certain task. The input (cause) is then acted on by the individual's mental and psychological processes to produce a particular outcome. The outcome that the manager prefers is, of course, compliance with the directive, but depending on the states of the individual's processes, the outcome could be noncompliance. Similarly, you can describe the behavior of a group in systems theory terms. For example, the behavior of a group of employees to unionize (outcome) could be explained in terms of perceived managerial unfairness in the assignment of work (input) and the state of the group's cohesiveness (process). We use the term **systems theory** throughout this text to describe and explain the behavior of individuals and groups in organizations.

Systems Theory and Feedback

The concept of the organization as a system related to a larger system introduces the importance of feedback. As mentioned, the organization is dependent on the environment not only for its inputs but also for the acceptance of its outputs. It is critical, therefore, that the organization develop means for adjusting to environmental demands. The means for adjustment are information channels that enable the organization to recognize these demands. In business organizations, for example, market research is an important feedback mechanism. Other forms of feedback are customer complaints, employee comments, and financial reports.

In simplest terms, feedback refers to information that reflects the outcomes of an act or a series of acts by an individual, a group, or an organization. Throughout this text, you will see the importance of responding to the content of the feedback information.

Examples of the Input-Output Cycle

The business firm has two major categories of inputs: human and natural resources. Human inputs consist of the people who work in the firm. They contribute their time and energy to the organization in exchange for wages and other rewards, tangible and intangible. Natural resources consist of the nonhuman inputs processed or used in combination with the human element to provide other resources. A steel mill must have people and blast furnaces (along with other tools and machinery) to process iron ore into steel and steel products. An auto manufacturer takes steel, rubber, plastics, and fabrics and—in combination with people, tools, and equipment—uses them to make automobiles. A business firm survives as long as its output is purchased in the market in sufficient quantities and at prices that enable it to replenish its depleted stock of inputs.

Similarly, a university uses resources to teach students, to do research, and to provide technical information to society. The survival of a university depends on its ability to attract students' tuitions and taxpayers' dollars in sufficient amounts to pay the salaries of its faculty and staff as well as the costs of other resources. If a university's output is rejected by the larger environment, so that students enroll elsewhere and taxpayers support other public endeavors, or if a university is guilty of expending too great an amount of resources in relation to its output, it will cease to exist. Like a business firm, a university must provide the right output at the right price if it is to survive.[15]

Systems theory emphasizes two important considerations: (1) the ultimate survival of the organization depends on its ability to adapt to the demands of its environment, and (2) in meeting these demands, the total cycle of input-process-output must be the focus of managerial attention. Therefore, the criteria of effectiveness must reflect each of these two considerations, and you must define effectiveness accordingly. The systems approach accounts for the fact that resources have to be devoted to activities that have little to do with achieving the organization's primary goal.[16] In other words, adapting to the environment and maintaining the input-process-output flow require that resources be allocated to activities that are only indirectly related to that goal.

[15]Kim Cameron, "Measuring Organizational Effectiveness in Institutions of Higher Education," *Administrative Science Quarterly,* December 1978, pp. 604–29.

[16]Amitai Etzioni, "Two Approaches to Organizational Analysis: A Critique and a Suggestion," in *Assessment of Organizational Effectiveness,* ed. Jaisingh Ghorpade (Santa Monica, Calif.: Goodyear Publishing, 1971), p. 36.

THE TIME DIMENSION MODEL OF ORGANIZATIONAL EFFECTIVENESS

The concept of organizational effectiveness presented in this book relies on the previous discussion of systems theory, but we must develop one additional point: the dimension of time. Recall that two main conclusions of systems theory are: (1) effectiveness criteria must reflect the entire input-process-output cycle, not simply output and (2) effectiveness criteria must reflect the interrelationships between the organization and its outside environment. Thus:

1. Organizational effectiveness is an all-encompassing concept that includes a number of component concepts.
2. The managerial task is to maintain the optimal balance among these components.

Much additional research is needed to develop knowledge about the components of effectiveness. There is little consensus about these relevant components, about the interrelationships among them, and about the effects of managerial action on them.[17] In this textbook we attempt to provide the basis for asking the right questions about what constitutes effectiveness and how the qualities that characterize effectiveness interact.

According to systems theory, an organization is an element of a larger system, the environment. With the passage of time, every organization takes, processes, and returns resources to the environment. The ultimate criterion of organizational effectiveness is whether the organization survives in the environment. Survival requires adaptation, and adaptation often involves predictable sequences. As the organization ages, it probably will pass through different phases. It forms, develops, matures, and declines in relation to environmental circumstances. Organizations and entire industries rise and fall. Today, the personal-computer industry is on the rise, and the steel industry is declining. Marketing experts acknowledge the existence of product-market life cycles. Organizations also seem to have life cycles. Consequently, the appropriate criteria of effectiveness must reflect the stage of the organization's life cycle.[18]

Managers and others with interests in the organization must have indicators that assess the probability of the organization's survival. In actual practice, managers use a number of short-run indicators of long-run survival. Among these indicators are measurements of productivity, efficiency, accidents, turnover, ab-

---

[17]R. F. Zammuto, "A Comparison of Multiple Constituency Models of Organizational Effectiveness," *Academy of Management Review,* October 1984, pp. 606–16.

[18]Kim S. Cameron and David A. Whetten, "Perceptions of Organizational Effectiveness over Organizational Life Cycles," *Administrative Science Quarterly,* December 1981, pp. 525–44; and R. E. Quinn and Kim Cameron, "Organizational Life Cycles and Shifting Criteria of Effectiveness: Some Preliminary Evidence," *Management Science,* January 1983, pp. 33–51.

EXHIBIT 2-3

Time Dimension Model of Effectiveness

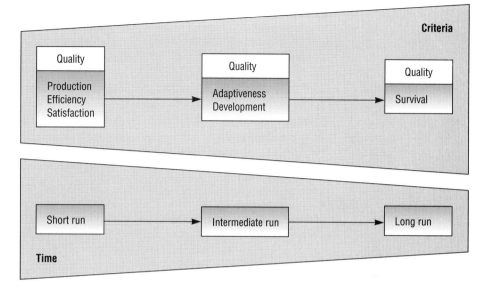

senteeism, quality, rate of return, morale, and employee satisfaction.[19] The overarching criterion that cuts across each time dimension is *quality*. Unless quality is perceived by customers, there will be no survival. Any of these criteria can be relevant for particular purposes. For simplicity, we will use four criteria of short-run effectiveness as representatives of all such criteria. They are quality, production, efficiency, and satisfaction.

Three intermediate criteria in the time dimension model are quality, adaptiveness, and development. The final two long-run criteria are quality and survival. The relationships between these criteria and the time dimension are shown in Exhibit 2-3.

CRITERIA OF EFFECTIVENESS

In the time dimension model, criteria of effectiveness typically are stated in terms of the short run, the intermediate run, and the long run. Short-run criteria are those referring to the results of actions concluded in a year or less. Intermediate-run criteria are applicable when you judge the effectiveness of an individual, group, or organization for a longer time period, perhaps five years. Long-run criteria are those for which the indefinite future is applicable. We will discuss six

[19]John P. Campbell, "On the Nature of Organizational Effectiveness," in *New Perspectives on Organizational Effectiveness,* ed. Paul S. Goodman and Johannes M. Pennings (San Francisco: Jossey-Bass, 1979), pp. 36–39.

general categories of effectiveness criteria, beginning with those of a short-run nature.

Quality

J. M. Juran and W. Edwards Deming, in 1950, were prophets without honor in their own country, the United States. These two Americans emphasized the importance of quality. There is now a belief that, in order to survive, organizations must design products, make products, and treat customers in a close-to-perfection way. Close-to-perfection means that quality is now an imperative.[20]

● R2–2   More than any other single event, the 1980 NBC White Paper, "If Japan Can . . . Why Can't We?" illustrates the importance of quality. The television show showed how, in 30 years, the Japanese had risen from the ashes of World War II to economic gianthood with products of superior quality. That is, Japanese organizational effectiveness centered on the notion of quality. The Japanese interpret quality as it relates to the customer's perception. Customers compare the actual performance of the product or evaluate the service being provided to their own set of expectations. The product or service either passes or fails. Thus, quality has nothing to do with how shiny or good looking something is or with how much it costs. **Quality** is defined as meeting customers' needs and expectations.

An American firm that has surfaced as one of the strongest advocates of quality is Motorola. Encounter 2-2 on page 33 points out how Motorola is working to achieve perfection. The firm believes that competing in the marketplace demands that quality be a major target.

In today's competitive internationalizing world, the effective company will be the one that provides customers with quality products or services. Retailers, bankers, manufacturers, lawyers, doctors, airlines, and others are finding out that, to stay in business (survival in effectiveness terms), the customer must be kept happy and satisfied.

Each of the criteria of effectiveness discussed above are significant. However, the one element that executives now recognize as being perhaps the most crucial is quality.

For more than four decades, W. Edwards Deming and J. M. Juran have been the advocates of quality.[21] Deming is the guru of statistical quality control (SQC). He is the namesake of Japan's most prestigious quality award, the Deming prize, created in 1951.

Juran is best known for his concept of total quality control (TQC). This is the application of quality principles to all company programs, including satisfying internal customers. In 1954 Juran first described his method in Japan. He has become an important inspiration to the Japanese because he applied quality to everyone from the top of the firm to the clerical staff.

[20]"The Quality Imperative," *Business Week*, October 25, 1991, pp. 7–11.

[21]W. Edwards Deming and J. M. Juran, "Dueling Pioneers," *Business Week*, October 25, 1991, p. 17.

ORGANIZATIONAL
ENCOUNTER • 2-2

MOTOROLA'S QUEST FOR QUALITY

Few United States companies can match Motorola's devotion to quality. In 1987 it set a five-year goal: It reached virtual perfection in manufacturing by slashing component defects to what's known in quality terms as the six-sigma level. That's 3.4 defects per million components. The target will be missed in 1992, but it looks like by 1993 it will be reached. By 2001 Motorola hopes that it will have a rate of defects of one per billion.

Motorola became quality conscious and smart the hard way: it lost market share to competitors. Other firms produced high quality and less expensive semiconductors, cellular phones, and pagers.

Motorola uses quality achievements as a centerpiece in achieving effectiveness. It is the core concept, but not the only one of importance. Motorola studies its customers and knows that quality is in the eye of the customer. To understand customers, Motorola has started to grade them. Those identified as the most demanding are then questioned in detail about their quality needs and expectations.

Motorola is also becoming a keen disciple of "robust quality," an idea proposed and implemented by Geni-chu Taguchi, a Japanese quality master. His credo is to create products so "robust" that they can withstand random fluctuations during manufacturing that might lead to defects. The MICROTAC foldable cellphone has only one-eighth the number of parts contained in its original 1978 portable telephone. Components snap together instead of being joined by screws or fasteners, and the company is trying to make its manufacturing variances more consistent on each component.

Taguchi was recruited by a research lab set up by General Douglas MacArthur in the postwar occupation to help fix Japan's chaotic phone system. He started developing and applying his "robust quality" approach to reduce the time and money wasted on hit-or-miss experiments. Taguchi has won four Deming awards. His "robust quality" principles have helped and improved such organizations as Hitachi, NEC, Toshiba, and Ford.

Another area Motorola is working on in order to stay ahead is attacking product cycles by shortening them. The firm strives to get quality right the first time, the logic being that, if a product is on the shelves for only six months, there is no time to correct defects discovered by customers. This spawns a second challenge, which is the transfer of knowledge. Motorola works at transferring what is learned about quality from old tasks (i.e., making last year's cellphone model) to new tasks (i.e., making this year's model).

Another requirement at Motorola is that responsibility for quality is pushed down the hierarchy. The firm spends over $30 million annually training employees to meet quality targets. The firm also insists that each of its 10,000 suppliers meet quality targets or lose the business.

Source: Adapted from "Future Perfect," *The Economist,* January 4, 1992, p. 61; "Dueling Pioneers," *Business Week,* October 25, 1991, p. 17; and "A Design Master's End Run around Trial and Error," *Business Week,* October 25, 1991, p. 24.

Today the Japanese, Europeans, Americans, and others who want to compete on the international level have learned a lot about Deming's, Juran's, and other quality improvement methods. Managers have learned that simply paying lip service to quality and what it means is not enough. If managers are to be effective over the short and long run, they must translate quality improvement into results: more satisfied customers, a more involved workforce, better designed products, and more creative approaches to solving problems. Competition is sparking a long overdue concern about quality. In many organizations, quality is now the top priority in the short, intermediate, and long run.[22]

Production

As used here, **production** reflects the ability of the organization to produce the quantity of output that the environment demands. The concept excludes any consideration of efficiency, which is defined below. The measures of production include profit, sales, market share, students graduated, patients released, documents processed, clients served, and the like. These measures relate directly to the output consumed by the organization's customers and clients.

Efficiency

Efficiency is defined as the ratio of outputs to inputs. This short-run criterion focuses attention on the entire input-process-output cycle, yet it emphasizes the input and process elements. Among the measures of efficiency are rate of return on capital or assets, unit cost, scrappage and waste, downtime, occupancy rates, and cost per patient, per student, or per client. Measures of efficiency inevitably must be in ratio terms; the ratios of benefit to cost or to time are the general forms of these measures.

Satisfaction

The idea of the organization as a social system requires that some consideration be given to the benefits received by its participants as well as by its customers and clients. **Satisfaction** and *morale* are similar terms referring to the extent to which the organization meets the needs of employees. We use the term *satisfaction* to refer to this criterion. Measures of satisfaction include employee attitudes, turnover, absenteeism, tardiness, and grievances.

Adaptiveness

Adaptiveness is the extent to which the organization can and does respond to internal and external changes. Adaptiveness in this context refers to management's ability to sense changes in the environment as well as changes within the organization itself. Ineffectiveness in achieving production, efficiency, and satisfaction can signal the need to adapt managerial practices and policies. Or the environment may demand different outputs or provide different inputs, thus necessitating change. To the extent that the organization cannot or does not adapt, its survival is jeopardized.

[22]Thomas H. Berry, "Managing the Total Quality Transformation" (New York: McGraw-Hill, 1991), p. 2.

How can you really know whether the organization is effectively adaptive?

There are short-run measures of effectiveness, but there are no specific and concrete measures of adaptiveness. Management can implement policies that encourage a sense of readiness for change, and certain managerial practices, if implemented, facilitate adaptiveness. For example, managers can invest in employee-training programs and career counseling. They can encourage and reward innovation and risk-taking behavior. Yet, when the time comes for an adaptive response, the organization either adapts or it does not adapt—and that is the ultimate measure.

Development

This criterion measures the ability of the organization to increase its capacity to deal with environmental demands. An organization must invest in itself to increase its chances of survival in the long run. The usual **development** efforts are training programs for managerial and nonmanagerial personnel. More recently the range of organizational development has expanded to include a number of psychological and sociological approaches.

Time considerations enable you to evaluate effectiveness in the short, intermediate, and long run. For example, you could evaluate a particular organization as effective in terms of production, satisfaction, and efficiency criteria but as ineffective in terms of adaptiveness and development. A manufacturer of buggy whips may be optimally effective because it can produce buggy whips better and faster than any other producer in the short run but still have little chance of survival because no one wants to buy its products. Thus, maintaining optimal balance means, in part, balancing the organization's performance over time.

The time dimensions model of effectiveness enables us to understand the work of managers in organizations. The basic job of managers is to identify and influence the causes of individual, group, and organizational effectiveness in the short, intermediate, and long run. Let us examine the nature of managerial work in that light.

MANAGEMENT FUNCTIONS AND EFFECTIVENESS

Whether the focus is on a Fortune 500 firm such as Procter & Gamble, on Quad Graphics, a fast-growing Pewaukee, Wisconsin, firm, or on a small Oakland, California, based ice cream company, Dreyer's Grand Ice Cream, Inc., two factors are important—understanding people and managing effectively.[23] People in any organization want to be treated as more than just faceless employees. Douglas McGregor informed the public about the importance of recognizing people decades ago. People want attention and recognition. Federal Express has a rule that

---

[23]H. John Storey, *Inside America's Fastest Growing Companies* (New York: John Wiley & Sons, 1989), pp. 135–36.

managers will not sit idly at their desks. They must, as Peters and Waterman encourage, walk around, talk to employees, and above all else, listen to what people are saying.

There are four basic types of organizations, large, medium, and small, in which people work and managers practice the art and science of management. Procter & Gamble is a large firm, while Dreyer's Grand Ice Cream is a small firm. They both are private for-profit firms that must use and efficiently manage their employee talents to earn a profit. The size of these two firms as well as the markets in which they conduct business are significantly different. Myron Fottler has provided a framework as displayed in Exhibit 2-4 for considering how management is practiced similarly and differently across organizations.[24] His framework identified four categories:

1. Private for-profit—business firms dependent on the market environment (Procter & Gamble, Quad Graphics, Dreyer's Grand Ice Cream, Inc.)
2. Private nonprofit—organizations dependent on public contributions and/or government grants to operate (St. Mark's Episcopal Church, Notre Dame University)
3. Private quasi-public—organizations created by legislatures to provide goods and services (New York Water District 873, South Texas Power Station in Bay City)
4. Public—government agency (Internal Revenue Service, Department of Education)

In each of these four types of organizations, managers are faced with environmental constraints; legal requirements; customer, client, or public demands; and resource needs. Consequently, how to manage demands, resources, environmental changes, and people effectively may differ. Even within each category managing people differs. For example, at Procter & Gamble the huge size of operations requires specific control systems and rigid reporting relationships for workers and managers. However, Dreyer's Ice Cream has less control and little adherence to structure. This looser atmosphere at Dreyer's is highlighted by such activities as an "all-you-can-eat" ice cream break every Wednesday afternoon.[25]

Managing people effectively in any of the four types of organizations involves the application of the planning, organizing, leading, and controlling functions of management. These functions are portrayed in Exhibit 2-4. The managerial responses to macro and micro environmental factors will be unique for the particular organization. However, exactly how planning or leading is done is largely determined by the type of organization and environment in which the manager must operate to survive.

[24]Myron D. Fottler, "Is Management Really Generic?" *Academy of Management Review,* January 1981, pp. 1–12.

[25]Storey, *Inside America's Fastest Growing Companies,* p. 136.

EXHIBIT 2-4

Organization Types, Environmental Dependencies, and Management Response

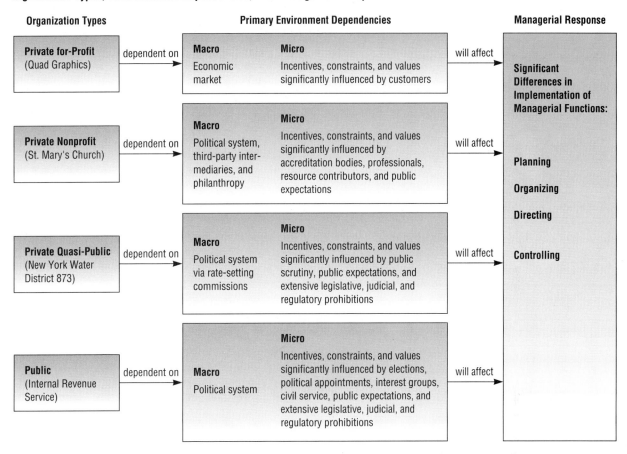

Source: Myron D. Fottler, "Is Management Really Generic?" *Academy of Management Review,* January 1981, p. 4.

Management is defined as a process, a series of actions, activities, or operations that lead to some end. The concept of management developed here is based on the assumption that the necessity for managing arises whenever work is specialized and is undertaken by two or more persons. Under such circumstances, the specialized work must be coordinated, and this creates the necessity for performing managerial work. The nature of managerial work in any organization, then, is to coordinate the work of others by performing four management functions: planning, organizing, leading, and controlling. In each case, the desired outcome of the function is to improve work performance.

Planning Effective Performance

The planning function includes defining the ends to be achieved and determining appropriate means to achieve the defined ends. Planning activities can be complex or simple, implicit or explicit, impersonal or personal. For example, the sales manager who is forecasting the demand for the firm's major product may rely on complex econometric models or on casual conversations with salespersons in the field. The intended outcomes of planning activities are mutual understandings about what the members of the organization should be attempting to achieve. These understandings may be reflected in the form of complicated plans that specify the intended results, or they may be reflected in a general agreement among the members.

Discussions of planning often are hampered by the absence of definitions of such terms as *mission, goal,* and *objective.* In some instances, the terms are used interchangeably, particularly *goal* and *objective.* In other instances, the terms are defined specifically, but there is no general agreement over the definitions. Depending on their backgrounds and purposes, managers and authors use the terms differently. However, the pivotal position of planning as a management function requires us to make very explicit the meanings of these key concepts.

Mission

Society expects organizations to serve specific purposes. These purposes are the missions of organizations. **Missions** are criteria for assessing the long-run effectiveness of an organization. Effective managers state the mission of their organization in terms of those conditions that, if realized, will assure the organization's survival. Statements of mission are found in laws, articles of incorporation, and in other extraorganizational sources. Mission statements are broad, abstract, and value-laden and thus are subject to various interpretations. For example, the mission of a state public health department—as expressed in the law that created it—mandates the agency to "protect and promote the health and welfare of the citizens of the Commonwealth." It is from this source that the organization will create its specific programs.

Goals

Goals are future states or conditions that contribute to the fulfillment of the organization's mission. A goal is somewhat more concrete and specific than a mission. Goals can be stated in terms of production, efficiency, and satisfaction. For example, one goal of a public health agency could be stated as "the eradication of measles as a health hazard by the end of 1993." In a business setting, a goal might be "to have viable sales outlets established in every major population center of the country by the end of 1994." It is entirely possible for an organization to have multiple goals that contribute to its mission. For example, a hospital may pursue patient care, research, and training. Universities typically state three significant goals: teaching, research, and community service. The existence of multiple goals places great pressure on managers not only to coordinate the routine operations of the units that strive for these goals but also to plan and allocate scarce resources to the goals.

Objectives

Objectives refer to statements of accomplishment that are to be achieved in the short run, usually one year. The public health agency's objective can be stated as "to reduce the incidence of measles from 6 per 10,000 to 4 per 10,000 by the end of the current year." The firm seeking to have sales outlets in all major population centers could state its current year's objective as "to have opened and begun operations in Chicago, Los Angeles, Louisville, and New York." Thus, goals are derived from the organization's mission, and objectives are derived from the goals.

A coherent set of missions, goals, and objectives defines the scope and direction of the organization's activities. Planning involves specifying not only where the organization is going, but also how it is to get there. Alternatives must be analyzed and evaluated in terms of criteria that follow from the mission, goals, and objectives. Thus, managers by their own decisions can affect how they and their organizations will be evaluated. Managers determine what ends are legitimate and, therefore, what criteria are relevant. And once the determination of appropriate means has been completed, the next managerial function—organizing—must be undertaken.

Organizing Effective Performance

The organizing function includes all managerial activities that are taken to translate the required planned activities into a structure of tasks and authority. In a practical sense, the organizing function involves specific activities.

Defining the Nature and Content of Each Job in the Organization

The tangible results of this activity are job specifications, position descriptions, or task definitions. These indicate what is expected of jobholders in terms of responsibilities, outcomes, and objectives. In turn, the skills, abilities, and training required to meet the defined expectations are also specified.

Determining the Bases for Grouping Jobs Together

The essence of defining jobs is specialization, that is, dividing the work. But once the overall task has been subdivided into jobs, the jobs must be put into groups, or departments. The managerial decision involves selecting the appropriate bases. For example, all of the jobs that require similar machinery may be grouped together, or the manager may decide to group all of the jobs according to the product or service they produce.

Deciding the Size of the Group

The purpose of grouping jobs is to enable a person to supervise the group's activities. Obviously, there is a limit to the number of jobs that one person can supervise, but the precise number will vary depending on the situation. For example, it is possible to supervise more jobs that are similar and simple than jobs that are dissimilar and complex. The supervisor of hourly workers can manage up to 25 or 30 employees, but the director of research scientists can manage far fewer, perhaps only 8 to 10.

Delegating Authority to the Assigned Manager

The preceding activities create groups of jobs with defined tasks. It then becomes necessary to determine the extent to which managers of the groups are allowed to make decisions and use the resources of the group without higher approval. This is **authority**.

Once the structure of task and authority is in place, it must be given life. People perform jobs, and management must recruit and select the appropriate individual who will perform the jobs. The process of finding and placing people in jobs is termed *staffing*. In some large organizations, specialized units such as personnel perform staffing activities. An important cause of individual effectiveness is a good fit between job requirements and individual abilities. Thus, even when staffing is performed by a specialized unit, the activity remains an important management responsibility.

The interrelationships between planning and organizing are apparent. The planning function results in the determination of organizational ends and means; that is, it defines the "whats" and "hows." The organizing function results in the determination of the "whos"; that is who will do what with whom to achieve the desired end results. The structure of tasks and authority should facilitate the fulfillment of planned results if the next management function, leading, is performed properly.

Leading Effective Performance

Leading involves the manager in close, day-to-day contact with individuals and groups. Thus, leading is uniquely personal and interpersonal. Even though planning and organizing provide guidelines and directives in the form of plans, job descriptions, organization charts, and policies, it is people who do the work. And people frequently are unpredictable. They have unique needs, aspirations, personalities, and attitudes. Thus, they each perceive the workplace and their jobs differently. Managers must take into account these unique perceptions and behaviors and somehow direct them toward common purposes.

Leading places the manager squarely in the arena of individual and group behavior. To function in this arena, the manager must have knowledge of individual differences and motivation, group behavior, power, and politics. In short, being a leader requires knowledge of ways to influence individuals and groups to accept and pursue organizational objectives, often at the expense of personal objectives.

Leading involves the day-to-day interactions between managers and their subordinates. In these interactions the full panorama of human behavior is evident: individuals work, play, communicate, compete, accept and reject others, join groups, leave groups, receive rewards, and cope with stress. Of all the management functions, leading is the one most humanly oriented.

Controlling Effective Performance

The controlling function includes activities that managers undertake to assure that actual outcomes are consistent with planned outcomes. Three basic conditions must exist to undertake control: standards, information, and corrective action.

Standards

Norms of acceptable outcomes, standards, must be spelled out. These standards reflect goals and objectives and usually are found in accounting, production, marketing, financial, and budgeting documents. In more specific ways standards are reflected in procedures, performance criteria, rules of conduct, professional ethics, and work rules. Standards therefore reflect desirable levels of achievement.

Interestingly, ethical standards in a world becoming more internationally connected can raise some dilemmas. Foreign companies have been using intelligence-gathering units for years to collect data on competitors. American businesses claim that they are losing competitive advantage because of foreign intelligence units. Encounter 2-3 poses some ethical questions about American standards versus foreign standards.

Information

Actual and planning outcomes must be compared using appropriate and reliable information. Many organizations have developed sophisticated information systems that provide managers with control data. Prime examples are standard cost accounting and quality control systems used extensively by modern manufacturing firms. In other instances the sources of information consist of nothing more than managers' observations of the behavior of people assigned to their departments.

Corrective Action

If actual outcomes are ineffective, managers must take corrective action. Without the ability to take corrective action, the controlling function has no point or purpose. Corrective action is made possible through the organizing function—if managers have been assigned the authority to take action.

Simply stated, managers undertake control to determine whether intended results are achieved and if not, why not. The conclusions managers reach because of their controlling activities are that the planning function is faulty or that the

ETHICS

E N C O U N T E R · 2-3

THE SPY BUSINESS IN BUSINESS

Foreign governments have teamed up with firms to gather data, statistics, and eavesdrop on competitors from other countries. There is also evidence that foreign intelligence services plant moles (spies or agents) in high-tech American firms. There is also evidence that American businesspeople have their briefcases examined and that information is collected when they travel to other countries.

The culprit list includes France, Japan, Germany, and Israel. American firms appear to be hurt in terms of performance and effectiveness by foreign spy machines. Is this fair, and should American firms be helped by U.S. spy agencies to return the favor? Foreign competitors do not play fair or by the rules. They steal what they can to help their firms succeed and survive.

If the government is not the place to seek intelligence help, then perhaps private firms should be used. Evidence shows that the Japanese, French, Russian, and Chinese government agencies have regularly passed along economic intelligence to business, placing American companies at a disadvantage.

What should American firms do? What would you do if you owned a small firm and foreign competitors were collecting data and spying on your business?

Source: Adapted from Karen Roebuck, "Companies Getting Smarter in Gathering of Intelligence Data," *The Houston Post,* January 5, 1992, pp. D1–D2; and Karen Roebuck, "Should U.S. Spy on Foreign Businesses?" *The Houston Post,* January 2, 1992, pp. D1–D2.

organizing function is faulty, or both. Controlling, then, is the completion of a logical sequence. The activities that controlling comprises include employee selection and placement, materials inspection, performance evaluation, financial statement analysis, and other well-recognized managerial techniques.

Describing management in terms of the four functions of planning, organizing, leading, and controlling is certainly not complete. Nothing in this description indicates the specific behaviors or activities associated with each function. Nor is there any recognition of the relative importance of these functions for overall organizational effectiveness. However, these four functions conveniently and adequately define management.

STUDYING ORGANIZATIONAL EFFECTIVENESS

The literature has revealed that the majority of organizational effectiveness studies have used quantitative research designs. Case studies, field studies, and occasionally field experiments have been used to analyze effectiveness.[26] On the

[26]Edward E. Lawler III, Alan M. Mohrman, Jr., Susan A. Mohrman, Gerald E. Ledford, Jr., and Thomas G. Cummings and Associates, *Doing Research That Is Useful for Theory and Practice* (San Francisco: Jossey-Bass, 1985).

other hand, qualitative research methods have been employed for the most part to study and learn about organizational culture. Using archival data, researching material artifacts, interpreting language, and using on-site participants to research stories and myths are popular qualitative procedures.[27] Appendix 2–A presents specific techniques that are used by researchers to study organizations. Even though years of research have been conducted, there are still many unanswered questions about behavior within organizational settings.

Practicing managers are still searching for answers about what to do or how to proceed so that effectiveness is the result. They also must learn about when and where to intervene to change and use culture to accomplish goals. The manager needs "road maps" that only reliable and valid research can help provide. The techniques provided in Appendix 2–A offer some general research guidelines for scientifically studying to understand effectiveness, culture, and other important variables.

Each reader of this book has already formed opinions about the behavior of people. It is common practice to watch the behaviors of others and to reach a conclusion about why a person behaved in a particular way. There is also a lot of guessing about what a person will do next. Hopefully, by studying, learning, and coming into contact with theory and research about organizational behavior, some of the guessing will be replaced by educated opinions, logic, and learning of principles. Guessing, hoping for the best, and casual approaches to explaining and predicting behavior in organizations are not sufficient in a world that has become economically competitive. Managers can't afford to rely on guesses. A statement made years ago captures the notion that behavior is not always some random event:

> *Behavior generally is predictable if we know how the person perceived the situation and what is important to him or her . . . An observer often sees behavior as nonrational because the observer does not have access to the same information or does not perceive the environment in the same way.*[28]

■ **E2–1**   Before going on to other chapters in the text, you may wish to complete Exercise 2–1 at the end of this chapter. The exercise will assess your initial view of organizational behavior, as well as your viewpoints about relevant topics. When you complete the course, complete the exercise again and see if your views have changed.

[27]J. Van Mannen, J. M. Dabbs, Jr., and R. R. Faulkner, eds., *Varieties of Qualitative Research* (Beverly Hills, Calif.: Sage Publications, 1982).

[28]E. E. Lawler III and J. G. Rhode, *Information and Control in Organizations* (Pacific Palisades, Calif.: Goodyear, 1976), p. 22.

SUMMARY OF KEY POINTS

- Quality definitions are abundant. We opted for a straightforward definition: Quality is meeting customers' needs and expectations. The perception of customers (e.g., patients, clients, or students) is the focal point of our definition. The technological aspects of a product or the elegance of providing a service are not included in our definition. Instead, needs and expectations being met is the key.

  The importance of quality is that it is the core concept that overarches any effectiveness criteria. Production in terms of quantity is important, but the quality of this output is more important. The crumbled Soviet Union found this out in that it produced large quantities of goods, but they were generally of low quality. The results of 70-plus years of this type of production thinking are still unfolding in what is now called the Commonwealth of Independent States (C.I.S.).

- The goal approach is based on the idea that organizations are rational, purposive entities that pursue specific missions, goals, and objectives. For example, how well Delta Airlines is performing—that is, how effective they are— is reviewed and analyzed in terms of how the mission, goals, and objectives are being accomplished in the short, intermediate, and long run.

- Managers do not generally walk around handing out behavioral science-type questionnaires or attitude surveys to determine satisfaction. They do, however, engage in observation, listening, and talking with employees. Attempting to acquire insight about attitudes, feelings, and emotions coupled with examining records of absenteeism, tardiness, accident rates, turnover, and grievances

  provides managers with a general picture of the degree and type of satisfaction among workers.

- The mission statement is considered a long-term guide-post to measure effectiveness. The mission is usually worded, presented, and implemented with the intention of enhancing the survival probability of the firm. One problem with instilling this kind of orientation is that writing an inspiring and meaningful mission statement is difficult. The state public health department mission statement is clear, but is it inspiring?

- A plan hopefully provides a map to "what" and "how" the organization is to proceed. The organizing function provides a guide to "who" will do the jobs to accomplish the plans. Planning initiates a call, a signal that individuals must be assembled, instructed, and provided with resources to achieve the mission, goals, and objectives of the institution.

- The text will attempt to convince you that intuition is practiced by everyone, but, in terms of dealing with the behavior of employees, it is better to learn more on a systematic approach. One systematic approach starts with thinking about the effectiveness criteria of an organization. What are they and how do we accomplish them? We are firm advocates of the fact that managing people is an art. However, knowing what the literature has to say, what other managers have learned, and how people interact in organizations has a scientific basis. The educated man or woman who will manage others in the future needs a lot of intuition, but he or she also needs to use any scientifically-derived hints, pointers, or principles that are available.

REVIEW AND DISCUSSION QUESTIONS

1. Why is perception such an important factor when the quality of a product or of a service is being considered?

2. Why are mission statements so difficult to compose and put down in writing?

3. There have been many success stories reported in literature about how someone achieved business, career, or personal goals by using intuition. Is there any place for the systematic study of achieving success as a man-

ager in an organization such as Quad Graphics (Exhibit 2-4)?

4. What are the main differences in taking a goal or a systems approach when interpreting organizational effectiveness?

5. What would be some of the potential negative consequences for a person who does not plan for his/her career?

6. Can a manager ever conclude that she has accurately measured and knows the job satisfaction of her 15 employees? Explain.

7. How would you determine whether a large public hospital in your city (community or regional) is effective?

8. "People are paid to be productive, not to be satisfied." Do you agree with this statement? What are its implications in terms of achieving organizational effectiveness?

9. Why is quality considered such an important, overarching concept throughout the industrialized world?

10. Today in the fast-paced, globalizing environment, it is important for an organization of any size to be adaptive. What does this mean now to a firm like General Motors, who, in 1991, experienced a 12 percent reduction in new car sales in the United States?

●

READINGS

READING 2–1   TEACHING THE WORK OF MANAGEMENT

Peter F. Drucker

A very old story tells of Phidias, the sculptor who created some 2400 years ago the statues that grace the roof of Athens's Parthenon. When he presented his bill, the Athenian Accounting Office—staffed, of course, by bright young MBAs trained in quantitative analysis—refused to pay. "You are charging for carving the statues in the full, even though they stand on the roof where no one sees their backsides," they argued. "You are wrong," Phidias wrote back. "The gods see them."

I am quite sure that Phidias lost that argument. Accountants always win the first round. But Phidias was right, of course. He was right because *workmanship counts*. Mediocrity will never become genius through conscientiousness. But it can beome effective. And genius without conscientiousness and workmanship soon degenerates into something well below mediocrity: It becomes cheating and fakery. Few tasks in any discipline require genius, but all require conscientiousness.

No century before ours, at least not in Western history, has had a large number of powerful, charismatic leaders. But since the declining years of the Roman Republic, there has been no century with more clamor for "leadership," more talk of "charisma," more shameless deification of mere mortals.

But if civilization—both in its material and in its aesthetic aspects—has survived this century full of world wars, concentration camps, torture, holocausts, and mass murder of millions in the name of "scientific theory" and "progress," it is not because of these great charismatic leaders, but despite them. Civilization has not flourished because of Stalin, Hitler, and Mao—and no more charismatic triad has been known in history. Civilization has been preserved by ordinary, uncharismatic people who kept on doing ordinary uncharismatic tasks—making and selling things, healing the sick, teaching students, preaching sermons—and doing them conscientiously. Every time a great, charismatic leader has finished turning the world into a charnel house, they have resumed their humdrum tasks. Unheroically, again and again, they "saved the sum

of things for pay," (as A. E. Houseman said of the expeditionary force of World War I).

Therefore, the greatest advances in human competence and human knowledge—whether in medicine or in technology, in science or in management—lay in developing the tools of workmanship, the tools that enable common people to do uncommon things.

WORKMANSHIP AS EXCELLENCE

Developing those tools is, I believe, the true aim of education, and especially of professional education, of education for responsible leadership. Of course, this is nothing new—it has been preached by all the truly wise men, by Socrates and Confucius and the Buddha. But we are prone, both in academia and in management, to forget it, and to mistake the surface gloss of brilliance for the essence of performance.

It is so easy to fall for sophistry—to mistake clever techniques for understanding, footnotes for scholarship, and fashions for truth—that it is doubly important to remind ourselves of the wisdom of Phidias, to remember that "the gods see it." This approach to workmanship is the only true definition of the much-abused term *excellence*.

The word *workmanship* refers to work, of course. To apply it to management therefore implies that managing is work. This belief is common today. But while I was by no means the first person to call managing "work" (that honor belongs to Henry Fayol, a Frenchman who published during World War I), the idea was still novel, and indeed almost heretical, when I first asserted it in the 40s. Management had been seen as rank, as power, as income, rather than as work. But only if managing is seen as work can we have a discipline of management.

Managing is, however, highly specific work. It is the work needed in and by the new phenomenon of this century, the organized "institution." By definition, management is carried out in—and only in—an institution. And by definition its concern is the institution and its performance. This all sounds obvious, if not trite. But it has profound implications that were by no means understood—or even anticipated—when we began and that are

Source: *New Management*, Winter 1988, pp. 2–5.

still not widely understood, let alone accepted. One implication concerns the scope of management; another, the nature of management, or what you might call the paradox of management.

MANAGEMENT IS MORE THAN BUSINESS

Most people hear "business management" when anyone says "management." Typically, management is taught in business schools, and the degree given is not in management but in business administration. But it was an historical accident that we started the study of management with business management and that, 40 years ago, we lodged the teaching of management in business schools.

Now we know that management is a generic function: the governance of the modern institution, or to put it more precisely, the governance of any institution in modern pluralist society. Now we are as much concerned with the management of the hospital, of the university, of the city, of the labor union, of the large Protestant congregation, of the Air Force, of the Catholic Diocese, of the symphony orchestra, of the not-for-profit, voluntary community service as we are with the management of a business. Each of these institutions needs to be managed just as much as the business enterprise.

We also know that the problems all of these institutions face are in large measure the same problems. They include matching people and jobs, motivating people, communication, the definition of mission, purpose, goals, and results, the function and structure of top management, the succession to it, the organization's social responsibilities. They equally include planning, budgeting, cash flow, and marketing.

We also know that the nonbusiness institutions are going to be increasingly important for the study and understanding of management. As the business organization is restructuring itself around knowledge and information, it will increasingly come to resemble nonbusiness—the hospital, the university, the symphony, or the opera—rather than the manufacturing company of 1920, in which there were a few generalists called managers and a great many unskilled and unknowing "hands" doing as they were told.

Nevertheless, society—and most especially the nonbusiness organizations themselves—expect, even demand, that management and its teaching be grounded in the experience of business management. The Protestant pastor who participated in a recent seminar of mine for CEOs of large and rapidly growing institutions had no difficulty applying the lessons of a business case to the problem of becoming an effective CEO of a large and rapidly growing suburban church. The vicar-general of a large Catholic diocese, another participant in this same seminar, had no difficulty applying the lessons of a business case to thinking through his priorities in allocating scarce resources of people and money.

The head of a nationwide charitable organization, another nonbusiness member of this same seminar, had no difficulty in translating business experience with kindling and quenching motivation to her own situation in which she had to attract and manage large numbers of volunteers. But the business people in the seminar found it very difficult indeed to translate into meaningful business language what these nonbusiness executives told them.

You may think this is an American phenomenon that signifies the American "business culture." But things are no different in the rest of the world—in Germany, in France, in Brazil, or in Japan. Business management, for better and worse, is seen as the archetype of modern management and as the locus for the paradigms, the principles, the policies, and the techniques to make *all* our social institutions effective and productive, and with them, modern society altogether.

I don't pretend to understand this. But it is fact. And it entails great responsibilities for those of us who teach management. We must never forget that our impact goes far beyond the fairly small and confined social sector that is "business." It even goes beyond the "private sector." We are expected to develop, to teach, and to exemplify the values, the methods, and the tools for *all* leadership groups in our society of organizations.

This is also a tremendous opportunity. As far as "business management" goes, the present schools are probably at their peak, or perhaps past it. To grow from now on, we will have to be able to reach and to satisfy the even larger but still largely untapped market of the nonbusiness organizations of society, preparing their future leaders, offering continuing education and self-development to their present leaders, and developing and disseminating the management tools they need.

MANAGEMENT AS PRACTICE

Finally, the paradox of management: Management is both *techne*—that is, empirical skills and indeed often almost a bag of tricks and rules of thumb—and, in itself, a liberal art.

Management is a practice. There is always a specific job to be done. There is always the unique management challenge of balancing results today and results tomorrow. There is, of course, more than one "bottom line." And the one commonly stressed, net profit over a short period, is of all the "bottom lines" the least reliable and the most easily manipulated.

Still, what counts in management, as in every practice, is performance and results. And what every practitioner in every practice including management therefore needs first are skills, a good many of them quite mundane, whether taking a patient's pulse or doing cash-flow analysis. Any school of management, exactly like any school of law, any school of engineering, any school of medicine, must be close to practice and practitioner. Both its teachers and its students need to get their hands dirty. They must have the "feel" for the practice that comes only with actual experience. They are, to be sure, concerned with knowledge. But there is no knowledge in a practice unless it has utility.

The work that comes out of even the most abstract mathematical model of a business strategy is always work that must be done by people. Thus, management is of necessity based on, and applies, all the liberal arts, all the humanities, and all the social sciences.

To an old liberal-arts man like me, the emergence of management creates a new horizon for the liberal arts. They were—and they still are—in danger of being seen as luxuries and ornaments, praiseworthy precisely because they have no function. Indeed, 50 years ago, in the Great Books movement, there was high pressure promotion of the liberal arts as being untainted by anything as sordid as utility and relevance, to be worshipped precisely because everyone of the exemplars was safely dead.

In management, however, the liberal arts again become what they have always been when they flourished: kinetic energy and guide to action.

MANAGEMENT AS LIBERAL ART

We do not know yet precisely how to link the liberal arts and management. We do not know yet what impact this linkage will have on either party—and marriages, even bad ones, always change both partners. We do know that the liberal arts must be an organic part in the teaching of management.

More than that, management is by itself a liberal art. It *has* to be. It cannot be techne alone. It cannot be concerned solely with results and performance.

Management always lives, works, and practices in and for an institution, which is a human community held together by the bond that, next to the tie of family, is the most powerful human bond: the work bond. And precisely because the object of management is a human community held together by the work bond for a common purpose, management always deals with the Nature of Man, and (as all of us with any practical experience learned) with Good and Evil as well. I have learned more theology as a practicing management consultant than I did when I taught religion.

That means there have to be values, commitment, convictions in management—even passion. Without them, there will be no performance and no results. Indeed, since management deals with people and not with things, management without values, commitments, convictions, can only do harm.

What characterized the West—the spirit, the embodiment of which is the university—rests on one sentence written 750 years ago by one of the greatest theologians and philosophers of Western tradition. Fighting the fundamentalists of his own day (and incidentally of his own Franciscan Order), who wanted to ban all secular learning and everything but the study of the Bible, St. Bonaventure wrote, paraphrasing the Epistle of St. James, "All knowledge leads back to the Source of All Light and to the Knowledge of Ultimate Truth."

I must admit that I am not quite sure how cost accounting, or the study of tax loopholes, or brand marketing, will lead back to the Source of All Light, let alone to the knowledge of Ultimate Truth. But I am quite sure that the spirit of St. Bonaventure's short sentence must animate all we do if management is to have results.

READING 2–2   WINS OF CHANGE

Ellen Freeman Roth

If an award were handed out to the country that hands out the greatest number of frivolous awards, the United States would certainly be a shoo-in to win. The assorted industries that produce trophies, plaques, and loving cups are presumably doing very well indeed. But now and then an award comes along that serves a real purpose, and the Malcolm Baldrige National Quality Award clearly fits that bill.

Named for the late Commerce Secretary Malcolm Baldrige, the award was established by Congress in 1987 to recognize U.S. companies that practice and promote quality. Administration of the program is handled by the American Society for Quality Control. The Foundation for the Malcolm Baldrige National Quality Award pays most of the costs with privately contributed funds. The remainder is covered by applicants' fees.

Firms applying for the award must undergo a rigorous evaluation by an independent board of examiners composed of private and public sector experts in quality, and the examination includes on-site visits for those passing the second of four screenings. A maximum of two awards is given annually in each of three categories: manufacturers, small businesses, and service companies. Winners are required to promote the award, disseminate information on their own quality programs, and share the approach they take on total quality management.

The award has taken some heat lately, with critics arguing that the pursuit of the award requires too much time, effort, and expense. But the general consensus seems to be that the application process, whether it produces a trophy or not, can be most instructive. Filling out the demanding 32-part application typically requires companies to ask tough questions of themselves, reevaluate their strengths and weaknesses, and then seek to implement improvements. The application can also serve as a useful working tool for those companies that don't actually apply for the award.

Out of the tens of thousands of companies that have requested the guidelines for applications, a mere 309 have actually applied, and only 9 have won. A score of 1,000 is conceivable, but very few firms have topped 750. Last year only 21.7 percent scored above 600, with close to half falling in the 401–600 range.

"The criteria are becoming more stringent each year as we continue to apply the lessons learned from past winners," explains Curt W. Reimann, director of the Baldrige program at the National Institute of Standards and Technology. "For instance, we want companies to be more specific in reporting and analyzing the results of quality efforts. Our purpose is not just to reward, but to *define*, quality."

The profiles of the nine winners of the Baldrige Award that follow will, we hope, help illuminate this continuing quest for a definition of quality.

Motorola, Inc. *(1988, manufacturing category), a Schaumburg, Ill.-based manufacturer of electronic equipment, systems, and components for U.S. and international markets.*

Motorolans are out to disprove the old saying "Nobody's perfect," and they're getting closer every day. They expect that by 1992, their company will achieve 99.9999997 percent perfect quality. Pretty impressive, especially considering that 12 years ago an executive who ran the firm's best division announced to 75 executives and managers, "Our quality levels really stink."

When then-chairman and CEO Robert W. Galvin witnessed the high quality performance in Japanese factories—and saw the payoff as Japanese competitors captured U.S. markets for pagers and cellular phones—he asked one Motorola division to focus on improving quality. Early in 1987 he instituted that group's proposed six sigma program—just 3.4 defects per million parts or, as Motorola calls them, opportunities for error—throughout the organization.

Now Motorola's goal of six sigma in all divisions by 1992 seems to be a holy grail among Motorolans. So far, the five-year plan is right on schedule. The company achieved a tenfold improvement by 1989 and expects to reach a hundredfold improvement by the end of this year. Defects are down more than 99 percent from nearly 6,000 per million opportunities for error in 1986. "We've saved $550 million in manufacturing costs in 1990 and some $1.5 billion over four years since starting our thrust for six sigma," says Richard C. Buetow, senior vice president and Motorola director of quality.

Such success requires tightly controlling every operation—"so you don't produce defects that need to be re-

Source: Ellen Freeman Roth, "Wins of Change," *World—The Magazine for Decision Makers*, No. 2, 1991, pp. 10–18.

paired," notes Buetow. "You need to rethink the process, starting from scratch. Then you set a goal for each part of the process and stick as close to it as possible." And that involves measuring everything, from defects in manufacturing to grammatical errors in marketing brochures.

Those concepts have also helped Motorola achieve its second initiative: reducing cycle time. For instance, Motorola completely changed the way it makes cellular telephones. Its new Micro-TAC phone has one-third fewer components than an earlier model. In addition, the company developed a short-cycle factory using just-in-time manufacturing to produce the phone and eliminated sample testing of parts through cooperation with suppliers. As a result, total cycle time was reduced thirtyfold and reliability improved tenfold. Motorola cellular phones now hold at least 30 percent of the world market.

"Short-cycle manufacturing isn't a new concept," notes George M. C. Fisher, Motorola's chairman and CEO. "It's back-to-basics manufacturing. Sixty years ago, Henry Ford could turn iron ore into a finished car in less than 48 hours."

Getting back to basics is also at the heart of another initiative in Motorola's quality program: education. Every year, the company spends some $60 million on employee education, and every employee receives 40 hours of training in a job-related area.

Motorola's intensive efforts are now legend. But statistics and strategy aside, quality still comes down to individual commitment, notes Galvin, now chairman of the executive committee. "It's a very personal obligation. If you can't talk with humility about quality, then you have not moved to the level of involvement that is absolutely essential."

Westinghouse Electric Corporation, Commercial Nuclear Fuel Division *(1988, manufacturing category), a Pittsburgh, Pa.-based maker and supplier of nuclear fuel assemblies and components.*

In 1980 foreign competition was forcing the Westinghouse Electric Corporation to make dramatic changes. "Our state of mind," says John H. Fooks, vice president, corporate productivity and quality at Westinghouse, "could be summed up by Samuel Johnson's eighteenth century remark, 'Nothing concentrates a man's mind so wonderfully as the prospect of being hanged in the morning.' "

Top management took a firsthand look at how its Japanese licensees and other firms were improving their product quality. "It was like visiting another planet," says Westinghouse chairman and CEO Paul E. Lego. "The idea of

no workplace inventory was a radical concept then. But we knew we couldn't just copy the Japanese. We had a to create our own culture."

In 1980 Westinghouse formed the Productivity and Quality Center (PQC) to lead the charge. Initially the center trained quality circle leaders and taught value analysis and other tools to boost office and factory efficiency. But realizing that those techniques had only localized influence, the company began to more closely examine processes rather than problems. After Westinghouse applied a time-based methodology in 1982 to improve factory operations, inventory dropped from 24 percent of sales to 15 percent in 1990, a savings of some $920 million. Those techniques also enabled the Commercial Nuclear Fuel Division to improve product reliability from 99.95 percent in 1982 to 99.9995 percent in 1991.

After seeing results in manufacturing, Westinghouse began to focus on quality performance in all operations. The PQC developed a method to continuously monitor 12 key quality areas—called conditions of excellence—from product performance to customer satisfaction. Each condition is measured and reported using graphs that show monthly actual and targeted performance. These graphs provide a running score sheet for all Westinghouse operations.

The PQC also answers requests from business units throughout the company to conduct total quality fitness reviews. Reviews are based on 12 criteria relating to the customer, human resources, product and process initiatives, and management leadership. In a review, a team of senior managers from other Westinghouse units, led by a PQC consultant, interviews a cross-section of employees from the unit and surveys customers, probing performance and results in the 12 key areas. At the end of the week-long process, the business unit manager—but not the manager's boss—is given a scorecard, an analysis of strengths and weaknesses, and recommendations for improving quality. PQC staff also provide continuing advice and measure performance improvement results. The center has led more than 450 reviews over the decade, from the CEO's office to the factory floor.

Most teams are multifunctional, composed of employees from finance to engineering, sometimes representing various sites. For instance, the Commercial Nuclear Fuel Division, with some 2,200 employees, has had up to 75 percent involvement in quality teams.

"Employee participation is essential," notes Fooks. "Our basic rule of thumb is: People whose behavior must change should be involved in planning as well as implementing change. The other critical ingredient is recognition of performance—it builds momentum, keeping the whole process moving." Westinghouse has a complex structure of awards for both individual and team performance.

Westinghouse has clearly gained momentum. Since the Commercial Nuclear Fuel Division won the Baldrige Award in 1988, two other units have been finalists. Corporate operating profits has more than doubled, from 5 percent in 1985 to more than 11 percent in 1990. And management is confident the company will reach the 15 percent operating profit level targeted by CEO Lego.

Globe Metallurgical Inc. *(1988, small business category), a privately held Cleveland-based manufacturer of silicon metal for the chemical and aluminum industries and iron-based metals for the foundry industry.*

Globe Metallurgical Inc. saw many competitors in the nation's smokestack industries go up in smoke in the early 1980s. Refusing to lose its legacy to cheap, imported, commodity-grade metals, Globe initiated a quality, efficiency, and cost (QEC) campaign in 1985 to become the lowest cost, highest quality producer of ferroalloys and silicon metal in the United States.

Within a year, QEC goals, from strategic planning to manufacturing, were integrated throughout the company. In manufacturing, the QEC program is built on careful monitoring and evaluation of all processes through statistical process control. All 260 employees at three locations are trained in this process. Using computer-controlled systems that provide constant feedback about whether targets for processing variables are being met, workers monitor and quantify such factors as the chemical and physical characteristics of the product.

Statistical evaluation, known as failure mode effects analysis, helps identify steps in the production process that are prone to failure. If a customer wants no chromium in its product, for instance, Globe analyzes the probability of chromium contamination. Evaluation is based on risk priority numbers and assesses such factors as how serious a failure might occur, its probability of occurrence, and the ability to detect such a failure before the process is under way. A QEC committee meets daily to review the previous day's performance and assess measures to correct fluctuations in quality. "We establish controls that are much stricter than what the customer requires," says James C. Cline, Globe quality manager.

Color control charts produced by a computer system developed by Globe detail every key characteristic of each product. The charts not only give employees a process performance appraisal, but also help customers understand Globe's manufacturing process. For instance, after conducting a two-year analysis of Globe's process and product improvement, one major customer stopped analyzing Globe's shipments. "Many of our customers don't check the quality of our products anymore," says Arden C. Sims, Globe president and CEO. "They know from their audits that our product is consistent.

"We've reached that level because we consider each downstream manufacturing process a customer of the previous process," adds Sims, "and we try to satisfy all our internal as well as external customers."

Through these measures, Globe has virtually eliminated out-of-specification shipments. Improved consistency of manufacturing operations has increased production and reduced energy consumption, a big cost savings for Globe. As a result of quality improvements and waste reduction, Globe cut costs by $17 million—or 15 percent of sales revenue—from 1986 to 1990. And the company expects $4 million in savings this year. "For every dollar we've spent on quality, we've gotten a return of $40," says Sims.

At the same time that it launched QEC, Globe shifted its focus from commodity markets such as steel manufacturing to higher value-added markets in the foundry, chemical, and aluminum industries, including manufacturers of safety items for the automotive industry and producers of therapeutic body implants for the medical industry. By improving quality and targeting market segments that demand superior product consistency, Globe has seen a "phenomenal increase in annual sales," according to Cline. "We've reached U.S. and foreign markets we hadn't even touched in 1985."

Milliken & Company *(1989, manufacturing category), a privately owned textile manufacturer headquartered in Spartanburg, S.C.*

"There are three obstacles to implementing a successful quality improvement process," notes Roger Milliken, chairman and CEO of Milliken & Company. "They are top management, middle management, and first-line management."

It's no surprise, then, that one of the company's first moves to weave quality into its processes was to flatten the management structure. Milliken has retrained almost 700 milddle managers as process improvement specialists since 1981. Reassigned production managers have helped cut costs company-wide—by, for one, helping reduce the company's off-quality goods by 52 percent.

Milliken began its restructuring in 1981 as part of an organization-wide Pursuit of Excellence program that makes commitment to customer service the focus of all operations. Company management developed this initiative after seeing Japanese competitors achieve higher productivity and quality with older and less technology than that in U.S. firms. And Pursuit of Excellence has reshaped Milliken, especially in the area of human resources.

Employees throughout the company, who are known as associates, were reorganized into autonomous self-managed teams. Production work teams undertake training, schedule work, and establish individual performance objectives—and any associate who finds safety hazards or deviations in the quality of products or processes may halt production. Upwards of 4,000 corrective action teams address specific manufacturing or other internal business problems and have improved customer service and cycle time. More than 300 supplier action teams help improve company relationships with suppliers. And some 300 customer action teams address customer needs, including new product development.

The team-driven structure is supported by a range of programs such as cross-training (Milliken annually spends about $1,300 in training per employee) and weekly and even daily rotations. Job descriptions and pay rates were condensed from 19 to 4. Team incentives replaced individual ones—a departure from the textile industry's reliance on piece rates. Not everyone favored changing the reward system: Some plant managers feared that without individual incentives, factories would decrease productivity. But strong results quickly allayed such concerns. One plant increased efficiency from 84 percent to 92 percent within five weeks.

Another tool that promotes employee involvement is an idea system and "24–72" rule: Managers who receive an idea must acknowledge it within 24 hours and, within 72 hours, must act on it or provide a plan of action. In 1990 each associate submitted an average of 39 "opportunities for improvement," compared with 1/2 an idea per associate before the rule. "We've come a long way, but we still have further to go," adds CEO Milliken. "Employees at leading Japanese companies submit some 50 to 100 suggestions each."

"One way to create that kind of environment is through recognition," he continues. "Management used to mean catching others doing something wrong. Now it means catching them doing something right and applauding them in many different ways."

The Pursuit of Excellence program encompasses a range of other efforts. For instance, advanced technology gives customers access to state-of-the-art computer-automated design, a system that has reduced cycle time for new product development and has sped up delivery of sample material to textile users 50 percent. The company has also improved its record of on-time delivery from 75 percent in 1984 to 98.4 percent today.

Now the company is halfway to its goal of achieving a tenfold increase in customer-focused quality measures in four years and has already met some safety and environmental goals set for 1993. And the firm's efforts will undoubtedly continue beyond that because, as CEO Milliken says, "In pursuit of quality improvement, we recognize that good is the enemy of best, and best the enemy of better."

Xerox Business Products and Systems *(1989, manufacturing category), a producer and supplier of document-processing products, systems, and services, which is part of the Xerox Corporation headquartered in Stamford, Conn.*

"We had grown complacent because we could sell almost anything for any price," says former Xerox Corporation chairman David T. Kearns, now deputy secretary of the U.S. Department of Education. Xerox faced virtually no competition in the late 1960s and early 1970s. But complacency vanished when Kearns saw Japanese competitors selling small copiers for what it cost Xerox to make them. "The Japanese simply managed better than we did," says Mark V. Shimelonis, vice president, quality, at Xerox Business Products and Systems.

So in 1979, Xerox introduced competitive benchmarking to measure company processes and operations against the best external standards. Xerox sent managers in search of better performance measurement standards in 240 areas: to Milliken & Company for employee programs; to Procter & Gamble for marketing; to American Express for billing procedures; and the list goes on. Today Xerox benchmarks everything, recognizing that the best place to learn is from the experts.

The company also learned that the experts aren't just outside the organization. In 1980 Xerox spent $50 million to recall a substandard copier designed to compete with low-cost Japanese machines. At a meeting shortly thereafter, a plant worker announced to Kearns, "I could have told you the copier wouldn't work. Why didn't you ask me?"

When the company's Japanese partner, Fuji Xerox Ltd., attributed much of its success in garnering the 1980 Deming Prize to involving the entire organization, Kearns saw the value of employee participation. That same year, Xerox and the union representing its manufacturing work force agreed to explore the use of a team approach to solve work-related problems. In 1983 Xerox adopted a no-layoff policy for union workers. The union partnership is still considered a model for U.S. industry. Employees have the opportunity to join assembly teams designing the work flow on the factory floor and determining how to manage various processes. Under this team arrangement, the company and union have a much less adversarial relationship than had existed historically.

The team concept was carried into design, engineering, and production processes. At the same time, Xerox adopted just-in-time manufacturing, no easy task with the company's worldwide procurement. Suppliers were cut from 5,000 ten years ago to 400 today. Inventory is down from a three-month to a three-week supply. And the company inspects less than 15 percent of incoming shipments, down from 80 percent a decade ago.

These initiatives brought significant wins, but, believing something was still missing, in 1984 Xerox launched Leadership Through Quality, a 34-step strategy making customer satisfaction central to every element of corporate life. "Too many of our initial quality projects were internal," says Kearns. "We should have made customer satisfaction the top priority at the outset."

In 1986, after about two-thirds of employees had been trained in the quality process, the company showed a 7.8 percent return on assets followed by an increase to 9.9 percent the next year. But Xerox was still at least a year behind schedule in meeting its quality objectives, so in 1987 the organization instituted further changes, including a Customer Obsession Program to measure customer satisfaction. If the customer satisfaction score didn't improve, some top managers received smaller bonuses—or none at all. And promotions were tied with dedication to quality initiatives.

The customer survey process, handled by a third-party organization, invites every customer to grade the company at least annually. The information helps Xerox develop measurable targets for quality improvement, change design and operations to meet customer needs, and assess demand for new technologies. The 40,000 monthly surveys showed that customer satisfaction rose 38 percent by 1989.

"All these efforts really paid off," notes quality vice president Shimelonis. "Profitability increased annually as the quality process took root. Return on assets reached 14.6 percent in 1990. And revenues increased from $9.42 billion in 1986 to $12.69 billion in 1990."

Now continuous improvement is a way of life, according to Shimelonis. "We have a saying at Xerox that we are in a race without a finish line. That's because, as we improve, so does our competition. And the better we get, the more our customers expect from us."

Cadillac Motor Car Division *(1990, manufacturing category), the Detroit, Mich.-based flagship division of General Motors North American Automotive Operations.*

The Cadillac Motor Car Division hit a few potholes in the mid-1980s. One assembly center got off to a bumpy start, and two more closed. At the same time, the company was losing the élan associated with "Cadillac style." The firm had compromised the distinctiveness of its cars by scaling down the size and making many of the parts interchangeable with other GM cars in anticipation of more costly, less available gasoline and more stringent fuel economy requirements and emission standards.

In 1989 the company returned to the longer "Cadillac look" by adding nine inches to DeVille and Fleetwood sedans. That was part of a major overhaul that Cadillac began in 1985 to change its corporate culture. The company sharpened its focus on customer satisfaction and product and service quality. And management developed a framework to guide decision making and business processes.

First, Cadillac implemented simultaneous engineering, an approach for product development that dramatically departs from methods commonly used in the industry. In the traditional sequential process, the product progresses from designers to engineers, to manufacturing, to the sales staff, with each department functioning largely in isolation. Simultaneous engineering combines all these disciplines, enabling staff to understand how changes in one functional area affect other areas. This approach makes it easier to prevent problems, determine how to monitor production processes, and identify opportunities to improve manufacturing and product quality.

The effectiveness of simultaneous engineering hinges on teamwork. Some 60 percent of employees participate on teams, sometimes with supplier representatives, to define, engineer, market, and continuously improve products. The program has already proven highly efficient: Cadillac has cut about one year off development time for a new car.

The success of simultaneous engineering teams was the springboard for complete cultural transformation at Cadillac. Now the company's constituencies are involved throughout the organization. For instance, United Auto Worker union leaders serve on UAW-GM Quality Network plant councils with Cadillac executives and plant managers; automotive suppliers and dealers are members of product development and improvement teams; and dealers and consumers participate in market assessment programs. In fact, the company showed the 1992 Seville model to more than 8,000 potential owners and modified the design in response to their feedback.

"One of the toughest challenges is translating the customer's often vague suggestions into engineering terms," says John O. Grettenberger, Cadillac general manager and General Motors vice president. "We use a tool called quality function deployment to identify the features most valued by customers and the design specifications that meet those requests. And to continuously improve our cars and manufacturing process, employees on the assembly line study, assemble, and disassemble prototype models and suggest alterations in parts or features."

These programs were well under way in 1989, earning Cadillac a place among the Baldrige finalists but no trophy. "The examiners said we needed more plant-customer connections," says Bill Howey, a Cadillac assembly-line veteran and member of Cadillac's World Class Quality Council, whose members serve as goodwill ambassadors to dealers and customers. "So we developed a program whereby we in the plant called new Cadillac owners who after three months hadn't returned their Gold Key customer satisfaction surveys. We fed that information back into the system, closing an important loop."

By all accounts, Cadillac's approach is working. "The main measure of quality in the automotive industry is warranty claims—costs for reworking items gone bad," explains Grettenberger. "We increased coverage, yet our warranty claims costs dropped by almost 30 percent over the last five years. During the same period, warranty-related problems decreased by almost 70 percent, and productivity has risen 60 percent."

International Business Machines Corporation, Rochester, Minn. *(1990, manufacturing category), manufacturer of intermediate computer systems and disk storage products.*

"By the mid-1980s, IBM had become bureaucratic and out of touch with the marketplace," says Stephen B. Schwartz, IBM's senior vice president for market-driven quality. "We were viewed as order takers, selling boxes while our customers wanted solutions."

When customers attending a high-level planning session in 1986 told IBM it wasn't meeting new demands, the company started transforming. It eliminated two layers of management and divested from businesses that were diverting resources from its core strengths. And it aimed to refocus on customers and excellence.

IBM Rochester serves as a model in the company's recently instituted market-driven quality program. Rochester set out in 1981 to improve product reliability and expanded its efforts twice, focusing on manufacturing cycle time, planning and development cycle, and other processes before setting the goal in 1989 to achieve total customer satisfaction. "That's essential in a business where a product is considered 'mature' after two years and downright decrepit at five," notes Schwartz. "And the way to reduce cycle time is to eliminate defects and simplify processes."

IBM is doing both. Until 1986 the development cycle time for mid-range computers was four to five years. IBM Rochester produced its AS/400 computer system—from defining customer requirements to shipping the product—in just over two years, at the same time increasing the product warranty period from three months to one year.

One major factor in that achievement is a good understanding of customer requirements. IBM Rochester conducts an extensive global market analysis and then detailed analyses of target markets to identify the features that customers want. Items are prioritized into short-term (two-year) and long-term (five-year) projects, and the plan is adjusted in response to customer feedback.

Another success factor is IBM's defect-prevention strategy. Early in the design process, teams isolate and remove potential defects using a high-powered computer that simulates the results of various designs. Repeating simulations until the team developed a virtually defect-free design cut cycle time for the AS/400 by ten months. Rochester's milestone process helped reduce cycle time in developing software for the AS/400, which was the most complex in IBM's history. Software development groups worked on segments of the software, they merged and tested them at each checkpoint.

Early Manufacturing Involvement teams, with design and manufacturing staff as well as IBM Rochester suppliers, helped simplify the manufacturing process and reduce product cost. For instance, the AS/400 uses about 4,000 parts, down from its predecessor's 10,000 parts.

IBM as a whole has invested more than $300 million since 1986 to improve processes and information systems. Meanwhile, IBM Rochester's capital spending on equipment for defect detection declined 75 percent, while write-offs as a proportion of manufacturing output dropped 55 percent.

Throughout the quality process at Rochester, customer feedback is solicited and integrated. Of approximately 40 data sources analyzed to guide improvement efforts, most either provide information on customers' product and service requirements or help parlay these expectations into specifications for new products. IBM Rochester's Software Partner Lab, for example, allows customers and business partners to jointly develop solutions for future product releases.

An integral component of Rochester's quality effort is empowering its work force. Rochester encourages leadership and invests an amount equal to 5 percent of its payroll in education and training. Managerial and nonmanagerial employees "own" or assume responsibility for quality improvement plans and head project teams. "Leadership makes the whole process work," reports Schwartz.

IBM Rochester has set the stage for IBM's aggressive, market-driven quality program. Now all lines of business in IBM are establishing a system of measurements to gauge their quality status and progress. The goal: six sigma by 1994.

Wallace Co., Inc. *(1990, small business category), a family-owned Houston, Tex.-based distribution company primarily serving the chemical and petrochemical industries.*

The Wallace Co., Inc., founded in 1942, has long enjoyed an excellent reputation. But even Wallace wasn't immune to the Gulf Coast energy slump in the early 1980s: The company's profits dropped 50 percent, forcing the shutdown of three distribution stores.

A visit from a major client in 1984 pointed the way to a new strategic plan. The client said it would be measuring suppliers' quality and concentrating business with select vendors. That prompted Wallace in 1985 to embark on a program of continuous quality improvement.

Wallace senior executives set out to educate themselves about quality and pass those lessons along to their staff. When that route won limited success, the company hired a quality training firm that taught, among other concepts, statistical process control (SPC)—a system it uses to track deliveries, customer credits, and other measurement processes.

SPC data collection is integrated into operations companywide. For example, truck drivers track delivery problems, salespeople compare time spent with each customer with gross profit generated by that customer, the quotations department tracks the number of quotes made versus orders received, and corporate headquarters assesses service performance for its top ten customers. Some 15 SPC coordinators chart trends, conduct analysis to isolate real and potential problems, and evaluate progress in accomplishing quality objectives. "Data collection is invaluable," says company CEO and vice chairman of the board John W. Wallace. "It doesn't take much time—and some of our people actually track data for their own enlightenment. They're proud of their records."

After implementing SPC to measure performance, the company prioritized the areas needing immediate attention by conducting an SPC analysis of customer credits; an outside survey of employees' skills, training needs, and attitudes; and an examination of tasks involving the most employees, where systemic inefficiencies would have the highest impact.

"We were issuing a large number of credits, so we attacked that area first," says CEO Wallace. "SPC gave us valuable direction, indicating that the trouble emanated not from the order fillers, as we had assumed, but from the order takers. The problem was systemic."

The company set up teams closest to areas targeted for improvement to solve problems and accomplish quality-related objectives. This approach brought scores of gains. For instance, in 1987 Wallace was going to be placed in the state's high-risk insurance pool, raising worker compensation premiums from $250,000 to $700,000 annually. After a staff team helped develop training programs to improve worker safety, accident rates plunged, and Wallace saved more than $500,000 in premiums in just one year.

"Teams now make all company decisions," notes Wallace. "In fact, the quality management steering committee hasn't overruled a single team decision. This program proves itself time and again."

Another component of Wallace's quality program is customer focus. The company uses such customer feedback channels as surveys, "partnering" meetings between company representatives and customers, and a customer service network that must respond to all inquiries and complaints within 60 minutes. Wallace also invites scrutiny, providing customers with access to some data bases as well as computer-generated reports of how well the company services its accounts.

Wallace has reaped numerous dividends from its efforts. Volume increased by 69 percent from 1987 to 1990, and market share grew from 10.4 percent to 18 percent. During that same period, on-time deliveries jumped from 75 percent to 94 percent and are expected to reach 99 percent this year. Wallace actually refunds its profit if it fails to meet the guaranteed delivery date.

Finally, Wallace is passing the torch by requiring

vendors to provide product guarantees and statistical evidence of quality. Representatives from Wallace, its suppliers, and its customers have established criteria for Wallace to certify vendors. The company has reduced its number of suppliers from more than 2,000 in 1987 to 325 today. And it provides training for suppliers in continuous quality improvement. Last year, 15 suppliers initiated programs based on Wallace's model.

Federal Express Corporation *(1990, service category), a global package delivery company based in Memphis, Tenn.*

After earning a failing grade on a business plan submitted during business school, Frederick W. Smith nonetheless forged ahead with that plan, forming the Federal Express Corporation in 1973. And that may have been the last time Smith chose not to listen, because he has made listening to employees and customers the keystone of FedEx's approach to quality.

"Customer satisfaction begins with employee satisfaction," says Smith, FedEx chairman and CEO. "That's why we adhere to the philosophy that if we put our employees first, they'll deliver impeccable service, and profit will naturally follow."

Profit has, indeed, followed. FedEx is number one in the express market, with 46 percent of market share. To stay there, Smith intends to keep moving, because, as he quotes Will Rogers, "Even if you're on the right track, you'll get run over if you just sit there."

So FedEx strives for continuous improvement. Twelve years ago the company installed a sophisticated worldwide computer tracking system that provides real time information on every customer transaction. Since then, FedEx has been consistently updating its technology.

While some might argue that you can't measure quality in a service company, FedEx says you must. Rapid growth forced the air express delivery giant to develop a more accurate way to measure performance than determining the percentage of packages delivered on time. "We deliver more than 1.4 million packages daily," notes John West, FedEx manager of quality assurance. "So 99.1 percent success equals over three million failures annually. That's unacceptable."

To pinpoint service failures and assess performance, in 1989 FedEx developed Service Quality Indicators (SQI), based on a list of 12 potential problems in delivering a package. Under the SQI, which grew out of a system nicknamed the "hierarchy of horrors," a package delivered even five minutes late on the correct day registers one negative point. Wrong-day delivery costs five points. And a lost package or missed pickup rates ten points, the highest on the chart. FedEx's goal: one fifth fewer "horrors" by the end of the program's fifth year. In addition to that internal rating system, FedEx conducts an average of 100 customer phone surveys daily.

Time, of course, is essential to FedEx's performance—and "empowering people is key to managing time," says Smith. "Empowerment allows employees to act immediately, fix problems, and do what it takes to keep customers happy. Empowered employees have shared goals and power, making turf irrelevant and teamwork imperative."

That all figures into FedEx's 1-10-100 rule: It costs $1 or one hour to resolve a problem immediately, ten times more to fix a mistake caught downstream in another department or location, and 100 times more if an error reaches a customer.

The company reinforces that principle in several ways. "To help create as secure environment that stimulates risk taking and innovation, we make no layoffs," says Smith. "We stuck to that even when we discontinued electronic mail service, affecting 1,300 jobs."

FedEx rates management through its Survey Feedback Action (SFA) program, annual anonymous surveys of all employees. After results are tabulated, managers hold staff meetings to discuss and resolve problems identified in the surveys. Some action plans have led to company-wide programs such as the Leadership Evaluation and Awareness Process, a program geared to evaluate employees' management potential.

And to tie the corporate culture to the bottom line, management bonuses hinge on meeting three corporate goals: people goals, measured by the SFA; service goals, based on low SQI; and profit goals. The stakes are high—up to 40 percent of salary can be bonus. And if the company doesn't reach all three of its goals, no one, not even the CEO, earns a bonus.

But so far, this year looks good for bonuses: The company recently reached its highest service level and lowest cost per package.

■

EXERCISE

EXERCISE 2–1   INITIAL VIEW OF ORGANIZATIONAL BEHAVIOR

Now that you have completed two chapters that set the tone for the book *Organizational Behavior and Management,* complete the following exercise. This should be used as your beginning *baseline* assumptions, opinions, and understanding of organizational behavior. Once you have completed the course (book), we will again take another look at your assumptions, opinions, and understanding.

This exercise contains 20 pairs of statements about organizational behavior. For each pair, circle the letter preceding the statement which you think is most accurate. Circle only *one* letter in each pair.

After you have circled the letter, indicate how certain you are of your choice by writing 1, 2, 3, or 4 on the line following each item according to the following procedure.

Place a "1" if you are *very uncertain* that your choice is correct.
Place a "2" if you are *somewhat uncertain* that your choice is correct.
Place a "3" if you are *somewhat certain* that your choice is correct.
Place a "4" if you are *very certain* that your choice is correct.
Do not skip any pairs.

1. *a.* A supervisor is well advised to treat, as much as possible, all members of his/her group exactly the same way.
   b. A supervisor is well advised to adjust his/her behavior according to the unique characteristics of the members of his/her group. _____

2. *a.* Generally speaking, individual motivation is greatest if the person has set goals for himself/herself that are *difficult* to achieve.
   b. Generally speaking, individual motivation is greatest if the person has set goals for himself/herself that are *easy* to achieve. _____

3. *a.* A major reason why organizations are not so productive as they could be these days is that managers are too concerned with managing the work group rather than the individual.
   b. A major reason why organizations are not so productive as they could be these days is that managers are too concerned with managing the individual rather than the work group. _____

4. *a.* Supervisors who, sometime prior to becoming a supervisor, have performed the job of the people they are currently supervising are apt to be more effective supervisors than those who have never performed that particular job.
   b. Supervisors who, sometime prior to becoming a supervisor, have performed the job of the people they are currently supervising are apt to be less effective supervisors than those who have never performed that particular job. _____

5. *a.* On almost every matter relevant to the work, managers are well advised to be completely honest and open with their subordinates.
   b. There are very few matters in the work place where managers are well advised to be completely honest and open with their subordinates. _____

6. *a.* One's need for power is a better predictor of managerial advancement than one's motivation to do the work well.
   b. One's motivation to do the work well is a better predictor of managerial advancement than one's need for power. _____

7. *a.* When people fail at something, they try harder the next time.

Source: Adapted from Robert Weinberg and Walter Nord, "Coping with 'It's All Common Sense,'" *Exchange: The Organizational Behavior Teaching Journal 7,* no. 2 (1982), pp. 29–32. Used with permission.

    b. When people fail at something, they quit trying. _____

8. *a.* Performing well as a manager depends most on how much education you have.

    b. Peforming well as a manager depends most on how much experience you have. _____

9. *a.* The most effective leaders are those who give more emphasis to getting the work done than they do to relating to people.

    b. The effective leaders are those who give more emphasis to relating to people than they do to getting the work done. _____

10. *a.* It is very important for a leader to "stick to his/her guns."

    b. It is *not* very important for a leader to "stick to his/her guns." _____

11. *a.* Pay is the most important factor in determining how hard people work.

    b. The nature of the task people are doing is the most important factor in determining how hard people work. _____

12. *a.* Pay is the most important factor in determining how satisfied people are at work.

    b. The nature of the task people are doing is the most important factor in determining how satisfied people are at work. _____

13. *a.* Generally speaking, it is correct to say that a person's attitudes cause his/her behavior.

    b. Generally speaking, it is correct to say that a person's attitudes are primarily rationalizations for his/her behavior. _____

14. *a.* Satisfied workers produce more than workers who are not satisfied.

    b. Satisfied workers produce no more than workers who are not satisfied. _____

15. *a.* The notion that most semiskilled workers desire work that is interesting and meaningful is most likely incorrect.

    b. The notion that most semiskilled workers desire work that is interesting and meaningful is most likely correct. _____

16. *a.* People welcome change for the better.

    b. Even if change is for the better, people will resist it. _____

17. *a.* Leaders are born, not made.

    b. Leaders are made, not born. _____

18. *a.* Groups make better decisions than individuals.

    b. Indiviudals make better decisions than groups. _____

19. *a.* The statement, "A manger's authority needs to be commensurate with his/her responsibility" is, practically speaking, a very meaningful statement.

    b. The statement, "A manager's authority needs to be commensurate with his/her responsibility" is, practically speaking, a basically meaningless statement. _____

20. *a.* A major reason for the relative decline in North American productivity is that the division of labor and job specialization have gone too far.

    b. A major reason for the relative decline in North American productivity is that the division of labor and job specialization have not been carried far enough. _____

▲

CASE

CASE 2-1   THE CASE OF THE MSWD

Changing the culture of an organization is a difficult, time-consuming, often gut-wrenching process. This is as true in public corporations as it is in the private domain. In fact, effecting such change in a public institution is, if anything, more difficult because of the number of legitimate constituencies—the public, legislators, unions, employees, special-interest groups—that can raise barriers to change. But change can be accomplished if a sufficient level of commitment is applied to the process for a long enough time. One example will reveal all the expenditures—of time, money, and morale—that are involved.

Metropolitan Sewer & Water District (MSWD—a major public wholesaler of these essential services to a large American city) is a public-sector corporation. It employs 2,500 people, has an annual budget of $75 million, and spends $200 million a year on capital improvements. MSWD is one of the oldest public agencies of its kind in the country.

Throughout the years, the MSWD carried out its mandate in fine fashion. Its accomplishments were not achieved without difficulty and controversy, however. At times in the history of MSWD, senior officials were charged and convicted of misuse of public funds.

A second problems MSWD faced both internally and in the eyes of the public was patronage. Over the years, administration after administration had found ways to plant favorite sons on MSWD's modest operating-budget payroll.

The third problem MSWD faced was one of rampant bureaucracy—a problem that organization theorist Henry Mintzberg suggests affects all older organizations. The average contract required 72 separate signatures and took close to nine months to wind its way through the bureaucracy before being let. Even a minor contract involved a foot-high pile of forms.

Despite the presence of a modern computer system, there were at least six separate manual personnel record

Source: Terrence Deal and Allan Kennedy, *Corporate Culture* (Reading, Mass.: Addison-Wesley Publishing, 1982), pp. 169–74. Reprinted with permission. This case is based on a real consulting assignment carried out by the authors. Names, titles, and a few facts have been changed in the interest of respecting the confidential interests of the client.

systems operating in MSWD. And even with these systems, no one could say with certainty how many people were on the payroll at any time.

All business was conducted by memo, and usually in a prescribed official format rather than face-to-face. Everything was done by the book. If it wasn't on paper, it wouldn't get done. A classic case of the process culture gone awry.

Still, this bureaucracy would not have been a serious problem except for some issues that recently surfaced. Water usage continued to rise and gradually began to exceed the design capacity of the system. Moreover, federal EPA regulations that were enacted required MSWD to upgrade its facilities. Confronted with these problems, the state secretary of the environment was determined to "bring the MSWD into the 20th century." He recognized that it would be almost irresponsible to launch the MSWD into these major capital expenditures with the organization in its current state of apparent bureaucratic ineptitude. He knew, however, that revitalizing this moribund culture would be difficult and would have to be accomplished without major infusions of new management talent. Nevertheless, he and his new general manager, Ken Dillon (not his real name), were determined to take on the challenge.

Ken Dillon was a key figure in changing MSWD. Dillon was in his mid-50s, semiretired, and a successful entrepreneur when he took over the reins at MSWD. He was used to getting things done and making things happen. When he brought this attitude to the career-oriented bureaucratic environment of MSWD, it was like a breath of fresh air.

During the first several months in revitalizing MSWD, Dillon familiarized himself with the organization. What he found was not encouraging. The MSWD's extremely cumbersome superstructure made Dillon officially responsible for running the organization, but most major and many minor decisions were subject to the review of an advisory committee. Decisions required a majority vote of the committee although Dillon did have veto power.

Further crimping his style was the fact that this highly centralized organization reported to a chief operating officer—a career civil servant. Originally this post was intended to help insulate MSWD from self-serving initiatives by politically minded general managers. In practical terms, it meant that Dillon had little direct authority in the day-to-day management of MSWD, since everyone else reported to the chief operating officer who could, in turn, go over Dillon's head to the advisory committee.

In terms of the MSWD's people, there were grounds for encouragement and disappointment. The biggest problem was the average age of the staff: 55 or older. The people in the agency had, for the most part, joined right after the war and spent their whole careers with it. The threat of impending retirements and the accompanying loss of the knowledge and skills of those who retired was a serious long-term problem for Dillon to deal with. On the positive side, the loyalty and motivation of the vast majority of the staff was remarkable. Despite public perceptions of a patronage-ridden bureaucracy, these people were dedicated public servants who were sincerely interested in making the MSWD work as well as possible.

Dillon's objective in this change was nothing short of changing MSWD from a reactive, bureaucratic culture to the proactive can-do attitude he was familiar with in his own company—a shift from a process culture to a work hard/play hard culture.

After six months of study, Dillon decided the time had come to act. To reshape the culture, he began by taking two major steps: he engaged consultants to supplement his staff in an aggressive change process, and he announced in a memo to MSWD's permanent complement of 2,500 employees that there would be no firings or layoffs as a result of the process he was launching. His objective, he said, was to work with the talented people of MSWD to improve its effectiveness. This second step turned out to be very significant later in the process since it helped buy time for some basic changes to take hold.

THE CHANGE PROCESS

The team of four consultants spent its first six weeks learning about MSWD. In a meeting at the end of this period, the first gesture in the change process was decided on—to set up three major task forces of MSWD employees to work with the consultants on three commonly agreed-upon problem areas. The three areas selected were:

- **Contracting** Everyone generally agreed something should be done to speed up contract processing.
- **Operations and maintenance** (O&M) Over the objections of the chief operating officer's functional managers, a second task force was assigned responsibility for O&M.

- **Personnel** All managers in MSWD used personnel constraints as their argument for why things couldn't be done differently no matter what the issue. The chief operating officer, for example, was convinced this task force would prove that nothing could be done.

In all, 25 professional and/or middle managers were assigned to these task forces full-time for their indeterminate duration—a gesture that in itself caused great consternation in the agency. Reservations aside, people in the MSWD were used to following orders, so all 25 members dutifully showed up for the initial group meeting that launched their efforts.

Meanwhile, Dillon initiated a weekly series of staff meetings with the chief operating officer, functional officer, functional manager, and their assistants. He specifically excluded these people from membership on the task forces; he would work with them himself.

During their first week of work, the task forces accomplished little. Members were not used to working in this fashion; many of them felt uncomfortable in this new role. By the second week the members began to open up in their meetings. For example, engineers on the contracting task force admitted disappointment when projects they had worked on were not received warmly by operation personnel. They were astonished to learn that the operations people were often distressed when the engineers didn't consult them about projects they were working on and when they delivered equipment that was hard to operate and maintain. Both sides agreed that better communications on projects between the two sides were definitely called for. In the other task forces, similar revelations were occurring—to everyone's amazement.

By the third week, all three task forces were hard at work trying to formulate recommendations to deal with the problems they had identified. Their recommendations—delivered during the seventh week—were reviewed by Dillon, senior management, and the advisory committee.

Awaiting management's response, the task forces had gone back to work on their recommendations. A half dozen more members were added to the task forces. Everyone seemed more and more committed to the change process as time went on.

Six weeks later, the task forces presented their final recommendations—essentially offering details on their original plans. Senior management raised some objections, and modifications were discussed. Then attention turned toward the consultants' recommendations for significant streamlining and decentralization of MSWD. They suggested (1) the elimination of the job of chief operating officer, (2) elimination of the jobs of the assistant functional managers, (3) establishment of a line of business (in other words, sewer and water structure), (4) a reassignment of the staffs of major functions such as engineering and environmental planning to create the nucleus of real engineering functions within both the sewer and water divisions, (5) creation of a new director of planning position to run the new planning system, and (6) creation of an office of contract administration to run the new project-management and contracting systems. After some review the package was finally endorsed.

THE IMPLEMENTATION OF CHANGE

With the endorsement in hand, Dillon moved quickly. True to his original pledge, no member of the organization was fired; all were slotted into new jobs. The reorganization was comprehensive enough that, in effect, a new management team was put in place.

Offices were moved on a Monday. On Tuesday, Dillon launched the new planning process that was designed to get the new management groups of each division working together as a team.

The planning process was designed to dovetail with the state budget process, thus creating very tight scheduling. However, despite weekend and late evening flurries, both divisions made it under the wire. The head of the sewer division, exhausted by the process, said to one of the consultants just after the advisory committee had approved his proposed budget: "This is the best thing that ever happened to the MSWD . . . and the most exhilarating experience I have ever had. We'll never go back to the old way again."

Six months later, no one could doubt that the MSWD was significantly different. There were still too much paper and too much conformance to the book, but there was also a clear set of agreed-upon priorities, a sense of real urgency in pursuing these priorities, and the beginnings of a "we can make it happen" mentality. Dillon believed that with one more year of operation in this new mode, the new culture would really take hold.

The secretary of the environment, the person who launched the whole process, claims it is the greatest organization turnaround he has witnessed in his 25 years as a public-sector manager.

CASE QUESTIONS

1. Describe the role of Dillon in the change effort.
2. What internal and external threats existed in the change process?
3. What role did training play in the change effort?
4. What potential problems do you see down the road as the change process takes hold?

Quantitative and Qualitative Research Techniques for Studying Organizational Behavior and Management Practice

SOURCES OF KNOWLEDGE ABOUT ORGANIZATIONS

The vast majority of the research reports and writing on organizations are contained in technical papers known as journals. Some of these journals, such as the *Academy of Management Review,* are devoted entirely to topics of management and organization, while journals such as *Organizational Behavior and Human Decision Processes* are devoted largely to the results of laboratory studies. Such journals as the *Harvard Business Review* are general business journals, while the *American Sociological Review* and the *Journal of Applied Psychology* are general behavioral science journals. These business and behavioral science journals often contain articles of interest to studies of management. Exhibit 2-5 presents a selective list of journals.

The sources in Exhibit 2-5 provide information, data, and discussion about what is occurring within and among organizations. This knowledge base provides managers with available research information that could prove useful in their own organizations or situations.

HISTORY AS A WAY OF KNOWING ABOUT ORGANIZATIONS

The oldest approach to the study of organizations is through the history of organizations, societies, and institutions. Throughout human history, people have joined with others to accomplish their goals, first in families, later in tribes and other, more sophisticated political units. Ancient peoples constructed pyramids, temples, and ships; they created systems of government, farming, commerce, and warfare. For example, Greek historians tell us that it took 100,000 men to build the great pyramid of Khufu in Egypt. The project took more than 20 years to

EXHIBIT 2-5

Selected Sources of Writing and Research on Organizations

1. Academy of Management Journal
2. Academy of Management Review
3. Academy of Management Executive
4. Administrative Science Quarterly
5. Advanced Management Journal
6. American Sociological Review
7. Business Horizons
8. Business Management
9. California Management Review
10. Decision Sciences
11. Fortune
12. Hospital and Health Services Administration
13. HR Focus
14. Human Organization
15. Human Resource Management
16. Industrial and Labor Relations Review
17. Industrial Engineering
18. Industrial Management Review
19. Journal of Applied Behavioral Science
20. Journal of Applied Psychology
21. Journal of Business
22. Journal of International Business Studies
23. Journal of Management
24. Journal of Management Studies
25. Management International Review
26. Management Review
27. Management Science
28. Organizational Behavior and Human Decision Processes
29. Organizational Dynamics
30. Personnel
31. Personnel Journal
32. Personnel Psychology
33. Public Administration Review
34. Sloan Management Review
35. Strategic Management Journal
36. Training and Development Journal

complete. It was almost as high as the Washington Monument and had a base that would cover eight football fields. Remember, these people had no construction equipment or computers. One thing they did have, though, was organization. While these "joint efforts" did not have formal names such as "XYZ Corporation," the idea of "getting organized" was quite widespread throughout early civilizations. The literature of the times refers to such managerial concepts as planning, staff assistance, division of labor, control, and leadership.[29]

The administration of the vast Roman Empire required the application of organization and management concepts. In fact, it has been said that "the real secret of the greatness of the Romans was their genius for organization."[30] This is because the Romans used certain principles of organization to coordinate the diverse activities of the empire.

If judged by age alone, the Roman Catholic Church would have to be considered the most effective organization of all time. While its success is the result of many factors, one of these factors is certainly the effectiveness of its organization and management. For example, a hierarchy of authority, a territorial organization, specialization of activities by function, and use of the staff principle were integral parts of early church organization.

Finally, it is not surprising that some important concepts and practices in modern organizations can be traced to military organizations. This is because,

---

[29]For an excellent discussion of organizations in ancient societies, see Claude S. George, Jr., *The History of Management Thought* (Englewood Cliffs, N.J.: Prentice-Hall, 1968), pp. 3–26.

[30]James D. Mooney, *The Principles of Organization* (New York: Harper & Row, 1939), p. 63.

like the church, military organizations were faced with problems of managing large, geographically dispersed groups. As did the church, military organizations adopted early the concept of staff as an advisory function for line personnel.

Knowledge of the history of organizations in earlier societies can be useful for the future manager. In fact, many of the early concepts and practices are being utilized successfully today. However, you may ask whether heavy reliance on the past is a good guide to the present and future. We shall see that time and organizational setting have much to do with what works in management.

EXPERIENCE AS A WAY OF KNOWING ABOUT ORGANIZATIONS

Some of the earliest books on management and organizations were written by successful practitioners. Most of these individuals were business executives, and their writings focused on how it was for them during their time with one or more companies. They usually put forward certain general principles or practices that had worked well for them. Although using the writings and experiences of practitioners sounds "practical," it has its drawbacks. Successful managers are susceptible to the same perceptual phenomena as each of us. Their accounts, therefore, are based on their own preconceptions and biases. No matter how objective their approaches, the accounts may not be entirely complete or accurate. In addition, the accounts also may be superficial since they often are after-the-fact reflections of situations in which, when the situations were occurring, the managers had little time to think about how or why they were doing something. As a result, the suggestions in such accounts often are oversimplified. Finally, as with history, what worked yesterday may not work today or tomorrow.[31]

SCIENCE AS A WAY OF KNOWING ABOUT ORGANIZATIONS

We have noted that a major interest in this book was the behavioral sciences which have produced theory, research, and generalizations concerning the behavior, structure, and processes of organizations. The interest of behavioral scientists in the problems of organizations is relatively new, becoming popular in the early 1950s. At that time, an organization known as the Foundation for Research on Human Behavior was established. The objectives of this organization were to promote and support behavioral science research in business, government, and other types of organizations.

Many advocates of the scientific approach believe that practicing managers and teachers have accepted prevalent practices and principles without the benefit of scientific validation. They believe that scientific procedures should be used

---

[31]Ian I. Mitroff, "Why Our Old Pictures of the World Do Not Work Anymore," in *Doing Research that Is Useful for Theory and Research*, ed. E. E. Lawler III, et al. (San Francisco: Jossey-Bass, 1985), pp. 18–44.

whenever possible to validate practice. Because of their work, many of the earlier practices and principles have been discounted or modified, and others have been validated.

Research in the Behavioral Sciences

Present research in the behavioral sciences is extremely varied with respect to the scope and methods used. One common thread among the various disciplines is the study of human behavior through the use of scientific procedures. Thus, it is necessary to examine the nature of science as it is applied to human behavior. Some critics believe that a science of human behavior is unattainable and that the scientific procedures used to gain knowledge in the physical sciences cannot be adapted to the study of humans, especially humans in organizations.

The authors do not intend to become involved in these arguments. However, we believe that the scientific approach is applicable to management and organizational studies.[32] Furthermore, as we have already pointed out, there are means other than scientific procedures that have provided important knowledge concerning people in organizations.

The manager of the future will draw from the behavioral sciences just as the physician draws from the biological sciences. The manager must know what to expect from the behavioral sciences, their strengths and weaknesses, just as the physician must know what to expect from bacteriology and how it can serve as a diagnostic tool. However, the manager, like the physician, is a practitioner. He or she must make decisions in the present, whether or not science has all the answers, and certainly cannot wait until it finds them before acting.

The Scientific Approach

Most current philosophers of science define "science" in terms of what they consider to be its one universal and unique feature: *method.* The greatest advantage of the scientific approach is that it has one characteristic not found in any method of attaining knowledge: *self-correction.*[33] The scientific approach is an objective, systematic, and controlled process with built-in checks all along the way to knowledge. These checks control and verify the scientist's activities and conclusions to enable the attainment of knowledge independent of the scientist's own biases and preconceptions.

[32]A similar debate has taken place for years over the issue of whether management is a science. For relevant discussions, the interested reader should consult R. E. Gribbons and S. D. Hunt, "Is Management a Science?" *Academy of Management Review,* January 1978, pp. 139–43; O. Behling, "Some Problems in the Philosophy of Science of Organizations," *Academy of Management Review,* April 1978, pp. 193–201; and O. Behling, "The Case for the Natural Science Model for Research in Organizational Behavior and Organization Theory," *Academy of Management Review,* October 1980, pp. 483–90.

[33]See Fred N. Kerlinger, *Foundations of Behavioral Research* (New York: Holt, Rinehart & Winston, 1973), p. 6.

EXHIBIT 2-6

Characteristics of the Scientific Approach

1. *The procedures are public.* A scientific report contains a complete description of what was done to enable other researchers in the field to follow each step of the investigation as if they were actually present.

2. *The definitions are precise.* The procedures used, the variables measured, and how they were measured must be clearly stated. For example, if examining motivation among employees in a given plant, it would be necessary to define what is meant by motivation and how it was measured (for example, number of units produced, number of absences).

3. *The data collecting is objective.* Objectivity is a key feature of the scientific approach. Bias in collecting and interpreting data has no place in science.

4. *The finding must be replicable.* This enables another interested researcher to test the results of a study by attempting to reproduce them.

5. *The approach is systematic and cumulative.* This relates to one of the underlying purposes of science, to develop a unified body of knowledge.

6. *The purposes are explanation, understanding, and prediction.* All scientists want to know "why" and "how." If they determine "why" and "how" and are able to provide proof, they can then predict the particular conditions under which specific events (human behavior in the case of behavioral sciences) will occur. Prediction is the ultimate objective of behavioral science as it is of all science.

Source: Bernard Berelson and Gary A. Steiner, *Human Behavior: An Inventory of Scientific Findings* (New York: Harcourt Brace Jovanovich, 1964), pp. 16–18.

Most scientists agree that there is no single scientific method. Instead, there are several methods that scientists can and do use. Thus, it probably makes more sense to say that there is a scientific approach. Exhibit 2-6 summarizes the major characteristics of this approach. While only an "ideal" science would exhibit all of them, they are nevertheless the hallmarks of the scientific approach. They exhibit the basic nature—objective, systematic, controlled—of the scientific approach, which enables others to have confidence in research results. What is important is the overall fundamental idea that the scientific approach is a controlled rational process.

Methods of Inquiry Used by Behavioral Scientists

How do behavioral scientists gain knowledge about the functioning organizations?[34] Just as physical scientists have certain tools and methods for obtaining information, so do behavioral scientists. These usually are referred to as research designs. In broad terms, three basic designs are used by behavioral scientists: the case study, the field study, and the experiment.

[34]A cross section of papers on gaining knowledge about organizations can be found in Thomas S. Bateman and Gerald R. Ferris, *Methods and Analysis in Organizational Research* (Reston, Va.: Reston Publishing, 1984).

Case Study

A case study attempts to examine numerous characteristics of one or more people, usually over an extended time period. For years, anthropologists have studied the customs and behavior of various groups by actually living among them. Some organizational researchers have done the same thing. They have worked and socialized with the groups of employees they were studying.[35] The reports on such investigations usually are in the form of a case study. For example, a sociologist might report the key factors and incidents that led to a strike by a group of blue-collar workers.

The chief limitations of the case-study approach for gaining knowledge about the functioning of organizations are:

1. Rarely can you find two cases that can be meaningfully compared in terms of essential characteristics. In other words, in another firm of another size, the same factors might not have resulted in a strike.
2. Rarely can case studies be repeated or their findings verified.
3. The significance of the findings is left to the subjective interpretation of the researcher. Like the practitioner, the researcher attempts to describe reality, but it is reality as perceived by one person (or a very small group). The researcher has training, biases, and preconceptions that inadvertently can distort the report. A psychologist may give an entirely different view of a group of blue-collar workers than would be given by a sociologist.
4. Since the results of a case study are based on a sample of one, the ability to generalize from them may be limited.[36]

Despite these limitations, the case study is widely used as a method of studying organizations. It is extremely valuable in answering exploratory questions.

Field Study

In attempts to add more reality and rigor to the study of organizations, behavioral scientists have developed several systematic field research techniques such as personal interviews, observation, archival data, and questionnaire surveys. These methods are used individually or in combination. They are used to investigate current practices or events, and with these methods, unlike with some other methods, the researcher does not rely entirely on what the subjects say. The researcher may personally interview other people in the organization—fellow

---

[35]See E. Chinoy, *The Automobile Worker and the American Dream* (Garden City, N.Y.: Doubleday, 1955); and D. Roy, "Banana Time—Job Satisfaction and Informal Interaction," *Human Organization,* 1960, pp. 158–69.

[36]Based in part on Robert J. House, "Scientific Investigation in Management," *Management International Review,* 1970, pp. 141–42. The interested reader should see G. Morgan and L. Smircich, "The Case for Qualitative Research," *Academy of Management Review,* October 1980, pp. 491–500; and L. R. Jauch, R. N. Osborn, and T. N. Martin, "Structured Content Analysis of Cases: A Complementary Method for Organizational Research," *Academy of Management Review,* October 1980, pp. 517–26.

workers, subordinates, and superiors—to gain a more balanced view before drawing conclusions.[37] In addition, archival data, records, charts, and statistics on file may be used to analyze a problem or hypothesis.

A very popular field study technique involves the use of expertly prepared questionnaires. Not only are such questionnaires less subject to unintentional distortion than personal interviews, but they also enable the researchers to greatly increase the number of individuals participating. Exhibit 2-7 presents part of a questionnaire used in organizations to evaluate ratee perceptions of a performance appraisal interview program. The questionnaire enables the collection of data on particular characteristics that are of interest (for example, equity, accuracy, and clarity). The seven-point scales measure a person's perceptions of the degree to which the performance appraisal interviews possess a given characteristic.

In most cases, surveys are limited to a description of the current state of the situation. However, if researchers are aware of factors that may account for survey findings, they can make conjectural statements (known as hypotheses) about the relationship between two or more factors and relate the survey data to those factors. Thus, instead of just describing perceptions of performance evaluation, the researchers could make finer distinctions (for example, distinctions regarding job tenure, salary level, or education) among groups of ratees. Comparisons and statistical tests could then be applied to determine differences, similarities, or relationships. Finally, longitudinal studies involving observations made over time are used to describe changes that have taken place. Thus, in the situation described here, we can become aware of changes in overall ratee perceptions of appraisal interviews over time, as well as ratee perceptions relating to individual managers.[38]

Despite their advantages over many of the other methods of gaining knowledge about organizations, field studies are not without problems. Here again, researchers have training, interests, and expectations that they bring with them.[39] Thus, a researcher inadvertently may ignore a vital technological factor when conducting a study of employee morale while concentrating only on behavioral factors. Also, the fact that a researcher is present may influence how the individual responds. This weakness of field studies has long been recognized and is noted in some of the earliest field research in organizations.

---

[37]See G. R. Salancik, "Field Stimulations for Organizational Behavior Research," *Administrative Science Quarterly,* December 1979, pp. 638–49, for an interesting approach to field studies.

[38]The design of surveys and the development and administration of questionnaires are better left to trained individuals if valid results are to be obtained. The interested reader might consult Seymour Sudman and Norman M. Bradburn, *Asking Questions: A Practical Guide to Questionnaire Design* (San Francisco: Jossey-Bass, 1982).

[39]For an excellent article on the relationship between what researchers want to see and what they do see, consult G. Nettler, "Wanting and Knowing," *American Behavioral Scientist,* July 1973, pp. 5–26.

EXHIBIT 2-7

**Scale for Assessing
GANAT Appraisal
Interviews**

Part A: Appraisal Interview

The following items deal with the formal appraisal interview used in conjuction with the GANAT project program. Please circle the number that best describes your opinion of the most recent interview session.

	Very False						Very True
1. The appraisal interview covered my entire job.	1	2	3	4	5	6	7
2. The discussion of my performance during the appraisal interview was covered equitably.	1	2	3	4	5	6	7
3. The appraisal interview was accurately conducted.	1	2	3	4	5	6	7
4. I didn't have to ask for any clarification.	1	2	3	4	5	6	7
5. The interview was fair in every respect.	1	2	3	4	5	6	7
6. The interview really raised my anxiety level.	1	2	3	4	5	6	7
7. The interview's purpose was simply not clear to me.	1	2	3	4	5	6	7
8. The appraisal interview really made me think about working smarter on the job.	1	2	3	4	5	6	7
9. The interview was encouraging to me personally.	1	2	3	4	5	6	7
10. I dreaded the actual interview itself.	1	2	3	4	5	6	7
11. The boss was totally aboveboard in all phases of the interview.	1	2	3	4	5	6	7
12. The interview gave me some direction and purpose.	1	2	3	4	5	6	7
13. The interview really pinpointed areas for improvement.	1	2	3	4	5	6	7
14. The interview was disorganized and frustrating.	1	2	3	4	5	6	7
15. I disliked the interview because the intent was not clear.	1	2	3	4	5	6	7

(continued)

		Very False						Very True
16.	The appraisal interviewer (boss) was not well trained.	1	2	3	4	5	6	7
17.	The interview has been my guide for correcting weaknesses.	1	2	3	4	5	6	7
18.	I understood the meaning of each performance area better after the interview.	1	2	3	4	5	6	7
19.	The interview time was too rushed.	1	2	3	4	5	6	7
20.	I received no advanced notice about the interview.	1	2	3	4	5	6	7
21.	The interview analyzed my performance fairly.	1	2	3	4	5	6	7
22.	I was often upset because the interview data were not accurate.	1	2	3	4	5	6	7
23.	My record as it was introduced in the interview contained no errors.	1	2	3	4	5	6	7

Source: This interview appraisal form was developed by John M. Ivancevich and sponsored by research funds provided by the GANAT Company.

Experiment

The experiment is potentially the most rigorous of scientific techniques. For an investigation to be considered an experiment, it must contain two elements—manipulation of some independent variable and observation or measurement of the results (dependent variable) while maintaining all other factors unchanged. Thus, in an organization, a behavioral scientist could change one organizational factor and observe the results while attempting to keep everything else unchanged.[40] There are two general types of experiments.

In a **laboratory experiment**, the environment is created by the researcher. For example, a management researcher may work with a small, voluntary group in a classroom. The group may be students or managers. They may be asked to communicate, perform tasks, or make decisions under different sets of conditions

[40]For a volume devoted entirely to experiments in organizations, see W. M. Evan, ed., *Organizational Experiments: Laboratory and Field Research* (New York: Harper & Row, 1971). Also see J. A. Walters, P. F. Salipante, Jr., and W. W. Notz, "The Experimenting Organization: Using the Results of Behavioral Science Research," *Academy of Management Review*, July 1978, pp. 483–92.

designated by the researcher. The laboratory setting permits the researcher to control closely the conditions under which observations are made. The intention is to isolate the relevant variables and to measure the response of dependent variables when the independent variable is manipulated. Laboratory experiments are useful when the conditions required to test a hypothesis are not practically or readily obtainable in natural situations and when the situation to be studied can be replicated under laboratory conditions. For such situations, many schools of business have behavioral science laboratories where such experimentation is done.

In a **field experiment**, the investigator attempts to manipulate and control variables in the natural setting rather than in a laboratory. Early experiments in organizations included manipulating physical working conditions such as rest periods, refreshments, and lighting. Today, behavioral scientists attempt to manipulate a host of additional factors.[41] For example, a training program might be introduced for one group of managers but not for another. Comparisons of performance, attitudes, and so on could be obtained later at one point or at several different points (a longitudinal study) to determine what effect, if any, the training program had on the managers' performances and attitudes.

The experiment is especially appealing to many researchers because it is the prototype of the scientific approach. It is the ideal toward which every science strives. However, while its potential is still great, the experiment has not produced a great breadth of knowledge about the functioning of organizations. Laboratory experiments suffer the risk of artificiality. The results of such experiments often do not extend to real organizations. Teams of business administration or psychology students working on decision problems may provide a great deal of information for researchers. Unfortunately, it is questionable whether this knowledge can be extended to a group of managers or nonmanagers making decisions under severe time constraints.[42]

Field experiments also have drawbacks. First, researchers cannot control every possible influencing factor (even if they knew them all) as they can in a laboratory. Here again, the fact that a researcher is present may make people behave differently, especially if they are aware that they are participating in an experiment. Experimentation in the behavioral sciences and, more specifically, experimentation in organizations are complex matters.

In a **true experiment**, the researcher has complete control over the experiment: the who, what, when, where, and how. A **quasi-experiment**, on the other hand, is an experiment in which the researcher lacks the degree of control over conditions

[41]See an account of the classic Hawthorne studies in Fritz J. Roethlisberger and W. J. Dickson, *Management and the Worker* (Boston: Division of Research, Harvard Business School, 1939). The original purpose of the studies, which were conducted at the Chicago Hawthorne Plant of Western Electric, was to investigate the relationship between productivity and physical working conditions.

[42]For a discussion of this problem, see K. W. Weick, "Laboratory Experimentation with Organizations: A Reappraisal," *Academy of Management Review,* January 1977, pp. 123–27.

that is possible in a true experiment. In the vast majority of organizational studies, it is impossible to completely control everything. Thus, quasi-experiments typically are the rule when organizational behavior is studied via an experiment.

Finally, with each of the methods of inquiry utilized by behavioral scientists, some type of measurement usually is necessary. For knowledge to be meaningful, it often must be compared with or related to something else. As a result, research questions (hypotheses) usually are stated in terms of how differences in the magnitude of some variable are related to differences in the magnitude of some other variable.

The variables studied are measured by research instruments. Those instruments may be psychological tests, such as personality or intelligence tests; questionnaires designed to obtain attitudes or other information, such as the questionnaire shown in Exhibit 2-7; or in some cases, electronic devices to measure eye movement or blood pressure.

It is very important that a research instrument be both **reliable** and **valid** Reliability is the consistency of the measure. In other words, repeated measures with the same instrument should produce the same results or scores. Validity is concerned with whether the research instrument actually measures what it is supposed to be measuring. Thus, it is possible for a research instrument to be reliable but not valid. For example, a test designed to measure intelligence could yield consistent scores over a large number of people but not be measuring intelligence.

RESEARCH DESIGNS

A number of designs are used in experiments to study organizational behavior. To illustrate some of the available designs, we shall use the example of a training program being offered to a group of first-line supervisors. Suppose the task of the researchers is to design an experiment that will permit the assessment of the degree to which the program influenced the performance of the supervisors. We will use the following symbols in our discussion:

S = The subjects, the supervisors participating in the experiment.

O = The observation and measurement devices used by the researcher (that is, ratings of supervisors' performance by superiors).

X = The experimental treatment, the manipulated variable (that is, the training program).

R = The randomization process.[43]

[43]R. H. Helmstader, *Research Concepts in Human Behavior* (New York: Appleton-Century-Crofts, 1970); William C. Scott and Terence R. Mitchell, *Organization Theory: A Structural and Behavioral Analysis* (Homewood, Ill.: Richard D. Irwin, 1976); and D. W. Emory, *Business Research Methods* (Homewood, Ill.: Richard D. Irwin, 1980).

One-Shot Design

If we assume that all supervisors go through the training program, it will be difficult for the researchers to evaluate it. This is because the researchers cannot compare the group with another group that did not undergo the training program. This design is called a one-shot design and is diagrammed as follows:

$$X \quad O$$

The letter X stands for the experimental treatment (that is, the training program), and the letter O, for the observation of performance on the job. The measure of performance could be in the form of an average score based on ratings of superiors. However, the researchers in no way can determine whether performance was influenced at all by the training program. This experimental design is rarely used because of its weaknesses.

One-Group Pretest-Posttest Design

The previous design can be improved upon by first gathering performance data on the supervisors, instituting the training program, then remeasuring their performance. This is diagrammed as follows:

$$O_1 \quad X \quad O_2$$

Thus, a pretest is given in time period 1, the program is administered, and a posttest is administered in time period 2. If $O_2 > O_1$, the differences can be attributed to the training program.

Numerous factors can confound the results obtained with this design. For example, suppose new equipment has been installed between O_1 and O_2. This could explain the differences in the performance scores. Thus, a **history factor** may have influenced our results. Other factors could influence our results. The most recurrent factors are listed along with their definitions in Exhibit 2-8.[44] Examination of Exhibit 2-8 indicates that results achieved in this design also may be confounded by **maturation** (the supervisors may learn to do a better job between O_1 and O_2, which would increase their performance regardless of training), **testing** (the measure of performance in O_1 may make the supervisors aware that they are being evaluated, which may make them work harder and increase their performance), and **instrumentation** (if the performance observations are made at different times of the day, the results could be influenced by fatigue). Each of these factors offers explanations for changes in performance other than the training program. Obviously, this design can be improved upon.

[44]Ibid.

EXHIBIT 2-8

Some Sources of Error in Experimental Studies

Factor	Definition
1. History	Events other than the experimental treatment (X) that occurred between pretest and posttest.
2. Maturation	Changes in the subject group with the passage of time that are not associated with the experimental treatment (X).
3. Testing	Changes in the performance of the subjects because measurement of their performance makes them aware that they are part of an experiment (that is, measures often alter what is being measured).
4. Instrumentation	Changes in the measures of participants' performance that are the result of changes in the measurement instruments or the conditions under which the measuring is done (for example, wear on machinery, boredom, fatigue on the part of observers).
5. Selection	When participants are assigned to experimental control groups on any basis other than random assignment. Any selection method other than random assignment will result in systematic biases that will result in differences between groups that are unrelated to the effects of the experimental treatment (X).
6. Mortality	If some participants drop out of the experiment before it is completed, the experimental and control groups may not be comparable.
7. Interaction effects	Any of the above factors may interact with the experimental treatment, resulting in confounding effects on the results. For example, the types of individuals withdrawing from a study (mortality) may differ for the experimental group and the control group.

Static-Group Comparison Design

In this design, half of the supervisors would be allowed to enroll for the training. Once the enrollment reached 50 percent of the supervisors, the training program would begin. After some period of time, the group of supervisors who enrolled in the program would be compared with those who did not enroll. This design is diagrammed as follows:

X O

O

Since the supervisors were not randomly assigned to each group, it is highly possible that the group that enrolled consists of the more highly motivated or more intelligent supervisors. Thus, *selection* is a major problem with this design. However, note that the addition of a **control group** (comparison group) has eliminated many of the error factors associated with the first two designs. The problem here is that the subjects were not randomly assigned to the experimental group (undergoing training) and the control group (no training). Therefore, it is possible that differences may exist between the two groups that are not related to the training.

The three designs discussed thus far (one-shot, one-group pretest-posttest, and static-group comparisons) have been described as "pseudo-experimental" or "quasi-experimental" designs. When true experimentation cannot be achieved, these designs (especially the last two) are preferred over no research at all or over relying on personal opinion. The following three designs can be considered true experimental designs because the researcher has complete control over the situation in the sense of determining precisely who will participate in the experiment and which subjects will or will not receive the experimental treatment.

Pretest-Posttest Control Group Design

This design is one of the simplest forms of true experimentation used in the study of human behavior. It is diagrammed as follows:

$$R \quad O_1 \quad X \quad O_2$$
$$R \quad O_1 \quad \quad O_2$$

Note that this design is similar to the one-group pretest-posttest design except that a control group has been added and the participants have been randomly assigned to both groups. Which group is to receive the training (experimental group) and which will not (control group) is also randomly determined. The two groups may be said to be equivalent at the time of the initial observations and at the time the final observations are made and are different only in that one group has received training while the other has not. In other words, if the change from O_1 to O_2 is greater in the experimental group than in the control group, we can attribute the difference to the training program rather than selection, testing, maturation, and so forth.

The major weakness of the pretest-posttest control group design is one of **interaction** (selection and treatment), where individuals are aware that they are participating in an experiment. In other words, being observed the first time makes all of the participants work more diligently, both those who are in the training group and those who are in the control group. Here, the participants in the training program will be more receptive to training because of the pretest. This problem of interaction can be overcome by using a posttest-only control group design.

Posttest-Only Control Group Design

In this design, the participants are randomly assigned to two groups, the training is administered to one group, and the scores on the posttests are compared (performance envaluated). It is diagrammed as follows:

$$R \quad X \quad O$$
$$R \quad \quad O$$

This eliminates the problem of the previous design by not administering a pretest. However, the dependent variable (performance) is an ultimate rather than a relative measure of achievement. Also, the researcher does not have a group that was pretested and posttested without receiving the experimental treatment (training program). Such a group can provide valuable information on the effects of history, maturation, instrumentation, and so on. However, where a pretest is difficult to obtain or where its use is likely to make the participants aware that an experiment is being carried on, this approach may be much preferred to the pretest-posttest control group design.

Solomon Four-Group Design

This design is a combination of the previous two designs and is diagrammed as follows:

Group 1	R	O_1	X	O_2
Group 2	R	O_1		O_2
Group 3	R		X	O_2
Group 4	R			O_2

Where gain or change in behavior is the designed dependent variable, this design should be used. This design is the most desirable of all the designs examined here. While it does not control any more sources of invalid results, it does permit the estimation of the extent of the effects of some of the sources of error. In our example here, the supervisors are randomly assigned to four groups, two of which will receive the training, one with a pretest and one without. Therefore, the researcher can examine, among other things, the effects of history (Group 1 to Group 2), testing (Group 2 to Group 4), and testing-treatment interaction (Group 2 to Group 3). Clearly, this design is the most complex, utilizing more participants, and it will be more costly. The added value of the additional information will have to be compared to the additional costs.[45]

QUALITATIVE RESEARCH

Instead of using experimental designs and concentrating on measurement issues, some researchers use qualitative research procedures. The notion of applying qualitative research methods to studying behavior within organizations recently has been addressed in leading research outlets.[46] The term **qualitative methods** is used to describe an array of interpretative techniques that attempt to describe and clarify the meaning of naturally occurring phenomena. It is by design rather

[45]For a complete coverage of this area, see Kerlinger, *Foundations of Behavioral Research*, pp. 300–76; Helmstader, *Research Concepts in Human Behavior*, pp. 91–121; and Emory, *Business Research Methods*, pp. 330–65.

[46]John Van Maanen, ed., *Qualitative Methodology* (Beverly Hills, Calif.: Sage Publications, 1983).

open-ended and interpretative. The researcher's interpretation and description are the significant data collection acts in a qualitative study. In essence, qualitative data are defined as those (1) whose meanings are subjective, (2) that are rarely quantifiable, and (3) that are difficult to use in making quantitative comparisons.

Using both quantitative and qualitative methods in the same study can, in some cases, achieve a comprehensiveness that neither approach, if used alone, could achieve.[47] Another possible advantage of the combined use of the quantitative and qualitative methods is that the use of multiple methods could help check for congruence in findings. This is extremely important, especially when prescribing management interventions on the base of research.[48]

The quantitative approach to organizational behavior research is exemplified by precise definitions, control groups, objective data collection, use of the scientific method, and replicable findings. These characteristics are presented in Exhibit 2–6. The importance of reliability, validity, and accurate measurement is always stressed. On the other hand, qualitative research is more concerned with the meaning of what is observed. Since organizations are so complex, a range of quantitative and qualitative techniques can be used side by side to learn about individual, group, and organizational behavior.[49]

Qualitative methodology uses the experience and intuition of the researcher to describe the organizational processes and structures being studied. The data collected by a qualitative researcher requires him or her to become very close to the situation or problem being studied. For example, one qualitative method used is called the ethnographic method by anthropologists.[50] Here the researcher typically studies a phenomenon for long periods of time as a participant-observer. The researcher becomes part of the situation being studied to feel what it is like for the people in that situation. The researcher becomes totally immersed in other people's realities.

Participant observation usually is supplemented by a variety of quantitative data collection tools such as structured interviews and self-report questionnaires. A variety of techniques is used so that the researcher can cross-check the results obtained from observation and recorded in field notes.

In training researchers in the ethnographic method, it is a common practice to place them in unfamiliar settings. A researcher may sit with and listen to workers on a production line, drive around in a police car to observe police officers, or do cleanup work in a surgical operating room. The training is designed to improve the researcher's ability to record, categorize, and code what is being observed.

[47]Christopher Stone, "Qualitative Reserch: A Viable Psychological Alternative," *Psychological Reports,* Winter 1985, pp. 63–75.

[48]Laura D. Goodwin and William L. Goodwin, "Qualitative vs. Quantitative Research, or Qualitative and Quantitative Research," *Nursing Research,* November–December 1984, pp. 378–80.

[49]Richard L. Daft, "Learning the Craft of Organizational Research," *Academy of Management Review,* October 1983, pp. 539–46.

[50]Anthony F. C. Wallace, "Paradigmatic Processes in Cultural Change," *American Anthropologist,* 1972, pp. 467–78.

An example of qualitative research involvement is present in Van Maanen's participant-observer study of a big-city police department. He went through police academy training and then accompanied police officers on their daily rounds. He functioned with police officers in daily encounters. Thus, he was able to provide vivid descriptions of what police work was like.[51]

Other qualitative techniques include content analysis (e.g., the researcher's interpretation of field notes), informal interviewing, archival data surveys and historical analysis, and the use of unobtrusive measures (e.g., data whose collection is not influenced by a researcher's presence). An example of the last would be the wear and tear on a couch in a cardiologist's office. As reported in the discussion of Type A Behavior Pattern in Chapter 6, the wear and tear was on the edges of the couch, which suggested anxiety and hyperactive behavior. Qualitative research appears to rely more on multiple sources of data than on any one source. The current research literature suggests a number of characteristics associated with qualitative research.[52]

1. *Analytical induction.* Qualitative research begins with the closeup, first-hand inspection of organizational life.
2. *Proximity.* Researchers desire to witness firsthand what is being studied. If the application of rewards is what is being studied, the researcher would want to observe episodes of reward distribution.
3. *Ordinary behavior.* The topics of research interest should be ordinary, normal, routine behaviors.
4. *Descriptive emphasis.* Qualitative research seeks descriptions for what is occurring in any given place and time. The aim is to disclose and reveal, not merely to order data and to predict.
5. *Shrinking variance.* Qualitative research is geared toward the explanation of similarity and coherence. Greater emphasis is placed on commonality and on things shared in organizational settings than on things not shared.
6. *Enlighten the consumer.* The consumer of qualitative research could be a manager. A major objective is to enlighten without confusing him or her. This is accomplished by providing commentary that is coherent and logically persuasive.

Researchers and managers do not have to choose either quantitative or qualitative research data and interpretation. There are convincing and relevant arguments that more than one method of research should be used when studying organizational behavior. Quantitative and qualitative research methods and procedures have much to offer practicing managers. Blending and integrating quantitative and qualitative research are what researchers and managers must do in the years ahead to better understand, cope with, and modify organizational behavior.

[51]John Van Maanen, J. M. Dobbs, Jr., and R. R. Faulkner, *Varieties of Qualitative Research* (Beverly Hills, Calif.: Sage Publications, 1982).

[52]Van Maanen, *Qualitative Methodology,* pp. 255–56.

PART

II

All achievers experience
their goals in vivid detail.

—Joe L. Whitley
Management Consultant

THE INDIVIDUAL IN
THE ORGANIZATION

C H A P T E R

3

Individual Differences and Work Behavior

LEARNING OBJECTIVES

IDENTIFY the major individual variables that influence work behavior.

DESCRIBE how attributions influence our behavior.

DISTINGUISH between stereotyping and prejudice.

EXPLAIN what an attitude is and identify its three components.

DISCUSS the relationship between job satisfaction and performance.

DESCRIBE the major forces influencing personality.

IDENTIFY several important personality factors.

Any attempt to learn why people behave as they do in organizations requires some understanding of individual differences. Managers spend considerable time making judgments about the fit between individuals, job tasks, and effectiveness. Such judgments are influenced typically by both the manager's and the subordinate's characteristics. Making decisions about who will perform what tasks in a particular manner—without some understanding of behavior—can lead to irreversible long-run problems.

Each employee is different in many respects. A manager needs to ask how such differences influence the behavior and performance of subordinates. This chapter highlights some of the individual differences that can explain why one person is a significantly better performer than another person. Differences among people require forms of adjustment for both the individual and those for whom he or she will work. Managers who ignore such differences often become involved in practices which hinder achieving organizational and personal goals.

THE BASIS FOR UNDERSTANDING WORK BEHAVIOR

A manager's observation and analysis of individual behavior and performance require the consideration of at least two sets of variables which directly influence individual behavior or what an employee does (e.g., produces output, sells automobiles, services machines). The two sets of variables are classified as being *individual* and *organizational*. Within each set are a number of subsets. For example, the individual variables include abilities and skills, perception, and personality. Exhibit 3-1 suggests that an employee's behavior is complex because it is affected by such diverse variables, experiences, and events. In fact, human behavior is far too complex to be explained by a generalization that applies to all people. Consequently, only a sampling of some of the relevant variables that influence human behavior in organizations are presented in the exhibit.

Exhibit 3-1 suggests that effective managerial practice requires that individual behavior differences be recognized and, when feasible, taken into consideration while carrying out the job of managing organizational behavior. To understand **individual differences,** a manager must (1) observe and recognize the differences, (2) study relationships between variables that influence individual behavior, and (3) discover relationships. For example, a manager is in a better position to make optimal decisions if he or she knows what the attitudes, perceptions, and mental abilities of employees are as well as how these and other variables are related. It also is important to know how each variable influences performance. Being able to observe differences, understand relationships, and predict linkages can facilitate

▲ C3–1

managerial attempts to improve performance. The Bob Knowlton Case at the end of the chapter demonstrates how individual differences can arise among several individual-level variables discussed in the chapter and illustrates the impact of these differences on organizational effectiveness.

Work behavior is anything a person does in the work environment. *Talking* to a manager, *listening* to a co-worker, *filing* a report, *typing* a memo, *placing* a completed unit in inventory, and *learning* how to use the firm's accounting system are all work behaviors. However, so are *daydreaming* about being on the golf course, *socializing with friends* around the water cooler, and *sabotaging* a new piece of equipment. Some of these behaviors contribute to productivity; others are nonproductive or even counterproductive. Nonetheless, they are all examples of behaviors engaged in by individuals in work settings. In the remainder of this chapter we will attempt to provide a basis for better understanding why these behaviors occur.

INDIVIDUAL VARIABLES

The individual variables presented in Exhibit 3-1 are classified as demographic factors, abilities and skills, perception, attitudes, and personality. We will briefly discuss the first two and examine in greater detail the latter three.

EXHIBIT 3-1

**Variables that Influence
Work Behavior**

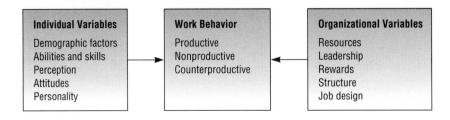

Demographic Factors

Demographic factors is a term used to include a number of individual differences that influence behavioral choices. These include such factors as socioeconomic background, nationality, educational attainment level, age, race, and sex, to name a few of the potentially more significant ones. Consider age for example. A 60-year-old nearing career's end will most likely have significantly different goals, experiences, and perhaps beliefs and values, than a 25-year-old just beginning a career. It would be surprising if these age-related differences *did not* occasionally lead these two individuals to choose different behaviors in otherwise similar situations. This is not to suggest that one's behavior is likely to be "better" than the other's, but it sometimes will be different. Effective management requires awareness of these differences.

Another example of an important demographic difference is that of sex, or gender. Possible gender-related differences have received particular attention in regard to professional and managerial careers. It has been argued, for example, that men will make better managers because they are more assertive, that women are less committed to organizational careers because of family considerations, or that men are less sensitive to the feelings of others. While it is true that examples supporting each of these generalizations can be found, so also can one find multiple examples which refute them. Indeed, research suggests that most of the stereotypical differences frequently used to describe males and females in organizations are simply not valid.[1]

It is important to understand, however, that the perception that these differences exist influences the behavior of both men and women in work settings. A male manager, for example, who assumes a female employee is less committed to the organization because of family responsibilities is likely—perhaps unconsciously—to behave differently toward her than he otherwise would. In turn, the female employee's behavior will likely be influenced—again, perhaps unconsciously—by the manager's behavior.

Many of the demographic factors that influence behavior do so not because there are true, innate differences between, for example, men and women, 60-

[1]G. N. Powell, "One More Time: Do Female and Male Managers Differ?," *Academy of Management Executive,* August 1990, pp. 68–75.

year-olds and 25-year-olds, or North Americans and Europeans. Rather, because there are different patterns of experiences, needs, and consequently goals, beliefs, and values, individuals in one of these categories behave differently than their counterparts in another category.

Abilities and Skills

Some employees, though highly motivated, simply do not have the abilities or skills to perform well. Abilities and skills play a major role in individual behavior and performance.[2] An **ability** is a trait (innate or learned) that permits a person to do something mental or physical. For example, various mental abilities such as inductive reasoning, number facility, verbal comprehension, memory span, spatial orientation, and deductive reasoning make up what is commonly referred to as intelligence. **Skills**, on the other hand, are task-related competences such as the skill to operate a lathe or a computer. Exhibit 3-2 presents a number of physical skills. In most cases, the terms *abilities* and *skills* are used interchangeably in this book.

Managers must attempt to match a person with abilities and skills to the job requirements. The matching process is important since no amount of leadership, motivation, or organizational resources can make up for deficiencies in abilities or skills. **Job analysis** is a widely used technique that takes some of the guesswork out of matching. Job analysis is the process of defining and studying a job in terms of tasks or behaviors and specifying the responsibilities, education, and training needed to perform the job successfully.[3]

Perception

Perception is the cognitive process by which an individual gives meaning to the environment. Because each person gives his or her own meaning to stimuli, different individuals will "see" the same thing in different ways. The way an employee sees the situation often has much greater meaning for understanding behavior than does the situation itself.

Since perception refers to the acquisition of specific knowledge about objects or events at any particular moment, it occurs whenever stimuli activate the senses. Perception involves cognition (knowledge). Thus, perception includes the interpretation of objects, symbols, and people in the light of pertinent experiences. In other words, perception involves receiving stimuli, organizing the stimuli, and translating or interpreting the organized stimuli so as to influence behavior and form attitudes.

[2]For a discussion of the nature of ability-performance relationships, see W. M. Coward and P. R. Sackett, "Linearity of Ability-Performance Relationships: A Reconfirmation," *Journal of Applied Psychology,* June 1990, pp. 297–300.

[3]For a complete discussion of job analysis, see J. M. Ivancevich, *Human Resource Management* (Homewood, Ill.: Richard D. Irwin, 1992), pp. 170–207.

EXHIBIT 3-2

**Sample of
Physical Skills**

Physical Skill	Description
1. Dynamic strength	Muscular endurance in exerting force continuously or repeatedly
2. Extent flexibility	The ability to flex or stretch trunk and back muscles
3. Gross body coordination	The ability to coordinate the action of several parts of the body while the body is in motion
4. Gross body equilibrium	The ability to maintain balance with nonvisual cues
5. Stamina	The capacity to sustain maximum effort requiring cardiovascular exertion

Source: Adapted from Edwin A. Fleishman, "On the Relation between Abilities, Learning, and Human Performance," *American Psychologist*, November 1972, pp. 1017–32.

Each person selects various cues that influence his or her perceptions of people, objects, and symbols. Because of these factors and their potential for imbalance, people often misperceive another person, group, or object. To a considerable extent, people interpret the behavior of others in the context of the setting in

■ E3–1   which they find themselves. Exercise 3–1 provides you with an opportunity to experience the influence of various assumptions on your own perceptions.

The following are some organizational examples that point out how perception influences behavior:

1. A subordinate's response to a supervisor's request is based on what she thought she heard the supervisor say, not on what was actually requested.
2. The manager considers the product sold to be of high quality, but the customer making a complaint feels that it is poorly made.
3. An employee is viewed by one colleague as a hard worker who gives good effort and by another colleague as a poor worker who expends no effort.
4. The salesperson regards her pay increase as totally inequitable, while the sales manager considers it a very fair raise.
5. A supervisor who regards an employee as an outstanding performer assigns her additional responsibilities as a reward, but she feels the supervisor is simply dumping more work in her lap.

A study clearly showing that managers and subordinates often have different perceptions was reported to Likert. He examined the perceptions of superiors and subordinates to determine the amounts and types of recognition that subordinates received for good performance. Both supervisors and subordinates were asked how often superiors provided rewards for good work. The results are presented in Exhibit 3-3.

There were significant differences in what the two groups perceived. Each group viewed the type of recognition being given at a different level. The subordinates in most cases reported that very little recognition was being provided by their supervisors and that rewards were provided infrequently. The superiors

EXHIBIT 3-3

The Perceptual Gap between Supervisors and Subordinates

Types of Recognition	Frequency with Which Supervisors Say They Give Various Types of Recognition for Good Performance	Frequency with Which Subordinates Say Supervisors Give Various Types of Recognition for Good Performance
Gives privileges	52%	14%
Gives more responsibility	48	10
Gives a pat on the back	82	13
Gives sincere and thorough praise	80	14
Trains for better jobs	64	9
Gives more interesting work	51	5

Source: Adapted from Rensis Likert, *New Patterns in Management* (New York: McGraw-Hill, 1961), p. 91.

saw themselves as giving a wide variety of rewards for good performance. The study points out that marked differences existed between the superiors' and the subordinates' perceptions of the superiors' behavior.

Perceptual Organization

An important aspect of what is perceived involves organization.[4] One of the most elemental organizing principles of perception is the tendency to pattern stimuli in terms of *figure-ground* relationships. Not all stimuli reach one's awareness with equal clarity. The factor focused on is called the **figure**. That which is experienced and is out of focus is called the **ground**. As you read this text, your perceptions are organized in terms of figure and ground. In every perceptual act, the figure-ground principle is operating.[5] A figure-ground workplace example is a union organizer who stands out more than other workers. As the union pushes to organize the work force, the organizer stands out more and more to management. In most cases, a union organizer would stand out and be considered a troublemaker by management.

The organizing nature of perception is also apparent when similar stimuli are grouped together and when stimuli in close proximity are grouped. Another grouping principle that shapes perceptual organization is called **closure** and refers to the tendency to want to close something with missing parts. Some individuals have a strong need to complete a configuration, a job, or a project. For example, if a person with a high need for closure is prevented from finishing a job or task, this could lead to frustration or a more drastic behavior such as quitting.

[4]M. W. Levine and J. M. Shefner, *Fundamentals of Sensation and Perception* (Reading, Mass.: Addison-Wesley Publishing, 1981), p. 17.

[5]B. V. H. Gilmer, *Applied Psychology* (New York: McGraw-Hill, 1975), p. 229.

Stereotyping

Stereotyping is a process employed to assist individuals in dealing with massive information processing demands. In this regard it represents a useful, even essential, way of categorizing individuals (or events, organizations, etc.) on the basis of limited information or observation. The process of forming stereotypes and placing individuals in certain categories on the basis of these stereotypes is a perceptual one. When we speak of the Germans as efficient, the Italians as great lovers, or the French as outstanding cooks, we are engaging in nationality stereotyping. Since many stereotypes relate to ethnic group membership it is important to distinguish between a stereotype and a prejudice. A prejudice is a stereotype that refuses to change when presented with information indicating the stereotype is inaccurate. Stereotypes can be helpful; prejudice is never helpful.

It is often assumed that stereotyping is inherently bad or wrong. This is not the case, however. Stereotyping is a useful process that greatly increases our efficiency in making sense out of our environment. Nonetheless, stereotyping can and does lead to inaccuracies and negative consequences.[6] To the extent that stereotypes create social injustice, result in poorer decision making, stifle innovation, or cause underutilization of organizational human resources they contribute to ineffectiveness and inefficiency. The solution to perceptual bias created by stereotypes is not to resist forming stereotypes; this is neither practical nor desirable. Rather, it is to (1) be alert to the fact that stereotypes are frequently formed on the basis of very little information and can be extremely inaccurate; (2) be receptive to new, additional information that can improve the accuracy of existing stereotypes; and (3) understand that stereotypes rarely apply well to a specific individual. Judgments based on personal knowledge of a specific individual are inevitably more accurate than reference to a broad category to which the individual belongs.

■ E3–2   Exercise 3–2 asks you to engage in some "occupational" stereotyping and provides a good illustration of assumptions you may make about both people and occupations. With this exercise you may also compare your stereotypes with those of others in the class completing the exercise.

Selective Perception

The concept of **selective perception** is important to managers since they often receive large amounts of information and data. Consequently, they may tend to select information that supports their viewpoints. People tend to ignore information or cues that might make them feel discomfort. For example, a skilled manager may be concerned primarily with an employee's final results or output. Since the employee is often cynical and negative when interacting with the manager, other managers may conclude that the employee will probably receive a poor performance rating. However, this manager selects out the negative features

---

[6]Loren Falkenberg, "Improving the Accuracy of Stereotypes in the Workplace," *Journal of Management,* March 1990, pp. 107–18.

or cues and rates the subordinate on the basis of results. This is a form of selective perception.

The Manager's Characteristics

People frequently use themselves as benchmarks in perceiving others. Research suggests that (1) knowing oneself makes it easier to see others accurately,[7] (2) one's own characteristics affect the characteristics identified in others,[8] and (3) persons who accept themselves are more likely to see favorable aspects of other people.[9]

Basically, these conclusions suggest that managers perceiving the behavior and individual differences of employees are influenced by their own traits. If they understand that their own traits and values influence perception, they probably can perform a more accurate evaluation of their subordinates. A manager who is a perfectionist tends to look for perfection in subordinates, while a manager who is quick in responding to technical requirements looks for this ability in his subordinates.

Situational Factors

The press of time, the attitudes of the people a manager is working with, and other situational factors will all influence perceptual accuracy. If a manager is pressed for time and has to immediately fill an order, then her perceptions will be influenced by the time constraints. The press of time literally will force the manager to overlook some details, to rush certain activities, and to ignore certain stimuli such as requests from other managers or from superiors.

Needs and Perceptions

Perceptions are influenced significantly by needs and desires. In other words, the employee, the manager, the vice president, and the director see what they want to see. Like the mirrors in the fun house at the amusement park, the work can be distorted; the distortion is related to needs and desires.

The influence of needs in shaping perceptions has been studied in laboratory settings. For instance, subjects at various stages of hunger were asked to report what they saw in ambiguous drawings flashed before them. It was found that as hunger increased up to a certain point, the subjects saw more and more of the ambiguous drawings as articles of food. The hungry subjects saw steaks, salads,

[7]R. D. Norman, "The Interrelationships among Acceptance-Rejection, Self-Other Identity, Insight into Self, and Realistic Perception of Others," *Journal of Social Psychology,* May 1953, pp. 205–35.

[8]J. Bossom and A. H. Maslow, "Security of Judges as a Factor in Impressions of Warmth in Others," *Journal of Abnormal and Social Psychology,* July 1957, pp. 147–48.

[9]K. T. Omivake, "The Relation between Acceptance of Self and Acceptance of Others Shown by Three Personality Inventories," *Journal of Consulting Psychology,* 1954, pp. 443–46.

and sandwiches, while the subjects who recently had eaten saw nonfood images in the same drawings.[10]

Emotions and Perceptions

A person's emotional state has a lot to do with perceptions. A strong emotion, such as total distaste for an organizational policy, can make a person perceive negative characteristics in most company policies and rules. Determining a person's emotional state is difficult. Yet managers need to be concerned about what issues or practices trigger strong emotions within subordinates. Strong emotions often distort perceptions.

Perception and Behavior

It is often said that perception *is* reality. That is, what an employee perceives to be real is, in fact for that employee, reality. Since behavior is greatly influenced by our personal interpretation of reality, it is easy to understand why our perceptual processes are potent determinants of behavior. One approach that provides a basis for understanding the relationship between perception and behavior is **attribution theory**. Attribution theory is concerned with the process by which individuals interpret events around them as being caused by a relatively stable portion of their environment.[11] In short, attribution theory attempts to explain the *why* of behavior. Exhibit 3-4 displays the attribution process.

According to attribution theory, it is the perceived causes of events, not the actual ones, that influence people's behavior. More specifically, individuals will attempt to analyze why certain events have occurred, and the results of that analysis will influence their behavior in the future. As the example in Exhibit 3-4 indicates, an employee who receives a raise will attempt to attribute the raise to some underlying cause. If the employee perceives the explanation for the raise to be the fact that she is a hard worker and consequently concludes that working hard leads to rewards in this organization, she would decide to continue working hard in the future. Another employee may attribute his raise to the fact that he participates in the company's bowling team and decides it makes sense to continue bowling for that reason. Thus, in both cases employees have made decisions affecting their future behaviors on the basis of their attributions. Subsequent events will be interpreted by these two employees based on their attributions of why these events happened and will be either reinforced or modified depending on future events.

The attribution process also can be important in understanding the behavior of other people. The behavior of a subordinate, for example, can be examined on the basis of its consensus, consistency, and distinctiveness. **Consensus** is the

---

[10]J. A. Deutsch, W. G. Young, and T. J. Kalogeris, "The Stomach Signals Satiety," *Science,* April 1978, pp. 23–33.

[11]H. H. Kelly, "Attribution Theory in Social Psychology," in *Nebraska Symposium on Motivation,* ed. D. Levine (Lincoln: University of Nebraska Press, 1967).

EXHIBIT 3-4

The Attribution Process

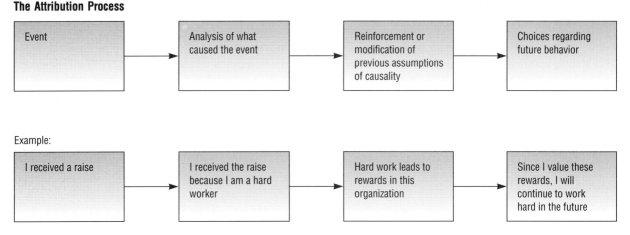

Source: Adapted from Abraham Korman, *Organizational Behavior* (Englewood Cliffs, N.J.: Prentice-Hall, 1977), p. 273.

degree to which other subordinates engage in the same behavior. **Consistency** is the degree to which the person in question engages in the same behaviors at different times. **Distinctiveness** is the degree to which the subordinate behaves similarly in other situations. For example, you might observe that a particular subordinate is taking extended rest breaks. If he is the only one in the work group doing this (low consensus), if he is doing this regularly (high consistency), and if he has a history of having taken extended breaks in other work groups he has been part of (low distinctiveness) you might reasonably attribute his behavior to internal factors (within the employee himself).

On the other hand, you might observe something quite different. Maybe most members of the work group are taking extended breaks (high consensus), and although this subordinate has been doing this regularly (high consistency) you have never known him to do this in other work groups of which he has been a member (high distinctiveness). A reasonable attribution in this scenario might be that there are external factors (in the work group environment) causing this behavior. We are not suggesting that the behavior is more or less appropriate in one scenario or the other, or that the subordinate should be held more or less accountable. The point is that whatever attributions the manager makes have direct implications for attempts to correct the problem.

The managerial implications of an attributional approach to understanding work behavior are important. In order to influence employee behavior, the manager must understand the attributions employees make. Further, the manager must be aware that his own attributions may be different from theirs. For example, if a manager perceives employee poor performance to be the result of lack of effort, she may attempt to increase motivation levels. On the other hand, if employees perceive performance problems to be attributable to lack of supervisory guidance, the efforts made by the manager are not likely to have the desired effect on performance. Managers cannot assume that their attributions will be the same as their employees'. Knowing this, coupled with an effort to understand what attributions employees make, can greatly enhance the manager's ability to have a positive effect on employee behavior.

Attitudes

Attitudes are determinants of behavior, because they are linked with perception, personality, and motivation. An **attitude** is a mental state of readiness, learned and organized through experience, exerting a specific influence on a person's response to people, objects, and situations with which it is related. Each of us has attitudes on numerous topics—unions, jogging, restaurants, friends, jobs, religion, the government, income taxes.

This definition of attitude has certain implications for the manager. First, attitudes are learned. Second, attitudes define one's predispositions toward given aspects of the world. Third, attitudes provide the emotional basis of one's interpersonal relations and identification with others. And fourth, attitudes are organized and are close to the core of personality. Some attitudes are persistent and enduring. Yet, like each of the psychological variables, attitudes are subject to change.[12]

Attitudes are intrinsic parts of a person's personality. However, a number of theories attempt to account for the formation and change of attitudes. One such theory proposes that people "seek a congruence between their beliefs and feelings toward objects" and suggests that the modification of attitudes depends on changing either the feelings or the beliefs.[13] The theory proposes that cognition, affect, and behavior determine attitudes and that attitudes, in turn, determine cognition, affect, and behavior. The **cognitive** component of an attitude consists of the person's perceptions, opinions, and beliefs. It refers to the thought processes with special emphasis on rationality and logic. An important element of cognition is the evaluative beliefs held by a person. Evaluative beliefs are manifested in the form of favorable or unfavorable impressions that a person holds toward an object or person.

Affect, the emotional or "feeling" component of an attitude, is learned from parents, teachers, and peer group members. One study displays how the affective component can be measured. A questionnaire was used to survey the attitudes of a group of students toward the church. The students then listened to tape recordings that either praised or disparaged the church. At the time of the tape recordings, the emotional responses of the students were measured with a galvanic skin response (GSR) device. Both prochurch and antichurch students responded

[12]D. J. Bem, *Attitudes, Beliefs, and Human Affairs* (Reading, Mass.: Brooks-Cole, 1982).

[13]M. J. Rosenberg, "A Structural Theory of Attitudes," *Public Opinion Quarterly,* Summer 1960, pp. 319–40.

EXHIBIT 3-5

**The Three Components
of Attitudes**

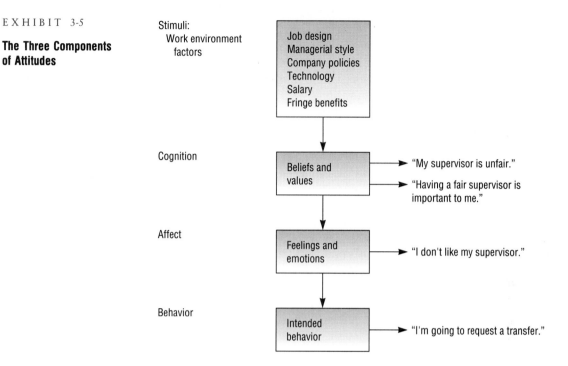

with greater emotion (displayed by GSR changes) to statements that contradicted their attitudes than to statements that reflected their attitudes.[14]

The behavioral component of an attitude refers to the tendency of a person to act in a certain way toward someone or something. A person can act toward someone or something in a friendly, warm, aggressive, hostile, or apathetic way or in any of a number of other ways. Such actions could be measured or assessed to examine the behavioral component of attitudes.

Exhibit 3-5 presents the three components of attitudes in terms of work environment factors such as job design, company policies, and fringe benefits. These stimuli trigger cognitive (thought), affective (emotional), and behavioral responses. In essence, the stimuli result in the formation of attitudes which then lead to one or more responses.

The theory of cognitive, affective, and behavioral components as determinants of attitudes has a significant implication for managers. The theory implies that the manager must be able to demonstrate that the positive aspects of contributing to the organization outweigh the negative aspects. It is through attempts to develop generally favorable attitudes toward the organization and the job that many managers achieve effectiveness.

[14]H. W. Dickson and E. McGinnies, "Affectivity and Arousal of Attitudes as Measured by Galvanic Skin Responses," *American Journal of Psychology*, October 1966, pp. 584–89.

Functions of Attitudes

From a managerial perspective, understanding employee attitudes and the cognitions and affect that help shape those attitudes is important in predicting behavior and in modifying attitudes. Critical to a fuller understanding of attitudes is knowing that various work-related attitudes serve important functions for employees. That is, attitudes are useful to people in a variety of ways. One way of describing the utility of attitudes has been advanced by Katz, who has suggested attitudes serve at least four functions: adjustment, ego-defensive, value-expressive, and knowledge.[15] (See Exhibit 3-6.)

The **adjustment** function of attitudes serves to enable people to more easily and effectively come to terms with their environment. Attitudes may assist individuals in adjusting to new or changing situations and may also provide a justification or rationale for their behaviors. Thus, a decision to change employers which greatly increases an individual's commuting time can become more easily rationalized if that individual holds a positive attitude toward the new employer because, for example, the opportunities for rapid advancement are much greater.

● R3–1   The article by Chris Argyris which is part of this chapter discusses problems of mutual adjustment between individuals and organizations. The development of attitudes which serve an adjustment function can contribute to resolving the problems identified in this article.

The **ego-defensive** function of attitudes allows people to protect themselves from having to acknowledge negative or otherwise unwanted truths about themselves. In this way threats to one's self-esteem or ego can be minimized. A lazy employee, for example, might develop an attitude that his supervisor does not like him, not because he is not a hard worker but because he frequently expresses disagreement with the supervisor. Thus, the employee is spared from the ego-threatening admission that he is not very committed to his job. Unfortunately, ego-defensive attitudes are frequently counterproductive for both the individual who holds them and for the organization because they reinforce distorted perceptions of reality. Encounter 3–1 describes some attributions regarding the relationship between productivity declines and worker attitudes that you may feel reflect ego-defensive attitudes.

Many attitudes provide an opportunity for individuals to express beliefs and values that are very important to them. When this is the case, attitudes are serving a **value-expressive** function. Attitudes expressed about issues such as nuclear disarmament, curbing drug abuse, and the role of church and state are examples of value expression; the attitude the individual holds regarding these issues represents a vehicle for expressing important central values. In an organizational context, an attitude expressed by an employee that other departments in the company ought to develop the degree of teamwork found in the employee's

---

[15]D. Katz, "Determinants of Attitude Arousal and Attitude Change," *Journal of Personality* 24 (1960), p. 81.

EXHIBIT 3-6

**Functions Served
by Attitudes**

Function	Description	Example
1. Adjustment	Facilitates coming to terms with the environment and changes in environments.	"The additional promotion opportunities available with my new employer make up for the increased time I spend commuting."
2. Ego-defensive	Facilitates protecting one's self from knowledge that one would find threatening.	"My supervisor doesn't like me because I disagree with him, even though I work as hard as everyone else."
3. Value-expressive	Facilitates the expression of values that are important to the individual.	"Every department in this company should develop the degree of team work we have in this department."
4. Knowledge	Facilitates explaining and organizing the environment.	"Management cannot be trusted."

department represents an attitude that expresses the value he or she places on cohesiveness and cooperation.

Finally, attitudes may fill a **knowledge function.** Such attitudes assist individuals in structuring their environment and bringing a greater degree of order to what otherwise might be a chaotic world. Stereotypes, which are a form of attitudes, are representative of the knowledge function. For example, the attitude held by some union members that management cannot be trusted reflects a way in which the holder of that attitude can simplify his world; having such an attitude allows the holder to deal with all management the same way and negates the need to evaluate the position of individual managers.

Changing Attitudes

Managers are often faced with the task of changing attitudes because previously structured attitudes hinder job performance. Although many variables affect attitude change, they all can be described in terms of three general factors: trust in the sender, the message itself, and the situation.[16] If employees do not trust the manager, they will not accept the manager's message or change an attitude. Similarly, if the message is not convincing, there will be no pressure to change.

The greater the prestige of the communicator, the greater the attitude change that is produced.[17] A manager who has little prestige and is not shown respect

---

[16]Jonathan L. Freedman, J. Merrill Carlsmith, and David O. Sears, *Social Psychology* (Englewood Cliffs, N.J.: Prentice-Hall, 1974), p. 271. Also see D. Coon, *Introduction to Psychology* (St. Paul, Minn.: West Publishing, 1977), pp. 626–29.

[17]Ibid, p. 272.

PRODUCTIVITY DECLINES AND WORKER ATTITUDES: IS MANAGEMENT EGO-DEFENSIVE?

A growing concern over the last decade among organizational researchers, executives, boards of directors, and various public and private interest groups has been the country's declining productivity rate. Public pronouncements by executives regarding the cause—particularly when they know their remarks will be attributed to them by name—tend to identify a host of factors contributing to the decline. On the other hand, when executives are responding *anonymously* to a survey, the outcome is much different.

When such a survey was conducted recently by First Pennsylvania Bank, almost 70 percent of the several hundred executives from the eastern and northeastern parts of the country who responded attributed the cause of productivity declines in large part to the poor attitudes and resulting bad habits of the work force. Not lack of capital investment, not technology, not bad management. Bad attitudes. Unfortunately, workers were not queried regarding their opinions for the decline.

What is interesting here is that the executives' attributions that poor worker attitudes are responsible for the productivity decline is itself an attitude. In the context of the text discussion on the functions of attitudes, a case may be made for suggesting such an attitude held by managers serves an ego-defensive function. "Blaming" the workers protects management from knowledge that could be somewhat threatening. What's threatening in this situation? If someone in the organization is responsible and it isn't the workers, who is left? Management!

In reality, productivity declines are a function of numerous interacting factors, one of which probably is poor worker attitudes; another of which is probably ineffective management. Also, in fairness, it should be pointed out that had workers been surveyed they may have had some ego-defensive attitudes of their own: They may have blamed management.

by peers and superiors will be in a difficult position if the job requires changing the attitudes of subordinates so they will work more effectively.

Liking the communicator can lead to attitude change because people try to identify with a liked communicator and tend to adopt attitudes and behaviors of the liked person. Not all managers, however, are fortunate enough to be liked by each of their subordinates. Therefore, it is important to recognize the importance of trust in the manager as a condition for liking the manager.

Even if a manager is trusted, presents a convincing message, and is liked, the problems of changing people's attitudes are not easily solved. An important factor is the strength of the employee's commitment to an attitude. A worker who has decided not to accept a promotion is committed to the belief that it is better to remain in his or her present position than to accept the promotion. Attitudes that have been expressed publicly are more difficult to change because the person has shown commitment, and to change would be to admit a mistake.

How much you are affected by attempts to change your attitude depends in part on the situation. When people are listening to or reading a persuasive message, they sometimes are distracted by other thoughts, sounds, or activities. Studies indicate that if people are distracted while they are listening to a message, they will show more attitude change because the distraction interferes with silent counterarguing.[18]

Distraction is just one of many situational factors that can increase persuasion. Another factor that makes people more susceptible to attempts to change attitudes is pleasant surroundings. The pleasant surroundings may be associated with the attempt to change the attitude.

Attitudes and Job Satisfaction

Job satisfaction is an attitude that individuals have about their jobs. It results from their perception of their jobs and the degree to which there is a good fit between the individual and the organization.[19] Thus job satisfaction stems from various aspects of the job such as pay, promotion opportunities, supervisors, and co-workers. Job satisfaction also stems from factors of the work environment such as the supervisor's style; policies and procedures; work group affiliation; working conditions; and fringe benefits. While numerous dimensions have been associated with job satisfaction, five in particular have crucial characteristics.[20] These five dimensions are:

Pay—the amount of pay received and the perceived equity of pay.
Job—the extent to which job tasks are considered interesting and provide opportunities for learning and for accepting responsibility.
Promotion opportunities—the availability of opportunities for advancement.
Supervisor—the abilities of the supervisor to demonstrate interest in and concern about employees.
Co-workers—the extent to which co-workers are friendly, competent, and supportive.

These five job satisfaction dimensions have been measured in some studies by using the Job Descriptive Index (JDI). Employees are asked to respond "yes," "no," or "?" (can't decide) in describing whether a word or phrase reflects their attitudes about their jobs. Of the 72 items on the JDI, 20 are presented in Exhibit 3-7. A scoring procedure is used to arrive at a score for each of the five dimensions. These five scores then are totaled to provide a measure of overall satisfaction.

A major reason for studying job satisfaction is to provide managers with ways to improve employee attitudes. Many organizations use attitude surveys to determine the levels of employee job satisfaction. National surveys indicate that, in

[18]R. A. Osterhouse and T. C. Brock, "Distraction Increases Yielding to Propaganda by Inhibiting Counterarguing," *Journal of Personality and Social Psychology*, March 1977, pp. 344–58.

[19]C. A. Reilly III, J. Chatman, and D. F. Caldwell, "People and Organizational Culture: A Profile Comparison Approach to Assessing Person-Organizational Fit," *Academy of Management Journal*, September 1991, pp. 487–516.

[20]P. C. Smith, L. M. Kendall, and C. L. Hulin, *The Measurement of Satisfaction in Work and Retirement* (Skokie, Ill.: Rand McNally, 1969).

EXHIBIT 3-7

Sample Items from the 72-Item Job Descriptive Index with "Satisfied" Responses Indicated

Work		Supervision	
N	Routine	Y	Asks my advice
Y	Creative	Y	Praises good work
N	Tiresome	N	Doesn't supervise enough
Y	Gives sense of accomplishment	Y	Tells me where I stand

People		Pay	
Y	Stimulating	Y	Income adequate for normal expenses
Y	Ambitious	N	Bad
N	Talk too much	N	Less than I deserve
N	Hard to meet	N	Highly paid

Promotions	
Y	Good opportunity for advancement
Y	Promotion an ability
N	Dead-end job
N	Unfair promotion policy

Source: The Job Descriptive Index is copyrighted by Bowling Green State University. The complete forms, scoring key, instructions, and norms can be obtained from Dr. Patricia C. Smith, Department of Psychology, Bowling Green State University, Bowling Green, Ohio 43404. Reprinted with permission.

general, workers are satisfied with their jobs.[21] These types of surveys, though interesting, may not reflect the actual degree of job satisfaction in a specific department or organization. There is also a problem that arises simply from asking people how satisfied they are. There is a bias toward giving a positive answer, since declaring anything less indicates that the person is electing to stay in a dissatisfying job. Additionally, to say that workers generally are satisfied with their jobs does not identify the fact that there are differences in satisfaction levels across diverse groups.

[21]Karen E. DeBats, "The Continuing Personnel Challenge," *Personnel Journal,* May 1982, pp. 332–44.

EXHIBIT 3-8

Satisfaction-Performance Relationships: Three views

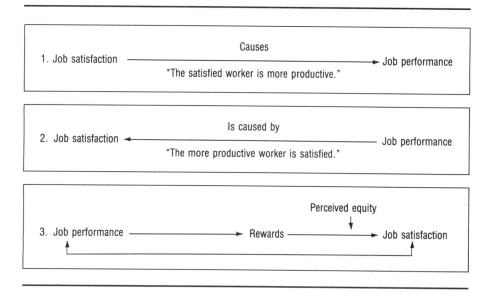

Satisfaction and Job Performance

One of the most widely debated and controversial issues in the study of job satisfaction is its relationship to job performance. Three general views of this relationship have been advanced: (1) satisfaction causes performance; (2) performance causes satisfaction; and (3) the satisfaction-performance relationship is moderated by other variables such as rewards.[22]

The first two views are supported weakly by research. A review of 20 studies dealing with the performance-satisfaction relationship found a low association between performance and satisfaction.[23] This evidence is rather convincing that a satisfied worker is not necessarily a high performer. Managerial attempts to make everyone satisfied will not yield high levels of production. Likewise, the assumption that a high-performing employee is likely to be satisfied is not supported.

The third view suggests that satisfaction and performance are related only under certain conditions. A number of other factors, such as pressure for production, supervisory level, task difficulty, and self-esteem, have been posited as moderating the relationship. Most attention, however, has focused on rewards as a key moderator. Generally, this view suggests that the rewards one receives as a consequence of good performance, and the degree to which these rewards are perceived as reasonable or equitable, affect both the extent to which satis-

[22]M. M. Petty, Gail McGee, and Jerry Cavender, "A Meta-Analysis of the Relationship between Individual Job Satisfaction and Individual Performance," *Academy of Management Review*, October 1984, pp. 712–21.

[23]Victor H. Vroom, *Work and Motivation* (New York: John Wiley & Sons, 1964).

faction results from performance and the extent performance is affected by satisfaction. Exhibit 3-8 shows all three of these viewpoints.

Personality

The relationship between behavior and personality is perhaps one of the most complex matters that managers have to understand. Personality is influenced significantly by cultural and social factors. Regardless of how personality is defined, however, certain principles generally are accepted among psychologists. These are:

1. Personality is an organized whole; otherwise, the individual would have no meaning.
2. Personality appears to be organized into patterns which are, to some degree, observable and measurable.
3. Although personality has a biological basis, its specific development is a product of social and cultural environments.[24]
4. Personality has superficial aspects, such as attitudes toward being a team leader, and a deeper core, such as sentiments about authority or the Protestant work ethic.
5. Personality involves both common and unique characteristics. Every person is different from every other person in some respects and similar to other persons in other respects.

These five ideas are included in the following definition of personality:

An individual's personality is a relatively stable set of characteristics, tendencies, and temperaments that have been significantly formed by inheritance and by social, cultural, and environmental factors. This set of variables determines the commonalities and differences in the behavior of the individual.[25]

The third idea points out some of the forces that are major determinants of personality. These forces are presented in Exhibit 3-9. Studies of family history, of identical twins, and of early childhood behavior indicate the importance of hereditary factors in personality formation. The importance of heredity varies from one personality trait to another. For example, heredity generally is more important in determining a person's temperament than values and ideals.

The degree to which every person is molded by culture is enormous. We frequently do not comprehend the impact of culture in shaping our personalities. It happens gradually, and usually there is no alternative but to accept the culture. The stable functioning of a society requires that there be shared patterns of behavior among its members and that there be some basis for knowing how to

[24]R. A. Price, S. G. Vandenberg, H. Dyer, and J. S. Williams, "Components of Variation in Normal Personality," *Journal of Personality and Social Psychology* 43 (1982), pp. 328–40.

[25]This definition is based on Salvatore R. Maddi, *Personality Theories: A Comparative Analysis* (Homewood, Ill.: Dorsey Press, 1980), p. 41.

EXHIBIT 3-9

**Some Major Forces
Influencing Personality**

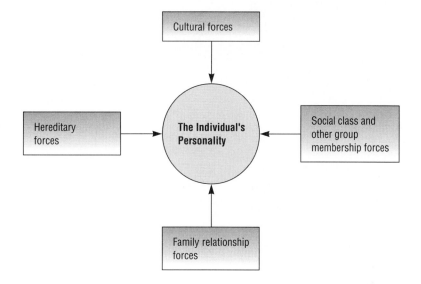

behave in certain situations. To ensure this, the society institutionalizes various patterns of behavior. The institutionalization of some patterns of behavior means that most members of a culture will have many common personality characteristics. At the same time, however, there is a great deal of cultural diversity within our society. The effective management of such diversity, and the differences that may exist within an organization's workforce because of it, is a critical and challenging task. The second reading selection of the chapter, "Managing Cultural Diversity: Implications for Organizational Competitiveness," provides a more detailed perspective on this important issue.

● **R3–2**

Increasingly in today's world, business operations are international in scope. This means they are frequently multicultural as well. Thus while most members of a culture will share similar personality characteristics, there may be significant differences across cultures. One of the challenges of doing business in a global economy is understanding and respecting cultural differences, particularly as they may affect personality and behavior. Encounter 3–2 cites some specific examples.

Social class also is important in shaping personality. The various neighborhoods of cities and towns tend to be populated by different social classes, each with its own mores. The neighborhood or community where a child grows up is the setting in which he or she learns about life. Social class influences the person's self-perception, perception of others, and perceptions of work, authority, and money. In terms of such pressing organizational problems as adjustment, quality of work life, and dissatisfaction, the manager attempting to understand employees must give attention to social class factors.

The nature of a person's expectations of others, the ways a person attempts to derive satisfaction, and the manner used to express feelings and resolve emotional conflicts are all formed in an interpersonal context. Family or parent-child

INTERNATIONAL

E N C O U N T E R · 3–2

CULTURAL FORCES AND PERSONALITY

One of the important forces working to shape personality is that of culture. Consequently, because nations differ in their cultural values, the personality and behavior of their citizens may differ as well. One stream of research that has identified differences in cultural values related to behavior in organizations is that of Geert Hofstede. Three of the cultural dimensions he describes relate to (1) the value placed on *individual* effort and accomplishment versus a collective or *group* orientation; (2) the degree to which uncertainty and ambiguity is accepted (*tolerance*) versus the extent to which it is unwanted (*avoidance*); and (3) the degree to which traditional male values are accepted by the society (*masculine*) versus traditional female values (*feminine*). Hofstede has collected data from 40 different countries. The differences found among a sample of six countries are shown below. The descriptions were

determined by dividing the distribution of scores on each dimension in half.

	Ind/ Group	Uncertainty	Masc/ Fem
France	Individual	Avoidance	Feminine
Hong Kong	Group	Tolerance	Masculine
India	Group	Tolerance	Masculine
Japan	Group	Avoidance	Masculine
Sweden	Individual	Tolerance	Feminine
United States	Individual	Tolerance	Masculine

In light of these cultural differences we should not be at all surprised that there are resulting personality differences. In conducting business in an international environment, individuals who are aware of and sensitive to these culturally shaped nuances will have a competitive advantage over those who are not.

Source: Based in part on information in G. Hofstede, *Culture's Consequence: International Differences in Work Related Values* (Beverly Hills: Sage Publications, 1980).

relationships are a key factor in this context. They set a pattern of behavior that leaves a significant imprint on all later behavior in the work organization.

A review of each of the determinants that shapes personality (Exhibit 3-9) will indicate that managers have little control over these determinants. However, no manager should conclude that personality is an unimportant factor in workplace behavior simply because it is formed outside the organization. The behavior of an employee cannot be understood without considering the concept of personality. In fact, personality is so interrelated with perception, attitudes, learning, and motivation that any analysis of behavior or any attempt to understand behavior is grossly incomplete unless personality is considered.

● R3–1   The importance of personality in shaping organizational behavior is illustrated by Argyris in the chapter readings selection, "The Individual and Organization: Some Problems of Mutual Adjustment." In this article Argyris argues that a basic incongruency exists between the personality of a mature adult and the demands of the organization. This incongruency explains a great deal of the counterproductive behavior that takes place in work settings.

Personality and Behavior

■ **E3–3**

An issue of interest to behavioral scientists and researchers is whether personality factors such as those measured by inventories or projective tests can predict behavior or performance in organizations. Exercise 3–3 is a demonstration example of a personality inventory that attempts to assess four aspects of personality. A total inventory or projective test rarely is employed in organizational behavior research. Typically, a few select personality factors such as locus of control, Machiavellianism, self-efficacy, or creativity are used, instead, to examine behavior and performance.

Locus of Control

The **locus of control** of individuals determines the degree to which they believe their behaviors influence what happens to them.[26] Some people believe they are autonomous—that they are masters of their own fate and bear personal responsibility for what happens to them. They see the control of their lives as coming from inside themselves. Rotter calls these people **internalizers**.[27]

Rotter also holds that many people view themselves as helpless pawns of fate, controlled by outside forces over which they have little, if any, influence. Such people believe that the locus of control is external rather than internal. Rotter calls them **externalizers**.

Rotter devised a scale containing 29 items to identify whether people are internalizers or externalizers.[28] The statements are concerned with success, failure, misfortune, and political events. One statement reflects a belief in internal control, and the other reflects a belief in external control. Four pairs of statements on the Rotter scale are shown in Exhibit 3-10.

A study of 900 employees in a public utility found that internally controlled employees were more satisfied with their jobs, more likely to be in managerial positions, and more satisfied with a participative management style than were employees who perceived themselves to be externally controlled.[29] Other research suggests locus of control is related to moral behavior, with internalizers doing what they think is right and being willing to suffer the consequences for doing so.[30] Encounter 3–3 demonstrates a possible relationship between locus of control and ethical behavior.

[26]P. E. Spector, "Behavior in Organizations as a Function of Employee's Locus of Control," *Psychological Bulletin* 91 (1982), pp. 482–97.

[27]J. R. Rotter, "Generalized Expectancies for Internal versus External Control of Reinforcement," *Psychological Monographs* 1, no. 609 (1966), p. 80.

[28]J. R. Rotter, "External Control and Internal Control," *Psychology Today,* June 1971, p. 37.

[29]T. R. Mitchell, C. M. Smyser, and S. E. Weed, "Locus of Control: Supervision and Work Satisfaction," *Academy of Management Journal,* September 1975, pp. 623–31.

[30]L. K. Trevino and S. A. Youngblood, "Bad Apples in Bad Barrels: A Causal Analysis of Ethical Decision-Making Behavior," *Journal of Applied Psychology,* August 1990, pp. 378–85.

Sample Items from an Early Version of Rotter's Test of Internal-External Locus of Control

1a   Promotions are earned through hard work and persistence.
1b   Making a lot of money is largely a matter of getting the right breaks.

2a   When I am right, I can convince others.
2b   It is silly to think that one can really change another person's basic attitudes.

3a   In my case, the grades I make are the results of my own efforts; luck has little or nothing to do with it.
3b   Sometimes I feel that I have little to do with the grades I get.

4a   Getting along with people is a skill that must be practiced.
4b   It is almost impossible to figure out how to please some people.

Machiavellianism

Imagine yourself in the following situation with two other people. Thirty new $1 bills are on the table to be distributed in any way the group decides. The game is over as soon as two of you agree to how it will be divided. Obviously, the fairest distribution would be $10 each. However, a selfish party could cut out the third person, and the other two would each end up with $15. Suppose that one person suggests this alternative to you and that before you can decide, the left-out person offers to give you $16, taking $14 as his or her share and cutting out the other person. What would you do?

Machiavellianism, a concept derived from the writings of Niccolò Machiavelli, helps answer the question. Machiavelli was concerned with the manipulation of people and with the orientations and tactics used by manipulators versus non-manipulators.[31]

From anecdotal descriptions of power tactics and the nature of influential people, various scales have been constructed to measure Machiavellianism. In one scale, the questions are organized around a cluster of beliefs about tactics, people, and morality. The person completing the scale is asked to indicate the extent of his or her agreement with statements such as: "The best way to handle people is to tell them what they want to hear"; "Anyone who completely trusts someone is asking for trouble"; and, "It is safe to assume that all people have a vicious streak and it will come out when given a chance."[32] In the money allocation game, the individuals who get the lion's share are those who score high on this scale. The low scorers get only slightly less than would be expected by a fair, one-third split.

[31]R. Christie and F. L. Geis, eds. *Studies in Machiavellianism* (New York: Academic Press, 1970).
[32]Ibid.

ETHICS
E N C O U N T E R • 3–3

CAN LOCUS OF CONTROL PREDICT UNETHICAL BEHAVIOR?

In recent years we have seen a varied array of media reports of wrongdoing and unethical behavior in business, government, and education. Savings & Loan institutions, Wall Street firms, universities with government contracts, and military procurement agencies are but a few of the entities that have made headlines. Are there personality factors that are related to choices individuals make to behavior ethically or unethically? Some recent research on ethical decision making sheds some light on this question. A partial description of a portion of this research follows.

In this study individuals with an average of five years work experience participated in an in-basket exercise in which they played the role of Pat Sneed, a national sales manager for an electronics firm. Among the dozen or so items in the in-basket were two that required decisions involving ethical concerns. In one, a regional sales director informs Sneed that one of his sales representatives is paying kickbacks. Sneed must decide whether or not to put an end to the kickbacks. In the second situation, Sneed receives a memo from the vice president of production which indicates the vice president has decided to change the material used in a product to save production costs. The memo advises that customers should not be informed of this change despite problems it might create. Sneed must decide what, if anything, to do. Responses by study participants to these two situations were judged on the basis of preestablished criteria to be either ethical or unethical.

Internal locus of control participants (as measured by the Rotter instrument discussed in the text) demonstrated more ethical behavior than their *external* counterparts. In fact, locus of control showed nearly twice as much effect on ethical decision making as did the combination of all of the several other variables which were included. The researchers suggest organizations may wish to assess locus of control when selecting managers for positions involving ethical decision making, although they acknowledge potential problems in doing so.

Source: The research described is reported in L. K. Trevino and S. A. Youngblood, "Bad Apples in Bad Barrels: A Causal Analysis of Ethical Decision-Making Behavior," *Journal of Applied Psychology,* August 1990, pp. 378–86.

Self-Efficacy

Self-efficacy relates to personal beliefs regarding competencies and abilities. Specifically, it refers to one's belief in one's ability to successfully complete a task. Individuals with a high degree of self-efficacy firmly believe in their performance capabilities. Self-efficacy is an important part of Bandura's social learning theory and comprises three dimensions: magnitude, strength, and generality.[33]

Magnitude refers to the level of task difficulty that individuals believe they can attain. For example, Jim may believe he can put an arrow in the archery range target 6 times in 10 attempts. Sara may feel she can hit the target 8 times; thus,

---

[33]A. Bandura, "Self-Efficacy: Toward a Unifying Theory of Behavioral Change," *Psychological Review* 84 (1977), pp. 191–215.

Sara has a higher magnitude of self-efficacy regarding this task than Jim. **Strength** refers to whether the belief regarding magnitude is strong or weak. If in the previous example Jim is moderately certain he can hit the target six times, while Sara is positive she can achieve eight hits, Sara is displaying greater strength of belief in her ability than is Jim. Finally, **generality** indicates how generalized across different situations the belief in capability is. If Jim thinks he can hit the target equally well with a pistol and rifle and Sara does not think she can, Jim is displaying greater generality than is Sara.

Beliefs regarding self-efficacy are learned. The most important factor in the development of self-efficacy appears to be past experiences. If over a period of time we attempt a task and are increasingly successful in our performance, we are likely to develop self-confidence and an increasing belief in our ability to perform the task successfully; conversely, if we repeatedly fail in our attempts to perform a task well, we are not as likely to develop strong feelings of self-efficacy. It is important to realize, however, that self-efficacy tends to be task specific; that is, a belief that we can perform very well in one job does not necessarily suggest a corresponding belief in our ability to excel in other jobs.

Feelings of self-efficacy have a number of managerial and organizational implications. Gist suggests that the self-efficacy concept has a number of theoretical and practical implications for organizational behavior and human resource management.[34] Included in the implications she suggests are important relationships between feelings of self-efficacy and performance appraisals, goal setting, and the use of incentives. Self-efficacy beliefs may also be important to consider in employee selection and training decisions and in identifying candidates for leadership positions.

Creativity

There are a number of ways to view **creativity**. First, you can consider the creative person as mad. Research evidence, however, offers no support for this view. Second, you can see the creative person as being disconnected from the art of creativity. Creativity, in this view, is a mystical act. Third, you can conclude that to be creative a person must be highly intelligent. Once again, however, the research showing a link between superior intelligence and creativity is generally negative. Finally, you can view creativity as a possibility open to every person—an expression of personality that can be developed.[35]

Many studies have examined creativity. Life histories, personality characteristics, and creativity tests often are scrutinized to determine a person's degree of creativity. In a typical test, subjects might be asked to examine a group of drawings

---

[34]M. E. Gist, "Self-Efficacy: Implications for Organizational Behavior and Human Resource Management," *Academy of Management Review*, July 1987, pp. 472–85.

[35]S. S. Gryskiewicz, "Restructuring for Innovation," *Issues and Observations*, November 1981, p. 1; and Isaac Asimov, "Creativity Will Dominate Our Time after the Concepts of Work and Fun Have Been Blurred by Technology," *Personal Administrator*, December 1983, p. 42.

and then indicate what the drawings represent. Novel and unusual responses are rated as being creative.

If creativity is viewed as a personality factor that can be developed, organizations can do a number of things to foster the developmental process.[36] These include:

1. *Buffering*—Managers can look for ways to absorb the risks of creative decisions.
2. *Organizational time-outs*—Give people time off to work on a problem and allow them to think things through.
3. *Intuition*—Give half-baked ideas a chance.
4. *Innovative attitudes*—Encourage everyone to think of ways to solve problems.
5. *Innovative organizational structures*—Let employees see and interact with many managers and mentors.

Motivation and Behavior

Now that we have explored the notion of individual differences, it is time we addressed a specific behavioral concern—motivation (Chapter 4). In order to understand such topics as motivation, rewards, and stress, the psychological and other variables discussed in this chapter must be a part of the manager's knowledge base. Attempting to motivate employees or to distribute meaningful rewards or to help subordinates cope with the stresses of work life is like groping in the dark if you do not have a sound, fundamental grasp of and insight into abilities, skills, perception, attitudes, and personality. The uninformed manager eventually may find his way, but there will be a lot of bumps, bruises, and wrong turns. The knowledgeable manager, on the other hand, possesses the insight and wisdom needed to move efficiently, to make better decisions, and to be on the lookout for inevitable, individual differences among his or her subordinates. As we proceed through the next four individual-level chapters, think about how abilities, skills, perception, attitudes, and personality help shape the behavior and performance of employees.

SUMMARY OF KEY POINTS

• Major individual variables that influence work behavior include demographic factors (e.g., age, sex, race), abilities and skills, perception, attitudes, and personality. These combine with various organizational variables (resources, leadership, rewards, job design, structure) to shape productive, nonproductive, and counterproductive work behaviors.

• Attributions we make about why an event occurs influence our behavior. The process involves analyzing why

[36]Ibid., p. 3.

something has happened (attributing a cause to the event), and fitting that explanation into a general framework which provides a basis for subsequent behavior. Thus our behavior is shaped by our perception of *why* certain things happen.

• Stereotyping is a process employed to assist us in dealing more efficiently with massive information processing demands. It can be a useful, even necessary, perceptual process. A prejudice is a particular form of stereotyping that resists change even in the face of contrary information. Many stereotypes can be helpful; prejudice is never helpful.

• An attitude is a learned predisposition to respond favorably or unfavorably to people, objects, and situations with which it is related. An attitude consists of a cognitive component (beliefs), an affect component (feelings), and a behavioral component which consists of the individuals' behavioral intentions.

• Although the job satisfaction-job performance relation-

ship is a complex one that is not fully understood, it seems clear that these two variables are related under certain conditions. One current view is that the rewards one receives as a consequence of good performance, and the degree to which these rewards are perceived as reasonable, affect both the extent to which satisfaction results from performance and the extent performance is affected by satisfaction.

• Major forces influencing the nature of an individual's personality include (1) hereditary factors, (2) parent-child and family relationships, (3) social class and other group membership forces, and (4) cultural factors. The latter is particularly critical as cross-cultural interactions increase in today's global business environment.

• There are numerous personality facets or factors which operate to influence behavior. Four that are frequently identified as being important in explaining behavior and performance are locus of control, Machiavellianism, self-efficacy, and creativity.

REVIEW AND DISCUSSION QUESTIONS

1. It seems evident that managers should attempt to match an employee's abilities and skills with job requirements. Is that also true with regard to attitudes and personality? Is it true with regard to demographic factors?

2. In what ways can stereotyping be a helpful process? Can a stereotype be useful even if it is not entirely accurate? Are we better off by getting rid of our stereotypes or by making them more accurate?

3. From the standpoint of managing people effectively, which is more important to the manager: subordinates' perceptions of their behavior or the actual behavior itself? Explain.

4. Can you identify attitudes you have about work or school (or this particular course) that affect your job or class performance? How were these attitudes developed and how easily might they be modified?

5. It is frequently said that we see what we want to see. How does attribution theory explain why this statement may be true?

6. Teri and Kimberly have the same ability and experience and are both average performers. Teri is an in-

ternalizer; Kimberly an externalizer. Gretchen, their boss, knows all this and hopes to improve their performance. Should she use a different strategy with each of them? Is she likely to have the same degree of success with both of them?

7. A criticism of some organizations is that all its members have the same personality. Why might this be desirable from the organization's perspective? How might this be counterproductive?

8. What sorts of difficulties might be encountered in doing business in a different culture? What might an organization do to minimize these difficulties?

9. As a manager, how might you increase a subordinate's feelings of self-efficacy regarding a job assignment? How might you attempt to increase the creativity of your subordinates?

10. So many factors influence an individual's behavior that it is impossible to accurately predict what their behavior will be in most situations. Why then should managers take time to understand individual differences?

•

READINGS

READING 3–1   THE INDIVIDUAL AND ORGANIZATION: SOME PROBLEMS OF MUTUAL ADJUSTMENT
Chris Argyris

It is a fact that most industrial organizations have some sort of formal structure within which individuals must work to achieve the organization's objectives.[1] Each of these basic components of organization (the formal structure and the individuals) has been and continues to be the subject of much research, discussion, and writing. An extensive search of the literature leads us to conclude, however, that most of these inquiries are conducted by persons typically interested in one or the other of the basic components. Few focus on both the individual and the organization.

Since in real life the formal structure and the individuals are continuously interacting and transacting, it seems useful to consider a study of their simultaneous impact upon each other. It is the purpose of this paper to outline the beginnings of a systematic framework by which to analyze the nature of the relationship between formal organization and individuals and from which to derive specific hypotheses regarding their mutual impact.[2] Although a much more detailed definition of formal organization will be given later, it is important to emphasize that this analysis is limited to those organizations whose original formal structure is defined by such traditional principles of organization as "chain of command," "task specialization," "span of control," and so forth. Another limitation is that since the nature of individuals varies from culture to culture, the conclusions of this paper are limited to those cultures wherein the proposed model of personality applies (primarily American and some Western European cultures).

The method used is a simple one designed to take advantage of the existing research on each component. The first objective is to ascertain the basic properties of each component. Exactly what is known and agreed upon by the experts about each of the components? Once this information has been collected, the second objective follows

logically. When the basic properties of each of these components are known, what predictions can be made regarding their impact upon one another once they are brought together?

SOME PROPERTIES OF HUMAN PERSONALITY

The research of the human personality is so great and voluminous that it is indeed difficult to find agreement regarding its basic properties.[3] It is even more difficult to summarize the agreements once they are inferred from the existing literature. Because of space limitations it is only possible to discuss in detail one of several agreements which seems to the writer to be the most relevant to the problem at hand. The others may be summarized briefly as follows. Personality is conceptualized as (1) being an organization of parts where the parts maintain the whole and the whole maintains the parts; (2) seeking internal balance (usually called adjustment) and external balance (usually called adaptation); (3) being propelled by psychological (as well as physical) energy; (4) located in the need systems; and (5) expressed through the abilities. (6) The personality of the organization may be called the self which (7) acts to color all the individual's experiences, thereby causing him to live in "private worlds" and which (8) is capable of defending (maintaining) itself against threats of all types.

The self, in this culture, tends to develop along specific trends which are operationally definable and empirically observable. The basic developmental trends may be described as follows. The human being, in our culture:

1. Tends to develop from a state of being passive as an infant to a state of increasing activity as an adult. (This is what E. H. Erikson has called self-initiative and Urie Bronfenbrenner has called self-determination.[4])

2. Tends to develop from a state of dependence upon others as an infant to a state of relative independence as an adult. Relative independence is the ability to "stand on one's own two feet" and simultaneously to acknowledge healthy dependencies.[5] It is characterized by the individual's freeing himself from his childhood determiners of behavior (e.g., the family) and developing his own set of behavioral determiners. The individual does not tend to

Source: Reprinted from "The Individual and Organization: Some Problems of Mutual Adjustment," by Chris Argyris, published in *Administrative Science Quarterly*, Vol. 2, No. 1 (June 1957), pp. 1–24, by permission of *The Administration Science Quarterly*, Copyright © 1957 *The Administrative Science Quarterly*.

react to others (e.g., the boss) in terms of patterns learned during childhood.[6]

3. Tends to develop from being capable of behaving in only a few ways as an infant to being capable of behaving in many different ways as an adult.[7]

4. Tends to develop from having erratic, casual, shallow, quickly dropped interests as an infant to possessing a deepening of interests as an adult. The mature state is characterized by an endless series of challenges where the reward comes from doing something for its own sake. The tendency is to analyze and study phenomena in their full-blown wholeness, complexity, and depth.[8]

5. Tends to develop from having a short time perspective (i.e., the present largely determines behavior) as an infant to having a much longer time perspective as an adult (i.e., the individual's behavior is more affected by the past and the future).[9]

6. Tends to develop from being in a subordinate position in the family and society as an infant to aspiring to occupy at least an equal and/or superordinate position relative to his peers.

7. Tends to develop from having a lack of awareness of the self as an infant to having an awareness of and control over the self as an adult. The adult who experiences adequate and successful control over his own behavior develops a sense of integrity (Erikson) and feelings of self-worth (Carl R. Rogers).[10]

These characteristics are postulated as being descriptive of a basic multidimensional developmental process along which the growth of individuals in our culture may be measured. Presumably every individual, at any given moment in time, could have his degree of development plotted along these dimensions. The exact location on each dimension will probably vary with each individual and even with the same individual at different times. Self-actualization may now be defined more precisely as the individual's plotted scores (or profile) along the above dimensions.[11]

A few words of explanation may be given concerning these dimensions of personality development:

1. They are only one aspect of the total personality. All the properties of personality mentioned above must be used in trying to understand the behavior of a particular individual. For example, much depends upon the individual's self-concept, his degree of adaptation and adjustment, and the way he perceives his private world.

2. The dimensions are continua, where the growth to be measured is assumed to be continuously changing in degree. An individual is presumed to develop continuously in degree from infancy to adulthood.

3. The only characteristic assumed to hold for all individuals is that, barring unhealthy personality development, they will move from the infant toward the adult end of each continuum. This description is a model outlining the basic growth trends. As such, it does not make any predictions about any specific individual. It does, however, presume to supply the researcher with basic developmental continua along which the growth of any individual in our culture may be described and measured.

4. It is postulated that no individual will ever obtain maximum expression of all these developmental trends. Clearly all individuals cannot be maximally independent, active, and so forth all the time and still maintain an organized society. It is the function of culture (e.g., norms, mores, and so forth) to inhibit maximum expression and to help an individual adjust and adapt by finding his optimum expression.

A second factor that prevents maximum expression and fosters optimum expression are the limits set by the individual's own personality. For example, some people fear the same amount of independence and activity that others desire, and some people do not have the necessary abilities to perform certain tasks. No given individual is known to have developed all known abilities to their full maturity.

5. The dimensions described above are constructed in terms of latent or genotypical characteristics. If one states that an individual needs to be dependent, this need may be ascertained by clinical inference, because it is one that individuals are not usually aware of. Thus, one may observe an employee acting as if he were independent, but it is possible that if one goes below the behavioral surface the individual may be quite dependent. The obvious example is the employee who always seems to behave in a manner contrary to that desired by management. Although this behavior may look as if he is independent, his contrariness may be due to his great need to be dependent upon management which he dislikes to admit to himself and to others.

One might say that an independent person is one whose behavior is not caused by the influence others have over him. Of course, no individual is completely independent. All of us have our healthy dependence (i.e., those which help us to be creative and to develop). One operational criterion to ascertain whether an individual's desire to be, let us say, independent and active is truly a mature manifestation is to ascertain the extent to which he permits others to express the same needs. Thus, an autocratic leader may say that he needs to be active and independent; he may also say that he wants subordinates who are the same. There is ample research to suggest, however, that his leadership pattern only makes him and his subordinates more dependence-ridden.

SOME BASIC PROPERTIES OF FORMAL ORGANIZATION

The next step is to focus the analytic spotlight on the formal organization. What are its properties? What are its basic "givens"? What probable impact will they have upon the human personality? How will the human personality tend to react to this impact? What sorts of chain reactions are probable when these two basic components are brought together?

Formal Organizations as Rational Organizations

Probably the most basic property of formal organization is its logical foundation or, as it has been called by students of administration, its essential rationality. It is the planners' conception of how the intended consequences of the organization may best be achieved. The underlying assumptions made by the creators of formal organization is that within respectable tolerances man will behave rationally, that is, as the formal plan requires him to behave. Organizations are formed with particular objectives in mind, and their structures mirror these objectives. Although man may not follow the prescribed paths, and consequently the objectives may never be achieved, Herbert A. Simon suggests that by and large man does follow these prescribed paths:

> *Organizations are formed with the intention and design of accomplishing goals; and the people who work in organizations believe, at least part of the time, that they are striving toward these same goals. We must not lose sight of the fact that however far organizations may depart from the traditional description . . . nevertheless most behavior in organizations is intendedly rational behavior. By "intended rationality," I mean the kind of adjustment of behavior to goals of which humans are capable—a very incomplete and imperfect adjustment, to be sure, but one which nevertheless does accomplish purposes and does carry out programs.*[12]

In an illuminating book, L. Urwick eloquently describes this underlying characteristic.[13] He insists that the creation of a formal organization requires a logical "drawing-office" approach. Although he admits that "9 times out of 10 it is impossible to start with a clean sheet," the organizer should sit down and in a "cold-blooded, detached spirit . . . draw an ideal structure." The section from which I quote begins with Urwick's description of how the formal structure should be planned. He then continues:

> *Manifestly that is a drawing-office job. It is a designing process. And it may be objected with a great deal of experience to support the contention that organization is never done that way . . . human organization. Nine times out of 10 it is impossible to start with a clean sheet. The organizer has to make the best possible use of the human material that is already available. And in 89 out of those 90 percent of cases he has to adjust jobs around to fit the man; he can't change the man to fit the job. He can't sit down in a cold-blooded, detached spirit and draw an ideal structure, an optimum distribution of duties and responsibilities and relationships, and then expect the infinite variety of human nature to fit into it.*
>
> *To which the reply is that he can and he should. If he has not got a clean sheet, that is no earthly reason why he should not make the slight effort of imagination required to assume that he has a clean sheet. It is not impossible to forget provisionally the personal facts— that old Brown is admirably methodical but wanting in initiative, that young Smith got into a mess with Robinson's wife and that the two men must be kept at opposite ends of the building, that Jones is one of those creatures who can think like a Wrangler about other people's duties but is given to periodic amnesia about certain aspects of his own.*[14]

The task of the organizer, therefore, is to create a logically ordered world where, as Fayol suggests, there is a "proper order" and in which there is a "place for everything (everyone)."[15]

The possibility that the formal organization can be altered by personalities, as found by Conrad M. Arensberg and Douglas McGregor[16] and Ralph M. Stogdill and Katheleen Koehler,[17] is not denied by formal organizational experts. Urwick, for example, states in the passage below that the planner must take into account the human element. But it is interesting to note that he perceives these adjustments as "temporary deviations from the pattern in order to deal with idiosyncrasy of personality." If possible, these deviations should be minimized by careful preplanning.

He [the planner] should never for a moment pretend that these (human) difficulties don't exist. They do exist, they are realities. Nor, when he has drawn up an ideal plan of organization, it is likely that he will be able to fit in all the existing human material perfectly. There will be small adjustments of the job to the man in all kinds of directions. But those adjustments are deliberate and temporary deviations from the pattern in order to deal with idiosyncrasy. There is a world of difference between such modification and drifting into an unworkable organization because Green has a fancy for combining bits of two incompatible functions, or White is "empire-building" ... or Black has always looked after the canteen, so when he is promoted to Sales Manager, he might as well continue to sell buns internally, though the main product of the business happens to be battleships.

What is suggested is that problems of organization should be handled in the right order. Personal adjustments must be made, insofar as they are necessary. But fewer of them will be necessary and they will present fewer deviations from what is logical and simple, if the organizer first makes a plan, a design—to which he would work if he had the ideal human material. He should expect to be driven from it here and there. But he will be driven from it far less and his machine will work much more smoothly if he starts *with a plan. If he starts with a motley collection of human oddities and tries to organize to fit them all in, thinking first of their various shapes and sizes and colors, he may have a patchwork quilt; he will not have an organization.*[18]

The majority of experts on formal organization agree with Urwick. Most of them emphasize that no organizational structure will be ideal. None will exemplify the maximum expression of the principles of formal organization. A satisfactory aspiration is for optimum expression, which means modifying the ideal structure to take into account the individual (and any environmental) conditions. Moreover, they urge that the people must be loyal to the formal structure if it is to work effectively. Thus, Taylor emphasizes that scientific management would never succeed without a "mental revolution."[19] Fayol has the same problem in mind when he emphasizes the importance of *esprit de corps.*

It is also true, however, that these experts have provided little insight into *why* they believe that people should undergo a "mental revolution," or why an *esprit de corps* is necessary if the principles are to succeed. The only hints found in the literature are that resistance to scientific management occurs because human beings "are what they are" or "because it's human nature." But *why* does "human nature" resist formal organizational principles? Perhaps there is something inherent in the principles which causes human resistance. Unfortunately, too little research specifically assesses the impact of formal organizational principles upon human beings.

Another argument for planning offered by the formal organizational experts is that the organization created by logical, rational design, in the long run, is more human than one created haphazardly. They argue that it is illogical, cruel, wasteful, and inefficient not to have a logical design. It is illogical because design must come first. It does not make sense to pay a large salary to an individual without clearly defining his position and its relationship to the whole. It is cruel because, in the long run, the participants suffer when no clear organizational structure exists. It is wasteful because, unless jobs are clearly predefined, it is impossible to plan logical training, promotion, resigning, and retiring policies. It is inefficient because the organization becomes dependent upon personalities. The personal touch leads to playing politics, which Mary Follett has described as a "deplorable form of coercion."[20]

Unfortunately, the validity of these arguments tends to be obscured in the eyes of the behavioral scientist because they imply that the only choice left, if the formal, rational, predesigned structure is not accepted, is to have no organizational structure at all, with the organizational structure left to the whims, pushes, and pulls of human beings. Some human-relations researchers, on the other hand, have unfortunately given the impression that formal structures are "bad" and that the needs of the individual participants should be paramount in creating and administering an organization. A recent analysis of the existing research, however, points up quite clearly that the importance of the organization is being recognized by those who in the past have focused largely upon the individual.[21]

In the past, and for the most part in the present, the traditional organizational experts based their "human architectural creation" upon certain basic principles or assumptions about the nature of organization. These principles have been described by such people as Urwick,[22] Mooney, Holden et al., Fayol, Dennison, Brown, Gullick, White, Gaus, Stene, Hopf, and Taylor. Although these principles have been attacked by behavioral scientists, the assumption is made in this paper that to date no one has defined a more useful set of formal organization principles. Therefore, the principles are accepted as givens. This frees us to inquire about their probable impact upon people, *if they are used as defined.*

Task (Work) Specialization

As James J. Gillespie suggests, the roots of these principles of organization may be traced back to certain principles of industrial economics, the most important of which is the basic economic assumption held by builders of the industrial revolution that "the concentration of effort on a limited field of endeavor increases quality and quantity of output."[23] It follows from the above that the necessity for specialization should increase as the quantity of similar things to be done increases.

If concentrating effort on a limited field of endeavor increases the quality and quantity of output, it follows that organizational and administrative efficiency is increased by the specialization of tasks assigned to the participants of the organization.[24] Inherent in this assumption are three others. The first is that the human personality will behave more efficiently as the task that it is to perform becomes specialized. Second is the assumption that there can be found a one best way to define the job so that it is performed at greater speed.[25] Third is the assumption that any individual differences in the human personality may be ignored by transferring more skill and thought to machines.[26]

A number of difficulties arise concerning these assumptions when the properties of the human personality are recalled. First, the human personality we have seen is always attempting to actualize its unique organization of parts resulting from a continuous, emotionally laden, ego-involving process of growth. It is difficult, if not impossible, to assume that this process can be choked off and the resultant unique differences of individuals ignored. This is tantamount to saying that self-actualization can be ignored. The second difficulty is that task specialization requires the individual to use only a few of his abilities. Moreover, as specialization increases, the less complex motor abilities are used more frequently. These, research suggests, tend to be of lesser psychological importance to the individual. Thus, the principle violates two basic givens of the healthy adult human personality. It inhibits self-actualization and provides expression for few, shallow, superficial abilities that do not provide the "endless challenge" desired by the healthy personality.

Harold L. Wilensky and Charles N. Lebeaux correctly point out that task specialization causes what little skill is left in a job to become very important.[27] Now small differences in ability may make enormous differences in output. Thus, two machine-shovel operators or two drill-press operators of different degrees of skill can produce dramatically different outputs. Ironically, the increasing importance of this type of skill for the healthy, mature worker means that he should feel he is performing self-satisfying work while using a small number of psychologically unchallenging abilities, when in actuality he may be predisposed to feel otherwise. Task specialization, therefore, requires a healthy adult to behave in a less mature manner, but it also requires that he feel good about it!

Not only is the individual affected, but the social structure as well is modified as a result of the situation described above. Wilensky and Lebeaux, in the same analysis, point out that placing a great emphasis on ability makes "Who you are" become less important that "What you can do." Thus, the culture begins to reward relatively superficial, materialistic characteristics.

Chain of Command

The principle of task specialization creates an aggregate of parts, each performing a highly specialized task. An aggregate of parts, each busily performing its particular objective, does not form an organization, however. A pattern of parts must be formed so that all the interrelationships among the parts create the organization. Following the logic of specialization, the planners create a new function (leadership) the primary responsibility of which is to control, direct, and coordinate the interrelationships of the parts and to make certain that each part performs its objective adequately. Thus, the planner makes the assumption that administrative and organizational efficiency is increased by arranging the parts in a determinate hierarchy of authority in which the part on top can direct and control the part on the bottom.

If the parts being considered are individuals, then they must be motivated to accept direction, control, and coordination of their behavior. The leader, therefore, is assigned formal power to hire, discharge, reward, and penalize the individuals in order to mold their behavior in the pattern of the organization's objectives.

The impact of such a state of affairs is to make the individuals dependent upon, passive, and subordinate to the leader. As a result, the individuals have little control over their working environment. At the same time their time perspective is shortened because they do not control the information necessary to predict their futures. These requirements of formal organization act to inhibit four of the growth trends of the personality, because to be passive, subordinate, and to have little control and a short time perspective exemplify in adults the dimensions of immaturity, not adulthood.

The planners of formal organization suggest three basic ways to minimize this admittedly difficult position. First, ample rewards should be given to those who perform well and who do not permit their dependence, subordination, passivity, and so forth to influence them in a negative manner. The rewards should be material and psychological. Because of the specialized nature of the worker's job, however, few psychological rewards are possible. It becomes important, therefore, that adequate material rewards are made available to the productive employee. This practice can lead to new difficulties, since the solution is, by its nature, not to do anything about the on-the-job situation (which is what is causing the difficulties) but to pay the individual for the dissatisfactions he experiences. The result is that the employee is paid for his dissatisfaction while at work and his wages are given to him to gain satisfactions outside his work environment.

Thus, the management helps to create a psychological set which leads the employees to feel that basic causes of dissatisfaction are built into industrial life, that the rewards they receive are wages for dissatisfaction, and that if satisfaction is to be gained, the employee must seek it outside the organization.

To make matters more difficult, there are three assumptions inherent in the above solution that also violate the basic givens of human personality. First, the solution assumes that a whole human being can split his personality so that he will feel satisfied in knowing that the wages for his dissatisfaction will buy him satisfaction outside the plant. Second, it assumes that the employee is primarily interested in maximizing his economic gains. Third, it assumes that the employee is best rewarded as an individual producer. The work group in which he belongs is not viewed as a relevant factor. If he produces well, he should be rewarded. If he does not, he should be penalized even though he may be restricting production because of informal group sanctions.

The second solution suggested by the planners of formal organization is to have technically competent, objective, rational, loyal leaders. The assumption is made that if the leaders are technically competent presumably they cannot have "the wool pulled over their eyes" and that therefore the employees will have a high respect for them. The leaders should be objective and rational and personify the rationality inherent in the formal structure. Being rational means that they must avoid becoming emotionally in-

volved. As one executive states, "We try to keep our personality out of the job." The leader must also be impartial; he must not permit his feelings to operate when he is evaluating others. Finally, the leader must be loyal to the organization so that he can inculcate the loyalty in the employees that Taylor, Fayol, and others believe is so important.

Admirable as this solution may be, it also violates several of the basic properties of personality. If the employees are to respect an individual for what he does rather than for who he is, the sense of integrity based upon evaluation of the total self which is developed in people is lost. Moreover, to ask the leader to keep his personality out of his job is to ask him to stop actualizing himself. This is not possible as long as he is alive. Of course, the executive may want to feel that he is not involved, but it is a basic given that the human personality is an organism always actualizing itself. The same problem arises with impartiality. As has been shown, the self concept always operates when we are making judgments. In fact, as Rollo May has pointed out, the best way to be impartial is to be as partial as one's needs predispose one to be but to be aware of this partiality in order to correct for it at the moment of decision.[28] Finally, if a leader can be loyal to an organization under these conditions, there may be adequate grounds for questioning the health of his personality makeup.

The third solution suggested by many adherents to formal organizational principles is to motivate the subordinates to have more initiative and to be more creative by placing them in competition with one another for the positions of power that lie above them in the organizational ladder. This solution is traditionally called "the rabble hypothesis." Acting under the assumption that employees will be motivated to advance upward, the adherents of formal organizations further assume that competition for the increasingly (as one goes up the ladder) scarcer positions will increase the effectiveness of the participants. D. C. S. Williams, conducting some controlled experiments, shows that the latter assumption is not necessarily valid. People placed in competitive situations are not necessarily better learners than those placed in noncompetitive situations.[29] M. Deutsch, as a result of extensive controlled experimental research, supports Williams' results and goes much further to suggest that competitive situations tend to lead to an increase in tension and conflict and a decrease in human effectiveness.[30]

Unity of Direction

If the tasks of everyone in a unit are specialized, then it follows that the objective or purpose of the unit must be specialized. The principle of unity of direction states that organizational efficiency increases if each unit has a single activity (or homogeneous set of activities) that are planned and directed by the leader.[31]

This means that the goal toward which the employees are working, the path toward the goal, and the strength of the barriers they must overcome to achieve the goal are defined and controlled by the leader. Assuming that the work goals do not involve the egos of the employees (i.e., they are related to peripheral, superficial needs), then ideal conditions for psychological failure have been created. The reader may recall that a basic given of a healthy personality is the aspiration for psychological success. Psychological success is achieved when each individual is able to define his own goals, in relation to his inner needs and the strength of the barriers to be overcome in order to reach these goals. Repetitive as it may sound, it is nevertheless true that the principle of unity of direction also violates a basic given of personality.

Span of Control

The principle of span of control[32] states that administrative efficiency is increased by limiting the span of control of a leader to no more than five or six subordinates whose work interlocks.[33]

It is interesting to note that Ernest Dale, in an extensive study of organizational principles and practices in 100 large organizations, concludes that the actual limits of the executive span of control are more often violated than not,[34] while in a recent study, James H. Healey arrives at the opposite conclusion.[35] James C. Worthy reports that it is formal policy in his organization to extend the span of control of the top management much further than is theoretically suggested.[36] Finally, W. W. Suojanen, in a review of the current literature on the concept of span of control, concludes that it is no longer valid, particularly as applied to the larger government agencies and business corporations.[37]

In a recent article, however, Urwick criticizes the critics of the span-of-control principle.[38] For example, he notes that in the case described by Worthy, the superior has a large span of control over subordinates whose jobs do not interlock. The buyers in Worthy's organization purchase a clearly defined range of articles; thereby, they find no reason to interlock with others.

Simon criticizes the span-of-control principle on the grounds that it increases the "administrative distance" between individuals. An increase in administrative distance violates, in turn, another formal organizational principle

that administrative efficiency is enhanced by keeping at a minimum the number of organizational levels through which a matter must pass before it is acted on.[39] Span of control, continues Simon, inevitably increases red tape, since each contact between agents must be carried upward until a common superior is found. Needless waste of time and energy result. Also, since the solution of the problem depends upon the superior, the subordinate is in a position of having less control over his own work situation. This places the subordinate in a work situation in which he is less mature.

Although the distance between individuals in different units increases (because they have to find a common superior), the administrative distance between superior and subordinate within a given unit decreases. As Whyte correctly points out, the principle of span of control, by keeping the number of subordinates at a minimum, places great emphasis on close supervision.[40] Close supervision leads the subordinates to become dependent upon, passive toward, and subordinate to, the leader. Close supervision also tends to place the control in the superior. Thus, we must conclude that span of control, if used correctly, will tend to increase the subordinate's feelings of dependence, submissiveness, passivity, and so on. In short, it will tend to create a work situation which requires immature, rather than mature, participants.

AN INCONGRUENCY BETWEEN THE NEEDS OF A MATURE PERSONALITY AND OF FORMAL ORGANIZATION

Bringing together the evidence regarding the impact of formal organizational principles upon the individual, we must conclude that there are some basic incongruencies between the growth trends of a healthy personality in our culture and the requirements of formal organization. If the principles of formal organization are used as ideally defined, then the employees will tend to work in an environment where (1) they are provided minimal control over their work-a-day world, (2) they are expected to be passive, dependent, subordinate, (3) they are expected to have a short-time perspective, (4) they are induced to perfect and value the frequent use of a few superficial abilities, and (5) they are expected to produce under conditions leading to psychological failure.

All of these characteristics are incongruent to the ones healthy human beings are postulated to desire. They are much more congruent with the needs of infants in our culture. In effect, therefore, formal organizations are willing to pay high wages and provide adequate seniority if mature adults will, for eight hours a day, behave in a less mature manner. If this analysis is correct, this inevitable incongruency increases (1) as the employees are of increasing maturity, (2) as the formal structure (based upon the above principles) is made more clear-cut and logically tight for maximum formal organizational effectiveness, (3) as one goes down the line of command, and (4) as the jobs become more and more mechanized (i.e., take on assembly-line characteristics).

As in the case of the personality developmental trends, this picture of formal organization is also a model. Clearly, no company actually uses the formal principles of organization exactly as stated by their creators. There is ample evidence to suggest that they are being modified constantly in actual situations. Those who expound these principles, however, probably would be willing to defend their position that this is the reason that human-relations problems exist; the principles are not followed as they should be.

In the model of the personality and the formal organization, we are assuming the extreme of each in order that the analysis and its results can be highlighted. Speaking in terms of extremes helps us to make the position sharper. In doing this, we make no assumption that all situations in real life are extreme (i.e., that the individuals will always want to be more mature and that the formal organization will always tend to make people more dependent, passive, and so forth, all the time).[41] The model ought to be useful, however, to plot the degree to which each component tends toward extremes and then to predict the problems that will tend to arise.

Returning to the analysis, it is not difficult to see why some students of organization suggest that immature and even mentally retarded individuals probably would make excellent employees in certain jobs. There is very little documented experience to support such a hypothesis. One reason for this lack of information is probably the delicacy of the subject. Examples of what might be obtained if a systematic study were made may be found in a recent work by Mal Brennan.[42] He cites the Utica Knitting Mill, which made arrangements during 1917 with the Rome Institution for Mentally Defective Girls to employ 24 girls whose mental age ranged from 6 to 10 years of age. The girls were such excellent workers that they were employed after the war emergency ended. In fact, the company added 40 more in another of their plants. It is interesting to note that the managers praised the subnormal girls highly. According to Brennan, in several important reports they said that:

when business conditions required a reduction of the working staff, the hostel girls were never "laid off" in disproportion to the normal girls; that they were more punctual, more regular in their habits, and did not indulge in as much "gossip and levity." They received the same rate of pay, and they had been employed successfully at almost every process carried out in the workshops.

In another experiment reported by Brennan, the Works Manager of the Radio Corporation, Ltd., reported that of five young morons employed, "the three girls compared very favourably with the normal class of employee in that age group. The boy employed in the store performed his work with satisfaction. . . . Although there was some doubt about the fifth child, it was felt that getting the most out of him was just a matter of right placement." In each of the five cases, the morons were reported to be quiet, respectful, well behaved, and very obedient. The Works Manager was especially impressed by their truthfulness. A year later the same Works Manager was still able to advise that "in every case, the girls proved to be exceptionally well-behaved, particularly obedient, and strictly honest and trustworthy. They carried out work required of them to such a degree of efficiency that *we were surprised they were classed as subnormals for their age.*"[43]

SUMMARY OF FINDINGS

If one were to put these basic findings in terms of propositions, one could state:

Proposition I. *There Is a Lack of Congruency between the Needs of Healthy Individuals and the Demands of the Formal Organization.*

If one uses the traditional formal principles of organization (i.e., chain of command, task specialization, and so on) to create a social organization, and if one uses as an input agents who tend toward mature psychological development (i.e., who are predisposed toward relative independence, activeness, use of important abilities, and so on), then one creates a disturbance, because the needs of healthy individuals listed above are not congruent with the requirements of formal organization, which tends to require the agents to work in situations where they are dependent, passive, use few and unimportant abilities, and so forth.

Corollary 1. The disturbance will vary in proportion to the degree of incongruency between the needs of the individuals and the requirements of the formal organization.[44]

An administrator, therefore, is always faced with a tendency toward continual disturbance inherent in the work situation of the individuals over whom he is in charge.

Drawing on the existing knowledge of the human personality, a second proposition can be stated.

Proposition II. *The Results of This Disturbance Are Frustration, Failure, Short-Time Perspective, and Conflict.*[45]

If the agents are predisposed to a healthy, mature self-actualization, the following results will occur:

1. They will tend to experience frustration because their self-actualization will be blocked.

2. They will tend to experience failure because they will not be permitted to define their own goals in relation to their central needs, the paths to these goals, and so on.

3. They will tend to experience short-time perspective, because they have no control over the clarity and stability of their future.

4. They will tend to experience conflict, because, as healthy agents, they will dislike the frustration, failure, and short-time perspective which is characteristic of their present jobs. If they leave, however, they may not find new jobs easily, and even if new jobs are found, they may not be much different.[46]

Based upon the analysis of the nature of formal organization, one may state a third proposition.

Proposition III. *The Nature of the Formal Principles of Organization Cause the Subordinate, at Any Given Level, to Experience Competition, Rivalry, Intersubordinate Hostility, and to Develop a Focus toward the Parts Rather than the Whole.*

1. Because of the degree of dependence, subordination, and so on of the subordinates upon the leader, and because the number of positions above any given level always tends to decrease, the subordinates aspiring to perform effectively and to advance will tend to find themselves in competition with, and receiving hostility from, each other.[47]

2. Because, according to the formal principles, the subordinate is directed toward and rewarded for performing his own task well, the subordinate tends to develop an orientation toward his own particular part rather than toward the whole.

3. This part-orientation increases the need for the leader to coordinate the activity among the parts in order to maintain the whole. This need for the leader, in turn, increases the subordinates' degree of dependence, subordination, and so forth. This is a circular process whose impact is to maintain and/or increase the degree of dependence, subordination, and so on, as well as to stimulate rivalry and competition for the leader's favor.

A BIRD'S-EYE, CURSORY PICTURE OF SOME OTHER RELATED FINDINGS

It is impossible in the short space available to present all of the results obtained from the analysis of the literature. For example, it can be shown that employees tend to adapt to the frustration, failure, short-term perspective, and conflict involved in their work situations by any one or a combination of the following acts:

1. Leaving the organization.
2. Climbing the organizational ladder.
3. Manifesting defense reactions such as daydreaming, aggression, ambivalence, regression, projection, and so forth.
4. Becoming apathetic and disinterested toward the organization, its makeup, and its goals. This leads to such phenomena as: *(a)* employees reducing the number and potency of the needs they expect to fulfill while at work; *(b)* employees goldbricking, making errors, cheating, slowing down, and so on.
5. Creating informal groups to sanction the defense reactions and the apathy, disinterest, and lack of self-involvement.
6. Formalizing the informal group.
7. Evolving group norms that perpetuate the behavior outlined in (3), (4), (5), and (6) above.
8. Evolving a psychological set in which human or nonmaterial factors become increasingly unimportant while material factors become increasingly important.
9. Acculturating youth to accept the norms outlined in (7) and (8).

Furthermore, it can also be shown that many managements tend to respond to the employees' behavior by:

1. Increasing the degree of their pressure-oriented leadership.
2. Increasing the degree of their use of management controls.
3. Increasing the number of "pseudo"-participation and communication programs.

These three reactions by management actually compound the dependence, subordination, and so on that the employees experience, which in turn cause the employees to increase their adaptive behavior, the very behavior management desired to curtail in the first place.

Is there a way out of this circular process? The basic problem is the reduction in the degree of dependency, subordination, submissiveness, and so on experienced by the employee in his work situation. It can be shown that job enlargement and employee-centered (or democratic or participative) leadership are elements which, if used correctly, can go a long way toward ameliorating the situation. These are limited, however, because their success depends upon having employees who are ego-involved and highly interested in the organization. This dilemma between individual needs and organization demands is a basic, continual problem posing an eternal challenge to the leader. How is it possible to create an organization in which the individuals may obtain optimum expression and, simultaneously, in which the organization itself may obtain optimum satisfaction of its demands? Here lies a fertile field for future research in organizational behavior.

NOTES

1. Temporarily, "formal structure" is defined as that which may be found on the organization charts and in the standard operating procedures of an organization.

2. This analysis is part of a larger project whose objectives are to integrate by the use of a systematic framework much of the existing behavioral-science research related to organization. The total report will be published by Harper & Brothers as a book, tentatively entitled *The Behavioral Sciences and Organization*. The project has been supported by a grant from the Foundation for Research on Human Behavior, Ann Arbor, Michigan, for whose generous support the writer is extremely grateful.

3. The relevant literature in clinical, abnormal, child, and social psychology and in personality theory, sociology, and anthropology was investigated. The basic agreements inferred regarding the properties of personality are assumed to be valid for most contemporary points of view. Allport's "trait theory," Cattell's factor analytic approach, and Kretschmer's somatotype framework are not included. For lay description see the author's *Personality Fundamentals for Administrators*, rev. ed. (New Haven, 1954).

4. E. H. Erikson, *Childhood and Society* (New York, 1950); Urie Bronfenbrenner, "Toward an Integral Theory of Personality," in Robert R. Blake and Glenn V. Ramsey, *Perception* (New York, 1951), pp. 206–57. See also R. Kotinsky, *Personality in the Making* (New York, 1952), pp. 8–25.

5. This is similar to Erikson's sense of autonomy and Bronfenbrenner's state of creative interdependence.

6. Robert W. White, *Lives in Progress* (New York, 1952), pp. 339 ff.

7. Lewin and Kounin believe that as the individual develops needs and abilities the boundaries between them become more rigid. This explains why an adult is better able than a child to be frustrated in one activity and behave constructively in another. See Kurt Lewin, *A Dynamic Theory of Personality* (New York, 1935); and Jacob S. Kounin, "Intellectual Development and Rigidity," in R. Barker, J. Kounin, and H. R. Wright, eds., *Child Behavior and Development* (New York, 1943), pp. 179–98.

8. White, *Lives in Progress*, p. 347 ff.

9. Lewin reminds those who may believe that a long-time perspective is not characteristic of the majority of individuals of the billions of dollars that are invested in insurance policies. Kurt Lewin, *Resolving Social Conflicts* (New York, 1948), p. 105.

10. Carl R. Rogers, *Client-Centered Therapy* (New York, 1951).

11. Another related but discrete set of developmental dimensions may be constructed to measure the protective (defense) mechanisms individuals tend to create as they develop from infancy to adulthood. Exactly how these would be related to the above model is not clear.

12. Herbert A. Simon, *Research Frontiers in Politics and Government* (Washington, D.C., 1955), ch. ii, p. 30.

13. L. Urwick, *The Elements of Administration* (New York, 1944).

14. Ibid., pp. 36–39; quoted by permission of Harper & Brothers.

15. Cited in Harold Koontz and Cyril O'Connell, *Principles of Management* (New York, 1955), p. 24.

16. Conrad M. Arensberg and Douglas McGregor," Determination of Morale in an Industrial Company," *Applied Anthropology*. 1 (January–March 1942), pp. 12–34.

17. Ralph M. Stogdill and Katheleen Koehler, *Measures of Leadership Structure and Organization Change* (Columbus, Ohio, 1952).

18. Ibid., pp. 36–39; quoted by permission of Harper & Brothers.

19. For a provocative discussion of Taylor's philosophy, see Reinhard Bendix, *Work and Authority in Industry* (New York, 1956), pp. 274–319.

20. Quoted in ibid., pp. 36–39.

21. Chris Argyris, *The Present State of Research in Human Relations* (New Haven, 1954), ch. i.

22. Urwick, *The Elements of Administration*.

23. James J. Gillespie, *Free Expression in Industry* (London, 1948), pp. 34–37.

24. Herbert A. Simon, *Administrative Behavior* (New York, 1947), pp. 80–81.

25. For an interesting discussion, see Georges Friedman, *Industrial Society* (Glencoe, Ill, 1955), p. 54 ff.

26. Ibid., p. 20. Friedman reports that 79 percent of Ford employees had jobs for which they could be trained in one week.

27. Harold L. Wilensky and Charles N. Lebeaux, *Industrialization and Social Welfare* (New York, 1955), p. 43.

28. Rollo May, "Historical and Philosophical Presuppositions for Understanding Therapy," in O. H. Mowrer, *Psychotherapy Theory and Research* (New York, 1953), pp. 38–39.

29. D. C. S. Williams, "Effects of Competition between Groups in a Training Situation," *Occupational Psychology* 30 (April 1956), pp. 85–93.

30. M. Deutsch, "An Experimental Study of the Effects of Cooperation and Competition upon Group Process," *Human Relations* 2 (1949), pp. 199–231.

31. The sacredness of these principles is questioned by a recent study. Gunnar Heckscher concludes that the principles of unity of command and unity of direction are formally violated in Sweden: "A fundamental principle of public administration in Sweden is the duty of all public agencies to cooperate directly without necessarily passing through a common superior. This principle is even embodied in the constitution itself, and in actual fact it is being employed daily. It is traditionally one of the most important characteristics of Swedish administration that especially central agencies, but also central and local agencies of different levels, cooperate freely and that this is being regarded as a perfectly normal procedure" [*Swedish Public Administration at Work* (Stockholm, 1955), p. 12].

32. First defined by V. A. Graicunas in an article entitled "Relationship in Organization," in L. Gulick and L. Urwick, eds., *Papers on the Science of Administration,* 2nd ed. (New York, 1947), pp. 184–87.

33. L. Urwick, *Scientific Principles and Organization* (New York, 1938), p. 8.

34. Ernest Dale, *Planning and Developing the Company Organization Structure* (New York, 1952), ch. xx.

35. James H. Healey, "Coordination and Control of Executive Functions," *Personnel* 33 (September 1956), pp. 106–17.

36. James C. Worthy, "Organizational Structure and Employee Morale," *American Sociological Review* 15 (April 1950), pp. 169–79.

37. W. W. Suojanen, "The Span of Control—Fact or Fable?" *Advanced Management* 20 (1955), pp. 5–13.

38. L. Urwick, "The Manager's Span of Control," *Harvard Business Review* 34 (May–June 1956), pp. 39–47.

39. Simon, *Research Frontiers,* pp. 26–28.

40. William Whyte, "On the Evolution of Industrial Sociology" (Mimeographed paper presented at the 1956 meeting of the American Sociological Society).

41. In fact, much evidence is presented in the book from which this article is drawn to support contrary tendencies.

42. Mal Brennan, *The Making of a Moron* (New York, 1953), pp. 13–18.

43. Mr. Brennan's emphasis.

44. This proposition does not hold under certain conditions.

45. In the full analysis, specific conditions are derived under which the basic incongruency increases or decreases.

46. These points are taken, in order, from: Roger G. Barker, T. Dembo, and K. Lewin, "Frustration and Regression: An Experiment with Young Children," *Studies in Child Welfare,* Vol. XVIII, No. 2 (Iowa City, Iowa, 1941); John Dollard et al., *Frustration and Aggression* (New Haven, 1939); Kurt Lewin et al., "Level of Aspiration," in J. McV. Hunt, ed., *Personality and the Behavior Disorders* (New York, 1944), pp. 333–78; Ronald Lippitt and Leland Bradford, "Employee Success in Work Groups," *Personnel Administration* 8 (December 1945), pp. 6–10; Kurt Lewin, "Time Perspective and Morale," in Gertrud Weiss Lewin, ed., *Resolving Social Conflicts* (New York, 1948), pp. 103–24; and Theodore M. Newcomb, *Social Psychology* (New York, 1950), pp. 361–73.

47. These problems may not arise for the subordinate who becomes apathetic, disinterested, and so on.

READING 3–2　MANAGING CULTURAL DIVERSITY: IMPLICATIONS FOR ORGANIZATIONAL COMPETITIVENESS

Workforce demographics for the United States and many other nations of the world indicate that managing diversity will be on the agendas of organizational leaders throughout the 90s. For example, a recent report on the workforces of 21 nations shows that nearly all of the growth in the labor force between now and 2000 will occur in nations

Source: Taylor H. Cox and Stacy Blake, "Managing Cultural Diversity: Implications for Organizational Competitiveness," **Academy of Management Executive,** August 1991, pp. 45–56.

with predominately non-Caucasian populations. Behind these statistics are vastly different age and fertility rates for people of different racioethnic groups. In the United States for example, the average white female is 33 years old and has (or will have) 1.7 children. Corresponding figures for blacks are 28 and 2.4, and for Mexican-Americans, 26 and 2.9.[1]

Leading consultants, academics and business leaders have advocated that organizations respond to these trends with a "valuing diversity" approach. They point out that

EXHIBIT 3-11

Spheres of Activity in the Management of Cultural Diversity

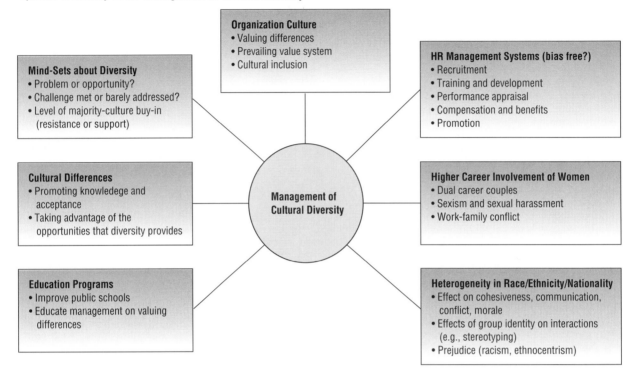

a well managed, diverse workforce holds potential competitive advantages for organizations.[2] However, the logic of the valuing diversity argument is rarely made explicit, and we are aware of no article that reviews actual data supporting the linkage of managing diversity and organizational competitiveness. This article reviews the arguments and research data on this link, and offers suggestions on improving organizational capability for managing cultural diversity. As shown in Exhibit 3-11, the term managing diversity refers to a variety of management issues and activities related to hiring and effective utilization of personnel from different cultural backgrounds.

DIVERSITY AS A COMPETITIVE ADVANTAGE

Social responsibility goals of organizations is only one area that benefits from the management of diversity. We will focus on six other areas where sound management can create a competitive advantage: (1) cost, (2) resource ac-

quisition, (3) marketing, (4) creativity, (5) problem solving, (6) organizational flexibility.[3] Exhibit 3-12 briefly explains their relationship to diversity management.

The first two items of the exhibit, the cost and resource acquisition arguments, are what we call the "inevitability-of-diversity" issues. Competitiveness is affected by the *need* (because of national and cross-national workforce demographic trends) to hire more women, minorities, and foreign nationals. The marketing, creativity, problem-solving, and system flexibility arguments are derived from what we call the "value-in-diversity hypothesis"—that diversity brings net-added value to organization processes.

Cost

Organizations have not been as successful in managing women and racioethnic minorities (racially and/or ethnically different from the white/Anglo majority) as white males. Date shows that turnover and absenteeism are often higher among women and racioethnic minorities than for white males. For example, one study reported that the

EXHIBIT 3-12

Managing Cultural Diversity Can Provide Competitive Advantage

1. Cost argument	As organizations become more diverse, the cost of a poor job in integrating workers will increase. Those who handle this well, will thus create cost advantages over those who don't.
2. Resource-acquisition argument	Companies develop reputations on favorability as prospective employers for women and ethnic minorities. Those with the best reputations for managing diversity will win the competition for the best personnel. As the labor pool shrinks and changes composition, this edge will become increasingly important.
3. Marketing argument	For multinational organizations, the insight and cultural sensitivity that members with roots in other countries bring to the marketing effort should improve these efforts in important ways. The same rationale applies to marketing to subpopulations within domestic operations.
4. Creativity argument	Diversity of perspectives and less emphasis on conformity to norms of the past (which characterize the modern approach to management of diversity) should improve the level of creativity.
5. Problem-solving argument	Heterogeneity in decision and problem-solving groups potentially produces better decisions through a wider range of perspectives and more thorough critical analysis of issues.
6. System flexibility argument	An implication of the multicultural model for managing diversity is that the system will become less determinant, less standardized, and therefore more fluid. The increased fluidity should create greater flexibility to react to environmental changes (i.e., reactions should be faster and at less cost).

overall turnover rate for blacks in the United States workforce is forty percent higher than for whites. Also, Corning Glass recently reported that between 1980–87, turnover among women in professional jobs was double that of men, and the rates for blacks were 2.5 times those of whites. A two-to-one ratio for women/men turnover was also cited by Felice Schwartz in her article on multiple career tracks for women in management.[4]

Job satisfaction levels are also often lower for minorities. A recent study that measured job satisfaction among black and white MBAs revealed that blacks were significantly less satisfied with their overall careers and advancement than whites.[5]

Frustration over career growth and cultural conflict with the dominant, white-male culture may be the major factor behind the different satisfaction levels. Two recent surveys of male and female managers in large American companies found that although women expressed a much higher probability of leaving their current employer than men, and had higher actual turnover rates, their primary reasons for quitting were lack of career growth opportunity or dissatisfaction with rates of progress. One of the surveys also

discovered that women have higher actual turnover rates at all ages, and not just during the child-bearing and child-rearing years.[6]

Organizations' failure to manage women and racioethnic minorities as successfully as white males translates into unnecessary costs. Since 85 percent of net additions to the workforce during the decade of the 90s are expected to be women and racioethnic minorities, these costs will escalate in the coming years.

Organizations that fail to make appropriate changes to more successfully use and keep employees from different backgrounds can expect to suffer a significant competitive disadvantage compared to those that do. Alternatively, organizations quick to create an environment where all personnel can thrive should gain a competitive cost advantage over nonresponsive or slowly responding companies.

Cost implications in managing diversity also occur in benefits and work schedules. In one study, companies were assigned an "accommodation score" based on the adoption of four benefit-liberalization changes associated with pregnant workers. Analysis revealed that the higher a company's accommodation score, the lower the number of sick days taken by pregnant workers and the more willing they were to work overtime during pregnancy.[7]

Two other studies investigated the effect of company investment in day care on human resource cost variables. In one study, turnover and absenteeism rates for working mothers using a company-sponsored child development center were compared to those who either had no children or had no company assistance. Absenteeism for the day-care users versus the other groups was 38 percent lower and the turnover rate was less than 2 percent compared to more than 6 percent for the nonbenefit groups. The second study showed that in a company that initiated an in-house child care facility, worker attitudes improved on six measures including organizational commitment and job satisfaction. In addition, turnover declined by 63 percent.[8]

Greater use of flextime work scheduling is another type of organizational accommodation to diversity. A recent field experiment assessing the impact of flextime use on absenteeism and worker performance found that both short- and long-term absence declined significantly. Three out of four worker efficiency measures also increased significantly.[9]

Cost savings of organizational changes must be judged against the investment. Nevertheless, the data strongly suggests that managing diversity efforts have reduced absenteeism and turnover costs, as cited earlier.

Research evidence relevant to cost implications of managing diversity on some dimensions other than benefit and work-schedule changes comes from a UCLA study of the productivity of culturally heterogeneous and culturally homogeneous work teams. Among the heterogeneous teams, some were more and some were less productive than the homogeneous teams.[10] This research suggests that if work teams "manage" the diversity well, they can make diversity an asset to performance. For example, all members should have ample opportunity to contribute and potential communications, group cohesiveness, and interpersonal conflict issues need to be successfully addressed. Alternatively, if diversity is ignored or mishandled, it may detract from performance.

Actual cost savings from improving the management of diversity are difficult to determine. It is, however, possible to estimate those related to turnover. For example, let us assume an organization has 10,000 employees in which 35 percent of personnel are either women or racioethnic minorities. Let us also assume a white male turnover rate of 10 percent. Using the previous data on differential turnover rates for women and racioethnic minorities of roughly

double the rate for white males, we can estimate a loss of 350 additional employees from the former groups. If we further assume that half of the turnover rate difference can be eliminated with better management, and that total turnover cost averages $20,000 per employee, the potential annual cost savings is $3.5 million. This example only addresses turnover, and additional savings may be realized from other changes such as higher productivity levels.

Although accurate dollar cost savings figures from managing diversity initiatives of specific companies are rarely published, Ortho Pharmaceuticals has calculated its savings to date at $500,000, mainly from lower turnover among women and ethnic minorities.[11]

Resource Acquisition

Attracting and retaining excellent employees from different demographic groups is the second "inevitability"-related competitiveness issue. As women and racioethnic minorities increase in proportional representation in the labor pool, organizations must compete to hire and retain workers from these groups. Recently published accounts of the "best companies" for women and for blacks have made public and highlighted organizations which are leaders in organizational change efforts to effectively manage diversity.[12] In addition to listing the best companies, the publications also discuss why certain companies were excluded from the list.

The impact of these publications on recruitment of quality personnel has already begun to surface. Merck, Xerox, Syntex, Hoffmann-La Roche, and Hewlett-Packard have been aggressively using favorable publicity to recruit women and racioethnic minorities. According to company representatives, the recognitions are, in fact, boosting recruiting efforts. For example, Merck cites its identification as one of the 10 best companies for working mothers as instrumental in recent increases in applications.[13]

As these reputations grow, and the supply of white males in the labor market shrinks, the significance of the resource acquisition issue for organizational competitiveness will be magnified.

Marketing

Markets are becoming as diverse as the workforce. Selling goods and services is facilitated by a representational workforce in several ways. First, companies with good reputations have correspondingly favorable public relations. Just as people, especially women and racioethnic minorities, may prefer to work for an employer who values diversity, they may also prefer to buy from such organizations.

Second, there is evidence that culture has a significant effect on consumer behavior. For example, in the Chinese culture, values such as a tradition of thrift, and teenagers' deference to their parents' wishes in making purchases, have been identified as affecting consumer behavior.[14] While much of the research on cross-cultural differences in consumer behavior has focused on cross-national comparisons, this research is also relevant to intra-country ethnic group differences.

Immigration from Latin America and Asia will continue to be high in the 90's. This represents a large influx of first-generation Americans having strong ties to their root cultures. Acculturation patterns among Asian and Hispanic Americans indicate that substantial identity with the root cultures remain even after three or more generations of United States citizenship. This implies that firms may gain competitive advantage by using employee insight to understand culture effects on buying decisions and map strategies to respond to them.

USA Today provides a good example. Nancy Woodhull, president of Gannett News Media, maintains that the newspaper's marketing success is largely attributable to the presence of people from a wide variety of cultural backgrounds in daily news meetings. Group diversity was planned and led to a representation of different viewpoints because people of different genders and racioethnic backgrounds have different experiences shaped by group identities.

Avon Corporation used cultural diversity to turn around low profitability in its inner-city markets. Avon made personnel changes to give Black and Hispanic managers substantial authority over these markets. These formerly unprofitable sectors improved to the point where they are now among Avon's most productive U.S. markets. Avon President Jim Preston commented that members of a given cultural group are uniquely qualified to understand certain aspects of the world view of persons from that group.

In some cases, people from a minority culture are more likely to give patronage to a representative of their own group. For at least some products and services, a multicultural salesforce may facilitate sales to members of minority culture groups.

Cultural diversification of markets is not limited to U.S. companies. Globalization is forcing major companies from many nations to address cultural difference effects among consumers. The fact that the U.S. contains one of the most culturally heterogeneous populations in the world represents a possible advantage in "national" competitiveness. Just having diversity, however, is not sufficient to produce benefits. We must also manage it.

Creativity

Advocates of the value-in-diversity hypothesis suggest that work team heterogeneity promotes creativity and innovation (see note 1). Research tends to support this relationship. Kanter's study of innovation in organizations revealed that the most innovative companies deliberately establish heterogeneous teams to "create a marketplace of ideas, recognizing that a multiplicity of points of view need to be brought to bear on a problem." Kanter also specifically noted that companies high on innovation had done a better job than most on eradicating racism, sexism, and classism and tended to employ more women and racioethnic minorities than less innovative companies.[15]

Research by Charlene Nemeth found that minority views can stimulate consideration of non-obvious alternatives in task groups. In a series of experiments, participants were asked to form as many words as possible from a string of 10 letters. Individual approaches to the task were determined and then groups formed that were either majority (all members subscribed to the strategy for forming letters advocated by the majority of participants) or minority (nonmajority individuals were present in the groups). Nemeth found that the "minority" groups adopted multiple strategies and identified more solutions than the "majority" groups. She concluded that the groups exposed to minority views were more creative than the more homogeneous, majority groups. She further concluded that persistent exposure to minority viewpoints stimulates creative thought processes.

Another experiment compared the creativity of teams that were homogeneous on a series of attitude measures against teams with heterogeneous attitudes. Problem solution creativity was judged on originality and practicality. Results indicated that as long as the team members had similar ability levels, the heterogeneous teams were more creative than the homogeneous ones.[16] If people from different gender, nationality, and racioethnic groups hold different attitudes and perspectives on issues, then cultural diversity should increase team creativity and innovation.

Attitudes, cognitive functioning, and beliefs are not randomly distributed in the population but tend to vary systematically with demographic variables such as age, race, and gender.[17] Thus, an expected consequence of increased cultural diversity in organizations is the presence of different perspectives for problem solving, decision making and creative tasks.

Specific steps must be taken however, to realize this benefit. The research shows that in order to obtain the performance benefits, it was necessary for heterogeneous team members to have awareness of the attitudinal differences of other members. Similarly, diversity needs to be managed in part, by informing work-group members of their cultural differences. In recognition of this, cultural awareness training has become a standard element of organization change projects focusing on managing diversity.

Problem Solving

Diverse groups have a broader and richer base of experience from which to approach a problem. Thus, managing diversity also has the potential to improve problem solving and decision making.

In the 1960s, several University of Michigan studies discovered that heterogeneous groups produced better quality solutions to assigned problems than homogeneous groups. Dimensions of group diversity included personality measures and gender. In one study, 65 percent of heterogeneous groups produced high quality solutions (solutions that provided either new, modified, or integrative approaches to the problem) compared to only 21 percent of the homogeneous groups. This difference was statistically significant. The researchers noted that "mixing sexes and personalities appears to have freed these groups from the restraints of the solutions given in the problem."[18]

Later studies also confirmed the effects of heterogeneity on group decision quality. The same conclusion is indirectly indicated by research on the "groupthink" phenomenon—the absence of critical thinking in groups caused partly by excessive preoccupation with maintaining cohesiveness. Most of the examples of groupthink cited in the literature, such as the decision of the Kennedy administration to invade Cuba in 1961, portray decision processes as producing disastrous results. Because group cohesiveness is directly related to degrees of homogeneity, and groupthink only occurs in highly cohesive groups, the presence of cultural diversity in groups should reduce its probability.[19]

Decision quality is best when neither excessive diversity nor excessive homogeneity are present. This point has been well summarized by Shepard: "Similarity is an aid to developing cohesion; cohesion in turn, is related to the success of a group. Homogeneity, however, can be detrimental if it results in the absence of stimulation. If all members

are alike, they may have little to talk about, they may compete with each other, or they may all commit the same mistake. Variety is the spice of life in a group, so long as there is a basic core of similarity."[20]

A core of similarity among group members is desirable. This theme is similar to the "core value" concept advocated in the organization culture literature.[21] Our interpretation is that all members must share some common values and norms to promote coherent actions on organizational goals. The need for heterogeneity, to promote problem solving and innovation, must be balanced with the need for organizational coherence and unity of action.

Additional support for the superior problem solving of diverse workgroups comes from the work of Nemeth cited earlier. In a series of studies, she found that the level of critical analysis of decision issues and alternatives was higher in groups subjected to minority views than in those which were not. The presence of minority views improved the quality of the decision process regardless of whether or not the minority view ultimately prevailed. A larger number of alternatives were considered and there was a more thorough examination of assumptions and implications of alternative scenarios.[22]

In sum, culturally diverse workforces create competitive advantage through better decisions. A variety of perspectives brought to the issue, higher levels of critical analysis of alternatives through minority-influence effects, and lower probability of groupthink all contribute.

System Flexibility

Managing diversity enhances organizational flexibility. There are two primary bases for this assertion. First, there is some evidence that women and racioethnic minorities tend to have especially flexible cognitive structures. For example, research has shown that women tend to have a higher tolerance for ambiguity than men. Tolerance for ambiguity, in turn, has been linked to a number of factors related to flexibility such as cognitive complexity, and the ability to excel in performing ambiguous tasks.[23]

Studies on bilingual versus monolingual subpopulations from several nations show that compared to monolinguals, bilinguals have higher levels of divergent thinking and of cognitive flexibility.[24] Since the incidence of bilingualism is much greater among minority culture groups (especially Hispanics and Asians) than the majority-white Anglo group, this research strongly supports the notion that cognitive flexibility is enhanced by the inclusion of these groups in predominantly Anglo workforces.

The second way that managing cultural diversity may enhance organizational flexibility is that as policies and procedures are broadened and operating methods become less standardized, the organization becomes more fluid and adaptable. The tolerance for different cultural viewpoints should lead to greater openness to new ideas in general. Most important of all, if organizations are successful in overcoming resistance to change in the difficult area of accepting diversity, it should be well positioned to handle resistance to other types of change.

SUGGESTIONS FOR ORGANIZATION CHANGE

We have reviewed six ways in which the presence of cultural diversity and its effective management can yield a competitive advantage. Organizations wishing to maximize the benefits and minimize the drawbacks of diversity, in terms of workgroup cohesiveness, interpersonal conflict, turnover, and coherent action on major organizational goals, must create "multicultural" organizations. The typical organization of the past has been either monolithic (homogeneous membership with a culture dominated by one cultural group) or plural (ostensively diverse membership but still culturally monolithic and without valuing and using differences to benefit the organization). By contrast, the multicultural organization is one where members of nontraditional backgrounds can contribute and achieve to their fullest potential.

The multicultural organization's specific features are as follows: (1) pluralism: reciprocal acculturation where all cultural groups respect, value, and learn from one another; (2) full structural integration of all cultural groups so that they are well represented at all levels of the organization; (3) full integration of minority culture-group members in the informal networks of the organization; (4) an absence of prejudice and discrimination; (5) equal identification of minority- and majority-group members with the goals of the organization, and with opportunity for alignment of organizational and personal career goal achievement; (6) a minimum of intergroup conflict which is based on race, gender, nationality, and other identity groups of organization members.[25]

Five key components are needed to transform traditional organizations into multicultural ones.

1. Leadership
2. Training
3. Research
4. Analysis and change of culture and human resource management systems
5. Follow up

Each of these are briefly discussed.

Leadership

Top management's support and genuine commitment to cultural diversity is crucial. Champions for diversity are needed—people who will take strong personal stands on the need for change, role model the behaviors required for change, and assist with the work of moving the organization forward. Commitment must go beyond sloganism. For example, are human, financial, and technical resources being provided? Is this item prominently featured in the corporate strategy and consistently made a part of senior level staff meetings? Is there a willingness to change human resource management systems such as performance appraisal and executive bonuses? Is there a willingness to keep mental energy and financial support focused on this for a period of years, not months or weeks? If the answer to all of these questions is yes, the organization has genuine commitment, if not, then a potential problem with leadership is indicated.

Top management commitment is crucial but not sufficient. Champions are also needed at lower organizational levels, especially key line managers. Many organizations are addressing the leadership requirement by the formation of task forces or advisory committees on diversity, often headed by a senior manager. Some companies also have a designated manager for diversity who oversees the work company-wide (examples include Corning Inc. and Allstate Insurance). We advise using the manager of diversity in addition to, rather than as a substitute for, a broader involvement team such as a diversity task force. This is especially important in the early stages of the work.

Training

Managing and valuing diversity (MVD) training is the most prevalent starting point for managing diversity. Two types of training are popular: awareness training and skill-building training. Awareness training focuses on creating an understanding of the need for, and meaning of management and valuing diversity. It is also meant to increase participants' self awareness on diversity related issues such as stereotyping and cross-cultural insensitivity. Skill-building training educates employees on specific cultural differences and how to respond to differences in the workplace. Often the two types are combined. Avon, Ortho Pharmaceuticals, Procter & Gamble, and Hewlett-Packard are examples of companies with extensive experience with training programs.

Training is a crucial first step. However, it has limitations as an organization change tool and should not be used in isolation. It is also important to treat training as an on-going education process rather than a one-shot seminar.

Research

Collection of information about diversity related-issues is the third key component. Many types of data are needed including traditional equal-opportunity profile data, analysis of attitudes and perceptions of employees, and data which highlights the career experiences of different cultural groups (e.g., are mentors equally accessible to all members?).

Research has several important uses. First, it is often helpful for identifying issues to be addressed in the education process. For example, data indicating differences of opinion about the value in diversity based on culture group can be used as a launching point for mixed-culture discussion groups in training sessions. Second, research helps identify areas where changes are needed and provides clues about how to make them. Third, research is necessary to evaluate the change effort. Baseline data on key indicators of the valuing diversity environment needs to be gathered and periodically updated to assess progress.

Culture and Management Systems Audit

A comprehensive analysis of the organization culture and human resource systems such as recruitment, performance appraisal, potential assessment and promotion, and compensation should be undertaken. The primary objectives of this audit are: (1) to uncover sources of potential bias unfavorable to members of certain cultural groups, and (2) to identify ways that corporate culture may inadvertently put some members at a disadvantage.

It is important to look beyond surface data in auditing systems. For example, research that we reviewed or conducted indicates that even when average performance ratings for majority versus minority culture members are essentially the same, there may be differences in the relative priority placed on individual performance criteria, the distribution of the highest ratings, or the relationship between performance ratings and promotion.[26] The audit must be

an in-depth analysis, and the assistance of an external cultural diversity expert is strongly advised.

To identify ways that corporate culture may put some members at a disadvantage, consider a scenario where a prominent value in the organization culture is "aggressiveness." Such a value may place certain groups at a disadvantage if the norms of their secondary or alternative culture discouraged this behavior. This is indeed the case for many Asians and for women in many countries including the United States. While it is conceivable that the preservation of this value may be central to organizational effectiveness (in which case the solution may be to acknowledge the differential burden of conformity that some members must bear and to give assistance to them in learning the required behaviors), it may also be that the organizational values need to change so that other styles of accomplishing work are acceptable and perhaps even preferred. The point is that the prevailing values and norms must be identified and then examined critically in light of the diversity of the workforce.

The results of the audit must be translated into an agenda for specific changes in the organization culture and systems which management must then work to implement.

Follow-up

The final component, follow-up, consists of monitoring change, evaluating the results, and ultimately institutionalizing the changes as part of the organization's regular on-going processes. Like other management efforts, there is a need for accountability and control for work on diversity. Accountability for overseeing the change process might initially be assigned to the diversity task force, or if available, manager of diversity. Ultimately, however, accountability for preserving the changes must be established with every manager. Changes in the performance appraisal and reward processes are often needed to accomplish this.

Follow-up activities should include additional training, repetition of the systems audit, and use of focus groups for on-going discussions about diversity issues.[27]

CONCLUSION

Organizations' ability to attract, retain, and motivate people from diverse cultural backgrounds, may lead to competitive advantages in cost structures and through maintaining the highest quality human resources. Further capitalizing on the potential benefits of cultural diversity in work groups, organizations may gain a competitive advantage in creativity, problem solving, and flexible adaptation to change. We have identified steps that organizations can take toward accomplishing this.

While this article has reviewed a significant amount of relevant research, additional work clearly needs to be done, especially on the "value-in-diversity" issues. Nevertheless, the arguments, data, and suggestions presented here should be useful to organizations to build commitment and promote action for managing diversity efforts in the 1990s and beyond.

NOTES

1. See William B. Johnston, Global Work Force 2000, *Harvard Business Review,* March–April, 1991 and "Middle-Age at 26," *The Wall Street Journal,* April 10, 1990.

2. For examples of the competitive advantage argument, see R. Roosevelt Thomas Jr., "From Affirmative Action to Affirming Diversity," *Harvard Business Review,* 2 (March/April 1990), pp. 107–17; Lennie Copeland, "Learning to Manage a Multicultural Workforce," *Training,* May 1988, pp. 48–56; Barbara Mandrell and Susan Kohler-Gray, "Management Development that Values Diversity," *Personnel,* 67 (March 1990), pp. 41–47; Katherine Etsy, "Diversity Is Good for Business," *Executive Excellence,* 5 (1988), pp. 5–6; and A.G. Sodano and S.G. Baler, "Accommodation to Contrast: Being Different in the Organization," *New Directions in Mental Health,* 20 (1983), pp. 25–36.

3. This focus is not intended to undermine the importance of social, moral, and legal reasons for attention to diversity. We have chosen to address its relevance for other types of goals, such as worker productivity and quality of decision making, because the impact of diversity in these areas has received relatively little attention in the past compared to the equal-opportunity related goals.

4. See the following sources for details on the turnover data: B.R. Bergmann and W.R. Krause, "Evaluating and Forecasting Progress in Racial Integration of Employment," *Industrial and Labor Relations Review,* 1968, pp. 399–409; Carol Hymowitz, "One Firm's Bid to Keep Blacks, Women," *Wall Street Journal,* February 16, 1989, Sec. B, 1; Felice Schwartz, "Management Women and the New Facts of Life," *Harvard Business Review,* January/February 1989, pp. 65–76.

5. Taylor Cox, Jr. and Stella Nkomo, "A Race and Gender Group Analysis of the Early Career Experience of MBA's," *Work and Occupations,* 18, no. 4, pp. 431–46.

6. These surveys were reviewed by Cathy Trost, "Women Managers Quit Not for Family but to Advance Their Corporate Climb," *Wall Street Journal,* May 2, 1990. For additional evidence on this point, including discussions of the cultural-

conflict issue, see Schwartz, Endnote 3; A.M. Morrison, R.P. White and E. Van Velsor, "Executive Women: Substance Plus Style," *Psychology Today,* August 1987, pp. 18–25; and Gail DeGeorge, "Corporate Women: They're About to Break Through to the Top," *Business Week,* June 22, 1987, pp. 72–77.

7. "Helping Pregnant Workers Pays Off," *USA Today,* December 2, 1987.

8. Stewart A. Youngblood and Kimberly Chambers-Cook, "Child Care Assistance Can Improve Employee Attitudes and Behavior," *Personnel Administrator,* February 1984, pp. 93–95+.

9. Jay S. Kim and Anthony F. Campagna, "Effects of Flextime on Employee Attendance and Performance: A Field Experiment," *Academy of Management Journal,* December 14, 1981, pp. 729–41.

10. Reported in Nancy Adler, *International Dimensions of Organizational Behavior* (Boston: Kent Publishing Co., 1986), p. 111.

11. The figure of $20,000 is based on computations of Michael Mercer for turnover costs of a computer programmer. Readers may wish to consult one of the following sources for turnover cost formulas and then use their own job structure to determine cost factors for the actual turnover costs: Michael Mercer, "Turnover: Reducing the Costs," *Personnel,* Vol. 5 (1988), pp. 36–42; Rene Darmon, "Identifying Sources of Turnover Costs, *Journal of Marketing,* 1990, Vol. 54, pp. 46–56. The data on Ortho is provided in Juliane Bailey, "How to Be Different but Equal," *Savvy Woman,* November 1989, pp. 47+.

12. Examples of these publications include Baila Zeitz and Lorraine Dusky, *Best Companies for Women* (New York: Simon and Schuster, 1988); and "The 50 Best Places for Blacks to Work," *Black Enterprise,* February 1989, pp. 73–91.

13. Selwyn Feinstein, "Being the Best on Somebody's List Does Attract Talent," *Wall Street Journal,* October 10, 1989. For other examples supporting the resource acquisition argument, see Joel Dreyfuss, "Get Ready for the New Work Force," *Fortune,* April 23, 1990, pp. 165–81.

14. S.G. Redding, "Cultural Effects on the Marketing Process in Southeast Asia," *Journal of Market Research Society,* Vol. 24, 19, pp. 98–114.

15. Rosabeth Moss-Kanter, *The Change Masters.* (New York: Simon and Schuster, 1983).

16. For details on the research in this section, readers should see: Charlan Jeanne Nemeth, "Differential Contributions of Majority and Minority Influence," *Psychological Review,* 93 (1986), pp. 23–32 and H.C. Triandis, E.R. Hall, and R.B. Ewen, "Member Homogeneity and Dyadic Creativity," *Human Relations,* 18 (1965), pp. 33–54.

17. Susan E. Jackson, "Team Composition in Organizational Settings: Issues in Managing a Diverse Workforce," in *Group Process & Productivity,* J. Simpson, S. Warchel and W. Wood (eds), (Beverly Hills, Calif.: Sage Publications, 1989).

18. L. Richard Hoffman and Norman R.F. Maier, "Quality and Acceptance of Problem Solving by Members of Homogeneous and Heterogeneous Groups," *Journal of Abnormal and Social Psychology*, 62 (1961), pp. 401–7. The quote in the text is from page 404.

19. For reviews of research on the effect of group heterogeneity on problem solving, see M.E. Shaw, *Group Dynamics: The Psychology of Small Group Behavior*, (New York: McGraw-Hill, 1981); J.E. McGrath, *Groups: Interaction and Performance* (Englewood Cliffs, N.J.: Prentice-Hall, 1984); and Irving Janis, *Victims of Groupthink*, (Boston: Houghton Mifflin Co., 1972).

20. C.R. Shepard, *Small Groups*, (San Francisco: Chandler Publishing Co., 1964), p. 118.

21. See Ed Schein, "Organizational Socialization and the Profession of Management," in D.A. Kolb, I.M. Rubin, and J.M. McIntyre (Eds.), *Organizational Psychology*, Englewood Cliffs: Prentice-Hall, 1984, pp. 7–21; and Y. Weiner, "Forms of Value Systems: A Focus on Organizational Effectiveness and Cultural Change and Maintenance," *Academy of Management Review*, 13 (1988), pp. 534–45.

22. See Charlan Jeanne Nemeth, "Dissent, Group Process, and Creativity," *Advances in Group Processes*, 2 (1985), pp. 57–75; and Charlan Jeanne Nemeth and Joel Wachter, "Creative Problem Solving as a Result of Majority versus Minority Influence," *European Journal of Social Psychology*, 13 (1983), pp. 45–55.

23. See Naomi G. Rotter and Agnes N. O'Connell, "The Relationships among Sex-Role Orientation, Cognitive Complexity, and Tolerance for Ambiguity," *Sex Roles*, 8(12), (1982), pp. 1209–20; and David R. Shaffer et al., "Interactive Effects of Ambiguity Tolerance and Task Effort on Dissonance Reduction," *Journal of Personality*, 41(2), (June, 1973), pp. 224–33.

24. These research studies are reviewed by Wallace Lambert, "The Effects of Bilingualism on the Individual: Cognitive and Sociocultural Consequences," in Peter A. Hurnbey (Ed.), *Bilingualism: Psychological, Social, and Educational Implications* (New York: Academic Press, 1977), pp. 15–27.

25. This discussion of traditional versus multicultural organizations is based on Taylor Cox's article, "The Multicultural Organization" which appeared in the May, 1991 issue of *The Executive*.

26. For a specific example of race differences in priorities of performance rating criteria, see Taylor Cox and Stella Nkomo, "Differential Performance Appraisal Criteria," *Group and Organization Studies*, 11 (1986), pp. 101–19. For an example of subtle bias in performance rating distributions see Asya Pazy's article: "The Persistence of Pro-Male Bias," *Organization Behavior and Human Decision Processes*, 38, (1986), pp. 366–77.

27. For additional discussion of organization change processes to manage diversity including specific examples of what pioneering companies are doing in this area, please see Taylor Cox's article "The Multicultural Organization" (note 24).

■

EXERCISES

EXERCISE 3–1   TESTING YOUR ASSUMPTIONS ABOUT PEOPLE

To enable you to examine your assumptions about people, their work, and how to get them to do the work that is expected, the following test will be helpful. Simply check the appropriate column beside each of the 15 statements that are presented. Read each statement and *immediately* place a check in one of the four columns. Because the test is designed to measure your assumptions, not your carefully reasoned responses, answer at once, not after "qualifying" the statement or looking for the "right" answer. There are no right or wrong answers, and the "best" answer is the one that describes what you actually believe; any other answer will only cloud the picture this test is trying to obtain—your instinctive pattern of behavior.

Think of "people" in a rather general sense, not as specific individuals. You are trying to analyze your general pattern of behavior—the image that you project to others. It should take you no more than 3 to 4 minutes to complete the quiz.

Source: Adapted from Roger Fritz, *Rate Your Executive Potential* (New York: John Wiley and Sons, 1988), pp. 61–64.

	Strongly Disagree	Disagree	Agree	Strongly Agree
1. Almost everyone could improve their job performance considerably if they really wanted to.	_____	_____	_____	_____
2. It is unrealistic to expect people to show the same enthusiasm for their work as for their leisure activities.	_____	_____	_____	_____
3. Even when given encouragement by the boss, very few people show the desire to improve themselves on the job.	_____	_____	_____	_____
4. If you give people enough money, they are less likely to worry about such intangibles as status or recognition.	_____	_____	_____	_____
5. When people talk about wanting more responsible jobs, they usually mean they want more money and status.	_____	_____	_____	_____
6. Because most people don't like to make decisions on their own, it is hard to get them to assume responsibility.	_____	_____	_____	_____
7. Being tough with people usually will get them to do what you want.	_____	_____	_____	_____
8. A good way to get people to do more work is to crack down on them once in awhile.	_____	_____	_____	_____
9. It weakens people's prestige whenever they have to admit that a subordinate has been right and they have been wrong.	_____	_____	_____	_____
10. The most effective manager is one who gets the results expected, regardless of the methods used in handling people.	_____	_____	_____	_____
11. It is too much to expect that people will try to do a good job without being prodded by their boss.	_____	_____	_____	_____

	Strongly Disagree	Disagree	Agree	Strongly Agree
12. The boss who expects people to set their own standards for performance probably will find that they don't set them very high.	_____	_____	_____	_____
13. If people don't use much imagination and ingenuity on the job, it's probably because relatively few have much of either.	_____	_____	_____	_____
14. One problem in asking for the ideas of subordinates is that their perspective is too limited for their suggestions to be of much practical value.	_____	_____	_____	_____
15. It is only human nature for people to try to do as little work as they can get away with.	_____	_____	_____	_____
TOTAL FOR EACH COLUMN	_____	_____	_____	_____
"WEIGHTING" EACH COLUMN	× 1_____	× 2_____	× 3_____	× 4_____
TOTAL SCORE				_____

TO SCORE THE TEST

Total the number of marks in each column. Obviously, unless you have skipped a question, the four totals should add up to 15.

Now "weigh" your answer by multiplying each column total by the figure given (that is, the total in the *strongly disagree* column × 1, the *disagree* column total × 2, the *agree* column total × 3, and the *strongly agree* column × 4). Enter the answers at the ends of the appropriate columns.

Add the four weighted column totals together to obtain your total score. The total should fall somewhere between 15 and 60. The theory is that your assumptions about people and their work leads you to develop a certain style of management.

Now determine where your score would fall in Table 1, record it there, and circle it.

The range from A to D at the top of the table provides for all possible sets of assumptions regarding people and their work. The segment from A to M represents various degrees of autocratic or authoritarian management styles while the segment from M to D covers different levels of democratic or developmental styles of management.

TABLE 1

Your Leadership Style

Style	60 A	Autocratic	33–30 M	Developmental	15 D
Often called . . .		Boss		Leader	
Motivates from . . .		Fear		Inspiration	
Supervision is . . .		Close		General	

EXERCISE 3–2   ASSUMPTIONS THAT COLOR PERCEPTIONS

OBJECTIVES

1. To gain awareness of the influence of our assumptions on perceptions and evaluations of others.
2. To compare our perceptions with others and to find similarities and differences.

STARTING THE EXERCISE

1. Read the descriptions of the four individuals provided in the *Personal Descriptions* below.
2. Decide which occupation is most likely for each person and place the name by the corresponding occupation in the *Occupations* list which follows. Each person is in a different occupation and no two people hold the same one.
3. Divide the class into groups of five to seven students each.
4. Share and compare your choices.
5. Compare your choices to the actual occupations. You will receive answers from your instructor.

Personal Descriptions

R. B. Red is a trim, attractive women in her early 30s. She holds an undergraduate degree from an eastern woman's college and is active in several professional organizations. She is an officer (on the national level) of Toastmistress International.

Her hobbies include classical music, opera, and jazz. She is an avid traveler, who is planning a sojourn to China next year.

Source: Jerri L. Frantzve, *Behaving in Organizations* (Boston: Allyn & Bacon, 1983), pp. 63–65.

W. C. White is a quiet, meticulous person. W. C. is tall and thin with blond hair and wire-framed glasses. Family, friends, and church are very important and W. C. devotes any free time to community activities.

W. C. is a wizard with figures but can rarely be persuaded to demonstrate this ability to do mental calculations.

G. A. Green grew up on a small farm in rural Indiana. He is an avid hunter and fisherman. In fact, he and his wife joke about their "deer-hunting honeymoon" in Colorado.

One of his primary goals is to "get back to the land," and he hopes to be able to buy a small farm before he is fifty. He drives a pickup truck and owns several dogs.

B. E. Brown is the child of wealthy professionals who reside on Long Island. Mr. Brown, B. E.'s father, is a "self-made" financial analyst who made it a point to stress the importance of financial security as B.E. grew up.

B. E. values the ability to structure one's use of time and can often be found on the golf course on Wednesday afternoons. B. E. dresses in a conservative upper-class manner and professes to be "allergic to polyester."

Occupations

Choose the occupation that seems most appropriate for each person described. Place the names in the spaces next to the corresponding occupations.

_____   Banker
_____   Labor negotiator
_____   Production manager

_____ Travel agent
_____ Accountant
_____ Teacher
_____ Computer operations manager
_____ Clerk
_____ Army general
_____ Salesperson
_____ Physician
_____ Truck driver
_____ Financial analyst

Discussion

1. What assumptions were made about each person?
2. What assumptions were made about each occupation?
3. Gender was not specified for White or Brown. What gender was assumed? What difference did that make?
4. How could such assumptions influence evaluations?

Your instructor has the identification of theoretical occupations.

EXERCISE 3–3 PERSONALITY INSIGHTS

The following 27 statements are designed to provide some insights regarding how you see yourself. In the blank space next to each of these statements, write the number which best describes how strongly you agree or disagree with the statement, or how true or false the statement is as it applies to you. The numbers represent the following:

5 = Strongly Agree, or Definitely True
4 = Generally Agree, or Mostly True
3 = Neither Agree nor Disagree, Neither True nor False
2 = Generally Disagree, or Mostly False
1 = Strongly Disagree, or Definitely False

Example:
__2__   You enjoy playing "bridge."

(The "2" in the space next to the statement indicates that you generally disagree: you are more negative than neutral about enjoying "bridge.")

_____ 1. In some circumstances in the past you have taken the lead.
_____ 2. Everyone should place trust in a supernatural force whose decisions he or she always obeys.
_____ 3. You like to perform activities involving selling or salesmanship.
_____ 4. As a rule you assess your previous actions closely.

_____ 5. You often observe those around you to see how your words and actions affect them.
_____ 6. What you earn depends on what you know and how hard you work.
_____ 7. Generally, those in authority do their share of the unpleasant jobs without passing them on to others.
_____ 8. The remedy for social problems depends on eliminating dishonest, immoral, and mentally inferior people.
_____ 9. Most people today earn their pay by their own work.
_____ 10. The lowest type of person is the one who does not love and respect his parents.
_____ 11. There are two kinds of people: the weak and the strong.
_____ 12. You are the kind of person who tends to look into and analyze himself or herself.
_____ 13. Your promotions depend more on whom you know than on how well you do your job.
_____ 14. All children should be taught obedience and respect for authority.
_____ 15. Those who are in public offices usually put their own interest ahead of the public interest.
_____ 16. Many bosses actually deserve lower pay than their employees.
_____ 17. Taking on important responsibilities like starting your own company is something you would like to do.
_____ 18. An insult to your good name should never go unpunished.
_____ 19. In a meeting you will speak up when you disagree with someone you are convinced is wrong.
_____ 20. Thinking about complex problems is enjoyable for you.

Source: This self-feedback experiential exercise is reprinted with permission from the *Subordinates' Management Styles Survey* by Bernard M. Bass, Enzo R. Valenzi, and Larry D. Eldridge.

_____ 21. Generally, people are well paid for their contributions to society.

_____ 22. It is better to work for a good boss than for yourself.

_____ 23. Many times you would like to know the real reasons why some people behave as they do.

_____ 24. In the long run, we each get what we deserve.

_____ 25. Most organizations believe in paying a fair day's wages for a fair day's work.

_____ 26. Getting ahead is based more on your performance than your politics.

_____ 27. You can't expect to be treated fairly by those above you unless you insist on it.

Take your answers to the above questions and enter them below in the appropriate space. In those cases where there is an asterisk before the number, use *reverse scoring* by subtracting your score from six, that is, a 1 becomes a 5, a 4 becomes a 2, and so forth. Asterisks indicate that you must change originally high scores to low ones and vice versa.

Group 1	Group 2	Group 3	Group 4
6. _____	1. _____	*2. _____	4. _____
7. _____	3. _____	*8. _____	5. _____
9. _____	17. _____	*10. _____	12. _____
*13. _____	19. _____	*11. _____	20. _____
*15. _____	*22. _____	*14. _____	23. _____
*16. _____	Total _____	*18. _____	Total _____
21. _____		Total _____	
24. _____			
25. _____			
26. _____			
*27. _____			
Total _____			

Now take each of your totals and divide by the number of answers so as to obtain your average responses, that is 2.3, 3.2, 4.1, and so forth. On a scale of 1–5, this measures how you see yourself in each of these four areas.

Average Score

The four areas, represented by Groups 1–4, respectively, are:

_____ 1. Fair—this score measures the extent to which you see the world as treating you fairly.

_____ 2. Assertive—this score measures the extent to which you see yourself as aggressive.

_____ 3. Equalitarian—this score measures the extent to which you see yourself as nonauthoritarian.

_____ 4. Introspective—this score measures the extent to which you see yourself as thinking about things that go on around you and trying to determine why they occur.

▲

CASE

CASE 3–1 BOB KNOWLTON

Bob Knowlton was sitting alone in the conference room of the laboratory. The rest of the group had gone. One of the secretaries had stopped and talked for a while about her husband's coming induction into the army and had finally left. Bob, alone in the laboratory, slid a little further down in his chair, looking with satisfaction at the results of the first test run of the new photon unit.

He liked to stay after the others had gone. His appointment as project head was still new enough to give him a deep sense of pleasure. His eyes were on the graphs before him, but in his mind he could hear Dr. Jerrold, the project head, saying again, "There's one thing about this place you can bank on. The sky is the limit for a man who can produce!" Knowlton felt again the tingle of happiness and embarrassment. Well, dammit, he said to himself, he had produced. He wasn't kidding anybody. He had come to the Simmons Laboratories two years ago. During a routine testing of some rejected Clanson components, he had stumbled on the idea of the photon correlator, and the rest just happened. Jerrold had been enthusiastic: A separate project had been set up for further research and development of the device, and he had gotten the job of running it. The whole sequence of events still seemed a little miraculous to Knowlton.

He shrugged out of the reverie and bent determinedly over the sheets when he heard someone come into the room behind him. He looked up expectantly; Jerrold often stayed late himself and now and then dropped in for a chat. This always made the day's end especially pleasant for Bob. It wasn't Jerrold. The man who had come in was a stranger. He was tall, thin, and rather dark. He wore steel-rimmed glasses and had a very wide leather belt with a large brass buckle. Lucy remarked later that it was the kind of belt the Pilgrims must have worn.

The stranger smiled and introduced himself. "I'm Simon Fester. Are you Bob Knowlton?" Bob said yes, and they shook hands. "Doctor Jerrold said I might find you in. We

were talking about your work, and I'm very much interested in what you are doing." Bob waved to a chair.

Fester didn't seem to belong in any of the standard categories of visitors: customer, visiting fireman, stockholder. Bob pointed to the sheets on the table. "There are the preliminary results of a test we're running. We've got a new gadget by the tail and we're trying to understand it. It's not finished, but I can show you the section we're testing."

He stood up, but Fester was deep in the graphs. After a moment, he looked up with an odd grin. "These look like plots of a Jennings surface. I've been playing around with some autocorrelation functions of surfaces—you know that stuff." Bob, who had no idea what he was referring to, grinned back and nodded, and immediately felt uncomfortable. "Let me show you the monster," he said, and led the way to the workroom.

After Fester left, Knowlton slowly put the graphs away, feeling vaguely annoyed. Then, as if he had made a decision, he quickly locked up and took the long way out so that he would pass Jerrold's office. But the office was locked. Knowlton wondered whether Jerrold and Fester had left together.

The next morning, Knowlton dropped into Jerrold's office, mentioned that he had talked with Fester, and asked who he was.

"Sit down for a minute," Jerrold said. "I want to talk to you about him. What do you think of him?" Knowlton replied truthfully that he thought Fester was very bright and probably very competent. Jerrold looked pleased.

"We're taking him on," he said. "He's had a very good background in a number of laboratories, and he seems to have ideas about the problems we're tackling here." Knowlton nodded in agreement, instantly wishing that Fester would not be placed with him.

"I don't know yet where he will finally land," Jerrold continued, "but he seems interested in what you are doing. I thought he might spend a little time with you by way of getting started." Knowlton nodded thoughtfully. "If his interest in your work continues, you can add him to your group."

"Well, he seemed to have some good ideas even without

Source: This case was prepared by Professor Alex Bavelas for courses in management of research and development conducted at the School of Industrial Management, Massachusetts Institute of Technology, Cambridge, and is used with his permission.

knowing exactly what we are doing," Knowlton answered. "I hope he stays; we'd be glad to have him."

Knowlton walked back to the lab with mixed feelings. He told himself that Fester would be good for the group. He was no dunce; he'd produce. Knowlton thought again of Jerrold's promise when he had promoted him—"the man who produces gets ahead in this outfit." The words seemed to carry the overtones of a threat now.

That day Fester didn't appear until midafternoon. He explained that he had had a long lunch with Jerrold, discussing his place in the lab. "Yes," said Knowlton, "I talked with Jerry this morning about it, and we both thought you might work with us for awhile."

Fester smiled in the same knowing way that he had smiled when he mentioned the Jennings surfaces. "I'd like to," he said.

Knowlton introduced Fester to the other members of the lab. Fester and Link, the mathematician of the group, hit it off well together and spent the rest of the afternoon discussing a method of analysis of patterns that Link had been worrying over the last month.

It was 6:30 when Knowlton finally left the lab that night. He had waited almost eagerly for the end of the day to come—when they would all be gone and he could sit in the quiet rooms, relax, and think it over. "Think what over?" he asked himself. He didn't know. Shortly after 5 P.M. they had almost all gone except Fester, and what followed was almost a duel. Knowlton was annoyed that he was being cheated out of his quiet period and finally resentfully determined that Fester should leave first.

Fester was sitting at the conference table reading, and Knowlton was sitting at his desk in the little glass-enclosed cubby he used during the day when he needed to be undisturbed. Fester had gotten the last year's progress reports out and was studying them carefully. The time dragged. Knowlton doodled on a pad, the tension growing inside him. What the hell did Fester think he was going to find in the reports?

Knowlton finally gave up and they left the lab together. Fester took several of the reports with him to study in the evening. Knowlton asked him if he thought the reports gave a clear picture of the lab's activities.

"They're excellent," Fester answered with obvious sincerity. "They're not only good reports; what they report is damn good, too!" Knowlton was surprised at the relief he felt and grew almost jovial as he said good-night.

Driving home, Knowlton felt more optimistic about Fester's presence in the lab. He had never fully understood the analysis that Link was attempting. If there was anything wrong with Link's approach, Fester would probably spot it. "And if I'm any judge," he murmured, "he won't be especially diplomatic about it."

He described Fester to his wife, who was amused by the broad leather belt and brass buckle.

"It's the kind of belt that Pilgrims must have worn," she laughed.

"I'm not worried about how he holds his pants up," he laughed with her. "I'm afraid that he's the kind that just has to make like a genius twice each day. And that can be pretty rough on the group."

Knowlton had been asleep for several hours when he was jerked awake by the telephone. He realized it had rung several times. He swung off the bed muttering about damn fools and telephones. It was Fester. Without any excuses, apparently oblivious of the time, he plunged into an excited recital of how Link's patterning problem could be solved.

Knowlton covered the mouthpiece to answer his wife's stage-whispered "Who is it?" "It's the genius," replied Knowlton.

Fester, completely ignoring the fact that it was 2:00 in the morning, proceeded in a very excited way to start in the middle of an explanation of a completely new approach to certain of the photon lab problems that he had stumbled on while analyzing past experiments. Knowlton managed to put some enthusiasm in his own voice and stood there, half-dazed and very uncomfortable, listening to Fester talk endlessly about what he had discovered. It was probably not only a new approach but also an analysis which showed the inherent weakness of the previous experiment and how experimentation along that line would certainly have been inconclusive. The following day Knowlton spent the entire morning with Fester and Link, the mathematician, the customary morning meeting of Bob's group having been called off so that Fester's work of the previous night could be gone over intensively. Fester was very anxious that this be done, and Knowlton was not too unhappy to call the meeting off for reasons of his own.

For the next several days Fester sat in the back office that had been turned over to him and did nothing but read the progress reports of the work that had been done in the last six months. Knowlton caught himself feeling apprehensive about the reaction that Fester might have to some of his work. He was a little surprised at his own feelings. He had always been proud—although he had put on a convincingly modest face—of the way in which new ground in the study of photon measuring devices had been broken in his group. Now he wasn't sure, and it seemed to him that Fester might easily show that the line of research they had been following was unsound or even unimaginative.

The next morning (as was the custom) the members of the lab, including the girls, sat around a conference table. Bob always prided himself on the fact that the work of the lab was guided and evaluated by the group as a whole, and he was fond of repeating that it was not a waste of time to include secretaries in such meetings. Often, what started out as a boring recital of fundamental assumptions to a naive listener, uncovered new ways of regarding these assumptions that would not have occurred to the researcher who had long ago accepted them as a necessary basis for his work.

These group meetings also served Bob in another sense. He admitted to himself that he would have felt far less secure if he had had to direct the work out of his own mind, so to speak. With the group meeting as the principle of leadership, it was always possible to justify the exploration of blind alleys because of the general educative effect on the team. Fester was there; Lucy and Martha were there; Link was sitting next to Fester, their conversation concerning Link's mathematical study apparently continuing from yesterday. The other members, Bob Davenport, George Thurlow, and Arthur Oliver, were waiting quietly.

Knowlton, for reasons that he didn't quite understand, proposed for discussion this morning a problem that all of them had spent a great deal of time on previously with the conclusion that a solution was impossible, that there was no feasible way of treating it in an experimental fashion. When Knowlton proposed the problem, Davenport remarked that there was hardly any use of going over it again, that he was satisfied that there was no way of approaching the problem with the equipment and the physical capacities of the lab.

This statement had the effect of a shot of adrenalin on Fester. He said he would like to know what the problem was in detail and, walking to the blackboard, began setting down the "factors" as various members of the group began discussing the problem and simultaneously listing the reasons why it had been abandoned.

Very early in the description of the problem it was evident that Fester was going to disagree about the impossibility of attacking it. The group realized this, and finally the descriptive materials and their recounting of the reasoning that had led to its abandonment dwindled away. Fester began his statement which, as it proceeded, might well have been prepared the previous night although Knowlton knew this was impossible. He couldn't help being impressed with the organized and logical way that Fester was presenting ideas that must have occurred to him only a few minutes before.

Fester had some things to say, however, which left Knowlton with a mixture of annoyance, irritation, and at the same time, a rather smug feeling of superiority over Fester in at least one area. Fester was of the opinion that the way that the problem had been analyzed was really typical of group thinking, and with an air of sophistication which made it difficult for a listener to dissent, he proceeded to comment on the American emphasis on team ideas, satirically describing the ways in which they led to a "high level of mediocrity."

During this time Knowlton observed that Link stared studiously at the floor, and he was very conscious of George Thurlow's and Bob Davenport's glances toward him at several points of Fester's little speech. Inwardly, Knowlton couldn't help feeling that this was one point at least in which Fester was off on the wrong foot. The whole lab, following Jerry's lead, talked if not practiced the theory of small research teams as the basic organization for effective research. Fester insisted that the problem could be approached and that he would like to study it for a while himself.

Knowlton ended the morning session by remarking that the meetings would continue and that the very fact that a supposedly insoluble experimental problem was now going to get another chance was another indication of the value of such meetings. Fester immediately remarked that he was not at all averse to meetings for the purpose of informing the group of the progress of its members—that the point he wanted to make was that creative advances were seldom accomplished in such meetings, that they were made by the individual "living with" the problem closely and continuously, a sort of personal relationship to it.

Knowlton went on to say to Fester that he was very glad that Fester had raised these points and that he was sure the group would profit by reexamining the basis on which they had been operating. Knowlton agreed that individual effort was probably the basis for making the major advances but that he considered the group meetings useful primarily because of the effect they had on keeping the group together and on helping the weaker members of the group keep up with the ones who were able to advance more easily and quickly in the analysis or problems.

It was clear as days went by and meetings continued that Fester came to enjoy them because of the pattern which the meetings assumed. It became typical for Fester to hold forth, and it was unquestionably clear that he was more brilliant, better prepared on the various subjects which were germane to the problem being studied, and more capable of going ahead than anyone there. Knowlton grew increasingly disturbed as he realized that his leadership of the group had been, in fact, taken over.

Whenever the subject of Fester was mentioned in occasional meetings with Dr. Jerrold, Knowlton would comment only on the ability and obvious capacity for work that Fester had. Somehow he never felt that he could mention his own discomforts, not only because they revealed a weakness on his own part but also because it was quite clear that Jerrold himself was considerably impressed with Fester's work and with the contacts he had with him outside the photon laboratory.

Knowlton now began to feel that perhaps the intellectual advantages that Fester had brought to the group did not quite compensate for what he felt were evidences of a breakdown in the cooperative spirit he had seen in the group before Fester's coming. More and more of the morning meetings were skipped. Fester's opinion concerning the abilities of others of the group, with the exception of Link, was obviously low. At times during morning meetings or in smaller discussions he had been on the point of rudeness, refusing to pursue an argument when he claimed it was based on another person's ignorance of the facts involved. His impatience of others led him to also make similar remarks to Dr. Jerrold. Knowlton inferred this from a conversation with Jerrold in which Jerrold asked whether Davenport and Oliver were going to be continued on; and his failure to mention Link, the mathematician, led Knowlton to feel that this was the result of private conversations between Fester and Jerrold.

It was not difficult for Knowlton to make a quite convincing case on whether the brilliance of Fester was sufficient recompense for the beginning of this breaking up of the group. He took the opportunity to speak privately with Davenport and with Oliver, and it was quite clear that both of them were uncomfortable because of Fester. Knowlton didn't press the discussion beyond the point of hearing them in one way or another say that they did feel awkward and that it was sometimes difficult for them to understand the arguments he advanced, but often embarrassing to ask him to fill in the background on which his arguments were based. Knowlton did not interview Link in this manner.

About six months after Fester's coming into the photon lab, a meeting was scheduled in which the sponsors of the research were coming to get some idea of the work and its progress. It was customary at these meetings for project heads to present the research being conducted in their groups. The members of each group were invited to other meetings which were held later in the day and open to all, but the special meetings were usually made up only of project heads, the head of the laboratory, and the sponsors.

As the time for the special meeting approached, it seemed to Knowlton that he must avoid the presentation at all cost. His reasons for this were that he could not trust himself to present the ideas and work that Fester had advanced because of his apprehension as to whether he could present them in sufficient detail and answer such questions about them as might be asked. On the other hand, he did not feel he could ignore these newer lines of work and present only the material that he had done or that had been started before Fester's arrival. He felt also that it would not be beyond Fester at all, in his blunt and undiplomatic way—if he were present at the meeting, that is—to make comments on his [Knowlton's] presentation and reveal Knowlton's inadequacy. It also seemed quite clear that it would not be easy to keep Fester from attending the meeting, even though he was not on the administrative level of those invited.

Knowlton found an opportunity to speak to Jerrold and raised the question. He remarked to Jerrold that with the meetings coming up and with the interest in the work and with the contributions that Fester had been making, he would probably like to come to these meetings, but there was a question of the feelings of the others in the group if Fester alone were invited. Jerrold passed this over very lightly by saying that he didn't think the group would fail to understand Fester's rather different position and that he thought that Fester by all means should be invited. Knowlton immediately said he had thought so, too; that Fester should present the work because much of it was work he had done; and as Knowlton put it, that this would be a nice way to recognize Fester's contributions and to reward him, as he was eager to be recognized as a productive member of the lab. Jerrold agreed, and so the matter was decided.

Fester's presentation was very successful and in some ways dominated the meeting. He attracted the interest and attention of many of those who had come, and a long discussion followed his presentation. Later in the evening—with the entire laboratory staff present—in the cocktail period before the dinner, a little circle of people formed about Fester. One of them was Jerrold himself, and a lively discussion took place concerning the application of Fester's theory. All of this disturbed Knowlton, and his reaction and behavior were characteristic. He joined the circle, praised

Fester to Jerrold and to others, and remarked on the brilliance of the work.

Knowlton, without consulting anyone, began at this time to take some interest in the possibility of a job elsewhere. After a few weeks he found that a new laboratory of considerable size was being organized in a nearby city and that the kind of training he had would enable him to get a project-head job equivalent to the one he had at the lab with slightly more money.

He immediately accepted it and notified Jerrold by a letter, which he mailed on a Friday night to Jerrold's home. The letter was quite brief, and Jerrold was stunned. The letter merely said that he had found a better position; that there were personal reasons why he didn't want to appear at the lab any more; that he would be glad to come back at a later time from where he would be, some 40 miles away, to assist if there was any mixup at all in the past work; that he felt sure that Fester could, however, supply any leadership that was required for the group; and that his decision to leave so suddenly was based on some personal problems—he hinted at problems of health in his family, his mother and father. All of this was fictitious, of course. Jerrold took it at face value but still felt that this was very strange behavior and quite unaccountable, for he had always felt his relationship with Knowlton had been warm and that Knowlton was satisfied and, as a matter of fact, quite happy and productive.

Jerrold was considerably disturbed, because he had already decided to place Fester in charge of another project that was going to be set up very soon. He had been wondering how to explain this to Knowlton, in view of the obvious help Knowlton was getting from Fester and the high regard in which he held him. Jerrold had, as a matter of fact, considered the possibility that Knowlton could add to his staff another person with the kind of background and training that had been unique in Fester and had proved so valuable.

Jerrold did not make any attempt to meet Knowlton. In a way, he felt aggrieved about the whole thing. Fester, too, was surprised at the suddenness of Knowlton's departure, and when Jerrold, in talking to him, asked him whether he had reasons to prefer to stay with the photon group instead of the project for the Air Force which was being organized, he chose the Air Force project and went on to that job the following week. The photon lab was hard hit. The leadership of the lab was given to Link with the understanding that this would be temporary until someone could come in to take over.

CASE QUESTIONS

1. What was the major problem that faced Knowlton?
2. What ego-defense mechanisms did Knowlton personally use?
3. Could Rotter's notion of locus of control be used to analyze Bob Knowlton's situation?

4

Motivation

LEARNING OBJECTIVES

DESCRIBE the three distinct components of motivation.

IDENTIFY the need levels in Maslow's hierarchy.

COMPARE motivators with hygiene factors.

DISCUSS the factors that reflect a high need for achievement.

DEFINE the key terms in expectancy theory.

DISTINGUISH between inputs and outputs in equity theory.

IDENTIFY the key steps in goal setting.

DESCRIBE the concept of the psychological contract.

No one questions the central role motivation plays in shaping behavior and specifically, in influencing work performance in organizations. Nonetheless, as important as motivation is, it is not the only factor that determines performance. Over the years a variety of other variables thought to play an important role in performance have been suggested. These include ability, instinct, and aspiration level as well as personal factors such as age, education, and family background.

One way of conceptualizing the various determinants of performance is illustrated in Exhibit 4-1. As can be seen from this exhibit, job performance may be viewed as a function of the **capacity** to perform, the **opportunity** to perform, and the **willingness** to perform. The capacity to perform relates to the degree to which an individual possesses task-relevant skills, abilities, knowledges, and experiences. Unless an employee knows what is supposed to be done and how to do it, high levels of job performance are not possible. Having the opportunity to perform is also a critical ingredient in the performance recipe. An employee assembling a product in a manufacturing plant who constantly experiences equipment failures

EXHIBIT 4-1

Determinants of Job Performance

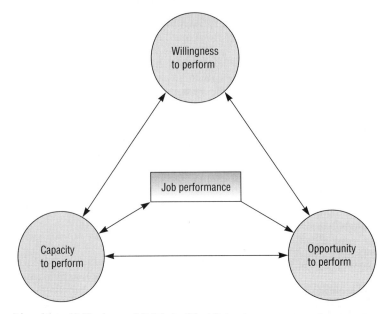

Source: Adapted from M. Blumberg and C. Pringle, "The Missing Opportunity in Organizational Research: Some Implications for a Theory of Work Performance," *Academy of Management Review*, October 1982, p. 565.

● R4–1

and a shortage of needed components is clearly going to be unable to perform at the same level as a worker who does not encounter those difficulties. Similarly, an accountant who must make entries in a hand ledger does not have the same opportunity to perform as one who has access to an electronic spreadsheet. Sometimes employees may lack the opportunity to perform not because of poor equipment or outdated technology, but because of poor decisions and outdated attitudes. Encounter 4-1 illustrates this problem, as does the more detailed examination that is the theme of the first reading selection in the chapter.

The third factor, willingness to perform, relates to the degree to which an individual both desires and is willing to exert effort toward attaining job performance. It is, in other words, motivation, and it is what this chapter is about. No combination of capacity and opportunity will result in high performance in the absence of some level of motivation, or willingness to perform.

From a managerial perspective, it is important to realize that the presence of motivation per se, coupled with a capacity and opportunity to perform does not ensure high performance levels. It is a rare manager who has not at some point concluded that performance would be much higher if "I could just get my people motivated." In all likelihood, those individuals are already motivated; what that manager really wants is motivation that results in more or different kinds of behaviors. To understand this distinction it is helpful to think of motivation as being made up of at least three distinct components: direction, intensity, and persistence.

ETHICS

E N C O U N T E R • 4-1

DO ORGANIZATIONS DISCOURAGE WOMEN MANAGERS?

Is it unethical to restrict upper-level management positions to only men? Virtually everyone would agree that it is, not to mention illegal and just poor business practice as well. Yet the Department of Labor's recently released "glass ceiling" report found that entrenched attitudes in organizations prevented women from moving very far up the corporate management ladder. What kind of attitudes? Consider, for example, a 1990 survey completed by a New York research firm which found that almost half of human resource managers thought women had less initiative and were less willing to take risks than men. Mary Mattis, vice president of the research firm says women are also perceived as being less committed, especially if they are mothers. "They're seen as people who will not stick around or who will not relocate" says Mattis.

These perceptions are incorrect. Another 1990 report indicates that it is frustration with lack of career progress rather than concern with home and family issues that accounts for the overwhelming majority of departures by women. This survey found that almost three-quarters of women who left large organizations moved to another company. Only 7 percent quit working. Indeed, women are just as tough and committed as men concludes Marilyn Loden, co-author of the book *Workforce America!* But, she says, male managers have to understand that men and women have different management styles. While men tend to depend on hierarchical arrangements for accomplishing results, women tend to use inspiration and involvement in decision making, and this makes women seem indecisive or unwilling to assert themselves.

How can the lack of opportunity for women to perform in managerial roles be overcome? Writing in *Business Week,* Susan Garland suggests that male managers would be smart to re-examine the politics of advancement. According to Garland, "women may have more difficulty developing the alliances that are as important as doing a job well, because older male managers often prefer proteges who are junior versions of themselves, i.e., young men." Companies should also review the way they conduct external searches for management talent. Male managers must make it clear to recruiters that they are not necessarily looking for their mirror image.

A few companies are implementing ways of rewarding those who help overcome the traditional stereotypes. For example, Tenneco Inc., a broad-based energy company, ties a portion of an executive's bonus to his or her progress in promoting women and minorities. This policy, in force since 1989, has led to a 25 percent rise in the numbers hired.

Source: Susan B. Garland, "How to Keep Women Managers on the Corporate Ladder." *Business Week,* September 2, 1991, p. 64.

Direction relates to what an individual chooses to do when presented with a number of possible alternatives. When faced with the task of completing a report requested by management, for example, an employee may choose to direct effort toward completing the report or toward solving the crossword puzzle in the morning newspaper (or any number of other possible activities). Regardless of which option is selected, the employee is motivated. If the employee selects the first alternative, the direction of his or her motivation is consistent with that desired by management. If the employee chooses the second alternative, the direction is counter to that desired by management, but the employee is none-theless motivated.

The **intensity** component of motivation refers to the strength of the response once the choice (direction) is made. Using the previous example, the employee may choose the proper direction (working on the report) but respond with very little intensity. Intensity, in this sense, is synonymous with effort. Two people may focus their behavior in the same direction, but one may perform better because he or she exerts more effort than the other. An attribute frequently used to describe an outstanding professional athlete is intensity. When coaches speak of an athlete as playing with a great deal of intensity, they are describing the amount of effort the player invests in the game.

Finally, **persistence** is an important component of motivation. Persistence refers to the staying power of behavior or how long a person will continue to devote effort. Some people will focus their behavior in the appropriate direction and do so with a high degree of intensity but only for a short period of time. Individuals who tackle a task enthusiastically but quickly tire of it, or burn out and seldom complete it, lack this critical attribute in their motivated behavior. Thus, the manager's real challenge is not so much one of increasing motivation per se but of creating an environment wherein employee motivation is channeled in the right direction at an appropriate level of intensity and continues over time.

Motivation is an explanatory concept we use to make sense out of the behaviors we observe. It is important to note that motivation is inferred. Instead of mea-suring it directly, we manipulate certain conditions and observe how behavior changes.[1] From the changes we observe, we improve our understanding of the underlying motivation. You assumed that your best friend had made a quick stop to eat lunch when you saw his car parked outside a fast-food restaurant. But your inference was not correct because your friend actually was talking to the manager about a weekend job. The lesson is clear: we must always be cautious when making motivational inferences. As more and more information is accu-mulated, however, our inferences become more accurate because we can eliminate alternative explanations.

THE STARTING POINT: THE INDIVIDUAL

Most managers must motivate a diverse and, in many respects, unpredictable group of people. The diversity results in different behavioral patterns that are in some manner related to needs and goals.

Needs refer to deficiencies an individual experiences at a particular time. The deficiencies may be physiological (e.g., a need for food), psychological (e.g., a need for self-esteem), or sociological (e.g., a need for social interaction). Needs are viewed as energizers or triggers of behavioral responses. The implication is

[1]Herbert Petri, *Motivation: Theory and Research* (Belmont, Calif.: Wadsworth Publishing, 1979), p. 4.

EXHIBIT 4-2

**The Motivational Process:
An Initial Model**

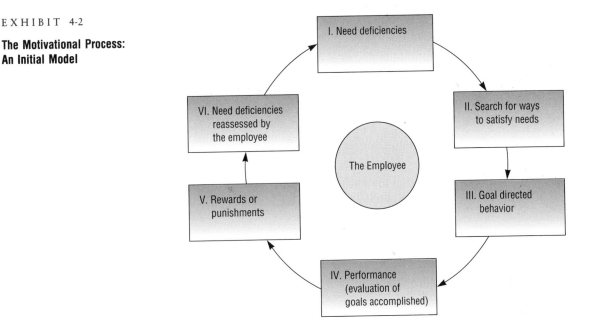

that when need deficiencies are present, the individual is more susceptible to a manager's motivational efforts.

The importance of goals in any discussion of motivation is apparent. The motivational process, as interpreted by most theorists, is goal directed. The goals, or outcomes, that an employee seeks are viewed as forces that attract the person. The accomplishment of desirable goals can result in a significant reduction in need deficiencies.

As illustrated in Exhibit 4-2, people seek to reduce various need deficiencies. Need deficiencies trigger a search process for ways to reduce the tension caused by the deficiencies. A course of action is selected, and goal-directed (outcome-directed) behavior occurs. After a period of time, managers assess that behavior, and the performance evaluation results in some type of reward or punishment. Such outcomes are weighed by the person, and the need deficiencies are reassessed. This, in turn, triggers the process, and the circular pattern is started once again.

MOTIVATION THEORIES: A CLASSIFICATION SYSTEM

Each person is attracted to some set of goals. If a manager is to predict behavior with any accuracy, he or she must know something about an employee's goals and about the actions the employee will take to achieve them. There is no shortage of motivation theories and research findings that attempt to provide explanations of the behavior-outcome relationship. Two categories can be used to classify

EXHIBIT 4-3

Managerial Perspective of Content and Process Theories of Motivation

Theoretical Base	Theoretical Explanation	Founders of the Theories	Managerial Application
Content	Factors within the person that energize, direct, sustain, and stop behavior. These factors can only be inferred.	Maslow—five-level need hierarchy. Herzberg—two major factors called hygiene-motivators. McClelland—three learned needs acquired from the culture: achievement, affiliation, and power.	Managers need to be aware of differences in needs, desires, and goals because each individual is unique in many ways.
Process	Describes, explains, and analyzes how behavior is energized, directed, sustained, and stopped.	Vroom—an expectancy theory of choices. Adams—equity theory based on comparisons that individuals make. Locke—goal-setting theory that conscious goals and intentions are the determinants of behavior.	Managers need to understand the process of motivation and how individuals make choices based on preferences, rewards, and accomplishments.

theories of motivation.[2] The **content theories** focus on the factors within the person that energize, direct, sustain, and stop behavior. They attempt to determine the specific needs that motivate people. The second category includes what we called the **process theories**. These theories provide a description and analysis of how behavior is energized, directed, sustained, and stopped. Exhibit 4-3 summarizes the basic characteristics of content and process theories of motivation from a managerial perspective.

Both categories of theories have important implications for managers, who are—by the nature of their jobs—involved with the motivational process. Three important content theories of motivation are: (1) Maslow's need hierarchy, (2) Herzberg's two-factor theory, and (3) McClelland's learned needs theory. Each of these three theories has had an impact on managerial practices and will be considered in the paragraphs that follow. Later in the chapter we shall examine some of the important process approaches.

[2]John P. Campbell, Marvin D. Dunnette, Edward E. Lawler III, and Karl E. Weick, *Managerial Behavior, Performance, and Effectiveness* (New York: McGraw-Hill, 1970), pp. 340–56.

Maslow's Need Hierarchy

The crux of Maslow's theory is that needs are arranged in hierarchy.[3] The lowest-level needs are the physiological needs, and the highest-level needs are the self-actualization needs. These needs are defined to mean the following:

1. **Physiological:** The need for food, drink, shelter, and relief from pain.
2. **Safety and security:** The need for freedom from threat, that is, the security from threatening events or surroundings.
3. **Belongingness, social, and love:** The need for friendship, affiliation, interaction, and love.
4. **Esteem:** The need for self-esteem and for esteem from others.
5. **Self-actualization:** The need to fulfill oneself by making maximum use of abilities, skills, and potential.

Maslow's theory assumes that a person attempts to satisfy the more basic needs (physiological) before directing behavior toward satisfying upper-level needs. Several other crucial points in Maslow's thinking are important to understanding the need-hierarchy approach.

1. A satisfied need ceases to motivate. For example, when a person decides that he or she is earning enough pay for contributing to the organization, money loses its power to motivate.
2. Unsatisfied needs can cause frustration, conflict, and stress. From a managerial perspective, unsatisfied needs are dangerous because they may lead to undesirable performance outcomes.
3. Maslow assumes that people have a need to grow and develop and, consequently, will strive constantly to move up the hierarchy in terms of need satisfaction. This assumption may be true for some employees but not others.

Maslow proposed that the typical adult in society has satisfied about 85 percent of the physiological need; 70 percent of the safety and security needs; 50 percent of the belongingness, social, and love needs; 40 percent of the esteem need; and 10 percent of the self-actualization need. Many critics disagree with these figures, however, particularly the 10 percent figure for self-actualization. These critics suggest that for blue-collar workers, many of whom are simply trying to survive, the true figure is far closer to zero. Exhibit 4-4 displays, in the form of a bar chart, Maslow's assertions regarding the degree of satisfaction of the five need types.

A number of research studies have attempted to test the need-hierarchy theory. The first reported field research that tested a modified version of Maslow's need hierarchy was performed by Porter.[4] At the time of the initial studies, Porter

[3]A. H. Maslow "A Theory of Human Motivation," *Psychological Review,* July 1943, pp. 370–96; and A. H. Maslow, *Motivation and Personality* (New York: Harper & Row, 1954).

[4]Lyman W. Porter, "A Study of Perceived Need Satisfaction in Bottom and Middle-Management Jobs," *Journal of Applied Psychology,* February 1961, pp. 1–10.

EXHIBIT 4-4

**The Typical Person's
Degree of Need Satisfaction**

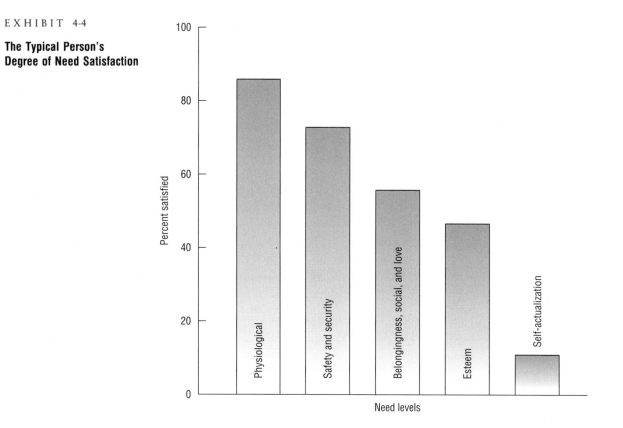

assumed that physiological needs were being adequately satisfied for managers, so he substituted a higher-order need called autonomy, defined as the person's satisfaction with opportunities to make independent decisions, set goals, and work without close supervision.

Since the early Porter studies, other studies have reported:

1. Managers higher in the organization chain of command place greater emphasis of self-actualization and autonomy.[5]
2. Managers at lower organizational levels in small firms (less than 500 employees) are more satisfied than their counterpart managers in large firms (more than 5,000 employees); however, managers at upper levels in large companies are more satisfied than their counterparts in small companies.[6]

[5]Lyman W. Porter, *Organizational Patterns of Managerial Job Attitudes* (New York: American Foundation for Management Research, 1964).

[6]Lyman W. Porter, "Job Attitudes in Management Perceived Deficiencies in Need Fulfillment as a Function of Size of the Company." *Journal of Applied Psychology,* December 1963, pp. 386–97.

3. American managers overseas are more satisfied with autonomy opportunities than are their counterparts working in the United States.[7]

Despite these findings, a number of issues remain regarding the need-hierarchy theory. First, data from managers in two different companies provided little support that a hierarchy of needs exits.[8] The data suggested that only two levels of needs exist: one is the physiological level, and the other is a level which includes all other needs. Further evidence also disputes the hierarchy notions.[9] Researchers have found that as managers advance in an organization, their needs for security decrease, with a corresponding increase in their needs for social interaction, achievement, and self-actualization.

Herzberg's Two-Factor Theory

Herzberg developed a content theory known as the two-factor theory of motivation.[10] The two factors are called the dissatisfiers-satisfiers or the hygiene motivators or the extrinsic-intrinsic factors, depending on the discussant of the theory. The original research which led to the theory gave rise to two specific conclusions. First, there is a set of **extrinsic** conditions, the job context, which result in dissatisfaction among employees when the conditions are not present. If these conditions are present, this does not necessarily motivate employees. These conditions are the **dissatisfiers** or **hygiene** factors, since they are needed to maintain at least a level of "no dissatisfaction." They include:

1. Salary.
2. Job security.
3. Working conditions.
4. Status.
5. Company procedures.
6. Quality of technical supervision.
7. Quality of interpersonal relations among peers, with superiors, and with subordinates.

Second, a set of **intrinsic** conditions, the job content—when present in the job, builds strong levels of motivation that can result in good job performance. If these conditions are not present, they do not prove highly satisfying. The factors in this set are called the *satisfiers* or *motivators* and include:

[7]John M. Ivancevich, "Perceived Need Satisfaction of Domestic versus Overseas Managers," *Journal of Applied Psychology,* August 1969, pp. 274–78.

[8]Edward E. Lawler III and J. L. Suttle, "A Causal Correlation Test of the Need Hierarchy Concept," *Organizational Behavior and Human Performance,* April 1972, pp. 265–87.

[9]Douglas T. Hall and K. E. Nougaim, "An Examination of Maslow's Need Hierarchy in an Organizational Setting," *Organizational Behavior and Human Performance,* February 1968, pp. 12–35.

[10]Frederick Herzberg, B. Mausner, and B. Snyderman, *The Motivation to Work,* (New York: John Wiley & Sons, 1959).

EXHIBIT 4-5

Traditional versus Herzberg View of Job Satisfaction

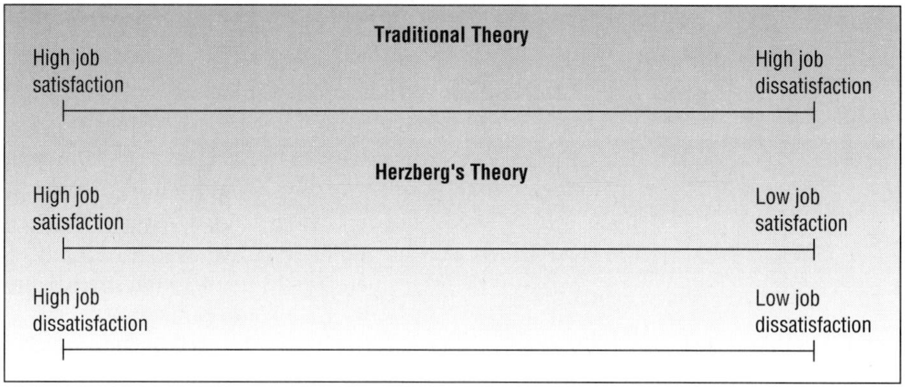

Traditional Theory

High job satisfaction ————————————————————————— High job dissatisfaction

Herzberg's Theory

High job satisfaction ————————————————————————— Low job satisfaction

High job dissatisfaction ————————————————————————— Low job dissatisfaction

1. Achievement.
2. Recognition.
3. Responsibility.
4. Advancement.
5. The work itself.
6. The possibility of growth.

These motivators are directly related to the nature of the job or task itself. When present they contribute to satisfaction. This, in turn, can result in intrinsic task motivation.[11]

Herzberg's model basically assumes that job satisfaction is not a unidimensional concept. His research leads to the conclusion that two continua are needed to correctly interpret job satisfaction. Exhibit 4-5 presents two different views of job satisfaction. Prior to Herzberg's work, those studying motivation viewed job satisfaction as a unidimensional concept; that is, they placed job satisfaction at one end of a continuum and job dissatisfaction at the other end of the same continuum. This meant that if a job condition caused job satisfaction, removing it would cause job dissatisfaction. Similarly, if a job condition caused job dissatisfaction, removing it would cause job satisfaction.

One appealing aspect of Herzberg's explanation of motivation is that the terminology is work-oriented. There is no need to translate psychological terminology into everyday language. Despite this important feature, Herzberg's work has been criticized for a number of reasons. For example, some researchers believe that Herzberg's work oversimplifies the nature of job satisfaction.[12] Other critics focus on Herzberg's methodology, which requires people to look at themselves

---

[11]For a discussion of the importance of intrinsic task motivation, see K. W. Thomas and B. A. Velthouse, "Cognitive Elements of Empowerment: An 'Interpretive' Model of Intrinsic Task Motivation," *Academy of Management Review*, October 1990, pp. 666–81.

[12]Marvin Dunnette, John Campbell, and M. Hakel, "Factors Contributing to Job Dissatisfaction in Six Occupational Groups," *Organizational Behavior and Human Performance*, May 1967, p. 147.

ORGANIZATIONAL

E N C O U N T E R • 4–2

INCREASING SATISFIERS CAN ENHANCE PERFORMANCE

Many organizations have attempted to implement the kind of job enrichment activities Herzberg argues are so important for enhancing motivation and performance. A few examples are the following:

- A large telephone company restructured the job of employees who handled correspondence with stockholders. Before the enrichment program, the workers had little autonomy, close supervision, low work quality, and high turnover. The restructuring reduced supervision, allowed the employees to compose their own correspondence, and encouraged them to become "experts" in the kinds of stockholder questions that appealed to them. Under the program, turnover, absenteeism, and costs were reduced, and a quality measurement index climbed from the 30s to the 90s.
- When it opened a new plant, a large manufacturer of pet foods decided to increase employee opportunities

for responsibility and task interest. Plant management allowed workers greatly increased participation in how the work was to be organized and assigned and gave them a significant voice in decisions regarding hiring, termination, and allocation of rewards. The plant experienced higher levels of productivity, lower costs, and lower absenteeism, turnover, and grievances than other plants within the company.

- A major hospital chain found that errors and the absenteeism rate dropped dramatically when it allowed employees to draw up their own work assignments. Meeting in small groups, employees with similar duties allocated assignments for each two-week period. They, rather than supervisors, were also responsible for ensuring that assignments were executed properly. Another positive outcome of the change was enhanced patient interaction. Patients reported the hospital staff was more sensitive to their needs and generally displayed a more positive and caring attitude.

retrospectively.[13] Still other critics charge that Herzberg has directed little attention toward testing the motivational and performance consequences of the theory. In his original study, only self-reports of performance were used, and in most cases, the respondents described job activities that had occurred over a long period of time.

Although the list of criticisms for Herzberg's model is long, the impact of the theory on practicing managers should not be underestimated. Many managers feel very comfortable about many of the things Herzberg includes in his two-factor discussion. From a scientific vantage point, this satisfaction presents some dangers of misuse, but from a very important, organizational-world perspective, it is appealing to managers. Encounter 4-2 provides some examples of organizational efforts to restructure jobs to increase the number of satisfiers and, consequently, enhance motivation.

[13]Abraham K. Korman, *Industrial and Organizational Psychology* (Englewood Cliffs, N.J.: Prentice-Hall, 1971), pp. 148–50.

McClelland's Learned Needs Theory

McClelland has proposed a theory of motivation that is closely associated with learning concepts. He believes that many needs are acquired from the culture.[14] Three of these learned needs are the need for achievement (n Ach), the need for affiliation (n Aff), and the need for power (n Pow).

McClelland contends that when a need is strong in a person, its effect is to motivate the person to use behavior that leads to its satisfaction. For example, having a high n Ach encourages an individual to set challenging goals, to work hard to achieve the goals, and to use the skills and abilities needed to achieve them.

Based on research results, McClelland developed a descriptive set of factors that reflect a high need for achievement. These are:

1. The person likes to take responsibility for solving problems.
2. The person tends to set moderate achievement goals and is inclined to take calculated risks.
3. The person desires feedback on performance.

The need for affiliation reflects a desire to interact socially with people. A person with a high need for affiliation is concerned about the quality of important personal relationships, and thus, social relationships take precedence over task accomplishment. A person with a high need for power, meanwhile, concentrates on obtaining and exercising power and authority. He or she is concerned with influencing others and winning arguments. Power has two possible orientations according to McClelland. It can be negative in that the person exercising it emphasizes dominance and submission. Or power can be positive in that it reflects persuasive and inspirational behavior.

The main theme of McClelland's theory is that these needs are learned through coping with one's environment. Since needs are learned, behavior which is rewarded tends to recur at a higher frequency. Managers who are rewarded for achievement behavior learn to take moderate risks and to achieve goals. Similarly, a high need for affiliation or power can be traced to a history of receiving rewards for sociable, dominant, or inspirational behavior. As a result of the learning process, individuals develop unique configurations of needs that affect their behavior and performance. Consider, for example, how a high need for achievement

▲ C4–1   might lead to the behaviors discussed in Case 4-1.

There are a number of criticisms of McClelland's theory. Not the least of these criticisms is that most of the evidence available which supports the theory has been provided by McClelland or his associates. McClelland's use of projective psychological personality tests has been questioned as being unscientific. Furthermore, McClelland's claim that n Ach can be learned runs counter to a large body of literature that argues that the acquisition of motives normally occurs in

---

[14]David C. McClelland, "Business Drive and National Achievement," *Harvard Business Review,* July–August 1962, pp. 99–112.

childhood and is very difficult to alter in adulthood. Finally, McClelland's theory is questioned on grounds of whether the needs are permanently acquired. Research is needed to determine whether acquired needs last over a period of time. Can something learned in a training-and-development program be sustained on the job?[15] This is an issue that McClelland and others have not been able to clarify.

A SYNOPSIS OF THE THREE CONTENT THEORIES

Each of the three content theories just discussed attempts to explain behavior from a slightly different perspective. None of the theories has been accepted as the sole basis for explaining motivation. Although some critics are skeptical, it appears that people have innate and learned needs and that various job factors result in a degree of satisfaction. Thus, each of the theories provides the manager with some understanding of behavior and performance.

The three theories are compared in Exhibit 4-6. McClelland has proposed no lower-order needs. However, the needs for achievement and power he has identified are not identical with Herzberg's motivators or Maslow's higher-order needs, but there are some similarities. A major difference between the three content theories is McClelland's emphasis on socially acquired needs. The Maslow theory offers a need classification system, and Herzberg discusses intrinsic and extrinsic job factors.

PROCESS THEORIES

The content theories we have examined focus mainly on the needs and incentives that cause behavior. They are concerned primarily about which specific things motivate people. The process theories of motivation are concerned with answering the questions of how individual behavior is energized, directed, maintained, and stopped. This section examines three process theories: expectancy theory, equity theory, and goal-setting theory. In discussing each of these in the paragraphs that follow, we will show how the motivational process works in organizational settings.

Expectancy Theory

One of the more popular explanations of motivation was developed by Victor Vroom.[16] Numerous studies have been done to test the accuracy of expectancy

---

[15]Paul R. Lawrence and Jay W. Lorsch, *Developing Organizations: Diagnosis and Action* (Reading, Mass.: Addison-Wesley Publishing, 1969).

[16]Victor H. Vroom, *Work and Motivation* (New York: John Wiley & Sons, 1964). For earlier work, see Kurt Lewin, *The Conceptual Representation and the Measurement of Psychological Forces* (Durham, N.C.: Duke University Press, 1938); and E. C. Tolman, *Purposive Behavior in Animals and Men* (New York: Appleton-Century-Crofts, 1932).

EXHIBIT 4-6

A Graphic Comparison of Three Content Theories of Motivation

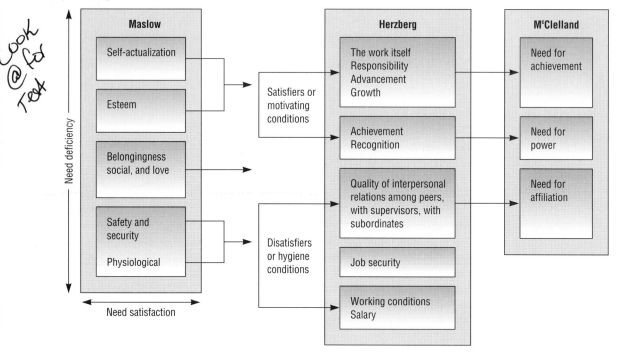

theory in predicting employee behavior, and direct tests have been generally supportive.[17] Vroom defines *motivation* as a process governing choices among alternative forms of voluntary activity. In his view, most behaviors are considered to be under the voluntary control of the person and consequently are motivated. In order to understand expectancy theory, it is necessary to define the terms of the theory and explain how they operate. The four most important terms are: *first-* and *second-level outcomes, instrumentality, valence,* and *expectancy.*

First-Level and Second-Level Outcomes

First-level outcomes resulting from behavior are those associated with doing the job itself and include productivity, absenteeism, turnover, and quality of productivity. The second-level outcomes are those events (rewards or punishments) that the first-level outcomes are likely to produce such as merit pay increases, group acceptance or rejection, promotion, and termination.

[17]J. I. Klein, "Feasibility Theory: A Resource-Munificence Model of Work Motivation and Behavior," *Academy of Management Review,* October 1990, pp. 646–65.

Instrumentality

This is the perception by an individual that first-level outcomes are associated with second-level outcomes. It refers to the strength of a person's belief that attainment of a particular outcome will lead to (be instrumental in) attaining one or more second-level outcomes. Instrumentality can be negative, suggesting that attaining a second-level outcome is less likely if a first-level outcome has occurred, or positive, suggesting that the second-level outcome is more likely if the first-level outcome has been attained.

Valence

Valence refers to the preferences for outcomes as seen by the individual. For example, a person may prefer a 10 percent merit raise over a relocation to a new facility. An outcome is positively valent when it is preferred and negatively valent when it is not preferred or is avoided. An outcome has a valence of zero when the individual is indifferent to attaining or not attaining it. The valence concept applies to both first- and second-level outcomes. Thus, a person may prefer to be a high-performing employee (first-level outcome) because she believes this will lead to a desired merit raise in pay (second-level outcome).

Expectancy

Expectancy refers to the individual's belief regarding the likelihood or subjective probability that a particular behavior will be followed by a particular outcome, and it is most easily thought of as a single probability statement. That is, it refers to a perceived chance of something occurring because of the behavior. Expectancy can take values ranging from 0, indicating no chance that an outcome will occur after the behavior or act, to +1, indicating perceived certainty that a particular outcome will follow a behavior or act.

In the work setting, individuals hold an effort-performance expectancy. This expectancy represents the individual's perception of how hard it will be to achieve a particular behavior (say, completing the budget on time) and the probability of achieving that behavior. There is also a performance-outcome expectancy. In the individual's mind, every behavior is associated with outcomes (rewards or punishments). For example, an individual may have an expectancy that if the budget is completed on time, he or she will receive a day off next week. Exhibit 4-7 presents the general expectancy model and includes the two expectancy points (E→P and P→O).

Expectancy theory attempts to provide a framework for answering the question "What determines an employee's willingness to expend effort on the job toward the accomplishment of organizational goals and objectives?" To put it another way, the theory assumes that "people will do what they can do when they want to."[18] That is, motivation is determined by people's beliefs about

[18]G. Salancik and J. Pfeffer, "A Social Information Processing Approach to Job Attitudes and Task Design," *Administrative Science Quarterly*, June 1978, pp. 224–53.

EXHIBIT 4-7

Expectancy Theory

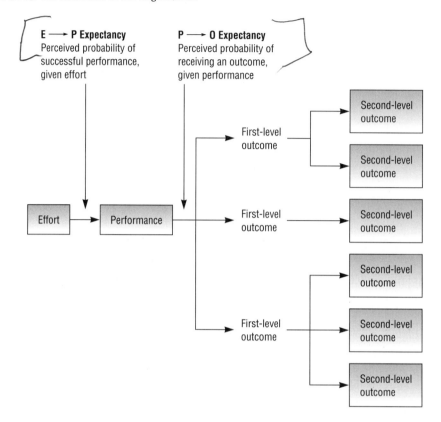

effort-performance relationships and the attractiveness of various work outcomes that may result from good (or poor) performance.

From a managerial perspective, expectancy theory suggests that the manager should develop on awareness of employee thought processes and, based on that awareness, take actions that will influence those processes in a manner that facilitates the attainment of positive organizational outcomes.

Exhibit 4-8 summarizes the potential applications of expectancy theory. As can be seen from the exhibit, the manager can play an active role in influencing employee expectancies, instrumentalities, and valences. Exerting such influence encompasses a variety of activities from the initial selection and training of employees through the administration of rewards. To do this effectively requires good (and continuing) communication and listening skills, and knowledge of and sensitivity to employee needs. An important implication here is that motivation programs should be designed with a sufficient degree of flexibility to address the kinds of individual differences discussed in Chapter 3, as well as need differences described earlier in this chapter in the discussion of content approaches to motivation.

EXHIBIT 4-8

Summary of Managerial Applications of Expectancy Theory

Expectancy Concept	Employee Question	Managerial Action
Expectancy	"Can I attain the desired level of performance?"	Select high ability employees. Provide adequate training. Provide necessary resource support. Identify desired performance.
Instrumentality	"What outcomes will I attain as a result of my performance?"	Clarify the reward system. Clarify performance-reward possibilities. Ensure rewards are contingent upon performance.
Valence	"What value do I place on available performance outcomes?"	Identify individual needs and preferences for outcomes. Match available rewards with these. Construct additional rewards as possible and feasible.

Research on Expectancy

The empirical research to test expectancy theory continues each year. A few studies have used students in laboratory experiments. However, most of the research has been conducted in field settings. For example, one interesting study examined performance-outcome instrumentality in a temporary organization.[19] The experiment used either an hourly rate of pay (low instrumentality) or a piece rate (high instrumentality). After individuals had worked for three four-hour days under one pay system, they were shifted to the other system and worked three more days. Immediately following the shift in pay systems, and for all three subsequent days, the performance of the subjects who were shifted to the high-instrumentality system was higher than their own performance under the low-instrumentality system and higher than the performance of the subjects who were shifted to the low-instrumentality system.

Another area that has been researched focuses on the valence and behavior portion of the expectancy theory model. The results have been mixed. However, it appears that three conditions must hold for the valence of outcomes to be related to effort. Performance-outcome instrumentalities must be greater than zero; effort-performance expectancies must be greater than zero; and there must be some variability in the valence of outcomes.[20]

[19]R. D. Pritchard and P. J. DeLeo, "Experimental Test of the Valence-Instrumentality Relationships in Job Performance," *Journal of Applied Psychology,* April 1973, pp. 264–79.

[20]J. P. Campbell and R. D. Pritchard, "Motivation Theory in Industrial and Organizational Psychology," in *Handbook of Industrial and Organizational Psychology,* ed. M. D. Dunnette (Skokie, Ill.: Rand McNally, 1976), pp. 84–95.

While expectancy theory is interesting, two very crucial questions remain unanswered: (1) Can behavioral scientists completely test it? and (2) Can managers use their findings? With respect to the second question, Nadler and Lawler have some definite opinions regarding managerial applications. Later in the chapter, in the readings selection titled "Motivation: A Diagnostic Approach," these authors identify a number of specific implications that expectancy theory has for organizations in general and managers specifically.

● R4–2

Equity Theory

The essence of **equity** theory is that employees compare their efforts and rewards with those of others in similar work situations. This theory of motivation is based on the assumption that individuals are motivated by a desire to be equitably treated at work. The individual works in exchange for rewards from the organization.

Four important terms in this theory are:

1. *Person:* The individual for whom equity or inequity is perceived.
2. *Comparison other:* Any group or persons used by Person as a referent regarding the ratio of inputs and outcomes.
3. *Inputs:* The individual characteristics brought by Person to the job. These may be achieved (e.g., skills, experience, learning) or ascribed (e.g., age, sex, race).
4. *Outputs:* What Person received from the job (e.g., recognition, fringe benefits, pay).

Equity exists when employees perceive that the ratios of their inputs (efforts) to their outputs (rewards) are equivalent to the ratios of other employees. Inequity exists when these ratios are not equivalent; an individual's own ratio of inputs to outcomes could be greater than, or less than, that of others.[21] Exhibit 4-9 illustrates the equity theory of motivation.

Change Procedures to Restore Equity

Equity theory suggests a number of alternative ways that can be used to restore a feeling or sense of equity. Some examples of restoring equity are:

1. *Changing inputs:* The employee may decide that he or she will put less time or effort into the job.
2. *Changing outputs:* The employee may decide to produce more units since a piece-rate pay plan is being used.
3. *Changing attitudes:* Instead of changing inputs or outputs, the employee may simply change the attitude he or she has. Instead of actually putting

---

[21]J. Stacy Adams, "Toward an Understanding of Equity," *Journal of Abnormal and Social Psychology*, November 1963, pp. 422–36.

EXHIBIT 4-9

The Equity Theory of Motivation

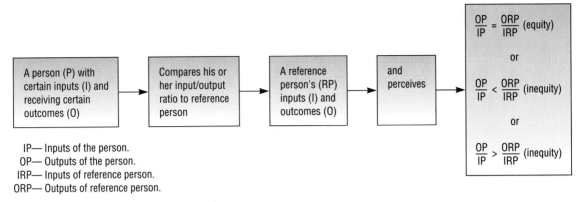

IP— Inputs of the person.
OP— Outputs of the person.
IRP— Inputs of reference person.
ORP— Outputs of reference person.

in more time at work, the employee may decide that "I put in enough time" to make a good contribution.

4. *Changing the reference person:* The reference person can be changed by making comparisons with the input/output ratios of some other person. This change can restore equity.

5. *Changing the inputs or outputs of the reference person:* If the reference person is a co-worker, it might be possible to attempt to alter his or her inputs or outputs as a way to restore equity.

Research on Equity

Most of the research on equity theory has focused on pay as the basic outcome. The failure to incorporate other relevant outcomes limits the impact of the theory in work situations. A review of the studies also reveals that the comparison person is not always clarified. A typical research procedure is to ask a person to compare his or her inputs and outcomes with those of a specific person. In most work situations, an employee selects the comparison person after working for some time in the organization. Two issues to consider are whether comparison persons are within the organization and whether comparison persons change during a person's work career.

Several individuals have questioned the extent to which inequity that results from overpayment (rewards) leads to perceived inequity. Locke argues that employees seldom are told they are overpaid. He believes that individuals are likely to adjust their idea of what constitutes an equitable payment to justify their pay.[22] Campbell and Pritchard point out that employer-employee exchange relationships

[22]Edwin A. Locke, "The Nature and Causes of Job Satisfaction," in *Handbook of Industrial and Organizational Psychology*, ed. M. Dunnette (Skokie, Ill.: Rand McNally, 1976), pp. 1297–1349.

are highly impersonal when compared to exchanges between friends. Perceived overpayment inequity may be more likely when friends are involved. Thus, individuals probably will react to overpayment inequity only when they believe that their actions have led to a friend's being treated unfairly. The individual receives few signals from the organization that it is being treated unfairly.[23]

Despite limitations, equity theory provides a relatively insightful model to help explain and predict employee attitudes about pay. The theory also emphasizes the importance of comparisons in the work situation. The identification of comparison persons seems to have some potential value when attempting to restructure a reward program. The theory has been shown to be a useful framework for examining the growing number of two-tier wage structures.[24] Equity theory also raises the issue of methods for resolving inequity, which can cause problems with morale, turnover, and absenteeism.

Goal Setting

There has been considerable and growing interest in applying goal setting to organizational problems and issues since Locke presented what is now considered a classic paper in 1968.[25] Locke proposed that **goal setting** is a cognitive process of some practical utility. His view is that an individual's conscious goals and intentions are the primary determinants of behavior.[26] It has been noted that "one of the commonly observed characteristics of intentional behavior is that it tends to keep going until it reaches completion."[27] That is, once a person starts something (e.g., a job, a new project), he or she pushes on until a goal is achieved. Also, goal-setting theory places specific emphasis on the importance of conscious goals in explaining motivated behavior. Locke has used the notion of intentions and conscious goals to propose and provide research support for the thesis that harder conscious goals will result in higher levels of performance if these goals are accepted by the individual.[28]

Descriptions of Goal Setting

A goal is the object of an action. For example, the attempt to produce four units on a production line or to cut direct costs by $3,000 or to decrease absenteeism

---

[23] Campbell and Pritchard, "Motivation Theory," pp. 63–130.

[24] J. E. Martin and M. M. Perterson, "Two-Tier Wage Structures: Implications for Equity Theory," *Academy of Management Journal*, June 1987, pp. 286–315.

[25] Edwin A. Locke, "Toward a Theory of Task Motivation and Incentives," *Organizational Behavior and Human Performance*, May 1968, pp. 157–89.

[26] For a discussion of the relationship between goals and intentions in motivated behavior, see M. E. Tubbs and S. E. Ekeberg, "The Role of Intentions in Work Motivation: Implications for Goal-Setting Theory and Research," *Academy of Management Review*, January 1991, pp. 180–99.

[27] Thomas A. Ryan, *Intentional Behavior* (New York: Ronald Press, 1970), p. 95.

[28] E. A. Locke and G. P. Latham, *A Theory of Goal Setting and Task Performance* (Englewood Cliffs, N.J.: Prentice-Hall, 1990).

in a department by 12 percent are goals. Locke has carefully described the attributes or the mental (cognitive) processes of goal setting. The attributes he highlights are goal specificity, goal difficulty, and goal intensity.

Goal **specificity** is the degree of quantitative precision (clarity) of the goal. Goal **difficulty** is the degree of proficiency or the level of performance that is sought. Goal **intensity** pertains to the process of setting the goal or of determining how to reach it.[29] To date, goal intensity has not been widely studied, although a related concept, goal **commitment,** has been considered in a number of studies. Goal commitment is the amount of effort used to achieve a goal.

Exhibit 4-10 portrays applied goal setting from a managerial perspective and the sequence of events for such a goal-setting program. The key steps in applying goal setting are: (1) diagnosis for readiness (determining whether the people, the organization, and the technology are suited for goal setting); (2) preparing employees via increased interpersonal interaction, communication, training, and action plans for goal setting; (3) emphasizing the attributes of goals that should be understood by a manager and subordinates; (4) conducting intermediate reviews to make necessary adjustments in established goals; and (5) performing a final review to check the goals set, modified, and accomplished. Each of these steps needs to be carefully planned and implemented if goal setting is to be an effective motivational technique. In too many applications of goal setting, steps outlined in—or issues suggested by—Exhibit 4-10 are ignored. Exercise 4–1 is designed to let you experience the goal-setting process first hand.

■ E4–1

Goal-Setting Research

Between 1968 and 1992 the amount of research on goal setting increased considerably. Locke's 1968 paper certainly contributed to the increase in laboratory and field research on goal setting. Another force behind the increase in interest and research was the demand of managers for practical and specific techniques that they could apply in their organizations. Goal setting offered such a technique for some managers and it thus became an important management tool for enhancing work performance.[30]

Empirical research findings from a variety of managerial and student samples have provided support for the theory that conscious goals regulate behavior. Yet a number of important issues concerning goal setting still must be examined more thoroughly. One area of debate concerns the issue of how much subordinate participation in goal setting is optimal.[31] A field experiment of skilled technicians

[29]Edwin A. Locke, Karyll N. Shaw, Lise M. Saari, and Gary P. Latham, "Goal Setting and Task Performance: 1969–1980," *Psychological Bulletin,* July 1981, p. 129.

[30]P. C. Early, G. B. Northcraft, C. Lee, and T. R. Lituchy, "Impact of Process and Outcome Feedback on the Relation of Goal Setting to Task Performance," *Academy of Management Journal,* March 1990, pp. 87–105.

[31]Miriam Erez, P. Christopher Earley, and Charles Hulin, "The Impact of Participation on Goal Acceptance and Performance : A Two-Step Model," *Academy of Management Journal,* March 1985, pp. 50–66.

EXHIBIT 4-10

Goal Setting as Applied in Organizations

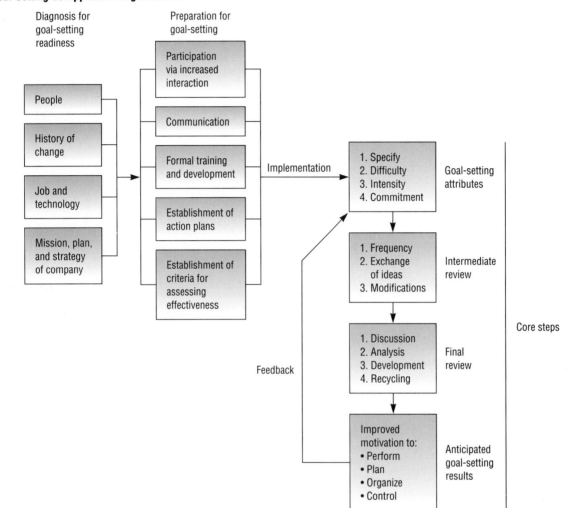

compared three levels of subordinate participation: full (the subordinates were totally involved); limited (the subordinates made some suggestions about the goals the superior set); and none.[32] Measures of performance and satisfaction were taken over a 12-month period. The groups with full or limited participant involvement in goal setting showed significantly more performance and satisfaction

[32]John M. Ivancevich, "Different Goal-Setting Treatments and Their Effects on Performance and Job Satisfaction," *Academy of Management Journal*, September 1977, pp. 406–19.

improvements than did the group that did not participate in goal setting. Interestingly, these improvements began to dissipate six to nine months after the program was started. Some research, however, has failed to find significant relationships between performance and participation in the goal-setting process.[33]

Research has found that specific goals lead to higher output than do vague goals such as "Do your best."[34] Field experiments using clerical workers, maintenance technicians, marketing personnel, truckers, engineering personnel, typists, and manufacturing employees have compared specific versus do-your-best goal-setting conditions.[35] The vast majority of these studies support—partly or totally—the hypothesis that specific goals lead to better performance than do vague goals. In fact, in 99 out of 100 studies reviewed by Locke and his associates, specific goals produced better results.[36]

Certain aspects of goal setting need to be subjected to scientific examination. One such area centers on individual differences and their impact on the success of goal-setting programs. Such factors as personality, career progression, training background, and personal health are important individual differences that should be considered when implementing goal-setting programs. Goal-setting programs also should be subjected to ongoing examination to monitor attitudinal and performance consequences. Some research has demonstrated that goal-setting programs tend to lose their potency over time, so there is a need to discover why this phenomenon occurs in organizations. Sound evaluation programs would assist management in identifying success, problems, and needs.

Goal setting can be a very powerful technique for motivating employees. When used correctly, carefully monitored, and actively supported by managers, goal setting can improve performance. However, neither goal setting nor any other technique can be used to correct every problem. No applied motivational approach can be *the* technique to solve all performance problems. This, unfortunately, is what some enthusiastic advocates have turned goal setting into—a panacea for everything.

MOTIVATION AND THE PSYCHOLOGICAL CONTRACT

A conceptual framework that provides a useful perspective for viewing the topic of motivation is **exchange theory**.[37] In a very general sense, exchange theory suggests that members of an organization engage in reasonably predictable give-and-take relationships (exchanges) with each other. For example, an employee

---

[33]C. Shalley, G. Oldham, and J. Porac, "Effects of Goal Difficulty, Goal-Setting Method, and Expected External Evaluation on Intrinsic Motivation," *Academy of Management Journal,* September 1987, pp. 553–63.

[34]Locke, "The Task Motivation and Incentives."

[35]For a complete analysis, see Locke et al., "Goal Setting."

[36]Ibid.

[37]P. Ekeh, *Social Exchange Theory* (Cambridge, Mass.: Harvard University Press, 1974).

gives time and effort in exchange for pay; management provides pleasant working conditions in exchange for employee loyalty. Schein suggests that the degree to which employees are willing to exert effort, commit to organizational goals, and derive satisfaction from their work is dependent on two conditions.[38]

1. The extent to which employee expectations of what the organization will give them and what they owe the organization in return matches the organization's expectations of what it will give and receive.
2. Assuming there is agreement on these expectations, the specific nature of what is exchanged (effort for pay, for example).

These mutual expectations regarding exchanges constitute part of the psychological contract. The **psychological contract** is an unwritten agreement between the individual and the organization which specifies what each expects to give to and receive from the other. While some aspects of an employment relationship, such as pay, may be explicitly stated, many others are not. These implicit agreements which may focus on exchanges involving satisfaction, challenging work, fair treatment, loyalty, and opportunity to be creative may take precedence over written agreements.

In the ideal psychological contract, those contributions the individual was willing to give would correspond perfectly to what the organization wanted to receive; similarly, what the organization wanted to give would correspond totally with what the individual wished to receive. In reality, however, this seldom if

▲ C4–1   ever occurs. A good illustration of this may be found in Case 4-1: FAB Sweets Limited. Additionally, psychological contracts are not static; either party's expectations can change as can either party's ability or willingness to continue meeting expectations.

When there are few or a decreasing number of matches between what each party expects to give and receive in the contract, work motivation suffers. The psychological contract provides a perspective for why this is true. Looking at motivation from a content theory approach, the psychological contract suggests that in return for time, effort, and other considerations, individuals desire to receive need gratification. Using Maslow's need hierarchy as an example, if an employee is operating at the self-actualization level and fails to receive a challenging job which allows for the application of all the capabilities that employee has, motivation will suffer. In other words, the satisfaction of needs are part of the contract; when the expectation of need satisfaction is not matched with the opportunity to achieve such satisfaction, the contract is violated and motivation is negatively affected.

The perspective on motivation provided by the concept of the psychological contract is not limited to content approaches to motivation, however; it is equally applicable to process explanations as well. Adam's equity theory is, in fact, a form of exchange theory. The notion of inputs and outcomes within equity theory

---

[38]H. Schein, *Organizational Psychology*, 2nd ed. (Englewood Cliffs, N.J.: Prentice-Hall, 1980).

MEETING EMPLOYEE EXPECTATIONS
JAPANESE STYLE

While it is not uncommon for an "us versus them" mindset to characterize labor relations in this country, such an attitude is extremely rare in Japan. Although there are numerous factors involved, it is clear that one reason this is far less often a problem in Japanese companies is that the Japanese do an especially effective job in meeting employee needs and expectations. Japanese executives are unlikely to forget that their organization's employees—not their equipment or technology—are their most valuable asset. Japanese companies understand that the best way to get employees to meet the company's expectations is to meet their employee expectations. In other words, Japanese executives are very skillful in building and maintaining what we have called the psychological contract. Japanese workers cooperate with management because management cooperates with them. The welfare of both is inseparable from that of the organization.

Princeton professor Alan Blinder makes the point that economics identifies an incentive issue known as the principal-agent problem. An example can be found in the relationship between a home owner and the real estate agent hired to sell the home. In whose interest will the agent act? Blinder suggests two major principal-agent problems are common in organizations. How do corporate boards ensure that executives serve the stockholders, and how do managers get workers to put forth their best efforts?

Primarily through large stock options that cause executives and shareholder to have the same interests, U.S. companies have solved the first problem. The Japanese, however, have taken the lead in solving the second problem. They do this by making employees both principals and agents. To a large extent Japanese organizations are run for the benefit of their employees rather than their stockholders. This means, among other things, relatively small salary differentials between executives and workers, managers who start out on the factory floor, and pursuit of growth—even when it is unprofitable—to provide employee job security. These are the types of things Japanese workers expect—and get. In turn management gets what it expects, highly motivated workers. When Toyota workers thinks in terms of "us versus them," "them" is far more likely to be General Motors or Honda than their own management.

Source: Based, in part, on Alan S. Blinder, "How Japan Puts the 'Human' in Human Capital," *Business Week,* November 11, 1991, p. 22.

is very similar to expectations of giving and receiving in the psychological contract. In the context of an expectancy approach to motivation, performance-outcome expectancies relate directly to the exchange of performance for pay, advancement, satisfaction, or other outcomes in the psychological contract; likewise, the desire to receive certain considerations in the context of the contract is analogous to positively valent outcomes in expectancy theory.

Managing the psychological contract successfully is one of the more important and challenging aspects of most managers' jobs. The more attuned the manager is to needs and expectations of subordinates, the greater the number of matches that are likely to exist and be maintained in the psychological contract. This, in turn, can positively impact the direction, intensity, and persistence of motivation in the organization. Encounter 4-3 provides an illustration of how the Japanese enhance motivation by maximizing the number of matches with employee needs and expectations.

REVIEWING MOTIVATION

In this chapter, six popular theories of motivation are portrayed. The theories typically are pitted against one another in the literature. This is unfortunate since each approach can help managers better understand workplace motivation. Each approach attempts to organize, in a meaningful manner, major variables associated with explaining motivation in work settings. The content theories are individual-oriented in that they place primary emphasis on the characteristics of people. Each of the process theories has a specific orientation. Expectancy theory places emphasis on individual, job, and environmental variables. It recognizes differences in needs, perceptions, and beliefs. Equity theory primarily addresses the relationship between attitudes toward inputs and outputs and reward practices. Goal-setting theory emphasizes the cognitive processes and the role of intentional behavior in motivation.

If anything, this chapter suggests that instead of ignoring motivation, managers must take an active role in motivating their employees. Four specific conclusions are offered here:

1. Managers can influence the motivation state of employees. If performance needs to be improved, then managers must intervene and help create an atmosphere that encourages, supports, and sustains improvement.
2. Managers should be sensitive to variations in employees' needs, abilities, and goals. Managers also must consider differences in preferences (valences) for rewards.
3. Continual monitoring of needs, abilities, goals, and preferences of employees is each individual manager's responsibility and is not the domain of personnel/human resources managers only.
4. Managers need to work on providing employees with jobs that offer task challenge, diversity, and a variety of opportunities for need satisfaction.

In simple terms, the theme of our discussion of motivation is that the *manager needs to be actively involved.* If motivation is to be energized, sustained, and directed, managers must know about needs, intentions, preferences, goals, and comparisons, and they must act on that knowledge. Failure to do so will result in many missed opportunities to help motivate employees in a positive manner.

■ **E4–2**   You may wish to complete Exercise 4-2 to assess your own motivation to manage, and to develop a program for increasing your motivation.

SUMMARY OF KEY POINTS

- Motivation is made up of at least three distinct components. *Direction* refers to what an individual chooses to do when presented with a number of possible alternative courses of action. *Intensity* relates to the strength of the individual's response once the choice (direction) is made. Finally, *persistence* refers to the staying power of behavior, or how long a person will continue to devote effort.

- Maslow's theory of motivation suggests that individuals' needs are arranged in a hierarchical order of importance and that a person will attempt to satisfy the more basic (lower level) needs before directing behavior toward satisfying higher level needs. Maslow's five need levels, from lowest to highest, are (1) physiological, (2) safety and security, (3) belongingness, social, and love, (4) esteem, and (5) self-actualization.

- Herzberg's research suggests that there are two important sets of factors. *Motivators* are intrinsic conditions and include achievement, recognition, and responsibility. *Hygienes* are extrinsic conditions and include salary, working conditions, and job security. In Herzberg's view, it is only the motivators that contribute to satisfaction and thus have the power to provide motivation.

- McClelland has developed a descriptive set of factors that reflect a high need for achievement. These are: (1) the person likes to take responsibility for solving problems; (2) the person tends to set moderate achievement goals and is inclined to take calculated risks; and (3) the person desires feedback on performance.

- Key terms in expectancy theory include instrumentality, valence, and expectancy. *Instrumentality* refers to the strength of a person's belief that achieving a specific result or outcome will lead to attaining a secondary outcome. *Valence* refers to a person's preference for attaining or avoiding a particular outcome. *Expectancy* refers to a person's belief regarding the likelihood or subjective probability that a particular behavior will be followed by a particular outcome.

- The essence of equity theory is that employees compare their job inputs and outputs with those of others in similar work situations. *Inputs* are what an individual brings to the job and include skills, experiences, and effort, among others. *Outputs* are what a person receives from a job and include recognition, pay, fringe benefits, and satisfaction, among others.

- The key steps in applying goal setting are: (1) diagnosis for readiness; (2) preparing employees via increased interpersonal interaction, communication, training, and action plans for goal setting; (3) emphasizing the attributes of goals that should be understood by a manager and subordinates; (4) conducting intermediate reviews to make necessary adjustments in established goals; and (5) performing a final review to check the goals set, modified, and accomplished.

- Employee expectations of what the organization will give them and what they owe the organization and the organization's expectation of what it will give to and receive from employees constitute the psychological contract. A *psychological contract* is an unwritten agreement between the individual and the organization which specifies what each expects to give to and receive from the other.

REVIEW AND DISCUSSION QUESTIONS

1. Why is it important for a manager to consider the various components of motivation when diagnosing motivation problems? Is any one of the components more or less important than any of the others?

2. Which of the content theories discussed in the chapter do you believe offers the best explanation of motivation? Which of the process theories? Overall, do you feel that the content approach or the process approach best explains motivation? Explain.

3. Motivation is just one of several factors that influence productivity. What other factors were discussed in this chapter? What is the relationship between these factors and motivation?

4. What implications does Herzberg's two-factor theory have for the design of organizational reward systems? How can the theory be used to explain differences in the three components of motivation?

5. Describe the sequence of events involved in the individual motivational process. What would happen to this process if no need deficiencies existed?

6. As a manager, would you rather the people for whom you are responsible be extrinsically or intrinsically motivated? Explain.

7. What would it be like to manage an organization where all the employees were self-actualized? What kinds of opportunities and problems would this situation present to management?

8. How important a role does perception play in determining whether an employee is receiving equitable treatment? What kinds of things might a manager do to influence those perceptions?

9. Goal-setting can be a difficult system to implement effectively. What kinds of problems might be encountered in attempting to install a goal-setting program in an organization? As a manager, what would you do to minimize the likelihood you would encounter these problems.

10. Is there a psychological contract between the students enrolled in this course and the instructor? What are some of the specifics of this contract? How was the contract determined?

●

READINGS

READING 4–1   ONE MORE TIME: DO FEMALE AND MALE MANAGERS DIFFER?

Gary N. Powell

Do female and male managers differ in the personal qualities they bring to their jobs? Yes, if you believe two recent articles in influential business magazines. Jan Grant, in a 1988 *Organizational Dynamics* article entitled "Women as Managers: What They Can Offer to Organizations,"[1] asserted that women have unique qualities that make them particularly well-suited as managers. Instead of forcing women to fit the male model of managerial success, emphasizing such qualities as independence, competitiveness, forcefulness, and analytical thinking, Grant argued that organizations should place greater emphasis on such female qualities as affiliation and attachment, cooperativeness, nurturance, and emotionality.

Felice Schwartz's 1989 *Harvard Business Review* article, "Management Women and the New Facts of Life,"[2] triggered a national debate over the merits of "mommy tracks" (though she did not use this term herself). She proposed that corporations (1) distinguish between "career-primary women" who put their careers first and "career-and-family" women who seek a balance between career and family, (2) nurture the careers of the former group as potential top executives, and (3) offer flexible work arrangements and family supports to the latter group in exchange for lower opportunities for career advancement. Women were assumed to be more interested in such arrangements, and thereby less likely to be suitable top executives than men; there has been less discussion over the merits of "daddy tracks."

Male and female managers certainly differ in their success within the managerial ranks. Although women have made great strides in entering management since 1970, with the overall proportion of women managers rising from 16 percent to 40 percent, the proportion of women who hold top management positions is less than 3 percent.[3] This could be due simply to the average male manager being older and more experienced than the average female manager. After all, managerial careers invariably start at the bottom. If there were no basic differences between male and female managers, it would be just a matter of time until the proportion of women was about the same at all managerial levels.

But are there basic differences between male and female managers? Traditional sex role stereotypes state that males are more masculine (e.g., self-reliant, aggressive, competitive, decisive) and females more feminine (e.g., sympathetic, gentle, shy, sensitive to the needs of others).[4] Grant's views of male-female differences mirrored these stereotypes. However, there is disagreement over the applicability of these stereotypes to managers. Three distinct points of view have emerged:

1. **No differences.** Women who pursue the nontraditional career of manager reject the feminine stereotype and have needs, values, and leadership styles similar to those of men who pursue managerial careers.
2. **Stereotypical differences.** Female and male managers differ in ways predicted by stereotypes, as a result of early socialization experiences that reinforce masculinity in males and femininity in females.
3. **Nonstereotypical differences.** Female and male managers differ in ways opposite to stereotypes, because women managers have to be exceptional to compensate for early socialization experiences that are different from those of men.

I recently conducted an extensive review of research on sex differences in management to determine the level of support for each of these viewpoints.[5] I considered four types of possible differences: in behavior, motivation, commitment, and subordinates' responses (see Exhibit 4-11).

THE REVIEW

The two most frequently studied types of managerial behavior are task-oriented and people-oriented behavior.[6] **Task-oriented behavior** is directed toward subordinates' performance and includes initiating work, organizing it, and setting deadlines and standards. **People-oriented behavior** is directed toward subordinates' welfare and

Source: Gary N. Powell, "One More Time: Do Female and Male Managers Differ?" *Academy of Management Executive*, August 1990, pp. 68–75.

EXHIBIT 4-11

**Sex Differences
in Management:
Selected Results**

Dimension	Results
Behavior:	
Task-oriented	No difference
People-oriented	No difference
Effectiveness ratings	Stereotypical difference in evaluations of managers in laboratory studies: Males favored
	No difference in evaluations of actual managers
Response to poor performer	Stereotypical difference: Males use norm of equity, whereas females use norm of equality.
Influence strategies	Stereotypical difference: Males use a wider range of strategies, more positive strategies, and less negative strategies. This difference diminishes when women managers have high self-confidence.
Motivation	No difference in some studies
	Nonstereotypical difference in other studies: Female motivational profile is closer to that associated with successful managers.
Commitment	Inconsistent evidence regarding difference
Subordinates responses	Stereotypical difference in responses to managers in laboratory studies: Managers using style that matches sex role stereotype are favored.
	No difference in responses to actual managers

includes seeking to build their self-confidence, making them feel at ease, and soliciting their input about matters that affect them.

There have been numerous studies of whether female and male leaders differ in these two types of behavior, including 1) laboratory studies in which individuals are asked to react to a standardized description of a female or male leader or are led by a female or male leader on a simulated work task, and 2) field studies comparing female and male leaders in actual organizational settings. Laboratory studies control the variable under investigation better, but they provide less information about the manager. Thus, they are more likely to yield results that support stereotypes of managers than field studies.

Sex role stereotypes suggest that men, being masculine, will be higher in task-oriented behavior and women, being feminine, will be higher in people-oriented behavior. However, sex role stereotypes are not supported when the results of different studies are considered as a whole. According to a "meta-analysis" of research studies, male and female leaders exhibit similar amounts of task-oriented and people-oriented behavior regardless of the type of study.

Male leaders have been rated as more effective in laboratory studies, but male and female leaders are seen as similarly effective in the "the real world".[7]

There are some possible sex differences in managerial behavior that are under investigation. For example, some evidence supporting the "stereotypical differences" view suggests that female and male managers differ in their responses to poor performers. Males may follow a norm of **equity**, basing their response on whether they believe the poor performance is caused by lack of ability or lack of effort, and females a norm of **equality**, treating all poor performers alike regardless of the assumed cause.[8] Other evidence suggests that female and male managers differ in the strategies they use to influence subordinates (see Exhibit 4-12), but that this difference diminishes as women managers gain self-confidence in their jobs.[9] Overall, though, the pattern of research results on sex differences in managerial behavior favors the "no differences" view.

Female managers are at least as motivated as male managers. Some studies have found that female and male managers score essentially the same on psychological tests of motives that predict managerial success, supporting the

EXHIBIT 4-12

The Basic Motivation-Behavior Sequence

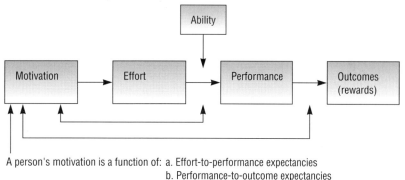

A person's motivation is a function of: a. Effort-to-performance expectancies
b. Performance-to-outcome expectancies
c. Perceived valence of outcomes

"no differences" view. When sex differences have been found, they have supported the "nonstereotypical differences" view. For example, in a study of nearly 2,000 managers, women managers reported lower basic needs and higher needs for self-actualization. Compared with males, female managers were more concerned with opportunities for growth, autonomy, and challenge and less concerned with work environment and pay. The women managers were judged to exhibit a "more mature and higher-achieving motivational profile" than their male counterparts.[10]

There is disagreement about whether female and male managers possess different levels of commitment.[11] Some studies have found that women are more committed as a group than males; other studies have found that women are less committed; and still other studies have found no sex difference in commitment. Instead, factors other than sex have been linked more conclusively to commitment. For example, age and education are positively associated with commitment. Greater job satisfaction, more meaningful work, and greater utilization of skills also are associated with stronger commitment.[12]

Even if male and female managers did not differ in any respect, their subordinates still could react to them differently. Subordinates' responses to managers have varied according to the type of study. Some laboratory studies have found that managers are judged more favorably when their behavior fits the appropriate sex role stereotype. Female managers using a people-oriented leadership style have been evaluated more positively than male managers using that style; and the male managers using a task-oriented style have been evaluated more positively than female managers using that style. However, subordinates do not respond differently to actual male and female man-

agers, supporting the "no differences" view. Once subordinates have worked for both female and male managers, the effects of stereotypes disappear and managers are treated as individuals rather than representatives of their sex.[13]

In summary, sex differences are absent in task-oriented behavior, people-oriented behavior, effectiveness ratings of actual managers, and subordinates' responses to actual managers. Stereotypical differences in some types of managerial behavior and in some ratings of managers in laboratory studies favor male managers. On the other hand, where differences in motivational profiles appear, they are nonstereotypical and favor female managers. Although results regarding sex differences in commitment are inconclusive, sex differences are not as extensive as other types of differences.

This review supports the "no differences" view of sex differences in management. There is not much difference between the needs, values, and leadership styles of male and female managers. The sex differences that have been found are few, found in laboratory studies more than field studies, and tend to cancel each other out.

IMPLICATIONS FOR ORGANIZATIONS

The implications of this review are clear: *If there are no differences between male and female managers, companies should not act as if there are.* Instead they should follow two principles in their actions:

1. To be gender-blind in their decisions regarding open managerial positions and present or potential managers, except when consciously trying to offset the effects of past discrimination.

2. To try to minimize differences in the job experiences of their male and female managers, so that artificial sex differences in career success do not arise.

Grant based her recommendations on a "stereotypical differences" view. She argued that organizations will benefit from placing greater value on women's special qualities:[14]

These "human resources" skills are critical in helping to stop the tide of alienation, apathy, cynicism, and low morale in organizations. . . . If organizations are to become more humane, less alienating, and more responsive to the individuals who work for them, they will probably need to learn to value process as well as product. Women have an extensive involvement in the processes of our society—an involvement that derives from their greater participation in the reproductive process and their early experience of family life. . . . Thus women may indeed be the most radical force available in bringing about organizational change.

Human resources skills are certainly essential to today's organizations. Corporations that are only concerned with getting a product out and pay little attention to their employees' needs are unlikely to have a committed work force or to be effective in the long run. However, women are at risk when corporations assume that they have a monopoly on human resource skills. The risk is that they will be placed exclusively in managerial jobs that particularly call for social sensitivity and interpersonal skills in dealing with individuals and special-interest groups, e.g., public relations, human resources management, consumer affairs, corporate social responsibility. These jobs are typically staff functions, peripheral to the more powerful line functions of finance, sales, and production and seldom regarded in exalted terms by line personnel. Women managers are disproportionately found in such jobs, outside the career paths that most frequently lead to top management jobs.[15] Corporations that rely on Grant's assertions about women's special abilities could very well perpetuate this trend. Thus it is very important that the facts about sex differences in management be disseminated to key decision-makers. When individuals hold onto stereotypical views about sex differences despite the facts, either of two approaches may be tried:

1. Send them to programs such as cultural diversity workshops to make them aware of the ways in which biases related to sex (as well as race, age, etc.) can affect their decisions and to learn how to keep these biases from occurring. For example, Levi Strauss put all of its executives, including the president, through an intensive three-day program designed to make them examine their attitudes toward women and minorities on the job.[16]

2. Recognize that beliefs and attitudes are difficult to change and focus on changing behavior instead. If people are motivated to be gender-blind in their decision-making by an effective performance appraisal and reward system backed by the CEO, they often come to believe in what they are doing.[17]

Organizations should do whatever they can to equalize the job experience of equally-qualified female and male managers. This means abandoning the model of a successful career as an uninterrupted sequence of promotions to positions of greater responsibility heading toward the top ranks. All too often, any request to take time out from career for family reasons, either by a woman or a man, is seen as evidence of lack of career commitment.

Schwartz based her recommendations on a real sex difference: More women than men leave work for family reasons due to the demands of maternity and the differing traditions and expectations of the sexes. However, her solution substitutes a different type of sex difference, that such women remain at work with permanently reduced career opportunities. It does not recognize that women's career orientation may change during their careers. Women could temporarily leave the fast track for the mommy track, but then be ready and able to resume the fast track later. Once they were classified as career-and-family, they would find it difficult to be reclassified as career-primary even if their career commitment returned to its original level.

Corporations could offer daddy tracks as well as mommy tracks and accurately believe that they were treating their female and male employees alike. However, if women tended to opt for such programs more than men and anyone who opted for one was held back in pursuing a future managerial career, the programs would contribute to a sex difference in access to top management positions. Automatic restrictions should not be placed on the later career prospects of individuals who choose alternative work arrangements. Those who wish to return to the fast track should be allowed to do so once they demonstrate the necessary skills and commitment.

There are other ways by which organizations can minimize sex differences in managers' job experiences. For example, the majority of both male and female top executives have had one or more mentors, and mentorship has been critical to their advancement and success.[18] However, as Kathy Kram, an expert on the mentoring process, observed, "It's easier for people to mentor people like themselves."[19] Lower-level female managers have greater difficulty in finding mentors than male managers at equivalent levels, due to the smaller number of female top executives. Unless companies do something, this gives lower-level male managers an advantage in getting ahead.

Some companies try to overcome barriers of sex by assigning highly-placed mentors to promising lower-level managers. For example, at the Bank of America, senior executives are asked to serve as mentors for three or four junior managers for a year at a time. Formal mentoring programs also have been implemented at the Jewel Companies, Aetna, Bell Labs, Merrill Lynch, and Federal Express. Such programs do not guarantee career success for the recipients of mentoring, of course. However, they do contribute to making mentors more equally available for male and female managers.[20]

Companies also influence job experiences through the training and development programs that they encourage or require their managers to take. These programs contribute to a sex difference in job experiences if 1) men and women are systematically diagnosed to have different developmental needs and thereby go through different programs, or 2) men and women are deliberately segregated in such programs. Both of these conditions have been advocated and met in the past. For example, in a 1972 article in *Personnel Journal,* Marshall Brenner concluded that[21]

> . . . *women will, for the immediate future, generally require different managerial development activities than men. This is based on research showing that, in general, they have different skills and different attitudes toward the managerial role than men do.*

This review suggests the opposite, particularly for women and men who are already in management positions. Women managers do not need to be sent off by themselves for "assertiveness training"—they already know how to be assertive. Instead, they need access to advanced training and development activities, such as executive MBAs or executive leadership workshops, just like male managers do.

Some of the available activities, such as the Executive Women Workshop offered by the Center for Creative Leadership (CCL), are open only to women. In addition, some companies, such as Northwestern Bell, have their own executive leadership programs for women only. Such programs, when attended voluntarily, provide women managers a useful opportunity to "share experiences and ideas with other executive women in a unique environment," as the CCL's catalogue puts it, as well as provide valuable executive training.[22] In general, though, women and men should be recommended for training and development programs according to their individual needs rather than their sex. Almost half of the companies regarded as "the best companies for women" in a recent book rely on training and workshops to develop their high-potential managerial talent. However, many of these companies, including Bidermann Industries, General Mills, Hewitt Associates, Neiman-Marcus, and PepsiCo, have no special programs for women: they simply assign the best and brightest people regardless of sex.[23]

In conclusion, organizations should not assume that male and female managers differ in personal qualities. They also should make sure that their policies, practices, and programs minimize the creation of sex differences in managers' experiences on the job. There is little reason to believe that either women or men make superior managers, or that women and men are different types of managers. Instead, there are likely to be excellent, average, and poor managerial performers within each sex. Success in today's highly competitive marketplace calls for organizations to make best use of the talent available to them. To do this, they need to identify, develop, encourage, and promote the most effective managers, regardless of sex.

NOTES

1. J. Grant, "Women as Managers: What They Can Offer to Organizations," *Organizational Dynamics,* Winter 1988, pp. 56–63.
2. F.N. Schwartz, "Management Women and the New Facts of Life," *Harvard Business Review,* January-February 1989, pp. 65–76.
3. U.S. Department of Labor, Bureau of Labor Statistics, *Employment and Earnings,* (October 1989), Table A-22, p. 29; *Handbook of Labor Statistics,* Bulletin 2175 (December 1983), Table 16. pp. 44–46; J.B. Forbes, J.E. Piercy, and T.L. Hayes. "Women Executives: Breaking Down Barriers?", *Business Horizons,* November-December 1988, pp. 6–9.
4. For a review of research on sex role stereotypes, see D.N. Ruble and T.N. Ruble, "Sex Stereotypes," in A.G. Miller (Ed.), *In the Eye of the Beholder* (New York: Praeger, 1982).
5. For a full report of this review with complete references, see G.N. Powell, Chapter 5. "Managing People," in *Women and Men in Management* (Newbury Park, Calif.: Sage, 1988).
6. The technical terms used by researchers for these types of behavior are "initiating structure behavior" and "consideration behavior."

7. G.H. Dobbins and S.J. Platz, "Sex Differences in Leadership: How Real Are They?" *Academy of Management Review,* 11, 1986, pp. 118–27.

8. G.H. Dobbins, "Effects of Gender on Leaders' Responses to Poor Performers: An Attributional Interpretation." *Academy of Management Journal* 28, 1985, pp. 587–98.

9. D. Instone, B. Major, and B.B. Bunker, "Gender, Self-Confidence, and Social Influence Strategies: An Organizational Simulation," *Journal of Personality and Social Psychology* 44, 1983, pp. 322–33.

10. S.M. Donnell and J. Hall, "Men and Women as Managers: A Significant Case of No Significant Difference." *Organizational Dynamics,* Spring 1980, p. 71.

11. Commitment to work, job, career, and organizations have all been examined in different streams of research. This article simply refers to commitment in general, since each type of commitment suggests a greater degree of involvement in work in spite of fine difference among them.

12. L.H. Chusmir, "Job Commitment and the Organizational Woman," *Academy of Management Review* 7, 1982, pp. 595–602.

13. K.M. Bartol and D.A. Butterfield, "Sex Effects in Evaluating Leaders," *Journal of Applied Psychology* 61, 1976, pp. 446–54; J. Adams, R.W. Rice, and J. Instone, "Follower Attitudes toward Women and Judgments concerning Performance by Female and Male Leaders," *Academy of Management Journal* 27, 1984, pp. 636–43.

14. Grant, p. 62.

15. G.N. Powell, Career Development and the Woman Manager: A Social Power Perspective," *Personnel,* May-June 1980, pp. 22–32.

16. P. Watts, "Bias Busting: Diversity Training in the Workplace," *Management Review,* December 1987, pp. 51–54; B. Zeitz and L. Dusky, "Levi Strauss," in *The Best Companies for Women* (New York: Simon and Schuster, 1988).

17. L. Festinger. *A Theory of Cognitive Dissonance* (Evanston, Ill.: Row, Peterson, 1957).

18. *The Corporate Woman Officer* (New York: Heidrich & Struggles, 1986); G.R. Roche, "Much Ado about Mentors," *Harvard Business Review,* January-February 1979, pp. 14–28; D.M. Hunt and C. Michael, "Mentorship: A Career Training and Development Tool," *Academy of Management Review* 8, 1983, pp. 475–85; R.N. Noe, "Women and Mentoring: A Review and Research Agenda," *Academy of Management Review* 13, 1988, pp. 65–78.

19. "Women and Minority Workers in Business Find a Mentor Can Be a Rare Commodity." *Wall Street Journal,* November 11, 1987, p. 39.

20. K.E. Kram, Chapter 7, "Creating Conditions that Encourage Mentoring," in *Mentoring at Work* (Glenview, Ill.: Scott, Foresman, 1985).

21. M.H. Brenner, "Management Development for Women." *Personnel Journal,* March 1972, p. 166.

22. *Programs: Center for Creative Leadership.* Greensboro, N.C. 15. July 1988-June 1989.

23. Zeitz & Dusky.

READING 4–2   MOTIVATION: A DIAGNOSTIC APPROACH

David A. Nadler
Edward E. Lawler III

- What makes some people work hard while others do as little as possible?
- How can I, as a manager, influence the performance of people who work for me?
- Why do people turn over, show up late to work, and miss work entirely?

These important questions about employees' behavior can only be answered by managers who have a grasp of what motivates people. Specifically, a good understanding of motivation can serve as a valuable tool for **understanding** the causes of behavior in organizations, for **predicting** the effects of any managerial action, and for **directing** behavior so that organizational and individual goals can be achieved.

Source: J. R. Hackman and E. E. Lawler, *Perspectives on Behavior in Organizations* (New York: McGraw-Hill, 1977).

EXISTING APPROACHES

During the past 20 years, managers have been bombarded with a number of different approaches to motivation. The terms associated with these approaches are well known— **human relations, scientific management, job enrichment, need hierarchy, self-actualization,** etc. Each of these approaches has something to offer. On the other hand, each of these different approaches also has its problems in theory and practice. Running through almost all of the approaches with which managers are familiar are a series of implicit but clearly erroneous assumptions.

Assumption 1: All employees are alike. Different theories present different ways of looking at people, but each of them assumes that all employees are basically similar in their makeup: Employees all want economic gains, or all want a pleasant climate, or all aspire to be self-actualizing, etc.

Assumption 2: All situations are alike. Most theories assume that all managerial situations are alike, and that the managerial course of action for motivation (for example, participation, job enlargement, etc.) is applicable in all situations.

Assumption 3: One best way. Out of the other two assumptions there emerges a basic principle that there is "one best way" to motivate employees.

When these "one best way" approaches are tried in the "correct" situation they will work. However, all of them are bound to fail in some situations. They are therefore not adequate managerial tools.

A NEW APPROACH

During the past 10 years, a great deal of research has been done on a new approach to looking at motivation. This approach, frequently called expectancy theory, still needs further testing, refining, and extending. However, enough is known that many behavioral scientists have concluded that it represents the most comprehensive, valid, and useful approach to understanding motivation. Further, it is apparent that it is a very useful tool for understanding motivation in organizations.

The theory is based on a number of specific assumptions about the causes of behavior in organizations.

Assumption 1: Behavior is determined by a combination of forces in the individual and forces in the environment. Neither the individual nor the environment alone determines behavior. Individuals come into organizations with certain "psychological baggage." They have past experiences and a developmental history which has given them unique sets of needs, ways of looking at the world, and expectations about how organizations will treat them. These all influence how individuals respond to their work environment. The work environment provides structures (such as a pay system or a supervisor) which influence the behavior of people. Different environments tend to produce different behavior in similar people just as dissimilar people tend to behave differently in similar environments.

Assumption 2: People make decisions about their own behavior in organizations. While there are many constraints on the behavior of individuals in organizations, most of the behavior that is observed is the result of individuals' conscious decisions. These decisions usually fall into two categories. First, individuals make decisions about *membership behavior*—coming to work, staying at work, and in other ways being a member of the organization. Second, individuals make decisions about the amount of

effort they will direct *towards performing their jobs.* This includes decisions about how hard to work, how much to produce, at what quality, etc.

Assumption 3: Different people have different types of needs, desires, and goals. Individuals differ on what kinds of outcomes (or rewards) they desire. These differences are not random; they can be examined systematically by an understanding of the differences in the strength of individuals' needs.

Assumption 4: People make decisions among alternative plans of behavior based on their perceptions (expectancies) of the degree to which a given behavior will lead to desired outcomes. In simple terms, people tend to do those things which they see as leading to outcomes (which can also be called rewards) they desire and avoid doing those things they see as leading to outcomes that are not desired.

In general, the approach used here views people as having their own needs and mental maps of what the world is like. They use these maps to make decisions about how they will behave, behaving in those ways which their mental maps indicate will lead to outcomes that will satisfy their needs. Therefore, they are inherently neither motivated nor unmotivated; motivation depends on the situation they are in, and how it fits their needs.

THE THEORY

Based on these general assumptions, expectancy theory states a number of propositions about the process by which people make decisions about their own behavior in organizational settings. While the theory is complex at first view, it is in fact made of a series of fairly straightforward observations about behavior. (The theory is presented in more technical terms in Appendix A.) Three concepts serve as the key building blocks of the theory:

Performance-Outcome Expectancy

Every behavior has associated with it, in an individual's mind, certain outcomes (rewards or punishments). In other words, the individual believes or expects that if he or she behaves in a certain way, he or she will get certain things. Examples of expectancies can easily be described. An individual may have an expectancy that if he produces 10 units he will receive his normal hourly rate while if he produces 15 units he will receive his hourly pay rate plus a bonus. Similarly an individual may believe that certain levels of performance will lead to approval or disapproval from members of her work group or from her supervisor. Each performance can be seen as leading to a number of different kinds of outcomes, and outcomes can differ in their types.

Valence

Each outcome has a "valence" (value, worth, attractiveness) to a specific individual. Outcomes have different valences for different individuals. This comes about because valences result from individual needs and perceptions, which differ because they in turn reflect other factors in the individual's life.

For example, some individuals may value an opportunity for promotion or advancement because of their needs for achievement or power, while others may not want to be promoted and leave their current work group because of needs for affiliation with others. Similarly, a fringe benefit such as a pension plan may have great valence for an older worker but little valence for a young employee on his first job.

Effort-Performance Expectancy

Each behavior also has associated with it in the individual's mind a certain expectancy or probability of success. This expectancy represents the individual's perception of how hard it will be to achieve such behavior and the probability of his or her successful achievement of that behavior.

For example, you may have a strong expectancy that if you put forth the effort, you can produce 10 units an hour, but that you have only a so-so chance of producing 15 units an hour if you try.

Putting these concepts together, it is possible to make a basic statement about motivation. In general, the motivation to attempt to behave in a certain way is greatest when:

a. The individual believes that the behavior will lead to outcomes (performance-outcome expectancy).
b. The individual believes that these outcomes have positive value for him or her (valence).
c. The individual believes that he or she is able to perform at the desired level (effort-performance expectancy).

Given a number of alternative levels of behavior (10, 15, and 20 units of production per hour, for example) the individual will choose that level of performance which has the greatest motivational force associated with it, as indicated by the expectancies, outcomes, and valences.

In other words, when faced with choices about behavior, the individual goes through a process of considering questions such as, "Can I perform at that level if I try?" "If I perform at that level, what will happen?" "How do I feel about those things that will happen?" The individual then decides to behave in that way which seems to have the best chance of producing positive, desired outcomes.

A General Model

On the basis of these concepts, it is possible to construct a general model of behavior in organizational settings (see Exhibit 4-12). Working from left to right in the model, motivation is seen as the force on the individual to expend effort. Motivation leads to an observed level of effort by the individual. Effort, alone, however, is not enough. Performance results from a combination of the effort that an individual puts forth and the level of ability which he or she has (reflecting skills, training, information, etc.). Effort thus combines with ability to produce a given level of performance. As a result of performance, the individual attains certain outcomes. The model indicates this relationship in a dotted line, reflecting the fact that sometimes people perform but do not get desired outcomes. As this process of performance-reward occurs, time after time, the actual events serve to provide information which influences the individual's perceptions (particularly expectancies) and thus influence motivation in the future.

Outcomes, or rewards, fall into two major categories. First, the individual obtains outcomes from the environment. When an individual performs at a given level, he or she can receive positive or negative outcomes from supervision, co-workers, the organization's rewards systems, or other sources. These environmental rewards are thus one source of outcomes for the individual. A second source of outcomes is the individual. These include outcomes which occur purely from the performance of the task itself (feelings of accomplishment, personal worth, achievement, etc.). In a sense, the individual gives these rewards to himself or herself. The environment cannot give them or take them away directly; it can only make them possible.

Supporting Evidence

Over 50 studies have been done to test the validity of the expectancy-theory approach to predicting employee behavior.[1] Almost without exception, the studies have confirmed the predictions of the theory. As the theory predicts, the best performers in organizations tend to see a strong relationship between performing their jobs well and receiving rewards they value. In addition they have clear performance goals and feel they can perform well. Similarly, studies using the expectancy theory to predict how people choose jobs also show that individuals tend to interview for and actually take those jobs which they feel will provide the rewards they value. One study, for example, was able to correctly predict for 80 percent of the people studied which of several jobs they would take.[2] Finally, the theory correctly predicts that beliefs about the outcomes associated with performance (expectancies) will be better predictors of performance than will feelings of job satisfaction since expectancies are the critical causes of performance and satisfaction is not.

Questions about the Model

Although the results so far have been encouraging, they also indicate some problems with the model. These problems do not critically affect the managerial implications of the model, but they should be noted. The model is based on the assumption that individuals make very rational decisions after a thorough exploration of all the available alternatives and on weighing the possible outcomes of all these alternatives. When we talk to or observe individuals, however, we find that their decision processes are frequently less thorough. People often stop considering alternative behavior plans when they find one that is at least moderately satisfying, even though more rewarding plans remain to be examined.

People are also limited in the amount of information they can handle at one time, and therefore the model may indicate a process that is much more complex than the one that actually takes place. On the other hand, the model does provide enough information and is consistent enough with reality to present some clear implications for managers who are concerned with the question of how to motivate the people who work for them.

Implications for Managers

The first set of implications is directed toward the individual manager who has a group of people working for him or her and is concerned with how to motivate good performance. Since behavior is a result of forces both in the person and in the environment, you as manager need to look at and diagnose both the person and the environment. Specifically, you need to do the following:

Figure out what outcomes each employee values. As a first step, it is important to determine what kinds of outcomes or rewards have valence for your employees. For each employee you need to determine "what turns him or her on." There are various ways of finding this out, including (*a*) finding out employees' desires through some structured method of data collection, such as a questionnaire, (*b*) observing the employees' reactions to different situations or rewards, or (*c*) the fairly simple act of asking them what kinds of rewards they want, what kind of career goals they have, or "what's in it for them." It is important to stress here that it is very difficult to change what people want, but fairly easy to find out what they want. Thus, the skillful manager emphasizes diagnosis of needs, not changing the individuals themselves.

Determine what kinds of behavior you desire. Managers frequently talk about "good performance" without really defining what good performance is. An important step in motivating is for you yourself to figure out what kinds of performances are required and what are adequate measures or indicators of performance (quantity, quality, etc.). There is also a need to be able to define those performances in fairly specific terms so that observable and measurable behavior can be defined and subordinates can understand what is desired of them (e.g., produce 10 products of a certain quality standard—rather than only produce at a high rate).

Make sure desired levels of performance are reachable. The model states that motivation is determined not only by the performance-to-outcome expectancy but also by the effort-to-performance expectancy. The implication of this is that the levels of performance which are set as the points at which individuals receive desired outcomes must be reachable or attainable by these individuals. If the employees feel that the level of performance required to get a reward is higher than they can reasonably achieve, then their motivation to perform well will be relatively low.

Link desired outcomes to desired performances. The next step is to directly, clearly, and explicitly link those outcomes desired by employees to the specific performances desired by you. If your employee values external rewards, then the emphasis should be on the rewards systems concerned with promotion, pay, and approval. While the linking of these rewards can be initiated through your making statements to your employees, it is extremely important that employees see a clear example of the reward process working in a fairly short period of time if the motivating "expectancies" are to be created in the employees' mind. The linking must be done by some concrete public acts, in addition to statements of intent.

If your employee values internal rewards (e.g., achievement), then you should concentrate on changing the nature of the person's job, for he or she is likely to respond well to such things as increased autonomy, feedback, and challenge, because these things will lead to a situation where good job performance is inherently rewarding. The best way to check on the adequacy of the internal and external reward system is to ask people what their perceptions of the situation are. Remember it is the perceptions of people that determine their motivation, not reality. It doesn't matter for example whether you feel a subordinate's pay is related to his or her motivation. Motivation will be present only if the subordinate sees the relationship. Many managers are misled about the behavior of their subordinates because they rely on their own perceptions of the situation and forget to find out what their subordinates feel. There is only one way to do this: ask. Questionnaires can be used here, as can personal interviews. (See Appendix B for a short version of a motivation questionnaire).

Analyze the total situation for conflicting expectancies. Having set up positive expectancies for employees, you then need to look at the entire situation to see if other factors (informal work groups, other managers, the organization's reward systems) have set up conflicting expectancies in the minds of the employees. Motivation will only be high when people see a number of rewards associated with good performance and few negative outcomes. Again, you can often gather this kind of information by asking your subordinates. If there are major conflicts, you need to make adjustments, either in your own performance and reward structure, or in the other sources of rewards or punishments in the environment.

Make sure changes in outcomes are large enough. In examining the motivational system, it is important to make sure that changes in outcomes or rewards are large enough to motivate significant behavior. Trivial rewards will result in trivial amounts of effort and thus trivial improvements in performance. Rewards must be large enough to motivate individuals to put forth the effort required to bring about significant changes in performance.

Check the system for its equity. The model is based on the idea that individuals are different and therefore different rewards will need to be used to motivate different individuals. On the other hand, for a motivational system to work it must be a fair one—one that has equity (not equality). Good performers should see that they get more desired rewards than do poor performers, and others in the system should see that also. Equity should not be confused with a system of equality where all are rewarded equally, with no regard to their performance. A system of equality is guaranteed to produce low motivation.

Implications for Organizations

Expectancy theory has some clear messages for those who run large organizations. It suggests how organizational structures can be designed so that they increase rather than decrease levels of motivation of organization members. While there are many different implications, a few of the major ones are as follows:

Implication 1: The design of pay and reward systems. Organizations usually get what they reward, not what they want. This can be seen in many situations, and pay systems are a good example.[3] Frequently, organizations reward people for membership (through pay tied to seniority, for example) rather than for performance. Little wonder that what the organization gets is behavior oriented towards "safe," secure employment rather than effort directed at performing well. In addition, even where organizations do pay for performance as a motivational device, they frequently negate the motivational value of the system by keeping pay secret, therefore preventing people from observing the pay-to-performance relationship that would serve to create positive, clear, and strong performance-to-reward expectancies. The implication is that organizations should put more effort into rewarding people (through pay, promotion, better job opportunities, etc.) for the performances which are desired, and that to keep these rewards secret is clearly self-defeating. In addition, it underscores the importance of the frequently ignored performance evaluation or appraisal process and the need to evaluate people based on how they perform clearly defined specific behaviors, rather than on how they score on ratings of general traits such as "honesty," "cleanliness," and other, similar terms which frequently appear as part of the performance appraisal form.

Implication 2: The design of tasks, jobs, and roles. One source of desired outcomes is the work itself. The expectancy-theory model supports much of the job enrichment literature, in saying that by designing jobs which enable people to get their needs fulfilled, organizations can bring about higher levels of motivation.[4] The major difference between the traditional approaches to job enlargement or enrichment and the expectancy-theory approach is the recognition by expectancy theory that different people have different needs, and therefore, some people may not want enlarged or enriched jobs. Thus, while the design of tasks that have more autonomy, variety, feedback, meaningfulness, etc., will lead to higher motivation in some, the organization needs to build in the opportunity for individuals to make choices about the kind of work they will do so that not everyone is forced to experience job enrichment.

Implication 3: The importance of group structures. Groups, both formal and informal, are powerful and potential sources of desired outcomes for individuals. Groups can provide or withhold acceptance, approval, affection, skill training, needed information, assistance, etc. They are a powerful force in the total motivational environment of individuals. Several implications emerge from the importance of groups. First, organizations should consider the structuring of at least a portion of rewards around group performance rather than individual performance. This is particularly important where group members have to cooperate with each other to produce a group product or service, and where the individual's contribution is often hard to determine. Second, the organization needs to train managers to be aware of how groups can influence individual behavior and to be sensitive to the kinds of expectancies which informal groups set up and their conflict or consistency with the expectancies that the organization attempts to create.

Implication 4: The supervisor's role. The immediate supervisor has an important role in creating, monitoring, and maintaining the expectancies and reward structures which will lead to good performance. The supervisor's role in the motivation process becomes one of defining clear goals, setting clear reward expectancies, and providing the right rewards for different people (which could include both organizational rewards and personal rewards such as recognition, approval, or support from the supervisor). Thus, organizations need to provide supervisors with an awareness of the nature of motivation as well as the tools (control over organizational rewards, skill in administering those rewards) to create positive motivation.

Implication 5: Measuring motivation. If things like expectancies, the nature of the job, supervisor-controlled outcomes, satisfaction, etc., are important in understanding how well people are being motivated, then organizations need to monitor employee perceptions along these lines. One relatively cheap and reliable method of doing this is through standardized employee questionnaires. A number of organizations already use such techniques, surveying employees' perceptions and attitudes at regular intervals (ranging from once a month to once every year and a half) using either standardized surveys or surveys developed specifically for the organization. Such information is useful both to the individual manager and to top management in assessing the state of human resources and the effectiveness of the organization's motivational systems.[5] (Again, see Appendix B for excerpts from a standardized survey.)

Implication 6: Individualizing organizations. Expectancy theory leads to a final general implication about a possible future direction for the design of organizations. Because different people have different needs and therefore have different valences, effective motivation must come through the recognition that not all employees are alike and that organizations need to be flexible in order to accommodate individual differences. This implies the "building in" of choice for employees in many areas, such as reward systems, fringe benefits, job assignments, etc., where employees previously have had little say. A successful example of the building in of such choice can be seen in the experiments at TRW and the Educational Testing Service with "cafeteria fringe-benefits plans" which allow employees to choose the fringe benefits they want, rather than taking the expensive and often unwanted benefits which the company frequently provides to everyone.[6]

SUMMARY

Expectancy theory provides a more complex model of man for managers to work with. At the same time, it is a model which holds promise for the more effective motivation of individuals and the more effective design of organizational systems. It implies, however, the need for more exacting and thorough diagnosis by the manager to determine (*a*) the relevant forces in the individual and (*b*) the relevant forces in the environment, both of which combine to motivate different kinds of behavior. Following diagnosis, the model implies a need to act—to develop a system of pay, promotion, job assignments, group structures, supervision, etc.—to bring about effective motivation by providing different outcomes for different individuals.

Performance of individuals is a critical issue in making organizations work effectively. If a manager is to influence work behavior and performance, he or she must have an understanding of motivation and the factors which influence an individual's motivation to come to work, to work hard, and to work well. While simple models offer easy answers, it is the more complex models which seem to offer more promise. Managers can use models (like expectancy theory) to understand the nature of behavior and build more effective organizations.

APPENDIX A: THE EXPECTANCY THEORY MODEL IN MORE TECHNICAL TERMS

A person's motivation to exert effort towards a specific level of performance is based on his or her perceptions of associations between actions and outcomes. The critical perceptions which contribute to motivation are graphically presented in Exhibit 4-13. These perceptions can be defined as follows:

A. The effort-to-performance expectancy (E→P): This refers to the person's subjective probability about the likelihood that he or she can perform at a given level, or that effort on his or her part will lead to successful performance. This term can be thought of as varying from 0 to 1. In general, the less likely a person feels that he or she can perform at a given level, the less likely he or she will be to try to perform at that level. A person's E→P probabilities are also strongly influenced by each situation and by previous experience in that and similar situations.

B. The performance-to-outcomes expectancy (P→O) and valence (V): This refers to a combination of a number of beliefs about what the outcomes of successful performance will be and the value or attractiveness of these outcomes to the individual. Valence is considered to vary from +1 (very desirable) to −1 (very undesirable) and the performance-to-outcomes probabilities vary from +1 (performance sure to lead to outcome) to 0 (performance not related to outcome). In general, the more likely a person feels that performance will lead to valent outcomes, the more likely he or she will be to try to perform at the required level.

C. Instrumentality: As Exhibit 4-13 indicates, a single level of performance can be associated with a number of different outcomes, each having a certain degree of valence. Some outcomes are valent because they have direct value or attractiveness. Some outcomes, however, have valence because they are seen as leading to (or being "instrumental" for) the attainment of other "second-level" outcomes which have direct value or attractiveness.

D. Intrinsic and extrinsic outcomes: Some outcomes are seen as occurring directly as a result of performing the task itself and are outcomes which the individual thus gives to himself (i.e., feelings of accomplishment, creativity, etc.). These are called intrinsic outcomes. Other outcomes that are associated with performance are provided or mediated by external factors (the organization, the supervisor, the work group, etc.). These outcomes are called extrinsic outcomes.

Along with the graphic representation of these terms presented in Exhibit 4-13, there is a simplified formula for combining these perceptions to arrive at a term expressing the relative level of motivation to exert effort towards performance at a given level. The formula expresses these relationships:

A. The person's motivation to perform is determined by the P→O expectancy multiplied by the valence (V) of the outcome. The valence of the first order outcome subsumes the instrumentalities and valences of second outcomes. The relationship is multiplicative since there is no motivation to perform if either of the terms is zero.

B. Since a level of performance has multiple outcomes associated with it, the products of all probability-times-valence combinations are added together for all the outcomes that are seen as related to the specific performance.

C. This term (the summed P→O expectancies times valences) is then multiplied by the E→P expectancy. Again the multiplicative relationship indicates that if either term is zero, motivation is zero.

D. In summary, the strength of a person's motivation to perform effectively is influenced by (1) the person's belief that effort can be converted into performance and (2) the net attractiveness of the events that are perceived to stem from good performance.

So far, all the terms have referred to the individual's perceptions which result in motivation and thus an intention to behave in a certain way. Exhibit 4-14 is a simplified representation of the total model, showing how these intentions get translated into actual behavior.[7] The model envisions the following sequence of events:

A. First, the strength of a person's motivation to perform correctly is most directly reflected in his or her effort—how hard he or she works. This effort expenditure may or may not result in good performance, since at least two factors must be right if effort is to be converted into performance. First, the person must possess the necessary abilities in order to perform the job well. Unless both ability and effort are high, there cannot be good performance. A second factor is the person's perception of how his or her effort can best be converted into performance. It is assumed that this perception is learned by the individual on the basis of previous experience in similar situations. This "how to do it" perception can obviously vary widely in accuracy, and—where erroneous perceptions exist—performance is low even though effort or motivation may be high.

EXHIBIT 4-13

Major Terms in Expectancy Theory

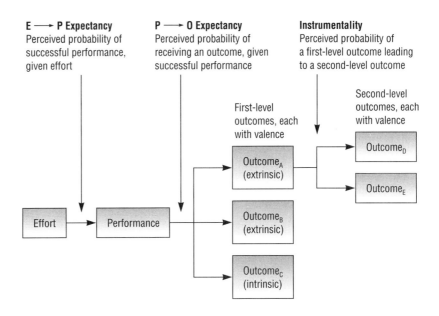

E ⟶ P Expectancy
Perceived probability of successful performance, given effort

P ⟶ O Expectancy
Perceived probability of receiving an outcome, given successful performance

Instrumentality
Perceived probability of a first-level outcome leading to a second-level outcome

First-level outcomes, each with valence

Second-level outcomes, each with valence

Effort → Performance

Outcome$_A$ (extrinsic) → Outcome$_D$, Outcome$_E$

Outcome$_B$ (extrinsic)

Outcome$_C$ (intrinsic)

Motivation is expressed as follows: M * [E→P] X > [(P→O) (V)]

EXHIBIT 4-14

Simplified Expectancy-Theory Model of Behavior

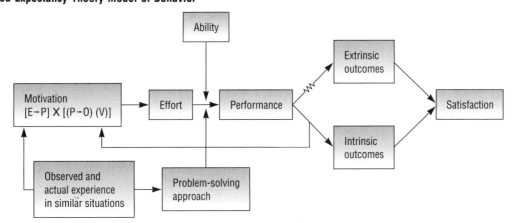

Ability

Motivation [E→P] X [(P→O) (V)] → Effort → Performance → Extrinsic outcomes / Intrinsic outcomes → Satisfaction

Observed and actual experience in similar situations → Problem-solving approach

EXHIBIT 4-15

Question 1: Here are some things that could happen to people if they do their jobs especially well. How likely is it that each of these things would happen if you performed your job especially well?

	Not at All Likely		Somewhat Likely		Quite Likely		Extremely Likely
a. You will get a bonus or pay increase	(1)	(2)	(3)	(4)	(5)	(6)	(7)
b. You will feel better about yourself as a person	(1)	(2)	(3)	(4)	(5)	(6)	(7)
c. You will have an opportunity to develop your skills and abilities	(1)	(2)	(3)	(4)	(5)	(6)	(7)
d. You will have better job security	(1)	(2)	(3)	(4)	(5)	(6)	(7)
e. You will be given chances to learn new things	(1)	(2)	(3)	(4)	(5)	(6)	(7)
f. You will be promoted or get a better job	(1)	(2)	(3)	(4)	(5)	(6)	(7)
g. You will get a feeling that you've accomplished something worthwhile	(1)	(2)	(3)	(4)	(5)	(6)	(7)
h. You will have more freedom on your job	(1)	(2)	(3)	(4)	(5)	(6)	(7)
i. You will be respected by the people you work with	(1)	(2)	(3)	(4)	(5)	(6)	(7)
j. Your supervisor will praise you	(1)	(2)	(3)	(4)	(5)	(6)	(7)
k. The people you work with will be friendly with you	(1)	(2)	(3)	(4)	(5)	(6)	(7)

B. Second, when performance occurs, certain amounts of outcomes are obtained by the individual. Intrinsic outcomes, not being mediated by outside forces, tend to occur regularly as a result of performance, while extrinsic outcomes may or may not accrue to the individual (indicated by the wavy line in the model).

C. Third, as a result of the obtaining of outcomes and the perceptions of the relative value of the outcomes obtained, the individual has a positive or negative affective response (a level of satisfaction or dissatisfaction).

D. Fourth, the model indicates that events which occur influence future behavior by altering the E→P, P→O, and V perceptions. This process is represented by the feedback loops running from actual behavior back to motivation.

APPENDIX B: MEASURING MOTIVATION USING EXPECTANCY THEORY

Expectancy theory suggests that it is useful to measure the attitudes individuals have in order to diagnose motiva-

tional problems. Such measurement helps the manager to understand why employees are motivated or not, what the strength of motivation is in different parts of the organization, and how effective different awards are for motivating performance. A short version of a questionnaire used to measure motivation in organizations is included here.[8] Basically, three different questions need to be asked (see Exhibits 4-15, 4-16, and 4-17).

Using the Questionnaire Results

The results from this questionnaire can be used to calculate a **work-motivation score**. A score can be calculated for each individual and scores can be combined for groups of individuals. The procedure for obtaining a work-motivation score is as follows:

A. For each of the possible positive outcomes listed in questions 1 and 2, multiply the score for the outcome in question 1 (P→O expectancies) by the corresponding score

EXHIBIT 4-16

Question 2: Different people want different things from their work. Here is a list of things a person could have on his or her job. How *important* is each of the following to you?

	Moderately Important or Less			Quite Important		Extremely Important	
How Important Is . . . ?							
a. The amount of pay you get	(1)	(2)	(3)	(4)	(5)	(6)	(7)
b. The chances you have to do something that makes you feel good about yourself as a person	(1)	(2)	(3)	(4)	(5)	(6)	(7)
c. The opportunity to develop your skills and abilities	(1)	(2)	(3)	(4)	(5)	(6)	(7)
d. The amount of job security you have	(1)	(2)	(3)	(4)	(5)	(6)	(7)
How Important Is . . . ?							
e. The chances you have to learn new things	(1)	(2)	(3)	(4)	(5)	(6)	(7)
f. Your chances for getting a promotion or getting a better job	(1)	(2)	(3)	(4)	(5)	(6)	(7)
g. The chances you have to accomplish something worthwhile	(1)	(2)	(3)	(4)	(5)	(6)	(7)
h. The amount of freedom you have on your job	(1)	(2)	(3)	(4)	(5)	(6)	(7)
How Important Is . . . ?							
i. The respect you receive from the people you work with	(1)	(2)	(3)	(4)	(5)	(6)	(7)
j. The praise you get from your supervisor	(1)	(2)	(3)	(4)	(5)	(6)	(7)
k. The friendliness of the people you work with	(1)	(2)	(3)	(4)	(5)	(6)	(7)

EXHIBIT 4-17

Question 3: Below you will see a number of pairs of factors that look like this:

Warm weather → sweating   (1) (2) (3) (4) (5) (6) (7)

You are to indicate by checking the appropriate number to the right of each pair how often it is true for you personally that the first factor leads to the second on *your job*. Remember, for each pair, indicate how often it is true by checking the box under the response which seems most accurate.

	Never	Sometimes			Often		Almost Always
a. Working hard → high productivity	(1)	(2)	(3)	(4)	(5)	(6)	(7)
b. Working hard → doing my job well	(1)	(2)	(3)	(4)	(5)	(6)	(7)
c. Working hard → good job performance	(1)	(2)	(3)	(4)	(5)	(6)	(7)

on question 2 (valences of outcomes). Thus, score 1*a* would be multiplied by score 2*a*, score 1*b* by score 2*b*, etc.

B. All of the 1 times 2 products should be added together to get a total of all expectancies times valences.

C. The total should be divided by the number of pairs (in this case, 11) to get an average expectancy-times-valence score.

D. The scores from question 3 (E→P expectancies) should be added together and then divided by three to get an average effort-to-performance expectancy score.

E. Multiply the score obtained in step C (the average expectancy times valence) by the score obtained in step D (the average E→P expectancy score) to obtain a total work-motivation score.

Additional Comments on the Work-Motivation Score

A number of important points should be kept in mind when using the questionnaire to get a work-motivation score. First, the questions presented here are just a short version of a larger and more comprehensive questionnaire. For more detail, the articles and publications referred to here and in the text should be consulted. Second, this is a general questionnaire. Since it is hard to anticipate in a general questionnaire what may be valent outcomes in each situation, the individual manager may want to add additional outcomes to questions 1 and 2. Third, it is important to remember that questionnaire results can be influenced by the feelings people have when they fill out the questionnaire. The use of the questionnaire as outlined above assumes a certain level of trust between manager and subordinates. People filling out questionnaires need to know what is going to be done with their answers and usually need to be assured of the confidentiality of their responses. Finally, the research indicates that, in many cases, the score obtained by simply averaging all the responses to question 1 (the P→O expectancies) will be as useful as the fully calculated work-motivation score. In each situation, the

manager should experiment and find out whether the additional information in questions 2 and 3 aid in motivational diagnosis.

NOTES

1. For reviews of the expectancy theory research see T. R. Mitchell. Expectancy models of job satisfaction, occupational preference, and effort: A theoretical, methodological, and empirical appraisal. *Psychological Bulletin,* 1974, 81, 1053–1077. For a more general discussion of expectancy theory and other approaches to motivation see E. E. Lawler, *Motivation in Work Organizations.* (Belmont, Calif.: Brooks/Cole, 1973).
2. E. E. Lawler, W. J. Kuleck, J. G. Rhode, and J. F. Sorenson. Job Choice and Post-Decision Dissonance. *Organizational Behavior and Human Performance* 13, 1975, pp. 133–45.
3. For a detailed discussion of the implications of expectancy theory for pay and reward systems, see E. E. Lawler, *Pay and Organizational Effectiveness: A Psychological View.* (New York: McGraw-Hill), 1971.
4. A good discussion of job design with an expectancy theory perspective is in J. R. Hackman, G. R. Oldham, R. Janson, and K. Purdy. A New Strategy for Job Enrichment. *California Management Review.* Summer, 1975, p. 57.
5. The use of questionnaires for understanding and changing organizational behavior is discussed in D. A. Nadler, *Feedback and Organizational Development. Using Data-Based Methods.* (Reading, Mass.: Addison-Wesley Publishing, 1977).
6. The whole issue of individualizing organizations is examined in E. E. Lawler, The Individual Organization: Problems and Promise, *California Management Review* 17(2), 1974, pp. 31–39.
7. For a more detailed statement of the model see E. E. Lawler, Job Attitudes and Employee Motivation: Theory, Research, and Practice, *Personal Psychology* 23, 1970, pp. 223–37.
8. For a complete version of the questionnaire and supporting documentation see D. A. Nadler, C. Cammann, G. D. Jenkins, and E. E. Lawler, (Eds.) *The Michigan Organizational Assessment Package* (Progress Report II) (Ann Arbor: Survey Research Center, 1975).

■

EXERCISES

EXERCISE 4–1   GOAL SETTING—HOW TO DO IT

Each person is to work alone for at least 30 minutes with this exercise. After sufficient time has elapsed for each person to work through the exercise, the instructor will go over each goal and ask for comments from the class or

group. The discussion should display the understanding of goals that each participant has and what will be needed to improve his or her goal-writing skills.

Writing and evaluating goals seem simple, but they are

often not done well in organizations. The press of time, previous habits, and little concern about the attributes of a goal statement are reasons why goals are often poorly constructed. Actually, a number of guidelines should be followed in preparing goals.

1. A well-presented goal statement contains four elements:
   a. An action or accomplishment verb.
   b. A single and measurable result.
   c. A date of completion.
   d. A cost in terms of effort, resources, or money or some combination of these factors.
2. A well-presented goal statement is short; it is not a paragraph. It should be presented in a sentence.
3. A well-presented goal statement specifies only what and when and doesn't get into how or why.
4. A well-presented goal statement is challenging and attainable. It should cause the person to stretch his or her skills, abilities, and efforts.
5. A well-presented goal statement is meaningful and important. It should be a priority item.
6. A well-presented goal statement must be acceptable to you so that you will try hard to accomplish the goal.

The goal statement model should be:

To (action or accomplishment verb) (single result) by (a date—keep it realistic) at (effort, use of what resource, cost).

An example for a production operation:

To reduce the production cost per unit of Mint toothpaste by at least 3 percent by March 1, at a changeover of equipment expense not to exceed $45,000.

Examine the next four statements that are presented as goal statements. Below each goal write a critique of the statement. Is it a good goal statement? Why? Discuss your viewpoints in the class group discussion.

To reduce my blood pressure to an acceptable level.

_____
_____
_____
_____
_____
_____
_____
_____

To make financial investments with a guaranteed minimum return of at least 16 percent.

_____
_____
_____
_____
_____
_____
_____

To spend a minimum of 45 minutes a day on a doctor-approved exercise plan, starting Monday, lasting for six months, at no expense.

_____
_____
_____
_____
_____
_____
_____

To spend more time reading non-work-related novels and books during the next year.

_____
_____
_____
_____
_____
_____
_____

EXERCISE 4–2 YOUR MOTIVATION TO MANAGE

How motivated are you to manage? It is your motivation to manage that will provide some indication of how likely you are to be satisfied with a management position. There is no ideal formula for having a desire to manage, but one indication can be obtained by answering a few questions.

The "Motivation to Manage" (MTM) scale is subjective assessment and you may have some error, but at least it will sensitize you to the key variables and encourage you to think about these issues.

Activities that are performed and enjoyed are very different for the person with a high versus a low Motivation to Manage (MTM). Jobs with given characteristics are better and less well suited to each managerial type. The table below indicates those job characteristics that are best matched with people with high MTM and low MTM.

MTM/Job Fit

In order for you to be satisfied and successful in an organizational role, you must first attempt to match your basic motivation to the job. Does your job fit your Mo-

tivation to Manage? Different jobs require different levels of MTM. Look at Exhibit 4-18 and try to determine if you are in a high or low MTM job. Suppose that you have just concluded that you have low Motivation to Manage? What should you do?

You have two alternatives:

1. Select jobs that are more appropriate to your MTM
2. Attempt to change your MTM

In order for you to be happy, fulfilled, and successful in your job, you must fit the job requirements. There must be a match between your motivation and the characteristics of the job, the activities you like to do and those demanded by the job. Thorough and accurate self-assessment regarding your Motivation to Manage is very important information as you make career choices.

Changing Your Motivation to Manage

It is generally accepted in psychology that a certain amount of motivation is learned. McClelland has claimed the ability to teach people to increase their need for achievement. He has also concluded that successful managers have a

Source: "Motivation to Manage" is an exercise developed by Dennis P. Slevin, *Executive Survival Manual,* Innodyne, Inc., P.O. Box 11386, Pittsburgh, Pa. 15238.

MOTIVATION TO MANAGE AUDIT

How Motivated to Manage Are You?

Complete this instrument by circling the number for each item that represents your best estimate of your current level.

	Well below Average				Average				Well above Average	
1. Favorable attitude toward authority	0	1	2	3	4	5	6	7	8	9	10
2. Desire to compete	0	1	2	3	4	5	6	7	8	9	10
3. Assertive motivation	0	1	2	3	4	5	6	7	8	9	10
4. Desire to exercise power	0	1	2	3	4	5	6	7	8	9	10
5. Desire for a distinctive position	0	1	2	3	4	5	6	7	8	9	10
6. A sense of responsibility	0	1	2	3	4	5	6	7	8	9	10

TOTAL MOTIVATION TO MANAGE = _____

Now place a check mark next to the number for each item that represents your best estimate of where you would *like to be*. The difference between your *desired* and *actual* score for each item is your Motivation to Manage deficit on that factor. It will be used in completing your Motivation to Manage Action Plan (Motivation 2).

higher need for power than their need for affiliation. This seems compatible with the MTM in that one must be prepared to exercise power over others in order to succeed as a manager.

Is it possible to increase a person's Motivation to Manage? Perhaps. Little research has been done in this area. There are no figures to cite. However, look at the six components of Motivation to Manage. They are *learned* motives. Therefore, one should be able to change them. Is it possible to change your Motivation to Manage? Definitely. If you want to.

Do you *want* to change your Motivation to Manage? If yes, you will need to formulate an action plan for changing each of the components of managerial motivation.

Go back to the Motivation to Manage Audit. Look at your desired level for each of the factors in the Motivation to Manage in your present position. The difference between the desired level and your actual level provides a **managerial motivation** deficit for each factor. Specify on the Motivation to Manage Action Plan the specific steps that you might take to increase your MTM on each factor to remove the deficit.

MOTIVATION TO MANAGE ACTION PLAN

Record your Motivation to Manage deficit (desired–actual) for each factor below. Then specify appropriate action steps you might take to increase your Motivation to Manage on each factor and remove the deficit.

1. Favorable Attitude Toward Authority   Deficit: _____
   Action Plan: _____
   _____
   _____
   _____ Probability of Success: _____

EXHIBIT 4-18

**Job Characteristics
Associated with
Motivation to
Manage (MTM)**

Low MTM	High MTM
Relatively small span of control	Large span of control
Small number of subordinates	Large number of subordinates
High technical/engineering component	High people/budgetary component
Maintain "hands-on" expertise	Surround oneself with technical experts
Limited number of activities per day	As many as 200 activities per day
Few interruptions	Many interruptions
Time for reading, analyzing	Time for interactions
Serve as facilitator to staff	Serve as "boss" to staff
Career progression—Increase in technical expertise	Career progression—Managerial advancement
Little exercise of power is required	Much intervention in lives of others
Lower stress position	Higher stress position

2. Desire to Compete   Deficit: _____
   Action Plan: _____
   _____
   _____
   _____ Probability of Success: _____

3. Assertive Motivation   Deficit: _____
   Action Plan: _____
   _____
   _____
   _____ Probability of Success: _____

4. Desire to Exercise Power   Deficit: _____
   Action Plan: _____
   _____
   _____
   _____ Probability of Success: _____

5. Desire for Distinctive Position   Deficit: _____
   Action Plan: _____
   _____
   _____
   _____ Probability of Success: _____

6. A Sense of Responsibility   Deficit: _____
   Action Plan: _____
   _____
   _____
   _____ Probability of Success: _____

EXHIBIT 4-19

Motivating Yourself and Others

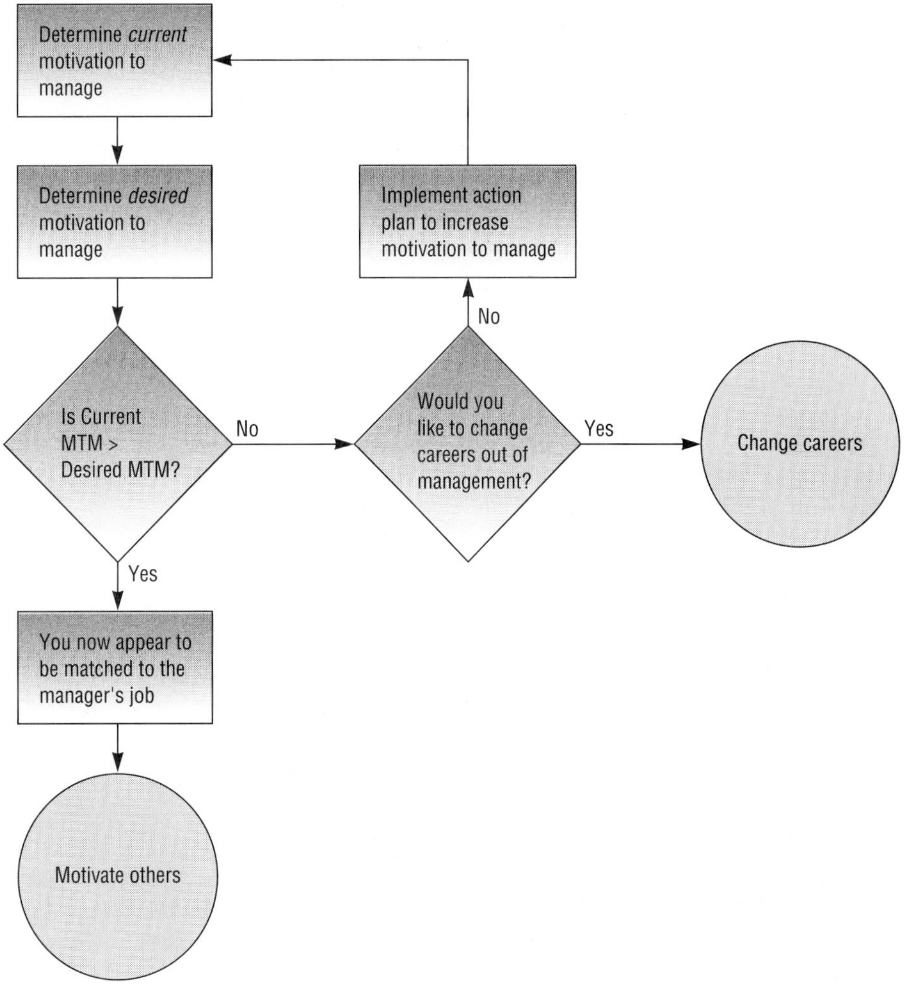

You have now had an opportunity to assess in a personal way your Motivation to Manage. The logical steps in this assessment are portrayed in the flow chart shown in Exhibit 4-19. Try to accomplish this in as perceptive a way as possible. It's fun to consider your own personal motivational structures and to talk to others about career, job, and personal needs. If you can better understand where you are concerning your Motivation to Manage, you will be in a better position to perform your job at peak effi- ciency. If your Motivation to Manage is insufficient for your current or future job prospects, then you must seriously consider changing these needs or changing your career. Millions of people get matched to millions of jobs through ad hoc and almost accidental sequences of events. In this exercise you are provided with a framework for consciously and analytically attempting to assess the match between your motivation structure and the manager's job.

▲

CASES

CASE 4–1   ENTREPRENEURS' MOTIVATIONS: DO THEORIES EXPLAIN THEM?

Thinking about starting or buying a business? If so, you have probably heard many times that most new business ventures fail within five years and that the two most common causes of failure are lack of financing and poor management. If you think this assessment sounds unduly pessimistic, we have good news for you. Most of what you have heard about the chances of succeeding in small business is more myth than reality, painting a far more dismal picture than actually exists.

Reflecting back on American business history, you should not be surprised by this. Alfred P. Sloan, the guiding genius behind General Motors, graduated at the top of his class from Massachusetts Institute of Technology. On the other hand, Ray Kroc, the founder of McDonald's, did not graduate from high school. We have similar difficulties predicting success using such other descriptive characteristics as age, sex, and prior work experience.

At a time when the Fortune 500 firms are aggressively downsizing to become more "entrepreneurial," newly formed companies have become the principal creators of jobs in the American economy. And the trend is growing. In 1965, there were 204,000 business start-ups in the country; by 1988, that annual figure had grown to nearly 700,000.

But how realistic is the entrepreneurial dream? Does the potential to create a successful business lie within each of us? Is it the predominant need that drives us, or does it take some special combination of traits? Research into these questions is beginning to yield answers, but as yet there is nearly unanimous agreement on only one fact: the need for money is not the driving force. Rather, says psychologist and management consultant Harry Levinson, president of the Levinson Institute in Belmont, Massachusetts, entrepreneurs work with such single-minded intensity because they are psychologically compelled to.

Other researchers argue that, regardless of gender, enterprise often proceeds from deep psychic disruption. As author George Gilder remarks, "It's really hard to be an entrepreneur. You have to commit yourself obsessively to

a project that might well fail, and you have to forgo all kinds of gratifications and do all kinds of jobs that other people don't want to do."

John J. Kao, an associate professor of business administration at the Harvard Business School, highlights the importance of self-actualization. "This model posits entrepreneurship as a desire for personal growth and development," and "above all else the desire to create something, whether a new product or process, a new organization or new way of doing business." When Sandra Kurtzig describes creating ASK Computer Systems, for example, she speaks fondly of "nurturing an idea, taking a seed and growing it into a baby." She also recalls the pleasure she took in hiring "good people and feeling responsible for them."

Other researchers also emphasize the entrepreneur's creative drive. David McClelland, the author of the learned needs theory discussed in this chapter found that entrepreneurs, like artists, tend to be strongly invested in their work. They are motivated by the need for achievement, challenge, and the opportunity to be innovative.

Entrepreneurs have also been likened to juvenile delinquents. "It's not that they break the law or are dishonest," says psychoanalyst Abraham Zaleznik, a professor at Harvard Business School. "But they do have one thing in common: they don't have the normal fear or anxiety mechanisms." Often, in fact, they seem to act on impulse, to be reckless.

Fred Smith's story of tide bucking is among the best known. He researched and wrote the basic plan for Federal Express as a paper in college. His professor derided the very idea of a next-day air express company and flunked him on the paper. But Smith went ahead anyway and—after some very lean years—proved his vision to be spectacularly right.

Entrepreneurs have often been members of a religious or racial minority who have had to build their own innovative paths to achievement and recognition. And it is no accident that Liz Claiborne, the first female Fortune 500 CEO who didn't inherit her position through family connections, took what *Working Woman* magazine dubbed "the outside route to the top" by starting her own firm.

In our time, the greatest source of entrepreneurial ma-

Source: Henry H. Beam and Thomas A. Carey, "Could You Succeed in Small Business?" *Business Horizons,* September-October 1989, pp. 65–69; Diane Cole, "The Entrepreneurial Self," *Psychology Today,* June 1989, pp. 60–63.

terial has been politics, war, and the resulting international caravan of refugees. Gilder writes:

In nearly every nation, many of the most notable entrepreneurs are immigrants. Immigration usually entails violation of ancestral ties and parental obligations. Dealing in their youths with convulsive change, thrown back on their own devices to create a productive existence . . . immigrants everywhere suffer the guilt of disconnection from their home and families and ally easily with the forces of the future against the claims of the past.

Perhaps the prototypical immigrant success story is Jack Tramiel, chairman of Atari, Inc. (the computer company), who came to America after surviving the horrors of Auschwitz in World War II. The Polish-born Tramiel turned a former typewriter repair shop into the Commodore International computer corporation. He frankly regards the practice of business as a battle for survival, the equivalent of war. Characterized by *Forbes* magazine as "abrasive and autocratic" when he was forced out of Commodore in 1984, Tramiel rebuilt Atari into a force in the personal computer industry after it had been given up for dead by its previous owner.

Nonetheless, for every immigrant like Tramiel, schooled in the harshest adversity, there is a comfortable, middle-class American—Steve Jobs (Apple and NEXT computers) or Sandra Kurtzig—who simply felt compelled to realize a vision or an ambition. So is there, after all, a distinct entrepreneurial personality? Many experts have looked at the available evidence and are not convinced the species is distinct.

But the lives entrepreneurs lead are observably different, and so are their achievements. As Joseph Schumpeter, one of the earliest economists to recognize and extol the place of the entrepreneur within capitalist society, once wrote,

"To act with confidence beyond the range of familiar beacons and to overcome . . . resistance requires aptitudes that are present in only a small fraction of the population." And it is a simple fact that most of us choose lives that are less intense, less perilous, and not so filled with grand ambition.

Entrepreneurship is as varied as human ingenuity and enterprise, and so are the needs, goals, and motives that drive it. Its prevalence among those uprooted by political upheaval, victimized by discrimination, or oppressed by the daily grind suggest that the entrepreneur, like the artist or the intellectual, is simply looking for freedom—of expression and of the spirit.

Just as there is no one explanation of an entrepreneur's motivation (that internal drive), no specific set of principles found in motivational theories will help us understand entrepreneurship. But it is safe to predict that, whatever the next decade holds for the economies of the Soviet Union, East Germany, Poland, Hungary, Bulgaria, and Czechoslovakia, the self-motivation of citizens will be important. After years of being controlled and not being able to express themselves freely, the people of the Eastern bloc are about to unleash a tremendous wave of self-motivation. Are there entrepreneurs lurking in these countries? We think there are, and the content motivation theories will help us understand their behavior.

CASE QUESTIONS

1. How can content theories be used to understand entire nations that are attempting to unleash entrepreneurial practices?
2. What role does self-actualization play in entrepreneurship?
3. Can a person be trained or educated to become an entrepreneur? Explain.

CASE 4–2 FAB SWEETS LIMITED

ORGANIZATIONAL SETTING

FAB Sweets Limited is a manufacturer of high quality sweets (candies). The company is a medium-sized, family-owned, partially unionized and highly successful confectionery producer in the north of England. The case study is set

Source: Case prepared by N. Kemp, C. Clegg, T. Wall. *Case Studies in Organizational Behaviour,* ed. C. Clegg, N. Kemp, and K. Legge (London: Harper & Row, 1985).

within a single department in the factory where acute problems were experienced.

BACKGROUND TO THE CASE

The department (hereafter called HB) produces and packs over 40 lines of hard-boiled sweets on a batch-production system. It is organized in two adjacent areas, one for production staffed by men and one for packing staffed by

EXHIBIT 4-20

The HB Department: Physical Layout and Work Flow

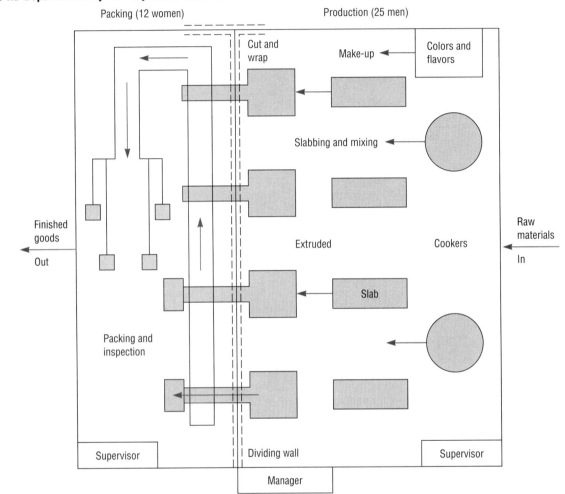

Packing (12 women)   Production (25 men)

Cut and wrap   Make-up   Colors and flavors

Slabbing and mixing

Finished goods   Extruded   Cookers   Raw materials

Out   In

Slab

Packing and inspection

Supervisor   Dividing wall   Supervisor

Manager

women. The areas are separated by a physical barrier, allowing the packing room to be air conditioned and protected from the humidity resulting from production. Management believed this was necessary to stop the sweets from sweating (thus sticking to their wrappers) during storage. Each room has a chargehand and a supervisor who reports to the department manager, who himself is responsible to the factory manager. In total, 37 people work in the department (25 in production, 12 in packing), the majority

of whom are skilled employees. Training takes place on the job, and it normally takes two years to acquire the skills necessary to complete all the production tasks. Exhibit 4-20 presents an outline of the physical layout of the department and the work flow.

The production process is essentially quite simple. Raw materials, principally sugar, are boiled to a set temperature, with "cooking time" varying from line to line. The resulting batches are worked on by employees who fold and manipulate them so as to create the required texture, while adding coloring and flavorings ("slabbing" and "mixing"). Different batches are molded together to create the flavor mixes and patterns required ("make up"). The batch, which by now is quite cool, is then extruded through a machine which cuts it into sweets of individual size. Some products at this stage are automatically wrapped and then passed by conveyor belt to the packing room where they are inspected, bagged, and boxed ready for dispatch to retail and wholesale outlets. Other products progress unwrapped into the packing room where they are fed into a wrapping machine, inspected, bagged and dispatched. Several different product lines can be produced at the same time. The most skilled and critical tasks occur early in the process; these include "cooking" mixtures for different products and "make up" (e.g., for striped mints). These skills are gradually learned until the operator is able to "feel" the correct finish for each of the 40 lines. All the tasks are highly interdependent such that any one individual's performance affects the ease with which the next person down the line can successfully achieve his/her part of the production process. Although the work appears quite simple and the management of the process straightforward, the department nevertheless experienced acute problems. These are outlined below.

THE PROBLEM

In objective terms the problems in HB were manifest in a high level of labor turnover, six new managers in eight years, production which consistently fell below targets based on work study standards, and high levels of scrap. The department was known as the worst in the factory, and its problems were variously characterized in terms of "attitude," "atmosphere" and "climate." Moreover, employees had few decision-making responsibilities, low motivation, low job satisfaction, and received little information on their performance. Finally there were interpersonal problems between the employees in the production and packing rooms, between the two supervisors, and also among the operators, and there were a number of dissatisfactions relating to grading and payment levels.

EXPERIENCE OF THE METHOD OF WORKING

To understand how HB works and how people experienced their work, it is necessary to recognize the strong drive throughout the organization for production. Departmental managers are judged primarily in terms of their production levels (against targets) and the efficiency (against work study standards) at which they perform. In HB this pressure was transmitted to the two supervisors. In practice, production levels were the number of batches of sweets processed, and efficiency was the ratio of batches produced to hours used by direct labor.

The production supervisor responded to the pressure for production in a number of ways. First, in an attempt to maximize production, he always allocated people to the jobs at which they performed best. He also determined the cooker speeds. In effect, this set the pace of work for both production and packing. Buffer stocks were not possible in production because the sweets needed processing before they cooled down. If he was falling behind the target, the supervisor responded by speeding up the pace of work. In addition, he regarded his job purely in terms of processing batches and ignored problems in the packing room which may in fact have resulted directly from his actions or from those of this staff. The supervisory role thus involved allocating people to tasks, setting machine speeds (and hence the pace of work), organizing reliefs and breaks, monitoring hygiene, safety and quality standards, maintaining discipline and recording data for the management information systems. The chargehand undertook these responsibilities in the absence of a supervisor, spending the rest of his time on production.

The men in production complained that they were bored with always doing the same jobs, especially as some were physically harder than others (for example, "slabbing" involved manual manipulation of batches of up to 50 kilograms). Several claimed that their greater efforts should receive financial recognition. Furthermore, this rigidity of task allocation was in direct conflict with the grading system which was designed to encourage flexibility. To be on the top rate of pay in the department, an operator had to be capable of performing all the skills for all the lines and hence be able to cover any job. Training schedules matched this. In practice, however, people rarely used more than one or two of their skills. The others decayed through disuse. All the staff recognized that the grading system was at odds with how the department actually worked and tended to be dissatisfied with both. The production supervisor's strict control over the pace of work also proved suboptimal in other ways. For example, he sometimes pushed the pace to a level regarded as impossible by the staff. Whether this was true or self-fulfilling is a moot point—the net result was an increase in the level of scrap. Also he ignored the wishes of the staff to work less hard in the afternoon when they were tired: again scrap resulted. In addition the feeling was widespread among the men in production that management and supervision organized the work badly and would do better if they took advice from the shop floor. Their own perceived lack of control over the job led them to abrogate responsibility when things went wrong ("We told them so!!"). And finally, although the processes of production were highly interdependent, operators adopted an insular perspective and the necessary cooperation between workers was rarely evident, and then only on the basis of personal favors between friends.

The equivalent pressure on the packing supervisor was to pack the sweets efficiently. As her section could pack no more than was produced, her only manipulable variable was hours worked. Thus to increase her efficiency she could only transfer the packers to "other work" within her room (e.g., cleaning) or to another department.

The packers for their part resented being asked to work flat out when HB was busy, only to be moved elsewhere when things were slacker. As described above, their own work flow was basically controlled by the speed at which the men were producing. When in difficulty, direct appeals to the men to slow down were unsuccessful and so they channeled their complaints through their supervisor. Because of the insular perspective adopted by the production supervisor (in rational support of his own targets), her approaches were usually ignored ("It's my job to produce sweets"), and the resulting intersupervisory conflict took up much of the department manager's time. In addition the packing room was very crowded and interpersonal conflicts were common.

Finally, production problems throughout the factory were created by seasonal peaks and troughs in the market demand for sweets. These "busy" and "slack" periods differed between production departments. In order to cope with market demands the production planning department transferred staff, on a temporary basis, between production departments. In HB this typically meant that, when they were busy, "unskilled" employees were drafted in to help, whereas when demand was low HB employees were transferred to other departments where they were usually given the worst jobs. Both of these solutions were resented by the employees in HB.

This description of the department is completed when one recognizes the complications involved in scheduling over 40 product lines through complex machinery, all of it over 10 years old. In fact, breakdowns and interruptions to smooth working were common. The effects of these on the possible levels of production were poorly understood and in any case few operators were aware of their targets or of their subsequent performance. More immediately the breakdowns were a source of continual conflict between the department and the maintenance engineers responsible to an engineering manager. The department laid the blame on poor maintenance, the engineers on abuse or lack of care by production workers in handling the machinery. Much management time was spent in negotiating "blame" for breakdowns and time allowances resulting since this affected efficiency figures. Not surprisingly, perhaps, the factory-wide image of the department was very poor on almost all counts, and its status was low.

PARTICIPANTS' DIAGNOSES OF THE PROBLEMS

Shopfloor employees, chargehands, supervisors, the department manager and senior management were agreed that much was wrong in HB. However, there was no coherent view of the causes and what should be done to make improvements. Many shopfloor employees placed the blame on supervision and management for their lack of technical and planning expertise and their low consideration for subordinates. The production supervisor favored a solution in terms of "getting rid of the troublemakers," by transferring or sacking his nominated culprits. The department manager wanted to introduce a senior supervisor to handle the conflicts between the production and packing supervisors and further support the pressure for production. The factory manager thought the way work was organized and managed might be at the core of the difficulties.

CASE QUESTIONS

1. Why is turnover often considered a motivation problem?
2. How would you analyze the department problem using expectancy theory?
3. How would you solve the motivation problem? Be specific.

C H A P T E R

5

Evaluating and Rewarding Individual Behavior

LEARNING OBJECTIVES

DESCRIBE several purposes of performance evaluation

IDENTIFY a variety of different evaluation methods

DISCUSS reinforcement theory

DESCRIBE the elements in a model of individual rewards

COMPARE intrinsic and extrinsic rewards

UNDERSTAND the role rewards play in turnover and absenteeism

DISCUSS the relationship between rewards and performance

IDENTIFY several innovative reward systems

Organizations use a variety of rewards to attract and retain people and to motivate them to achieve their personal and organizational goals.[1] The manner and timing of distributing rewards are important issues that managers must address almost daily. Managers distribute such rewards as pay, transfers, promotions, praise, and recognition. They also can help create the climate that results in more challenging and satisfying jobs. Because these rewards are considered important by employees, they have significant effects on behavior and performance. In this chapter we are concerned with how rewards are distributed by managers. We

[1] J.H. Donnelly, J.L. Gibson, and J.M. Ivancevich, *Fundamentals of Management,* 5th ed. (Homewood, Ill.: Richard D. Irwin, 1992).

discuss the reactions of people to rewards and examine the response of employees to rewards received in organizational settings. Additionally, we present the role of rewards in organizational membership, absenteeism, turnover, and commitment.

Before individuals can be rewarded there must be some basis for distributing rewards. Some rewards may accrue to all individuals simply by virtue of their employment with the organization. These are what are known as universal or across-the-board rewards. Other rewards may be a function of tenure or seniority. Many rewards, however, are related to job performance. To distribute these rewards equitably it is necessary to evaluate employee performance. Thus, we begin this chapter with a look at performance evaluation. Developing effective evaluation systems is just as critical to organizational success as is developing effective reward systems. Both systems represent efforts to influence employee behavior. To achieve maximum effectiveness it is necessary to carefully link employee evaluation systems with reward systems.

EVALUATING PERFORMANCE

Virtually every organization of at least moderate size has a formal employee performance evaluation system. Assessing and providing feedback about performance is considered essential to an employee's ability to perform job duties effectively.[2] In discussing this topic we will identify the purposes performance evaluation may serve, and examine what the focus of evaluations should be. We will also take a look at a number of different performance evaluation methods, examining their strengths and weaknesses.

Purposes of Evaluation

The basic purpose of evaluation, of course, is to provide information about work performance. More specifically, however, such information can serve a variety of purposes. Some of the major ones are:

1. Provide a basis for reward allocation, including raises, promotions, transfers, layoffs, and so on.
2. Identify high-potential employees.
3. Validate the effectiveness of employee selection procedures.
4. Evaluate previous training programs.
5. Facilitate future performance improvement.
6. Develop ways of overcoming obstacles and performance barriers.
7. Identify training and development opportunities.
8. Establish supervisor-employee agreement on performance expectations.

[2]B.R. Nathan, A.M. Mohrman, Jr., and J. Milliman, "Interpersonal Relations as a Context for the Effects of Appraisal Interviews on Performance and Satisfaction: A Longitudinal Study," *Academy of Management Journal,* June 1991, pp. 352–69.

CULTURAL DIFFERENCES IN PERFORMANCE EVALUATIONS

Performance evaluations, like many other management procedures, are not universally the same across all cultures. The primary purpose served by evaluations, the procedures used to conduct evaluations, and the manner in which information is communicated, are just a few of the components of performance evaluation that may differ as a function of the culture in which the evaluation is being conducted. Below are a few examples of some of the differences that exist between the United States, Saudi Arabia, and Japan. For each country, the descriptions of the various components reflect usual or typical practice. Clearly within any single country there will be variations between organizations and, less frequently, within organizations.

Component	United States	Saudi Arabia	Japan
Purpose	Fairness, employee development	Placement	Employee development
Who conducts evaluation	Supervisor	Manager several layers higher	Mentor and supervisor
Frequency	Once a year or periodically	Once a year	Developmental appraisal once a month. Evaluation appraisal after 12 years
Assumptions	Objective appraiser is fair	Subjective more important than objective	Objective and subjective equal importance
Manner of communication and feedback	Criticism direct and may be in writing	Criticism subtle and will not be in writing	Criticism subtle and given orally
Rebuttals	Employee will feel free to rebutt	Employee will feel free to rebutt	Employee will rarely rebutt
Praise	Given individually	Given individually	Given to entire group

Source: Adapted from a report of the Association of Cross-Cultural Trainers in Industry, Southern California, 1984; and from P.R. Harris, and R.T. Moran, *Managing Cultural Differences,* 3rd ed. (Houston: Gulf Publishing, 1991).

These eight specific purposes can be grouped into two broad categories. The first four have a **judgmental orientation**; the last four have a **developmental orientation**. Evaluations with a judgmental orientation focus on past performance and provide a basis for making judgments regarding which employee should be rewarded, and how effective organizational programs—such as selection and training—have been. Evaluations with a developmental orientation are more concerned with improving future performance by insuring expectations are clear and by identifying ways to facilitate employee performance through training. These two broad categories are, of course, not mutually exclusive. Performance evaluation systems can, and do, serve both general purposes.

The general purpose for which performance evaluations are conducted will also vary across different cultures. So also will the frequency with which evaluations are conducted, who conducts them, and a variety of other components. Encounter 5-1 illustrates some cultural differences in typical performance evaluations across three different countries.

Focus of Evaluation

Effective performance evaluation is a continuous, ongoing process and simply stated involves asking two questions: Is the work being done effectively? and, Are employee skills and abilities being fully utilized? The first question tends toward a judgmental orientation, while the second is more developmental in nature. Generally, evaluations should focus on translating the position responsibilities into each employees' day-to-day activities. Position responsibilities are determined on the basis of a thorough job analysis, a procedure that is discussed in more detail in Chapter 12. Additionally, the evaluation should assist the employee in understanding these position responsibilities, the work goals associated with them, and the degree to which the goals have been accomplished.

Performance evaluations should focus on job performance, not individuals. If a word processor operator's work comes to her by written communication and she forwards the completed work to persons with whom she has no personal contact, should the fact that she cannot express herself well when talking to someone be an important factor in judging her performance? If we focus on her verbal ability we are concerned about her as an individual, and are evaluating *her*. But if we look at this in relation to its effect on how well she does her job, we are evaluating her **performance**.

When evaluating employee behavior it is necessary to ensure not only that the focus of the appraisal remains on job performance, but that it also has proper weighting of relevant behaviors. Relevancy, in the context of performance evaluation has three aspects—deficiency, contamination, and distortion. **Deficiency** occurs when the evaluation does not focus on all aspects of the job. If certain job responsibilities and activities are not considered, the evaluation is deficient. **Contamination** can be said to be the reverse of deficiency. It occurs when activities *not* part of the job are included in the evaluation. If we evaluate the word processor mentioned in the previous paragraph on her verbal skills, this would be a form of contamination. Finally, **distortion** takes place in the evaluation process when an improper emphasis is given to various job elements. If, for example, placing the phones on automatic answering at the close of each business day is only a small element of a secretary's job, making that activity the major factor in evaluating his performance would be distorting that particular job element. Well-focused performance evaluations avoid deficiencies, contaminations, and distortions. Case 5–1 "The Politics of Performance Appraisal," provides an opportunity to consider further the issue of what the evaluation should focus on.

▲ C5–1

PERFORMANCE EVALUATION METHODS

Most managers can provide at least a general assessment of their employees' performance, even in the absense of a formal system of evaluation. Having a formal system, however, promotes the systematic and equitable collection of performance information, and helps ensure timely and useful feedback. After you complete Exercise 5–1 you will also see that evaluation can facilitate the effective diagnosis of performance problems.

■ E5–1

There are a number of different methods available for evaluating employee performance. Each has its own adherents and detractors. In the next few paragraphs we will describe a few of the more commonly used techniques.[3]

Checklists

A checklist, as the name implies, provides a list of job-related behaviors and requires that the individual doing the evaluation check those behaviors that best describe the employee. In some cases, certain behaviors on the list are weighted more heavily than others because of their greater significance or importance in contributing to overall successful performance. Separate checklists are frequently developed for different jobs since required behaviors vary across jobs. Alternatively, the same form may be used across many jobs, while the behaviors on the checklist that are scored for a particular job are varied.

Critical Incidents

The critical incident technique focuses the evaluator's attention on particularly significant behaviors. These behaviors may be either positive or negative. A real value of the critical incident technique is that it identifies specific behavioral events, not vague impressions, that affected performance. A list of critical incidents can be extremely effective in demonstrating both desired and undesired behaviors. Since the incidents comprise actual behavior, it is usually easy for the employee to relate to them and understand how they affected the overall performance evaluation. Essential to the success of the critical incident technique is the willingness of the supervisor to maintain an ongoing log of relevant incidents. Otherwise, many of the incidents might be forgotten.

Graphic Rating Scales

Graphic rating scales are one of the oldest and most popular evaluation techniques. In a typical graphic rating scale a set of dimensions related to successful job performance are listed. Such dimensions might include quantity of work,

[3]For a full discussion of various evaluation methods, see J.M. Ivancevich, *Human Resource Management,* 5th ed. (Homewood Ill.: Richard D. Irwin, 1992).

quality of work, initiative, willingness to accept responsibility, knowledge of job, and attendance, to name a few. For each of these dimensions, the employee is rated along a four to seven point scale (five point is the most common) reflecting the extent to which the behavior or characteristic being rated was exhibited during the period covered by the evaluation. If desired, a quantitative total rating can be computed by summing the point values of the ratings received on each dimension.

The popularity of this technique stems from its ease of use, its efficiency in the use of time to complete evaluations, and that it can be applied to a wide variety of different jobs. Like other subjective ratings, however, it is subject to the biases of the rater, including the tendency toward leniency.

Behaviorally Anchored Rating Scales (BARS)

The BARS approach combines elements of two previously discussed techniques: graphic rating scales and critical incidents. BARS resemble graphic rating scales in that both include a number of dimensions to be rated. Unlike the graphic scales, however, the BARS dimensions result from a thorough study to determine specific important areas of performance for a particular job. Each dimension is then anchored with a series of equally specific behaviors representing a range of excellent to unacceptable levels of performance. The anchors are examples of critical incidents which have been shown to be related to various levels of performance. Exhibit 5-1 shows an example of a BARS dimension for an engineer.

BARS advantages include their ease of use, relatively high reliability between raters, and a focus on specific job-related behaviors rather than general traits or characteristics. This latter characteristic tends to make evaluation feedback more acceptable than if a supervisor talked in vague generalities.[4] Also, since the job holders themselves are frequently involved in obtaining examples of relevant critical incidents, there tends to be greater acceptance of the form itself. On the downside, a BARS system can be expensive to develop and maintain. Development takes a great deal of time and must be done for each different job. Additionally, since most jobs change over time, BARS forms must be continually updated to reflect relevant job changes.

Multiperson Comparisons

In multiperson comparisons the job performance of one employee is evaluated in comparison with one or more other employees. It is, therefore, a relative rather than absolute appraisal method. In its simplest form, a straight ranking is used. In a 12-employee group, for example, each person would be ranked from number one, the best performer, to number 12, the poorest performer. A variation is the **group order ranking**, in which the rater is required to place employees into

---

[4]T.J. Klein, "Performance Reviews that Rate an 'A'," *Personnel,* May 1990, pp. 38–40.

EXHIBIT 5-1

A BARS Peformance Dimension for an Engineer

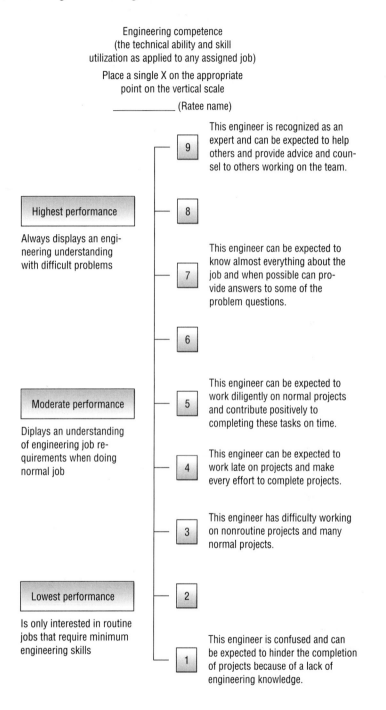

Engineering competence
(the technical ability and skill
utilization as applied to any assigned job)

Place a single X on the appropriate
point on the vertical scale

_____ (Ratee name)

9 — This engineer is recognized as an expert and can be expected to help others and provide advice and counsel to others working on the team.

Highest performance

8

Always displays an engineering understanding with difficult problems

7 — This engineer can be expected to know almost everything about the job and when possible can provide answers to some of the problem questions.

6

Moderate performance

5 — This engineer can be expected to work diligently on normal projects and contribute positively to completing these tasks on time.

Diplays an understanding of engineering job requirements when doing normal job

4 — This engineer can be expected to work late on projects and make every effort to complete projects.

3 — This engineer has difficulty working on nonroutine projects and many normal projects.

Lowest performance

2

Is only interested in routine jobs that require minimum engineering skills

1 — This engineer is confused and can be expected to hinder the completion of projects because of a lack of engineering knowledge.

predetermined groups, such as the top quarter, middle half, or bottom quarter. Still another variation is the **paired comparison** method, in which each employee is compared with every other employee. This method can become quite cumbersome as the total number of employees being compared increases.

A potentially important advantage of multiperson comparison methods is that they force raters to make distinctions between employees. A frequent problem in performance evaluation is the tendency to rate everyone as "above average" or "superior." This is particularly true when the rater must provide feedback to the employee being evaluated.[5] On the other hand, multiperson comparisons provide little or no specific information regarding *why* an employee's performance is rated the way it is. To learn that you are ranked 20th out of 24 employees may tell you your performance is not highly regarded, but provides you with no information you can use to improve it.

Improving Evaluations

Developing an effective performance evaluation system constitutes a critical and challenging task for management. This means, among other things, maximizing the use and acceptance of the evaluations while minimizing dissatisfaction with any aspect of the system. A full treatment of performance evaluation problems and methods of overcoming them is beyond the scope of our discussion here. We offer, however, the following suggestions for improving the effectiveness of virtually any evaluation system.

1. Higher levels of employee participation in the evaluation process leads to more satisfaction with the system.
2. Setting specific performance goals to be met results in greater performance improvement than discussions of more general goals.
3. Evaluating subordinates' performance is an important part of a supervisor's job; they should receive training in the process, and they should be evaluated on how effectively they discharge this part of their own job responsibilities.
4. Systematic evaluation of performance does little good if the results are not communicated to employees.
5. Performance evaluation feedback should not focus solely on problem areas; good performance should be actively recognized and reinforced.
6. Remember that while formal performance evaluation may take place on a set schedule (for example, annually), effective evaluation is a continuous ongoing process.

To the extent that performance is linked with the organization's reward system, then performance evaluation represents an attempt to influence the behavior of

[5] H.H. Meyer, "A Solution to the Performance Appraisal Feedback Enigma," *Academy of Management Executive*, February 1991, pp. 68–76.

organizational members. That is, it is an attempt to *reinforce* the continuation or elimination of certain actions. The basic assumption is that behavior is influenced by its consequences and that it is possible to affect behavior by controlling such consequences. Consequently, we begin our discussion of rewarding individual behavior by examining the topic of reinforcement.

REINFORCEMENT THEORY

Attempts to influence behavior through the use of rewards and punishments that are consequences of the behavior are called **operant conditioning**. Operants are behaviors that can be controlled by altering the consequences that follow them. Most workplace behaviors such as performing job-related tasks, reading a budget report, or coming to work on time are operants. A number of important principles of operant conditioning can aid the manager in attempting to influence behavior.

Reinforcement

Reinforcement is an extremely important principle of conditioning. Managers often use **positive reinforcers** to influence behavior. A positive reinforcer is a stimulus which, when added to the situation, strengthens the probability of a behavioral response. Thus, if the positive reinforcer has value to the person, it can be used to improve performance. (It should be noted, however, that a positive reinforcer which has value to one person may not have value to another person.) Sometimes **negative reinforcers** may be used. Negative reinforcement refers to an increase in the frequency of a response following removal of the negative reinforcer immediately after the response. As an example, exerting high degrees of effort to complete a job may be negatively reinforced by not having to listen to the "nagging" boss. That is, completing the job through increased effort (behavior) minimizes the likelihood of having to listen to a nagging stream of unwanted advice (negative reinforcer) from a superior.

Punishment

Punishment is defined as presenting an uncomfortable or unwanted consequence for a particular behavioral response. Some work-related factors that can be considered punishments include a superior's criticism, being fired, being suspended, receiving an undesirable transfer or assignment, or being demoted. Being laid off ■ E5–2 may be viewed as a punishment by some who complete Exercise 5–2 at the end of the chapter. While punishment can suppress behavior if used effectively, it is a controversial method of behavior modification in organizations. It should be employed only after careful and objective consideration of all the relevant aspects ▲ C5–2 of the situation. The Bob Collins case at the end of this chapter provides the reader with an opportunity to decide whether—and how—a particular act performed by Bob Collins should be punished.

Extinction

Extinction reduces unwanted behavior. When positive reinforcement for a learned response is withheld, individuals will continue to practice that behavior for some period of time. However, after a while, if the nonreinforcement continues, the behavior will decrease in frequency and intensity and will eventually disappear. The decline and eventual cessation of the response rate is known as extinction.

Reinforcement Schedules

It is extremely important to properly time the rewards or punishments used in an organization. The timing of these outcomes is called **reinforcement scheduling**. (See Exhibit 5-2) In the simplest schedule, the response is reinforced each time it occurs. This is called **continuous reinforcement**. If reinforcement occurs only after some instances of a response and not after each response, an **intermittent reinforcement** schedule is being used. From a practical viewpoint, it is virtually impossible to reinforce continually every desirable behavior. Consequently, in organizational settings, almost all reinforcement is intermittent in nature.

An intermittent schedule means that reinforcement does not occur after every acceptable behavior. The assumption is that learning is more permanent when correct behavior is rewarded only part of the time. Ferster and Skinner have presented four types of intermittent reinforcement schedules.[6] Briefly, the four are

1. **Fixed interval.** A reinforcer is applied only when the desired behavior occurs after the passage of a certain period of time since the last reinforcer was applied. An example would be to only praise positive performance once a week and not at other times. The fixed interval is one week.
2. **Variable interval.** A reinforcer applied at some variable interval of time. A promotion is an example.
3. **Fixed ratio.** A reinforcer is applied only if a fixed number of desired responses has occurred. An example would be paying a lathe operator a $10 bonus when the operator has produced 50 consecutive pieces which pass quality control inspection.
4. **Variable ratio.** A reinforcer is applied only after a number of desired responses, with the number of desired responses changing from situation to situation, around an average. For a classic example of a variable ratio schedule, consider Encounter 5-2.

Research on reinforcement schedules has shown that higher rates of response usually are achieved with ratio rather than interval schedules. This finding is understandable since high response rates do not necessarily speed

---

[6]C. B. Ferster and B. F. Skinner, *Schedules of Reinforcement* (New York: Appleton-Century-Crofts, 1957).

EXHIBIT 5-2

**Reinforcement Schedules
and Their Effects
on Behavior**

Schedule	Description	When Applied to Individual	When Removed by Manager	Organizational Example
Continuous	Reinforcer follows every response	Faster method for establishing new behavior	Faster method to cause extinction of new behavior	Praise after every response, immediate recognition of every response
Fixed interval	Response after specific time period is reinforced	Some inconsistency in response frequencies	Faster extinction of motivated behavior than variable schedules	Weekly, bimonthly, monthly paycheck
Variable interval	Response after varying period of time (an average) is reinforced	Produces high rate of steady responses	Slower extinction of motivated behavior than fixed schedules	Transfers, promotions, recognition
Fixed ratio	A fixed number of responses must occur before reinforcement	Some inconsistency in response frequenices	Faster extinction of motivated behavior than variable schedules	Piece rate, commission on units sold
Variable ratio	A varying number (average) of responses must occur before reinforcement	Can produce high rate of response that is steady and resists extinction	Slower extinction of motivated behavior than fixed schedules	Bonus, award, time off

Source: Adapted from O. Behling, C. Schriesheim, and J. Tolliver, "Present Theories and New Directions in Theories of Work Effort," *Journal of Supplement Abstract Service of the American Psychological Association*, 1974, p. 57.

up the delivery of a reinforcer in an interval schedule as they do with ratio schedules. Occasionally, however, reinforcement schedule research has produced unexpected findings. For example, one study compared the effects of continuous and variable ratio piece rate bonus pay plans. Contrary to predictions, the continuous schedule yielded the highest level of performance. One reason cited for the less-than-expected effectiveness of the variable ratio schedules was that some employees working on these schedules were opposed to the pay plan. They perceived the plan as a form of gambling, and this was not acceptable to them.[7]

Of the many reported applications of the principles of reinforcement, the most publicized has been the program at Emery Air Freight Company under

[7]G. Yukl, K. N. Wexley, and J. E. Seymore, "Effectiveness of Pay Incentives under Variable Ratio and Continuous Reinforcement Schedules," *Journal of Applied Psychology*, February 1977, pp. 19–23.

202   *Part II / The Individual in the Organization*

O R G A N I Z A T I O N A L
E N C O U N T E R • 5–2

REINFORCEMENT THEORY AND THE CASINO BOTTOM LINE

Reinforcement theory is alive and well among casino owners in Atlantic City, New Jersey, and Las Vegas, Nevada. These owners know how people react to reinforcement.

Most players of slot machines assume that jackpots occur according to some random reinforcement schedule. If the casino owners set the machines to pay off on a fixed-ratio schedule, then counting the number of pulls between each jackpot would be a successful technique. If the slots were on a fixed-interval schedule, then the player simply would have to watch the clock and time the occurrence of jackpots. The casino owners know that players are more likely to stay with the machine and feed in coins if there is a random-reinforcement schedule. Then the players have no idea when they will strike it rich. They must keep playing to win,

even once or twice. Thus, what we find in Atlantic City and Las Vegas is a program of random reinforcement.

The casino owners also know the value of atmosphere in keeping players at the machine. An atmosphere of excitement is created because people all around seem to be winning. The owners have accomplished this excitement by connecting each slot machine to a central control. Why? So that when any single slot machine hits a jackpot, sirens wail, lights flash, bells sound off, and screams of joy and displays of pleasure are heard and seen by everyone. The sights and sounds inform everyone that it pays to keep playing.

Does it work? Absolutely. Above all else, casino owners are business people. Their objective is to make a profit. They have learned that what keeps the slot machine player coming back more effectively than anything else is a variable ratio schedule of reinforcement.

---

the direction of Edward Feeney, a company executive.[8] The approach he used was (1) to regularly inform employees of how well they were meeting specific goals related to shipping-container usage and then (2) to reinforce improvement with praise and recognition. The results of the program were impressive. In 80 percent of the situations where it was applied, container usage increased from 45 percent to 95 percent. Savings from container usage alone amounted to over $500,000 a year and increased to $2 million during the first three years. As a result of these findings, Emery began using a similar reinforcement system for handling customer problems on the telephone and for estimating the container sizes needed for shipment of lightweight packages.

In addition to Emery, the list of companies relying on various schedules of reinforcement to reward employees includes Michigan Bell Telephone, Ford Motor Company, American Can Company, United Air Lines, Connecticut General Life Insurance Company, Chase Manhattan Bank, General Electric, Standard Oil of Ohio, and B. F. Goodrich Company. The results of some of these applications are summarized in Exhibit 5-3.

---

[8]At Emery Air Freight: Positive Reinforcement Boosts Performance," *Organizational Dynamics,* Winter 1973, p. 43.

EXHIBIT 5-3

Examples of the Use of Reinforcement Principles in Organizations

The Organization	Types of Employees	Goals of Program	Frequency of Feedback	Positive Reinforcers Applied	Results
Michigan Bell Telephone	Operating level (e.g., mechanics, maintenance workers)	Decrease turnover and absenteeism Increase productivity Improve union-management relations	Lower level — daily and weekly Higher level — monthly and quarterly	Praise and recognition Opportunity to see oneself improve	Attendance performance has improved by 50 percent Productivity and efficiency have continued to be above standard where positive reinforcement is being used
Connecticut General Life Insurance Company	Clerical and first-line supervisors	Decrease absenteeism Decrease lateness	Immediate	Self-feedback System feedback Earned time off	Chronic absenteeism and lateness have been drastically reduced Some divisions refused to use positive reinforcement because it was "outdated"
General Electric Company	Employees at all levels	Meet EEO objectives Decrease absenteeism and turnover Improve training Increase productivity	Immediate — uses modeling and role play as training tools to teach users	Praise Rewards Constructive feedback	Cost savings Increased productivity Increased self-esteem in minority groups Decreased direct labor cost
B. F. Goodrich Company	Manufacturing employees at all levels	Improve meeting of schedules Increase productivity	Weekly	Praise Recognition Freedom to choose one's own activity	Productivity increases of over 300 percent

Source: Adapted from W. Clay Hammer and Ellen P. Hammer, "Behavior Modification on the Bottom Line," *Organizational Dynamics*, Spring 1976, pp. 12–14.

A MODEL OF INDIVIDUAL REWARDS

A model that illustrates how rewards fit into the overall policies and programs of an organization can prove useful to managers. The main objectives of reward programs are: (1) to attract qualified people to *join* the organization, (2) to *keep* employees coming to work, and (3) to *motivate* employees to achieve high levels of performance. Exhibit 5-4 presents a model that attempts to integrate satisfaction, motivation, performance, and rewards. Reading the exhibit from left to right suggests that the motivation to exert effort is not enough to cause acceptable performance. Performance results from a combination of the effort of an individual and the individual's level of ability, skill, and experience. The performance results of the individual are evaluated either formally or informally by management, and two types of rewards can be distributed: intrinsic or extrinsic. The rewards are evaluated by the individual, and to the extent the rewards are satisfactory and equitable, the individual achieves a level of satisfaction.

A significant amount of research has been done on what determines whether individuals will be satisfied with rewards. Lawler has summarized five conclusions based on the behavioral science research literature. They are:

1. *Satisfaction with a reward is a function both of how much is received and of how much the individual feels should be received.* This conclusion is based on the comparisons that people make. When individuals receive less than they feel they should, they are dissatisfied.

2. *An individual's feelings of satisfaction are influenced by comparisons with what happens to others.* People tend to compare their efforts, skills, seniority, and job performance with those of others. They then attempt to compare rewards. That is, they compare their own inputs with the inputs of others relative to the rewards received. This input-outcome comparison was discussed when the equity theory of motivation was introduced in Chapter 4.

3. *Satisfaction is influenced by how satisfied employees are with both intrinsic and extrinsic rewards.* Intrinsic rewards are valued in and of themselves; they are related to performing the job. Examples would be feelings of accomplishment and achievement. Extrinsic rewards are external to the work itself; they are administered externally. Examples would be salary and wages, fringe benefits, and promotions. There is some debate among researchers as to whether intrinsic or extrinsic rewards are more important in determining job satisfaction. The debate has not been settled because most studies suggest that both rewards are important.[9] One clear message from the research is that extrinsic and intrinsic rewards satisfy different needs.

[9]T. R. Mitchell, "Motivation: New Directions for Theory, Research, and Practice," *Academy of Management Review,* January 1982, pp. 80–88.

EXHIBIT 5-4

The Reward Process

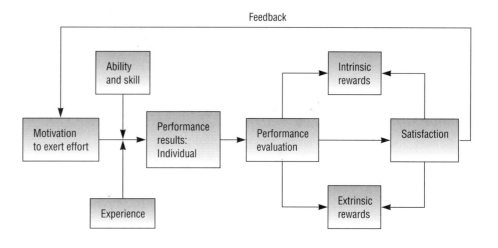

4. *People differ in the rewards they desire and in how important different rewards are to them.* Individuals differ on what rewards they prefer. In fact, preferred rewards vary at different points in a person's career, at different ages, and in various situations.

5. *Some extrinsic rewards are satisfying because they lead to other rewards.* For example, a large office or an office that has carpeting or drapes is often considered a reward because it indicates the individual's status and power. Money is a reward that leads to such things as prestige, autonomy and independence, security, and shelter.[10]

The relationship between rewards and satisfaction is not perfectly understood, nor is it static. It changes because people and the environment change. There are, however, some important considerations that managers could use to develop and distribute rewards. First, the rewards available must be sufficient to satisfy basic human needs. Federal legislation, union contracts, and managerial fairness have provided at least minimal rewards in most work settings. Second, individuals tend to compare their rewards with those of others. If inequities are perceived, dissatisfaction occurs. People make comparisons regardless of the quantity of the rewards they receive. Finally, the managers distributing rewards must recognize individual differences. Unless individual differences are considered, invariably the reward process is less effective than desired. Any reward package should (1) be sufficient to satisfy basic needs (e.g., food, shelter, clothing), (2) be considered equitable, and (3) be individually oriented.[11] To these could be added the very

---

[10] E. E. Lawler III, "Reward Systems," in *Improving Life at Work*, ed. J. R. Hackman and J. L. Suttle (Santa Monica, Calif.: Goodyear Publishing, 1977), pp. 163–226.

[11] Ibid., p. 168.

● **R5–1**   important point made by Steven Kerr in his article accompanying this chapter (Reading 5–1). For rewards to have their desired effect, they must reward the behavior that management wishes to encourage. Too often, as Kerr points out, what actually get rewarded are behaviors which the manager is trying to discourage.

INTRINSIC AND EXTRINSIC REWARDS

The rewards shown in Exhibit 5-3 are classified into two broad categories, extrinsic and intrinsic. Whether rewards are extrinsic or intrinsic, it is important to first consider the rewards valued by the person since an individual will put forth little effort unless the reward has value. Both extrinsic and intrinsic rewards

■ **E5–3**   can have value. Exercise 5–3 helps illustrate the facts that both intrinsic and extrinsic rewards are considered important, and that different individuals value different rewards.

Extrinsic Rewards

Financial Rewards: Salary and Wages

Money is a major extrinsic reward. It has been said, "Although it is generally agreed that money is the major mechanism for rewarding and modifying behavior in industry . . . very little is known about how it works."[12] To really understand how money modifies behavior, the perceptions and preferences of the person being rewarded must be understood. Of course, this is a challenging task for a manager to complete successfully. Unless employees can see a connection between performance and merit increases, money will not be a powerful motivator.

Many organizations utilize some type of incentive pay plan to motivate employees. Lawler presents the most comprehensive summary of the various pay plans and their effectiveness as motivators.[13] Each plan is evaluated on the basis of the following questions:

1. How effective is it in creating the perception that pay is related to performance?
2. How well does it minimize the perceived negative consequences of good performance?

---

[12]R. L. Opsahl and M. D. Dunnette, "The Role of Financial Compensation in Industrial Motivation," *Psychological Bulletin,* August 1966, p. 114.

[13]Edward E. Lawler III, Pay and Organizational Effects (New York: McGraw-Hill, 1971), pp. 164–70.

EXHIBIT 5-5

Evaluation of Pay-Incentive Plans in Organizations

Type of Pay Plan	Performance Criteria	Perceived Pay-Performance Linkage	Minimization of Negative Consquences	Perceived Relationship between Other Rewards and Performance
Salary plan:				
For individuals	Productivity	Good	Neutral	Neutral
	Cost effectiveness	Fair	Neutral	Neutral
	Superiors' rating	Fair	Netural	Fair
For group	Productivity	Fair	Neural	Fair
	Cost effectiveness	Fair	Neutral	Fair
	Superiors' rating	Fair	Neutral	Fair
For total organization	Productivity	Fair	Neutral	Fair
	Cost effectiveness	Fair	Neutral	Fair
	Profits	Neutral	Neutral	Fair
Bonus plan:				
For individuals	Productivity	Excellent	Poor	Neutral
	Cost effectiveness	Good	Poor	Neutral
	Superiors' rating	Good	Poor	Neutral
For group	Productivity	Good	Neutral	Fair
	Cost effectiveness	Good	Neutral	Fair
	Superiors' rating	Good	Neutral	Fair
For total organization	Productivity	Good	Neutral	Fair
	Cost effectiveness	Good	Neutral	Fair
	Profits	Fair	Neutral	Fair

Source: Adapted from Edward E. Lawler III, *Pay and Organizational Effectiveness* (New York: McGraw-Hill, 1971), table 9-3, p. 165.

3. How well does it contribute to the perception that important rewards other than pay (e.g., praise and interest shown in the employee by a respected superior) result in good performance? A summary of Lawler's ideas is presented in Exhibit 5-5.

Financial Rewards: Fringe Benefits

In the United States, organizations spend approximately $610 billion annually on employee benefits. In most cases, fringe benefits are primarily financial. Some fringe benefits, however, such as IBM's recreation program for employees and General Mills's picnic grounds, are not entirely financial. The major financial fringe benefit in most organizations is the pension plan, and for most employees, the opportunity to participate in the pension plan is a valued reward. Fringe benefits such as pension plans, hospitalization, and vacations usually are not contingent on the performance of employees, but are based on seniority or attendance.

Interpersonal Rewards

The manager has some power to distribute such interpersonal rewards as status and recognition. By assigning individuals to prestigious jobs, the manager can attempt to improve or remove the status a person possesses. However, if co-workers do not believe that a person merits a particular job, it is likely that status will not be enhanced. By reviewing performance, managers can, in some situations, grant what they consider to be job changes to improve status. The manager and co-workers both play a role in granting job status.

Promotions

For many employees, promotion does not happen often; some employees never experience it in their careers. The manager making a promotion reward decision attempts to match the right person with the job. Criteria often used to reach promotion decisions are performance and seniority. Performance, if it can be accurately assessed, is often given significant weight in promotion reward allocations.

Intrinsic Rewards

Completion

The ability to start and finish a project or job is important to some individuals. These people value what is called **task completion**. Some people have a need to complete tasks, and the effect that completing a task has on a person is a form of self-reward. Opportunities that allow such people to complete tasks can have a powerful motivating effect.

Achievement

Achievement is a self-administered reward that is derived when a person reaches a challenging goal. McClelland has found that there are individual differences in striving for achievement.[14] Some individuals seek challenging goals, while others tend to seek moderate or low goals. In goal-setting programs, it has been proposed that difficult goals result in a higher level of individual performance than do moderate goals. However, even in such programs, individual differences must be considered before reaching conclusions about the importance of achievement rewards.

Autonomy

Some people want jobs that provide them with the right and privilege to make decisions and operate without being closely supervised. A feeling of autonomy could result from the freedom to do what the employee considers best in a

---

[14]David C. McClelland, *The Achieving Society,* (New York: D. Van Nostrand, 1961).

particular situation. In jobs that are highly structured and controlled by management, it is difficult to create tasks that lead to a feeling of autonomy.

Personal Growth

The personal growth of any individual is a unique experience. An individual who is experiencing such growth senses his or her development and can see how his or her capabilities are being expanded. By expanding capabilities, a person is able to maximize or at least satisfy skill potential. Some people often become dissatisfied with their jobs and organizations if they are not allowed or encouraged to develop their skills.

The Interaction of Intrinsic and Extrinsic Rewards

The general assumption has been that intrinsic and extrinsic rewards have an independent and additive influence on motivation. That is, motivation is determined by the sum of the person's intrinsic and extrinsic sources of motivation.[15] This straightforward assumption has been questioned by several researchers. Some have suggested that in situations in which individuals are experiencing a high level of intrinsic rewards, the addition of extrinsic rewards for good performance may cause a decrease in motivation.[16] Basically, the person receiving self-administered feelings of satisfaction is performing because of intrinsic rewards. Once extrinsic rewards are added, feelings of satisfaction change because performance is now thought to be due to the extrinsic rewards. The addition of the extrinsic rewards tends to reduce the extent to which the individual experience self-administered intrinsic rewards.[17]

The argument concerning the potential negative effects of extrinsic rewards has stimulated a number of research studies. Unfortunately, these studies report contradictory results. Some researchers report a reduction in intrinsic rewards following the addition of extrinsic rewards for an activity.[18] Other researchers have failed to observe such an effect.[19] A review of the literature found that 14 of 24 studies reported the theory that extrinsic rewards reduced intrinsic

---

[15]D. C. Feldman and H. J. Arnold, *Managing Individual and Group Behavior in Organizations* (New York: McGraw-Hill, 1983), p. 164.

[16]E. L. Deci, "The Effects of Externally Mediated Rewards on Intrinsic Motivation," *Journal of Personality and Social Psychology*, 1971, pp. 105–15. Also, E. L. Deci, *Intrinsic Motivation* (New York: Plenum Press, 1975).

[17]B. M. Staw, *Intrinsic and Extrinsic Motivation* (Morristown, N.J.: General Learning Press, 1975).

[18]B. M. Staw, "The Attitudinal and Behavior Consequences of Changing a Major Organizational Reward," *Journal of Personality and Social Psychology*, June 1974, pp. 742–51.

[19]C. D. Fisher, "The Effects of Personal Control, Competence, and Extrinsic Reward Systems on Intrinsic Motivation," *Organizational Behavior and Human Performance*, June 1978; pp. 273–87. Also, J. S. Phillips and R. G. Lord, "Determinants of Intrinsic Motivation: Locus of Control and Competence Information as Components of Deci's Cognitive Evaluation Theory," *Journal of Applied Psychology*, April 1980, pp. 211–18.

motivation.[20] However, 10 of the 24 studies found no support for the reducing effect theory. Of the 24 studies reviewed, only two used actual employees as subjects. All of the other studies used college students or grade school students. In studies of telephone operators and clerical employees, the reducing effect theory was not supported.[21] Managers need to be aware that no scientifically based and reported study substantiates that extrinsic rewards have a negative effect on intrinsic motivation.

Administering Rewards

Managers are faced with the decision of how to administer rewards. Three major theoretical approaches to reward administration are: (1) positive reinforcement, (2) modeling and social imitation, and (3) expectancy.[22]

Positive Reinforcement

In administering a positive reinforcement program, the emphasis is on the desired behavior that leads to job performance rather than performance alone. The basic foundation of administering rewards through positive reinforcement is the relationship between behavior and its consequences. This relationship was discussed earlier in the chapter. While positive reinforcement can be a useful method of shaping desired behavior, other considerations concerning the type of reward schedule to use are also important. This relates to the discussion of continuous and intermittent schedules presented earlier. Suffice it to say that management should explore the possible consequences of different types of reward schedules for individuals. It is important to know how employees respond to continuous, fixed-interval, and fixed-ratio schedules.

Modeling and Social Imitation

There is little doubt that many human skills and behaviors are acquired by observational learning or, simply, imitation. Observational learning equips a person to duplicate a response, but whether the response actually is imitated depends on whether the model person was rewarded or punished for particular behaviors. If a person is to be motivated, he or she must observe models receiving reinforcements that are valued. In order to use modeling to administer rewards, managers

---

[20]K. B. Boone and L. L. Cummings, "Cognitive Evaluation Theory: An Experimental Test of Processes and Outcomes," *Organizational Behavior and Human Performance,* December 1981, pp. 289–310.

[21]E. M. Lopez, "A Test of Deci's Cognitive Evaluation Theory in an Organizational Setting" (Paper presented at the 39th annual convention of the Academy of Management, Atlanta, Georgia, August 1979).

[22]Lyman W. Porter "Turning Work into Nonwork. The Rewarding Environment," in *Work and Nonwork in the Year 2001,* ed. M. D. Dunnette (Belmont, Calif.: Wadsworth Publishing, 1973), p. 122, suggests three approaches. Porter introduces operant conditioning. We believe that when rewards are being discussed, positive reinforcement should be used.

must determine who responds to this approach. In addition, selecting appropriate models is a necessary step. Finally, the context in which modeling occurs needs to be considered. That is, if high performance is the goal and it is almost impossible to achieve that goal because of limited resources, the manager should conclude that modeling is not appropriate.[23]

Expectancy Theory

Some research suggests that expectancy theory constructs provide an important basis for classifying rewards.[24] From a rewards administration perspective, the expectancy approach, like the other two methods of administering rewards, requires managerial action. Managers must determine the kinds of rewards employees desire and do whatever is possible to distribute those rewards. Or they must create conditions so that what is available in the form of rewards can be applied. In some situations, it simply is not possible to provide the rewards that are valued and preferred. Therefore, managers often have to increase the desirability of other rewards.

A manager can, and often will, use principles from each of the three methods of administering rewards—positive reinforcement, modeling, and expectancy. Each of these methods indicates that employee job performance is a result of the application of effort. To generate the effort to perform, managers can use positive reinforcers, modeling, and expectations.

What combination of methods to use is not, of course, the only issue in administering rewards. Organizational resources, competitive influences, labor market constraints, and government regulations are but a few of the many factors which must be considered in developing and maintaining reward programs. One particular issue which is receiving increasing attention is that of gender equity in reward administration. As Encounter 5-3 illustrates, women's salaries still trail those of men, and to the extent this reflects gender differences within the same jobs it becomes at least an ethical issue if not a legal one.

REWARDS, TURNOVER, AND ABSENTEEISM

Some managers assume that high turnover is a mark of an effective organization. This view is somewhat controversial because a high quit rate means more expense for an organization. However, some organizations would benefit if disruptive and low performers quit.[25] Thus, the issue of turnover needs to focus on the *frequency* and on *who* is leaving.

---

[23]The discussion of Porter, "Turning Work into Nonwork," was used in the development of this section.

[24]R. Kanungo and J. Hartwick, "An Alternative to the Intrinsic-Extrinsic Dichotomy of Work Rewards," *Journal of Management*, Fall 1987, pp. 751–66.

[25]Dan. R. Dalton, David M. Krackhardt, and Lyman W. Porter, "Functional Turnover. An Empirical Assessment," *Journal of Applied Psychology*, December 1982, pp. 716–21.

ETHICS

ENCOUNTER · 5-3

ARE WOMEN RECEIVING EQUITABLE PAY TREATMENT?

There is no question that, on the average, employed women receive less pay than employed men. Based on 1990 U.S. Census Bureau figures, the average median yearly earnings for full-time women workers was only 71 percent of the comparable men's figures. This, of course, does not necessarily mean women are being treated inequitably or unethically; it could merely reflect differences in the types of jobs held by women and men.

But it most likely doesn't. This is because significant pay differentials exist *within* job categories, as well as across them. For example, based on the same 1990 figures, women's earnings as a percent of men's within job categories included the following: 66 percent for service workers, machine operators, assemblers, and inspectors; 65 percent for transportation workers; 64 percent for executives and managers; and 57 percent for sales. While other gaps are somewhat smaller, they exist for virtually every category of jobs. The gender gap in what are considered the prime earning years of age 35–44 is even larger; across all full-time workers in that age category, women's pay is equal to only 69 percent of men's.

The 1963 amendment to the Fair Labor Standards Act known as the Equal Pay Act requires equal pay for equal work for men and women. Equal work is defined as work requiring equal skills, effort, and responsibility under similar working conditions. Since the passage of this legislation, the female-male pay gap has clearly narrowed. As the figures cited above indicate, however, just as clearly there is a great deal that remains to be done.

A 1984 Supreme Court ruling permits women to bring suit on the grounds that they are paid less than men holding jobs of comparable worth based on job content evaluation. In this suit Washington County, Oregon, prison matrons claimed sex discrimination because male prison guards, whose jobs were somewhat different, received substantially higher pay. The county had evaluated the male's jobs as having 5 percent more job content than the female's jobs, but paid the males 35 percent more. That same year, the state of Washington began wage adjustments to approximately 15,000 employees. This was the first of several adjustments aimed at eliminating state pay differentials between predominately female and male jobs by 1993.

While there are frequently legitimate reasons for pay differentials between women and men in comparable jobs (length of service in the position, for example), unfair differences still exist. To reward job employees differently, based solely on gender, is not only unethical and illegal, it is poor business practice as well.

Ideally, if managers could develop reward systems that retained the best performers and caused poor performers to leave, the overall effectiveness of an organization would improve.[26] To approach this ideal state, an equitable and favorably compared reward system must exist. The feeling of **equity** and **favorable comparison** has an external orientation. That is, the equity of rewards and favorableness involves comparisons with external parties. This orientation is used because quitting most often means that a person leaves one organization for an alternative elsewhere.

[26]Dan R. Dalton and William D. Tudor, "Turnover: A Lucrative Hard Dollar Phenomenon," *Academy of Management Review,* April 1982, p. 212.

There is no perfect means for retaining high performers. It appears that a reward system based on **merit** should encourage most of the better performers to remain with the organization. There also has to be some differential in the reward system that discriminates between high and low performers, the point being that the high performers must receive significantly more extrinsic and intrinsic rewards than the low performers.

Absenteeism, no matter for what reason, is a costly and disruptive problem facing managers.[27] It is costly because it reduces output and disruptive because it requires that schedules and programs be modified. It is estimated that absenteeism in the United States results in the loss of more than 400 million workdays per year, or about 5.1 days per employee.[28] Employees go to work because they are motivated to do so. The level of motivation will remain high if an individual feels that attendance will lead to more valued rewards and fewer negative consequences than alternative behaviors.

Managers appear to have some influence over attendance behavior. They have the ability to punish, establish bonus systems, and allow employee participation in developing plans. Whether these or other approaches will reduce absenteeism is determined by the value of the rewards perceived by employees, the amount of the rewards, and whether employees perceive a relationship between attendance and rewards. These same characteristics appear every time we analyze the effects of rewards on organizational behavior.

REWARDS AND JOB PERFORMANCE

Behaviorists and managers agree that extrinsic and intrinsic rewards can be used to motivate job performance. It is also clear that certain conditions must exist if rewards are to motivate good job performance: the rewards must be valued by the person, and they must be related to the level of job performance that is to be motivated.[29]

In Chapter 4, expectancy motivation theory was presented. It was stated that, according to the theory, every behavior has associated with it (in a person's mind) certain outcomes or rewards or punishments. In other words, an assembly-line worker may believe that by behaving in a certain way, he or she will get certain things. This is a description of the **performance-outcome expectancy**. The worker may expect that a steady performance of 10 units a day eventually will result in transfer to a more challenging job. On the other hand, the worker may expect

---

[27]G. J. Blau and B. B. Kimberly, "Conceptualizing How Job Involvement and Organizational Commitment Affect Turnover and Absenteeism," *Academy of Management Review,* April 1987, pp. 288–300.

[28]Richard M. Steers and Susan R. Rhodes, "A New Look at Absenteeism," *Personnel,* November-December, 1980, pp. 60–65.

[29]Michael W. Spicer, "A Public Choice Approach to Motivating People in Bureaucratic Organizations," *Academy of Management Review,* July 1985, pp. 518–26.

that a steady performance of 10 units a day will result in being considered a rate-buster by co-workers.

Each outcome has a **valence** or value to the person. Outcomes such as pay, promotion, a reprimand, or a better job have different values for different people because each person has different needs and perceptions. Thus, in considering which rewards to use, a manager has to be astute at considering individual differences. If valued rewards are used to motivate, they can result in the exertion of effort to achieve high levels of performance. Reading 5–2, "Rewards and Recognition," at the end of this chapter emphasizes the relationship between rewards and performance. It cites, for example, a review of 300 studies which concluded that when pay is linked to performance, motivation, productivity, and satisfaction are all higher.

● **R5–2**

REWARDS AND ORGANIZATIONAL COMMITMENT

There is little research on the relationship between rewards and organizational commitment. **Commitment** to an organization involves three attitudes: (1) a sense of identification with the organization's goals, (2) a feeling of involvement in organizational duties, and (3) a feeling of loyalty for the organization.[30] Research evidence indicates that the absence of commitment can reduce organizational effectiveness.[31] People who are committed are less likely to quit and accept other jobs. Thus, the costs of high turnover are not incurred. In addition, committed and highly skilled employees require less supervision. Close supervision and a rigid monitoring control process are time-consuming and costly. Furthermore, a committed employee perceives the value and importance of integrating individual and organizational goals. The employee thinks of his or her goals and the organization's goals in personal terms.

Intrinsic rewards are especially important for the development of organizational commitment. Organizations able to meet employee needs by providing achievement opportunities and by recognizing achievement when it occurs have a significant impact on commitment. Thus, managers need to develop intrinsic reward systems that focus on personal importance or self-esteem, to integrate individual and organizational goals, and to design challenging jobs.

Innovative Reward Systems

The typical list of rewards that managers can and do distribute in organizations has been discussed. We all know that pay, fringe benefits, and opportunities to achieve challenging goals are considered rewards by most people. It is also gen-

[30]Amon E. Reichers, "A Review and Reconceptualization of Organizational Commitment," *Academy of Management Review*, July 1985, pp. 465–76.

[31]R. T. Mowday, L. W. Porter, and R. M. Steers, *Employee-Organization Linkages* (New York: Academic Press, 1982).

Reward Approach	Major Strengths	Major Weaknesses	Research Support
Cafeteria-style fringe benefits	Since employees have different desires and needs, programs can be tailored to fit individuals	Administration can become complex and costly. The more employees involved, the more difficult it is to efficiently operate the approach.	Limited since only a few programs have been scientifically examined.
Banking time off	Can be integrated with performance in that time-off credits can be made contingent on performance achievements.	Requires that an organization have valid, reliable, and equitable performance appraisal program.	Extremely limited.
All-salaried teams	Eliminates treating some employees as insiders and some as outsiders. Everyone is paid a salary and is a member of the team.	Assumes that everyone wants to be a team member and paid a salary. Some individuals value being nonmanagers and nonsalaried.	None available.
Skill-based pay	Employees must clearly demonstrate skill before receiving any pay increases.	Training costs to upgrade employee skills are higher than under conventional pay systems.	Very limited with no direct skill-based versus conventional pay compensation studies available.

erally accepted that rewards are administered by managers through such processes as reinforcement, modeling, and expectancies. What are some of the newer and innovative, yet largely untested, reward programs that some managers are experimenting with? Four different approaches to rewards that are not widely tested are cafeteria-style fringe benefits, banking time off, paying all employees a salary, and skill-based pay. The strengths and weaknesses of these four approaches are summarized in Exhibit 5-6.

Cafeteria-Style Fringe Benefits

In a cafeteria-style plan, management places an upper limit on how much the organization is willing to spend to fringe benefits. Employees then decide how they would like to receive the total fringe benefit amount and develop individual, personally attractive fringe benefit packages. Some employees take all of the fringes in cash; others purchase special medical protection plans. The cafeteria plan provides individuals with the benefits they prefer rather than the benefits that someone else establishes for them.

Using a cafeteria-style plan has some distinct advantages. First, it allows employees to play an active role instead of a passive role in making decisions about the allocation of fringe benefits. Second, employees receive benefits that have the greatest personal value to them. This provides many people with a psychologically uplifting feeling. Third, the cafeteria-style plan makes the economic value of fringe benefits obvious to each employee. It highlights the value of fringes. In many situations, employees grossly underestimate the value of their employer's fringe benefits.

Some administrative problems are associated with cafeteria plans.[32] Because of the different preferences of employees, records become more complicated. For a large organization with a cafeteria plan, a computer system is almost essential to do the record keeping. Another problem involves group insurance premium rates. Most life and medical insurance premiums are based on the number of employees participating. It is difficult to predict the participation level under a cafeteria plan.

TRW Inc. has placed approximately 12,000 employees on a cafeteria plan. It allows employees to rearrange and redistribute their fringe benefit packages every year. Over 80 percent of the TRW participants have changed their benefit packages since the plan was initiated.[33]

Banking Time Off

Time off from work is attractive to most people. In essence, most companies have a time-off system built into their vacation programs. Employees receive different amounts of time off based on the years they have worked for the organization. An extension of such a time-off reward could be granted for certain levels of performance. That is, a bank of time-off credits could be built up contingent on performance achievements.

Today, some organizations are selecting their best performers to attend educational and training programs. One company in Houston selects the best performers and provides them with an opportunity to attend an executive educational program. Being eligible is largely contingent on the performance record of the individual. Those finally selected are given two Fridays off a month to attend classes.

The All-Salaried Team

In most organizations, managers are paid salaries, and nonmanagers receive hourly wages. The practice of paying all employees a salary is supposed to improve loyalty, commitment, and self-esteem. The notion of being a part of a team is projected by the salary-for-everyone practice. One benefit of the all-salary practice considered important by nonmanagers is that it eliminates punching a time clock. To date, rigorous investigations of the influence, if any, of the all-salary practice are not available. It does seem to have promise when applied to some employees.

---

[32]J. H. Shea, "Cautions about Cafeteria-Style Benefit Plans," *Personnel Journal,* January 1981, p. 37.

[33]Lawler, "Reward Systems," p. 182.

The link between the performance evaluation system and reward distribution was shown in Exhibit 5-3. The discussion of this and other linkages in the reward process suggests the complexity of using rewards to motivate better performance. Managers need to use judgment, diagnosis, and the resources available to reward their subordinates. Administering rewards is perhaps one of the most challenging and frustrating tasks that managers must perform.

Skill-Based Pay

Skill-based pay is being used by a growing number of firms.[34] In traditional compensation systems, workers are paid on the basis of their jobs. The hourly wage rate depends primarily on the job performed. In a skill-based plan, employees are paid at a rate based on their personal skills. Typically, employees start at a basic initial rate of pay; they receive increases as their skills develop. Their pay rates are based on skill levels, no matter which jobs they are assigned.

In conventional pay systems, the job determines the pay rate and range. In the skill-based plan, however, the skills developed by employees are the key pay determinants. The skill-based pay plan approximates how professionals are compensated. In many organizations, professionals who do similar work are difficult to separate in terms of contributions made. Thus, surveys of what other firms pay professionals are used to establish pay grades and maturity curves. In skill-based plans, pay increases are not given at any specific time because of seniority.[35] Instead, a raise is granted when employees demonstrate their skills to perform particular jobs.

One study of two firms, a U.S. automobile manufacturer and a container manufacturer, suggests that skill-based pay plans have some unique motivational value. Workers in these plants displayed more motivation to develop their job skills, were more satisfied with pay, identified more closely with their job tasks, and were rotated more frequently from job to job.

SUMMARY OF KEY POINTS

- Among the major purposes which performance evaluation can serve are (1) providing a basis for reward allocation, (2) identifying high-potential employees, (3) validating the effectiveness of employee selection procedures, (4) evaluating previous training programs, and (5) facilitating future performance improvement.

- There are a number of different methods available for evaluating employee performance. Some of the more frequently used methods include checklists, critical incidents, graphic rating scales, and behaviorally anchored rating scales. Additional methods, available for making multiperson comparisons, include straight rankings, group order rankings, and paired comparisons.

- Reinforcement theory suggests that behavior is influenced by its consequences and that it is possible to affect behavior by controlling such consequences. Desired

[34]H. Tosi and L. Tosi, "What Managers Need to Know about Knowledge-Based Pay," *Organizational Dynamics,* Winter 1986, p. 52–64.

[35]G. E. Ledford, Jr., "Skill-Based Pay: A Concept that's Catching On," *Personnel,* September 1985, pp. 20–26.

behaviors are reinforced through the use of rewards, while undesired behaviors can be extinguished through punishment. The timing of rewards and punishments is extremely critical and is controlled through the use of various *reinforcement schedules.*

- A useful model of individual rewards would include the suggestion that ability, skill, and experience, in addition to motivation, result in various levels of individual performance. The resulting performance is then evaluated by management, who can distribute two types of rewards: intrinsic and/or extrinsic. These rewards are evaluated by the individual receiving them, and to the extent they result in satisfaction, motivation to perform is enhanced.

- Organizational rewards can be classified as either extrinsic or intrinsic. Extrinsic rewards include salary and wages, fringe benefits, promotions, and certain types of interpersonal rewards. Extrinsic rewards can include such things as a sense of completion, achievement, autonomy, and personal growth.

- An effective reward system would encourage the best performers to remain with the organization, while causing the poorer performers to leave. To accomplish this the system must be perceived as equitable. Additionally, the reward system should minimize the incidents of absenteeism. Generally, absenteeism will be less if an employee feels that attendance will lead to more valued rewards and fewer negative consequences.

- Both extrinsic and intrinsic rewards can be used to motivate job performance. For this to occur, certain conditions must exist: the rewards must be valued by the employee, and they must be related to the level of job performance that is to be motivated.

- In addition to standard organizational rewards such as pay, fringe benefits, advancement, and opportunities for growth, some organizations are experimenting with more innovative reward programs. Examples of such approaches include cafeteria-style benefits, banking time off, all-salaried teams, and skill-based pay.

REVIEW AND DISCUSSION QUESTIONS

1. What are the major organizational purposes served by formal performance evaluation systems? Are different methods of performance evaluation best suited for each major purpose? Explain.

2. If you were designing a system to evaluate the performance of the instructor in this class, what method, or combination of methods, discussed in this chapter would you use? Why?

3. Evaluations of employees should not only focus on job performance, but should include proper weighting of relevant behaviors. What are the three aspects of relevancy in the context of performance evaluations? Are any one of these more or less important than the others?

4. From a managerial perspective, why is it impractical to provide continuous reinforcement in work environments? If it were practical, would it be a good idea? Why or why not?

5. The degree of employee satisfaction with the organization's reward system will significantly affect how successful the system is in influencing performance. Based on the research literature, what do we know

about what influences whether individuals will be satisfied with the rewards they receive?

6. What are some of the problems that must be overcome to successfully administer a merit pay plan in an organization? What solutions can you offer for these problems?

7. What are the three major approaches to reward administration discussed in the chapter? Give an example of each of them.

8. Do you think rewards are more important in attracting people to the organization, keeping people in the organization, or motivating people to higher levels of performance? Explain.

9. What are the examples of innovative reward systems discussed in the chapter? Can you suggest other innovative approaches organizations might use? Identify potential problems with the approaches you suggest and try to find ways of overcoming them.

10. Given its costs, under what conditions do you think a BARS evaluation system is a justified approach to evaluating employees? Explain.

●

READINGS

READING 5-1 ON THE FOLLY OF REWARDING A, WHILE HOPING FOR B

Steven Kerr

Whether dealing with monkeys, rats, or human beings, it is hardly controversial to state that most organisms seek information concerning what activities are rewarded, and then seek to do (or at least pretend to do) those things, often to the virtual exclusion of activities not rewarded. The extent to which this occurs of course will depend on the perceived attractiveness of the rewards offered, but neither operant nor expectancy theorists would quarrel with the essence of this notion.

Nevertheless, numerous examples exist of reward systems that are fouled up in that behaviors which are rewarded are those which the rewarded is trying to *discourage,* while the behavior he desires is not being rewarded at all.

In an effort to understand and explain this phenomenon, this paper presents examples from society, from organizations in general, and from profit-making firms in particular. Data from a manufacturing company and information from an insurance firm are examined to demonstrate the consequences of such reward systems for the organizations involved, and possible reasons why such reward systems continue to exist are considered.

SOCIETAL EXAMPLES

Politics

Official goals are "purposely vague and general and do not indicate . . . the host of decisions that must be made among alternative ways of achieving official goals and the priority of multiple goals . . ." They usually may be relied on to offend absolutely no one, and in this sense can be considered high-acceptance, low-quality goals. An example might be "build better schools." Operative goals are higher in quality but lower in acceptance, since they specify where the money will come from, what alternative goals will be ignored, etc.

The American citizenry supposedly wants its candidates for public office to set forth operative goals, making their

proposed programs "perfectly clear," specifying sources and uses of funds, etc. However, since operative goals are lower in acceptance, and since aspirants to public office need acceptance (from at least 50.1 percent of the people), most politicians prefer to speak only of official goals, at least until after the election. They of course would agree to speak at the operative level if "punished" for not doing so. The electorate could do this by refusing to support candidates who do not speak at the operative level.

Instead, however, the American voter typically punishes (withholds support from) candidates who frankly discuss where the money will come from, rewards politicians who speak only of official goals, but hopes that candidates (despite the reward system) will discuss the issues operatively. It is academic whether it was moral for Nixon, for example, to refuse to discuss his 1968 "secret plan" to end the Vietnam war, his 1972 operative goals concerning the lifting of price controls, the reshuffling of his cabinet, etc. The point is that the reward system made such refusal rational.

It seems worth mentioning that no manuscript can adequately define what is "moral" and what is not. However, examination of costs and benefits, combined with knowledge of what motivates a particular individual, often will suffice to determine what for him is "rational."[1] If the reward system is so designed that it is irrational to be moral, this does not necessarily mean that immorality will result. But is this not asking for trouble?

War

If some oversimplification may be permitted, let it be assumed that the primary goal of the organization (Pentagon, Luftwaffe, or whatever) is to win. Let it be assumed further that the primary goal of most individuals on the front lines is to get home alive. Then there appears to be an important conflict in goals—personally rational behavior by those at the bottom will endanger goal attainment by those at the top.

But not necessarily! It depends on how the reward system is set up. The Vietnam war was indeed a study of disobedience and rebellion, with terms such as *fragging*

Source: Reprinted with permission from *Academy of Management Journal,* December 1975, pp. 769–83.

(killing one's own commanding officer) and *search and evade* becoming part of the military vocabulary. The difference in subordinates' acceptance of authority between World War II and Vietnam is reported to be considerable, and veterans of the Second World War often have been quoted as being outraged at the mutinous actions of many American soldiers in Vietnam.

Consider, however, some critical differences in the reward system in use during the two conflicts. What did the GI in World War II want? To go home. And when did he get to go home? When the war was won! If he disobeyed the orders to clean out the trenches and take the hills, the war would not be won and he would not go home. Furthermore, what were his chances of attaining his goal (getting home alive) if he obeyed the orders compared to his chances if he did not? What is being suggested is that the rational soldier in World War II, *whether patriotic or not,* probably found it expedient to obey.

Consider the reward system in use in Vietnam. What did the man at the bottom want? To go home. And when did he get to go home? When his tour of duty was over! This was the case *whether or not* the war was won. Furthermore, concerning the relative chance of getting home alive by obeying orders compared to the chance if they were disobeyed, it is worth noting that a mutineer in Vietnam was far more likely to be assigned rest and rehabilitation (on the assumption that fatigue was the cause) than he was to suffer any negative consequence.

In his description of the "zone of indifference," Barnard stated that "a person can and will accept a communication as authoritative only when . . . at the time of his decision, he believes it to be compatible with his personal interests as a whole." In light of the reward system used in Vietnam, would it not have been personally irrational for some orders to have been obeyed? Was not the military implementing a system which *rewarded* disobedience, while *hoping* that soldiers (despite the reward system) would obey orders?

Medicine

Theoretically, a physician can make either of two types of error, and intuitively one seems as bad as the other. A doctor can pronounce a patient sick when he is actually well, thus causing him needless anxiety and expense, curtailment of enjoyable foods and activities, and even physical danger by subjecting him to needless medication and surgery. Alternatively, a doctor can label a sick person well, and thus avoid treating what may be a serious, even fatal ailment. It might be natural to conclude that physicians seek to minimize both types of error.

Such a conclusion would be wrong.[2] It is estimated that numerous Americans are presently afflicted with iatrogenic (physician **caused**) illnesses. This occurs when the doctor is approached by someone complaining of a few stray symptoms. The doctor classifies and organizes these symptoms, gives then a name, and obligingly tells the patient what further symptoms may be expected. This information often acts as a self-fulfilling prophecy, with the result that from that day on the patient for all practical purposes is sick.

Why does this happen? Why are physicians so reluctant to sustain a type 2 error (pronouncing a sick person well) that they will tolerate many type 1 errors? Again, a look at the reward system is needed. The punishments for a type 2 error are real: guilt, embarrassment, and the threat of a lawsuit and scandal. On the other hand, a type 1 error (labeling a well person sick) "is sometimes seen as sound clinical practice, indicating a healthy conservative approach to medicine." Type 1 errors also are likely to generate increased income and a stream of steady customers who, being well in a limited physiological sense, will not embarrass the doctor by dying abruptly.

Fellow physicians and the general public therefore are really *rewarding* type 1 errors and at the same time *hoping* fervently that doctors will try not to make them.

GENERAL ORGANIZATIONAL EXAMPLES

Rehabilitation Centers and Orphanages

In terms of the prime beneficiary classification, organizations such as these are supposed to exist for the "public-in-contact," that is, clients. The orphanage therefore theoretically is interested in placing as many children as possible in good homes. However, often orphanages surround themselves with so many rules concerning adoptions that it is nearly impossible to pry a child out of the place. Orphanages may deny adoption unless the applicants are a married couple, both of the same religion as the child, without history of emotional or vocational instability, with a specified minimum income and a private room for the child, etc.

If the primary goal is to place children in good homes, then the rules ought to constitute means toward that goal. Goal displacement results when these "means become ends-in-themselves that displace the original goals."

To some extent these rules are required by law. But the influence of the reward system on the orphanage's management should not be ignored. Consider, for example, that the:

1. Number of children enrolled often is the most important determinant of the size of the allocated budget.
2. Number of children under the director's care also will affect the size of his staff.
3. Total organizational size will determine largely the director's prestige at the annual conventions, in the community, etc.

Therefore, to the extent that the staff size, total budget, and personal prestige are valued by the orphanage's executive personnel, it becomes rational for them to make it difficult for children to be adopted. After all, who wants to be the director of the smallest orphanage in the state?

If the reward system errs in the opposite direction, paying off only for placements, extensive goal displacement again is likely to result. A common example of vocational rehabilitation in many states, for example, consists of placing someone in a job for which he has little interest and few qualifications, for two months or so, and then "rehabilitating" him again in another position. Such behavior is quite consistent with the prevailing reward system, which pays off for the number of individuals placed in any position for 60 days or more. Rehabilitation counselors also confess to competing with one another to place relatively skilled clients, sometimes ignoring persons with few skills who would be harder to place. Extensively disabled clients found that counselors often prefer to work with those whose disabilities are less severe.[3]

Universities

Society *hopes* that teachers will not neglect their teaching responsibilities but *rewards* them almost entirely for research and publications. This is most true at the large and prestigious universities. Clichés such as "good research and good teaching go together" notwithstanding, professors often find that they must choose between teaching and research-oriented activities when allocating their time. Rewards for good teaching usually are limited to outstanding teacher awards, which are given to only a small percentage of good teachers and which usually bestow little money and fleeting prestige. Punishments for poor teaching are also rare.

Rewards for research and publications, on the other hand, and punishments for failure to accomplish these, are commonly administered by universities at which teachers are employed. Furthermore, publication-oriented resumés usually will be well received at other universities, whereas teaching credentials, harder to document and quantify, are much less transferable. Consequently it is rational for university teachers to concentrate on research, even if to the detriment of teaching and at the expense of their students.

By the same token, it is rational for students to act based upon the goal displacement which has occurred within universities concerning what they are rewarded for. If it is assumed that a primary goal of a university is to transfer knowledge from teacher to student, then grades become identifiable as a means toward that goal, serving as motivational, control, and feedback devices to expedite the knowledge transfer. Instead, however, the grades themselves have become much more important for entrance to graduate school, successful employment, tuition refunds, parental respect, etc., than the knowledge or lack of knowledge they are supposed to signify.

It therefore should come as no surprise that information has surfaced in recent years concerning fraternity files for examinations, term-paper writing services, organized cheating at the service academies, and the like. Such activities constitute a personally rational response to a reward system which pays off for grades rather than knowledge.

BUSINESS-RELATED EXAMPLES

Ecology

Assume that the president of XYZ Corporation is confronted with the following alternatives:

1. Spend $11 billion for antipollution equipment to keep from poisoning fish in the river adjacent to the plant; or
2. Do nothing, in violation of the law, and assume a 1 in 10 chance of being caught, with a resultant $1 million fine plus the necessity of buying the equipment.

Under this not unrealistic set of choices, it requires no linear program to determine that XYZ Corporation can maximize its probabilities by flouting the law. Add the fact that XYZ's president is probably being rewarded (by creditors, stockholders, and other salient parts of his task environment) according to criteria totally unrelated to the number of fish poisoned, and his probable course of action becomes clear.

Evaluation of Training

It is axiomatic that those who care about a firm's well-being should insist that the organization get fair value for its expenditures. Yet it is commonly known that firms seldom bother to evaluate a new GRID, MBO, job enrichment program, or whatever, to see if the company is getting its money's worth. Why? Certainly it is not because people have not pointed out that this situation exists; numerous practitioner-oriented articles are written each year to just this point.

The individuals (whether in personnel, manpower planning, or wherever) who normally would be responsible for conducting such evaluations are the same ones often charged with introducing the change effort in the first place. Having convinced top management to spend the money, they usually are quite animated afterwards in collecting arigorous vignettes and anecdotes about how successful the program was. The last thing many desire is a formal, systematic, and revealing evaluation. Although members of top management may actually *hope* for such systematic evaluation, their reward systems continue to *reward* ignorance in this area. And if the personnel department abdicates its responsibility, who is to step into the breach? The change agent himself? Hardly! He is likely to be too busy collecting anecdotal "evidence" of his own, for use with his next client.

Miscellaneous

Many additional examples could be cited of systems which in fact are rewarding behaviors other than those supposedly desired by the rewarder A few of these are described briefly below.

Most coaches disdain to discuss individual accomplishments, preferring to speak of teamwork, proper attitude, and a one-for-all spirit. Usually, however, rewards are distributed according to individual performance. The college basketball player who feeds his teammates instead of shooting will not compile impressive scoring statistics and is less likely to be drafted by the pros. The ballplayer who hits to right field to advance the runners will win neither the batting nor home run titles, and will be offered smaller raises. It therefore is rational for players to think of themselves first, and the team second.

In business organizations where rewards are dispensed for unit performance or for individual goals achieved, without regard for overall effectiveness, similar attitudes often are observed. Under most Management by Objectives (MBO)

systems, goals in areas where quantification is difficult often go unspecified. The organization therefore often is in a position where it *hopes* for employee effort in the areas of team building, interpersonal relations, creativity, etc., but it formally *rewards* none of these. In cases where promotions and raises are formally tied to MBO, the system itself contains a paradox in that it "asks employees to set challenging, risky goals, only to face smaller paychecks and possibly damaged careers if these goals are not accomplished."

It is *hoped* that administrators will pay attention to long-run costs and opportunities and will institute programs which will bear fruit later on. However, many organizational reward systems pay off for shorter-run sales and earnings only. Under such circumstances it is personally rational for officials to sacrifice long-term growth and profit (by selling off equipment and property, or by stifling research and development) for short-term advantages. This probably is most pertinent in the public sector, with the result that many public officials are unwilling to implement programs which will not show benefits by election time.

As a final, clear-cut example of a fouled-up reward system, consider the cost-plus contract or its next of kin, the allocation of next year's budget as a direct function of this year's expenditures. It probably is conceivable that those who award such budgets and contracts really hope for economy and prudence in spending. It is obvious, however, that adopting the proverb "to him who spends shall more be given," rewards not economy, but spending itself.

TWO COMPANIES' EXPERIENCE

A Manufacturing Organization

A midwest manufacturer of industrial goods had been troubled for some time by aspects of its organizational climate it believed dysfunctional. For research purposes, interviews were conducted with many employees and a questionnaire was administered on a companywide basis, including plants and offices in several American and Canadian locations. The company strongly encouraged employee participation in the survey, and made available time and space during the workday for completion of the instrument. All employees in attendance during the day of the survey completed the questionnaire. All instruments were collected directly by the researcher, who personally administered each session. Since no one employed by the firm handled the questionnaire, and since respondent names were not asked for, it seems likely that the pledge of anonymity given was believed.

A modified version of the Expect Approval scale was included as part of the questionnaire. The instrument asked respondents to indicate the degree of approval or disapproval they could expect if they performed each of the described actions. A seven-point Likert scale was used, with 1 indicating that the action would probably bring strong disapproval and 7 signifying likely strong approval.

Although normative data for this scale from studies of other organizations are unavailable, it is possible to examine fruitfully the data obtained from this survey in several ways. First, it may be worth noting that the questionnaire data corresponded closely to information gathered through interviews. Furthermore, as can be seen from the results summarized in Exhibit 5-7, sizable differences between various work units, and between employees at different job levels within the same work unit, were obtained. This suggests that response bias effects (social desirability in particular loomed as a potential concern) are not likely to be severe.

Most importantly, comparisons between scores obtained on the Expect Approval scale and a statement of problems which were the reason for the survey revealed that the same behaviors which managers in each division thought dysfunctional were those which lower level employees claimed were rewarded. As compared to job levels 1 to 8 in Division B (see Exhibit 5-7), those in Division A claimed a much higher acceptance by management of "conforming" activities. Between 31 and 37 percent of Division A employees at levels 1–8 stated that going along with the majority, agreeing with the boss, and staying on everyone's good side brought approval; only once (level 5–8 responses to one of the three items) did a majority suggest that such actions would generate disapproval.

Furthermore, responses from Division A workers at levels 1–4 indicate that behaviors geared toward risk avoidance were as likely to be rewarded as to be punished. Only at job levels 9 and above was it apparent that the reward system was positively reinforcing behaviors desired by top management. Overall, the same "tendencies toward conservatism and apple-polishing at the lower levels" which divisional management had complained about during interviews were those claimed by subordinates to be the most rational course of action in light of the existing reward system. Management apparently was not getting the behaviors it was *hoping* for, but it certainly was getting the behaviors it was perceived by subordinates to be *rewarding*.

An Insurance Firm

The Group Health Claims Division of a large eastern insurance company provides another rich illustration of a reward system which reinforces behaviors not desired by top management.

Attempting to measure and reward accuracy in paying surgical claims, the firm systematically keeps track of the number of returned checks and letters of complaint received from policyholders. However, underpayments are likely to provoke cries of outrage from the insured, while overpayments often are accepted in courteous silence. Since it often is impossible to tell from the physician's statement which of two surgical procedures, with different allowable benefits, was performed, and since writing for clarifications will interfere with other standards used by the firm concerning "percentage of claims paid within two days of receipt," the new hire in more than one claims section is soon acquainted with the informal norm: "When in doubt, pay it out!"

The situation would be even worse were it not for the fact that other features of the firm's reward system tend to neutralize those described. For example, annual "merit" increases are given to all employees, in one of the following three amounts:

1. If the worker is "outstanding" (a select category, into which no more than two employees per section may be placed): 5 percent
2. If the worker is "above average" (normally all workers not "outstanding" are so rated): 4 percent
3. If the worker commits gross acts of negligence and irresponsibility for which he might be discharged in many other companies: 3 percent.

Now, since (*a*) the difference between the 5 percent theoretically attainable through hard work and the 4 percent attainable merely by living until the review date is small and (*b*) since insurance firms seldom dispense much of a salary increase in cash (rather, the worker's insurance benefits increase, causing him to be further overinsured), many employees are rather indifferent to the possibility of obtaining the extra 1 percent reward and therefore tend to ignore the norm concerning indiscriminant payments.

However, most employees are not indifferent to the rule which states that, should absences or latenesses total three or more in any six-month period, the entire 4 or 5 percent due at the next "merit" review must be forfeited. In this sense the firm may be described as *hoping* for performance, while *rewarding* attendance. What it gets, of course, is

EXHIBIT 5-7

**Summary of Two Divisions'
Data Relevant to
Conforming and Risk-
Avoidance Behaviors
(extent to which
subjects expect approval)**

Dimension	Item	Division and Sample	Total Responses	Percentage of Workers Responding		
				1, 2, or 3 (Disapproval)	4	5, 6, or 7 (Approval)
Risk avoidance	Making a risky decision based on the best information available at the time, but which turns out wrong.	A, levels 1–4 (lowest)	127	61	25	14
		A, levels 5–8	172	46	31	23
		A, levels 9 and above	17	41	30	30
		B, levels 1–4 (lowest)	31	58	26	16
		B, levels 5–8	19	42	42	16
		B, levels 9 and above	10	50	20	30
Risk	Setting extremely high and challenging standards and goals, and then narrowly failing to make them.	A, levels 1–4	122	47	28	25
		A, levels 5–8	168	33	26	41
		A, levels 9 +	17	24	6	70
		B, levels 1–4	31	48	23	29
		B, levels 5–8	18	17	33	50
		B, levels 9 +	10	30	0	70
	Setting goals which are extremely easy to make and then making them.	A, levels 1–4	124	35	30	35
		A, levels 5–8	171	47	27	26
		A, levels 9 +	17	70	24	6
		B, levels 1–4	31	58	26	16
		B, levels 5–8	19	63	16	21
		B, levels 9 +	10	80	0	20
	Being a "yes man" and always agreeing with the boss.	A, levels 1–4	126	46	17	37
		A, levels 5–8	180	54	14	31
		A, levels 9 +	17	88	12	0
		B, levels 1–4	32	53	28	19
		B, levels 5–8	19	68	21	11
		B, levels 9 +	10	80	10	10
	Always going along with the majority.	A, levels 1–4	125	40	25	35
		A, levels 5–8	173	47	21	32
		A, levels 9 +	17	70	12	18
		B, levels 1–4	31	61	23	16
		B, levels 5–8	18	68	11	21
		B, levels 9 +	10	80	10	10
	Being careful to stay on the good side of everyone, so that everyone agrees that you are a great guy.	A, levels 1–4	124	45	18	37
		A, levels 5–8	173	45	22	33
		A, levels 9 +	17	64	6	30
		B, levels 1–4	31	54	23	23
		B, levels 5–8	19	73	11	16
		B, levels 9 +	10	80	10	10

attendance. If the absence-lateness rule appears to the reader to be stringent, it really is not. The company counts "times" rather than "days" absent, and a 10-day absence therefore counts the same as one lasting 2 days. A worker in danger of accumulating a third absence within six months merely has to remain ill (away from work) during his second absence until his first absence is more than six months old. The limiting factor is that at some point his salary ceases, and his sickness benefits take over. This usually is sufficient to get the younger workers to return, but for those with 20 or more years' service, the company provides sickness benefits of 90 percent of normal salary, tax-free! Therefore. . . .

Causes

Extremely diverse instances of systems which reward behavior A although the rewarder apparently hopes for behavior B have been given. These are useful to illustrate the breadth and magnitude of the phenomenon, but the diversity increases the difficulty of determining commonalities and establishing causes. However, four general factors may be pertinent to an explanation of why fouled-up reward systems seem to be so prevalent.

Fascination with an "Objective" Criterion

It has been mentioned elsewhere that:

> Most "objective" measures of productivity are objective only in that their subjective elements are (*a*) determined in advance, rather than coming into play at the time of the formal evaluation, and (*b*) well concealed on the rating instrument itself. Thus industrial firms seeking to devise objective rating systems first decide, in an arbitrary manner, what dimensions are to be rated, . . . usually including some items having little to do with organization effectiveness while excluding others that do. Only then does Personnel Division churn out official-looking documents on which all dimensions chosen to be rated are assigned point values, categories, or whatever.

Nonetheless, many individuals seek to establish simple, quantifiable standards against which to measure and reward performance. Such efforts may be successful in highly predictable areas within an organization, but are likely to cause goal displacement when applied anywhere else. Overconcern with attendance and lateness in the insurance firm and with number of people placed in the vocational re-

habilitation division may have been largely responsible for the problems described in those organizations.

Overemphasis on Highly Visible Behaviors

Difficulties often stem from the fact that some parts of the task are highly visible while other parts are not. For example, publications are easier to demonstrate than teaching, and scoring baskets and hitting home runs are more readily observable than feeding teammates and advancing base runners. Similarly, the adverse consequences of pronouncing a sick person well are more visible than those sustained by labeling a well person sick. Team-building and creativity are other examples of behaviors which may not be rewarded simply because they are hard to observe.

Hypocrisy

In some of the instances described the rewarder may have been getting the desired behavior, notwithstanding claims that the behavior was not desired. This may be true, for example, for management's attitude toward apple-polishing in the manufacturing firm (a behavior which subordinates felt was rewarded, despite management's avowed dislike of the practice). This also may explain politicians' unwillingness to revise the penalties for disobedience of ecology laws, and the failure of top management to devise reward systems which would cause systematic evaluation of training and development programs.

Emphasis on Morality or Equity Rather than Efficiency

Some consideration of other factors prevents the establishment of a system which rewards behaviors desired by the rewarder. The felt obligation of many Americans to vote for one candidate or another, for example, may impair their ability to withhold support from politicians who refuse to discuss the issues. Similarly, the concern for spreading the risks and costs of wartime military service may outweigh the advantage to be obtained by committing personnel to combat until the war is over.

It should be noted that only with respect to the first two causes are reward systems really paying off for other than desired behaviors. In the case of the third and fourth causes the system is rewarding behaviors desired by the rewarder, and the systems are fouled up only from the standpoints of those who believe the rewarder's public statements (cause 3), or those who seek to maximize efficiency rather than other outcomes (cause 4).

CONCLUSIONS

Modern organization theory requires a recognition that the members of organizations and society possess divergent goals and motives. It therefore is unlikely that managers and their subordinates will seek the same outcomes. Three possible remedies for this potential problem are suggested.

Selection

It is theoretically possible for organizations to employ only those individuals whose goals and motives are wholly consonant with those of management. In such cases the same behaviors judged by subordinates to be rational would be perceived by management as desirable. State-of-the-art reviews of selection techniques, however, provide scant grounds for hope that such an approach would be successful.

Training

Another theoretical alternative is for the organization to admit those employees whose goals are not consonant with those of management and then, through training, socialization, or whatever, alter employee goals to make them consonant. However, research on the effectiveness of such training programs, though limited, provides further grounds for pessimism.

Altering the Reward System

What would have been the result if:

1. Nixon had been assured by his advisors that he could not win reelection except by discussing the issues in detail?
2. Physicians' conduct was subjected to regular examination by review boards for type 1 errors (calling healthy people ill) and to penalties (fines, censure, etc.) for errors of either type?
3. The President of XYZ Corporation had to choose between (*a*) spending $11 billion for antipollution equipment, and (*b*) incurring a 50-50-chance of going to jail for five years?

Managers who complain that their workers are not motivated might do well to consider the possiblity that they have installed reward systems which are paying off for behaviors other than those they are seeking. This, in part, is what happened in Vietnam, and this is what regularly frustrates societal efforts to bring about honest politicians, civic-minded managers, etc. This certainly is what happened in both the manufacturing and the insurance companies.

A first step for such managers might be to find out what behaviors currently are being rewarded. Perhaps an instrument similar to that used in the manufacturing firm could be useful for this purpose. Chances are excellent that these managers will be surprised by what they find—that their firms are not rewarding what they assume they are. In fact, such undesirable behavior by organizational members as they have observed may be explained largely by the reward systems in use.

This is not to say that all organizational behavior is determined by formal rewards and punishments. Certainly it is true that in the absence of formal reinforcement some soldiers will be patriotic, some presidents will be ecology-minded, and some orphanage directors will care about children. The point, however, is that in such cases the rewarder is not *causing* the behaviors desired but is only a fortunate bystander. For an organization to *act* upon its members, the formal reward system should positively reinforce desired behaviors, not constitute an obstacle to be overcome.

It might be wise to underscore the obvious fact that there is nothing really new in what has been said. In both theory and practice these matters have been mentioned before. Thus in many states Good Samaritan laws have been installed to protect doctors who stop to assist a stricken motorist. In states without such laws it is commonplace for doctors to refuse to stop, for fear of involvement in a subsequent lawsuit. In college basketball additional penalties have been instituted against players who foul their opponents deliberately. It has long been argued by Milton Friedman and others that penalties should be altered so as to make it irrational to disobey the ecology laws, and so on.

By altering the reward system the organization escapes the necessity of selecting only desirable people or of trying to alter undesirable ones. In Skinnerian terms, "As for responsibility and goodness—as commonly defined—no one . . . would want or need them. They refer to a man's behaving well despite the absence of positive reinforcement that is obviously sufficient to explain it. Where such reinforcement exists, 'no one needs goodness.' "

NOTES

1. In Simon's terms, a decision is "subjectively rational" if it maximizes an individual's valued outcomes so far as his knowl-

edge permits. A decision is "personally rational" if it is oriented toward the individual's goal.

2. In one study (4) of 14,867 films for signs of tuberculosis, 1,216 positive readings turned out to be clinically negative; only 24 negative readings proved clinically active, a ratio of 50 to 1.

3. Personal interviews conducted during 1972–73.

REFERENCES

1. Chester I. Barnard, *The Functions of the Executive.* (Cambridge, Mass.: Harvard University Press, 1964).
2. Peter M. Blau, and W. Richard Scott, *Formal Organizations.* (San Francisco, Chandler, 1962).
3. Fred E. Fiedler, Predicting the Effects of Leadership Training and Experience from the Contingency Model, *Journal of Applied Psychology* 56, pp. 114–19, 1972.
4. L. H. Garland, Studies of the Accuracy of Diagnostic Procedures. *American Journal Roentgenological, Radium Therapy Nuclear Medicine,* 82, 25–38, 1959.
5. Steven Kerr, Some Modifications in MBO as an OD Strategy, *Academy of Management Proceedings,* 1973, pp. 39–42.
6. Steven Kerr, What Price Objectivity? *American Sociologist* 8, 1973, pp. 92–93.
7. G. H. Litwin and R. A. Stringer, Jr., *Motivation and Organizational Climate.* (Boston: Harvard University Press, 1968).
8. Charles Perrow, The Analysis of Goals in Complex Organizations. In *Readings on Modern Organizations,* ed. A. Etzioni (Englewood Cliffs, N.J.: Prentice-Hall, 1969).
9. Thomas Scheff, Decision Rules, Types of Error, and Their Consequences in Medical Diagnosis. In *Mathematical Explorations in Behavioral Science,* ed. F. Massarik and P. Ratoosh (Homewood, Ill.: Irwin, 1965).
10. Herbert A. Simon, *Administrative Behavior* (New York: Free Press, 1957).
11. G. E. Swanson, Review Symposium: Beyond Freedom and Dignity. *American Journal of Sociology* 78, 1972, pp. 702–5.
12. E. Webster, *Decision Making in the Employment Interview* (Montreal: Industrial Relations Center, McGill University, 1964).

READING 5–2   REWARDS AND RECOGNITION: YES, THEY REALLY WORK

Ron Zemke

Money may not make the world go around, but managers in exemplary service-sector organizations firmly believe that recognition and rewards are powerful twin engines for employee motivation. In the eyes of managers from 101 such organizations profiled for a new book on service quality, recognizing and praising employees for a job well done isn't superfluous or magnanimous. It's necessary. It confirms accomplishment and reinforces commitment.

In these organizations there is a positive payoff for employees who meet the service standards, and additional financial rewards and psychic accolades for those who exceed them. Employees who go one step further for the customers become "service heroes." They are held up as role models and rewarded accordingly, because their managers know that the celebration of organizational, group and individual service accomplishments is essential if the delivery of high-quality service is to be the norm, not the exception.

Source: Reprinted with permission from *Training,* November 1988, pp. 49–53.

COMPENSATION AND MOTIVATION

People don't work just for the fun of it. They work mostly for the money they need to buy the necessities and luxuries of life. Money is a powerful motivator—and a generalized one. It is a means to a vast number of ends and makes possible the fulfillment of any number of dreams.

We need to know, first and foremost, that our paychecks will keep the wolf from the door. But as pay rises, so do visibility, prestige, personal pride and self-esteem. Those attributes can be harnessed to motivate continuing good performance. Consequently, great service organizations often pay above-average wages for their industry. They make that distinction a point of internal pride and a prominent feature in their recruiting efforts.

Exemplary companies in the service sector realize that while pay may ensure attendance, it typically doesn't produce strategic alignment, personal enthusiasm or outstanding performance. So many of them use the carrot of monetary incentives as well. Mississippi Management Corp., an extremely successful hotel management company based in Jackson, Mississippi, pays regular bonuses for such mundane tasks as carving prime rib properly or making more beds (correctly of course) than the norm. Shuttle-bus drivers for Los Angeles-based SuperShuttle Inc. can earn a paid day off, which is compensated according to a variable rate based on their own typical performance. So the more they hustle and the better they serve, the more they earn on the job and the more valuable their time off becomes.

At first Union National Bank of Charlotte, North Carolina, branch employees are "shopped" by a specialized research company up to three times a quarter. The payoff for an employee who scores a perfect "6" is instant cash in hand, as much as $200. According to First Union Corp.'s chairman and CEO Edward E. Crutchfield, Jr., instantaneous rewards are crucial. "Recognition and reward have to be done on a very short-interval basis—given immediately after the service has been rendered. It's not something that you'd get in your pension 35 years from now; it's money you can buy bread with on Monday." Federal Express employees, from the couriers on the streets each day to the parcel sorters in the Memphis hub each night, can buy lots of bread. Sorters start at well over $9 an hour, and even part-timers are eligible for profit-sharing bonuses. At Nordstrom Department Stores, salespeople earn about $2 an hour above local retail wages plus a sales commission of 6 percent or more. A top sales associate can gross $50,000 to $60,000 a year, the kind of money usually reserved only for managers in the retail industry.

It's a little puzzling that more companies don't use financial incentives at the front line. Personal pay tied to organizational performance has long been a valued executive perk, generally with sound results. A 1983 McKinsey & Co. study found that in the most profitable companies in the $25 million sales range, for example, 40 percent of CEO compensation and 36 percent of senior management pay is tied to organizational performance. A study conducted in the late 1970s for the National Science Foundation noted that among the 1,100 companies then listed on the New York Stock Exchange, those with formal incentive plans for managers earned an average 43.6 percent more pre-tax profit than companies that did not use incentives.

Executives aren't the only ones who respond well to such programs. The same National Science Foundation report also reviewed 300 studies of productivity, pay and job satisfaction, and concluded that when pay is linked to performance, employees' motivation to work is raised, their productivity is higher, and they're usually more satisfied with their work. One study cited in the report examined 400 companies and found that those that switched from a system that didn't measure work to one that measured work and included performance feedback raised productivity an average of 43 percent. When both performance feedback and *incentives* were instituted, productivity rose 63.8 percent on average.

The study's authors concluded that increased productivity depends on two things. First is motivation: Arousing and maintaining the will to work effectively means having workers who are productive not because they are coerced but because they are committed. Second is reward: Of all the factors that help to create highly motivated and satisfied workers, the principal one appears to be that effective performance is recognized and rewarded in terms that are meaningful to the individual, whether financial, psychological or both.

That message traditionally has been better understood in manufacturing companies than in service organizations. *People, Performance and Pay,* a recent study by the American Productivity Center in Houston and the American Compensation Association, found that 48 percent of manufacturers, but only 19 percent of service companies, use performance incentive systems. In the service businesses that use these compensation tactics, the most successful techniques are reportedly productivity gain-sharing, pay-for-knowledge, and small-group incentives.

Incentive systems aren't automatic performance generators, of course. They can even backfire. Sometimes organizations will "readjust" a system when it becomes obvious that salespeople are going to greatly exceed their sales goals. The excuse is always that the program "needs some fine-tuning." The real reason is that someone in senior management has decided it would be unseemly for some of the troops to earn so much more than others "at *their* level." Translation: "Who do they think they are, earning as much for front-line work as I do as a manager?" Invariably, the front-line people get the message and never again do anything remotely productive enough to get them "rate busted."

It's a natural impulse to make sure the troops' wages don't compare too closely to those of the leaders, says Harvard University's Rosabeth Moss Kanter. "Social psychologists have shown that the maintenance of an authority relationship depends on a degree of inequality," she says. "If the distance between boss and subordinate—social, economic or otherwise—declines, so does automatic deference and respect.

"This is further aided by the existence of objective measures of contribution. Once high performance is established, once the measures are clear and clearly achieved, the subordinate no longer needs the good will of his or her boss quite so much. One more source of dependency is reduced, and power again becomes more equalized. Proven achievement reflected in higher earnings than the boss's produces security. Security produces risk taking. Risk taking produces speaking up and pushing back," Kanter concludes.

The instinct to preserve traditional forms of hierarchy and bureaucracy is understandable, but it's worth suppressing when the goal is superior service. Managers are only free to lead when they are able to free their employees to think and act—to understand and do something about the problems encountered in day-to-day business. Nothing signals the sincerity of that message like an incentive for exceptional customer service.

It is vital, however, to think through all the implications of an incentive plan before you institute it. Brokerage houses have long provided incentives to stockbrokers based on their individual performance, typically calculated in terms of sales. Of course, large individual revenues accumulate into large corporate revenues, which can make the organization more hungry for record-breaking quarterly reports than for customer satisfaction.

Even before the October 1987 stock market crash, the business press had begun to question some of the practices in vogue on Wall Street. At some houses, every possible sort of incentive was dangled before the brokers—furs, Mercedes-Benzes, yachts, dinner for two anyplace on the planet, you name it. The question was whether these practices—notable by their absence in firms such as Goldman Sachs and A.G. Edwards & Sons—were causing brokers to work *against* their clients' best interests, churning accounts and pushing people into questionable ventures because those activities boosted the brokers' own compensation and rewards so remarkably.

To be effective over the long term, incentives must be based on the customer's best interests as well as their effects on the individual's paycheck and the company's quarterly revenues. They should emphasize legitimate customer satisfaction. An incentive program that subordinates an organization's long-term relationship with the customer to an individual's short-term gain—whether that individual is a salesperson, a stockholder or a highly placed executive—is a dangerous narcotic.

REWARD AND CORPORATE CULTURE

Reward systems are both a product and an influence on an organization's culture. Professor Jeffrey Kerr of the Edwin L. Cox School of Business at Southern Methodist University believes that "who gets rewarded and why is an unequivocal statement of the corporation's values and beliefs." Kerr and his colleagues suggest that there are two opposite extremes in organizational reward "systems." Those extremes illustrate just how heavily various types of systems can influence an organization's culture and its people's behavior.

The hierarchy-based reward system, as the name implies, is a top-down model. Superiors define and evaluate the performance of subordinates. Performance is defined in both qualitative and quantitative terms, with qualitative performance parameters often as important as—or even more important than—quantitative measures. Evaluation of performance is usually quite subjective. Even in quantifiable areas, superiors sometimes use their own knowledge and experiences to interpret the numbers.

That bare-bones description makes working in an organization with a hierarchy-based reward system sound about as pleasant as being a serf on a medieval estate; any alternative would be an improvement, right? Don't be so sure. Hierarchical structures lead to formal salary systems, like a Hay system, that rewards tenure as well as performance. Bonuses tend to represent only a small slice of compensation and are usually based on group and team performance rather than individual performance. Belonging, cooperation, teamwork and loyalty have high value in the hierarchy system. Activities such as employee training, career development, frequent promotions, lateral movement for developmental purposes and the awarding of special perquisites characterize organizations with these reward systems.

The resulting culture, says Kerr, is very much what *Theory Z* author Bill Ouchi describes as a clan: a familiar or fraternal group in which all members acknowledge an obligation beyond the contractual exchange of labor for salary. The individual's long-term commitment to the organization is traded for the organization's long-term commitment to the individual. "The relationship," Kerr explains, "is predicated on mutual interests."

At the other extreme of organizational reward systems, says Kerr, is the "performance-based reward system." Numbers are paramount. The qualitative aspects of performance don't affect evaluations, especially at the managerial level. Performance objectives are precise and tend to be primarily numeric. Results matter, and the methods for achieving them are usually up to the local managers and their subordinates. Performance evaluation and feedback focus on the immediate, not the long term. High levels of autonomy and reward characterize the performance-based organization. Concepts such as mentoring, socialization, development, promotability and career planning play little part in the performance-based organization.

In Ouchi's scheme of things this is a market culture. Relationships are contractual and mutually exploitive. Level of performance and level of reward are the only guarantees in the contract. When a juicy job opens up, the company is as likely to bring in someone from the outside as to promote an insider.

Are there any pluses in this dog-eat-dog culture? Certainly. For instance, earning potential is unlimited. The profit pool is established among a small number of people, usually a division-sized unit, and is independent of the larger organization. Symbols of rank and status are almost nonexistent, and being a member of the "right clique" or the right family is not a factor in getting ahead.

Kerr also points out that the market culture "does generate personal initiative, a strong sense of ownership and responsibility for operators and decisions, and an entrepreneurial approach to management. The individual is free to pursue goals with a minimum of organizational constraints."

The point of making the distinction between the two systems carriers more than mere academic interest. When you are thinking about ways to improve performance through reward and recognition, you must be guided not only by the art and science of incentive motivation but also by an understanding of the culture and values of your organization.

SYMBOLIC REWARD

Money isn't everything—although many continue to insist that it's ahead of whatever is in second place. Still, effective incentive and reward programs can be created from a combination of dollars, trips to exotic locales, merchandise and purely psychological payoffs. American Airlines takes much of the reward methodology of its frequent-flyer program and plugs it into an employee incentive program for individual and small-group service achievements. At Ryder Systems, the Miami-based transportation company, a similar program is in place for rewarding the dealers who rent Ryder's trucks to customers.

Exclusivity can lend appeal to programs whose actual goods range from simple to awe-inspiring. Employees at Southern Bell often ask where they can buy the designer-style jackets and sports apparel the company awards to outstanding service providers. They're told the items aren't

for sale—the only way to get a jacket is to earn a jacket. Similarly, executives at Acura's U.S. headquarters in Gardena, California, can only envy the limited-edition crystal sculptures awarded to the best dealerships; the contract calls for the artist to produce only enough for the winners.

A little spontaneity is often an effective ingredient in choosing an award or making one out of something at hand. With the St. Louis Cardinals playing in the 1987 World Series, a Citicorp manager in that town knew exactly how to reward the service accomplishments of his branch's people. The cruise-for-two promos accumulated from wholesalers in 1987 by Ukrop's Super Markets in Richmond, Virginia, became highly sought-after prizes for exceptional front-line performance within the small supermarket chain. Auto mechanics at Don Beyer Volvo, a car dealership in Falls Church, Virginia, regularly compete for a month's worth of driving around in a luxury model right off the showroom floor.

Little rewards can be as effective as big ones if they're used in the right way. Lapel-style pins and special name tags are tactics common to service leaders such as Federal Express, Lenscrafters and First Federal/Osceola. At Citicorp Retail Services in Denver, good suggestions for new or better ways to serve customers warrant a "Bright Ideas" coffee mug or similar keepsake. The employee who submits the month's best idea wins temporary possession of a circulating trophy—a three-foot-high light bulb.

It's a lighthearted approach, but the underlying thought is what's important. According to Lauren O'Connell, Citicorp's assistant vice president of operations, "The point of these contests and recognition programs and service evaluations and checklists is that they make everyone feel that quality service is his or her individual responsibility. That not only leads to better service quality for the customer, it also means higher morale. People do care bout their jobs when they know that their managers consider those jobs to be important. And caring about one's job and knowing that it's important is where service quality really starts."

CELEBRATION

Often entwined with recognition and reward is a sense of celebration. That's clearly apparent when American Express assembles its Great Performers in New York City each year so executives and colleagues can glow upon them for a job exceptionally done. BellSouth, parent of Southern Bell and LensCrafters, also brings its service award winners into corporate headquarters at annual meetings to laud their achievements. Pizza Hut and Domino's Pizza do the same for managers and franchises at national meetings.

Organization-development consultant Cathy DeForest writes that, like the leaders of any army, managers must "recognize that the act of celebrating provides a way to nourish the spirit of an organization as well as create a moment in time when a glimpse of a transformed organization can be seen and felt."

Recognition and celebrations also are ways of reaffirming to people that they are an important part of something that matters. These little ceremonies can be significant motivators for people in any organization, but especially so in a service organization, where "pride in the product" is essentially pride in personal performance. Two recent studies make the point.

In 1987 *Inc.* magazine and the Hay Group consulting company compared opinions and feelings of employees in the relatively small companies that form the "*Inc. 500*" with those of employees in the large corporations that make up the "*Fortune 500*." Employees in small companies rated their pay and benefits as poorer, their opportunity for advancement as less promising, and company communication as worse than did their counterparts in the larger companies. But surprise! Overall job satisfaction in small companies was significantly, even spectacularly higher.

Why? According to the *Inc.*/Hay survey, employees of the smaller companies tended to believe they were important to their organizations and to feel that their organizations were doing something significant. More specifically, people in the smaller companies felt their work was more challenging, said their ideas were more likely to be adopted, reported a higher sense of accomplishment from what they did, and thought they were treated with more respect.

Focus group discussions validated the survey findings, *Inc.* reported: "These are employees who talked about the company in first-person plural, as in, 'We can serve our customers faster' or 'We may look like we're disorganized, but we're not.' Said another: 'The quality is personal—the product is us.' "

The second confirmation of the importance of feeling involved in something worthwhile comes from a study done by the Forum Corp., a Boston-based consulting company. Forum found that employees who believed their organizations served customers well were much less likely to say they planned to leave their current jobs within the next year than those who felt they worked for a company that was doing a poor job of serving the customer.

The concept of being part of something valuable, worthwhile and important often is expressed most forcefully by the executives at the top of an organization. Fred Smith, founder of Federal Express, has the iron-jawed, fiery look of the true believer when he tells an interviewer, "Our corporate philosophy is people, service, profit. We do something important. We carry the most important commerce in the history of the world." It is no accident that one often hears that sentiment repeated with similar fervor by couriers and managers throughout the FedEx system.

Marriott employees, when asked about their unusual corporate loyalty, say, "We're part of a family here. The name Marriott is a person's name, and it stands for something." That same sense of pride and belonging becomes evident when you talked to people at a lot of organizations that routinely receive high marks from customers for service quality and performance: Lands' End, Dun & Bradstreet, United Van Lines, Southern Bell, CompuServe, Delta Air Lines, Miller Business Systems, Kinder-Care, Chubb, Northwestern Mutual Life Insurance Co., 3M, H.B. Fuller, Beth Israel Hospital, The Mayo Clinic . . . the list could stretch on.

But the most memorable way I have heard it expressed was at Walt Disney World, where I asked a young groundskeeper, "How do you like being a street sweeper in a theme park?" He stepped back, stood up tall, looked me square in the eye, and shot back: "I'm not a street sweeper. I'm in show business. I'm part of the Act."

To front-line workers in any organization with ambitions of providing distinctive service to its customers, the feeling of being a part of something important may be the most important motivational principle of all.

■

EXERCISES

EXERCISE 5-1   DIAGNOSING A WORK PERFORMANCE PROBLEM

BACKGROUND

Proper diagnosis is a critical aspect of effective motivation management. Oftentimes managers become frustrated because they don't understand the causes of observed performance problems. They might experiment with various "cures," but the inefficiency of this trial-and-error process often simply increases their frustration level. In addition, the accompanying misunderstanding adds extra strain to the manager-subordinate relationship. This generally makes the performance problem even more pronounced, which prompts the manager to resort to more drastic responses, and a vicious, downward spiral ensues.

The performance diagnosis model in Exhibit 5-8 offers a systematic way for managers and subordinates to collaboratively pinpoint the cause(s) of dissatisfaction and performance problems. It assumes that employees will work hard and be good performers if the work environment encourages these actions. Consequently, rather than jumping to conclusions about poor performance stemming from deficiencies in personality traits or a bad attitude, this diagnostic process helps managers focus their attention on improving the selection, job design, performance evaluation, and reward allocation systems. In this manner, the specific steps necessary to accomplish work goals and management's expectations are examined to pinpoint why the worker's performance is falling short.

The manager and low-performing subordinate should follow the logical discovery process in the model, step by step. They should begin by examining the current perceptions of performance as well as the understanding of performance expectations and then proceed through the model until the performance problems have been identified. The model focuses on seven of these problems.

A. Perception Problem: "Do you agree your performance is below expectations?" A perception problem suggests that the manager and subordinate have different views of the subordinate's current performance level. Unless this disagreement is resolved, it is futile to continue the diag-

Source: Adapted from David A. Whetten and Kim S. Cameron, "Exercises for Diagnosing Work Performance Problems," *Developing Management Skills* (HarperCollins Publishers, 1991), pp. 379–83.

nostic process. The entire problem-solving process is based on the premise that both parties recognize the existence of a problem and are interested in solving it. If agreement does not exist, the manager should focus on resolving the discrepancy in perceptions, including clarifying current expectations (Problem E).

B. Resources Problem: "Do you have the resources necessary to do the job well?" (Ability has three components, and these should be explored in the order shown in the model. This order reduces a subordinate's defensive reactions.) Poor performance may stem from a lack of resource support. Resources include material and personnel support as well as cooperation from interdependent work groups.

C. Training Problem: "Is a lack of training interfering with your job performance?" Individuals may be asked to perform tasks that exceed their current skill or knowledge level. Typically this problem can be overcome through additional training or education.

D. Aptitude Problem: "Do you feel this is the right job/blend of work assignments for you?" This is the most difficult of the three ability problems to resolve because it is the most basic. If the **resupply** (providing additional resources) and **retraining** solutions have been explored without success, then more drastic measures may be required. These include **refitting** the person's current job requirements, **reassigning** him to another position, or, finally, **releasing** him from the organization.

E. Expectations Problem: "What are your performance expectations for this position? What do you think my expectations are?" This problem results from poor communications regarding job goals or job requirements. In some cases, the stated goals may be different from the desired goals. In other words, the employee is working toward one goal while the supervisor desires another. This often occurs when subordinates are not sufficiently involved in the goal- or standard-setting process. When this results in unrealistic, imposed expectations, motivation suffers.

F. Incentive Problem: "Do you believe rewards are linked to your performance in this position?" Either the individual does not believe that "performance makes a difference" or insufficient performance feedback and reinforcement have

EXHIBIT 5-8

Performance Diagnosis Model

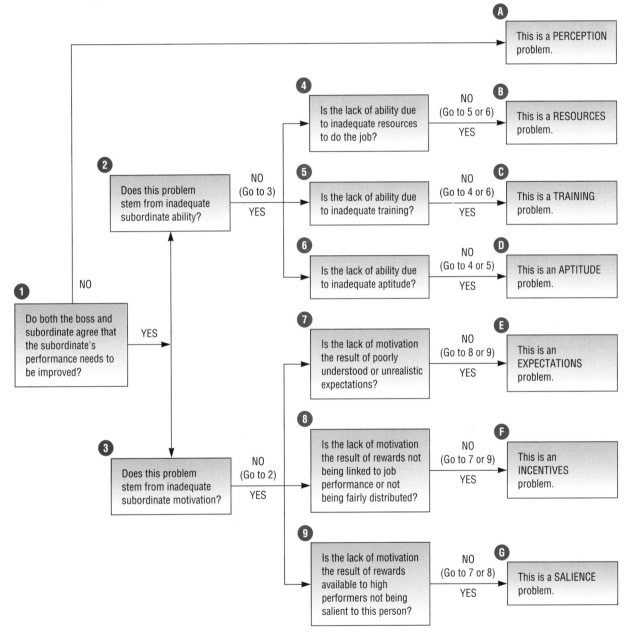

been given. The manager should also ask, "Do you feel rewards are being distributed equitably?" This provides an opportunity to discuss subordinates' criteria for judging fairness. Often, unrealistic standards are being used.

G. *Salience Problem:* "Are the performance incentives attractive to you?" Salience refers to the importance an individual attaches to available rewards. Oftentimes the incentives offered to encourage high performance simply aren't highly valued by a particular individual. The salience problem points out the need for managers to be creative in generating a broad range of rewards and flexible in allowing subordinates to choose among rewards.

Assignment

Option 1: Read the case, "Joe's Performance Problems", and privately use the diagnostic model Exhibit 5-8 to pinpoint plausible performance problems. Next, in small groups discuss your individual assessments and list the specific questions you should ask Joe to accurately identify, from his point of view, the obstacles to his high performance. Finally, brainstorm ideas for plausible solutions. Be prepared to represent your group in role-playing a problem-solving interview with Joe.

JOE'S PERFORMANCE PROBLEMS

Joe joined your architectural firm two years ago as a draftsman. He is thirty-five years old and has been a draftsman since graduating from a two-year technical school right after high school. He is married and has four children. He has worked for four architectural firms in twelve years.

Joe came with mediocre recommendations from his previous employer, but you hired him anyway because you needed help desperately. Your firm's workload has been extremely high due to a local construction boom. The result

is that a lot of the practices that contribute to a supportive, well-managed work environment have tended to be overlooked. For instance, you can't remember the last time you conducted a formal performance review or did any career counseling. Furthermore, the tradition of closing the office early on Friday for a social hour was dropped long ago. Unfortunately, the tension in the office runs pretty high some days due to unbearable time pressures and the lack of adequate staff. Nighttime and weekend work have become the norm rather than the exception.

Overall, you have been pleasantly surprised by Joe's performance. Until recently he worked hard and consistently produced high-quality work. Furthermore, he frequently volunteered for special projects, made lots of suggestions for improving the work environment, and has demonstrated an in-depth practical knowledge of architecture and the construction business. However, during the past few months, he has definitely slacked off. He doesn't seem as excited about his work, and several times you have found him daydreaming at his desk. In addition, he has gotten into several heated arguments with architects about the specifications and proper design procedures for recent projects.

After one of these disagreements, you overheard Joe complaining to his office-mate, "No one around here respects my opinion. I'm just a lowly draftsman. I know as much as these hotshot architects, but because I don't have the degree, they ignore my input, and I'm stuck doing the grunt work. Adding insult to injury, my wife has had to get a job to help support our family. I must be the lowest-paid person in this firm." In response to a question from a co-worker regarding why he didn't pursue a college degree in architecture, Joe responded, "Do you have any idea how hard it is to put bread on the table, pay a Seattle mortgage, work overtime, be a reasonably good father and husband, plus go to night school? Come, on, be realistic!"

EXERCISE 5–2   REWARD OR PUNISHMENT: THE LAY-OFF DECISION

OBJECTIVES

1. To acquire an understanding of how difficult it is to make a lay-off decision.
2. To examine how you weigh various personal and job-related behaviors to make a lay-off decision.

STARTING THE EXERCISE

Read the employee descriptions and develop your own sequence of laying employees off. Number 1 would be the first laid off, Number 2 would be the second laid off, and so forth. There is no perfect answer, but you should be able to defend your lay-off sequence array. Is being the last person laid off a reward? For what?

After you have arrayed the employees in order of lay off, the class will be divided into groups of five to eight students each to share and compare choices and reasons.

J. J. Miller, Inc. is a small job shop that manufactures parts for electronic equipment. The firm is a major supplier to a number of large equipment manufacturers. As a result of recent orders and demand, Miller's management has met on two occasions to consider cutting costs and even laying off some workers. Miller is a nonunion firm that is located in Mesquite, a suburb of Dallas, Texas. The company has prided itself on being a fair employer that has rewarded employees with bonuses and jobs without ever having to lay employees off. However, for today's meeting, the president has asked you to rank order from first to seventh the employees in the production bay that will experience the first voluntary cutbacks in the firm's history.

A description of the employees are as follows:

- Don Dombroski—White male; age 34; married, three children. Has worked at Miller's for six years; generally good performer who has had some incidents of absence and tardiness in the last 12 months.
- Lu Wong Chen—Oriental male; age 35; married, one child. Has only been at Miller's for 18 months but is considered top technician in the shop. Has a tendency to stay by himself and stay away from coworkers.

- Nancy Carlatta—White female; age 42; husband recently disabled. Has two college-age children she is helping through school. Volunteers for everything, says that she must work. Does acceptable work and has been at Miller's for seven years.
- Tito Guereba—Hispanic male; age 24; worked at Miller's for three years; is single. Does above average work and was being considered for training courses to improve skills.
- Mitchell Green—Black male; age 33; married with two children. Wife was recently laid off. Has a good, steady performance record. Has been talking about attempting to unionize Miller. Worked for five years in the company.
- Jack Aremian—White male; age 49; married with five children. Has been at Miller's since it opened 11 years ago. Is a chronic complainer and has an alcohol problem that causes him to be excessively absent. When he is sober, his work is steady and is considered good.
- Mary Lou Cisneros—Hispanic female; age 30; divorced, single parent with two children. Has four years of tenure. Is considered a good performer. Because of difficulties raising a handicapped child, is considered to be quite moody. Flies off the handle when asked to do some jobs.

EXERCISE 5–3 MAKING CHOICES ABOUT REWARDS

OBJECTIVES

1. To illustrate individual differences in reward preferences.
2. To emphasize how both extrinsic and intrinsic rewards are considered important.
3. To enable people to explore the reasons for the reward preferences of others.

STARTING THE EXERCISE

Initially individuals will work alone establishing their own list of reward preferences after reviewing Exhibit 5-8. Then the instructor will set up groups of four to six students to examine individual preferences and complete the exercise.

The Facts

It is possible to develop an endless list of on-the-job rewards. Presented in a random fashion in Exhibit 5-9 are some of the rewards that could be available to employees.

Exercise Procedures

Phase I: 25 minutes

1. Each individual should set up from Exhibit 5-9 a list of extrinsic and intrinsic rewards.
2. Each person should then rank-order from most important to least important the two lists.
3. From the two lists, rank the eight most important rewards. How many are extrinsic, and how many are intrinsic?

EXHIBIT 5-9

Some Possible Rewards for Employees

Company picnics	Smile from manager	Vacation trips for performance
Watches	Feedback on performance	Manager asking for advice
Trophies	Feedback on career progress	Informal leader asking for advice
Piped-in-music	Larger office	
Job challenge	Club privileges	Office with a window
Achievement opportunity	More prestigious job	The privilege of completing a job from start to finish
Time off for performance	More job involvement	
Vacation	Use of company recreation facilities	
Autonomy	Participation in decisions	
Pay increase	Stock options	
Recognition		

Phase II: 30 minutes

1. The instructor will set up groups of four to six individuals.
2. The two lists in which the extrinsic and intrinsic categories were developed should be discussed.

3. The final rank orders of the eight most important rewards should be placed on a board or chart at the front of the room.
4. The rankings should be discussed within the groups. What major differences are displayed?

▲

CASES

CASE 5–1   THE POLITICS OF PERFORMANCE APPRAISAL

Every Friday, Max Steadman, Jim Coburn, Lynne Sims, and Tom Hamilton meet at Charley's after work for drinks. The four friends work as managers at Eckel Industries, a manufacturer of arc-welding equipment in Minneapolis. The one-plant company employs about 2,000 people. The four managers work in the manufacturing division. Max, 35, manages the company's 25 quality control inspectors. Lynne, 33, works as a supervisor in inventory management, Jim, 34, is a first-line supervisor in the metal coating

Source: Kim A. Stewart, University of Denver. Several perspectives were drawn from an insightful study reported in Clinton O. Longenecker, Henry P. Sims, Jr, and Dennis A. Gioia, "Behind the Mask: The Politics of Employee Appraisal," *Academy of Management Executive*, August 1987, pp. 183–91.

department. Tom, 28, supervises a team of assemblers. The four managers' tenure at Eckel Industries ranges from 1 year (Tom) to 12 years (Max).

The group is close-knit; Lynne, Jim, and Max's friendship stems from their years as undergraduate business students at the University of Minnesota. Tom, the newcomer, joined the group after meeting the three at an Eckel management seminar last year. Weekly get-togethers at Charley's have become a comfortable habit for the group and provide an opportunity to relax, exchange the latest gossip heard around the plant, and give and receive advice about problems encountered on the job.

This week's topic of discussion: performance appraisal, specifically the company's annual review process, which the plant's management conducted in the last week. Each of the four managers completed evaluation forms (graphic rating scales) on all of his or her subordinates and met with each subordinate to discuss the appraisal.

TOM: This was the first time I've appraised my people, and I dreaded it. For me, it's been the worst week of the year. Evaluating is difficult; it's highly subjective and inexact. Your emotions creep into the process. I got angry at one of my assembly workers last week, and I still felt the anger when I was filling out the evaluation forms. Don't tell me that my frustration with the guy didn't bias my appraisal. I think it did. And I think the technique is flawed. Tell me—what's the difference between a five and a six on "cooperation"?

JIM: The scales are a problem. So is memory. Remember our course in personnel in college? Philips said that according to research, when we sit down to evaluate someone's performance in the past year, we will only be able to actively recall and use 15 percent of the performance we actually observed.

LYNNE: I think political considerations are always a part of the process. I know I consider many other factors besides a person's actual performance when I appraise him.

TOM: Like what?

LYNNE: Like the appraisal will become part of his permanent written record that affects his career. Like the person I evaluate today, I have to work with tomorrow. Given that, the difference between a five and a six on cooperation isn't that relevant, because frankly, if a five makes him mad and he's happy with a six . . .

MAX: Then you give him the six. Accuracy is important, but I'll admit it—accuracy isn't my primary objective when I evaluate my workers. My objective is to motivate and reward them so they'll perform better. I use the review process to do what's best for my people and my department. If that means fine-tuning the evaluations to do that, I will.

TOM: What's an example of fine-tuning?

MAX: Jim, do you remember three years ago when the company lowered the ceiling on merit raises? The top merit increase that any employee could get was 4 percent. I boosted the ratings of my folks to get the best merit increases for them. The year before that, the ceiling was 8 percent. The best they could get was less than what most of them received the year before. I felt they deserved the

4 percent, so I gave the marks that got them what I felt they deserved.

LYNNE: I've inflated ratings to encourage someone who is having personal problems but is normally a good employee. A couple of years ago, one of my better people was going through a painful divorce, and it was showing in her work. I don't think it's fair to kick someone when they're down, even if their work is poor. I felt a good rating would speed her recovery.

TOM: Or make her complacent.

LYNNE: No, I don't think so. I felt she realized her work was suffering. I wanted to give her encouragement; it was my way of telling her she had some support and that she wasn't in danger of losing her job.

JIM: There's another situation where I think fine-tuning is merited—when someone's work has been mediocre or even poor for most of the year, but it improves substantially in the last two, three months or so. If I think the guy is really trying and is doing much better, I'd give him a rating that's higher than his work over the whole year deserves. It encourages him to keep improving. If I give him a mediocre rating, what does that tell him?

TOM: What if he's really working hard, but not doing so great?

JIM: If I think he has what it takes, I'd boost the rating to motivate him to keep trying until he gets there.

MAX: I know of one or two managers who've inflated ratings to get rid of a pain in the neck, some young guy who's transferred in and thinks he'll be there a short time. He's not good, but thinks he is and creates all sorts of problems. Or his performance is OK, but he just doesn't fit in with the rest of the department. A year or two of good ratings is a sure trick for getting rid of him.

TOM: Yes, but you're passing the problem on to someone else.

MAX: True, but it's no longer my problem.

TOM: All the examples you've talked about involve inflating evaluations. What about deflating them, giving someone less than you really think he deserves? Is that justified?

LYNNE: I'd hesitate to do that, because it can create problems. It can backfire.

MAX: But it does happen. You can lower a guy's ratings to shock him, to jolt him into performing better. Sometimes, you can work with someone, coach them, try to help them improve, and it just doesn't work. A basement-level rating can tell him you mean business. You can say that isn't fair, and for the time being, it isn't. But what if you feel that if the guy doesn't shape up he faces being fired in a year or two, and putting him in the cellar, ratingswise, will solve his problem? It's fair in the long run if the effect is that he improves his work and keeps his job.

JIM: Sometimes, you get someone who's a real rebel, who always questions you, sometimes even oversteps his bounds. I think deflating his evaluation is merited just to remind him who's the boss.

LYNNE: I'd consider lowering someone's true rating if they've had a long record of rather questionable performance, and I think the best alternative for the person is to consider another job with another company. A low appraisal sends him a message to consider quitting and start looking for another job.

MAX: What if you believe the situation is hopeless, and you've made up your mind that you're going to fire the guy as soon as you've found a suitable replacement. The courts have chipped away at management's right to fire. Today, when you fire someone, you'd better have a strong case. I think once a manager decides to fire, appraisals become very negative. Anything good that you say about the subordinate can be used later against you. Deflating the ratings protects yourself from being sued and sometimes speeds up the termination process.

TOM: I understand your points, but I still believe that accuracy is the top priority in performance appraisal. Let me play devil's advocate for a minute. First, Jim, you complained about our memory limitations introducing a bias into appraisal. Doesn't introducing politics into the process further distort the truth by introducing yet another bias? Even more important, most would agree that one key to motivating people is providing true feedback—the facts about how they're doing so they know where they stand. Then you talk with them about how to improve their per-

formance. When you distort an evaluation—however slightly—are you providing this kind of feedback?

MAX: I think you're overstating the degree of fine-tuning.

TOM: Distortion, you mean.

MAX: No, fine-tuning. I'm not talking about giving a guy a seven when he deserves a two or vice versa. It's not that extreme. I'm talking about making slight changes in the ratings when you think that the change can make a big difference in terms of achieving what you think is best for the person and for your department.

TOM: But when you fine-tune, you're manipulating your people. Why not give them the most accurate evaluation and let the chips fall where they may? Give them the facts and let them decide.

MAX: Because most of good managing is psychology. Understanding people, their strengths and shortcomings. Knowing how to motivate, reward, and act to do what's in their and your department's best interest. And sometimes, total accuracy is not the best path. Sometimes, it's not in anybody's best interest.

JIM: All this discussion raises a question. What's the difference between fine-tuning and significant distortion? Where do you draw the line?

LYNNE: That's about as easy a question as what's the difference between a five and a six. On the form, I mean.

QUESTIONS FOR CONSIDERATION

1. Based on your view of the objectives of performance evaluation, evaluate the perspectives about performance appraisal presented by the managers.
2. In your opinion, at what point does "fine-tuning" evaluations becomes unacceptable distortion?
3. Assume you are the vice president of personnel at Eckel Industries and that you are aware that fine-tuning evaluations is a prevalent practice among Eckel managers. If you disagree with this perspective, what steps would you take to reduce the practice?

CASE 5–2   BOB COLLINS

Bob Collins was employed by the Mansen Company, a division of Sanford, Barnes, Inc., a diversified company engaged mainly in the manufacture and sale of men's and women's apparel. The Miami plant of the Mansen Company is the largest of the 19 manufacturing locations and has, in its organization, an industrial engineering unit.

As department head of industrial engineering in the Miami plant, Jim Douglas also has the responsibility for all industrial engineering functions in the Florida Region. This includes three smaller plants within a 275-mile radius of Miami. Jim reports to the Miami plant manager, Mr. Scott, for local projects and to the Florida regional manager, Mr. Glenn, for projects of a regional nature. Mr. Glenn has been regional manager for many years, but only for the previous 23 months had this been his sole responsibility. Prior to this time, he was also the manager of the Miami plant, and he was still a dominant personality in the plant, partially because of Mr. Scott's indecisiveness.

Assisting Jim in Miami are two other industrial engineers, Bob Collins and Mark Douglas. Mark was hired in September, 1987, soon after his release from the army, and had been with Mansen about 27 months. Bob had been with the company for about 21 months since leaving his last position because of a conflict there regarding a heavy workload and a schedule requiring some night work. Bob had freely given this information during this preemployment interview, but no effort had been made to uncover the past employer's version of the situation.

Jim holds an associate degree in industrial engineering from a two-year technical school, while both Bob and Mark have bachelor's degrees, in history and business, respectively. All three men are army veterans. Jim and Mark had served as enlisted men for nine and two years, respectively, Jim becoming a staff sergeant and Mark, a sergeant. Bob served as an officer for four years reaching the rank of captain. Bob had displayed a talent for creative and imaginative thinking in regards to mechanical development and was assigned a majority of the projects that delved into the creation, installation, and improvement of mechanical innovations and devices. In addition, he and the local head of mechanical development, Ned Larson, worked together on many of their own original ideas, both in the planning and development. (See Exhibit 5-10.)

Used with permission of the authors, Richard E. Dutton and Rodney C. Sherman, University of South Florida.

EXHIBIT 5-10

Partial Organization Chart—The Mansen Company

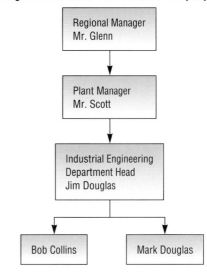

CURRENT SITUATION

One day Bob came upon an interoffice memo, in Jim's incoming mail box, containing a question from Mr. Glenn about a mechanical project on which Bob was working. Feeling that he could save time for Jim, he picked up the memo, read it, and proceeded to Mr. Glenn's office to answer the question. When he returned, he simply put the memo back in Jim's mail box and went on with other work.

Later in the day Jim returned to the office to answer his mail and came upon Mr. Glenn's memo. Jim sought out Bob and the following conversation ensued:

JIM: Bob, I've got a short note here from Mr. Glenn asking about the status of the cuff machine project I gave you. Where do we stand on that now?

BOB: Well, as I mentioned before, all we have to build is the automatic stacking device and then we should have the machine about ready to go. Some of the parts won't be in until the first of next week, but it should only take about a day after that to finish.

JIM: Okay, that's good. How about answering this memo to Mr. Glenn and we'll have him up-to-date on this thing?

BOB: I already have. I saw the memo earlier and went on in and brought him up on how the project stands.

JIM: Did you get a copy of this too?

BOB: No, I saw yours and decided to save you time so I went ahead and answered his question.

JIM: You mean you got this out of my box?

BOB: Yeah, I saw it as I was coming to my desk and decided to go ahead and get it out of the way.

JIM: Oh well, I'll just hold on to this for awhile then.

Several days later, Jim and Bob were discussing one of Bob's new ideas, and the discussion became very heated when Jim rejected the idea as too expensive, in both time and money.

JIM: And another thing. Bob, I don't want you going through my mail box again. What's in there is none of your business unless I assign it to you.

BOB: I was just trying to do you a favor and get the memo answered. If you don't want me to do that, then I won't.

JIM: You would have answered eventually, but I don't want you to do these things unless I tell you to. I'm in charge of the department, and I have to know what's going on. That reminds me of another thing. From now on, you tell me about all of the projects you're working on. I don't want any more secret projects being worked on without my knowing it. I feel pretty stupid when Mr. Scott or Mr. Glenn asks me a question about something I've never even heard of. From now on, you tell me about your ideas, and if we can work it into the schedule we will; otherwise it will have to wait until we can get to it. This also means not going to Mr. Glenn with your ideas first, and then telling me that he thinks it's a good idea and should be developed. I'll approve the ideas first, and then we'll check with him if necessary.

BOB: I know you're talking about the new sleeve hemming stacker, and I just happened to mention it to Mr. Glenn this morning at coffee break, and he wanted to know more about it. I had to tell him about it when he asked.

JIM: That's right. In that case you couldn't have done anything else, but from now on make sure you've cleared these ideas with me before going to him.

Mark came into the office, and the discussion was ended.

The following day, Bob and Mark were leaving the office together, and Bob told Mark about his discussion with Jim.

BOB: Mark, I'm so mad at Jim I'd like to quit and walk out of here right now. I know damn well I could make more money somewhere else and wouldn't have to put up with Jim. You know what really gets me down is the thousands of dollars that I can prove I've saved the company, and I can't get a decent raise. I know Jim is making about $26,000, and I feel I'm worth as much as he is, but I do realize that they have to pay him more because he's a department head. However, he's not worth the amount of difference in our salaries. I feel I should be able to get at least $1,000 a year more than I'm getting now, but the "Book" won't allow that much of a raise at one time. And besides that, I'd feel more like putting out more for the company. As it is, I want to do my best, but it's hard to feel that way when you aren't fairly paid for your work.

MARK: You know what chances you've got of getting *that* kind of a raise! What started all of this anyway?

BOB: Well, I was telling Jim about my idea for the fronts presser and he turned it down, just like he's done most of my ideas.

MARK: Did he tell you *why* he turned it down?

BOB: Said it would be too expensive and would take too much time. Mark, it would save us a penny a dozen which would be about $5,000 a year; they're just time studies to try and satisfy some operator who doesn't really want to work.

MARK: I know. My projects are like that too, and he turned down my idea for revamping the boxing department. You know what a bottleneck that had been. My first estimate, which was conservative, was savings of $50,000 a year plus being able to get out our weekly production. We're not anywhere near that now and spending twice the amount of money we need to. This would also allow the warehouse to have half of the present boxing area. But Jim says it can't be done because there would have to be too much coordination between departments, and that it would take someone with more authority than we have to make it work. I told him if we were to work up the proposal and send it to Mr. Scott, he couldn't pass up those savings on a system that's workable. Of course, you know how Scott hates to make decisions, but if Mr.

Glenn knew about it, it would be our main project until it was installed. You know how he likes those dollar signs.

BOB: Yeah, I know. Jim doesn't seem to understand that these little projects don't save us any money and yet he turns down ideas that will save us thousands of dollars a year. You know he doesn't know anything about mechanical development. And besides that, when you try to explain something to him and he doesn't understand it, he says it won't work. But I know that he takes some of these ideas and mentions them to Mr. Scott and Mr. Glenn and takes credit for them. I don't like that one little bit, and I'm going to tell him so one of these days. Then, after telling me my idea for the fronts presser wasn't any good, he chewed me out for going through his mail box. That happened a couple of days ago. When I tried to do him a favor by answering a question Mr. Glenn had asked in a memo, he got all upset. He didn't know anything about it anyway, so what's the difference?

MARK: Well, do you think it was right to go through his mail?

BOB: Well, I just happened to see the subject of the memo and I knew it was concerned with my project so I went ahead and answered the question. I didn't go through his mail; the memo was right on top, and I just happened to see it on my way to my desk.

MARK: Yes, but you *did* get into his personal mail box and went ahead without him knowing about it. Do you see what I mean, Bob? I mean he *is* the head of the department, and he needs to know what goes on within the department.

BOB: But he doesn't have to know *everything* I'm working on. It's none of his business. Most of the things Ned and I do are our own ideas, and he doesn't have a thing to do with them—he doesn't even understand them. Anyway, he told me he didn't want me working on any "secret" projects, that I was to tell him about all of my ideas before I did anything with them. Well, I'll tell you, I'm going ahead and do the projects he assigns me, but I'm still going to work on my own ideas whenever I get a chance. Here comes Mr. Scott, I'll see you later.

After closing hours that night and after Bob had left, Jim and Mark were still in the office.

JIM: Mark, did Bob tell you about our little discussion yesterday afternoon?

MARK: He said you had a few words.

JIM: Bob's just getting too big for his own britches. If he doesn't like something I say or do, he acts like a little child. Goes around pouting and gloomy for two or three days. He's just going to have to learn that he's not running the department, although I'm sure he feels he could do a better job than I'm doing. But the thing is that he can't take any criticism. Some of his ideas are good, but others are just too far out and we don't have the time for them. He's going to have to realize that we have other things to do besides mechanical development. I know a lot of our projects cost us more to carry out than can be saved in terms of dollars, but if we can show an operator what is being done is right—or if it's wrong—admit the error and correct the situation, then that can be worth as much as saving several thousand of dollars a year. Although we are becoming increasingly automated, we have to remember that people are still our main source of production and that without their cooperation, we're out of business. Besides, mechanical development isn't even his job, but because he has had some good ideas, I've let him work with Ned on them. I know he's sensitive, and that he is worth a lot to the company because some of his ideas are worthwhile, but if he doesn't change his ways, I'm going to have to talk to Mr. Glenn about letting him go. I've got to run this department, and we can't do our best when he acts up like he does.

CASE QUESTIONS

1. Should Bob be disciplined or punished for going through Jim's mail? Why?
2. Suppose that Jim decides to punish Bob for going through his personal mail. What approach should be used to make the punishment effective?
3. What role could Mr. Glenn have played when Bob came directly to him to respond to the memo?

C H A P T E R

6

Occupational Stress:
An Individual View

LEARNING OBJECTIVES

UNDERSTAND that the term stress can be defined in a number of different ways,
depending on one's perspective

DESCRIBE the General Adaptation Syndrome

DISCUSS the major variables in an integrative model of stress

DISTINGUISH between several categories of stressors

IDENTIFY three important variables which moderate the relationship between
stressors and stress

COMPARE clinical with organizational approaches to stress management programs

DISCUSS several individual approaches to managing stress

Interest in occupational stress has become widespread. However, the experience
of stress is not new. Our cave-dwelling ancestors faced stress every time they left
their caves and encountered their enemy, the saber-toothed tigers. The tigers of
yesteryear are gone, but they have been replaced by other predators—work overload, a nagging boss, time deadlines, excessive inflation, poorly designed jobs,
marital disharmony, the drive to keep up with the Joneses. These work and
nonwork predators interact and create stress for individuals on and off the job.

This chapter focuses primarily on the individual at work in organizations and
on the stress created in this setting. Much of the stress experienced by people in

our industrialized society originates in organizations; much of the stress that originates elsewhere affects our behavior and performance in these same organizations.

● **R6–1**   In the article "Who Beats Stress—and How" which is part of this chapter, the author, Alan Farnham, points out that what we do not understand about stress would fill volumes. His point is well taken. One of the complicating issues in understanding stress is the fact that it has been defined in a multitude of ways. We begin this chapter with our definition of stress.

WHAT IS STRESS?

Stress means different things to many different people. The businessperson thinks of stress as frustration or emotional tension; the air traffic controller thinks of it as a problem of alertness and concentration; the biochemist thinks of it as a purely chemical event. In an uncomplicated way, it is best to consider stress as something that involves the interaction of the individual with the environment.[1] Most definitions of stress recognize the individual and the environment in terms of a stimulus interaction, a response interaction, or a stimulus-response interaction.

Stimulus Definition

A stimulus definition of stress would be the following: Stress is the force or stimulus acting on the individual that results in a response of strain, where strain is pressure or, in a physical sense, deformation. One difficulty with this definition is that it fails to recognize that two people subjected to the same stress may show far different levels of strain.

Response Definition

A response definition of stress would be the following: Stress is the physiological or psychological response of an individual to an environmental stressor, where a **stressor** is a potentially harmful external event or situation. In the stimulus definition, stress is an external event; here it is an internal response. This definition fails to enable anyone to predict the nature of the stress response or even whether there will be a stress response.

Stimulus-Response Definition

An example of a stimulus-response definition is that stress is the consequence of the interaction between an environmental stimulus and the individual's response.

[1]M. T. Matteson and J. M. Ivancevich, *Controlling Work Stress* (San Francisco: Jossey-Bass, 1987).

Viewed as more than either a stimulus or a response, stress is the result of a unique interaction between stimulus conditions in the environment and the individual's predisposition to respond in a particular way.

A Working Definition

Each of the three definitions offers important insights into what constitutes stress. Consequently, we will borrow from each to develop a working definition for this chapter. We define stress as:

An adaptive response, mediated by individual differences and/or psychological processes, that is a consequence of any external (environmental) action, situation, or event that places excessive psychological and/or physical demands on a person.

This working definition portrays stress in a more negative light than do many definitions. Note, however, that we have included the term **excessive** in the definition. Clearly, not all stress is negative. The positive stress that Dr. Hans Selye referred to as eustress (from the Greek *eu,* meaning good, as in *euphoria*) is stimulating in a positive sense. Eustress provides the challenge that may serve as the basis for motivation.

The above working definition allows us to focus attention on specific environmental conditions that are potential sources of stress. Whether stress is felt or experienced by a particular individual will depend on that individual's unique characteristics. Furthermore, the definition emphasizes an adaptive response. The great majority of our responses to stimuli in the work environment do not require adaptation and thus are not really potential sources of stress.

An important point to keep in mind is that a variety of dissimilar situations— work effort, fatigue, uncertainty, fear, emotional arousal—are capable of producing stress. Therefore, it is extremely difficult to isolate a single factor as the sole cause.[2]

THE GENERAL ADAPTATION SYNDROME

Stress includes both psychological and physiological components. Dr. Hans Selye, the pioneer of stress research, was the first to conceptualize the psychophysiological responses to stress.[3] Selye considered stress a nonspecific response to any demand made upon an organism. He labeled the three phases of the defense reaction that a person establishes when stressed as the general adaptation syndrome (GAS). Selye called the defense reaction general because stressors had effects on several areas of the body. Adaptation refers to a stimulation of defenses designed to help the body adjust to or deal with the stressors. And syndrome

[2]Rita E. Numerof, *Managing Stress,* (Rockville, Md.: Aspen Publications, 1983), p. 7.

[3]Hans Selye, *The Stress of Life* (New York: McGraw-Hill, 1976); and Hans Selye, *Stress without Distress* (Philadelphia, Pa.: J. B. Lippincott, 1974).

indicates that individual pieces of the reaction occur more or less together. The three distinct phases are called *alarm*, *resistance*, and *exhaustion*.

The **alarm stage** is the initial mobilization by which the body meets the challenge posed by the stressor. When a stressor is recognized, the brain sends forth a biochemical message to all of the body's systems. Respiration increases, blood pressure rises, pupils dilate, muscles tense up, and so forth.

If the stressor continues, the GAS proceeds to the **resistance stage**. Signs of being in the resistance stage include fatigue, anxiety, and tension. The person is now fighting the stressor. While resistance to a particular stressor may be high during this stage, resistance to other stressors may be low. A person has only finite sources of energy, concentration, and ability to resist stressors. Individuals often are more illness-prone during periods of stress than at other times.[4]

The final GAS stage is **exhaustion**. Prolonged and continual exposure to the same stressor may eventually use up the adaptive energy available, and the system fighting the stressor becomes exhausted.

It is important to keep in mind that the activation of the GAS places extraordinary demands on the body. Clearly, the more frequently the GAS is activated and the longer it remains in operation, the more wear and tear there is on the psychophysiological mechanisms. The body and mind have limits. The more frequently a person is alarmed, resists, and becomes exhausted by work, nonwork, or the interaction of these activities, the more susceptible he or she becomes to fatigue, disease, aging, and other negative consequences.

STRESS AND WORK: A MODEL

For most employed individuals, work and work-related activities and preparation time represent more than a 40-hour-a-week commitment. Work is a major part of our lives, and work and nonwork activities are strongly interdependent. The distinction between stress at work and stress at home is an artificial one at best. Nonetheless, our main concern here is with stressors at work.

To better illustrate the link between stressors, stress, and consequences, we have developed an integrative model of stress and work. A managerial perspective is used to develop the parts of the model shown in Exhibit 6-1. The model divides stressors at work into four categories: physical, individual, group, and organizational. The model also presents five potential categories of the effects of stress. In this book, we are concerned primarily with the effects that influence job performance.

The model introduces moderators.[5] The moderator variables that have been investigated by occupational stress researchers include age, sex, work addiction, self-esteem, and community involvement. We have elected to discuss three

[4]Selye, *Stress without Distress*, p. 5.

[5]Robert R. Holt, "Occupational Stress," in *Handbook of Stress*, ed. L. Goldberger and S. Breznitz (New York: Free Press, 1982), pp. 419–44.

EXHIBIT 6-1

Stress and Work: A Working Model

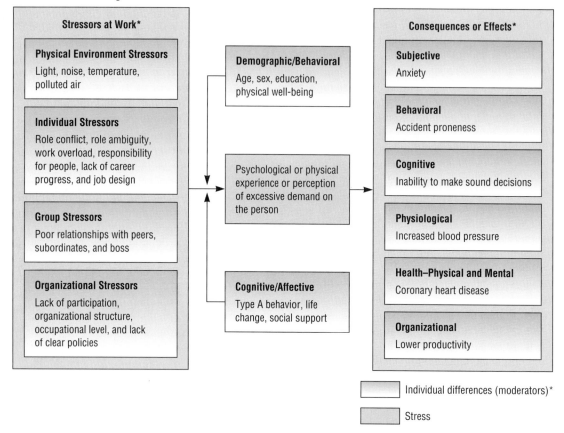

*Only some of these variables are discussed in this chapter. For a more complete discussion of these stressors and moderators, see Michael T. Matteson and John M. Ivancevich, *Controlling Work Stress* (San Francisco: Jossey-Bass, 1987).

moderators that have received the most research attention: Type A behavior pattern, social support, and life-change events. These are defined and explored later in this chapter.

Consequences of Stress

The mobilization of the body's defense mechanisms are not the only potential consequences of contact with stressors. The effects of stress are many and varied. Some effects, of course, are positive, such as self-motivation, stimulation to work harder, and increased inspiration to live a better life. However, many effects of stress are disruptive and potentially dangerous. Cox has identified five potential consequences of the effects of stress.[6] His categories include:

1. **Subjective effects:** Anxiety, aggression, apathy, boredom, depression, fatigue, frustration, loss of temper, low self-esteem, nervousness, feeling alone.
2. **Behavioral effects:** Accident proneness, alcoholism, drug abuse, emotional outbursts, excessive eating, excessive smoking, impulsive behavior, nervous laughter.
3. **Cognitive effects:** Inability to make sound decisions, poor concentration, short attention span, hypersensitivity to criticism, mental blocks.
4. **Physiological effects:** Increased blood glucose levels, increased heart rate and blood pressure, dryness of the mouth, sweating, dilation of pupils, hot and cold flashes.
5. **Organizational effects:** Absenteeism, turnover, low productivity, alienation from co-workers, job dissatisfaction, reduced organizational commitment and loyalty.

These five types are not all-inclusive, nor are they limited to effects on which there is universal agreement and for which there is clear scientific evidence. They merely represent some of the potential effects that frequently are associated with stress. It should not be inferred, however, that stress always causes the effects listed above.

Not all individuals will experience the same consequences. Research suggests, for example, that one of many factors influencing stress consequences is type of employment. In one study, conducted at the Institute for Social Research at the University if Michigan, a sample of 2,010 employees were chosen from 23 occupations to examine the relationship between stress and stress consequences. The occupations were combined into four specific groups—blue-collar workers (skilled and unskilled) and white-collar workers (professional and nonprofessional).

Blue-collar workers reported the highest subjective effects, including job dissatisfaction; white-collar workers, the lowest. The unskilled workers reported the most boredom and apathy with their job conditions. They specifically identified a number of major stressors that created their psychological state: underutilization of skills and abilities, poor fit of the job with respect to desired amounts of responsibility, lack of participation, and ambiguity about the future. Skilled blue-collar workers shared some of these stressors and consequences with their unskilled counterparts, but not all; they reported above-average utilization of their skills and abilities but had less responsibility and more ambiguity. White-collar professionals reported the fewest negative consequences. In all groups, however, there were indications that job performance was affected.[7]

---

[6]T. Cox, *Stress* (Baltimore: University Park Press, 1978), p. 92.

[7]J. French, W. Rogers, and S. Cobb, "A Model of Person-Environment Fit," in *Coping and Adaptation,* eds. G. Coelho, D. Hamburgh, and J. Adams (New York: Basic Books, 1974).

Each of the five categories of stress effects shown in Exhibit 6-1 is important from a managerial perspective. In both human and monetary terms, the costs of stress are great and growing. Based on a variety of estimates and projections from government, industry, and health groups, we place the costs of stress at approximately $100 billion annually. This estimate, which probably is conservative, attempts to take into account the dollar effects of reductions in operating effectiveness resulting from stress. These effects include poorer decision making and decreases in creativity. The huge figure also reflects the costs associated with mental and physical health problems arising from stress conditions, including hospital and medical costs, lost work time, turnover, sabotage, and a host of other variables that may contribute to stress costs.

Physical and Mental Health

Among the potential consequences of stress, those classified as physiological are perhaps the most controversial and organizationally dysfunctional. Those who hypothesize a link between stress and physical health problems are, in effect, suggesting that an emotional response is responsible for producing a physical change in an individual. In fact, most medical textbooks attribute between 50 and 75 percent of illness to stress-related origins.[8]

Perhaps the most significant of the potential stress and physical illness relationships is that of coronary heart disease (CHD). Although virtually unknown in the industrialized world 60 years ago, CHD now accounts for half of all deaths in the United States. The disease is so pervasive that American males who are now between the ages of 45 and 55 have one chance in four of dying from a heart attack in the next 10 years. Traditional risk factors such as obesity, smoking, heredity, high cholesterol, and high blood pressure can account for no more than about 25 percent of the incidence of coronary heart disease. There is growing medical opinion that job and life stress may be a major contributor in the remaining 75 percent.[9] Several studies have found, for example, a relationship between changes in blood pressure and job stress.[10]

Closely allied with the health consequences of stress are the mental health effects. Kornhauser studied extensively the mental health of industrial workers.[11] He did not find a relationship between mental health and such factors as salary, job security, and working conditions. Instead, clear associations between mental health and job satisfaction emerged. Poor mental health was associated with

[8]M. H. Brenner, "The Stressful Price of Prosperity," *Science News,* March 18, 1978, p. 166.

[9]David C. Glass, *Behavior Patterns, Stress, and Coronary Disease* (Hillsdale, N.J.: Erlbaum Associates, 1977), pp. 5–6.

[10]See, for example, Karen Matthews, Eric Cottington, Evelyn Talbott, Lewis Kuller, and Judith Siegel, "Stressful Work Conditions and Diastolic Blood Pressure among Blue-Collar Factory Workers," *American Journal of Epidemiology,* 1987, pp. 280–91.

[11]A. Kornhauser, *Mental Health of the Industrialized Worker* (New York: John Wiley & Sons, 1965).

JAPANESE WORKERS FEAR *KAROSHI*

A major Japanese insurer (Fukoku Life Insurance Co.) recently completed a survey of Japanese workers which clearly indicates work-related stress is pervasive in cultures outside the United States.

Surveying 500 employees with more than 15 years work experience at the same companies in metropolitan Tokyo, the researchers found that the fabled workaholism of Japanese white-collar workers takes its toll: Many of them dread and fear their jobs. The poll revealed a strong fear of *karoshi*—death from overwork.

There are several indications that the number of such deaths among Japanese businessmen is growing rapidly. Dr. Kiyoyasu Arikawa, who advises executives on how to reduce their risk, reports that the number of *karoshi* grew from 10 in 1969 to 150 in 1987. The Labor Ministry received 777 applications for compensation because of "sudden death" at work in 1990, a 55 percent increase from three years earlier.

The survey revealed that 70 percent of the respondents felt they were "stressed," with almost one-quarter of them experiencing "a frequent desire to call in sick." When asked if they feared death by overwork, 43 percent said yes. Fierce competition among employees, as well as a strong sense of responsibility to their companies, lead many workers to stay at the office well into the night and to refuse to take all their vacation time.

Additionally, 60 percent reported their jobs are boring and 57 percent found relationships at work stressful. What is the solution to these difficulties? Eighty-five percent of the respondents "just want to sleep more."

Source: Based on a November 29, 1990, Association Press wire release.

frustration growing out of not having a satisfying job. Similarly, a comprehensive survey of American workers concluded that a third of them experienced job stress related depression.[12] Nor are such consequences restricted to American workers, as Encounter 6-1 demonstrates.

In addition to frustration, the anxiety and depression that may be experienced by individuals under a great deal of stress may manifest itself in the form of alcoholism (about 5 percent of the adult population are problem drinkers), drug dependency (more than 150 million tranquilizer prescriptions are written in the United States annually), hospitalization (more than 25 percent of occupied hospital beds have people with psychological problems), and, in extreme cases, suicide.[13] Even the relatively minor mental disruptions produced by stress, such as the inability to concentrate or reduced problem-solving capabilities, may prove very costly to an organization.[14]

[12]*Employee Burnout: America's Newest Epidemic,* Northwestern National Life Insurance Company, 1991, p. 8.

[13]Herbert Peyser, "Stress and Alcohol," in *Handbook of Stress,* eds. L. Goldberger and S. Breznitz (New York: Free Press, 1982), p. 586.

[14]For a comprehensive review of physical and mental health outcomes of stress, see Daniel Ganster and John Schaubroeck, "Work Stress and Employee Health," *Journal of Management,* June 1991, pp. 235–72.

Before we examine parts of the stress and work model in more detail, several caveats are in order. This model, or any model attempting to integrate stress and work phenomena, is not totally complete. There are so many important variables that a complete treatment would require much more space. Furthermore, the variables we discuss are offered only as ones that provide managerial perspectives on stress. They certainly are not the only appropriate variables to consider. Finally, accurate and reliable measurement is extremely important. Management-initiated programs to manage stress at optimal levels will depend on how well these and other variables are measured.

Physical Environmental Stressors

Physical environment stressors often are termed **blue-collar stressors** because they are more a problem in blue-collar occupations.[15] More than 14,000 workers die annually in industrial accidents (nearly 55 a day, or 7 people every working hour); more than 100,000 workers are permanently disabled every year; and employees report more than 5 million occupational injuries annually.[16] New estimates of the toll of workplace chemicals, radiation, heat stress, pesticide, and other toxic materials has led the National Institute of Occupational Safety and Health (NIOSH) to estimate that about 100,000 workers may die annually from industry-related diseases that could have been prevented. With less extreme consequences, studies have linked temperature extremes, inadequate lighting, and crowding to measures of job stress.[17]

Many blue-collar workers are nervous and stressed by the alleged health consequences of working in their present jobs. Since the passage in 1970 of the Occupational Safety and Health Act (OSHA), some of the stress experienced by individuals has been reduced. Gains can be traced to employers' increased acceptance of OSHA regulations. In addition, many unions enthusiastically support the act. Problems still exist, and management now is being held responsible by the courts for stress that is related to the physical and general work environment. The number of jury compensation awards is growing, and the court's role can be expected to become even more significant in the future.[18] Encounter 6-2 illustrates the increasing role being played both by courts and by workers' compensation boards in job stress cases.

---

[15]Arthur B. Shostak, *Blue-Collar Stress* (Reading, Mass.: Addison-Wesley Publishing, 1980).

[16]Ibid., p. 19.

[17]R. L. Sutton and A. Rafaeli, "Characteristics of Work Stations as Potential Occupational Stressors," *Academy of Management Journal*, June 1987, pp. 260–76.

[18]John M. Ivancevich, Michael T. Matteson, and Edward Richards III, "Who's Liable for Stress on the Job?" *Harvard Business Review*, March–April 1985, pp. 60–72.

EMPLOYEE DAMAGE CLAIMS INCREASING

According to the July 22, 1991 issue of *Business Week,* 30 percent of the workers laid off in the last few years by Security Metal Products Corp. have filed mental stress claims. Typically, the company's insurance carrier has settled quickly because "the way the law was written we couldn't win by fighting them." In the same state in1990, $380 million was paid to workers claiming job-related stress problems. Increasingly, employees are turning to workers' compensation boards and the courts to recover damages suffered as a result of job-related stress. Consider the following cases in which employees asked for, and won, compensation:

1. A company executive alleged that the pressure of managing his unit during a time when his company was in bankruptcy led to severe depression and caused him to become an alcoholic. He filed for workers' compensation and when the claim was denied went to court. The state court ordered the company to pay.

2. A Raytheon Company employee experienced a nervous breakdown when she learned she would be transferred to another department. A state supreme court ruled she was entitled to compensation, saying her breakdown was a "personal injury arising out of and in the course of . . . employment."

3. A nurse won her case for job-related stress damages by convincing the court that the physician for whom she worked made her do all the distasteful work in the office such as telling patients the results of positive cancer tests.

4. A state trooper's duties involved cruising around a quiet rural area. He became very depressed, however, because he was on call 24 hours a day. He claimed that because he never knew when the phone would ring, his sex life deteriorated. The state supreme court approved the officer's claim for total, permanent disability. When the attorney general asked the court to reconsider, the trooper settled for a smaller monetary award.

5. A department store executive shot himself in his office. His secretary went into a state of depression after entering the office and finding him laying in a pool of blood. One year and $20,000 worth of psychiatrist bills later, she recovered. Insurance and workers' compensation refused to pay; a civil court ruled in her favor.

These are but a few examples of a rapidly growing trend. As state workers' compensation laws are becoming more liberal in their definition of what constitutes an "injury," and as the link between stress and various physical and mental health problems becomes better understood, more and more companies are finding themselves being held liable for employee stress. According to the National Council on Compensation Insurance, stress claims now account for almost 15 percent of occupational disease claims, a percentage that has tripled since 1980. Some law firms are even beginning to specialize in job stress litigation, with one having undertaken an advertising campaign which opens with the question: "Does your job make you sick?"

And what has Security Metal Products done in response to the claims they experienced? They have relocated to another state where the law is less hospitable to stress claims and their workers' compensation premiums are significantly lower.

Individual Stressors

Stressors at the individual level have been studied more than any other category presented in Exhibit 6-1. Role conflict is perhaps the most widely examined individual stressor.[19] Role conflict is present whenever compliance by an individual to one set of expectations about the job is in conflict with compliance to another set of expectations.[20] Facets of role conflict include being torn by conflicting demands from a supervisor about the job and being pressured to get along with people with whom you are not compatible. Regardless of whether role conflict results from organizational policies or from other persons, it can be a significant stressor for some individuals. For example, a study at Goddard Space Flight Center determined that about 67 percent of employees reported some degree of role conflict. The study further found that employees who experienced more role conflict also experienced lower job satisfaction and higher job-related tension.[21] It is interesting to note that the researchers also found that the greater the power or authority of the people sending the conflicting role messages, the greater was the job dissatisfaction produced by role conflict.

In order to perform their jobs well, employees need certain information regarding what they are expected to do and not to do. Employees need to know their rights, privileges, and obligations. **Role ambiguity** is a lack of understanding about the rights, privileges, and obligations that a person has for doing the job. In the study at Goddard Space Flight Center, administrators, engineers, and scientists completed a role ambiguity stress scale. The results showed that role ambiguity was significantly related to low job satisfaction and to feelings of job-related threat to people's mental and physical well-being. Furthermore, the more ambiguity a person reported, the lower was the person's utilization of intellectual skills, knowledge, and leadership skills.

Everyone has experienced **work overload** at one time or another. Overload may be of two different types: quantitative or qualitative. Having too many things to do or insufficient time to complete a job is **quantitative overload**. **Qualitative overload**, on the other hand, occurs when individuals feel that they lack the ability needed to complete their jobs or that performance standards are too high.

From a health standpoint, studies as far back as 1958 established that quantitative overload might cause biochemical changes, specifically elevations in blood cholesterol levels.[22] One study examined the relationship of overload, underload, and stress among 1,540 executives of a major corporation. Those executives in the low and high ends of the stress ranges reported and had more significant

[19]Stephen J. Havlovic and John P. Keenan, "Coping with Work Stress: The Influence of Individual Differences," *Journal of Social Behavior and Personality* 6, no. 7 (1991), pp. 199–212.

[20]J. Leigh, G. Lucas, Jr., and R. Woodman, "Effects of Perceived Organizational Factors on Role Stress-Job Attitude Relationships," *Journal of Management,* March 1988, pp. 41–58.

[21]R. L. Kahn, D. M. Wolfe, R. P. Quinn, J. D. Snoek, and R. A. Rosenthal, *Organizational Stress: Studies in Role Conflict and Ambiguity* (New York: John Wiley & Sons, 1964), p. 94.

[22]B. L. Margolis, W. M. Kroes, and R. P. Quinn, "Job Stress: An Untested Occupational Hazard," *Journal of Occupational Medicine,* October 1974, pp. 659–61.

EXHIBIT 6-2

The Underload Overload Continuum

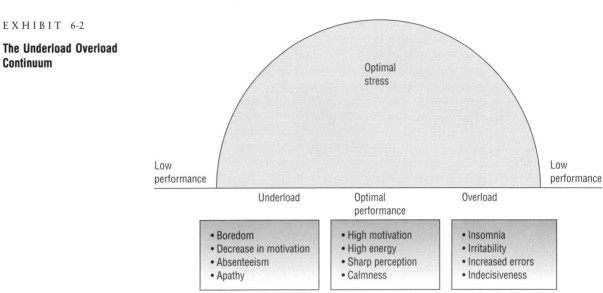

medical problems. This study suggests that the relationship between stressors, stress, and disease may be curvilinear. This is, those who are underloaded and those who are overloaded represent two ends of a continuum, each with a significantly elevated number of medical problems.[23] The underload/overload continuum is presented in Exhibit 6-2. The optimal stress level provides the best balance of challenge, responsibility, and reward. Case 6–1, "The Case of the Missing Time," portrays a situation in which overload appears to be a major problem. As you work through this case, it may be helpful to keep in mind that reducing the amount of work that must be completed may not be the only way to deal positively with overload.

▲ C6–1

Any type of responsibility can be a burden for some people. Different types of responsibility apparently function differently as stressors. One way of categorizing this variable is in terms of responsibility for people versus responsibility for things. The intensive care unit nurse, the neurosurgeon, and the air traffic controller each have a high responsibility for people. One study found support for the hypothesis that responsibility for people contributes to job-related stress.[24] The more responsibility for people reported, the more likely the employee was to smoke heavily, have high blood pressure, and show elevated cholesterol levels. Conversely, the more responsibility for things the employee reported, the lower were these indicators.

[23]Clinton Weiman, "A Study of Occupational Stressors and the Incidence of Disease/Risk," *Journal of Occupational Medicine,* February 1977, pp. 119–22.

[24]John R. P. French and Robert D. Caplan, "Psychosocial Factors in Coronary Heart Disease," *Industrial Medicine,* September 1970, pp. 383–97.

Group Stressors

The effectiveness of any organization is influenced by the nature of the relations among groups. Many group characteristics can be powerful stressors for some individuals. A number of behavioral scientists have suggested that good relationships among the members of a work group are a central factor in individual well-being.[25] Poor relations include low trust, low supportiveness, and low interest in listening to and trying to deal with the problems that confront an employee.[26] Studies in this area have reached the same conclusion: mistrust of the person one works with is positively related to high role ambiguity, which leads to inadequate communications among people and low job satisfaction.

Organizational Stressors

A problem in the study of organizational stressors is identifying which are the most important ones. Participation in decision making is considered an important part of working within organizations for some individuals. **Participation** refers to the extent that a person's knowledge, opinions, and ideas are included in the decision process. Participation can contribute to stress. Some people may be frustrated by the delays often associated with participative decision making. Others may view shared decision making as a threat to the traditional right of a supervisor or manager to have the final say.

Organizational structure is another stressor that rarely has been studied. One available study of trade salespersons examined the effects of tall (bureaucratically structured), medium, and flat (less rigidly structured) arrangements on job satisfaction, stress, and performance. It was determined that salespersons in the least bureaucratically structured arrangement experienced less stress and more job satisfaction and performed more effectively than did salespersons in the medium and tall structures.[27]

A number of studies have examined the relationship of organizational level to health effects. The majority of these studies suggest the notion that the risk of contracting such health problems as coronary heart disease increases with organizational level.[28] Not all researchers, however, support the notion that the higher one is in an organization hierarchy, the greater is the health risk. A study

---

[25]Chris Argyris, *Integrating the Individual and the Organization* (New York: John Wiley & Sons, 1964); and Cary L. Cooper, *Group Training and Organizational Development* (Basel, Switzerland: Karger, 1973).

[26]French and Caplan, "Psychosocial Factors."

[27]John M. Ivancevich and James H. Donnelly, "Relation of Organizational Structure to Job Satisfaction, Anxiety-Stress, and Performance," *Administrative Science Quarterly*, June 1975, pp. 272–80.

[28]R. V. Marks, "Social Stress and Cardiovascular Disease," *Milbank Memorial Found Quarterly*, April 1976, pp. 51–107.

of Du Pont employees found that the incidence of heart disease was inversely related to salary level.[29]

The nature of the classifications used in these studies has contributed to the confusion of the results.[30] The trend now is to look in more detail at significant job components as a way of explaining the effects of stress. Several studies, for example, have tried to assess whether inactivity or increased intellectual and emotional job demands contribute most to the increased risk of coronary heart disease. One early study contributed to this form of analysis in that it found that downtown bus drivers (sedentary jobs) and conductors (active jobs) had higher coronary heart disease than did their suburban counterparts.[31] More research is needed to determine whether emotional job demands are more powerful than inactivity in explaining the incidence of health problems.

We have considered only a very small sample of the tremendous amount of behavioral and medical research that is available on stressor, stress, and effects linkages. The information available, like other organizational research, is contradictory in some cases. However, what is available implies a number of important points. These points are:

1. There is a relationship between stressors at work and physical, psychological, and emotional changes in individuals.
2. The adaptive responses to stressors at work have been measured by self-rating, performance appraisals, and biochemical tests. Much more work must be done in properly measuring stress at work.
3. There is no universally acceptable list of stressors. Each organization has its own unique set that should be examined.
4. Individual differences explain why the same stressor that is disruptive and unsettling to one person is challenging to another person.

MODERATORS

Stressors evoke different responses from different people. Some individuals are better able to cope with a stressor than others. They can adapt their behavior in such a way as to meet the stressor head-on. On the other hand, some individuals are predisposed to stress; that is, they are not able to adapt to the stressor.

The model presented in Exhibit 6-1 suggests that various factors moderate the relationship between stressors and stress. A moderator is a condition, behavior,

[29]S. Pell and C. A. D'Alonzo, "Myocardial Infarction in a One-Year Industrial Study," *Journal of the American Medical Association,* June 1958, pp. 332–37.

[30]Cary L. Cooper and Judi Marshall, "Occupational Sources of Stress: A Review of the Literature Relating to Coronary Heart Disease and Mental Ill Health," *Journal of Occupational Psychology,* March 1976, pp. 11–28.

[31]J. N. Morris et al., "Coronary Heart Disease and Physical Activity at Work: Coronary Heart Disease in Different Occupations," *Lancet,* October 1953, pp. 1053–57.

or characteristic that qualifies the relationship between two variables. The effect may be to intensify or weaken the relationship. The relationship between the number of gallons of gasoline used and total miles driven, for example, is affected by the variable speed (a moderator). Likewise, an individual's personality may moderate or affect the extent to which that individual experiences stress as a consequence of being in contact with a particular stressor. We will briefly examine three of many possible moderators: (1) Type A behavior pattern (TABP), (2) social support, and (3) life-change events.

Type A Behavior Pattern (TABP)

Cardiovascular disease is the leading cause of death in the United States. Nearly 1 million Americans die of cardiovascular disease each year, and more than 40 million Americans are afflicted with some form of the disease.[32]

In the 1950s two medical cardiologists and researchers, Meyer Friedman and Ray Rosenman, discovered what they called the **Type A behavior pattern (TABP)**.[33] They searched the medical literature and found that traditional coronary risk factors such as dietary cholesterol, blood pressure, and heredity could not totally explain or predict coronary heart disease (CHD). **Coronary heart disease** is the term given to cardiovascular diseases that are characterized by an inadequate supply of oxygen to the heart. Other factors seemed to the two researchers to be playing a major role in CHD. Through interviews with and observation of patients, they began to uncover a pattern of behavior or traits. They eventually called this the Type A behavior pattern (TABP).

The person with TABP has these characteristics:

- Chronically struggles to get as many things done as possible in the shortest time period.
- Is aggressive, ambitious, competitive, and forceful.
- Speaks explosively, rushes others to finish what they are saying.
- Is impatient, hates to wait, considers waiting a waste of precious time.
- Is preoccupied with deadlines and is work-oriented.
- Is always in a struggle with people, things, events.

The converse, Type B individual, mainly is free of the TABP characteristics and generally feels no pressing conflict with either time or persons. The Type B may have considerable drive, wants to accomplish things, and works hard, but the Type B has a confident style that allows him or her to work at a steady pace and not race against the clock. The Type A has been likened to a racehorse; the Type B, to a turtle. Exercise 6–1 will provide you with an opportunity to assess your Type A or B characteristics.

■ E6–1

[32]Virginia, A. Price, *Type A Behavior Pattern* (New York: Academic Press, 1982), p. 3.

[33]Meyer Friedman and Diane Ulmer, *Treating Type A Behavior and Your Heart* (New York: Alfred A. Knopf, 1984).

Since the early work of Friedman and Rosenman on TABP, a number of studies have examined whether Type A is a predictor of CHD.[34] Some of these follow.

Western Collaborative Group Study

The first major prospective study designed to examine the coronary risk associated with Type A behavior was the Western Collaborative Study.[35] The study used a double blind design in that the researchers assessing Type A had no knowledge of the 3,154 men's health status. Those researchers assessing coronary heart disease risk (e.g., blood pressure, cholesterol level, triglycerides, and family history) had no knowledge of the men's Type A behavior. Structured interviews (SI) were used to assess Type A at the beginning and also 8.5 years later. The men assessed as Type A had a risk ratio of 2.2 for development of coronary heart disease compared to Type Bs. The 2-to-1 risk ratio remained after multivariate statistical adjustment for the traditional risk factors.

MRFIT Study

The Multiple Risk Factor Intervention Trial (MRFIT) was a large-scale clinical trial designed to alter behaviors associated with the traditional coronary heart disease factors.[36] A subset of MRFIT participants (n = 3,110) were recruited to determine whether the prospective findings of the Western Collaborative Group Study would be replicated.[37] Rosenman trained and certified the SI interviewers. Eight centers from different regions of the United States followed the assessment and seven-year follow-up phases of the study. All assessments were done blind to Type A behavior of participants. Final results revealed no relationship between SI-defined Type A or self-report-defined Type A and any clinical manifestations of coronary heart disease.

Subcomponent Research

The MRFIT research pointed to the need to move beyond assessing only global Type A behavior. An increasing number of researchers are attempting to determine which aspects of Type A are the most "toxic."[38] Thus, instead of examining a

[34]For a thorough review and appraisal, see Suzanne G. Haynes and Karen A. Matthews, "Review and Methodologic Critique of Recent Studies on Type A Behavior and Cardiovascular Disease," *Annals of Behavioral Medicine*, 1988, pp. 47–59.

[35]R. H. Rosenman, R. J. Brand, C. D. Jenkins et al. "Coronary Heart Disease in the Western Collaborative Group Study: Final Follow-Up Experience of 8 and 1/2 Years." *Journal of American Medical Association* 233 (1975), pp. 872–77.

[36]R. B. Shekelle, S. B. Hulley, J. D. Neaton et al. "The MRFIT Behavior Pattern Study: II. Type A Behavior and Incidence of Coronary Heart Disease," *American Journal of Epidemiology* 122 (1985), pp. 559–70.

[37]J. Stamler, "Type A Behavior Pattern: An Established Major Risk Factor for Coronary Heart Disease," in *Current Controversies in Cardiovascular Disease*, ed. E. Rappaport (Philadelphia: W. B. Saunders, 1980).

[38]R. B. Williams, Jr., "Type A Behavior and Coronary Heart Disease: Something Old, Something New," *Behavior Medicine Update* 6 (1984), pp. 29–33.

global Type A factor, these researchers are assessing subcomponents of Type A or behavioral factors not associated with Type A. Williams proposes that hostility and anger are the most damaging components of Type A in terms of coronary heart disease.[39] He has used the Cook-Medley Ho Scale as a measure of hostility. The Ho scale consists of 50 Minnesota Multiphasic Personality Inventory items that can be answered in either a hostile or nonhostile direction. Ho scores increase as a function of increasing Type A behavior as assessed by SI. Among Duke Medical Center patients with Ho scores of 10 or less, only 48 percent had significant coronary heart disease problems. Among those with scores above 10, 70 percent had problems. The relationship of Type A to coronary heart disease is significant in both men and women. Other studies employing hostility measures have yielded similar results.[40]

Other subcomponent research has focused on the achievement orientation portion of Type A behavior, and on the finding that Type As tend to display impatience and irritability when the pace of events is not moving rapidly enough for their liking. One such study found no negative health consequences associated with the achievement component, but did demonstrate significant relationships between impatience-irritability and depression.[41] As researchers learn more about the individual components that comprise Type A behavior further refinements in our understanding of the toxic portion of the behavior pattern can be expected.

The accumulated evidence at this point suggests strongly that managers attempting to manage stress should include TABP in their assessments. Failure to do so would ignore some of the better interdisciplinary research (behavioral and medical) that has been conducted over the past 25 years. Of all the moderators that could or should be included in a stress model, TABP seems to be one of the most promising for additional consideration.

Social Support

Numerous studies have linked social support with many aspects of health, illness, and quality of life.[42] The literature offers a number of definitions of social support. Some of these definitions focus on the exchange of information or material, the availability of a confidant, and gratification of basic social needs. Social support is defined as the comfort, assistance, or information one receives through formal or informal contacts with individuals or groups.[43] This definition would apply

[39]Ibid.

[40]Timithy W. Smith and Mary K. Pope, "Cynical Hostility as a Health Risk: Current Status and Future Directions," in *Type A Behavior,* ed. M. Strube (Newbury Park, Calif.: Sage, 1991).

[41]S. D. Bluen, J. Barling, and W. Burns, "Predicting Sales Performance, Job Satisfaction, and Depression by Using the Achievement Strivings and Impatience-Irritability Dimensions of Type A Behavior," *Journal of Applied Psychology* 75, 1990, pp. 212–16.

[42]See for example James G. Anderson, "Stress and Burnout among Nurses: A Social Network Approach," *Journal of Social Behavior and Personality* 6, no. 7 (1991), pp. 251–72.

[43]Barbara S. Wallston, Sheryle W. Alagna, Brenda M. DeVellis, and Robert F. DeVellis, "Social Support and Physical Health," *Health Psychology,* Fall 1983, pp. 367–91.

to a co-worker listening to a friend who failed to receive a desired promotion, a group of recently laid-off workers helping each other find new employment, or an experienced employee helping a new hiree learn a job.

Social support has been operationalized as the number of people one interacts with, the frequency of contact with other individuals, or the individual's perceptions about the adequacy of interpersonal contact. The limited amount of research using these factors suggests that social support protects or buffers individuals from the negative consequences of stressors. One study showed significant interactions of social support and work stress for factory workers. The support of co-workers moderated the relationship between role conflict and health complaints.[44] The higher the level of social support reported, the fewer were the health complaints reported.

A recent study examined the relationship between social support and a personality variable discussed previously in Chapter 3, locus of control, on job stress. In a sample of over 300 police officers and firefighters, the researchers found that social support buffered the effects of job stress on physical health complaints. They further found that the buffering effect of social support was much greater for internal locus-of-control participants than for externals.[45]

The best evidence to date on the importance of social support derives from the literature on rehabilitation, recovery, and adaptation to illness.[46] For example, better outcomes have been found in alcohol treatment programs when the alcoholic's family is supportive and cohesive.[47] Managerial use of social support research in reducing stress will be expanded as more organizationally based research is conducted.[48]

Life-Change Events

Common sense holds that when individuals undergo extremely stressful changes in their lives, their personal health likely will suffer at some point. Research work on this intriguing proposition was initiated by Holmes and Rahe.[49] Their work led to the development of the Schedule of Recent Life Events, of which a later version was titled the Social Readjustment Rating Scale (SRRS). Through research

[44]J. M. LaRocco, J. S. House, and J. R. P. French, "Social Support, Occupational Stress, and Health," *Journal of Health and Social Behavior,* June 1980, pp. 202–18.

[45]M. R. Fusilier, D. C. Ganster, and B. T. Mayes, "Effects of Social Support, Role Stress, and Locus of Control on Health," *Journal of Management,* Fall 1987, pp. 517–28.

[46]R. E. Mitchell, A. G. Billings, and R. H. Moos, "Social Support and Well Being: Implications for Prevention Programs," *Journal of Primary Prevention,* February 1982, pp. 77–98; and E. L. Cowen, "Help Is Where You Find It: Four Informal Helping Groups," *American Psychologist,* April 1982, pp. 385–95.

[47]Benjamin H. Gottlieb, *Social Support Strategies* (Beverly Hills, Calif.: Sage Publications, 1983).

[48]James J. House, *Work Stress and Social Support* (Reading, Mass.: Addison-Wesley Publishing, 1981).

[49]T. H. Holmes and R. H. Rahe, "Social Readjustment Scale," *Journal of Psychosomatic Research,* 1967, pp. 213–18.

and analysis, Holmes and Rahe weighted the SRRS. An individual is asked to indicate which of the listed events has happened to him or her in the past 12 months. The SRRS is presented in Exhibit 6-3.

Holmes and Rahe found that individuals reporting life-change units totaling 150 points or less generally had good health the following year. However, those reporting life-change units totaling between 150 and 300 points had about a 50 percent chance of developing a serious illness the following year. And among individuals scoring 300 or more points, there was at least a 70 percent chance of contracting a major illness the following year.

The relationships found between life-change event scores and personal health problems have not been overwhelming.[50] The correlations in most studies between the total score and major health problems the following year have been relatively low.[51] Of course, many individuals who are exposed to many life changes show absolutely no subsequent health problems. That is, they are hardy enough to withstand the consequences of life changes.

Kobasa proposed that individuals who experienced high life-change unit scores without becoming ill might differ, in terms of personality, from individuals who had subsequent health problems.[52] She refers to the personality characteristic as "hardiness." The individuals with the hardiness personality seem to possess three important characteristics. First, they believe that they can control the events they encounter. Second, they are extremely committed to the activities in their lives. Third, they treat change in their lives as a challenge.

In a longitudinal study to test the three-characteristic theory of hardiness, managers were studied over a two-year period. It was determined that the more managers possessed hardiness characteristics, the smaller was the negative impact of life change units on their personal health.[53] Hardiness appeared to buffer the negative impact of life changes.

ORGANIZATIONAL PROGRAMS TO MANAGE STRESS

An astute manger never ignores a turnover or absenteeism problem, work-place drug abuse, a decline in performance, reduced quality in production, or any other sign that the organization's performance goals are not being met. The effective manager, in fact, views these occurrences as symptoms and looks beyond them

[50]Scott M. Monroe, "Major and Minor Life Events as Predictors of Psychological Distress: Further Issues and Findings," *Journal of Behavioral Medicine,* June 1983, pp. 189–205.

[51]David V. Perkins, "The Assessment of Stress Using Life Events Scales," in *Handbook of Stress,* eds. L. Goldberger and S. Breznitz (New York: Free Press, 1982), pp. 320–31.

[52]Suzanne C. Kobasa, "Conceptualization and Measurement of Personality in Job Stress Research," In *Occupational Stress: Issues and Developments in Research,* ed. Joseph J. Hurrell, Jr., Lawrence R. Murphy, Steven L. Sauter, and Cary L. Cooper (New York: Taylor & Francis, 1988), pp. 100–109.

[53]S. C. Kobasa, S. R. Maddi, and S. Kahn, "Hardiness and Health: A Prospective Study," *Journal of Personality and Social Psychology,* January 1982, pp. 168–77.

EXHIBIT 6-3

**Social
Readjustment
Rating Scale**

Rank	Life Event	Mean Value
1	Death of spouse	100
2	Divorce	73
3	Marital separation	65
4	Jail term	63
5	Death of close family member	63
6	Personal injury or illness	53
7	Marriage	50
8	Fired at work	47
9	Marital reconciliation	45
10	Retirement	45
11	Change in health of family member	44
12	Pregnancy	40
13	Sex difficulties	39
14	Gain of new family member	39
15	Business readjustment	39
16	Change in financial state	38
17	Death of close friend	37
18	Change to different line of work	36
19	Change in number of arguments with spouse	35
20	Mortgage over $10,000	31
21	Foreclosure of mortgage or loan	30
22	Change in responsibilities at work	29
23	Son or daughter leaving home	29
24	Trouble with in-laws	29
25	Outstanding personal achievement	28
26	Spouse beginning or stopping work	26
27	Beginning or ending school	26
28	Change in living conditions	25
29	Revision of personal habits	24
30	Trouble with boss	23
31	Change in work hours or conditions	20
32	Change in residence	20
33	Change in schools	20
34	Change in recreation	19
35	Change in church activities	19
36	Change in social activities	18
37	Mortgage or loan less than $10,000	17
38	Change in sleeping habits	16
39	Change in number of family get-togethers	15
40	Change in eating habits	15
41	Vacation	13
42	Christmas	12
43	Minor violations of the law	11

The amount of life stress that a person has experienced in a given period of time, say one year, is measured by the total number of life change units (LCUs). These units result from the addition of the values (shown in the right-hand column) associated with events that the person has experienced during the target period.

Source: Thomas H. Holmes and Richard H. Rahe, "The Social Readjustment Rating Scale," *Journal of Psychosomatic Research*, 1967, pp. 213–18.

to identify and correct the underlying causes. Yet most managers today likely will search for traditional causes such as poor training, detective equipment, or inadequate instructions on what needs to be done. In all likelihood, stress is not on the list of possible problems. Thus, the very first step in any program to manage stress so that it remains within tolerable limits is recognition that it exists. Any intervention program to manage stress first must determine whether stress exists and what is contributing to its existence.

Some programs indicate the specific problem on which they are focused: alcohol or drug abuse program, job relocation program, career counseling program, and so forth. Others are more general: the Emotional Health Program of Equitable Life, the Employee Assistance Center at B. F. Goodrich, the Illinois Bell Health Evaluation Program, and the Caterpillar Tractor Special Health Services.

Originally, labels such as mental health were used. However, to get away from the connotation of serious psychiatric disease, companies have changed the names of their programs. Today, a popular name is stress management, and two prototypes of stress-management programs appear to be in use: clinical and organizational. The former is initiated by the firm and focuses on individual problems. The latter deals with units or groups in the work force and focuses on problems of the group or the total organization.

Clinical Programs

These programs are based on the traditional medical approach to treatment. Some of the elements in the programs include:

- **Diagnosis:** Person with problem asks for help. Person or people in employee health unit attempt to diagnose problem.
- **Treatment:** Counseling or supportive therapy is provided. If staff within company can't help, employee is referred to professionals in community.
- **Screening:** Periodic examination of individuals in highly stressful jobs is provided to detect early indications of problems.
- **Prevention:** Education and persuasion are used to convince employees at high risk that something must be done to help them cope with stress.

Clinical programs, or employee-assistance programs as they are frequently called, may be internal company-run programs or external efforts in which the organization contracts with a private firm to provide services to company employees. The previously cited Emotional Health Program at Equitable Life is typical of such programs. It is concerned with prevention, treatment, and referral of employees. Staffed by a clinical psychologist, a physician, a psychology intern, and a counselor, it focuses on individual intervention. Offered are biofeedback, relaxation training, and counseling. When appropriate, referrals are made to external mental health practitioners and hospitals.[54] All such programs must be

---

[54]J. M. Ivancevich, M. T. Matteson, S. M. Freedman, and J. S. Phillips, "Worksite Stress Management Interventions," *American Psychologist*, February 1990, pp. 252–61.

staffed by competent personnel if they are to provide benefits. The trust and respect of users must be earned, and this is possible only if a qualified staff exists to provide diagnosis, treatment, screening, and prevention services.

Organizational Programs

Organizational programs are aimed more broadly at an entire employee population. Sometimes extensions of the clinical program, they are often stimulated by problems identified in a group or a unit or by some impending change such as the relocation of a plant, the closing of a plant, or the installation of new equipment. Such programs are found at IBM, Dow Chemical, Control Data, and Equitable Life. In many of these programs, health appraisals like the one found in Exercise 6–2, "Health Risk Appraisal," are administered.

■ **E6–2**

A variety of organizational programs can be used to manage work stress, including management by objectives, organizational development programs, job enrichment, redesigning the structure of the organization, establishing autonomous work groups, establishing variable work schedules, and providing employee health facilities. For example, such companies as Xerox, Rockwell International, Weyerhaeuser, and PepsiCo are spending thousands of dollars for gyms equipped with treadmills, exercise bicycles, jogging tracks, and full-time physical education and health care staffs. One of the more impressive programs is found at Kimberly-Clark, where $2.5 million has been invested in a 7,000-square-foot health-testing facility and a 32,000-square-foot physical fitness facility staffed by 15 full-time health care personnel.[55]

Ensuring Program Success

Simply offering a clinical or organization-type stress management program does not guarantee positive results for either employees or the sponsoring organization. While many factors will determine how successful any particular program will be, a number of recommendations, if followed, will increase the likelihood of beneficial outcomes. Among the more important ones are:

1. Top-management support, including both philosophical support and support in terms of staff and facilities, is necessary.
2. Unions should support the program and participate in it where appropriate.
3. The greatest payoff from stress management comes not from one-shot activities but from ongoing and sustained effort; thus, long-term commitment is essential.
4. Extensive and continuing employee involvement would include involvement not only in the initial planning but in implementation and maintenance as well. This is one of the most critical factors for ensuring representative employee participation.

[55]J. M. Ivancevich and M. T. Matteson, "*Stress at Work,*" (Glenview, Ill.: Scott, Foresman, 1980), p. 215.

5. Clearly stated objectives lay a solid foundation for the program. Programs with no or poorly defined objectives are not likely to be effective or achieve sufficient participation to make them worthwhile.
6. Employees must be able to participate freely, without either pressure or stigma.
7. Confidentiality must be strictly adhered to. Employees must have no concerns that participation will in any way affect their standing in the organization.

The last point, that of confidentiality, is particularly critical. Not only is it essential for program success, it helps illustrate that there are important ethical issues involved in the operation of corporate stress management programs. Encounter 6-3 discusses confidentiality and some other important ethical issues as well.

INDIVIDUAL APPROACHES TO STRESS

There are also many individual approaches to managing stress. To see this, all you have to do is visit any bookstore and look at the self-improvement section. It will be stocked with numerous how-to-do-it books for reducing stress. We have selected only a few of the more popularly cited methods for individually managing stress. They have been selected because (1) some research is available on their impact, (2) they are widely cited in both the scientific literature and the popular press, and (3) scientifically sound evaluations of their effectiveness are under way.

Cognitive Techniques

The basic rationale for some individual approaches to stress management, known collectively as cognitive techniques, is that people's responses to stressors are mediated by cognitive processes, or thoughts.[56] The underlying assumption of these techniques is that people's thoughts, in the form of expectations, beliefs, and assumptions, are labels they apply to situations, and these labels elicit emotional responses to the situations. Thus, for example, if an individual labels the loss of a promotion a catastrophe, the stress response is to the label, not to the situation. Cognitive techniques of stress management focus on changing labels or cognitions so that people appraise situations differently. This reappraisal typically centers on removing cognitive distortions such as magnifying, overgeneralizing, and personalization.[57] All cognitive techniques have a similar objective: to help individuals gain more control over their reactions to stressors by modifying their cognitions.

[56]C. P. Kimble, "Stress and Psychosomatic Illness," *Journal of Psychosomatic Research*, 1982, pp. 63–71.
[57]H. R. Beech, L. Burns, and B. Sheffield, *A Behavioral Approach to the Management of Stress*, (New York: John Wiley & Sons, 1984).

E N C O U N T E R • 6-3

ETHICAL ISSUES IN CORPORATE STRESS MANAGEMENT PROGRAMS

There are aspects of stress management programs that necessitate making decisions which may involve significant ethical issues. While there are others, three important kinds of ethical concerns include:

1. *Confidentiality.* While maintaining confidentiality is critical to program success, is it inviolate? What if an employee admits to a counselor to drinking on the job and the safety of other workers is compromised? What are the ethics of maintaining confidentiality in that situation? Of not maintaining confidentiality?
2. *Should programs be compulsory or voluntary?* If a particular program has been shown to have a significant positive effect, should participation be mandatory for all employees, or for all employees who are known to have the problem the program addresses? Or, should employees have the right to participate or not as they see fit? While it may seem

clear that individuals should not be "forced" to participate, is it really? Companies require individuals to come to work, to participate in training programs, to get annual physical exams; is stress management participation different?

3. *Program scope and coverage.* In a way this is the reverse of the previous issue. If a particular program is known to be beneficial to participants, should not everyone who wishes be allowed to participate? In other words, what are the ethical considerations involved in restricting participation to only those with certain job titles or responsibilities, or to those from whom the organization expects to receive the greatest payoff?

There may be no concrete universal answers to these questions. Nonetheless, they are important issues which organizations must be prepared to address when designing and implementing stress management programs.

Evaluative research of cognitive techniques to stress management is not extensive, although the studies reported to date are generally positive. Representative occupational groups where research has indicated positive outcomes with the use of cognitive approaches include nurses, teachers, athletes, and air traffic controllers.[58] The positive research, coupled with the wide range and scope of situations and stressors amenable to such an approach, make cognitive techniques particularly attractive as an individual stress management strategy.

Relaxation

The general purpose of relaxation training is to reduce the individual's arousal level and bring about a calmer state of affairs from both psychological and physiological perspectives. Psychologically, successful relaxation results in enhanced feelings of well-being, peacefulness, a sense of being in control, and a reduction in felt tension and anxiety; physiologically, decreases in blood pressure,

[58]Donald Meichenbaum, *Stress Inoculation Training,* (New York: Pergamon Press, 1985).

respiration, and heart rate should take place. Relaxation techniques include breathing exercises; muscle relaxation; autogenic training, which combines elements of muscle relaxation and meditation; and a variety of mental relaxation strategies, including imagery and visualization.[59]

Just as stress is an adaptive response of the body, there is also an adaptive antistress response, "a relaxation response."[60] Benson reports that in this response, muscle tension decreases, heart rate and blood pressure decrease, and breathing slows.[61] The stimuli necessary to produce relaxation include (a) a quiet environment, (b) closed eyes, (c) a comfortable position, and (d) a repetitive mental device.

Meditation

Transcendental meditation, or TM, is a form of meditation that has attracted many individuals. Its originator, Maharishi Mahesh Yogi, defines TM as turning the attention toward the subtler levels of thought until the mind transcends the experience of the subtlest state of thought and arrives at the source of thought.[62] The basic procedure used in TM is simple, but the effects claimed for it are extensive. One simply sits comfortably with closed eyes and engages in the repetition of a special sound (a mantra) for about 20 minutes twice a day. Studies available indicate that TM practices are associated with reduced heart rate, lowered oxygen consumption, and decreased blood pressure.[63]

Not everyone who mediates experiences positive payoffs. A sufficiently large number of people report meditation to be effective in managing stress, however, that a number of organizations have started, supported, or approved of meditation programs for employees. They include, among others, Coors Brewing, Monsanto Chemicals, Xerox, Connecticut General Life Insurance Company, and the U.S. Army.

Biofeedback

Individuals can be taught to control a variety of internal body processes by using a technique called biofeedback. In biofeedback, small changes occurring in the body or brain are detected, amplified, and displayed to the person. Sophisticated recording and computer technology makes it possible for a person to attend to subtle changes in heart rate, blood pressure, temperature, and brain-wave patterns that normally would be unobservable.[64] Most of these processes are affected by stress.

---

[59]M. T. Matteson and J. M. Ivancevich, "Individual Stress Management Interventions: Evaluation of Techniques," *Journal of Management Psychology* 1 (1987), pp. 24–30.

[60]Herbert Benson, *The Relaxation Response* (New York: William Morrow, 1975).

[61]Herbert Benson and Robert L. Allen, "How Much Stress Is Too Much?" *Harvard Business Review*, September–October 1980, p. 88.

[62]P. Carrington, *Freedom in Meditation* (New York: Anchor Press, 1978).

[63]D. Kuna, "Meditation and Work," *Vocational Guidance Quarterly*, June 1975, pp. 342–46.

[64]Philip G. Zimbardo, *Psychology and Life* (Glenview, Ill.: Scott, Foresman, 1979), p. 551.

The potential role of biofeedback as an individual stress management technique can be seen from the bodily functions that can, to some degree, be brought under voluntary control. These include brain waves, heart rates, muscle tension, body temperature, stomach acidity, and blood pressure. Most if not all of these processes are affected by stress. The potential of biofeedback, then, is its ability to help induce a state of relaxation and restore bodily functions to a nonstressed state. One advantage of biofeedback over nonfeedback techniques is that it gives precise data about bodily functions. By interpreting the feedback, individuals know how high their blood pressure is, for example, and discover, through practice, means of lowering it. When they are successful, the feedback provides instantaneous information to that effect.

Biofeedback training has been useful in reducing anxiety, lowering stomach acidity (and thus, reducing the likelihood of ulcer formation), controlling tension and migraine headaches, and in general, reducing negative physiological manifestations of dysfunctional stress. Despite these positive results in controlled situations, individuals using biofeedback devices must remain cautious. It is unlikely that the average employee could effectively alter any biological process without proper training and expensive equipment.

■ **E6–3** It should be noted that none of these individual approaches to stress management was utilized by Mr. Dana in Exercise 6–3. In completing this exercise, you may wish to consider how these approaches might make a positive contribution to Mr. Dana's coping.

SUMMARY OF KEY POINTS

- Stress may be viewed as either a stimulus or a response. We view it as an **adaptive** response, mediated by individual factors, that is the result of a situation which makes unusual demands on a person.

- As individuals, we establish a defense reaction to stress. This reaction is termed the **general adaptation syndrome** (GAS). The three phases of the GAS are alarm, resistance, and exhaustion.

- Major variables in an integrative model of stress are 1) **stressors** (individual, group, organizational, and physical environment), 2) stress itself, 3) consequences (subjective, behavioral, cognitive, physiological, health, organizational), and 3) individual differences (demographic/behavioral, cognitive/affective).

- Three important variables which moderate the relationship between stressors and stress are 1) the Type A behavior pattern, 2) social support, and 3) significant life-change events.

- Numerous programs initiated and sponsored by organizations are available for managing work-related stress. Most of these programs may be characterized as being either clinical or organizational in nature. Clinical programs are based on the traditional medical approach to treatment and include employee assistance programs. Organizational programs are aimed more broadly at all employees and may include management by objectives, job enrichment, organizational development programs, and a variety of other approaches.

- Individual intervention programs for managing stress are numerous. The more promising programs of this kind include cognitive techniques, relaxation training, meditation, and biofeedback.

REVIEW AND DISCUSSION QUESTIONS

1. Does the kind of definition of stress an organization uses have implications for its stress management programs? Can you give an example?

2. Think of a stressful experience that might commonly occur in a work setting. Explain what is happening to the individual experiencing the stress using the General Adaptation Syndrome model.

3. Why would achieving the goal of eliminating all stress in the workplace be counterproductive for organizations?

4. Exhibit 6-1 suggests that there are several levels of work stressors. The same figure indicates that a number of individual factors moderate the relationship between stressors and stress. Are certain individual factors more or less likely to moderate the effects of certain stressors? Explain.

5. With very few exceptions unions have not been receptive to, or supportive of, stress management programs. Why do you suppose this is true? As a manager, how would you gain the union's cooperation in an organizationally sponsored stress management program?

6. What subcomponents of the Type A behavior pattern appear to be the most toxic?

7. Many different aspects of one's life may contribute to the formation and maintenance of Type A behavior. Discuss how each of the following might contribute: the work environment, school, television, home life as a child.

8. How should an organization decide whether to offer stress management programs? What sort of issues should be taken into consideration in deciding between a clinical or organization approach to such programs?

9. Chapter 3 examined several personality characteristics or traits. How might those act as moderators of the stress-stressor relationship? What other aspects of personality might serve as moderators.

10. Increasingly, American workers are being sent on overseas assignments. What stressors might be unique to such assignments. What might organizations do to minimize their impact?

•

READING

READING 6-1 WHO BEATS STRESS BEST—AND HOW
Alan Farnham

In a faster-spinning world, managers are finding new ways to ease stress in workers and themselves. Wisdom comes from surprising sources—like the Army—and pays off.

What we don't understand about stress could fill volumes. And it does. Some books say stress is an invigorating tonic; others, that it's lethal. Stress stands implicated in practically every complaint of modern life, from equipment downtime to premature ejaculation, from absenteeism to sudden death. Some workers in high-stress occupations—bomb deactivators, for example—suffer its effects hardly at all. Yet a man who tastes port for a living lies awake some nights worried that "the whole business is riding on my palate." There's enough apparently contradictory information about stress to make any honest seeker after truth, well, anxious.

Isn't there more stress today than ever before? There might be. There might be more love. But neither condition is quantifiable. Diseases to which stress contributes—hypertension, heart attack, ulcers, the common cold—are quantifiable, but since stress isn't their only cause, an increase in them doesn't necessarily signal an increase in stress.

Ask people if they *feel* more stressed, and, of course, they say yes. Who would admit, even if it were true, that he feels *less* stressed than he did a year ago? Inner peace is seen to be the prerogative of dweebs. It's hip to be stressed. Earlier this year Northwestern National Life Insurance questioned a random sample of 600 U.S. workers. Almost half (46%) said their jobs were highly stressful; 34% said they felt so much stress they were thinking of quitting.

Some of then were telling the truth. Commutes really are growing longer, highways more congested. In more families, both husbands and wives have jobs. And with upsizings, downsizings, rightsizings, takeovers, and mergers, the corporate world in recent years has turned upside down more times than James Dean's roadster.

Source: "Who Beats Stress Best—And How," *Fortune*, October 7, 1991, pp. 71–86.

The number of stress-related workers' compensation claims has ballooned in states such as California that compensate for so-called mental-mental injuries. In these, an intangible (mental) injury results from an intangible (mental) cause, such as stress. California courts have awarded compensation to workers who just say they feel hurt. Judith Bradley, a former cake decorator with Albertson's, a supermarket chain, won compensation in part because she said her supervisor had been "very curt" with her. He had told her to "get the lead out" and to "get your butt in high gear," and had reprimanded her for leaving cakes out of the freezer. She was distressed, sued, and won.

Though recently the number of stress-related claims has begun to decline in California, dollar costs nationally continue to rise. Donna Dell, manager of employee relations for Wells Fargo Bank, says workers suffering from stress "typically are out a long, long time, and they need lots of rehabilitation," including costly visits to psychiatrists. In medical treatment and time lost, stress cases cost, on average, twice as much as other workplace injuries: more than $15,000 each.

Perhaps the most telling sign of stress's apparent rise: strong business for purveyors of relief. Psychologist Stanley Fisher, a Manhattan hypnotist, says the demise of New York's boom-boom real estate market has sent many relief-seeking former brokers and developers his way. Gene Cooper, a partner at Corporate Counseling Associates (a supplier of corporate employee assistance programs), says, "It used to be, 3% to 5% of our calls for counseling were stress related. Now, more like 8% to 14%." They come from all levels, clerks to VPs.

There are stress-fighting tapes, goggles that send pulses of white light into your head, vibrating music beds ("not quite like the first time you had sex," says one manufacturer, "but maybe the second"). Morgan Fairchild has a video out (*Morgan Fairchild Stress Management*, $19.95).

Whenever the status quo gets a good shaking—even where that shaking eventually results in grater opportunity and freedom of choice—stress goes up, as people scramble to adapt. Yet if change is a constant, and if everyone is susceptible to stress, why doesn't everyone suffer from it equally? Why do some maddeningly healthy people appear not to suffer from it at all?

Not everyone finds the same event stressful. Drop a scorpion into a box of puppies, and you get stressed puppies. But drop it into a box of elf owls, which eat scorpions, and you get satisfaction. If a tree falls in the rain forest and nobody from Ben & Jerry's hears it, is there stress? No. Perhaps you think drinking port is fun. Peter Ficklin, wine master of Ficklin Vineyards, a California portmaker, says, "Sure, it's a pleasure to taste port. But the fortified wine category is down. There's increased competition. In the busy season, sometimes, I have trouble sleeping. The whole business is riding on my palate."

Some people are protected from stress by buffers. For example, the more mastery or control a person feels he has over circumstances, the less stress he's apt to feel, even if his control extends no further than the power to decide how he's going to feel about change. A surefire recipe for creating stress is to put someone in a job that affords him little decision-making power but carries great responsibility or imposes heavy psychological demands.

Rare is the job where an employee has complete control. Wally Goelzer, a flight attendant for Alaska Airlines, has plenty of control over his schedule—he's got 11 years' seniority. But the workplace limits his freedom: "Probably the worst incident in the last six months was an alcohol situation. The plane was full of a mixture of tourists and commercial fishermen. I had to tell this guy, one of the fishermen, that we wouldn't serve him any more alcohol. Now these fisherman are out on their boat sometimes six or eight weeks. He wasn't pleased. Yelling. Profanities. People around him were not having an ideal travel experience. 'What you're doing,' I told him, 'is you're being loud now.' I didn't want to stir him up too much, since we're all trapped in a tube at 29,000 feet."

The most potent buffer against stress may well be membership in a stable, close-knit group or community. Example: the town of Roseto, Pennsylvania. Stress researcher Dr. Stewart Wolf wondered 25 years ago why Roseto's residents, though they smoked, drank, ate fat, and otherwise courted doom, lived free from heart disease and other stress-related ills. He suspected their protection sprang from the town's uncommon social cohesion and stability: It was inhabited almost entirely by descendants of Italians who had moved there 100 years previously from Roseto, Italy. Few married outside the community; the firstborn was always named after a grandparent; ostentation or any display of superiority was avoided, since that would invite "the evil eye" from one's neighbor.

Wolf predicted Rosetians would start dying like flies if the modern world intruded. It did. They did. By the mid-1970s, Rosetians had Cadillacs, ranch-style homes, mixed marriages, new names, and a rate of coronary heart disease the same as any other town's.

The U.S. Army tries to instill a Rosetian cohesion prophylactically. Says Dr. David Marlowe, chief of the department of military psychiatry at the Walter Reed Army Institute of Research: "If a bond trader feels stress, he can go meditate for 20 minutes. A soldier facing enemy fire can't. So we have to give him the maximum protection ahead of time." Marlowe says that where stress is concerned, Army research shows the primary issues are organizational. "You want to build cohesion into a group, by making sure soldiers have good information, that they aren't faced with ambiguity, that they have solid relationships with leaders. If a man feels his squad is listening to him, if he can talk to it about his hopes, fears, anxieties, he's not likely to experience stress." The Army's No. 1 psychological discovery from World War II, he says, was "the strength imparted by the small, primary work group."

Keeping group cohesion strong *after* battle is crucial, too, since members, by collectively reliving their experience and trying to put it in perspective, get emotions off their chests that otherwise might leave them stressed out for months or years. The process is called debriefing. Squad members, for example, are encouraged to use travel time en route home from a war zone to talk about their battlefield experience. "It helps them detoxify," says Marlowe. "That's why we brought them back in groups from Desert Storm. Epidemiologically, we know it works." Thus, the group emerges both as the primary protection against stress and as the means for relief after a stressful event.

In light of the Army's approach, much of what passes for stress management in U.S. industry looks superficial. Most FORTUNE 500 companies offer employees either an employee assistance program (EAP), a wellness promotion program, or both. Some of these emphasize stress management. At Liz Claiborne, for example, well-attended lunchtime seminars explain how workers can relax by using mental imagery, muscle relaxation, and a variety of other proven techniques. Why the big turnout? "Misery loves company," says Sharon Quilter, Claiborne's director of benefits. Honeywell has offered a 45-minute program called Wellness and Your Funny Bone, taught by Sister Mary Christelle Macaluso, R.S.M. (Religious Sister of Mercy), Ph.D., "a lecturer/humorist with a Ph.D. in anatomy."

Ted Barash, president of a company that provides wellness programs, dismisses such approaches to stress reduction as "Band-Aid happy hours and traveling humor shows." Professor Paul Roman, a University of Georgia expert on behavioral health who has surveyed EAP programs, says most "never address the source of the stress. They blame the victim. Our studies at Southwestern Bell and other companies show the single biggest source of stress is poorly trained and inept supervisors."

External suppliers of EAP programs, such as Corporate Counseling Associates, purveyors of counseling to Time Warner, Digital Equipment, Liz Claiborne, and others, are understandably reluctant to tell clients how to run their own businesses. Says CPA partner Gene Cooper: "We help employees develop coping mechanisms. We don't reduce the stress itself." One of Cooper's counselors, asked if she ever suggests stress-relieving organizational changes to employers, says no, "that would be presumptuous."

Stress experts who advocate a more interventionist approach ask how it can possibly make sense for a company to soothe employees with one hand—teaching them relaxation through rhythmic breathing—while whipping them like egg whites with the other, moving up deadlines, increasing overtime, or withholding information about job security. Any company serious about stress management should consider the following steps:

- **Audit stress.** Dr. Paul J. Rosch, president of the American Institute of Stress, thinks any intelligent program must begin and end with a stress audit. Questionnaires typically ask workers and managers to list conditions they find most stressful. Answers can illuminate areas where workers are stressed by boredom, as well as those where they are stressed by overwork. (Rustout, stressmeisters are fond of saying, can be as anxious-making as burnout.) Rosch says, "An audit may show a need for programs not generally thought of as stress reducing, though they serve that function." Examples: child care and flextime. Follow-up audits show results.
- **Use EAPs aggressively.** Try to catch stress before it blooms. At McDonnell Douglas, EAP director Daniel Smith uses a program called Transitions to prepare workers for potentially traumatic organizational changes. "You tell people what they're going to feel before they feel it," he says. "It prevents more significant problems downstream."

 Case in point: Pete Juliano, head of McDonnell Douglas's 2,000-person facilities management operation, knew he would have to flatten and streamline his division to make it more responsive. Specifically, he would have to strip five levels of management with 260 managers down to three levels with 170.

 "Nobody was going out the door," he says, "and nobody was getting a pay cut. They'd all be staying on, though not all as managers. Still, that's a tough nut to crack: One day you're a manager. The next, you're carrying tools. How do you tell your wife and kids? How do you go to work each day and face not being a manager?"

 Juliano called in the Transitions team, whose members made a two-hour presentation to the department. They covered such topics as how to face your spouse and peers if you don't continue as a manager, how to recognize denial, how to cope with anger. The counselors also told listeners about career options if they decided to leave the division or McDonnell Douglas. "It gave them a chance to vent," says Juliano. "There have been cases of guys committing suicide when they had to go back to carrying tools. But we didn't have any serious problems."

- **Examine EAP usage.** If you've got an EAP program, study the usage data that counselors collect: How many employees from what departments are requesting help, and for what? For example, if you know that (1) in the past five years nobody from your tax department has ever used the EAP program, (2) half the accountants signed up for stress counseling last week, and (3) it's not mid-April, then you might be seeing evidence of a problem.
- **Give employees information.** They can't feel in control of circumstances if they lack it. When Donna Dell became manager of employee relations at Wells Fargo Bank last November, she saw there were about 3,000 workers' competition cases outstanding. Accidents accounted for 80%; another 10% were from workers claiming various injuries from working at video display terminals; and 10% were from stress. She wanted to know where the stress claims came from. Were they, for instance, from employees who had been laid off or who had just been through a performance review? There was no correlation to either event. "I was surprised," says Dell. "Venegance, apparently, was not the issue."

 Asbestos was. "We don't have any claims for asbestosis per se," she says, "but we get stress claims from people who *fear* they may have been exposed. You don't have to prove you were exposed to get workers' comp. The fear is enough. Now we provide instruction at sites where toxic material construction has been scheduled. We go in, in advance, with trainers and explain to the employees what's going to happen. Since we implemented this program about a year and a half ago, we haven't had any more such claims."

- **Match employees with jobs they can master.** In his bestselling book, *Flow,* Mihaly Csikszentmihalyi, a psychology professor at the University of Chicago, points out that the least stressed people often are those who are working flat out on some task that *they* have selected—something they really love to do. They give themselves so completely that they achieve a kind of precision and grace—what the author calls "flow." The chance of your getting such performance from workers goes up, and their stress down, the more choice you give them over assignments.

- **Be prepared for trauma.** It's easy to forget that stress isn't always the result of a thousand tiny cuts. "Having a gun put to your head can be upsetting," says Chris Dunning, a trauma expert at the University of Wisconsin at Milwaukee. She ought to know. Her business is de-stressing shot cops, crews of crashed airliners, and, at this writing, the forensic examiners in the Jeffrey Dahmer case ("they're having trouble eating meat").

Abrupt and upsetting things happen in offices. Homicide and suicide—not accidents—now account for 14 percent of male on-the-job deaths and 46 percent of female, reports psychologist James Turner, an expert on workplace mayhem. At the emergency department of Oakland's Highland Hospital, says chief resident Linda Jenks, mounting stress—with no end in sight—precipitated two suicides. "A young intern got into her car, numbed up her neck with lidocaine, took out a scalpel, and dissected herself in her rearview mirror. Within a week, a night nurse started an i.v. on herself—injected potassium, which stopped her heart immediately. After that, the hospital said, 'Okay, we're ignoring a problem here.' It's as if to admit it is a sign of failure." A suicide, an industrial accident, or any other traumatic event, says Dunning, leaves a lingering psychological strain on survivors: "It usually takes a good three months to get an organization back on track."

But, says Mark Braverman, president of Crisis Management Group, a Massachusetts consulting firm, these traumas present management with opportunities as well as problems. "Management sometimes won't talk about the event or face up to it directly," he says. "We try to tell them that if they do face up

to it and answer workers' questions, they can build a bond that lasts longer afterward." Even if you can't talk, he says, talk: "If you can't tell them much because OSHA is still completing an investigation, tell them that."

Braverman cites an example of trauma handled right: "A computer company had had a helicopter crash. They'd also had a work site shooting. So they decided, within the structure of their EAP, to create a protocol for dealing with traumatic stress. Later a safety system failed in a plant with 2,000 people, killing one. Every work group got together. The international manager of facilities was flown in to answer questions, including the ones on everybody's minds: Why did the system fail? Could it happen again? EAP counselors were available, but it was the information itself that was most stress-relieving."

Traumatic stress tends to be infectious. Since large numbers of employees are involved, clusters of stress-based workers' comp suits can result. In court the cases are much harder to defend against than less dramatic stress cases. Says Jim Turner: "It behooves you greatly to go in early with counselors, since this will reduce your overall long-term cots."

At Wells Fargo, where bank robberies rose 37% in this year's first quarter, tellers have been traumatized. "We do get stress claims from robbery incidents, and we don't dispute them," says Donna Dell. Instead, the bank dispatches EAP counselors to affected branches, where they conduct group debriefings, much the way the Army does.

Bryan Lawton, head to Wells Fargo's debriefing program, explains how it works: "The professional asks them things like, where were you when the incident happened, how did you respond, how did the others act? When the employees start to talk, they find out they're not alone, not the only ones who feel the way they do. Everybody else feels guilty or angry over the event. They're told these are normal emotions." The professional then tells them how they can expect to feel weeks later.

Nobody is sure why debriefings work, but they do. And they are cost-effective. "All it takes," says Lawton, "is one case to lead to a significant expense. One person's trauma can wind up costing the bank $100,00." The figure includes lost time, medical treatment, and retraining cost.

O'Dell Williams, with the bank 16 years, has survived ten robbery situations, the most recent one as a branch manager in Vallejo, California, on May 20.

The robbery attempt scared more than 20 of his employees. "I was afraid we'd lose some afterward," he says. But EAP counselors intervened quickly, and so far nobody has quit. And nobody has filed a workers' comp claim.

- **Don't forget the obvious.** Managers who want to reduce stress should make sure workers have the tools and training they need to get job done. Says John Murray, a police bomb deactivator in Florida: "I'm lucky. I've got the best equipment and the best training. There are departments where all they used to give you was a mattress and a fishhook." Managers should set realistic deadlines and go out of their way not to change deadlines, once set. What works well for the Army works just as well in the office: Build cohesion through communication. Straighten out managers who like to play the Charles Boyer part from *Gaslight*—who hold sway over subordinates by keeping them confused, by withholding information, or by keeping roles and responsibilities ill-defined.

Do all these things, behave flawlessly, and your exposure to stress-based lawsuits still remains almost unimaginably broad. Chris Dunning cites a case where an employee, as part of some lunchroom high jinks, got silly and taped a co-worker's arm to a chair—very lightly, not so it restrained her. She started screaming. Other workers looked at each other in disbelief: What was the woman's problem? It turned out that, as a child, she had been forcibly restrained and raped. The taping of the arm caused her to reexperience the trauma of that, and her subsequent disability was judged to be 100 percent the employer's responsibility.

At least this worker's distress was real. Some employees undoubtedly abuse the system, and there are lawyers and doctors eager to help them. Listen to Joseph Alibrandi, chairman of Whittaker Corp., an aerospace manufacturer: "We try to minimize the problems in the physical workplace, to do all we can to reduce *true* stress. But a lot of that seems frustratingly irrelevant, There's always an epidemic of 'sore back' after a layoff. Or they say they can't perform sexually. How the hell are you going to defend against that?"

It's almost impossible, of course, but you can try to flag potential claimants early on. New hires can be asked, as part of their medical evaluation, "Have you ever been off work due to a stress-related illness?" A "yes" may indicate to the doctor that the employee's assignment should be changed.

Performing a periodic stress audit, or making stress management part of your EAP or wellness program, can pay off in court. Says John M. Ivancevich, dean of the business school at the University of Houston: "Even a sloppy attempt at stress management can be a legal defense."

Finally: you. Feeling stressed? Not sure what to do? The first rule, says Dr. James Turner, is, Don't quit your job. "They build these fantasies," he says of stressed-out executives. "They'll go sailing. They'll open a copy center. Lately, for some reason, they all want to open copy centers." But sooner or later everyone wants to come back.

Instead of quitting, learn the techniques of coping. You'll find plenty of experts willing to teach them to you for a price, but they're not too complex, and many stressed workers have discovered them without help. Flight attendant Wally Goelzer and plenty of other people use them daily without knowing it. "Sometimes I put my hands out like a scale," he says. "I ask myself: How much does this problem matter? I think of a friend of mine who was killed in a plane crash. 'Life is too short,' I can hear her say. She used to say that, and I can see her face."

Emergency room resident Jenks and bomb deactivator Murray know the stress-relieving power of humor, even when it's of the gallows type. Says Murray: "Yeah, I get a certain amount of kidding. I've got three daughters, and when Father's Day comes around they give me a card with a fuse in it." Says Jenks: "We use black humor at work so much that it's gotten so I have to remember to clean up my act when I'm around normal people.,"

Then again, you might want to put aside the tricks and strategies, since these change like frocks. You might think about your life. Is it the way you wanted? If not, all the perspective and joking in the world will get you only so far. Mihaly Csikszentmihalyi, who lectures occasionally to 40-ish managers, notes that those who insist on regaining control of their lives, even at what temporarily may seem the peril of their careers, often see an unexpected payoff down the line. "There comes a point where they're working 70 hours a week, and they're not sure why. Their family lives are suffering. Maybe they've never given any thought to setting priorities. Some decide they can't do everything—that they have to step off the fast track to get back their family life or take better care of their health. And then a most interesting thing happens: The ones who do it, most of them, in a year or two, they get promoted." Dare to be second-rate, if that's how you have to think of it. It may not be what you imagine.

■

EXERCISES

EXERCISE 6–1   BEHAVIOR ACTIVITY PROFILE—A TYPE A MEASURE

Each of us displays certain kinds of behaviors, thought patterns of personal characteristics. For each of the 21 sets of descriptions below, circle the number which you feel best describes where you are between each pair. The best answer for each set of descriptions is the response that most nearly describes the way you feel, behave, or think. Answer these in terms of your regular or typical behavior, thoughts, or characteristics.

1. I'm always on time for appointments.   7 6 5 4 3 2 1   I'm never quite on time.
2. When someone is talking to me, chances are I'll anticipate what they are going to say, by nodding, interrupting, or finishing sentences for them.   7 6 5 4 3 2 1   I listen quietly without showing any impatience.
3. I frequently try to do several things at once.   7 6 5 4 3 2 1   I tend to take things one at a time.
4. When it comes to waiting in line (at banks, theaters, etc.), I really get impatient and frustrated.   7 6 5 4 3 2 1   It simply doesn't bother me.
5. I always feel rushed.   7 6 5 4 3 2 1   I never feel rushed.
6. When it comes to my temper, I find it hard to control at times.   7 6 5 4 3 2 1   I just don't seem to have one.

TOTAL SCORE 1–7 _____ = S

7. I tend to do most things like eating, walking and talking rapidly.   7 6 5 4 3 2 1   Slowly.
8. Quite honestly, the things I enjoy most are job-related activities.   7 6 5 4 3 2 1   Leisure-time activities.
9. At the end of a typical work day, I usually feel like I needed to get more done than I did.   7 6 5 4 3 2 1   I accomplished everything I needed to.
10. Someone who knows me very well would say that I would rather work than play.   7 6 5 4 3 2 1   I would rather play than work.
11. When it comes to getting ahead at work nothing is more important.   7 6 5 4 3 2 1   Many things are more important.
12. My primary source of satisfaction comes from my job.   7 6 5 4 3 2 1   I regularly find satisfaction in non-job pursuits, such as hobbies, friends, and family.

13. Most of my friends and social ac-
    quaintances are people I know from
    work.

7　6　5　4　3　2　1

Not connected with my work.

14. I'd rather stay at work than take a
    vacation.

7　6　5　4　3　2　1

Nothing at work is important
enough to interfere with my
vacation.

TOTAL SCORE 8–14 _____ = J

15. People who know me well would de-
    scribe me as hard driving and com-
    petitive.

7　6　5　4　3　2　1

Relaxed and easygoing.

16. In general, my behavior is governed
    by a desire for recognition and
    achievement.

7　6　5　4　3　2　1

What I want to do — not by
trying to satisfy others.

17. In trying to complete a project or
    solve a problem I tend to wear my-
    self out before I'll give up on it.

7　6　5　4　3　2　1

I tend to take a break or quit if
I'm feeling fatigued.

18. When I play a game (tennis, cards,
    etc.) my enjoyment comes from win-
    ning

7　6　5　4　3　2　1

The social interaction.

19. I like to associate with people who
    are dedicated to getting ahead.

7　6　5　4　3　2　1

Easygoing and take life as it
comes.

20. I'm not happy unless I'm always
    doing something.

7　6　5　4　3　2　1

Frequently, "doing nothing" can
be quite enjoyable.

21. What I enjoy doing most are compet-
    itive activities.

7　6　5　4　3　2　1

Noncompetitive pursuits.

TOTAL SCORE 15–21 _____ = H

Impatience (S)	Job Involvement (J)	Hard Driving and Competitive (H)	Total Score (A) = S + J + H

The Behavior Activity Profile attempts to assess the three Type A coronary-prone behavior patterns, as well as provide a total score. The three a priori types of Type A coronary-prone behavior patterns are shown:

Items	Behavior Pattern		Characteristics
1–7	Impatience	(S)	Anxious to interrupt Fails to listen attentively Frustrated by waiting (e.g., in line, for others to complete a job)
8–14	Job Involvement	(J)	Focal point of attention is the job Lives for the job Relishes being on the job Immersed by job activities
15–21	Hard driving/ Competitive	(H)	Hardworking, highly competitive Competitive in most aspects of life, sports, work etc. Racing against the clock
1–21	Total score	(A)	Total of S + J + H represents your global Type A behavior

Score ranges for total score are:

Score	Behavior Type
122 and above	Hard-core Type A
99–121	Moderate Type A
90–98	Low Type A
80–89	Type X
70–79	Low Type B
50–69	Moderate Type B
40 and below	Hard-core Type B

Percentile Scores

Now you can compare your score to a sample of over 1,200 respondents

Percentile Score _____   *Raw Score* _____

Percent of Individuals Scoring Lower	Males	Females
99%	___ 140	___ 132
95%	___ 135	___ 126
90%	___ 130	___ 120
85%	___ 124	___ 112
80%	___ 118	___ 106
75%	___ 113	___ 101
70%	___ 108	___ 95
65%	___ 102	___ 90
60%	___ 97	___ 85
55%	___ 92	___ 80
50%	___ 87	___ 74
45%	___ 81	___ 69
40%	___ 75	___ 63
35%	___ 70	___ 58
30%	___ 63	___ 53
25%	___ 58	___ 48
20%	___ 51	___ 42
15%	___ 45	___ 36
10%	___ 38	___ 31
5%	___ 29	___ 26
1%	___ 21	___ 21

EXERCISE 6–2   HEALTH RISK APPRAISAL

The Health Risk Appraisal form was developed by the Department of Health and Welfare of the Canadian government. Their initial testing program indicated that approximately one person out of every three who completed the form would modify some unhealthy aspects of lifestyle for at least a while. Figuring the potential payoff was worth it, the government mailed out over 3 million copies of the questionnaire to Canadians who were on social security.

Subsequent checking indicated that their initial projections of the number of recipients altering their behavior was correct. Perhaps you will be among the one third.

Choose from the three answers for each question the one answer which most nearly applies to you. The plus and minus signs next to some numbers indicate more than (+) and less than (−). Note that a few items have only two alternatives.

Exercise

_____ 1. Physical effort expended during the workday: mostly?
(a) heavy labor, walking, or housework; (b) —; (c) deskwork

_____ 2. Participation in physical activities—skiing, golf, swimming, etc., or lawn mowing, gardening, etc.?
(a) daily? (b) weekly; (c) seldom

_____ 3. Participation in vigorous exercise program?
(a) three times weekly; (b) weekly; (c) seldom

_____ 4. Average miles walked or jogged per day?
(a) one or more; (b) less than one; (c) none

_____ 5. Flights of stairs climbed per day?
(a) 10 +; (b) 10 −; (c) —

Nutrition

_____ 6. Are you overweight?
(a) no; (b) 5 to 19 lbs; (c) 20 + lbs.

_____ 7. Do you eat a wide variety of foods, something from each of the following five food groups: (1) meat, fish, poultry, dried legumes, eggs, or nuts; (2) milk or milk products; (3) bread or cereals; (4) fruits; (5) vegetables?
(a) each day; (b) three times weekly; (c) —

Alcohol

_____ 8. Average number of bottles (12 oz.) of beer per week?
(a) 0 to 7; (b) 8 to 15; (c) 16 +

_____ 9. Average number of hard liquor (1½ oz.) drinks per week?
(a) 0 to 7; (b) 8 to 15; (c) 16 +

_____ 10. Average number of glasses (5 oz.) of wine or cider per week?
(a) 0 to 7; (b) 8 to 15; (c) 16 +

_____ 11. Total number of drinks per week including beer, liquor or wine?
(a) 0 to 7; (b) 8 to 15; (c) 16 +

Drugs

_____ 12. Do you take drugs illegally?
(a) no; (b) —; (c) yes

_____ 13. Do you consume alcoholic beverages together with certain drugs (tranquilizers, barbiturates, illegal drugs)?
(a) no; (b) —; (c) yes

_____ 14. Do you use pain-killers improperly or excessively?
(a) no; (b) —; (c) yes

Tobacco

_____ 15. Cigarettes smoked per day?
(a) none; (b) 10 −; (c) 10 +

_____ 16. Cigars smoked per day?
(a) none; (b) 5 −; (c) 5 +

_____ 17. Pipe tobacco pouches per week?
(a) none; (b) 2 −; (c) 2 +

Personal Health

_____ 18. Do you experience periods of depression?
(a) seldom; (b) occasionally; (c) frequently

_____ 19. Does anxiety interfere with your daily activities?
(*a*) seldom; (*b*) occasionally;
(*c*) frequently

_____ 20. Do you get enough satisfying sleep?
(*a*) yes; (*b*) no; (*c*) —

_____ 21. Are you aware of the causes and dangers of VD?
(*a*) yes; (*b*) no; (*c*) —

_____ 22. Breast self-examination? (if not applicable, do not score)
(*a*) monthly; (*b*) occasionally; (*c*) —

Road and Water Safety

_____ 23. Mileage per year as driver or passenger?
(*a*) 10,000 −; (*b*) 10,000 +; (*c*) —

_____ 24. Do you often exceed the speed limit?
(*a*) no; (*b*) by 10 mph +;
(*c*) by 20 mph +

_____ 25. Do you wear a seat belt?
(*a*) always; (*b*) occasionally; (*c*) never

_____ 26. Do you drive a motorcylce, moped, or snowmobile?
(*a*) no; (*b*) yes; (*c*) —

_____ 27. If yes to the above, do you always wear a regulation safety helmet?
(*a*) yes; (*b*) —; (*c*) no

_____ 28. Do you ever drive under the influence of alcohol?
(*a*) never; (*b*) —; (*c*) occasionally

_____ 29. Do you ever drive when your ability may be affected by drugs?
(*a*) never; (*b*) —; (*c*) occasionally

_____ 30. Are you aware of water safety rules?
(*a*) yes; (*b*) no; (*c*) —

_____ 31. If you participate in water sports or boating, do you wear a life jacket?
(*a*) yes; (*b*) no; (*c*) —

General

_____ 32. Average time watching TV per day (in hours)?
(*a*) 0 to 1; (*b*) 1 to 4; (*c*) 4 +

_____ 33. Are you familiar with first-aid procedures?
(*a*) yes; (*b*) no; (*c*) —

_____ 34. Do you ever smoke in bed?
(*a*) no; (*b*) occasionally; (*c*) regularly

_____ 35. Do you always make use of equipment provided for your safety at work?
(*a*) yes; (*b*) occasionally; (*c*) no

To Score: Give yourself 1 point for each *a* answer; 3 points for each *b* answer; 5 points for each *c* answer. *Total Score:* _____

—A *total score of 35–45 is excellent.* You have a commendable lifestyle based on sensible habits and a lively awareness of personal health.

—A total score of 45–55 is *good.* With some minor change, you can develop an excellent lifestyle.

—A total score of 56–65 is *risky.* You are taking unnecessary risks with your health. Several of your habits should be changed if potential health problems are to be avoided.

—A total score of 66 and over is *hazardous.* Either you have little personal awareness of good health habits or you are choosing to ignore them. This is a danger zone.

EXERCISE 6–3   MR. DANA'S COPING MECHANISM

OBJECTIVES

1. To emphasize that negative coping mechanisms are used by individuals.
2. To enable individuals to compare their interpretation of coping effectiveness with others.

STARTING THE EXERCISE

There is no one set way to prevent work stress or guarantee effective coping in stressful situations. Listed below is a personal history of how one individual copes with the stresses of work. After reading the history, list some of the cognitive, emotional, and physical responses experienced by Mr. Dana. How effective is he in coping with the situation? After you individually consider the issue of effectiveness, the instructor will form small groups to discuss why or why not Mr. Dana is effective in coping with stress.

Once the group has read the personal history, evaluate the effectiveness of Mr. Dana's coping and also discuss why Mr. Dana is experiencing the amounts and types of stress portrayed in the incident.

Mr. Dana is a 49-year-old store manager. He expresses to anyone that will listen that he is stressed by the job. As he puts it: "A lot of managers haven't made it, but I've been here for 19 years." He feels that his difficult job should earn him respect off the job. He has constant arguments with his wife because she doesn't seem sympathetic about how tough his work is.

His marriage of 23 years is going through a transition because his wife has returned to school and is "growing more independent." The Danas have two teenage children. The children expect to receive some financial help from their parents when they begin college in the near future.

Mr. Dana runs an excellent business, but he feels that he hasn't progressed well in the company. He has been offered the managerial position in larger stores but has turned down offers because he did not want to move his family. He seems to always lament the fact that he didn't become a dentist like his father encouraged him to become as a child.

Mr. Dana behaves as if every incident on the job is a major issue. He believes that a store manager should make no errors. Making an error is the same as being unworthy or unreliable. He always questions his worth and ability and tests it against the errors he made. He refers to himself as always being on guard against making stupid mistakes. This striving for perfection irritates a lot of his subordinates because many believe that making mistakes is a part of life that can't be avoided.

A lot of things that top management does bothers Mr. Dana. For example, he was told on Friday that he had to begin training two assistant managers next week. He is particularly upset at the timing of the directive and not being asked his opinion about the assistants' schedule of training. At this time, Mr. Dana was overloaded with other commitments and found the training assignment to be ill-timed. When the assistants arrived on Monday, they were introduced to a tense, irritated store manager who didn't hide his feelings. That evening Mr. Dana unloaded his frustration on his son who didn't move fast enough to clean up his room. A 20-minute shouting and screaming match occurred that eventually involved the entire family. After things settled down. Mr. Dana was unhappy with himself for losing control. He became withdrawn and depressed for the next week at home and on the job.

▲

CASE

CASE 6–1   THE CASE OF THE MISSING TIME

At approximately 7:30 A.M. on Tuesday, June 23, 1959, Chet Craig, manager of the Norris Company's Central Plant, swung his car out of the driveway of his suburban home and headed toward the plant located some six miles away, just inside the Midvale city limits. It was a beautiful day. The sun was shining brightly and a cool fresh breeze was blowing. The trip to the plant took about twenty minutes and sometimes gave Chet an opportunity to think about plant problems without interruption.

The Norris Company owned and operated three printing plants. Norris enjoyed a nationwide commercial business, specializing in quality color work. It was a closely held company with some 350 employees, nearly half of whom were employed at the Central Plant, the largest of the three Norris production operations. The company's main offices were also located in the Central Plant building.

Chet had started with the Norris Company as an expediter in its Eastern Plant in 1948, just after he graduated

Source: "The Case of the Missing Time," by Thomas J. McNichols, Northwestern University Business School, 1973, pp. 143–48. Reprinted by permission.

from Ohio State. After three years Chet was promoted to production supervisor, and two years later he was made assistant to the manager of the Eastern Plant. Early in 1957 he was transferred to the Central Plant as assistant to the plant manager and one month later was promoted to plant manager when the former manager retired.

Chet was in fine spirits as he relaxed behind the wheel. As his car picked up speed, the hum of the tires on the newly paved highway faded into the background. Various thoughts occurred to him, and he said to himself, "This is going to be the day to really get things done."

He began to run through the day's work, first one project, then another, trying to establish priorities. After a few minutes he decided that the open-end unit scheduling was probably the most important, certainly the most urgent. He frowned for a moment as he recalled that on Friday the vice president and general manager had casually asked him if he had given the project any further thought. Chet realized that he had not been giving it much thought lately. He had been meaning to get to work on this idea for over three months, but something else always seemed to crop up. "I haven't had much time to sit down and really work it out," he said to himself. "I'd better get going and hit this one today for sure." With that he began to break down the objectives, procedures, and installation steps of the project. He grinned as he reviewed the principles involved and calculated roughly the anticipated savings. "It's about time," he told himself. "This idea should have been followed up long ago." Chet remembered that he had first conceived of the open-end unit scheduling idea nearly a year and a half ago, just prior to his leaving Norris's Eastern Plant. He had spoken to his boss, Jim Quince, manager of the Eastern Plant, about it then, and both agreed that it was worth looking into. The idea was temporarily shelved when he was transferred to the Central Plant a month later.

A blast from a passing horn startled him, but his thoughts quickly returned to other plant projects he was determined to get under way. He started to think through a procedure for simpler transport of dies to and from the Eastern Plant. Visualizing the notes on his desk, he thought about the inventory analysis he needed to identify and eliminate some of the slow-moving stock items, the packing controls that needed revision, and the need to design a new special-order form. He also decided that this was the day to settle on a job printer to do the simple outside printing of office forms. There were a few other projects he couldn't recall offhand, but he could tend to them after lunch, if not before. "Yes, sir," he said to himself, "this is the day to really get rolling."

Chet's thoughts were interrupted as he pulled into the company parking lot. When he entered the plant Chet knew something was wrong as he met Al Noren, the stockroom foreman, who appeared troubled. "A great morning, Al," Chet greeted him cheerfully.

"Not so good, Chet; my new man isn't in this morning," Noren growled.

"Have you heard from him?" asked Chet.

"No, I haven't," replied Al.

Chet frowned as he commented, "These stock handlers assume you take it for granted that if they're not here, they're not here, and they don't have to call in and verify it. Better ask Personnel to call him."

Al hesitated for a moment before replying. "Okay, Chet, but can you find me a man? I have two cars to unload today."

As Chet turned to leave he said, "I'll call you in half an hour, Al, and let you know."

Making a mental note of the situation, Chet headed for his office. He greeted the group of workers huddled around Marilyn, the office manager, who was discussing the day's work schedule with them. As the meeting broke up, Marilyn picked up a few samples from the clasper, showed them to Chet, and asked if they should be shipped that way or if it would be necessary to inspect them. Before he could answer, Marilyn went on to ask if he could suggest another clerical operator for the sealing machine to replace the regular operator, who was home ill. She also told him that Gene, the industrial engineer, he called and was waiting to hear from Chet.

After telling Marilyn to go ahead and ship the samples, he made a note of the need for a sealer operator for the office and then called Gene. He agreed to stop by Gene's office before lunch and started on his routine morning tour of the plant. He asked each foreman the types and volumes of orders they were running, the number of people present, how the schedules were coming along, and the orders to be run next; helped the folding-room foreman find temporary storage space for consolidating a carload shipment; discussed quality control with a pressman who had been running poor work; arranged to transfer four people temporarily to different departments, including two for Al in the stockroom; and talked to the shipping foreman about pickups and special orders to be delivered that day. As he continued through the plant, he saw to it that reserve stock was moved out of the forward stock area, talked to another pressman about his requested change of vacation schedule, had a "heart-to-heart" talk with a press helper who seemed to need frequent reassurance, and approved two type and one color-order okays for different pressmen.

Returning to his office, Chet reviewed the production reports on the larger orders against his initial productions and found that the plant was running behind schedule. He called in the folding-room foreman and together they went over the lineup of machines and made several necessary changes.

During this discussion, the composing-room foreman stopped in to cover several type changes, and the routing foreman telephoned for approval of a revised printing schedule. The stockroom foreman called twice, first to inform him that two standard, fast-moving stock items were dangerously low, later to advise him that the paper stock for the urgent Dillion job had finally arrived. Chet made the necessary subsequent calls to inform those concerned.

He then began to put delivery dates on important and difficult inquiries received from customers and salesmen. (The routine inquiries were handled by Marilyn). While he was doing this he was interrupted twice, once by a sales correspondent calling from the West Coast to ask for a better delivery date than originally scheduled, once by the personnel vice president asking him to set a time when he could hold an initial training and induction interview with a new employee.

After dating the customer and salesmen inquiries, Chet headed for his morning conference in the executive offices. At this meeting he answered the sales vice president's questions in connection with "hot" orders, complaints, and the status of large-volume orders and potential new orders. He then met with the general manager to discuss a few ticklish policy matters and to answer "the old man's" questions on several specific production and personnel problems. Before leaving the executive offices, he stopped at the office of the secretary-treasurer to inquire about delivery of cartons, paper, and boxes and to place a new order for paper.

On the way back to his own office, Chet conferred with Gene about two current engineering projects concerning which he had called earlier. When he reached his desk, he lit a cigarette and looked at his watch. It was ten minutes before lunch, just time enough to make a few notes of the details he needed to check in order to answer knotty questions raised by the sales manager that morning.

After lunch Chet started again. He began by checking the previous day's production reports, did some rescheduling to get out urgent orders, placed appropriate delivery dates on new orders and inquiries received that morning, and consulted with a foreman on a personal problem. He spent some twenty minutes at the TWX going over mutual problems with the Eastern Plant.

By midafternoon Chet had made another tour of the plant, after which he met with the personnel director to review with him a touchy personal problem raised by one of the clerical employees, the vacation schedules submitted by his foremen, and the pending job-evaluation program. Following this conference, Chet hurried back to his office to complete the special statistical report for Universal Waxing Corporation, one of Norris's best customers. As he finished the report, he discovered that it was ten minutes after six and he was the only one left in the office. Chet was tired. He put on his coat and headed through the plant toward the parking lot; on the way he was stopped by both the night supervisor and night layout foremen for approval of type and layout changes.

With both eyes on the traffic, Chet reviewed the day he had just completed. "Busy?" he asked himself. "Too much so—but did I accomplish anything?" His mind raced over the day's activities. "Yes and no" seemed to be the answer. "There was the usual routine, the same as any other day. The plant kept going and I think it must have been a good production day. Any creative or special-project work done?" Chet grimaced as he reluctantly answered, "No."

With a feeling of guilt, he probed further. "Am I an executive? I'm paid like one, respected like one, and have a responsible assignment with the necessary authority to carry it out. Yet one of the greatest values a company derives from an executive is his creative thinking and accomplishments. What have I done about it? An executive needs some time for thinking. Today was a typical day, just like most other days, and I did little, if any, creative work. The projects that I so enthusiastically planned to work on this morning are exactly as they were yesterday. What's more, I have no guarantee that tomorrow night or the next night will bring me any closer to their completion. This is the real problem and there must be an answer."

Chet continued, "Night work? Yes, occasionally. This is understood. But I've been doing too much of this lately. I owe my wife and family some of my time. When you come down to it, they are the people for whom I'm really working. If I am forced to spend much more time away from them, I'm not meeting my own personal objectives. What about church work? Should I eliminate that? I spend a lot of time on this, but I feel I owe God some time, too. Besides, I believe I'm making a worthwhile contribution in this work. Perhaps I can squeeze a little time from my fraternal activities. But where does recreation fit in?"

Chet groped for the solution. "Maybe I'm just rationalizing because I schedule my own work poorly. But I don't think so. I've studied my work habits carefully and I think I plan intelligently and delegate authority. Do I need an assistant? Possibly, but that's a long-term project and I don't believe I could justify the additional overhead expenditure. Anyway, I doubt whether it would solve the problem."

But this time Chet had turned off the highway onto the side street leading to his home—the problem still uppermost in his mind. "I guess I really don't know the answer," he told himself as he pulled into his driveway. "This morning everything seemed so simple, but now . . . " His thoughts were interrupted as he saw his son running toward the car calling out, "Mommy, Daddy's home."

To lead the people,
walk behind them.

—**Lao-tzu**

INTERPERSONAL INFLUENCE
AND GROUP BEHAVIOR

CHAPTER

7

Group Behavior

LEARNING OBJECTIVES

UNDERSTAND that the term *group* can be viewed from several different perspectives

IDENTIFY the elements in the process of group formation and development

COMPARE formal and informal groups

DISCUSS the reasons why people form groups

DESCRIBE the stages of group development

IDENTIFY several important characteristics of groups

DISCUSS the concept of role

SPECIFY relevant criteria for group effectiveness

This chapter examines groups in organizations. The existence of groups in organizations can alter the individual's motivation or needs and influence the behavior of individuals in an organizational setting. Organizational behavior is more than simply the logical composite of the behavior of individuals. It is not their sum or product but rather a much more complex phenomenon, a very important part of which is the group. The chapter provides a model for understanding the nature of groups in organizations. It explores the various types of groups, the reasons for their formation, their characteristics, and some end results

■ E7–1 of group membership. Once you have completed this chapter, Exercise 7–1 can provide an excellent opportunity to experience many of the group concepts discussed throughout the chapter.

THE NATURE OF GROUPS

No generally accepted definition of a group exists. Instead, a range of available views can be presented, and from these a comprehensive definition can be developed. Even with a comprehensive definition, there will be overlap among the interpretations offered. It should be noted that the originators of the various definitions worked in different disciplines or held diverse perspectives. Ultimately, the group in a work setting provided the focus for attempting to clarify and interpret group behavior.

A Group in Terms of Perception

Many behavioral scientists believe that to be considered a group, the members of a group must perceive their relationship to others. For example:

A small group is defined as any number of persons engaged in interaction with one another in a single face-to-face meeting or series of such meetings, in which each member receives some impression or perception of each other member distinct enough so that he can, either at the time or in late questioning, give some reaction to each of the others as an individual person, even though it may be only to recall that the other was present.[1]

This view points out that the members of a group must perceive the existence of each member as well as the existence of the group.

A Group in Terms of Organization

Sociologists view the group primarily in terms of organizational characteristics. For example, according to a sociological definition, a group is:

an organized system of two or more individuals who are interrelated so that the system performs some function, has a standard set of role relationships among its members, and has a set of norms that regulate the function of the group and each of its members.[2]

This view emphasizes some of the important characteristics of groups, such as roles and norms, which are discussed later in this chapter.

A Group in Terms of Motivation

A group that fails to help its members satisfy their needs will have difficulty remaining viable. Employees who are not satisfying their needs in a particular group will search for other groups to aid in important need satisfactions. This view defines a group as:

[1]R. F. Bales, *Interaction Process Analysis: A Method for the Study of Small Groups* (Reading, Mass.: Addison-Wesley Publishing, 1950), p. 33.

[2]J. W. McDavid and M. Harari, *Social Psychology: Individuals, Groups, Societies* (New York: Harper & Row, 1968), p. 237.

a collection of individuals whose existence as a collection is rewarding to the individuals.[3]

As pointed out in an earlier chapter, it is difficult to ascertain clearly what facets of the work organization are rewarding to individuals. The problem of identifying individual needs is a shortcoming of defining a group solely in terms of motivation.

A Group in Terms of Interaction

Some theorists assume that interaction in the form of interdependence is the core of "groupness." A view that stresses interpersonal interactions is the following:

We mean by a group a number of persons who communicate with one another often over a span of time, and who are few enough so that each person is able to communicate with all the others, not at secondhand, through other people, but face-to-face.[4]

All of these four views are important since they each point to key features of groups. Furthermore, it can be stated that if a group exists in an organization, its members:

1. Are motivated to join.
2. Perceive the group as a unified unit of interacting people.
3. Contribute in various amounts to the group processes (i.e., some people contribute more time or energy to the group).
4. Reach agreements and have disagreements through various forms of interaction.

In this textbook, a group is defined as:

two or more employees who interact with each other in such a manner that the behavior and/or performance of a member is influenced by the behavior and/or performance of other members.[5]

AN INTEGRATED MODEL OF GROUP FORMATION AND DEVELOPMENT

Although every group is different, possessing its own unique attributes and dynamics, it is also true that in many important ways groups tend to display similar patterns of evolution. Exhibit 7-1 presents a model of group formation and

[3]Bernard M. Bass, *Leadership Psychology and Organizational Behavior* (New York: Harper & Row, 1960), p. 39.

[4]G. C. Homans, *The Human Group* (New York: Harcourt Brace Jovanovich, 1950), p. 1

[5]See M. E. Shaw, *Group Dynamics: The Psychology of Small Group Behavior*, 2nd ed. (New York: McGraw-Hill, 1976).

EXHIBIT 7-1

A Model of Group Formation and Development

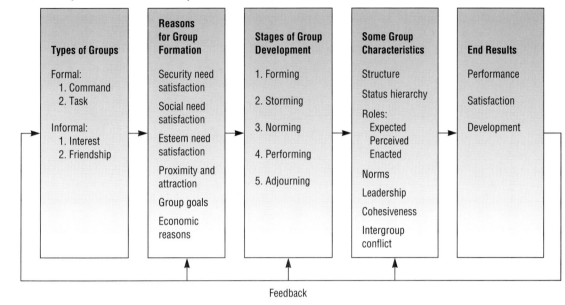

Types of Groups	Reasons for Group Formation	Stages of Group Development	Some Group Characteristics	End Results

Formal:
1. Command
2. Task
 	
Informal:
1. Interest
2. Friendship
	Security need satisfaction
	
	Social need satisfaction
	
	Esteem need satisfaction
	
	Proximity and attraction
	
	Group goals
	
	Economic reasons
		1. Forming
		
		2. Storming
		
		3. Norming
		
		4. Performing
		
		5. Adjourning
			Structure
			
			Status hierarchy
			
			Roles:
			  Expected
			  Perceived
			  Enacted
			
			Norms
			
			Leadership
			
			Cohesiveness
			
			Intergroup conflict
				Performance
				
				Satisfaction
				
				Development

Feedback

development that we will follow in this chapter in discussing this important organizational behavior and management topic. The model suggests that the end results of group activity are shaped by a number of antecedent variables, each category of which we will examine in this chapter. Indeed, each segment of the model can (and, in reality, does) influence each of the other segments.

TYPES OF GROUPS

An organization has technical requirements that arise from its stated goals. The accomplishment of these goals requires that certain tasks be performed and that employees be assigned to perform these tasks. As a result, most employees will be members of a group based on their position in the organization. These are **formal groups**. On the other hand, whenever individuals associate on a fairly continuous basis, there is a tendency for groups to form whose activities may be different from those required by the organization. These are **informal groups**. Both formal groups and informal groups, it will be shown, exhibit the same general characteristics.

Formal Groups

The demands and processes of the organization lead to the formation of different types of groups. Specifically, two types of formal groups exist: command and task.

Command Group

The command group is specified by the organization chart and is made up of the subordinates who report directly to a given supervisor. The authority relationship between a department manager and the supervisors, or between a senior nurse and her subordinates, is an example of a command group.

Task Group

A task group comprises the employees who work together to complete a particular task or project. For example, the activities of clerks in an insurance company when an accident claim is filed are required tasks. These activities create a situation in which several clerks must communicate and coordinate with one another if the claim is to be handled properly. These acquired tasks and interactions facilitate the formation of a task group.[6] The nurses assigned to duty in the emergency room of a hospital usually constitute a task group since certain activities are required when a patient is treated.

Informal Groups

Informal groups are natural groupings of people in the work situation in response to social needs. In other words, informal groups do not arise as a result of deliberate design. They evolve naturally. Two specific types of informal groups exist: interest and friendship.

Interest Groups

Individuals who may not be members of the same command or task group may affiliate to achieve some mutual objective. Examples of interest groups include employees grouping together to present a unified front to management for more benefits and waitresses "pooling" their tips. Note that the objectives of such groups are not related to those of the organization but are specific to each group.

Friendship Groups

Many groups form because the members have something in common such as age, political beliefs, or ethnic background. These friendship groups often extend their interaction and communication to off-the-job activities.

---

[6]Connie J. G. Gersick, "Marking Time: Predictable Transitions in Task Groups," *Academy of Management Journal*, June 1989, pp. 274–309.

A distinction has been made between two broad classifications of groups—formal and informal. The major difference between them is that formal command and task groups are designated by the formal organization as a means to an end. Informal interest and friendship groups are important for their own sake. They satisfy a basic human need for association. If employees' affiliation patterns were documented, it would become rapidly apparent that they belong to numerous and often overlapping groups. Why so many groups exist is the question to which we turn next.

WHY PEOPLE FORM GROUPS

Formal and informal groups form for various reasons.[7] Some of the reasons involve needs, proximity, attraction, goals, and economics.

The Satisfaction of Needs

One of the most compelling reasons why people join groups is because they believe membership in a particular group will help them satisfy one or more important needs. Typical employee needs that can be satisfied to a degree by the affiliation with groups include security, social, and esteem needs.

Security needs may be partially met, for example, by membership in an employee group that acts as a buffer between employees and the organizational system. Without such a group, an individual may feel alone in facing management and organizational demands. This "aloneness" leads to a degree of insecurity which can be offset by group membership. **Social needs** can be satisfied through groups, because the group provides a vehicle for an individual to interact with others. Indeed, it is difficult to imagine being able to fulfill general social needs without participating in at least some groups. **Esteem needs** may be partially met by belonging to a high-status or prestige group, membership in which is difficult to obtain or is based on some noteworthy achievement. An example would be the million-dollar round table in the life insurance business. For people with high esteem needs, membership in such a group can provide much need satisfaction.

Proximity and Attraction

Interpersonal interaction can result in group formation. Two important facets of interpersonal interaction are proximity and attraction. **Proximity** involves the physical distance between employees performing a job. **Attraction** designates the attraction of people to each other because of perceptual, attitudinal, performance, or motivational similarity.

---

[7]Seth Alcorn, "Understanding Groups at Work," *Personnel*, August 1989, pp. 28–36.

The greater the number of individuals in close proximity to one another, the greater the social density. Social density is a measure of the number of people within a certain walking distance (for example, 35 feet) of each other. Walking distance, rather than straight-line distance, is a better predictor of the amount of interaction that will occur. It is much easier, for example, to interact with a co-worker 10 yards away and separated by two desks than it is to interact with someone 1 yard away but separated by a wall. Individuals who work in close proximity have numerous opportunities to exchange ideas, thoughts, and attitudes about various on- and off-the-job activities. These exchanges often result in some type of group formation. This proximity also makes it possible for individuals to learn about the characteristics of other people. To sustain the interaction and interest, a group is often formed. Facilitating the exposure to one another of people who work in close proximity may be a deliberate strategy by management, as illustrated in Encounter 7-1.

Group Goals

A group's goals, if clearly understood, can be reasons why an individual is attracted to it. For example, an individual may join a group that meets after work to become familiar with a new personal computer system. Assume that this system is to be implemented in the work organization over the next two years. The person who voluntarily joins the after-hours group believes that learning the new system is a necessary and important goal for employees.

It is not always possible to identify group goals. The assumption that formal organizational groups have clear goals must be tempered by the understanding that perception, attitudes, personality, and learning can distort goals. For example, a new employee may never be formally told the goals of the unit that he or she has joined. By observing the behavior and attitudes of others, individuals may conclude what they believe the goals to be. These perceptions may or may not be accurate. The same can be said about the goals of informal groups.

Economic Reasons

In many cases groups form because individuals believe they can derive greater economic benefits from their jobs if they organize. For example, individuals working at different points on an assembly line may be paid on a group-incentive basis where the production of the group determines the wages of each member. By working and cooperating as a group, the individual may obtain higher economic benefits.

In numerous other instances, economic motives lead to group formation: workers in nonunion organizations form a group to exert pressure on top management for more benefits; top executives in a corporation form a group to review executive compensation. Whatever the circumstances, the group members have a common interest—increased economic benefits—that leads to group affiliation.

ORGANIZATIONAL

E N C O U N T E R · 7-1

REMOVING THE PHYSICAL BARRIERS

Research has repeatedly demonstrated that when proximity and density are increased in work settings, positive outcomes increase. In a research and development laboratory, for example, the flow of technical information increased when employee desks were moved closer together. In another situation employees reported greater feedback, friendship opportunities, and general work satisfaction after a move to a new building with increased social density. Other studies have found increases in performance and decreases in stress can accompany closer proximity. It is not surprising then that some companies deliberately attempt to increase proximity and density. An example is the Hewlett-Packard (HP) plant in Waltham, Massachusetts.

The Waltham plant is a huge bullpen with only four-foot-high dividers splitting up the floor space. The idea is that by minimizing physical barriers that may separate personnel, closer cooperation and a sense of common purpose can be achieved among workers, supervisors, and managers. A HP division manager's office ($100 million unit) is a small, wall-less space directly on the factory floor and shared with a secretary. This type of close physical proximity helps also in getting different specialists, such as product design people and manufacturing types, to work together. In short, everyone is accessible to everyone else. HP clearly believes that promoting group effort this way pays dividends in terms of increased performance and loyalty.

STAGES OF GROUP DEVELOPMENT

Groups learn just as individuals do. The performance of a group depends both on individual learning and on how well the members learn to work with one another. For example, a new product committee formed for the purpose of developing a response to a competitor may evolve into a very effective team, with the interests of the company being most important. However, it may also be very ineffective if its members are more concerned about their individual departmental goals than about developing a response to a competitor. This section describes some general stages through which groups evolve and points out the sequential development process involved.[8]

One widely cited model of group development assumes that groups proceed through as many as five stages of development: (1) forming, (2) storming, (3) norming, (4) performing, and (5) adjourning.[9] Although identifying the stage a

---

[8]For a recent review of group development stages see K. L. Bettenhausen, "Five Years of Group Research: What We Have Learned and What Needs To Be Addressed," *Journal of Management,* June 1991, pp. 345–81.

[9]B. W. Tuckman, "Developmental Sequence in Small Groups," *Psychological Bulletin,* November 1965, pp. 384–99; and B. W. Tuckman and M. Jensen, "Stages of Small Group Development Revisited," *Groups and Organization Studies,* 1977, pp. 419–27.

group is in at a specific time can be difficult, it is nonetheless important to understand the development process. At each stage group behaviors differ, and consequently each stage can influence the group's end results.

Forming

The first stage of group development is **forming**, and it is characterized by un-certainty (and frequently, confusion) about the purpose, structure, and leadership of the group. Activities tend to focus on group members' efforts to understand and define their objectives, roles, and assignments within the group. Patterns of interaction among group members are tried out and either discarded or adopted, at least temporarily. The more diverse the group is, the more difficult it is to maneuver through this stage and the longer it takes. That is why this is a par-ticularly sensitive stage in the formation of multicultural groups. Generally, this stage is complete when individuals begin to view themselves as part of a group.

Storming

The **storming** stage of group development tends to be marked with conflict and confrontation. This generally emotionally intense stage may involve competition among members for desired assignments and disagreements over appropriate task-related behaviors and responsibilities. A particularly important part of storming can involve redefinition of the groups' specific tasks and overall goals.

Individually, group members are likely to begin to decide the extent to which they like the group tasks and their degree of commitment to them. While members may accept the group at one level, at another level there may be resistance to the control the group imposes on them. Some group members may begin to withdraw during storming, making this stage a particularly critical one for group survival and effectiveness. It is essential that the conflict that typifies storming be managed, as opposed to being suppressed. Suppression of conflict at this point is likely to create negative effects that can seriously hinder group functioning in later stages.

Norming

While storming is marked by conflict and confrontation, **norming** is characterized by cooperation and collaboration. It is also the stage where group cohesion begins significant development. There tends to be an open exchange of information, acceptance of differences of opinion, and active attempts to achieve mutually agreed upon goals and objectives. There is a strong degree of mutual attraction and commitment, and feelings of group identity and camaraderie. Behavioral norms are established and accepted by the completion of this stage, as are lead-ership and other roles in the group. The specific important impact of norms on group functioning is addressed in a subsequent section on group characteristics.

Performing

The fourth, and what may be the final stage, is performing. **Performing** is that stage where the group is fully functional. The group structure is set, and the roles of each member are understood and accepted. The group focuses its energies, efforts, and commitments on accomplishing the tasks it has accepted.

For some groups this stage marks the attainment of a level of effectiveness that will remain more or less constant. For others, the process of learning and development will be ongoing so that group effectiveness and efficiency continue. In the former case, group performance will be maintained at a level sufficient to insure survival; in the latter case, the group will record increasingly higher levels of achievement. Which way any particular group will go will depend on a number of variables, particularly how successfully the group completed earlier development stages.

Adjourning

The **adjourning** stage involves the termination of group activities. Many groups, of course, are permanent and never reach the adjourning stage. For temporary groups, however, such as committees, project groups, task forces, and similar entities, this stage includes disbandment. Customary task activities are complete and the group focuses on achieving closure. This stage can be marked by very positive emotions centering on successful task accomplishment and achievement. It may also be a source of feelings of loss, disappointment, even anger. The latter may be especially true in the case of permanent groups which fail to survive because of organizational downsizing or bankruptcy.

Of course, not all groups progress smoothly and predictably through these stages. Numerous factors can either hinder or facilitate the process. For example, if new members are constantly entering the group while others are leaving, the group may never complete the performing stage. Other factors that may influence the pattern of group development include the context or environment in which the group operates and group members' awareness of time and deadlines.

CHARACTERISTICS OF GROUPS

▲ C7–1

As groups evolve through their various stages of development. they begin to exhibit certain characteristics. To understand group behavior, you must be aware of these general characteristics. They are: structure, status hierarchy, roles, norms, leadership, cohesiveness, and conflict. Case 7–1, "Banana Time Case," provides an excellent opportunity to identify many of these characteristics in a real work group.

Structure

Within any group some type of structure evolves over a period of time. The group members are differentiated on the basis of such factors as expertise, aggressiveness, power, and status. Each member occupies a position in the group, and the pattern of relationships among the positions constitutes a group structure. Most groups have some type of status differences among positions such that the group structure is hierarchical. Status in formal groups usually is based on the position in the formal organization, while in informal groups, status can be based on anything relevant to the group (e.g., golf scores, ability to communicate with management).

Status Hierarchy

Status and **position** are so similar that the terms often are used interchangeably. The status assigned to a particular position is typically a consequence of certain characteristics that differentiate one position from other positions. In some cases a person is given status because of such factors as job seniority, age, or assignment. For example, the oldest worker may be perceived as being more technically proficient and is attributed status by a group of technicians. Thus, assigned status may have nothing to do with the formal status hierarchy.

The status hierarchy, and particularly the deference paid to those at the top of the hierarchy, may sometimes have unintended—and undesirable—effects on performance. A vivid example occurred several years ago when a commercial jetliner ran out of fuel and crash-landed short of the runway in Portland, Oregon, killing 10 of the 189 persons aboard. The plane ran out of fuel while flight crew members were preoccupied with a landing gear problem that had forced them to circle Portland for some time. The Air Transportation Safety Board's report of the accident showed that both the copilot and the flight engineer knew the fuel situation was becoming critical, but they did not do enough to warn the captain. A study of the transcript of the cockpit conversation that took place prior to the crash confirms that warnings were made but were subtle, gentle, and extremely deferential to the senior captain in his position at the top of the status hierarchy.[10]

Roles

Each position in the group structure has an associated role that consists of the behaviors expected of the occupant of that position.[11] For example, the director of nursing services in a hospital is expected to organize and control the department of nursing. The director is also expected to assist in preparing and administering

[10]Douglas B. Feaver, "Pilots Learn to Handle Crises—and Themselves," *Washington Post*, September 12, 1982, p. A6.

[11]For an excellent discussion on this and related topics, see Dennis Organ, *Organizational Citizenship Behavior: The Good Citizen Syndrome* (Lexington, Mass.: Lexington Books, 1988).

the budget for the department. A nursing supervisor, on the other hand, is expected to supervise the activities of nursing personnel engaged in specific nursing services such as obstetrics, pediatrics, and surgery. These expected behaviors generally are agreed on not only by the occupants, the director of nursing and the nursing supervisor, but by other members of the nursing group and other hospital personnel.

In addition to an **expected role** are also a perceived role and an enacted role. The **perceived role** is the set of behaviors that a person in a position believes he or she should enact. As discussed in Chapter 3, perception can, in some instances, be distorted or inaccurate. The **enacted role**, on the other hand, is the behavior that a person actually carries out. Thus, three possible role behaviors can result. Conflict and frustration may arise from differences in these three role types. In fairly stable or permanent groups, there typically is a good agreement between expected and perceived roles. When the enacted role deviates too much from the expected role, the person either can become more like the expected role or leave the group.

Through membership in different groups, individuals perform multiple roles. For example, first-line supervisors are members of the management team but also are members of the group of workers they supervise. These multiple roles result in a number of expected role behaviors. In many instances, the behaviors specified by the different roles are compatible. When they are not, however, the individual experiences role conflict. Several types of role conflict exist with some important consequences. Role conflict is discussed later in this chapter.

Norms

Norms are the standards shared by members of a group, and they have certain characteristics that are important to group members. First, norms are formed only with respect to things that have significance for the group. They may be written, but very often they can be verbally communicated to members. In many cases they may never be formally stated but somehow are known by group members. If production is important, then a norm will evolve. If helping other group members complete a task is important, then a norm will develop. Second, norms are accepted in various degrees by group members. Some norms are completely accepted by all members while other norms are only partially accepted. And third, norms may apply to every group member, or they may apply to only some group members. For example, every member may be expected to comply with the production norm, while only group leaders may be permitted to disagree verbally with a management directive.

Groups develop norms for regulating many different aspects of their members' behavior.[12] In work groups, however, the most common norm relates to

[12]K. L. Bettenhausen and J. K. Murnighan, "The Development and Stability of Norms in Groups Facing Interpersonal and Structural Challenge," *Administrative Science Quarterly*, 1991, pp. 20–35.

EXHIBIT 7-2

**Hypothetical Production
Norm and Its Zone
of Acceptance**

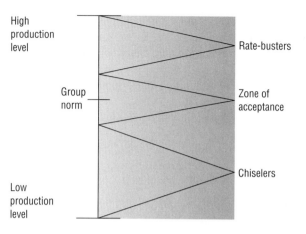

productivity and group productivity norms specify "acceptable" production behavior. It is important to understand that the group's perception of what is an
acceptable level of production may be significantly different from management's
perception. The group's production norm may differ from management's for a
number of reasons including a fear of rate-cutting if production is too high or a
fear of reprisal if production falls too low.

Exhibit 7-2 illustrates where a group's production norm might fall on a productivity continuum. The zone of acceptance depicted in the exhibit represents
minor deviations above and below the group's norm which would be deemed
acceptable to the group. Group members greatly exceeding the norm might be
referred to as rate-busters, while those producing well below group expectations
might be known as chiselers.

Norm Conformity

An issue of concern to managers is why employees conform to group norms.[13]
This issue is especially important when a person with skill and capability is
performing significantly below his or her capacity so that group norms are not
violated. A number of variables may influence conformity to group norms. The
personal characteristics of the individual play a role. For example, research indicates that persons of high intelligence are less likely to conform than less intelligent individuals, and authoritarian personality types conform more than do
nonauthoritarians.[14] **Situational factors** such as group size and structure may
influence conformity. For example, conformity may become more difficult in

---

[13]Daniel C. Feldman, "The Development and Enforcement of Group Norms," *Academy of Management Review,* January 1984, pp. 47–53.

[14]Salvatore R. Maddi, *Personality Theories: A Comparative Analysis* (Homewood, Ill.: Dorsey
Press, 1980), chap. 7.

NONCONFORMITY COSTLIER FOR JAPANESE EXECS THAN AMERICAN

How costly is a failure to conform to expected norms? In one instance at least, the answer is it's far more costly if you work for Mazda than it is if you work for Ford.

Here is what happened. A defect was discovered in a switch that affected the operation of brake lights and cruise control mechanisms in approximately 3,500 Mazdas. The company attempted to keep news of the defect under wraps. Mazda quietly replaced the switches on the automobiles of customers who complained, but— initially at least—did not notify other customers of the potential problem. It is not known if the defect has been responsible for any injuries or deaths.

The problem was made public after a series of articles in Japan's most prestigious daily newspaper criticized the company for failing to conduct a total recall. This in turn led to a public criticism of the company by the Japanese Transport Ministry.

One day later Mazda announced a recall program. Additionally, it was announced, Mazda chairman Kenichi Yamamoto and 17 other executives received salary cuts of 5 percent to 10 percent for the first three months of 1991. Japanese executives' salaries are much smaller than those of their American counterparts, and thus the cuts represented a significant penalty.

Although the company was severely criticized in Japan for failing to conform to acceptable standards of behavior, U.S. observers praised the willingness of senior management to accept the blame for its poor decision. "Mazda is doing what it ought to do," said Clarence Ditlow, executive director of the Center for Auto Safety, a Ralph Nader group. "We would doubt that American companies would do the same."

Ditlow drew a parallel with an earlier incident at Ford Motor Company. When the company was fined several million dollars for falsifying auto exhaust test reports, according to Ditlow "Ford's shareholders paid the fine instead of the executives."

The contrast in the two incidents is not unusual. Japanese executives frequently take the blame for problems in their organizations. It is consistent with the emphasis placed upon the group and the responsibility of the leadership to set the example.

Source: Based in part on an article by Leslie Helm, "Top Mazda Officials to Have Pay Docked," *Houston Chronicle,* December 27, 1990.

larger groups or in those whose members are geographically separated. **Intergroup relationships,** which include such factors as the kind of pressure the group exerts and the degree to which the member identifies with the group, are another potentially important variable.

The degree of conformity with group norms may also be influenced by cultural factors. Some cultures with a more collective tradition may place greater emphasis on the group, and conformity with norms, than might cultures with a more individualistic orientation. Typical examples of these two orientations are Japan and the United States. Groups have traditionally played a far greater role in Japanese society than in American. Consequently, conformity to group norms is given greater emphasis in Japanese organizations. Likewise, so is nonconformity. Encounter 7-2 provides a telling illustration of this latter point, while demonstrating an important cultural difference.

Potential Consequences of Conforming to Group Norms

The research on conformity distinctly implies that conformity is a requirement of sustained group membership. The member who does not conform to important norms often is punished by a group such as by being isolated or ignored. Conformity has some potential negative and positive consequences. On the negative side, conformity can result in a loss of individuality and the establishment of only moderate levels of performance. This type of behavior can be costly to an organization that needs above-average levels of performance to remain competitive. Positive consequences can also occur from conformity to group norms. If no conformity existed, a manager would have a difficult, if not impossible, time in predicting a group's behavior patterns. This inability to estimate behavior could result in unsuccessful managerial attempts to channel the group's efforts toward the accomplishment of organizational goals.

■ **R7–1**   In one article accompanying this chapter, "The Development and Enforcement of Group Norms," Daniel Feldman examines in some detail how group norms develop and why they are enforced. In this article note particularly the four conditions under which norms are most likely to be enforced.

Leadership

The leadership role is an extremely crucial characteristic of groups as the leader of a group exerts some influence over the other members of the group. In the formal group, the leader can exercise legitimately sanctioned power. That is, the leader can reward or punish members who do not comply with the orders or rules. Sometimes, however, there is no formal leader, even in a formal group. Such a condition exists in self-managed teams (SMTs), an increasingly popular concept that we will discuss in Chapter 12.

The leadership role also is a significant factor in an informal group. The person who becomes an informal group leader generally is viewed as a respected and high-status member who embodies the values of the group, aids the group in accomplishing its goals, and enables members to satisfy needs. Additionally, the leader is the choice of group members to represent their viewpoint outside the group and usually is concerned with maintaining the group as a functioning unit.

Cohesiveness

Formal and informal groups seem to possess a closeness or commonness of attitude, behavior, and performance. This closeness has been referred to as cohesiveness. Cohesiveness typically is regarded as a force. It acts on the members to remain in a group and is greater than the forces pulling the members away from the group. A cohesive group, then, involves individuals who are attracted to one another. A group that is low in cohesiveness does not possess interpersonal attractiveness for the members.

Since highly cohesive groups are composed of individuals who are motivated to be together, there is a tendency on the part of management to expect effective group performance. This logic is not supported conclusively by research evidence. In general, as the cohesiveness of a work group increases, the level of conformity to group norms also increases. But these norms may be inconsistent with those of organization. The group pressures to conform are more intense in the cohesive group. The question of whether managers should encourage or discourage group cohesiveness is examined later in this chapter.

There are, of course, numerous sources of attraction to a group. These might include:

1. The goals of the group and the members are compatible and clearly specified.
2. The group has a charismatic leader.
3. The reputation of the group indicates that the group successfully accomplishes its tasks.
4. The group is small enough to permit members to have their opinions heard and evaluated by others.
5. The members are attractive in that they support one another and help one another overcome obstacles and barriers to personal growth and development.[15]

Cohesiveness and Performance

The concept of cohesiveness is important for understanding groups in organizations, as is the recognition of the impact of groups on performance.[16] The degree of cohesiveness in a group can have positive or negative effects, depending on how group goals match up with those of the formal organization.[17] In fact, four distinct possibilities exist, as illustrated in Exhibit 7-3.

Exhibit 7-3 indicates that if cohesiveness is high and the group accepts and agrees with formal organizational goals, then group behavior probably will be positive from the formal organization's standpoint. However, if the group is highly cohesive but has goals that are not congruent with those of the formal organization, then group behavior probably will be negative from the formal organization's standpoint.

---

[15]C. Cartwright and A. Zander, *Group Dynamics: Research and Theory* (New York: Harper & Row, 1968).

[16]J. M. George and K. L. Bettenhausen, "Understanding Prosocial Behavior, Sales Performance, and Turnover: A Group Level Analysis in a Service Context," *Journal of Applied Psychology*, October, 1990, pp. 698–709.

[17]It should be noted, of course, that cohesiveness is not the only factor which may influence performance. For just one example, see Wendy Wood, Darlene Polek, and Cheryl Aiken, "Sex Differences in Group Task Performance," *Journal of Personality and Social Psychology*, January 1985, pp. 63–71.

EXHIBIT 7-3

The Relationship between Group Cohesiveness and Agreement with Organizational Goals

		Agreement with Organizational Goals	
		Low	High
Degree of Group Cohesiveness	**Low**	Performance probably oriented away from organizational goals.	Performance probably oriented toward achievement of organizational goals.
	High	Performance oriented away from organizational goals.	Performance oriented toward achievement of organizational goals.

Exhibit 7-3 also indicates that if a group is low in cohesiveness and the members have goals that are not in agreement with those of management, then the results probably will be negative from the standpoint of the organization. Behavior will be more on an individual basis than on a group basis because of the low cohesiveness. On the other hand, it is possible to have a group low in cohesiveness where the members' goals agree with those of the formal organization. Here, the results probably will be positive, although again more on an individual basis than on a group basis.

When the goals of a cohesive group conflict with those of management, some form of intervention by management usually is necessary. Intervention techniques are discussed in detail in the next chapter.

Groupthink

Highly cohesive groups are very important forces in organizational behavior. In other words, it is a good idea to place people with many similarities in an isolated setting, give them a common goal, and reward them for performance. On the surface, this may look like a good idea. One author has provided a very provocative account about highly cohesive groups.[18] In his book, Irving Janis has analyzed foreign policy decisions made by a number of presidential administrations and concluded that these groups were highly cohesive and close-knit. He has labeled their decision-making process groupthink. Janis defines groupthink as the "deterioration of mental efficiency, reality testing, and moral judgement" in the interest of group solidarity.[19] According to Janis, groups suffering from

---

[18]Irving Janis, *Victims of Groupthink: A Psychological Study of Foreign Policy Decisions and Fiascos,* 2nd ed. (Boston: Houghton Miffin, 1982).

[19]Ibid., p. 9.

groupthink tend to display a number of characteristics. Among these characteristics are the following.

Illusion of Invulnerability. Members of one group believed that they were invincible. For example, on the eve of the disastrous attempt to invade Cuba in April 1961 (the Bay of Pigs invasion), Robert Kennedy stated that with the talent in the group, they could overcome whatever challenged them with "common sense and hard work" and "bold new ideas."

Tendency to Moralize. The group studied had a general tendency to view the United States as the leader of the free world. Any opposition to this view was characterized by the group's members as weak, evil, or unintelligent.

Feeling of Unanimity. The group reported that each member of the executive committee supported the president's decisions. Later on, however, members indicated that they had had serious doubts at the time the decisions were being made. For example, Arthur Schlesinger and Theodore Sorensen both reported that they had reservations about the decisions being made with respect to Southeast Asia during the Kennedy years. Both men admitted regretting their hesitancy to let their views be known at the time. However, at the time they believed that everyone else was in total agreement and that they had the only differing view. Rather than appear weak or soft, each kept his view to himself. This indicates how the pressure toward group solidarity can distort the judgment of individual members.

Pressure to Conform. Occasionally, President John F. Kennedy would bring in an expert to respond to questions that members of the group might have. The purpose was to have the expert in effect silence the critic instead of actively encouraging discussion of divergent views. Other informal pressures to conform were also used on cabinet and staff members. In one instance Arthur Schlesinger reported that Robert Kennedy has mentioned informally to him that while he could see some problems associated with a particular decision, the president needed unanimous support on the issue. There was a strong perceived need for group solidarity. Thus, groups can exert great pressure to conform on individual members.

Opposing Ideas Dismissed. Any individual or outside group that criticized or opposed a decision or policy received little or no attention from the group. Even valid ideas and relevant arguments were often dismissed prematurely. Janis notes that much evidence indicated strongly that the invasion of Cuba would fail, but it was given little consideration. Thus, information conflicting with group goals can be distorted or ignored as individual members strive for agreement and solidarity.

Certainly, some level of group cohesiveness is necessary for a group to tackle a problem. If seven individuals from seven different organizational units are assigned a task, the task may never be completed effectively. The point, however, is that more cohesiveness may not necessarily be better. While members of task groups may redefine solving a problem to mean reaching agreement rather than making the best decision, members of cohesive groups may redefine it to mean preserving relations among group members and preserving the image of the group. Some research suggests that even among highly cohesive groups, groupthink is not a factor if the group is composed of highly dominant individuals.[20]

Intergroup Conflict

An important characteristic of groups is that they frequently conflict with other groups in an organization. There are many reasons why groups conflict with one another, and the consequences of this conflict can be good for the organization or can be extremely negative. This chapter is concerned mainly with what happens *within* groups: the types of characteristics of groups as they develop. What happens *between* groups (intergroup behavior) is the subject of the next chapter.

▲ C7–2   The second case in this chapter, "Work Group Ownership of an Improved Tool," provides an excellent opportunity to examine how several of the group characteristics just discussed may have an effect—not always positive—on group and organizational effectiveness. In this case note particularly the effects of roles, norms, leadership, and cohesiveness.

THE CONCEPT OF ROLE

The concept of role is very important to the understanding of organizational behavior. Role refers to the expected behavior patterns attributed to a particular position in an organization.

The roles of wife and husband are familiar to everyone. Those roles are culturally defined expectations associated with particular positions. A role may include attitudes and values as well as specific kinds of behavior. It is what an individual must do in order to validate his or her occupancy of a particular position. In other words, what kind of a husband or wife an individual is depends a great deal on how he or she performs the culturally defined role associated with the position.

Certain activities are expected of every position in the formal organization. These activities constitute the role for that position from the standpoint of the organization. The organization develops job descriptions that define the activities of a particular position and how it relates to other positions in the organization. However, roles may not be set forth explicitly and yet be clearly understood by group members. For example, members of the marketing department in a bank

[20]Michael Callaway, Richard Marriott, and James Esser, "Effects of Dominance on Group Decision Making: Toward a Stress-Reduction Explanation of Groupthink," *Journal of Personality and Social Psychology*, October 1985, pp. 949–52.

may know that only the director of marketing represents the bank at national conventions and that they have no chance of attending even though this has never been explicitly stated. This is true both for formal (task and command) groups and for informal (interest and friendship) groups. Thus, whether they are formally or informally established, status hierarchies and accompanying roles are integral parts of every organization.

■ **E7–2**   Exercise 7–2, "What To Do with Johnny Rocco," provides an opportunity to experience first hand many of the role concepts discussed in the following sections.

Multiple Roles and Role Sets

Most of us play many roles simultaneously. This is because we occupy many different positions in a variety of organizations—home, work, church, civic, and so forth. Within each of these organizations, we occupy and perform certain roles. Most individuals perform **multiple roles**. We may simultaneously be playing the role of parent, mate, supervisor, and subordinate. Each position may have different role relationships. For example, the position of college professor involves not only the role of teacher in relation to students but also numerous other roles relating the position to administrators, peers, the community, and alumni. Each group may expect different things. Students may expect good classroom performance; administrators may expect classroom performance, research, and publication; the college community may expect community service; and alumni may expect help in recruiting students and athletes. This we term the **role set**. A role set refers to those individuals who have expectations for the behavior of the individual in the particular role. The more expectations, the more complex is the role set. For example, a college professor probably has a more complex role set than that of a forest ranger but one less complicated than that of a politician.

Multiple roles refers to different roles, while role set refers to the different expectations associated with one role. Therefore, an individual involved in many different roles, each with a complex role set, faces the ultimate in complexity of individual behavior. The concepts of multiple roles and role sets are important because there may be complications that make it extremely difficult to define specific roles, especially in organizational settings.[21] This can often result in role conflict for the individual. As we saw in Chapter 6, role conflict is a major cause of individual stress in organizations.

Role Perception

You can understand how different individuals have different perceptions of the behavior associated with a given role. In an organizational setting, accuracy in

---

[21]An important work in this field is R. L. Kahn, D. M. Wolfe, R. P. Quinn, and J. D. Snoek, *Organizational Stress: Studies in Role Conflict and Ambiguity* (New York: John Wiley & Sons, 1964), pp. 12–26.

role perception can have a definite impact on performance. This matter is further complicated in an organization because there may be three different perceptions of the same role: that of the formal organization, that of the group, and that of the individual. For example, a college dean has perceptions of the role of professors, as do students and the professors themselves. As we saw in our discussion of role sets above, student perceptions of the role of a professor may be very different from those of the college administrators. This increases even further the possibility of role conflict.

The Organization

The positions that individuals occupy in an organization are the sum total of the organizationally defined roles. This includes the position in the chain of command, the amount of authority associated with the position, and the functions and duties of the position. These roles are defined by the organization and relate to the position and not to a particular individual.

The Group

Role relationships develop that relate individuals to the various groups to which they belong. These may be formal and informal groups; the expectations evolve over time and may or may not match up with the organization's perception of the role. In a group of salespeople, for example, the individual with the longest time in the field may be expected to represent the group to the district manager, although this person may not be the most successful salesperson in the company. In this respect, the role relationships are similar to group norms.

The Individual

Every individual who occupies a position in an organization or group has a clearly defined perception of his or her role. This perception is influenced greatly by background and social class since they affect the individual's basic values and attitudes. These are brought to the organization and affect individuals' perception of their roles. For example, because of social class background and values, a newly promoted first-line supervisor may perceive his or her role as being that of a representative of the group "to" management rather than that of a representative "of" management to the group.

Role Conflict

Because of the multiplicity of roles and role sets, it is possible for an individual to face a situation where there is simultaneous occurrence of two or more role requirements and the performance of one precludes the performance of the others. When this occurs, the individual faces a situation known as **role conflict**. Several forms of role conflict can occur in organizations.

Person-Role Conflict

Person-role conflict occurs when role requirements violate the basic values, attitudes, and needs of the individual occupying the position. A supervisor who finds it difficult to dismiss a subordinate with a family and an executive who resigns rather than engage in some unethical activity are examples of individuals experiencing this type of role conflict.[22]

Intrarole Conflict

Intrarole conflict occurs when different individuals define a role according to different sets of expectations, making it impossible for the person occupying the role to satisfy all of them. This is more likely to occur when a given role has a complex role set (many different role relationships.) The supervisor in an industrial situation has a rather complex role set and thus may face intrarole conflict. On one hand, top management has a set of expectations that stresses the supervisor's role in the management hierarchy. However, the supervisor may have close friendship ties with members of the command group who may be former working peers. This is why supervisors often are described as being "in the middle."[23]

Interrole Conflict

Interrole conflict can result from facing multiple roles. It occurs because individuals simultaneously perform many roles, some of which have conflicting expectations. A scientist in a chemical plant who also is a member of a management group might experience role conflict of this kind. In such a situation, the scientist may be expected to behave in accordance with the expectations of management as well as the expectations of professional chemists. A physician placed in the role of hospital administrator also may experience this type of role conflict. Sometimes, the conflict is between the individual's role as a group member on the one hand and a member of the larger organization on the other. Encounter 7-3 is a case in point. In the next chapter you will see that interrole conflict often is also the cause of conflict between groups in many organizations.

---

[22]For example, see N. Keeley, "Subjective Performance Evaluation and Person-Role Conflict under Conditions of Uncertainty," *Academy of Management Journal,* June 1977, pp. 301–14. For an analysis of some of the organizational implications of this type of conflict, see L. Roos and F. Starke, "Roles in Organizations," in *Handbook of Organizational Design,* ed. W. Starbuck and P. Nystrom (Oxford, England: Oxford University Press, 1980).

[23]For classic discussions of the conflict-laden position of foremen, see F. J. Roethlisberger, "The Foreman: Master and Victim of Double Talk," *Harvard Business Review,* September–October 1965, pp. 23 ff; and F. C. Mann and J. K. Dent, "The Supervisor: Member of Two Organizational Families," *Harvard Business Review,* November–December 1954, pp. 103–12.

THE ETHICS OF ROLE CONFLICT: USING EMPLOYEES AS INFORMANTS

Is it ethical for an organization to create role conflict by using employees as paid informants? Law enforcement agencies rely on paid informants routinely. These snitches (as they are known in the business) frequently provide information essential to solving a crime. But while their use by the police is not unusual, the use by management of employees in the role of paid informants is most unusual.

A California department store decided to do just that, however. Emporium-Capwell offered a "bounty" to store employees. One pay period when employees opened their pay envelopes they found a second check in the amount of $300. A close inspection revealed the check to be nonnegotiable. An attached note from management, however, promised to reward employees for reporting co-workers who shoplift or commit other dishonest acts.

"Would you like to have this check?" read the note. "If so, simply provide the loss prevention department with information which leads to the termination of a dishonest employee. All information is treated with strict confidence and thoroughly investigated before any action is taken."

When asked, many Emporium employees indicated that they resented the move and definitely would not cooperate with management. "I've worked here 18 years, and this is the lousiest thing I've ever seen here," said one distressed employee. "Everyone was mad. On the one hand, they want you to work as a team and respect your co-workers. On the other, they want you to stab them in the back. I just think it's lousy."

Richard Hedges, president of the union which represents many of the Emporium-Capwell employees, agreed most emphatically. Hedges was quoted as saying, "It's one thing to say, 'If you have knowledge that someone is violating the law, contact us.' It's another to put out a bounty and encourage people to call with their suspicions. I think this may backfire. It will create ill will and paranoia."

Paying informants as the Emporium-Capwell plan did is different from programs such as those at Nynex and Pacific Bell, where whistle-blower hotlines have been set up to facilitate transmission of information regarding illegal activities. No cash rewards are offered, however. While role conflict may be engendered in these latter examples as well, the absence of a "bounty hunter" feature raised far fewer ethical questions.

Source: Based in part on articles appearing in the *Houston Chronicle,* November 9, 1985, sec. 1, p. 4; and *Business Week,* September 23, 1991, p. 65.

The Results of Role Conflict

Behavioral scientists agree that an individual confronted with role conflict will experience psychological stress that may result in emotional problems and indecision. These problems were outlined in detail in Chapter 6. While there are certain kinds of role conflict that managers can do little to avoid, many role conflicts can be minimized. For example, some types of role conflict (especially intrarole conflict) can be the result of violations of the classical principles of chain of command and unity of command. The rationale of the early management writers for these two principles was that violation probably would cause conflicting pressures on the individual. In other words, when individuals are faced with conflicting expectations or demands from two or more sources, the likely result will be a decline in performance.

In addition, interrole conflict can be generated by conflicting expectations of formal or informal groups, with results similar to those of intrarole conflict. Thus, a highly cohesive group with goals not consistent with those of the formal organization can cause a great deal of interrole conflict for the group's members.

END RESULTS

Groups exist to accomplish objectives. In the case of work groups, those objectives are generally related to the performance of specific tasks which in turn are designed to result in attainment of formal organizational outcomes. Measurable production (e.g., number of units assembled, percent of market captured, number of customers served) is perhaps the most obvious, but certainly not the only, end result of work group activities.

One of the attractive attributes of groups is their potential synergism. Synergism is the cooperative action of discrete entities such that the total effect is greater than the sum of the effects taken independently. In the case of groups, discrete entities are individual members of the group. Synergistic groups can create something that is more than the sum total of that produced by individuals. Thus,

Potential Group Performance = Individual Performance + Synergy

Actual performance, however, may be different. Actual group performance may be expressed by the following equation:

Actual Group Performance = Potential Performance − Faulty Group Process

What this suggests is that synergistic gains from groups may be offset by operating failures within the group. If there is intragroup conflict, communication breakdowns, insufficient interaction, political maneuvering, lack of role clarity, poor decision making, inept leadership, or any number of other counterproductive conditions, group performance will most likely be negatively affected. No groups operate smoothly and efficiently all of the time. Insuring that instances of faulty process are minimized is a constant, and extremely critical, challenge for managers and group members alike.

While some form of production output (goods, services, ideas, etc.) is typically an important measure of group performance and effectiveness, it is not the only consideration. Organizational researcher Richard Hackman identifies three important criteria of group effectiveness.[24]

1. *The extent to which the group's productive output meets the standard of quantity, quality, and timeliness of the users of the output.* For example,

[24]J. Richard Hackman, ed, "Groups that Work (and Those that Don't)," (San Francisco: Jossey-Bass Publishers, 1990), pp. 6–7.

a group which produced a product that was unacceptable to a customer could not be considered effective no matter what the group or others thought about the product.

2. *The extent to which the group process of actually doing the work enhances the capability of group members to work together interdependently in the future.* This suggests that even though the group might produce a product meeting the standards mentioned in the first criterion, if that end result was obtained in a manner destructive to future working relationships, the group is not effective. The fact that a group is a temporary one, such as a task force or project team, does not negate the importance of this criterion of effectiveness.

3. *The extent to which the group experience contributes to the growth and well-being of its members.* This criterion relates to the end results of development and satisfaction which were specified in Exhibit 7-1 at the beginning of the chapter. Note that it is not necessary for a group to have member development and satisfaction as a stated objective for this to be a legitimate test of group effectiveness. When group participation does not contribute to personal or professional development and/or does not lead to any personal need satisfaction, this may have negative consequences. It suggests group productivity may not continue over an extended period of time, and it may have implications for the quality of group members' participation in subsequent groups.

● **R7–2**   In the second article accompanying this chapter, "Teamwork at General Foods: New and Improved," Marc Bassim shows, with a real life example, how groups organized into interfuctional work teams can be a significant factor in establishing an environment that contributes to maximizing end results.

SUMMARY OF KEY POINTS

- The term group can be viewed from many different perspectives. A group can be thought of in terms of perception, organization, motivation, interaction, or any combination of these. For our purposes a group may be thought of as two or more employees who interact with each other in such a manner that the behavior and/or performance of one member is influenced by the behavior and/or performance of other members.

- The model of the process of group formation and development presented in the chapter has a number of elements. These include the different types of groups, the reasons why group are formed, stages in group development, important characteristics of groups, and end results of group activity.

- Formal groups are created to facilitate the accomplishment of an organization's goal. Command groups, specified by the organization chart, and task groups, comprised of employees working together to complete a specific project are two types of formal groups. Informal groups are associations of individuals in the work situation in response to social needs. Interest groups and friendship groups are two types of informal groups.

- Formal and informal groups exist for a number of reasons. Need satisfaction may be a compelling reason to join a group. Security, social, and esteem needs are typical examples. Proximity and attraction may be another reason. That is, people may form groups because their physical location encourages interaction and they enjoy such interaction. People may also form groups to facilitate the accomplishment of common goals. Finally, some groups form because individuals believe they can derive economic benefits from group membership.

- As groups form and develop, they tend to go through several sequential stages. These are (1) *forming,* characterized by uncertainty and confusion, (2) *storming,* marked by conflict and confrontation, (3) *norming,* where group cohesion begins significant development, (4) *performing,* where the group becomes fully functional, and for some groups (5) *adjourning,* which involves the termination of group activities.

- To understand group behavior it is essential to be aware that formal and informal groups exhibit certain characteristics. These include the type of structure that evolves over time in the group; the status hierarchy that exists and the basis used for determining member status; the norms or behaviors the group expects its member to adhere to; the type of leadership in the group; the degree of cohesiveness that exists within the group; and role conflict, which may take the form of person-role conflict, interrole conflict, or intrarole conflict.

- The concept of role is vital to an understanding of group behavior. A role is the expected behavior patterns attributed to a particular position. Most individuals perform multiple roles, each with its own role set (expectations of others for the role). An individual involved in many different roles, each having a complex role set, faces the ultimate in complexity of individual behavior.

- Relevant criteria for group effectiveness include (1) the extent to which group output meets expected standards of quantity, quality, and timeliness; (2) the extent to which the group process enhances the capability of group members to work together interdependently in the future; and (3) the extent to which the group experience contributes to the growth and well-being of its members.

REVIEW AND DISCUSSION QUESTIONS

1. Why is it important for managers to be familiar with the concepts of group behavior?

2. Why is groupthink something to be avoided? How might a manager attempt to ensure that groupthink doesn't occur in his or her group?

3. Are the factors that influence group behavior the same or different from those that influence individual behavior. Explain.

4. Describe a case of person-role conflict, intrarole conflict, or interrole conflict that you have experienced personally. How did you resolve the conflict? Was the resolution satisfactory?

5. Is it always important for satisfactory end results to be achieved with respect to performance, satisfaction, and development? Can you think of a situation where satisfaction and/or development might be more important than performance?

6. Under what circumstances might an organization encourage the formation of informal employee groups? When might they discourage such groups?

7. Think of a formal group to which you belong. Describe the group in terms of the characteristics of groups discussed in the chapter.

8. Repeat the process in the previous question, this time for an informal group to which you belong.

9. What is the relationship between group norms and group cohesiveness? What roles do both cohesiveness and norms play in shaping group performance?

10. Would you expect the membership of informal groups in organizations to overlap that of formal groups? Why or why not?

•

READINGS

READING 7–1   THE DEVELOPMENT AND ENFORCEMENT OF GROUP NORMS
Daniel C. Feldman

Group norms are the informal rules that groups adopt to regulate and regularize group members' behavior. Although these norms are infrequently written down or openly discussed, they often have a powerful, and consistent, influence on group members' behavior (Hackman, 1976).

Most of the theoretical work on group norms has focused on identifying the types of group norms (March, 1954) or on describing their structural characteristics (Jackson, 1966). Empirically, most of the focus has been on examining the impact that norms have on other social phenomena. For example, Seashore (1954) and Schachter, Ellertson, McBride, and Gregory (1951) use the concept of group norms to discuss group cohesiveness; Trist and Bamforth (1951) and Whyte (1955a) use norms to examine production restriction; Janis (1972) and Longley and Pruitt (1980) use norms to illustrate group decision making; and Asch (1951) and Sherif (1936) use norms to examine conformity.

This paper focuses on two frequently overlooked aspects of the group norms literature. First, it examines *why* group norms are enforced. Why do groups desire conformity to these informal rules? Second, it examines *how* group norms develop. Why do some norms develop in one group but not in another? Much of what is known about group norms comes from post hoc examination of their impact on outcome variables; much less has been written about how these norms actually develop and why they regulate behavior so strongly.

Understanding how group norms develop and why they are enforced is important for two reasons. First, group norms can play a large role in determining whether the group will be productive or not. If the work group feels that management is supportive, groups norms will develop that facilitate—in fact, enhance—group productivity. In contrast, if the work group feels that management is antagonistic, group norms that inhibit and impair group performance are much more likely to develop. Second, managers can play a major role in setting and changing group norms. They can use their influence to set task-facilitative norms; they can monitor whether the group's norms are functional; they can explicitly address counterproductive norms with subordinates. By understanding how norms develop and why norms are enforced, managers can better diagnose the underlying tensions and problems their groups are facing, and they can help the group develop more effective behavior patterns.

WHY NORMS ARE ENFORCED

As Shaw (1981) suggests, a group does not establish or enforce norms about every conceivable situation. Norms are formed and enforced only with respect to behaviors that have some significance for the group. The frequent distinction between task maintenance duties and social maintenance duties helps explain why groups bring selected behaviors under normative control.

Groups, like individuals, try to operate in such a way that they maximize their chances for task success and minimize their chances of task failure. First of all, a group will enforce norms that facilitate its very survival. It will try to protect itself from interference from groups external to the organization or harassment from groups internal to the organization. Second, the group will want to increase the predictability of group members' behaviors. Norms provide a basis for predicting the behavior of others, thus enabling group members to anticipate each other's actions and prepare quick and appropriate responses (Shaw, 1981; Kiesler & Kiesler, 1970).

In addition, groups want to ensure the satisfaction of their members and prevent as much interpersonal discomfort as possible. Thus, groups also will enforce norms that help the group avoid embarrassing interpersonal problems. Certain topics of conversation might be sanctioned, and certain types of social interaction might be openly discouraged. Moreover, norms serve an expressive function for groups (Katz & Kahn, 1978). Enforcing group norms gives group members a chance to express what their central

Source: Reprinted from "The Development and Enforcement of Group Norms," by Daniel C. Feldman, published in *Academy of Management Review*, Vol. 9, No. 1 (January 1984), pp. 47–53 by permission of the *Academy of Management Review*.

values are, and to clarify what is distinctive about the group and central to its identity (Hackman, 1976).

Each of these four conditions under which group norms are most likely to be enforced is discussed in more detail below.

1. **Norms are likely to be enforced if they facilitate group survival.** A group will enforce norms that protect it from interference or harassment by members of other groups. For instance, a group might develop a norm not to discuss its salaries with members of other groups in the organization, so that attention will not be brought to pay inequities in its favor. Groups might also have norms about not discussing internal problems with members of other units. Such discussions might boomerang at a later date if other groups use the information to develop a better competitive strategy against the group.

Enforcing group norms also makes clear what the "boundaries" of the group are. As a result of observation of deviant behavior and the consequences that ensue, other group members are reminded of the **range** of behavior that is acceptable to the group (Dentler & Erikson, 1959). The norms about productivity that frequently develop among piecerate workers are illustrative here. By observing a series of incidents (a person produces 50 widgets and is praised; a person produces 60 widgets and receives sharp teasing; a person produces 70 widgets and is ostracized), group members learn the limits of the group's patience. "This far, and no further." The group is less likely to be "successful" (i.e., continue to sustain the low productivity expectations of management) if it allows its jobs to be reevaluated.

The literature on conformity and deviance is consistent with this observation. The group is more likely to reject the person who violates group norms when the deviant has not been a "good" group member previously (Hollander, 1958, 1964). Individuals can generate "idiosyncrasy credits" with other group members by contributing effectively to the attainment of group goals. Individuals extend these credits when they perform poorly or dysfunctionally at work. When a group member no longer has a positive "balance" of credits to draw on when he or she deviates, the group is much more likely to reject that deviant (Hollander, 1961).

Moreover, the group is more likely to reject the deviant when the group is failing in meeting its goals successfully. When the group is successful, it can afford to be charitable or tolerant towards deviant behavior. The group may disapprove, but it has some margin for error. When the group is faced with failure, the deviance is much more sharply punished. Any behavior that negatively influences the success of the group becomes much more salient and threatening to group members (Alvarez, 1968; Wiggins, Dill, & Schwartz, 1965).

2. **Norms are more likely to be enforced if they simplify, or make predictable, what behavior is expected of group members.** If each member of the group had to decide individually how to behave in each interaction, much time would be lost performing routine activities. Moreover, individuals would have more trouble predicting the behaviors of others and responding correctly. Norms enable group members to anticipate each other's actions and to prepare the most appropriate response in the most timely manner (Hackman, 1976; Shaw, 1981).

For instance, when attending group meetings in which proposals are presented and suggestions are requested, do the presenters really want feedback or are they simply going through the motions? Groups may develop norms that reduce this uncertainty and provide a clearer course of action, for example, make suggestions in small, informal meetings but not in large, formal meetings.

Another example comes from norms that regulate social behavior. For instance, when colleagues go out for lunch together, there can be some awkwardness about how to split the bill at the end of the meal. A group may develop a norm that gives some highly predictable or simple way of behaving, for example, split evenly, take turns picking up the tab, or pay for what each ordered.

Norms also may reinforce specific individual members' roles. A number of different roles might emerge in groups. These roles are simply expectations that are shared by group members regarding who is to carry out what types of activities under what circumstances (Bales & Slater, 1955). Although groups obviously create pressure toward uniformity among members, there also is a tendency for groups to create and maintain **diversity** among members (Hackman, 1976). For instance, a group might have one person whom others expect to break the tension when tempers become too hot. Another group member might be expected to keep track of what is going on in other parts of the organization. A third member might be expected to take care of the "creature" needs of the group—making the coffee, making dinner reservations, and so on. A fourth member might be expected by others to take notes, keep minutes, or maintain files.

None of these roles are **formal** duties, but they are activities that the group needs accomplished and has somehow parcelled out among members. If the role expectations are not met, some important jobs might not get done, or other group members might have to take on additional responsibilities. Moreover, such role assignments reduce individual members' ambiguities about what is expected specifically of them. It is important to note, though, that who takes what role in a group also is highly influenced by individuals' personal needs. The person with a high need for structure often wants to be in the note-taking role to control the structuring activity in the group; the person who breaks the tension might dislike conflict and uses the role to circumvent it.

3. **Norms are likely to be enforced if they help the group avoid embarrassing interpersonal problems.** Goffman's work on "facework" gives some insight on this point. Goffman (1955) argues that each person in a group has a "face" he or she presents to other members of a group. This "face" is analogous to what one would call "self-image," the person's perceptions of himself or herself and how he or she would like to be seen by others. Groups want to ensure that no one's self-image is damaged, called into question, or embarrassed. Consequently, the group will establish norms that discourage topics of conversation or situations in which face is too likely to be inadvertently broken. For instance, groups might develop norms about not discussing romantic involvements (so that differences in moral values do not become salient) or about not getting together socially in people's homes (so that differences in taste or income do not become salient).

A good illustration of Goffman's facework occurs in the classroom. There is always palpable tension in a room when either a class is totally unprepared to discuss a case or a professor is totally unprepared to lecture or lead the discussion. One part of the awkwardness stems from the inability of the other partner in the interaction to behave as he or she is prepared to or would like to behave. The professor cannot teach if the students are not prepared, and the students cannot learn if the professors are not teaching. Another part of the awkwardness, though, stems from self-images being called into question. Although faculty are aware that not all students are serious scholars, the situation is difficult to handle if the class as a group does not even show a pretense of wanting to learn. Although students are aware that many faculty are mainly interested in research and consulting, there is a problem if the professor does not even show a pretense of caring to teach. Norms almost always develop between professor and students about what level of preparation and interest is expected by the other because both parties want to avoid awkward confrontations.

4. **Norms are likely to be enforced if they express the central values of the group and clarify what is distinctive about the group's identity.** Norms can provide the social justification for group activities to its members (Katz & Kahn, 1978). When the production group labels rate-busting deviant, it says: "We care more about maximizing group security than about individual profits." Group norms also convey what is distinctive about the group to outsiders. When an advertising agency labels unstylish clothes deviant, it says: "We think of ourselves, personally and professionally, as trend-setters, and being fashionably dressed conveys that to our clients and our public."

One of the key expressive functions of group norms is to define and legitimate the power of the group itself over individual members (Katz & Kahn, 1978). When groups punish norm infraction, they reinforce in the minds of group members the authority of the group. Here, too, the literature on group deviance sheds some light on the issue at hand.

It has been noted frequently that the amount of deviance in a group is rather small (Erikson, 1966; Schur, 1965). The group uses norm enforcement to show the *strength* of the group. However, if a behavior becomes so widespread that it becomes impossible to control, then the labeling of the widespread behavior as deviance becomes problematic. It simply reminds members of the *weakness* of the group. At this point, the group will redefine what is deviant more narrowly, or it will define its job as that of keeping deviants **within bounds**, rather than that of obliterating it altogether. For example, though drug use is and always has been illegal, the widespread use of drugs has led to changes in law enforcement over time. A greater distinction now is made between "hard" drugs and other controlled substances; less penalty is given to those apprehended with small amounts than large amounts; greater attention is focused on capturing large scale smugglers and traffickers than the occasional user. A group, unconsciously if not consciously, learns how much behavior it is capable of labeling deviant and punishing effectively.

Finally, this expressive function of group norms can be seen nicely in circumstances in which there is an inconsistency between what group members **say** is the group norm and how people actually **behave**. For instance, sometimes groups will engage in a lot of rhetoric about how much independence its managers are allowed and how much it values entrepreneurial effort; yet the harder data suggest that the more conservative, deferring, or dependent managers get rewarded. Such an inconsistency can reflect conflicts among the group's expressed values. First, the group can be ambivalent about independence; the group knows it needs to encourage more entrepreneurial efforts to flourish, but such efforts create competition and threaten the status quo. Second, the inconsistency can reveal major subgroup differences. Some people may value and encourage entrepreneurial behavior, but others do not—and the latter may control the group's rewards. Third, the inconsistency can reveal a source of the group's self-consciousness, a dichotomy between what the group is really like and how it would like to be perceived. The group may realize that it is too conservative, yet be unable or too frightened to address its problem. The expressed group norm allows the group members a chance to present a "face" to each other and to outsiders that is more socially desirable than reality.

HOW GROUP NORMS DEVELOP

Norms usually develop gradually and informally as group members learn what behaviors are necessary for the group to function more effectively. However, it also is possible for the norm development process to be short-cut by a critical event in the group or by conscious group decision (Hackman, 1976).

Most norms develop in one or more of the following four ways: explicit statements by supervisors or co-workers; critical events in the group's history; primacy; and carryover behaviors from past situations.

1. **Explicit statements by supervisors or co-workers.** Norms that facilitate group survival or task success often are set by the leader of the group or powerful members (Whyte, 1955b). For instance, a group leader might explicitly set norms about not drinking at lunch because subordinates who have been drinking are more likely to have problems dealing competently with clients and top management or they are more likely to have accidents at work. The group leader might also set norms about lateness, personal phone calls, and long coffee breaks if too much productivity is lost as a result of time way from the work place.

Explicit statements by supervisors also can increase the predictability of group members' behavior. For instance, supervisors might have particular preferences for a way of analyzing problems or presenting reports. Strong norms will be set to ensure compliance with these preferences. Consequently, supervisors will have increased certainty about receiving work in the format requested, so they can plan accordingly; workers will have increased certainty about

what is expected, so they will not have to outguess their boss or redo their projects.

Managers or important group members also can define the specific role expectations of individual group members. For instance, a supervisor or a co-worker might go up to a new recruit after a meeting to give the proverbial advice: "New recruits should be seen and not heard." The senior group member might be trying to prevent the new recruit from appearing brash or incompetent or from embarrassing other group members. Such interventions set specific role expectations for the new group member.

Norms that cater to supervisor preferences also are frequently established even if they are not objectively necessary to task accomplishment. For example, although organizational norms may be very democratic in terms of everybody calling each other by their first names, some managers have strong preferences about being called Mr., Ms., or Mrs. Although the form of address used in the work group does not influence group effectiveness, complying with the norm bears little cost to the group member, whereas noncompliance could cause daily friction with the supervisor. Such norms help group members avoid embarrassing interpersonal interactions with their managers.

Fourth, norms set explicitly by the supervisor frequently express the central values of the group. For instance, a dean can set very strong norms about faculty keeping office hours and being on campus daily. Such norms reaffirm to members of the academic community their teaching and service obligations, and they send signals to individuals outside the college about what is valued in faculty behavior or distinctive about the school. A dean also could set norms that allow faculty to consult or do executive development two or three days a week. Such norms, too, legitimate other types of faculty behavior and send signals to both insiders and outsiders about some central values of the college.

2. **Critical events in the group's history.** At times there is a critical event in the group's history that established an important precedent. For instance, a group member might have discussed hiring plans with members of other units in the organization, and as a result new positions were lost or there was increased competition for good applicants. Such indiscretion can substantially hinder the survival and task success of the group; very likely the offender will be either formally censured or informally rebuked. As a result of such an incident, norms about secrecy might develop that will protect the group in similar situations in the future.

An example from Janis's *Victims of Groupthink* (1972) also illustrates this point nicely. One of President

Kennedy's closest advisors, Arthur Schlesinger, Jr., had serious reservations about the Bay of Pigs invasion and presented his strong objections to the Bay of Pigs plan in a memorandum to Kennedy and Secretary of State Dean Rusk. However, Schlesinger was pressured by the President's brother, Attorney General Robert Kennedy, to keep his objections to himself. Remarked Robert Kennedy to Schlesinger: "You may be right or you may be wrong, but the President has made his mind up. Don't push it any further. Now is the time for everyone to help him all they can." Such critical events led group members to silence their views and set up group norms about bounds of disagreeing with the president.

Sometimes group norms can be set by conscious decision of a group after a particularly good or bad experience the group has had. To illustrate, a group might have had a particularly constructive meeting and be very pleased with how much it accomplished. Several people might say, "I think the reason we got so much accomplished today is that we met really early in the morning before the rest of the staff showed up and the phone started ringing. Let's try to continue to meet at 7:30 A.M." Others might agree, and the norm is set. On the other hand, if a group notices it accomplished way too little in a meeting, it might openly discuss setting norms to cut down on ineffective behavior (e.g., having an agenda, not interrupting others while they are talking). Such norms develop to facilitate task success and to reduce uncertainty about what is expected from each individual in the group.

Critical events also can identify awkward interpersonal situations that need to be avoided in the future. For instance, a divorce between two people working in the same group might have caused a lot of acrimony and hard feeling in a unit, not only between the husband and wife but also among various other group members who got involved in the marital problems. After the unpleasant divorce, a group might develop a norm about not hiring spouses to avoid having to deal with such interpersonal problems in the future.

Finally, critical events also can give rise to norms that express the central, or distinctive, values of the group. When a peer review panel finds a physician or lawyer guilty of malpractice or malfeasance, first it establishes (or reaffirms) the rights of professionals to evaluate and criticize the professional behavior of their colleagues. Moreover, it clarifies what behaviors are inconsistent with the group's self-image or its values. When a faculty committee votes on a candidate's tenure, it, too, asserts the legitimacy of influence of senior faculty over junior faculty. In addition, it sends (hopefully) clear messages to junior faculty about its values in terms of quality of research, teaching, and service. There are important "announcement effects" of peer reviews; internal group members carefully reexamine the group's values, and outsiders draw inferences about the character of the group from such critical decisions.

3. **Primacy.** The first behavior pattern that emerges in a group often sets group expectations. If the first group meeting is marked by very formal interaction between supervisors and subordinates, then the group often expects future meetings to be conducted in the same way. Where people sit in meetings or rooms frequently is developed through primacy. People generally continue to sit in the same seats they sat in at their first meeting, even though those original seats are not assigned and people could change where they sit at every meeting. Most friendship groups of students develop their own "turf" in a lecture hall and are surprised/dismayed when an interloper takes "their" seats.

Norms that develop through primacy often do so to simplify, or make predictable, what behavior is expected of group members. There may be very little task impact from where people sit in meetings or how formal interactions are. However, norms develop about such behaviors to make life much more routine and predictable. Every time a group member enters a room, he or she does not have to "decide" where to sit or how formally to behave. Moreover, he or she also is much more certain about how other group members will behave.

4. **Carry-over behaviors from past situations.** Many group norms in organizations emerge because individual group members bring set expectations with them from other work groups in other organizations. Lawyers expect to behave towards clients in Organization I (e.g., confidentiality, setting fees) as they behaved towards those in Organization II. Doctors expect to behave toward patients in Hospital I (e.g., "bedside manner," professional distance) as they behaved in Hospital II. Accountants expect to behave towards colleagues at Firm I (e.g., dress code, adherence to statutes) as they behaved towards those at Firm II. In fact, much of what goes on in professional schools is giving new members of the profession the same standards and norms of behavior that practitioners in the field hold.

Such carryover of individual behaviors from past situations can increase the predictability of group members' behaviors in new settings and facilitate task accomplishment. For instance, students and professors bring with them fairly constant sets of expectations from class to class. As a result, students do not have to relearn continually their roles from class to class; they know, for instance, if they come in late to take a seat quietly at the back of the room without being told. Professors also do not have to relearn continually their roles; they know, for instance, not to mumble, scribble in small print on the blackboard, or be vague when making course assignments. In addition, presumably the most task-successful norms will be the ones carried over from organization to organization.

Moreover, such carryover norms help avoid embarrassing interpersonal situations. Individuals are more likely to know which conversations and actions provoke annoyance, irritation, or embarrassment to their colleagues. Finally, when groups carry over norms from one organization to another, they also clarify what is distinctive about the occupational or professional role. When lawyers maintain strict rules of confidentiality, when doctors maintain a consistent professional distance with patients, when accountants present a very formal physical appearance, they all assert: "These are the standards we sustain *independent* of what we could 'get away with' in this organization. This is *our* self-concept."

SUMMARY

Norms generally are enforced only for behaviors that are viewed as important by most group members. Groups do not have the time or energy to regulate each and every action of individual members. Only those behaviors that ensure group survival, facilitate task accomplishment, contribute to group morale, or express the group's central values are likely to be brought under normative control. Norms that reflect these group needs will develop through explicit statements of supervisors, critical events in the group's history, primacy, or carryover behaviors from past situations.

Empirical research on norm development and enforcement has substantially lagged descriptive and theoretical work. In large part, this may be due to the methodological problems of measuring norms and getting enough data points either across time or across groups. Until such time as empirical work progresses, however, the usefulness of group norms as a predictive concept, rather than as a post hoc explanatory device, will be severely limited. Moreover, until it is known more concretely why norms develop and why they are strongly enforced, attempts to *change* group norms will remain haphazard and difficult to accomplish.

REFERENCES

R. Alvarez, "Informal Reactions to Deviance in Stimulated Work Organizations: A Laboratory Experiment," *American Sociological Review 33*, 1968, pp. 895–912.

S. Asch, "Effects of Group Pressure upon the Modification and Distortion of Judgment," in *Group Leadership, and Men,* ed. M. H. Guetzkow (Pittsburg: Carnegie, 1951), pp. 117–90.

R. F. Bales and P. E. Slater, "Role Differentiation in Small Groups," in *Family, Socialization, and Interaction Process,* eds. T. Parsons, R. F. Bales, J. Olds, M. Zelditch, and P. E. Slater (Glencoe, Ill.: Free Press, 1955), pp. 35–131.

R. A. Dentler and K. T. Erikson, "The Functions of Deviance in Groups. *Social Problems 7,* 1959, pp. 98–107.

K. T. Erikson, *Wayward Puritans.* (New York: Wiley, 1966).

E. Goffman, On Face-Work: An Analysis of Ritual Elements in Social Interaction, *Psychiatry 18,* 1955, pp. 213–31.

J. R. Hackman, "Group Influences on Individuals," *Handbook of Industrial and Organizational Psychology,* ed. M. Dunnette (Chicago: Rand McNally, 1976), pp. 1455–1525.

E. P. Hollander, Conformity, Status, and Idiosyncrasy Credit, *Psychological Review 65,* 1958, pp. 117–27.

E. P. Hollander, Some Effects of Perceived Status on Responses to Innovative Behavior, *Journal of Abnormal and Social Psychology 63,* 1961, pp. 247–50.

E. P. Hollander, *Leaders, Groups, and Influence.* (New York: Oxford University Press, 1964).

J. A. Jackson, Conceptual and Measurement Model for Norms and Roles. *Pacific Sociological Review 9,* 1966, pp. 35–47.

I. Janis, *Victim of Groupthink: A Psychological Study of Foreign-Policy Decisions and Fiascos.* (New York: Houghton-Mifflin, 1972).

D. Katz and R. L. Kahn, *The Social Psychology of Organizations,* 2nd ed. (New York: Wiley, 1978).

C. A. Kiesler and S. B. Kiesler, *Conformity.* (Reading, Mass.: Addison-Wesley, 1970).

J. Longley and D. C. Pruitt, "Groupthink: A Critique of Janis' Theory," in *Review of Personality and Social Psychology* ed. Ladd Wheeler (Beverly Hills: Sage, 1980). pp. 74–93.

J. March, "Group Norms and the Active Minority," *American Sociological Review 19,* 1954, pp. 733–41.

S. Schachter, N. Ellertson, D. McBride, and D. Gregory, "An Experimental Study of Cohesiveness and Productivity," *Human Relations 4,* 1951, pp. 229–38.

E. M. Schur, *Crimes without Victims.* (Englewood Cliffs, N.J.: Prentice-Hall, 1965).

S. Seashore, *Group Cohesiveness in the Industrial Work Group.* (Ann Arbor: Institute for Social Research, University of Michigan, 1954).

M. Shaw, *Group Dynamics,* 3rd ed (New York: Harper, 1936).

E. L. Trist and K. W. Bamforth, "Some Social and Psychological Consequences of the Longwall Method of Coal-Getting," *Human Relations 4,* 1951, pp. 1–38.

W. F. Whyte, *Money and Motivation.* (New York: Harper, 1955).

W. F. Whyte, *Street Corner Society*. (Chicago: University of Chicago Press, 1955).

J. A. Wiggins, F. Dill, and R. D. Schwartz, "On Status-Liability," *Sociometry* 28, 1965, pp. 197–209.

READING 7–2   TEAMWORK AT GENERAL FOODS: NEW AND IMPROVED

Mark Bassin

Human resources are any organization's primary asset. Yet most larger organizations continue to organize their people in basic work patterns that inhibit or limit their employee's contributions. General Foods decided to change that pattern and establish interfunctional work teams as a strategic approach to maximizing its human resources in a wide variety of settings.

The company's contention is that organizing its work force into interfunctional work teams is, in general, the single most critical factor in creating a work environment that enables and promotes the achievement of peak performance. General Foods' experiences in this area are equally applicable in a wide variety of organizational settings, in both the private and public sectors, where there are high levels of dependence.

Peak performance usually is used to describe extraordinary achievement in an individual athletic context. Similarly, group peak performance is a group's ability to sustain superior output, quality and member satisfaction in terms of its principal goals. It's important to note that these three conditions are closely interrelated, each contributing to and supporting the others.

The athlete reaches his or her peak level by harnessing a perfect balance of physical capacity, mental conditioning and inner energy. Likewise, for the group it's the unique synergy created by the integration of the various resources and capacities of its members, focused against a clearly understood and deeply valued goal that make extraordinary outputs possible.

The most exciting point about peak performance is that it does not require a company of individual superstars. It's not the gifted individuals who make peak performance possible as much as the dynamics of belief, collaboration, and support. Thus, the power of peak performance lies in its availability to large numbers of employees currently in the organization.

Peak performance, however, is not something easily achieved—it requires several specific conditions. General Foods, for example, found that its best chances for approaching levels of peak performance are by establishing interfunctional business-work teams.

These teams, multidisciplinary groups of individuals, are focused on and fully dedicated to a specific business, groups of businesses or a fairly major long-term project within the organization. The key ingredient in such a team is the strengthened sense of ownership, involvement and responsibility for business results by all team members.

Unlike most resource roles in which individuals are asked to contribute to their area of functional expertise only, team members are expected to focus their energies on the total business or project needs, as if the business were their own.

The financial resource on the Minute Rice team, for example, is expected to contribute to all aspects of that business, such as advertising, strategy, package design, and product quality, as well as its financial structure and status. Thus, these teams are not temporary project groups or task forces.

Teams are the most effective vehicle to stimulate member participation and involvement. Their benefits include:

- More sharing and integration of individual skills and resources.
- Untapping and use of unknown member resources.
- More stimulation, energy and endurance by members working jointly than is usual when individuals work alone.
- More emotional support among team members.
- Better performance, in terms of quantity and quality, more wins, more innovation.
- More ideas for use in problem solving.
- More commitment and ownership by members around the team goals, i.e., higher motivation.
- More sustained effort directed at team goals.
- More team member satisfaction, higher motivation, and more fun.
- The sense of being a winner, greater confidence, and the ability to achieve more.

Japan's cultural team orientation and its positive impact on productivity is well known. Likewise, recent studies on innovation in large companies show that most successful

Source: *Personnel Journal*, May 1988, pp. 62–70.

development work is accomplished through fairly autonomous interfunctional work teams.

The potential for higher output and quality through teamwork is woven into the basic fabric of our social structure. Our evolution as a species into tightly knit interdependent groups—families—is no accident. By combining the resources and skills of team members with the higher energy and motivation level that the group provides, employees can reach extraordinary levels of achievement.

It is precisely the ability of a team to create a cycle of positive dynamics, each impacting and reinforcing the other, that usually enables individual team members to reach higher levels of performance than if they worked individually. Teams provide an opportunity to achieve more with less or, in the case of development, to move more quickly.

Teams are powerful vehicles for building and maintaining loyalty by becoming important cornerstones or anchors of identity for their members. It's difficult for most individuals to feel a strong sense of identity or loyalty to an organization if their perceived impact upon the firm is minimal. As team members, their impact is more direct, noticeable, and appreciated, which usually intensifies each member's feelings of identity and loyalty. In today's complex world of mergers and acquisitions, this need by individuals to feel connected to something they can control and impact appears to be increasing.

The combination of fulfilling the social need many individuals have to belong, coupled with the additional energy team members provide for each other, results in more excitement and enthusiasm in the workplace. Having fun at work is an essential ingredient for a productive work force. Winning teams are fun, and the opportunity to help make a team a winner can be a powerful and long-term motivator.

Teams can become powerful self-perpetuating systems to achieve greater outputs, strong identity and member satisfaction. They offer an exciting approach to the problem of providing more output with less resources, yet at the same time they increase member satisfaction. It's possible, therefore, that teams might emerge as the basic organizational structural unit of the future.

For a company to reach extraordinary levels of achievement, it must establish high-performing team characteristics, which include:

- Goals. They must be clear, important missions, with well-ordered, agreed-upon objectives. In addition, they must have clearly understood priorities based on member discussion and negotiation, as well as recognition and value for accomplishing results within a distinct timeframe.
- Roles. The team is a diverse representation of skills and perspectives. Individuals should have the authority to act. Likewise, each member's growth and accomplishment within the framework of team output and interdependence is recognized and valued. Members must understand each other's involvement.
- Leadership. The leader must champion the team and maintain a broad multifunctional project viewpoint. He or she must be attentive to the working climate of the team and work to establish a positive operating environment. The leader, whose leadership approach is modified to fit changing needs of the team (from directive to participative), also obtains needed resources for the unit.
- Team relations. The rules and norms of behavior are openly discussed and agreed upon, establishing a climate of trust, mutual respect, excellence, and innovation. The team has a work-hard-play-hard attitude, in which members participate and are committed to the project's output. Members are as attentive to how they work as they are to the final results (process and content).
- Rewards and recognition. The team is given the recognition and latitude needed to perform efficiently. Informal team celebrations might be held during the life of project. In addition, the company must ensure that the individual's contributions to the team's output are expected, valued, and always rewarded.

IT DOESN'T TAKE MAGIC TO BUILD A HIGH-PERFORMANCE TEAM

In most cases peak-performance teams don't occur or develop naturally, even if members possess strong skills or abilities. Some athletic teams, although composed of exceptionally gifted individuals, never seem to reach their full potential as a team. For most teams, like individual athletes, reaching levels of peak performance requires considerable devotion, concentration, and energy directed specifically at this issue.

On the other hand, building a high-performance team is not a magical or mystical experience. Five requirements, which link together to form the team's foundation, characterize most high-performance teams. If one link is weak or missing, the entire team's performance is seriously impaired, which makes peak performance doubtful.

Vision is the starting point for any team; vision is the team's overriding purpose for existence. The team's vision is its agenda, and as such it must be greater, more important or stronger than the private agendas of each member if it is to provide the impetus for the team's power. At the very least, it must be compatible with the individual agendas of each member.

Vision is only effective when it is held and shared by all team members. Such ownership is critical for achieving peak performance from the group.

The team's vision becomes its energy, as well as its source of power and motivation. To achieve this power, the vision must be anchored to a job worth doing in the eyes of each team member. They must be able to see, touch, feel, and express information to each other. Visions are most successful when they are imagined with sufficient detail to create a living picture. Without such a vision, extraordinary performance is unlikely.

But a vision by itself is not enough. Accompanying it must be a perceived dependent need. Team members must overtly realize that the vision is not achievable without their combined talents. This is the difference between teams, and less cohesive interdependent groups. If there is no dependent need to achieve a vision, the team will not be the correct vehicle to pursue the problem, and less intensive forms of cooperation and teamwork usually will suffice.

The team leader has primary responsibility for formulating, communicating, and behaviorally representing the vision that is to be shared by all members. This vision requires distinct, but interrelated, steps, including:

- It must be worthy of ownership by the group.
- It must be communicated continually to members in a way that gives it vitality and life.
- The leader must embody and model the vision in his or her behavior with the group. This demonstrates a serious commitment to the vision, which enables the leader to expect similar commitment from other team members.

Such a leadership is impossible without the leader's strong belief in and commitment to the vision, as well as to his or her teammates' ability to achieve it. In nearly all cases, teams face occasions when the obstacles to forward movement seem overwhelming. Therefore, they must possess the ability to recover, profit from mistakes, continue to move forward and endure, with the leader's behavior setting the tone or standard. It is the leader's ability to use such critical incidents as opportunities to strengthen a team

that comprises an essential element of his or her leadership skills.

It's absolutely true that leaders need to be present at moments of crisis to lead by example. However, the leader must slowly transfer the responsibility for team development to all team members and as this responsibility is shared, groups transform into teams.

The fourth critical element in building a team is coordination, which is a process for effectively using and integrating members' resources. Without a clearly defined process for working together, good intentions often fail to produce exceptional results. The purpose of a coordination process is to focus and integrate resources at critical junction points, or milestones, along the road to the vision. Teams work best when some regular system of planning for setting priorities and integrating resources is used so activities are organized around clearly defined outcomes.

Similar to the huddle in a football game, coordination systems generally work best when the team sets aside the time to meet regularly for this exact purpose. At such meetings, team members look beyond their functional areas of expertise at the general health of the team.

During the meetings, progress against objectives is assessed openly and honestly, and new priorities are identified in behavioral terms. Team members are assigned responsibilities in relation to these priorities and working relationships, and moral and other issues regarding team performance are aired.

The quality of these meetings is critical to the team's success. The leader plays a crucial role in facilitating open communications, problem solving, and decision making. Effective leaders use these meetings to reenergize team members, and care for the maintenance needs of members, as well as the task requirements.

It's important that the teams learn to meet and plan together effectively so they can reach levels of peak performance. Without such a coordination process, sustained peak performance by teams is virtually impossible.

Similar to all other living systems, teams need to be able to adjust and respond to changing conditions (from within themselves or their environment) to remain effective. The better they adjust and respond, the more effective the team will be.

Consider, for example, how effective sports teams adjust and modify their performance as circumstances change through a game or during a single play. This is not to imply that effective teams don't need to stop the action to regroup and replan. They do. Both functions are critical. In general, as teams mature their ability to use feedback and readjust as they go improves.

In peak-performance teams, this function is shared by all members and becomes almost second nature. It happens quickly and informally, often with members anticipating each other's changing needs and requirements. In fact, peak performance is not achieved until a team is able to respond automatically.

Combined, the five elements of vision, dependent need, leadership, coordinating process, and the ability to adjust and adapt form the foundation of team peak performance. These elements, or subsystems, are interrelated and interdependent; a change in one affects the others often in dramatic ways.

As in any kind of development, aligning, integrating, and balancing these elements to produce optimum effectiveness is a difficult task. It requires significant commitment, time, energy, and skill on the part of all team members. However, when achieved, it leads to actions and satisfaction well worth the effort.

CONSIDER THE OBSTACLES IN BUILDING PEAK PERFORMANCE TEAMS

Expectation. Most individuals have never experienced peak performance and, therefore, they don't expect it of themselves or others. First they must be introduced to the expectations of peak performance before anything can happen. That's why vision and leadership are so critical; without an expectation, there can be no achievement.

Most individual team members think of themselves as functional experts, and identify their sphere of potential contributions within that area. As team members, individuals' expectations must be significantly stretched so they think of themselves as businesspeople concerned with all aspects of the business, not limited only to their areas of functional knowledge or expertise.

Although it would be ludicrous to ignore their strengths as areas for contribution, it is equally ludicrous to limit potential inputs to these specific areas. This requires a significant change in expectation regarding contributions and input on the part of team members.

Business team peak performance is a group phenomenon; however, most business organizations are structured around individual performance and competition. Reward systems, promotions and a sense of identity are individually geared and generated. The individual and his or her contribution is the fundamental unit in work cultures, not the group.

This is a different basic assumption than what is required for a peak-performing team. In such a team, the group vision must be stronger than individual agendas. The opportunities for group members to help one another must be unencumbered by competition among them.

If personal competition interferes with group cooperation, the possibilities for peak performance diminish. As in a sports team, if one member values his or her personal performance above the team's, team cohesion is lessened and team performance suffers.

This does not imply there isn't room for extraordinary individual performance in a team context. On the contrary, it's often team support that helps individuals achieve such levels of performance.

Compensation. In terms of support for team activity, nothing is symbolically more important than compensation. The way in which a company actually pays its employees says more than nearly anything about what the firm values. It's simply not enough to support teamwork with rhetoric and good wishes. Compensation programs that directly link the compensation for individuals on teams with team output must be developed to truly support the group. This is relatively simple to do, especially with business teams whose performance can be clearly measured in quantitative terms.

Teams that exceed objectives should share directly in the rewards. There are many formulas available specifying how this can be done that offer a wide degree of flexibility to accommodate different team structures. Plans can vary from total team compensation programs to partial plan programs in which team performance makes up a specified portion of an individual's compensation.

Nor do team incentive programs limit recognizing the contributions of individual members. Part of an individual's compensation can be based on individual performance while the rest depends on team outputs. These compensation programs, in addition, can be designed on a short- or long-term combined basis. Achievement of critical milestones can be rewarded, as well as more significant payouts for long-range achievements. What is critical here is the reinforcement of the team concept that these compensation programs can offer.

Continuity. Even with sustained effort and attention, considerable time is required to establish identity, build trust, work out roles and procedures, solve problems, and gain confidence before the team begins operating near optimum levels. Six months to a year is not an unrealistic timeframe for this type of development.

Because small, fully dedicated peak-performance teams are so dependent on the unique contributions and synergies of each individual, changes in membership can be quite disruptive. Continuity serves as a prime motivator when team members know they will be working together for several years. The stakes are high, the interdependent need is clear, and it makes sense to strive together to achieve high levels of performance.

From a day-to-day and long-term commitment perspective, a relatively high degree of continuity is essential for building peak-performance business teams. This is an issue for many organizations, in which individuals, particularly strong ones, expect to move every two years or so.

One option for building teams in this type of environment is to require a three-to-five-year commitment for membership on such a team. This is more easily accomplished if there is a corresponding compensation program tied to long-range results that make it worthwhile for members to remain with the team.

Another alternative is to staff the team primarily with more experienced, slightly older, less upwardly mobile members for whom such a commitment does not pose a problem. A third option is to balance the team with enough key "long termers" so some membership movement isn't a major problem. In any case, continuity is clearly an issue to address up front in attempting to establish peak performance business teams.

Career movement. In the past, general survey data continued to pinpoint what has almost become a preoccupation with careers. Traditionally, in most business settings careers are functionally driven or determined. Individuals basically belong to and identify with a particular area of functional expertise.

The use of teams challenges a number of these functional notions of career movement, among them loyalty and identity. Because the purpose of teams is to focus more member attention directly on the business, functional identity becomes secondary.

Teams offer an alternative sequence of career movement. Once an employee becomes part of the team, and is exposed to all aspects of a business, a logical move for the stronger team members is to team leader. In that position the individual has a unique opportunity to act as a mini general manger and develop the perspectives and skills necessary for higher levels of general management.

Thus, by presenting an alternative path to general management, as well as broadening career possibilities, teams pose a threat to those employees who feel more comfortable with more traditional, functionally dominant notions of career movement and value. For example, at General Foods, marketing was once the only path to general management. With team leaders beginning to emerge from all functions, this dominance is no longer assured.

Power, authority, and organization layers. A critical issue surrounding teams concerns power, authority, and layers in the organization. Basically, teams are empowering vehicles, and as they mature and succeed, team members naturally begin to gain confidence and desire more responsibility. (At General Foods, Brand Teams which have focused most of their earlier attention on execution, have pushed for a larger role in strategy formulation. This is a natural and healthy tendency.)

A problem is likely to occur when this extended role or scope of responsibility on the part of the team overlaps those in the next level of management. As teams mature, it becomes clear they often are quite capable of assuming the role of this next layer of management, which can lead to confusion and frustration.

Generally, as companies move toward leaner organizational structures, teams that function in such a manner are exactly what is needed. However, in the transition period, teams are likely to raise sensitive questions about whether value is really being added in the organization management structure.

A new General Foods factory, for example, is being built to produce products for a particular venture team. At issue is whether the team should report, as usual, to the operations manager who is in that team's division or directly to the team leader. Such challenges to the traditional notions of power and authority are inevitable as teams develop.

ARE TEAMS FOR EVERY COMPANY?

How broadly should teams be used, and how formally should they be structured? Are teams a more effective way to organize work, and should they be available to everyone? Or, should the group have an elitist positioning, available only to the best and brightest, as with other key organizational positions? Should teams be used only in certain business situations, such as development, in which speed is critical, and not much is known about a business? These

EXHIBIT 7-4

Options for Business Teams

Informal Teams	Communication Teams	Formalized Business Brand Teams	Development/Venture Teams
Product manager as informal leader	Product manager as formal leader	Product manager as formal leader	Team regarded as a self-autonomous, fairly independent unit
Informal communication with functional resources	Ongoing formal team communications and postings	Fully dedicated functional resources	Leader designated according to venture
Informal brainstorming and problem solving	Formal brainstorming and problem solving	Team sets yearly objectives and quarterly priorities	Leader has input into selection of other fully dedicated resources
Situational task forces	Situational task forces	Team results evaluated by staff on quarterly basis	Resources (functional representatives) fully dedicated for 3–5-year time period and report to venture team leader
Resources (functional representatives) assigned but not necessarily fully dedicated	Resources (functional representatives) assigned but not necessarily fully dedicated	Ongoing formal meetings, postings and problem solving	Team sets yearly objectives and priorities
		Product manager has some formalized input into functional members' evaluation	Ongoing formal meetings, postings and problem solving
		Reward system that supports team achievement	Reward system that supports team achievement — significant short- and long-range incentives
		Secretaries on team	Team responsible all aspects of business development, from strategy through implementation
		Staff sets strategy, but within the strategy guidelines team makes most business decisions	
		Gradually eliminate unnecessary layers from organization	
		Teams are clearly the foundation of the division — impact promotions and career movement	

fundamental, value-laden decisions regarding teams and their uses are critical, and they must be considered carefully as the teams are formed.

A related, and equally complex, decision regarding team formation concerns the degree of formalization. How formal and structured, or how autonomous are the teams to be? They can be molded along a wide continuum, ranging from informal, loosely held informational groupings to highly structured, independent, fully dedicated, fairly autonomous entities.

Although the unique power and energy of teams increase as they move toward the more autonomous, fully dedicated model, clearly this is not appropriate for all settings. Matching the need, setting and model to use is critical for the team's success. (See Exhibit 7-4.)

It's not surprising there are so many complex issues surrounding the development of high-performance teams. These groups are exceptional entities to be valued and treasured, and it's fitting that they require a great deal of effort to create. However, the payback derived by the organization and to those involved is clearly worth the effort.

Although teams might not be for every organization or employee, or for every situation, they offer a certain amount of promise as a basic pattern for approaching work in most organizations. It's possible that future organizations will resemble loosely coupled circles that can move and adjust quickly, rather than the stable, bureaucratic pyramids of today. For such an organization, the ability to create peak-performance teams will be a critical, competitive advantage.

REFERENCES

A. Carson, "Participatory Management Beefs Up the Bottom Line," *Personnel 4* (1985), pp. 45–48.

C. Garfield, *Peak Performance Mental Training Techniques of the World's Greatest Athletes* (Los Angeles, Calif.: Warner Books, 1984).

R. M. Kanter, *The Change Masters, Innovation for Productivity in the American Corporation* (New York: Simon & Schuster, 1983).

J. Naisbitt, *Megatrends: Ten New Directions Transforming Our Lives* (New York: Warner Books, 1982).

J. Naisbitt and P. Aberdine, *Re-inventing the Corporation* (New York: Warner Books, 1985).

■

EXERCISES

EXERCISE 7–1   PARTICIPATING IN AND OBSERVATIONS OF GROUP PROCESSES

OBJECTIVES

1. To provide experience in participating in and observing groups undertaking a specific task.
2. To generate data that can be the focus of class discussion and analysis.

STARTING THE EXERCISE

The Situation

You are appointed to a personnel committee in charge of selecting a manager for the department that provides administrative services to other departments. Before you begin interviewing candidates, you are asked to develop a list of the personal and professional qualifications the

Source: Kae H. Chung and Leon C, Megginson, *Organizational Behavior* (New York: Harper & Row, 1981), pp. 241–44. Used by permission

manager needs. The list will be used as the selection criteria.

The Procedure

1. Select five to seven members to serve on the committee.
2. Ask the committee to rank the items in the following list in their order of importance in selecting the department head.
3. The students not on the committee should observe the group process. Some should observe the whole group, and others individual members. The observers can use observation guides A and B.
4. The observers should provide feedback to the participants.
5. The class should discuss how the committee might improve its performance.

Selection Criteria

_____ Strong institutional loyalty	_____ High intelligence
_____ Ability to give clear instructions	_____ Ability to grasp the overall picture
_____ Ability to discipline subordinates	_____ Ability to get along well with people
_____ Ability to make decisions under pressure	_____ Familiarity with office procedures
_____ Ability to communicate	_____ Professional achievement
_____ Stable personality	_____ Ability to develop subordinates

A. Group Process Observation Guide

Instructions: Observe the group behavior in the following dimensions. Prepare notes for feedback.

Group Behaviors	Description	Impact
Group Goal: Are group goals clearly defined?		
Decision Procedure: Is the decision procedure clearly defined?		
Communication Network: What kind of communication network is used? Is it appropriate?		
Decision Making: What kind of decision process is used? Is it appropriate?		
Group Norm: Observe the degrees of cohesiveness, compatibility, and conformity.		
Group Composition: What kind of group is it?		
Other Behavior: Is there any behavior that influences the group process?		

B. Individual Role Observation Guide

Instructions: Observe one committee member. Tabulate (or note) behaviors that he or she exhibits as the group works.

Initiating Ideas: Initiates or clarifies ideas and issues.	**Confusing Issues:** Confuses others by bringing up irrelevant issues or by jumping to other issues.
Managing Conflicts: Explores, clarifies, and resolves conflicts and differences.	**Mismanaging Conflicts:** Avoids or suppresses conflicts, or creates "win-or-lose" situations.
Influencing Others: Appeases, reasons with, or persuades others.	**Forcing Others:** Gives orders or forces others to agree.
Supporting Others: Reinforces or helps others to express their opinions.	**Rejecting Others:** Deflates or antagonizes others.
Listening Attentively: Listens and responds to others' ideas and opinions.	**Showing Indifference:** Does not listen or brushes off others.
Showing Empathy: Shows the ability to see things from other people's viewpoint.	**Self-Serving Behavior:** Exhibits behavior that is self-serving.
Exhibiting Positive Nonverbal Behaviors: Pays attention to others, maintains eye contact, composure, and other signs.	**Exhibiting Negative Nonverbal Behaviors:** Tense facial expression, yawning, little eye contact, and other behaviors.

EXERCISE 7–2   WHAT TO DO WITH JOHNNY ROCCO

OBJECTIVES

1. Participating in a group assignment playing a particular role.

2. Diagnosing the group decision process after the assignment has been completed.

Source: Adapted from David A. Whetton and Kim S. Cameron, *Developing Management Skills* (Glenview, Ill.: Scott, Foresman and Company, 1984), pp. 450–53.

STARTING THE EXERCISE

After reading the material relating to Johnny Rocco, a committee is formed to decide the fate of Johnny Rocco. The chairperson of the meeting is Johnny's supervisor, who should begin by assigning roles to the group members. These roles (shop steward, head of production, Johnny's co-worker, director of personnel, and social worker who helped Johnny in the past) represent points of view the chairperson feels should be included in this meeting. (Johnny is not to be included.) Two observers should be assigned.

After the roles have been assigned, each role-player should complete the personal preference part of the worksheet, ordering the alternatives according to their appropriateness from the vantage point of his or her role.

Once the individual preferences have been determined, the chairperson should call the meeting to order. The following rules govern the meeting: (1) the group must reach a consensus ordering of the alternatives; (2) the group cannot use a statistical aggregation, or majority vote, decision-making process; (3) members should stay "in character" throughout the discussion. Treat this as a committee meeting consisting of members with different backgrounds, orientations, and interests who share a problem.

After the group has completed the assignment, the two observers should conduct a discussion of the group process using the Group Process Diagnostic Questions as a guide. Group members should not look at these questions until after the group task has been completed.

JOHNNY ROCCO

Johnny has a grim personal background. He is the third child in a family of seven. He has not seen his father for several years and his recollection is that his father used to come home drunk and beat up every member of the family; everyone ran when he came staggering home.

His mother, according to Johnny, wasn't much better. She was irritable and unhappy and she always predicted that Johnny would come to no good end. Yet she worked when her health allowed her to do so in order to keep the family in food and clothing. She always decried the fact that she was not able to be the kind of mother she would like to be.

WORKSHEET

Personal Preference	Group Decision	
_____	_____	Give Johnny a warning that at the next sign of trouble he will be fired.
_____	_____	Do nothing, as it is unclear that Johnny did anything wrong.
_____	_____	Create strict controls (do's and don'ts) for Johnny with immediate strong punishment for any misbehavior.
_____	_____	Give Johnny a great deal of warmth and personal attention and affection (overlooking his present behavior) so he can learn to depend on others.
_____	_____	Fire him. It's not worth the time and effort spent for such a low-level position.
_____	_____	Talk over the problem with Johnny in an understanding way so he can learn to ask others for help in solving his problems.
_____	_____	Give Johnny a well-structured schedule of daily activities with immediate and unpleasant consequences for not adhering to the schedule.
_____		Do nothing now, but watch him carefully and provide immediate punishment for any future misbehaviors.
_____	_____	Treat Johnny the same as everyone else, but provide an orderly routine so he can learn to stand on his own two feet.
_____	_____	Call Johnny in and logically discuss the problem with him and ask what you can do to help him.
_____	_____	Do nothing now, but watch him so you can reward him the next time he does something good.

Johnny quit school in the seventh grade. He had great difficulty conforming to the school routine—misbehaving often, acting as a truant quite frequently, and engaging in numerous fights with schoolmates. On several occasions he was picked up by the police and, along with members of his group, questioned during several investigations into cases of both petty and grand larceny. The police regarded him as "probably a bad one."

The juvenile officer of the court saw in Johnny some good qualities that no one else seemed to sense. This man, Mr. O'Brien, took it on himself to act as a "big brother" to Johnny. He had several long conversations with Johnny, during which he managed to penetrate to some degree Johnny's defensive shell. He represented to Johnny the first semblance of personal interest in his life. Through Mr. O'Brien's efforts, Johnny returned to school and obtained a high school diploma. Afterwards, Mr. O'Brien helped him obtain a job.

Now at age twenty, Johnny is a stockroom clerk in one of the laboratories where you are employed. On the whole Johnny's performance has been acceptable, but there have been glaring exceptions. One involved a clear act of insubordination on a fairly unimportant matter. In another Johnny was accused, on circumstantial grounds, of destroying some expensive equipment. Though the investigation is still open, it now appears that the destruction was accidental.

Johnny's supervisor wants to keep him on for a least a trial period, but he wants "outside" advice as to the best way of helping him grow into greater responsibility. Of course, much depends on how Johnny behaves in the next few months. Naturally, his supervisor must follow personnel policies that are accepted in the company as a whole. It is important to note that Johnny is not an attractive young man. He is rather weak and sickly, and shows unmistakable signs of long years of social deprivation.

A committee is formed to decide the fate of Johnny Rocco. The chairperson of the meeting is Johnny's supervisor, and should begin by assigning roles.

GROUP PROCESS DIAGNOSTIC QUESTIONS

Communications

1. Who responded to whom?
2. Who interrupted? Was the same person interrupted consistently?
3. Were there identifiable "communication clusters"? Why or why not?
4. Did some members say very little? If so, why? Was level of participation ever discussed?
5. Were efforts made to involve everyone?

Decision Making

1. Did the group decide how to decide?
2. How were decisions made?
3. What criterion was used to establish agreement?
   a. Majority vote?
   b. Consensus?
   c. No opposition interpreted as agreement?
4. What was done if people disagreed?
5. How effective was your decision-making process?
6. Does every member feel his or her input into the decision-making process was valued by the group, or were the comments of some members frequently discounted? If so, was this issue ever discussed?

Leadership

1. What type of power structure did the group operate under?
   a. One definite leader?
   b. Leadership functions shared by all members?
   c. Power struggles within the group?
   d. No leadership supplied by anyone?
2. How does each member feel about the leadership structure used? Would an alternative have been more effective?
3. Did the chairperson provide an adequate structure for the discussion?
4. Was the discussion governed by the norms of equity?
5. Was the chairperson's contribution to the content of the discussion overbearing?

Awareness of Feelings

1. How did members in general react to the group meetings? Were they hostile (toward whom or what?), enthusiastic, apathetic?

2. Did members openly discuss their feelings toward each other and their role in the group?
3. How do group members feel now about their participation in this group?

Task Behavior

1. Who was most influential in keeping the group task oriented? How?

2. Did some members carry the burden and do most of the work, or was the load distributed evenly?
3. If some members were not contributing their fair share, was this ever discussed? If so, what was the outcome? If not, why?
4. Did the group evaluate its method of accomplishing a task during or after the project? If so, what changes were made?
5. How effective was our group in performing assigned tasks? What improvements could have been made?

▲

CASES

CASE 7–1   BANANA TIME CASE

This paper undertakes description and explanatory analysis of the social interaction which took place within a small work group of factory machine operatives during a two-month period of participant observation.

My fellow operatives and I spent our long days of simple, repetitive work in relative isolation from other employees of the factory. Our line of machines was sealed off from other work areas of the plant by the four walls of the clicking room. The one door of this room was usually closed. Even when it was kept open during periods of hot weather, the consequences were not social; it opened on an uninhabited storage room of the shipping department. Not even the sounds of work activity going on elsewhere in the factory carried to this isolated workplace. There were occasional contacts with outside employees, usually on matters connected with the work; but, with the exception of the daily calls of one fellow who came to pick up finished materials for the next step in processing, such visits were sporadic and infrequent.

The clickers were of the genus punching machines; of mechanical construction similar to that of the better-known

Source: Exerpted from Donald F. Roy, " 'Banana Time,' Job Satisfaction, and Informal Interaction." Reproduced by permission of the Society for Applied Anthropology from *Human Organization* 18, no. 4 (Winter 1959–60), pp. 151–68.

punch presses, their leading features were hammer and block. The hammer, or punching head, was approximately 8 inches by 12 inches at its flat striking surface. The descent upon the block was initially forced by the operator, who exerted pressure on a handle attached to the side of the hammer head. A few inches of travel downward established electrical connection for a sharp power-driven blow. The hammer also traveled by manual guidance in a horizontal plane to and from, and in an arc around, the central column of the machine. Thus, the operator, up to the point of establishing electrical connections for the sudden and irrevocable downward thrust, had flexibility in maneuvering his instrument over the larger surface of the block. The latter, approximately 24 inches wide, 18 inches deep, and 10 inches thick, was made, like a butcher's block, of inlaid hardwood; it was set in the machine at a convenient waist height. On it the operator placed his materials, one sheet at a time if leather, stacks of sheets if plastic, to be cut with steel dies of assorted sizes and shapes. The particular die in use would be moved, by hand, from spot to spot over the materials each time a cut was made; less frequently, materials would be shifted on the block as the operator saw need for such adjustment.

Introduction to the new job, with its relatively simple machine skills and work routines, was accomplished with what proved to be, in my experience, an all-time minimum of job training. The clicking machine assigned to me was situated at one end of the row. Here the superintendent and one of the operators gave a few brief demonstrations, accompanied by bits of advice, which included a warning to keep hands clear of the descending hammer. After a short practice period, at the end of which the superintendent expressed satisfaction with progress and potentialities, I was left to develop my learning curve with no other supervision than that afforded by members of the work group. Further advice and assistance did come from time to time from my fellow operatives, sometimes upon request, sometimes unsolicited.

THE WORK GROUP

Absorbed at first in three related goals of improving my clicking skill, increasing my rate of output, and keeping my left hand unclicked, I paid little attention to my fellow operatives save to observe that they were friendly, middle-aged, foreign born, full of advice, and very talkative. Their names, according to the way they addressed each other, were George, Ike, and Sammy. George, a stocky fellow in his late 50s, operated the machine at the opposite end of the line; he, I later discovered, had emigrated in early youth from a country in southeastern Europe. Ike, stationed at George's left, was tall, slender, in his early 50s, and Jewish; he had come from eastern Europe in his youth. Sammy, number-three man in the line and my neighbor, was heavy-set, in his late 50s, and Jewish; he had escaped from a country in eastern Europe just before Hitler's legions had moved in. All three men had been downwardly mobile in occupation in recent years. George and Sammy had been proprietors of small businesses; the former had been "wiped out" when his uninsured establishment burned down; the latter had been entrepreneuring on a small scale before he left all behind him to flee the Germans. According to his account, Ike had left a highly skilled trade which he had practiced for years in Chicago.

THE WORK

It was evident to me before my first workday drew to a weary close that my clicking career was going to be a grim process of fighting the clock, the particular timepiece in this situation being an old-fashioned alarm clock that ticked away on a shelf near George's machine. I had struggled through many dreary rounds with the minutes and hours

during the various phases of my industrial experience, but never had I been confronted with such a dismal combination of working conditions as the extra-long workday, the infinitesimal cerebral excitation, and the extreme limitation of physical movement. The contrast with a recent stint in the California oil fields was striking. This was no eight-hour day of racing hither and yon over desert and foothills with a rollicking crew of "roustabouts" on a variety of repair missions at oil wells, pipelines, and storage tanks. Here there were no afternoon dallyings to search the sands for horned toads, tarantulas, and rattlesnakes or to climb old wooden derricks for raven's nests with an eye out, of course, for the telltale streak of dust in the distance, which gave ample warning of the approach of the boss. This was standing all day in one spot beside three old codgers in a dingy room looking out through barred windows at the bare walls of a brick warehouse, leg movements largely restricted to the shifting of body weight from one foot to the other, hand and arm movements confined, for the most part, to a simple repetitive sequence of place the die—punch the clicker—place the die—punch the clicker, and intellectual activity reduced to computing the hours to quitting time. It is true that from time to time a fresh stack of sheets would have to be substituted for the clicked-out old one; but the stack would have been prepared by someone else, and the exchange would be only a minute or two in the making. Now and then a box of finished work would have to be moved back out of the way, and an empty box brought up, but the moving back and the bringing up involved only a step or two. And there was the half hour for lunch and occasional trips to the lavatory or the drinking fountain to break up the day into digestible parts. But after each momentary respite, hammer and die were moving again: click—move die—click—move die.

I developed a game of work. The game developed was quite simple, so elementary, in fact, that its playing was reminiscent of rainy-day preoccupations in childhood when attention could be centered by the hour on colored bits of things of assorted sizes and shapes. But this adult activity was not mere pottering and piddling; what it lacked in the earlier imaginative content, it made up for in clean-cut structure. Fundamentally involved were: (a) variation in color of the materials cut, (b) variation in shapes of the dies used, and (c) a process called "scraping the block." The basic procedure which ordered the particular combination of components employed could be stated in the form: "As soon as I do so many of these, I'll click some brown ones." And with success in attaining the objective of working with brown materials, a new goal of "I'll get to do the white ones" might be set. Or the new goal might involve switching dies.

INFORMAL SOCIAL ACTIVITY OF THE WORK GROUP: TIMES AND THEMES

I began to take serious note of the social activity going on around me; my attentiveness to this activity came with growing involvement in it. What I heard at first, before I started to listen, was a stream of disconnected bits of communication that did not make much sense. Foreign accents were strong, and referents were not joined to coherent contexts of meaning. It was just "jabbering." What I saw at first, before I began to observe, was occasional flurries of horseplay that were so simple and unvarying in pattern and so childish in quality that they made no strong bid for attention. For example, Ike would regularly switch off the power at Sammy's machine whenever Sammy made a trip to the lavatory or the drinking fountain. Correlatively, Sammy invariably fell victim to the plot by making an attempt to operate his clicking hammer after returning to the shop. And as the simple pattern went, this blind stumbling into the trap was always followed by indignation and reproach from Sammy, smirking satisfaction from Ike, and mild paternal scolding from George. My interest in this procedure was at first confined to wondering when Ike would weary of his tedious joke or when Sammy would learn to check his power switch before trying the hammer.

Most of the breaks in the daily series were designated as "times" in the parlance of the clicker operators, and they featured the consumption of food or drink of one sort or another. There was coffee time, peach time, banana time, fish time, Coke time, and, of course, lunch time. Other interruptions that formed part of the series but were not verbally recognized as times were window time, pickup time, and the staggered quitting times of Sammy and Ike. These latter unnamed times did not involve the partaking of refreshments.

My attention was first drawn to this times business during my first week of employment when I was encouraged to join in the sharing of two peaches. It was Sammy who provided the peaches; he drew them from his lunch box after making the announcement, "Peach time!" On this first occasion I refused the proffered fruit but thereafter regularly consumed my half peach. Sammy continued to provide the peaches and to make the "Peach time!" announcement, although there were days when Ike would remind him that it was peach time, urging him to hurry up with the midmorning snack. Ike invariably complained

about the quality of the fruit, and his complaints fed the fires of continued banter between peach donor and critical recipient. I did find the fruit a bit on the scrubby side but felt, before I achieved insight into the function of peach time, that Ike was showing poor manners by looking a gift horse in the mouth. I wondered why Sammy continued to share his peaches with such an ingrate.

Banana time followed peach time by approximately an hour. Sammy again provided the refreshments—namely, one banana. There was, however, no four-way sharing of Sammy's banana. Ike would gulp it down by himself after surreptitiously extracting it from Sammy's lunch box, kept on a shelf behind Sammy's work station. Each morning, after making the snatch, Ike would call out, "Banana time!" and proceed to down his prize while Sammy made futile protests and denunciations. George would join in with mild remonstrances, sometimes scolding Sammy for making so much fuss. The banana was one that Sammy brought for his own consumption at lunch time; he never did get to eat his banana but kept bringing one for his lunch. At first this daily theft startled and amazed me. Then I grew to look forward to the daily seizure and the verbal interaction which followed.

Window time came next. It followed banana time as a regular consequence of Ike's castigation by the indignant Sammy. After "taking" repeated references to himself as a person badly lacking in morality and character, Ike would "finally" retaliate by opening the window that faced Sammy's machine to let the "cold air" blow in on Sammy. The slandering which would, in its echolalic repetition, wear down Ike's patience and forbearance usually took the form of the invidious comparison: "George is a good daddy. Ike is a bad man! A very bad man!" Opening the window would take a little time to accomplish and would involve a great deal of verbal interplay between Ike and Sammy, both before and after the event. Ike would threaten, make feints toward the window, then finally open it. Sammy would protest, argue, and make claims that the air blowing in on him would give him a cold; he would eventually have to leave his machine to close the window. Sometimes the weather was slightly chilly, and the draft from the window unpleasant, but cool or hot, windy or still, window time arrived each day. (I assume that it was originally a cold-season development.) George's part in this interplay, in spite of the "good daddy" laudations, was to encourage Ike in his window work. He would stress the tonic values of fresh air and chide Sammy for his unappreciativeness.

THEMES

To put flesh, so to speak, on this interactional frame of times, my work group had developed various "themes" of verbal interplay, which had become standardized in their repetition. These topics of conversation ranged in quality from an extreme of nonsensical chatter to another extreme of serious discourse. Unlike the "times," these themes flowed one into the other in no particular sequence of predictability. Serious conversation could suddenly melt into horseplay, and vice versa. In the middle of a serious discussion on the high cost of living, Ike might drop a weight behind the easily startled Sammy or hit him over the head with a dusty paper sack. Interaction would immediately drop to a low comedy exchange of slaps, threats, guffaws, and disapprobations, which would invariably include a 10-minute echolalia of "Ike is a bad man, a very bad man! George is a good daddy, a very fine man!" Or, on the other hand, a stream of such invidious comparisons as followed a surreptitious switching-off of Sammy's machine by the playful Ike might merge suddenly into a discussion of the pros and cons of saving for one's funeral.

"Kidding themes" were usually started by George or Ike, and Sammy was usually the butt of the joke. Sometimes Ike would have to "take it," seldom George. One favorite kidding theme involved Sammy's alleged receipt of $100 a month from his son. The points stressed were that Sammy did not have to work long hours or did not have to work at all, because he had a son to support him. George would always point out that he sent money to his daughter; she did not send money to him. Sammy received occasional calls from his wife, and his claim that these calls were requests to shop for groceries on the way home were greeted with feigned disbelief. Sammy was ribbed for being closely watched, bossed, and henpecked by his wife, and the expression, "Are you man or mouse?" became an echolalic utterance, used both in and out of the original context.

Serious themes included the relating of major misfortunes suffered in the past by group members. George referred again and again to the loss by fire of his business establishment. Ike's chief complaints centered around a chronically ill wife who had undergone various operations and periods of hospital care. Ike spoke with discouragement of the expenses attendant upon hiring a housekeeper for himself and his children; he referred with disappointment and disgust to a teenage son, an inept lad who "couldn't even fix his own lunch. He couldn't even make himself a sandwich!" Sammy's reminiscences centered on the loss of a flourishing business when he had to flee Europe ahead of the Nazi invasion.

There was one theme of especially solemn import, the "professor theme." This theme might also be termed "George's daughter's marriage theme," for the recent marriage of George's only child was inextricably bound up with George's connection with higher learning. The daughter had married the son of a professor, who instructed in one of the local colleges. This professor theme was not in the strictest sense a conversation piece; when the subject came up, George did all the talking. The two Jewish operatives remained silent as they listened with deep respect, if not actual awe, to George's accounts of the Big Wedding, which, including the wedding pictures, entailed an expense of $1,000. It was monologue, but there was listening, there was communication, the sacred communication of a temple, when George told of going for Sunday afternoon walks on the Midway with the professor or of joining the professor for a Sunday dinner. Whenever he spoke of the professor, his daughter, the wedding, or even of the new son-in-law, who remained for the most part in the background, a sort of incidental like the wedding cake, George was complete master of the interaction. His manner, in speaking to the rank-and-file of clicker operators, was indeed that of master deigning to notice his underlings. I came to the conclusion that it was the professor connection, not the straw-boss-ship or the extra nickel an hour, that provided the fount of George's superior status in the group.

CASE QUESTIONS

1. What type of group has evolved and is reported in the "Banana Time Case"?
2. Describe what you consider to be important group characteristics observed in this work group.
3. Is this work group cohesive? Explain.

CASE 7–2   WORK GROUP OWNERSHIP OF AN IMPROVED TOOL

The Whirlwind Aircraft Corporation was a leader in its field and especially noted for its development of the modern supercharger. Work in connection with the latter mechanism called for special skill and ability. Every detail of the supercharger had to be perfect to satisfy the exacting requirements of the aircraft industry.

In 1941 (before Pearl Harbor), Lathe Department 15-D was turning out three types of impeller, each contoured to within 0.002 inch and machined to a mirrorlike finish. The impellers were made from an aluminum alloy and finished on a cam-back lathe.

The work was carried on in four shifts, two men on each. The personnel in the finishing section were as follows:

1. *First Shift*—7 A.M. to 3 P.M. Sunday and Monday off.
    a. Jean Latour, master mechanic, French Canadian, 45 years of age. Latour had set up the job and trained the men who worked with him on the first shift.
    b. Pierre DuFresne, master mechanic, French Canadian, 36 years of age. Both these men had trained the workers needed for the other shifts.
2. *Second Shift*—3 P.M. to 11 P.M. Friday and Saturday off.
    a. Albert Durand, master mechanic, French Canadian, 32 years of age; trained by Latour and using his lathe.
    b. Robert Benet, master mechanic, French Canadian, 31 years of age; trained by DuFresne and using his lathe.
3. *Third Shift*—11 P.M. to 7 A.M. Tuesday and Wednesday off.
    a. Philippe Doret, master mechanic, French Canadian, 31 years of age; trained by Latour and using his lathe.
    b. Henri Barbet, master mechanic, French Canadian, 30 years of age; trained by Dufresne and using his lathe.
4. *Stagger Shift*—Monday, 7 A.M. to 3 P.M.; Tuesday, 11 P.M. to 7 A.M.; Wednesday, 11 P.M. to 7 A.M.; Thursday off; Friday, 3 P.M. to 11 P.M.; Saturday 3 P.M. to 11 P.M.; Sunday, off.

    a. George MacNair, master mechanic, Scottish, 32 years of age; trained by Latour and using his lathe.
    b. William Reader, master mechanic, English, 30 years of age, trained by DuFresne and using his lathe.

Owing to various factors (such as the small number of workers involved, the preponderance of one nationality, and the fact that Latour and DuFresne had trained the other workers), these eight men considered themselves as members of one work group. Such a feeling of solidarity is unusual among workers on different shifts, despite the fact that they use the same machines.

The men received a base rate of $1.03 an hour and worked on incentive. Each man usually turned out 22 units a shift, thus earning an average of $1.19 an hour. Management supplied Rex 95 High-Speed Tool-Bits, which workers ground to suit themselves. Two tools were used: one square bit with a slight radius for recess cutting, the other bit with a 45-degree angle for chamfering and smooth finish. When used, both tools were set close together, the worker adjusting the lathe from one operation to the other. The difficulty with this setup was that during the rotation of the lathe, the aluminum waste would melt and fuse between the two toolbits. Periodically the lathe had to be stopped so that the toolbits could be freed from the welded aluminum and reground.

At the request of the supervisor of Lathe Department 15-D, the methods department had been working on his tool problem. Up to the time of this case, no solution had been found. To make a firsthand study of the difficulty, the methods department had recently assigned one of its staff, Mr. MacBride, to investigate the problem in the lathe department itself. Mr. MacBride's working hours covered parts of both the first and second shifts. MacBride was a young man, 26 years of age, and a newcomer to the methods department. For the three months prior to this assignment, he had held the post of "suggestion man," a position which enabled newcomers to the methods department to familiarize themselves with the plant setup. The job consisted in collecting, from boxes in departments throughout the plant, suggestions submitted by employees and making a preliminary evaluation of these ideas. The current assignment of studying the tool situation in Lathe Department 15-D, with a view to cutting costs, was his first special task. He devoted himself to this problem with great zeal but did not succeed in winning the confidence of the workers. In pursuance of their usual philosophy, "Keep your mouth shut if you see anyone with a suit on," they volunteered no information and took the stand that, since the methods man had been given this assignment, it was up to him to carry it out.

While MacBride was working on this problem, Pierre DuFresne hit upon a solution. One day he successfully contrived a tool which combined the two bits into one. This eliminated the space between the two toolbits which in the past had caught the molten aluminum waste and allowed it to become welded to the cutting edges. The new toolbit had two advantages: it eliminated the frequent machine stoppage for cleaning and regrinding the old-type tools; and it enabled the operator to run the lathe at a higher speed. These advantages made it possible for the operator to increase his efficiency 50 percent.

DuFresne tried to make copies of the new tool, but was unable to do so. Apparently the new development had been a "luck accident" during grinding which he could not duplicate. After several unsuccessful attempts, he took the new tool to his former teacher, Jean Latour. The latter succeeded in making a drawing and turning out duplicate toolbits on a small grinding wheel in the shop. At first the two men decided to keep the new tool to themselves. Later, however, they shared the improvement with their fellow workers on the second shift. Similarly it was passed on to the other shifts. But all these men kept the new development a closely guarded secret as far as "outsiders" were concerned. At the end of the shift, each locked the improved toolbit securely in his toolchest.

Both DuFresne, the originator of the new tool, and Latour, its draftsman and designer, decided not to submit the idea as a suggestion but to keep it as the property of their group. Why was this decision made? The answer lies partly in the suggestion system and partly in the attitude of Latour and DuFresne toward other features of company work life and toward their group.

According to an information bulletin issued by the company, the purpose of the suggestion system was to "provide an orderly method of submitting and considering ideas and recommendations of employees to management; to provide a means for recognizing and rewarding individual ingenuity; and to promote cooperation." Awards for accepted suggestions were made in the following manner: "After checking the savings and expense involved in an adopted suggestion [the suggestion committee] determined the amount of the award to be paid, based upon the savings predicted upon a year's use of the suggestion. . . . It is the

intention of the committee . . . to be liberal in the awards, which are expected to adequately compensate for the interest shown in presenting suggestions." In pursuance of this policy, it was customary to grant the suggestor an award equivalent to the savings of an entire month.

As a monetary return, both DuFresne and Latour considered an award based on one months's saving as inadequate. They also argued that such awards were really taken out of the worker's pockets. Their reasoning was as follows: All awards for adopted suggestions were paid out of undistributed profits. Since the company also had a profit-sharing plan, the money was taken from a fund that would be given to the workers anyway, which merely meant robbing Peter to pay Paul. In any case, the payment was not likely to be large and probably would be less than they could accumulate if increased incentive payments could be maintained over an extended period without discovery. Thus there was little in favor of submitting the new tool as a suggestion.

Latour and DuFresne also felt that there were definite hazards to the group if their secret were disclosed. They feared that once the tool became company property, its efficiency might lead to layoff of some members in their group, or at least make work less tolerable by leading to an increased quota at a lower price per unit. They also feared that there might be a change in scheduled work assignments. For instance, the lathe department worked on three different types of impeller. One type was a routine job and aside from the difficulty caused by the old-type tool, presented no problem. For certain technical reasons, the other two types were more difficult to make. Even Latour, an exceptionally skilled craftsman, had sometimes found it hard to make the expected quota before the new tool was developed. Unless the work load was carefully balanced by scheduling easier and more difficult types, some of the operators were unable to make standard time.

The decision to keep the tool for their own group was in keeping with Latour's work philosophy. He had a strong feeling of loyalty to his own group and had demonstrated this in the past by offering for their use several improvements of his own. For example, he made available to all workers in his group a set of special gauge blocks which were used in aligning work on lathes. To protect himself in case mistakes were traced to these gauges, he wrote on them: "Personnel [*sic*] Property—Do not use. Jean Latour."

Through informal agreement with their fellow workers, Latour and DuFresne "pegged production" at an efficiency rate that in their opinion would not arouse management's suspicion or lead to a restudy of the job, with possible cutting of the rate. This enabled them to earn an extra 10 percent incentive earnings. The other 40 percent in additional efficiency was used as follows: The operators established a reputation for a high degree of accuracy and finish. They set a record for no spoilage and were able to apply the time gained on the easier type of impeller to work on the other types which required greater care and more expert workmanship.

The foreman of the lathe department learned about the new tool soon after it was put into use but was satisfied to let the men handle the situation in their own way. He reasoned that at little expense he was able to get out production of high quality. There was no defective work, and the men were contented.

Mr. MacBride was left in a very unsatisfactory position. He had not succeeded in working out a solution of his own. Like the foreman, he got wind of the fact that the men had devised a new tool. He urged them to submit a drawing of it through the suggestion system, but this advice was not taken, and the men made it plain that they did not care to discuss with him the reasons for this position.

Having no success in his direct contact with the workers, Mr. MacBride appealed to the foreman, asking him to secure a copy of the new tool. The foreman replied that the men would certainly decline to give him a copy and would resent as an injustice any effort on his part to force them to submit a drawing. Instead he suggested that MacBride should persuade DuFresne to show him the tool. This MacBride attempted to do, but met with no success in his efforts to ingratiate himself with DuFresne. When he persisted in his attempts, DuFresne decided to throw him off the track. He left in his lathe a toolbit which was an unsuccessful copy of the original discovery. At shift change, MacBride was delighted to find what he supposed to be the improved tool. He hastily copied it and submitted a drawing to the tool department. When a tool was made up according to these specifications it naturally failed to do what was expected of it. The workers, when they heard of this through the "grapevine," were delighted. DuFresne

did not hesitate to crow over MacBride, pointing out that his underhanded methods had met with their just reward.

The foreman did not take any official notice of the conflict between DuFresne and MacBride. Then MacBride complained to the foreman that DuFresne was openly boasting of his trick and ridiculing him before the workers. Thereupon, the foreman talked to DuFresne, but the latter insisted that his ruse had been justified as a means of self-protection.

When he was rebuffed by DuFresne, the foreman felt that he had lost control of the situation. He could no longer conceal from himself that he was confronted by a more complex situation than what initially he had defined as a "tool problem." His attention was drawn to the fact that the state of affairs in his department was a tangle of several interrelated problems. Each problem urgently called for a decision that involved understanding and practical judgment. But having for so long failed to see the situation as a whole, he now found himself in a dilemma.

He wished to keep the goodwill of the work group, but he could not countenance the continued friction between DuFresne and MacBride. Certainly, he could not openly abet his operators in obstructing the work of a methods man. His superintendent would now certainly hear of it and would be displeased to learn that a foreman had failed to tell him of such an important technical improvement. Furthermore, he knew that the aircraft industry was expanding at this time and that the demand for impellers had increased to such an extent that management was planning to set up an entire new plant unit devoted to this product.

CASE QUESTIONS

1. How mature or developed in terms of cohesiveness is Latour's group?
2. Why has McBride failed so miserably with Latour's group?
3. What can management do to correct the current problems?

Intergroup Behavior and Conflict

LEARNING OBJECTIVES

EXPLAIN the difference between traditional and contemporary views of conflict

DISTINGUISH between functional and dysfunctional conflict

DESCRIBE the relationship between intergroup conflict and organizational performance

DISCUSS why intergroup conflict occurs

IDENTIFY several consequences of dysfunctional intergroup conflict

DESCRIBE techniques for managing conflict through resolution

DISCUSS several approaches to stimulating conflict

For any organization to perform effectively, interdependent individuals and groups must establish working relationships across organizational boundaries, between individuals, and among groups. Individuals or groups may depend on one another for information, assistance, or coordinated action. But the fact is that they are interdependent. Such interdependence may foster cooperation or conflict.

For example, the production and marketing executives of a firm may meet to discuss ways to deal with foreign competition. Such a meeting may be reasonably free of conflict. Decisions get made, strategies are developed, and the executives return to work. Thus, there is intergroup cooperation to achieve a goal. However, this may not be the case if sales decline because the firm is not offering enough variety in its product line. The marketing department desires broad product lines to offer more variety to customers, while the production department desires narrow product lines to keep production costs at a manageable level and to increase productivity. Conflict is likely to occur at this point because each function has its own goals which, in this case, conflict. Thus, groups may cooperate on one point and conflict on another.

The focus of this chapter is on conflict that occurs between groups in organizations.[1] Intergroup problems are not the only type of conflict that can exist in organizations. Conflict between individuals, however, usually can be more easily resolved through existing mechanisms. Troublesome employees can be fired, transferred, or given new work schedules.

This chapter begins with an examination of attitudes toward conflict. Reasons for the existence of intergroup conflict and its consequences also are presented. Finally, we outline various techniques that have been used successfully to manage intergroup conflict.

TRADITIONAL VERSUS CONTEMPORARY PERSPECTIVES ON CONFLICT

Since the early part of this century, organizational scholars have gradually changed their perspectives on conflict. Much of this change in thinking relates to assumptions about whether conflict is positive or negative. Two relatively distinct perspectives on conflict can be identified, traditional and contemporary.

The traditional perspective asserts that all conflict is bad. Thus, the presence of conflict indicates that something is wrong. This perspective on conflict was probably reinforced by the violent struggles that took place between management and the young labor movement during the first 25 years of this century. One important consequence of this view is that since conflict is inherently bad, it must be eliminated. Typically, attempts to eliminate conflict took the form of suppression. Unfortunately, while suppression might remove the outward appearance of conflict, it does not contribute to resolving the underlying difficulties which led to it.

This traditional perspective on conflict is still held by many people today. Nonetheless, in recent years organizational theorists and practitioners have gradually changed their view of conflict in light of knowledge gained from both research and practice. This has led to what may be described as a more contemporary perspective on conflict.

The contemporary viewpoint describes conflict as neither inherently good nor bad but as inevitable. Too much conflict can have negative consequences because it requires time and resources to deal with it and diverts energy that could more constructively be applied elsewhere. Too little conflict, on the other hand, can also be negative in that such a state can lead to apathy and lethargy and provide little or no impetus for change and innovation. If everything is always going

---

[1]See Clayton Alderfer and Ken K. Smith, "Studying Intergroup Relations Embedded in Organizations," *Administrative Science Quarterly,* March 1982, pp. 35–64.

smoothly (that is, there is no conflict) people may become too comfortable to want to make changes that could improve organizational effectiveness.

Two important conclusions regarding conflict from the contemporary perspective follow:

1. In many situations conflict can be good because it can have positive results (for example, stimulating innovation and creativity).
2. Since conflict is inherently neither good nor bad and can lead to both positive and negative results, a primary concern should be the management of conflict, rather than its elimination or suppression. This suggests, among other things, that there may be times when conflict is created as a deliberate strategy to stimulate the search for new and better ways of doing things.

A REALISTIC VIEW OF INTERGROUP CONFLICT

Conflict is inevitable in organizations. Intergroup conflict, however, can be both a positive and a negative force, so management should not strive to eliminate all conflict, only conflict that will have disruptive effects on the organization's efforts to achieve goals. Some type or degree of conflict may prove beneficial if it is used as an instrument for change or innovation. For example, evidence suggests conflict can improve the quality of decision making in organizations.[2] Thus, the critical issue is not conflict itself but how conflict is managed. Using this approach, we can define conflict in terms of the effect it has on the organization. In this respect, we shall discuss both *functional* and *dysfunctional* conflict.[3]

Functional Conflict

A functional conflict is a confrontation between groups that enhances and benefits the organization's performance. For example, two departments in a hospital may be in conflict over the most efficient and adaptive method of delivering health care to low-income rural families. The two departments agree on the goal but not on the means to achieve it. Whatever the outcome, low-income rural families probably will end up with better medical care once the conflict is settled. Without this type of conflict in organizations, there would be little commitment to change, and most groups likely would become stagnant.

Thus, functional conflict can be thought of as a type of "creative tension."

■ E8–1   Exercise 8–1 provides an illustration of functional conflict. On the other hand, the situation in this exercise may sometimes lead to dysfunctional conflict.

[2]R. A. Cosier and C. R. Schwenk, "Agreement and Thinking Alike: Ingredients for Poor Decisions," *Academy of Management Executive,* February 1990, pp. 69–74.

[3]S. P. Robbins, *Essentials of Organizational Behavior* (Englewood Cliffs, N.J.: Prentice-Hall, 1992), pp. 182–84.

Dysfunctional Conflict

A **dysfunctional conflict** is any confrontation or interaction between groups that harms the organization or hinders the achievement of organizational goals. Management *must* seek to eliminate dysfunctional conflict. Beneficial conflict often can turn into bad conflicts, but in most cases, the point at which functional conflict becomes dysfunctional is impossible to identify precisely. Certain levels of stress and conflict may help create a healthy and positive movement toward goals in one group. Those same levels, however, may prove extremely disruptive and dysfunctional in another group (or at a different time for the former group). A group's tolerance for stress and conflict can also depend on the type of organization it serves. Automobile manufacturers, professional sports teams, and crisis organizations such as police and fire departments would have different points where functional conflict becomes dysfunctional than would organizations such as universities, research and development firms, and motion picture production firms.

Conflict and Organizational Performance

As was indicated earlier, the contemporary perspective on conflict suggests that conflict may have either positive or negative consequences for the organization, depending on how much exists and how it is managed. Every organization has an optimal level of conflict that can be considered highly functional—it helps generate positive performance. When the conflict level is too low, performance can also suffer. Innovation and change are less likely to take place, and the organization may have difficulty adapting to its changing environment. If a low conflict level continues, the very survival of the organization can be threatened. On the other hand, if the conflict level becomes too high, the resulting chaos also can threaten the organization's survival. An example is the popular press coverage of the results of "dissension" in labor unions and its impact on performance. If fighting between rival factions in the union becomes too great, it can render the union less effective in pursuing its mission of furthering its members' interests. A further example may be found in the first case at the end of this chapter. The

▲ C8–1 Evergreen Willows case illustrates a number of conflict issues to be discussed in this chapter. The relationship between the level of intergroup conflict and organizational performance that is consistent with a contemporary perspective is presented in Exhibit 8-1 and explained for three hypothetical situations.

Views toward Intergroup Conflict in Practice

Some organizational researchers contend that dysfunctional conflict should be eliminated and functional conflict encouraged. In reality, however, this is not what actually happens in most organizations. In practice, and consistent with the traditional perspective on conflict, many managers attempt to eliminate all types

EXHIBIT 8-1

Relationship between Intergroup Conflict and Organizational Performance

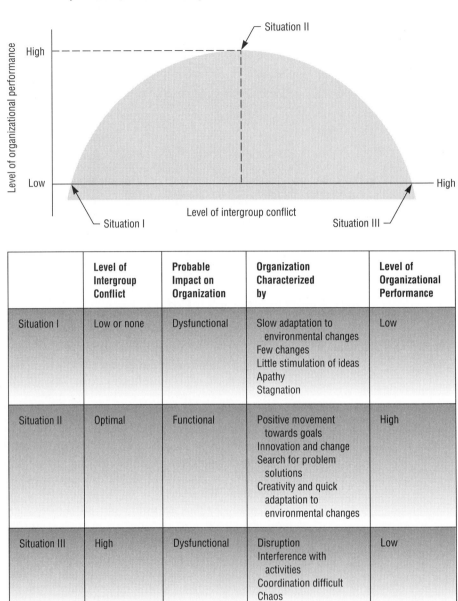

	Level of Intergroup Conflict	Probable Impact on Organization	Organization Characterized by	Level of Organizational Performance
Situation I	Low or none	Dysfunctional	Slow adaptation to environmental changes Few changes Little stimulation of ideas Apathy Stagnation	Low
Situation II	Optimal	Functional	Positive movement towards goals Innovation and change Search for problem solutions Creativity and quick adaptation to environmental changes	High
Situation III	High	Dysfunctional	Disruption Interference with activities Coordination difficult Chaos	Low

of conflict, whether dysfunctional or functional. Why is this the case? Some reasons are:

1. Many of the important institutions in our society (for example, the home, schools, and churches) are operated on the traditional view of conflict. Traditionally, conflict between children or between children and parents

has, for the most part, been discouraged. In school systems, conflict has been discouraged; teachers had all the answers, and both teachers and children were rewarded for orderly classrooms. Finally, most religious doctrines stress cooperation and acceptance without questioning.

2. Managers often are evaluated and rewarded for the lack of conflict in their areas of responsibility. Anticonflict values, in fact, become part of the "culture" of the organization. Harmony and satisfaction are viewed positively, while conflicts and dissatisfaction are viewed negatively. Under such conditions, managers seek to avoid conflicts—functional or dysfunctional—that could disturb the status quo.

WHY INTERGROUP CONFLICT OCCURS

Every group comes into at least partial conflict with every other group with which it interacts. This tendency is known as "the law of interorganizational conflict."[4] In this section we examine four factors that contribute to group conflict: work interdependence, differences in goals, differences in perceptions, and the increased demand for specialists.

Interdependence

Work interdependence occurs when two or more organizational groups must depend on one another to complete their tasks. The conflict potential in such situations is high. Three distinct types of interdependence among groups have been identified.[5]

Pooled Interdependence

Pooled interdependence requires no interaction among groups because each group, in effect, performs separately. However, the pooled performances of all the groups determine how successful the organization is. For example, the staff of an IBM sales office in one region may have no interaction with their peers in another region. Similarly, two bank branches will have little or no interaction. In both cases, however, the groups are interdependent because the performance of each must be adequate if the total organization is to thrive. The conflict potential in pooled interdependence is relatively low, and management can rely on standard rules and procedures developed at the main office for coordination.

Sequential Interdependence

Sequential interdependence requires one group to complete its task before another group can complete its task. Tasks are performed in a sequential fashion. In a manufacturing plant, for example, the product must be assembled before it can

[4]See Anthony Downs, *Inside Bureaucracy* (Boston: Little, Brown, 1968).

[5]J. Thompson, *Organizations in Action* (New York: McGraw-Hill, 1967).

be painted. Thus, the assembling department must complete its task before the painting department can begin painting.

Under these circumstances, since the output of one group serves as the input for another, conflict between the groups is more likely to occur. Coordinating this type of interdependence involves effective use of the management function of planning.

Reciprocal Interdependence

Reciprocal interdependence requires the output of each group to serve as input to other groups in the organization. Consider the relationships that exist between the anesthesiology staff, nursing staff, technician staff, and surgeons in a hospital operating room. This relationship creates a high degree of reciprocal interdependence. The same interdependence exists among groups involved in space launchings. Another example is the interdependence among airport control towers, flight crews, ground operations, and maintenance crews. Clearly, the potential for conflict is great in any of these situations. Effective coordination involves management's skillful use of the organizational processes of communication and decision making.

All organizations have pooled interdependence among groups. Complex organizations also have sequential interdependence. The most complicated organizations experience pooled, sequential, and reciprocal interdependence among groups. The more complex the organization, the greater are the potentials for conflict and the more difficult is the task facing management.

Differences in Goals

As the subunits of an organization become specialized, they often develop dissimilar goals. A goal of a production unit may include low production costs and few defective products. A goal of the research and development unit may be innovative ideas that can be converted into commercially successful new products. These different goals can lead to different expectations among the members of each unit. Because of their goals, production engineers may expect close supervision, while research scientists may expect a great deal of participation in decision making. Because of the different goals of these two groups, conflict can result when they interact. Finally, marketing departments usually have a goal of maximum gross income. On the other hand, credit departments seek to minimize credit losses. Depending on which department prevails, different customers might be selected. Here again, conflict can occur because each department has a different goal. There are certain conditions that foster intergroup conflict because of differences in goals.

Limited Resources

When resources are limited and must be allocated, mutual dependencies increase and any differences in group goals become more apparent. If money, space, the labor force, and materials were unlimited, each group could pursue, at least to a relative degree, its own goals. But in virtually all cases, resources must be allocated or shared. When groups conclude that resources have not been allocated in an equitable manner, pressures toward conflict increase.[6]

Reward Structures

Intergroup conflict is more likely to occur when the reward system is related to individual group performance rather than to overall organizational performance. When rewards are related to individual group performance, performance is, in fact, viewed as an independent variable, although the performance of the group is in reality very interdependent. For example, in the situation described above, suppose that the marketing group is rewarded for sales produced and that the credit group is rewarded for minimizing credit losses. In such a situation, competition will be directly reinforced and dysfunctional conflict will, inadvertently, be rewarded.

Intergroup conflict arising from differences in goals can be dysfunctional to the organization as a whole. Depending on the type of organization, intergroup conflicts also can be dysfunctional to third-party groups—usually the clients the organization serves. An example of this is the controversy in many teaching hospitals over the conflict between meeting the goals of quality health care for patients and meeting the teaching needs of future physicians.

A particular type of conflict related to differences in goals is somewhat similar to what is frequently called a conflict of interest. Conflicts of interest generally suggest there is a moral or ethical dimension involved in the dispute. Encounter 8-1 provides an example of such a situation.

Differences in Perceptions

▲ C8–2

The differences in goals can be accompanied by differing perceptions of reality, and disagreements over what constitutes reality can lead to conflict. For instance, a problem in a hospital may be viewed in one way by the administrative staff and in another way by the medical staff. Alumni and faculty may have different perceptions concerning the importance of a winning football program. Many factors cause groups in organizations to form differing perceptions of reality.[7] The major factors include different goals, different time horizons, status incongruency, and inaccurate perceptions. The L.E.S., Inc. Case, which accompanies this chapter, is an excellent study in how differences in perceptions can be the

[6]B. Kabanoff, "Equity, Equality, Power, and Conflict," *Academy of Management Review*, April 1991, pp. 416–41.

[7]Karen Brown and Terence Mitchell, "Influence of Task Interdependence and Number of Poor Performers on Diagnosis of Causes of Poor Performance," *Academy of Management Journal*, June 1986, pp. 412–23.

ETHICS

E N C O U N T E R • 8-1

CONFLICT AT GENERAL DYNAMICS: MORE FOR A FEW, NOTHING FOR MANY

Increasingly of late, the large amounts of compensation received by a handful of top executives in many large corporations has come under fire. Critics have charged that executive performance does not warrant such lofty rewards, and there is growing unrest among organizational members who receive far, far less compensation for their services. At General Dynamics however, one of the country's largest defense contractors, the conflict has an added twist. Here is the situation:

In 1991 General Dynamics shareholders approved a "Gain/Sharing" executive compensation plan for the top 25 managers in the company. The plan provides for these executives to receive bonuses equal to predetermined multiples of their salaries for every 10-point jump above the $25.56 price of the company's shares on February 15 of that year. In May, when the plan was adopted, this meant the executives received $6 million in bonuses. With General Dynamics stock continuing to climb, the plan entitled these same executives to an additional $12 million in bonus payments. Thus, in the first six months of the plan's operation, these 25 executives earned an average of over $700,000 each in bonuses. And while the rank and file General Dynamics worker may question whether the company's executives

are worth that much money, the real conflict centers around why the price of the company's stock—which is what kicked in the bonuses—rose so much in such a short period of time.

The answer to that question is that investors are excited that the company's cash position is growing so rapidly—around $600 million by the end of 1991, and the CEO recently announced that the cash position is far more than the company needs and that "excess" cash will be returned to shareholders. Much of the cash has accumulated as a result of management decisions to cut spending, including the layoff of 12,000 employees in the last year. From a worker's perspective the whole deal stinks: Management awards itself bonuses for achieving stock price increases which it brings about by letting go 13 percent of the work force.

"Why is there just Gain/Sharing for the 25—most of them relative newcomers—while people who have worked in the trenches for many years are losing their jobs?" asks Dean L. Girardot, a General Dynamics coordinator for the International Association of Machinists, which represents company workers in Texas and California plants. Graef S. Crystal of the University of California, Berkeley, and formerly a General Dynamics executive, observes that "This ill-conceived plan smacks of the Marie Antoinette School of management."

Source: Based on J. E. Ellis, Layoffs on the Line, Bonuses in the Executive Suite, *Business Week,* October 21, 1991, p. 34.

underlying cause of conflicts. At least two of the factors discussed here (different goals and inaccurate perceptions) contribute to the conflicts in this case.

Different Goals

Differences in group goals are an obvious contributor to differing perceptions. For instance, if the goal of marketing is to maximize sales, that department's personnel will certainly view a major breakdown in production differently than will the staff of the production department, whose goal is to minimize costs.

Different Time Horizons

Time perspectives influence how a group perceives reality. Deadlines influence the priorities and importance that groups assign to their various activities. Research scientists working for a chemical manufacturer may have a time perspective of several years, while the same firm's manufacturing engineers may work within time frames of less than a year. A bank president might focus on 5- and 10-year time spans, while middle managers might concentrate on much shorter spans. With such differences in time horizons, problems and issues deemed critical by one group may be dismissed as not important by another, and conflicts may erupt.

Status Incongruency

Conflicts concerning the relative status of different groups are common and influence perceptions. Usually, many different status standards are found in an organization, rather than an absolute one. The result is many status hierarchies. For example, status conflicts often are created by work patterns—which group initiates the work and which group responds. A production department, for instance, may perceive a change as an affront to its status because it must accept a salesperson's initiation of work. This status conflict may be aggravated deliberately by the salesperson. Academic snobbery is certainly a fact of campus life at many colleges and universities. Members of a particular academic discipline perceive themselves, for one reason or another, as having a higher status than others.

Inaccurate Perceptions

Inaccurate perceptions often cause one group to develop stereotypes about other groups. While the differences between groups may actually be small, each group will tend to exaggerate them. Thus, you will hear that "all women executives are aggressive" or "all bank trust officers behave alike." When the differences between the groups are emphasized, the stereotypes are reinforced, relations deteriorate, and conflict develops.

The Increased Demand for Specialists

Conflicts between staff specialists and line generalists are probably the most common type of intergroup conflict. With the growing necessity for technical expertise in all areas of organizations, staff roles can be expected to expand, and line and staff conflicts can be expected to increase. Line and staff persons simply view one another and their roles in the organization from different perspectives.[8] Exhibit 8-2 summarizes some additional causes of conflict between staff

[8]For a classic discussion, see L. A. Allen, "The Line-Staff Relationship," *Management Record*, September 1955, pp. 346–49.

EXHIBIT 8-2

**Causes of Line/
Staff Conflict**

Perceived Diminution of Line Authority. Line managers fear that specialists will encroach on their jobs and thereby diminish their authority and power. As a result, specialists often complain that line executives do not make proper use of staff specialists and do not give staff members sufficient authority.

Social and Physical Differences. Often, major differences exist between line managers and staff specialists with respect to age, education, dress, and attitudes. In many cases, staff specialists are younger than line managers and have higher educational levels or training in a specialized field.

Line Dependence on Staff Knowledge. Since line generalists often do not have the technical knowledge necessary to manage their departments, they are dependent on the specialist. The resulting gap between knowledge and authority may be even greater when the staff specialist is lower in the organizational hierarchy than the manager, which is often the case. As a result, staff members often complain that line managers resist new ideas.

Different Loyalties. Divided loyalties frequently exist between line managers and staff specialists. The staff specialist may be loyal to a discipline, while the line manager may be loyal to the organization. The member of the product development group may be a chemist first and a member of the organization second. The production manager's first loyalty, however, may be to the organization. When loyalties to a particular function or discipline are greater than loyalties to the overall organization, conflict is likely to occur.

specialists and line generalists.[9] With the growth of sophistication, specialization, and complexity in most organizations, line/staff conflicts will continue to be a major concern in the management of organizational behavior.

THE CONSEQUENCES OF DYSFUNCTIONAL INTERGROUP CONFLICT

Behavioral scientists have spent more than three decades researching and analyzing how dysfunctional intergroup conflict affects those who experience it.[10]

[9]See M. Dalton, "Conflicts between Staff and Line Managerial Officers," *American Sociological Review,* June 1950, pp. 342–51; A W. Gouldner, "Cosmopolitans and Locals: Toward an Analysis of Latent Social Roles," *Administrative Science Quarterly,* December 1957, pp. 281–306; A. Etzioni, ed., *Complex Organizations* (New York: Holt, Rinehart & Winston, 1961); A. Etzioni, *Modern Organization* (Englewood Cliffs, N.J.: Prentice-Hall, 1964); R. W. Scott, "Professionals in Bureaucracies: Areas of Conflict," in *Professionals,* ed. H. M. Vollmer and D. L. Mills (Englewood Cliffs, N.J.: Prentice-Hall, 1966); P. R. Lawrence and J. W. Lorsch, *Organization and Environment: Managing Differentiation and Integration* (Boston: Graduate School of Business Administration, Harvard University, 1967); J. A. Balasco and J. A. Alutto, "Line and Staff Conflicts: Some Empirical Insights," *Academy of Management Journal,* March 1969, pp. 469–77; E. Rhenman, *Conflict and Cooperation in Business* (New York: John Wiley & Sons, 1970); P. K. Berger and A. J. Grimes, "Cosmopolitan-Local: A Factor Analysis of the Construct," *Administrative Science Quarterly,* June 1973, pp. 223–35; and J. E. Sorensen and T. L. Sorensen, "The Conflict of Professionals in Bureaucratic Organizations," *Administrative Science Quarterly,* March 1974, pp. 98–106.

[10]The classic work is M. Sherif and C. Sherif, *Groups in Harmony and Tension* (New York: Harper & Row, 1953). Their study was conducted among groups in a boys' camp. They stimulated conflict between the groups and observed the changes that occurred in group behavior. Also see their "Experiments in Group Conflict," *Scientific American,* March 1956, pp. 54–58.

They have found that groups placed in a conflict situation tend to react in fairly predictable ways. We shall now examine a number of the changes that occur *within groups* and *between groups* as a result of dysfunctional intergroup conflict.

Changes within Groups

Many changes are likely to occur within groups involved in intergroup conflict. Unfortunately, these changes generally result in either a continuance or an escalation of the conflict.

Increased Group Cohesiveness

It is clear that when groups are engaged in a conflict their cohesion tends to increase. Competition, conflict, or perceived external threat usually result in group members putting aside individual differences and closing ranks. Members become more loyal to the group, and group membership becomes more attractive. This increase in cohesion is necessary to mobilize group resources in dealing with the "enemy" and tends to result in the suppression of internal disagreements. This tendency toward increased cohesion in the face of threat can be seen in the Middle East. Arab nations have historically had difficulties getting along with each other except when a common threat (in the form of Israel) is the focus of their attention.

Emphasis on Loyalty

The tendency of groups to increase in cohesiveness suggests that conformity to group norms becomes more important in conflict situations. In reality it is not unusual for groups to overconform to group norms in conflict situations. This may take the form of blind acceptance of dysfunctional solutions to the conflict and result in groupthink, as discussed in the previous chapter. In such situations group goals take precedence over individual satisfaction as members are expected to demonstrate their loyalty. In major conflict situations interaction with members of "the other group" may be completely outlawed.

Rise in Autocratic Leadership

In extreme conflict situations where threats are perceived, democratic methods of leadership are likely to become less popular. The members want strong leadership. Thus, the leaders are likely to become more autocratic. In the National Football League players' strike in 1987 and the PATCO strike discussed in the next chapter, the heads of each union had tremendous authority.

Focus on Activity

When a group is in conflict, its members usually emphasize doing what the group does and doing it very well. The group becomes more task-oriented. Tolerance for members who "goof off" is low, and there is less concern for individual member satisfaction. The emphasis is on accomplishing the group's task and defeating the "enemy" (the other group in the conflict).

Changes between Groups

During conflicts, certain changes will probably occur between the groups involved.

Distorted Perceptions

During conflicts, the perceptions of each group's members become distorted. Group members develop stronger opinions of the importance of their units. Each group sees itself as superior in performance to the other and as more important to the survival of the organization than other groups. In a conflict situation, nurses may conclude that they are more important to a patient than physicians, while physicians may consider themselves more important than hospital administrators. The marketing group in a business organization may think, "Without us selling the product, there would be no money to pay anyone else's salary." The production group, meanwhile, will say, "If we don't make the product, there is nothing to sell." Ultimately, none of these groups is more important, but conflict can cause their members to develop gross misperceptions of reality.

Negative Stereotyping

As conflict increases and perceptions become more distorted, all of the negative stereotypes that may have ever existed are reinforced. A management representative may say, "I've always said these union guys are just plain greedy. Now they've proved it." The head of a local teacher's union may say, "Now we know that what all politicians are interested in is getting reelected, not the quality of education." When negative stereotyping is a factor in a conflict, the members of each group see less differences within their unit and greater differences between the groups than actually exist.

Decreased Communication

Communications between the groups in conflict usually break down. This can be extremely dysfunctional, especially where sequential interdependence or reciprocal interdependence relationships exist between groups. The decision-making process can be disrupted, and the customers or others whom the organization serves can be affected. Consider the possible consequences to patients, for instance, if a conflict between hospital technicians and nurses continues until it lowers the quality of health care.

While these are not the only dysfunctional consequences of intergroup conflict, they are the most common, and they have been well documented in the research literature.[11] Other consequences, such as violence and aggression, are less common

---

[11]For additional discussion, see J. Litterer, "Conflict in Organizations: A Re-Examination," *Academy of Management Journal*, September 1966, pp. 178–86; J. W. Lorsch and J. J. Morse, *Organizations and Their Members: A Contingency Approach* (New York: Harper & Row, 1974); and E. Schein, "Intergroup Problems in Organizations," in *Organization Development: Theory, Practice, and Research*, 2nd. ed. W. French, C. Bell, and R. Zawacki (Plano, Tex.: Business Publications, 1983), pp. 106–10.

■ **E8–2**   but also occur. Exercise 8–2 serves as an excellent example of many of the changes that occur between groups when conflict is present. When intergroup conflicts take place, some form of managerial intervention is usually necessary. How managers can deal with these situations is the subject of the next section.

MANAGING INTERGROUP CONFLICT THROUGH RESOLUTION

Since managers must live with intergroup conflict, they must confront the problem of managing it.[12] In this section, you will examine techniques that have been used successfully in resolving intergroup conflicts that have reached levels dysfunctional to the organization. Most of these techniques involve some type of exchange between the conflicting parties, suggesting that resolution may be facilitated by

● **R8–1**   constructive negotiation, a topic treated in detail in the next chapter. Reading 8–1 also presents the attributes of a conflict resolution process.

Problem Solving

The confrontation method of problem solving seeks to reduce tensions through face-to-face meetings of the conflicting groups. The purpose of the meetings is to identify conflicts and resolve them. The conflicting groups openly debate various issues and bring together all relevent information until a decision has been reached. Effective problem solving requires that the conflicting parties display a willingness to work collaboratively toward an integrative solution that satisfies the needs of all concerned. Problem solving is particularly effective in increasing commitment to a solution through incorporating everyone's concerns into a consensual decision.

Problem solving is a desirable approach to conflict resolution but one that can be extremely difficult to implement effectively. The greatest obstacle which must be overcome is the win-lose mentality that so often characterizes conflicting groups. Unless the parties involved can rise above this kind of thinking, problem solving is not likely to be successful.

Superordinate Goals

In the resolution of conflicts between groups, the **superordinate goals** technique involves developing a common set of goals and objectives. These goals and objectives cannot be attained without the cooperation of the groups involved. In fact, they are unattainable by one group singly and supersede all other goals of

---

[12]For an examination of specific devices for assessing how managers manage conflict see, E. van de Vlert and B. Kabanoff, "Toward Theory-Based Measures of Conflict Management," *Academy of Management Journal,* March 1990, pp. 199–209.

any of the individual groups involved in the conflict.[13] For example, several unions in the automobile and steel industries have, in recent years, agreed to forgo increases and in some cases to accept pay reductions because the survival of their firm or industry was threatened.[14] When the crisis is over, demands for higher wages undoubtedly will return, as they have at once-struggling Chrysler Corporation.

Expansion of Resources

As noted earlier, a major cause of intergroup conflict is limited resources. Whatever one group succeeds in obtaining is gained at the expense of another group. The scarce resource may be a particular position (e.g., the presidency of the firm), money, space, and so forth. For example, one major publishing firm decided to expand by establishing a subsidiary firm. Most observers believed that the major reason for the expansion was to allow the firm to become involved in other segments of the market. While this was partially correct, a stronger reason was to enable the firm to stem the exit of valued personnel. By establishing the subsidiary, the firm was able to double its executive positions, since the subsidiary needed a president, various vice presidents, and other executives. Expanding resources is a very successful technique for solving conflicts in many cases since this technique may enable almost everyone to be satisfied. In reality, however, resources usually are not easily expanded.

Avoidance

Frequently, some way can be found to avoid conflict. While avoidance may not bring any long-run benefits, it can be an effective and appropriate strategy in some situations. Foremost among these is when avoidance is used as a temporary alternative. When the conflict is a particularly heated one, for example, temporary avoidance gives the involved parties an opportunity to cool down and regain perspective. Avoidance may also buy time needed to gather additional information necessary for a longer range solution. Avoidance might also be appropriate when other parties are in a better position to resolve the conflict or when other matters that are more important need to be addressed. Unfortunately, people have a great temptation to overuse avoidance; the number of situations where avoidance is an effective approach to conflict resolution are typically less than we would like them to be.

[13]See M. Sherif and C. Sherif, *Social Psychology* (New York: Harper & Row, 1969), pp. 228–62, for a detailed discussion of this method. Sherif and Sherif conducted a number of sociopsychological experiments designed to determine effective ways of resolving conflict. Based on this research, they developed the concept of superordinate goals. Also see J. D. Hunger and L. W. Stern, "An Assessment of the Functionality of the Superordinate Goal in Reducing Conflict," *Academy of Management Journal,* December 1976, pp. 591–605.

[14]J. B. Arthur and J. B. Dworkin, "Current Issues in Industrial and Labor Relations," *Journal of Management,* September 1991, pp. 515–52.

Forcing

As its name suggests, forcing is a technique whereby a resolution to a conflict is "forced" upon the conflicting parties. Forcing is the approach used in our judicial system. When two parties have a disagreement and one sues the other, both parties appear in court, and the resolution is imposed by the judge. One or both parties may be unhappy with the decision, but the conflict is at least officially resolved. Arbitration is another form of formal forcing. While it is most frequently associated with union-management conflict, arbitration is finding growing acceptance in nonunion environments as well. Encounter 8-2 details a proposal to submit a particular form of conflict—termination of an employee—to formal arbitration procedures.

In a work environment, a manager may informally accept the role of judge or act as arbitrator and force a resolution on two workers who have a conflict. Without question this technique can lead to a quick resolution, but since it imposes an external solution on the parties, there may be a lack of commitment to making it work. Additionally, the losing party may feel mistreated, develop negative attitudes, and in the extreme, might seek some form of revenge. It is important to remember that forcing focuses on the results of conflict and not on the causes. Thus, if the causes of the conflict are still present, the conflict is likely to recur.

Smoothing

The technique known as smoothing emphasizes the common interests of the conflicting groups and de-emphasizes their differences. The basic belief behind smoothing is that stressing shared viewpoints on certain issues facilitates movement toward a common goal. If the differences between the groups are serious, smoothing—like avoidance—is a short-run solution at best. Smoothing also may contribute to low-quality decisions whose full implications are not realized.[15]

Compromise

Compromise is a traditional method for resolving intergroup conflicts. With compromise, there is no distinct winner or loser, and the decision reached probably is not ideal for either group. Compromise can be used very effectively when the goal sought (for example, money) can be divided equitably. If this is not possible, one group must give up something of value as a concession.

Compromise might be useful when two conflicting parties with relatively equal power are both strongly committed to mutually exclusive goals. It may also represent a way of gaining a temporary settlement to particularly complex and difficult issues. We saw earlier that problem solving was a very desirable but difficult approach to conflict resolution. Compromise is a good "back-up"

---

[15]Dean Tjosvold, "Implications of Controversy Research for Management," *Journal of Management,* Fall/Winter 1985, pp. 21–37.

ARBITRATING TERMINATION DISPUTES

You have just received notice that you are being terminated by your employer for reasons you feel are entirely unjustified. You are not a member of an equal employment opportunity legislation protected group. Nor are you a union member working under a labor agreement which specifies in detail under what circumstances an employee may be terminated. What means do you have for resolving this conflict? The answer is, you can sue. Other than taking your employer to court, however, there really is not a widely acceptable way of resolving the dispute. That may soon change, however. The National Conference of Commissioners on Uniform State Laws has proposed a new employment statute that would let most fired workers take their case to a neutral arbitrator.

Under the legal doctrine of employment-at-will, organizations can fire employees for any reason—or no reason at all. In recent years, however, thousands of discharged workers have filed law suits claiming unfair dismissal. Courts in 45 states have accepted such cases, undercutting the employment-at-will doctrine. The result are jury trials and large damage awards for a growing number of workers. In California, for example, where workers win 70 percent of the jury trials, awards average between $300,000 to $500,000. Dismissed workers, on the other hand, may have to spend up to $40,000 on legal fees to press their lawsuits, which could take a year or more to resolve.

Under the commission's proposal the case could be decided in a few weeks and would cost about $15,000 total. The proposed system of arbitration would work something like this:

1. With suits no longer permitted, a fired worker would file a complaint.
2. Each side in the conflict would make its case before an arbitrator.
3. If the employer won, the firing would stand. If the employee won, he or she would be reinstated or get up to three years' severance pay.

Individual states would decide for themselves whether or not to go to this system. Thus, it will be many years before most workers would be covered. Nonetheless, it represents a means for resolving conflict that has potential advantages for both sides in the dispute.

Source: Based in part on material from A. Bernstein and Z. Schiller, "Tell It to the Arbitrator," *Business Week,* November 4, 1991, p. 109.

strategy, which conflicting parties can fall back on if their attempts at problem solving are unsuccessful. Compromise may involve third-party interventions as well as total group or representative negotiating.[16]

Altering the Human Variable

Altering the human variable involves trying to change the behavior of the members of the groups involved. This method focuses on the cause or causes of the conflict and on the attitudes of the people involved. While the method is certainly difficult,

[16]M. A. Neale and Max H. Bazerman, "The Effects of Framing and Negotiator Overconfidence on Bargaining Behavior and Outcomes," *Academy of Management Journal,* March 1985, pp. 34–49.

EXHIBIT 8-3

An Overview of Intergroup Conflict

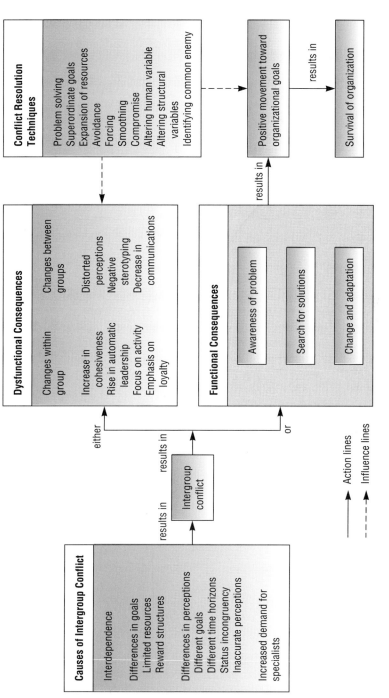

it does center on the cause of the conflict. Chapter 16 of this book focuses specifically on changing behavior. In the chapter, we shall see that while altering the human variable is slower than other methods and often costly, the results can be significant in the long run.

Altering the Structural Variables

Another way to resolve intergroup disputes is to alter the structural variables. This involves changing the formal structure of the organization. Structure refers to the fixed relationships among the jobs of the organization and includes the design of jobs and departments. Altering the structure of the organization to resolve intergroup conflict involves such things as transferring, exchanging, or rotating members of the groups or having someone serve as a coordinator, liaison, or go-between who keeps groups communicating with one another.

Identifying a Common Enemy

In some respects, identifying a common enemy is the negative side of superordinate goals. Groups in conflict may temporarily resolve their differences and unite to combat a common enemy. The common enemy may be a competitor that has just introduced a clearly superior product. Conflicting groups in a bank suddenly may work in close harmony when government bank examiners make a visit. The common-enemy phenomenon is very evident in domestic conflicts. Most police officers prefer not to become involved in heated domestic conflicts because, in far too many cases, the combatants close ranks and turn on the police officer.

Whatever the techniques utilized to deal with intergroup conflict (and there are others in addition to those discussed here), the important point is that managers must learn how to recognize both the existence and the causes of intergroup conflict. They must also develop skills to deal with it.

The most commonly used methods for managing intergroup conflict have strengths and weaknesses and are effective or ineffective under different conditions and situations. What this chapter has said thus far about intergroup conflict is summarized in Exhibit 8-3. The exhibit illustrates the relationship between causes and types of conflict, the consequences of conflict, and techniques for resolution. It is also important to keep in mind that views of conflict and approaches to conflict resolution vary across cultures. Encounter 8-3 provides an illustration.

MANAGING INTERGROUP CONFLICT THROUGH STIMULATION

Throughout this chapter we have stressed that some conflict is beneficial. This point was first made in the discussion of the contemporary perspective on conflict and is noted again in Exhibit 8-3, which focuses on some of the functional consequences of intergroup conflict. We have already examined the situation where conflict is dysfunctional because it is too high; we have said little, however, regarding situations in which there is an insufficient amount of conflict. If groups

INTERNATIONAL
E N C O U N T E R • 8-3

CONFLICT RESOLUTION: HOW JAPANESE AND AMERICANS DIFFER

Rensis Likert, the renowned social scientist and management expert, once observed that the strategies used by a society and its organizations for dealing with conflict reflect the basic values and philosophy of that society. In ideal circumstances conflicts can be difficult to resolve; once the confounding variable of intercultural differences is added, conflict resolution becomes even more complex. Consider, for example, Japanese and American differences.

Of course, these are broad generalizations which may well not apply in specific situations or with specific individuals or groups. Nonetheless, they serve to point out the fact that intercultural conflicts—and successful intercultural conflict resolution—are affected by differing cultural perspectives, values, and styles of interacting. All of these are significant factors which cannot be ignored in the conflict resolution process.

Japanese	American	Japanese	American
Resolution involves long-term perspective	Short-term perspective	Takes time, process is important; win-win approach	Time is money; win-lose approach
Cooperation based on team spirit	Spirit of competition and rivalry	Emotional sensitivity highly valued	Emotional sensitivity not highly valued
Disagreement with superior often, but polite	Disagreement with superior seldom, but violent	Good of the group is ultimate aim	Profit motive or good of individual ultimate aim
Disputes settled through conferral and trust	Disputes settled through contracts and bringing arbitration	Face-saving crucial; decisions often made to save someone from embarrassment	Decision made on cost-benefit basis; face-saving not always important

Source: Based on materials from P. Casse, *Training for the Multicultural Manager: A Practical and Cross-Cultural Approach to the Management of People* (Washington D.C.: Society of Intercultural Education, Training and Research, 1982), and B. J. Punnett, *Experiencing International Management* (Boston: PWS-Kent, 1989).

become too complacent because everything always operates smoothly, management might benefit from stimulating conflict. Lack of any disagreement can lead to suboptimum performance, including inferior decision making.

A variety of research supports this conclusion. In one laboratory study, experimental and control groups were formed to solve a problem. The experimental groups had a member, a confederate of the researcher, whose job was to challenge the majority view of the groups he or she had been planted in as the group attempted to solve the problem. The control groups had no such member. In every case, the experimental groups out-performed the control groups.[17]

[17]E. Boulding, "Further Reflections on Conflict Management," in *Power and Conflict in Organizations,* ed. R. Kahn and E. Boulding (New York: Basic Books, 1964), pp. 146–50.

What can management do to stimulate conflict for constructive purposes? The next section examines four techniques that have been used successfully to stimulate conflict to a functional level, thereby contributing positively to organizational performance.

Communication

By intelligent use of the organization's communication channels, a manager can stimulate beneficial conflict. Information can be placed carefully into formal channels to create ambiguity, reevaluation, or conformation. Information that is threatening (e.g., a proposed budget cut) can stimulate functional conflict in a department and improve performance. Carefully planted rumors also can serve a useful purpose. For example, a hospital administrator may start a rumor about a proposed reorganization of the hospital. His purpose if twofold: (1) to stimulate new ideas on how to more effectively carry out the mission of the hospital and (2) to reduce apathy among the staff.

Bringing Outside Individuals into the Group

A technique widely used to "bring back to life" a stagnant organization or subunit of an organization is to hire or transfer in individuals whose attitudes, values, and backgrounds differ from those of the group's present members. Many college faculties consciously seek new members with different backgrounds and often discourage the hiring of graduates of their own programs. This is to ensure a diversity of viewpoints on the faculty. The technique of bringing in outsiders is also used widely in government and business. Recently, a bank president decided not to promote from within for a newly created position of marketing vice president. Instead, he hired a highly successful executive from the very competitive consumer products field. The bank president felt that while the outsider knew little about marketing financial services, her approach to, and knowledge of, marketing was what the bank needed to become a strong competitor.

Altering the Organization's Structure

Changing the structure of the organization cannot only help resolve intergroup conflict; it is also excellent for *creating* conflict. For example, a school of business typically has several departments. One, named the Department of Business Administration, includes all of the faculty members who teach courses in management, marketing, finance, production management, and so forth. Accordingly, the department is rather large, with 32 members under one department chairman, who reports to the dean. A new dean recently has been hired, and he is considering dividing the business administration unit into several separate departments (e.g., departments of marketing, finance, management), each with five or six members and a chairperson. The reasoning is that reorganizing in this manner will create competition among the groups for resources, students, faculty, and so forth, where none existed before because there was only one group. Whether this change will improve performance remains to be seen.

Stimulating Competition

Many managers utilize various techniques to stimulate competition among groups. The use of a variety of incentives, such as awards and bonuses for outstanding performance, often stimulates competition. If properly utilized, such incentives can help maintain a healthy atmosphere of competition that may result in a functional level of conflict. Incentives can be given for least defective parts, highest sales, best teacher, greatest number of new customers, or in any area where increased conflict is likely to lead to more effective performance.

SUMMARY OF KEY POINTS

- The traditional perspective of conflict holds that all organizational conflict is bad, and thus should be eliminated or minimized to the fullest extent possible. The more contemporary view recognizes that conflict is neither inherently good nor bad but can be either depending on how it is dealt with. Rather than eliminating conflict, this view stresses that what is important is that conflict be effectively managed.

- A functional conflict is a confrontation between groups that enhances and benefits the organization's performance. Functional conflict can contribute to creativity, innovation, and improved decision making, among other benefits. Dysfunctional conflict, on the other hand, is that which harms the organization or hinders the achievement of organizational goals.

- Levels of conflict can be related to overall organizational performance. Too much conflict can be disruptive, creating chaos and damaging interpersonal relations. Too little conflict can also detract from performance. If conflict levels are too low innovation and change are less likely to take place. Each organization has an optimal level of conflict that can be extremely functional.

- Conflict is inevitable. Every group will sometime come into conflict with one or more other groups. There are numerous factors that contribute to intergroup conflict. Four particularly important ones are (1) the interdependent nature of the relationship between work groups; (2) differences between goals of organizational subunits;

(3) different perceptions of people, situations, and events; and (4) the increased demand for specialists which contributes to increasing the incidence of the three factors.

- Groups involved in dysfunctional conflict tend to react in fairly predictable ways. Some changes occur *within* the groups involved in conflict; others take place *between* the groups. Within group changes include increased cohesiveness, emphasis on group loyalty, a rise in autocratic leadership, and a focus on task-oriented activity. Between group changes include an increase in perceptual distortion, negative stereotyping of the other group, and decreased communications.

- A number of techniques exist for resolving intergroup conflict that has become dysfunctional. Among them are problem solving, creating superordinate goals, expanding available resources, avoidance, forcing (in which a third party mandates a resolution), smoothing (emphasizing the common interests of the conflicting parties), compromise, changing the behavior of conflicting parties, changing the structure of the organization, and attempting to identify a common enemy.

- Sometimes conflict levels are too low, and the objective becomes stimulating functional conflict between groups. Techniques available for stimulating conflict include intelligent use of communication channels, bringing outsiders into the group, altering the organization's structure, and creating competition between groups.

REVIEW AND DISCUSSION QUESTION

1. What are the differences between the traditional and contemporary perspectives on organizational conflict? What are the management implications of these two different perspectives?

2. What is the difference between functional and dysfunctional conflict? Can conflict which starts off as functional become dysfunctional? Can dysfunctional conflict be changed to functional?

3. Is there a relationship between the level of intergroup conflict and organizational performance? How can an organization achieve the optimal level of conflict?

4. What are some of the major reasons why intergroup conflict occurs? In your personal experience, what is the most frequent reason?

5. There are a number of possible consequences of dysfunctional conflict. What are these? Are some of these consequences more or less likely to occur in organizational conflict situations?

6. As organizations grow in size and complexity, interdependence increases, goal differences grow, and work and people become more specialized. Does this suggest conflict in organizations must increase? Does knowledge that these changes are occurring help us better prepare for them. How?

7. Identify and describe the three types of work interdependence discussed in the chapter. Which type is most likely to generate conflict? Which type is least likely to result in conflict?

8. When intergroup conflict occurs, changes take place both within and between the conflicting groups. What are these changes? Which changes generally are positive ones? Which are generally negative?

9. What are the major differences between resolution and stimulation in managing conflict? Could both be appropriate with the same groups at the same time? Explain.

10. How important are individual differences such as abilities, personality, and attitudes in causing or resolving conflict? Why is it important for a manager to be aware of these differences in dealing with conflict situations?

●

READING

READING 8-1   HOW TO DESIGN A CONFLICT MANAGEMENT PROCEDURE THAT FITS YOUR DISPUTE

Danny Ertel
Conflict Management, Inc.
Harvard Negotiation Project

In ancient Greece, a tale was told of a road-side inn where a traveler might find lodging for the night, and although the traveler might be tall, short, fat, or thin, the inn's bed fit all just the same. The innkeeper, of course, was Procrustes, a giant who tied travelers to the bedstead and either stretched them or chopped their legs to make them fit. Many business disputes seem to be approached this way today: no matter how diverse the parties, issues, or stakes, litigation is the answer. And even those managers or counsel who, unlike Procrustes' guests, perceive a choice among several available "beds"—litigation, arbitration, or even mini-trials—rarely make further attempts to tailor the dispute resolution process to the conflict at hand. Instead they allow the parties to be realigned, the issues reframed, or the stakes redefined.

Managers must deal with a broad range of conflicts, many of which involve parties external to the organization: valuable business partners, threatening competitors, or inquisitive regulators. But scorched-earth litigation followed by an on-the-courthouse-steps settlement is clearly not the answer to every dispute. Dealing with a competitor turned potential alliance partner whose third-level subsidiary may be infringing on a patent calls for a different approach than does responding to a "professional plaintiff" who has filed a frivolous shareholder derivative suit. Both of these may be different still from how one might want to manage the plausible antitrust claim of a disgruntled distributor.

Sensing the need for a better approach to process selection, both in-house and outside counsel have begun, with the help of academics and specialized professionals, to serve up a choice between traditional litigation and ADR—alternative dispute resolution. But that either-or choice is hardly confidence inspiring: expensive and disruptive litigation on the one hand, and an enigmatic acronym on the other.

Source: Reprinted from Danny Ertel, "How to Design a Conflict Management Procedure That Fits Your Dispute," *Sloan Management Review,* Summer 1991, pp. 29–42.

Those who do opt for ADR face another vexing choice: should we go into arbitration, mediation, or a mini-trial? The standard, if somewhat unfair, criticisms of each process are well known: "arbitrators split the baby in half"; "mediators never resolve really difficult cases"; "there is more 'trial' than 'mini' in mini-trials." At the other end of the spectrum, ADR partisans indiscriminately and somewhat disingenuously extol the virtues of all ADR processes as uniformly cheaper, faster, and more confidential than the litigation strawman. The choice among the two or three most commercially established ADR mechanisms often feels like the choice offered at a "new and improved" Procrustean Inn: not one, but three beds, accompanied by the familiar promise of "an exacting fit."

Of course, not every dispute requires a custom designed process any more than every ancient traveler required stretching or hacking. But misdirected attempts to fit the problem to the process exact high tolls in both human and economic terms: wasted time and money, damaged morale, lost opportunity, and unwanted publicity, to name a few. Effective dispute management requires more informed decision making, based on a careful analysis of the conflict and of the means available to resolve it. The manager responsible for the conflict, whether the disputant or a superior, should probably make these decisions and subsequently design and implement the appropriate process, with the advice and support of legal counsel. This essay, then, is directed at such individuals or teams—the conflict managers.

If no single dispute resolution process can effectively, fairly, and efficiently address all concerns raised by the rich universe of external business disputes, what the conflict managers need is a consistent analytical framework. Instead of refining questionnaires or checklists for choosing between litigation and ADR, and instead of sorting through the benefits and drawbacks of standard litigation alternatives, thoughtful managers should change the question. They should ask not **which** process should we use (suggesting a choice among discrete options), but how can we resolve **this** conflict? They should try to understand the

EXHIBIT 8-4

**Overview of
Methodology**

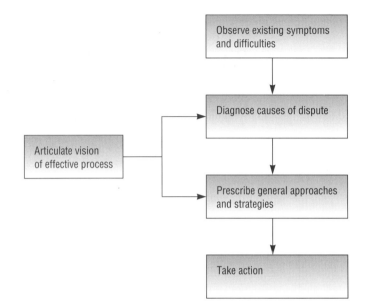

dispute and determine whether designing a more well-suited resolution process is cost effective. Borrowing problem-solving tools from engineering and medicine, conflict managers should attempt to understand what about the conflict has prevented its being quickly and effectively resolved. Only then will they be well equipped to make an informed decision about how to proceed, and if appropriate, to devise a process capable of resolving the conflict.

In this essay, I propose a methodology to allow managers and their counsel to consider systematically either particular conflicts or categories of disputes and then to devise, refine, and implement appropriate procedures for dealing with them.[1] The method, structured as a set of inquiries that the disputants may attempt to answer independently or jointly, starts by positing a standard against which one might measure success. It is a vision of what a good conflict resolution process should look like. The conflict managers can then consider existing difficulties or symptoms against the backdrop of that clear objective. Next they can then try to formulate a diagnosis based on their real-world understanding of business disputes and try to prescribe some general approaches or strategies. Finally, they can specify procedures and an implementation plan. At each step of the way, the conflict managers can rely on the articulated measure of success to instruct their analysis and evaluate their prescriptions. Exhibit 8-4 offers a schematic view of the process.[2]

This methodology should prove useful at different levels. Industry groups or professional associations, for example, might devise and publish model procedures for broad classes of disputes. Indeed, the Center for Public Resources, Inc., a New York-based coalition of general counsel, private practitioners, judges, and academics has adopted this methodology for designing alternatives to certain types of securities litigation. Parties entering a long-term business relationship such as a strategic alliance have used it to draft sophisticated dispute resolution protocols in anticipation of potential disputes. Ultimately, if disputants either lack or are dissatisfied with available model procedures, they can use this approach to negotiate an appropriate process.

ATTRIBUTES OF AN EFFECTIVE CONFLICT MANAGEMENT PROCESS

Mechanisms for resolving conflict always incorporate some implicit tradeoffs, such as between accuracy and cost, creativity and enforceability, speed and thoroughness. Different conflicts, parties, and relationships require different choices. For example, a disagreement among joint venture partners may call for a highly confidential, forward-looking process that focuses primarily on preventing similar incidents in the future, whereas a dispute with product end users might require litigation to finality, so as to establish a firm precedent. Establishing consensus among disputants early on with respect to the attributes of a good process will facilitate discussion of the design.

I propose the following interest-oriented process for managing business disputes, based in part on the body of theory being developed at the Harvard Negotiation Project.[3] This seven-element framework is a set of categories for organizing information and ideas about process and for analyzing the tradeoffs between competing priorities. It should help conflict managers diagnose the current process and prescribe a fresh approach. The sidebar summarizes the attributes.

CLARIFIES INTERESTS

An effective dispute resolution process should help the parties understand their own and each other's interests. Without understanding the basic wants, needs, or fears motivating the dispute, the parties will find it difficult to obtain anything but zero-sum, purely distributive results. A process that focuses on the parties' stated positions or demands will inevitably leave the parties feeling somewhat dissatisfied with both the process and the outcome. A bluffing contest, however entertaining it may be for buying a used car, cannot be the best way to resolve complex, multi-issue disputes.

While positions may be in conflict, underlying interests need not be. There may be room for dovetailing those interests in such a way that both parties can gain, or at least find themselves distributing a great deal more value than they initially thought was at stake. For example, an engineer who has developed an innovative stamping tool was preparing to retire. He demanded a 3 percent royalty from his former employer for its use. The company, after carefully analyzing the value added to the production process by the tool, and on the advice of its accountants and investment bankers, extended a firm offer of 1.5 percent. After months of haggling, they were no closer.

With some work, a facilitator learned that the engineer has sought 3 percent as a means of insuring himself should he be held personally liable for a young shop worker sustaining injuries from the high-speed stamping tool. After further discussions, the facilitator discovered that the company could bring the engineer under its corporate liability policy, at nominal cost to the company. The company had never offered to do so because it did not understand the interest underlying the engineer's bargaining position. The engineer, upon learning that his retirement could be pro-

tected against the unlikely but catastrophic event, was quite satisfied to accept a royalty of around 1 percent.

While most experienced negotiators intuitively recognize the difference between their stated position and their underlying interests, they are often reluctant to disclose their real interests for fear of exposing themselves to extortion. An effective resolution process should allow the parties to share this kind of information without unduly subjecting themselves to such a risk. Absent such a process, the parties may fail to uncover a range of possible agreements that would satisfy their interests without the need to compromise between initial positions.

BUILDS A GOOD WORKING RELATIONSHIP

The parties to a conflict have some sort of relationship, if only for the purposes of the dispute. And whatever that relationship is, it could probably be better. A good working relationship should enable them to deal effectively and efficiently with the disagreements, large and small, that inevitably arise in any complex interaction between institutions.

A well-designed dispute resolution process should serve two relationship functions. First, it should fill in where the working relationship is breaking down, facilitating the parties' ability to resolve the problem on its merits, as they might have been able to do but for the current breakdown. That might mean, for example, that the process would include mechanisms that temporarily replace the parties' need to trust each other by guaranteeing performance in some easily enforceable manner, or that it would specify use of a third party to help set aside personality issues.

Second, an effective process should also help the parties work purposely toward the kind of relationship they want to have. It may be that the parties want to have no relationship at all and the process should facilitate closure. But if they want a long-term, cooperative relationship in which each feels consulted and accepted, they should probably not follow a purely retrospective process designed to allocate blame.

Both relationship functions add up to the same thing: the process should leave the parties at least slightly better able to deal with each other next time, whenever that happens to be. That need not mean the corporate equivalent of a long-term love affair, but parties who would find it mutually beneficial to work together should not be prevented from doing so because their dispute resolution process has made it even harder for them to speak to each other.

GENERATES GOOD OPTIONS

Most managers would prefer to choose the best course of action from among several options than from a list of one. The more options on the table (within limits, of course), the greater the likelihood of discovering a productive path. What may seem like a foolish or risky approach at first glance may, after reconsideration and refinement by others, develop into a mutually profitable one. An effective dispute resolution process should spur the parties, perhaps with external support or advice, to generate a list of such options before evaluating and choosing among them.

To the extent possible, the process should also orient the parties toward designing options that create value, rather than merely distribute it. By making mutual gain the ex-

pressed goal, the options generated are likely to be more creative and value generating.

IS PERCEIVED AS LEGITIMATE

Costly and inefficient as it may be, litigation does incorporate certain norms and rules that society believes are essential to the social order. For example, some liability standards and burdens of proof have been tilted in favor of one party or the other in support of legislative policy goals. For an "alternate" process to succeed, the parties must believe it will produce a good solution without requiring them to give up substantial rights they would have had in litigation. An alternate process that seemed to shift

---

Attributes of an Effective Conflict Resolution Process

1. **Clarifies Interests**
   - by encouraging the parties to explore the interests underlying their respective bargaining positions
   - by facilitating the exploration of common and nonconflicting interests
   - by communicating each party's interests to the other without unduly exposing anyone to extortion on the basis of such interests

2. **Builds a Good Working Relationship**
   - by enabling the parties to deal effectively with their differences in the current dispute
   - by fostering the type of relationship the parties would have wanted to have but for the present dispute
   - by making it easier for the parties to deal with each other next time

3. **Generates Good Options**
   - by spurring the parties to brainstorm many options before evaluating them and choosing among them
   - by encouraging the parties to devise ways to create value for mutual gain

4. **Is Perceived as Legitimate**
   - by not being seen to cause the parties to forfeit legal or other rights disproportionately (i.e., the process should not be seen as itself tilting the balance of power)
   - by not being perceived as contrary to the public interest
   - by instilling in the parties a sense that the solutions it produces will be fair and equitable

5. **Is Cognizant of the Parties' Procedural Alternatives**
   - by allowing both sides to develop realistic assessments of their own and the other side's procedural and substantive alternatives
   - by being more attractive to the parties along whatever axis is most important to them (e.g., costs, time, degree of disclosure, nature of outcomes, and quality of compliance)

6. **Improves Communication**
   - by encouraging the questioning and testing of underlying assumptions
   - by facilitating the understanding and discussion of partisan perceptions
   - by establishing effective two-way communication between decision makers

7. **Leads to Wise Commitments**
   - by enabling the parties to devise commitments that are realistic, operational, and compliance-prone
   - by positioning the parties with efficient recourse to litigation in the event they fail to reach agreement or in the event of non-compliance

the balance of power dramatically would most likely meet resistance from at least one party—including possibly their refusal to participate in the process, or failure to comply fully with any result. Similarly, an alternate process that negated advantages conferred by the legislature on certain classes of parties might well come under powerful criticism as being contrary to the public interest.[4]

No one likes being taken advantage of. A desirable dispute resolution process should instill in the parties a sense that the solution is fair and equitable and was arrived at in a principled fashion. If the new process requires voluntary participation by the disputants, neither the procedures nor the solutions they produce may be perceived as partisan or arbitrary.

IS COGNIZANT OF THE PARTIES' PROCEDURAL ALTERNATIVES

Notwithstanding prior commitments to arbitration, mediation, or some other process, few conflicts arise that cannot at some point and in some form lead to litigation. Given that state of affairs, a good process permits the parties to assess realistically their own and their counterpart's litigation alternative. In order to be effective, the process must appear, along whatever axis the parties consider most important, to be preferable to litigation. If cost is of principal concern, the new process should be less expensive than litigation; if confidentiality is at issue, it should afford the parties greater control over disclosure; if a long-term relationship is at stake, then perhaps the process should produce forward-looking solutions rather than allocate blame. Ultimately what this means is that the process should generate solutions that are more efficient and satisfying for each side than what they expect litigation could produce. For instance, in a consent-based process the parties might well agree to take more constructive steps than anything a court could order them to do.

IMPROVES COMMUNICATION

Many a dispute escalates because one side misunderstands what the other has said or done. If such misunderstandings are common enough among trusted business partners, they are legion among adversaries and especially their zealous advocates. In the middle of litigation, a simple request for information can be perceived as an attempt to blackmail or coerce, an innocent joke can be taken as an insult, and an attempt to reschedule a meeting as an example of bad

faith. Why do we inevitably see the others' actions in the worst possible light and expect them to give us the benefit of the doubt? Part of the reason is that we all operate on the basis of many unstated assumptions. One common assumption about adversaries is that they want what we want and that if something is good for them, it must be bad for us. Regardless of whether those assumptions have merit in any given case, acting on them without articulating and testing them is simply unwise. A good dispute resolution process should help the parties articulate and examine their assumptions before they act on them.

Similarly, a great many of us tend to see the facts in the way most favorable to our own side. Once we make up our mind about something, we tend systematically to filter out inconsistent data and to gather as much supporting evidence as possible. It is an inclination well worth resisting, and a good dispute resolution process should facilitate a discussion of those partisan perceptions and how they might be biasing each side's assessment of the situation. One partner in a large national law firm periodically instructs his young associates to begin research on a particular side of a case without telling them they have actually been engaged to represent the opposite side. When they report back to him with their preliminary research (which is usually quite favorable), he tells them, "Remember this well, because this is how strong our opponents think their case is; now prepare our case in response."

Understanding someone's concerns need not make us agree with them; it should, however, help us persuade them that they do not have to meet their needs at our expense. Good communication between decision makers is essential to effective conflict management. If an executive cannot make herself understood, how can she influence anyone? And if she does not understand her counterpart, how can she craft a persuasive proposition? A good process for resolving disputes should establish and maintain effective communication channels.

LEADS TO WISE COMMITMENTS

A good process should enable the disputants to craft wise commitments after they have carefully considered all the relevant information and a number of possible options, and after they have determined that their alternatives away from the table are not as good as what they can obtain through a negotiated agreement. Only then will they be able to craft a commitment that is realistic, operational, and compliance-prone. To minimize the risk that one party will use the process as an expensive dilatory tactic, an

EXHIBIT 8-5

Designing the Process

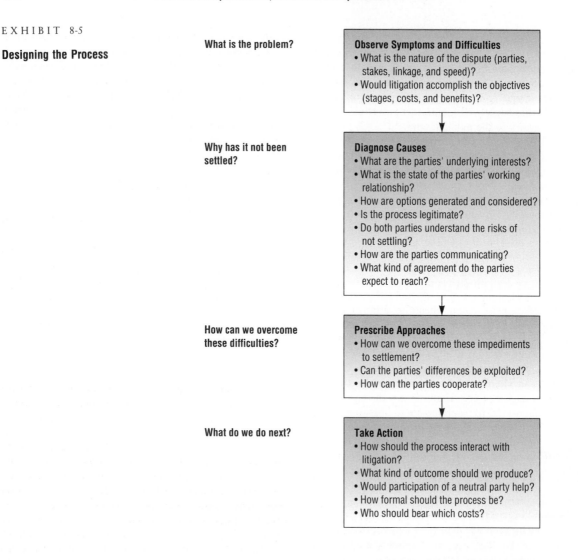

What is the problem?

Observe Symptoms and Difficulties
- What is the nature of the dispute (parties, stakes, linkage, and speed)?
- Would litigation accomplish the objectives (stages, costs, and benefits)?

Why has it not been settled?

Diagnose Causes
- What are the parties' underlying interests?
- What is the state of the parties' working relationship?
- How are options generated and considered?
- Is the process legitimate?
- Do both parties understand the risks of not settling?
- How are the parties communicating?
- What kind of agreement do the parties expect to reach?

How can we overcome these difficulties?

Prescribe Approaches
- How can we overcome these impediments to settlement?
- Can the parties' differences be exploited?
- How can the parties cooperate?

What do we do next?

Take Action
- How should the process interact with litigation?
- What kind of outcome should we produce?
- Would participation of a neutral party help?
- How formal should the process be?
- Who should bear which costs?

effective process should also position the disputants with efficient recourse to litigation or some other self-help alternative in the event they fail to reach agreement or one party fails to comply with its obligations.

Having identified the attributes of the dispute resolution procedure, the conflict manager can begin examining the problem at hand—whether it is an ongoing or an anticipated dispute or class of disputes—and to craft procedures for dealing with it. The design process should be structured and systematic: observe the existing difficulties or symptoms, diagnose their possible causes, and then prescribe general approaches to dealing with them. Finally, make an

informed decision about what specific actions to pursue. Exhibit 8-5 illustrates this methodology.

OBSERVE SYMPTOMS AND DIFFICULTIES

Before a doctor attempts a diagnosis, she gathers information. She asks the patient to describe his symptoms, to explain in some detail what has brought him into her office in search of a remedy. Good managers, before launching into conflict resolution, should try to understand the conflict as well as possible. Before they can put something right, they must identify what is wrong; in doing so, they should consider both the nature of the dispute and the traditional means of resolving it.

Although categorizing complex business conflicts is no easier than describing everything that can be physically or psychologically wrong with a human being, conflicts do have some characteristics in common that may instruct the resolution design. The methodology described here poses a series of inquiries concerning the parties and the issues. No single answer to a question will determine conclusively the "best" process to follow; each response will, however, help to identify concerns that should somehow be acknowledged.

THE NATURE OF THE DISPUTE

The questions that follow are designed to help conflict managers gather and structure information.[5] They should also challenge conflict managers to question their assumptions about their own interests, the other side's intentions, the likely perceptions of third parties, and so forth.

Parties

How many parties are there? Are they individuals or institutions? How sophisticated (financially and legally) are they? Is either party a "repeat player" with respect to this type of conflict, or is this likely to be a one-shot experience for both?

By knowing something about the number and relative sophistication and experience of the disputants, the conflict manager can better design a process that addresses each of their interests. Large institutional entities with experienced in-house or outside counsel, for example, may be less likely to require a process that provides education and reality testing than would individuals who have never litigated previously or who may be ill equipped to evaluate complex settlement proposals.

Stakes

Do the parties agree about what is at stake? Is this a dispute over money? If so, is the conflict over a fixed sum, or will a subjective determination of the amount be required? Is this a dispute about assigning blame for past conduct, or is the primary goal to define permissible future conduct? Is publicity a major concern for either party? Does this dispute primarily concern the relative competitive posture of the parties? Is this merely "strategic" litigation, with no substantive goal other than to delay or distract?

Understanding what is at stake requires more than reading the prayer for relief in a civil complaint. Without developing a clear sense of the disputants' underlying interests, it will be difficult, if not impossible, to design a procedure that allows each to feel confident that his or her interests can and will be addressed.

Linkage

How is the resolution of this conflict tied to other pending or contemplated disputes between the parties or with others? What collateral consequences will either adjudication or settlement have for one or both parties?

The collateral consequences, whether real or imagined, of resolving a particular dispute are often at least as important as the issue at hand. In designing a procedure, care must be taken to consider whether one or both parties would want the results exported to other disputes, or whether confidentiality of the outcome and avoidance of setting a precedent is the key to resolving the conflict.

Speed

Is speedy resolution important to either party? Would either benefit from delay? Why? Is it simply a matter of the stakeholder enjoying the time value of the money or are other factors at play?

Speed is often one of the first items on the list of ADR advantages. But is it always a good thing? Although overcrowded dockets generally cause some of the delay associated with litigation, litigants are themselves responsible for substantial delay. Conflict managers must consider the relevance of the passing of time to one or both disputants, whether to allow tempers to cool, fiscal years or reporting periods to close, or key personnel to turn over. These can be as important, in some cases, as the time value of money or the urge to bring unpleasant situations to a prompt conclusion.

THE LITIGATION PATH

Conflict managers must generally face the reality that litigation is readily available to the disputants. In order to craft a better process for managing a particular dispute or class of disputes, they should become familiar with the traditional litigation process and learn from litigation's flaws and virtues.

Stages

What are the various stages through which the litigation must go? What is the intended purpose of each? In practice, what happens at each stage? How much time typically passes between each phase? At what points are these suits typically settled, if at all?

Dispute resolution procedures need not be wholly divorced from litigation, nor need they be a complete substitute. The judicial process offers the most effective means of dealing with some issues. Alternative procedures may actually complement litigation, for example, by streamlining discovery and reducing the number of disputed questions of law or fact. By developing an understanding of the various stages of the traditional litigation path, parties can better design a process tailored to their needs.

Costs and Benefits

How expensive is litigation in expended fees and lost productivity? How are expenses incurred over the dispute's life (front-weighted, evenly distributed, end-weighted)? Are the costs evenly borne by the parties? Aside from the actual court award, what other benefits does either party expect from litigation (public vindication, blame shifting, fulfilling fiduciary duty in attempting to recover funds)? Do the costs have proportional impact or significance to the parties?

Litigation, like any other product or service a manager buys, delivers some value. It may produce a favorable outcome, but even it if does not, it at least provides some finality and generally delivers a credible and legitimate result. At a minimum it often succeeds in shifting responsibility for the outcome from the line executive to the legal department. The key question, however, is at what cost does it accomplish these objectives? Is this a product worth buying, or could the same interests be met for less? The decision to litigate is a business decision. A manager charged with that decision must consider the alternatives and compare how litigation fares with other means of meeting personal and institutional interests.

DIAGNOSE CAUSES

Depending on how one defines ADR, the term may well encompass ordinary negotiation between the parties in the course of preparing to litigate. In that sense, there is nothing new, different, or unusual about it—90 percent to 95 percent of all civil lawsuits are settled. The key to designing a procedure that will help disputants make better decisions

about whether and how to settle, and to generate more attractive choices in the majority of cases, is to focus on what has kept the parties from resolving their conflict until now. Having developed a picture of the conflict, the conflict manager should now ask, "Why haven't the parties settled yet?"

The range of possible answers to this question is very broad. Any given conflict will generally have multiple barriers to settlement. One or more impediments to resolution may leap out as obvious; others may be more subtle, yet nonetheless significant. The framework for an effective process may serve as an analytical guide to sort through and organize these diagnoses. By comparing the current process with the target process, the conflict manager can generate ideas for remedying the deficiencies.

Interests versus Positions

Have negotiations to date focused on demands and concessions? Are the parties being forthcoming about their underlying interests? If pressed, could each party answer the following questions in a manner to which the other would agree: "What do your counterparts really hope to accomplish in this dispute?" and "For what purpose?"

One exceedingly common cause of breakdowns in negotiations is that both parties get locked into extreme positions from which neither can easily make concessions. One telltale sign is a pattern of negotiating along single, highly quantifiable variables, such as money. A process that encourages such negotiation exacerbates the zero-sum mentality that generally accompanies bitter disputes. For example, as long as the engineer and the manufacturing company were locked into a positional haggle over the royalty percentage, they could make no progress without one side or the other feeling that it had backed down.

Relationship Problems

What relationship did the parties have prior to the dispute? Are they likely to have future dealings? Has one party threatened to terminate the business relationship unless the other gives in?

Another possible cause for the negotiation breakdown could be the parties' working relationship. All too often, personality problems keep the parties from discussing the problem's merits. Sometimes personal trust has broken down so far that the parties cannot even agree to disagree, for fear that the other is trying to pull a fast one. In diagnosing why the dispute has not yet been resolved, it

might be useful to know whether the real problem has become the people involved.

Limited Generation of Options

Who has introduced the options that have been considered so far? Does one party typically take the lead in presenting proposals, or do the parties share the burden? Are the parties reluctant to put the first offer on the table? Do time constraints operate differently on them? Do cost constraints affect the settlement (e.g., might it be easier to settle a suit in a particular fiscal year or under another project's budget)?

Another consequence of negotiation on the basis of positions rather than interests is a relative poverty of good options to choose from. If the negotiators perceive their preparation as girding themselves for battle, and their proposals as starting positions to be defended but eventually modified, they will more likely than not craft proposals that are highly favorable to their own side, expecting to make some concessions later. As both sides do this, blithely ignoring their counterpart's interests and constraints as "their problem," no one is devoting any energy to inventing mutually advantageous options that might bring added value to the table.

Fear of Arbitrary, Illegitimate Outcomes

Do the negotiators have critical constituencies to which they must report their handling of the dispute? Do those constituents expect their agents to follow certain rituals? Are there readily available standards, within the industry or otherwise, that cover how disputes such as this one are settled?

One reason a party refuses to settle a dispute may have more to do with the dispute resolution process than with the settlement's content. If the process feels arbitrary or coercive, the party may devalue an outcome that it might otherwise have accepted. In baseball, for example, players and owners both accept an arbitrator's award that coincides with their counterpart's final offer more readily than they do if that same salary figure is proposed by the other side in a blustering "take it or leave it" fashion. Similarly, a party may reject an attractive offer if the terms seem unrelated to any external standards or somehow conjured up out of thin air. Without some supporting rationale, the party might well wonder whether through more strategic negotiating it could do better. A party's inability to explain the logic of a particular settlement to its constituents may well stand in the way of a profitable resolution.

Overestimation of the Litigation Alternative

Do the negotiators have access to an objective assessment of the dispute, whether internally or outside their institution? Have they done any systematic analysis of the litigation risk? How carefully have they thought through the nonmonetary consequences of not settling?

Sometimes the principal impediment to settlement stems from one or both parties' limited understanding of their procedural alternatives. A failure to grasp the true costs and benefits of litigation can keep one or both parties from settling a case that should never have been litigated. An interesting example arose in an intellectual property dispute. Two parties that shared a profitable market sued and countersued each other over a number of aggressive trade practices, challenging the validity of one's right to exclude the other from certain market segments or from certain applications of the intellectual property. Only after careful analysis did they realize that if **either** prevailed in court on its principal theories, they would open the market to a host of new competitors, to the detriment of both. Without that understanding, however, there had been little room for settlement: each viewed its chances of prevailing at trial optimistically enough that no settlement offer or counteroffer that either could reasonably propose was likely to be acceptable to the other.

Poor Communication

What channels do the decision makers use to communicate? Do they always go through lawyers or other agents or do they sometimes communicate directly? How does each party perceive the other's motives? Do the parties disagree on the facts or on the inferences to be drawn therefrom?

If the parties have very different pictures of the conflict and consequently have drawn very different conclusions as to how to resolve it, it may be impossible for them to reach an agreement. A debtor and a creditor may look at the distribution of proceeds from asset liquidation in the same way the pessimist and the optimist observe the proverbial glass of water: one perceives the glass as half empty, posing the problem of how to refill it, while the other perceives it as half full, presenting an opportunity to distribute its contents between the parties.

Differing perceptions may be formed a number of ways—an individual's psychological makeup or a career of working on an emotionally charged issue. Or perhaps each side has access to only part of the information necessary to understand the situation and its context. Depending on the primary reasons for the differing perceptions, the conflict managers might devise procedures for gathering information, testing the objectivity of the parties' perceptions, or facilitating their discussion of such perceptions. To get past the unproductive clash of perceptions, each party must be helped to understand how the other sees it, without feeling that to understand that perspective means it has also to agree with it.

Unclear Commitments

Assuming some agreement could be reached, would it require a one-time act, such as a cash payment, or would compliance involve an ongoing commitment to a more complicated program? What issues must a settlement address? Who would have to cooperate in order to make the agreement operational?

If the parties have not considered or discussed with each other what the outline of an agreement would look like, they may develop very different ideas. The more different these images are, the more difficult it will be for them to arrive at a workable resolution. If one views the problem as an imminently bursting dam in need of an immediate stop-gap solution, while the other thinks the dispute is really about the long-term management of a complex navigation and irrigation system, they will be working toward radically different objectives and each will have a tough time understanding the other. Unless the process can help them clarify the nature and scope of the final commitment, they will probably escalate the conflict in an effort to impose a solution. The international diplomacy analogue makes the front pages all too often: in most armed conflicts, the opponents eventually talk about whether and how to cease hostilities. Unless those operational terms are clearly understood by both sides, one side may find its efforts to work toward an interim cease fire frustrated by the other's perception of the demand as a permanent cessation and full demobilization. Consequently, both sides increase combat, to "remind" the other side of how bad things can be in the absence of an agreement.

PRESCRIBE APPROACHES

Now the conflict managers are better prepared to devise a process that can overcome, or at least mitigate, the effect of the impediments described above. They can systematically review their particular diagnoses and devise general approaches to build a process that approximates their view of effective dispute resolution. A few illustrations should help capture the flavor of the task.

Overcome Impediments

If the parties are locked into a positional bargaining battle in which substantial concessions seem unlikely, mechanisms to clarify their interests, as distinguished from their positions, may be of value. The classic object of single-variable positional bargaining is money, but underlying a demand for a particular sum are usually other interests that could perhaps be satisfied some other way. An outside facilitator may be able to solicit this kind of information confidentially. When a highly leveraged entrepreneur was attempting to sell one of his magazine properties, his bottom-line asking price was $400,000. No amount of haggling could get him to move, even though no buyer had offered more than $325,000, and independent appraisals had estimated the property's fair market value as somewhere between $280,000 and $325,000. Only after extensive prodding by an outside facilitator did he admit that his problem was not that he needed $400,000, or that he thought the magazine was worth that much. Rather, he felt constrained by a financing clause that treated any write down of more than $100,000 on any asset as a condition of default. Since all of his financing had cross-default provisions, he could not possibly accept less than $400,000 for a property he had initially purchased at $500,000. Once they understood that, the parties, in consultation with their lawyers and accountants, devised a creative financing scheme that would not trigger a default, but that nonetheless represented real cost to the purchasers of about $310,000.

If both sides are much too willing to take their chances in court, a helpful prescription might afford them a confidential way to develop a realistic assessment of their litigation prospects. The decision-tree and risk-analysis tools long familiar to business decision makers are now being used with some success in analyzing litigation decisions.[6] Such an analysis, carried out independently and confidentially for each side by an outside expert, might inject a useful dose of reality into the process.

If partisan perceptions arising from a disparity in the parties' experience and access to information are impeding communication, the conflict managers may want to devise an information-sharing process that enables one party to "catch up." If neither party has sufficient information, perhaps a joint or neutral fact-finding process would help. If one side is concerned that the terms of an agreement will be disclosed, the conflict managers might incorporate into the process some means of managing the flow of information about the agreement.

Sometimes, the greatest impediment to settling a dispute comes from the way in which the conflict has been framed, which in turn constrains the types of options the parties consider. To the extent that the parties view the problem as principally involving the distribution of something—money, liability, kudos, or blame—they will conclude that more for one necessarily means less for the other and will proceed to address the problem on that basis. While it is not always possible to settle a dispute by "enlarging the pie," experience teaches that truly adversarial disputants can always produce a result that leaves less for both, a "negative sum." Some conflicts, because of the parties' needs and resource constraints, may never be settled unless someone attempts to generate mutual gains. The small trade magazine that grievously but wholly unintentionally libels the fast-rising entrepreneur may simply not have the ability to make him whole through cash compensation. If he insists on a lump sum payment equivalent to what he might expect to be awarded in court, he may well end up with an unenforceable judgment against a bankrupt company. But a cover story on his visionary leadership in an emerging industry might net him valuable exposure and the publisher an interesting article, made richer and more credible by the subject's full cooperation.

One of the conflict managers' goals, and potentially their greatest contribution, is identifying opportunities for turning the dispute into a positive-sum game. By orienting the parties toward joint problem solving instead of adversarial posturing, and by facilitating communication and information exchange, a well-designed process can help the parties resolve their dispute more profitably for both sides. Two rich sources of value-enhancing potential are the parties' differences and their ability to cooperate.[7]

Exploit Differences

Do the parties place different values on possible outcomes or on different goods and services? Do they face different tax or other incentives? Do they have different concerns about publicity? Do the parties have different expectations about contingent events, different attitudes toward risk? Do they have different preferences about the resolution's timing or the performance of the settlement?

One school of thought suggests that the best way to resolve a dispute is to minimize the parties' differences. The more alike the two disputants seem, the more likely they are to reach some accommodation. While that may

sometimes be true, it is not always possible to accomplish. Some parties may just have too diverse a set of interests and expectations to be homogenized. Besides, many differences are valuable and worth preserving. Many a business alliance is struck not because the parties are similar, but precisely because the parties have different strengths or perspectives that they believe make a good fit. A good process for managing conflict should facilitate the way the parties deal with their differences rather than paper over them.

Facilitate Cooperation

Is cooperation between the parties a desirable and efficient manner of resolving the problem? Are economies of scale possible? Do the parties have shared interests in some substantive outcome, public good, or public perception of their handling of the dispute? Can one side take steps to benefit the other significantly at minimal cost to itself?

Cooperation with the enemy is usually the last thing disputants consider. Yet it is precisely because that whole class of solutions is so often overlooked that it should be systematically considered in almost every dispute. Sometimes the best way to resolve a problem about past performance is jointly to devise a better mechanism for encouraging, facilitating, and monitoring future performance. Perhaps the prior OEM agreement was not fulfilled because it would have worked better as a full-fledged joint venture. In most business conflicts, there is usually some way that one side could confer substantial value on the other at comparatively low cost, if only in business referrals or good public relations, or more tangibly in at-cost supply contracts or third-party guarantees. The failure to systematically consider those options costs money.

In many business conflicts there are also activities that both sides would agree constitute a good use of resources and from which both would derive at least indirect benefit; they should consider committing part of what is at stake in the conflict to some such mutually beneficial activity instead of squandering more resources in fighting over how to allocate the nominal stakes between them.

TAKE ACTION

The analysis thus far has proceeded through the classic problem-solving stages. The first step defined a desired outcome—an effective process for managing business disputes. Second, the conflict managers were encouraged to make observations of the conflict, as yet unresolved by traditional means. The third step encouraged them to diagnose the causes for the parties' failure to settle the case thus far. Fourth, based on these diagnoses, they were to prescribe some general approaches for dealing with the identified problems. Now is the time to take action. What should the conflict managers do next? How do they go from scratchpad to an action plan for resolving this conflict?

Making Process Choices

Designing a custom dispute resolution process requires making some specific decisions about types of mechanisms to use and how they might fit together. These decisions will vary significantly from one case to another.

The Interaction with Litigation

If the process replaces traditional litigation, should it aim primarily at facilitating settlement, or would some sort of partial or streamlined adjudication be preferable? How should the alternative procedures interact with the traditional litigation track? Should litigation be temporarily stayed? Should judicial approval of the alternative procedures be sought in advance?

Sometimes the only way to apply sufficient pressure on the parties to reach a productive settlement is to keep litigation going full steam ahead while someone else tries to settle the case on a "second track." Indeed, this is one way to make the parties more comfortable with trying a new approach; they don't have to surrender any perceived advantage in court. Although such an approach does seem to require committing additional resources to the conflict, it may still pay off handsomely in the efficiency and quality of the outcome. If the "second track" succeeds, the savings from early termination of the "litigation track" alone will easily outweigh the additional expenditures.[8] Other times, in order for an innovative dispute resolution procedure to have a real chance of success, the parties must agree to a temporary cease-fire on the legal battlefield, to enable the negotiators to explore a problem-solving approach and exchange information safely.

Expected Product

Should the outcome be binding on the parties, or merely advisory? What will be gained or lost in the flexibility of the process, the seriousness with which parties participate, or their willingness to accept the process at all?

The procedures should help the parties craft a solution that meets their interests, feels legitimate, and is preferable to their best alternative away from the table. Such procedures need not impose an outcome on any party; indeed, by definition any such solution will enjoy the support and consent of every party. Yet some nonbinding procedures may lend themselves to bad faith manipulation and may be used solely for delay and intelligence-gathering. For such situations, dispute resolution procedures can be designed to generate a resolution to which all parties will be bound, even if none would have advocated it.

Participation by a Neutral

Would a neutral party be of some help? In what capacity? Should a neutral facilitate communication between the parties, evaluate their positions, generate settlement proposals, or ascertain facts? Each of these involves different degrees of intrusion into the process by a stranger to the conflict.

The intervention of a neutral is often charged with tension and anxiety. Some will worry about how the neutral will perceive them and their position and will seek the neutral's approval. Some will worry that outsiders will see the use of a neutral as an admission that they cannot solve their own problems; they will either try to conceal the request for intervention or show public disdain for the neutral's efforts. Often such public posturing becomes a self-fulfilling prophecy and the neutral, stripped of credibility and trust, cannot help but fail. Before seeking intervention, try to visualize the neutral's role. What procedural deficiencies might the neutral address? Is there some other way of addressing them effectively?

Many of the tasks neutrals undertake actually require only someone who does not have a vested interest in the resolution of the conflict, rather than a wholly nonpartisan stranger. In many contexts it is possible and desirable to overcome barriers to settlement by using "internal neutrals," that is, individuals within one or both organizations who are not directly involved in the dispute and whose primary interest is in helping manage the conflict. So-called "wise men" procedures, whereby senior executives within two organizations are designated as process resources to help jointly resolve, for example, a dispute between line managers, are worth considering for any complex, long-term business relationship.

Formality

How formal or informal a process seems best suited to the parties and the dispute? Should rules be specified concerning the stages of the process or their timing? What rules of discovery, if any, should be incorporated? How should the presentation of evidence and testimony (whether to each other or to a neutral) proceed? Should there be avenues of review?

At the risk of turning the design process into a legislative drafting exercise, it is important that the conflict managers think carefully through the operational aspects of the process and the consultative and verification mechanisms that will be necessary to resolve the inevitable procedural disputes. Not only must they think about what process would best help the parties resolve their substantive conflict, but they must consider how to deal with disputes about the process itself. During the discovery phase of traditional litigation, for example, counsel are expected to work out their differences, but if they are unable to do so, they may seek a ruling from the judge, magistrate, or special master presiding over that aspect of the case. While that is not to say that one should adopt an adversarial litigious process to resolve disputes about the process, it does mean that these mechanisms require careful attention, and that the participation of legal counsel may be especially useful.

Costs

Who should bear the cost of a failure to reach agreement under the new process? In the event the parties reach an agreement, how should costs be allocated among them?

Much has been written about the importance of cost incentives in dispute resolution, both for counsel and their clients.[9] The parties can decide whether they will cover their own costs or allocate costs some other way. Although there may not be an easily identifiable winner in the sense there is in litigation, it may be worth considering whether those responsible for making the parties incur additional costs should bear them. Some dispute resolution mechanisms in litigation, for example, place the burden on the party declining a good faith settlement offer to "do better" by forcing them to bear the risk (in the form of a redistribution of litigation costs) of failing to do so.

Getting Started

As noted earlier, the method described in this essay can be applied by professional organizations to draft model procedures for classes of disputes, or by parties to a business venture who want to draft dispute resolution protocols for future conflicts between them, or by a manager facing a problem that has not been resolved earlier in the

process. Whichever the case, conflict managers should make use of as much information as is available.

Although once a conflict arises it may be more difficult to establish the kind of joint problem-solving relationship that might have been available earlier, more facts may be known at that time, and these should permit the parties to devise a process better suited to the specific dispute than to a hypothetical conflict. Mutual consent will generally be required to undertake anything but traditional litigation. The parties will have to negotiate procedures and details, and such negotiations may provide an opportunity for the parties to begin to cooperate.

The analysis described here should enable managers facing an escalating conflict to do several things: first, they should be able to decide whether it is worthwhile to structure a custom dispute resolution process and to discuss the option clearly and systematically with legal counsel; second, even if the conflict managers choose not to negotiate about the process, by having diagnosed the existing problem they should be better prepared to think about how to settle it on the merits; and third, if they decide to approach their counterparts to discuss the possibility of a better process, they will be prepared for negotiating over it.

To initiate such negotiation, managers might try to schedule a meeting with their counterparts to explore conflict management procedures, making it clear that the substance of the dispute is not on the agenda for that meeting. Accompanying the invitation to such a meeting might be a draft of what an effective process should be able to accomplish (rather than what it should look like), along the lines of the attributes described in the sidebar, and an invitation to revise the draft. A list of attributes of a good dispute resolution process is sufficiently removed from the substance of the conflict that the managers may well be able to approach the problem of designing appropriate procedures much the way they might handle a less adversarial problem-solving session: whatever their respective views of the dispute itself, they have a shared interest in using a process that is tailored to the problem, and that might be less painful than letting Procrustes help them into one of those "one size fits all" beds.

REFERENCES

1. Based on their experience with labor-management disputes in the coal industry, Ury and Goldberg have come up with a useful and somewhat different checklist of steps that should be included in systems for managing recurring conflicts within an

organization. See: W. Ury, J. Brett, and S. Goldberg, *Getting Disputes Resolved* (San Francisco: Jossey-Bass, 1988).

2. This diagnostic approach to designing a dispute resolution process is based in part on the Circle Chart described in: R. Fisher and W. Ury, *Getting to Yes* (Boston: Houghton Mifflin, 1981), pp. 68–71.

3. The seven elements of the framework have been described in different forms in a variety of published and unpublished papers. The use of this framework for designing alternatives to litigation is, to my knowledge, original to this essay. For a brief definition, see: R. Fisher, "Negotiating Inside Out," *Negotiation Journal 5* (1989), pp. 33–41.

4. O. M. Fiss, "Against Settlement," *Yale Law Journal 93* (1984), pp. 1073–1090.

5. These inquiries have evolved from a related set of considerations outlined in S. Goldberg, E. Green, and F. Sander, *Dispute Resolution* (Boston: Little, Brown & Co., 1985), pp. 545–48; H. Raiffa, *The Art and Science of Negotiation* (Cambridge, Massachusetts: Belknap Press, 1982), pp. 14–19; and other works that attempt to identify the "ADR potential" of a dispute or to produce a classification scheme for disputes.

6. Raiffa (1982); M. Raker, " The Application of Decision Analysis and Computer Modeling to the Settlement of Complex Litigation" (Cambridge, Massachusetts: ILP Symposium, MIT, 1987).

7. D. Lax and J. Sebenius, *The Manager as Negotiator* (New York: The Free Press, 1986), pp. 88–116.

8. R. Fisher, "He Who Pays the Piper," *Harvard Business Review,* March-April 1985, pp. 150–59; P. Mode and D. Siemer, "The Litigation Partner and the Settlement Partner," *Litigation,* Summer 1986, pp. 33–35.

9. S. Shavell, "Suit, Settlement, and Trial: A Theoretical Analysis under Alternative Methods for the Allocation of Legal Costs," *Journal of Legal Studies* 11 (1982), pp. 55–81; J. C. Coffee, Jr., "Understanding the Plaintiff's Attorney: The Implications of Economic Theory for Private Enforcement of Law through Class and Derivative Actions," *Columbia Law Review* 86 (1986), pp. 669–727.

■

EXERCISES

EXERCISE 8–1   THE OLD STACK PROBLEM

OBJECTIVES

1. To closely examine the dynamics of intergroup competition.
2. To illustrate how effectively a group is in developing a solution to a problem.

Step 1: Group Problem Solving
(30 minutes)

Divide into groups of from four to six persons each. Each group member should read "The Problem" below. The best procedure is for each person to develop a solution independently and for the group to spend a period of time discussing these solutions without evaluating them. Then the solutions should be evaluated and the best solution adopted.

The problem may be assigned in advance of class in order to give students more time to develop solutions.

The original source for this exercise could not be identified.

However, the final discussion and selection process should be done as a group in the classroom.

Step 2: Select Judges and Spokespeople
(5 minutes)

Each group should select one member to serve on a panel of judges to select the best solution. A spokesperson must also be selected to present the solution to the panel of judges.

Step 3: Present Solutions
(15 minutes)

Spokespersons for each group will present their group solution to the judges and the remainder of the class. A chalkboard or flip chart should be used to illustrate the solution along with the spokesperson's explanation. The explanation should be brief and concise, and spokespeople may not criticize other solutions. The spokespeople should provide quality arguments in support of their solutions.

Step 4: Straw Vote
(5 minutes)

After all group solutions are presented, the judges may think about the solutions for one or two minutes, then judges will state in turn which solution they prefer. **Judges must make their judgments independently, without discussion among themselves.** Judges are asked simply to state the solution they prefer. They do not explain their reasons for voting. The instructor should record the number of votes given to each solution on the chalkboard or flip chart next to that solution.

Step 5: Modified Problem Solving
(10 minutes)

Student groups re-form and discuss their approach. Judges and spokespersons return to their original groups. At this time, the groups may not change the basic strategy of their solution, but they may provide refinements. Groups are encouraged to compare their solution to other solutions at this point and may instruct the spokesperson to present weaknesses in other solutions as well as strengths of their own. The group also has the freedom to nominate a new spokesperson or judge at this time.

Step 6: Restate Solutions
(10 minutes)

The group spokespeople briefly restate the solutions using the earlier illustration. Minor modifications can be made. Spokespersons are encouraged to point out the strengths of their group's solutions and to criticize other solutions. The goal of the spokespeople is to persuade the judges that their group's solution is best.

Step 7: Final Vote

The judges are given one or two minutes to individually decide for which solution to vote. Judges may not discuss the solutions among themselves, and they must state their vote out loud. The instructor will indicate the number of votes next to each solution's illustration. The solution that receives the most votes is the winner.

Step 8: Discussion
(15 minutes)

The class as a whole should reflect back over their experience and discuss what happened. Students are encouraged to be self-reflective about their feelings toward their own group's solution, toward the judges, and so on. Judges are encouraged to express their feelings about any pres-

sures they felt from the group to vote in a certain way. The instructor or student may also wish to compare their observations to theories of intergroup behavior as illustrated in lectures or readings. The following questions may help guide that discussion.

1. Did any examples of scapegoating occur? Did losing groups express dissatisfaction or unfairness with the judges or the evaluation process?
2. Did any groups put pressure on the judges to act as a representative of their group rather than to vote in an unbiased fashion? Did judges feel pressure to represent their group even if pressure was not overtly expressed?
3. Did any groups develop a superiority complex, wherein they truly believed that their own group solution was best although from an objective perspective the solution may not have been best?
4. What was the reaction of winning versus losing groups? Did winners seem happy and satisfied while losers seemed discontented with one another or with the exercise?
5. During the second round of presentations, were certain solutions singled out for more criticism? Were these solutions the ones that received the most votes in the straw ballot, as if people were trying to tear down the strongest contender?
6. How does this group exercise compare to functioning of groups in the real world? These groups existed temporarily, while groups in the real world engage in real competitions and have strong and lasting commitments. Would representatives of real-world groups tend to reflect group wishes or to reach unbiased decisions? How might intergroup difficulties be overcome in organizations?

The Problem

An explosion has ripped a hole in a brick smokestack. The stack appears to be perfectly safe, but a portion of the access ladder has been ripped away and the remainder loosened. Your engineers need to inspect the damage immediately to determine whether the stack may collapse. How do you get one of your engineers up to inspect the hole safely and efficiently?

The smokestack is 140 feet high. The structure next to the smokestack is a water tower. In your solution you should use only those materials in Exhibit 8-6, including what you assume to be in the truck and sporting goods store.

EXHIBIT 8-6

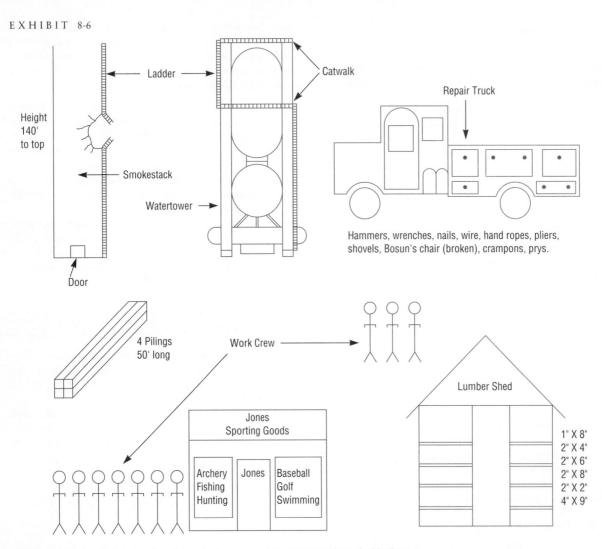

All fixed objects, with the exception of Jones's store, are spatially related as shown in this diagram.

EXERCISE 8–2   WORLD BANK: AN EXERCISE IN INTERGROUP NEGOTIATION

Step 1. The class is divided into two groups. The size of each of the groups should be no more than 10. Those not in one of the two groups are designated as observers. How-

Source: Adapted from John E. Jones and J. William Pfeiffer, eds. *The 1975 Annual Handbook for Group Facilitators.* (San Diego, Calif.: University Associates, 1975).

ever, groups should not have less than six members each. The instructor will play the role of the referee/ banker for the World Bank.

Step 2. Read the World Bank Instruction Sheet.

Step 3. Each group or team will have 15 minutes to organize itself and plan strategy before beginning. Before the first round each team must choose *(a)* two negotiators, *(b)* a representative, *(c)* a team recorder, *(d)* a treasurer.

Step 4. The referee/banker will signal the beginning of round one and each following round and also end the exercise in about one hour.

Step 5. Discussion. In small groups or with the entire class, answer the following questions.

1. What occurred during the exercise?
2. Was there conflict? What type?
3. What contributed to the relationships among groups?
4. Evaluate the power, leadership, motivation, and communication among groups.
5. How could the relationships have been more effective?

WORLD BANK GENERAL INSTRUCTION SHEET

This is an intergroup activity. You and your team are going to engage in a task in which money will be won or lost. *The objective is to win as much as you can.* There are two teams involved in this activity, and both teams receive identical instructions. After reading these instructions, your team has 15 minutes to organize itself and plan its strategy.

Each team represents a country. Each country has financial dealings with the World Bank. Initially, each country contributed $100 million to the World Bank. Countries may have to pay further monies or may receive money from the World Bank in accordance with regulations and procedures described below under sections headed Finance and Payoffs.

Each team is given 20 cards. These are your *weapons.* Each card has a marked side (X) and an unmarked side. The marked side of the card signifies that the weapon is armed. Conversely, the blank side shows the weapon to be unarmed.

At the beginning, each team will place 10 of its 20 weapons in their armed positions (marked side up) and the remaining 10 in their unarmed positions (marked side down). These weapons will remain in your possession and out of sight of the other team at all times.

There will be **rounds** and **moves.** Each round consists of seven moves by each team. There will be two or more rounds in this simulation. The number of rounds depends on the time available. Payoffs are determined and recorded after each round.

1. A move consists of turning two, one, or none of the team's weapons from armed to unarmed status, or vice versa.
2. Each team has two minutes to move. There are 30-second periods between moves. At the end of two minutes, the team must have turned two, one, or none of its weapons from armed to unarmed status, or from unarmed to armed status. If the team fails to move in the alloted time, no change can be made in weapon status until the next move.
3. The length of the $2\frac{1}{2}$-minute periods between the beginning of one move and the beginning of the next is fixed and unalterable.

Each new round of the experiment begins with all weapons returned to their original positions, 10 armed and 10 unarmed.

Finances

The funds you have contributed to the World Bank are to be allocated in the following manner:

$60 million will be returned to each team to be used as your team's treasury during the course of the decision-making activities.

$40 million will be retained for the operation of the World Bank.

Payoffs

1. *If there is an attack:*
   a. Each team may announce an attack on the other team by notifying the referee/banker during the 30 seconds following *any* 2-minute period used to decide upon the move (including the seventh, or final, decision period in any round). The choice of each team during the decision period just ended counts as a move. An attack may not be made during negotiations.
   b. If there is an attack (by one or both teams), two things happen: (1) the round ends and (2) the World Bank levies a penalty of $5 million for each team.
   c. The team with the greater number of armed weapons wins $3 million for each armed weapon it has over and above the number of armed weapons of the other team. These funds are paid

directly from the treasury of the losing team to the treasury of the winning team. The referee/bankers will manage this transfer of funds.

2. *If there is no attack:* At the end of each round (seven moves), each team's treasury receives from the World Bank $2 million for each of its weapons that is at that point unarmed, and each team's treasury pays to the World Bank $2 million for each of its weapons remaining armed.

Negotiations

Between moves each team has the opportunity to communicate with the other team through its negotiators.

Either team may call for negotiations by notifying the referee/bankers during any of the 30-second periods between decisions. A team is free to accept or reject any invitation to negotiate.

Negotiators from both teams are *required* to meet after the third and sixth moves (after the 30-second period following that move, if there is no attack).

Negotiations can last no longer than three minutes. When the two negotiators return to their teams, the two-minute decision period for the next move begins once again.

Negotiators are bound only by: *(a)* the three-minute time limit for negotiations and *(b)* their required appearance after the third and sixth moves. They are otherwise free to say whatever is necessary to benefit themselves or their teams. The teams similarly are not bound by agreements made by their negotiators, even when those agreements are made in good faith.

Special Roles

Each team has 15 minutes to organize itself to plan team strategy. During this period before the first round begins, each team must choose persons to fill the following roles. (Each team must have each of the following roles, which can be changed at any time by a decision of the team.)

- *Negotiators*—activities stated above.
- A *representative*—to communicate team decisions to the referee/bankers.
- A *recorder*—to record the moves of the team and to keep a running balance of the team's treasury.
- A *treasurer*—to execute all financial transactions with the referee/bankers.

▲

CASES

CASE 8–1 EVERGREEN WILLOWS

Evergreen Willows, a new convalescent home, had been in operation for several months. The large one-story building, which had been specially constructed for its purpose, was divided into two identical wings designated A and B. In the center of the building, separating the wings, was a large living room, a chapel, offices, and a middle wing which included the kitchen, patients' dining room, and employees' dining room. A and B wings consisted of a nurse's station in the center with a corridor of patients' rooms to each side (see Exhibit 8-7).

Source: Allan R Cohen, Stephen L. Fink, Herman Gadon, and Robin D. Willits, *Effective Behavior in Management* (Homewood, Ill.: Richard D. Irwin, 1984), pp. 596–600.

Each nurse's station served the patients for its wing, and each was under the direction of a charge nurse. Other nurses and nurse's aides worked under the charge nurse. From the opening day, each wing had been staffed separately. The director of nurses had assigned the more experienced, older aides to A wing, where she planned to locate sicker patients. She assigned the less experienced aides to B wing, which was to have patients who were more ambulatory. Except on rare occasions, A-wing staff did not work on B wing nor B-wing staff on A wing.

The day shift on B wing consisted of one charge nurse and four nurse's aides. Normally the charge nurse was Jenny, a young registered nurse who had had no previous experience as a charge nurse before working at the home. On her days off, she was replaced by Sue, a licensed prac-

EXHIBIT 8-7

Evergreen Willows Floor Plan

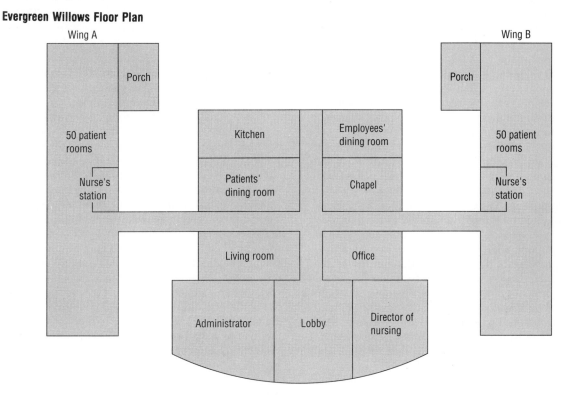

tical nurse who worked part-time. The nurse's aides had rotating days off each week so that, except when someone was sick and had to be replaced, the same aides were usually on duty at the same time. The B-wing aides were of similar age and experience, having been hired at the same time. All lived in the local community and tended to see one another socially after hours.

Jenny's duties as charge nurse included dispensing medications, keeping charts and records up-to-date, and supervising the work of the aides. Actual patient care was the responsibility of the aides. Most of the B-wing patients were at least partially ambulatory. Caring for them involved assisting them in bathing, dressing, walking, and feeding, or what nurses call activities of daily living. The aides also liked to visit with the lonelier patients whenever time permitted. A number of the patients wandered around during the day, and it was often necessary for the aides to look for them, which consumed a great deal of time con-

sidering the size of the building. Jenny, in giving her medications, ranged all over the building in search of patients and was not always to be found on the wing.

From the opening of the home, Jenny had found that there was barely enough time in the day for the work she had to do. She did not give detailed instructions to the aides, and they developed their own routines in caring for the patients. One new aide even said that "it took me weeks before I felt I knew what I was supposed to be doing." Usually they would separate by corridor, each doing the work they saw needing to be done. All helped in passing out breakfast and dinner trays, feeding patients, and in answering lights when a patient called for assistance. All of the B-wing aides kept busy, although sometimes there were complaints by some who felt they were "getting stuck" with the more unpleasant jobs because no one else would do them.

Nonetheless the atmosphere on the wing was friendly.

The aides often spoke of how much they enjoyed the patients. While most of the aides had not sought a job working with older patients, even those who might have preferred a job in a hospital caring for younger patients soon discovered that the "old folks" were interesting people. Consequently, there was much friendly contact between patients and aides as well as among aides and among patients. The patients enjoyed the atmosphere, although sometimes their families worried about the way they were allowed to wander about.

In contrast, A-wing patients were for the most part bedridden and required more actual nursing care. In fact, if a patient on B wing took sick, the home's policy was to transfer the patient to A wing where there was a larger staff/patient ratio. The staff consisted of a charge nurse, Elizabeth, and two or three R.N.s or L.P.N.s and six aides. The charge nurse took care of duties at the nurse's station and drug room, while the other nurses dispensed drugs and did treatments. The nurses's aides did patient care. Many of the patients were unable to walk or stand and helping them to a chair involved heavy lifting. Fewer patients than on B wing were dressed, most wearing johnnies and bathrobes, and most remained in their rooms. Many of the patients who were confined to their rooms rang for the aides frequently throughout the day, often for only minor requests.

Elizabeth was an older, more experienced nurse than Jenny and supervised the aides working under her in a strict manner. Each morning the aides were paired in teams of two and assigned to 16 specified patients. The assignments were standardized, and the A-wing aides usually worked systematically and on a schedule to complete their work. There was little change from day to day, and patients were generally taken care of at the same time each day and were accustomed to this. Working in teams of two gave each aide someone to assist her when lifting was necessary. Assignments included patients located far apart on the floor, but aides usually cared only for the patients on their assignment sheets. When another patient asked for assistance they would often answer "Wait until your nurse gets here." Elizabeth kept a close watch on her aides and was very critical of the work they did. Sometimes she could be heard over the intercom saying something like, "Girls, there are five lights on A wing." She insisted that the girls maintain a professional relationship with the patients. While the atmosphere on the wing was far from homey, the sick patient received good technical care, and their families felt a good deal of confidence in the quality of care provided on A wing.

The administrator and director of nurses were cheerful and apparently well liked by the nursing staff. They appeared at meetings held approximately every other week for in-service educational training or to update employees on issues of importance. Their response to the work done by the nurses and the aides was favorable. However, they were rarely seen on the wings, and they delegated a great deal of responsibility to the charge nurses.

After several months the director of nurses announced at one of the in-service meetings that the aides would now have assignments alternating them between the two wings. While she felt completely satisfied with the performance of both wings, she felt the aides should be more versatile and experienced with all types of patients.

When this new plan went into effect, a series of problems began to develop between the head nurses and aides of the two wings. B-wing aides on A wing found themselves answering lights not belonging to their own patients and falling behind in their own scheduled work. While working on one corridor, an aide would often forget those patients on the other corridor assigned to her, and those patients frequently had their lights on and unanswered for long periods of time. They complained to the head nurse when they had to wait. Thus the B-wing aides were under constant criticism from Elizabeth, but when they tried to talk to her they found she was not listening.

The help Elizabeth had from the other nurses allowed her more free time than Jenny had. She was often seen laughing and talking with the other nurses, but she did not socialize with the aides.

When on their own wing, the B-wing aides now found they had to do even more work than usual. Most of the aides from A wing were lost on B and needed much help in caring for the B-wing patients. Nothing was written down, and Jenny was too busy or not around to help them; so the responsibility of orienting them fell to the B-wing aides.

Stating that there was "nothing to do" on B wing, a few of the A-wing aides took frequent coffee breaks. The regular aides from B wing could not find them when they needed help or did not have the time to go to the employees' dining room to get them. One incident on B wing occurred when an aide was assisting a patient to bed, and the patient slipped to the floor. There was no one nearby, nor did anyone answer the emergency light when the aide called. The aide had to leave the patient to get help. When this situation was reported to Jenny, she reprimanded the A-wing aide who was not on the floor where she was supposed to be and recommended to the director of nurses that she be fired. It was the decision of the director that she "should be entitled to a second chance." The situation did not improve.

A great deal of resentment developed among the nursing staff. Several of the aides, including those considered to be the best workers, quit or began looking for other jobs. The attitude of the administrator and director of nurses was one of little concern. In the words of the director of nursing: "We have many applicants for each vacancy. Anyone can be replaced. Our turnover rate of employees here is better than in most nursing homes."

CASE QUESTIONS

1. How does the work that a person must perform contribute to problems or conflict?
2. How would you analyze a situation in which an experienced aide forgot about patients on the other corridor assigned to her? Is this an indication of a problem?
3. Is the A-wing/B-wing situation an example of competition or conflict? Explain.

CASE 8-2 L. E. S., INC.

BACKGROUND

L. E. S., Inc., is a large U.S. company engaged in the manufacture and sales of a wide range of electrical products. Headquarters are in Ohio, with five regional sales and marketing offices. L. E. S. has 17 manufacturing facilities mainly concentrated in the Northeast, with newer plants in the Southwest. There is a national network of warehouses to service the U.S. market. The manufacturing operations are organized on a divisional basis: power and transmission, electrical components, and small appliances. There are three plants manufacturing electrical components, such as switches, sockets, and relays. One of these plants is L. E. S. (Worcester).

The site of Worcester consists of a manufacturing plant where low-cost, high-volume electrical components are assembled for the computer and electrical industry. Over the last three years, Worcester Plant has doubled its work force in response to rapid sales growth. (See organization chart in Exhibit 8-8.)

There are six production sections:

Section 1—connector and cable assemblies.

Sections 2 and 3—switches, relays, and timers.

Sections 4 and 5—circuit board components.

Sections 6—circuit breaker assemblies.

Sections 2 through 6 work two shifts, Section 1 operates three shifts, and each shift has its own supervisor. Half of the production operators have less than one year with the company. Only four section shift supervisors have more

Source: Copyright © Ann Cunliffe, March 1991. Reproduced with permission.

than two years' service, and only two of these have had any supervisory training.

Key Characters

Manufacturing Manager

Martin Collins; M.B.A.; age 44. Overall responsibility for Worcester Plant. Reports to the divisional vice president in Ohio. Mike has been manufacturing manager for six years, having been appointed to the position from a job at headquarters.

Production Manager

John Drummond; no formal qualifications; age 49. John has worked in the plant for 15 years, 4 as a supervisor, and the last 11 as a production manager. Responsible for the six production sections and their maintenance. This involves planning work schedules, dealing with day-to-day production issues, and the maintenance of equipment and a workshop to build and modify equipment according to plans drawn by the design department.

Quality Manager

Mike Peterson; degree in electrical engineering; age 43. Mike has worked in quality in the plant for the last 12 years, and he insures that products meet quality standards by the inspection of finished products prior to dispatch to the warehouse. He also is responsible for the inspection of incoming new materials.

Engineering Manager

Chris Brooks; degree in electrical engineering; M.B.A.; age 35. The only woman on the management team, she was

EXHIBIT 8-8

Organization Chart L. E. S., Inc. (Worcester): 236 Employees

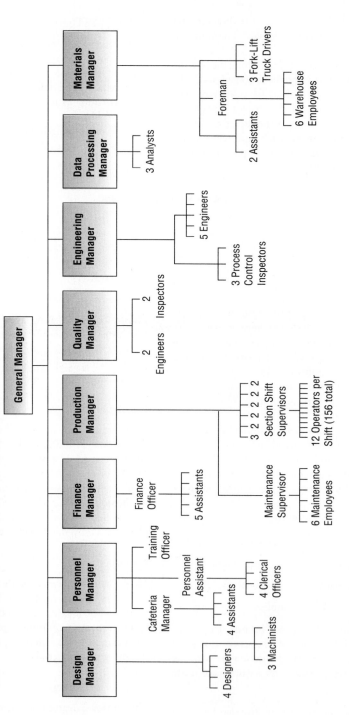

recruited by the manufacturing manager, three years ago, from outside the company. She is responsible for the development of new products, the improvement of existing manufacturing methods, and technical problem solving in the production departments. There is also a responsibility for process control. Most of the projects relating to the former two activities are self-generated and important in maintaining the competitiveness of L. E. S. The production department relies heavily on the technical expertise of the engineering department in maintaining a smooth flow of operations.

Materials Manager

Rich Sweeney; experience; age 39. He has spent six years in this job. He plans production and insures the required amount of materials are in stock to manufacture customer orders. Responsible also for implementing the manufacturing requirements planning (MRP) to optimize and control material inventories.

Design Manager

Bob Lemire; degree in mechanical engineering; age 30. Worked for L. E. S. (Worcester) for one year. He is responsible for the design of new equipment and the modification of existing equipment. This department works closely with the maintenance department.

Team Objectives

Objectives for each year are set at an annual seminar for the management team listed above. These objectives were identified by the manufacturing manager and agreed to by the team after a brief discussion. Extracts from the annual plan show the main priorities of the company this year:

We are in a very competitive era in which we must reduce costs to survive. Part of this activity is increasing productivity through the introduction of more efficient manufacturing activity. Specifically, this involves the introduction of new equipment and processes, the modification of existing equipment, and the more effective use of that equipment to improve output, quality, and reduce wastage.

It is extremely important to our overall success that we carry out our activities on a team basis. The company will only maintain and improve its product leadership through commitment to a team effort.

Currently, a number of production problems exist in the plant, resulting in late deliveries to customers. These problems have been identified by the management team as:

1. A high scrap rate: 15 percent of wasted products and materials over all sections.
2. Section 1 being fully utilized, 24 hours a day. This results in no leeway in meeting excess demands.
3. Quality problems, requiring products to be reworked to meet quality standards.

Last week, the following memorandum was sent:

Memorandum

From: M. Collins

To: J. Drummond
M. Peterson
C. Brooks
R. Sweeney
B. Lemire

MANUFACTURING MEETING

As you are aware, we have a number of problems affecting plant performance. I have organized a meeting for next Monday, 2 P.M., to assess the situation and identify some solutions to our problems. This situation is reaching a critical point and we need to take action fast. Please insure that you attend.

THE MANAGEMENT MEETING

Martin Collins (manufacturing manager): "Thanks for coming. As you know, we have a number of problems that we need to resolve if we are to improve productivity levels and meet current and future market demands. We need to improve manufacturing efficiency, and there are two main problems we need to consider: One, productivity is falling. We have more people but they seem to be less effective. Second, there are a number of projects that have not and will not be completed in the time scale we would like them to be.

"In today's climate we cannot afford to continue like this. We need to address these issues—and fast! Perhaps we can start by assessing the current situation."

"The problem is, we've just got too much to do," said John (production manager). "We've got to produce more and more with the same number of sections. Section 1 is running to capacity, 24 hours a day, seven days a week. We need more equipment. Maintenance and design are working on improving our existing equipment, but it's a slow job with the breakdowns they keep having to deal with. Bob and I have discussed this and agree it would help us both."

Bob (design manager) nodded in agreement.

"I don't think it's only that, John; we have got quality problems as well, which need to be ironed out," said Chris (engineering manager).

"We can't afford to buy more equipment until we've dealt with our existing problems," said Martin. "The emphasis is on cost reduction as well as on maintaining our market share."

John replied, "The other problem is that half the employees only started with us less than a year ago, so they haven't much experience. The supervisors haven't much idea about work scheduling, as most of them have had no training in supervision. I have to keep on their backs all the time to make sure they get the job done."

"Why don't we get the personnel department down to look at the possibility of training those who need it?" asked Chris. "We could use training as a base for increasing individual efficiency."

"When do you think we have time to take them off production?" John replied. "We have enough trouble meeting targets with everyone working."

"That's true," said Martin.

"Give me some more operators and I might have the time," added John.

"I think it would be worthwhile looking at equipment and staffing implications, as well as at operator and supervisor competence," said Chris. "It's no use saying we need more operators until we know we are utilizing the people and equipment we've got—effectively."

"It's an idea. I'll get personnel to look into the possibilities; after all, its job is to assess staffing needs," said Martin.

"The other problem is that we are not focusing on quality and volume of output for each particular product." Chris paused. "The operators do, but no one else does. We are all more concerned with our own individual functions—we see things in a compartmentalized way, rather than focusing on the product as a whole."

"Yes," agreed Mike (quality manager). "Take quality. Chris and I provided a procedure and control chart for supervisors to work to—but it won't work unless we have some formal mechanism for the engineer, the process control technician, and the supervisor to modify it for each

line. There seems to be a lack of communication between these people at the shop floor level, no matter how we try to encourage it."

"I agree," added Chris. "There seems to be a number of solutions to problems that have been improvised or implemented by various people—supervisors, maintenance, quality engineers, and engineers who just happened to get involved. Because these aren't documented, the next person to deal with the problem is unaware of them and has to start dealing with the problem from scratch. We need some formalization of procedures and problem solving."

"It would certainly help," said Mike.

"Look, I've said before that we need to be more flexible in production," said John firmly. He turned to Mike. "You know what it was like when we first started: there were no written job descriptions, everyone knew what they were doing, and did it—we had no problems then."

"But things have changed," said Mike.

"We just got bigger," replied John. "So we need to be more flexible—I'm sure Rick would agree, we were talking about it yesterday."

"Sure," said Rick (materials manager), "and Martin is always saying we need to be more flexible."

"I accept that in our business we need to be able to adapt quickly to customer demands, if we are to remain competitive; but we can still have structure and flexibility. . . ." began Chris.

"Is that what you learned on your business course?" interrupted John. "Well, Mike knows that production can only be effective if we've got that space to maneuver. He's worked with us for 12 years and knows we've had some very good workers who have come up with some creative solutions."

"Well . . . I suppose so," Mike reluctantly agreed.

"That's fine," said Chris. "But because those solutions aren't documented or formalized, we get changes on changes that can mask the original problem. One of the supervisors was telling me yesterday that they rarely get the same maintenance person dealing with problems in her section. When they eventually arrive, they do something—go away—and no one is any the wiser. When the next problem occurs, it's a different maintenance employee who starts again. She says, it's the same on other sections, and that the maintenance people can't wait to get back to their workshop to get on with their job there. That is one area that would benefit from formalization. . . ."

"My maintenance department people do their jobs!" interrupted John.

"They do see themselves as a 'cut above the rest,' John," said Mike.

"They have an important job to do," replied John. "They like things as they are."

"But it takes them time to deal with any problems, because they are not thoroughly familiar with the detail of that particular section," said Chris. "They've no allegiance to a product."

"Look, I'll say it again—we need to be flexible," said John.

"Well, there is something in that. What about the problem we have with the overrunning of projects?" asked Martin. "It's particularly a problem in engineering and in quality."

"I'm glad to hear it's not only production having problems!" said John, in a loud aside to Rick. "Guess an M.B.A. doesn't give you all the answers!" Ignoring this comment, Chris began, "My engineers are just as frustrated as we are that they aren't meeting the deadlines. Their jobs are becoming fragmented, and they are having to move from one task to another because of the day-to-day problems that arise. This obscures the more long-term projects, and it's only the urgent jobs that get attention. The conflict arises because the same people are dealing with long-term improvement projects and day-to-day problems, and the latter have to take precedence. What do you think, Mike?"

"I agree. We have the same problems and for basically the same reasons," replied Mike. "We can't concentrate on long-term quality problems because of the day-to-day ones . . . "

"We are here to get the product out, Mike," interrupted John. "That's got to be our priority. We need to meet customer orders."

"Yes, but don't forget we also have to retain those customers and meet the quality specifications. We need to consider the medium to long-term, as well," said Martin.

"We really need to look at how to balance the two and minimize the conflicting demands. Mike and I have been discussing the problem and think it may be useful to separate development and day-to-day problems." Chris looked at Mike for support.

"That's impossible!" retorted John.

"It can be done," replied Chris. "We need to develop a team approach. A small development group could be established to deal with medium to long-term projects. We could organize production on a team basis, each section having a team consisting of the appropriate shift supervisor or supervisors, someone from maintenance who would have a permanent assignment to that section, an engineer, and quality input."

"One quality inspector could cover each product group," added Mike.

"We would need more staff for that, " said Rick, "and John and I have more than enough problems to deal with without trying to get a team to work together!"

"Anyway, we need more operators, not engineers and quality people—it's *producers* we need," said John.

"It would give us more time to study our quality problems. . . ." began Mike.

Martin said, "It would also need more money and an immediate cost increase."

Mike looked around the group. "Well, . . . maybe it is a nonstarter." He looked apologetically at Chris.

Chris tried again. "I believe we should be looking at the way we are organized and staffed. We are obviously going wrong somewhere, and I don't believe it's all based on technical problems. I'm sure we could run more efficiently, even if we only reorganized our existing resources. We also need to stress the importance of quality; the operators can't be very motivated when they see such a high scrap rate—that we are doing little about."

"The only way I'll produce more is with more operators," said John.

Chris gave up, feeling frustrated that no one was open to the points she was making.

"Okay," said Marin. "I'll get personnel to look at staffing levels. Can you liaise with them, John, and report back to our next meeting? I'll also get them to look at the supervisors' training needs, although I doubt we'll have time to release them. Meanwhile, let's try and solve some of those quality problems."

The meeting finished.

Chris caught up with Mike outside. "What happened, Mike? I thought we'd agreed to push for the team approach?" "There isn't much you can do when John gets started," said Mike. "Anyway, things aren't going to change."

"Not if we all take the short-term expedient view," replied Chris. "Martin knows we need to do something but he's not sure what. We could have put forward those alternatives we discussed—I thought you were all for them?"

"I was . . ." said Mike.

CASE QUESTIONS

1. What are some of the main causes of conflict at L. E. S., Inc.?
2. Why do each of the participants attending the meeting view the problems differently?
3. How should the situation and conflict be resolved?

Organizational Power, Politics, and Negotiations

LEARNING OBJECTIVES

DISTINGUISH between the terms influence and power

IDENTIFY five interpersonal power bases

DESCRIBE three forms of structural power

DISCUSS the concepts of powerlessness and empowerment

IDENTIFY the contingencies that influence subunit power

EXPLAIN what is meant by the term *the illusion of power*

DESCRIBE five political games played in organizations

DISCUSS the criteria for determining ethical behavior

DISTINGUISH between win-win and win-lose negotiation

IDENTIFY the major types of third party negotiations

Power is a pervasive part of the fabric of organizational life. Managers and nonmanagers use it. They manipulate power to accomplish goals and, in many cases, to strengthen their own positions.[1] A person's success or failure in using or reacting to power is determined largely by understanding power, knowing

[1]Edwin Cornelius III and Frank Love, "The Power Motive and Managerial Success in a Professionally Oriented Service Industry Organization," *Journal of Applied Psychology*, February 1984, pp. 32–39.

how and when to use it, and being able to anticipate its probable effects. The purpose of this chapter is to examine power and its uses in organizations. We will look at the sources (bases) of power, how power is used, and the relationship between power and organizational politics.

THE CONCEPT OF POWER

The study of power and its effects is important to understanding how organizations operate. It is possible to interpret every interaction and every social relationship in an organization as involving power.[2] How organizational subunits and individuals are controlled is related to the issue of power and influence. The terms **power** and **influence** are frequently used interchangeably in the organizational behavior literature; however, there is a subtle, yet important difference. Influence is a transaction in which person B is induced by person A to behave in a certain way. For example, if an employee works overtime at the boss's request, that employee has been *influenced* by the boss.

Like influence, power involves a relationship between two people. Robert Dahl, a political scientist, captures this important relational focus when he defines power as "A has power over B to the extent that he can get B to do something B would not otherwise do."[3] What is the difference in this definition of power and our earlier definition of influence? Power represents the capability to get someone to do something; influence is the exercise of that capability. Another way of stating the distinction is to say that power is the potential to influence, while influence is power in action. Thus, an individual may have power (the capacity to influence) but not exercise it; on the other hand, an individual cannot influence (induce certain behaviors in another) without power.

As was the case in the definition of power above, we frequently speak of someone having power over someone else. While this is correct, it is important to stress that power is not an attribute of a particular person. Rather, it is an aspect of the relationship that exists between two (or more) people. No individual or group can have power in isolation; power must exist in relation to some other person or group. If A has power over B, it is, in part, because B is willing for that to be an aspect of the relationship between them. If and when B no longer desires that to be part of his or her relationship with A, A will no longer have power over B and no longer be able to influence B's behavior. Thus, *obtaining, maintaining,* and *using* power are all essential to influencing the behavior of people in organizational settings.

There is one other aspect in the concept of power that should be noted. When power is one of the attributes of a relationship, then so also is **dependency**. It was noted above that A has power with respect to B only so long as B is willing

[2]Henry Mintzberg, "Power and Organizational Life Cycles," *Academy of Management Review,* October 1984, pp. 207–24.

[3]Robert Dahl, "The Concept of Power," *Behavioral Science,* July 1957, pp. 202–3.

to allow A to exert influence. B is likely to continue to allow this as long as outcomes B wants can be effected by A. Thus, the amount of power one person has over another is a product of the net dependence of the one over the other. If B depends on A more than A depends on B, A holds the power. If Sam, a night shift worker who wishes a transfer to the day shift, knows that his boss can veto the request, then he is dependent on the boss with respect to that outcome. Consequently, all else being equal, he is more likely to agree to be influenced by his boss.

POWER AND AUTHORITY

In organizations the use of power frequently involves the application of authority. **Authority** is the *formal* power a person has because of the position he or she holds in the organization. Orders from a manager in an authority position are followed because they must be followed. That is, persons in higher positions have legal authority over subordinates in lower positions. Not following orders subjects the offender to disciplinary action just as not following society's legal directives subjects one to disciplinary action in the form of arrest and penalty. Organizational authority has the following characteristics:

1. *It is invested in a person's position.* An individual has authority because of the position he or she holds, not because of any specific personal characteristics.
2. *It is accepted by subordinates.* The individual in a legal authority position exercises authority and can gain compliance because he or she has a legitimate right.
3. *Authority is used vertically.* Authority flows from the top down in the hierarchy of an organization.

Possessing formal power, or authority, does not mean that all orders will be followed by those who are subordinate to the individual in authority. For a subordinate to comply with an order from a superior requires that the order fall within the subordinate's zone of indifference. The term **zone of indifference** may be explained as follows: If all possible orders which might be directed to an individual from a superior were arranged in the order of their acceptability to the individual, some would be clearly acceptable while others might be clearly unacceptable. For example, a request by a manager that a subordinate complete her expense report might be an acceptable order. It would lie within her zone of indifference; that is, she is relatively indifferent to the request as far as the question of her boss's authority is concerned.

However, if the boss were to request that she record expenses she did not incur, or that she otherwise "pad" the expense report, such a request might well fall outside her zone of indifference. She may elect not to comply because she is no longer indifferent with respect to such an order. A person's zone of indifference may be wider or narrower depending on a number of factors such as the extent

INTERNATIONAL

E N C O U N T E R • 9-1

POWER DIFFERENCES ACROSS CULTURES

Significant differences in work-related values, attitudes, and behaviors exist across a wide variety of different cultures. Geert Hofstede, a Dutch researcher, surveyed managers and nonmanagers in 40 countries and concluded that national culture explained more value, attitude, and behavior differences in organizations than did any other variable. One of the dimensions on which Hofstede found important cross cultural differences between managers and subordinates was what is referred to as *power distance*.

Power distance is a measure of the extent to which organizational members accept the unequal distribution of power. Specifically, to what extent do subordinates accept that their boss has more power than they do? In high power distance cultures subordinates are likely to do what the boss asks, without question, because he or she is the boss. In low power distance cultures, on the other hand, the boss's orders are more likely to be questioned. Low power distance cultures, because they are more egalitarian, tend to be less accepting of the overt use of power. All else being equal, employees in these societies would be expected to have a narrower zone of indifference.

The United States is a low power distance country, as are Israel, Denmark, Australia, Ireland, New Zealand, and Canada. Large and high power distance countries, where subordinates might be expected to have wide zones of indifference, include Mexico, Philippines, Venezuela, India, Yugoslavia, Singapore, and Hong Kong.

Source: Based in part on information in G. Hofstede, *Culture's Consequences: International Differences in Work Related Values* (Beverly Hills: Sage Publications, 1980).

to which the boss has a source of power other than authority. Zone of indifference size may also be shaped by cultural factors, as illustrated in Encounter 9-1.

POWER BASES

Power facilitates the organization's adaptation to its environment. The subunits (individuals, departments) able to assist in that adaptation are the ones which will hold power. Power can be derived from many source. How power is obtained in an organization depends to a large extent on the type of power being sought. Power can be derived from interpersonal, structural, and situational bases.

Interpersonal Power

French and Raven suggested five interpersonal bases of power: legitimate, reward, coercive, expert, and referent.[4]

[4]John R. P. French and Bertram Raven, "The Basis of Social Power," in *Studies in Social Power*, ed. D. Cartwright (Ann Arbor: Institute for Social Research, University of Michigan, 1959), pp. 150–67.

Legitimate Power

This signifies a person's ability to influence because of position. A person at a higher level has **legitimate power** over people below. In theory, organizational equals (e.g., all first-line supervisors) have equal, legitimate power. However, each person with legitimate power uses it with a personal flair. The terms *legitimate power* and *authority* frequently are used interchangeably.

Reward Power

This type of power is based on a person's ability to reward a follower for compliance. **Reward power** is used to back up the use of legitimate power. If followers value the rewards or potential rewards the person can provide (recognition, a good job assignment, a pay raise, additional resources to complete a job), they may respond to orders, requests, and directions.

Coercive Power

The opposite of reward power is **coercive power**, power to punish. Followers may comply out of fear. A manager may block a promotion or harass a subordinate for poor performance. These practices and the fear they will be used are coercive power.

Expert Power

A person has **expert power** when he or she possesses special expertise that is highly valued. Experts have power even when their rank is low. An individual may possess expertise on technical, administrative, or personal matters. The more difficult it is to replace the expert, the greater is the degree of expert power he or she possesses. Occasionally, individuals' expertise does not bestow upon them as much ability to influence as they think it does. This is vividly illustrated in Encounter 9-2 "Misjudging Power Results in 11,500 Terminations." Expert power is a personal characteristic while legitimate, reward, and coercive power are largely prescribed by the organization.

Referent Power

Many individuals identify with and are influenced by a person because of the latter's personality or behavioral style. The charisma of the person is the basis of **referent power**. A person with charisma is admired because of his or her characteristics. The strength of a person's charisma is an indication of his or her referent power. *Charisma* is a term that is often used to describe politicians, entertainers, or sports figures. However, some managers are regarded as extremely charismatic by their subordinates. Certain aspects of charismatic leadership will be discussed in more detail in chapter 10.

The five bases of interpersonal power can be divided into two major categories: organizational and personal. Legitimate, reward, and coercive power are primarily prescribed by the organization, the position, formal groups, or specific interaction

**MISJUDGING POWER RESULTS IN
11,500 TERMINATIONS**

On August 31, 1981, 11,500 air traffic controllers, members of the Professional Air Traffic Controllers Organization (PATCO) walked off the job. Conflicts between PATCO and the Federal Aviation Administration reached their peak during that summer. Instead of open and constructive bargaining, there were threats, hostility, and disruptive actions. Despite the fact that the controllers were legally prohibited from striking, the vast majority of PATCO members took a walk.

It was perhaps the greatest single example in modern times of miscalculating power.

When President Reagan announced that after a 48-hour grace period all remaining striking controllers would be fired, only a handful returned to work. The same assessment of their degree of "expert power," which had led them to strike in the first place, led the vast majority to call the president's bluff. Indications were that PATCO felt its members, because of their special-

ized knowledge and skill and the essential role they played in aviation, held the balance of power. Their assumption appeared to be that with no controllers, air traffic in the United States would come to a standstill and no president (especially one who had been on the job for only seven months) could afford to let that happen.

It was clearly a miscalculation. The president carried out his intentions, and more than 11,000 controllers lost their jobs. PATCO lost its right to represent the controllers and simply ceased to exist. In a case of legitimate power versus expert power, the expert power side not only lost but was totally destroyed. There were in fact no real winners. Air travelers were stranded for days; airline schedules were in chaos for months; the air traffic controllers lost their jobs; and the government had to hire and train new air traffic controllers, a process that literally took years and millions of dollars to complete.

patterns. A person's legitimate power can be changed by transferring the person, rewriting the job description, or reducing the power by restructuring the organization. On the other hand, expert and referent power are very personal. They are the result of an individual's personal expertise or style and, as such, are grounded in the person and not the organization.

These five types of interpersonal power are not independent. On the contrary, a person can use these power bases effectively in various combinations. Also, the use of a particular power base can affect the others. Some research has suggested, for example, that when subordinates believe a manager's coercive power is increasing, they also perceive a drop in reward, referent, and legitimate power held by the manager. Other research suggests that legitimate and reward power are positively related while coercive power is inversely related to legitimate and reward power. The end-of-chapter case "Missouri Campus Bitterly Divided over How to Reallocate Funds" provides an opportunity to examine the role of several different types of interpersonal power in an organizational setting.

▲ **C9–1**

It was suggested earlier that obtaining or building power (along with maintaining and using it) was essential to influencing the behavior of organizational

● **R9–1**　members. As the first article in this chapter, "Power and Influence: The View from Below," suggests, the use of different types of power will influence different behaviors.

NEED FOR POWER

Throughout history human beings have always been fascinated by power. In ancient Chinese writings, concern about power is clearly expressed—the taming power of the great, the power of light, the power of the dark. Early religious writings also contain numerous references to the person who possesses or acquires power. Historical records show that there have been differences in the extent to which individuals have pursued, feared, enjoyed, and misused power. Currently, the image of those who seek power is for the most part quite negative. For example, power seekers have been portrayed as:

Neurotics who are covering up feelings of inferiority, anxiety, hatred.
Substituting power for lack of affection, being alone, being deprived of friendship.
Attempting to compensate for some childhood deprivation.[5]

The power seeker has been labeled as being weak, neurotic, and troubled. This, of course, may be true for some power seekers (e.g., Adolf Hitler), but to place every power seeker in this category seems too broad sweeping and general.

McClelland proposes that power can be responsibly sought and used.[6] In addition to examining the need for achievement (discussed in Chapter 4), McClelland examined the **need for power,** or as he refers to it, n Pow. McClelland defined *n Pow* as the desire to have an impact on others. This type of impact may be shown basically in three ways: (1) by strong action, by giving help or advice, by controlling someone; (2) by action that produces emotion in others; and (3) by a concern for reputation.

Research has been devoted to attempts at determining how people high in n Pow behave as contrasted with people low in n Pow. In general, individuals high in n Pow (1) are competitive and aggressive, (2) are interested in prestige possessions (e.g., a car), (3) prefer action situations, and (4) join a number of groups. Research on n Pow conducted by McClelland and his associates has revealed that the most effective organizational managers share these characteristics:

They have a high n Pow.
They use their power to achieve organizational goals.

---

[5]David Kipnis, *The Powerholders* (Chicago: University of Chicago Press, 1976), pp. 149–56. Kipnis doesn't present these characteristics as fitting all power seekers but only as a summarization of the ugly and bland face of power seekers.

[6]David C. McClelland, *Power: The Inner Experience* (New York: Irvington Publishers, 1975), p. 7.

They practice a participative or "coaching" style when interacting with followers.

They do not concentrate on developing close relations with others.[7]

The effective managers in McClelland's research were designated as *institutional managers* because they used their power to achieve organizational (institutional) goals. The institutional managers were more effective than the *personal power managers*, who used their power for personal gain, and the *affiliative managers*, who were more concerned with being liked than with using their power.

McClelland has also found that men who score high in n Pow, are low in need for affiliation, and are high in self-control are very effective. Young managers who displayed these characteristics when they entered AT&T were more likely to have been promoted to higher levels of management in the company after 16 years than were young managers who did not display these characteristics.[8]

The research work stimulated and conducted by McClelland presents evidence that is contrary to the negative image that has historically been attached to all power seekers. Stating that all power seekers are weak, neurotic, and troubled is as ridiculous as stating that all power seekers are effective, well adjusted, and highly motivated. There are what McClelland refers to as the "two faces of power." One face depicts power seekers in negative terms. The other face suggests that power can be used to accomplish goals, use resources efficiently, and help followers feel more powerful themselves. McClelland's view seems to be more realistic and correct than the view that all power seekers are weak and neurotic.

STRUCTURAL AND SITUATIONAL POWER

Power is primarily prescribed by structure within the organization.[9] The structure of an organization is the control mechanism by which the organization is governed. In the organization's structural arrangements, decision-making discretion is allocated to various positions. Also the structure establishes the patterns of communication and the flow of information. Thus, organizational structure creates formal power and authority by specifying certain individuals to perform specific job tasks and make certain decisions. Structure also encourages informal power through its effect on information and communication within the system.

We have already discussed how formal position is associated with power and authority. Certain rights, responsibilities, and privileges accrue from a person's

[7]David C. McClelland and David H. Burnham, "Power Is the Great Motivator," *Harvard Business Review,* March–April 1976, pp. 100–110.

[8]David C. McClelland, "Understanding Psychological Man," *Psychology Today,* May 1982, pp. 55–56.

[9]Jeffrey Pfeffer, *Power in Organizations* (Marshfield, Mass.: Pitman Publishing, 1981), p. 117; and Dean Tjosvold, "Power and Social Context in Superior-Subordinate Interaction," *Organizational Behavior and Human Decision Process,* Summer 1985, pp. 281–93.

position. Other forms of structural power exist because of resources, decision making, and information.[10]

Resources

Kanter argues quite convincingly that power stems from (1) access to resources, information, and support and (2) the ability to get cooperation in doing necessary work.[11] Power occurs when a person has open channels to resources—money, human resources, technology, materials, customers, and so on. In organizations, vital resources are allocated downward along the lines of the hierarchy. The top-level manager has more power to allocate resources than do other managers further down in the managerial hierarchy. The lower level manager receives resources that are granted by top-level managers. In order to assure compliance with goals, top-level managers (e.g., presidents, vice presidents, directors) allocate resources on the basis of performance and compliance. Thus, a top-level manager usually has power over a lower level manager because the lower level manager must receive resources from above to accomplish goals.

Decision-Making Power

The degree to which individuals or subunits (e.g., a department or a special project group) can affect decision making determines the amount of power acquired. A person or subunit with power can influence how the decision-making process occurs, what alternatives are considered, and when a decision is made.[12] For example, when Richard Daley was mayor of Chicago, he was recognized as a power broker. He not only influenced the decision-making process, but he also had the power to decide which decision would be given priority in the city council and when decisions would be made.[13] He was a powerful politician because he was considered to be an expert at controlling each step in important decisions.

Information Power

Having access to relevant and important information is power. Accountants generally do not have a particularly strong or apparent interpersonal power base in an organization. Rather, accountants have power because they control important information. Information is the basis for making effective decisions. Thus, those

---

[10]Pfeffer, *Power,* pp. 104–22; Rosabeth M. Kanter, "Power Failures in Management Circuits," *Harvard Business Review,* July–August 1979, pp. 65–75; and Hugh R. Taylor, "Power at Work," *Personnel Journal,* April 1986, pp. 42–49.

[11]Kanter, "Power Failures."

[12]For an organizationally oriented, concise, and excellent discussion of structural and situationally oriented sources of power, see Don Hellriegel, John W. Slocum, Jr., and Richard W. Woodman, *Organizational Behavior* (St. Paul, Minn.: West Publishing, 1986), pp. 465–68.

[13]Mike Royko, *Boss: Richard J. Daley of Chicago* (New York: E. P. Dutton, 1971).

EXHIBIT 9-1

Symptoms and Sources of Powerlessness

Position	Symptoms	Sources
First-line supervisors (e.g., foreman, line supervisor)	Supervise too closely Fail to train subordinates Not sufficiently oriented to the management team Inclined to do the job themselves	Routine, rule-minded jobs Limited lines of communication Limited advancement oppportunities for themselves and their subordinates
Staff professional (e.g., corporate lawyer, personnel/ human resources specialist)	Create islands and set themselves up as experts Use professional standards as basis for judging work that distinguishes them from others Resist change and become conservative risk takers	Their routine tasks are only adjuncts to real line job Blocked career advancement Replaced by outside consultants for nonroutine work
Top-level managers (e.g., chief executive officer, vice president)	Short-term horizon Top-down communication systems emphasized Reward followers to think like the manager, do not welcome bearers of bad news	Uncontrollable lines of supply Limited or blocked lines of information about lower managerial levels Diminished lines of support because of challenges to legitimacy

Source: Reprinted by permission of the *Harvard Business Review*. Adapted from "Power Failures in Management Circuits," by Rosabeth Moss Kanter (July–August 1979), p. 73. Copyright © 1979 by the President and Fellows of Harvard College; all rights reserved.

who possess information needed to make optimal decisions have power. The accountant's position in the organization structure may not accurately portray the amount of power that he or she wields. A true picture of a person's power is provided not only by the person's position but also by the person's access to relevant information.

A number of organizational situations can serve as the source of either power or powerlessness (not acquiring power). The powerful manager exists because he or she allocates required resources, makes crucial decisions, and has access to important information.[14] He or she is likely to make things happen. The powerless manager, however, lacks the resources, information, and decision-making prerogatives needed to be productive. Exhibit 9-1 presents some of the common symptoms and sources of powerlessness of first-line supervisors, staff professionals, and top-level managers. This exhibit indicates that a first-line manager, for example, may display a number of symptoms of powerlessness such as supervising very closely and not showing much concern about training or developing subordinates. If these symptoms persist, it is likely that the individual is powerless.

[14]Anthony T. Cobb, "An Episodic Model of Power: Toward an Integration of Theory and Research," *Academy of Management Review*, July 1984, pp. 482–93.

EMPOWERMENT

Managers at any level in the organization can increase the power of subordinates (managers or nonmanagers) who report to them. This is accomplished through the process of **empowerment.** Empowerment has been defined by Conger and Kanungo as "a process of enhancing feelings of self-efficacy among organizational members through the identification of conditions that foster powerlessness and through their removal by both formal organizational practices and informal techniques of providing efficacy information."[15] These researchers suggest that empowerment is a process consisting of five stages.

The first stage involves identifying the conditions existing in the organization that lead to feelings of powerlessness on the part of organizational members. These conditions could find their origin in organizational factors (such as poor communications or highly centralized resources), management styles (such as authoritarianism), reward systems (nonmerit based rewards, low incentive value rewards), or in the nature of the jobs (low task variety, unrealistic performance goals).

The diagnoses completed in the first stage lead to the implementation of empowerment strategies and techniques in the second stage. Use of participative management, establishing goal-setting programs, implementing merit-based pay systems, and job enrichment through redesign, are examples of possible empowerment activities. The use of these programs is designed to accomplish two objectives in the third stage. One is simply to remove the conditions identified in the first stage as contributing to powerlessness. The second, and more important, is to provide self-efficacy information to subordinates. Self-efficacy describes a belief in one's effectiveness. Individuals high in self-efficacy tend to be confident and self-assured and feel they are likely to be successful in whatever endeavors they undertake.

Receiving such information results in feelings of empowerment in the fourth stage. This is because increasing self-efficacy strengthens effort-performance expectancies. You will recall from the discussion of expectancy theory in chapter 4, that this means increasing the perceived probability of successful performance, given effort. Finally, the enhanced empowerment feelings from stage 4 are translated into behaviors in the fifth and final stage. These behavioral consequences of empowerment include increased activity directed toward task accomplishment.[16]

Thus by helping organizational members feel more assured of their capability to perform well, and by increasing the linkages between effort and performance, empowerment can result in positive individual and organizational payoffs.

---

[15]J. A. Conger and R. N. Kanungo, "The Empowerment Process: Integrating Theory and Practice," *The Academy of Management Review,* July 1988, p. 4747.

[16]Ibid, pp. 471–82.

■ **E9–1** Exercise 9–1 can be completed to provide you with information regarding your personal empowerment profile.

INTERDEPARTMENTAL POWER

The primary focus to this point has been on individual power and how it is obtained. However, it is also important to consider subunit or interdepartmental power. Subunit power is the focus of the strategic contingency theory developed by Hickson. A strategic contingency is an event that is extremely important for accomplishing organizational goals.[17] Crozier, a French sociologist, provided insight into the idea of strategic contingencies. He studied the relationships between workers in the production and maintenance departments of French tobacco-processing plants. Crozier found that the production workers enjoyed job security because of tenure, were protected against unfair disciplinary action, and were not replaced or transferred arbitrarily. The production workers were less skilled than the maintenance workers. The maintenance workers were highly skilled and were recruited and selected only after going through a rigorous screening process.

The production workers were dependent on the maintenance workers. This power differential was explained in terms of the control exercised by the maintenance workers over an important contingency. If machines were shut down, the entire plant came to a halt. Efficiently functioning machines were needed to accomplish output goals. Since the maintenance workers, at the request of the production workers, repaired machines that were down, they possessed significant power.

When machines were down, the job performance of the production workers suffered. Stoppages totally disrupted the workflow and the output of the production workers. Crozier proposed that the maintenance workers controlled a strategically contingent factor in the production process. Crozier's study provided clear evidence of subunit power differences. The study also stimulated other studies that eventually resulted in a strategic contingencies explanation of power differences.[18]

Using the work of Crozier and Hickson and his associates, it is possible to develop a concise explanation of strategic contingencies. The model presented in Exhibit 9-2 suggests that subunit power, the power differential between subunits,

---

[17]Michel Crozier, *The Bureaucratic Phenomenon* (Chicago: University of Chicago Press, 1964).

[18]It should be noted that the strategic contingency theory was developed by D. J. Hickson and his colleagues. Other theorists and researchers have modified and discussed this approach. However, the reader is urged to use the original sources for a discussion of the complete and unmodified theory. See D. J. Hickson, C. R. Hinnings, C. A. Lee, R. E. Schneck, and J. M. Pennings, "A Strategic Contingency Theory of Intraorganizational Power," *Administrative Science Quarterly*, June 1971, pp. 216–29; and C. R. Hinnings, D. J. Hickson, J. M. Pennings, and R. E. Schneck, "Structural Conditions of Intraorganizational Power," *Administrative Science Quarterly*, March 1974, pp. 22–44.

EXHIBIT 9-2

**A Strategic Contingency
Model of Subunit Power**

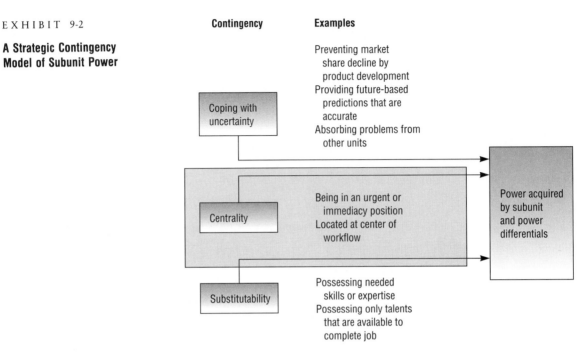

This figure is based on the detailed research work conducted by D J. Hickson, C. R. Hinnings, C. A. Lee, R. E. Schneck, and J. M. Pennings, "A Strategic Contingency Theory of Intraorganizational Power," *Administrative Science Quarterly,* June 1971, pp. 216–29; and C. R. Hinnings, D. J. Hickson, J. M. Pennings, and R. E. Schneck, "Structural Conditions of Intraorganizational Power," *Administrative Science Quarterly,* March 1974, pp. 22–44.

is influenced by (1) the degree of ability to cope with uncertainty, (2) the centrality of the subunit, and (3) the substitutability of the subunit.

Coping with Uncertainty

Unanticipated events can create problems for any organization or subunit. It is, therefore, the subunits most capable of coping with uncertainty that typically acquire power. There are three types of coping activities. First is *coping by prevention.* Here a subunit works at reducing the probability that some difficulty will arise. One example of a coping technique is designing a new product to prevent lost sales because of new competition in the marketplace.

Second is *coping by information.* The use of forecasting is an example. Possessing timely forecasting information enables a subunit to deal with such events as competition, strikes, shortages of materials, and consumer demand shifts. Planning departments conducting forecasting studies acquire power when their predictions prove accurate.

Third is *coping by absorption.* This coping approach involves dealing with uncertainty as it impacts the subunit. For example, one subunit might take a problem employee from another subunit and attempt to retrain and redirect that employee. This is done as a favor so that the other subunit will not have to go through the pain of terminating or continuing to put up with the employee. The subunit that takes in the problem employee gains the respect of other subunits, which results in an increase in power.

The relation of coping with uncertainty to power was expressed by Hickson as follows: "The more a subunit copes with uncertainty, the greater its power within the organization."[19]

Centrality

The subunits that are most central to the flow of work in an organization typically acquire power.[20] No subunit has zero centrality since all subunits are somehow interlinked with other subunits. A measure of centrality is the degree to which the work of the subunit contributes to the final output of the organization.[21] Since a subunit is in a position to affect other subunits, it has some degree of centrality and therefore power.

Also a subunit possesses power if its activities have a more immediate or urgent impact than that of other subunits. For example, Ben Taub is a major public hospital in Houston. The emergency and trauma treatment subunit is extremely important and crucial, and it contains significant power within the hospital. Failures in this subunit could result in the death of emergency victims. On the other hand, the psychiatric subunit does important work but not of the crucial and immediate type. Therefore, it has significantly less subunit power than the emergency and trauma treatment subunit.

Substitutability

Substitutability refers to the ability of other subunits to perform the activities of a particular subunit. If an organization has or can obtain alternative sources of skill, information, and resources to perform the job done by a subunit, the subunit's power will be diminished. Training subunits lose power if training work can be done by line managers or outside consultants. On the other hand, if a subunit has unique skills and competencies (e.g., the maintenance workers in Crozier's study discussed above) that would be hard to duplicate or replace, this would tend to increase the subunit's power over other subunits.

Hickson et al. capture the importance of substitutability power when they

---

[19]Hickson et al., "Strategic Contingency Theory."

[20]L. C. Freeman, D. Roeder, and R. R. Mulholland, "Centrality in Social Networks: II. Experimental Results," *Social Networks,* June 1980, pp. 119–42.

[21]Richard L. Daft, *Organization Theory and Design* (St. Paul, Minn.: West Publishing, 1983), pp. 392–98. This source contains an excellent discussion of this strategic contingency perspective in terms of managerial and organizational theory. Daft's discussion is a concise and informative presentation of the original Hickson et al. theory and research.

propose that the lower the substitutability of the activities of a subunit, the greater is its power within the organization.[22]

THE ILLUSION OF POWER

Admittedly, some individuals and subunits have vast amounts of power to get others to do things the way they want them done. However, there are also illusions of power. Imagine that one afternoon your supervisor asks you to step into his office. He starts the meeting: "You know we're really losing money using that Beal stamping machine. I'd like you to do a job for the company. I want you to destroy the machine and make it look like an accident." Would you comply with this request? After all, this is your supervisor, and he is in charge of everything—your pay, your promotion opportunities, your job assignments. You might ask yourself, "Does my supervisor have this much power over me?"

Where a person or subunit's power starts and stops is difficult to pinpoint. You might assume that the supervisor in the hypothetical example has the specific power to get someone to do this unethical and illegal "dirty work." However, even individuals who seemingly possess only a little power can influence others. A series of studies conducted by Milgram focused on the illusion of power. In these studies, subjects who had been voluntarily recruited thought they were administering electrical shocks of varying intensity to other subjects.[23] Ostensibly the experiment was designed to study the effects of punishment on learning. In reality the studies focused on obedience to authority. Exhibit 9-3 displays the surprising results.

At the experimenter's direction, 26 of 40 subjects, or 65 percent, continued to increase the intensity of the shocks they thought they were administering to another person all the way to the maximum voltage. This was in spite of the fact that the control panel indicated increasing voltage dosages as "intense," "extreme," "danger," and "severe shock." Additionally, screams could be heard coming from the booth, and the subject allegedly receiving the shock begged the experimenter to stop the project. In spite of this, and even though the subjects were uncomfortable administering the shocks, they continued. Milgram stated:

> *I observed a mature and initially poised businessman enter the laboratory, smiling and confident; within 20 minutes he was reduced to a twitching, stuttering wreck, who was rapidly approaching a point of nervous collapse . . . yet he continued to respond to every word of the experimenter and obeyed to the end.*[24]

Why did the subjects obey the experimenter? Although the experimenter possessed no specific power over the subjects, he appeared to be a powerful person.

---

[22]Ibid., p. 40.

[23]S. Milgram, "Behavioral Study of Obedience," *Journal of Abnormal and Social Psychology*, October 1963, pp. 371–78; and S. Milgram, *Obedience to Authority* (New York: Harper & Row, 1974).

[24]Milgram, "Behavioral Study of Obedience," p. 377.

EXHIBIT 9-3

**Results of
Milgram's Classic
Experiment on
Obedience**

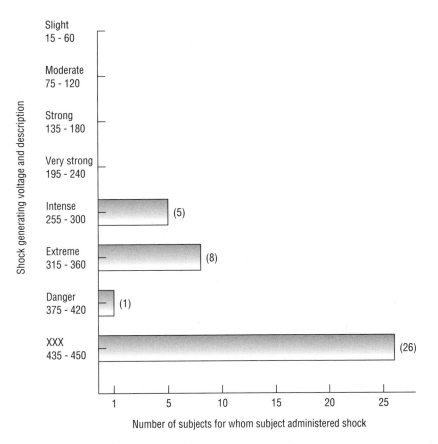

Source: Based on descriptions and data presented in S. Milgram, "Behavioral Study of Obedience," *Journal of Abnormal and Social Psychology,* October 1963, pp. 371–78.

He created an illusion of power. The experimenter, dressed in a white lab coat, was addressed by others as "doctor" and was very stern. The subjects perceived the experimenter as possessing legitimacy to conduct the study. The experimenter apparently did an excellent job of projecting the illusion of having power.

The Milgram experiments indicate that possessing power in a legitimate way is not the only way power can be exerted. Individuals who are perceived to have power may also be able to significantly influence others. Power is often exerted by individuals who have only minimum or no actual power. The "eye of the beholder" plays an important role in the exercise of power.[25]

[25]S. H. Ng, *The Social Psychology of Power* (New York: Academic Press, 1980), p. 119; Dean Tjosvold, "The Dynamics of Positive Power," *Training and Development Journal,* June 1984, pp. 72–76; K. Macher, "The Politics of People," *Personal Journal,* January 1986, pp. 50–53.

POLITICAL STRATEGIES AND TACTICS

Individuals and subunits continually engage in **politically oriented behavior**.[26] By politically oriented behavior we mean a number of things:

1. Behavior that usually is outside the legitimate, recognized power system.
2. Behavior that is designed to benefit an individual or subunit, often at the expense of the organization in general.
3. Behavior that is intentional and is designed to acquire and maintain power.

■ **E9–2**

As a result of politically oriented behaviors, the formal power that exists in an organization often is sidetracked or blocked. In the language of organizational theory, political behavior results in the displacement of power. Exercise 9–2 allows you to make some judgments regarding the extent to which political processes are involved in organizational decisions and to compare your judgments with others completing the exercise.

Research on Politics

A number of studies have been conducted to explore political behavior and perceptions in organizations.[27] A study of 142 purchasing agents examined their political behavior. The job objective of the purchasing agents was to negotiate and fill orders in a timely manner. However, the purchasing agents also viewed their jobs as being a crucial link with the environment—competition, price changes, market shifts.[28] Thus, the purchasing agents considered themselves information processors. The vital link of the purchasing agents with the external environment placed them in conflict with the engineering department. As a result of the conflict, attempts to influence the engineering subunit were a regular occurrence.

A variety of political tactics used by the purchasing agents were discovered in this study. They included:

1. *Rule evasion:* Evading the formal purchase procedures in the organization.
2. *Personal-political:* Using friendships to facilitate or inhibit the processing of an order.

---

[26]Manual Velasquez, Dennis J. Moberg, and Gerald F. Cavanagh, "Organizational Statesmanship and Dirty Politics: Ethical Guidelines for the Organizational Politician," *Organizational Dynamics,* Autumn 1983, pp. 65–79; and David Yoffie and Sigrid Bergenstein, "Creating Political Advantage: The Rise of Corporate Enterpreneurs," *California Management Review,* Fall 1985, pp. 124–39.

[27]Dan L. Madison, Robert W. Allen, Lyman W. Porter, Patricia A. Renwick, and Bronston T. Mayes, "Organizational Politics: An Exploration of Managers' Perceptions," *Human Relations,* February 1980, pp. 79–100; Jeffrey Gantz and Victor V. Murray, "The Experience of Workplace Politics," *Academy of Management Journal,* June 1980, pp. 237–51; and Robert W. Allen, Dan L. Madison, Lyman W. Porter, Patricia A. Renwick, and Bronston T. Mayes, "Organizational Politics: Tactics and Characteristics of Its Actors," *California Management Review,* 1979, pp. 77–83.

[28]George Strauss, "Tactics of the Lateral Relationship: The Purchasing Agent," *Administrative Science Quarterly,* 1962, pp. 161–86.

EXHIBIT 9-4

Managerial Perceptions of Organizational Political Behavior

Tactic	Combined Groups	Chief Executive Officers	Staff Managers	Supervisors
Attacking or blaming others	54.0%	60.0%	50.0%	51.7%
Use of information	54.0	56.7	57.1	48.3
Image building/impression management	52.9	43.3	46.4	69.0
Developing base of support	36.8	46.7	39.3	24.1
Praising others, ingratiation	25.3	16.7	25.0	34.5
Power coalitions, strong allies	25.3	26.7	17.9	31.0
Associating with the influential	24.1	16.7	35.7	20.7
Creating obligations/reciprocity	12.6	3.3	14.3	30.7

Source: R. W. Allen, D. L. Madison, L. W. Porter, P. A. Renwick, and B. T. Mayes, "Organizational Politics: Tactics and Characteristics of Its Actors." Copyright 1979 by the Regents of the University of California. Reprinted from *California Management Review*, December 1979, p. 79, by permission of the Regents.

3. *Educational:* Attempting to persuade engineering to think in purchasing terms.
4. *Organizational:* Attempting to change the formal or informal interaction patterns between engineering and purchasing.

These political tactics, used by the purchasing agents to accomplish their goals, (1) were outside the legitimate power system, (2) occasionally benefited the purchasing agent at the expense of the rest of the organization, and (3) were intentionally developed so that more power was acquired by the purchasing agent.

Another study of political behavior was conducted in the electronics industry in southern California. A total of 87 managers (30 chief executive officers, 28 higher level staff managers, and 29 supervisors) were interviewed and asked about political behavior.[29] Exhibit 9-4 presents a summary of the eight categories of political tactics (behavior) that were mentioned most frequently by each of the three managerial groups.

The managers also were asked to describe the personal characteristics of the individuals who used political behavior effectively. Thirteen personal characteristics were identified as important. These characteristics are presented in Exhibit 9-5.

The managers in this study were aware of political behavior because it was a part of their organizational experiences. As the researchers noted, the research was not designed to praise or disparage political behavior. Instead, it was intended to show that politics is a fact of organizational existence.

[29]Allen et al., "Organizational Politics."

EXHIBIT 9-5

Personal Characteristics of Effective Politicians

Personal Characteristics	Combined Groups	Chief Executive Officers	Staff Managers	Supervisor
Articulate	29.9%	36.7%	39.3%	12.8%
Sensitive	29.9	50.0	21.4	17.2
Socially adept	19.5	10.0	32.1	17.2
Competent	17.2	10.0	21.4	20.7
Popular	17.2	16.7	10.7	24.1
Extroverted	16.1	16.7	14.3	17.2
Self-confident	16.1	10.0	21.4	17.2
Aggressive	16.1	10.0	14.3	24.1
Ambitious	16.1	20.0	25.0	3.4
Devious	16.1	13.3	14.3	20.7
"Organization person"	12.6	20.0	3.6	13.8
Highly intelligent	11.5	20.0	10.7	3.4
Logical	10.3	3.3	21.4	6.9

Source: R. W. Allen, D. L. Madison, L. W. Porter, P. A. Renwick, and B. T. Mayers, "Organizational Politics: Tactics and Characteristics of Its Actors." Copyright 1979 by the Regents of the University of California. Reprinted from *California Management Review,* December 1979, p. 78, by permission of the Regents.

Playing Politics

If anything, the available (yet scanty) research indicates that politics exists in organizations and that some individuals are very adept at political behavior. Mintzberg and others describe these adept politicians as playing games.[30] The games that managers and nonmanagers engage in are intended to (1) resist authority (the insurgency game), (2) counter the resistance to authority (the counterinsurgency game), (3) build power bases (the sponsorship game and the coalition-building game), (4) defeat rivals (the line-versus-staff game), and (5) effect organizational change (the whistle-blowing game). In all, Mintzberg describes and discusses 13 types of political games. Five of these are briefly presented.

The Insurgency Game

This game is played to resist authority. For example, suppose that a plant foreman is instructed to reprimand a particular worker for violating company policies. The reprimand can be delivered according to the foreman's feelings and opinions

[30]This discussion of games relies on the presentation in Henry Mintzberg, *Power in and around Organizations* (Englewood Cliffs, N.J.: Prentice-Hall, 1983), chap. 13, pp. 171–271. Please refer to the source for a complete and interesting discussion of political games.

about its worth and legitimacy. If the reprimand is delivered in a halfhearted manner, it probably will have no noticeable effect. On the other hand, if it is delivered aggressively, it may be effective. Insurgency in the form of not delivering the reprimand as expected by a higher level authority would be difficult to detect and correct. Insurgency as a game to resist authority is practiced in organizations at all levels.

The Sponsorship Game

This is a rather straightforward game in that a person attaches himself or herself to someone with power. The sponsor typically is the person's boss or someone else with higher power and status than those of the person. Typically, individuals attach themselves to someone who is on the move. There are a few rules involved in playing this game. First, the person must be able to show commitment and loyalty to the sponsor. Second, the person must follow each sponsor-initiated request or order. Third, the person must stay in the background and give the sponsor credit for everything. Finally, the person must be thankful and display gratitude to the sponsor. The sponsor is not only a teacher and trainer for the person but also a power base. Some of the sponsor's power tends to rub off on the person because of his or her association with the sponsor.

The Coalition-Building Game

A subunit such as a personnel/human resources management department or a research and development department may be able to increase its power by forming an alliance or coalition with other subunits. The strength in numbers idea is encouraged by coalition building.[31] When such alliances are formed within the organization, there is an emphasis on common goals and common interests. However, forming coalitions with groups outside the organization can also enhance the power of a subunit.

This example of building an internal coalition illustrates how power can be acquired. In most organizations the personnel/human resources department typically has limited power. However, current litigation involving employee relations and employee health problems associated with disability triggered by job stress is becoming a costly expense. Consequently, legal staffs in organizations have acquired power. These legal staffs do not have the information, daily contact with employees, and records needed to legally serve the firm. Skills, abilities, and information to cope with employee-based uncertainties are more in the domain of the personnel/human resources department. Therefore, an alliance between the legal staff and the personnel/human resources department would enhance both their power bases. The coalition would enable the organization to effectively address legal issues.

Building a coalition with an external group can also enhance the power of

---

[31]William B. Stevenson, Jane L. Pearce, and Lyman W. Porter, "The Concept of Coalition in Organization Theory and Research," *Academy of Management Review*, April 1985, pp. 256–68.

various groups. The alumni office of most state universities interacts with alumni in fund raising, projecting a positive image, and providing service on community projects. The donations of alumni are extremely important for funding and supporting research programs conducted within a university. The alumni office would acquire more power by forming an alliance with major donors who actively support it. The university would be hard-pressed to ignore requests that major donors made to the administration to support the alumni office, the implication being that failing to support the alumni office and its personnel would cause these donors to withhold funds.

The Line-versus-Staff Game

The game of line manager versus staff adviser has existed for years in organizations. In essence, it is a game that pits line authority to make operating decisions against the expertise possessed by staff advisers. There are also value differences and a clash of personality. Line managers typically are more experienced, more oriented to the bottom line, and more intuitive in reaching decisions. On the other hand, staff advisers tend to be younger, better educated, and more analytical decision makers.[32] These differences result in viewing the organizational world from slightly different perspectives.

Withholding information, having access to powerful authority figures, creating favorable impressions, and identifying with organizational goals are tactics used by line and staff personnel. The line-versus-staff clash must be controlled in organizations before it reaches the point at which organizational goals are not being achieved because of the disruption.

The Whistle-Blowing Game

Whistle-blowing behavior is receiving increasing attention.[33] This game is played to bring about organizational change. If a person in an organization identifies a behavior that violates his or her sense of fairness, morals, ethics, or law, then he or she may blow the whistle. **Whistle-blowing** means that the person informs someone—a newspaper reporter, a government representative, a competitor—about an assumed injustice, irresponsible action, or violation of the law. The whistle-blower is attempting to correct the behavior or practice. By whistle-blowing, the person is bypassing the authority system within the organization. This is viewed in a negative light by managers who possess position power. Often, whistle-blowing is done secretly to avoid retribution by the authority system.

Whistle-blowers come from all levels in the organization.[34] For example, an

---

[32]S. S. Hammond III, "The Roles of the Manager and Management Scientist in Successful Implementation," *Sloan Management Review,* Winter 1974, pp. 1–24.

[33]J. P. Near and Marcia Miceli, "Organizational Dissonance: The Case for Whistle-Blowing," *Journal of Business Ethics,* 1985, pp. 1–16.

[34]Janelle Dozier and Marcia Miceli, "Potential Predictors of Whistle-Blowing: A Prosocial Behavior Perspective," *Academy of Management Review,* October 1985, pp. 823–36.

Eastern Airlines pilot complained to management first and then to the public about defects in his plane's automatic pilot mechanisms. His complaints were attacked by management as being groundless. In another example, a biologist reported to the Environmental Protection Agency that his consulting firm had submitted false data to the agency on behalf of an electric utility company; he was fired. In still another publicized case, an engineer at Ford complained about the faulty design of the Pinto. Unfortunately, this whistle-blower was demoted. Many of the legal costs and settlements from Pinto crash victims might have been avoided if the whistle-blower's message had been taken more seriously.[35]

These five examples of political game playing are not offered as always being good or bad for the organization. They are games that occur in organizations with various degrees of frequency. They occur within and between subunits, and they are played by individuals representing themselves or a subunit. Certainly, political behaviors carried to an extreme can hurt individuals and subunits. However, it is unrealistic to assume that all political behavior can or should be eliminated through management intervention. Even in the most efficient, profitable, and socially responsible organizations and subunits, political behaviors and games are being acted out.

ETHICS, POWER, AND POLITICS

Issues of power and politics often involve ethical issues as well. For example, if power is used within the formal boundaries of a manager's authority and within the framework of organizational policies, job descriptions, procedures, and goals, it is really nonpolitical power and most likely does not involve ethical issues. When the use of power is outside the bounds of formal authority, politics, procedures, job descriptions, and organizational goals, it is political in nature. When this occurs, ethical issues are likely to be present. Some examples might include bribing government officials, lying to employees and customers, polluting the environment, and a general "ends justify the means" mentality.

Managers confront ethical dilemmas in their jobs because they frequently use power and politics to accomplish their goals. Each manager, therefore, has an ethical responsibility. Recently, researchers have developed a framework that allows a manager to integrate ethics into political behavior. Researchers recommend that a manager's behavior must satisfy certain criteria to be considered ethical.[36]

[35]Alice L. Priest, "When Employees Think Their Company Is Wrong," *Business Week,* November 24, 1980, p. 2; and Andy Pasztor, "Speaking up Gets Biologist into Big Fight," *The Wall Street Journal,* November 26, 1980, p. 29.

[36]Gerald F. Cavanagh, Denis J. Moberg, and Manual Velasquez, "The Ethics of Organizational Politics," *Academy of Management Review,* July 1981, pp. 363–74; and Velasquez, Moberg, and Cavanagh, "Organizational Statesmanship and Dirty Politics."

USING AN ETHICS DECISION TREE

Political behavior is pervasive. As the text indicates, such behavior is inherently neither good nor bad. In determining whether a particular choice of behaviors is ethical or unethical, based on the criteria discussed in the text, a manager might find the decision tree in Exhibit 9-6 useful.

Application of this decision tree approach is certainly not a panacea. There may be situations in which one or more of these criteria cannot be employed, or in which there is a conflict between criteria. Making the ethically correct political behavior choice is neither always easy nor possible. However, models such as this one can be of assistance to managers in their decision making.

Source: Adapted from G. F. Cavanagh, D. J. Moberg, and M. Velasquez, "The Ethics of Organizational Politics," *Academy of Management Review,* July 1981, p. 368.

1. *Criterion of utilitarian outcomes:* The manager's behavior results in optimization of satisfactions of people inside and outside the organization. In other words, it results in the greatest good for the greatest number of people.
2. *Criterion of individual rights:* The manager's behavior respects the rights of all affected parties. In other words, it respects basic human rights of free consent, free speech, freedom of conscience, privacy, and due process.
3. *Criterion of distributive justice:* The manager's behavior respects the rules of justice. It does not treat people arbitrarily but rather equitably and fairly.

What does a manager do when a potential behavior cannot pass the three criteria? Researchers suggest that it may still be considered ethical in the particular situation if it passes the *criterion of overwhelming factors.* To justify the behavior, it must be based on tremendously overwhelming factors in the nature of the situation such as conflicts among criteria (e.g., the manager's behavior results in both positive and negative results), conflicts within the criteria (e.g., a manager uses questionable means to achieve a positive result), and/or an incapacity to employ the first three criteria (e.g., the manager acts with incomplete or inaccurate information). Encounter 9-3 presents a decision tree approach to the application of these criteria.

NEGOTIATIONS

Negotiations are a fact of life. Whether they take place between leaders of superpowers in the context of arms control deliberations, attorneys in the process of plea-bargaining for their clients, car buyer and salesperson, supervisor and subordinate, or parent and child, we are all affected every day by negotiations.

EXHIBIT 9-6

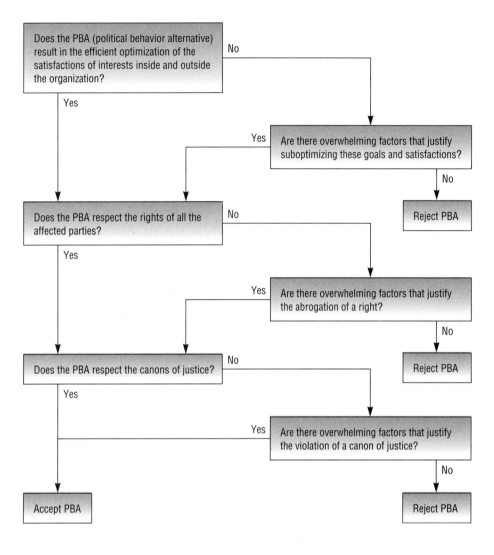

Negotiation may be viewed as a process in which two or more parties attempt to reach acceptable agreement in a situation characterized by some level of real or potential disagreement. In an organizational context negotiation may take place (1) between two people (as when a manager and subordinate decide on the completion date for a new project the subordinate has just received), (2) within a group (most group decision-making situations), and (3) between groups (such as the purchasing department and a supplier regarding price, quality, or delivery date).

Regardless of the setting or the parties involved, negotiations usually have at least four elements.[37] There is some degree of *interdependence* between the parties. That is, each party is in some way affected by, or depends on, the other. This strongly suggests a power relationship exists between the negotiators. Second, some disagreement or *conflict* exists. This may be real or simply perceived conflict. Third, the situation must be conducive to *opportunistic interaction*. This means that each party has both the means and inclination to attempt to influence the other. Finally, there exists some *possibility of agreement*. In the absence of this latter element of course, negotiations cannot bring about a positive resolution.

Win-Lose Negotiating

The classical view suggests negotiations are frequently a form of a zero-sum game. That is, to whatever extent one party wins something the other party loses. In a zero-sum situation there is an assumption of limited resources, and the negotiation process is to determine who will receive these resources. This is also known as distributive negotiating. The term refers to the process of dividing, or "distributing" scarce resources. Such a win-lose approach characterizes numerous negotiating situations. Buying an automobile is a classic example. As the buyer, the less you pay the less profit the seller makes; your "wins" (in the form of fewer dollars paid) are the seller's "losses" (in the form of fewer dollars of profit). Note that in win-lose negotiating one party does not necessarily "lose" in an absolute sense. Presumably the party selling the car still made a profit, but to the extent the selling price was lowered to make the sale, the profit was lower.

In organizations win-lose negotiating is quite common. It characterizes most bargaining involving material goods, such as the purchase of supplies or manufacturing raw materials. Win-lose negotiating can be seen in universities where each college attempts to negotiate the best budget for itself, invariably at the expense of some other college. Frequently, the most variable example of distributive negotiations in organizations are those that take place between labor and management. Issues involving wages, benefits, working conditions, and related matters, are seen as a conflict over limited resources.

Win-Win Negotiating

Win-win, or integrative, negotiating brings a different perspective to the process. Unlike the zero-sum orientation in win-lose, win-win negotiating is a positive-sum approach. Positive-sum situations are those where each party gains without a corresponding loss for the other party. This does not necessarily mean that everyone gets everything they wanted, for seldom does that occur. It simply means that an agreement has been achieved which leaves all parties better off than they were prior to the agreement.

---

[37]D. A. Lax and J. K. Sebenius, *The Manager as Negotiator* (New York: Free Press, 1986).

It may seem as if a win-win approach is always preferable to a win-lose one. Why should there be a winner and a loser if instead there can be two winners? Realistically, however, not every negotiating situation has an integrative payoff. Some situations really are distributive; a gain for one side must mean an offsetting loss for the other. In the automobile purchase example cited earlier, it is true that both the purchaser and the seller can "win" in the sense that the purchaser obtains the car and the seller makes a profit. Nonetheless, this is essentially a distributive situation. The purchaser can obtain a better deal *only* at the loss of some profit by the seller. There is simply no way the purchaser can get the lowest price while the seller obtains the highest profit.

Even if the nature of what is being negotiated lends itself to a win-win approach, the organization of the negotiators may not. Win-win, or integrative, negotiating can work only when the issues are integrative in nature, and all parties are committed to an integrative process. Typically, union and management bargaining includes issues that are both distributive and integrative in nature. However, because negotiators for both sides so frequently see the total process as distributive, even those issues which truly may be integrative become victims of a win-lose attitude, to the detriment of both parties.

INCREASING NEGOTIATION EFFECTIVENESS

Just as there is no one best way to manage, neither is there one best way to negotiate. The selection of specific negotiation strategies and tactics depend on a number of variables. The nature of the issues being negotiated is a critical consideration. For example, how one approaches negotiating distributive issues may be quite different than the strategy employed for negotiating integrative ones. The context or environment in which the negotiations are taking place may also be an important consideration, as may be the nature of the outcomes that are desired from the negotiating process. In many negotiating situations this last consideration may be the most important.

One useful way to think about desired outcomes is to distinguish between *substantive* and *relationship* outcomes.[38] **Substantive outcomes** have to do with how the specific issue is settled. To strive to end up with a bigger piece of the pie than the other party is to focus on a substantive outcome. On the other hand, to negotiate in a manner designed primarily to maintain good relations between the parties—irrespective of the substantive result—is to focus on **relationship outcomes.** While the two concerns are not mutually exclusive, the relative importance assigned them will affect a manager's choice of negotiation strategies.

● R9–2 The second reading selection accompanying this chapter examines the issue of substantive and relationship outcomes in more detail. The article offers a decision

[38]G. T. Savage, J. D. Blair, and R. L. Sorenson, "Consider Both Relationships and Substance When Negotiating Strategically," *Academy of Management Executive,* February 1989, pp. 37–48.

tree approach for deciding on the most appropriate approach to negotiations, depending on the nature of the desired outcomes.

One model for increasing negotiating effectiveness is found in the work of the Dutch management practitioner Willem Mastenbroek. Although the model is extremely comprehensive, the key focus is on four activities:[39]

1. *Obtaining substantial results.* This refers to activities which focus on the content of what is being negotiated. Desirable outcomes cannot be achieved if the negotiations do not stay constructively focused on the real issues. A judicious exchange of information regarding goals and expectations of the negotiating process is an example of this type of activity.

2. *Influencing the balance of power.* The final outcome of negotiations is almost always directly related to the power and dependency relationships between the negotiators. Neither attempts to increase your power through dominance, nor responding with total deference to the other party's attempt to increase their power represents the most effective means of dealing with power issues. Achieving subtle shifts in the balance of power through the use of persuasion, facts, and expertise, are almost always more effective.

3. *Promoting a constructive climate.* This relates to activities which are designed to facilitate progress by minimizing the likelihood that tension or animosity between the parties becomes disruptive. Specific activities might include attending to each party's opinions, acting in a predictable and serious manner, treating each party with respect, and showing a sense of humor. Being on different sides of an issue does not have to mean being at odds personally.

4. *Obtaining procedural flexibility.* These are activities which allow a negotiator to increase negotiating effectiveness through increasing the type and number of options available for conducting the negotiations. The longer a negotiator can keep the widest variety of options open, the greater the likelihood of reaching a desirable outcome. Examples include judicious choice of one's initial position, dealing with several issues simultaneously, and putting as many alternatives on the table as possible.

Third Party Negotiations

Negotiations do not always take place only between the two parties directly involved in the disagreement. Sometimes third parties are called in when negotiations between the main parties have broken down or reached an impasse. At other times, third parties may be part of the negotiations process from the beginning. In some instances third party involvement is imposed on the disputing parties; in others, the parties themselves voluntarily seek out third party assistance. In any event, the instances of third party negotiations appear to be increasing.

[39]W. Mastenbroek, *Negotiate* (Oxford, United Kingdom: Basil Blackwell, Inc., 1989).

There are different kinds of third party interventions, and third party involvement has been characterized in many different ways. One such typology suggests there are four basic kinds of interventions.[40] **Mediation,** where a neutral third party acts as a facilitator through the application of reasoning, suggestion, and persuasion. Mediators facilitate resolution by affecting how the disputing parties interact. Mediators have no binding authority; the parties are free to ignore mediation efforts and recommendations. **Arbitration** is where the third party has the power (authority) to impose an agreement. In conventional arbitration, the arbitrator selects an outcome that is typically somewhere between the final positions of the disputing parties. In final-offer arbitration, the arbitrator is mandated to choose one or the other of the parties' final offers, and thus, has no real control over designing the agreement.[41] **Conciliation** occurs where the third party is someone who is trusted by both sides and serves primarily as a communication link between the disagreeing parties. A conciliator has no more formal authority to influence the outcome than does a mediator. Finally, **consultation** is where a third party trained in conflict and conflict-resolution skills attempts to facilitate problem solving by focusing more on the relations between the parties than on the substantive issues. The chief role of the consultant is to improve the negotiating climate so that substantive negotiations can take place at some point in the future.

It is not uncommon for managers to serve as third parties in negotiations. Situations in which this could occur would include two subordinates who are having a disagreement, an employee and a dissatisfied customer, or disputes between two departments, both of which report to the manager. As a third party, the manager could be called upon to assume any and all of these four types of roles.

Improving Negotiations

In one form or another negotiations is becoming an increasingly important part of the manager's job. A recent review of the topic of negotiations concluded with a set of recommendations for managers on how to improve the negotiation process. The following suggestions were offered:[42]

1. Begin the bargaining with a positive overture—perhaps a small concession—and then reciprocate the opponent's concessions.
2. Concentrate on the negotiation issues and the situational factors, not on the opponent or his or her characteristics.
3. Look below the surface of your opponent's bargaining and try to determine his or her strategy.

[40]R. J. Fisher, *The Social Psychology of Intergroup and International Conflict Resolution* (New York: Springer-Verlag, 1990).

[41]M. H. Bazerman and M. A. Neale, *Negotiating Rationality* (New York: The Free Press, 1992).

[42]J. A. Wall and M. W. Blum, "Negotiations," *Journal of Management,* June 1991, p. 296.

4. Do not allow accountability to your constituents or surveillance by them to spawn competitive bargaining.
5. If you have power in a negotiation, use it—with specific demands, mild threats, and persuasion—to guide the opponent toward an agreement.
6. Be open to accepting third-party assistance.
7. In a negotiation, attend to the environment and be aware that the opponent's behavior and power are altered by it.

SUMMARY OF KEY POINTS

• Power is the capability one party has to affect the actions of another party. Influence is transaction in which one party induces another party to behave in a certain way. Another way of making a distinction is to think of power as the potential to influence, and influence as power in action.

• French and Raven introduced the notion of five interpersonal power bases: legitimate (position based), reward, coercive (punishment based), expert, and referent (charismatic). These five bases can be divided into two major categories: organizational and personal. Legitimate, reward, and coercive power are primarily prescribed by an organization, while expert and referent power are based on personal qualities.

• Organizational structure creates power by specifying certain individuals to perform certain tasks. Three important forms of structural power include (1) access to resources, (2) ability to affect decision-making processes, and (3) having access to relevant and important information.

• Powerlessness occurs when an individual has little or no access to the bases of interpersonal or structural power. Empowerment refers to a process whereby conditions that contribute to powerlessness are identified and removed. Two important factors in empowerment are helping organizational members feel confident of their ability to perform well, and increasing the linkages between effort and performance.

• The strategic contingency approach addresses subunit power. A strategic contingency is an event or activity that is extremely important for accomplishing organi-

zational goals. The strategic contingency factors that have been disclosed by research include coping with uncertainty, centrality, and substitutability.

• Individuals with very little or no real power may still influence others because they *appear* to be powerful. This is the illusion of power that was clearly illustrated in the Milgram experiments on obedience.

• Mintzberg introduced the notion of political game playing in organizations. Examples of political games include *insurgency* (resisting authority), *sponsorship* (attaching oneself to someone with power, *coalition-building (building power-bases), line-versus-staff* (defeating rivals), and *whistle-blowing* (effecting organizational change).

• A manager's behavior should satisfy certain criteria to be considered ethical. These include the (1) *criterion of utilitarian outcomes* (the greatest good for the greatest number), (2) *criterion of individual rights,* (respecting rights of free consent, speech, privacy, and due process).

• Win-lose negotiating is a form of a zero-sum game. That is, to the extent one party wins something the other party loses. Win-win negotiating is a positive-sum approach, wherein each party gains without a corresponding loss for the other party.

• There is an increasing use of third parties in negotiations. In some cases third parties may be part of the entire process, in others they may be called in only when an impasse is reached. Different types of third party negotiations include mediation, arbitration, conciliation, and consultation.

REVIEW AND DISCUSSION QUESTIONS

1. Power is an aspect of a relationship between two or more persons. What implications does this fact have for organizational members who wish to increase their power? Decrease the power of others?

2. Is there one particular form of power that is best to have in organizations? Are some forms of power easier (or more difficult) to acquire in organizations?

3. What steps are involved in the empowerment process? Describe how they might be carried out in a situation with which you are familiar.

4. What changes in an organization's or department's environment would bring about changes in strategic contingencies? How might changes in these contingencies affect power relationships in the unit?

5. How the illusion of power can be just as effective as actual power was clearly illustrated in the "obedience to authority" experiments conducted by Milgram. Can you think of other examples where people have responded to the illusion of power? Does this happen in organizations?

6. Sometimes "playing politics" is the most effective way of achieving objectives. Why is this the case? Should organizations be concerned about it?

7. Five of Mintzberg's political games are described in the chapter. How many of them have you witnessed being played in organizations of which you were a member? What other games have you seen played? Which games have you played?

8. The use of power and politics often involve ethical issues. What are the criteria that may be used to determine the extent to which a manager's behavior is ethical? Are there ever legitimate exceptions to these criteria?

9. What are the four elements typically part of all negotiations? Are there likely to be differences in these elements depending on whether the negotiations are of a win-win or a win-lose nature?

10. What suggestions were given for improving negotiations? What additional suggestions can you make?

●

READINGS

READING 9–1   POWER AND INFLUENCE: THE VIEW FROM BELOW

Timothy R. Hinkin
Chester A. Schriesheim

More than most of their colleagues, human resources professionals find themselves in situations involving power and influence. After all, they interact with everyone in the organization hierarchy. Often, too, they must arbitrate between supervisors and employees in situations that developed from the use (or misuse) of power.

Thus to do their jobs effectively, human resources professionals need to understand the nature of power and influence in work organizations. Equally important, they need to share that knowledge with every member of the organization who has responsibility for supervising—and consequently exerting power and influence—over other employees.

TWO SCHOOLS OF THOUGHT

In most human interactions, behavior is based largely on role expectations. Certain behaviors are expected and accepted as legitimate; deviance from those behaviors can lead to conflict or misunderstanding. When dining at an expensive restaurant, for example, customers expect to be seated by a host or hostess and to be served by a waiter or waitress. If they are not seated within a given period of time, they may become irritable. Role expectations have been violated, and depending on situational factors such as hunger, they may complain or decide to leave.

In the workplace, employees have role expectations for themselves and their co-workers; violation of those expectations may also have negative effects. Employees' role expectations are based on behaviors expected of a worker in a particular position as well as on characteristics unique to that person. The role expectations created by a worker's position are based on job content, the behavior of previous job incumbents, and organizational goals. The role expectations created by the worker are based on what is known about that person, and the person may alter expected role behavior over time.

Source: Timothy R. Hinkin and Chester A. Schriesheim, *Personnel*, May 1988, pp. 47–50. Reprinted with permission.

Similarly, a certain degree of power is inherent in every position in an organization; that power can be increased or decreased by the jobholder as a result of his or her behavior. Typically, power is viewed as the potential to exert influence, whereas influence is thought of in active terms, involving the actual modification of another person's behavior. Perhaps the best known and accepted framework of power is that of John R. P. French and Bertram Raven. In their article, "The Bases of Social Power," published in *Studies in Social Power* (edited by Dorwin Cartwright, Institute for Social Research, University of Michigan, 1959), they discuss the relationships between various power bases and organizational "outcomes" such as employee satisfaction. In contrast, many recent studies, such as the work of David Kipnis, Stuart M. Schmidt, and Ian Wilkinson ("Interorganizational Influence Tactics: Explorations in Getting One's Way," *Journal of Applied Psychology* 65, 1980), focus on the influence tactics chosen by individual managers when they attempt to gain compliance from others in their organizations.

Many researchers have criticized the literature on the bases of social power for not attempting to link the study of managerial power to the literature on influence tactics. On the other hand, researchers who have investigated the influence tactics used by managers in various situations have given little attention to the antecedents to or consequences of those tactics. Thus further investigation of the relationships between the various bases of power, influence tactics, and important organizational consequences is needed.

A DIFFERENT APPROACH

For our exploration of the relationships between managerial power and influence and organizational outcomes, we decided to take an approach different from that used by most researchers to date. We decided to measure power and influence from the viewpoint of the target of influence attempts—the supervised employees. We believe that this approach makes sense for two reasons: First, people do not react to "objective" facts but rather to their individual

EXHIBIT 9-7

**Definitions of Power
Bases and Illustrative
Survey Items**

Reward power — the ability to administer to another person things that person desires or to remove or decrease things that person does not desire.

Examples:
My supervisor can increase my pay level.
My supervisor can provide me with special benefits.

Coercive power — the ability to administer to another person things that person does not desire or to remove or decrease things that person desires.

Examples:
My supervisor can give me undesirable job assignments.
My supervisor can make my work difficult for me.

Legitimate power — the ablity to administer to another person feelings of obligation or responsibility.

Examples:
My supervisor can make me feel that I have commitments to meet.
My supervisor can give me the feeling that I have responsibilities to fulfill.

Expert power — the ability to administer to another person information, knowledge, or expertise.

Examples:
My supervisor can provide me with sound job-related advice.
My supervisor can share with me his or her considerable experience and/or training.

Referent power — the ability to administer to another person feelings of personal acceptance or approval.

Examples:
My supervisor can make me feel like he or she approves of me.
My supervisor can make me feel valued.

EXHIBIT 9-8

**Influence Tactics and
Illustrative Survey Items**

Position and organization sanctions:
My supervisor threatened my job security (that is, hinted at firing me or having me fired).
My supervisor filed a report about me with higher-ups (that is, his or her supervisor).

Exchange (striking a bargain):
My supervisor offered me an exchange. (That is, "If you do this for me, I will do something for you.")
My supervisor did personal favors for me.

Rational explanation and clarification:
My supervisor explained the reasons for his or her request.
My supervisor presented information to support his or her point of view.

Personal assertiveness:
My supervisor repeatedly reminded me about his or her request.
My supervisor simply ordered me to do what was asked.

Coalitions:
My supervisor obtained the support of the employees he or she supervises to back up his or her request.
My supervisor obtained the support of co-workers to back up his or her request.

Ingratiation:
My supervisor acted very humbly while making his or her request.
My supervisor acted in a friendly manner before asking for what he or she wanted.

perceptions. Second, a substantial amount of research indicates that considerable discrepancy often exists between what managers do and what they say they do.

In our study, we asked 251 middle managers in a wide variety of organizations to assess the power and influence tactics of their supervision as well as their own satisfaction and commitment. Through a multistep, multisample procedure, we developed conceptual definitions for the bases of power identified by French and Raven and generated survey items for each measure. The survey items were evaluated to ensure content validity and were then subjected to a series of analyses to obtain final scales with adequate reliability. Definitions of the power bases as well as some illustrative items for each survey measure are shown in Exhibit 9-7.

The influence measures used in this survey were based on the work of Kipnis and his colleagues. A series of statistical (factor) analyses suggested that employees' perceptions of their supervisor's influence tactics fall into six categories, which are listed in Exhibit 9-8 along with some illustrative survey items for each measure.

The "outcome" measures that we examined were overall job satisfaction, satisfaction with supervisor's technical skill, satisfaction with supervisor's human relations skill, and commitment to the organization. All of the measures have been used in prior studies and have been shown to have adequate reliability and validity.

SOME CLEAR PATTERNS

The results of our study reveal a clear pattern of relationships between the way employees perceive their supervisor's base of power and the employees' level of satisfaction and commitment. Reward power had a strong positive correlation with the satisfaction measures (though not commitment), while legitimate, expert, and referent power had a strong positive correlation with all of the outcome measures. Coercive power had the opposite effect—a strong negative correlation with all of the outcome measures. The overall pattern of our results suggests that coercive power is perceived negatively by employees, while the other power bases are viewed positively—a pattern consistent with previous theory and research.

We noted some interesting correlations between specific influence tactics used by an employee's supervisor and the employee's level of satisfaction and commitment. For example, several influence tactics used by supervisors (ingratiation, exchange, and coalitions) had no correlation with an employee's level of satisfaction and commitment. Al-

though employees may have perceived those tactics to be acceptable with respect to the behavior expected of their supervisor, the tactics were ineffective—at least in terms of increasing employees' satisfaction and commitment to the organization. (Further, even though these influence tactics are commonly used by managers, they were not correlated with any of the perceived bases of power.)

In contrast, a supervisor's use of personal assertiveness had a strong negative correlation with both employee satisfaction and commitment. Organization sanctions also had a strong negative correlation with the measures of satisfaction, although the negative effects were substantially less than those of personal assertiveness. Clearly, employees do not like to be threatened or strong-armed. However, they seem to react less negatively to influence tactics that they perceive as being sanctioned by the organization than those that they perceive as stemming from their supervisor's personal assertiveness. Nevertheless, both influence tactics were perceived as outside the domain of expected or desired supervisor role behavior.

Moreover, personal assertiveness had a strong positive correlation with coercive power (which research suggests should be used only as the "power of last resort"). It also had strong negative relationships with expert and referent power. Similarly, organizational sanctions had strong negative correlations with legitimate, expert, and referent power.

One influence tactic had a very strong positive correlation with employees' satisfaction and commitment. Employees greatly preferred being given a rational explanation for complying with the directives of their supervisor. That is, they preferred to understand the purpose of their actions; when their supervisor attempted to do this, they responded positively. Further, use of rational explanation had a strong positive correlation with both legitimate and referent power as well as a moderate positive correlation with reward and expert power. Apparently, supervisors with these bases of power are more likely to clarify the reasons behind their requests, a supervisory behavior that may be both desired and expected by employees.

COMPLIANCE AND ACCEPTANCE

Employees often comply with the demands of supervisors because they are required to do so. However, researchers have found that with the use of certain influence tactics, performance is likely to deteriorate over time or in the absence of continued direct supervision. Conversely, if employees accept an influence tactic as legitimate and consistent with their expectations of supervisory behavior, they

EXHIBIT 9-9

Correlations between Supervisor's Influence Tactics, Employee's Perceptions of Supervisor's Power Base, and Employee Satisfaction, Compliance, and Acceptance

Supervisor's Influence Tactic	Employee's Perception of Supervisor's Power Base*	Employee Satisfaction	Employee Compliance†	Employee Acceptance†
Ingratiation	No correlation	No correlation	Unpredictable	Negative
Exchange	No correlation	No correlation	Unpredictable	Negative
Coalitions	No correlation	No correlation	Unpredictable	Negative
Sanctions	$-L$, $-E$, $-F$	Negative	Positive	Negative
Assertiveness	$+C$, $-E$, $-F$	Negative	Positive	Negative
Rationality	$+L$, $+F$, $+E$, $+R$	Positive	Positive	Positive

*Definitions of symbols: $(-)$ negative, $(+)$ positive, (L) legitimate power, (E) expert power, (F) referent power, (C) coercive power, (R) reward power.

†Findings are based on the research of Bernard M. Bass, *Stogdill's Handbook of Leadership,* rev. ed. (New York: Free Press, 1981); Miriam Erez and Yesayaha Rim, "The Relationship between Goals, Influence Tactics, and Personal and Organizational Variables," *Human Relations* 35 (1982); John R. P. French and Bertram Raven, "The Bases of Social Power, in *Studies in Social Power,* ed. Donald Cartwright (Ann Arbor: Institute of Social Research, University of Michigan, 1959); and David Kipnis and Stuart M. Schmidt, *Profile of Organizational Influence Strategies* (University Associates, 1982).

EXHIBIT 9-10

The Influence Process

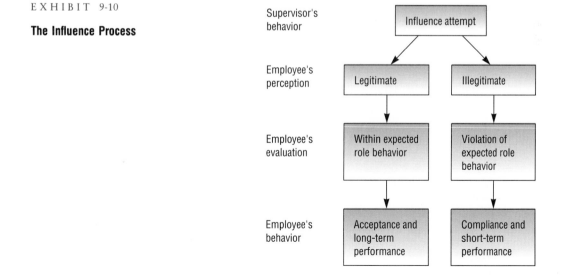

are likely to accept the directive and continue to perform without direct supervision. The results of our study and prior theoretical and empirical research suggest that the relationships shown in Exhibit 9-9 exist.

The way employees view their supervisor's power base is correlated with the supervisor's influence tactics. And employees will evaluate the influence tactics as being legitimate or illegitimate and within or outside the limits of expected supervisory behavior. Ultimately, influence tactics affect employees' feelings and behavior, as illustrated in Exhibit 9-10.

Because our study was not experimental, cause-and-effect conclusions cannot be considered as "demonstrated." However, the strong positive correlations between rational explanation, employee satisfaction and commitment, and the positively perceived bases of power suggest that a supervisor's power and effectiveness may be enhanced by using a strategy of clarification.

On the other hand, personal assertiveness and organizational sanctions have a negative correlation with employee satisfaction and commitment as well as with the positively perceived bases of power. Yet short-term employee compliance may result if the consequences of noncompliance are sufficiently severe. The correlations suggest that personal assertiveness and organizational sanctions are associated with negative outcomes for the organization and may be outside the bounds of expected (and acceptable) supervisory behavior.

Certain types of influence tactics (namely, ingratiation, exchange, and coalitions) are not correlated with any perceived base of power or with employee satisfaction and commitment. These behaviors may be seen as "normal" for the supervisor, but apparently they are of little use in influencing employees.

THE POWER OF INFORMATION

Many of the current management trends, such as quality circles, emphasize employee participation in the decision-making process. The underlying premise of these programs is that employees will be more motivated (and satisfied) if they have a voice in shaping policy and influencing decisions. Unfortunately, employee participation in decision making is not always possible—or desirable. The results of our study suggest that an organization may benefit simply if supervisors *explain* to their employees why things are being done and thereby help employees understand their work roles and what is taking place around them.

Recent popular and academic literature has focused on the power of information, suggesting that people who have information have power. Although empirical support for this notion is scarce, the work that has been done has supported it, and the idea is also intuitively appealing. If information is a source of power, can it be harnessed by supervisors and, if so, how?

The results of our study strongly suggest that supervisors should share information with their employees. They should take the time to explain their actions and requests to their staff members. Training may be necessary to help supervisors develop this capacity. Although several different influence tactics can be used to gain short-term employee compliance, only the use of rational explanations has positive effects that may benefit both the supervisor and the organization in the long run. The classic assumption that people are rational may be truer than we think, and as rational entities people prefer to be influenced in a rational manner.

READING 9–2   CONSIDER BOTH RELATIONSHIPS AND SUBSTANCE WHEN NEGOTIATING STRATEGICALLY

Grant T. Savage
John D. Blair
Ritch L. Sorenson

When David Peterson, director of services for Dickerson Machinery, arrives at his office, he notes four appointments on his schedule. With his lengthy experience in negotiating

Source: Grant T. Savage, John D. Blair, and Ritch L. Sorenson, "Consider Both Relationships and Substance when Negotiating Strategically," *Academy of Management Executive*, February 1989, pp. 37–47.

important contracts for this large-equipment repair service, he does not take long to identify the agenda for each appointment.[1]

A steering clutch disk salesman from Roadworks will arrive at 8:30 A.M. Peterson has relied for years on disks supplied by Caterpillar and knows those disks can provide the 8,000 hours of service Dickerson guarantees. Price is an issue in Peterson's selection of a supplier, but more important is a guarantee on the life span of the part.

A meeting is scheduled at 9:30 with a mechanic who has swapped a new company battery for a used battery from his own truck. This "trade" is, of course, against company policy, and the employee has been reprimanded and told his next paycheck will be docked. However, the mechanic wants to discuss the matter.

A representative for Tarco, a large road-building contractor, is scheduled for 10:00 A.M. Peterson has been interested in this service contract for a couple of years. He believes that if he can secure a short-term service contract with Tarco, Dickerson's high-quality mechanical service and guarantees will result in a long-term service relationship with the contractor. The night before, Peterson had dinner with Tarco's representative, and this morning he will provide a tour of service facilities and discuss the short-term contract with him.

A meeting with management representatives for union negotiations is scheduled for 1:00 P.M. That meeting will probably last a couple of hours. Peterson is concerned because the company has lost money on the shop undergoing contract talks, and now the union is demanding higher wages and threatening to strike. The company cannot afford a prolonged strike, but it also cannot afford to increase pay at current service production rates. Negotiating a contract will not be easy.

CHOOSING NEGOTIATION STRATEGIES

Peterson's appointments are not unique. Researchers and scholars have examined similar situations. What strategic advice does the negotiation literature offer for handling these four situations?

One of the best developed approaches is *game theory*, which focuses on maximizing substantive outcomes in negotiations.[2] Peterson would probably do well by focusing on only the best possible outcome for Dickerson Machinery in his meetings with the salesman and the employee: He already has a good contract for a steering wheel clutch, but if the salesman can offer a better deal, Peterson will take it; and in the case of the employee, Peterson will hear him out but foresees no need to deviate from company policy.

In contrast, an exclusive focus on maximizing the company's substantive outcomes would probably not work in the other two situations: Tarco may continue being serviced elsewhere unless enticed to try Dickerson; and during the union negotiations, strategies to maximize outcomes for management only could force a strike.

Another well-developed strategic approach is *win-win problem solving*. It is designed to maximize outcomes for both parties and maintain positive relationships.[3] This approach could work in the union negotiation, but the outcome would probably be a compromise, not a true win-win solution.

Win-win negotiation probably is not the best strategy in the other three situations. Either Roadwork's salesman meets the guarantee and beats current prices, or he does not; trying to find a win-win solution would probably be a waste of time. Similarly, because the meeting with the employee will occur after company rules have been applied, a win-win solution is probably not in the company's best interest. Lastly, an attempt to maximize the company's substantive outcomes in a short-term service contract with Tarco could hinder long-term contract prospects.

Any one approach to negotiation clearly will not work in all situations. Executives need a framework for determining what strategies are best in different situations. We believe the best strategy depends on desired outcomes. In this article, we characterize the two major outcomes at issue in the previous examples as *substantive* and *relationship outcomes*. Although both types of outcomes have been discussed in the literature, relationship outcomes have received much less attention. Our contention is that a systematic model of strategic choice for negotiation must account for both substantive and relationship outcomes. In articulating such a model, we suggest that executives can approach negotiation strategically by assessing the negotiation context; considering unilateral negotiation strategies; transforming unilateral into interactive negotiation strategies; and monitoring tactics and reevaluating negotiation strategies.

ASSESSING THE NEGOTIATION CONTEXT

A crucial context for any negotiation is the manager's current and desired relationship with the other party. Unfortunately, in their rush to secure the best possible substantive outcome, managers often overlook the impact of the negotiation on their relationships. This oversight can hurt a manager's relationship with the other party, thus limiting his or her ability to obtain desired substantive outcomes now or in the future.

Each interaction with another negotiator constitutes an *episode* that draws from current and affects future relationships. Intertwined with pure concerns about relationships are concerns about substantive outcomes. Many times negotiators are motivated to establish or maintain positive relationships and willingly "share the pie" through mutually beneficial collaboration. Other negotiations involve substantive outcomes that can benefit one negotiator only at the expense of the other (a fixed pie). These cases often motivate negotiators to discount the relationship and claim as much of the pie as possible.

Most negotiations, however, are neither clearly win-win nor win-lose situations, but combinations of both (an indeterminate pie). Such mixed-motive situations, in which both collaboration and compensation may occur, are particularly difficult for managers to handle strategically.[4] The relationship that exists prior to the negotiation, the relationship that unfolds during negotiations, and the desired relationship often will determine whether either negotiator will be motivated to share the pie, grab it, or give it away.

In any case, managers should keep existing and desired relationships in mind as they bid for substantive outcomes. For example, when negotiators are on the losing end of a win-lose negotiation, they should examine the implications of taking a short-term loss. During his third appointment, Peterson's willingness to make only minimal gains in service contracts for the short term may create a positive relationship that will lead to a lucrative, long-term contract with Tarco. The relative importance of possible substantive and relationship outcomes should help executives decide whether and how to negotiate. To guide their decision process, managers should begin by assessing their relative power and the level of conflict between them and the other party. Both are key determinants of their current relationship with the other party.

Exhibit 9-11 illustrates the negotiation context, showing those aspects of the situation and negotiation episode that shape relationship and substantive outcomes. Existing levels of power and conflict influence (1) the relationship between the executive and the other party and (2) the negotiation strategies they choose. These strategies are implemented through appropriate tactics during a negotiation episode—a one-on-one encounter, a telephone call, or a meeting with multiple parties—and result in substantive and relationship outcomes.

The multiple arrows linking strategies, tactics, and the negotiation episode in Exhibit 9-11 show the monitoring process through which both the manager and the other party refine their strategies and tactics during an episode. A complex and lengthy negotiation, such as a union contract negotiation, may include many episodes; a simple negotiation may be completed within one episode. Each episode, nonetheless, influences future negotiations by changing the manager's and the other party's relative power, the level of conflict between them, and their relationship.

Relative Power

The relative power of the negotiators establishes an important aspect of their relationship: the extent of each party's dependence on the other. Researchers have found that individuals assess their power in a relationship and choose whether to compete, accommodate, collaborate, or withdraw when negotiating with others.[5] Managers can assess their power relative to the other party by comparing their respective abilities to induce compliance through the control of human and material resources. To what extent do they each control key material resources? To what extent do they each control the deployment, arrangement, and advancement of people within the organization?[6]

These questions will help managers determine whether their relationship with the other party is based on independence, dependence, or interdependence. Additionally, these questions should help executives consider how **and** whether their relationship with the other party should be strengthened or weakened. Often managers will find themselves or their organizations in interdependent relationships that have both beneficial and detrimental aspects. These relationships are called mixed-motive situations in the negotiation literature because they provide incentives for both competitive and cooperative actions.

In his relationship with the Roadwork salesman, Peterson has considerable power. He is satisfied with his current vendor and has other vendors wanting to sell him the same product. The numerous choices available allow him to make demands on the salesman. Similarly, Peterson has more relative power than the mechanic. On the other hand, he has relatively little power with Tarco, since the contractor can choose from a number of equipment-service shops. Moreover, Tarco's representative did not make the initial contact and has not actively sought Dickerson's services.

Level of Conflict

The level of conflict underlying a potential negotiation establishes how the negotiators perceive the effective dimension of their relationship—that is, its degree of supportiveness or hostility. Managers can assess the relationship's level of conflict by identifying the differences between each party's interests. On what issues do both parties agree?

EXHIBIT 9-11

**Assessing the
Negotiation Context**

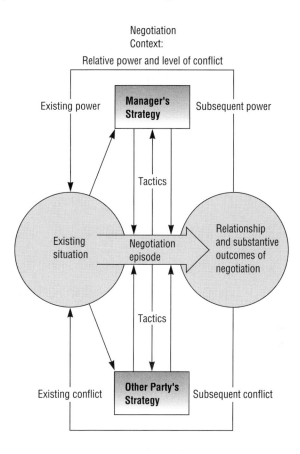

On what issues do they disagree? How intense and how ingrained are these differences?[7]

Answers to these questions will reveal whether negotiations will easily resolve differences and whether the relationship is perceived as supportive or hostile. These questions, like the questions about relative power, should also help executives consider how **and** whether the relationship should be strengthened or weakened. Very few negotiations begin with a neutral relationship. Indeed, the affective state of the relationship may be a primary reason for negotiating with a powerful other party, especially if the relationship has deteriorated or been particularly supportive.

In Peterson's case, neutral to positive relationships exist with the Roadwork salesman and the Tarco representative. However, his relationships with the mechanic and the union are potentially hostile. For example, management and union representatives have already had confrontations. Their conflict may escalate if the relationship is not managed and both sides are not willing to make concessions.[8]

Considering a Unilateral Negotiation Strategy

Before selecting a strategy for negotiation, a manager should consider his or her interests and the interests of the organization. These interests will shape the answers to two basic questions: (1) Is the substantive outcome very important to the manager? and (2) Is the relationship outcome very important to the manager?

Four *unilateral* strategies (see Exhibit 9-12) emerge from the answers: *trusting collaboration, firm competition, open subordination,* and *active avoidance.*[9] We call these unilateral strategies because in using them, managers consider only their own interests or the interests of their

EXHIBIT 9-12

**Considering a Unilateral
Negotitation Strategy**

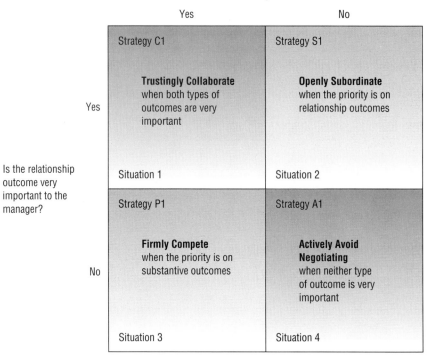

Is the substantive
outcome very important
to the manager?

	Yes	No
Yes	Strategy C1 **Trustingly Collaborate** when both types of outcomes are very important Situation 1	Strategy S1 **Openly Subordinate** when the priority is on relationship outcomes Situation 2
No	Strategy P1 **Firmly Compete** when the priority is on substantive outcomes Situation 3	Strategy A1 **Actively Avoid Negotiating** when neither type of outcome is very important Situation 4

Is the relationship
outcome very
important to the
manager?

organization, ignoring for the time being the interests of the other party.

The unilateral strategies presented in Exhibit 9-12 are similar to the conflict management styles suggested by the combined works of Blake and Mouton, Hall, and Kilmann and Thomas.[10] However, while we agree that personalities and conflict-management preferences influence a person's ability to negotiate, our selection of terms reflects our focus on strategies instead of styles. For example, Johnston uses the term *subordination* to refer to a strategy similar to the conflict-management style variously termed *accommodation* (Kilmann and Thomas), *smoothing* (Blake and Mouton), or *yield-lose* (Hall).[11] We, however, see using the openly subordinative strategy as more than simply "rolling over and playing dead" or "giving away the store." Rather, this strategy is designed to strengthen long-term relational ties, usually at the expense of short-term substantive outcomes. Our discussion below also gets beyond Johnston's conception, showing how a negotiator can focus the openly

subordinative group according to his or her substantive goals.

Our view is consistent with research that suggests that individuals adopt different strategies in different relational contexts.[12]

We anticipate the managers' success with these unilateral strategies depends on their ability to exhibit a variety of conflict styles. To highlight the role of relationship and substantive priorities, we describe these four unilateral strategies in their most extenuated, ideal form, and articulate their underlying assumptions. In many ways our descriptions are classic depictions of each type of strategy. Two of these strategies—competition and collaboration—are frequently discussed in the conflict and negotiation literature.

1. *Trusting Collaboration (C1)*. In general, if both relationship and substantive outcomes are important to the organization, the manager should consider *trusting col-*

laboration. The hallmark of this strategy is openness on the part of both parties. By encouraging cooperation as positions are asserted, the executive should be able to achieve important relationship and substantive outcomes. The executive seeks a win-win outcome both to achieve substantive goals *and* maintain a positive relationship.

Trustingly collaborative strategies generally are easiest to use and most effective when the manager's organization and the other party are interdependent and mutually supportive. These circumstances normally create a trusting relationship in which negotiators reciprocally disclose their goals and needs. In this climate, an effective problem-solving process and a win-win settlement typically result.

2. *Open Subordination (S1).* If managers are more concerned with establishing a positive relationship with another party than obtaining substantive outcomes, they should openly subordinate. We use the term *subordination* instead of *accommodation* to differentiate this strategic choice from a conflict-management style. An openly subordinative strategy is a yield-win strategy that usually provides desired substantive outcomes to the other party but rarely to the manager. A subordinative strategy may be used regardless of whether the manager exercises more, less, or equal power relative to the other party. Our argument is that subordination can be an explicit strategic negotiation behavior—not simply a reflection of power. If the manager has little to lose by yielding to the substantive interests of the other party, open subordination can be a key way for him or her to dampen hostilities, increase support, and foster more interdependent relationships.

3. *Firm Competition (P1).* If substantive interests are important but the relationship is not, the manager should consider *firmly competing.* This situation often occurs when managers have little trust for the other party or the relationship is not good to begin with. In such situations, they may want to exert their power to gain substantive outcomes. To enact this competitive strategy, they may also become highly aggressive, bluffing, threatening the other party, or otherwise misrepresenting their intentions. Such tactics hide the manager's actual goals and needs, preventing the other party from using that knowledge to negotiate its own substantive outcomes. Not surprisingly, the credibility of the executive's aggressive tactics and, thus, the success of the firmly competitive strategy often rests on the organization's power vis-à-vis the other party. When following a firmly competitive strategy, the manager seeks a win-lose substantive outcome and is willing to accept a neutral or even a bad relationship.

4. *Active Avoidance (A1).* Managers should consider *actively avoiding negotiation* if neither the relationship nor the substantive outcomes are important to them or the organization. Simply *refusing* to negotiate is the most direct and active form of avoidance. Executives can simply tell the other party they are not interested in or willing to negotiate. Such an action, however, will usually have a negative impact on the organization's relationship with the other party. Moreover, managers must determine which issues are a waste of time to negotiate. We treat avoidance, like subordination, as an explicit, strategic behavior rather than as an option taken by default when the manager is uncertain about what to do.

However, we recognize that these unilateral strategies are most successful only in a limited set of situations. In the next section we include various *interactive* modifications that make these classic, unilateral strategies applicable to a wider set of negotiation situations.

INTERACTIVE NEGOTIATION STRATEGIES

Before using the unilateral strategies suggested by Exhibit 9-12, the executive should examine the negotiation from each party's perspective. The choice of a negotiation strategy should be based not only on the interests of the executive or organization but also on the interests of the other party. The manager should anticipate the other party's substantive and relationship priorities, assessing how the negotiation is likely to progress when the parties interact. This step is crucial because the unilateral strategies described above could lead to grave problems if the other party's priorities differ. For example, when using either trusting collaboration or open subordination, the manager is vulnerable to exploitation if the other party is concerned only about substantive outcomes. When anticipating the other party's substantive and relationship priorities, executives should consider the kinds of actions the other party might take. Are those actions likely to be supportive or hostile? Will they represent short-term reactions or long-term approaches to the substantive issues under negotiation? Are those actions likely to change the party's degree of dependence on, or interdependence with, the organization? The answers will depend on (1) the history of the executive's relations with the other party and (2) the influence of key individuals and groups on the manager and of key individuals and groups on the manager and the other party.

In short, executives should take into account both their own and the other party's substantive and relationship priorities in choosing a negotiating strategy. Exhibit 9-13 is a decision tree designed to help managers decide which strategy to use. The left side represents, in a different form, the analysis in Exhibit 9-11; thus, Exhibit 9-12 also shows how the manager's substantive and relationship priorities lead to *unilateral strategies* based solely on the manager's position. The right side illustrates how these unilateral strategies may be continued, modified, or replaced after the manager considers the other party's potential or apparent priorities.[13]

Managers should examine the appropriateness of a unilateral negotiation strategy by accounting for the other party's priorities before they use it. Sometimes such scrutiny will simply justify its use. For example, when both substantive and relationship outcomes are important to an executive, the appropriate unilateral strategy is trusting collaboration. If the manager anticipates that the other party also values both substantive and relationship outcomes (see Exhibit 9-12, Situation 1), he or she would continue to favor this strategy. At other times, scrutiny of the other party's priorities may suggest some modifications. We discuss next each of the interactive variations of the classic, unilateral strategies.

1. *Principled Collaboration (C2)*. The C1 collaborative strategy assumes that the other party will reciprocate whenever the executive discloses information. However, if the manager negotiates openly and the other party is not open or is competitive, the manager could be victimized. Under such circumstances, the manager should use the modified collaborative strategy of principal collaboration.[14] Rather than relying on only trust and reciprocity, the manager persuades the other party to conduct negotiations based on a set of mutually agreed upon principles that will benefit each negotiator.

2. *Focused Subordination (S2)*. The openly subordinative strategy (S1) assumes that the substantive outcome is of little importance to the organization. Sometimes, however, an organization has both substantive and relationship interests, but the other party has little stake in either interest. By discovering and then acquiescing to those key needs that are of interest only to the other party, the manager can still gain some substantive outcomes for the organization while assuring a relatively positive relationship outcome. Here, managers both create substantive outcomes for the other party and achieve substantive outcomes for themselves or their organization.

3. *Soft Competition (P2)*. Under circumstances the directness of the firmly competitive strategy (P1) may need

to be softened. For example, even though the manager may place little importance on the relationship outcome, this relationship may be very important to the other party. If the other party is powerful and potentially threatening, the manager would be wise to use a competitive strategy that maintains the relationship. Here the executive would avoid highly aggressive and other "dirty" tactics.

4. *Passive Avoidance (A2)*. If the manager does not consider either the relationship or the substantive outcome important but the other party views the negotiation as important for a relationship outcome, the manager probably should *delegate* the negotiation. By passively avoiding the negotiation, the manager allows someone else within the organization to explore possible outcomes for the organization and keep the relationship from becoming hostile. Delegating ensures that possible opportunities are not ignored while freeing the executive from what appears to be a low-priority negotiation.

5. *Responsive Avoidance (A3)*. By contrast, if the manager considers neither the relationship nor the substantive outcome important and the other party considers the substantive outcome important and the relationship unimportant, the manager should *regulate* the issue. Direct interaction with the other party is not necessary; the manager can be responsive but still avoid negotiating by either applying standard operating procedures or developing new policies that address the other party's concern.

Transforming Unilateral Strategies

The model of strategic choice in Exhibit 9-13 connects unilateral and interactive negotiation strategies. In many instances the interactive strategies are modifications of the unilateral strategies. We base the decision to modify or replace a unilateral strategy almost exclusively on the manager's and other party's differing outcome priorities. Three outcome conditions and three sets of assumptions influence the choice of interactive strategies.

1. *Outcome Condition One: The manager may value the relationship, but the other party may not.* For example, a manager who assumes that trust and cooperation will result in a fair outcome may be taken advantage of by another party who is concerned with only substantive outcomes.[15] Hence, we suggest either principled collaboration or soft competition for such cases to ensure that the other party does not take advantage of the manager (see Exhibit 9-13, Situation 2). On the other hand, the manager may simply want to create a long-term business relationship with someone who currently is interested in neither sub-

EXHIBIT 9-13

Selecting an Interactive Strategy

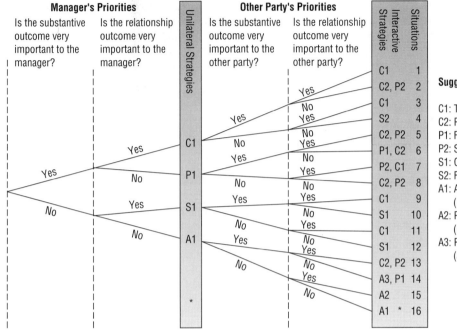

stantive nor relationship outcomes. In these cases the manager should choose to subordinate in a focused fashion—rather than to trustingly collaborate—to establish a relationship with the other party (see Exhibit 9-13, Situation 4).

2. *Outcome Condition Two: The manager may not value the relationship, but the other party may.* Given only their own substantive priorities, managers would firmly compete or actively avoid negotiation under these circumstances. However, if the other party is interested in the relationship, the manager may not have to compete firmly to obtain desired substantive outcomes. The manager may collaborate or softly compete and still gain substantive goals without alienating the other party (see Exhibit 9-13, Situations 5–8). Such strategies may also foster a long-term relationship with substantive dividends for the manager.

Similarly, in situations where neither substantive nor relationship outcomes are important to the manager but

the relationship is important to the other party, the manager may choose an interactive strategy other than avoidance. The other party is in a position to choose a subordinative strategy and may offer substantive incentives to the manager. If the manager chooses principled collaboration or soft competition, he or she may gain some positive substantive outcomes (see Exhibit 9-13, Situation 13).

3. *Outcome Condition Three. Both parties may value the relationship, but the manager may not value substantive outcomes.* In these cases, whether or not the other party is interested in substantive outcomes, the manager may choose a trustingly collaborative strategy to maintain positive ties with the other party (see Exhibit 9-13, Situations 9 and 11).

4. *Transformation Assumptions.* Underlying these three outcome conditions are three sets of assumptions. First, we assume that most relationships will involve some mixture of dependence and interdependence as well as some degree of supportiveness and hostility. Second, we assume

that most negotiators will view the relationship outcome as important under four separate conditions—high interdependence, high dependence, high supportiveness, or high hostility—or possible combinations of those conditions. Third, from a manager's perspective, each of the basic strategies has a different effect with regard to power and conflict: (1) collaborative strategies strengthen the interdependence of the manager and the other party while also enhancing feelings of supportiveness, (2) subordinative strategies increase the other party's dependence on the manager while also deemphasizing feelings of hostility, and (3) competitive strategies decrease the manager's dependence on the other party but may also escalate feelings of hostility.

Thus, many of the interactive negotiation strategies in Exhibit 9-13 seek to enhance interdependent relationships or favorably shift the balance of dependence within a relationship. These same strategies also attempt to dampen feelings of hostility or heighten feelings of supportiveness.

Illustrations of Negotiation-Strategy Transformations

To demonstrate more concretely how Exhibit 9-13 works, we will examine how Dickerson's Peterson might act if he were to follow the decision tree to choose his negotiation strategies.

1. *From Avoidance to Collaboration or Competition.* In planning to meet with the steering clutch salesman, Peterson first considers whether the substantive outcome is very important to Dickerson Machinery. Because the company already has a satisfactory source for clutch disks, the substantive outcome is not very important. Second, Peterson considers the importance of the relationship outcome. Given that Dickerson Machinery currently has no ties with Roadworks and Peterson foresees no need to establish a long-term relationship, the relationship outcome is not very important either. Based on Peterson's priorities only, unilateral avoidance strategy (A1) seems appropriate.

However, Peterson now considers the salesman's priorities. First, is the substantive outcome important to the salesman? Obviously it is—Roadworks is a struggling, new company and needs new clients. Second, is the relationship outcome important to Roadworks? Because the salesman works on a commission with residuals, he probably desires a long-term sales contract, so the relationship outcome is important. The salesman's priorities suggest that he would probably collaborate trustingly (C1).

After answering the questions forming the decision tree in Exhibit 9-13 (see Situation 13), Peterson has two options for an interactive strategy. Since he is in a position of power, he does not need to make concessions. Moreover, the salesman may have products worthy of consideration. Thus, Peterson can engage in principled collaboration (C2) or softly compete (P2). In other words, he can collaborate based on principles, taking a strong stand on what he expects in a sales contract; or he can softly compete by making product demands that do not offend the salesman.

2. *From Collaboration to Subordination.* For the situation with the contractor, the relationship outcome is very important to Dickerson Machinery but the immediate, substantive outcome is not. Peterson realizes that Dickerson needs Tarco's business for long-term stability but does not need to make a profit in the short term. Therefore, his unilateral strategy would be to subordinate openly (S1). He decides to change his strategy from the trustingly collaborative (C1) approach he has used in past dealings with Tarco.

As Peterson considers the contractor's priorities, he anticipates that the substantive outcome is important to Tarco but the relationship outcome is not. Tarco's representative has made clear the need for reliable service at the lowest possible price; conversely, Tarco has not responded to Peterson's bid to provide service for more than two years. Peterson recognizes, based on Exhibit 9-12, that Tarco can compete firmly (P1). After assessing both parties' priorities using the decision tree (see Exhibit 9-13, Situation 10), he decides he should continue with an interactive strategy of open subordination (S1). Such a strategy is more likely to induce Tarco's representative to offer a contract than the trustingly collaborative strategy he has used previously. For example, he is prepared to subordinate by offering a "winter special" to reduce labor costs by 10 percent, cutting competitive parts costs by 15 percent, and providing a new paint job at 50 percent the normal costs or providing a six-month deferment on payment, all in addition to paying for the trip to the plant.

3. *From Competition to Collaboration.* Peterson's analysis of the negotiation with the labor union includes an assessment of the recent history of and level of conflict between the union and the company. Previous episodes in this contract negotiation have led both the union and Dickerson Machinery to change their priorities. During the first few episodes, both parties focused on only substantive outcomes and ignored relationship outcomes, using firmly competitive strategies. Also, during these earlier episodes,

both sides' demands hardened to the point where the union threatened to strike and management threatened to give no increases in wages or benefits.

Now, however, Peterson believes that both substantive and relationship outcomes are important to Dickerson. The company wants to find a way to increase productivity without giving much of an increase in pay and benefits. It also does not want to lose good mechanics or stimulate a strike. Dickerson's unilateral strategy under these conditions should be trustingly collaborative (C1).

From analyzing the union's position, Peterson realizes that both the substantive and relationship outcomes should be important to the union. His informal discussions with union representatives have assured him that both sides are now concerned about maintaining the relationship. Nonetheless, the union clearly wants an increase in pay and benefits even though it also does not want a strike. In short, the union now is likely to trustingly collaborate but could easily shift its priorities and choose to firmly compete.

As he enters the negotiation strategy session this afternoon, Peterson plans to recommend to the management negotiation team the use of a principled collaborative (C2) strategy (see Exhibit 9-13, Situation 2). because of the current instability in the relationship, he does not want to provide the union with any opportunity to exploit a perceived weakness that a more trustingly collaborative strategy might create.

Monitoring and Reevaluating Strategies

After implementing their interactive strategy, managers should monitor the other party's tactics. How the other party acts will signal its strategy. Based on the other party's tactics, executives can (1) determine if their assumptions and expectations about the other party's strategy are accurate and (2) modify, if needed, their strategies during this and subsequent negotiation episodes. Exhibit 9-11 provides an overview of this process. The arrows linking strategies to tactics and the negotiation episode represent how tactics (1) are used to implement a strategy (first arrow), (2) provide information to each party (second, reversed arrow), and (3) may affect the choice of alternative strategies during a negotiation episode (third arrow).

Monitoring Tactics

More specifically, we view tactics in two ways: (1) as clusters of specific actions associated with the implementation of one strategy or another and (2) as actions that derive their strategic impact from the particular phase of the negotiation in which they are used. In Exhibit 9-14, we combine these two perspectives to provide executives with descriptions of competitive, collaborative, and subordinative tactics across various phases of negotiation. We suggest that most negotiations go through four phases: (1) the search for an arena and agenda formulation, (2) the stating of demands and offers, (3) a narrowing of differences, and (4) final bargaining.[16] Not every negotiation will involve all of these phases. Rather, these phases characterize typical negotiations in mixed-motive situations. Hence, a specific phase may be skipped or never attained.[17]

For example, the search for an arena in which to carry out discussions may be unnecessary for some ongoing negotiations; however, most negotiations will initially involve some Phase 1 interaction about the items to be discussed. During the second phase, both the manager and the other party express their preferences and establish their commitments to specific issues and outcomes. The third phase may be skipped, although it usually occurs if the manager and the other party are far apart in their preferences and commitments. Both sides may add or delete bargaining items or shift preferences to avoid an impasse. The fourth phase completes the negotiation: The manager and the other party reduce their alternatives, making joint decisions about each item until a final agreement is reached.

Exhibit 9-14 should help managers recognize (1) how using certain tactics during various phases of a negotiation is essential to implementing their strategy and (2) how the tactics of the other party reflect a particular strategic intent. An unanticipated strategy implemented by the other party may indicate that the executive inaccurately assessed the negotiation context or under- or over-estimated the strength of the other party's priorities. Hence, once the manager recognizes the other party's actual strategy, he or she should reassess the negotiation, repeating the process discussed in previous sections to check the appropriateness of his or her strategies.

Sometimes, however, the other party's use of an unanticipated strategy does not mean the executive's assessment of the negotiation context was inaccurate. In Exhibit 9-13, some combinations of the manager's and other party's priorities result in the listing of two interactive strategies. Managers should normally use the first (left-hand) strategies in these listings. The secondary (right-hand) strategies are suggested as countermoves the executive should use if the other party uses a strategy different from the one expected, but the executive remains convinced that his or her diagnosis is accurate.

EXHIBIT   9-14

Using Tactics across Negotiation Phases

Negotiation Phases	Negotiation Tactics		
	Competitive	**Collaborative**	**Subordinative**
The search for an arena and agenda formulation	• Seek to conduct negotiations on manager's home ground. • Demand discussion of manager's agenda items; curtail discussions of other party's items. • Ignore or discount the other party's demands and requests.	• Seek to conduct negotiations on neutral ground. • Elicit the other party's agenda items and assert manager's items; incorporate both. • Consider other party's demands and requests.	• Seek to conduct negotiations on the other party's ground. • Elicit the other party's agenda items and subvert manager's items. • Concede to the other party's demands and requests.
The stating of demands and offers	• Insist other party make initial offers or demands on all items. • Respond with very low offers or very high demands. • Commit to each item; exaggerate manager's position and discredit other party's.	• Alternate initial offers and demands on items with other party. • Respond with moderate offers or moderate demands. • Indicate reasons for manager's commitment to item outcomes; probe the other party's reasons.	• Make initial offers or demands on all other party-relevant items. • Make high offers or low demands. • Accept the other party's commitments to items; explain manager's commitments.
A narrowing of differences	• Demand that other party make concessions; back up demand with threats. • Delete, add, or yield only on low manager-interest items. • Magnify degree of manager's concessions; downplay other party's.	• Seek equitable exchange of concessions with the other party. • Delete, add, or yield items if mutal interests converge. • Honestly assess manager's and other party's concessions.	• Concede to the other party's demands. • Delete, add, or yield to any other party-relevant item. • Acknowledge the other party's concessions; downplay manager's concessions.
Final bargaining	• Seek large concessions from the other party. • Concede only minimally on high manager-interest items. • Use concessions on low manager-interest items as bargaining chips.	• Seek equitable exchange of concessions from the other party. • Seek mutually beneficial outcomes when conceding or accepting concessions on items.	• Yield to the other party's relevant preferences by accepting low offers and making low demands.

Reevaluating Negotiation Strategies

Take, for example, Peterson's appointment with the mechanic who has swapped a battery from a company truck with his own used battery. Going into the negotiation, Peterson decides that his unilateral strategy should be trusting collaboration: The mechanic is highly skilled and would be hard to replace, yet the infraction is a serious matter. He also anticipates that the employee will be interested primarily in retaining a good relationship with Dickerson's management. Hence, Peterson decides to stick with trusting collaboration as his interactive strategy (see Exhibit 9-13, Situation 3).

However, during the first five minutes of the meeting, Peterson's efforts to discuss returning the battery to the company and removing the infraction from the mechanic's personnel record are repeatedly rebuffed by the employee. Instead, the mechanic threatens to retire early from Dickerson and collect the benefits due him unless Peterson transfers him. Peterson recognizes that the mechanic is employing competitive tactics to set the agenda, which reflects an interest in substantive outcomes but little concern for relationship outcomes.

As the negotiation enters the next phase, Peterson considers the mechanic's apparent priorities and reevaluates his own priorities. Now neither the substantive nor the relationship outcomes are very important to him. He knows that Dickerson has no opening for the mechanic at any other shop; moreover, if the employee wants to leave, the relationship is of little value. Based on this reassessment (see Exhibit 9-13, Situation 14), Peterson sees that he has two interactive strategic options: He can regulate the matter (A3) by pressing criminal charges or compete firmly (P1) with the employee.

Rather than withdraw from the interaction, Peterson decides to compete firmly and tells the mechanic that unless the battery is returned, he will do everything he can legally do to prevent the mechanic from receiving optimal severance benefits. If the employee refuses to return the battery, Peterson can still request Dickerson's legal department to file criminal charges against him (A3) as a way to publicize and enforce a legitimate regulatory approach designed to help the company avoid this kind of negotiation.

DISCUSSION

Most of the negotiation literature focuses on substantive outcomes without systematically considering the ways negotiations affect relationships. The approach we have taken underscores how negotiation strategies should address both parties' substantive and relationship priorities. Further, we encourage executives proactively to view negotiation as an indeterminate, reiterative, and often confusing process. It requires them to anticipate and monitor the other party's actions. The other party's tactics will inform managers as to whether their assumptions about the other party's priorities and strategy are correct. Based on this assessment, managers can modify their negotiation strategies as needed during current or future episodes.

Managers should heed, however, a few caveats about our advice:

1. Underlying the strategic choice model in Exhibit 9-13 is the assumption that most negotiations are of the mixed-motive sort; that is, the manager and other party usually negotiate over several substantive items. Some items have potential outcomes that can benefit both negotiators; others have potential outcomes that can benefit only one negotiator. Under these conditions, collaborative, competitive, and subordinative strategies may all come into play as the negotiators seek either win-win, win-lose or yield-win substantive outcomes. Our emphasis in the model is on win-win substantive outcomes brought about through collaborative strategies (C1 and C2).

2. We assume that most relationships will involve some mixture of dependence and interdependence. Furthermore, we posit that most negotiators will view the relationship outcome as important when it is characterized by either high interdependence or high dependence. Collaborative strategies will strengthen the interdependence of the organization and the other party, subordinate strategies will increase the other party's dependence on the organization, and competitive strategies will decrease the organization's dependence on the other party. Our advice about negotiation strategies is directed particularly toward managers who want to enhance relationships of interdependence or favorably shift the balance of dependence within a relationship.

3. We also recognize that the history and level of conflict between an organization and another party strongly influence each negotiator's attitude toward the existing relationship. Feelings of hostility, we assume, will be escalated by a competitive strategy; in contrast, feelings of hostility will be deemphasized by a subordinative strategy. Following this same logic, feelings of supportiveness will be enhanced by a collaborative strategy. Several of the strategies suggested in Exhibit 9-13—trusting collaboration, soft competition, open subordination, and passive

and responsive avoidance—attempt to dampen hostilities and increase supportiveness between the manager and the other party.

4. Our advice to executives is simultaneously well supported and speculative. On one hand, the classic (unilateral) strategies suggested in Exhibit 9-13 are fairly well supported within the negotiation literature; the link between these strategies and both relationship and substantive outcomes is the special focus of our approach. On the other hand, the effectiveness of the interactive strategies suggested in Exhibit 9-13 remains open to continuing empirical investigation. We have developed this interactive model of strategic choice by linking our concerns about relationship outcomes with what is currently known about the basic strategies of negotiation.

Although the three sets of assumptions we make about relationships are usually warranted in most organization-related negotiations, executives should carefully consider whether their situations fit with these constraints before using our strategic choice model (Exhibit 9-13). However, regardless of the situation, we believe that managers will generally be more effective negotiators when they carefully assess both (1) the relationship and the substantive aspects of any potential negotiation and (2) what is important to the other party and what is important to them.

NOTES

The authors wish to thank the three anonymous Editorial Review Board members who reviewed an earlier draft of this article for their developmental critiques and constructive suggestions for improving the manuscript.

1. The incidents reported in this vignette and throughout the article are based on actual experiences in a multistate machinery servicing company.
2. See H. Raiffa's *The Art and Science of Negotiation* (Cambridge, Mass.: Harvard University Press, 1982), for a discussion of how game theory can help negotiations maximize their substantive outcomes under a diverse set of situations.
3. Both R. Fisher and W. Ury's *Getting to Yes: Negotiating Agreements without Giving in* (Boston: Houghton-Mifflin, 1981), and A. C. Filley's "Some Normative Issues in Conflict Management," *California Management Review* 21, no. 2 (1978), pp. 61–65, treat win-win problem solving as a principled, collaborative process.
4. See S. Bacharach and E. J. Lawler, *Power and Politics in Organizations: The Social Psychology of Conflict, Coalitions, and Bargaining* (San Francisco, Calif.: Jossey-Bass, 1980), for a recent discussion of mixed-motive negotiation situations.

5. See L. Putnam and C. E. Wilson, "Communicative Strategies in Organizational Conflicts: Reliability and Validity of a Measurement Scale," in *Communication Yearbook* 6, ed. M. Burgoon, (Newbury Park, Calif.: Sage Publications, 1982), pp. 629–52. See also R. A. Cosier and T. L. Ruble, "Research on Conflict-Handling Behavior: An Experimental Approach," *Academy of Management Journal* 24 (1981) pp. 816–31.
6. Power as the ability to induce compliance is discussed in J. March and H. Simon, *Organizations* (New York: John Wiley & Sons, 1958); and in P. Blau, *Exchange and Power in Social Life* (New York: John Wiley & Sons, 1964). Two recent books discussing power from a material-resource perspective are H. Mintzberg, *Power in and around Organizations* (Englewood Cliffs, N.J.: Prentice-Hall, 1983); and J. Pfeffer, *Power in Organizations* (Marshfield, Mass.: Pitman, 1981). A. Giddens' *The Constitution of Society: Outline of the Theory of Structuration* (Berkeley: University of California Press, 1984), discusses power from a critical-theory perspective within the field of sociology, emphasizing how power involves control over human resources.
7. For discussions of conflict intensity and durability, see I. R. Andrews and D. Tjosvold, "Conflict Management under Different Levels of Conflict Intensity," *Journal of Occupational Behaviour* 4 (1983), pp. 223–28; and C. T. Brown, P. Yelsma, and P. W. Keller, "Communication-Conflict Predisposition: Development of a Theory and an Instrument," *Human Relations* 34 (1981), pp. 1103–17.
8. See M. Deutsch, *The Resolution of Conflict* (New Haven, Conn.: Yale University Press, 1973), for a discussion of how spiraling conflicts can be both inflamed and controlled.
9. For further discussions on these basic strategies, see C. B. Derr, "Managing Organizational Conflict: Collaboration, Bargaining, and Power Approaches," *California Management Review* 21 (1978), pp. 76–82; Filley, Note 3; Fisher and Ury, Note 3; R. Johnston, "Negotiation Strategies: Different Strikes for Different Folks," in *Negotiation: Readings, Exercises, and Cases,* ed. R. Lewicki and J. Litterer (Homewood, Ill.: Richard D. Irwin, 1985), pp. 156–64; D. A. Lax and J. K. Sebenius, *The Manager as Negotiator: Bargaining for Cooperation and Competitive Gain* (New York: The Free Press, 1986); and D. G. Pruitt, "Strategic Choice in Negotiation," *American Behavioral Scientist* 27 (1983), pp. 167–94.
10. For an overview of the contributions by these and other conflict-management researchers, see the special issue on "Communication and Conflict Styles in Organizations," L. L. Putnam, ed., *Management Communication Quarterly* 1, no. 3 (1988), pp. 291–445. See also R. Blake and J. Mouton, "The Fifth Achievement," *Journal of Applied Behavioral Science* 6 (1970), pp. 413–26; J. Hall, *Conflict Management Survey: A Survey of One's Characteristic Reaction to and Handling of Conflicts between Himself and Others* (Conroe, Tex.: Teleometrics, 1986); and R. H. Kilmann and K. W. Thomas, "Interpersonal Conflict-Handling Behavior as Re-

flections of Jungian Personality Dimensions," *Psychological Reports* 37 (1975), pp. 971–80; and "Developing a Forced-Choice Measure of Conflict-Handling Behavior: The 'Mode' Instrument," *Educational & Psychological Measurement* 37 (1977), pp. 309–25.

11. See Note 10 above; especially see Johnston.

12. M. L. Knapp, L. L. Putnam, and L. J. Davis, "Measuring Interpersonal Conflict in Organizations: Where Do We Go from Here?" *Management Communication Quarterly* 1 (1988), pp. 414–29; Putnam and Wilson, Note 5; and J. Sullivan, R. B. Peterson, N. Kameda, and J. Shimada, "The Relationship between Conflict Resolution Approaches and Trust—A Cross-Cultural Study," *Academy of Management Journal* 24 (1981), pp. 803–15.

13. We call these strategies *interactive* because they take into account the interactive effect of the manager's and the other party's anticipated or actual priorities concerning substantive and relationship outcomes. Interactive strategies based on anticipating the other party's priorities, as we later discuss in some length, may be changed to reflect more closely the actual priorities of the other party, as revealed through the interaction during a negotiation episode.

14. See Fisher and Ury, Note 3.

15. See, for example, L. L. Cummings, D. L. Harnett, and O. J. Stevens, "Risk, Fate, Conciliation and Trust: An International Study of Attitudinal Differences among Executives," *Academy of Management Journal* 14 (1971), pp. 285–304.

16. Different researchers offer varying descriptions of negotiation phases. See L. Putnam, "Bargaining as Organizational Communication," in *Organizational Communication: Traditional Themes and New Directions,* ed. R. D. McPhee and P. K. Tompkins (Beverly Hills, Calif.: Sage Publications, 1985), for a summary of this research. Ann Douglas proposed the first three-step model in "The Peaceful Settlement of Industrial and Intergroup Disputes," *Journal of Conflict Resolution* 1 (1957), pp. 69–81. However, this model and subsequent three-stage models do not consider the search for the arena as a component phase of a negotiation. P. Gulliver's *Disputes and Negotiations: A Cross-Cultural Perspective* (New York: Academic Press, 1979), proposes an eight-stage model of negotiation, remedying that oversight. Our proposed four-phase model condenses and draws extensively from Gulliver's work.

17. Additionally, we view the phases of negotiation as conceptually separate from our notion of negotiation episodes (see Exhibit 9–11). All four phases may take place during one episode, particularly if the negotiation involves a single issue of low concern to one or another negotiator. On the other hand, during very complex negotiations stretching over a period of months, numerous episodes may constitute each phase.

■

EXERCISES

EXERCISE 9–1   EMPOWERMENT PROFILE

Step 1: Complete the following questionnaire.*

For each of the following items, select the alternative with which you feel more comfortable. While for some items you may feel that both a and b describe you or neither is ever applicable you should select the alternative that better describes you most of the time.

1. When I have to give a talk or write a paper, I . . .
    _____ a. Base the content of my talk or paper on my own ideas.
    _____ b. Do a lot of research, and present the findings of others in my paper or talk.

Source: "The Empowerment Profile" from *The Power Handbook* by Pamela Cuming. Copyright © 1980 by CBI Publishing. Reprinted by permission by Van Nostrand Reinhold Co., Inc.

2. When I read something I disagree with, I . . .
    _____ a. Assume my position is correct.
    _____ b. Assume what's presented in the written word is correct.

3. When someone makes me extremely angry, I . . .
    _____ a. Ask the other person to stop the behavior that is offensive to me.
    _____ b. Say little, not quite knowing how to state my position.

4. When I do a good job, it is important to me that . . .
    _____ a. The job represents the best I can do.
    _____ b. Others take notice of the job I've done.

5. When I buy new clothes, I . . .
    _____ a. Buy what looks best on me.
    _____ b. Try to dress in accordance with the latest fashion.

6. When something goes wrong, I . . .
   _____ a. Try to solve the problem.
   _____ b. Try to find out who's at fault.

7. As I anticipate my future, I . . .
   _____ a. Am confident I will be able to lead the kind of life I want to lead.
   _____ b. Worry about being able to live up to my obligations.

8. When examining my own resources and capacities, I . . .
   _____ a. Like what I find.
   _____ b. Find all kinds of things I wish were different.

9. When someone treats me unfairly, I . . .
   _____ a. Put my energies into getting what I want.
   _____ b. Tell others about the injustice.

10. When someone criticizes my efforts, I . . .
    _____ a. Ask questions in order to understand the basis for the criticism.
    _____ b. Defend my actions or decisions, trying to make my critic understand why I did what I did.

11. When I engage in an activity, it is very important to me that . . .
    _____ a. I live up to my own expectations.
    _____ b. I live up to the expectations of others.

12. When I let someone else down or disappoint them, I . . .
    _____ a. Resolve to do things differently next time.
    _____ b. Feel guilty, and wish I had done things differently.

13. I try to surround myself with people . . .
    _____ a. Whom I respect.
    _____ b. Who respect me.

14. I try to develop friendships with people who . . .
    _____ a. Are challenging and exciting.
    _____ b. Can make me feel a little safer and a little more secure.

15. I make my best efforts when . . .
    _____ a. I do something I want to do when I want to do it.
    _____ b. Someone else gives me an assignment, a deadline, and a reward for performing.

16. When I love a person, I . . .
    _____ a. Encourage him or her to be free and choose for himself or herself.
    _____ b. Encourage him or her to do the same thing I do and to make choices similar to mine.

17. When I play a competitive game, it is important to me that I . . .
    _____ a. Do the best I can.
    _____ b. Win.

18. I really like being around people who . . .
    _____ a. Can broaden my horizons and teach me something.
    _____ b. Can and want to learn from me.

19. My best days are those that . . .
    _____ a. Present unexpected opportunities.
    _____ b. Go according to plan.

20. When I get behind in my work, I . . .
    _____ a. Do the best I can and don't worry.
    _____ b. Worry or push myself harder than I should.

Step 2: Score your responses as follows:

Total your a responses: _____
Total your b responses: _____

Step 3: Discussion. In small groups or with the entire class, answer the following questions:

1. What did you learn about yourself?
2. Would your closest friend agree with the scores or the scoring for a and b?
3. How could an organization use information gathered from this type of empowerment profile?

EXERCISE 9–2   POLITICAL PROCESSES IN ORGANIZATIONS

OBJECTIVES

1. To review the type of political behavior used in reaching decisions.

2. To examine student versus practicing manager perceptions of politics.

The purpose of this exercise is to analyze and predict when political behavior is used in organizational decision making and to compare participants' ratings of politically based decisions with ratings of practicing managers.

Politics is the use of influence to make decisions and obtain preferred outcomes in organizations. Surveys of

Source: Richard L. Daft and Kristen M. Dahlen, "Political Processes in Organizations," *Organization Theory* (St. Paul, Minn.: West Publishing, 1984), pp. 252–54.

managers show that political behavior is a fact of life in virtually all organizations. Every organization will confront situations characterized by uncertainty and disagreement, hence standard rules and rational decision models can't necessarily be used. Political behavior and rational decision process act as substitutes for one another, depending upon the degree of uncertainty and disagreement that exists among managers about specific issues. Political behavior is used and is revealed in informal discussions and unscheduled meetings among managers, arguments, attempts at persuasion, and eventual agreement and acceptance of the organizational choice.

START THE EXERCISE

In the following exercise, please evaluate the extent to which politics will play a part in decisions that are made in organizations.

Step 1: Individual Ranking
(5 minutes)

Rank the 11 organizational decisions listed on the scoring sheet below according to the extent you think politics plays a part. The most political decision would be ranked 1, the least political decisions would be ranked 11. Enter your ranking on the first column of the scoring sheet.

Step 2: Team Ranking
(20 minutes)

Divide into teams of from three to five people. As a group, rank the 11 items according to your group's consensus on the amount of politics used in each decision. Use good group decision-making techniques to arrive at a consensus. Listen to each person's ideas and rationale fully before reaching a decision. Do not vote. Discuss items until agreement is reached. Base your decisions on the underlying logic provided by group members rather than on personal preference. After your team has reached a consensus, record the team rankings in the second column on the scoring sheet.

Step 3: Correct Ranking
(5 minutes)

After all teams have finished ranking the 11 decisions, your instructor will read the correct ranking based on a survey of managers. This survey indicates the frequency with which politics played a part in each type of decision. As the instructor reads each item's ranking, enter it in the "correct ranking" column on the scoring sheet.

Step 4: Individual Score
(5 minutes)

Your individual score is computed by taking the difference between your individual ranking and the correct ranking for each item. Be sure to use the *absolute* difference between your ranking and the correct ranking for each item (ignore pluses and minuses). Enter the difference in column 4 labeled "Individual Score." Add the numbers in column 4 and insert the total at the bottom of the column. This score indicates how accurate you were in assessing the extent to which politics plays a part in organizational decisions.

Step 5: Team Score
(5 minutes)

Compute the difference between your group's ranking and the correct ranking. Again, use the *absolute* difference for each item. Enter the difference in column 5, labeled "Team Score." Add the numbers in column 5 and insert the total at the bottom of the column. The total is your team score.

Step 6: Compare Teams
(5 minutes)

When all individual and team scores have been calculated, the instructor will record the data from each group for class discussion. One member of your group should be prepared to provide both the team score and the lowest individual score on your team. The instructor may wish to display these data so that team and individual scores can be easily compared as illustrated on the bottom of the scoring sheet. All participants may wish to record these data for further reference.

Step 7: Discussion
(15 minutes)

Discuss this exercise as a total group with the instructor. Use your experience and the data to try to arrive at some conclusions about the role of politics in real-world organizational decision making. The following questions may facilitate the total group discussion.

1. Why did some individuals and groups solve the ranking more accurately than others? Did they have more experience with organizational decision making? Did they interpret the amount of uncertainty and disagreement associated with decisions more accurately?

Decisions	1. Individual Ranking	2. Team Ranking	3. Correct Ranking	4. Individual Score	5. Team Score
1. Management promotions and transfers					
2. Entry level hiring					
3. Amount of pay					
4. Annual budgets					
5. Allocation of facilities, equipment, offices					
6. Delegation of authority among managers					
7. Interdepartmental coordination					
8. Specification of personnel policies					
9. Penalties for disciplinary infractions					
10. Performance appraisals					
11. Grievances and complaints					

	Team Number						
	1	2	3	4	5	6	7
Team Scores:							
Lowest individual score on each team:							

The scoring sheet is based on Jeffrey Gandz and Victor V. Murray, "The Experience of Workplace Politics," *Academy of Management Journal* 23 (1980), pp. 237–51.

2. If the 11 decisions were ranked according to the importance of rational decision processes, how would that ranking compare to the one you've completed above? To what extent does this mean both rational and political models of decision making should be used in organizations?

3. What would happen if managers apply political processes to logical, well understood issues? What would happen if they applied rational or quantitative techniques to uncertain issues about which considerable disagreement existed.?

4. Many managers believe that political behavior is greater at higher levels in the organization hierarchy. Is there any evidence from this exercise that would explain why more politics would appear at higher rather than lower levels in organizations?

5. What advice would you give to managers who feel politics is bad for the organization and should be avoided at all costs?

CASE

CASE 9–1 MISSOURI CAMPUS BITTERLY DIVIDED OVER HOW TO REALLOCATE FUNDS

On the campus of the University of Missouri here, the signs of spring came late and were decidedly makeshift: a white sheet bearing the spray-painted legend "SOCIAL WORK IS HERE TO STAY" draped from windows in Clark Hall; a crudely lettered placard taped to a glass door in Memorial Union defiantly announcing, "HELL NO, HOME EC WON'T GO!"

Hasty construction accounted for the homemade quality of the signs, for as the academic year drew quickly to a close, many students and faculty members were surprised to find themselves fighting for their academic lives—the survival of their programs.

In a year in which this campus has had to contend with a host of financial problems—some fabricated, critics allege—April was the cruelest month. It was on April 2 that proposals to "reallocate" nearly $12 million in operating funds over the next three years were announced. Among them were recommendations to eliminate two of the university's 14 colleges and to reduce substantially the offerings in five others.

The ensuing controversy divided the campus. "It has set department against department and colleague against colleague," says one dean. "It's civil war, with everyone trying to gore everyone else's bull."

In mid-April, the faculty voted to call for the resignation of Chancellor Barbara S. Uehling if she did not withdraw the proposals.

By the time graduating students were preparing for last week's commencement exercises, the subject of their conversations—whether or not they had jobs—also seemed to be a prime topic of talk among many members of the faculty and staff.

What led to this course of events was a decision last summer by President James C. Olson to take action "to preserve and even enhance the quality of the university in a time of severely limited resources."

"The university has coped with 10 years of inadequate funding by making cuts across the board," he says. "It became clear that a continuation of that policy was a prescription for mediocrity."

Mr. Olson announced last July that the university would attempt to save approximately $16 million over the next three years to finance pay raises as well as library, laboratory, and other improvements. He told the chancellors of the four Missouri campuses that their first priority was to be the development of an adequate compensation plan for the university staff. His plan was supported by the university's Board of Curators.

President Olson's goal is to bring salaries at the university up to the average of those at member institutions of the Big 8 and Big 10 athletic conferences—institutions that, he says, "are comparable to Missouri in mission." At the start of the 1981–82 academic year, Missouri had the lowest salary average in that comparison group, 8.9 percent below the midpoint.

Mr. Olson instructed the chancellors to find money for salary adjustments "by reducing the quantity of what you do rather than the quality."

That met with approval on the Columbia campus, where Chancellor Uehling has said "the concept of shared poverty is not viable for a competitive university," and where the faculty has been on the record for five years in opposition to across-the-board budget cuts.

The 24,000-student campus, biggest in the system, is scheduled for the largest reductions: as much as $12 million, or about 5 percent of its operating budget.

The curators adopted procedures for the "discontinuance" of program, and the university established four criteria for reviewing them: overall quality, contribution to the university's mission, need for the program, and financial considerations. Application of the criteria was left up the individual campuses.

"On two occasions I identified to the deans the ways in which we might go about this task," says Provost Ronald F. Bunn, who is faced with reducing the budget for academic programs by $7 million.

"A QUALITY MATRIX"

According to Mr. Bunn, most of the deans suggested that he take on the task. The Faculty Council recommended the same. "This was an administrative job," says David West, the council chairman and a professor of finance.

Source: Written by Paul Desruisseaux. Reprinted with permission of *The Chronicle of Higher Education,* copyright © 1982.

"We wanted the administration to make its proposals, and then we'd take shots at it."

Mr. Bunn reviewed all of the campus's academic programs himself, rating them according to the four criteria established by the president. He compiled what he calls "a quality matrix," which resembles the box score of a baseball game. The programs that ranked lowest he proposed reducing.

Specifically, the provost recommended the elimination of the School of Library and Informational Science and the College of Public and Community Services (with the possible retention of its masters-in-social-work program). He also recommended major reductions in the College of Education, the College of Engineering, the School of Nursing, the College of Home Economics, and the School of Health Related Professions. In some cases the reductions would mean the eliminations of one or more departments within those colleges.

All told, campus officials estimated that the cuts in academic programs would affect 2,500 students and as many as 200 faculty and staff members. Since tenure regulations require the university to give tenured faculty members 13 months' notice of plans to eliminate their jobs, the reduction proposals would have little effect on the 1982–83 budget.

When university administrators announced their plans on April 2, those in the academic programs predictably provoked the greatest response.

"IT INFURIATES ME"

An ad hoc committee of faculty members and students was charged with reviewing the provost's recommendations and conducting hearings.

Individuals in the targeted programs have been outspokenly critical of Provost Bunn's judgment.

"We are the only accredited library-science program in Missouri, and it infuriates me—as a citizen as much as anything—that the campus, unilaterally, has made the decision to eliminate programs that exist nowhere else in the state," says Edward P. Miller, dean of the library school. "I don't think the provost could have done a worse job of abrogating the criteria for review if he tried."

Bob G. Woods, dean of the College of Education, who supported the idea of programmatic cuts, says he was prepared to reduce his budget by as much as $500,000, but when he learned that reductions of $1.2 million were required, he changed his mind. "I want the process to be refuted as unnecessary at this time," he says.

Officials in the College of Home Economics charge that the recommendations to eliminate two departments there were based on outdated information. "The decision regarding my program was based on a three-year-old internal-review document," says Kitty G. Dickerson, chairman of the department of clothing and textiles, who is in her first year at Missouri. "I was brought here to strengthen this department. There were 35 recommendations in that internal review, and we have already addressed all but three. But there was never an opportunity to let it be known that we have made this enormous progress."

Martha Jo Martin, assistant dean of home economics, says that eliminating the two departments would cost the college its accreditation and half of its enrollment.

Opposition was not limited to those in programs proposed for reduction. Says Andrew Twaddle, a professor of sociology, "My main concern is not with the actual targeting of programs but the fact that the administration made these decisions with little input from the faculty, except for a select group of its supporters.

"I honestly don't know what the university's real fiscal situation is—there are so many conflicting figures flying around, and no one is backing them up very well," he adds. "But according to the bylaws of this campus, the faculty is supposed to make academic policy, and when you're talking about what is or is not to be taught at the university, you're talking about policy."

Others are concerned about the impact of the proposals on women and minorities.

"We are assuming that the university is aware of its commitment to affirmative action," says W. L. Moore, an assistant professor of education and chairman of the Black Faculty and Staff Organization. "But we have not been kept informed, and we are very skeptical of all that is being done in this area."

Mr. Moore says his organization has determined that the proposed cuts would affect 63 percent of the black faculty members. The university's Office of Equal Opportunity says the figure is 33 percent. This discrepancy is due to the administration's inclusion of nonteaching blacks in its figures, says Mr. Moore. "But the precise number doesn't matter, because even 33 percent is too high a price to pay," he adds.

Of the campus's 620 black undergraduates, 255 are enrolled in targeted programs, says H. Richard Dozier, coordinator of minority-student services. "Blacks weren't admitted to this institution until 1950, and they make up only 3.7 percent of the student body," he says. "These cuts would be regressive."

Blacks on the campus have asked the administration for assurances that the university's five-year affirmative-action goals will be met.

There is also some feeling on the campus that faculty salary raises are being used as, in the words of one dean, "a smokescreen" for an attempt to change the institution from a multipurpose university to a research university. One reduction target, home economics, is, according to officials of that college, one of only two areas of study identified in federal farm-bill legislation as being part of the educational responsibility of a land-grant institution.

While some opponents of the proposals were testifying before the review committee, others were mustering support for them. Students, faculty members, and alumni mounted massive letter-writing and phone-calling campaigns aimed at state legislators and the university's curators. Rallies were held, petitions circulated, press conferences staged. The Missouri State Teachers Association expressed outrage. The State Senate's Education Committee held a hearing.

On April 7, the Columbia campus's student senate passed a resolution denouncing the academic review.

On April 19, the faculty voted 237 to 70 to call for the resignations of the chancellor and the provost if the reduction proposals were not withdrawn. The vote, however, has been criticized—by, among others, Chancellor Uehling herself—for not being a true representation of the sentiments of the campus's 2,038-member faculty. Last November, when the faculty voted against midyear salary increases if they were to come at the expense of campus jobs, more than 800 members cast ballots.

THE "POINT MAN"

The author of the resignation resolution, George V. Boyle, says he believes the vote was representative.

"We should not be cannibalizing ourselves in order to give people raises," says Mr. Boyle, director of labor education, a program not affected by the provost's proposal. "When you encounter heavy seas and the best plan the captain offers is to lighten the load by throwing crew members overboard, I think the crew has to try and come up with something better."

"Our approach to these reductions," says Provost Bunn, "required that I become the 'point man,' and the discussion stage has subsequently become an adversarial one: The source of the recommendations—me—has become as much a subject of debate as the recommendations themselves. It

has also become a highly political one, and I think it's unfortunate that the debate has been brought to the legislature and the curators before we have completed the review process on campus."

Chancellor Uehling also came in for some personal criticism when the campus learned that she was among the final candidates for the chancellorship of the 19-campus California State University system. She took herself out of the running for that job last week and announced that she was committed to working for policies that would enable the Columbia campus "not simply to survive but to carry into the future even greater strength than before."

The chancellor says she is not surprised by the demonstrations of hostility. "It's a very frightening and painful process," she says. "I can understand the anger on the part of some, but I still think our greater obligation is to the institution as a whole."

Ms. Uehling says that while she will not review or comment on the recommended proposals until they come to her in their final form, she supports the process and is convinced of its necessity.

"For the past five years, the State of Missouri has provided the university with budget increases that have amounted to only one half the rate of inflation," she says. "When I came, the faculty was already on the record in opposition to across-the-board cuts to provide salary raises, and we must bring salaries up to attract and retain quality people. We **have** lost some good people.

"We have no hidden agenda. Our only agenda is our determination to take charge of our own fate. We are trying to anticipate the future so that we won't have to engage in crisis kind of planning. There are enough signs of an impending erosion of our quality to make us want to get ahead and start doing what we do smaller and better."

There have also been signs that the state can't afford to support the university to any greater extent. Missouri voters in 1980 passed an amendment prohibiting the legislature from increasing appropriations unless there were corresponding growth in the state economy. In 1981, Missouri ranked 46th in state-tax revenue growth, one of the reasons the governor, on two occasions, withheld portions of the university's budget totaling 13 percent.

Nevertheless, some critics charge that salary increases—if they are essential now—could be provided for next year without eliminating programs, since there has been a slight increase in the state appropriation from what was originally expected, and a 17 percent hike in student fees.

"If you take a short-term view, it's possible to conclude that we could have an acceptable level of salary adjustment for the coming year," says Mr. Bunn. "That isn't the case if you're looking ahead. Some on campus feel that it isn't important for us to strengthen our salary structure, but in my judgment that is a very narrow view of the aspirations this campus should have for itself."

To be sure, there is faculty support for the administration. "I think the faculty who approved of this strategy previously ought to be heard from again," says John Kuhlman, a professor of economics. "I don't think we can afford to sit back and watch a few departments create the big fight with the provost."

Adds Sam Brown, chairman of the psychology department, "It would be difficult to find anyone to say they'd favor the cannibalization of their colleagues' jobs for the sake of a salary raise. But ignoring the source of funds, I can say as a department chairman that one of the major problems I face is insufficient salary increments for faculty."

OTHER IMPROVEMENTS SOUGHT

According to Provost Bunn, when salary raises are given out, they will not be distributed uniformly but will be based on individual merit and the salary market in the particular field.

While salaries will have the highest claim on the "reallocated" funds, the provost also hopes there will be enough money to strenghten equipment and expense budgets—"to bring them back to at least the real-dollar level of three years ago."

The provost said he would consider seriously the advice offered by the committee reviewing his proposals. What is not an option, in his view, is to back away from the $7 million in savings that his proposals would provide.

When it reported to the provost May 6, however, the review committee announced that it had voted to weaken the effect of all but one of the proposed reductions. Mr. Bunn is expected to submit his final recommendations to the chancellor by the end of this week.

The Board of Curators, at meetings on May 6 and 7, conducted lengthy discussions of the reallocation process underway at the Columbia campus. The result, William T. Doak, president of the board, told the press, was that the curators were so divided on the question that had a vote been taken on the proposals they would have been rejected.

"We are trying to plan for a very uncertain future," says President Olson, "and I'm not sure we've yet found the mechanism for doing that. We are seeking it."

Chancellor Uehling is expected to submit her reallocation proposals to President Olson sometime in June. The curators are scheduled to vote on the proposals in July.

"The board's resistance to any program eliminations has certainly given those who favor such a course of action cause for pause," says the Faculty Council's David West, who has supported the process from the outset. "There has been much more visible and vocal opposition to the process in the past four weeks than there had been support for it up to that time."

On the Columbia campus, faculty members were circulating petitions calling for votes of confidence and of no confidence in the administration. Mr. West says he is advising those faculty members not to call for campuswide votes at this time.

"There has already been too much confrontation, and faculty votes would just prolong it," he says. "I think everyone should try to gather additional information and rethink his position. And try to find some means by which all of this division can be mitigated."

CASE QUESTIONS

1. How much and what type of power does the faculty possess at the University of Missouri?
2. What does Provost Bunn mean when he claims that he played the role as a "point man" in this situation?
3. What type of politics is being played in this case? Give and explain examples.

CHAPTER

10

Leadership

LEARNING OBJECTIVES

DEFINE the terms leadership and self-leadership.

DISCUSS the accuracy of what is called the trait theory of leadership.

DISCUSS The Vroom-Jago model and how it is used to study leadership.

DESCRIBE the difference in the interpretation of what is referred to as transitional and transformational leadership.

EXPLAIN the debate concerning whether charismatic qualities of leadership can be learned.

DESCRIBE what role *perceptions* play in the attribution theory of leadership.

In all of the groups to which you have belonged—family, sports team, social club, study group, work unit—there typically was a person who was more influential than the others. The most influential person in these groups is usually called a leader. Leaders are extremely important in a variety of organizational settings. Indeed, organizations would be less efficient without leaders, and in extreme cases, they would be unable to accomplish purposeful goals. For these and similar reasons, leadership has been the center of attention of theorists, researchers, and practitioners.

Although leadership is important and has been studied by behavioral scientists for decades, it is still somewhat of a mystery.[1] Even after thousands of studies, there is still a lack of consensus among the experts on exactly what leadership is and how it should be analyzed. Further reflecting this ambiguity, this chapter examines a number of somewhat distinct perspectives of leadership.

[1]Bernard M. Bass, *Stogdill's Handbook of Leadership* (New York: Free Press, 1982).

437

LEADERSHIP DEFINED

The five bases of interpersonal power discussed in Chapter 9 suggest that power can be defined as the ability to influence another person's behavior. Where one individual attempts to affect the behavior of a group without using the coercive form of power, we describe the effort as leadership. More specifically, "**leadership** is an attempt at influencing the activities of followers through the communication process and toward the attainment of some goal or goals."[2] This definition implies that leadership involves the use of influence and that all relationships can involve leadership. A second element in the definition involves the importance of the communication process. The clarity and accuracy of communication affect the behavior and performance of followers.

Another element of the definition focuses on the accomplishment of goals. The effective leader may have to deal with individual, group, and organizational goals. Leader effectiveness typically is considered in terms of the degree of accomplishment of one or a combination of these goals.

Exhibit 10–1 represents a model of leadership based upon the above definition. The model summarizes the key sources and perceived bases of interpersonal power and also presents some of the possible moderating factors between the sources and perceived bases of power and outcomes (goals). The model suggests that (1) a successful leader is one who is aware of sources of power and the importance of perceived power; (2) the leader does not rely on coercive power; (3) the sources of a leader's power include place, time, information, and personality characteristics; and (4) the accomplishment of goals depends not only on power sources and perceptions but also on follower needs, the situation, and the experience of the leader.[3] A leader is a person who has the ability to influence followers while at the same time commanding the respect of his or her followers. Mahatma Gandhi, Martin Luther King, Jr., and Franklin D. Roosevelt fit this interpretation of a leader.

TRAIT THEORIES

● **R10–1**

Much of the early work on leadership focused on identifying the traits of effective leaders. This approach was based on the assumption that a finite number of individual traits of effective leaders could be found. Thus, most research was designed to identify intellectual, personality, and physical traits of successful leaders.

---

[2]Edwin A. Fleishman, "Twenty Years of Consideration and Structure," in *Current Developments in the Study of Leadership,* eds. Edwin A. Fleishman and James G. Hunt (Carbondale, Ill.: Southern Illinois University Press, 1973), p. 3.

[3]See Arthur G. Jago, "Leadership: Perspectives in Theory and Research," *Management Science,* March 1982, pp. 315–36.

EXHIBIT 10-1

A Leadership Model: Sources, Moderators, Outcomes

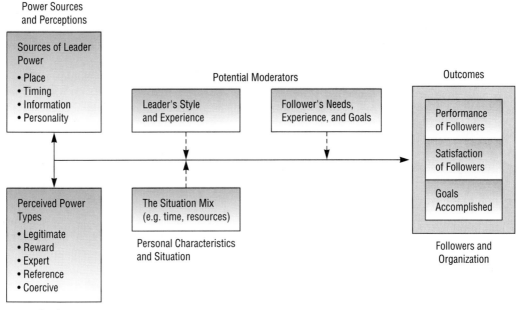

Intellectual Traits

Dimensions of intelligence that have been associated with leadership effectiveness include decisiveness, judgmental ability, knowledge, and verbal abilities. In a review of 35 studies, Stogdill found a general trend indicating that leaders were somewhat more intelligent than their followers but not exceedingly more so.[4] Extreme intelligence differences tended to be dysfunctional.

Personality Traits

Some research suggests that personality traits such as alertness, originality, personal integrity, and self-confidence are associated with effective leadership.[5] Still other investigators identify creativity, emotional balance, nonconformity, and diplomacy.[6] A major difficulty in attempts to relate personality and leadership

---

[4]Ralph M. Stogdill, *Handbook of Leadership* (New York: Free Press, 1974), pp. 43–44.

[5]For example, see Chris Argyris, "Some Characteristics of Successful Executives," *Personnel Journal,* June 1955, pp. 50–63; and J. A. Hornaday and C. J. Bunker, "The Nature of the Entrepreneur," *Personnel Psychology,* Spring 1970, pp. 47–54.

[6]Bass, *Stogdill's Handbook of Leadership,* pp. 75–76.

has been finding valid ways to measure personality traits. Progress, however, although slow, is being made.[7]

Physical Traits

Studies of the relationship between effective leadership and physical characteristics such as age, height, weight, and appearance provide contradictory results. Being taller and heavier than the average of a group certainly is not a requirement for achieving a leader position.[8] However, many organizations believe that a physically large person is required to secure compliance from followers. This notion relies heavily on the coercive or fear basis of power. On the other hand, Truman, Gandhi, Napoleon, and Stalin are examples of individuals of small stature who rose to positions of leadership.

Although traits such as these have, in some studies, differentiated effective from ineffective leaders, many contradictory findings still exist. Consequently, after years of speculation and research, we are not even close to identifying a specific set of leadership traits. Thus, the trait approach, while interesting and intuitively appealing, does not seem to be very different for identifying and predicting leadership potential.

The driving force behind Slim-Fast's success is S. Daniel Abraham. Predicting his success would have been difficult since it took him over 46 years to build his business. However, he has parlayed intelligence, a strong personality, high energy, and enthusiasm into a profitable business. The Encounter describes his situation and also raises some potential ethical issues that he will eventually have to face.

PERSONAL-BEHAVIORAL THEORIES

In the late 1940s researchers began to explore the notion that how a person acts determines that person's leadership effectiveness. Instead of searching for traits, these researchers examined behaviors and their impact on the performance and satisfaction of followers. Today there are a number of well-known personal-behavior theories of leadership. We examine two of the more prominent ones in this chapter.

---

[7]For example, see James Conley, "Longitudinal Stability of Personality Traits: A Multiact-Multimethod-Multioccasion Analysis," *Journal of Personality and Social Psychology*, November 1985, pp. 1266–82.

[8]Ralph M. Stogdill, "Personal Factors Associated with Leadership," *Journal of Applied Psychology*, January 1948, pp. 35–71.

ORGANIZATIONAL
E N C O U N T E R · 10-1

TRAITS OF SLIM FAST'S LEADER

S. Daniel Abraham—intelligent, creative, self-confident, hardworking, and goal-oriented. Who is he? He is the president of Slim-Fast. The hot-selling meal replacement provider that has become synonymous with easy weight loss is Abraham's empire. He controls more than 70 percent of the estimated $4.3 billion appetite-suppressant and meal-replacement wholesale market.

Slim-Fast's sales total an estimated $650 million annually. Abraham also owns West Palm Beach-based Thompson Medical Co., which markets diet drugs like Dexatrim and Appedrine. In 1956 Abraham introduced his first diet product, Slim-Mint gum. In 1976 he brought out Dexatrim. Slim-Fast appeared in 1977, but was pulled from the shelves that same year when 59 dieters died from liquid protein diets. Some of the diets had as few as 300 calories per day. Slim-Fast was not involved in the deaths, since it is a 1,200-calorie-per-day plan, but its sales disappeared.

Abraham is a hands-on leader making almost every decision himself. He closely supervises the design of packages and products. He personally signed Tommy Lasorda, the Los Angeles Dodgers manager, to appear in Slim-Fast ads in 1989.

Is Slim-Fast or any quick-fix diet protein for real? The Federal Trade Commission told three liquid-diet makers to get rid of false promises in their ads. Abraham may be next on the list. The FTC may require Slim-Fast and others to disclose in their ads the probability of regaining weight. Abraham is moving his company into health food and to areas for the spot dieter (a person who wants to lose at most five pounds). His vision is to control the destiny of his firm. The government hasn't pointed a finger at Slim-Fast, and Abraham wants it to stay that way. If they do, however, he will have a line of products from quick-fix diets, to spot diets, to health food. Something for everyone is the way this hard-working, self-confident man operates. Abraham has a vision and is driven to accomplish his goals.

Source: Adapted from Phyllis Berman and Amy Feldman, "An Extraordinary Peddler," *Forbes,* December 9, 1991, p. 136.

The University of Michigan Studies

In 1947 Rensis Likert began studying how best to manage the efforts of individuals to achieve desired performance and satisfaction objectives.[9] The purpose of most of the leadership research of the Likert-inspired team at the University of Michigan has been to discover the principles and methods of effective leadership. Through interviewing leaders and followers, the researchers identified two distinct styles of leadership, referred to as *job-centered* and *employee-centered.* The job-centered leader practices close supervision so that subordinates perform their tasks using specified procedures. This type of leader relies on coercion, reward, and legitimate power to influence the behavior and performance of followers. The concern of people is viewed as important but as a luxury that a leader cannot always afford.

[9]For a review of this work, see Rensis Likert, *New Patterns of Management* (New York: McGraw-Hill, 1961); and Rensis Likert, *The Human Organization* (New York: McGraw-Hill, 1967).

The employee-centered leader believes in delegating decision making and aiding followers in satisfying their needs by creating a supportive work environment. The employee-centered leader is concerned with followers' personal advancement, growth, and achievement. These actions are assumed to be conducive to the support of group formation and development.

The Michigan series of studies does not clearly show that one particular style of leadership is always the most effective. Moreover, it only examines two aspects of leadership—task and people behavior.

The Ohio State Studies

Among the several large research programs on leadership that developed after World War II, one of the most significant was headed by Fleishman and his associates at Ohio State University. This program resulted in a two-factor theory of leadership.[10] The studies isolated two leadership factors, referred to as *initiating structure* and *consideration*. The definitions of these factors are as follows: Initiating structure involves behavior in which the leader organizes and defines the relationships in the group, tends to establish well-defined patterns and channels of communication, and spells out ways of getting the job done. Consideration involves behavior indicating friendship, mutual trust, respect, warmth, and rapport between the leader and the followers.

Since the original research, there have been numerous studies of the relationship between these two leadership dimensions and various effectiveness criteria. Many of the early results stimulated the generalization that leaders above average in both consideration and initiating structure were more effective. In a study of supervisors at International Harvester, however, the researchers began to find some more complicated interpretations of the two dimensions. They found that those scoring higher on initiating structure had higher proficiency ratings (ratings received from superiors) but also had more employee grievances. The higher consideration score was related to lower proficiency ratings and lower absences.[11]

The Michigan and Ohio State theories each attempt to isolate broad dimensions of leadership behavior. In so doing, they have provided practitioners with information on what behaviors leaders should possess. This knowledge has resulted in the establishment of training programs for individuals who perform leadership tasks. Each of the approaches also is associated with highly respected theorists, researchers, or consultants, and each has been studied in different organizational

---

[10]For a review of the studies, see Stogdill, *Handbook of Leadership,* chap. 11. Also see Edwin A. Fleishman, "The Measurement of Leadership Attitudes in Industry," *Journal of Applied Psychology,* June 1953, pp. 153–58; C. L. Shartle, *Executive Performance and Leadership* (Englewood Cliffs, NJ: Prentice-Hall, 1956); Edwin A. Fleishman, E. F. Harris, and H. E. Burtt, *Leadership and Supervision in Industry* (Columbus: Bureau of Educational Research, Ohio State University, 1955); and Fleishman, "Twenty Years of Consideration and Structure."

[11]Fleishman, Harris, and Burtt, *Leadership and Supervision.*

settings. Yet the linkage between leadership and such important performance indicators as production, efficiency, and satisfaction has not been conclusively resolved by either of the two personal-behavioral theories.[12]

SITUATIONAL THEORIES

For the most part the previously discussed trait and behavioral approaches to leadership represent a search for the "one best way" to lead. To the extent that any approach to leadership focuses on identifying a style of behavior or mix of traits that will be effective in all situations, it may be thought of as a "universalist" theory. The failure of universalist approaches, be they trait or behavioral in nature, has led to the evolution of "situational" theories that suggest that leadership effectiveness is a function of a variety of factors that will vary depending on the nature of the leadership situation. As the importance of situational factors became better recognized, leadership research became more systematic, and contingency models of leadership began to appear in the organizational behavior and management literature. Among the well-publicized and researched situation-oriented leadership approaches, the most prominent are the Fiedler contingency model, the Vroom-Jago model, and the path-goal theory. Each of these approaches has its advocates, and each attempts to identify the leader behaviors most appropriate for a variety of different leadership situations. Also, each model attempts to identify the leader-situation patterns that are important for effective leadership.

THE CONTINGENCY LEADERSHIP MODEL

The contingency model of leadership effectiveness was developed by Fiedler[13] and postulates that the performance of groups is dependent on the interaction between leadership style and situational favorableness. Leadership style is measured by the *Least-Preferred Co-Worker Scale (LPC)*, an instrument developed by Fiedler which assesses the degree of positive or negative feelings held by a person toward someone with whom he or she least prefers to work. Low scores on the LPC are thought to reflect a *task-oriented*, or controlling, structuring leadership style. High scores are associated with a *relationship-oriented*, or passive, considerate leadership style.

Fiedler proposes three factors which determine how favorable the leadership environment is, or the degree of situational favorableness. *Leader-member relations* refers to the degree of confidence, trust, and respect the followers have in

---

[12]For a discussion of the relationship between leadership and performance, see, for example, James Meindl and Sanford Ehrlich, "The Romance of Leadership and the Evaluation of Organizational Performance," *Academy of Management Journal*, March 1987, pp. 91–109.

[13]Fred E. Fiedler, *A Theory of Leadership Effectiveness* (New York: McGraw-Hill, 1967).

their leader. This is the most important factor. *Task structure* is the second most important factor and refers to the extent to which the tasks the followers are engaged in are structured. That is, is it clearly specified and known what followers are supposed to do, how they are to do it, when and in what sequence it is to be done, and what decision options they have (high structure)? Or are these factors unclear, ambiguous, unspecifiable (low structure)? *Position power* is the final factor and refers to the power inherent in the leadership position. Generally, greater authority equals greater position power.

Together, these three factors determine how favorable the situation is for the leader. Good leader-member relations, high task structure, and strong position power constitute the most favorable situation. Poor relations, low degree of structure, and weak position power represent the least favorable situation. The varying degrees of favorableness and the corresponding appropriate leadership style are shown in Exhibit 10-2.

Fiedler contends that a permissive, more lenient (relationship-oriented) style is best when the situation is moderately favorable or moderately unfavorable. Thus, if a leader is moderately liked and possesses some power, and the job tasks for subordinates are somewhat vague, the leadership style needed to achieve the best results are relationship-oriented. In contrast, when the situation is highly favorable or highly unfavorable, a task-oriented approach generally produces the desired performance. Fiedler bases his conclusion regarding the relationship between leadership style and situational favorableness on more than two decades of research in business, educational, and military settings.[14]

Fiedler is not particularly optimistic that leaders can be trained successfully to change their preferred leadership style. Consequently, he sees changing the favorableness of the situation as a better alternative. In doing this, a first step recommended by Fiedler is to determine whether leaders are task- or relationship-oriented. Next, the organization needs to diagnose and classify the situational favorableness of its leadership positions. Finally, the organization must select the best strategy to bring about improved effectiveness. If leadership training is selected as an option, then it should devote special attention to teaching participants how to modify their environments and their jobs to fit their styles of leadership. That is, leaders should be trained to change their leadership situations. Fiedler suggests that when leaders can recognize the situations in which they are most successful, they can then begin to modify their own situations.

Not everyone would agree with Fiedler's contention that leaders cannot be trained to modify their leadership style. Training leaders is a multibillion-dollar business every year. Organizations continue to search for the best candidates and the most effective training programs to prepare leaders. More and more firms are searching for flexibility within the candidates.

---

[14]Fred E. Fiedler, "How Do You Make Leaders More Effective? New Answers to an Old Puzzle," *Organizational Dynamics,* Autumn 1972, pp. 3–8.

EXHIBIT 10-2

Summary of Fiedler's Situational Variables and Their Preferred Leadership Styles

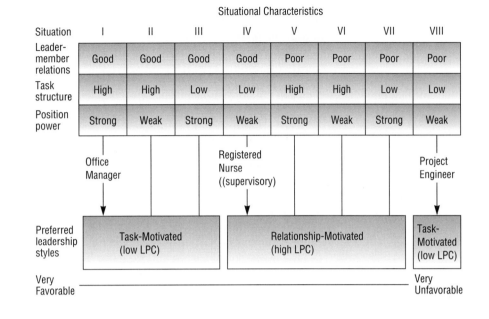

Situational Characteristics

Situation	I	II	III	IV	V	VI	VII	VIII
Leader-member relations	Good	Good	Good	Good	Poor	Poor	Poor	Poor
Task structure	High	High	Low	Low	High	High	Low	Low
Position power	Strong	Weak	Strong	Weak	Strong	Weak	Strong	Weak

Office Manager

Registered Nurse ((supervisory))

Project Engineer

Preferred leadership styles	Task-Motivated (low LPC)	Relationship-Motivated (high LPC)	Task-Motivated (low LPC)

Very Favorable   Very Unfavorable

THE VROOM-JAGO MODEL OF LEADERSHIP

Victor Vroom and Philip Yetton initially developed a leadership decision-making model that indicated the situations in which various degrees of participative decision making would be appropriate.[15] In contrast to Fiedler, Vroom and Yetton attempted to provide a **normative model** that a leader could use in making decisions. Their approach assumed that no single leadership style was appropriate. Unlike Fiedler, Vroom and Yetton assumed that leaders must be flexible enough to change their leadership styles to fit situations. In developing their model, Vroom and Yetton made these assumptions:

1. The model should be of value to leaders or managers in determining which leadership styles they should use in various situations.
2. No single leadership style is applicable to all situations.
3. The main focus should be the problem to be solved and the situation in which the problem occurs.
4. The leadership style used in one situation should not constrain the styles used in other situations.
5. Several social processes influence the amount of participation by subordinates in problem solving.

After a number of years of research and application, the original model has been revised by Vroom and Arthur Jago in order to further improve its accuracy

[15]V. Vroom and P. Yetton, *Leadership and Decision Making* (Pittsburgh: University of Pittsburgh Press, 1973).

and predictability.[16] To understand the Vroom-Jago leadership model it is important to consider three elements that are critical components of the model: (1) specification of the criteria by which decision effectiveness is judged, (2) a framework for describing and categorizing specific leader behaviors or styles, and (3) key diagnostic variables that describe aspects of the leadership situation.

Decision Effectiveness

Selection of the appropriate decision-making process involves considering two criteria of decision effectiveness: decision quality and subordinate commitment. **Decision quality** refers to the extent to which the decision impacts job performance. For example, deciding whether to paint the stripes in the employee parking lot yellow or white requires low decision quality because it has little or no impact on job performance. On the other hand, a decision regarding at what level to set production goals requires high decision quality. **Subordinate commitment** refers to how important it is that subordinates be committed to or accept the decision in order that it may be successfully implemented. Deciding which color paint to use in the parking lot does not really require employee commitment to be successfully implemented; just as clearly, setting production goals at a particular level does require commitment.

In addition to quality and commitment considerations, decision effectiveness may be influenced by time considerations. A decision is not an effective one, regardless of quality and commitment, if it takes too long to make. Even a decision made relatively quickly, if it is a participative one involving a number of people, may be costly in terms of total time spent. Thus, a decision made at a meeting of 15 department members and the department manager that takes two hours has used 32 workhours. In terms of overall organizational effectiveness, this may represent a larger opportunity cost than can be justified.

Decision Styles

The Vroom-Jago model makes a distinction between two types of decision situations facing leaders: individual and group. Individual decision situations are those whose solutions affect only one of the leader's followers. Decision situations that affect several followers are classified as group decision. Five different leadership decision styles that fit individual and group situations are available. These are defined in Exhibit 10-3. In the exhibit, A stands for autocratic, C for consultative, G for group, and D for delegative. The Roman numerals indicate variants of the same process.

---

[16]V. Vroom and A. Jago, *The New Leadership: Managing Participation in Organizations* (Englewood Cliffs, N.J.: Prentice-Hall, 1988).

EXHIBIT 10-3

Decision Styles for Leadership: Individuals and Groups

Individual Level	Group Level
AI. You solve the problem or make the decision yourself, using information available to you at that time.	**AI.** You solve the problem or make the decision yourself, using information available to you at that time.
AII. You obtain any necessary information from the subordinate then decide on the solution to the problem yourself. You may or may not tell the subordinate what the problem is in getting the information from him. The role played by your subordinate in making the decision is clearly one of providing specific information that you request rather than generating or evaluating alternative solutions.	**AII.** You obtain any necessary information from subordinates then decide on the solution to the problem yourself. You may or may not tell the subordinates what the problem is in getting the information from them. The role played by your subordinates in making the decision is clearly one of providing specific information that you request rather than generating or evaluating solutions.
CI. You share the problem with the relevant subordinate, getting ideas and suggestions. Then *you* make the decision. This decision may or may not reflect your subordinate's influence.	**CI.** You share the problem with the relevant subordinates individually, getting their ideas and suggestions without bringing them together as a group. Then *you* make the decision. This decision may or may not reflect your subordinates's influence.
GI. You share the problem with one of your subordinates, and together you analyze the problem and arrive at a mutually satisfactory solution in an atmosphere of free and open exchange of information and ideas. You both contribute to the resolution of the problem, with the relative contribution of each being dependent knowledge rather than formal authority.	**CII.** You share the problem with your subordinates in a group meeting. In this meeting you obtain their ideas and suggestions. Then *you* make the decision, which may or may not reflect your subordinates' influence.
DI. You delegate the problem to one of your subordinates, providing him or her with any relevant information that you possess but giving him or her responsibility for solving the problem alone. Any solution that the person reaches will receive your support.	**GII.** You share the problem with your subordinates as a group. Together you generate and evaluate alternatives and attempt to reach agreement (consensus) on a solution. Your role is much like that of chairman, coordinating the discussion, keeping it focused on the problem, and making sure that the critical issues are discussed. You do not try to influence the group to adopt "your" solution, and you are willing to accept and implement any solution that has the support of the entire group.

Diagnostic Procedure

To determine the most appropriate decision-making style for a given situation, Vroom and Jago suggest that leaders perform a *situational diagnosis*. To accomplish this they have identified a series of questions that can be asked about the situation.[17] Eight of these questions that pertain to our discussion of the model are as follows:

1. How important is the technical quality of this decision?
2. How important is subordinate commitment to the decision?
3. Do you have sufficient information to make a high-quality decision?
4. Is the problem well structured?
5. If you were to make the decision by yourself, it is reasonably certain that your subordinates would be committed to the decision?
6. Do subordinates share the organizational goals to be attained in solving this problem?
7. Is conflict among subordinates over preferred solutions likely?
8. Do subordinates have sufficient information to make a high-quality decision?

Each of these questions may be thought of as representing a dichotomy. That is, they may be answered yes or no, or high or low. It is also possible, however, within the framework of the model for responses to fall between the dichotomized extremes. Answers of "probably" and "maybe" may reflect subtle differences among situations, particularly those which in some way may be ambiguous or unclear.

Application of the Model

Actual application of the Vroom-Jago model can vary significantly in its degree of complexity, sophistication, and specificity, depending on the particular purpose for which it is used and the needs of the decision maker. In its simplest form, application of the model can be expressed as a set of decision-making heuristics or rules of thumb. Exhibit 10-4 lists the 8 rules of thumb (out of a total of 11) that apply to the model as discussed here. In contrast, in its most complex form the model requires the use of mathematical formulas too complex to describe here. Using the manager's analysis of the situation represented by the manager's responses to the diagnostic questions, the formulas predict the most appropriate way of handling the situation, the second best way, and so forth. The complexity of this approach, however, requires the use of a personal computer and specially developed software.

In between these two approaches is the use of decision trees. Such decision trees can represent the operation of the more complex equations in the model if certain simplifying assumptions are made. Exhibit 10-5 shows one of these trees. The first simplifying assumption is that each question, or problem attribute, can be given a clear yes or no (or high or low) response. The second simplifying assumption is that 4 of the 12 possible problem attributes are held constant. The decision tree depicted in this figure is what Vroom and Jago label a "time-driven"

---

[17]Ibid.

EXHIBIT 10-4

Rules of Thumb Underlying the Vroom-Jago Model

Rules to improve decision quality:
1. Avoid the use of AI when:
   a. The leader lacks the necessary information.
2. Avoid the use of GII when:
   a. Subordinates do not share the organizational goals.
   b. Subordinates do not have the necessary information.
3. Avoid the use of AII and CI when:
   a. The leader lacks the necessary information.
   b. The problem is unstructured.
4. Move toward GII when:
   a. The leader lacks the necessary information.
   b. Subordinates share the organizational goals.
   c. There is conflict among subordinates over preferred solutions.

Rules to improve decision commitment:
1. Move toward GII when:
   a. Subordinates are not likely to become committed to the leader's decision.
   b. There is conflict among coordinates over preferred solutions.

Rules to reduce decision costs (time):
1. Move toward AI especially if:
   a. A severe time constraint exists.
   b. The problem is unstructured.
2. Avoid use of CII and GII if:
   a. Subordinates are geographically dispersed.
   b. There is conflict among subordinates over preferred solutions.

Source: Abridged from V. Vroom and A. Jago, *The New Leadership* (Englewood Cliffs, N.J.: Prentice-Hall, 1988). Copyright 1987 by V. Vroom and A. Jago. Used with permission of the authors.

decision tree. It is designed for the manager who places maximum weight on saving time. Other trees are available for managers who weight time (and other factors) differently. Exhibit 10-5 is used in completing the end-of-chapter exercise, "Leadership Style Analysis," in which you can apply the Vroom-Jago model to the leadership situation.

■ **E10–1**

When the Vroom-Jago model is used in leadership training and development settings, it is not unusual for all three approaches to be used. The rules of thumb help convey the basic logic of the model, the decision trees provide a vehicle for representing various trade-offs among objectives, and the use of a computer efficiently allows for answering numerous "what if" questions once the basic model itself is understood.

Validity of the Model

As was the case with the original model in 1973, the revised model currently lacks complete empirical evidence establishing its validity. Certainly the model is thought to be consistent with what we now know about the benefits and costs

EXHIBIT 10-5

Time-Driven Decision Tree

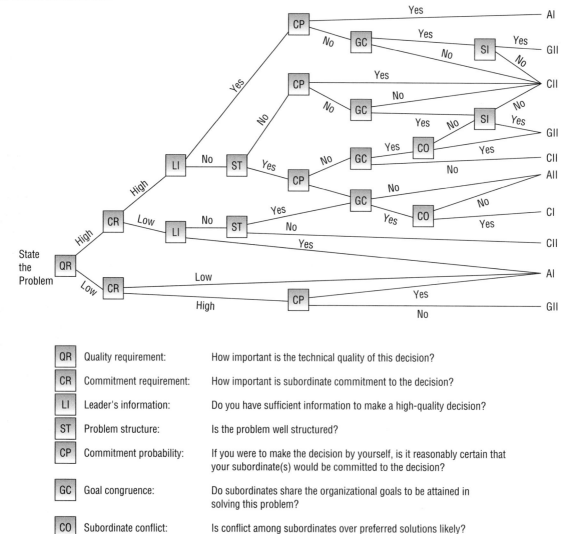

QR	Quality requirement:	How important is the technical quality of this decision?
CR	Commitment requirement:	How important is subordinate commitment to the decision?
LI	Leader's information:	Do you have sufficient information to make a high-quality decision?
ST	Problem structure:	Is the problem well structured?
CP	Commitment probability:	If you were to make the decision by yourself, is it reasonably certain that your subordinate(s) would be committed to the decision?
GC	Goal congruence:	Do subordinates share the organizational goals to be attained in solving this problem?
CO	Subordinate conflict:	Is conflict among subordinates over preferred solutions likely?
SI	Subordinate information:	Do subordinates have sufficient information to make a high-quality decision?

of participation. Moreover, it represents a direct extension of the original 1973 model for which ample validation evidence does exist. Nonetheless, without extensive evidence that the use of the model can improve decision effectiveness—and, by extension, leadership success, its value as a theoretical contribution and as a practical tool remains open to question.

▲ **C10–1** The L. J. Summers Company case at the end of the chapter can provide an opportunity to use the Vroom-Jago model (and decision tree) to determine the level of subordinate participation in decisions concerning changes to cut costs and boost performance.

PATH-GOAL MODEL

Like the other situational or contingency leadership approaches, the **path-goal model** attempts to predict leadership effectiveness in different situations. According to this model, leaders are effective because of their positive impact on followers' motivation, ability to perform, and satisfaction. The theory is designated path-goal because it focuses on how the leader influences the followers' perceptions of work goals, self-development goals, and paths to goal attainment.[18]

The foundation of path-goal theory is the expectancy motivation theory discussed in Chapter 4. Some early work on the path-goal theory asserts that leaders will be effective by making rewards available to subordinates and by making those rewards contingent on the subordinates' accomplishment of specific goals.[19] It is argued by some that an important part of the leader's job is to clarify for subordinates the kind of behavior most likely to result in goal accomplishment. This activity is referred to as *path clarification.*

The early path-goal work led to the development of a complex theory involving four specific styles of leader behavior (directive, supportive, participative, and achievement) and three types of subordinate attitudes (job satisfaction, acceptance of the leader, and expectations about effort-performance-reward relationships).[20] The *directive leader* tends to let subordinates know what is expected of them. The *supportive leader* treats subordinates as equals. The *participative leader* consults with subordinates and uses their suggestions and ideas before reaching a decision. The *achievement-oriented leader* sets challenging goals, expects subordinates to perform at the highest level, and continually seeks improvement in performance.

Two types of situational or contingency variables are considered in the path-goal theory. These variables are the *personal characteristics of subordinates* and the *environmental pressures and demands* with which subordinates must cope in order to accomplish work goals and derive satisfaction.

---

[18]Robert J. House, "A Path-Goal Theory of Leadership Effectiveness," *Administrative Science Quarterly,* September 1971, pp. 32–39. Also see Robert J. House and Terence R. Mitchell, "Path-Goal Theory of Leadership," *Journal of Contemporary Business,* Autumn 1974, pp. 81–98, which is the basis for the discussion.

[19]Martin G. Evans, "The Effects of Supervisory Behavior on the Path-Goal Relationship," *Organizational Behavior and Human Performance,* May 1970, pp. 277–98. Also see Martin G. Evans, "Effects of Supervisory Behavior: Extensions of Path-Goal Theory of Motivation," *Journal of Applied Psychology,* April 1974, pp. 172–78.

[20]Robert J. House and Gary Dessler, "The Path-Goal Theory of Leadership: Some Post Hoc and A Priori Tests," in *Contingency Approaches to Leadership,* ed. James G. Hunt (Carbondale: Southern Illinois University Press, 1974).

An important personal characteristic is subordinates' perception of their own ability. The higher the degree of perceived ability relative to the task demands, the less likely the subordinate is to accept a directive leader style. This directive style of leadership would be viewed as unnecessarily close. In addition, it has been discovered that a person's *locus of control* also affects responses. Individuals who have an internal locus of control (they believe that rewards are contingent on their efforts) are generally more satisfied with a participative style, while individuals who have an external locus of control (they believe that rewards are beyond their personal control) are generally more satisfied with a directive style.[21]

The environmental variables include factors that are not within the control of the subordinate but are important to satisfaction or to the ability to perform effectively.[22] These include the tasks, the formal authority system of the organization, and the work group. Any of these environmental factors can motivate or constrain the subordinate. The environmental forces may also serve as a reward for acceptable levels of performance. For example, the subordinate could be motivated by the work group and receive satisfaction from co-workers' acceptance for doing a job according to group norms.

The path-goal theory proposes that leader behavior will be motivational to the extent that it helps subordinates cope with environmental uncertainties. A leader who is able to reduce the uncertainties of the job is considered to be a motivator because he or she increases the subordinate's expectations that their efforts will lead to desirable rewards. Exhibit 10-6 summarizes the basic features of the path-goal approach.

A Critique of the Path-Goal Model

The path-goal model, like the Vroom-Jago model, warrants further study because some questions remain about its predictive power. One researcher suggested that subordinate performance might be the cause of changes in leader behavior instead of, as predicted by the method, the other way around.[23] A review of the path-goal approach suggested that the model has resulted in the development of only a few hypotheses. These reviewers also point to the record of inconsistent research results associated with the model. Additionally, much of the research to date has involved only partial tests of the model.[24]

On the positive side, however, the path-goal model is an improvement over the trait and personal-behavioral theories. It attempts to indicate which factors affect the motivation to perform. In addition, the path-goal approach introduces both situational factors and individual differences when examining leader be-

[21]House and Mitchell, "Path-Goal Theory of Leadership."

[22]Ibid.

[23]C. Green, "Questions of Causation in the Path-Goal Theory of Leadership," *Academy of Management Journal,* March 1979, pp. 22–41.

[24]J. Faulk and E. Wendler, "Dimensionality of Leader-Subordinate Interactions: A Path-Goal Approach," *Organizational Behavior and Human Performance,* 1982, pp. 241–64.

EXHIBIT 10-6

The Path-Goal Model

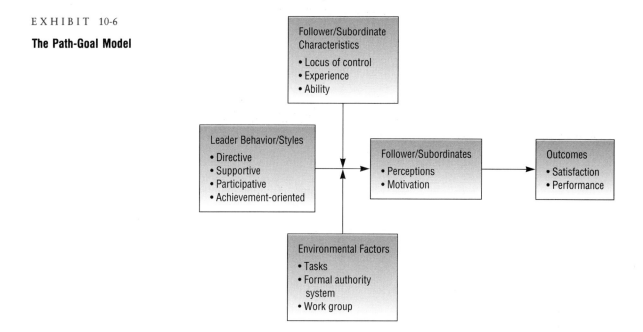

havior and outcomes such as satisfaction and performance. The path-goal approach makes an effort to explain why a particular style of leadership works best in a given situation. As more research accumulates, this type of explanation will have practical utility for those interested in the leadership process in work settings.

COMPARISON OF THE SITUATIONAL APPROACHES

Three current models for examining leadership have been presented. These models have similarities and differences. They are similar in that they (1) focus on the dynamics of leadership, (2) have stimulated research on leadership, and (3) remain controversial because of measurement problems, limited research testing, or contradictory research results.

The themes of each model are summarized in Exhibit 10-7. Fiedler's model has been the most tested and perhaps the most controversial. His view of leader behavior centers on task- and relationship-oriented tendencies and how these tendencies interact with task and position power. Vroom and Jago view leader behavior in terms of autocratic, consultative, or group styles. Finally, the path-goal approach emphasizes the instrumental actions of leaders and four styles for conducting these actions—directive, supportive, participative, and achievement-oriented.

EXHIBIT 10-7

A Comparison of Three Situational Approaches to Leadership

Approach	Leader Behavior/Style	Situational Factors	Outcome Criteria
Fiedler's contingency model	Task-oriented (low LPC) Relationship-oriented (high LPC)	Task-structure Leader-member relations Position power	Group's effectiveness
Vroom-Jago	Autocratic Consultive Group	Quality of decision Information requirement Problem structure Followers' acceptance of decision Mutuality of follower and organizational goals Level of follower conflict	Quality of decision Acceptance of decision by followers Time to make decisions
Path-goal	Directive Supportive Participative Achievement-oriented	Follower characteristics Environmental factors	Satisfaction Performance

Source: Adapted from Edwin P. Hollander, *Leadership Dynamics* (New York: Free Press, 1978).

The situational variables discussed in each approach differ somewhat. There is also a different view of outcome criteria for assessing how successful the leader behavior has been. Fiedler discusses leader effectiveness; Vroom and Jago discuss the quality of a decision, follower acceptance, and the timeliness of the decision; the path-goal approach focuses on satisfaction and performance.

The Attribution Theory of Leadership

In our discussion of perception in Chapter 3 we introduced the concept of attributions. Attribution theory, we said, was concerned with the process by which individuals interpret events around them and attribute causes to these events. It was suggested that people's behavior is influenced by the perceived, rather than the actual, causes of events. In short, attribution theory attempts to explain the *why* of behavior. Similarly, the emphasis of attribution leadership theory is on why some behavior has occurred.

The attributional approach in leadership starts with the position that the leader is essentially an *information processor.*[25] In other words, the leader is searching

---

[25]S. G. Green and T. R. Mitchell, "Attributional Processes of Leaders in Leader-Member Interactions," *Organizational Behavior and Human Performance*, June 1979, pp. 429–58.

EXHIBIT 10-8

An Attributional Leadership Model

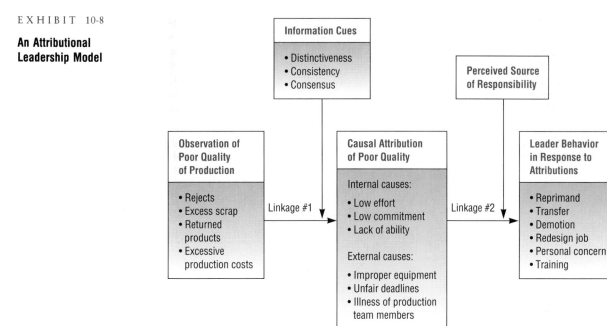

Source: Adapted from Terence R. Mitchell and Robert E. Wood, "An Empirical Test of an Attributional Model of Leader's Responses to Poor Performance," in *Academy of Management Proceedings,* 1979, ed. Richard C. Houseman, p. 94.

for information cues that explain why something is happening. From these cues, the leader attempts to construct causal explanations that guide his or her leadership behavior. The process in simple terms appears to be follower behavior → leader attributions → leader behavior. A somewhat more detailed schema of an attributional model of leadership can be found in Exhibit 10-8.

Two important linkages are emphasized in Exhibit 10-8. At the first linkage point, the leader attempts to make attributions about poor performance. These attributions are moderated by three information sources—distinctiveness, consistency, and consensus. The second linkage point suggests that the leader's behavior or response is determined by the types of attributions he or she makes. This relationship between attribution and leader behavior is moderated by the leader's perception of responsibility. For example, the more a behavior is seen as caused by some characteristic of the follower (i.e., an internal cause) and the more the follower is judged to be responsible for the behavior, the more likely the leader is to take some action toward the follower.

Currently, the research support for the attributional approach to leadership, while positive, is limited, and additional testing of the model is needed, particularly in applied organizational settings.[26] Understanding the causes of leader behavior, or at least searching for these causes, seems more promising for managerial use than does simply adding another trait or descriptive theory to the already large leadership literature.[27]

ALTERNATIVE EXPLANATIONS OF LEADERSHIP

The theoretical, empirical, and application work provided by the trait, personal-behavior, and situational approaches have advanced the understanding of leadership in work settings. However, a number of gaps, differences in opinions, and changes in the nature of work, diversity in the work force, and internationally inspired approaches concerning leadership still remain. Such questions and issues as the following are still being debated: (1) Are leaders really needed? (2) Are there substitutes for leadership that affect the performance of followers? and (3) Are leader-follower interaction patterns significant?

Are Leaders Necessary?

There are some academic researchers who propose that leadership has become irrelevant in organizations.[28] Even the chief executive officer is depicted as a person with little control over most resources. For example, Lee Iacocca at Chrysler, Jack Welch at General Electric, and John Sculley at Apple Computer must seek and receive the approval of others to make major investment, product design, and hiring decisions. Committees, boards, and review panels enter into decision making. Shareholders, consumers, and government regulators all impose constraints on the chief executive officer.

The environment in which a firm operates affects a leader's span of discretion. For example, a chief executive officer in the public utility industry must operate within the rules, policies, and constraints imposed by a public utility board or commission. School superintendents have very little control over the enrollments in their district.[29] Birth rates and the district's economic status influence the school budget more than a superintendent's vision or wisdom.

The concept of self-managed work groups also raises the issue of whether leaders are that important. Self-management is defined as the set of strategies a person uses to influence him- or herself. Included in the discussion of strategies

---

[26]M. Martinko and W. L. Gardner, "The Leader/Member Attribution Process," *Academy of Management Review*, April 1987, pp. 235–49.

[27]D. Giola and H. Sims, Jr., "Cognitive-Behavior Connections: Attributions and Verbal Behavior in Leader-Subordinate Interactions," *Organizational Behavior and Human Decision Processes*, April 1986, pp. 197–229.

[28]Jeffrey Pfeffer, "The Ambiguity of Leadership," *Academy of Management Review*, January 1977, pp. 104–11.

[29]A. B. Thomas, "Does Leadership Make a Difference to Organizational Performance?" *Administrative Science Quarterly*, September 1988, pp. 388–400.

I N T E R N A T I O N A L
E N C O U N T E R • 10-2

EMPOWERMENT RULES AT PEPSICO

The "Cola Wars" is big business in and outside the United States. Pepsi Cola and Coca-Cola are the two biggest warriors in this ongoing battle for market share. Dr. Wayne (Red) Calloway is at the head of the Pepsi team. His leadership style is now legendary. He practices, preaches, and supports empowered leadership. A bottom-up approach to leading is what Calloway wants as a part of Pepsi's organizational culture.

To make sure Pepsi hires managers who can be empowered to lead, Calloway meets with everyone who is interviewing for a vice presidential position or higher. He interviews about 75 executives a year. He is also involved in twice-yearly evaluations of management-level employees—about 600 people.

Calloway is always on the search for new ways to get employees more involved. He puts together the company's "Share Power Rally," at which employees from every division discuss individual initiative. He also initiated a "Great Pepsi Co. Brainstorm" in which employees won prizes for contributing ideas on how to do business better.

Calloway is also asking his management team to look through overseas opportunities. Pepsi Co. already operates in 60 countries, and its snack business operates in 24 countries. In soft drinks, however, Coke remains the king overseas, outselling Pepsi by 3 to 1. Calloway wants to find the right people to manage the overseas war with Coke and other competitors. He is looking for bold, creative, free-thinking, and self-confident men and women who can properly handle authority while working outside the United States.

Source: Adapted from Andrea Rothman, "Can Wayne Calloway Handle the Pepsi Challenge," *Business Week*, January 27, 1992, pp. 90–98.

are behavioral and cognitive approaches.[30] Behavioral strategies deal with actions such as setting job goals, interpreting feedback, and personally rewarding oneself for completing a task. Cognitive strategies involve thinking carefully about a job and even producing mental images of how to perform a job well.

Self-management can apply to individuals and to work groups. The self-managed work group could be involved with accomplishing an entire job without any formal supervisors checking or overseeing the work.

Manz and Sims believe that self-leadership will play a growing role because of the changes in technology that have already and will continue to occur.[31] Workers will have to motivate themselves in the increasingly complex and higher technology work settings. Manz and Sims coined the word *superleadership* to describe the type of leader who leads others to lead themselves. Superleaders have the ability to create in subordinates the desire, skill, and persistence needed

[30]Henry P. Sims, Jr., and Peter Lorenzi, *The New Leadership Paradigm* (Newbury Park, Calif.: Sage, 1992), pp. 180–81.

[31]Charles C. Manz and Henry P. Sims, Jr., *Superleadership: Leading Others to Lead Themselves* (New York: Prentice-Hall, 1989).

to be self-leaders.[32] At PepsiCo, Chief Executive Officer Wayne Calloway is attempting to encourage and find self-leaders to make an impact in international markets. He wants to empower them to perform well at PepsiCo.

Substitutes for Leadership

A wide variety of individual, task, environmental, and organizational characteristics have been identified as factors that influence relationships between leader behavior and follower satisfaction and performance. Some of these variables (e.g., follower expectations of leader behavior) appear to influence which leadership style will enable the leader to motivate and direct followers. Others function, however, as *substitutes for leadership*. Substitute variables tend to negate the leader's ability either to increase or decrease follower satisfaction or performance.[33] Some people claim that substitutes for leadership are prominent in many organizational settings.

Exhibit 10-9, based on previously conducted research, provides substitutes for only two of the more popular leader behavior styles—relationship-oriented and task-oriented. For each of these leader behavior styles, Kerr and Jermier present which substitutes (characteristics of the subordinate, the task, or the organization) will serve to neutralize the style.[34] For example, an experienced, well-trained, and knowledgeable employee does not need a leader to structure the task (e.g., a task-oriented leader). Likewise, a job (task) that provides its own feedback does not need a task-oriented leader to inform the employee how he or she is doing. Also, an employee in a very cohesive group does not need a supportive, relationship-oriented leader. The group is a substitute for this type of leader.

Admittedly, we do not fully understand the leader-follower relationship in organizational settings. The need to continue searching for guidelines and principles is apparent. Such searching now seems to be centered on more careful analysis of a situational perspective of leadership and on issues such as the cause-effect question, the constraints on leader behavior, and substitutes for leadership. We feel that it is better to study leaders and substitutes for leaders than to use catchy descriptions to identify leaders. This type of study and analysis can result in the development of program to train, prepare, and develop employees for leadership roles.[35]

---

[32]Charles C. Manz and Henry P. Sims, Jr., Superleadership beyond the Myth of Heroic Leadership," *Organizational Dynamics,* Spring 1991, pp. 18–25.

[33]Steven Kerr and John M. Jermier, "Substitutes for Leadership: Their Meaning and Measurement," *Organizational Behavior and Human Performance,* December 1978, pp. 376–403.

[34]Ibid.

[35]C. C. Manz, "Self-Leadership: Toward an Expanded Theory of Self-Influence Processes in Organizations," *Academy of Management Review,* July 1986, pp. 585–600.

EXHIBIT 10-9

Substitutes for Leadership

	Will Tend to Neutralize	
Characteristic	**Relationship-Oriented**	**Task-Oriented**
Of the subordinate:		
1. Ability experience, training, knowledge		X
2. Need for independence	X	X
3. "Professional" orientation	X	X
4. Indifference toward organizational rewards	X	X
Of the task:		
5. Unambiguous and routine		X
6. Methodologically invariant		X
7. Provides its own feedback concerning accomplishment		X
8. Intrinsically satisfying	X	
Of the organization:		
9. Formalization (explicit plans, goals, and areas of responsibility)		X
10. Inflexibility (rigid, unbending rules and procedures)		X
11. Highly specified and active advisory and staff functions		X
12. Close-knit, cohesive work groups	X	X
13. Organizational rewards not within the leader's control	X	X
14. Spatial distance between superior and subordinates	X	X

Source: Adapted from Steven Kerr and John M. Jermier, "Substitutes for Leadership: Their Meaning and Measurement," *Organizational Behavior and Human Performance,* December 1978, p. 378.

Vertical Dyad Linkage (VDL) Approach

In the personal-behavioral explanation of leadership, it is assumed that the leader's behavior is the same across all followers.[36] This thinking is similar to assuming that a parent treats or interacts with each of her three children the same. Graen has proposed the vertical dyad linkage theory of leadership (VDL) which proposes that there is no such thing as consistent leader behavior across subordinates. A leader may be very considerate and relaxed toward one follower and very rigid

[36]George Graen, "Role-Making Processes with Complex Organizations," in *Handbook of Industrial Organizational Psychology,* M. D. Dunnette ed. (Chicago: Rand McNally, 1976), pp. 1210–59.

and structured with another subordinate. Each relationship has a uniqueness, and it is the one-on-one relationships that determine the behaviors of subordinates.

The VDL approach suggests that leaders classify subordinates in *in*-group members and *out*-group members. The in-group members share a common bond and value system and interact with the leader. Out-group members have less in common with the leader and do not share much with him or her. The Leader-Member Exchange Questionnaire partially presented in Exhibit 10-10 can be used to measure in-group versus out-group status.[37]

The VDL explanation suggests that in-group members are likely to receive more challenging assignments and more meaningful rewards. The performance consequences of being in the out-group are likely to be poor. An out-group member is not considered to be the type of person the leader prefers to work with, and this attitude is likely to become a self-fulfilled prophecy. The out-group members receive less challenging assignments, receive little positive reinforcement, become bored with the job, and often quit.

The VDL approach rests on the assumption that the leader's perception of followers influences the leader's behavior, which then influences the follower's behavior. This exchange or mutual influence explanation is also found in the equity theory explanation of motivation.

Charismatic Leadership

Individuals such as John Kennedy, Winston Churchill, and Walt Disney possessed an attractiveness that enabled them to make a difference with citizens, employees, or followers. Their leadership approach is referred to as *charismatic leadership*. Max Weber suggested that some leaders have a gift of exceptional qualities—a charisma—that enables them to motivate followers to achieve outstanding performance.[38] Such a charismatic leader is depicted as being able to play a vital role in creating change.

Steven Jobs, cofounder of Apple Computers, provides an example of how charisma works to inspire others. Job's impact, attraction, and inspiration when he was with the firm were described as follows:

> *When I walked through the Macintosh building with Steve, it became clear that he wasn't just another general manager bringing a visitor along to meet another group of employees. He and many of Apple's leaders weren't managers at all; they were impresarios. . . . Not unlike the director of an opera company, the impresario must cleverly deal with the creative temperaments of artists. . . . His gift is to merge powerful ideas with the performance of his artists.[39]*

[37]George Graen, R. Liden, and W. Hoel, "Role of Leadership in the Employee Withdrawal Process," *Journal of Applied Psychology*, 1982, pp. 868–72.

[38]Max Weber, *The Theory of Social and Economic Organization*, trans. A. M. Henderson and T. Parsons (New York: Free Press, 1947, originally published 1924).

[39]John Sculley, "Sculley's Lessons from Inside Apple," *Fortune*, September 14, 1987, pp. 108–11.

EXHIBIT 10-10

**Items That Assess
Leader-Member Exchange**

1. How flexible do you believe your supervisor is about evolving change in *your* job?
   4 = Supervisor is enthused about change; 3 = supervisor is lukewarm to change; 2 = supervisor sees little need to change; 1 = Supervisor sees no need for change.

2. Regardless of how much formal organizational authority your supervisor has built into his/her position, what are the chances that he/she would be personally inclined to use his/her power to help you solve problems in your work? 4 = He certainly would; 3 = Probably would; 2 = Might or might not; 1 = No.

3. To what extent can *you* count on your supervisor to "bail you out" at his/her expense when *you* really need him/her? 4 = Certainly would; 3 = Probably; 2 = Might or might not; 1 = No.

4. How often do you take suggestions regarding your work to your supervisor? 4 = Almost always; 3 = Usually; 2 = Seldom; 1 = Never.

5. How would *you* charcterize *your* working relationship with your supervisor? 4 = Extremely effective; 3 = Better than average; 2 = About average; 1 = Less than average.

The five items are summed for each participant, resulting in a possible range of scores from 5 to 20.

Lee Iacocca, chairperson of Chrysler, is cited as a person who has charismatic qualities. However, he has been so publicly visible that certain events like those cited in the following Encounter may have damaged his charismatic influence as the leader of Chrysler.

Defining Charismatic Leadership

Charisma is a Greek word meaning "gift." Powers that could not be clearly explained by logical means were called charismatic. Presently, no definitive answer has been given on what constitutes charismatic leadership behavior. House suggests that charismatic leaders are those who have charismatic effects on their followers to an unusually high degree.[40]

Conger's Model.   Jay Conger has proposed a model that illustrates how charisma evolves.[41] Exhibit 10-11 presents his four-stage model of charismatic leadership. In stage one, the leader continuously assesses the environment, adapts, and formulates a vision of what must be done. The leader's goals are established. In stage two, the leader communicates his or her vision to followers, using whatever means are necessary. The stage-three segment is highlighted by working on trust and commitment. Doing the unexpected, taking risk, and being technically proficient are important in this stage. In stage four, the charismatic leader serves as

[40]Robert J. House "A 1976 Theory of Charismatic Leadership," in *Leadership: The Cutting Edge,* ed. J. G. Hunt and L. L. Larson (Carbondale: Southern Illinois University Press, 1977), pp. 189–207.

[41]His views of charismatic leadership are clearly presented in Jay A. Conger, *The Charismatic Leader* (San Francisco: Jossey-Bass, 1989). Also see David A. Nadler and Michael L. Tushman, "Beyond the Charismatic Leader: Leadership and Organizational Change," *California Management Review,* Winter 1990, pp. 77–97.

ENCOUNTER • 10-3

CHIPPING AWAY AT CHARISMA

In 1987 Chrysler Corp. faced criminal charges of tampering with odometers on new cars. Two Chrysler executives were accused of disconnecting or replacing odometers on 60,000 vehicles. It seems that company employees drove new cars and trucks with odometers disconnected for as long as five weeks. The vehicles were then shipped to dealers, who sold them as new cars. Also, about 40 vehicles shipped as new had actually been involved in accidents.

The high-profile leader at Chrysler at the time was Lee Iacocca. When charges were brought against the company, Iacocca at first accused the government of misinterpreting a legal and routine test-drive program. Test drives are necessary to determine a car's quality.

About one week after the indictments, Chrysler announced it was discontinuing the disconnect program. Iacocca then issued a public apology announcing that

Chrysler had made a mistake. He promised that the practice would not be repeated. The firm then placed a two-page advertisement in national newspapers stating that Chrysler would extend the warranties on test cars and replace cars that had been damaged during test drives and then later sold as new.

Did the odometer incident damage Iacocca's image as a charismatic leader? Some think that he never reclaimed his image as a person who is attractive and charismatic. In 1992 Iacocca was in the news again while traveling to Japan with President Bush. Iacocca was attempting to persuade the Japanese to allow more American products into their markets. He railed on television about unfair Japanese practices. Again, some leadership watchers claim that he damaged his "charisma quotient" by whining and groveling. Charisma is an elusive attribute to acquire and, apparently, an attribute that can also be damaged or lost.

Source: Adapted from O. C. Ferrell and John Fraedich, *Business Ethics* (Boston: Houghton Mifflin, 1991), pp. 173–75; and John Bussey, "Lee Iacocca Calls Odometer Policy Dumb," *The Wall Street Journal*, July 2, 1987, p. 2.

a role model and motivator. The charismatic leader uses praise and recognition to instill within followers the belief that they can achieve the vision.

What Constitutes Charismatic Leadership Behavior? What behavioral dimensions distinguish charismatic leaders from noncharismatic leaders? A criticism of the early work on charismatic leadership is that the explanations of it lacked specificity. Some limited attempts have been made to develop and test specific charismatic qualities such as vision, acts of heroism, and the ability to inspire.[42] However, in most cases, clarifying what specifically constitutes charismatic behavior has been generally ignored.

A number of empirical studies have examined behavior and attributes of charismatic leaders, such as articulation ability, affection for the leader, ability to

---

[42]See A. R. Willner, *The Spellbinders: Charismatic Political Leadership* (New Haven, Conn.: Yale University Press, 1984).

EXHIBIT 10-11

Stages in Charismatic Leadership

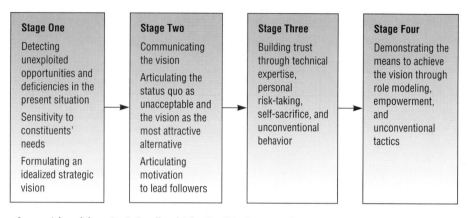

Stage One	Stage Two	Stage Three	Stage Four
Detecting unexploited opportunities and deficiencies in the present situation	Communicating the vision	Building trust through technical expertise, personal risk-taking, self-sacrifice, and unconventional behavior	Demonstrating the means to achieve the vision through role modeling, empowerment, and unconventional tactics
Sensitivity to constituents' needs	Articulating the status quo as unacceptable and the vision as the most attractive alternative		
Formulating an idealized strategic vision	Articulating motivation to lead followers		

Source: Adapted from O. C. Ferrell and John Fraedich, *Business Ethics* (Boston: Houghton Mifflin, 1991), pp. 173–75; and John Bussey, "Lee Iacocca Calls Odometer Policy Dumb," *The Wall Street Journal*, July 2, 1987, p. 2.

inspire, dominating personality, and need for influence.[43] However, no specific set of behaviors and attributes is universally accepted by theorists, researchers, and practitioners. A descriptive behavioral framework that builds upon empirical work has been offered. The framework, presented in Exhibit 10-12 assumes that charisma must be viewed as an attribution made by followers within the work context.

Two Types of Charismatic Leaders

In most discussions of charismatic leadership, the term *vision* is highlighted. It is argued that the first requirement for exercising charismatic leadership is expressing a shared vision of what the future could be. Through communication ability, the visionary, charismatic leader links followers' needs and goals to job or organizational goals. Linking followers with the organization's direction, mission, and goals is easier if they are dissatisfied or not challenged by the current situation.

Crisis-based charismatic leaders have an impact when the system must handle a situation for which existing knowledge, resources, and procedures are not adequate.[44] The crisis-produced charismatic leader communicates clearly and

[43]Bernard M. Bass, *Leadership Performance beyond Expectations* (New York: Academic Press, 1985); Warren G. Bennis and Burt Nanes, *Leaders* (New York: Harper & Row, 1985); Robert J. House and M. L. Baetz, "Leadership: Some Empirical Generalizations and New Research Directions," in *Research in Organizational Behavior*, ed. Barry M. Staw (Greenwich, Conn.: JAI Press, 1979), pp. 399–401.

[44]J. M. Bryson, "A Perspective on Planning and Crisis in the Public Sector," *Strategic Management Journal*, 1981, pp. 181–96.

EXHIBIT 10-12

Behavioral Components of Charismatic and Noncharismatic Leaders

Component	Charismatic Leader	Noncharismatic Leader
Relation to status quo	Essentially opposed to status quo and strives to change it (Steve Jobs at Apple).	Essentially agrees with status quo and strives to maintain it.
Future goal	Idealized vision highly discrepant from status quo (Tom Monaghan with the Domino's Pizza concept).	Goal not too discrepant from status quo.
Likableness	Shared perspective and idealized vision makes him or her a likable and honorable hero worthy of identification and imitation (Lee Iacocca in first three years at Chrysler).	Shared perspective makes him or her likable.
Expertise	Expert in using unconventional means to transcend the existing order (Al Davis, owner of the Los Angeles Raiders).	Expert in using available means to achieve goals within the framework of the existing order.
Environmental sensitivity	High need for environmental sensitivity for changing the status quo (Edgar Woolard at Du Pont).	Low need for environmental sensitivity to maintain status quo.
Articulation	Strong articulation of future vision and motivation to lead (Ross Perot at EDS).	Weak articulation of goals and motivation to lead.
Power base	Personal power, based on expertise, respect, and admiration for a unique hero (Jan Carlzon at Scandinavian Airlines System — SAS).	Position power and personal power (based on reward, expertise, and liking for a friend who is a similar other).
Leader-follower relationship	Elitist, entrepreneur, an exemplary (Mary Kay Ash of Mary Kay Cosmetics).	Egalitarian, consensus seeking, or directive.
	Transforms people to share the radical changes advocated (Edward Land, inventor of Polaroid camera).	Nudges or orders people to share his or her views.

Source: Adapted from Jay A. Conger and Rabindra Kanungo, "Toward a Behavioral Theory of Charismatic Leadership in Organizational Settings," *Academy of Management Review*, October 1987, pp. 637–47.

specifically what actions need to be taken and what will be the consequence of the action.

A number of crisis situations have required immediate action on the part of leaders. Do you recall some of them?

- In 1978, the Three Mile Island nuclear power plant accident.
- In 1982, the contamination of Tylenol capsules with cyanide, causing the deaths of eight people and a loss of $100 million in recalled packages for

Johnson & Johnson. In 1986, a second poisoning incident caused the recall of packages and another loss of $150 million.

- In 1984, the worst industrial accident in history in Bhopal, Indian, killing 3,000 people and injuring another 300,000.
- In 1986, a tragic explosion of the space shuttle *Challenger,* costing the lives of 7 astronauts.
- In 1989, a 10-million-gallon oil spill into Prince William Sound near Valdez, Alaska, by an Exxon oil tanker.
- In 1990, 72 million bottles of Perrier water were recalled by the company because of possible benzene contamination.

These events caught the attention of everyone. Each day, smaller but still significant crises occur throughout the world.

Crisis management is a growing field of study and inquiry.[45] The crises managers face enable charismatic leadership to emerge. First, under conditions of stress, ambiguity, and chaos, followers give power to individuals who have the potential to correct the crisis situation. The leader is empowered to do what is necessary to correct the situation or solve the problem. In many cases, the leader is unconstrained and is allowed to use whatever he or she thinks is needed.[46]

A crisis also permits the leader to promote nontraditional actions by followers. The crisis-based charismatic leader has greater freedom to encourage followers to search for ways to correct the crisis. Some of the methods, procedures, and tactics adopted by followers may be disorderly, chaotic, and outside the normal boundary of actions. However, the charismatic leader in a crisis situation encourages, supports, and usually receives action from followers.[47]

The present state of knowledge about charismatic leadership is still relatively abstract and ambiguous. Despite Weber's concept of charismatic authority, Conger's framework of how charismatic leadership evolves, House's definition and propositions about the characteristics of charismatic leaders, and some limited research results, much more theoretical and research work needs to be done. There is a void in understanding about whether charismatic leaders can be harmful in expressing visions that are unrealistic or inaccurate in the way they attack a crisis problem. Management scholar and writer Peter Drucker claims that "charisma becomes the undoing of leaders." How accurate is Drucker? No one knows at this time. However, evidence suggests that charismatic leaders (e.g., Hitler, Stalin, Jim Jones) can secure greater commitment of failing, personally demeaning,

[45]S. Fink, *Crisis Management* (New York: AMACOM, 1986); Ian I. Mitroff, Paul Shrivastava, and Firdaus E. Udivadia, "Effective Crisis Management," *Academy of Management Executive,* November 1987, pp. 283–92.

[46]N. Roberts, "Transforming Leadership: A Process of Collective Action," *Human Relations,* 1985, pp. 1023–46.

[47]B. Hedberg, "How Organizations Learn and Unlearn," in *Handbook of Organizational Design,* ed. P. C. Nystrom and W. H. Starbuck (London: Oxford University Press, 1980), pp. 3–27.

and tragic goals than can the average leader.[48] In the business world, John DeLorean was able to raise hundreds of millions of dollars for his failed automobile venture because of his powers of persuasion and impression management. He promoted himself as an innovative genius.

The positive and negative aspects of charismatic leadership need to be studied. Studying each theory of leadership with regard to its positive and negative impact on followers and situations should be a top priority. We raise questions here about the dark side of charismatic leadership but to be thorough, we must also ask whether there is a dark side to the other theories.

Transactional and Transformational Leadership

Transactional Leadership

The exchange role of the leader has been referred to as *transactional*. Exhibit 10-13 presents the *transactional leadership* roles. The leader helps the follower identify what must be done to accomplish the desired results: better-quality output, more sales or services, reduced cost of production. In helping the follower identify what must be done, the leader takes into consideration the person's self-concept and esteem needs. The transactional approach uses the path-goal concepts as its framework.

In using the transaction style, the leader relies on contingent reward and on management by exception. Research shows that when contingent reinforcement is used, followers exhibit an increase in performance and satisfaction:[49] followers believe that accomplishing objectives will result in their recovering desired rewards. Using management by exception, the leader will not be involved unless objectives are not being accomplished.

Transactional leadership is not often found in organizational settings. One national sample of U.S. workers showed that only 22 percent of the participants perceived a direct relationship between how hard they worked and how much pay they received.[50] That is, the majority of workers believed that good pay was not contingent on good performance. Although workers prefer a closer link between pay and performance, it was not present in their jobs. Why? There are probably a number of reasons, such as unreliable performance appraisal systems, subjectively administered rewards, poor managerial skills in showing employees the pay-performance link, and conditions outside the manager's control. Also, managers often provide records that are not perceived by followers to be meaningful or important.

[48]Conger, *Charismatic Leader*, p. 137.

[49]P. M. Podsakoff, W. D. Tudor, and R. Skov, "Effect of Leader Contingent and Non-Contingent Reward and Punishment Behaviors on Subordinate Performance and Satisfaction," *Academy of Management Journal*, 1982, pp. 810–21.

[50]D. Yankelovich and J. Immerivoki, *Putting the Work Ethic to Work* (New York: Public Agenda Foundation, 1983).

EXHIBIT 10-13

Transactional Leadership

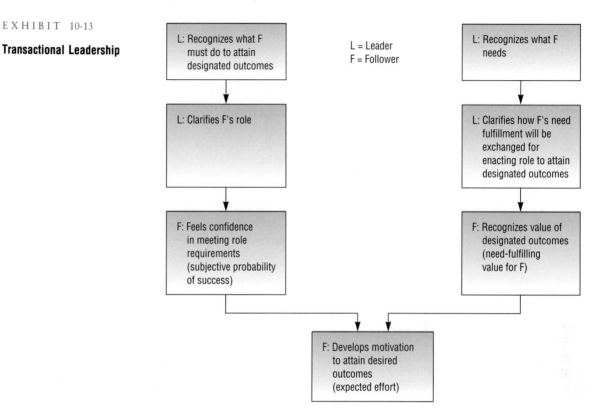

Source: Bernard M. Bass, *Leadership and Performance beyond Expectations* (New York: Free Press, 1985), p. 12.

A small pay increase, a personal letter from the boss, or a job transfer may not be what employees want in the form of a contingent reward. Until managers understand what the employee wants, administer the rewards in a timely manner, and emphasize the pay-performance link, there is likely to be confusion, uncertainty, and minimal transactional impact in leader-follower relationships.

The Transformational Theme

An exciting new kind of leader, referred to as the *transformational leader,*[51] motivates followers to work for transcendental goals instead of short-term self-interest and for achievement and self-actualization instead of security.[52] In transformational leadership, viewed as a special case of transactional leadership, the

● **R10–2**

---

[51]James M. Burns, *Leadership* (New York: Harper & Row, 1978).

[52]Brice J. Avolio and Bernard M. Bass, "Transformational Leadership, Charisma and Beyond," in *Emerging Leadership Vistas,* ed. James G. Hunt, B. Rajaram Baliga, H. Peter Dachler, and Chester A. Schriesheim (Lexington, Mass.: Lexington Books, 1988), pp. 29–49.

employee's reward is internal. By expressing a vision, the transformational leader persuades followers to work hard to achieve the goals envisioned. The leader's vision provides the follower with motivation for hard work that is self-rewarding (internal).

Transactional leaders will adjust goals, direction, and mission for practical reason. Transformational leaders, on the other hand, make major changes in the firm's or unit's mission, way of doing business, and human resource management in order to achieve their vision. The transformational leader will overhaul the entire philosophy, system, and culture of an organization.

Names that come to mind when we think about transformational leaders are Michael Eisner at Walt Disney, Jack Welch at General Electric, and, of course, Lee Iacocca at Chrysler. Under Eisner's leadership, for example, Disney has moved into movies (some R-rated), syndicated a business show for television, introduced a television channel, introduced new cartoon characters, and licensed new apparel products. Eisner took risks and pushed the company along a path that was unheard of for 40 years. He transformed Walt Disney Company from a conservative into an assertive, proactive company.[53]

A framework that helps describe how Eisner, Welch, and Iacocca transformed their organizations is presented in Exhibit 10-14. Note that the transactional approach is incorporated into the transformational leadership model. As noted by Tosi, most successful charismatic/transforming leaders have the ability to transact with subordinates the day-to-day routine requirements and actions.[54] The transformational leader must possess transactional leadership skills.

The development of transformational leadership factors has evolved from research by Bass.[55] He identified five factors (first three apply to transformational and last two apply to transactional leadership) that describe transformational leaders. They are:

- *Charisma.* The leader is able to instill a sense of value, respect, and pride and to articulate a vision.[56]
- *Individual attention.* The leader pays attention to followers' needs and assigns meaningful projects so that followers grow personally.
- *Intellectual stimulation.* The leader helps followers rethink rational ways to examine a situation. Encourages followers to be creative.
- *Contingent reward.* The leader informs followers about what must be done to receive the rewards they prefer.

---

[53]Jay Clarke, "Disney World Grows like Pinocchio's Nose," *Houston Chronicle,* March 6, 1988, p. 9.

[54]Henry J. Tosi, Jr., "Toward a Paradigm Shift in the Study of Leadership," in *Leadership: Beyond Establishment Views,* ed. James G. Hung, V. Sekraran, and Chester A. Schriesheim (Carbondale: Southern Illinois University Press, 1982), pp. 222–23.

[55]Bass, *Leadership Performance.*

[56]Jay C. Conger, "Inspiring Others: The Language of Leadership," *Academy of Management Executive,* February 1991, pp. 31–45.

EXHIBIT 10-14

Transformation Leadership

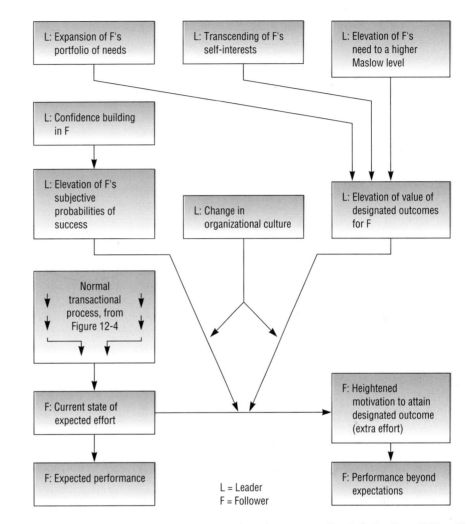

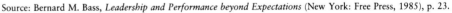

Source: Bernard M. Bass, *Leadership and Performance beyond Expectations* (New York: Free Press, 1985), p. 23.

- *Management by exception.* The leader permits followers to work on the task and does not intervene unless goals are not being accomplished in a reasonable time and at a reasonable cost.

One of the most important characteristics of the transformational leader is charisma. However, charisma by itself is not enough for successful transformational leadership, as Bass clearly states:

The deep emotional attachment which characterizes the relationship of the charismatic leader to followers may be present when transformational leadership occurs, but we can distinguish a class of charismatics who are not at all transformational in their influence. Celebrities may be identified as charismatic by a large segment of the public. Celebrities are held in awe and reverence by the masses who are developed by them. People will be emotionally aroused in the presence of celebrities and identify with them in their fantasy, but the celebrities may not be involved at all in any transformation of their public. On the other hand, with charisma, transformational leaders can play the role of teacher, mentor, coach, reformer, or revolutionary. Charisma is a necessary ingredient of transformational leadership, but by itself it is not sufficient to account for the transformational process.[57]

In addition to charisma, transformational leaders need assessment skills, communication abilities, and a sensitivity to others. They must be able to articulate their vision, and they must be sensitive to the skill deficiencies of followers.

Is Leader Behavior a Cause or an Effect?

We have implied that leader behavior has an effect on the follower's performance and job satisfaction. There is, however, a sound basis from which one can argue that follower performance and satisfaction cause the leader to vary his or her leadership style. It has been argued that a person will develop positive attitudes toward objects that are instrumental to the satisfaction of his or her needs.[58] This argument can be extended to leader-follower relationships. For example, organizations reward leaders (managers) based on the performance of followers (subordinates). If this is the case, leaders might be expected to develop positive attitudes toward high-performing followers. Let us say that an employee, Joe, because of outstanding performance, enables his boss, Mary, to receive the supervisory excellence award, a bonus of $1,000. The expectation then is that Mary would think highly of Joe and reward him with a better work schedule or job assignment. In this case, Joe's behavior leads to Mary's being rewarded, and she in turn rewards Joe.

In a field study data were collected from first-line managers and from two of each manager's first-line supervisors. The purpose of this research was to assess the direction of causal influence in relationships between leader and follower variables. The results strongly suggested that (1) leader consideration behavior caused subordinate satisfaction and (2) follower performance caused changes in the leader's emphasis on both consideration and the structuring of behavior-performance relationships.[59]

The research available on the cause-effect issue is still quite limited. It is premature to conclude that all leader behavior, or even a significant portion of

[57]Ibid., p. 31.

[58]D. Katz and E. Stotland, "A Preliminary Statement to a Theory of Attitude Structure and Change," in *Psychology: A Study of Science*, ed. S. Koch (New York: McGraw-Hill, 1959).

[59]Charles N. Greene, "The Reciprocal Nature of Influence between Leader and Subordinate," *Journal of Applied Psychology*, April 1975, pp. 187–93.

such behavior, is a response to follower behavior. However, there is a need to examine the leader-follower relationship in terms of reciprocal causation. That is, leader behavior causes follower behavior and follower behavior causes leader behavior.

This chapter has presented the idea that a single, universally accepted theory of leadership is not available. Each of the perspectives covered in the chapter provides insight into leadership. The fact is that various traits of leaders (e.g., intelligence, personality) influence how they behave with followers. Also, situational variables and follower characteristics (e.g., needs, abilities, experience) affect a leader's behavior. Therefore, trait, personal-behavioral, and situational characteristics must be considered when attempting to understand leadership in organizational settings.

SUMMARY OF KEY POINTS

- Leadership is defined in many different ways. In concise terms, leadership is an attempt to influence the activities (work-related) of followers through the communication process and toward the attainment of some goal or goals. Self-leadership is the concept that individuals will lead themselves or will be self-initiators of acceptable workplace behavior.

- Trait theory has for years attempted to identify, classify, and apply the traits of effective leaders. Originally, it was assumed that a finite number of individual traits could be identified. This has not been the case. Thus, in terms of accuracy, the trait approach is somewhat questionable.

- The Vroom-Jago extended a normative model that provides guidance to leaders in presenting appropriate styles to fit specific situations. The model suggests that the amount of subordinate participation depends on the leader's skill and knowledge, whether a quality decision is needed, the degree of structure of the problem, and whether acceptance by followers is needed to implement the decision.

- Transformational leadership is considered a special case of transactional leadership. The transactional leader helps the follower identify what must be done to accomplish the desired results. He or she uses the path-goal concepts and approach. Transformational leaders express a vision and are able to persuade followers to work hard to accomplish the goals envisioned.

- Whether charismatic qualities can be learned is unknown. There are no specific scientific studies that clearly show that charisma can be acquired via training or executive development.

- Perception plays a major role in the attribution leadership theory. How the leader interprets cues such as worker performance (output or quantity) influences how the leader will respond toward the worker. Interpretation involves the leader's perception.

REVIEW AND DISCUSSION QUESTIONS

1. Over time the various theories proposed to explain leadership have become increasingly complex. Why has this happened?

2. What are the major differences between attributional and personal-behavioral explanations of leader behavior?

3. Do organizations do a good job in selecting people for leadership positions? Are there ways in which they could do a better job?

4. Organizations annually spend a great deal of money on leadership training. Is this a wise investment? Are there other, less costly ways of improving leadership?

5. Are leaders really necessary? Does the superleadership concept suggest that leaders are not needed?

6. Realistically, how much control does a leader have over situational favorableness? How might a leader go about trying to improve favorableness?

7. What type of research is needed to validate and further develop the Vroom-Jago model?

8. What charismatic qualities would be important to learn and practice while serving as a leader?

9. The vertical dyad linkage theory is considered an exchange approach to leadership. Why?

10. Is there a cause-and-effect relationship between leader behavior and follower performance? What is the nature, or direction, of the relationship?

•

READINGS

READING 10–1 LEADERSHIP: DO TRAITS MATTER?

Shelley A. Kirkpatrick
Edwin A. Locke

Few issues have a more controversial history than leadership traits and characteristics. In the 19th and early 20th centuries, "great man," leadership theories were highly popular. These theories asserted that leadership qualities were inherited, especially by people from the upper class. Great men were born, not made (in those days, virtually all business leaders were men). Today, great man theories are a popular foil for so-called superior models. To make the new models plausible, the "great men" are endowed with negative as well as positive traits. In a recent issue of the *Harvard Business Review,* for example, Slater and Bennis write,

> *"The passing years have . . . given the coup de grace to another force that has retarded democratization—the 'great man' who with brilliance and farsightedness could preside with dictatorial powers as the head of a growing organization."*[1]

Such great men, argue Slater and Bennis, become "outmoded" and dead hands on "the flexibility and growth of the organization." Under the new democratic model, they argue, "the individual is of relatively little significance."

Early in the 20th century, the great man theories evolved into trait theories. ("Trait" is used broadly here to refer to people's general characteristics, including capacities, motives, or patterns of behavior.) Trait theories did not make assumptions about whether leadership traits were inherited or acquired. They simply asserted that leaders' characteristics are different from non-leaders. Traits such as height, weight, and physique are heavily dependent on heredity, whereas others such as knowledge of the industry are dependent on experience and learning.

The trait view was brought into question during the mid-century when a prominent theorist, Ralph Stogdill, after a thorough review of the literature concluded that "A person does not become a leader by virtue of the possession of some combination of traits."[2] Stogdill believed

this because the research showed that no traits were universally associated with effective leadership and that situational factors were also influential. For example, military leaders do not have traits identical to those of business leaders.

Since Stogdill's early review, trait theory has made a come back, though in altered form. Recent research, using a variety of methods, has made it clear that successful leaders are not like other people. The evidence indicates that there are certain core traits which significantly contribute to business leaders' success.

Traits alone, however, are not sufficient for successful business leadership—they are only a precondition. Leaders who possess the requisite traits must take certain actions to be successful (e.g., formulating a vision, role modeling, setting goals). Possessing the appropriate traits only makes it more likely that such actions will be taken and be successful. After summarizing the core leadership traits, we will discuss these important actions and the managerial implications.

THE EVIDENCE: TRAITS DO MATTER

The evidence shows that traits do matter. Six traits on which leaders differ from nonleaders include: drive, the desire to lead, honesty/integrity, self-confidence, cognitive ability, and knowledge of the business.[3] These traits are shown in Exhibit 10-15.

Drive

The first trait is labeled "drive" which is not to be confused with physical need deprivation. We use the term to refer to a constellation of traits and motives reflecting a high effort level. Five aspects of drive include achievement motivation, ambition, energy, tenacity, and initiative.

Achievement

Leaders have a relatively high desire for achievement. The need for achievement is an important motive among ef-

Source: Shelley A. Kirkpatrick and Edwin A. Locke, "Leadership: Do Traits Matter?" *Academy of Management Executive,* May 1991, pp. 48–60.

EXHIBIT 10-15

Leadership Traits

Drive: achievement, ambition, energy, tenacity, initiative

Leadership Motivation (personalized vs. socialized)

Honesty and Integrity

Self-confidence (including emotional stability)

Cognitive Ability

Knowledge of the Business

Other Traits (weaker support): charisma, creativity/originality, flexibility

---

fective leaders and even more important among successful entrepreneurs. High achievers obtain satisfaction from successfully completing challenging tasks, attaining standards of excellence, and developing better ways of doing things. To work their way up to the top of the organization, leaders must have a desire to complete challenging assignments and projects. This also allows the leader to gain technical expertise, both through education and work experience, and to initiate and follow through with organizational changes.

The constant striving for improvement is illustrated by the following manager who took charge of a $260 million industrial and office-products division:[4]

> *After twenty-seven months on the job. Tom saw his efforts pay off: the division had its best first quarter ever. By his thirty-first month, Tom felt he had finally mastered the situation. . . . [Tom] finally felt he had the structure and management group in place to grow the division's revenues to $400 million and he now turned his attention to divesting a product group which no longer fit in with the growth objectives of the division.*

Managers perform a large amount of work at an unrelenting pace. To perform well, a leader needs to constantly work toward success and improvement. Superior managers and executives are concerned with doing something better than they or others have ever done it. For example, at PepsiCo only "aggressive achievers" survive. Similarly, Thomas Watson of IBM has been described as "driven throughout by a personal determination to create a company larger than NCR."[5] This brings us to a second related motive: ambition.

Ambition

Leaders are very ambitious about their work and careers and have a desire to get ahead. To advance, leaders actively take steps to demonstrate their drive and determination. Ambition impels leaders to set hard, challenging goals for themselves and their organizations. Walt Disney, founder of Walt Disney Productions, had a "dogged determination to succeed" and C. E. Woolman of Delta Air Lines had "inexhaustible ambition."

Effective leaders are more ambitious than nonleaders. In their 20-year study, psychologists Ann Howard and Douglas Bray found that among a sample of managers at AT&T, ambition, specifically the desire for advancement, was the strongest predictor of success twenty years later. The following character sketches of two managers who successfully progressed illustrate the desire for advancement:[6]

> *I want to be able to demonstrate the things I learned in college and get to the top," said Al, "maybe even be president. I expect to work hard and be at the third level within 5 years, and to rise to much higher levels in the years beyond that. I am specifically working on my MBA to aid in my advancement. If I'm thwarted on advancement, or find the challenge is lacking, I'll leave the company.*

> *[He] had been promoted to the district level [after 8 years] and certainly expected to go further. Although he still wouldn't pinpoint wanting to be president (his wife's dream for him), he certainly had a vice presidency (sixth level) in mind as early as year 2 in the study, after his first promotion.*

The following sketches characterize two less ambitious individuals:

> *Even though Chet had the benefits of a college degree, his below-average scholastic performance did not fill him with confidence in his capabilities. He hedged a bit with his interviewer when asked about his specific as-*

pirations, saying he wasn't sure what the management levels were. When pressed further, he replied, "I'd like to feel no job is out of my reach, but I'm not really possessed of a lot of ambition. There are times when I just want to say, 'To hell with everything.' "

After [his] promotion to the second level, he looked more favorably upon middle management, but he sill indicated he would not be dissatisfied to stay at the second level. [He] just seemed to take each position as it came; if he ever looked ahead, he didn't appear to look up.

Energy

To sustain a high achievement drive and get ahead, leaders must have a lot of energy. Working long, intense work weeks (and many weekends) for many years, requires an individual to have physical, mental, and emotional vitality.

Leaders are more likely than nonleaders to have a high level of energy and stamina and to be generally active, lively, and often restless. Leaders have been characterized as "electric, vigorous, active, full of life" as well as possessing the "physical vitality to maintain a steadily productive work pace."[7] Even at age 70, Sam Walton, founder of Wal-Mart discount stores, still attended Wal-Mart's Saturday morning meeting, a whoop-it-up 7:30 a.m. sales pep rally for 300 managers.

The need for energy is even greater today than in the past, because more companies are expecting all employees, including executives, to spend more time on the road visiting the organization's other locations, customers, and suppliers.

Tenacity

Leaders are better at overcoming obstacles than nonleaders. They have the "capacity to work with distant objects in view" and have a "degree of strength of will or perseverance."[8] Leaders must be tirelessly persistent in their activities and follow through with their programs. Most organizational change programs take several months to establish and can take many years before the benefits are seen. Leaders must have the drive to stick with these programs, and persistence is needed to ensure that changes are institutionalized.

Determined to sink the Serapis, Jones spotted an open hatch on the Serapis' deck and ordered a young sailor to climb into the rigging and toss grenades into the hatch, knowing the English had stored their ammunitions there. After missing with the first two grenades, the third grenade

disappeared into the hatchway and was followed by a thunderous explosion aboard the Serapis. Engulfed in flames, the English captain surrendered to Jones. Even though the entire battle had gone against him, John Paul Jones was determined not to give up, and it was this persistence that caused him to finally emerge victorious.

It is not just the direction of action that counts, but sticking to the direction chosen. Effective leaders must keep pushing themselves and others toward the goal. David Glass, CEO of Wal-Mart, says that Sam Walton "has an overriding something in him that causes him to improve every day. . . . As long as I have known him, he has never gotten to the point where he's comfortable with who he is or how we're doing." Walt Disney was described as expecting the best and not relenting until he got it. Ray Kroc, of McDonald's Corporation, was described as a "dynamo who drove the company relentlessly."[9] Kroc posted this inspirational message on his wall:

Nothing in the world can take the place of persistence. Talent will not; nothing is more common than unsuccessful men with great talent.
Genius will not; unrewarded genius is almost a proverb.
Education will not; the world is full of educated derelicts.
Persistence, determination alone are omnipotent.

Persistence, of course, must be used intelligently. Dogged pursuit of an inappropriate strategy can ruin an organization. It is important to persist in the right things. But what are the right things? In today's business climate, they may include the following: satisfying the customer, growth, cost control, innovation, fast response time, and quality. Or, in Tom Peters' terms, a constant striving to improve just about everything.

Initiative

Effective leaders are proactive. They make choices and take action that leads to change instead of just reacting to events or waiting for things to happen; that is, they show a high level of initiative. The following two examples from consultant Richard Boyatzis of McBer and Company illustrate proactivity.[10]

I called the chief, and he said he couldn't commit the resources, so I called the budget and finance people, who gave me a negative response. But then I called a guy in another work group who said he was willing to make a trade for the parts I needed. I got the parts and my group was able to complete the repairs.

One of our competitors was making a short, half-inch component and probably making $30,000-$40,000 a year on it. I looked at our line: we have the same product and can probably make it better and cheaper. I told our marketing manager: "Let's go after that business." I made the decision that we would look at it as a marketplace rather than looking at it as individual customers wanting individual quantities. I said, here's a market that has 30,000 pieces of these things, and we don't give a damn where we get the orders. Let's just go out and get them. We decided we were going to charge a specific price and get the business. Right now we make $30,000-$40,000 on these things and our competitor makes zero.

Instead of sitting "idly by or [waiting] for fate to smile upon them," leaders need to "challenge the process."

Leaders are achievement-oriented, ambitious, energetic, tenacious, and proactive. These same qualities, however, may result in a manager who tries to accomplish everything alone, thereby failing to develop subordinate commitment and responsibility. Effective leaders must not only be full of drive and ambition, they must *want to lead others.*

Leadership Motivation

Studies show that leaders have a strong desire to lead. Leadership motivation involves the desire to influence and lead others and is often equated with the need for power. People with high leadership motivation think a lot about influencing other people, winning an argument, or being the greater authority. They prefer to be in a leadership rather than subordinate role. The willingness to assume responsibility, which seems to coincide with leadership motivation, is frequently found in leaders.

Sears psychologist Jon Bentz describes successful Sears executives as those who have a "powerful competitive drive for a position of . . . authority . . . [and] the need to be recognized as men of influence."[11] Astronauts John Glenn and Frank Borman built political and business careers out of their early feats as space explorers, while other astronauts did not. Clearly, all astronauts possessed the same opportunities, but is was their personal makeup that caused Glenn and Borman to pursue their ambitions and take on leadership roles.

Psychologist Warren Bennis and colleague Burt Nanus state that power is a leader's currency, or the primary means through which the leader gets things done in the organization. A leader must want to gain the power to exercise influence over others. Also, power is an "expand-able pie," not a fixed sum; effective leaders give power to others as a means of increasing their own power. Effective leaders do not see power as something that is competed for but rather as something that can be created and distributed to followers without detracting from their own power.

Successful managers at AT&T completed sentence fragments in the following manner:[12]

"When I am in charge of others I find my greatest satisfactions."
"The job I am best fit for is one which requires leadership ability."
"I depend on others to carry out my plans and directions."

A manager who was not as successful completed the sentence fragment "Taking orders . . ." with the ending "is easy for it removes the danger of a bad decision."

Successful leaders must be willing to exercise power over subordinates, tell them what to do, and make appropriate use of positive and negative sanctions. Previous studies have shown inconsistent results regarding dominance as a leadership trait. According to Harvard psychologist David McClelland, this may be because there are two different types of dominance: a personalized power motive, or power lust, and a socialized power motive, or the desire to lead.[13]

Personalized Power Motive

Although a need for power is desirable, the leader's effectiveness depends on what is behind it. A leader with a personalized power motive seeks power as an end in itself. These individuals have little self-control, are often impulsive, and focus on collecting symbols of personal prestige. Acquiring power solely for the sake of dominating others may be based on profound self-doubt. The personalized power motive is concerned with domination of others and leads to dependent, submissive followers.

Socialized Power Motive

In contrast, a leader with a socialized power motive uses power as a means to achieve desired goals, or a vision. Its use is expressed as the ability to develop networks and coalitions, gain cooperation from others, resolve conflicts in a constructive manner, and use role modeling to influence others.

Individuals with a socialized power motive are more emotionally mature than those with a personalized power motive. They exercise power more for the benefit of the whole organization and are less likely to use it for manipulation. These leaders are also less defensive, more willing to take advice from experts, and have a longer-range view. They use their power to build up their organization and make it successful. The socialized power motive takes account of followers' needs and results in empowered, independent followers.

Honesty and Integrity

Honesty and integrity are virtues in all individuals, but have special significance for leaders. Without these qualities, leadership is undermined. Integrity is the correspondence between word and deed and honesty refers to being truthful or non-deceitful. The two form the foundation of a trusting relationship between leader and followers.

In his comprehensive review of leadership, psychologist Bernard Bass found that student leaders were rated as more trustworthy and reliable in carrying out responsibilities than followers. Similarly, British organizational psychologists Charles Cox and Cary Cooper's "high flying" (successful) managers preferred to have an open style of management, where they truthfully informed workers about happenings in the company. Morgan McCall and Michael Lombardo of the Center for Creative Leadership found that managers who reached the top were more likely to follow the following formula: "I will do exactly what I say I will do when I say I will do it. If I change my mind, I will tell you well in advance so you will not be harmed by my actions."[14]

Successful leaders are open with their followers, but also discreet and do not violate confidences or carelessly divulge potentially harmful information. One subordinate in a study by Harvard's John Gabarro made the following remark about his new president: "He was so consistent in what he said and did, it was easy to trust him." Another subordinate remarked about an unsuccessful leader, "How can I rely on him if I can't count on him consistently?"[15]

Professors James Kouzes, Barry Posner, and W. H. Schmidt asked 1500 managers "What values do you look for and admire in your superiors?" Integrity (being truthful and trustworthy, and having character and conviction) was the most frequently mentioned characteristic. Kouzes and Posner conclude:

Honesty is absolutely essential to leadership. After all, if we are willing to follow someone, whether it be into battle or into the boardroom, we first want to assure ourselves that the person is worthy of our trust. We want to know that he or she is being truthful, ethical, and principled. We want to be fully confident in the integrity of our leaders.

Effective leaders are credible, with excellent reputations, and high levels of integrity. The following description (from Gabarro's study) by one subordinate of his boss exemplifies the concept of integrity: "By integrity, I don't mean whether he'll rob a bank, or steal from the till. You don't work with people like that. It's whether you sense a person has some basic principles and is willing to stand by them."

Bennis and Nanus warn that today credibility is at a premium, especially since people are better informed, more cautious, and wary of authority and power. Leaders can gain trust by being predictable, consistent, and persistent and by making competent decisions. An honest leader may even be able to overcome lack of expertise, as a subordinate in Gabarro's study illustrates in the following description of his superior: "I don't like a lot of the things he does, but he's basically honest. He's a genuine article and you'll forgive a lot of things because of that. That goes a long way in how much I trust him."

Self-Confidence

There are many reasons why a leader needs self-confidence. Being a leader is a very difficult job. A great deal of information must be gathered and processed. A constant series of problems must be solved and decisions made. Followers have to be convinced to pursue specific courses of action. Setbacks have to be overcome. Competing interests have to be satisfied. Risks have to be taken in the face of uncertainty. A person riddled with self-doubt would never be able to take the necessary actions nor command the respect of others.

Self-confidence plays an important role in decision-making and in gaining others' trust. Obviously, if the leader is not sure of what decision to make, or expresses a high degree of doubt, then the followers are less likely to trust the leader and be committed to the vision.

Not only is the leader's self-confidence important, but so is others' perception of it. Often, leaders engage in impression management to bolster their image of competence; by projecting self-confidence they arouse followers' self-confidence. Self-confident leaders are also more likely to be assertive and decisive, which gains others' confidence in the decision. This is crucial for effective implementation of the decision. Even when the decision turns out to be a poor one, the self-confident leader admits the mistake and uses it as a learning opportunity, often building trust in the process. Manor Care, Inc., for example, lost over $21 million in 1988 when it was caught holding a large portion of Beverly Enterprise's stock. Chairman and CEO Stewart Bainum, Jr. stated, "I take full and complete responsibility for making the acquisition."[16] Considered to be the "best managed company in the [nursing home] industry," Manor Care's stock has rebounded, and it seems to be making a comeback. Less successful managers are more defensive about failure and try to cover up mistakes.

Emotional Stability

Self-confidence helps effective leaders remain even-tempered. They do get excited, such as when delivering an emotionally-charged pep talk, but generally do not become angry or enraged. For the most part, as long as the employee did his/her homework leaders remain composed upon hearing that an employee made a costly mistake. For example, at PepsiCo, an employee who makes a mistake is "safe . . . as long as it's a calculated risk."

Emotional stability is especially important when resolving interpersonal conflicts and when representing the organization. A top executive who impulsively flies off the handle will not foster as much trust and teamwork as an executive who retains emotional control. Describing a superior, one employee in Gabarro's study stated, "he's impulsive and I'm never sure when he'll change signals on me."

Researchers at the Center for Creative Leadership found that leaders are more likely to "derail" if they lack emotional stability and composure. Leaders who derail are less able to handle pressure and more prone to moodiness, angry outbursts, and inconsistent behavior, which undermines their interpersonal relationships with subordinates, peers, and superiors. In contrast, they found the successful leaders to be calm, confident, and predictable during crisis.

Psychologically hardy, self-confident individuals consider stressful events interesting, as opportunities for development, and believe that they can influence the outcome. K. Labich in *Fortune* magazine argued that "By demonstrating grace under pressure, the best leaders inspire those around them to stay calm and act intelligently."[17]

Cognitive Ability

Leaders must gather, integrate, and interpret enormous amounts of information. These demands are greater than ever today because of rapid technological change. Thus, it is not surprising that leaders need to be intelligent enough to formulate suitable strategies, solve problems, and make correct decisions.

Leaders have often been characterized as being intelligent, but not necessarily brilliant and as being conceptually skilled. Kotter states that a "keen mind" (i.e., strong analytical ability, good judgment, and the capacity to think strategically and multidimensionally) is necessary for effective leadership, and that leadership effectiveness requires "above average intelligence," rather than genius.

An individual's intelligence and the perception of his or her intelligence are two highly related factors. Professors Lord, DeVader, and Alliger concluded that "intelligence is a key characteristic in predicting leadership perceptions."[18] Howard and Bray found that cognitive ability predicted managerial success twenty years later in their AT&T study. Effective managers have been shown to display greater ability to reason both inductively and deductively than ineffective managers.

Intelligence may be a trait that followers look for in a leader. If someone is going to lead, followers want that person to be more capable in *some* respects than they are. Therefore, the follower's perception of cognitive ability in a leader is a source of authority in the leadership relationship.

Knowledge of the Business

Effective leaders have a high degree of knowledge about the company, industry, and technical matters. For example, Jack Welch, president of GE has a PhD in engineering; George Hatsopolous of Thermo Electron Corporation, in the years preceding the OPEC boycott, had both the business knowledge of the impending need for energy-efficient appliances and the technical knowledge of thermodynamics to create more efficient gas furnaces. Technical expertise enables the leader to understand the concerns of subordinates regarding technical issues. Harvard Professor John Kotter argues that expertise is more important than formal education.

Effective leaders gather extensive information about the company and the industry. Most of the successful general managers studied by Harvard's Kotter spent their careers in the same industry, while less successful managers lacked industry-specific experience. Although cognitive ability is needed to gain a through understanding of the business, formal education is not a requirement. Only forty percent of the business leaders studied by Bennis and Nanus had business degrees. In-depth knowledge of the organization and industry allows effective leaders to make well-informed decisions and to understand the implications of those decisions.

Other Traits

Charisma, creativity/originality, and flexibility are three traits with less clear-cut evidence of their importance to leadership.[19] Effective leaders may have charisma, however, this trait may only be important for political leaders. Effective leaders also may be more creative than nonleaders, but there is no consistent research demonstrating this. Flexibility or adaptiveness may be important traits for a leader in today's turbulent environment. Leaders must be able to make decisions and solve problems quickly and initiate and foster change.

There may be other important traits needed for effective leadership, however, we believe that the first six that we discussed are the core traits.

THE REST OF THE STORY

A complete theory of leadership involves more than specifying leader traits. Traits only endow people with the potential for leadership. To actualize this potential, additional factors are necessary which are discussed in our forthcoming book *The Essence of Leadership* (written with additional authors).

Three categories of factors are discussed here: skills, vision, and implementing the vision. **Skills** are narrower in meaning than traits and involve specific capacities for action such as decision making, problem solving, and performance appraisal.

The core job of a leader, however, is to create a *vision*— a concept of what the organization should be. To quote Bennis and Nanus, "a vision articulates a view of a realistic, credible, attractive future for organization, a condition that is better in some important ways than what now exists. A vision is a target that beckons."[20] Next the leader must *communicate* this vision to followers through inspirational speeches, written messages, appeals to shared values and above all through acting as a role model and personally acting in a way that is consistent with the vision. Third, the leader must develop or at least help to develop a general *strategy* for achieving the vision (i.e. a strategic vision).

Implementing the vision requires at least six activities:

1. *Structuring.* Today's effective organizations have minimal bureaucracy: small corporate staffs, few layers of management and large spans of control. The leader must insure that the organization's structure facilitates the flow of information (downward, upward, and diagonally). Information from customers regarding product quality and services is especially crucial.

2. *Selecting and Training.* Leaders must make sure that people are hired who have the traits needed to accept and implement the vision. Maintaining and upgrading skills is assured by constant training, as is commitment to the organization's vision.

3. *Motivating.* Leaders cannot achieve the vision alone; they must stimulate others to work for it too. They must generate enthusiasm, commitment, and compliance. Besides communicating the vision, effective leaders use at least six procedures to motivate followers.

   a. *Formal authority.* The leader is the "boss" and must use his or her legitimate power constructively. The leader must start by asking directly for what he or she wants. *Thriving on Chaos* author Tom Peters said that if one wants something, then "Just ask for it."

   b. *Role Models.* Leaders must behave the way they wish their followers would behave. For example, if they want subordinates to be customer-oriented, they should spend time themselves talking to customers. This has far more influence on employees than just telling them that customers are important.

   c. *Build subordinate self-confidence.* If employees have been carefully selected and trained, such confidence will be justified. Jay Conger calls the process of strengthening subordinates' belief in their capabilities "empowerment."[21]

   d. *Delegation of authority.* Giving autonomy and responsibility to employees also creates empowerment. In their book *Superleadership,* Charles Manz and Henry Sims[22] argue that delegating authority actually enhances the power of leaders by helping their subordinates become capable of attaining organizational goals. Effective delegation, of course, pre-supposes that subordinates are capable of holding the responsibilities they are given (as a result of extensive training and experience).

   e. *Specific and challenging goals.*[23] Ensuring that subordinates have specific and challenging goals lead to higher performance than ambiguous goals.

Challenging goals are empowering, because they demonstrate the leader has confidence in the follower. Goals must be accompanied by regular feedback indicating progress in relation to the goals. Feedback, in turn, requires adequate performance measurement.

For goals to be effective employees must be committed to them. Inspiration, modeling, training, and delegation all facilitate commitment.

   f. *Rewards and punishments.* Effective leaders are *not* tolerant of those who reject the vision or repeatedly fail to attain reasonable goals. Rewards (and punishments) send messages not only to the employee in question but also to others; followers often direct their own actions by looking at what happens to their peers. People may learn as much or more by observing models than from the consequences of their own actions.[24] Rewards may include pay raises, promotions and rewards, as well as recognition and praise. Effective leaders do not just reward achievement, they celebrate it.

4. *Managing Information.* Leaders have a profound influence on how information is managed within the organization. Effective leaders are effective information gatherers because they are good listeners and encourage subordinates to express their opinions. They stay in contact with the rest of the organization by, in Tom Peters' terms, "wandering around." Leaders actively seek information from outside the organization. Good leaders also disseminate information widely so that followers will understand the reasons for decisions that are made and how their work fits into the organization's goals. At the same time, effective leaders try not to overwhelm subordinates with too much information.

5. *Team Building.* Achieving goals requires collaboration among many (in some cases, hundreds of thousands) individuals. Leaders need to help build effective teams, starting with the top management team.[25] While an effective leader cannot do everything, he or she can insure that everything gets done by hiring, training, and motivating skilled people who work together effectively. And they, in turn, can build effective teams of their own.

6. *Promoting Change and Innovation.* Finally, effective leaders must promote change and innovation. The vision, since it pertains to a desired future state, is the starting point of change. This must be reinforced by constant restructuring, continual retraining to develop new skills, setting specific goals for innovation and improvement, rewarding innovation, encouraging a constant information flow in all directions and emphasizing responsiveness to customer demands.

It is clear that leadership is a very demanding activity and that leaders who have the requisite traits—drive, desire to lead, self-confidence, honesty (and integrity), cognitive ability, and industry knowledge—have a considerable advantage over those who lack these traits. Without drive, for example, it is unlikely that an individual would be able to gain the expertise required to lead an organization effectively, let alone implement and work toward long-term goals. Without the desire to lead, individuals are not motivated to persuade others to work toward a common goal; such an individual would avoid or be indifferent to leadership tasks. Self-confidence is needed to withstand setbacks, persevere through hard times, and lead others in new directions. Confidence gives effective leaders the ability to make hard decisions and to stand by them. A leader's honesty and integrity form the foundation on which the leader gains followers' trust and confidence; without honesty and integrity, the leader would not be able to attract and retain followers. At least a moderate degree of cognitive ability is needed to gain and understand technical issues as well as the nature of the industry. Cognitive ability permits leaders to accurately analyze situations and make effective decisions. Finally, knowledge of the business is needed to develop suitable strategic visions and business plans.

MANAGEMENT IMPLICATIONS

Individuals can be selected either from outside the organization or from within non- or lower-managerial ranks based on their possession of traits that are less changeable or trainable. Cognitive ability (not to be confused with knowledge) is probably the least trainable of the six traits. Drive is fairly constant over time although it can change; it is observable in employees assuming they are given enough autonomy and responsibility to show what they can do. The desire to lead is more difficult to judge in new hires who may have had little opportunity for leadership early in life. It can be observed at lower levels of management and by observing people in assessment center exercises.

Two other traits can be developed through experience and training. Knowledge of the industry and technical knowledge come from formal training, job experience, and a mentally active approach toward new opportunities for learning. Planned job rotation can facilitate such growth. Self-confidence is both general and task specific. People differ in their general confidence in mastering life's challenges but task-specific self-confidence comes from mastering the various skills that leadership requires as well as the technical and strategic challenges of the industry. Such confidence parallels the individual's growth in knowledge.

Honesty does not require skill building; it is a virtue one achieves or rejects by choice. Organizations should look with extreme skepticism at any employee who behaves dishonestly or lacks integrity, and should certainly not reward dishonesty in any form, especially not with a promotion. The key role models for honest behavior are those at the top. On this issue, organizations get what they model, not what they preach.

CONCLUSIONS

Regardless of whether leaders are born or made or some combination of both, it is unequivocally clear that *leaders are not like other people*. Leaders do not have to be great men or women by being intellectual geniuses or omniscient prophets to succeed, but they do need to have the "right stuff" and this stuff is not equally present in all people. Leadership is a demanding, unrelenting job with enormous pressures and grave responsibilities. It would be a profound disservice to leaders to suggest that they are ordinary people who happened to be in the right place at the right time. Maybe the place matters, but it takes a special kind of person to master the challenges of opportunity. Let us not only give credit, but also use the knowledge we have to select and train our future leaders effectively. We believe that in the realm of leadership (and in every other realm), the individual does matter.

ENDNOTES

This article is based on a chapter of a forthcoming book by Edwin A. Locke, Shelley A. Kirkpatrick, Jill K. Wheeler, Jodi Schneider, Kathryn Niles, Harold Goldstein, Kurt Welsh, and Dong-Ok Chah, entitled *The Essence of Leadership*. We would like to thank Dr. Kathryn Bartol for her helpful comments on this manuscript.

1. P. Slater and W. G. Bennis, "Democracy Is Inevitable," *Harvard Business Review*, September–October 1990, pp. 170–71. For a summary of trait theories, see R. M. Stodgill's *Handbook of Leadership*, (New York: Free Press, 1974). For reviews and studies of leadership traits, see R. E. Boyatzis, *The Competent Manager* (New York: Wiley & Sons, 1982); C. J. Cox and C. L. Cooper, *High Flyers: An Anatomy of Managerial Success* (Oxford: Basil Blackwell); G. A. Yukl, *Leadership in Organizations* (Englewood Cliffs, N.J.: Prentice Hall, 1989), Chapter 9.

2. R. M. Stogdill, "Personal Factors Associated with Leadership: A Survey of the Literature," *Journal of Psychology* 25, p. 64 (1948).

3. See the following sources for evidence and further information concerning each trait: (1) drive: B. M. Bass's *Handbook of Leadership* (New York: The Free Press, 1990); K. G. Smith and J. K. Harrison, "In Search of Excellent Leaders" (in W. D. Guth's *The Handbook of Strategy,* New York: Warren, Gorham, & Lamont, 1986). (2) desire to lead: V. J. Bentz, "The Sears Experience in the Investigation, Description, and Prediction of Executive Behavior." (in F. R. Wickert and D. E. McFarland's *Measuring Executive Effectiveness,* (New York: Appleton-Century-Crofts, 1967); J. B. Miner, "Twenty Years of Research on Role-Motivation Theory of Managerial Effectiveness," *Personnel Psychology* 31, (1978), pp. 739–60. (3) honesty/integrity: Bass, op cit.; W. G. Bennis and B. Nanus, *Leaders: The Strategies for Taking Charge* (New York: Harper & Row, 1985); J. M. Kouzes and B. Z. Posner, *The Leadership Challenge: How to Get Things Done in Organizations* (San Francisco: Jossey-Bass); T. Peters, *Thriving on Chaos* (New York: Harper & Row, 1967); A. Rand, *For the New Intellectual* (New York: Signet, 1961). (4) self-confidence; Bass, op cit. and A. Bandura, *Social Foundations of Thought and Action: A Social Cognitive Theory,* (Englewood Cliffs, NJ: Prentice-Hall). Psychological hardiness is discussed by S. R. Maddi and S. C. Kobasa, *The Hardy Executive: Health Under Stress* (Chicago: Dorsey Professional Books, 1984); W. M. McCall Jr. and M. M. Lombardo, *Off the Track: Why and How Successful Executives Get Derailed* (Technical Report No. 21, Greensboro, N.C.: Center for Creative Leadership, 1983). (5) cognitive ability: R. G. Lord, C. L. DeVader, and G. M. Alliger, "A Meta-Analysis of the Relation between Personality Traits and Leadership Perceptions: An Application of Validity Generalization Procedures," *Journal of Applied Psychology* 61, 1986; pp. 402–10; A. Howard and D. W. Bray, *Managerial Lives in Transition: Advancing Age and Changing Times* (New York: Guilford Press, 1988). (6) knowledge of the business: Bennis and Nanus, op. cit.; J. P. Kotter, *The General Managers* (New York: MacMillan); Smith and Harrison, op. cit.

4. From J. J. Gabarro, *The Dynamics of Taking Charge* (Boston: Harvard Business School Press, 1987).

5. All PepsiCo references are from B. Dumaine, "Those High-flying Managers at PepsiCo." *Fortune,* April 10, 1989, pp. 78–86. The Watson quote is from Smith and Harrison, op. cit., as are the Disney and Woolman quotes in the following paragraph.

6. The four quotes are from Howard and Bray, op. cit.

7. From Kouzes and Posner, op. cit., pp. 122, and V. J. Bentz, op. cit. The Sam Walton quote is from J. Huey, "Wal-Mart: Will It Take Over the World?," *Fortune*, January 30, 1989, pp. 52–59.

8. From Bass, op. cit.

9. The Walton quote is from Huey, op. cit., and the Kroc quote is from Smith and Harrison, op. cit. The quote on Kroc's wall is taken from Bennis and Nanus, op. cit.

10. From Boyatzis, op. cit. Also, Kouzes and Posner, op. cit., stress the importance of leader initiative.

11. From Bentz, op. cit.

12. From Howard and Bray, op. cit.

13. The distinction between a personalized and a socialized power motive is made by D. C. McClelland, "N-achievement and entrepreneurship: A longitudinal study." *Journal of Personality and Social Psychology*. 1, (1965), pp. 389–92. These two power motives are discussed further by Kouzes and Posner, op. cit.

14. From McCall and Lombardo, op. cit.

15. From Gabarro, op. cit.

16. K. F. Girard examines Manor Care in "To the Manor Born," *Warfield's*, March, 1989, pp. 68–75.

17. From K. Labich, "The Seven Keys to Business Leadership," *Fortune*, October 24, 1988, pp. 58–66.

18. From Lord, DeVader, and Alliger, op. cit.

19. For research on charisma, see Bass, op. cit; and R. J. House, W. D. Spangler, and J. Woycke, "Personality and Charisma in the U.S. Presidency: A Psychological Theory of Leadership Effectiveness (Wharton School, University of Pennsylvania, 1969, unpublished manuscript); on creativity/originality, see Howard and Bray, op cit., and A. Zaleznik, *The Managerial Mystique* (New York: Harper and Row, 1989); on flexibility, see Smith and Harrison, op. cit.

20. From Bennis and Nanus, op. cit.

21. From J. A. Conger, *Charismatic Leadership: The Elusive Factor in Organizational Effectiveness* (San Francisco: Jossey-Bass, 1988).

22. C. Manz and H. P. Sims, *Superleadershp: Leading Others to Lead Themselves* (New York: Prentice Hall, 1989).

23. See E. A. Locke and G. P. Latham, *A Theory of Goal Setting & Task Performance* (Englewood Cliffs, NJ: Prentice Hall, 1990).

24. See Bandura, op. cit.

25. See D. C. Hambrick, "The Top Management Team: Keys to Strategic Success," *California Management Review*, 30, 1987, pp. 1–20.

READING 10–2   MANAGERS OF MEANING: FROM BOB GELDOF'S BAND AID TO AUSTRALIAN CEOS

David C. Limerick

An Irish pop singer, Bob Geldof, may be remembered more as a quintessential leader of the 1980s and 1990s than as a musician. Outraged by the ineffective response of governments worldwide to the Ethiopian famine, he decided to make a record. Not just any record, however. He enlisted the support and participation of many great pop artists, and the record made millions of dollars. He then arranged a concert. Again, not just any concert, but a concert on a scale never dreamed of by anyone else—performed by an array of pop stars never before assembled and watched by billions of people throughout the world. The money generated by "Band Aid" and "Live Aid," as those two projects were called, helped relieve starvation in Ethiopia.

Geldof's participation in the relief effort did not end

with fund raising. He maintained a vivid public image, meeting public figures worldwide and urging, bullying, and cajoling them until relief got through to Ethiopia. "Band Aid" and "Live Aid" were followed by "Sports Aid" and a host of other "Aids," which orchestrated interest groups throughout the world toward the same cause and kept up the momentum of aid to Ethiopia.

What Geldof achieved and the way he did it provide insights into the new challenges facing strategic managers. In a study of 50 Australian chief executive officers (CEOs), two colleagues and I found that they face the task that Geldof faced—of cutting across loosely coupled groups and individuals (who very often are stars in their own right) and getting them to collaborate in a common cause. Strategic managers no longer are the rational analysts of a few years ago: they are managers of vision, of mission, of identity, of culture. They are managers of meaning.

The research project on which I base much of my current thinking began in 1984. My colleagues and I set out

Source: David C. Limerick "Managers of Meaning: From Bob Geldof's Band Aid to Australian CEOs" *Organizational Dynamics*, Spring 1990, pp. 60–67.

EXHIBIT 10-16

Characteristics of the Geldof Era

Social and Organizational	New Managerial Priorities	Requiring the Use of	Requiring New Competencies
Loosely coupled organizations	Management of identity	Language and slogans	Holistic, empathetic abilities
Collaborative individualism	Management of corporate culture	Legends and models	Metastrategic vision
		Systems and sanctions	Mature, internal locus of control
			Networking skills

to look at linkages between strategy, structure, and culture in 50 Australian business and government organizations selected on the basis of either financial success over a number of years or reputation for good management. Although we analyzed newspaper and journal articles, company reports, and other literature on each of the organizations studied, the heart of the study was a series of in-depth interviews with their CEOs during which we teased out strategic and structural changes in their organizations and the CEOs' perceptions of the core values they would like to see their organizations have.

I have used the experiences of those Australian CEOs to look at (1) the social and organizational changes that have occurred during the past decade or so, (2) the new managerial priorities they imply, and (3) the techniques and competencies required for meeting those priorities. (See Exhibit 10-16 for a summary of the characteristic and demands of the Geldof era.) I believe that the Australian CEOs and Geldof are not alone in their management approach. Rather, their experiences will, I believe, strike a familiar chord in managers of other Western organizations as well.

ORGANIZATIONAL AND SOCIAL CHANGES DURING THE GELDOF ERA

During the 1960s and 1970s, managers and academics alike drove organizations hard toward "interlocking group" structures—organizational forms that were tightly linked and tightly controlled (sometimes the euphemism "facilitated" was used). More often than not, even divisionalized organizations had a sizable number of controllers/facilitators at their headquarters to keep the organization

integrated. ITT, with a 300-member staff at its Brussels headquarters alone, exemplified organizations of that time.

In contrast, the CEOs my colleagues and I talked to in the Geldof era deliberately rejected most of those models in favor of very loosely coupled systems with high levels of individualism. Most of them were transforming the tightly interlocked structures of their organizations into decentralized and cellular ones. As one CEO commented, "I don't want more relationships between people; I want fewer."

The CEO of an engineering firm provided, perhaps, the most complete expression of this change in direction: "So we decided to identify segments of the industry and to literally create freestanding units to deal with each. We said to them. This is your baby; you tell us what your market is, the resources you need, the strategy you're going to develop, the market share you're aiming at. Then we would turn a bunch of fellows loose on a dedicated specialty."

LOOSELY COUPLED ORGANIZATIONS

In general, loosely coupled organizations have three key characteristics. They have (1) smaller, autonomous units that are (2) innovative, proactive, and market-oriented and (3) led by a lean corporate headquarters.

One CEO expressed the views of most in our survey when he argued, "You have to be decentralized; the more we can create cells of people with a lot of autonomous delegated authority, the more successful we are." Those cells have to be customer-oriented, with "a determination to be in control of the environment instead of being pushed around by it," according to the CEO. Although they are smaller units, the cells are dedicated to specified market niches and are able to focus on "controlling" or, more realistically, influencing the environments of those niches.

To ensure autonomy and responsibility for action, loosely coupled organizations have to keep corporate headquarters very small. In many cases, widespread decimation of central staff positions may be needed. As one CEO remarked, "We discovered that we could not afford two personnel officers at $35,000 each; we could only afford one at $70,000!"

Geldof's fundamental management philosophy is very similar. In his autobiography *Is That It?* (Penguin, 1986), he stated, "Band Aid must never become what I have always most detested—an institution." Instead, he created a network of loosely coupled, dedicated units: "I told Kevin we could extend the value of what we did by setting up various 'Aids' in the industries most of our essential purchases for Africa would come from." He thus stimulated the formation of "Truckers for Band Aid," "Builders for Band Aid," and a host of special-interest groups such as "Sports Aid," "Actor Aid," and "Bush Aid." As Geldof observed, the list went on "longer than the alphabet."

The Australian CEOs we interviewed were developing organization structures much closer to Geldof's Band Aid than to the integrated bureaucracies of the 1970s: They were transformational leaders dedicated to needs and to doing something about them. They were supported by a lean, organic executive group as they attempted to orchestrate decentralized, autonomous individuals and groups toward a common vision and goal. Those parallels fascinated me but also raised a fundamental question: Why should such a widespread movement toward "chunked" organizations have emerged in Australia during the 1980s?

The notion that such movements are fads did not seem to make much sense. Indeed, most of the CEOs claimed to have invented the movement for themselves. A better answer lies in systems theory itself. *Loosely coupled systems handle change and turbulence more effectively.* Such systems have emerged as a pragmatic response to the extreme rate of change during recent times. Tightly coupled systems simply cannot adapt fast enough.

Geldof makes a similar point about Band Aid: Compared with larger, conventional charities, Band Aid was infinitely more adaptable. He wrote, "We were flexible and could look around to see where gaps were left by the other agencies and then plug them."

The very responsiveness of a loosely coupled organization enables it to pursue strategies of nichemanship. That characteristic, moreover, is reinforced by a second devel-

opment within the organization—the emergence of collaborative individualism.

COLLABORATIVE INDIVIDUALISM

Contrary to my expectations, the Australian CEOs did not mention teamwork during intensive questioning about the effectiveness of their organizations. In fact, only three or four references to teamwork were made during the entire series of interviews. We therefore broached the issue with the CEOs at the end of each discussion, at which point they usually reported that teamwork was vitally important to their organizations.

According to the CEOs, teamwork had been their dominant problematic issue during the 1970s, and during the decade they had poured resources into team development. However, by the 1980s teamwork had receded to the status of a *sine qua non* of effectiveness; the dominant problematic issue had become individualism. The CEOs were far more concerned about developing mature, proactive individuals with a self-driven capacity to transform systems. As the CEO of a large government organization put it: "I am looking for someone who will keep asking questions when the rest of the team has stopped."

Such individuals had to be collaborative, however. The CEOs desired a form of individualism that stood on the shoulders of teamwork. As another CEO stated, "I am looking for a team of individuals."

In this sense, collaborative individualism lies on the other side of teamwork. It stresses the need for individuals who are not imprisoned by the boundaries of the group and who will transform the group when the interests of the organization so dictate. Transformational leadership, as distinct from transactional leadership, is an important characteristic of the collaborative individual. As J. Burns in his book *Leadership* (Harper and Row, 1978) pointed out, transactional leaders work by increment, contracting and transacting with others to maintain a stable organization, whereas transformational leaders create new situations and processes. Independent, transforming individuals, they create a new vision of the possible and inspire others to follow.

Although individualistic values are part of the historical consciousness of Anglo-American-colonial society, the individualistic value of the 1980s are subtly different. The CEOs we interviewed did not seek the return of the corporate buccaneer of the 1960s, clawing his or her way through four levels of management to get to the top. Yet they did not want servants of collectivism either. They saw the collaborative individual as (1) individualistic, yet collaborative; (2) proactive, with an internal locus of control; and (3) politically aware and skilled. The CEO of a large Australian bank captured this image when he stated that he did not want a team of football players but rather a team of cricketers.

For American readers, baseball players can be substituted for cricketers in the CEO's metaphor; the meaning is the same. The CEO wanted individuals who would confront that 100-mile-an-hour-ball on their own yet adjust their styles—collaborate—when their teams were in trouble. They had to be able to solve their own problems as well as those of the group.

"The need is for . . . the will to **manage** . . . and so we are saying to people that you do not have to be reactive, you must go out and plan and act on the business," he explained.

Collaborative individualism applied to relationships with governments, too. As one CEO noted, "Our big breakthrough was in developing techniques for dealing with government." Another pointed out that such political responsiveness demanded that managers have "political skills" and a capacity for political infighting.

BOB GELDOF: THE COLLABORATIVE INDIVIDUAL

The characteristics of the collaborative individual are very close to those of Bob Geldof: individualistic yet collaborative, proactive, and internally driven but with rugged political skills. He values those same characteristics in the people he admires, as his recounting of a meeting with Mother Teresa in Africa demonstrates: "There was a certainty of purpose which left little patience. But she was totally selfless; every moment her aim seemed to be, how can I use this or that situation to help others. . . . She held my hand as she left and said, 'Remember this. I can do something you can't do and you can do something I can't do. But we both have to do it.'"

And Geldof did. His vision was clear. When asked why he was trying to organize something as impossible as a global telethon, he replied, "Because people are dying."

At the same time, Geldof was skilled at using political guile, or even force, when necessary. For example, he blocked the British government from taxing his Band Aid record sales by taking the matter into the public arena. And when a catering company at his charity concert wanted a profit,

he threatened to tell everyone to pack their own meals and boycott the company.

The characteristics of the collaborative individual and the task that confronted Geldof are essentially congruent. The "organization" he brought together was loosely coupled in the extreme, consisting of mature, proactive individuals, many of them stars, with the potential for collaboration. However, a collaborative individual, Geldof, was needed to transform this aggregate into a collaborative enterprise.

Other managers have confronted similar situations. Jimmy Pattison and Llew Edwards, for example, had to get hundreds of independent contributors to collaborate toward a common goal at the Vancouver and Brisbane Expo sites. Perhaps they, too, can be seen as pioneers of a new managerial era. Most of the organizations we studied were not as atomistic or as diffuse as Band Aid or the Vancouver and Brisbane Expos, but many seem headed in that direction. Some were beginning to franchise parts of their businesses or to engage in toll manufacturing (a process of subcontracting parts of, or even the whole of, manufacturing to other independent organizations).

A number of American and European companies have adopted similar structures. Lewis Galoob Toys Incorporated, for example, sold $58 million of "Golden Girl" action figures at a time when the company had only 115 employees. Galoob farmed out all manufacturing to contractors in Hong Kong and did not even collect its own accounts, selling receivables instead to a credit corporation. Sulzer Brothers Limited, a Swiss manufacturer of diesel engines, now licenses engine design to other firms and services engines made by licensees. Even large, long-established companies such as Firestone Tire & Rubber, Minnesota Mining & Manufacturing Co., and General Electric Co. sell finished products bought from foreign companies. Such organizations together with more loosely coupled organizations with widespread autonomous units (such as Johnson & Johnson, which has more than 130 business units) are facing many of the same challenges to strategic management as those confronted by Geldof. Thus we are at the beginning of a Geldof era, not the end.

NEW MANAGERIAL PRIORITIES AND TECHNIQUES

The problem with loose coupling and individualism is that they represent a centrifugal force that can endanger the survival of the whole. Whereas tightly coupled organizations can rely on a myriad of strategic and operational control systems to achieve integration, loosely coupled organizations have to rely on bottom-line information to evaluate divisional performance. That information, however, may come too late to prevent dangerous actions or even alert the organization to them. The recurrent nightmare of a natural resource-based company, for example, is that one of its divisions will act irresponsibly, destroying public confidence in the entire company and thereby endangering the long-term survival of the enterprise.

In the absence of more operational controls, CEOs of loosely coupled organizations have to rely on shared goals, values, and meanings to secure collaborative action. That is, they have to create "value-driven" systems. Our study suggests that the CEOs of loosely coupled organizations face two major interrelated challenges: the management of identity and the management of corporate culture.

MANAGEMENT OF IDENTITY

Recent thinking on corporate strategy has focused on identification of the organization's "mission" and the "vision" on which that mission is based. At the heart of these two issues is the very identity of the organization—its unique shape, boundaries, purpose, and values that differentiate the organization and its members from other organizations. I do not believe that this concern is an accidental fad. On the contrary, loosely coupled organizations depend for their very survival on a widespread acceptance of a clear vision and mission.

In the course of our interviews, most of the CEOs provided a cogent picture of the linkages between strategy, structure, and culture within their organizations, all of which were linked to deep-seated image of the identity of the organization. For a few, this "metastrategy" was perfectly conscious and coherent. The CEO of a large chemical company, for example, linked disappearing trade barriers and the maturing of the chemical industry to his company's attempt to move away from an engineering-oriented bureaucracy toward autonomous, market-oriented business units governed by a small corporate headquarters. His picture was coherent; the vision of the entrepreneurial organization, clear. For many of the other CEOs, the image was less accessible, although I was impressed by the fit between the elements of the identity they each espoused.

In many of the organizations we looked at, we spoke to senior managers who reported directly to the CEO. These managers did not always understand their organi-

zation's metastrategy as clearly as the CEO did. For the most part, the CEOs seemed aware of their failure to clearly communicate their overall vision of the organization.

During the interviews, no one statement or phrase communicated the CEO's vision. Rather it was revealed through a whole series of allegories, metaphors, slogans, legends, and myths. I have come to the conclusion that such a concept of identity is so much an empathetic and holistic phenomenon that it defies the linear logic of speech. As one CEO complained, "Every time I try to communicate the image, I cheapen it."

The difficult task that confronts strategic managers today parallels the one surmounted by Geldof—reaching across loosely coupled, autonomous individuals and providing a basis for collaboration by identifying and communicating a common vision and mission. For Geldof, the mission of Live Aid was clear: People were dying. He communicated this mission fearlessly to others. In trying to persuade the pop group The Who to participate in Live Aid, for example, he resorted to the ultimate argument: if they played, they would be responsible for saving a few people's lives. "It was true, but it sounded so corny," he wrote about the incident. "It came down in the end to personal responsibility."

It was difficult for Geldof not to cheapen his vision, not to make it sound corny. This same task confronts each CEO of loosely coupled systems. He or she has to establish and communicate the very *identity* (vision, mission) of the organization and manage the field of shared meanings, values and beliefs that surround the identity to make the vision credible and persuasive.

MANAGEMENT OF CORPORATE CULTURE

Our study provides abundant data on the continuing and almost obsessive attempts of CEOs to come to grips with and mold the field of meaning within the organization—to manage its culture. Many of those attempts were related to crises that had demanded not only radical structural change but also massive cultural change for the organization. For a major Australian bank facing the trauma of deregulation of the finance industry, a major problem was, in the CEO's words "the shape of our people." As he explained, "We have a culture which goes back 150 years. Now we are a financial conglomerate acting globally. And so now we are asking people to change their shape, to change their culture."

In moving toward new organizational forms and missions, the CEOs we interviewed were expanding and in some cases redefining the identity and shape of their enterprises. What did these new organizations look like? Almost all of them emphasized autonomy and proactivity, two characteristics central to loosely coupled systems and collaborative individualism. Companies had to move away from uncertain introspection and the reactivity that accompanies it. Said one CEO, "We definitely tend to be too inward looking. Somewhere deep down in our gut is an unspoken feeling that we can't do it as well as those other people." Instead, the companies had to move toward confident innovativeness. As one CEO noted, "We have to be entrepreneurial. It was almost a *cri de coeur* from members of an organization which had recently merged and was looking for a new identity."

For most CEOs we interviewed, the task of managing and transforming the values of their organizations was a challenge undertaken at an overt, conscious level. The strategies and variables they used to manage culture, however, were often more subtle, more elusive, and less conscious. They included language and slogans, legends and models, systems and sanctions, as well as self-modeling.

Language and Slogans

The CEOs used a variety of images couched in rich, expressive language to approximate the values they sought. Many of those images recurred a number of times during a CEO's interview. It became clear that the images had assumed the status of slogans and in all probability were used frequently in everyday contact with others in the organization.

For example, one CEO said, "One in five acquisitions don't work out, and there are lots of managers who look to me to make their divestment decisions for them. In effect, they continue to hold the dead baby to the breast." That rather shocking image of holding a dead baby to the breast recurred a number of times during the interview. Such phrases and slogans tend to become institutionalized. Managers at a large finance company we studied were dominated by the notion of "stretch objectives," a term inspired by Cecil Rhodes's (and Robert Browning's) maxim "Let every man's reach exceed his grasp." To the analytical outsider, such phrases may seem trite. Yet, when Brian Loton, CEO of Australia's largest company, BHP, said "Big is out. Good is in," I noted that he had an almost visceral identification with the phrase. The executives around him, too, nodded intensely.

Such identification may penetrate far down the line, according to the CEOs we interviewed. Yet it is not won easily. The CEO of a computer company commented, "The biggest danger is apathy . . . (but) there is a real dedication to this set of values. While to a certain extent apathy and cynicism blow them apart, respect for the values is stronger and more typical of the organization as a whole."

Language, on its own, is not enough to secure shared meaning. It has to be represented and reinforced in other organizational processes and symbols.

Legends and Models

Many organizations in the study had key figures in their history who had assumed legendary status and who were held up to others as models for action. The CEOs we interviewed were intimately aware of those legends and eager to tell us about them. A mining company's deeply held values of care for people in the organization were neatly wrapped up in the following legend told during our interview with its CEO: "There is the story that George Fisher, in the half an hour it took him to get to the gate of his factory from his car, would get to know absolutely everything that was happening simply by talking to various people. Legend also has it that Sir James, too, in driving down the streets of, say, Mt. Isa, would suddenly stop the car and say 'Isn't that so-and-so who was involved in training the winning cricket team yesterday?' "

A retail chain revered its founder as "a genius." An oil company hailed its founding explorer as "a dreamer" who created the "exploration culture" of the organization. Whether such stories are true in every detail is irrelevant; they are models and persuasive symbols of deeply held values.

Systems and Sanctions

The number of systems and sanctions available in loosely coupled organizations is not as great as the number of systems and sanctions available in more bureaucratic organizations. Nevertheless, the systems that are available are widely used to institutionalize values. In our study, organizations that had retained some staff strength at corporate headquarters used such human resources systems as orientation and training programs and performance appraisal to back up their values. Some regularly distributed throughout the organization videotapes of executives giving briefings or morale talks. Others used credos and charters to institutionalize their core values. Many moved employees around the organization to diffuse values.

Most CEOs, however, ultimately had to back up core values by resorting to the strongest sanctions of all: promoting, demoting, or firing. They used such sanctions only when all else had failed. One CEO, for example, had taken his highest-performing manager and put him into the "sin bin" (a research laboratory) because his behavior was not quite ethical enough. The CEO said he intended to keep him there until the manager learned "better manners"—that is, until the manager learned to conform to the central values of the organization.

Self-Modeling

Most of the CEOs preferred not to resort to such sanctions and attempted to use positive modeling whenever possible. Since the systems available to them were so scarce, most of them in the end relied on personal example. They networked extensively within their organizations, asserting their values and attempting to represent core values and meanings personally. Although some frustration could be sensed behind these limitations, not one of the CEOs was prepared to centralize to gain greater control. As one of them rather desperately said, "I just have to use the force of my own personality and style."

The extent of such networking was typified in one CEO's description of a senior manager's typical week at his company: "Thirty percent attending small, informal meetings; 20 percent visiting plants and project sites; 20 percent talking on the telephone; 10 percent attending scheduled meetings; and 5 percent on answering correspondence and reading."

As I listened to CEOs talking about their techniques for managing meaning, I was reminded most strongly of Bob Geldof—his traveling, networking, cajoling, building images of the possible, and, despite a lack of access to sanctions, succeeding in building a landmark collaborative enterprise. Overall, I gained a clear picture of the overwhelming attention given by CEOs to the task of creating and communicating meanings and values, a task they believed was central to the achievement of the organization's objectives.

The CEOs reported that in most organizations the chief executive plays a key role in the management culture. One CEO reflected, "The influence of the top person in the organization is quite frightening, really." Yet our data also suggest that this influence is not exerted from an isolated position. Most of the CEOs we spoke to had built around them a tight cohort of senior executives with whom they shared the problem of managing change. These groups aimed at creating a culture with its own momentum. Ideally it would "get to a point that even if the leader is not there, the culture will go on," as one CEO noted. The task of communicating a new vision and identity to even that group of senior executives, however, can be formidable and frustrating for the CEO.

From our study, we simply have no knowledge of how effective the CEOs and managers actually were at managing corporate culture (that is the subject of a second study now under way). For some analysts there is a question of whether culture can be managed at all. Certainly CEOs are not the sole influencers of fields of meaning in organizations; there are many other actors and subcultures and countercultures at work. But our CEOs are undeterred by the debate. They see themselves as being a vital force in the development of the values of their organizations, and our study gives ample evidence of the overwhelming amount of their time devoted to attempting to manage culture.

To create and sustain corporate cultures, even with the help of a top management cohort, is an enormous challenge that demands the exercise of competencies not generally considered centrally important to management in past decades. The sheer magnitude of the networking task can tax personal energy reserves to the point of exhaustion. The public image of the tired, emotional Geldof provides an index of how hard the road is to travel.

NEW COMPETENCIES FOR MANAGERS IN THE GELDOF ERA

The managers of the Geldof era are not the rational contingency analysts of past decades. Their roles as managers of meaning place a new emphasis on holistic, empathetic skills. Such skills, to be sure, have always been important to management, but they are vitally, critically important to managers of meaning. We explored with the CEOs in our study the competencies required by senior managers in today's organizations. The clusters they helped us identify reflect the new managerial role:

- *Skills in empathy.* The CEOs stressed that managers should be empathetic, warm, and able to supervise autonomous individuals. The capacity to communicate, often symbolically, also was important.
- *Skills in transformation.* The rapid pace of change requires skills in changing systems and values. Thus managers require transformational leadership skills;

they have to be strong and able to both mold and change their organizations.

- *Proactivity.* Using such phrases as "self-driven," "doers," "bias for action" and "ambitous," the CEO stressed the need for an ability to get things done. Pragmatic common sense, reflected in such phrases as "smell for the dollar," "common business sense" and "good knowledge of what the business is about," also is required.
- *Political skills.* Managers have to be able to understand the political climate and deal with the political environment.
- *Networking skills.* Managers need the capacity to network between the elements of the broader organizational picture, interpreting for them the mission and identity of the organization.
- *Intuitive, creative thinking.* The CEOs stressed creativity, intuition, imagination, innovation, lateral thinking, and the ability to ask "what if" questions rather than linear logical abilities.
- *Personal maturity.* The task of networking throughout very different autonomous systems makes enormous demands on the maturity of the individual, who is no longer able to cling to a specific role within a coherent structure for a sense of identity. Thus managers need both self understanding and a commitment to the values of the larger system. They must understand their strengths and weaknesses, continue learning by self-evaluation and have the capacity to cope with stress. They also must be mature, professional, loyal, and ethical in business practice.

The skills described above are characteristic of Geldof. He is empathetic but proactive, as his reaction to first seeing the dying children of Ethiopia demonstrates: "The eyes were looking at me. I began to cry. I was angry. Crying was useless and a waste of energy." He used his energy and political skills to transform the efforts of others and to achieve what others said could not be done. His actions were brilliant, creative, quirky, and entirely intuitive. As he explained, "but it **was** different. It **was** extraordinary. I am too close to it now to stand back and see it in all its unlikely power and glory, but in future years I know I will wonder how the hell it was possible and what it was that enabled me to do it. I never once stopped to consider what happened next. I acted intuitively all the time."

According to Geldof, these abilities were forged and tempered by his early experiences. But can they be developed through formal training and education? This was an issue we explored with the Australian CEOs.

In general, the CEOs cited the focus on rational analysis in traditional M.B.A. programs as inadequate for imparting empathetic skills. Many argued that the skills described above are **process** skills, distinct from the knowledge areas covered by most Australian management schools. The CEOs wanted more action/learning strategies, such as in-company M.B.A. programs or an emphasis on in-company projects and experiences.

Moreover, the CEOs were puzzled by the emphasis on conventional OD techniques preoccupied with teamwork—techniques they considered inadequate. They wanted increased attention focused on programs that help individuals map and understand themselves; stimulate symbolic thinking, intuition, and empathy; encourage the capacity to tolerate ambiguity and paradox; and develop networking and political skills. These characteristics are hard-won, and people with them are difficult to find. Thus, while the CEOs most frequently mentioned the "quality of human resources" as the key strength of their organizations, they also most often nominated it as their key area of threat and vulnerability.

The task of managing meaning is difficult and demanding, to be sure. Why else would chief executives need to devote so much of their time to it? Yet we sensed among the Australian CEOs in our study a certain confidence, even perhaps a touch of arrogance, in their capacity to conceive of and move their organizations toward new identities and new values. Without such confidence, "Saint Bob," as Geldof sometimes was called, could not have achieved what he did either.

A FINAL NOTE

Not all transformational leaders are as socially contributive as Geldof was. There must of necessity be a fine line between transformational leadership and autocracy. We believe that when there is a large power gap in organizations, transformation means autocracy. However, the essence of the loosely coupled system is the autonomy of the parts, and the essence of collaborative individualism is the empowerment of the individual. That, too, was the essence of the situation Geldof faced. Under such circumstances, the identification of mission and the mobilization of values are a contributive social act.

Implicit in this analysis is a warning. Management

theorists and practitioners alike must think more overtly about the management of corporate culture, about the social conditions in which it takes place, and about the controls and checks on "transformers" in our organiza- tions and our societies. The odds are that we will see the emergence of more managers of meaning, not fewer. As noted earlier, we are at the beginning of the Geldof era, not the end of it. It deserves very close attention.

■

EXERCISE

EXERCISE 10–1 LEADERSHIP STYLE ANALYSIS

OBJECTIVES

1. To learn how to diagnose different leadership situ- ations.
2. To learn how to apply a systematic procedure for analyzing situations.
3. To improve understanding of how to reach a deci- sion.

STARTING THE EXERCISE

Review the time-driven decision tree in Exhibit 10–5. The instructor will then form groups of four to five people to analyze each of the following three cases. Try to reach a group consensus on which decision style is best for the particular case. You are to select the best style based on use of the Vroom-Jago model, available decision styles, and decision rules. Each case should take a group between 30 and 45 minutes to analyze.

EXERCISE PROCEDURES

Phase I (10–15 minutes): Individually read case and select proper decision style, using Vroom-Jago model.

Phase II (30–45 minutes): Join group appointed by in- structor and reach group consensus.

Phase III (20 minutes): Each group spokesperson presents group's response and rationale to other groups.

These phases should be used for each of the cases.

Case I

Setting: Corporate headquarters
Your position: Vice president

As marketing vice president, you frequently receive non- routine requests from customers. One such request, from a relatively new customer, is for extended terms on a large purchase ($2.5 million) involving several of your product lines. The request is for extremely favorable terms that you would not consider except for the high inventory level of most product lines at the present time due to the unanti- cipated slack period that the company has experienced over the last six months.

You realize that the request is probably a starting point for negotiations, and you have proved your abilities to negotiate the most favorable arrangements in the past. As preparation for these negotiations, you have familiarized yourself with the financial situation of the customer, using various investment reports that you receive regularly.

Reporting to you are four sales managers, each of whom has responsibility for a single product line. They know of the order, and like you, they believe that it is important to negotiate terms with minimum risk and maximum re- turns to the company. They are likely to differ on what constitutes an acceptable level of risk. The two younger managers have developed a reputation of being "risk tak- ers," whereas the two more senior managers are substan- tially more conservative.

Case II

Setting: Toy manufacturer
Your position: Vice president, engineering and design

You are a vice president in a large toy manufacturing com- pany, and your responsibilities include the design of new products that will meet the changing demand in this un- certain and very competitive industry. Your design teams, each under the supervision of a department head, are therefore under constant pressure to produce novel, marketable ideas.

At the opposite end of the manufacturing process is the quality control department, which is under the authority of the vice president, production. When quality control has encountered a serious problem that may be due to design features, its staff has consulted with one or more of your department heads to obtain their recommendations for any changes in the production process. In the wake of consumer concern over the safety of children's toys, however, the responsibilities of quality control have recently been expanded to ensure not only the quality but also the safety of your products. The first major problem in this area has arisen. A preliminary consumer report has "blacklisted" one of your new products without giving any specific reason or justification. This has upset you and others in the organization since it was believed that this product would be one of the most profitable items in the coming Christmas season.

The consumer group has provided your company with an opportunity to respond to the report before it is made public. The head of quality control has therefore consulted with your design people, but you have been told that they became somewhat defensive and dismissed the report as "overreactive fanatic nonsense." Your people told quality control that, while freak accidents were always possible, the product was certainly safe as designed. They argued that the report should simply be ignored.

Since the issue is far from routine, you have decided to give it your personal attention. Because your design teams have been intimately involved in all aspects of the development of the item, you suspect that their response was extreme and was perhaps governed more by their emotional reaction to the report than by the facts. You are not convinced that the consumer group is totally irresponsible, and you are anxious to explore the problem in detail and to recommend to quality control any changes that may be required from a design standpoint. The firm's image as a producer of high-quality toys could suffer a serious blow if the report were made public and public confidence were lost as a result.

You will have to depend heavily on the background and experience of your design teams to help you in ana-

lyzing the problem. Even though quality control will be responsible for the decision to implement any changes that you may ultimately recommend, your own subordinates have the background of design experience that could enable you to set standards for what is "safe" and to suggest any design modifications that would meet these standards.

Case III

Setting: Corporate headquarters
Your position: Vice president

The sales executives in your home office spent a great deal of time visiting regional sales offices. As marketing vice president, you are concerned that the expenses incurred on these trips are excessive—especially now, when the economic outlook seems bleak and general belt-tightening measures are being carried out in every department.

Having recently been promoted from the ranks of your subordinates, you are keenly aware of some cost-saving measures that could be introduced. You have, in fact, asked the accounting department to review a sample of past expense reports, and it has agreed with your conclusion that several highly favored travel "luxuries" could be curtailed. For example, your sales executives could restrict first-class air travel to only those occasions when economy class is unavailable, and airport limousine service to hotels could be used instead of taxis where possible. Even more savings could be made if your personnel carefully planned trips such that multiple purposes could be achieved where possible.

The success of any cost-saving measures, however, depends on the commitment of your subordinates. You do not have the time (or the desire) to closely review the expense reports of these sales executives. You suspect, though, that they do not share your concerns over the matter. Having once been in their position, you know that they feel themselves to be deserving of travel amenities.

The problem is to determine which changes, if any, are to be made in current travel and expense account practices in light of the new economic conditions.

▲

CASES

CASE 10–1 L. J. SUMMERS COMPANY

Jon Reese couldn't think of a time in the history of L. J. Summers Company when there had been as much anti-company sentiment among the workers as had emerged in the past few weeks. He knew that Mr. Summers would place the blame on him for the problems with the production workers because Jon was supposed to be helping Mr. Summers' son, Blaine, to become oriented to his new position. Blaine had only recently taken over as production manager of the company (see Exhibit 10-17). Blaine was unpopular with most of the workers, but the events of the past weeks had caused him to be resented even more. This resentment had increased to the point that several of the male workers had quit and all the women in the assembly department had refused to work.

The programs that had caused the resentment among the workers were instituted by Blaine to reduce waste and lower production costs, but they had produced completely opposite results. Jon knew that on Monday morning he would have to explain to Mr. Summers why the workers had reacted as they did and that he would have to present a plan to resolve the employee problems, reduce waste, and decrease production costs.

COMPANY HISTORY

L. J. Summers Company manufactured large sliding doors made of many narrow aluminum panels held together by thick rubber strips, which allowed the door to collapse as it was opened. Some of the doors were as high as 18 feet and were used in buildings to section off large areas. The company had grown rapidly in its early years due mainly to the expansion of the building program of the firm's major customer, which accounted for nearly 90 percent of Summers' business.

When L. J. Summers began the business, his was the only firm that manufactured the large sliding doors. Recently, however, several other firms had begun to market similar doors. One firm in particular had been bidding to obtain business from Summers' major customer. Fearing

Source: Reprinted by permission from *Organization and People* (2nd Edition), by J. B. Ritchie and Paul Thompson; Copyright 1976, 1980, 1984, by West Publishing Company. All rights reserved. Pp 358–62.

that the competitor might be able to underbid his company, Mr. Summers began urging his assistant, Jon, to increase efficiency and cut production costs.

CONDITIONS BEFORE THE COST REDUCTION PROGRAMS

A family-type atmosphere had existed at Summers before the cost reduction programs were instituted. There was little direct supervision of the workers from the front office, and no pressure was put on them to meet production standards. Several of the employees worked overtime regularly without supervision. The foremen and workers often played cards together during lunchtime, and company parties after work were common and popular. Mr. Summers was generally on friendly terms with all the employees, although he was known to get angry if something displeased him. He also participated freely in the daily operations of the company.

As Mr. Summers's assistant, Jon was responsible for seeing to it that the company achieved the goals established by Mr. Summers. Jon was considered hard-working and persuasive by most of the employees and had a reputation of not giving in easily to employee complaints.

Blaine Summers had only recently become the production manager of Summers. He was in his early 20s, married, and had a good build. Several of the workers commented that Blaine liked to show off his strength in front of others. He was known to be very meticulous about keeping the shop orderly and neat, even to the point of making sure that packing crates were stacked "his way." It was often commented among the other employees how Blaine seemed to be trying to impress his father. Many workers voiced the opinion that the only reason Blaine was production manager was that his father owned the company. They also resented his using company employees and materials to build a swing set for his children and to repair his camper.

Blaine, commenting to Jon one day that the major problem with production was the workers, added that people of such caliber as the Summers' employees did not understand how important cost reduction was and that they would rather sit around and talk all day than work. Blaine

EXHIBIT 10-17

L. J. Summers Company Organization Chart

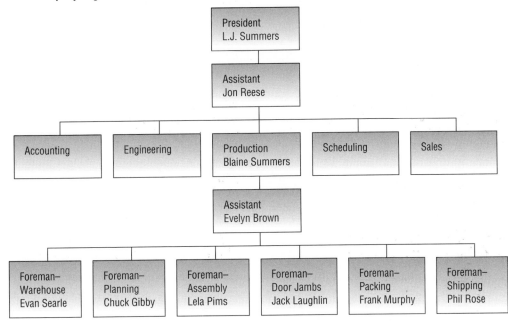

rarely spoke to the workers but left most of the reprimanding and firing up to his assistant, Evelyn Brown.

Summers employed about 70 people to perform the warehousing, assembly, and door-jamb building, as well as the packing and shipping operations done on the doors. Each operation was supervised by a foreman, and crews ranged from 3 men in warehousing to 25 women in the assembly department. The foremen were usually employees with the most seniority and were responsible for quality and on-time production output. Most of the foremen had good relationships with the workers.

The majority of the work done at Summers consisted of repetitive assembly tasks requiring very little skill or training; for example, in the pinning department the workers operated a punch press, which made holes in the panels. The job consisted of punching the hole and then inserting a metal pin into it. Workers commented that it was very tiring and boring to stand at the press during the whole shift without frequent breaks.

Wages at Summers were considered to be low for the

area. The workers griped about the low pay but said that they tried to compensate by taking frequent breaks, working overtime, and "taking small items home at night." Most of the workers who worked overtime were in the door-jamb department, the operation requiring the most skill. Several of these workers either worked very little or slept during overtime hours they reportedly worked.

The majority of the male employees were in their mid-20s; about half of them were unmarried. There was a great turnover among the unmarried male workers. The female employees were either young and single or older married women. The 25 women who worked in production were all in the assembly department under Lela Pims.

THE COST REDUCTION PROGRAMS

Shortly after Mr. Summers began stressing the need to reduce waste and increase production, Blaine called the foremen together and told them that they would be responsible for stricter discipline among the employees. Unless each foreman could reduce waste and improve production in his department, he would either be replaced or receive no pay increases.

The efforts of the foremen to make the workers eliminate wasteful activities and increase output brought immediate resistance and resentment. The employees' reactions were typified by the following comment: "What has gotten into Chuck lately? He's been chewing us out for the same old things we've always done. All he thinks about now is increasing production." Several of the foremen commented that they didn't like the front office making them the "bad guys" in the eyes of the workers. The workers didn't change their work habits as a result of the pressure put on them by the foremen, but a growing spirit of antagonism between the workers and the foremen was apparent.

After several weeks of no apparent improvement in production, Jon called a meeting with the workers to announce that the plant would go on a 4-day, 10-hour-a-day work week in order to reduce operating costs. He stressed that the workers would enjoy having a three-day weekend. This was greeted with enthusiasm by some of the younger employees, but several of the older women complained that the schedule would be too tiring for them and that they would rather work five days a week. The proposal was voted on and passed by a two-to-one margin. Next Jon stated that there would be no more unsupervised overtime and that all overtime had to be approved in advance by Blaine. Overtime would be allowed only if some specific job had to be finished. Those who had been working overtime protested vigorously, saying that this would only result in lagging behind schedule, but Jon remained firm on this new rule.

Shortly after the meeting, several workers in the doorjamb department made plans to stage a work slowdown so that the department would fall behind schedule and they would have to work overtime to catch up. One of the workers, who had previously been the hardest working in the department said, "We will tell them that we are working as fast as possible and that we just can't do as much as we used to in a five-day week. The only thing they could do would be to fire us, and they would never do that." Similar tactics were devised by workers in other departments. Some workers said that if they couldn't have overtime they would find a better paying job elsewhere.

Blaine, observing what was going on, told Jon, "They think I can't tell that they are staging a slowdown. Well,

I simply won't approve any overtime, and after Jack's department gets way behind I'll let him have it for fouling up scheduling."

After a few weeks of continued slowdown, Blaine drew up a set of specific rules, which were posted on the company bulletin board early one Monday morning (see Exhibit 10-18). This brought immediate criticism from the workers. During the next week they continued to deliberately violate the posted rules. On Friday two of the male employees quit because they were penalized for arriving late to work and for "lounging around" during working hours. As they left they said they would be waiting for their foreman after work to get even with him for turning them in.

That same day the entire assembly department (all women) staged a work stoppage to protest an action taken against Myrtle King, an employee of the company since the beginning. The action resulted from a run-in she had with Lela Pims, foreman of the assembly department. Myrtle was about 60 years old and had been turned in by Lela for resting too much. She became furious, saying she couldn't work 10 hours a day. Several of her friends had organized the work stoppage after Myrtle had been sent home without pay credit for the day. The stoppage was also inspired by some talk among the workers of forming a union. The women seemed to favor this idea more than the men.

When Blaine found out about the incident he tried joking with the women and in jest threatened to fire them if they did not begin working again. When he saw he was getting nowhere he returned to the front office. One of the workers commented, "He thinks he can send us home and push us around and then all he has to do is tell us to go back to work and we will. Well, this place can't operate without us."

Jon soon appeared and called Lela into his office and began talking with her. Later he persuaded the women to go back to work and told them that there would be a meeting with all the female employees on Monday morning.

Jon wondered what steps he should take to solve the problems at L. J. Summers Company. The efforts of management to increase efficiency and reduce production costs had definitely caused resentment among the workers. Even more disappointing was the fact that the company accountant had just announced that waste and costs had increased since the new programs had been instituted, and the company scheduler reported that Summers was farther behind on shipments than ever before.

EXHIBIT 10-18

Production Shop Regulations

1. Anyone reporting late to work will lose one half hour's pay for each five minutes of lateness. The same applies to punching in after lunch.

2. No one is to leave the machine or post without the permission of the supervisor.

3. Anyone observed not working will be noted, and if sufficient occurrences are counted the employee will be dismissed.

CASE QUESTIONS

1. Describe the cause of the problem that led to the production slowdown by employees at the Summers Company.

2. How might management's concern about production costs and waste have been handled in a way that would have avoided the problems that occurred?

3. What kind of leadership procedures are now needed to resolve the problems management now faces?

CASE 10–2   GRACE PASTIAK'S 'WEB OF INCLUSION'

Last fall, Tellabs Inc., a maker of sophisticated telephone equipment, received an important order that would have to be completed by the end of the year. Instead of simply posting overtime notices, as would happen in many factories, Grace Pastiak called a meeting of the plant's workers.

"I knew that it was getting into the holiday season and many of the people would have family demands," said Mrs. Pastiak, director of manufacturing for one of three operating divisions.

Standing on a ladder in the middle of the plant, she spoke to the workers. "I gave them some choices," she said. "I said we could tell marketing we could only do half. We could bring in contract labor, or we could shift some production outside. After we talked about it, they said, 'Go for it' and that's what we did." The workers readily put in overtime to get the job done on time.

Mrs. Pastiak appears to be not just another plant manager. Instead of writing memos or limiting her discussions to one or two lieutenants, she prefers a more personal approach. She communicates directly with her people on the plant floor, trying to infect them with a zeal for producing high-quality products. And she fiddles endlessly in search of a better production set-up.

It is a style that Judy B. Rosener, a professor at the University of California at Irvine, calls "interactive leadership" and that some researchers have suggested is distinctive to women. The female managers who exhibit it, Professor Rosener wrote in a December article in the Harvard Business Review, "encourage participation, share power and information, enhance other people's self-worth, and get others excited about their work."

Sally Helgesen, a journalist and author of the book "The Female Advantage—Women's Ways of Leadership," says the phenomenon affects the configurations of their staffs. She concludes that women tend to form flat organizations, rather than hierarchies, that emphasize frequent contacts among staff members and the sharing of information. She calls these networks "webs of inclusion."

AN EVOLVING ROLE

The developments, these researchers say, are an outgrowth of women's evolving role in the work force. While earlier generations of female executives seemed to delight in proving they were tougher than any man, "a second wave of women," Professor Rosener wrote, "is making its way into top management not by adopting the style and habits that have proved successful for men, but by drawing on the skills and attitudes they developed from their shared experience as women."

Grace Pastiak, who at the age of 35 is one of the rare female managers in manufacturing, may be representative

Source: John Holusha, *The New York Times*, May 5, 1991. Copyright © 1991 by The New York Times Company. Reprinted by permission.

of this new generation. But she says her style stems from reading and courses rather than from her orientation as a woman. "I don't think it is gender-specific," she said.

"I have the bias that people do better when they are happy," said Mrs. Pastiak, who attributes her style in part to her education in sociology and early jobs in social work. "The old style of beating on people to get things done does not work."

In fact, whether this more nurturing management style is more distinctive to women than to men is a controversial issue. Indeed, Professor Rosener's article touched off a spirited discussion in a subsequent issue of the Harvard Business Review.

One woman who is free to run a business as she chooses, Barbara Grogan, the owner of Western Industrial Contractors, a heavy-equipment moving company in Denver, said: "Women do lead and manage differently. There is no real hierarchy in my office, and we never have meetings. Nobody controls information and power. We just make it happen."

Ross Webber, a professor of management at the Wharton School of the University of Pennsylvania, thinks there is a general drift away from a hierarchical, military-style management style. "In the broadest-brush terms, the decline of the hierarchy as a source of power, and an emphasis on the ability to build coalitions, is the central management trend of the past 25 years," he said. "As such, it has been a helpful trend for women managers."

For her part, Mrs. Pastiak, as the supervisor of a work force of 170 people, provides a test case of whether the factories can work effectively without relying on the traditional rigid command structure.

Although high-ranking women are found in abundance in the professions and in important staff positions in large corporations, fewer have moved into jobs of authority in manufacturing. "It may be a supply-side problem," Professor Webber observed. "Women do not want to manage in blue-collar, union situations."

There is a culture of flexibility and innovation at Tellabs that has probably permitted Mrs. Pastiak to go further with soft management methods than might have been possible in more tradition-bound companies.

Founded in 1974, Tellabs employs 2,100 in a nonunion shop and has annual sales of about $200 million, which means it is still tiny to be competing with the likes of AT&T, Northern Telecom, Siemens, NEC, and Fujitsu.

The company operates at the intersection of the communications and computer industries. It produces products for the big long-distance and regional telephone companies as well as concerns that have their own telephone and data communications systems. A typical product is an echo canceler, which blocks out the mysterious third voice that can be a nuisance during long distance calls.

COMMITTED TO TRAINING

Mrs. Pastiak is regarded by both her bosses and subordinates as an effective manager, and the numbers seem to back this up. She meets production targets 98 percent of the time, compared with an industry standard that she puts near 96 percent. And it is a record she keeps without seeming to be preoccupied with the output, attendance, and cost reports that are the production manager's staples.

Instead, she is a champion of worker empowerment, worker education, and Japanese quality methods. She takes two full days each month, for example, to teach a course in what the company calls Total Quality Commitment—a task that she believes most male managers in her position would assign a subordinate.

Speaking to factory workers gathered in a conference room, she bubbles with enthusiasm as she goes over her personal formula for improving quality by systematic problem solving. An astute instructor making sure her students get the message, she repeatedly focuses their attention: "What is the purpose? What is the process? And what is the payoff?"

About a dozen workers are taken at a time from their usual task of assembling circuit boards to attend the hour-long sessions. Mrs. Pastiak considers it time well spent, despite the loss of production time. "I cannot think of anything more important that I should be doing than empowering people," she said in the flat twang of a native of northern Illinois. "I want people to have a sense of accomplishment."

Not that production is neglected. Sitting in her corner office, Mrs. Pastiak reaches for a thick red binder filled with documents listing output by shift. "I get daily reports on what we shipped and weekly reports on other key measures," she said.

But she says the staff's development means she does not need to spend as much time studying reports. "The stronger the teams become, the less they need you," she said.

WORKER SELF-RELIANCE

That throws more of the problem-solving to workers on the factory floor, said Tom Sharpe and Tim Murphy, two

of her subordinates. "We get daily reports on why things did not ship," said Mr. Sharpe. "Usually it is for a reason out of our control. If it is within our control, we fix it and then cut the boss in on what we have done."

The proof of the production line's self-reliance: its ability to fill 98 percent of its orders. "In another plant, something may need to be done, but people say, 'That's not my job' and the order goes unfilled," Mrs. Pastiak said. "Around here the attitude is 'what do we have to do to get the order to the customer.'"

Mrs. Pastiak said it helps if top management reinforces this every-person-matters mentality. Even though the recession has cut orders, no production workers have been laid off. Instead, workers have shifted to four-day weeks until orders picked up. (The company reported a loss of $968,000 for the first quarter, compared with a profit of $2.54 million last year.)

Most of Mrs. Pastiak's subordinate managers are men, many of whom say she manages differently than men in senior roles. Duane Dhamen, a project manager, said in referring to the head of another division, "he talks to one or two key people and lets the information filter down to the ranks." By contrast, Mrs. Pastiak "puts a stronger focus on the team and open communications," he said.

Another manager, David Gladstein, said: "If Grace left tomorrow, we would still be a team, at least for a while. But with a different individual, it could change."

Mrs. Pastiak did not know a capacitor from a resistor when she came to work at Tellabs as a buyer in 1977.

At that time, recalls Michael J. Birck, a former Bell Laboratories engineer who was one of the founders of Tellabs and remains its president, sales growth was rapid, but it was clear the company's manufacturing operations were dragging it down. "We had a 35.8 percent gross margin in 1985, which is no way to survive," he said, "At that level we could not invest enough in new products to grow." The aim was at least 45 percent before taxes and depreciation and interest costs.

In addition, there were serious quality problems, a significant threat in an industry that emphasizes reliability. "Mike Birck went into one of our stock-rooms and checked some of our products," recalled Edward McDevitt, a vice president. "Only 70 percent of the samples he chose performed to specs."

Rather than try to solve the problems by shifting production overseas, as some companies have done, Mr. Birck asked Mr. McDevitt to start applying Japanese manufacturing methods, like just-in-time inventory control and statistical quality control. Mr. McDevitt, in turn, chose Mrs.

Pastiak to lead a pilot project in the Lisle factory in mid-1986.

"I knew that Grace was good at teaching and training, and I knew she would move any roadblocks in her way," he said.

Under the new process, individual workers were trained to inspect their own work and given the right to shut down production until errors were corrected. Rather than working on parts of a product, like welders on an automobile assembly line, workers were organized into teams. Each team assembles a product from beginning to end, and each member of a team is trained to do multiple jobs.

The pilot project was successful. Work-in-process inventory went down 80 percent. The time it took to fill an order went from 22 days to 2. Financial margins improved as well. Last year the company, whose shares are traded over-the-counter, reported that its gross margin had widened to 44.9 percent.

While the project was under way, Mrs. Pastiak spent most of her days on the factory floor, changing the way the circuit boards were assembled, soldered, and tested. She rearranged so many machines that the maintenance crews would try to hide when she came around. "They would say, 'That woman is moving furniture again,'" Mrs. Pastiak recalled.

The success of the pilot led to companywide use of the technique and to Mrs. Pastiak's promotion to director of manufacturing in 1987, making her the highest-ranking woman line executive in the company. (Among staff jobs, women hold the titles of general counsel and the head of a software development project.)

A FEW MORE HURDLES

Grace Swanson met Robert Pastiak at Tellabs. "He actually worked for me for awhile, which was interesting," she said.

They have two small children: Annie, who is $2\frac{1}{2}$ years old and Brian, 17 months. Mrs. Pastiak said she drops the children at a day care center in the morning and picks them up in the evening. She concedes it is a less-than-ideal arrangement.

Nevertheless, being part of a two-income couple may also have given her more latitude to act than her male peers. "I may have more freedom to innovate, because my paycheck is not the sole support of the family," she said.

Still, even at Tellabs, some of her female colleagues doubt that a woman can go to the very top. They said that

EXHIBIT 10-19

**A Big Gap between
the Sexes**

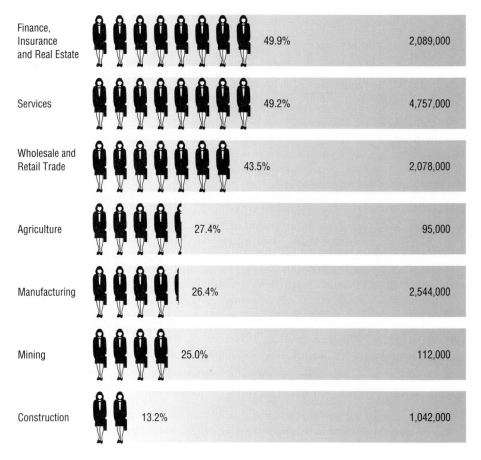

Finance, Insurance and Real Estate	49.9%	2,089,000
Services	49.2%	4,757,000
Wholesale and Retail Trade	43.5%	2,078,000
Agriculture	27.4%	95,000
Manufacturing	26.4%	2,544,000
Mining	25.0%	112,000
Construction	13.2%	1,042,000

Source: Women's Bureau, Department of Labor, 1990.

in general the men who control manufacturing companies need to become more comfortable with women as colleagues—and their styles—before they begin bestowing vice presidential titles on women.

"It is a comfort-level thing," said Diana Kreitling, a former manufacturing supervisor who is now in marketing. "Most of the male managers are in their mid-40s to 60s, which is about half a generation ahead of us. Their real concern is, 'Can I tell this joke? Can I go golfing with her? What about business trips?' "

CASE QUESTIONS

1. Do only female managers exhibit what is referred to as interactive leadership? Discuss.
2. What does Pastiak mean by total quality commitment?
3. What team-oriented approaches seem to be working for Pastiak?

ORGANIZATIONAL STRUCTURE
AND JOB DESIGN

Everything should be
made as simple as
possible, but not simpler.

—Albert Einstein

11

Organizational Structure and Design

LEARNING OBJECTIVES

IDENTIFY the choices which must be made in designing an organization structure

DEFINE what is meant by the term division of labor

DISCUSS the role of delegation of authority in design decisions

DESCRIBE several forms of departmentalization

EXPLAIN the importance of span of control

DEFINE three important dimensions of structure

COMPARE mechanistic and organic organizational design

IDENTIFY the major advantages of matrix organization design

DISCUSS multinational organization structure and design issues

Organizational structure and design have always been important factors influencing the behavior of individuals and groups that comprise the organization; the new rules of operating in today's global business environment make structure and design considerations even more critical.[1] Through the design of the structure, management establishes expectations for what individuals and groups will do to achieve the organization's purposes. But before these purposes can be accomplished, somebody must do some work. Not only must people do some work, they must do the right work. And that brings us to organizational structure,

---

[1]C. Borucki and C. K. Barnett, "Restructuring for Survival: The Navistar Case," *Academy of Management Executive*, February 1990, p. 36.

because through organization managers decide how the purposes will be accomplished.[2]

Managers achieve coordinated effort through the design of a structure of task and authority relationships.[3] Design, in this context, implies that managers make a conscious effort to predetermine the way employees do their work. Structure refers to relatively stable relationships and processes of the organization. Organizational structure is considered by many to be "the anatomy of the organization, providing a foundation within which the organization functions."[4] Thus, the structure of an organization, similar to the anatomy of a living organism, can be viewed as a framework. The idea of structure as a framework "focuses on the differentiation of positions, formulation of rules and procedures, and prescriptions of authority."[5] Therefore, the purpose of structure is to regulate, or at least reduce, uncertainty in the behavior of individual employees.

Organizations are purposive and goal-oriented, so it follows that the structure of organizations also is purposive and goal-directed. Our concept of organizational structure takes into account the existence of purposes and goals, and our attitude is that management should think of structure in terms of its contribution to organizational effectiveness, even though the exact nature of the relationship between structure and effectiveness is inherently difficult to know. Structure alone, however, is only one part of the organization. This chapter examines structural and design variables in the context of a total organization system.

DESIGNING AN ORGANIZATIONAL STRUCTURE

Managers who set out to design an organizational structure face difficult decisions. They must choose among a myriad of alternative frameworks of jobs and departments. The process by which they make these choices is termed *organizational design*, and it means quite simply the decisions and actions that result in an organizational structure. This process may be explicit or implicit, it may be "one-shot" or developmental, or it may be done by a single manager or by a team of managers.[6] However the actual decisions come about, the content of the decisions

---

[2]D. Miller, "The Genesis of Configuration," *Academy of Management Review,* October 1987, pp. 691–92.

[3]George P. Huber and Reuben R. McDaniel, "The Decision-Making Paradigm of Organizational Design," *Management Science,* May 1986, p. 573.

[4]Dan R. Dalton, William D. Todor, Michael J. Spendolini, Gordon J. Fielding, and Lyman W. Porter, "Organization Structure and Performance: A Critical Review," *Academy of Management Review,* January 1980, p. 49.

[5]Stewart Ranson, Bob Hinings, and Royston Greenwood, "The Structuring of Organizational Structures," *Administrative Science Quarterly,* March 1980, p. 2.

[6]Ronald A. Heiner, "Imperfect Decisions in Organizations: Toward a Theory of Internal Structures," *Journal of Economic Behavior and Organization,* January 1988, pp. 25–44.

is always the same. The first two decisions focus on individual jobs, and the next two decisions focus on departments, or groups of jobs.

1. Managers decide how to divide the overall task into successively smaller jobs—divide the total activities of the task into smaller sets of related activities. The effect of this decision is to define jobs in terms of specialized activities and responsibilities. Although jobs have many characteristics, the most important one is their degree of specialization.

2. Managers distribute authority among the jobs. Authority is the right to make decisions without approval by a higher manager and to exact obedience from designated other people. All jobs contain some degree of right to make decisions within prescribed limits, but not all jobs contain the right to exact obedience from others. The latter aspect of authority distinguishes managerial from nonmanagerial jobs. Managers can exact obedience; nonmanagers cannot.

   The outcomes of these two decisions are jobs which management assigns to individuals. The jobs will have two distinct attributes: activities and authority. The third and fourth decisions affect the manner in which the jobs are grouped into departments.

3. Managers decide the bases by which the individual jobs are to be grouped together. This decision is much like any other classification decision, and it can result in groups containing jobs which are relatively homogeneous or heterogeneous.

4. Finally, managers decide the appropriate size of the group reporting to each superior and this decision involves determining whether spans of control are relatively few or many.

Thus, organizational structures vary depending on the choices that managers make. If we consider each of the four design decisions to be a continuum of possible choices, the alternative structures can be depicted as follows:

Division of labor:	Specialization	
	High	Low
Authority:	Delegation	
	High	Low
Departmentalization:	Basis	
	Homogeneous	Heterogeneous
Span of control:	Number	
	Few	Many

Generally speaking, organizational structures will tend toward one extreme or the other along each continuum. Structures tending to the left are characterized by a number of terms including *classical, formalistic, structured, bureaucratic, System 1,* and *mechanistic.* Structures tending to the right are termed *neoclassical, informalistic, unstructured, nonbureaucratic, System 4,* and *organic.*[7] Exactly where along the continuum an organization finds itself has implications for its performance as well as for individual and group behavior.

DIVISION OF LABOR

Division of labor concerns the extent to which jobs are specialized. Managers divide the total task of the organization into specific jobs having specified activities which define what the person performing the job is to do. For example, the activities of the job "accounting clerk" can be defined in terms of the methods and procedures required to process certain types of quantities of transactions during a period of time. Using the same methods and procedures, one accounting clerk could be processing accounts receivable while others process accounts payable. Thus, jobs can be specialized both by method and by application of the method.

The economic advantages of dividing work into specialized jobs are the principal historical reasons for the creation of organizations.[8] As societies became more and more industrialized and urbanized, craft production gave way to mass production. Mass production depends on the ability to obtain the economic benefits of specialized labor, and the most effective means for obtaining specialized labor is through organizations. Although managers are concerned with more than the economic implications of jobs, they seldom lose sight of specialization as the

■ E11–1 rationale for dividing work among jobs.[9] Completing Exercise 11–1 provides an excellent illustration of the importance of an effective division of labor in completing work.

DELEGATION OF AUTHORITY

Managers decide how much authority is to be delegated to each job and each jobholder. As we have noted, authority refers to the right of individuals to make decisions without approval by higher management and to exact obedience from others. It is important to understand that delegation refers specifically to making

---

[7]Henry Tosi, *Theories of Organization* (New York: John Wiley & Sons, 1984).

[8]Richard E. Kopelman, "Job Redesign and Productivity: A Review of the Literature," *National Productivity Review,* Summer 1985, p. 239.

[9]Donald J. Campbell, "Task Complexity: A Review and Analysis," *Academy of Management Review,* January 1988, pp. 40–52.

decisions—not to doing work. A sales manager can be delegated the right to hire salespersons (a decision) and the right to assign them to specific territories (obedience). Another sales manager may not have the right to hire but may have the right to assign territories. Thus, the degree of delegated authority can be relatively high or relatively low with respect to both aspects of authority. For any particular job there is a range of alternative configurations of authority delegation and managers must balance the relative gains and losses of these alternatives. Let us evaluate some of them.

First, relatively high delegation of authority encourages the development of professional managers. As decision-making authority is pushed down (delegated) in the organization, managers have opportunities to make significant decisions and to gain skills that enable them to advance in the company. By virtue of their right to make decisions on a broad range of issues, managers develop expertise that enables them to cope with problems of higher management. Managers with broad decision-making power often make difficult decisions. Consequentially, they are trained for promotion into positions of even greater authority and responsibility. Upper management can readily compare managers on the basis of actual decision-making performance. The advancement of managers on the basis of demonstrated performance can eliminate favoritism and personality conflicts in the promotion process.

Second, high delegation of authority can lead to a competitive climate within the organization. Managers are motivated to contribute in this competitive atmosphere since they are compared with their peers on various performance measures. A competitive environment in which managers compete on how well they achieve sales, cost reduction, and employee development targets can be a positive factor in overall organizational performance. Competitive environments can also produce destructive behavior if the success of one manager occurs at the expense of another. But regardless of whether it is positive or destructive, significant competition exists only when individuals have authority to do those things which enable them to win.

Finally, managers who have relatively high authority are able to exercise more autonomy and thus satisfy their desires to participate in problem solving. This autonomy can lead to managerial creativity and ingenuity which contribute to the adaptiveness and development of the organization and managers. Opportunities to participate in setting goals can be positive motivators. But a necessary condition for goal setting is authority to make decisions.

These are only three of the benefits associated with delegated authority. But these advantages are not free of costs. Some of the costs are:

First, managers must be trained to make the decisions that go with delegated authority. Formal training programs can be quite expensive, and the costs can more than offset the benefits.

Second, many managers accustomed to making decisions resist delegating authority to their subordinates. Consequently, they may perform at lower levels of effectiveness because they believe that delegation of authority involves losing control.

Third, administrative costs are incurred because new or altered accounting, rating, and reporting systems must be developed to provide top management with information about the effects of their subordinates' decisions.

These are, of course, only some of the costs. As is usually the case in managerial decisions, whether to centralize or decentralize authority cannot be resolved simply and can be guided only by general questions.

DEPARTMENTALIZATION

The process of defining the activities and authority of jobs is analytical; that is, the total task of the organization is broken down into successively smaller ones. But then management must combine the divided tasks into groups of departments.

The rationale of grouping jobs rests on the necessity for coordinating them. The specialized jobs are separate, interrelated parts of the total task, and accomplishing the task requires the accomplishment of each of the jobs. But the jobs must be performed in the specific manner and sequence intended by management when they were defined. As the number of specialized jobs in an a organization increases, there comes a point when they can no longer be effectively coordinated by a single manager. Thus, to create manageable numbers of jobs, they are combined into smaller groups, and a new job is defined—that of manager of the group. The crucial managerial consideration when creating departments is the determination of the bases of grouping jobs. These bases are termed *departmentalization bases,* and some of the more widely used ones are described in the following sections.

Functional Departmentalization

Managers can combine jobs according to the functions of the organization. Every organization must undertake certain activities in order to do its work, and these necessary activities are the organization's functions. The necessary functions of a manufacturing firm include production, marketing, finance, accounting, and personnel—activities necessary to create, produce, and sell a product. The necessary functions of a commercial bank include taking deposits, making loans, and investing the bank's funds. The functions of a hospital include surgery, psychiatry, housekeeping, pharmacy, nursing, and personnel.[10] Each of these functions can be a specific department, and jobs can be combined according to them. The functional basis is often found in relatively small organizations providing a narrow range of products and services. It is also widely used as the basis of divisions of large multiproduct organizations.

---

[10]Peggy Leatt and Rodney Schneck, "Criteria for Grouping Nursing Subunits in Hospitals," *Academy of Management Journal,* March 1984, pp. 150–64.

The Oldsmobile Division of General Motors is structured on a functional basis as depicted in Exhibit 11-1. GM management decided on eight functions—engineering, manufacturing, reliability, distribution, finance, personnel, public relations, and purchasing—as the bases for combining the jobs of the Oldsmobile Division. Other divisions of General Motors use different functional bases depending on management decisions. The specific configuration of functions that appear as separate departments varies from organization to organization.

The principal advantage of the functional departmentalization basis is its efficiency. That is, it seems logical to have a department consisting of experts in a particular field such as production or accounting. By having departments of specialists, management creates highly efficient units. An accountant is generally more efficient when working with other accountants and other individuals who have similar backgrounds and interests. They can share expertise to get the work done.

A major disadvantage of this departmental basis is that because specialists are working with and encouraging each other in their area of expertise and interest, the organizational goals may be sacrificed in favor of departmental goals. Accountants may see only their problems and not those of production or marketing or the total organization. In other words, the culture of and identification with the department are often stronger than identification with the organization and

▲ C11–1   its culture. The Eagle Airlines case at the end of this chapter provides an opportunity to see some of the difficulties posed by functional departmentalization. Additionally, it offers a chance to recommend an alternative form of design.

Territorial Departmentalization

Another commonly adopted method for departmentalizing is to establish groups on the basis of geographical area. The logic is that all activities in a given region should be assigned to one manager who would be in charge of all operations in that particular geographical area.

In large organizations territorial arrangements are advantageous because physical dispersion of activities makes centralized coordination difficult. For example, it is extremely difficult for someone in New York to manage salespeople in Kansas City. It makes sense to assign the managerial job to someone in Kansas City.

R. H. Macy & Co., Inc., is organized along territorial lines, and its divisions reflect the locations of Macy stores in the several states in which they operate. The managers of individual stores in a specific city report to a regional president. For example, the manager of Macy's in Sacramento reports to the president of Macy's California with offices in San Francisco.

Territorial departmentalization provides a training ground for managerial personnel. The company is able to place managers in territories and then assess their progress in that geographical region. The experience that managers acquire in a territory away from headquarters provides valuable insights about how products and/or services are accepted in the field.

EXHIBIT 11-1

Organizational Structure of Oldsmobile Division

Product Departmentalization

Many large diversified companies group jobs on the basis of product where all jobs associated with producing and selling a product or product line are placed under the direction of one manager. As a firm grows by increasing the number of products it markets, it is difficult to coordinate the various functional departments, and it becomes advantageous to establish product units. This form of organization allows personnel to develop total expertise in researching, manufacturing, and distributing a product line. Concentration of the authority, responsibility, and accountability in a specific product department allows top management to coordinate actions.

The Consumer Products Division of Kimberly-Clark reflects product departmentalization. The specific product groups shown in Exhibit 11-2 include feminine hygiene, household, and commercial products. Within each of these units we find production and marketing personnel. Since managers of product divisions coordinate sales, manufacturing, and distribution of a product, they become the overseers of a profit center. In this manner profit responsibility is implemented in product-based organizations. Managers are often asked to establish profit goals at the beginning of a time period and then to compare actual profit with planned profit.

Product-based organizations foster initiative and autonomy by providing division managers with the resources necessary to carry out their profit plans. But such organizations face the difficult issue of deciding how much redundancy is necessary. Divisional structures contain some degree of redundancy because each division wants its own research and development, engineering, marketing, and production personnel. Thus, with technical and professional personnel found throughout the organization at the division levels, the cost can be exorbitant. In companies with a large number of divisions, coordination also can be extremely difficult. One major firm, 3M, has attempted to deal with these problems through its organization of the R&D function as described in Encounter 11-1.

EXHIBIT 11-2

Organizational Structure of Consumer Products Division, Kimberly-Clark Corporation

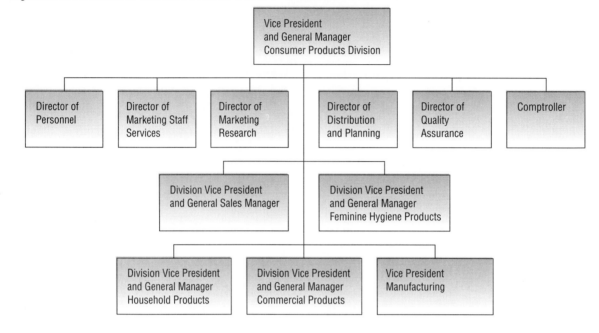

Customer Departmentalization

Customers and clients can be bases for grouping jobs.[11] For example, educational institutions have customer-oriented divisions such as regular (day and night) courses and extension divisions. In some instances a professor will be affiliated solely with one or the other. In fact, the titles of some faculty positions often specifically mention the extension division.

Another form of customer departmentalization is the loan department in a commercial bank. Loan officers are often associated only with industrial, commercial, or agricultural loans, and the customer will be served by one of these three loan officers.

Some department stores are set up to a degree on a customer basis with groupings such as university shops, men's and boys' clothing departments, and bargain floors. Organizations with customer-based departments are better able to satisfy customer-identified needs than organizations that base departments on noncustomer factors.[12]

---

[11]Richard B. Chase and David A. Tansik, "The Customer Contact Model for Organization Design," *Management Science,* September 1983, pp. 1037–50.

[12]Frank Cornish, "Building a Customer-Oriented Organization," *Long-Range Planning,* June 1988, pp. 105–7.

ORGANIZATIONAL
E N C O U N T E R • 11-1

ORGANIZING 3M'S R&D FUNCTION TO INNOVATE

How does an old-line manufacturing firm whose base products are sandpaper and tape become and remain a recognized leader in product innovation? 3M's success has inspired others to emulate its management practices and organizational structure. Although the firm uses many strategies to stimulate and reward innovative behavior throughout the firm, a cornerstone is its policy of keeping divisions small, with average sales of about $200 million each.

Of course, keeping divisions small means increasing the number of divisions. 3M has a divisional structure consisting of 89 divisions responsible for producing and marketing some 60,000 types and sizes of products. The divisions are grouped into sectors, and sector managers report to corporate headquarters. The company has found that coordinating product development and research in such a structure presents staggering problems. To manage the function, the company has created a structure that distinguishes between different R&D activities.

Research and development personnel at the divisional level concentrate attention on the existing products and markets. They are expected to investigate opportunities for modifying products the division has already developed and placed on the market. R&D personnel at the sector level function in scientific research laboratories and concentrate on the hard sciences, particularly chemistry. Their product development research is limited to those which are scheduled for introduction five years hence. The third group of R&D personnel are located at corporate headquarters. This unit conducts primary research on state-of-the art technology.

The advantages of splitting out a seemingly homogeneous function such as R&D are that differences in usage can be identified for each level of the organization. In addition the sector-level personnel act as coordinators of the day-to-day needs of division-level research and the blue-sky activities of the corporate researchers.

In addition to its structuring of the R&D function, 3M encourages innovation in other ways. Employees can spend up to 15 percent of their time on ideas that hold promise for becoming new products. And the firm has a policy that each division's sales revenue must be generated by products developed within the past five years. Other innovative firms such as Rubbermaid, Hewlett-Packard, and General Electric have similar polices and practices.

Source: Based on Alicia Johnson, "3M: Organized to Innovate," *Management Review,* July 1986, pp. 58–63.

Mixed and Changing Departmentalization

The bases for departments do not remain unchanged in organizations. Because of the importance of departments, managers change the bases as conditions warrant. An organization chart should be viewed much like a snapshot of a moving object. The action is frozen for a moment, but the viewer understands that the object continued in motion. Over time organizations will use a mix of bases—at some time using function and at other times using product, territory, and customer bases. Moreover, within the same organization will be different bases at different levels of management. For example, the departmental basis at the corporate level of General Motors is by product type—compact and full-size cars—with an executive vice president heading up each division. The general managers of the Chevrolet and Pontiac divisions report to the compact car vice president; the general managers of the Buick, Oldsmobile, and Cadillac divisions report to the full-size-car vice president. But below the general managers, function is on the departmental basis as we noted in Exhibit 11-1.

SPAN OF CONTROL

The determination of appropriate bases for departmentalization established the kinds of jobs that will be grouped together. But that determination does not establish the number of jobs to be included in a specific group. That determination is the issue of span of control. Generally, the issue comes down to the decision of how many people a manager can oversee; that is, will the organization be more effective if the span of control is relatively wide or narrow? The question is basically concerned with determining the volume of interpersonal relationships the department's manager is able to handle. Moreover, the span of control must be defined to include not only formally assigned subordinates but also those who have access to the manager. A manager may be placed in a position of being responsible not only for immediate subordinates but may also be the chairperson of several committees and task groups that take time.

The number of potential interpersonal relationships between a manger and subordinates increases geometrically as the number of subordinates increases arithmetically. This relationship holds because managers potentially contend with three types of interpersonal relationships: (1) direct single, (2) direct group, and (3) cross. Direct-single relationships occur between the manager and each subordinate individually in a one-on-one setting. Direct-group relations occur between the manager and each possible permutation of subordinates. Finally, cross relationships occur when subordinates interact with one another.

The critical consideration in determining the manager's span of control is not the number of potential relationships. Rather it is the frequency and intensity of the actual relationships that is important. Not all relationships will occur, and those which do will vary in importance. If we shift our attention from potential to actual relationships as the basis for determining optimum span of control, at least three factors appear to be important.

Required Contact

Research and development, medical, and production work have a need for frequent contact and a high degree of coordination between a superior and subordinates. The use of conferences and other forms of consultation often aid in the attainment of goals within a constrained time period. For example, the research and development team leader may have to consult frequently with team members so that a project is completed within a time period that will allow the organization to place a product on the market. Thus, instead of relying on memos and reports, it is in the best interest of the organization to have as many in-depth contacts with the team as possible. A large span of control would preclude contacting subordinates so frequently, and this could have detrimental effects on completing the project. In general, the greater the inherent ambiguity that exists in an individual's job, the greater the need for supervision to avoid conflict and stress.[13]

Degree of Specialization

The degree of employee specialization is a critical consideration in establishing the span of control at all levels of management. It is generally accepted that a manager at the lower organizational level (e.g., first-line supervisor) can oversee more subordinates because work at this level is more specialized and less complicated than at higher levels of management (e.g., president). Management can combine highly specialized and similar jobs into relatively large departments because the employees may not need close supervision.

Ability to Communicate

Instructions, guidelines, and policies must be communicated verbally to subordinates in most work situations. The need to discuss job-related factors influences the span of control. The individual who can clearly and concisely communicate with subordinates is able to manage more people than one who cannot do so.

Even though it is possible to identify some of the specific factors that relate to optimal spans of control, the search for the full answer continues.[14]

DIMENSIONS OF STRUCTURE

The four design decisions (division of labor, delegation of authority, departmentalization, and span of control) result in the structure of organizations. Researchers and practitioners of management have attempted to develop their understanding of relationships between structures and performance, attitudes, satisfaction, and other variables thought to be important, but this has been hampered by the complexity of the relationships themselves as well as by the difficulty of defining and measuring the concept of organizational structure.

Although universal agreement on a common set of dimensions that measure differences in structure is neither possible nor desirable, some suggestions can be

---

[13]Lawrence B. Chonko, "The Relationship of Span of Control to Sales Representatives, Experienced Role Conflict and Role Ambiguity," *Academy of Management Journal,* June 1982, pp. 452–56; and David D. Van Fleet, "Span of Management Research and Issues," *Academy of Management Journal,* September 1983, pp. 546–52.

[14]Robert D. Dewar and Donald P. Simet, "A Level-Specific Prediction of Spans of Control Examining the Effects of Size, Technology, and Specialization," *Academy of Management Journal,* March 1981, pp. 5–24.

made. At the present time three dimensions—formalization, centralization, and complexity—are often used in research and practice to describe structure.[15]

Formalization

The dimension of formalization refers to the extent to which expectations regarding the means and ends of work are specified and written. In a highly formalized organizational structure, rules and procedures prescribe what each individual should be doing. Such organizations would have written standard operating procedures, specified directives, and explicit policies.[16] In terms of the four design decisions, formalization is the result of high specialization of labor, high delegation of authority, the use of functional departments, and wide spans of control.

Although formalization is defined in terms of written rules and procedures, it is important to understand how these are viewed by the employees. In organizations with all the appearances of formalization—thick manuals of rules, procedures, and policies—employees may not perceive the manuals as affecting their behavior. Thus, even though rules and procedures exist, they must be enforced if they are to affect behavior.[17]

Centralization

Centralization refers to the location of decision-making authority in the hierarchy of the organization. More specifically, the concept refers to the delegation of authority among the jobs in the organization. Typically, researchers and practitioners think of centralization in terms of (1) decision making and (2) control.[18] But despite the apparent simplicity of the concept, it can be complex.

The complexity of the concept derives from three sources: First, people at the same level can have different decision-making authority. Second, not all decisions are of equal importance in organizations. For example, a typical management practice is to delegate authority to make routine operating decisions (i.e., decentralization) but retain authority to make strategic decisions (i.e., centralization). Third, individuals may not perceive that they really have authority even though their job descriptions include it. Thus, objectively they have authority, but subjectively they do not.[19]

[15]Richard S. Blackburn, "Dimensions of Structure: A Review and Reappraisal," *Academy of Management Review,* January 1982, pp. 59–66.

[16]James P. Walsh and Robert D. Dewar, "Formalization and the Organizational Life Cycle," *Journal of Management Studies,* May 1987, pp. 215–32.

[17]E. J. Walton, "The Comparison of Measures of Organization Structure," *Academy of Management Review,* January 1981, pp. 155–60.

[18]See, for example, J. A. Alexander, "Adaptive Change in Corporate Control Practices," *Academy of Management Journal,* March 1991, pp. 162–93.

[19]Jeffrey D. Ford, "Institutional versus Questionnaire Measures of Organizational Structure," *Academy of Management Journal,* September 1979, pp. 601–10.

Complexity

Complexity is the direct outgrowth of dividing work and creating departments. Specifically, the concept refers to the number of distinctly different job titles, or occupational groupings, and the number of distinctly different units, or departments. The fundamental idea is that organizations with a great many different kinds and types of jobs and units create more complicated managerial and organizational problems than those with fewer jobs and departments.

Complexity, then, relates to differences among jobs and units. It therefore is not surprising that differentiation is often used synonymously with complexity. Moreover, it has become standard practice to use the term horizontal differentiation to refer to the number of different units at the same level; vertical differentiation refers to the number of levels in the organization. The degree of vertical differentiation determines how "flat" or "tall" the organization will be. In recent years there has been a tendency to reduce vertical differentiation, or flatten organizations. Since this reduces the number of levels in the organization such restructuring activities can displace employees. Thus, important questions of company values and ethical issues may be involved in restructuring. Encounter 11-2 provides an example.

The discussion of the relationships between dimensions of organizational structure and the four design decisions is summarized in Exhibit 11-3. The figure notes only the causes of high formalization, centralization, and complexity. However, the relationships are symmetrical: the causes of low formalization, centralization, and complexity are the opposite of those shown. In completing Exercise 11–2, think about the dimensions of structure as you compete with other groups.

■ **E11–2**

ORGANIZATIONAL DESIGN MODELS

As we have seen, organizational design refers to managerial decision making aimed at determining the structure and processes that coordinate and control the jobs of the organization. The outcome of organizational design decisions is the framework or structure of the organization. However, design decisions are not permanent. Organization designs are continually adapted to deal more effectively with changing conditions.[20] Earlier in this chapter, we examined a number of factors and dimensions that influence the structure which ultimately emerges. In this section, we briefly examine two general organizational design models that have had significant impact on management theory and practice. While there is little uniformity in the terms used to designate the models, we refer to them as *mechanistic* and *organic*.[21] In a later section in the chapter, we review an emerging organizational design: the matrix.

[20]J. E. McCann, "Design Principles for an Innovating Company," *Academy of Management Executive,* May 1991, pp. 76–93.

[21]Tom Burns and G. M. Stalker, *The Management of Innovation* (London: Tavistock Publications, 1961).

ETHICS
E N C O U N T E R • 11-2

RESTRUCTURING AT MOTOROLA: MAINTAINING COMPANY VALUES

Competitive pressures from home and abroad have forced many business firms to consider ways to cut costs and eliminate waste. Many companies responded to these challenges by reducing the levels of management and increasing the spans of control. Among other benefits, these flatter structures reduced costs by eliminating managerial jobs.

Motorola was one of the companies that restructured. However, top management was particularly concerned with how efforts to reduce managerial personnel would affect the company's long-standing commitment to certain values, such as treating employees ethically and with respect and dignity, including protecting employees who had served the company well in the past. The company devised the following plan for dealing with the necessity to cut costs and, at the same time, adhere to high ethical standards and people-first values. The process consisted of five steps involving the managers and company human resource professionals in joint activities:

Step 1: Data Gathering
Each top manager drew an organization chart showing every reporting relationship down to the direct-labor level. These hand-drawn charts showed what really went on in the unit, as distinct from what was supposed to go on.

Step 2: Analysis
Human resource professionals analyzed the charts and identified issues for discussion with the managers. The analysis indicated instances of too many managerial levels, too narrow spans of control, and overlapping responsibilities.

Step 3: Discussion
The analysis was presented to the managers for discussion, and they were presented with the opportunity to explain and clarify the relationships shown on the charts.

Step 4: Goals Negotiation
As discussions between managers and the human resource staff revealed problems, managers were asked to propose solutions. When managers disagreed with the staff, they were challenged to present their own analyses and solutions.

Step 5: Implementation and Tracking
As managers implemented the changes in organizational structure, they documented the resultant cost savings. The source of these savings were salaries of managers not replaced on retirement or transfer.

Thus, through a program that directly included the people who would be affected in the decision-making process and which provided alternative options for employees, Motorola succeeded in maintaining its reputation for putting people first.

Source: Based on Phil Nienstedt and Richard Wintermantel, "Motorola Restructures to Improve Productivity," Management Review, January 1987, pp. 47–49.

The Mechanistic Model

During the early part of the 20th century a body of literature emerged that considered the problem of designing the structure of an organization as but one of a number of managerial tasks, including planning and controlling. The objective of the contributors to that body of literature was to define *principles* that could

EXHIBIT 11-3

Organization Dimensions and Organizational Decisions

Dimensions	Decisions
High formalization	1. High specialization 2. Delegated authority 3. Functional departments 4. Wide spans of control
High centralization	1. High specialization 2. Centralized authority 3. Functional departments 4. Wide spans of control
High complexity	1. High specialization 2. Delegated authority 3. Territorial, customer, and product departments 4. Narrow spans of control

guide managers in the performance of their tasks. Numerous theorists and management practitioners made contributions to this literature, including such names as Fayol, Follet, and Weber. While each contributor made a unique contribution, they all had a common thread. They each described the same type of organization, one that functioned in a machinelike manner to accomplish the organization's goals in a highly efficient manner. Thus, the term *mechanistic* aptly describes such organizations. **Mechanistic organizations** emphasize the importance of achieving high levels of production and efficiency through the use of extensive rules and procedures, centralized authority, and high specialization:

1. Activities are specialized into clearly defined jobs and tasks.
2. Persons of higher rank typically have greater knowledge of the problems facing the organization than those at lower levels. Unresolved problems are thus passed up the hierarchy.
3. Standardized policies, procedures, and rules guide much of the decision making in the organization.
4. Rewards are chiefly obtained through obedience to instructions from supervisors.[22]

The mechanistic model achieves high levels of efficiency due to its structural characteristics. It is highly complex because of its emphasis on specialization of labor; it is highly centralized because of its emphasis on authority and accountability; and it is highly formalized because of its emphasis on function as the primary basis of departmentalization.

[22]C. R. Gullet, "Mechanistic vs. Organic Organizations: What Does the Future Hold?" *Personnel Administrator*, 1975, p. 17.

The Organic Model

The **organic model** of organizational design stands in sharp contrast to the mechanistic model. The organizational characteristics and practices that underlie the organic model are distinctly different from those that underlie the mechanistic model. The most distinct differences between the two models result from the different effectiveness criteria that each seeks to maximize. While the mechanistic model seeks to maximize efficiency and production, the organic model seeks to maximize flexibility and adaptability:

1. There is a de-emphasis on job descriptions and specialization. Persons become involved in problem solving when they have the knowledge or skill that will help solve the problem.
2. It is not assumed that persons holding higher positions are necessarily better informed than those at lower levels.
3. Horizontal and lateral organizational relationships are given as much or more attention as vertical relationships.
4. Status and rank differences are de-emphasized.
5. The formal structure of the organization is less permanent and more changeable.[23]

The organic organization is flexible and adaptable to changing environmental demands because its design encourages greater utilization of the human potential. Managers are encouraged to adopt practices that tap the full range of human motivations through job design which stresses personal growth and responsibility. Decision making, control, and goal-setting processes are decentralized and are shared at all levels of the organization. Communications flow throughout the organization, not simply down the chain of command. These practices are intended to implement a basic assumption of the organic model, which states that an organization will be effective to the extent that its structure is "such as to ensure a maximum probability that in all interactions and in all relationships with the organization, each member, in the light of his background, values, desires, and expectations, will view the experience as supportive and one which builds and maintains a sense of personal worth and importance."[24]

An organizational design that provides individuals with this sense of personal worth and motivation and that facilitates flexibility and adaptability would have the following characteristics:

1. It would be relatively simple because of its de-emphasis on specialization and its emphasis on increasing job range.
2. It would be relatively decentralized because of its emphasis on delegation of authority and increasing job depth.

[23]Ibid.

[24]Rensis Likert, *New Patterns of Management* (New York: McGraw-Hill, 1961); and Rensis Likert, *The Human Organization* (New York: McGraw-Hill, 1967).

3. It would be relatively informalized because of its emphasis on product and customer as bases for departmentalization.

■ **E11–3**   Which model best describes your organization? Exercise 11–3 can help provide you with an answer to that question. Which of the two models is better? The answer is neither and both. Neither is better for any and all situations. Both can be better depending on the situation.[25] Because of management's interest in designing organizations that have the advantages of both models, the matrix model has emerged as a promising alternative.

MATRIX ORGANIZATION DESIGN

A **matrix organization** design attempts to maximize the strengths and minimize the weaknesses of both the mechanistic and organic designs. In practical terms the matrix design combines functional and product departmental bases.[26] Companies such as American Cyanamid, Avco, Carborundum, Caterpillar, Hughes Aircraft, ITT, Monsanto, NCR, Prudential Insurance, TWR, and Texas Instruments are only a few of the users of matrix organization. Public sector users include public health and social service agencies.[27] Although the exact meaning of matrix organization is not well established, the most typical meaning sees it as a balanced compromise between functional and product organization, between departmentalization by process and by purpose.[28]

The matrix organizational design achieves the desired balance by superimposing, or overlaying, a horizontal structure of authority, influence, and communication on the vertical structure. The arrangement can be described as in Exhibit 11-4. Personnel assigned in each cell belong not only to the functional department but also to a particular product or project. For example, manufacturing, marketing, engineering, and finance specialists will be assigned to work on one or more projects or products. As a consequence, personnel will report to two managers—one in their functional department and one in the project or product unit. The existence of a dual authority system is a distinguishing characteristic of matrix organization.

Matrix structures are found in organizations which require responses to rapid change in two or more environments, such as technology and markets; which

[25]Robert K. Kazanjian and Robert Drazin, "Implementing Internal Diversification: Contingency Factors for Organization Design Choices," *Academy of Management Review,* April 1987, pp. 342–54.

[26]Jay R. Galbraith and Robert K. Kazanjian, "Organizing to Implement Strategies of Diversity and Globalization: The Role of Matrix Organizations," *Human Resource Management,* Spring 1986, pp. 37–54; and Diane Krusko and Robert R. Cangemi, "The Utilization of Project Management in the Pharmaceutical Industry," *Journal of the Society of Research Administrators,* Summer 1987, pp. 17–24.

[27]Kenneth Knight, "Matrix Organization: A Review," *Journal of Management Studies,* May 1976, p. 111.

[28]Ibid., p. 114.

**Matrix
Organizations**

Project, Products	Functions			
	Manufacturing	Marketing	Engineering	Finance
Project or product A				
Project or product B				
Project or product C				
Project or product D				
Project or product E				

face uncertainties that generate high information-processing requirements; and which must deal with financial and human resources constraints.[29] Managers confronting these circumstances must obtain certain advantages which are most likely to be realized with matrix organization.[30]

Advantages of Matrix Organization

A number of advantages can be associated with the matrix design. Some of the more important ones are as follows:

Efficient Use of Resources

Matrix organization facilitates the utilization of highly specialized staff and equipment. Each project or product unit can share the specialized resource with other units rather than duplicating it to provide independent coverage for each. This advantage is particularly so when projects require less than the full-time efforts of the specialist. For example, a project may require only half a computer scientist's time. Rather than having several underutilized computer scientists assigned to each project, the organization can keep fewer of them fully utilized by shifting them from project to project.

Flexibility in Conditions of Change and Uncertainty

Timely response to change requires information and communication channels that efficiently get the information to the right people at the right time.[31] Matrix

---

[29]Paul R. Lawrence, Harvey F. Kolodny, and Stanley M. Davis, "The Human Side of the Matrix," *Organizational Dynamics,* September 1977, p. 47.

[30]The following discussion is based upon Knight, "Matrix Organization."

[31]Christopher K. Best, "Organizing for New Development," *Journal of Business Strategy,* July/August 1988, pp. 34–39.

structures encourage constant interaction among project unit and functional department members. Information is channeled vertically and horizontally as people exchange technical knowledge, resulting in quicker response to competitive conditions, technological breakthroughs, and other environmental conditions.

Technical Excellence

Technical specialists interact with other specialists while assigned to a project. These interactions encourage cross-fertilization of ideas such as when a computer scientist must discuss the pros and cons of electronic data processing with a financial accounting expert. Each specialist must be able to listen, understand, and respond to the views of the other. At the same time, specialists maintain ongoing contact with members of their own discipline because they are also members of a functional department.

Freeing Top Management for Long-Range Planning

An initial stimulus for the development of matrix organizations is that top management increasingly becomes involved with day-to-day operations. Environmental changes tend to create problems that cross functional and product departments and cannot be resolved by the lower level managers. For example, when competitive conditions create the need to develop new products at faster than previous rates, the existing procedures become bogged down. Top management is then called upon to settle conflicts among the functional managers. Matrix organization makes it possible for top management to delegate ongoing decision making, thus providing more time for long-range planning.

Improving Motivation and Commitment

Project and product groups are composed of individuals with specialized knowledge to whom management assigns, on the basis of their expertise, responsibility for specific aspects of the work. Consequently, decision making within the group tends to be more participative and democratic than in more hierarchical settings. This opportunity to participate in key decisions fosters high levels of motivation and commitment, particularly for individuals with acknowledged professional orientations.

Providing Opportunities for Personal Development

Members of matrix organizations are provided considerable opportunity to develop their skills and knowledge. Placed in groups consisting of individuals representing diverse parts of the organization, they come to appreciate the different points of view expressed and become more aware of the total organization. Moreover, the experience broadens each specialist's knowledge not only of the organization but of other scientific and technical disciplines—engineers develop knowledge of financial issues; accountants learn about marketing.

Different Forms of Matrix Organization

Matrix organization forms can be depicted as existing in the middle of a continuum with mechanistic organizations at one extreme and organic organizations at the other. Organizations can move from mechanistic to matrix forms or from organic to matrix forms. Ordinarily, the process of moving to matrix organization is evolutionary. That is, as the present structure proves incapable of dealing with rapid technological and market changes, management attempts to cope by establishing procedures and positions which are outside the normal routine.

This evolutionary process consists of the following steps:

Task Force

When a competitor develops a new product that quickly captures the market, a rapid response is necessary. Yet in a System 1 organization, new product development is often too time-consuming because of the necessity to coordinate the various units that must be involved. A convenient approach is to create a task force of individuals from each functional department and charge it with the responsibility to expedite the process. The task force achieves its objective then dissolves, and members return to their primary assignment.

Teams

If the product or technological breakthrough generates a family of products that move through successive stages of new and improved products, the temporary task force concept is ineffective. A typical next step is to create permanent teams consisting of representatives from each functional department. The teams meet regularly to resolve interdepartmental issues and to achieve coordination. When not involved with issues associated with new product development, the team members work on their regular assignments.

Product Managers

If the technological breakthrough persists so that new product development becomes a way of life, top management will create the roles of product managers. In a sense, product managers chair the teams, but they now are permanent positions. They have no formal authority over the team members but must rely on their expertise and interpersonal skill to influence them. Companies such as General Foods, Du Pont, and IBM make considerable use of the product management concept.

Product Management Departments

The final step in the evolution to matrix organization is the creation of product management departments with subproduct managers for each product line. In some instances the subproduct managers are selected from specific functional departments and would continue to report directly to their functional managers. Considerable diversity in the application of matrix organization exists, yet the

essential feature is the creation of overlapping authority and the existence of dual authority.

Exactly where along the continuum an organization stops in the evolution depends on factors in the situation. Specifically and primarily important are the rates of change in technological and product developments. The resultant uncertainty and information required vary.

MULTINATIONAL STRUCTURE AND DESIGN

As we have seen previously, four design decisions regarding division of labor, delegation of authority, departmentalization, and span of control shape the design of organizational structures. These decisions, in turn, are affected by a variety of factors. Foremost among them are the social, political, cultural, legal, and economic environments in which the organization is operating. Because of their very nature, multinational corporations frequently exist in very divergent environments. A multinational corporation may be categorized as consisting of a group of geographically dispersed organizations with different national subsidiaries.[32]

One approach to setting up a foreign subsidiary is that of *replication*. That is, the same organization structure and operating policies and procedures that exist in the existing domestic organization are used. For example, when establishing its foreign subsidiaries, Procter & Gamble created an "exact replica of the United States Procter & Gamble organization" because they believed that using "exactly the same policies and procedures which have given our company success in the United States will be equally successful overseas."[33] The potential difficulty with such a practice is that it may result in the reliance upon organizational designs and management practices that are simply unsuitable for the environment of the host country. This may explain why there is a tendency for foreign subsidiary organizational structures to evolve over time as the company becomes more internationalized.[34]

For multinational corporations there are a number of factors which may have important implications for structure and design decisions, as well as general operating policies. We will briefly examine four of these.[35]

1. *National boundaries are an important force in defining organizational environments.* This is similar to the point we made at the beginning of this

---

[32]S. Ghoshal and C. A. Bartlett, "The Multinational Corporation as an Interorganizational Network," *Academy of Management Review*, October 1990, pp. 603–25.

[33]C. A. Bartlett and S. Ghoshal, *Managing across Borders: The Transnational Solution* (Boston: Harvard Business School Press, 1989), p. 38.

[34]D. A. Ricks, B. Toyne, and Z. Martinez, "Recent Developments in International Management Research," *Journal of Management*, June 1990, pp. 219–53.

[35]The following discussion is based upon P. M. Rosenzweig and J. V. Singh, "Organizational Environments and the Multinational Enterprise," *Academy of Management Review*, April 1991, pp. 340–61.

discussion. For many elements of structure, crossing national boundaries creates a necessity for carefully assessing the nature and extent of environmental differences.

2. *National boundaries are of varying importance for different elements of organizational structure and process.* Not all effects are equal. Some aspects of an organization may be significantly affected by distinct aspects of the environment of the host country. Other aspects may be affected by global or regional factors that are independent of a particular nation. Still other aspects may be relatively environment free.

3. *Subsidiaries of multinational corporations can act as conduits that introduce changes into the host country's environment.* In some cases this may mean the direct replication of elements of a particular structure heretofore not used in the host country. More often, however, it relates to operating procedures that emanate from the subsidiary organization. An example would be Marriott Corporation's introduction of their five-day work week into Hong Kong, a setting in which a six-day work week is the norm.[36]

4. *Subsidiaries of multinational corporations can act as conduits by which features of the host country's environment are introduced throughout the organization.* This is the reverse of the previous point. It strongly suggests that beneficial changes can—and do—flow both ways. Organizations should be structured to facilitate both directions of change.

Of course, while there can be important cross-country differences that dictate making adaptations in structure, policy, and management practices, there can also be a great deal of similarity even between widely divergent countries. One of the challenges to organizational researchers is to provide data to help better understand the degree of similarity and difference across national boundaries that have implications for organizational operations. Encounter 11-3 provides an example.

A FINAL WORD

Managers must consider many complex factors and variables to design an optimal organizational structure. We have discussed several of the more important ones in this chapter. As we have seen, the key design decisions are division of labor, departmentalization, span of control, and delegation of authority. These decisions which reflect environmental and managerial interactions are complex, and matching the appropriate structure to these factors to achieve strategic performance outcomes is not an easy task.

Organizational design remains an important issue in the management of organizational behavior and effectiveness. As we approach the 21st century, organizational design will become even more important. As is apparent, strategies

[36]Ibid, p. 354.

INTERNATIONAL

E N C O U N T E R • 11-3

ARE IDEAL ORGANIZATIONAL DESIGN NORMS UNIVERSAL?

How different or similar are organizational design norms across different nations? Data from executives in three very different countries suggest that while there are some differences, there are also a number of similarities. Managers from three distinct national environments were surveyed: People's Republic of China, Hong Kong, and Canada. While Hong Kong and Canada both represent varying degrees of a market economy, China is a planned economy with tight social and economic controls. One of the main questions addressed in the study was the extent to which ideal organizational design considerations are subject to a process of globalization. Globalization is a convergence process through which cross-cultural and national differences are reduced.

Six different factors relating to organizational design considerations were identified: (1) Participation, which related to the extent organizations should be designed to facilitate consultation and participation; (2) Formal organization, relating to the degree of formality in operating procedures, authority structure, and evaluation and control systems; (3) Strategic adaptiveness, which defined technical characteristics of organizations relating to flexibility, efficiency, and adaptability; (4) Democratic organization, which related to the existence of democratic values in organizations; (5) Internal competition and risk taking, which focused on competition for internal promotions and encouragement of risk taking; and (6) Centralization, relating to authority structure.

To a great extent globalization had occurred. There were no real differences in organizational design variables between the three countries as they related to factors of strategic adaptiveness, democratic organization, and centralization. Only minor differences showed up with respect to participation, with China placing a slightly higher value on organization designs to encourage worker participation than Hong Kong and Canada. Somewhat larger differences existed with respect to formal structure, where China and Hong Kong managers indicated preferences for a higher degree of formal structure than managers from Canada. Significant differences also were found on the internal competition and risk taking factor, where Canada and Hong Kong were more desirous of designs to encourage these characteristics than was the People's Republic of China.

Although these findings indicate that total globalization has not occurred, they strongly suggest that, in these three disparate cultures at least, it is well on its way.

Source: I. Vertinsky, D. K. Tse, D. A. Wehrung, and K. Lee, "Organizational Design and Management Norms: A Comparative Study of Managers' Perceptions in the People's Republic of China, Hong Kong, and Canada," *Journal of Management,* December 1990, pp. 853–67.

which have been successful in the past will prove ineffectual in the face of the new international competition, technological change, and the shifting patterns of industrial development. As organizations experiment with new strategies, they will be forced to experiment with new configurations, such as triangular design.[37] These designs will bear closer resemblance to organic than to mechanistic designs.

[37]R. W. Keidel, "Triangular Design: A New Organizational Geometry," *Academy of Management Executive,* November 1990, pp. 21–37.

Organizations of the future are likely to be flatter, less hierarchical and more decentralized.[38]

● **R11-1**   Tom Peters' article "Restoring American Competitiveness: Looking at New Models of Organizations," which accompanies this chapter, makes a strong case for the argument that organization structure has a lot to do with organization performance. In fact, he states that American organizations have no choice but to move away from the mechanistic design model.

Organizational structures differ on many dimensions. Regardless of the specific configuration of the parts, however, the overriding purpose of organizational structures is to channel the behavior of individuals and groups into patterns which contribute to organizational performance. An extremely important factor in organizational structures is the jobs of individuals who comprise the organization. The topic of job design and its effects on performance and quality of work life are explored in the following chapter.

SUMMARY OF KEY POINTS

- Four key managerial decisions determine organization structures. These decisions are concerned with dividing the work, delegating authority, departmentalizing jobs into groups, and determining spans of control.

- The term division of labor concerns the extent to which jobs are specialized. Dividing the overall task of the organization into smaller related tasks provide the technical and economic advantages found in specialization of labor.

- Delegating authority enables an individual to make decisions and extract obedience without approval by higher management. Like other organizing issues, delegated authority is a relative, not absolute concept. All individuals in an organization have some authority. The question is whether they have enough to do their jobs.

- There are several forms, or bases, of departmentalization. *Functional* groups jobs by the function performed, i.e. marketing, production, accounting. *Territorial* groups on the basis of geographical location. *Product* groups on the basis of the department's output. *Customer* groups on the basis of the users of the good or service provided.

- Span of control relates to the decision regarding how many people a manager can oversee. It is an important variable because managerial effectiveness can be compromised if spans of control are too large. Additionally, span of control affects the number of levels in an organization; the wider the span, the fewer the levels.

- Three important dimensions of structure are formalization, centralization, and complexity. Formalization refers to the extent to which policies, rules, and procedures exist in written form; centralization refers to the extent to which authority is retained in the jobs of top management; and complexity refers to the extent to which the jobs in the organization are relatively specialized.

- Two important organizational design models are termed *mechanistic* and *organic*. Mechanistic design is characterized by highly specialized jobs, homogeneous departments, narrow spans of control, and relatively centralized authority. Organic designs, on the other hand, include relatively despecialized jobs, heterogeneous departments, wide spans of control, and decentralized authority.

[38]P. F. Drucker, "The Coming of the New Organization," *Harvard Business Review,* January-February 1988, pp. 45–53.

- Matrix designs offer a number of potential advantages. These include efficient use of resources, flexibility in conditions of change and uncertainty, technical excellence, freeing top management for long-range planning, improving motivation and commitment, and providing good opportunities for personal development.

- It is important to be particularly attentive to structure and design considerations in multinational organizations. Differences in the social, political, culture, legal, and economic environments of countries hosting subsidiaries of domestic organizations can dictate the need for different answers to design questions.

REVIEW AND DISCUSSION QUESTIONS

1. What choices must be made by management when designing an organization structure?

2. "The more authority that is delegated to nonmanagers, the less authority managers have." Is this necessarily a true statement? Explain.

3. What are the most common bases for departmentalization? On what basis is a university typically organized? What other type of departmentalization might you suggest for a university?

4. What are some of the factors which may have important implications for structure and design decisions in multinational corporations?

5. Characterize the following organizations on the basis of their degree of formalization, centralization, and complexity: The university you are attending, the federal government, and a local branch of a national fast-food franchise.

6. Can you think of a particular company or type of industry that tends toward a mechanistic design? What advantages and disadvantages could you see if that organization or industry adopted a more organic form?

7. What is the difference between organizational structure and design?

8. What cues might a manager have that suggest a problem with the design of an organization? Is changing an existing organization a different task from designing a brand new structure? Explain.

9. Changes in organizational size affect structure. In what ways might growth (increasing size) affect an organization's structure? In what ways might decreasing size affect structure?

10. What are some of the potential advantages of a matrix design? What are some of the potential problems of the dual authority concept of such designs?

●

READING

READING 11–1   **RESTORING AMERICAN COMPETITIVENESS: LOOKING FOR NEW MODELS OF ORGANIZATIONS**

Tom Peters
The Tom Peters Group

Every day brings new reports of lousy American product or service quality, vis-à-vis our foremost overseas competitors. The news of buyers rejecting our products pours in from Des Moines; Miami; Santa Clara County, California; Budapest; Zurich; and even Beijing. Industry after industry is under attack—old manufacturers and new, as well as the great hope of the future, the service industry. Change on an unimagined scale is a must, and islands of good news—those responding with alacrity—are available for our inspection. But it is becoming increasingly clear that the response is not coming fast enough. For instance, even the near-freefall of the dollar does not seem to be enough to make our exports attractive or reduce our passion for others' imports.

"Competitiveness is a microeconomic issue," the chairman of Toyota Motors stated recently. By and large, I agree. There are things that Washington, Bonn, Tokyo, Sacramento, Harrisburg, and Albany can do to help. But most of the answers lie within—that is, within the heads and hearts of our own managers.

NEEDED: NEW MODELS

If we are to respond to wildly altered business and economic circumstances, we need entirely new ways of thinking about organizations. The familiar "military model"—the hierarchical, or "charts and boxes" structure—is not bearing up. It is a structure designed for more placid settings, and derived in times when you knew who the enemy was (not today's nameless or faceless Libyan terrorists or religious fanatics led by an old man in Teheran), and had time to prepare a response to your problems. (It took us Americans several years to gear up to win World War II— a luxury we can no longer afford in this era of nuclear capability.)

Likewise, peacetime economic wars of yore were marked

by near certainty. Americans brought cheap energy to the fray, and were blessed by a vast "free trade" market at home. And for the first six decades of this century, we knew who our competitors were—a few big, domestic concerns. We knew where their leaders went to school, what cereals they ate for breakfast. Today, almost every U.S. industry has its competitors, from low-cost Malaysia to high-cost Switzerland, topped off by scores of tiny domestic competitors. Every industry now has—and keeps getting—new, unknown competitors. Moreover, the reality of exchange rates, interest rates, rates of inflation, prices of energy, and the ever-reconfigured microprocessor means that all of everything is up for grabs, unknown, constantly gyrating.

But remember that the American colonists broke away from their British masters in a war that featured the use of guerilla tactics. Popular mythology has it that the British insisted on lining up in rigid, straight-line formations to do battle, sporting bright red coats. By contrast, Ethan Allen and his fabled Green Mountain Boys eschewed formations, hid behind trees, and used their skill as crack shots while victoriously scampering through icy woods of the Hampshire Grants (now Vermont). Perhaps we again need organizations that evince the spunk and agility of the Green Mountain Boys rather than the formality of the British—a formality that was out of touch, then, with the new competitive reality in 18th century colonial wars and is out of touch, now, with the reality of the new economic wars.

Pictures, so it is said, are worth a thousand words. I believe that, and this article is devoted to describing two pictures, or "organizational maps." Neither looks much like a traditional organization chart; there is no square box at the top labeled "Chairman" (or "Vice Chairman," or "Chief Executive Officer," or "President," and so on). Both charts break tradition in that they include customers, suppliers, distributors, and franchisees. The layouts are circular, moving from customers in toward the corporate chieftains at the circle's center. But beyond the circular scheme, the two bear little resemblance to one another.

EXHIBIT 11-5

The Inflexible, Rule-Determined, Mass Producer of the Past: All Persons Know Their Place

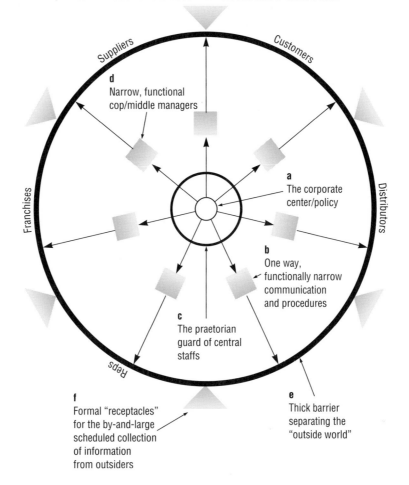

THE INFLEXIBLE, RULE-DETERMINED, MASS PRODUCER OF THE PAST

Let's begin with an assessment of Exhibit 11-5. Start with *a*, the corporate center/policy. This is the traditional, invisible, impersonal, generally out-of-touch corporate hub. The tininess of the circle representing the corporate center suggests both tightness and narrowness of scope; communications to the outside world (in or beyond the firm's official boundary) is usually via formal declaration—the policy manual or the multivolume plan, by and large determined on high—and communicated via the chain of command (i.e., downward). Within this tiny circle lie the "brains of the organization." It is here, almost exclusively,

that the long-term thinking, planning, and peering into the future take place.

Move on to *b*—one-way, functionally narrow communication via rules and procedures. Most communication in this generic organization type is highly channeled (hence the straight line) and top-down (note the direction of the arrowheads). So, communication and "control" are principally via rulebook, procedure manual, union contract, or the endless flow of memos providing guidance and demanding an endless stream of microinformation from the line. Moreover, the communication rarely "wobbles" around the circle (look at Exhibit 11-6 for a dramatic contrast); that is, the lion's share of the communicating is restricted to the narrow functional specialty (operations, engineering,

EXHIBIT 11-6

The Flexible, Porous, Adaptive, Fleet-of-Foot Organization of the Future: Every Person is "Paid" to be Obstreperous, a Disrespecter of Formal Boundaries, to Hustle and to Be Engaged Fully with Engendering Swift Action, Constantly Improving Everything

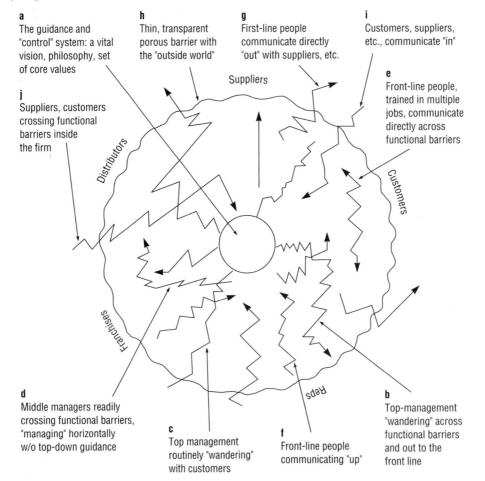

a The guidance and "control" system: a vital vision, philosophy, set of core values

j Suppliers, customers crossing functional barriers inside the firm

h Thin, transparent porous barrier with the "outside world"

g First-line people communicate directly "out" with suppliers, etc.

i Customers, suppliers, etc., communicate "in"

e Front-line people, trained in multiple jobs, communicate directly across functional barriers

Suppliers

Distributors

Customers

Franchises

Reps

d Middle managers readily crossing functional barriers, "managing" horizontally w/o top-down guidance

c Top management routinely "wandering" with customers

f Front-line people communicating "up"

b Top-management "wandering" across functional barriers and out to the front line

marketing, etc.), more or less represented by the individual arrows.

Then comes *c*, the praetorian guard of central corporate staffs. The corporate center is tightly protected (note the thick line) by a phalanx of brilliant, MBA-trained, virgin (no line-operating experience), analysis-driven staffs. If the isolation of the corporate chieftains in their plush-carpeted executive suites were not enough, this group seals them off once and for all. It masticates any input from below (i.e., the field) into 14-color, desk-top-published graphics, with all the blood, sweat, tears, and frustrated customer

feedback drained therefrom. On those occasions when the senior team attempts to reach out directly, the staff is as good at cutting its superiors off ("Don't bother, we'll do a study of that marketplace—no need to visit") as it is at cutting off unexpurgated flow from below to the chief and his or her most senior cohorts.

Next, per *d*, are the functionally narrow cop/middle managers. My graphic description is a lumpy (substantial) square, located in the midst of the linear communication flow between the top and the bottom (the bottom, as in last and least—the first line of supervision and the front line). The middle manager, as his or her role is traditionally conceived, sits directly athwart the virtually sole communication channel between the top and the bottom. He or she is, first and foremost, the guardian of functional turf and prerogatives and the *next* block in the communication channel—remember that the praetorian guard was substantial block #1. The "cop" notion is meant to be represented by both the solidity of the block and its direct positioning in the downward communication flow. The middle manager is a filter of data, coming both from the bottom (infrequently) and from the top (much more frequently). The middle manager's job, as depicted here, is seen as vertically oriented (largely confined to the function in question and to passing things up and down) rather than horizontally oriented.

A thick, opaque barrier—*e*—marks the transition from the firm to the outside world of suppliers, customers, distributors, franchisees, reps, and so on. The barrier is very impermeable. Communication, especially informal communication, does not flow readily across it, either from the customer "in" or from the front line of the organization "out."

Which leads directly to the idea of *f*—formal "receptacles" from the scheduled collection of information from outsiders. Of course the old, inflexible organization does communicate with the outside world. But the communication tends to be formal, coming mainly from market research or from orderly interaction via salespeople. Both the timing and the format of the communication is predetermined. Even competitive analysis is rigid, hierarchical, and focused—a formal competitive analysis unit that audits known competitors, mainly on a scheduled basis.

These six attributes are hardly an exhaustive examination of the old-style organization, but they do capture many of its outstanding attributes and orientations—static, formal, top-down oriented, and rule-and-policy determined. It is orderly to a fault (a dandy trait in a different world). To be sure, this depiction is stylized and therefore somewhat unfair, but my observations argue that it captures a frightening amount of the truth in today's larger organizations.

THE FLEXIBLE, POROUS, ADAPTIVE, FLEET-OF-FOOT ORGANIZATION OF THE FUTURE

It takes but a glance to appreciate the radically different nature of Exhibit 11-6—it's a mess! So, welcome to the real world in today's more innovative businesses: start-ups, mid-size firms, and the slimmed-down business units of bigger firms. To the world of The Limited, Benetton, or the Gap in retailing. To the world of Compaq, Sun Microsystems, or the ASIC divisions of Intel or Motorola in computer systems. To the world of steelmakers Worthington Industries, Chaparral, and Nucor. To the world of Weaver Popcorn, Johnsonville Sausage, Neutrogena, ServiceMaster, and University National Bank & Trust of Palo Alto, California. To the world of somewhat ordered chaos, somewhat purposeful confusion; the world, above all, of flexibility, adaptiveness, and action. Or to a new world violently turned upside down.

Begin with *a*—the new-look corporate guidance system, a vital vision, philosophy, set of core values, and an out-and-about senior management team (see *b* and *c*). First, the innermost circle depicting the corporate center in Exhibit 11-6 is obviously bigger than its counterpart in Exhibit 11-5. My point is frightfully difficult to describe. I pictured the traditional corporate center in Exhibit 11-5 as out of touch, shrivelled, formalistic, and ruled by very tight policy and a constraining rather than opportunistic plan, with contacts inside and outside the enterprise conveyed in written format, usually via brisk, impatient, and bloodless staffers (the praetorian guard). But the visual image that comes to mind for the center of Exhibit 11-6 is of a glowing, healthy, breathing corporate center. People from below regularly wander in without muss or fuss, and those at the top are more often than not out wandering. Customers and suppliers are as likely to be members of the executive floor (which, happily, doesn't really exist as a physical entity) as are the members of the senior team. But above all, the glow comes from management's availability, informality, energy, hustle, and the clarity of (and excitement associated with) the competitive vision, philosophy, or core values. Rule here is not written, but by example, by role model, by spirited behavior, and by fun—the vigorous pursuit of a worthwhile competitive idea, whether the firm is a bank, local insurance agency, or superconductor outfit.

Next, as previously anticipated, comes *b*—top management "wandering" across functional barriers and out to the front line in the firm. First, all the communication lines in Exhibit 11-6 are portrayed as zigzagging and wavy, with reason: To be as flexible and adaptive as required by tomorrow's competitive situation demands the wholesale smashing of traditional barriers and functional walls, both up and down and from side to side. So, this particular wavy line not only depicts the chief and his or her senior cohorts wandering about, but it shows them purposefully disrespecting those functional spokes (in fact, there are no formal functional spokes in this organization chart). And, of course, the even more significant point is that the chiefs' (and their lieutenants') wandering regularly takes them to where the action is—at the front line, in the distribution center at 2 A.M., at the reservation center, at the night clerk's desk, in the factory, in the lab, or on the operations center floor.

Top management's "somewhat aimless ambling," as I like to call it, is not just restricted to the inside portion of the chart. Therefore, *c* depicts top management "wandering" with customers. Of course, the primary point is that top management is out and about—hanging out in the dealerships, with suppliers, and in general with customers, both big and small. But, again, the waviness of the line suggests a clarification; that is, the senior management visit here is not restricted to the stilted, formal, "visit a customer a day" sort of affairs that mark all too many traditional top-management teams. Instead, it is the semi-unplanned visit; the drop-in to the dealer, supplier, or customer; or the largely unscheduled "ride around" with a salesperson on his or her normal, daily route.

As important as any of the contrasts between Exhibits 11-5 and 11-6 is *d*—middle managers routinely crossing functional barriers and managing horizontally without specific top-down guidance. Moving fast to implement anything, particularly engaging in fast-paced new product and service development, demands much faster, much less formal, and much less defensive communication across traditional organization boundaries. Thus, the chief role for the middle manager of the future (albeit much fewer in number than in today's characteristically bloated middle-management ranks) is horizontal management rather than vertical management. The latter, as suggested in Exhibit 11-5, principally involves guarding the sanctity of the functional turf, providing any number of written reasons why function *x* is already overburdened and can't help function *y* at this particular juncture. In the new arrangement, the middle manager is paid proactively to grease skids between functions; that is, to be out of the office working with other functions to accomplish, not block, swift action taking. Once more, the zigzag nature of the line is meant to illustrate an essential point: Communication *across* functional barriers should be natural, informal, proactive, and helpful, not defensive and not preceded by infinite checking with the next layer(s) of management.

Perhaps the biggest difference involves *e*—frontline people, trained in multiple jobs, also routinely communicating across previously impenetrable functional barriers. The frontline person in Exhibit 11-5 has not only been cut off

from the rest of the world by the button-down chieftains, praetorian guards, and turf-guarding middle managers, but also by a lack of training and cross-training, a history of not being listened to, and a last layer of cop—an old-school, Simon Legree, first-line supervisor. The role of the new-look frontline person sets all this on its ear. First, he or she is "controlled" not by a supervisor, middle management, or procedure book, but rather by the clarity and excitement of the vision, its daily embodiment by wandering senior managers, an extraordinary level of training, the obvious respect she or he is given, and the self-discipline that almost automatically accompanies exceptional grants of autonomy.

Not only is the frontline person encouraged to learn numerous jobs within the context of the work team, but she or he is also encouraged, at the frontline, to cross functional boundaries. Only regular frontline boundary crossing, in a virtually uninhibited fashion, will bring forth the pace of action necessary for survival today. More formally, in the new regime you would expect to see frontline people as members of quality or productivity improvement teams that involve four or five functions. Informally, you would routinely observe the frontline person talking with the purchasing officer, a quality expert, or an industrial engineer (who she or he called in for advice, not vice versa) or simply chatting with members of the team 75 feet down the line—always at work on improvement projects that disdain old divisions of labor/task.

Move on to *f* and *g*, which take this frontline person two nontraditional steps further. First, *f*—frontline people communicating "up." The key to unlocking extraordinary productivity and quality improvements lies within the heads of the persons who live with the task, the persons on the firing line. Thus, in the new-look organization it becomes *more* commonplace for the frontline person to be communicating up, perhaps even two or three levels of management up (and one prays that there are no more than that in total) or all the way to the top on occasion.

And then—virtually unheard of outside sales and service departments today—the "average" person, per *g*, will routinely be out and about; that is, frontline people communicating directly with suppliers, customers, etc. Who is the person who best knows the problem with defective supplier material? Obviously, it's the frontline person who lives with it eight hours a day. With a little bit of advice and counsel from team members, and perhaps some occasional help from a middle manager (and following a bunch of perpetual training), who is the best person to visit the supplier—yes, take on a multiday visit that includes discussions with senior supplier management? Answer: It's again obvious—the front-line person or persons who suffer daily at the scene of the supplier's crime.

Now let's turn to the boundary, *h*—a thin, transparent permeable barrier to the outside world. This is yet another extraordinary distinction between the old-look and the new-look outfit. Recall Exhibit 11-5: The external barrier was thick, impermeable, and penetrated only at formal "receptacles." The new barrier is thin and wavy. Both the thinness and the imprecision are meant to suggest that there will be regular movement across it, in both directions. Frontline people, and senior people without prior notification, will be heading out with only semiplanned routines. Likewise, "external" colleagues will be regularly hanging out inside the firm (see *i* and *j* below). To be sure, the firm does exist as a legal entity: It is incorporated, and people are on its payroll. But more than any other factor, the idea of the firm turned inside out—the tough, recalcitrant hide that separates it from "them" (customers, suppliers, etc.) ripped off—is the image I'm trying to convey. NIH (not invented here) is no longer tolerable. The firm must be permeable to (that is, listen to with ease and respect and act upon) ideas from competitors, both small and large, foreign and domestic; from interesting noncompetitors; from suppliers, customers, franchisees, reps, dealers, frontline people, and suppliers' frontline persons; and from joint venture partners. It must become virtually impossible to put one's finger on the outside organization boundary. Flow to and fro, by virtually everyone, all the time, and largely informally (i.e., leading to fast improvement without muss, fuss, and memos) must become the norm.

Next we move to *i*—customers, suppliers, etc., communicating (talking, hanging out, and participating) "in." The movement from adversarial to new nonadversarial/partnership relations with outsiders of all stripes is one of the biggest shifts required of American firms. Right now, the big (or small) business organization is typically the site of unabated warfare: top management versus lower management, management versus the union, function versus function, and—relative to outsiders—company versus customers, company versus franchisees, company versus dealers and, above all, company versus suppliers. This must stop—period. Cleaning out the bulk of the distracting praetorian guard and middle management will obviously help, but achieving an attitude of partnership is at the top of the list of requirements, truly "living" a permeable organizational barrier. Customers and suppliers (and their people at all levels) must be part of any new product or service design teams. Even more routinely, customers, suppliers,

franchisees, and reps ought to be part of day-to-day productivity and quality improvement teams. Once again, to compete today means to improve constantly, to invest fast; stripping away the impermeable barriers is the sine qua non of speedy implementation.

Which leads directly to *i*—suppliers, customers, etc., crossing functional barriers to work, and help, inside the firm. The idea of *i* was fine and dandy, but not enough. Customers shouldn't just be in the firm; they must be part of its most strategic internal dealings. The supplier shouldn't be shunted off to the purchasing person. Rather, he should be working with cost accountants, factory or operations center people, marketing teams, and new product and service design teams. Moreover, the wavy line suggests that the communication will be informal, not stilted.

There is no doubt that Exhibit 11-6, taken as a whole, appears anarchic. To a large extent, this must be so. To move faster in the face of radical uncertainty (competitors; energy, money, and currency costs; revolutionary technologies; and world instability) means that more chaos, more anarchy is required.[1] But that is only half the story. Return to Exhibit 11-6, idea *a*—the corporate guidance system in the new-look firm. Recall my halting effort to describe it as a glowing sun, an energy center. In fact, the control in Exhibit 11-6 may be much tighter than in the traditional Exhibit 11-5 organization. Instead of a bunch of stilted, formalistic baloney and out-of-reach leaders, the new control as noted is the energy, excitement, spirit, hustle, and clarity of the competitive vision that emanates from the corporate center. So when the newly empowered frontline person goes out to experiment—for example, to work with a supplier or with a multifunction team on quality or productivity improvement—she or he is, in fact, *tightly* controlled or guided by the attitudes, beliefs, energy, spirit, and so on, of the vital competitive vision. Moreover, that frontline person is extraordinarily well trained, unlike in the past, and remarkably well informed (for example, almost no performance information is kept secret from him or her). So, it's not at all a matter of tossing people out into a supplier's operation and saying. "We gotta be partners, now." The frontline person "out there" is someone who has seen senior management face to face (and smelled their enthusiasm); a person who has served on numerous multifunction teams; a person whose learning and training is continuous; a person who has just seen last month's divisional P&L in all its gory (or glorious) detail, following a year-long accounting course for all frontline "hands." Thus, there can be an astonishingly high degree of controlled flexibility and informality, starting with the front-line and outsiders, in our new-look (Exhibit 11-6) organization. But there is also an astonishing amount of hard work required—perpetually clarifying the vision, living the vision, wandering, chatting, listening, *and* providing extraordinary and continuous training, for example—that must precede and/or accompany all this. So, perhaps "purposeful chaos," or something closely akin, is the best description of the Exhibit 11-6/new-look firm.

The ultimate point that underlies this brief contrast between and description of the two models is the non-optional nature of the Exhibit 11-6 approach. Americans are getting kicked, battered, and whacked about in industry after industry. We must change, and change fast. The two charts discussed here are radically different, and although I'm not sure that Exhibit 11-6 is entirely "correct,"

I am sure that the radical difference between the two is spot on.

NOTE

1. See R. C. Conant and R. W. Ashby, "Every Good Regulator of a System Must Be a Model of that System," *International Journal of Systems Science* 1, no. 2 (1970), pp. 89–97. There is a compelling theoretical as well as pragmatic basis for the idea. In 1970, Conant and Ashby posited the Law of Requisite Variety, which has become the cornerstone of information theory. In layman's terms, it means that you have to be as messy as the surrounding situation. In a volatile world, we must have more sensors, processing information faster and leading to faster (and by definition more informal) action taking.

■

EXERCISES

EXERCISE 11–1   PAPER PLANE CORPORATION

OBJECTIVES

1. To illustrate how division of labor can be efficiently structured.
2. To illustrate how a competitive atmosphere can be created among groups.

STARTING THE EXERCISE

Unlimited groups of six participants each are used in this exercise. These groups may be directed simultaneously in the same room. Approximately a full class period is needed to complete the exercise. Each person should have assembly instructions and a summary sheet, which are shown on the following pages, and ample stacks of paper ($8\frac{1}{2}$ by 11 inches). The physical setting should be a room large enough so that the individual groups of six can work without interference from the other groups. A working space should be provided for each group.

- The participants are doing an exercise in production methodology.

Source: Louis Potheni in Fred Luthans, *Organizational Behavior* (New York: McGraw-Hill, 1985), p. 655.

- Each group must work independently of the other groups.
- Each group will choose a manager and an inspector, and the remaining participants will be employees.
- The objective is to make paper airplanes in the most profitable manner possible.
- The facilitator will give the signal to start. This is a 10-minute, timed event utilizing competition among the groups.
- After the first round, everyone should report their production and profits to the entire group. They also should note the effect, if any, of the manager in terms of the performance of the group.
- This same procedure is followed for as many rounds as there is time.

PAPER PLANE CORPORATION: DATA SHEET

Your group is the complete work force for Paper Plane Corporation. Established in 1943, Paper Plane has led the market in paper plane production. Presently under new management, the company is contracting to make aircraft for the U.S. Air Force. You must establish an efficient production plant to produce these aircraft. You must make your contract with the Air Force under the following conditions:

1. The Air Force will pay $20,000 per airplane.
2. The aircraft must pass a strict inspection made by the facilitator.
3. A penalty of $25,000 per airplane will be subtracted for failure to meet the production requirements.

4. Labor and other overhead will be computed at $300,000.
5. Cost of materials will be $3,000 per bid plane. If you bid for 10 but only make 8, you must pay the cost of materials for those you failed to make or which did not pass inspection.

Summary sheet

Round 1:
Bid: _____ Aircraft @ $20,000.00 per aircraft = _____
Results: _____ Aircraft @ $20,000.00 per aircraft = _____
Less: $300,000.00 overhead _____ × $3,000 cost of raw materials _____ × $25,000 penalty
Profit: _____

Round 2:
Bid: _____ Aircraft @ $20,000.00 per aircraft = _____
Results: _____ Aircraft @ $20,000.00 per aircraft = _____
Less: $300,000.00 overhead _____ × $3,000 cost of raw materials _____ × $25,000 penalty
Profit: _____

Round 3:
Bid: _____ Aircraft @ $20,000.00 per aircraft = _____
Results: _____ Aircraft @ $20,000.00 per aircraft = _____
Less: $300,000.00 overhead _____ × $3,000 cost of raw materials _____ × $25,000 penalty
Profit: _____

Step 1: Take a sheet of paper and fold it in half, then open it back up.

Step 2: Fold upper corners to the middle

Step 3: Fold the corners to the middle again.

Step 4: Fold in half.

Step 5: Fold both wings down.

Step 6: Fold tail fins up.

Completed aircraft

EXERCISE 11–2   DESIGNING ORGANIZATIONS TO COMPETE

OBJECTIVES

1. To design and operate an organization under conditions of competition.
2. To compare production and quality outputs under different organization structures.

STARTING THE EXERCISE

The class is divided into groups of five or six students. Approximately one and one-half hour is needed to complete the exercise. The room should be large enough so that each group can work without disturbing the other groups. The groups work independently of one another. After the groups are formed, the exercise begins with Step 1.

INTRODUCTION

In this exercise you will form a "miniorganization" with several other people. You will be competing with other companies in your industry.

Step 1: 10 minutes

Read the directions below and ask the instructor about any points that need clarification. Everyone should be familiar with the task before beginning Step 2.

DIRECTIONS

You are a small company that manufactures words and then packages them in meaningful (English language) sentences. Market research has established that sentences of at least three words but not more than six words each are in demand.

The "words-in-sentences" (WIS) industry is highly competitive; several new firms have recently entered what appears to be an expanding market. Since raw materials, technology, and pricing are all standard for the industry,

Source: Douglas T. Hall, Donald D. Bowen, Roy J. Lewicki, and Francine S. Hall, *Experiences in Management and Organizational Behavior*, 2nd ed. (New York: John Wiley & Sons, 1982), pp. 238–42.

your ability to compete depends on two factors: (1) volume and (2) quality.

Group Task   Your group must design and participate in running a WIS company. You should design your organization to be as effective as possible during each 10-minute production run. After the first production run, you will have an opportunity to reorganize your company if you want to.

Raw Materials   For each production run you will be given a raw material word or phrase. The letters found in the word or phrase serve as the raw materials available to produce new words in sentences. For example, if the raw material word is *organization,* you could produce the words and sentence: "Nat ran to a zoo."

Production Standards   There are several rules that have to be followed in producing words-in-sentences. If these rules are not followed, your output will not meet production specifications and will not pass quality-control inspection.

1. The same letter may appear only as often in a manufactured word as it appears in the raw material word or phrase; for example, "organization" has two *o*'s. Thus, "zoo" is legitimate, but "zoonosis" is not. It has too many *o*'s and *s*'s.
2. Raw material letters can be used again in different manufactured words.
3. A manufactured word may be used only once in a sentence and in only one sentence during a production run; if a word—for example, *a*—is used once in a sentence, it is out of stock.
4. A new word may not be made by adding *s* to form the plural of an already used manufactured word.
5. A word is defined by its spelling, not its meaning.
6. Nonsense words or nonsense sentences are unacceptable.
7. All words must be in the English language.
8. Names and places are acceptable.
9. Slang is not acceptable.

Measuring Performance   The output of your WIS company is measured by the total number of acceptable words that are packaged in sentences. The sentences must be legible, listed on no more than two sheets of paper, and handed to the Quality Control Review Board at the completion of each production run.

Delivery Delivery must be made to the Quality Control Review Board 30 seconds after the end of each production run.

Quality Control If any word or sentence does not meet the standards set forth above, *all* the words in the sentence will be rejected. The Quality Control Review Board (composed of one member of each company) is the final arbiter of acceptability. In the event of a tie vote on the Review Board, a coin toss will determine the outcome.

STEP 2: 15 minutes

Design your organizations to produce your words-in-sentences. There are many potential ways of organizing. Since some are more effective than others, you may want to consider the following:

1. What is your company's objective?
2. How will you achieve your objective? How should you plan your work, given the time allowed?
3. What division of labor, authority, and responsibility is most appropriate, given your objective, your task, and the technology?
4. Which group members are most qualified to perform certain tasks?

Assign one member of your group to serve on the Quality Control Review Board. This person may also participate in production runs.

STEP 3: 10 minutes—Production Run 1

1. The instructor will hand each WIS company a sheet with a raw material word or phrase.
2. When the instructor announces "Begin production," you are to manufacture as many words as possible and package them in sentences for delivery to the Quality Control Review Board. You will have 10 minutes.
3. When the instructor announces "Stop production," you will have 30 seconds to deliver your output to the Quality Control Review Board. Output received after 30 seconds does not meet the delivery schedule and will not be counted.

STEP 4: 10 minutes

1. The designated members from the companies of the Quality Control Review Board review output from each company. The total output should be recorded (after quality control approval).
2. While the board is completing its task, each WIS company should discuss what happened during Production Run 1.

STEP 5: 10 minutes

Each company should evaluate its performance and organization. Companies may reorganize for Run 2.

STEP 6: 10 minutes—Production Run 2.

1. The instructor will hand each WIS company a sheet with a raw material word or phrase.
2. Proceed as in Step 3. You will have 10 minutes for production.

STEP 7: 10 minutes

1. The Quality Control Review Board will review and record each company's output. The total for Runs 1 and 2 will be tallied.
2. While the board is completing its task, each WIS company should prepare an organization chart depicting its structure for both production runs.

STEP 8: 10 minutes

Discuss this exercise as a total group.

EXERCISE 11–3   ASSESSING ORGANIZATIONAL DIMENSIONS—MECHANISTIC/ORGANIC

The following assessment allows you to identify the extent to which an organization has organic-mechanistic char-

Source: Marshall Sashkin and William C. Morris, *Organizational Behavior* (Reston, Va.: Reston Publishing, 1984), pp. 360–61.

acteristics. Think of an organization that you work or have worked for and describe it using the following 10 items. You can then use the scoring key to locate the organization on the organic-mechanistic continuum.

Instructions: Describe the extent to which each of the following 10 statements is true of or accurately characterizes the organization in question.

	To a very great extent	To a considerable extent	To a moderate extent	To a slight extent	To almost no extent
1. This organization has clear rules and regulations that everyone is expected to follow closely.	☐	☐	☐	☐	☐
2. Polices in this organization are reviewed by the people they affect before being implemented.	☐	☐	☐	☐	☐
3. In this organization a major concern is that everyone be allowed to develop their talents and abilities.	☐	☐	☐	☐	☐
4. Everyone in this organization knows who their immediate supervisor is; reporting relationships are clearly defined.	☐	☐	☐	☐	☐
5. Jobs in this organization are clearly defined; everyone knows exactly what is expected of a person in any specific job position.	☐	☐	☐	☐	☐
6. Works groups are typically temporary and change often in this organization.	☐	☐	☐	☐	☐
7. All decisions in this organization must be reviewed and approved by upper level management.	☐	☐	☐	☐	☐
8. In this organization the emphasis is on adapting effectively to constant environmental change.	☐	☐	☐	☐	☐
9. Jobs in this organization are usually broken down into highly specialized, smaller tasks.	☐	☐	☐	☐	☐
10. Standard activities in this organization are always covered by clearly outlined procedures that define the sequence of actions that everyone is expected to follow.	☐	☐	☐	☐	☐

Scoring

On the scoring grid, circle the numbers that correspond to your response to each of the 10 questions. Enter the numbers in the boxes then add up all the numbers in boxes. This is your ORG MECH Score.

	Q1	Q2	Q3	Q4	Q5	Q6	Q7	Q8	Q9	Q10
Great	5	5	1	5	5	1	5	1	5	5
Considerable	4	4	2	4	4	2	4	2	4	4
Moderate	3	3	3	3	3	3	3	3	3	3
Slight	2	2	4	2	2	4	2	4	2	2
No	1	1	5	1	1	5	1	5	1	1
	☐	☐	☐	☐	☐	☐	☐	☐	☐	☐

Total Score ☐

Interpretation

High scores indicate high degrees of mechanistic/bureaucratic organizational characteristics. Low scores are associated with adaptive/organic organizational characteristics.

```
    10            20            30            40            50
  Highly                      Mixed                     Highly
  Organic                                             Mechanistic
```

▲

CASE

CASE 11–1   EAGLE AIRLINES

Eagle Airlines was a medium-sized regional airline serving the southwest quarter of the United States. The company had been growing rapidly in the last 15 years, partially as a result of dynamic company activity but also as a result of the rapid economic growth of the area which it served.

The most outstanding of the areas was Bartlett City. Bartlett City's growth since the middle 1940s had rested on two primary developments. One was the very rapid growth of manufacturing and research establishments concerned with defense work. Some firms located here at the urging of government agencies to build new defense plants and laboratories away from coastal areas. Others moved to this location because of the attractive climate and scenery, which was considered an advantage in attracting technicians, engineers, and scientists for work on advanced military projects. Once some plants and research laboratories were developed, smaller, independent firms sprang up in the community for the purpose of servicing and supplying those which were established first. These developments encouraged the rapid growth of local construction and the opening of numerous attractive housing developments. The second basis for growth was the completion, also in the 1940s, of a major irrigation project that opened a large area for intensive cultivation.

Source: Prepared by Joseph A. Litterer. Used by permission.

While the economy of Bartlett City had grown rapidly, it was in many ways tied to coastal areas, where parent firms or home offices of many of the local establishments existed. Also, since many of its industries serviced the national defense effort, they consequently had to be closely connected with matters decided on in Washington or other places distant from Bartlett City. Finally, it had many strong financial and business ties with major coastal cities, such as San Francisco and Los Angeles. As a result, executives, engineers, and scientists in Bartlett City industries were frequently in contact with the major business, political, and scientific centers of the country, particularly those on the West Coast. In making a trip, for example, to Los Angeles from Bartlett City, one was faced with using one of three alternative modes of travel: auto, private corporate jet, or commercial jet flight. Eagle Airlines had the sole route between Bartlett City and Los Angeles, which was found to be a most lucrative run and to which it gave a great deal of attention.

COMPANY MANAGEMENT

The rapid growth of Eagle Airlines was held by many to be in no small degree a result of the skill of its management. It should be pointed out that its top management had been particularly skillful in obtaining and defending its route structure and had been particularly successful in financing, at advantageous terms, the acquisition of modern aircraft, particularly jet-powered airplanes. Top management emphasized "decentralization," in which the lower members of management were given as much freedom as possible to fulfill their responsibilities in whatever way they thought best. This policy was though to have built a dynamic, aggressive, and extremely able group of middle- and lower-level executives who had been particularly imaginative in finding ways to expand and improve the operation of the firm. This decentralization had always been accompanied by the understanding that the individual manager must "deliver." This policy, or actually philosophy, was conveyed and reinforced through letters, personal conservations, and example. Executives who increased sales or reduced costs, or in some manner made their operations more efficient, were rewarded in a number of ways. Praise, both public and private, was given to executives who improved their unit's performance. Bonuses for increased sales or cost reduction were both generous and frequent, and promotions came rapidly to those who managed outstanding units. The chairman of the board, who was also chief

executive officer during this period of growth, frequently used words that were only half-jokingly claimed by other executives to be the company motto. "This company's success rests upon expansion and efficiency."

THE LOCAL UNIT

Eagle Airlines was organized as shown in Exhibit 11-7. The three major divisions were Operations, which was involved in scheduling and operating the planes over the entire route system; Sales, which was concerned with advertising all phases of airline service, maintaining ticket offices in all cities and airports, and also selling to institutional customers such as companies and government agencies; and Service, which was concerned with activities at the airport, maintenance, handling baggage, loading passengers, and similar functions.

For all practical purposes, operations had no local offices in that it had to operate the entire system. Sales and service had both district and local or regional offices. The sales manager in Bartlett City, for example, was responsible for the ticket sales at the airport and in maintaining a downtown ticket office, as well as for institutional sales to the local companies and agencies. Service was usually broken into a number of subdivisions at the local level, so that at Bartlett City there was a ramp service manager who was responsible for handling everything pertaining to the airplane while it was on the ground, but not while it was under maintenance. The manager would, therefore, be responsible for the loading and unloading of all baggage, mail, and passengers. That individual was also responsible for cleaning the planes between flights, having food put on board, getting baggage to the customers and picking up from them, guiding passengers on and off the aircraft, and checking their tickets when they arrived at the terminal.

Consistent with company policy of decentralization and individual accountability, each of these local people had an individual budget and standards of performance. A sales manager, for example, was given complete authority to hire, train, and fire whatever salespeople or any other personnel he or she thought necessary. The sales manager knew what his or her budget was and was expected to stick within it and reduce it if possible. Furthermore, the sales manager knew what the standards of performance relevant to sales volume were. The company placed great emphasis on an increase in sales rather than in absolute volume of sales. Hence, the sales manager at Bartlett City,

EXHIBIT 11-7

Partial Organization Chart of Eagle Airlines

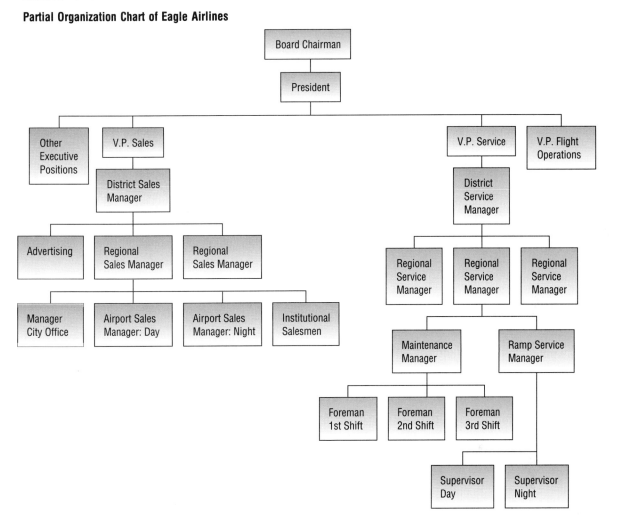

as at all other local units, knew that individual performance would be evaluated, not on matching past sales volume, but by increasing it a certain percentage. The percentage would vary from one location to another depending upon the number of conditions: market potential, absolute volume, and similar terms. Although the percentage increase might vary, it was always there and was known by the company as the "ratchet." The regional service manager had no actual sales figure to be held accountable for, but that manager did have costs that were expected to be controlled and, if at all possible, reduced. While there was no

similar "ratchet," such as a percentage reduction of costs expected each year, there was continual pressure on the local ramp manager in the form of exhortation, suggestions, and illustrations of managers who had successfully found ways to reduce costs.

PLAN OF THE SALES MANAGER

Carl Dodds, sales manager in Bartlett City, had been with Eagle Airlines seven years, during which time he had had three promotions. Upon graduation from a Western state university, he had started working for Eagle Airlines in the San Francisco office as a ticket clerk at the local airport. Within a year he had been made accounts sales representative, selling airline service to local companies and institutions. Within two years he had become a local sales manager at San Jose, the smallest of the company's sales offices. Six months ago he had received his promotion to Bartlett City, the second largest sales office, and, until recently, the one growing most rapidly. Dodds's superior looked at him as a particularly dynamic, inventive salesperson and sales manager. He seemed gifted at finding ways of substantially increasing sales. In previous positions he had developed a number of attention-getting promotion packages that met with spectacular results. Higher management looked to him to again increase sales at Bartlett City, which had leveled out about a year ago with the decline in the economy. It was not known how long the decline would continue.

Some of Dodds's previous associates in the other parts of the company agreed that he had been imaginative in developing some spectacular promotion schemes but also felt that success had always been of the short-run variety— he had made sudden bursts at the expense of long-term growth. They further claimed that he had been fortunate in always being promoted out of a position before the consequences of his activity caught up with him.

Since coming to Bartlett City, Dodds had been intensively studying the local market situation, making contacts with the various companies and big business executives, hiring some new salespeople, and training them after having, as he called it, weeded out some deadwood. He had also increased advertising and redecorated the downtown sales office. In spite of this activity, in his own mind, he had been largely getting ready for his major effort.

Dodds defined his sales situation this way. The airline had done well attracting customers who wanted speed and convenience. However, a considerable number of business executives drove or used a company plane. He adopted and embellished a popular local image of the Bartlett City executive as a dynamic, imaginative, administrator-scientist who represented a new type of business tycoon. In Dodds's mind, what he had to do was sell this young dynamic, new type of tycoon the comfort and gracious service that, apparently, such a person thought should come to him or her in this new role. His new plan then was to do everything possible to give the "new tycoons" this sort of service. He therefore developed a plan to set up *Tycoon*

Specials on certain of the flights carrying the greatest number of these business executives. This plan was to begin with the flight between Bartlett City and Los Angeles.

In this plan the customer-executive upon arriving at the ticket-checking counter for the *Tycoon Special* flight would be asked to select his or her own seat. This then would be reserved in the customer's name. Upon arriving at the ramp for boarding, the customer would be greeted by name by the gate attendant, usually dressed plainly but neatly in a white top, blue cap, and slacks, but now in a gold coat and a simulated turban. Stretching between the gate and the aircraft was to be a wide, rich-red carpet. Upon arrival, the customer's name would be announced through a special intercom to the plane. As the individual walked down the red carpet, the customer-executive would note that the flight hostess would appear smiling at the door, ready to greet him or her by name before being ushered to the appropriate seat, identified by a card with the executive's name, indicating, "This seat is reserved for Tycoon _____."

Once in flight this deluxe service would continue, with the hostesses changing into more comfortable and feminine-looking lounge dresses and serving a choice of champagne, wine, and cocktails along with exotic and varied hors d'oeuvres. There were other details to the plan, but this will give you some idea of its general nature. In this way, Dodds thought surely that he would be able to not only match but exceed the services and comfort some executives thought they obtained by alternative means of transportation.

Dodds's great problem was in getting the plan operational. Almost all the service had to be provided by people who did not report to him. This would be supplied by the local ramp service manager, to whom the gate clerk reported, and who would have to provide the red carpet, the additional gold uniforms, turbans, and the other paraphernalia necessary to create the impression that Dodds had in mind. The local ramp service manager, Chris Edwards, had been particularly abrupt in rejecting this proposal, insisting that it did not make sense and that he was going to have absolutely nothing to do with it. Dodds had in several meetings attempted to "sell," persuade, pressure, and finally threaten Edwards into accepting the plan. Edwards's refusal had become more adamant and pointed at every step. Relationships between the two, never close or cordial, had deteriorated until there was nothing but the most unrestrained hostility expressed between them.

REACTION OF THE SERVICE MANAGER

Chris Edwards was a graduate engineer who had worked for the company for about 10 years. He had first started in the maintenance department of the firm and had gradually risen through several supervisory positions before being given this position as service manager with Eagle. It was the first position he had had in which he had an independent budget and was held individually accountable. After three years in this capacity, he personally felt and had been led to believe by several higher executives in the company that he had acquired as much experience in this position as was necessary. He was, therefore, looking forward to a new assignment, which probably involved a promotion in the very near future. He realized that this promotion would probably be based upon his earlier proven technical competence and his more recent experience in his present position, where he had run a particularly efficient operation. This was evidenced by several reductions in his operating expenses, due to efficiencies he had installed, and by other measures of performance, such as reduction in the time necessary to service, fuel, and load aircraft.

After having met with increasingly adamant refusals by Edwards, Dodds had gone to his superior, pointing out that he was being hampered by Edwards in his effort to increase sales and advance the company. Dodds' supervisor had made a point of seeing his counterpart, in the service area, asking if something could not be done by the service people at Bartlett City to support the sales effort. Upon inquiry, Edwards's superior learned the details of the request from Edwards and the reasons for his refusal. Dodds kept insistent pressure on his superior, asking to have something done about the local service manager's obstinacy. Eventually, word of the continued arguments between Dodds and Edwards went up the chain of command to the vice president of sales and later to the vice president in charge of service. One day while discussing this issue, their conversation was overheard by the president. Upon hearing the story, he made the comment that these personality clashes would either have to be straightened out or one or both of the men either transferred or, for that matter, fired. He emphatically insisted that the company could not operate efficiently with an unnecessary expenditure of energy going into personal disputes.

CASE QUESTIONS

1. Evaluate the firm's organization design in terms of the important contingency factors which are relevant in this instance.
2. What changes would you recommend be made in the present organization design?
3. What do you believe will be the most important sources of resistance to changing the organization structure?

Job Design

LEARNING OBJECTIVES

IDENTIFY the key elements linking job design and performance

DEFINE the term job analysis

COMPARE the job design concepts of range and depth

DESCRIBE perceived job content

IDENTIFY the different types of job performance outcomes

DISCUSS motivational properties of jobs

COMPARE job rotation with job enlargement

EXPLAIN job enrichment

DISCUSS self-managed teams

The building blocks of organizational structures are the jobs people perform, and a major cause of organizational effectiveness is employee job performance. Job design refers to the process by which managers decide individual job tasks and authority. Apart from the very practical issues associated with job design—issues that relate to effectiveness in economic, political, and monetary terms, we can appreciate its importance in social and psychological terms. As noted in earlier chapters, jobs can be sources of psychological stress and even mental and physical impairment. On a more positive note, jobs can provide income, meaningful life experiences, self-esteem, esteem of others, regulation of our lives, and association with others. Thus, the well-being of organizations and people depend upon how well management is able to design jobs.

JOB DESIGN AND QUALITY OF WORK LIFE

In recent years the issue of designing jobs has gone beyond the determination of the most efficient way to perform tasks. The **quality of work life** (QWL) has become an important design ingredient, and the concept is now widely used to refer to "a philosophy of management that enhances the dignity of all workers, introduces changes in an organization's culture, and improves the physical and emotional well-being of employees."[1] Unfortunately, not all attempts to improve employee physical and/or emotional well-being have the desired effects. Sometimes there may be legal or ethical issues which are difficult to resolve, as Encounter 12-1 illustrates.

In some organizations QWL programs are intended to increase employee trust, involvement, and problem solving so as to increase both worker satisfaction and organizational effectiveness.[2] It is not surprising to find that the quality of work life concept embodies theories and ideas of the human relations movement of the 1950s and the job enrichment efforts of the 60s and 70s.

As America moves toward the 21st century, the challenge to managers is to provide for both quality of work life and improved production and efficiency through revitalization of business and industry. At the present time, the trade-offs between the gains in human terms from improved quality of work life and the gains in economic terms from revitalization are not fully known. Some believe it will be necessary to defer quality of work life efforts so as to make the American economy more productive and efficient,[3] while others observe that the sense of urgency to become more productive in domestic and overseas markets presents opportunities to combine the two.[4] In either event we agree that "it is a challenging task to design an effective job that satisfies the psychological needs of the worker, and, in concert with other jobs, allows for continuous improvement in productivity and quality."[5]

Job design and redesign techniques attempt to (1) identify the most important needs of employees and the organization and (2) remove obstacles in the

[1]Richard E. Kopelman, "Job Redesign and Productivity: A Review of the Evidence," *National Productivity Review,* Summer 1985, p. 239.

[2]Harry C. Katz, Thomas A. Kochan, and Mark R. Weber, "Assessing the Effects of Industrial Relations Systems and Efforts to Improve the Quality of Working Life on Organizational Effectiveness," *Academy of Management Journal,* September 1985, pp. 514–15.

[3]Amitai Etzioni, "Choose America Must—Between 'Reindustrialization and Quality of Life,' *Across the Board,* October 1980, pp. 43–49; and Marvin R. Weisbord, *Productive Workplaces: Organizing and Managing for Dignity, Meaning, and Community* (San Francisco: Jossey-Bass, 1987).

[4]D. J. Skrovan, ed., *Quality of Work Life* (Reading, Mass.: Addison-Wesley Publishing, 1983); and Noel M. Tichy and David Ulrich, "The Challenge of Revitalization," *New Management,* Winter 1985, pp. 53–59.

[5]M. H. Safizadeh, "Job Design: The Case of Workgroups in Manufacturing Operations," *California Management Review,* Summer 1991, p. 63.

JOB DESIGN AND ETHICS: THE CASE OF JOHNSON CONTROLS

There is little dispute that jobs should be designed in a way which eliminates, or at least minimizes, the likelihood that employees may experience adverse physical or health consequences from performing the job. Some jobs, however, even when properly designed, may still be inherently hazardous. For example, it may be impossible to completely eliminate exposure to toxic chemicals or hazardous substances even when jobs have been well designed. Such was the case at the battery manufacturing division of Johnson Controls, an automotive equipment supplier.

By its very nature, battery manufacturing entails possible exposure to high lead levels. Sufficiently high blood lead levels can be dangerous to anyone; even moderately elevated levels, however, can pose a particular risk for pregnant women and their unborn children. Thus, after having designed the manufacturing operation in a manner to minimize exposure, Johnson Controls instituted a policy to provide further safeguards for a particularly susceptible group: Women with childbearing capacity were essentially prohibited from working in high lead exposure positions in its battery facility. Fertile women already employed in such positions when the policy went into effect were permitted to stay as long as they maintained safe blood lead levels; otherwise they were transferred to another job with no loss of pay or benefits.

Most management students, when queried, indicate that this sounds like a reasonable policy, with many suggesting that it would be unethical (and perhaps should be illegal) for the company not to protect a particularly susceptible group of individuals—some of whom (unborn children) are powerless to protect themselves. At the same time however, virtually all of these students agree that sex discrimination in hiring and employment decisions is clearly unethical (and also illegal). And sex discrimination is what Johnson Controls was charged with as a result of this policy.

The initial determination in the case went against the company. Subsequently, the U.S. Court of Appeals for the Seventh Circuit ruled the policy was not in violation of Title VII. Five months later the California Court of Appeals ruled the company in violation of California fair employment statutes. Final resolution of this specific case came with the 1991 Supreme Court ruling that essentially upheld the illegality of the Company's policy. This case illustrates that what constitutes an "ethical" management decision may be subject to disagreement among those who have a stake in the decision.

Source: Based in part on information in G. P. Panaro, *Employment Law Manual* (Boston: Warren, Gorham & Lamont, 1991), p. S9–30.

workplace that frustrate those needs. Managers hope the results are jobs which (1) fulfill important individual needs and (2) contribute to individual, group, and organizational effectiveness. But whether the outcomes of those managerial actions are positive is debatable. Obviously, designing and redesigning jobs is complex. The remainder of this chapter reviews the important theories, research, and practices of job design. As will be seen, contemporary management has at its disposal a wide range of techniques that facilitate the achievement of personal and organizational performance.

A CONCEPTUAL MODEL OF JOB DESIGN

The conceptual model depicted in Exhibit 12-1 is based on the extensive research literature that has appeared in the last 20 years and includes the various terms and concepts that appear in the current literature. When linked together these concepts describe the important determinants of job performance and organizational effectiveness. The model takes into account a number of sources of complexity. It recognizes that individuals react differently to jobs. While one person may derive positive satisfaction from a job, another may not. It also recognizes the difficult trade-offs between organizational and individual needs. For example, the technology of manufacturing (an environmental difference) may dictate that management adopt assembly-line mass-production methods and low-skilled jobs to achieve optimal efficiency. Such jobs, however, may result in great unrest and worker discontent. Perhaps these costs could have been avoided by a more careful balancing of organizational and individual needs.

The ideas reflected in Exhibit 12-1 are the bases for this chapter. We will present each important factor that is the cause or the effect of job design, beginning with job analysis.

JOB ANALYSIS

Job analysis is the process of decision making which translates task, human, and technological factors into job designs. Either managers or personnel specialists undertake the process, and a number of approaches exist to assist them. Two of the more widely used approaches are functional job analysis and position analysis questionnaire.[6]

Functional Job Analysis

Functional job analysis (FJA) focuses attention on task and technological factors. It directs attention to the following four aspects of each job or class of jobs:

1. What the worker does in relation to data, people, and jobs.
2. What methods and techniques the worker uses.
3. What machines, tools, and equipment the worker uses.
4. What materials, products, subject matter, or services the worker produces.

The first three aspects relate to job activities; the fourth, to job performance. FJA provides job descriptions classifying them according to any one of the four dimensions. In addition to defining what activities, methods, and machines make

[6]John M. Ivancevich, *Human Resource Management*, 5th ed. (Homewood, Ill.: Richard D. Irwin, 1992).

EXHIBIT 12-1

**Job Design and
Job Performance**

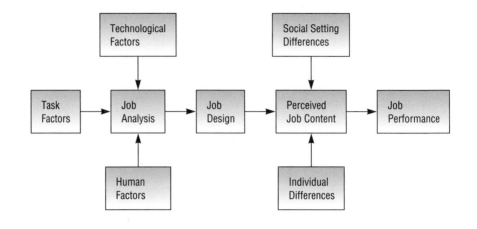

up the job, FJA also defines what the individual doing the job should produce. FJA can, therefore, be the basis for defining standards of performance.

FJA is the most popular and widely used of the job analysis methods.[7] In addition it is the basis for the most extensive available list of occupational titles.

Position Analysis Questionnaire

Position analysis questionnaire (PAQ) takes into account human as well as task and technological factors. PAQ has the been the object of considerable attention by researchers and practitioners alike who believe that accurate job analysis must take human factors into account. PAQ analysis attempts to identify the following six job aspects:

1. Information sources critical to job performance.
2. Information processing and decision making critical to job performance.
3. Physical activity and dexterity required of the job.
4. Interpersonal relationships required of the job.
5. Physical working conditions and the reactions of individuals to those conditions.
6. Other job characteristics such as work schedules and work responsibilities.

It is important to note that FJA and PAQ overlap considerably. Each attempts to identify job activities that are necessary given the task to be done and the technology to do it with. But PAQ includes the additional consideration of the individual's psychological responses to the job and its environment.

Numerous methods exist to perform job analysis, and different methods can give different answers to important questions such as "How much is the job

---

[7]Sidney Gael, *The Job Analysis Handbook for Business, Industry, and Government* (New York: John Wiley & Sons, 1988).

worth?"[8] Thus, the selection of the method for performing job analysis is not trivial and is one of the most important decisions to be made in job design. As we noted, PAC and FJA appear to be two of the most popular ones in practice and recent surveys of the opinions of expert job analysts bear out their popularity.[9]

JOB DESIGNS

Job designs are the results of job analysis and they specify three job characteristics: range, depth, and relationships.

Range and Depth

The range of a job refers to the number of tasks a jobholder performs. The individual who performs eight tasks to complete a job has a wider range than a person performing four. In most instances the greater the number of tasks performed, the longer it takes to complete the job.

A second job characteristic is depth, the amount of discretion an individual has to decide job activities and job outcomes. In many instances job depth relates to personal influence as well as delegated authority. An employee with the same job title and at the same organizational level as another employee may possess more, less, or the same amount of job depth because of personal influence.

▲ C12–1 Case 12–1, "The Hovey and Beard Company Case," describes a situation involving job depth issues, among others. As the case illustrates, job depth can play an important role in determining performance and satisfaction outcomes.

Job range and depth distinguish one job from another not only within the same organization but also among different organizations. To illustrate how jobs differ in range and depth, Exhibit 12-2 depicts the differences for selected jobs of business firms, hospitals, and universities. For example, business research scientists, hospital chiefs of surgery, and university presidents generally have high job range and significant depth. Research scientists perform a large number of tasks and are usually not closely supervised. Chiefs of surgery have significant job range in that they oversee and counsel on many diverse surgical matters. In addition, they are not supervised closely, and they have the authority to influence hospital surgery policies and procedures.

University presidents have a large number of tasks to perform. They speak to alumni groups, politicians, community representatives, and students. They

[8]Robert M. Madigan and David J. Hoover, "Effects of Alternative Job Evaluation Methods on Decisions Involving Pay Equity," *Academy of Management Journal*, March 1986, pp. 84–100; Edward H. Lawler III, "What's Wrong with Point-Factor Job Evaluation?" *Personnel*, January 1987, pp. 38–44.

[9]Jai V. Ghorpade, *Job Analysis: A Handbook for the Human Resource Director* (Englewood Cliffs, N.J.: Prentice-Hall, 1988); and Edward L. Levine, Ronald A. Ash, Hardy Hall, and Frank Sistrunk, "Evaluation of Job Analysis Methods by Experienced Job Analysts," *Academy of Management Journal*, June 1983, pp. 339–48.

548 Part IV / Organizational Structure and Job Design

EXHIBIT 12-2

Job Depth and Range

High Depth

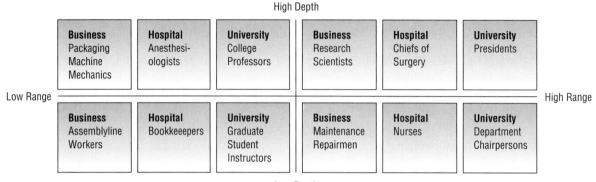

Low Range   High Range

Low Depth

develop, with the consultation of others, policies on admissions, fund raising, and adult education. They can alter the faculty recruitment philosophy and thus alter the course of the entire institution. For example, a university president may want to build an institution noted for high-quality classroom instruction and for providing excellent services to the community. This thrust may lead to recruiting and selecting professors who want to concentrate on these two specific goals. In contrast, another president may want to foster outstanding research and high-quality classroom instruction. Of course, another president may attempt to develop an institution noted for instruction, research, and service. The critical point is that university presidents have sufficient depth to alter the course of a university's direction.

Examples of jobs with high depth and low range are packaging machine mechanics, anesthesiologists, and faculty members. Mechanics perform the limited tasks that pertain to repairing and maintaining packaging machines. But they can decide how breakdowns on the packaging machine are to be repaired. The discretion means that the mechanics have relatively high job depth.

Anesthesiologists also perform a limited number of tasks. They are concerned with the rather restricted task of administering anesthetics to patients. However, they can decide the type of anesthetic to be administered in a particular situation, a decision indicative of high job depth.

University professors specifically engaged in classroom instruction have relatively low job range. Teaching involves comparatively more tasks than the work of the anesthesiologist but fewer tasks than that of the business research scientist. However, professors' job depth is greater than that of graduate student instructors because they determine how they will conduct the class, what materials will be presented, and the standards to be used in evaluating students. Graduate students typically do not have complete freedom in the choice of class materials and procedures. Professors decide these matters for them.

Highly specialized jobs are those that have few tasks to accomplish by pre-scribed means. Such jobs are quite routine; they also tend to be controlled by specified rules and procedures (low depth). A highly despecialized job (high range) has many tasks to accomplish within the famework of discretion over means and ends (high depth). Within an organization there typically are great differences among jobs in both range and depth. Although managers have no precise equa-tions to use in deciding job range and depth, they can follow this guideline: Given the economic and technical requirements of the organization's mission, goals, and objectives, what is the optimal point along the continuum of range and depth for each job?

Job Relationships

Job relationships are determined by managers' decisions regarding departmen-talization bases and spans of control. The resulting groups become the respon-sibility of a manager to coordinate toward organization purposes. These decisions also determine the nature and extent of jobholders' interpersonal relationships, individually and within groups. As we already have seen in the discussion of groups in organizations, group performance is affected in part by group cohe-siveness. And the degree of group cohesiveness depends on the quality and kind of interpersonal relationships of jobholders assigned to a task or command group.

The wider the span of control, the larger the group and consequently the more difficult it is to establish friendship and interest relationships. Simply, people in larger groups are less likely to communicate (and interact sufficiently to form interpersonal ties) than people in smaller groups. Without the opportunity to communicate, people will be unable to establish cohesive work groups, and an important source of satisfaction may be lost for individuals who seek to fulfill social and esteem needs through relationships with co-workers.

The basis for departmentalization that management selects also has important implications for job relationships. The functional basis places jobs with similar depth and range in the same groups; while product, territory, and customer bases place jobs with dissimilar depth and range together. Thus, in functional depart-ments people will be performing much the same specialty. Product, territory, and customer departments, however, are composed of jobs which are quite different and heterogeneous. Individuals who work in heterogeneous departments expe-rience feelings of dissatisfaction, stress, and involvement more intensely than those in homogeneous, functional departments. People with homogeneous back-grounds, skills, and training have more common interests than those with het-erogeneous ones. Therefore, it is easier for them to establish satisfying social relationships with less stress but also with less involvement in the department's activities.

Job designs describe the objective characteristics of jobs. Through job analysis techniques such as FJA and PAQ, managers can describe jobs in terms of re-quired activities to produce a specified outcome. But yet another factor must be considered before we can understand the relationship between jobs and performance—perceived job content.

PERCEIVED JOB CONTENT

Many managers no doubt believe that the way to improve job performance is to determine (1) the "best way" to do a job and (2) the standard time for completing it. Industrial engineers routinely practice motion and time analyses to determine preferred work activities in relation to raw materials, product design, order of work, tools, equipment, and workplace layout. Time studies determine the preferred time for performing each job activity. Through motion and time studies, jobs can be designed solely in terms of technical data.

However, the belief that job design can be based solely on technical data ignores the very large role played by the individual who performs the job. Individuals differ profoundly as we have noted in the chapter on individual differences. They come to work with different backgrounds, needs, and motivations. Once on the job they experience the social setting in which the work is performed in unique ways. It is not surprising to find that different individuals perceive jobs differently.

Perceived job content, then, refers to job characteristics as perceived by the jobholder. It is important to distinguish between the objective and subjective properties of a job as reflected in the perceptions of people who perform them.[10] Managers cannot understand the causes of job performance without consideration of individual differences such as personality, needs, and span of attention.[11] Nor can managers understand the causes of job performance without consideration of the social setting in which the job is performed.[12] According to Exhibit 12-1, perceived job content precedes job performance. Thus, if managers desire to increase job performance by changing perceived job content, they can change job design, individual perceptions, or social settings.

If management is to understand perceived job content, some method for measuring it must exist.[13] In response to this need, organization behavior researchers have attempted to measure perceived job content in a variety of work settings by using questionnaires that jobholders complete and which measure their perceptions of certain job characteristics.

---

[10]Kenneth R. Brousseau, "Toward a Dynamic Model of Job-Person Relationships: Findings, Research Questions and Implications for Work System Design," *Academy of Management Review,* January 1983, pp. 33–45.

[11]Donald P. Schwab and L. L. Cummings, "A Theoretical Analysis of the Impact of Task Scope on Employee Performance," *Academy of Management Review,* April 1976, pp. 31–32.

[12]James W. Dean and Daniel J. Brass, "Social Interaction and the Perception of Job Characteristics in an Organization," *Human Relations,* June 1985, pp. 571–82.

[13]Thomas W. Ferratt, Randall B. Dunham, and Jon L. Pierce, "Self-Report Measures of Job Characteristics and Affective Responses: An Examination of Discriminant Validity," *Academy of Management Journal,* December 1981, pp. 780–94.

Job Characteristics

The pioneering effort to measure perceived job content through employee responses to a questionnaire resulted in the identification of six characteristics: variety, autonomy, required interaction, optional interaction, knowledge and skill required, and responsibility.[14] The index of these six characteristics is termed the **Requisite Task Attribute Index** *(RTAI).* The original RTAI has been extensively reviewed and analyzed. One important development was the review by Hackman and Lawler who revised the index to include the six characteristics shown in Exhibit 12-3.[15]

Variety, task identity, and feedback are perceptions of job range. Autonomy is the perception of job depth, and dealing with others and friendship opportunities reflect perceptions of job relationships. Employees sharing similar perceptions, job designs, and social settings should report similar job characteristics. Employees with different perceptions, however, report different job characteristics for the same job. For example, an individual with a high need for social belonging would perceive friendship opportunities differently than another individual with a low need for social belonging.

Individual differences in need strength, particularly the strength of growth needs, influence the perception of task variety. Employees with relatively weak higher order needs are less concerned with performing a variety of tasks than are those with relatively strong growth needs. Thus, managers expecting higher performance from increased task variety would be disappointed if the jobholders did not have strong growth needs. Even individuals with strong growth needs cannot perform more and more tasks continuously because at some point, performance turns down as these individuals reach the limits imposed by their abilities and time. The relationship between performance and task variety even for individuals with high growth needs is likely to be curvilinear.[16]

Differences in social settings of work also affect perceptions of job content. Examples of social setting differences include leadership style and what other people say about the job. As has been pointed out by more than one research study, how a person perceives a job is greatly affected by what other people say about it. If a person's friends state their jobs are boring, that person is likely to

[14]Eugene F. Stone and Hal G. Gueuthal, "An Empirical Derivation of the Dimensions along which Characteristics of Jobs Are Perceived," *Academy of Management Journal,* June 1985, pp. 376–96, identifies Arthur N. Turner and Paul R. Lawrence, *Industrial Jobs and the Worker: An Investigation of Response to Task Attributes* (Cambridge, Mass.: Harvard University Press, 1965), to be the source of contemporary measures of perceived job characteristics.

[15]J. Richard Hackman and Edward W. Lawler III, "Employee Reactions to Job Characteristics," *Journal of Applied Psychology,* June 1971, pp. 259–86; and J. Richard Hackman and Greg R. Oldham, "Development of the Job Diagnostic Survey," *Journal of Applied Psychology,* April 1975, pp. 159–70.

[16]Joseph E. Champoux, "A Three Sample Test of Some Extensions to the Job Characteristics Model of Work Motivation," *Academy of Management Journal,* September 1980, pp. 466–78.

EXHIBIT   12-3

**Selected Job
Characteristics**

Variety. The degree to which a job requires employees to perform a wide range of operations in their work and/or the degree to which employees must use a variety of equipment and procedures in their work.

Autonomy. The extent to which employees have a major say in scheduling their work, selecting the equipment they use, and deciding on procedures to be followed.

Task identity. The extent to which employees do an entire or whole piece of work and can clearly identify with the results of their efforts.

Feedback. The degree to which employees, as they are working, receive information that reveals how well they are performing on the job.

Dealing with others. The degree to which a job requires employees to deal with other people to complete their work.

Friendship opportunities. The degree to which a job allows employees to talk with one another on the job and to establish informal relationships with other employees at work.

Source: Henry P. Sims, Jr., Andrew D. Szilagyi, and Robert T. Keller, "The Measurement of Job Characteristics," *Academy of Management Journal,* June 1976, p. 197.

■ **E12–1** state that his or her job is also boring and if the individual perceives the job as boring, job performance would no doubt suffer. Job content, then, results from the interaction of many factors in the work situation. To diagnose your personal preferences about job content characteristics, complete Exercise 12–1.

JOB PERFORMANCE

Job performance includes a number of outcomes. In this section we will discuss performance outcomes that have value to the organization and to the individual.

Objective Outcomes

Quantity and quality of output, absenteeism, tardiness, and turnover are objective outcomes that can be measured in quantitative terms. For each job implicit or explicit standards exist for each of these objective outcomes. Industrial engineering studies establish standards for daily quantity, and quality control specialists establish tolerance limits for acceptable quality. These aspects of job performance account for characteristics of the product, client, or service for which the jobholder is responsible.

Partly in response to perceived differences between foreign and domestic products, there has been a great deal of interest in recent years in the objective performance outcome of quality. A variety of programs have been instituted to improve the quality of both products and services. Foremost among these efforts have been the use of quality circles.[17] A quality circle is a small group of employees, usually 6–12, who meet on a regular basis on company time to recommend improvements and solve quality related problems.[18] Quality circles can be thought of as a form of self-managed teams, a concept that will be discussed later in this chapter. Although improving objectively measured quality outcomes is a primary objective of quality circles, participation in such groups can also contribute to intrinsic and job satisfaction outcomes as well.

Personal Behavior Outcomes

The jobholder reacts to the work itself by attending regularly or being absent, by staying with the job, or by quitting. Moreover, physiological and health-related problems can ensue as a consequence of job performance. Stress related to job performance can contribute to physical and mental impairment; accidents and occupationally related disease can also ensue.

Intrinsic and Extrinsic Outcomes

Job outcomes include intrinsic and extrinsic work outcomes and the distinction between the two is important for understanding the reactions of people to their jobs. In a general sense, intrinsic outcomes are objects or events that follow from the worker's own efforts and don't require the involvement of any other person. More simply it is an outcome clearly related to action on the worker's part. Although outcomes typically are thought to be solely in the province of professional and technical jobs, all jobs potentially have opportunities for intrinsic outcomes. Such outcomes involve feelings of responsibility, challenge, and recognition and result from such job characteristics as variety, autonomy, identity, and significance.

Extrinsic outcomes, however, are objects or events that follow from the workers' own efforts in conjunction with other factors or persons not directly involved in the job itself. Pay, working conditions, co-workers, and even supervision are potentially job outcomes but are not a fundamental part of the work. Dealing with others and friendship interactions are sources of extrinsic outcomes.

Most jobs provide opportunities for both intrinsic and extrinsic outcomes. It then becomes important to understand the relationship between the two. Generally, it is held that extrinsic rewards reinforce intrinsic rewards in a positive

---

[17]For an excellent recent review of quality circles, see R. P. Steel and R. F. Lloyd, "Cognitive, Affective, and Behavioral Outcomes of Participation in Quality Circles: Conceptual and Empirical Findings," *The Journal of Applied Behavioral Science* 1, 1988, pp. 1–17.

[18]E. E. Adam, Jr., "Quality Circle Performance," *Journal of Management,* March 1991, pp. 25–39.

direction when the individual can attribute the source of the extrinsic reward to his or her own efforts. For example, receiving a pay raise (extrinsic reward) increases feeling good about oneself if the cause of the pay raise is thought to be one's own efforts and competence and not favoritism extended by the boss. This line of reasoning explains why some individuals get no satisfaction out of sharing in the gains derived from group rather than individual effort.[19]

Job Satisfaction Outcomes

Job satisfaction depends on the levels of intrinsic and extrinsic outcomes and how the jobholder views those outcomes. These outcomes have different values for different people because people differ in the importance they attach to job outcomes. For some people, responsible and challenging work may have neutral or even negative value. For others, such work outcomes may have high positive values. Those differences alone would account for different levels of job satisfaction for essentially the same job tasks.

Another important individual difference is job involvement.[20] People differ in the extent that (1) work is a central life interest, (2) they actively participate in work, (3) they perceive work as central to self-esteem, and (4) they perceive work as consistent with self-concept. Persons who are not involved in their work cannot be expected to realize the same satisfaction as those who are. This variable accounts for the fact that two workers could report different levels of satisfaction for the same performance levels.

A final individual difference is the perceived equity of the outcome in terms of what the jobholder considers a fair reward. If the outcomes are perceived to be unfair in relation to those of others in similar jobs requiring similar effort, the jobholder will experience dissatisfaction and seek means to restore the equity, either by seeking greater rewards (primarily extrinsic) or by reducing effort.

Thus, we see that job performance includes many potential outcomes. Some are of primary value to the organization—the objective outcomes, for example. Other outcomes are of primary importance to the individual—job satisfaction. Job performance is without doubt a complex variable that depends on the interplay of numerous factors. Managers can make some sense of the issue by understanding the motivational implications of jobs.

[19]Hugh J. Arnold, "Task Performance, Perceived Competence, and Attributed Causes of Performance as Determinants of Intrinsic Motivation," *Academy of Management Journal*, December 1985, pp. 876–88.

[20]Sharon E. Beatty, Lynne R. Kahle, and Pamela Homer, "The Involvement-Commitment Model: Theory and Implications," *Journal of Business Research*, March 1988, pp. 149–68; and Gary J. Blau and Kimberly S. Boal, "Conceptualizing How Job Involvement and Organizational Commitment Affect Turnover and Absenteeism," *Academy of Management Review*, April 1987, pp. 288–300.

MOTIVATIONAL PROPERTIES OF JOBS AND JOB PERFORMANCE

Researchers and managers in the motivational properties of jobs base their interest of organization behavior on the understanding that job performance depends upon more than the ability of the jobholder. Specifically, job performance is determined by the interaction of ability and motivation as expressed by the equation:

$$\text{Job Performance} = \text{Ability} \times \text{Motivation}$$

The equation reflects the fact that one person's job performance can be greater than that of a second person because of greater ability, motivation, or both. It also reflects the possibility that job performance could be zero even if the jobholder has ability; in such instances, motivation would have to be zero. Thus, it is imperative that management consider the potential impact of job motivation.

● R12–1

The field of organization behavior has advanced a number of suggestions for improving the motivational properties of jobs. Invariably the suggestions, termed **job redesign strategies**, attempt to improve job performance through changes in actual job characteristics with the expectation that positive changes in work attitudes and motivation will follow.[21] In the next sections we review the more significant of these strategies. And, in the first readings selection at the end of the chapter, a unique approach to job redesign is offered: providing employees with the authority and responsibility for redesigning their own jobs.

REDESIGNING JOB RANGE: JOB ROTATION AND JOB ENLARGEMENT

The earliest attempts to redesign jobs date to the scientific management era. The efforts at that time emphasized efficiency criteria—the individual tasks that make up a job are limited, uniform, and repetitive.[22] This practice led to narrow job range and, consequently, reported high levels of job discontent, turnover, absenteeism, and dissatisfaction. Accordingly, strategies were devised which resulted in wider job range through increasing the requisite activities of jobs. Two of these approaches are job rotation and job enlargement.

---

[21]William H. Glick, G. Douglas Jenkins, Jr., and Nina Gupta, "Method versus Substance: How Strong Are Underlying Relationships between Job Characteristics and Attitudinal Outcomes?" *Academy of Management Journal,* September 1986, pp. 441–64.

[22]The literature of scientific management is voluminous. The original works and the subsequent criticisms and interpretations would make a large volume. Of special significance are the works of the principal authors including: Frederick W. Taylor, *Principles of Scientific Management* (New York: Harper & Row, 1911); Harrington Emerson, *The Twelve Principles of Efficiency* (New York: The Engineering Magazine, 1913); Henry L. Gantt, *Industrial Leadership* (New Haven, Conn.: Yale University Press, 1916); Frank B. Gilbreth, *Motion Study* (New York: D. Van Nostrand, 1911); and Lillian M. Gilbreth, *The Psychology of Management* (New York: Sturgis & Walton, 1914).

Job Rotation

Managers of organizations such as Western Electric, Ford, Bethlehem Steel, and TRW have utilized different forms of the job rotation strategy, a practice involving rotating an individual from one job to another. In so doing the individual is expected to complete more job activities since each job includes different tasks. Job rotation involves increasing the range of jobs and the perception of variety in the job content, and increasing task variety should, according to expectancy theory, increase the intrinsic valence associated with job satisfaction. However, the practice of job rotation does not change the basic characteristics of the assigned jobs. Critics state that this approach involves nothing more than having people perform several boring and monotonous jobs rather than one.

Nonetheless, job rotation continues to be widely utilized and is viewed quite positively by its adherents. For example, at G.S.I. Transcomm Data System job rotation is employed to reduce boredom. Since the job rotation plan went into effect annual turnover rates have dropped from 25 percent to 7 percent.[23] And at Corning, a job rotation system which allows weekly rotations and includes higher pay for each new job learned has been credited with helping reduce defects to three parts per million from 10,000 parts per million.[24]

Job Enlargement

The pioneering Walker and Guest study[25] was concerned with the social and psychological problems associated with mass production jobs in automobile assembly plants. They found that many workers were dissatisfied with their highly specialized jobs. In particular, they disliked mechanical pacing, repetitiveness of operations, and lack of a sense of accomplishment. Walker and Guest also found a positive relationship between job range and job satisfaction. The findings of this research gave early support for those motivation theories which predict that increases in job range will increase job satisfaction and other, objective, job outcomes. Job enlargement strategies focus on the opposite of dividing work— they are a form of despecialization or increasing the number of tasks an employee performs. For example, a job is designed such that the individual performs six tasks instead of three.

Although in many instances an enlarged job requires a longer training period, job satisfaction usually increases because boredom is reduced. The implication, of course, is that the job enlargement will lead to improvement in other performance outcomes.

The concept and practice of job enlargement have become considerably more sophisticated. In recent years effective job enlargement involves more than simply

---

[23]B. G. Posner, "Role Changes," *Inc.*, February 1990, pp. 95–98.

[24]K. H. Hammonds, "Corning's Class Act," *Business Week*. May 13, 1991, pp. 68–76.

[25]Charles R. Walker and Robert H. Guest, *The Man on the Assembly Line* (Cambridge, Mass.: Harvard University Press, 1952).

increasing task variety. In addition, it is necessary to redesign certain other aspects of job range, including providing the worker-paced (rather than machine-paced) control. Each of these changes involves balancing the gains and losses of varying degrees of labor division.

Some employees cannot cope with enlarged jobs because they cannot comprehend complexity; moreover, they may not have an attention span sufficiently long to stay with and complete an enlarged set of tasks. However, if employees are known to be amenable to job enlargement and if they have the requisite ability, then job enlargement should increase satisfaction and product quality and decrease absenteeism and turnover. These gains are not without costs, however, including the likelihood that employees will demand larger salaries in exchange for their performance of enlarged jobs. Yet these costs must be borne if management desires to implement the redesign strategy that enlarges job depth and job enrichment. Job enlargement is a necessary precondition for job enrichment.

REDESIGNING JOB DEPTH: JOB ENRICHMENT

The impetus for redesigning job depth was provided by Herzberg's two factor theory of motivation.[26] The basis of his theory is that factors which meet individuals' need for psychological growth, especially responsibility, job challenge, and achievement, must be characteristic of their jobs. The application of his theory is termed **job enrichment**. The implementation of job enrichment is realized through direct changes in job depth. Managers can provide employees with greater opportunities to exercise discretion by making the following changes:

1. *Direct feedback:* The evaluation of performance should be timely and direct.
2. *New learning:* A good job enables people to feel they are growing. All jobs should provide opportunities to learn.
3. *Scheduling:* People should be able to schedule some part of their own work.
4. *Uniqueness:* Each job should have some unique qualities or features.
5. *Control over resources:* Individuals should have some control over their job tasks.
6. *Personal accountability:* People should be provided with an opportunity to be accountable for the job.

As defined by the executive in charge of a pioneering job enrichment program at Texas Instruments, job enrichment is a process which (1) encourages employees to behave like managers in managing their jobs and (2) redesigns the job to make such behavior feasible.[27] The process as implemented in TI is continuous and pervades the entire organization. Every job in TI is viewed as subject to analysis to determine if it can be enriched to include managerial activities and thereby

[26]Frederick Herzberg, "The Wise Old Turk," *Harvard Business Review,* September–October 1974, pp. 70–80.

[27]M. Scott Myers, *Every Employee a Manager* (New York: McGraw-Hill, 1970), p. xxi.

made more meaningful. Moreover, as the jobs of nonmanagerial personnel are redesigned to include greater depth, the jobs of managers must be redesigned. The redesigned managerial jobs emphasize training and counseling of subordinates and de-emphasize control and direction. An application of job enrichment in a nonmanufacturing setting is illustrated in Encounter 12-2.

As the theory and practice of job enrichment have evolved, managers have become aware that successful applications require numerous changes in the way work is done. Some of the more important changes include delegating greater authority to workers to participate in decisions, to set their own goals, and to evaluate their (and their work groups') performance. Job enrichment also involves changing the nature and style of managers' behavior. Managers must be willing and able to delegate authority. Given the ability of employees to carry out enriched jobs and the willingness of managers to delegate authority, gains in performance can be expected. These positive outcomes are the result of increasing employees' expectancies that efforts lead to performance, that performance leads to intrinsic and extrinsic rewards, and that these rewards have power to satisfy needs. These significant changes in managerial jobs when coupled with changes in nonmanagerial jobs suggest the importance of a supportive work environment as a prerequisite for successful job enrichment efforts.

Job enrichment and job enlargement are not competing strategies. Job enlargement but not job enrichment may be compatible with the needs, values, and abilities of some individuals. Yet job enrichment, when appropriate, necessarily involves job enlargement. A promising approach to job redesign which attempts to integrate the two approaches is the job characteristic model devised by Hackman, Oldham, Janson, and Purdy.[28]

The model attempts to account for the interrelationships among (1) certain job characteristics, (2) psychological states associated with motivation, satisfaction, and performance, (3) job outcomes, and (4) growth need strength. Exhibit 12-4 describes the relationships among these variables. The core dimensions of the job consist of characteristics first described by Turner and Lawrence. Although variety, identity, significance, autonomy, and feedback do not completely describe perceived job content, they, according to this model, sufficiently describe those aspects which management can manipulate to bring about gains in productivity.

The steps management can take to increase the core dimensions include combining task elements, assigning whole pieces of work (i.e., work modules), allowing discretion in selection of work methods, permitting self-paced control, and opening feedback channels. These actions increase task variety, identity, and significance; consequently, the "experienced meaningfulness of work" psychological state is increased. By permitting employee participation and self-evaluation and creating autonomous work groups, the feedback and autonomy dimensions

---

[28]J. Richard Hackman, Greg Oldham, Robert Janson, and Kenneth Purdy, "New Strategy for Job Enrichment," *California Management Review,* Summer 1975, pp. 57–71; and Hackman and Oldham, "Development of the Job Diagnostic Survey," pp. 159–70.

ORGANIZATIONAL

E N C O U N T E R • 12-2

ENRICHING BANKING JOBS

Although many job enrichment programs have been implemented in manufacturing facilities, service jobs have also been enriched. Two recent enrichment programs at banks are illustrative.

When surveys revealed that Citibank rated very low on customer service, the bank determined the reason was that its employees didn't "feel like somebody." They were dissatisfied with their mundane jobs. Building on the idea that everybody wants to feel like somebody, the bank undertook extensive changes designed to enrich many of the jobs held by its employees. Among the many changes implemented were the following:

- Decentralizing operations so that one person could handle an entire transaction from the time it comes into the bank until it leaves.
- Putting the employees who do the job in direct contact with the customers and the computers.
- Undertaking considerable training and education for the entire work force.

Typical of the changes was the redesign of the letter of credit unit. Prior to redesign, the unit was organized on a functional basis, with the processes of payment examination, processing, filing, issuing and amending, customer service, and accounting each representing distinct organizational entities. The unit was reorganized under a work station concept in which a single individual now performed all of those operations for his or her group of customers. The redesign took place over a two-year period and was accompanied by training sessions which taught the new skills needed. It was also necessary to develop new skills among management, including the attitude that employee opinions are valuable and desirable inputs into decisions.

At another bank, with 38 locations in seven different metropolitan areas, the enrichment program focused on the job position of teller, of which there were over 1,000. Surveys indicated the tellers felt their jobs were boring and underutilized their skills, and they resented being treated as "glorified clerks." Job changes included:

- Increasing the range of activities performed. For example, previously they cashed checks and accepted deposits and loan payments, referring commercial and travelers check customers to special tellers. Under the new system they learned to perform all specialized teller activities.
- Increasing discretionary authority for immediate crediting of deposits and cashing large checks.
- Posting all their transactions through an on-line terminal. Previously, transactions were held in a tray until they were collected and taken to another area where bookkeeping employees posted them.
- Establishing a closer link between tellers and customers. For example, transaction receipts included a special message at the bottom giving the teller's name and urging the customer to contact that teller in the event of error or question. The teller could then handle the inquiry alone or refer it to someone else.

Among other benefits accruing from this job enrichment program was a significant increase in performance as measured 24 months and again 48 months after the redesign.

Sources: R. W. Walters, "The Citibank Project: Improving Productivity through Work Design," in D. L. Kirkpatrick, *How to Manage Change Effectively* (San Francisco: Jossey-Bass, 1985), pp. 195–208; and R. W. Griffin, "Effects of Work Redesign on Employee Perceptions, Attitudes, and Behaviors: A Long-Term Investigation," *Academy of Management Journal,* June 1991, pp. 425–35.

EXHIBIT 12-4

The Job Characteristics Model

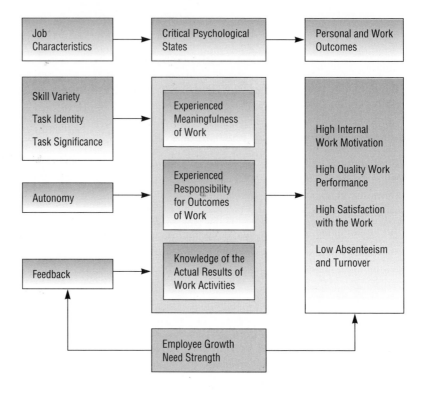

are increased along with the psychological states "experienced responsibility" and "knowledge of actual results."

The positive benefits of these redesign efforts are moderated by individual differences in the strength of employees' growth needs. That is, employees with strong need for accomplishment, learning, and challenge will respond more positively than those with relatively weak growth needs. In more familiar terms, employees who have high need for self-esteem and self-actualization are the more likely candidates for job redesign. Employees forced to participate in job redesign programs but who lack either the need strength or the ability to perform redesigned jobs may experience stress, anxiety, adjustment problems, erratic performance, turnover, and absenteeism.

The available research on the interrelationships between perceived job content and performance are meager. One recent survey of 30 actual applications of job redesign strategies confirms that failures are as frequent as successes.[29] It is apparent, however, that managers must cope with significant problems in matching

[29]Kopelman, "Job Redesign and Productivity."

employee needs and differences and organizational needs.[30] The problems associated with job redesign are several, including:

1. The program is time-consuming and costly.
2. Unless lower level needs are satisfied, people will not respond to opportunities to satisfy upper level needs. And even though our society has been rather successful in providing food and shelter, these needs regain importance when the economy moves through periods of recession and inflation.
3. Job redesign programs are intended to satisfy needs typically not satisfied in the workplace. As workers are told to expect higher order need satisfaction, they may raise their expectations beyond that which is possible. Dissatisfaction with the program's unachievable aims may displace satisfaction with the jobs.
4. Finally, job redesign may be resisted by labor unions who see the effort as an attempt to get more work for the same pay.

Practical efforts to improve productivity and satisfaction through implementation of job redesign strategy have emphasized autonomy and feedback. Relatively less emphasis has been placed on identity, significance, and variety.[31] Apparently it is easier to provide individuals with greater responsibility for the total task and increased feedback than to change the essential nature of the task itself. To provide identity, significance, and variety often requires enlarging the task to the point of losing the benefits of work simplification and standardization. But within the economic constraints imposed by the logic of specialization, it is possible to design work so as to give individuals complete responsibility for its completion to the end and at the same time to provide supportive managerial

■ **E12–2** monitoring. Drawing upon the job characteristics model, Exercise 12–2 demonstrates how to determine the level of each of the models' characteristics in a job and how the factors relate to individual motivation.

In general, the conclusions one reaches when considering the experience of job redesign approaches are that they are relatively successful in increasing quality, but not quantity, of output. This conclusion pertains, however, only if the reward system already satisfies lower level needs. If it presently does not satisfy lower level needs, employees cannot be expected to experience upper level need satisfaction (intrinsic rewards) through enriched jobs. Since a primary source of organizational effectiveness is job performance, managers should design jobs according to the best available knowledge. At present, the strategies for designing and redesigning jobs have evolved from scientific management approaches to work design with emphasis on quality of work-life issues in the context of rapidly changing technology.

---

[30]William E. Zierden, "Congruence in the Work Situation: Effects of Growth Needs, Management Style, and Job Structure on Job-Related Satisfactions," *Journal of Occupational Behavior*, October 1980, pp. 297–310.

[31]Kopelman, "Job Design and Productivity," p. 253.

JOB DESIGN, TECHNOLOGY, AND SOCIOTECHNICAL SYSTEM DESIGN

Job redesign strategy focuses on jobs in the context of individuals' needs for economic well-being and personal growth. A somewhat broader perspective is provided by sociotechnical theory which focuses on jobs in the context of work systems. Both perspectives are cognizant of the imperative of achieving organizational effectiveness. Sociotechnical theory and application of job design developed from studies undertaken in English coal mines from 1948 to 1958.[32] The studies became widely publicized for demonstrating the interrelationship between the social system and the technical system of organizations which was revealed when economic circumstances forced management to change the way the coal was mined (the technical system). Historically, the technical system consisted of small groups of miners (the social system) working together on "short faces," or seams of coal. But the advent of technological advancements improved roof control and safety and made long-wall mining possible. The new system required a change in the social system where groups would be disbanded in favor of one-person, one-task jobs. Despite the efforts of management and even the union, the miners eventually devised a social system that restored many of the characteristics of the group system. This experience has been completely described in organizational behavior literature, and it has stimulated a great deal of research and application.

Self-Managed Teams

There is no contradiction between sociotechnical theory and job redesign theory. Indeed, the two are entirely compatible. The compatibility relates to the demands of modern technology for self-directed and self-motivated job behavior made possible in jobs designed to provide autonomy and variety. This has led to a growing interest in **self-managed teams** (SMT). An SMT is a relatively small group of individuals who are empowered to perform certain activities based on procedures established and decisions made within the group, with minimum or no outside direction. SMTs can take many forms, including task forces, project teams, quality circles, and new venture teams.[33] They can be found in a growing number of organizations, including General Motors, Hewlett-Packard, Prudential, General Foods, Goodyear, and General Mills. Like a number of processes, SMTs are an example of what is essentially an American concept that was implemented outside the United States and "imported back" after demonstrating success. A pioneering effort in Sweden is described in Encounter 12-3.

---

[32]Eric Trist, "The Evolution of Sociotechnical Systems" (Occasional paper, Ontario Quality of Working Life Centre, June 1981).

[33]David Barry, "Managing the Bossless Team: Lessons in Distributed Leadership," *Organizational Dynamics,* Summer 1991, pp. 31–47.

INTERNATIONAL
E N C O U N T E R • 12-3

SOCIOTECHNICAL SYSTEM DESIGN AT VOLVO

When Pehr Gyllenhammar joined Volvo in 1971 as its managing director, performance indicators such as productivity, absenteeism, and turnover were unsatisfactory. A major milestone in changing this occurred in 1974 with the opening of Volvo's new Kalmar assembly plant. Gyllenhammar had been personally and visibly behind the design and construction phases of the new plant to assure that opportunities to provide enriched jobs were parts of the physical and technological layout. The plant incorporated a technology of assembly in which overhead carriers moved the auto body, chassis, and subassemblies to assembly team areas. There, work teams of 20 to 25 employees completed major segments of auto assembly—electrical systems, instrumentation, finishing, and so on. Each group was responsible for a whole piece of work, and they functioned as autonomous units. The results were good (productivity was higher than at Volvo's conventional assembly operation at Gothenburg), but not perfect (absenteeism ran at 17 percent, only slightly below the 20 percent at Gothenburg).

Fifteen years later in 1989, Volvo's newest facility in Uddevalla went into full production (it actually opened in 1987). The Uddevalla complex carries the innovations started at Kalmar much further. It is divided into six assembly plants, each of which has eight SMTs comprised of 7 to 10 workers. The teams are responsible for handling scheduling, quality control, work assignments, even hiring. There are no first-line supervisors. Each team has a spokesperson/ombudsman who reports to the plant manager.

Teams work in one area and assemble four cars per shift. Teams determine how long they will work on a car and they take responsibility for correcting any defects. Since all team members are trained to handle all jobs, each individual works an average of three hours before repeating an operation. Indeed, the training is extensive; each worker receives 16 weeks of training before they ever touch a car, and on-the-job orientation extends another 65 weeks. Volvo will not release productivity figures, but the company claims that Uddevalla produces automobiles with fewer labor hours and higher quality than other Volvo plants, including Kalmar. And what about the chronic Swedish absenteeism problem that even Kalmar didn't make much of a dent in? It has been reduced to 8 percent.

Sources: Berth Jansson and Alden Lank, "Volvo: A Report on the Workshop on Production Technology and Quality of Working Life," *Human Resource Management,* Winter 1985, pp. 455–65; "Volvo's Radical New Plant: The Death of the Assembly Line?" *Business Week,* August 28, 1989; and W. E. Nothdurft, "How to Produce Work-Ready Workers," *Across the Board,* September 29, 1990, pp. 74–84.

In a bold new endeavor, the Saturn Corporation, an independent subsidiary of General Motors, is using the team approach to producing a brand new automobile in a state-of-the-art plant in Spring Hill, Tennessee. Prior to plant construction, a team of 99 Saturn workers visited 160 different facilities around the world, traveling over 2 million miles to find what worked and what didn't.[34] The Saturn plant is organized around nearly 200 SMTs, each of which has the authority to decide how to do its job, including hiring team members. Most even

[34]S. C. Gwynne, "The Right Stuff," *Time,* October 29, 1990, pp. 74–84.

have budgetary responsibilities and can make decisions to change suppliers for parts team members use. Saturn has one of the most extensive worker training programs found in the automobile industry. Employees spend a minimum of 250 hours in training, with many receiving three times that much. Nor is training restricted to nuts and bolts of assembly. It includes topics such as awareness, conflict management, consensus-decision making, and group dynamics.

Rigorous research on the effectiveness of SMTs and similar arrangements is not extensive, but what exists is supportive, particularly in terms of their positive effect on employee attitudes.[35] Both the number of evaluation efforts and their rigor are rapidly increasing, however. Indications are that SMTs will become an

● R12–2   increasingly utilized job design tool. For a specific example, the second reading selection in the chapter describes how one company was able to attain significant productivity increases through the use of SMTs.

SUMMARY OF KEY POINTS

- Job design is based on an analysis of the job, taking into account technological, task, and human factors. In turn, job design, along with social setting differences and individual differences, contributes to perceived job content, which directly affects performance.

- Job analysis is a procedure for determining what is involved in a job, including identification of the activities engaged in to perform the job, the necessary characteristics the jobholder must possess to effectively do the job, the physical environment elements in which the job is performed, as well as outcomes or performance specifications.

- Job range and depth both refer to certain characteristics of any job. Job range is the total number of tasks that a jobholder performs. Job depth is the amount of discretion the jobholder has to determine job activities and outcomes.

- Perceived job content refers to job characteristics as perceived by the jobholder. This "subjective" judgment of what is involved in a job may be quite different from the "objective" determination of job content. Since perceived job content determines performance it is essential

- that these individual differences in perception be recognized.

- Job performance may involve several different types of outcomes. Among the more important are objective outcomes (quantity and quality of production, for example); personal behavior outcomes (stress and physical health outcomes); intrinsic (for example, feelings of responsibility) and extrinsic (for example, pay) outcomes; and job satisfaction outcomes.

- Job performance is determined by an interaction of ability and motivation. Consequently, job design strategies have arisen in an effort to increase the motivational properties of jobs. Such strategies include job rotation, enlargement, and enrichment.

- Job rotation involves moving an individual from one job to another in an effort to increase the number of activities a jobholder performs. Job enlargement involves redesigning a job so that it includes a larger number of activities. Both rotation and enlargement focus on increasing job range.

- Job enrichment is a redesign strategy which has as its major focus increasing job depth. While it almost always

---

[35]J. L. Codery, W. S. Mueller, and L. M. Smith, "Attitudinal and Behavioral Effects of Autonomous Group Working: A Longitudinal Field Study," *Academy of Management Journal,* June 1991, pp 464–76.

involves enlarging the job, it also seeks to increase the discretion the jobholder has and to provide a more challenging set of duties.

- Self-managed teams are groups empowered to perform certain activities based on procedures established and decisions made within the group, with a minimum of external direction.

REVIEW AND DISCUSSION QUESTIONS

1. How is quality of work life (QWL) related to job design? Should organizations be concerned about QWL issues? Why or why not?

2. What are the major differences between functional job analysis and the position analysis questionnaire? Would factors such as the type of job being analyzed or the nature of the workers who do the job favor one of those job analysis techniques over the other?

3. What are the core dimensions in the job characteristics model? What implications do these core dimensions have for job design efforts?

4. Explain the difference between job enlargement and job enrichment? Under what circumstances might an organization not wish to enlarge or enrich a job?

5. It has been suggested that we are training more and more people to do less and less. That is, more people have more capabilities to perform tasks that are requiring fewer capabilities. Do you agree? If so, what is the solution?

6. How might the range and depth of the following jobs be increased: letter carrier, pharmacist, college professor, parole officer?

7. What are the bases for the idea that job redesign and sociotechnology theories are compatible approaches for improving job performance?

8. From an organization's perspective, are some job performance outcomes more or less important than others? Is the same true from an individual employee's perspective?

9. "Self-managed teams are simply an attempt by management to get more out of an employee under the guise of improving the quality of work life." Do you agree or disagree with that statement? Explain.

10. Are job design strategies of rotation, enlargement, and enrichment more compatible with mechanistic or organic organizational designs? Explain.

●

READINGS

READING 12–1   EMPLOYEES REDESIGN THEIR JOBS
Stephen L. Perlman

This unique idea allows workers to be creative in outlining their job responsibilities and forces them to justify how the proposed changes will help them flourish—from an individual and organizational perspective.

Employee-centered work redesign is an innovative concept that may provide a practical solution to the organizational/individual gap by linking the mission and goals of the company with the individual job satisfaction needs of employees.

Without abandoning the successful team methods used in quality circles (QCs), self-directed teams (SDTs), and traditional work redesign, the employee-centered approach allows individuals to practice creative decision making. This is achieved because fundamental work enhancement (from satisfaction and quality improvement perspectives) is placed in the hands of the employees who develop and implement their ideas under the guidance of management. Employee-centered work redesign develops constructive means for employees to become involved in redefining work roles to benefit the organization as well as themselves.

What gives employee-centered work redesign its unique organizational-individual link is its emphasis on total accountability. Although employees are encouraged to be creative in redesigning their jobs, they must be able to justify how their proposed changes will improve quality and support the organization's vision and mission as well as have a positive impact on other employees and systems.

Employees also must be able to justify how their job redesigns will give them greater job satisfaction and provide decision-making control and a degree of autonomy, as well as an opportunity for professional growth. By making employees accountable from an organizational and individual perspective, they become challenged to take the responsibility of thinking, planning, and implementing ideas and to invest themselves in the organization.

Another critical factor in the employee-centered concept is recognizing the contributions of each employee, although individual ideas are part of an overall team mission. This recognition comes from establishing the redesign contribution within the organizational work structure and its daily functioning. Some ways to do this include:

- A redesigned job title, created by the employee
- A revised job description, based on the redesign
- A criteria-based performance evaluation in which the employee holds him- or herself accountable for the job.

Recognition in this sense tends to be permanent because the redesigned work role is acknowledged by management and staff daily. In turn, this sends a clear and powerful message to employees—the company considers their work to be meaningful.

Since employee-centered work redesign was introduced at several Southern California community hospitals in 1985, there has been strong evidence to support its ability to enhance quality of service and quality of work life. From an organizational standpoint, employee-centered groups (during a three-to-five-year period) representing 35 programs and involving 482 employees, had a 57 percent lower turnover ratio than nonemployee-centered groups. In addition, department managers consistently say that they've been able to retain valuable employees better through employee-centered work redesign.

Another benefit is that employee relations problems tend to decline and remain low for staff who participate in employee-centered programs. This may occur for several reasons. Perhaps most significantly, employees learn to be sensitive and appreciate other people's ideas, even if they're inconsistent with their own.

During an employee-centered program, workers have the opportunity to gain a better understanding of process and change. They realize that alterations must benefit the organization as well as their needs, and they recognize that they're accountable for facilitating that change.

Surveys taken after such programs reveal that employees most often increase their awareness of how change takes place and become more receptive to working productively with other individuals.

Stephen L. Perlman is president of Human Resource Innovators.

Source: Stephen L. Perlman, "Employees Redesign Their Jobs," *Personnel Journal,* November 1990, pp. 37–38, 40.

EXHIBIT 12-5

Employee-Centered Work Redesign

Critical Factors	Employee Benefits	Organizational Benefits
• Strong commitment from management to the program to ensure success • Teamwork between employees and their managers to redesign work functions • Organizational benefit in one or more of the following areas: 1) Work productivity. 2) Work quality. 3) Cost containment. • Demonstrate positive impact on staff and existing systems • Hands-on problem-solving format.	• Career and professional growth opportunities realized within the organization • Increased employee job satisfaction • Employees gain insights into the organization • Opportunity to contribute to organizational goals • Employees learn to communicate their needs, concerns and interests • Broaden organization perspective • Promotes career growth opportunities • Access to information • Identify critical skills.	• Greater use of employees • Taps into employee skills, knowledge and creativity • Increased productivity and improved quality • Reduced employee turnover • Employees become stakeholders, not job holders, in the organization • Increased accountability leads to cost-effective behavior • Promotes positive work attitude to discourage employee grievances • Supports cooperative teamwork between employees and management.

Similarly, performance scores for the same employee groups during a three- to five-year period (on a 0–100 scale), have averaged a 23 percent improvement during the first year following the program and have remained at approximately 19 percent above nonemployee-centered groups.

There also are numerous examples of previously mediocre performers participating in employee-centered programs and going on to achieve individual recognition. In the area of quality improvement, employee-centered changes have streamlined departmental operations, promoted commitment to organizational ideals and values, and encouraged task-oriented checks and balances.

Employee-generated ideas have resulted in new and/or improved programs and services that have produced additional revenue or contained costs. Of the 482 approved work redesign models, 31 percent saved more than $5,000 during the first year and 15 percent saved more than $13,500. Independent customer satisfaction and quality control surveys also have shown impressive results for groups that have participated in employee-centered programs.

From an individual perspective, employee-centered work redesign has been an effective mechanism to keep creative high performers in the organization by providing them with a work environment where they continually can be challenged and grow. In so doing, it has shown the ability to strengthen an organization's career development activities by facilitating a multitude of professional growth and advancement opportunities where few or none may have existed before. This is because the nature of work redesign allows new or modified jobs to be created based on changing organizational needs.

Employee-centered work redesign has proven to be an excellent method for employees to communicate their needs, concerns, and interests to management as well as to one another. It has been used effectively in helping employees identify skills, knowledge, and work experiences they wish to refine or gain and creates a practical method for incorporating these goals into a plan that also benefits the organization.

With its focus on work role identification, employee-centered work redesign has produced significant job expansion and modification, allowing greater control of individual work functions and thereby stimulating job accountability.

THE PROCESS STARTS WITH AN ORGANIZATIONAL MISSION

The employee-centered work redesign process begins with individuals learning about the vision and mission of their respective departments through informal yet in-depth discussions with their managers. In cases in which the mission has yet to be created or is undergoing revision (because of organizational or external conditions), ask high-performing employees who have demonstrated company loyalty to participate in mission development.

Workers then complete a needs assessment survey that helps them identify personal job satisfaction and professional development goals that are consistent with the mission and goals of the unit. To ensure consistency, the department manager and work redesign trainer review and discuss each individual goal with the employee (and modify it if necessary) before granting approval. Each employee is asked to specify at least three meaningful personal/professional goals before moving on to the next exercise.

Next, employees learn to identify potential obstacles to their goals and form strategic ways to eliminate or minimize such barriers through communicating concerns with their managers and peers, and by effective planning and intervention. Obstacle identification and intervention is a good form of reality testing that allows the worker to examine his or her goals from a practicality standpoint and to help reduce any anxieties produced in going through the process.

Employees then prepare inventories of their present work, separating major tasks into three distinct areas: work to be retained; work to be modified; and work to be eliminated. Employees also are asked to identify new work to be added to their positions. Where an employee places a current task is based on the need for a better functioning job as well as to meet job satisfaction and professional development goals better. The same accountability applies to any new tasks identified.

In the next stage, employees must identify preferred work roles for every modified or new task listed in the inventory. This identification should take the form of an action verb (i.e., coordinate, analyze, conduct, process, distribute, and so on). The preferred work role is a key component in the process of making employees accountable for their positions.

For example, an employee may have the general title of *clerk,* but through employee-centered work redesign he or she actually may coordinate or supervise a particular job function. Employees also must justify their work redesign changes by determining how each alteration will produce some benefit to the department in terms of quality improvement, productivity, and /or cost containment.

Although employees initially are left to come up with their own creative ideas for work redesign, there's the occasional need to provide assistance to facilitate thinking, such as learning how to use guided imagery to visualize or discover new work areas to develop. During this process, some employees will have valid suggestions for improving task functions, but need help from their peers, trainers or managers as to the mechanics of the redesign.

In addition, employees must identify how their ideas will impact other staff members and the department as a whole. Potentially negative discoveries are discussed candidly in group settings or in individual consultations with the trainer and manager. Modifications in the work redesign model are made accordingly.

During the entire program, employees, trainers, and managers work as a team, sharing the goal of facilitating total quality improvement with individual job satisfaction. The trainer's role is to teach the redesign process, help refine ideas, and offer support and guidance. The manager, while allowing ideas to originate with employees, stands ready to support or offer constructive criticism and direction when necessary to ensure a well thought-out design.

In most cases, employees working in groups will identify common goals and interventions to improve quality. What results may be viewed as a team project or even a team redesign. To retain individuality (and a sense of job accountability), however, each member of the group identifies a permanent role he or she wants to have in the redesign model. Eventually, this is added to the employee's new job description to ensure accountability.

All work redesign proposals must be reviewed carefully by management on a trial basis before implementation. During this time, new systems, tasks, or other changes are monitored for effectiveness and impact on all affected parties. If minor flaws in the design are identified, corrections can be made quickly. Redesign models that successfully pass the trial period are made permanent.

Developing and implementing an employee-centered program within an organization doesn't necessarily mean discarding all other HR strategies. What it does mean is viewing the overall strategy from the concept of building high performance/customer satisfaction together with a high quality of work life.

Strategies that already support the recognition of employees as major contributors to the development of the organization's desired culture should be retained. Firms that pride themselves on being innovative could incorporate the employee-centered approach (with its focus on creativity) and integrate employee-centered outcomes with a pay-for-performance merit plan.

These programs also can be used to help solve other productivity/quality problems and make better use of current talent through job sharing, flex-schedules, and so forth, which simultaneously satisfy diverse individual needs.

A well-administered, employee-centered plan can add multiple avenues for professional growth and advancement, and become a vital part of any company's career development effort. In fact, using employee-centered work redesign gives employees a reason to stay in a certain area as opposed to transferring out. Employee-centered ideas, approved by management and incorporated into the mainstream of the work structure and system, only can enhance a firm's recognition program.

Naturally, special care must be taken when designing these programs. Although a major goal of any employee-centered program is worker empowerment, that power must be monitored and channeled to ensure that: (1) There's sufficient organizational benefit in the proposed change; and (2) the change doesn't have an adverse impact on other employees, management and the system at large.

The process of initiating employee-centered work redesign ideally shoulders a part of a larger process in identifying or redefining the organization's vision, mission, goals and objectives, so that employees have a clear direction in assessing their roles. Furthermore, the most effective employee-centered programs have occurred when there is full and collaborative management participation.

No matter what change process an organization wants to use for its human resources strategies, it may need to alter its view of employees—perhaps regarding them less as subordinates and more as partners. In this manner, firms may find practical and realistic ways to deal with and solve their human resources and organizational problems.

READING 12–2   SELF-DIRECTED WORK TEAMS YIELD LONG-TERM BENEFITS

Anna Versteeg

A growing number of business experts advocate that workers should take on some management tasks. Many companies are already experimenting with self-managing work teams. Here's how one company was able to achieve record productivity gains through total employee involvement.

Harold and Jackie begin their workday the same way many other operations employees do: with a meeting of the cell or group in which they work. Harold discusses the day's work load and individual assignments with the group; Jackie notes a potential quality issue regarding one component. But Harold isn't a supervisor and Jackie isn't a quality inspector—both are simply team members.

Anna Versteeg is operations manager of Northern Telecom Canada Limited's Morrisville, North Carolina, plant. Northern Telecom is headquartered in Mississauga, Ontario.

Source: Anna Versteeg, "Self-Directed Work Teams Yield Long-Term Benefits," *The Journal of Business Strategy,* November/December 1990, pp. 9–12.

Other employees in the cell handle the ordering of materials, scheduling and tracking of overtime, calculation of cell productivity, and budget expenditures. Harold and Jackie are not smarter than other employees, nor are they better paid. Neither has a college degree. Yet each day they make business decisions that were once reserved for management.

Harold, Jackie, and more than 1,000 of their fellow employees at Research Triangle Park (RTP) in Morrisville, North Carolina, and at Creedmoor, Northern Telecom's Raleigh-area facilities, have begun a process that is transforming the work environment. They participate in the team-directed work force (TDWF).

Team direction has its roots in a number of employee involvement strategies popular as early as the 1940s—for example, sensitivity training, "T" groups, and quality circles. But team direction is distinct from all of them in its relentless focus on business performance.

"Let's be perfectly clear: We're here to run a business," says Debra Boggan, manager at the Morrisville plant. "What's driving us is the same thing that's driving every other Northern Telecom function: results. Senior management sets the targets; they don't tell us how to achieve them.

"In the 1990s, the companies that are going to succeed are the ones that are going to get innovation and spirit back into the workplace," she adds. "And I feel much more comfortable knowing that I have 420 people worried about my business than just ten or fifteen people worried about my business. Empowering employees—giving them the responsibility for the business—is the key."

Here are the results achieved to date by Northern Telecom as a result of TDWF. Business at the Morrisville repair facility was not expected to grow, but revenue has increased 63 percent since team direction began three years ago. Sales are up 26 percent, and earnings have grown 46 percent. Productivity per employee is up more than 60 percent; scrap is down 63 percent. Quality results have risen 50 percent, while the number of quality inspectors has dropped 40 percent. At Creedmoor, where team direction is still being introduced, one team-directed manufacturing cell has gone nine weeks—and still counting—without a quality defect.

According to the Creedmoor operations manager, Brent Stroud, such advances are the real purpose of team direction. "Our company is looking for quantum leaps in quality, productivity, and earnings. We can't achieve these with traditional management methods."

Adds Rich Rollinson of RTP: "This is a long-term change in management philosophy that's needed to ensure our survival."

Results like these are not a surprise to the company's managers, for example Morrisville's Joe Greene. Such results are a natural consequence of involving employees in setting goals and making decisions on how to achieve them. "Who knows better what it takes to do a job than the person who does it every day?" asks Greene. "But if you want to be the best, people will be challenged to do even more. If you let people set the goal and decide how to get there, they'll achieve more than managers ever dreamed of."

Team Direction: A Primer

If your company is thinking about implementing team direction, these are the major issues that need to be addressed:

Team direction is not a program. It is not an experiment — going back is virtually impossible. The process needs commitment from the top. Team direction is a new attitude. It is treating people with respect and empowering them with the responsibility for all functions of the business. It is using the collective brainpower of all as a competitive strategy.

Trust. Trust is a critical element for all employees. Management must be willing to let go and to delegate responsibility; employees must believe they will be allowed to have ownership and make *real* decisions. Earning trust is a long-term process. When risks are taken, mistakes will happen. However, more can be learned from mistakes than from success. A fear of failure should not be created.

Fear. At the outset, managers and supervisors fear loss of control because under the old system, control is power. With team direction, managers gain more support because everyone becomes responsible for the business, not just the managers. First-line managers may fear losing their jobs, as teams take on traditional managerial responsibilities.

Control vs. direction. One of the biggest changes in team direction involves the role of the manager or supervisor, transforming this person from boss-dictator to coach-facilitator. Facilitators help guide, direct, and support the team, but they do not control it. This is a difficult transition for some.

Fallout. Fear of change is natural, but do not write anyone off without *resolutely* trying to include him or her on the team. Typically, about 25 perent of first-line supervisors leave after a company adopts TDWF. However, one Northern Telecom facility found that it lost 75 percent of its first-line supervisors because they could not adapt to team direction.

Training. Training can make or break team direction. Training for all employees should be on two levels: skill-based training to make all employees cross-functional and communication training. Everyone must communicate openly and learn to deal with their feelings.

Stress. Emotions run high in the beginning. Issues that were buried for many years come out into the open.

Stress-management courses for all employees are very helpful.

Barriers. In a participatory workplace, reserved parking, executive dining rooms, ties, time clocks, and all other barriers that separate management from other employees should be critically examined.

Textbook definitions of team direction are hard to come by. Those involved say that is because it is not a program; it is a direction and a set of ideals. "More than anything," says one plant manager, "it's a mind-set change, and it starts with each one of us."

The evolution of the TDWF concept began at the Morrisville facility about three years ago with a videotape and a time clock. "The time clock sent a signal that management didn't trust us," relates one Morrisville employee.

At that time, plant management made available a number of videotapes for employees to view, in particular one by the management consultant Tom Peters that featured a segment on employee teams. "That segment was worn out because it had been viewed so many times," says Boggan. "Employees began to tell us that we could do better, and we started to ask ourselves why there were different standards for employees and management."

CHANGES IN ATTITUDE

As a first small step, the time clock in the plant was removed. Employees were told they were responsible for monitoring their own breaks, lunches, and work hours. There was one caveat: The change could not affect customer service or productivity.

"It was as simple as realizing that people are adults," says Boggan. "We basically stopped telling people to check their brains at the front door; we started treating them with respect."

Employees were suspicious at first. "I thought it was a setup," says Amanda Dunston. "I thought they'd still be watching us, that maybe it was just another way of getting rid of people. But that didn't happen." However, the trust had to be earned, day after day.

The next stage in the change process involved defining goals and operating parameters for the business unit, determining exactly what constituted "acceptable perfor-

mance," and researching employee involvement strategies used by other companies. It quickly became clear that the issue of trust had to be addressed directly in order to put in place some of the process changes, such as just-in-time and other cell-based manufacturing concepts, that were needed to meet production goals.

One of the most important elements in team direction is training all employees on all functions of the business. Creedmoor's operations manager, Brent Stroud, says, "We've planned for about fifty hours of training per person this year, which will be focused primarily on nonphysical skills: business knowledge, problem solving, and team dynamics."

The first, and some believe the most critical, need for training is in interpersonal skills. "To make these changes, we had to be real people—no games," remarks one employee. "We had to deal with feelings."

"And that meant communication skills," adds a Morrisville employee. "Traditional training focused on managers, as if other employees didn't need to know how to communicate."

The Working program, developed by Zenger-Miller, a training company headquartered in San Jose, California, is being used to teach basic peer relationship skills essential in a team environment. The program is taught in an 18-week sequence, with one two-hour module each week. Modules teach "skill units," which help people communicate more clearly and honestly and keep communication focused on business issues rather than on personal differences—on behavior rather than on the person.

These ideas are not earth shattering. The first reaction of most employees is usually "I know that!" But sometimes a dose of common sense is just what people say they need.

As team direction developed, Morrisville management found that employees asked to be more and more involved in making business decisions. Teams came forward with proposals to alter work schedules and steamline decision making. Some parameters had to be set. One of the first decision factors was the impact of a change on customers. There could be no negative impact, only a positive one.

The specific changes proposed by employees ranged from the simple to the profound. To break down one symbolic barrier between managers and employees, men stopped wearing ties. Production employees established direct customer contacts through face-to-face meetings, telephone surveys, and other methods. Employees began to evaluate one another in peer performance review sessions, first for feedback only, then to recommend merit salary increases.

PITFALLS OF THE PROCESS

Employees and managers involved in team direction are often passionate in their praise of the concepts. Even so, they readily admit that adopting this management philosophy is not easy. (See the sidebar, "Team Direction: A Primer," for a discussion of issues involved in the implementation of team direction.)

"Why aren't all companies doing this? Because it's hard," says Rick Gilbert of Morrisville. "We've all been taught certain ways of responding, and it's easy to become a dictator again."

When asked "What are the pitfalls of team direction?" Debra Boggan, a Morrisville plant manager, replies, "What are the pitfalls of the way you're managing now? They're no different; this is just new." She offers two caveats generally echoed by those experienced in team direction.

- **Move with caution.** "You can't start the process without commitment to see it through, because once you start there's no going back," she says.
- **Expect chaos at first.** "You're encouraging people to communicate openly, maybe for the first time. There will be conflicts in areas you thought were going pretty well. You expect these will work out after people develop trust in your intentions."

As team direction evolved, other Northern Telecom facilities throughout the United States and Canada expressed interest, but on their own terms. "We don't believe there is an exact recipe for team direction," says one employee at RTP. "It grows differently from facility to facility and from team to team."

Employees at the Morrisville plant described the TDWF process in a team-drafted statement: "At the heart of workplace transformation is a firm belief in and support of the team concept of democratic team functioning, of participatory decision making. The business team is thus the cornerstone on which the entire organization is constructed.

EXERCISES

EXERCISE 12–1 JOB DESIGN PREFERENCES

OBJECTIVES

1. To illustrate individual differences in preferences about various job design characteristics.
2. To illustrate how your preferences may differ from those of others.
3. To examine the most important and least important job design characteristics and how managers would cope with them.

STARTING THE EXERCISE

First you will respond to a questionnaire asking about your job design preferences and how you view the preferences of others. After working through the questionnaire *individually,* small groups will be formed. In the groups discussion will focus on the individual differences in preferences expressed by group members.

Job design is concerned with a number of attributes of a job. Among these attributes are the job itself, the requirements of the job, the interpersonal interaction opportunities on the job, and performance outcomes. There are certain attributes that are preferred by individuals. Some prefer job autonomy, while others prefer to be challenged by different tasks. It is obvious that individual differences in preferences would be an important consideration for managers. An exciting job for one person may be a demeaning and boring job for another individual. Managers could use this type of information in attempting to create job design conditions that allow organizational goals and individual goals and preferences to be matched.

The Job Preference form is presented below. Please read it carefully and complete it after considering each characteristic listed. Due to space limitations, not all job design characteristics are included for your consideration. Use only those that are included on the form.

Phase I: 15 minutes

1. Individually complete the A and B portions of the Job Design Preference form.

Phase II: 45 minutes

1. The instructor will form groups of four to six students.
2. Discuss the differences in the rankings individuals made on the A and B parts of the form.
3. Present each of the A rank orders of group members on a flip chart or the blackboard. Analyze the areas of agreement and disagreement.
4. Discuss what implications the A and B rankings would have to a *manager* who would have to supervise a group such as the group you are in. That is, what could a manager do to cope with the individual differences displayed in steps 1, 2, and 3 above?

JOB DESIGN PREFERENCES

A. Your Job Design Preferences

Decide which of the following is most important to you. Place a 1 in front of the most important characteristic. Then decide which is the second most important characteristic to you and place a 2 in front of it. Continue numbering the items in order of importance until the least important is ranked 10. There are no right answers since individuals differ in their job design preferences. Do not discuss your individual rankings until the instructor forms groups.

_____ Variety in tasks
_____ Feedback on performance from doing the job
_____ Autonomy
_____ Working as a team
_____ Responsibility
_____ Developing friendships on the job
_____ Task identity
_____ Task significance
_____ Having the resources to perform well
_____ Feedback on performance from others (e.g., the manager, co-workers)

B. Others' Job Design Preferences

In the A section you have provided your preferences. Now number the items as you think others would rank them. Consider others who are in your course, class, or program, that is, those who are also completing this exercise. Rank the factors from 1 (most important) to 10 (least important).

_____ Variety in tasks
_____ Feedback on performance from doing the job
_____ Autonomy
_____ Working as a team
_____ Responsibility
_____ Developing friendships on the job
_____ Task identity
_____ Task significance
_____ Having the resources to perform well
_____ Feedback on performance from others (e.g., the manager, co-workers)

EXERCISE 12–2   JOB DESIGN

PURPOSE

This exercise illustrates how particular characteristics of work relate to the motivation of those who perform it. Tasks can be thought of as being different on several characteristics:

Source: Henry L. Tosi and Jerald W. Young, *Management Experiences and Illustrations*, (Homewood, IL: Richard D. Irwin, Inc., 1982).

1. The amount of *task autonomy*.
2. The degree of *variety* of activities.
3. The extent to which one can *identify* their task as a whole unit of work.
4. The *significance* of the job's influence on other people—both within and outside the organization.
5. The *feedback* which the task itself provides about performance.

This exercise demonstrates how to determine the level of each of these characteristics in a job and how these factors relate to individual motivation.

TIME REQUIRED

10 minutes to read the work biography and 15 minutes to complete the questionnaire. This exercise may also be completed as a homework assignment and brought to class for discussion.

PREPARATION

There are two approaches to using this exercise. Your instructor will give you directions.

Either

1. Think about the job you now hold or one you have held. Respond to the items on the following questionnaires as they relate to that job.

Or

2. Read one of the work biographies at the end of this book (as assigned by your instructor) and complete the following items as they relate to the situation described.

JOB DESIGN

JOB TITLE _____
　　　　　　　　(Title of the job to be analyzed)

JOB DESCRIPTION:　Briefly describe the major responsibilities of the job.

_____

_____

This part of the questionnaire asks you to describe your (the) job, as *objectively* as you can. *Please do not use the questionnaire to show how much you like or dislike your job.* Questions about that will come later. Make your descriptions as accurate and as objective as you possibly can.

1. How much autonomy is there in your job? That is, to what extent does your job permit you to decide *on your own* how to go about doing the work?

$$1————2————3————4————5————6————7$$

Very little; the job gives me almost no personal say about how and when the work is done.	Moderate autonomy; many things are standardized and not under my control but I can make some decisions about the work.	Very much; the job gives me almost complete responsibility for deciding how and when the work is done.

2. To what extent does your job involve doing a *"whole" and identifiable piece of work?* That is, is the job a complete piece of work that has an obvious beginning and end? Or is it only a small *part* of the overall piece of work, which is finished by other people or by automatic machines?

My job is only a tiny part of the overall piece of work; the results of my activities cannot be seen in the final product or service.	My job is a moderately sized chunk of the overall piece of work; my own contribution can be seen in the final outcome.	My job involves doing the whole piece of work from start to finish; the results of my activities are easily seen in the final product of service.

3. How much variety is there in your job? That is, to what extent does the job require you to do *many different things* at work, using a *variety of your skills* and *talents*?

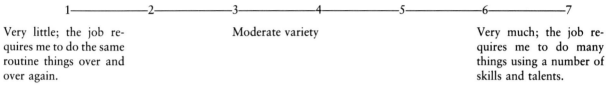

Very little; the job requires me to do the same routine things over and over again.	Moderate variety	Very much; the job requires me to do many things using a number of skills and talents.

4. In general, how much impact on others does your job have? That is, are the results of your work likely to significantly affect the lives or well-being of other people?

Not very significant; the outcomes of my work are *not* likely to have important effects on their people.	Moderately significant	Highly significant; the outcomes of the work can affect other people in very important ways.

5. To what extent does *doing the job itself* provide you with information about your work performance? That is, does the actual *work itself* provide clues about how well you are doing — aside from any "feedback" co-workers or supervisor may provide?

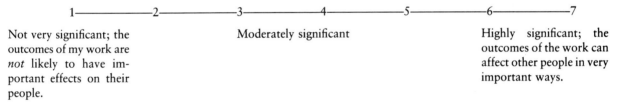

Very little; the job itself is set up so I could work forever without finding out how well I am doing.	Moderately; sometimes doing the job provides "feedback" to me; sometimes it does not.	Very much; the job is set up so that I get almost constant "feedback" as I work about how well I am doing.

Listed below are a number of statements which could be used to describe a job. You are to indicate whether each statement is an *accurate* or an *inaccurate* description of *your* job. Once again, please try to be as objective as you can in deciding how accurately each statement describes your job—regardless of whether you *like* or *dislike* your job.

Write a number in the blank beside each statement based on the following scale:

How accurate is the statement in describing your job?

1	2	3	4	5	6	7
Very inaccurate	Mostly inaccurate	Slightly inaccurate	Uncertain	Slightly accurate	Mostly accurate	Very accurate

_____ 6. The job requires me to use a number of complex or high-level skills.

_____ 7. The job is arranged so that I have the chance to do an entire piece of work from beginning to end.

_____ 8. Just doing the work required by the job provides many chances for me to figure out how well I am doing.

_____ 9. This job is not at all simple or repetitive.

_____ 10. This job is one where many other people can be affected by how well the work gets done.

_____ 11. The job allows me a chance to use my personal initiative or judgment in carrying out the work.

_____ 12. The job provides me the chance to completely finish the piece of work I begin.

_____ 13. The job itself provides many clues about whether or not I am performing well.

_____ 14. The job gives me considerable opportunity for independence and freedom in how I do the work.

_____ 15. The job itself is quite significant or important in the broader scheme of things.

Listed below are a number of characteristics which could be present on any job. People differ about how much they would like to have each one present in their own jobs. We are interested in learning *how much you personally would like* to have each one present in your job.

Using the scale below, please indicate the *degree* to which you *would like* to have each characteristic present in your job.

1————————2————————3————————4————————5————————6————————7

Would like having this
only a moderate amount
(or less)

Would like having this
very much

Would like having this
extremely much

_____ 16. Stimulating and challenging work.

_____ 17. Chances to exercise independent thought and action in my job.

_____ 18. Opportunities to learn new things from my work.

_____ 19. Opportunities to be creative and imaginative in my work.

_____ 20. Opportunities for personal growth and development in my job.

_____ 21. A sense of worthwhile accomplishment in my work.

Computation work sheet for internal motivating potential

I. Average identity (AVG IDENT)

    Question 2 = _____
    Question 7 = _____
    Question 12 = _____
         Total = _____

II. Average variety (AVG VAR)

    Question 3 = _____
    Question 6 = _____
    Question 9 = _____
         Total = _____

$\dfrac{\text{TOTAL}}{3}$ = _____ = AVG IDENT

$\dfrac{\text{TOTAL}}{3}$ = _____ = AVG VAR

III. Average significance (AVG SIG)

        Question 4 = _____
        Question 10 = _____
        Question 15 = _____
            Total = _____

$$\frac{TOTAL}{3} = \underline{\quad} = AVG\ SIG$$

IV. Average autonomy (AVG AUTO)

        Question 1 = _____
        Question 11 = _____
        Question 14 = _____
            Total = _____

$$\frac{TOTAL}{3} = \underline{\quad} = AVG\ AUTO$$

V. Average feedback from job (AVG FEED)

        Question 5 = _____
        Question 8 = _____
        Question 13 = _____
            Total = _____

$$\frac{TOTAL}{3} = \underline{\quad} = AVG\ FEED$$

Internal motivating Potential score $= \left[\dfrac{(AVG\ IDENT\ +\ AVG\ VAR\ +\ AVG\ SIG)^1}{3} \right] * AVG\ AUTO^2 * AVG\ FEED^3$

$= \left[\dfrac{(\text{------}\ +\ \text{------}\ +\ \text{------})}{3} \right] * \underline{\quad} * \underline{\quad}$

(Note: *means multiply by.)

$= \underline{\qquad\qquad\qquad}$

    1 = Meaningfulness score
    2 = Responsibility score
    3 = Knowledge of results score

Growth Need Strength (AVG GNS)

    Question 16 _____
    Question 17 _____
    Question 18 _____
    Question 19 _____
    Question 20 _____
    Question 21 _____
        Total = _____

    Total ÷ 6 = _____ = AVG GNS

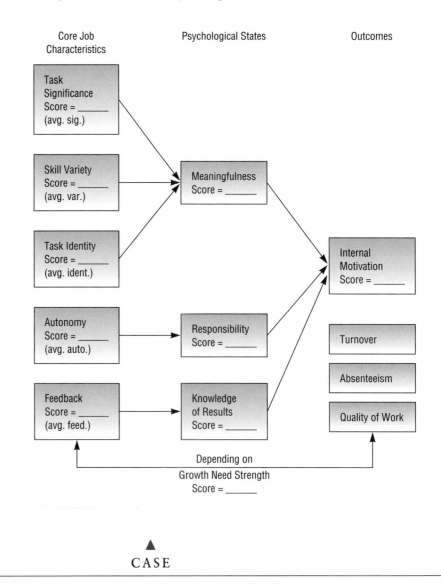

Core Job Characteristics — Psychological States — Outcomes

- Task Significance Score = _____ (avg. sig.)
- Skill Variety Score = _____ (avg. var.)
- Task Identity Score = _____ (avg. ident.)
- Autonomy Score = _____ (avg. auto.)
- Feedback Score = _____ (avg. feed.)
- Meaningfulness Score = _____
- Responsibility Score = _____
- Knowledge of Results Score = _____
- Internal Motivation Score = _____
- Turnover
- Absenteeism
- Quality of Work

Depending on Growth Need Strength Score = _____

▲
CASE

CASE 12–1   THE HOVEY AND BEARD COMPANY CASE

PART 1

The Hovey and Beard Company manufactures a variety of wooden toys, including animals, pull toys, and the like.

Source: Abridged and adapted from Chapter 10, Group Dynamics and Intergroup Relations, by George Strauss and Alex Bavelas (under the title "The Hovey and Beard Case"). From *Money and Motivation,* edited by William F. Whyte. Copyright © 1955 by Harper & Row Publishers, Inc.

The toys were manufactured by a transformation process that began in the wood room. There, toys were cut, sanded, and partially assembled. Then the toys were dipped into shellac and sent to the painting room.

In years past, the painting had been done by hand, with each employee working with a given toy until its painting was completed. The toys were predominantly two-colored, although a few required more than two colors. Now in response to increased demand for the toys, the painting operation was changed so that the painters sat in a line by an endless chain of hooks. These hooks moved continuously in front of the painters and passed into a long horizontal oven. Each painter sat in a booth designed to carry away fumes and to backstop excess paint. The painters would take a toy from a nearby tray, position it in a jig inside the painting cubicle, spray on the color according to a pattern, and then hang the toy on a passing hook. The rate at which the hooks moved was calculated by the engineers so that each painter, when fully trained, could hang a painted toy on each hook before it passed beyond reach.

The painters were paid on a group bonus plan. Since the operation was new to them, they received a learning bonus that decreased by regular amounts each month. The learning bonus was scheduled to vanish in six months, by which time it was expected that they would be on their own—that is, able to meet the production standard and earn a group bonus when they exceeded it.

QUESTIONS

1. Assume that the training period for the new job setup has just begun. What change do you predict in the level of output of the painters? Why?
   increase   decrease   stay the same
2. What other predictions regarding the behavior of these painters do you make based upon the situation described so far?

PART 2

By the second month of the training period, trouble developed. The painters learned more slowly than had been anticipated and it began to look as through their production would stabilize far below what was planned. Many of the hooks were going by empty. The painters complained that the hooks moved too fast and that the engineer had set the rates wrong. A few painters quit and had to be replaced with new ones. This further aggravated the learning problem. The team spirit that the management had expected to develop through the group bonus was not in evidence except as an expression of what the engineers called "resistance." One painter, whom the group regarded as its leader (and the management regarded as the ringleader), was outspoken in taking the complaints of the group to the supervisor. These complaints were that the

job was messy, the hooks moved too fast, the incentive pay was not correctly calculated, and it was too hot working so close to the drying oven.

PART 3

A consultant was hired to work with the supervisor. She recommended that the painters be brought together for a general discussion of the working conditions. Although hesitant, the supervisor agreed to this plan.

The first meeting was held immediately after the shift was over at 4 o'clock in the afternoon. It was attended by all eight painters. They voiced the same complaints again: the hooks went by too fast, the job was too dirty, and the room was hot and poorly ventilated. For some reason, it was this last item that seemed to bother them most. The supervisor promised to discuss the problems of ventilation and temperature with the engineers, and a second meeting was scheduled. In the next few days the supervisor had several talks with the engineers. They, along with the plant superintendent, felt that this was really a trumped-up complaint and that the expense of corrective measures would be prohibitively high.

The supervisor came to the second meeting with some apprehensions. The painters, however, did not seem to be much put out. Rather, they had a proposal of their own to make. They felt that if several large fans were set up to circulate the air around their feet, they would be much more comfortable. After some discussion, the supervisor agreed to pursue the idea. The supervisor and the consultant discussed the idea of fans with the superintendent. Three large propeller-type fans were purchased and installed.

The painters were jubilant. For several days the fans were moved about in various positions until they were placed to the satisfaction of the group. The painters seemed completely satisfied with the results, and the relations between them and the supervisor improved visibly.

The supervisor, after this encouraging episode, decided that further meetings might also prove profitable. The painters were asked if they would like to meet and discuss other aspects of the work situation. They were eager to do this. Another meeting was held and the discussion quickly centered on the speed of the hooks. The painters maintained that the engineer had set them at an unreasonably fast speed and that they would never be able to fill enough of them to make a bonus.

The discussion reached a turning point when the group's leader explained that it wasn't that the painters couldn't work fast enough to keep up with the hooks but that they couldn't work at that pace all day long. The supervisor explored the point. The painters were unanimous in their opinion that they could keep up with the belt for short periods if they wanted to. But they didn't want to because if they showed they could do this for short periods then they would be expected to do it all day long. The meeting ended with an unprecedented request by the painters: "Let us adjust the speed of the belt faster or slower depending on how we feel." The supervisor agreed to discuss this with the superintendent and the engineers.

The engineers reacted negatively to the suggestion. However, after several meetings it was granted that there was some latitude within which variations in the speed of the hooks would not affect the finished product. After considerable argument with the engineers, it was agreed to try out the painters' idea.

With misgivings, the supervisor had a control with a dial marked "low, medium, fast" installed at the booth of the group leader. The speed of the belt could now be adjusted anywhere between the lower and upper limits that the engineers had set.

QUESTIONS

1. What changes do you now expect in the level of output of the painters? Why?

   increase   decrease   stay the same

2. What changes do you expect in the feelings of the painters toward their work situation? Why?

   more positive   more negative   no change

3. What other predictions do you make about the behavior of the painters?

PART 4

The painters were delighted and spent many lunch hours deciding how the speed of the belt should be varied from hour to hour throughout the day. Within a week the pattern had settled down to one in which the first half hour of the shift was run on a medium speed (a dial setting slightly above the point marked "medium"). The next two

and a half hours were run at high speed, and the half hour before lunch and the half hour after lunch were run at low speed. The rest of the afternoon was run at high speed with the exception of the last 45 minutes of the shift, which was run at medium.

The constant speed at which the engineers had originally set the belt was actually slightly below the "medium" mark on the control dial: the average speed at which the painters were running the belt was on the high side of the dial. Few, if any, empty hooks entered the oven, and inspection showed no increase of rejects from the paint room.

Production increased, and within three weeks (some two months before the scheduled ending of the learning bonus) the painters were operating at 30 to 50 percent above the level that had been expected under the original arrangement. Naturally, their earnings were correspondingly higher than anticipated. They were collecting their base pay, earning a considerable piece-rate bonus, and still benefiting from the learning bonus. They were earning more now than many skilled workers in other parts of the plant.

QUESTIONS

1. How do you feel about the situation at this point?
2. Suppose that you were the supervisor. What would you expect to happen next? Why?

PART 5

Management was besieged by demands that the inequity between the earnings of the painters and those of other workers in the plant be taken care of. With growing irritation between the superintendent and the supervisor, the engineers and supervisor, and the superintendent and engineers, the situation came to a head when the superintendent revoked the learning bonus and returned the painting operation to its original status: the hooks moved again at their constant, time-studied, designated speed. Production dropped again and within a month all but two of the eight painters had quit. The supervisor stayed on for several months, but, feeling aggrieved, left for another job.

Success is turning
knowledge into positive
action.

—**Dorothy Leeds**

ORGANIZATIONAL PROCESSES

Decision Making

The focus of this chapter is on decision making. The quality of the decisions that managers reach is the yardstick of their effectiveness.[1] Indeed, it has been suggested that management *is* decision making, and because it is, the very essence of the entire managerial process is to be found in its study. Increasingly, however, important decisions are being made in organizations by nonmanagers. Thus, while decision making is an important management process, it is fundamentally a *people* process. This chapter, therefore, describes and analyzes decision making in terms that reflect the ways in which people make decisions upon their understanding of individual, group, and organizational goals and objectives.

[1]Barnard M. Bass, *Organizational Decision Making* (Homewood, Ill.: Richard D. Irwin, 1983).

TYPES OF DECISIONS

Managers in various kinds of organizations may be separated by background, lifestyle, and distance, but sooner or later, they must all make decisions. Even when the decision process is highly participative in nature, with full involvement by subordinates, it is the manager who ultimately is responsible for the outcomes of a decision. In this section, our purpose is to present a classification system into which various kinds of decisions can be placed, regardless of whether the manager makes the decision unilaterally or in consultation with, or delegation to, subordinates.

Specialists in the field of decision making have developed several ways of classifying different types of decisions. For the most part, these classification systems are similar, differing mainly in terminology. We use the widely adopted distinction suggested by Herbert Simon.[2] Simon distinguishes between two types of decisions:

1. *Programmed decisions.* If a particular situation occurs often, a routine procedure usually will be worked out for solving it. Decisions are **programmed** to the extent that they are repetitive and routine and a definite procedure has been developed for handling them.
2. *Nonprogrammed decisions.* Decisions are nonprogrammed when they are novel and unstructured. There is no established procedure for handling the problem, either because it has not arisen in exactly the same manner before or because it is complex or extremely important. Such decisions deserve special treatment.

While the two classifications are broad, they point out the importance of differentiating between programmed and nonprogrammed decisions. The managements of most organizations face great numbers of programmed decisions in their daily operations. Such decisions should be treated without expending unnecessary organizational resources on them. On the other hand the nonprogrammed decision must be properly identified as such since it is this type of decision that forms the basis for allocating billions of dollars worth of resources in our economy every year. Unfortunately, it is the human process involving this type of decision that we know the least about.[3] Exhibit 13-1 presents a breakdown of the different types of decisions, with examples of each type, in different kinds of organizations. The exhibit illustrates that programmed and nonprogrammed decisions require different kinds of procedures and apply to distinctly different types of problems.

---

[2]Herbert A. Simon, *The New Science of Management Decision* (New York: Harper & Row, 1960), pp. 5–6.

[3]Neil M. Agnew and John L. Brown, "Executive Judgment: The Institution/Rational Ratio," *Personnel*, December 1985, pp. 48–54.

EXHIBIT 13-1

Types of Decisions

	Programmed Decisions	Nonprogrammed Decisions
Type of problem	Frequent, repetitive, routine, much certainty regarding cause-and-effect relationships	Novel, unstructured, much uncertainty regarding cause-and-effect relationships
Procedure	Dependence on policies, rules, and definite procedures	Necessity for creativity, intuition, tolerance for ambiguity, creative problem solving
Examples	*Business firm:* Periodic reorders of inventory	*Business firm:* Diversification into new products and markets
	University: Necessary grade-point average for good academic standing	*University:* Construction of new classroom facilities
	Health care: Procedure for admitting patients	*Health care:* Purchase of experimental equipment
	Government: Merit system for promotion of state employees	*Government:* Reorganization of state government agencies

Traditionally, programmed decisions have been handled through rules, standard operating procedures, and the structure of the organization that develops specific procedures for handling them. Operations researchers—through the development of mathematical models—have facilitated the handling of these types of decisions.

On the other hand, nonprogrammed decisions usually have been handled by general problem-solving processes, judgment, intuition, and creativity. Unfortunately, the advances that modern management techniques have made in improving nonprogrammed decision making have not been nearly as great as the advances they have made in improving programmed decision making.[4]

Ideally, the main concern of top management should be nonprogrammed decisions, while first-level management should be concerned with programmed decisions. Middle managers in most organizations concentrate mostly on programmed decisions, although in some cases they will participate in nonprogrammed decisions. In other words, the nature, frequency, and degree of certainty surrounding a problem should dictate at what level of management the decision should be made.

Obviously, problems arise in those organizations where top management expends much time and effort on programmed decisions.[5] One unfortunate result

[4]Weston Agor, "The Logic of Institution: How Top Executives Make Important Decisions," *Organizational Dynamics,* Winter 1986, pp. 5–18.

[5]Anna Grandori, "A Prescriptive Contingency View of Organizational Decision Making," *Administrative Science Quarterly,* June 1984, pp. 192–209.

of this practice is a neglect of long-range planning, which is subordinated to other activities, whether the organization is successful or is having problems. If the organization is successful, this justifies continuing the policies and practices that have achieved success. If the organization experiences difficulty, its current problems have first priority and occupy the time of top management. In either case, long-range planning ends up being neglected.

Finally, the neglect of long-range planning usually results in an overemphasis on short-run control. This results in a lack of delegation of authority to lower levels of management, which often has adverse effects on motivation and satisfaction.

THE DECISION-MAKING PROCESS

Decisions should be thought of as a means rather than ends. They are the *organizational mechanisms* through which an attempt is made to achieve a desired state. They are, in effect, an *organizational response* to a problem. Every decision is the outcome of a dynamic process that is influenced by a multitude of forces. This process is diagrammed in Exhibit 13-2. The reader should not, however, interpret this outline to mean that decision making is a fixed procedure. It is a sequential process rather than a series of steps. This sequence diagram enables us to examine each element in the normal progression that leads to a decision.

Examination of Exhibit 13-2 reveals that it is more applicable to nonprogrammed decisions than to programmed decisions. Problems that occur infrequently, with a great deal of uncertainty surrounding the outcome, require that the manager utilize the entire process. For problems that occur frequently, however, this is not necessary. If a policy is established to handle such problems, it will not be necessary to develop and evaluate alternatives each time a similar problem arises.

Establishing Specific Goals and Objectives and Measuring Results

Goals and objectives are needed in each area where performance influences the effectiveness of the organization. If goals and objectives are adequately established, they will dictate what results must be achieved and the measures that indicate whether or not they have been achieved.

Problem Identification and Definition

A necessary condition for a decision is a problem—if problems did not exist, there would be no need for decisions. Problems typically result from a determination that a discrepancy exists between a desired state and current reality.[6] This

---

[6]David A. Cowan, "Developing a Classification Structure of Organizational Problems: An Empirical Investigation," *Academy of Management Journal,* June 1990, pp. 366–90.

EXHIBIT 13-2

The Decision-Making Process

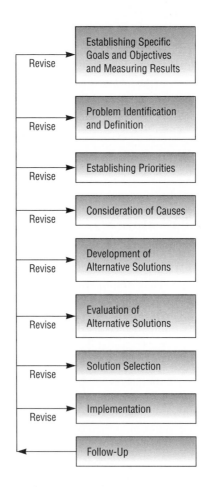

underscores the importance of establishing goals and objectives. How critical a problem is for the organization is measured by the gap between the levels of performance specified in the organization's goals and objectives and the levels of performance attained. Thus, a gap of 20 percent between a sales volume objective and the volume of sales actually achieved signifies that some problem exists. How

■ **E13–1** good are you at problem solving? Exercise 13–1 will assess your problem-solving style.

It is easy to understand that a problem exists when a gap occurs between desired results and actual results. However, certain factors often lead to difficulties in identifying exactly what the problem is.[7] These factors are:

1. *Perceptual problems.* As noted in Chapter 3, individual feelings may act in such a way as to protect or defend us from unpleasant perceptions. Negative

[7]See G. P. Huber, *Managerial Decision Making* (Glenview, Ill.: Scott, Foresman, 1980).

information may be selectively perceived in such a way as to distort its true meaning or it may be totally ignored. For example, a college dean may fail to identify increasing class sizes as a problem while at the same time being sensitive to problems faced by the president of the university in raising funds for the school.

2. *Defining problems in terms of solutions.* This is really a form of jumping to conclusions. For example, a sales manager may say, "The decrease in profits is due to our poor product quality." The sales manager's definition of the problem suggests a particular solution—the improvement of product quality in the production department. Certainly, other solutions may be possible. Perhaps the sales force has been inadequately selected or trained. Perhaps competitors have a superior product.

3. *Identifying symptoms as problems.* "Our problem is a 32 percent decline in orders." While it is certainly true that orders have declined, the decline in orders is really a symptom of the real problem. When the manager identifies the real problem, the cause of the decline in orders will be found.

Problems usually are of three types: opportunity, crisis, or routine.[8] Crisis and routine problems present themselves and must be attended to by the managers. Opportunities, on the other hand, usually must be found. They await discovery, and they often go unnoticed and eventually are lost by an inattentive manager. This is because, by their very nature, most crises and routine problems demand immediate attention. Thus, a manager may spend more time in handling problems than in pursuing important new opportunities. Many well-managed organizations try to draw attention away from crises and routine problems and toward longer range issues through planning activities and goal-setting programs.

Establishing Priorities

All problems are not created equal. Deciding whether to launch a new product in response to a competitor's move is probably a more significant decision than whether the employee lounge should be repainted. The process of decision making and solution implementation requires resources. Unless the resources the organization has at its disposal are unlimited, it is necessary to establish priorities for dealing with problems. This, in turn, means being able to make a determination of the significance level of the problem. Determining problem significance involves consideration of three issues: urgency, impact, and growth tendency.

Urgency relates to time. How critical is the time pressure? Putting out a fire in the office is probably more urgent that fixing a stalled elevator. On the other hand, the elevator is likely to be more urgent than repairing a broken copier. The potential for stopgap measures also impacts urgency. For example, if there are people in the stalled elevator who can be released before the elevator is repaired,

---

[8]Dean Tjosvold, "Effects of Crisis Orientation on Managers' Approach to Controversy in Decision Making," *Academy of Management Journal*, March 1984, pp. 130–38.

that reduces the urgency of making repairs. *Impact* describes the seriousness of the problem's effects. Effects may be on people, sales, equipment, profitability, public image, or any number of other organizational resources. Whether problem effects are short term or long term, and whether the problem is likely to create other problems are also questions related to impact. *Growth tendency* addresses future considerations. Even though a problem may currently be of low urgency and have little impact, if allowed to go unattended it may grow. The decision to cut back on routine preventive maintenance of plant equipment as a cost-cutting measure may not create a significant problem immediately. Over time, however, major difficulties may arise.

The more significant the problem, as determined by its urgency, impact, and growth tendency, the more important it is that it be addressed. A critical part of effective decision making is determining problem significance.

Consideration of Causes

While not impossible, it is ordinarily difficult and ill-advised to determine a solution to a problem when the problem cause is unknown. The practice of bloodletting and the use of leeches are examples of solutions that formerly were applied to a variety of medical problems. If the causes of the medical conditions had been known, other solutions would have been implemented. If an organization wishes to address the problem of declining sales, how can it decide on an appropriate solution if it does not know the reason for the decline? If sales are falling because the product is no longer price competitive, possible solutions will be quite different than if it is due to poor service after the sale. Proper identification of causes helps the decision maker to avoid solving the wrong problem.[9]

Frequently, the search for problem causes leads to a better definition of the real problem. Causes can be turned into new—and better—problem statements. For example, a large metropolitan bank recently began to experience an increase in the number of customers who closed out their accounts. Defining the problem as "loss of accounts" the bank determined the cause was increased customer dissatisfaction with service. This cause then became the basis for a restatement of the original problem. In an effort to determine the cause of the restated problem, the bank contacted several former customers and learned they felt the tellers handling their transactions had gone from being friendly and pleasant to grumpy and irritable. Thus, this cause became the even better defined problem: unfriendly tellers. The problem-to-cause-to-problem sequence was completed when it was determined that a poorly explained change in dress policy requiring all tellers to wear standard blazers was the *real* problem. It was easily addressed, and a special program for former customers who returned to the bank resulted in recouping virtually all the lost accounts.

---

[9]J. M. Dukerich and M. L. Nichols, "Causal Information Search in Managerial Decision Making," *Organizational Behavior and Human Decision Processes,* October 1991, pp. 106–22.

Development of Alternative Solutions

Before a decision is made, feasible alternatives should be developed (actually these are potential solutions to the problem), and the potential consequences of each alternative should be considered. This is really a search process in which the relevant internal and external environments of the organization are investigated to provide information that can be developed into possible alternatives.[10] Obviously, this search is conducted within certain time and cost constraints, since only so much effort can be devoted to developing alternatives.

For example, a sales manager may identify an inadequately trained sales force as the cause of declining sales. The sales manager then would identify possible alternatives for solving the problem such as (1) a sales training program conducted at the home office by management, (2) a sales training program conducted by a professional training organization at a site away from the home office, or (3) more intense on-the-job training.

Evaluation of Alternative Solutions

Once alternatives have been developed, they must be evaluated and compared. In every decision situation, the objective is to select the alternative that will produce the most favorable outcomes and the least unfavorable outcomes. This again points up the necessity of objectives and goals since in selecting from among alternatives, the decision maker should be guided by the previously established goals and objectives. The alternative-outcome relationship is based on three possible conditions:

1. *Certainty.* The decision maker has complete knowledge of the probability of the outcome of each alternative.
2. *Uncertainty.* The decision maker has absolutely no knowledge of the probability of the outcome of each alternative.
3. *Risk.* The decision maker has some probabilistic estimate of the outcomes of each alternative.

Decision making under conditions of risk is probably the most common situation.[11] It is in evaluating alternatives under these conditions that statisticians and operations researchers have made important contributions to decision making. Their methods have proved especially useful in the analysis and ranking of alternatives. Sometimes, however, as Encounter 13-1 illustrates, less "scientific" approaches are used.

In evaluating alternative solutions two cautions should be kept in mind. First, it is critical that this phase of the decision-making process be kept separate and

---

[10]David B. Jamison, "The Importance of Boundary Spanning Roles in Strategic Decision Making," *Journal of Management Studies,* April 1984, pp. 131–52.

[11]J. E. Hodder and H. E. Riggs, "Pitfalls in Evaluating Risky Projects," *Harvard Business Review,* January–February 1985, pp. 128–35.

ORGANIZATIONAL

E N C O U N T E R • 13-1

HUNCH PLAYING AND DECISION MAKING

On occasion, decision makers—when asked what led them to make a particular decision—admit they had a "feeling" or "played a hunch." Consider the following examples:

Robert Jensen, chairman of General Cable Corporation, has had to make strategic decisions regarding diversifying, which involved more than $300 million in sell-offs and acquisitions. He states: "On each decision, the mathematical analysis only got me to the point where my intuition had to take over."

The late Roy Kroc recounted how he decided to invest $2.7 million in 1960 to purchase the McDonald name, a decision considered to be a bad deal by his lawyer. Kroc said: "I closed my office door, cussed up and down, threw things out the window, called my lawyer back, and said: 'Take it.' I felt in my funny bone it was a sure thing."

Jean Paul Getty, the oil billionaire, in recalling his early days in the Texas oil fields, tells the story of how he sent his geologists to gather core samples in order to assess the likelihood of striking oil in a particular lease. The geologists performed their analyses and concluded there was no oil. Getty, however, just *felt* oil was there and ordered drilling anyway. The result was one of the richest fields with which Getty was ever associated.

So, while playing a hunch may pay dividends, keep in mind that planned, systematic approaches to decision making are, in the long run, going to produce the best decisions. For every story like those above, there are hundreds where a decision maker played a hunch—and lost.

Source: Based, in part, on an article by Ray Rowan, "Those Business Hunches Are More than Blind Faith," *Fortune,* April 23, 1979, pp. 111–14.

---

distinct from the previous step, identifying solutions. This is particularly true in a group decision-making context. When alternatives are evaluated as they are proposed, this may restrict the number of alternative solutions identified. If evaluations are positive, there may be a tendency to end the process prematurely by settling on the first positive solution. On the other hand, negative evaluations make it less likely for someone to risk venturing what may be an excellent solution for fear of being criticized or thought less of.

The second caution is to be wary of solutions that are evaluated as being "perfect." This is particularly true when the decision is being made under conditions of uncertainty. If a solution appears to have no drawbacks or if, in a group setting, there is unanimous agreement on a course of action, it may be useful to assign someone to take a devil's advocate position. The job of a devil's advocate is to be a thorough critic of the proposed solution. Research supports the benefits of devil's advocacy and the conflict a devil's advocate may cause, thus forcing a decision maker to reexamine assumptions and information.[12] A

---

[12]R. A. Cozier and C. R. Schwenk, "Agreement and Thinking Alike: Ingredients for Poor Decisions," *Academy of Management Executive,* February 1990, pp. 69–74.

● **R13–1** more comprehensive discussion of the dangers of agreement and the use of devil's advocacy can be found in reading selection R13–1 at the end of the chapter.

Solution Selection

The purpose of selecting a particular solution is to solve a problem in order to achieve a predetermined objective. This point is an extremely important one. It means that a decision is not an end in itself but only a means to an end. Although the decision maker chooses the alternative that is expected to result in the achievement of the objective, the selection of that alternative should not be an isolated act. If it is, the factors that led to and lead from the decision are likely to be excluded. Specifically, the steps following the decision should include implementation and follow-up. The critical point is that decision making is more than an act of choosing; it is a dynamic process.

Unfortunately for most managers, situations rarely exist in which one alternative achieves the desired objective without having some positive or negative impact on another objective. Situations often exist where two objectives cannot be optimized simultaneously. If one objective is *optimized,* the other is *suboptimized.* In business organization, for example, if production is optimized, employee morale may be suboptimized, or vice versa. Or a hospital superintendent optimizes a short-run objective such as maintenance costs at the expense of a long-run objective such as high-quality patient care. Thus, the multiplicity of organizational objectives complicates the real world of the decision maker.

A situation could also exist where attainment of an organizational objective would be at the expense of a societal objective. The reality of such situations is seen clearly in the rise of ecology groups, environmentalists, and the consumerist movement. Apparently, these groups question the priorities (organizational as against societal) of certain organizational decision makers. In any case, whether an organizational objective conflicts with another organizational objective or with a societal objective, the values of the decision maker will strongly influence the alternative chosen.

In managerial decision making, optimal solutions often are impossible. This is because the decision maker cannot possibly know all of the available alternatives, the consequences of each alternative, and the probability of occurrence of these consequences.[13] Thus, rather than being an *optimizer,* the decision maker is a *satisfier,* selecting the alternative that meets an acceptable (satisfactory) standard.

Implementation

Any decision is little more than an abstraction if it is not implemented, and it must be effectively implemented in order to achieve the objective for which it

---

[13]Paul Shrivastava and I. I. Mitroff, "Enhancing Organizational Research Utilization: The Role of Decision Makers' Assumptions," *Academy of Management Review,* January 1984, pp. 18–26.

was made. It is entirely possible for a "good" decision to be hurt by poor implementation. In this sense, implementation may be more important than the actual choice of the alternative.

Since, in most situations, implementing decisions involves people, the test of the soundness of a decision is the behavior of the people involved relative to the decision. While a decision may be technically sound, it can be undermined easily by dissatisfied subordinates. Subordinates cannot be manipulated in the same manner as other resources. Thus, a manager's job is not only to choose good solutions but also to transform such solutions into behavior in the organization. This is done by effectively communicating with the appropriate individuals and groups.[14]

Follow-Up

Effective management involves periodic measurements of results. Actual results are compared with planned results (the objective), and if deviations exist, changes must be made. Here again, we see the importance of measurable objectives. If such objectives do not exist, then there is no way to judge performance. If actual results do not match planned results, changes must be made in the solution chosen, in its implementation, or in the original objective if it is deemed unattainable. If the original objective must be revised, then the entire decision-making process will be reactivated. The important point is that once a decision is implemented, a manager cannot assume that the outcome will meet the original objective. Some system of control and evaluation is necessary to make sure the actual results are consistent with the results planned for when the decision was made.

Sometimes the result or outcome of a decision is unexpected or is perceived differently by different people, and dealing with this possibility is an important part of the follow-up phase in the decision process.

BEHAVIORAL INFLUENCES ON INDIVIDUAL DECISION MAKING

Several behavioral factors influence the decision-making process. Some of these factors influence only certain aspects of the process, while others influence the entire process. However, each may have an impact and, therefore, must be understood to fully appreciate decision making as a process in organizations. Four individual behavioral factors—values, personality, propensity for risk, and potential for dissonance—are discussed in this section. Each of these factors has been shown to have significant impact on the decision-making process.

---

[14]Teresa M. Harrison, "Communication and Participative Decision Making: An Exploratory Study," *Personnel Psychology,* Spring 1985, pp. 93–116.

Values

In the context of decision making, **values** can be thought of as the guidelines a person uses when confronted with a situation in which a choice must be made. Values are acquired early in life and are a basic (often taken for granted) part of an individual's thoughts. The influence of values on the decision-making process is profound:

- In *establishing objectives,* it is necessary to make value judgments regarding the selection of opportunities and the assignment of priorities.
- In *developing alternatives,* it is necessary to make value judgments about the various possibilities.
- In *choosing an alternative,* the values of the decision maker influence which alternative is chosen.
- In *implementing* a decision, value judgments are necessary in choosing the means for implementation.
- In the *evaluation and control* phase, value judgments cannot be avoided when corrective action is taken.

It is clear that values pervade the decision-making process. As one example, consider the issue of ethics in decision making. An ethical decision can be viewed as one that is legal and morally acceptable to society; an unethical decision is either illegal or morally unacceptable.[15] To a large extent, a decision maker's willingness to make ethical or unethical decisions will by influenced by his or her values. Well publicized scandals involving Wall Street insider trading, the savings and loan industry, defense contractor overcharges, the Iran-Contra affair, and many others, have heightened awareness of the critical role values play in decision making. Encounter 13-2 provides a powerful example. The incident related in this Encounter can be pursued in greater depth and detail in Case 13–1.

▲ C13–1

Personality

Decision makers are influenced by many psychological forces, both conscious and subconscious. One of the most important of these forces is the decision makers' personality, which is strongly reflected in the choices made. Some studies have examined the effect of selected personality variables on the process of decision making.[16] These studies generally have focused on the following sets of variables:

[15]T. M. Jones, "Ethical Decision Making by Individuals in Organizations: An Issue-Contingent Model," *Academy of Management Review,* April 1991, pp. 366–95.

[16]P. A. Renwick and H. Tosi, "The Effects of Sex, Marital Status, and Educational Background on Selected Decisions," *Academy of Management Journal,* March 1978, pp. 93–103; and A. A. Abdel-Halim, "Effects of Task and Personality Characteristics on Subordinates' Responses to Participative Decision Making," *Academy of Management Journal,* September 1983, pp. 477–84.

HOW ETHICAL WAS THE CHALLENGER DECISION?

While millions of horrified viewers watched on live television, on January 28, 1986, the space shuttle Challenger exploded less than two minutes after lift-off. All seven crew members perished. In retrospect, it was clear the launch should have been cancelled. Was it just as clear before the fact? Consider the following:

On the evening before the launch, a teleconference took place between representatives of Morton Thiokol (manufacturer of the booster rocket), the Marshall Space Flight Center (MSFC), and the Kennedy Space Center. Morton Thiokol engineers expressed concern over the integrity of the O-ring seals at temperatures below 53 degrees (temperatures at the launch site were below freezing). The Thiokol senior engineer concluded the data supported a no-launch decision. The director of space engineering at MSFC indicated he was "appalled" by the Thiokol recommendation but would not launch over the contractor's objections. At that point the MSFC chief of solid rockets gave his view, concluding that the data presented were inconclusive.

Based on NASA's rule that contractors and themselves had to prove it was safe to fly, the statement that the data were inconclusive should have stopped the launch. However, a Thiokol vice president who was also on the line requested an off-line caucus to reevaluate the data. During the caucus, two engineers attempted to make themselves heard as management representatives began a discussion. Their attempts were met with cold stares as management representatives struggled to compile data that would support a launch decision. Returning to the teleconference, the Thiokol VP read the launch support rationale and recommended that the launch proceed.

NASA, for its part, accepted the recommendation without any discussion or probing. It was consistent with their desires. Several launch delays had already taken place, and NASA feared loss of public and political support. Another delay would have jeopardized the politically important ASTRO mission in March. NASA may also have been hoping for a favorable mention by the president during his State of the Union address scheduled for the evening of launch day.

The text defines an ethical decision as one that is both legal and morally acceptable to society. Was this an ethical decision?

Source: Based in part on R. Marx, C. Stubbart, V. Traub, and M. Cavanaugh, "The NASA Space Shuttle Disaster: A Case Study," *Journal of Management Case Studies,* Winter 1987, pp. 300–18; and G. Whyte, "Decision Failures: Why They Occur and How to Prevent Them," *Academy of Management Executive,* August 1991, pp. 23–31.

1. *Personality variables.* These include the attitudes, beliefs, and needs of the individual.
2. *Situational variables.* These pertain to the external, observable situations in which individuals find themselves.
3. *Interactional variables.* These pertain to the momentary state of the individual as a result of the interaction of a specific situation with characteristics of the individual's personality.

The most important conclusions concerning the influence of personality on the decision-making process are as follows:

- It is unlikely that one person can be equally proficient in all aspects of the decision-making process. The results suggest that some people will do better in one part of the process, while others will do better in another part.
- Such characteristics as intelligence are associated with different phases of the decision-making process.
- The relation of personality to the decision-making process may vary for different groups on the basis of such factors as sex and social status.

An important contribution of this research is that it determined that the personality traits of the decision maker combine with certain situational and interactional variables to influence the decision-making process.

Propensity for Risk

From personal experience, you undoubtedly are aware that decision makers vary greatly in their propensity for taking risks. This one specific aspect of personality strongly influences the decision-making process. A decision maker who has a low aversion to risk will establish different objectives, evaluate alternatives differently, and select different alternatives than will another decision maker in the same situation who has a high aversion to risk. The latter will attempt to make choices where the risk or uncertainty is low or where the certainty of the outcome is high. You will see later in the chapter that many people are bolder and more innovative and advocate greater risk taking in groups than as individuals. Apparently, such people are more willing to accept risk as members of a group.

Risk propensity is also affected by whether potential outcomes are characterized in terms of losses or gains. This, in turn, depends on how the decision maker "frames" the decision. *Framing* refers to the decision maker's perception, in terms of gains or losses, of the decision's possible outcomes.[17] When the choice is perceived as being between losses, there is a greater propensity to take risks than when it is perceived as being between gains.

Potential for Dissonance

Much attention has been focused on the forces and influences affecting the decision maker before a decision is made and on the decision itself. But only recently has attention been given to what happens *after* a decision has been made. Specifically, behavioral scientists have focused attention on the occurrence of postdecision anxiety.

Such anxiety is related to what Festinger calls cognitive dissonance.[18] Festinger's **cognitive dissonance** theory states that there is often a lack of consistency

---

[17]Glen Whyte, "Decision Failures: Why They Occur and How To Prevent Them," *Academy of Management Executive,* August 1991, pp. 23–31.

[18]Leon Festinger, *A Theory of Cognitive Dissonance* (New York: Harper & Row, 1957), chap. 1.

or harmony among an individual's various cognitions (attitudes, beliefs, and so on) after a decision has been made). That is, there will be a conflict between what the decision maker knows and believes and what was done, and as a result the decision maker will have doubts and second thoughts about the choice that was made. In addition, there is a likelihood that the intensity of the anxiety will be greater when any of the following conditions exist:

1. The decision is an important one psychologically or financially.
2. There are a number of foregone alternatives.
3. The foregone alternatives have many favorable features.

Each of these conditions is present in many decisions in all types of organizations. You can expect, therefore, that postdecision dissonance will be present among many decision makers, especially those at higher levels in the organization.

When dissonance occurs, it can, of course, be reduced by admitting that a mistake has been made. Unfortunately, many individuals are reluctant to admit they have made a wrong decision and will be more likely to use one or more of the following methods to reduce their dissonance:

1. Seek information that supports the wisdom of their decision.
2. Selectively perceive (distort) information in a way that supports their decision.
3. Adopt a less favorable view of the foregone alternatives.
4. Minimize the importance of the negative aspects of the decision and exaggerate the importance of the positive aspects.

While each of us may resort to some of this behavior in our personal decision making, it is easy to see how a great deal of it could be extremely harmful in terms of organizational effectiveness. The potential for dissonance is influenced heavily by one's personality, specifically one's self-confidence and persuasibility. In fact, all of the behavioral influences are closely interrelated and are only isolated here for purposes of discussion.[19] For example, what kind of a risk taker you are and your potential for anxiety following a decision are very closely related, and both are strongly influenced by your personality, your perceptions, and your value system. Before managers can fully understand the dynamics of the decision-making process, they must appreciate the behavioral influences on themselves and other decision makers in the organization when they make decisions.

It should be noted that each of the behavioral influences we have just discussed—values, personality, propensity for risk, and potential for dissonance—are influenced by the culture to which the decision maker has been exposed. As organizational decision making transcends national boundries, cultural influences—and differences—become increasingly significant. Cultural differences that affect decision making abound. Encounter 13-3 provides some examples.

[19]Richard Harrison and James G. March, "Decision Making and Post-Decision Surprises," *Administrative Science Quarterly*, March 1984, pp. 26–42.

**CROSS-CULTURAL DIMENSIONS
OF DECISION MAKING**

Organizational decision making in the United States is presumed to be based on thorough and objective analysis of relevant information. Whether this is true in actual practice is arguable, but it does represent what is supposed to happen "ideally." This is not the ideal in every society, however. In some countries, it is inappropriate for senior executives to consult subordinates before making a decision; in other countries it is equally inappropriate for them not to consult subordinates. In almost every aspect of decision making, different cultural norms dictate different ways of proceeding. A few examples:

1. In some cultures (United States, for example) problems are more likely to be seen as requiring solutions, whereas in others (Thailand, for example) problems are more likely to be seen as situations requiring acceptance.
2. Americans value following the chain of command during the decision-making process. Swedes, on the other hand, will willingly go around or over someone in the chain if doing so is helpful to the decision process. Such behavior would be viewed as inappropriate in American organizations and perfectly acceptable in Swedish ones.
3. Italians, who value tradition and history, will tend to adopt tried and proven solutions to current problems. Australians are more present oriented—and more aggressive—and are more likely to try unique and innovative alternative solutions.

4. Germans tend to process their decisions through committees, frequently composed primarily of technical experts. The French, who tend to be highly centralized, would not likely use committees.
5. In high power-distance cultures like India, decisions are made at the highest level of the organization. In a low power-distance culture like Sweden, on the other hand, the lowest level employees expect to make their own decisions.

The differences between Japanese and American management practices are often subjects of debate and discussion. Decision making is a part of management practice, and many differences in the decision-making process exist between these two countries. For example, the Japanese are much more consensus oriented than are Americans. Japanese decision making is often described by the word *nemawaski*, which means root-binding. Each employee has a sense of running the organization because nothing gets done until everyone agrees. Many—if not most—American managers would find this approach frustrating and agonizingly slow. Japanese are also likely to spend much more time on deciding if there is even a need for a decision and on what the decision is about than their American counterparts. Because of this they tend to direct their attention to major decisions, in contrast to American managers who often focus (by Japanese thinking) on minutia.

These, and other, examples help illustrate the many cultural variations in decision making. They also explain why cross-cultural decision making can be so very difficult.

GROUP DECISION MAKING

The first parts of this chapter focused on individuals making decisions. In most organizations, however, a great deal of decision making is achieved through committees, teams, task forces, and other kinds of groups.[20] This is because

[20]H. W. Crott, K. Szilvas, and J. A. Zuber, "Group Decision, Choice Shift, and Polarization in Consulting, Political, and Local Political Scenarios: An Experimental Investigation and Theoretical Analysis," *Organizational Behavior and Human Decision Processes,* June 1991, pp. 22–41.

managers frequently face situations in which they must seek and combine judgments in group meetings. This is especially true for nonprogrammed problems, which are novel and have much uncertainty regarding the outcome. In most organizations, it is unusual to find decisions on such problems being made by one individual on a regular basis. The increased complexity of many of these problems requires specialized knowledge in numerous fields, usually not possessed by one person. This requirement, coupled with the reality that the decisions made eventually must be accepted and implemented by many units throughout the organization, has increased the use of the collective approach to the decision-making process.

Individual versus Group Decision Making

Considerable debate has occurred over the relative effectiveness of individual versus group decision making. Groups usually take more time to reach a decision than individuals do. But bringing together individual specialists and experts has its benefits since the mutually reinforcing impact of their interaction results in better decisions. In fact, a great deal of research has shown that consensus decisions with five or more participants are superior to individual decision making, majority vote, and leader decisions.[21] Unfortunately, open discussion has been found to be negatively influenced by such behavioral factors as the pressure to conform; the influence of a dominant personality type in the group; "status incongruity," as a result of which, lower status participants are inhibited by higher status participants and "go along" even though they believe that their own ideas are superior; and the attempt of certain participants to influence others because these participants are perceived to be expert in the problem area.[22] Additionally, framing effects occur more frequently in groups.[23]

Certain decisions appear to be better made by groups, while others appear better suited to individual decision making. Nonprogrammed decisions appear to be better suited to group decision making. Usually calling for pooled talent, the decisions are so important that they are frequently made by top management and, to a somewhat lesser extent, by middle managers.

---

[21]For examples, see B. M. Staw, "The Escalation of Commitment to a Course of Action," *Academy of Management Review,* October 1981, pp. 577–88; and Max H. Bazerman and Alan Appelman, "Escalation of Commitment in Individual and Group Decision Making," *Organizational Behavior and Human Decision Processes,* Spring 1984, pp. 141–52.

[22]Richard A. Guzzo and James A. Waters, "The Expression of Affect and the Performance of Decision-Making Groups," *Journal of Applied Psychology,* February 1982, pp. 67–74; D. Tjosvold and R. H. G. Field, "Effects of Social Context on Consensus and Majority Vote Decision Making," *Academy of Management Journal,* September 1983, pp. 500–06; and Frederick C. Miner, Jr., "Group versus Individual Decision Making: An Investigation of Performance Measures, Decision Strategies, and Process Losses/Gains," *Organizational Behavior and Human Decision Processes,* Winter 1984, pp. 112–24.

[23]Glen Whyte, "Escalating Commitment in Individual and Group Decision Making: A Prospect Theory Approach," *Organizational Behavior and Human Decision Processes,* In Press.

In terms of the decision-making process itself, the following points concerning group processes for nonprogrammed decisions can be made:

1. In *establishing objectives*, groups probably are superior to individuals because of the greater amount of knowledge available to groups.
2. In *identifying alternatives*, the individual efforts of group members are necessary to ensure a broad search in the various functional areas of the organization.
3. In *evaluating alternatives*, the collective judgment of the group, with its wider range of viewpoints, seems superior to that of the individual decision maker.
4. In *choosing an alternative*, it has been shown that group interaction and the achievement of consensus usually result in the acceptance of more risk than would be accepted by an individual decision maker. In any event, the group decision is more likely to be accepted as a result of the participation of those affected by its consequences.
5. *Implementation* of a decision, whether or not made by a group, usually is accompanied by individual managers. Thus, since a group cannot be held responsible, the responsibility for implementation necessarily rests with the individual manager.

Exhibit 13-3 summarizes the research on group decision making. It presents the relationship between the probable quality of a decision and the method utilized to reach the decision. It indicates that as we move from "individual" to "consensus," the quality of the decision improves. Note also that each successive method involves a higher level of mutual influence by group members. Thus, for a complex problem requiring pooled knowledge, the quality of the decision is likely to be higher as the group moves toward achieving consensus.[24]

Creativity in Group Decision Making

If groups are better suited to nonprogrammed decisions than individuals are, then an atmosphere fostering group creativity must be created. In this respect, group decision making may be similar to brainstorming in that discussion must be free-flowing and spontaneous. All group members must participate, and the evaluation of individual ideas must be suspended in the beginning to encourage participation. However, a decision must be reached, and this is where group decision making differs from brainstorming. Exhibit 13-4 presents guidelines for developing the permissive atmosphere that is important for creative decision making. Also, Exercise 13–2 will help you assess your own creativity.

■ **E13–2**

---

[24]For a discussion of group decision making in complex problems, see Stuart Hart, Mark Boroush, Gordon Enk, and William Hornick, "Managing Complexity through Consensus Mapping: Technology for the Structuring of Group Decisions," *Academy of Management Review,* July 1985, pp. 587–600.

EXHIBIT 13-3

Probable Relationship between Quality of Group Decision and Method Utilized

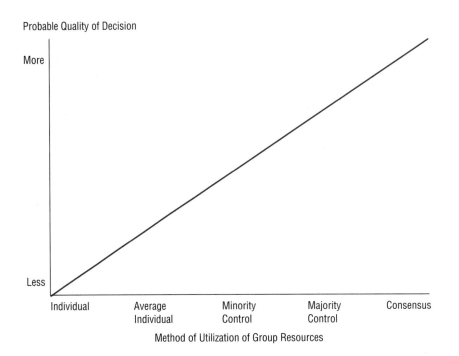

Probable Quality of Decision

More

Less

Individual   Average Individual   Minority Control   Majority Control   Consensus

Method of Utilization of Group Resources

Techniques for Stimulating Creativity

It seems safe to say that in many instances, group decision making is preferable to individual decision making. But we have all heard the statement "A camel is a racehorse designed by a committee." Thus, while the necessity and the benefits of group decision making are recognized, numerous problems also are associated with it, some of which already have been noted. Practicing managers are in need of specific techniques that will enable them to increase the benefits from group decision making while reducing the problems associated with it. Ned Norman in

▲ C13–2   Case 13–2 is going to have to be creative in moving his deadlocked committee.

We shall examine three techniques that when properly utilized have been found to be extremely useful in increasing the creative capability of a group in generating ideas, understanding problems, and reaching better decisions. Increasing the creative capability of a group is especially necessary when individuals from diverse sectors of the organization must pool their judgments and create a satisfactory course of action for the organization. The three techniques are known as brainstorming, the Delphi technique, and the nominal group technique.

Brainstorming

In many situations, groups are expected to produce creative or imaginative solutions to organizational problems. In such instances, **brainstorming** often has been found to enhance the creative output of the group. The technique of brain-

EXHIBIT 13-4

**Creative Group
Decision Making**

Group Structure

The group is composed of heterogeneous, generally competent personnel who bring to bear on the problem diverse frames of reference, representing channels to each relevant body of knowledge (including contact with outside resource personnel who offer expertise not encompassed by the organization), with a leader who facilitates the creative process.

Group Roles

Each individual explores with the entire group all ideas (no matter how intuitively and roughly formed) that bear on the problem.

Group Processes

The problem-solving process is characterized by:

1. Spontaneous communication between members (not focused on the leader).
2. Full participation from each member.
3. Separation of idea generation from idea evaluation.
4. Separation of problem definition from generation of solution strategies.
5. Shifting of roles, so that interaction that mediates problem solving (particularly search activities and clarification by means of constant questioning directed both to individual members and to the whole group) is not the sole responsibility of the leader.
6. Suspension of judgment and avoidance of early concern with solutions, so that the emphasis is on analysis and exploration rather than on early commitment to solutions.

Group Style

The social-emotional tone of the group is characterized by:

1. A relaxed, nonstressful environment.
2. Ego-supportive interaction, where open give-and-take between members is at the same time courteous.
3. Behavior that is motivated by interest in the problem rather than concern with short-run payoff.
4. Absence of penalties attached to any espoused idea or position.

Group Norms

1. Are supportive of originality and unusual ideas and allow for eccentricity.
2. Seek behavior that separates source from content in evaluating information and ideas.
3. Stress a nonauthoritarian view with a realistic view of life and independence of judgment.
4. Support humor and undisciplined exploration of viewpoints.
5. Seek openness in communication, where mature self-confident individuals offer "crude" ideas to the group for mutual exploration without threat to the individuals for "exposing" themselves.
6. Deliberately avoid giving credence to short-run results or short-run decisiveness.
7. Seek consensus but accept majority rule when consensus is unobtainable.

Source: Andre L. Delbecq, "The Management of Decision Making within the Firm: Three Strategies for Three Types of Decision Making," *Academy of Management Journal*, December 1967, pp. 334–35.

storming includes a strict series of rules. The purpose of the rules is to promote the generation of ideas while, at the same time, avoiding the inhibitions of members that usually are caused by face-to-face groups. The basic rules are:

- No idea is too ridiculous. Group members are encouraged to state any extreme or outlandish idea.

- Each idea presented belongs to the group, not to the person stating it. In this way, it is hoped that group members will utilize and build on the ideas of others.
- No idea can be criticized. The purpose of the session is to generate, not evaluate, ideas.

Brainstorming is widely used in advertising where it apparently is effective. In some other situations, it has been less successful because there is no evaluation or ranking of the ideas generated. Thus, the group never really concludes the problem-solving process.

The Delphi Technique

This technique involves the solicitation and comparison of anonymous judgments on the topic of interest through a set of sequential questionnaires that are interspersed with summarized information and feedback of opinions from earlier responses.[25]

The **Delphi process** retains the advantage of having several judges while removing the biasing effects that might occur during face-to-face interaction. The basic approach has been to collect anonymous judgments by mail questionnaires. For example, the members independently generate their ideas to answer the first questionnaire and return it. The staff members summarize the responses as the group consensus and feed this summary back along with a second questionnaire for reassessment. Based on this feedback, the respondents independently evaluate their earlier responses. The underlying belief is that the consensus estimate will result in a better decision after several rounds of anonymous group judgment. While it is possible to continue the procedure for several rounds, studies have shown essentially no significant change after the second round of estimation.

The Nominal Group Technique (NGT)

NGT has gained increasing recognition in health, social service, education, industry, and government organizations.[26] The term **nominal group technique** was adopted by earlier researchers to refer to processes that bring people together but do not allow them to communicate verbally. Thus, the collection of people is a group "nominally," or in name only. You will see, however, that NGT in its present form combines both verbal and nonverbal stages.

---

[25]Norman Dalkey, *The Delphi Method: An Experimental Study of Group Opinion* (Santa Monica, Calif.: Rand Corporation, 1969). This is a classic work on the Delphi methods.

[26]See Andre L. Delbecq, Andrew H. Van de Ven, and David H. Gustafson, *Group Techniques for Program Running* (Glenview, Ill.: Scott, Foresman, 1975). The discussion here is based on this work.

Basically, NGT is a structured group meeting that proceeds as follows: A group of individuals (7 to 10) sit around a table but do not speak to one another. Rather, each person writes ideas on a pad of paper. After five minutes, a structured sharing of ideas takes place. Each person around the table presents one idea. A person designated as recorder writes the ideas on a flip chart in full view of the entire group. This continues until all of the participants indicate that they have no further ideas to share. There is still no discussion.

The output of this phase is a list of ideas (usually between 18 and 25). The next phase involves structured discussion in which each idea receives attention before a vote is taken. This is achieved by asking for clarification or stating the degree of support for each idea listed on the flip chart. The next stage involves independent voting in which each participant, in private, selects priorities by ranking or voting. The group decision is the mathematically pooled outcome of the individual votes.

Both the Delphi technique and NGT have had an excellent record of successes. Basic differences between them are:

1. Delphi participants typically are anonymous to one another, while NGT participants become acquainted.
2. NGT participants meet face-to-face around a table, while Delphi participants are physically distant and never meet face-to-face.
3. In the Delphi process, all communication between participants is by way of written questionnaires and feedback from the monitoring staff. In NGT, communication is direct between participants.[27]

Practical considerations, of course, often influence which technique is used. For example, such factors as the number of working hours available, costs, and the physical proximity of participants will influence which technique is selected.

Our discussion here has not been designed to make the reader an expert in the Delphi process or NGT. Our purpose throughout this section has been to indicate the frequency and importance of group decision making in every type of organization. The three techniques discussed are practical devices whose purpose is to improve the effectiveness of group decisions.

Decision making is a common responsibility shared by all executives, regardless of functional area or management level. Every day, managers are required to make decisions that shape the future of their organization as well as their own futures. The quality of these decisions is the yardstick of the managers' effectiveness. Some of these decisions may have a strong impact on the organization's success, while others will be important but less crucial. However, all of the decisions will have some effect (positive or negative, large or small) on the organization.

[27]Ibid., p. 18.

SUMMARY OF KEY POINTS

- Decisions may be classified as programmed or nonprogrammed, depending on the type of problem. Decisions are *programmed* to the extent that they are repetitive and routine and a definite procedure has been developed for handling them. Decisions are *nonprogrammed* when they are novel and unstructured and there is no established procedure for handling the problem.

- The decision-making process entails following a number of steps. Sequentially, these are (1) establishing specific goals and objectives and measuring results, (2) problem identification and definition, (3) establishing priorities, (4) consideration of causes, (5) development of alternative solutions, (6) evaluation of alternative solutions, (7) solution selection, (8) implementation, and (9) follow-up.

- Because not all problems are of the same importance, it is necessary to prioritize them. How significant a problem is depends on at least three problem attributes: urgency, impact, and growth tendency. *Urgency* relates to time and how critical time pressures are in dealing with a problem. *Impact* describes the seriousness of the problem's effects. *Growth tendency* addresses the likelihood of future changes in problem urgency or impact.

- The relationship between alternatives and outcomes is based on three possible conditions. *Certainty* exists when the decision maker has complete knowledge of the probability of the outcome of each alternative. *Uncertainty* exists when absolutely no such knowledge is available. *Risk* is an intermediate condition, wherein some probabilistic estimate of outcomes can be made.

- The decision-making process is influenced by behavioral factors. Different decision makers may behave differently at any step in the decision-making process. Behavioral factors include values, propensity for risk, potential for dissonance, and personality.

- Research suggests that decisions made by groups are superior to those made by individuals. However, there are aspects of group decision making that tend to have negative effects. These include pressure to conform and the disproportionate influence exerted by a dominant group member.

- One of the advantages of group decision making is that it can facilitate the identification of creative and innovative solutions to problems. Three specific techniques for stimulating creativity in groups are brainstorming, the nominal group technique, and the Delphi process.

REVIEW AND DISCUSSION QUESTIONS

1. "The source of most of our problems is someone else's solution to an earlier problem." Do you agree with this statement? What implications does this statement have for organizational decision making?

2. Why is it important to establish priorities among different problems? Under what conditions might it be necessary to re-evaluate priorities?

3. Increasingly today, decisions are made in a global context. Can you think of some techniques that might be employed to reduce the likelihood of difficulties when decision makers from different cultures are working together to solve a problem?

4. Can individuals be trained to make better decisions? What aspects of decision making do you think could be most improved through training decision makers?

5. Think of a reasonably important nonprogrammed decision you have made recently. Did you employ an approach similar to the decision-making process outlined in Exhibit 13-2? How good was your decision? Could it have been improved by using the decision-making process? Explain.

6. How important a role should ethics play in decision making? Should managers—and organizations—be evaluated on the extent to which they make ethical decisions?

7. What role does personality play in decision making? Can you think of an example from your own experience where the personality of a decision maker clearly influenced his or her decision?

8. Creativity requires nonconformity of thinking. Does that explain why so many organizational decisions are noncreative? Aside from the specific techniques discussed in the chapter, what can be done to stimulate creative decision making in an organization?

9. What are the relative advantages and disadvantages of individual versus group decision making?

10. "Decisions should be thought of as means rather than ends." Explain what this statement means and what effect it should have on decision making.

●

READING

READING 13–1   AGREEMENT AND THINKING ALIKE: INGREDIENTS FOR POOR DECISIONS

Richard A. Cosier, Indiana University
Charles R. Schwenk, Indiana University

EXECUTIVE OVERVIEW

People frequently believe that conflict is to be avoided in organizations. They think that meetings and decisions should reflect agreement and consensus. This article suggests that fostering disagreement in a structured setting may actually lead to better decisions. Two techniques for programming conflict into the decision-making process are suggested— the devil's advocate decision program (DADP) and the dialectic method (DM). In particular, evidence indicates that larger firms operating in uncertain environments benefit from encouraging structured conflict in decision-making. This article challenges managers to consider either the devil's advocate or dialectic methods to program conflict into important organizational decisions.

ARTICLE

Most of us believe that a major objective in organizations is to foster agreement over decisions. After all, agreement indicates cohesion and homogeneity among employees. People who are in agreement with each other are satisfied and secure.

There is growing evidence that suggests conflict and dissent are what organizations really need to succeed.[1] Corporate decisions should be made after thoughtful consideration of counterpoints and criticism. People with different viewpoints must be encouraged to provide thoughts on important decisions. Widespread agreement on a key issue is a red flag, not a condition of good health.

There is an old story at General Motors about Alfred Sloan. At a meeting with his key executives, Sloan proposed a controversial strategic decision. When asked for comments, each executive responded with supportive comments and praise. After announcing that they were all in apparent agreement, Sloan stated that they were not going to proceed with the decision. Either his executives didn't know enough to point out potential downsides of the decision, or they were agreeing to avoid upsetting the boss and disrupting the cohesion of the group. The decision was delayed until a debate could occur over the pros and cons.

Some contemporary managers, however, recognize the benefits of conflict. Gavin Rawl, chief executive officer at Exxon, follows a policy of "healthy disrespect," according to *Business Week*.

Even as he rose through the Exxon hierarchy, however, Rawl always had a healthy disrespect for bureaucracy. The company was obsessed with consensus. Proposals would wend their way through a maze of committees and task forces, through layers of staff. As Senior Vice-President Charles R. Sitter says: "In a large organization, good ideas have lots of foster parents, and the bad decisions produce lots of orphans." Consensus, after all, is safer: The footprints are covered.[2]

Another example is the flamboyant Scott McNealy, Sun Microsystems' chief executive officer. McNealy encourages noisy, table-pounding meetings and debate among senior executives. Dissent and opinion is a natural part of the "controlled chaos."[3]

These managers, like others, have recognized the need to allow different view points and critical thinking into organizational decisions. The type of conflict that is encouraged involves different interpretations of common issues or problems.[4] This "cognitive conflict," was noted as functional many years ago by psychologist Irving Janis. Janis, in his famous writings on groupthink, pointed out that striving for agreement and preventing critical thought frequently leads to poor decisions such as those made during the Bay of Pigs invasion and the defense of Pearl Harbor.

Cognitive conflict can arise in two ways: (1) It can reflect true disagreement among managers and surface through an open environment which encourages participation, or (2) It can be programmed into the decision-making processes and forced to surface, regardless of managers' true feelings. Although both methods may be effective, the second is decidedly less common. Given the po-

Source: Richard A. Cosier and Charles R. Schwenk, "Agreement and Thinking Alike: Ingredients for Poor Decisions," *Academy of Management Executive*, February 1990, pp. 69–74.

tential benefits of programmed conflict in organizational decision-making, companies would do well to implement it. While elements of both methods of conflict generation are reviewed, means for encouraging programmed conflict is a major focus in this article.

ALLOWING TRUE DISAGREEMENT

Allowing disagreement to surface in organizations is exemplified by Jack Welch at General Electric. *Business Week* observed:

> *Welch, though, is convinced he can reach his aims. Like a man obsessed, he is driving G.E. through drastic fundamental change. Once formal, stable, gentlemanly, the new G.E. is tough, aggressive, iconoclastic. "It's a brawl," says Frank P. Doyle, senior vice president for corporate relations. "It's argumentative, confrontational" Working there can be a shock to newcomers. "There's a much higher decibel level here. I told Jack what passes for conversation here would be seen as a mugging by RCA people," Doyle says.[5]*

The planning process involves scrutiny and criticism at G.E. Suggestions are expected and frequently offered and people are encouraged by Welch to speak their minds. This is consistent with organizational case studies that note the value of "forthright discussion" versus behind the scenes politicking in determining organizational strategy. In one case, the vice president for manufacturing and finance at a company showing strong performance stated:

> *You don't need to get the others behind you before the meeting. If you can explain your view (at the meeting), people will change their opinions. Forefront (the fictitious name of the company) is not political at this point. But, you must give your reasons or your ideas don't count. (VP of manufacturing.)*
>
> *There is some open disagreement—it's not covered up. We don't gloss over the issues, we hit them straight on. (VP of finance.)[6]*

Several studies on strategic decision making show that in general, successful companies advocate open discussions, surfacing of conflict, and flexibility in adopting solutions. Other studies, however, suggest that strategy is facilitated by consensus. This contradiction raises an important issue. Consensus may be preferred for smaller, nondiversified, privately held firms competing in the same industry while larger firms dealing with complex issues of diversification may benefit from the dissent raised in open

discussions. Larger firms in uncertain environments need dissent while smaller firms in more simple and stable markets can rely on consensus. In addition, Dess concludes, "organizations competing within an industry experiencing high growth may benefit from a relatively high level of disagreement in assessing the relative importance of company objectives and competitive methods."[7]

Examples of the benefits of conflict in tactical problem solving (short-term) situations are also common. Bausch and Lomb have established "tiger teams" composed of scientists from different disciplines. Team members are encouraged to bring up divergent ideas and offer different points of view. Xerox uses round table discussions composed of various functional experts to encourage innovation. Compaq expects disagreement during all stages of new product development. Stuart Gannes, writing in *Fortune*, explains, "But at Compaq, instead of just arguing over who is right, we tear down positions to reasons. And when you get to reasons you find facts and assumptions."[8] Apple Computer, Ford Motor Co., Johnson and Johnson, and United Parcel Service are other examples of companies that tolerate conflict and debate during decisions.

In general, successful leaders seem to encourage managers to speak their minds. While this allows conflict into decision-making, it carries a potential high cost. Positions are frequently tied to people and competitive "zero-sum" situations in which perceived winners and losers are likely to develop. Clearly, "losers" are less likely in future discussions to give their opinions.

Also, unprogrammed conflict is likely to be emotional and involve personal feelings. Lingering dislikes and rivalries are possible after higher emotional interchanges. Coalitions form and long-term divisiveness ensues.

Corporate time and money may have to be diverted from problem solving to resolving emotional conflicts between managers.

What may, in fact, be needed is programmed conflict that raises different opinions *regardless of the personal feelings of the managers*. Although research exists supporting some options for programmed conflict, few, if any, examples exist in the corporate world.

PROGRAMMED CONFLICT

The Devil's Advocate

What can leaders do to experience the benefits associated with conflict in decision making, while minimizing the cost? Two options with potential are the devil's advocate and

EXHIBIT 13-5

**A Devil's Advocate
Decision Program**

1. A proposed course of action is generated.
   ↓
2. A devil's advocate (individual or group) is assigned to criticize the proposal.
   ↓
3. The critique is presented to key decision-makers.
   ↓
4. Any additional information relevant to the issues is gathered.
   ↓
5. The decision to adopt, modify, or discontinue the proposed course of action is taken.
   ↓
6. The decision is monitored.

dialectic methods for introducing programmed conflict into organizational decisions.

The usefulness of the devil's advocate technique was illustrated several years ago by psychologist Irving Janis when discussing famous fiascos. Janis attributes group-think—the striving for agreement instead of the best decision in a group—to decisions such as were made during The Bay of Pigs and Pearl Harbor.[9] Watergate and Vietnam are also often cited as examples. Janis recommends that everyone in the group assume the role of a devil's advocate and question the assumptions underlying the popular choice. Alternatively, an individual or subgroup could be formally designated as the devil's advocate and present a critique of the proposed course of action. This avoids the tendency of agreement interfering with problem solving. Potential pitfalls are identified and considered before the decision is final.

While Janis' observations are generally well known and accepted, corporate implementation of devil's advocacy as a formal element in decision making is rare. This is despite recent research that supports the benefits of devil's advocacy.[10] The conflict generated by the devil's advocate may cause the decision maker to avoid false assumptions and closely analyze the information. The devil's advocate raises questions that force an in-depth review of the problem-solving situation.

A devil's advocate decision program (DADP) can take several forms. However, all options require that an individual or group be assigned the role of critic. It needs to be clear that the criticism must not be taken personally, but is part of the organizational decision process.

The devil's advocate is assigned to identify potential pitfalls and problems with a proposed course of action.

The issue could relate to strategic planning, new product development, innovation, project development, or of other problems not amenable to programmed solutions. A formal presentation to the key decision makers by the devil's advocate raises potential concerns. Evidence needed to address the critique is gathered and the final decision is made and monitored. This DADP is summarized in Exhibit 13-5.

It is a good idea to rotate people assigned to devil's advocate roles. This avoids any one person or group being identified as the critic on all issues. The devil's advocate role may be advantageous for a person and the organization. Steve Huse, chairperson and CEO of House Food Group, states that the devil's advocate role is an opportunity for employees to demonstrate their presentation and debating skills. How well someone understands and researches issues is apparent when presenting a critique.[11] The organization avoids costly mistakes by hearing viewpoints that identify pitfalls instead of foster agreement.

Often, a devil's advocate is helpful in adopting expert advice from computer-based decision support systems. Behavioral scientists Cosier and Dalton suggest that computer-based decisions may be more useful if exposed to a critique than simply accepted by managers.[12]

The Dialectic

While the DADP lacks an "argument" between advocates of two conflicting positions, the dialetic method (DM) programs conflict into decisions, regardless of managers' personal feelings, by structuring a debate between conflicting views.

The dialectic philosophy, which can be traced back to

EXHIBIT 13-6

**The Dialectic
Decision Method**

1. A proposed course of action is generated.
   ↓
2. Assumptions underlying the proposal are identified.
   ↓
3. A conflicting counterproposal is generated based on different assumptions.
   ↓
4. Advocates of each position present and debate the merits of their proposals before key decision makers.
   ↓
5. The decision to adopt either position, or some other position, e.g. a compromise, is taken.
   ↓
6. The decision is monitored.

Plato and Aristotle, involves synthesizing the conflicting views of a thesis and an antithesis. More recently, it played a principle role in the writings of Hegel who described the emergence of new social orders after a struggle between opposing forces. While most of the world's modern legal systems reflect dialectic processes, Richard O. Mason was one of the first organization theorists to apply the dialectic to organizational decisions.[13] He suggested that the decision maker consider a structured debate reflecting a plan and a counterplan before making a strategic decision. Advocates of each point of view should present their assumptions in support of the argument.

The benefits of DM are in the presentation and debate of the assumptions underlying proposed courses of action. False or misleading assumptions become apparent and decisions based on these poor assumptions are avoided. The value of DM, shown in Exhibit 13-6, for promoting better understanding of problems and higher levels of confidence in decisions is supported by research.[14]

Critics of DM point to the potential for it to accentuate who won the debate rather than the best decision. Compromise, instead of optimal decisions, is likely. Managers will require extensive training in dialectic thinking and philosophy. Supporters of DADP argue that a critique focuses the decision-maker on issues while the dialectic focuses more on the process of structural debate. Nevertheless, Cosier and Dalton suggest that DM may be the best method to use under the worst decision-making condition—high uncertainty and low information availability. The dialectic may be a good way to define problems and generate needed information for making decisions under uncertainty. When information is available and causal re-

lationships are known, computer-assisted or devil's advocate methods are preferred.

PROGRAMMED AND UNPROGRAMMED CONFLICT

It is not a major breakthrough in management advice to suggest that conflict can improve decisions, although it is useful to remind managers of the need to allow dissent. It is, however, uncommon for managers to formally program conflict into the decision-making process. Thus, regardless of personal feelings, programmed conflict requires managers to challenge, criticize, and generate alternative ideas. Compared to conflict that is allowed to naturally surface, programmed conflict may reduce negative emotional by-products of conflict generation since dissent is no longer "personal." It also insures that a comprehensive decision framework is applied to important problems and issues.

Two options for implementing programmed conflict are based on the devil's advocate (DADP) and dialectic (DM) methods. We challenge managers to formally encourage controversy and dissent when making important choices under uncertain conditions. Encouraging "yes sayers" and complacency promotes poor decisions and lack of innovative thinking in organizations.

NOTES

1. Conflict has been frequently presented as a positive force in textbooks. See, for example, Peter P. Schoderbek, Richard A. Cosier, and John C. Aplin, *Management,*

(San Diego: Harcourt, Brace, and Jovanovich, 1988). pp. 511–12.

2. "The Rebel Shaking Up Exxon," *Business Week,* July 18, 1988, p. 107.

3. "Sun Microsystems Turns On the Afterburners," *Business Week,* July 18, 1988, p. 115.

4. Tjosvold uses the term "controversy" to describe this type of conflict. He differentiates controversy from conflicts of interest which involve the actions of one person blocking the goal attainment of another person. See Dean Tjosvold, "Implications of Controversy Research for Management," *Journal of Management* 11, 1985, pp. 22–23.

5. "Jack Welch: How good a manager?" *Business Week,* December 14, 1987, p. 94.

6. Kathleen M. Eisenhardt and L. J. Bourgeois III, "Politics of Strategic Decision Making in High-Velocity Environments," *Academy of Management Journal* 31, 1988, pp. 751–52.

7. Gregory G. Dess, "Consensus on Strategy Formulation and Organizational Performance: Competitors in a Fragmented Industry," *Strategic Management Journal* 8, 1987, p. 274.

8. Stuart Gannes, "America's Fastest-Growing Companies," *Fortune,* May 23, 1988, p. 29.

9. See Irving L. Janis, *Victims of Groupthink,* (Boston: Houghton-Mifflin, 1972).

10. See, for example, Richard A. Cosier, "Methods for Improving the Strategic Decision: Dialectic Versus the Devil's Advocate," *Strategic Management Journal* 16, 1982, pp. 176–184.

11. Steve Huse, chairperson and CEO of Huse Food Group Inc., shared these observations in an interview with the senior author.

12. A model is developed which recommends methods of presenting information based upon conditions of uncertainty and information availability in Richard A. Cosier and Dan R. Dalton, "Presenting Information Under Conditions of Uncertainty and Availability: Some Recommendations," *Behavioral Science* 33, 1988, 272–81.

13. Richard O. Mason, "A Dialectical Approach to Strategic Planning," *Management Science* 15, 1969, pp. B403–14.

14. Ian I. Mitroff and J. R. Emshoff, "On Strategic Assumption-Making: A Dialectical Approach to Policy and Planning," *Academy of Management Review,* 4, 1979, pp. 1–12.

■

EXERCISES

EXERCISE 13–1 PROBLEM-SOLVING QUESTIONNAIRE

Part I. Circle the response that comes closest to how you usually feel or act. There are no right or wrong responses to any of these items.

1. I am more careful about
   a. People's feelings.
   b. Their rights.
2. I usually get on better with
   a. Imaginative people.
   b. Realistic people.

3. It is a higher compliment to be called
   a. A person of real feeling.
   b. A consistently reasonable person.
4. In doing something with other people, it appeals more to me
   a. To do it in the accepted way.
   b. To invent a way of my own.
5. I get more annoyed at
   a. Fancy theories.
   b. People who do not like theories.

Source: Adapted from the Myers-Briggs Type indicator and a scale developed by Don Hellriegel, John Slocum, and Richard W. Woodman, *Organizational Behavior,* 3rd ed. (St. Paul, Minn.: West Publishing, 1983), pp. 127–41.

6. It is higher praise to call someone
   a. A person of vision.
   b. A person of common sense.
7. I more often let
   a. My heart rule my head.
   b. My head rule my heart.

8. I think it is a worse fault
   a. To show too much warmth.
   b. To be unsympathetic.
9. If I were a teacher, I would rather teach
   a. Courses involving theory.
   b. Fact courses.

Part II. Which in the following pair appeals to you more? Circle *a* or *b*.

10. *a.* Compassion	*b.* Foresight	14. *a.* Uncritical	*b.* Critical
11. *a.* Justice	*b.* Mercy	15. *a.* Literal	*b.* Figurative
12. *a.* Production	*b.* Design	16. *a.* Imaginative	*b.* Matter-of-fact
13. *a.* Gentle	*b.* Firm		

Scoring Key

Mark each of your responses on the following scales. Then use the point value column to arrive at your score. For example, if you answered *a* to the first question, you would check *1a* in the feeling column.

This response receives zero points when you add up the point value column. Instructions for classifying your scores are indicated below the scales.

Sensation	Point Value	Intuition	Point Value	Thinking	Point Value	Feeling	Point Value
2 *b* _____	1	2 *a* _____	2	1 *b* _____	1	1 *a* _____	0
4 *a* _____	1	4 *b* _____	1	3 *b* _____	2	3 *a* _____	1
5 *a* _____	1	5 *b* _____	1	7 *b* _____	1	7 *a* _____	1
6 *b* _____	1	6 *a* _____	0	8 *a* _____	0	8 *b* _____	1
9 *b* _____	2	9 *a* _____	2	10 *b* _____	2	10 *a* _____	1
12 *a* _____	1	12 *b* _____	0	11 *a* _____	2	11 *b* _____	1
15 *a* _____	1	15 *b* _____	1	13 *b* _____	1	13 *a* _____	1
16 *b* _____	2	16 *a* _____	0	14 *b* _____	0	14 *a* _____	1
Maximum Point Value	(10)		(7)		(9)		(7)

Classifying Total Scores

Write *intuition* if your intuition score is equal to or greater than your sensation score.
Write *sensation* if your sensation score is greater than your intuition score.
Write *feeling* if your feeling score is greater than your thinking score.
Write *thinking* if your thinking score is greater than your feeling score.

E X E R C I S E 13–2 HOW CREATIVE ARE YOU?

In recent years, several task-oriented tests have been developed to measure creative abilities and behavior. While certainly useful, they do not adequately tap the complex network of behaviors—the particular personality traits, attitudes, motivations, values, interests, and other variables that predispose a person to think creatively.

To arrive at assessment measures that would cover a broader range of creative attributes, our organization developed an inventory type of test. A partial version of this instrument is featured below.

After each statement, indicate with a letter the degree or extent with which you agree or disagree with it:

A = Strongly agree
B = Agree
C = In between or don't know
D = Disagree
E = Strongly disagree

Mark your answers as accurately and frankly as possible. Try not to "second guess" how a creative person might respond to each statement.

1. I always work with a great deal of certainty that I'm following the correct procedures for solving a particular problem.   _____
2. It would be a waste of time for me to ask questions if I had no hope of obtaining answers.   _____
3. I feel that a logical step-by-step method is best for solving problems.   _____
4. I occasionally voice opinions in groups that seem to turn some people off.   _____
5. I spend a great deal of time thinking about what others think of me.   _____
6. I feel that I may have a special contribution to give to the world.   _____
7. It is more important for me to do what I believe to be right than to try to win the approval of others.   _____
8. People who seem unsure and uncertain about things lose my respect.   _____
9. I am able to stick with difficult problems over extended periods of time.   _____
10. On occasion I get overly enthusiastic about things.   _____
11. I often get my best ideas when doing nothing in particular.   _____
12. I rely on intuitive hunches and the feeling of "rightness" or "wrongness" when moving toward the solution of a problem.   _____
13. When problem solving, I work faster analyzing the problem and slower when synthesizing the information I've gathered.   _____
14. I like hobbies which involve collecting things   _____
15. Daydreaming has provided the impetus for many of my more important projects.   _____
16. If I had to choose from two occupations other than the one I now have, I would rather be a physician than an explorer.   _____
17. I can get along more easily with people if they belong to about the same social and business class as myself.   _____
18. I have a high degree of aesthetic sensitivity.   _____
19. Intuitive hunches are unreliable guides in problem solving.   _____
20. I am much more interested in coming up with new ideas than I am in trying to sell them to others.   _____

21. I tend to avoid situations in which I might feel inferior. _____
22. In evaluating information, the source of it is more important to me than the content. _____
23. I like people who follow the rule "business before pleasure." _____
24. One's own self-respect is much more important than the respect of others. _____
25. I feel that people who strive for perfection are unwise. _____
26. I like work in which I must influence others. _____
27. It is important for me to have a place for everything and everything in its place. _____
28. People who are willing to entertain "crackpot" ideas are impractical. _____
29. I rather enjoy fooling around with new ideas, even if there is no practical payoff. _____
30. When a certain approach to a problem doesn't work, I can quickly reorient my thinking. _____
31. I don't like to ask questions that show ignorance. _____
32. I am able to more easily change my interests to pursue a job or career than I can change a job to pursue my interests. _____
33. Inability to solve a problem is frequently due to asking the wrong questions. _____
34. I can frequently anticipate the solution to my problems. _____
35. It is a waste of time to analyze one's failures. _____
36. Only fuzzy thinkers resort to metaphors and analogies. _____
37. At times I have so enjoyed the ingenuity of a crook that I hoped he or she would go scot-free. _____
38. I frequently begin work on a problem which I can only dimly sense and not yet express. _____
39. I frequently tend to forget things such as names of people, streets, highways, small towns, etc. _____
40. I feel that hard work is the basic factor in success. _____
41. To be regarded as a good team member is important to me. _____
42. I know how to keep my inner impulses in check. _____
43. I am a thoroughly dependable and responsible person. _____
44. I resent things being uncertain and unpredictable. _____
45. I prefer to work with others in a team effort rather than solo. _____
46. The trouble with many people is that they take things too seriously. _____
47. I am frequently haunted by my problems and cannot let go of them. _____
48. I can easily give up immediate gain or comfort to reach the goals I have set. _____
49. If I were a college professor, I would rather teach factual courses than those involving theory. _____
50. I'm attracted to the mystery of life. _____

Scoring Instructions. To compute your percentage score, circle and add up the values assigned to each item.

	Strongly Agree A	Agree B	In-between or Don't Know C	Disagee D	Strongly Disagree E
1.	−2	−1	0	+1	+2
2.	−2	−1	0	+1	+2
3.	−2	−1	0	+1	+2
4.	+2	+1	0	−1	−2
5.	−2	−1	0	+1	+2
6.	+2	+1	0	−1	−2
7.	+2	+1	0	−1	−2
8.	−2	−1	0	+1	+2
9.	+2	+1	0	−1	−2
10.	+2	+1	0	−1	−2
11.	+2	+1	0	−1	−2

	Strongly Agree A	Agree B	In-between or Don't Know C	Disagee D	Strongly Disagree E
12.	+2	+1	0	−1	−2
13.	−2	−1	0	+1	+2
14.	−2	−1	0	+1	+2
15.	+2	+1	0	−1	−2
16.	−2	−1	0	+1	+2
17.	−2	−1	0	+1	+2
18.	+2	+1	0	−1	−2
19.	−2	−1	0	+1	+2
20.	+2	+1	0	−1	−2
21.	−2	−1	0	+1	+2
22.	−2	−1	0	+1	+2
23.	−2	−1	0	+1	+2
24.	+2	+1	0	−1	−2
25.	−2	−1	0	+1	+1
26.	−2	−1	0	+1	+2
27.	−2	−1	0	+1	+2
28.	−2	−1	0	+1	+2
29.	+2	+1	0	−1	−2
30.	+2	+1	0	−1	−2
31.	−2	−1	0	+1	+2
32.	−2	−1	0	+1	+2
33.	+2	+1	0	−1	−2
34.	+2	+1	0	−1	−2
35.	−2	−1	0	+1	+2
36.	−2	−1	0	+1	+2
37.	+2	+1	0	−1	−2
38.	+2	+1	0	−1	−2
39.	+2	+1	0	−1	−2
40.	+2	+1	0	−1	−2
41.	−2	−1	0	+1	+2
42.	−2	−1	0	+1	+2
43.	−2	−1	0	+1	+2
44.	−2	−1	0	+1	+2
45.	−2	−1	0	+1	+2
46.	+2	+1	0	−1	−2
47.	+2	+1	0	−1	−2
48.	+2	+1	0	−1	−2
49.	−2	−1	0	+1	+2
50.	+2	+1	0	−1	−2

80 to 100	Very creative	20 to 39	Below average
60 to 79	Above average	−100 to 19	Noncreative
40 to 59	Average		

Further information about the test, "How Creative Are You?" is available from Princeton Creative Research, Inc., 10 Nassau St., P.O. Box 122, Princeton, NJ 08542.

▲

CASES

CASE 13-1 THE NASA SPACE SHUTTLE DISASTER: A CASE STUDY

In retrospect, Thiokol Inc.'s perfunctory green light unwittingly reads like a death warrant. For a breathless moment the reader is transfixed with the thought that the shuttle accident might have been avoided (Exhibit 13-7). But the lethal calculus of limited O-ring tolerances and subnormal Florida temperatures served not only as the immediate mechanical cause of the Challenger tragedy but also as a symptom of long-unresolved organizational issues. For example, besides advertising America's technological (and, derivatively, political) superiority, what, specifically, was the agency's actual scientific purpose? Was it reasonable to assume that a 14-year-old bureaucracy, driven by an exploratory ethos inspired by the futurology of H.G. Wells, could be readily adapted to a commercial schedule without creating serious organizational tensions? (From "Apollo" to "Shuttle"—the choice of project logos captures the essence of this radical reorientation). Given the institutionwide appropriation of the original astronauts' style (i.e., "Right Stuff"—an unflinching mix of high-tech, high-macho, and high-risk drama) and the virgin technology employed, did NASA and its galaxy of subcontractors operate with an attention to safety? Who and what defined the margin of error? What kind of adverse data interrupted a final countdown? How was it that after 25 elaborate countdowns and with onboard computers that routinely monitored 2,000 vital functions before every launch, the suspect integrity of the critical rocket joints was left un-"sensored"? Or did the collision of pioneering technology and unknown environmental factors make chance error inevitable? Risk could not be eliminated altogether and still allow spacecraft to be launched.

With the full backing of Presidents Kennedy and Johnson, James Webb, NASA's first and last entrepreneur, dreamed of fashioning an enlightened alliance between science and democratic tradition. Indeed, in light of the agency's dramatic accomplishments, it seemed that Webb's technocratic vision had been fulfilled. No order was too large, and, on the surface at least, the agency's partnership with the private sector produced spectacular results. NASA evoked a public image of detached reason; it was a beacon of order, competence, and hope for Americans jaded by generalized institutional decline. NASA appeared to stand outside the malignant politics, inefficiency, and crossed lines of responsibility that sabotaged the efforts of other major agencies both public and private.

Of course, image and reality do not always correspond. Recent revelations surrounding the decision and communication processes affecting the Challenger launch demonstrate that NASA was foremost a human institution with all the imperfection that this implies. And perhaps because of this rude shock, we harbor an ongoing sense of institutional loss in addition to the human loss of the seven crew members. Ultimately, beyond all its advances to American rocketry, NASA's most enduring legacy may be to organizational and managerial science.

NASA: A NARRATIVE HISTORY

The ongoing saga of America's space program and, particularly, the events surrounding the January 1986 loss of the shuttle Challenger can be better understood if divided into four successive periods: (1) a preliminary period of ad hoc and idiosyncratic research dating from Robert Goddard's pioneering experiments and ending abruptly with the Russian launch of Sputnik I; (2) a second period of public-funded and directed "command technology" commencing with the passage of the National Aeronautics and Space Act of 1958 and closing with the 1968 retirement of James Webb, NASA's first and only "big operator" (McDougall, 1985); (3) a subsequent chapter of organizational decline culminating in the January 1986 explosion of the ill-fated Challenger, a patronless period characterized by mounting national indifference to NASA, shrinking Congressional appropriations, and the unresolved organizational conflicts fueled by the agency's attempt to shift from an exploratory mode to a routine operation; and (4) following the Challenger loss, a self-searching period of mandated change and mission definition.

Source: Robert Marx, Charles Stubbart, Virginia Traub, and Michael Cavanaugh, "The Nasa Space Shuttle Disaster. A Case Study," *Journal of Management Case Studies*, Winter 1987, pp. 299–318.

Robert D. Marx is an Associate Professor of Management, Charles I. Stubbart is an Assistant Professor of Management, and Virginia Traub and Michael Cavanaugh are Ph.D. candidates, all at the University of Massachusetts at Amherst.

EXHIBIT 13-7

**Copy of Telefax Sent
to Kennedy and
Marshall Centers
by Thiokol**

MTI Assessment of Temperature Concern on SRM-25 (51L) Launch

- Calculations show that SRM-25 o-rings will be 20° colder than SRM-15 o-rings
- Temperature data not conclusive on predicting primary o-ring blow-by
- Engineering assessment is that:
  - Colder o-rings will have increased effective durometer ("harder")
  - "Harder" o-rings will take longer to "seat"
    - More gas may pass primary o-ring before the primary seal seats (relative to SRM-15)
      - Demonstrated sealing threshold is 3 times greater than 0.038° erosion experienced on SRM-15
  - If the primary seal does not seat, the secondary seal will seat
    - O-ring pressure leak check places secondary seal in outboard position which minimizes sealing time
- MTI recommends STS-51L launch proceed on 28 January 1986
  - SRM-25 will not be significantly different from SRM-15

Joe C. Kilminster, Vice President
Space Booster Programs

MORTON THIOKOL, INC.
WASATCH DIVISION

Source: Rogers Commission Report, 1986, p. 79.

Period I—Foundations

The interplanetary designs of Jules Verne and H.G. Wells served as principal inspiration for an entire generation of American and European backyard rocketeers. Yet, in every sense of the phrase, American rocketry was slow to get off the ground. Until World War II, the state remained disinterested. Invention and application of knowledge were generally acknowledged as the proper domain of private individuals and institutions. Indeed, dating from Robert Goddard's early experiments with liquid-fuel rockets in 1926 until the surprise attack on Pearl Harbor 15 years later, U.S. rocketry was relegated to an orphaned status. With the singular exception of the National Advisory Committee for Aeronautics (NACA), conceived at the end of World War I by Charles D. Walcott of the Smithsonian Institution to keep America abreast of advances in European aviation, large-scale government involvement in rocket (or most any other form of scientific) research languished.

World War II permanently altered this laissez-faire philosophy. Traditionally opposed to state assistance, Amer-

ica's political and scientific leadership closed ranks in recognizing the essential role of state-directed R&D in the conduct of modern warfare. Public funds, for instance, underwrote jet-assisted takeoffs and the development of antitank rockets (the bazooka). The war left its own special legacy to American rocket science, a fledgling aerospace industry. Ironically, the first private firm devoted to rocketry, Reaction Motors, Inc., founded in 1941, later became a division of Thiokol Chemical. Residual concerns about mixing politics and science swept aside, the war also facilitated public acceptance of a vast research consortium composed of government, industry, and university, thereby closing a long chapter in amateur invention. The efficacy of government-mobilized R&D was epitomized by the Manhattan Project and (exploiting the experience of captured German rocket scientists) a growing investment in the military applications of jet and rocket propulsion systems.

Although the war had served to resurrect and transform American rocketry, postwar rocket research lacked direc-

tion. Following demobilization, congressional and presidential interest waned. Constrained by parsimonious budgets, scientists tinkered with advanced versions of Von Braun's V-2 rocket. And satellite development, despite the promptings of the Rand Corporation, received low priority. Further developments awaited a crisis.

Period 2—Technocracy Achieved

In a 1954 report, Werner von Braun asked for $100,000 to build a space satellite because "a man-made satellite, no matter how humble (five pounds) would be a scientific achievement of tremendous impact." He prophesized that "it would be a blow to U.S. prestige if we did not do it first" (McDougall, 1985, p. 119). In a single stroke, the October 4, 1957 launch of Sputnik I overturned American assumptions about a U.S. technological monopoly and ignited a domestic political crisis. The U.S. response was rapid, however, and was waged along several fronts. The Congress promptly passed the National Defense Education Act to facilitate the recruitment of scientific and engineering talent. New and stricter criteria were promulgated for high school science curricula, backed by across-the-board increases in funding for basic science. On October 1, 1958, less than a full year after the first Soviet launch, the National Aeronautics and Space Act was signed into law creating a civilian bureaucracy to serve as the nation's foremost aeronautical contractor. (NASA performed only a small fraction of actual design and construction. Reviving cottage industry on an unprecedented scale, NASA contracted 80–90 percent of its work to private subcontractors.) Later, in 1961, impressed by the orbital flight of the Soviet cosmonaut, Yuri Gagarin, and in need of political ammunition to offset setbacks in Laos, the Congo, and the Bay of Pigs debacle, the new Kennedy Administration declared its commitment to place Americans on the moon within the decade: "This is the new ocean, and I believe the United States must sail on it and be in a position second to none" (John Kennedy, *Time*, Feb. 10, 1986). The young President would marshal American technology to extend America's landlocked frontier. Moreover, the Cold War now included outer space. Space science and the state were inextricably linked. Henceforth, space R&D budgets would be subject to the vicissitudes of superpower rivalry.

Under the energetic stewardship of James Webb, NASA underwrote the Mercury, Gemini, and Apollo programs, culminating in the Apollo 11 moon landing in July 1969. But even at the apex of its power—1964–1965—when the agency received money for the asking (1964 funding totaled $5.1 billion, nearly five times its 1961 budget), the

program's long-term objectives remained unclear. Even the NASA field centers failed to reach agreement on charting their own post-Apollo course. Moreover, in the face of the Johnson government's escalating commitments to the Great Society and Vietnam, Webb feared to press for new projects (a manned mission to Mars, a permanent moon base, orbiting space stations) that promised high and unpredictable costs. Not unlike the boom-or-bust revenues of the extractive economies within which it operated (the Gulf states), NASA funding began to evaporate in the second half of the decade. More pressing domestic problems and the relaxation of Cold War tensions undermined vital political support. And many had come to believe "that Apollo was the space program. Once the race was over and won, Americans could turn back to their selfish pursuits" (McDougall, 1985, p. 422).

Finally, in September 1969, the White House unveiled a new charter. A Space Task Group chaired by Spiro Agnew presented the President with three alternatives in descending order of cost. Nixon selected the least expensive—a space station with a shuttle. He later shelved the space station pending development of the shuttle. The message was clear. NASA, for all its technical achievements, was an institution without a coherent mission and was therefore expendable. Another Soviet first could have revived NASA. But having lost the race to the moon, Moscow seemed content to maintain a low profile.

Period 3—The Twilight Zone

"Apollo was a matter of going to the moon and building whatever technology would get us there: the Space Shuttle was a matter of building a technology and going wherever it could take us" (McDougall, 1985, p. 423). After Apollo 11, the agency and the aerospace industry languished. The agency's principal patrons had retired or died. Kennedy was dead. Both LBJ and Webb stepped down in 1968. (NASA chief administrators were replaced with every change in the White House). This was the situation until 1972, when the Nixon administration, convinced of the electoral fallout sure to result from an aerospace depression, agreed to fund the Space Shuttle (or Space Transportation System—STS).

The STS, however, represented a pyrrhic gain for the agency. Most of the original design was bargained away trying to accommodate competing military, commercial, and scientific interests. For instance, to meet Pentagon specifications, the orbiter's payload was increased. The vehicle's fully reusable technology was jettisoned. Furthermore, a zealous Office of Management and Budget trimmed original cost estimates by half. But perhaps most significantly, NASA bowed to Congressional pressure to transform the shuttle operation into a government version of Federal Express (Wilford, 1986, p. 102):

> To satisfy Congress, the system had to pay for itself, which meant that NASA, charted as a research and development agency, was put in the unaccustomed position of hustling business and running an orbital freight operation. The conflicting goals and pressures, as well as the complexity of the machines themselves, virtually assured that America's Space Transportation—as the shuttle is officially known—would not operate with the efficiency its original designers had planned.

The product of these compromises turned out to be an improvisational instrument useful for ferrying heavy (military) payloads into low earth orbit. But its technical limitations and the cost overruns associated with preflight preparations forfeited the high ground to foreign competition (comsats require higher earth orbits) and pushed the agency into chronic budget overruns.

There was another matter. For James Webb, space conquest was only a spinoff. NASA represented nothing less than a "revolution from above" (McDougall, 1985), an extraordinary opportunity to demonstrate the power of the technological revolution including projected advances in quantitative management. Modeled after the grand patterns of the Tennessee Valley Authority and Manhattan projects, NASA would serve as the prototypic administrative instrument for large-scale social and political change. Like McNamara's efforts to rationalize the Pentagon, Webb aimed to pioneer a new era in management science.

Period 4—Crossroads

Intermittent shuttle launchings notwithstanding, NASA has existed in a suspended state of animation since the spectacular voyage of Apollo 11 in 1969. The agency's most vital period was remarkably brief (1962–1968). In an odd turnabout of events, the American space program is viewed in much the same terms as in its formative, pre-World War II years—an exotic novelty, peripheral to mainstream national concerns.

Such is the power of television that recent American generations distinguish themselves by the media events they recollect. For some it was the Kennedy assassination, for others the Iranian hostage crisis. The haunting TV image of the disintegrating Challenger represents another generation's indelible memory. Measured against previous exploits, the "shuttle chapter" tells the story of an organization in decline. Fourteen years of development and 30 billion invested have produced only 25 flights since 1981. Sponsors were promised 30–60 profit-generating flights annually. NASA's romantic technology was inherently ill-suited for routine operations and commercial (cost-conscious) venture. The disappointment expressed by Dr. Alex Roland, a historian of technology at Duke University, seems almost mean-spirited at this stage: "The shuttle was an economic bust before the accident. It's just crazy to think, as some people in NASA do, that we can return to business as usual" (*New York Times*, Mar. 16, 1986). In the interim, with the shuttle program indefinitely grounded, the Pentagon's STS launch-dependent satellite program is stranded while foreign competitors eagerly vie for American commercial launch contracts.

NASA: A FUNCTIONAL ANALYSIS

NASA—The Organization

Officially, NASA is an agency of the Executive branch, under the control of the President, who directs space policy and appoints NASA's head administrator. Congress sets spending limits and can specify projects to be undertaken. The head administrator has several important tasks, including drawing up proposals and making decisions on future programs, resolving high-level personnel problems, and selling NASA to Congress and the U.S. public. Assistant administrators head various support functions and programs. During the Apollo program, and in the early days of the shuttle, astronauts, who had an appreciation of operations and flight safety, were regularly promoted to management. By the 1980s, this had stopped. NASA had nine field centers, each with its own special mission in support of the overall NASA effort. Private contractors work with, and report to, the field centers.

NASA has undergone several reorganizations in order to meet changing goals. A 1961 reorganization was made to develop a stronger headquarters team that could coordinate efforts among the field centers. In 1963, NASA decentralized to better meet the "man-on-the-moon" goal. After a tragic fire took the lives of three astronauts, organizational changes in 1967 created a centralized structure that could integrate decision making and increase emphasis on safety. Another reorganization occurred in 1983 when the shuttle program was reclassified from "developmental" to "operational." Exhibit 13-8 shows how NASA was organized as of January 1986.

EXHIBIT 13-8

NASA Organization

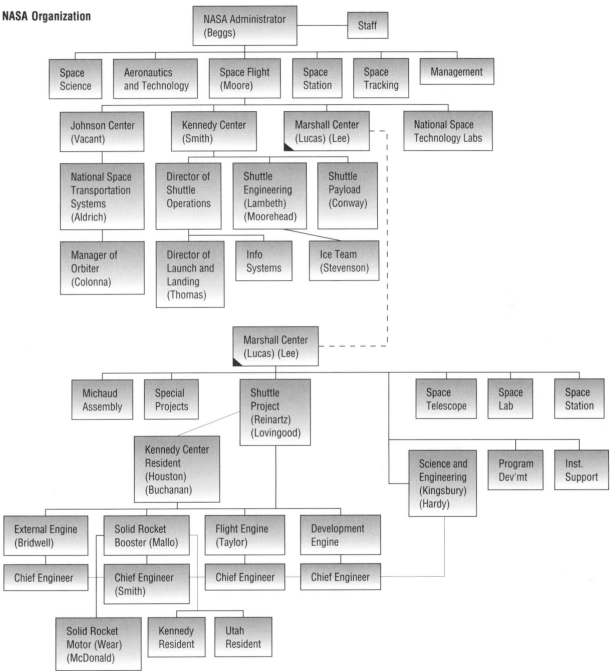

Constituencies

From the very beginning, many people feared that NASA would become more political and less scientific. Although it still has a highly scientific orientation, the goals and policies of the agency have been dictated by political considerations. Whether NASA must answer primarily to the Executive branch, Congress, or some other constituency is always a matter of debate. According to veteran observers of NASA, "NASA is a child of Congress, rather than that of the executive branch" (Hirsch and Trento, 1973, p. 126). On the other hand, former NASA Administrator James Beggs saw space-program support as a matter of "the mood of the country and a question of priorities" (*Sky and Telescope,* 1982, p. 333).

Without a doubt, each President set the tone for much of NASA's activities. It was during the Kennedy-Johnson administrations that NASA received its greatest support. In the post-Apollo days, NASA, fueled by the overwhelming technological success of its moon landings, pushed for manned space flight to Mars. One observer described NASA as "an organism that was more responsive to its own internal technological momentum than to externally developed objectives" (Logsdon, 1983, p. 86). The Nixon administration favored more practical goals. And politicians, who controlled matters of budget and set policy, pushed for a program with tangible benefits to science, the economy, and national security.

President Reagan's 1982 policy consisted of two priorities: maintaining U.S. leadership in space, and expanding private-sector involvement and investment. A less publicized policy was the increasing involvement of the Department of Defense and use of the space program for national defense. After three years of lobbying on the part of those supporting a space station, Reagan, in his 1984 State of the Union address, set a goal of an orbiting space station within 10 years. Administrator Beggs' push to make the shuttle "operational" may have been in part politically motivated; he recognized this was a necessary step in garnering support for the permanent, manned space station. Many people in NASA supported this goal. So did commercial, private enterprise.

Furthermore, the contracting companies who performed 80–90 percent of NASA's design and development work had active trade associations and lobbying efforts to promote their interests. With the shuttle in an "operational" state and the potential development of the manned space station, NASA was no longer its own customer. It now had to serve the needs of private industry. In short, there was a close-knit network between NASA, Congress, the Department of Defense, and private industry.

Public Relations

With so many different constituencies, NASA has always been acutely aware of the value of public relations and image. In its earliest days, NASA was particularly concerned with maintaining secrecy. The Kennedy administration felt that openness was a better approach to provide a counterattack to Soviet propaganda and secrecy. It was also a way of getting the most mileage out of the image of the U.S. as the underdog, steadily maintaining its effort to "catch up." The press was eager for involvement in the space program. They knew it made good copy—spaceships, astronaut heroes, patriotism, and American know-how. Engineers were "scientists" and words like "enhance" and "uprate" replaced the verb "improve." "Integrity" now described machines, and the press became members of an exclusive space-age fraternity.

The merits of manned versus unmanned space flight had been a continuing debate within and outside of NASA. Manned flights were criticized for being expensive, dangerous, and largely unnecessary, particularly in light of improving robotics and computer capabilities. Proponents countered that the intelligence and versatility that on-board humans brought to space missions could not be duplicated by any machine. Even more important was the use of manned missions to win support and bolster enthusiasm of both NASA personnel and the general public.

If anything represented the public's pride in the national space program, it was the original seven Mercury astronauts. They were the nation's "champions" at the same time they were the All-American boys next door. But as the number of astronauts and the size of missions increased, it became harder for the public to keep track of and identify with astronauts. Until the first manned moon flights, a rigid pecking order among the astronauts kept scientist and engineer astronauts on the ground while former fighter and test pilots were selected for moon missions.

Post-Apollo astronauts were selected for their capabilities as scientists. Racial and gender barriers were broken with the selection of female, black, and Asian astronauts. As NASA's programs became increasingly commercialized, it was difficult to retain the astronaut's pioneering and heroic image. Christa McAuliffe, selected as the first teacher in space, represented a new orientation toward the astronaut. The image of the fearless daredevil was no longer appropriate. Instead, outer space belonged to all and now the astronaut was Everyman and Everywoman.

Success and Failures

Even some of the most disastrous events in the agency's history were viewed as at least partial successes by NASA personnel. Prior to 1961, there were many rocket failures. In 1959, seven out of 17 launches failed. NASA saw these as necessary learning experiences, but there was much public criticism of their cost and delay.

By many accounts, however, the 1967 Apollo tragedy was an accident that should not have happened. In January 1967, during "routine" testing, a flash fire broke out in the command module, killing the three astronauts on board. The NASA review board acknowledged insufficient attention to crew safety. Some aspects of the investigation were suppressed by NASA and later revealed by a Congressional inquiry. Among the Congressional findings were "overconfidence" and "complacency" on the part of NASA and a lack of concern on the part of the prime contractor. A more critical review of the incident characterized Congressional findings as "ambiguous" and asserted that because of its close ties with NASA, Congress was reluctant to do anything that would implicate itself. The critique alleged that "sloppy workmanship and slipshod quality" had been with the program all along.

Despite "official" stringent safety standards, the agency was more concerned with meeting deadlines than with safety issues. NASA used this tragedy to its best advantage. Invoking the memory of the dead, they stressed the importance of getting on with the program because that's what the astronauts would have wanted. In spite of this setback, Kennedy's challenge to land a man on the moon was met.

The lives of three other astronauts were seriously endangered during the Apollo 13 mission. While enroute to the moon, the capsule's main oxygen tank exploded. Anderson, NASA's official biographer, believed that technology saved the day. The system contained sufficient flexibility and depth to permit the astronauts to ride safely back to earth. A review board investigating the incident had another perspective. They attributed the accident to a number of human errors and lack of proper monitoring and testing by NASA personnel and concluded that "the lessons of the Apollo 204 (fire) had not been fully applied" (Hirsch and Trento, 1973, p. 121).

Technical problems and failures with various Skylab and Shuttle missions called forth massive round-the-clock efforts by ground personnel and astronauts. Once again, failures became successes where problems were solved with "human ingenuity and courage" (Anderson, 1981, p. 83).

Finances and Budget

NASA's budget and employment figures are listed in Exhibit 13-9. In terms of both budget and employment, NASA enjoyed its greatest power in the mid 1960s with the buildup of the man-on-the-moon effort. Funding decreased steadily over the next ten years, as the nation turned its attention and priorities to other matters. Although funding improved with the shuttle, inflation-adjusted figures show little increase, and the watchword has been fiscal restraint.

NASA—Life on the Inside

Decision Making

Decisions had to be made about the agency's overall goals. But NASA could not be a good decision maker because "government policy is based on partisan and interest group politics instead of on business or technological grounds" (Goldman, 1985, pp. 48–49).

Decision making and problem solving around technical issues were accomplished by creating consensus. For example, one of Apollo's early tasks was to plan the mechanics of putting a man on the moon. A number of options were possible. A group of engineers came up with the idea of a lunar orbiter-lander combination. They spent two years refining the idea, arguing their case before various NASA groups, and they even went "out of channels" directly to NASA's general manager. Their idea gradually won adherents and was adopted.

In mid-1968, with the Apollo program seriously behind schedule, the head of the Manned Space Flight Center, George Low, decided that the scope of each mission should be broadened. Specifically, he believed the Apollo 8 mission should orbit the moon rather than the earth, as originally planned. This represented a bold new step in the Apollo program. He presented his idea to Robert Gilruth, the head of the space task group, who responded enthusiastically. Next they polled the senior project managers, who agreed that all current problems appeared to be solvable in time for the launch deadline. Within just a few months, the mission was reconfigured for its newly established goal.

By the mid-1980s, NASA administrators and engineers made a distinction between engineering and program management decisions. This represented a change from years

EXHIBIT 13-9

**NASA's Budget
and Employment**

Fiscal Year	Budget (in billions)		Employment	
	Nominal	**Real[a]**	**Government**	**Contractor**
1959	0.33	0.37	9,325	31,000
1960	0.51	0.57	10,286	36,500
1961	0.96	1.07	17,077	57,500
1962	1.83	2.02	22,156	115,000
1963	3.67	4.00	27,904	218,400
1964	5.10	5.49	31,984	347,100
1965	5.25	5.56	33,200	376,700
1966	5.18	5.33	33,924	360,000
1967	4.97	4.97	33,726	273,200
1968	4.59	4.40	32,471	235,400
1969	4.00	3.64	31,745	186,600
1970	3.75	3.22	31,223	136,580
1971	3.31	2.73	29,479	121,130
1972	3.36	2.68	27,428	117,540
1973	3.43	2.58	25,955	108,100
1974	3.04	2.06	24,854	100,200
1975	3.23	2.00	24,333	103,400
1976	3.51	2.06	24,039	108,000
1977	3.82	2.10	23,569	100,500
1978	4.06	2.08	23,237	102,800
1979	4.35	2.00	23,237	104,300
1980	5.24	2.12	22,563	101,800
1981	5.52	2.03	21,873	110,000
1982	6.02	2.08	21,652	105,000
1983	6.84	2.29	21,219	107,000

[a]Adjusted for inflation using the 1967 Consumer Price Index.

past. An engineer who had been with NASA since 1960 said (Bazell, 1986, p. 12):

> At the beginning, all the decisions were made at the lowest possible level. We worked together toward one goal. It was simply inconceivable that one person could have thought something was wrong—particularly if it was dangerous—and everyone else not know about it.

Another engineer echoed this perspective: "People making the decisions are getting farther and farther away from the people who get their hands dirty" (Bazell, 1986, p. 14).

A Changing Organization

What was clear was that NASA had changed in many ways over the past 25 years; in other ways it remained the same.

NASA at the start faced many challenges on many fronts dealing with rapid expansion and coordination of activities: leapfrogging the Soviets, dealing with the Executive branch and Congress, creating an environment good for scientific and technological creativity. The task was not merely to provide technical resources but also technical management so that a government-industry-university team could be built. The entire organization had to be geared toward flexibility to improve quality and reliability as the problems of space exploration were better understood. The emphasis was on avoiding "quick fixes" so that many small changes did not eventually add up to serious problems. The crash-program atmosphere of intense effort demanded by the program and by Kennedy's end-of-the-decade deadline was not without personal costs (divorces, heart attacks, and suicides) among NASA personnel.

At its 25th anniversary in 1983, NASA was facing a variety of issues, some of them new to the agency: commercialization of space activity; competition with Europe, Japan, and the Soviet Union; working closely with government military and civilian agencies as well as developing private-sector space activities; and meeting customer commitments. While the shuttle program had changed NASA's mandate, its field organizations retained their scientific and engineering orientations. Although this was appropriate for the Apollo era, observers felt this was currently causing problems for the agency.

Even before this time, NASA had shown resistance to certain changes. In 1973, one observer noted that there were difficulties associated with increasing the professional female and nonwhite staff and that the "overwhelming white domination of NASA is making it an increasingly conspicuous and embarrassing anomaly among government agencies" (Holden, 1973). Although NASA had hired a black woman for a top post in the agency's Affirmative Action department, the political realities of the Nixon administration made it a token gesture. She was dismissed for not fitting into the bureaucracy, but some felt her dismissal was precipitated by her refusal to play Nixon-era politics. It is not clear how much had changed by the mid 1980s, for in 1986 Robert Bazell described NASA insiders as a homogeneous group—white males in their fifties, career men with NASA or its contractors.

A 1979 shuttle management review team, headed by USAF General James Abrahmson, called for changes in management structure and philosophy. Some of the team's findings included the following:

The near-term potential for unanticipated technical problems, schedule slippage and cost growth is high and appropriate reserves should be included in all aspects of program planning.

There has been a lack of adequate long-range planning. . . . Emphasis has been on the current fiscal year, with only secondary attention to succeeding years. . . . Long range planning has not been performed to the extent required for a program as complex as the shuttle.

. . . The successive program changes and associated up and down expenditure rates have resulted in experienced contractor and subcontractor personnel being terminated. Recent and current aerospace industry demand for such personnel is such that experienced people do not remain available, resulting in the employment of inexperienced personnel at a cost to overall efficient performance. This constitutes a major cause for concern, especially for the production phase of the program.

. . . The space transportation system associate administrator (or Level 1 management) has, through an ever increasing personal participation in program activities, became the de facto program director . . . during the course of the fact finding, it became apparent that there was a broad and detailed involvement of Level 1 on technical issues with lesser attention given to cost and schedule.

In the effort to live with funding limitations while still progressing acceptably toward completion, shuttle management has generally set up work schedules that demanded more performance than could be delivered.

Members of the shuttle management review team also mentioned that NASA managers felt the way to keep shuttle costs down was to set up high work performance goals. One NASA manager said (Covault, 1979, pp. 20–21):

If we hadn't done it this way we could never have converted this thundering herd of Apolloites to more reasonable people. This program would have cost $10–$12 billion with the same philosophies we had in Apollo, and then there wouldn't have been any shuttle program.

A concern for costs persisted as the shuttle project progressed. Hans M. Mark, a NASA deputy administrator, reported that, "It is very unlikely that it will be possible to control costs of operations if the developmental attitudes that prevail at Johnson Space Center dominate after the shuttle becomes operational" (Covault, 1981, p. 13).

Despite a changing orientation toward the space program by the administration, many at NASA viewed the shuttle as another Apollo program. Therefore certain considerations, such as technical simplicity, minimizing operational costs, and meeting development schedules were seen by NASA people as less important than the technological development of the shuttle.

Heretofore, NASA had run with a single-flight focus. But because of the pressures of military needs and commercialization of shuttle flights, the program began to include several flights at various stages of readiness. It was becoming difficult to meet the flight schedule and maintain the overall efficiency of the system. By 1986, the schedule allowed for less than one month between flights. Furthermore, certain attitudes persisted from the resource-rich days of Apollo. There was still an inclination toward "can do" spontaneity in responding to crises and technological challenges and a very positive approach to problem solving. This type of enthusiasm was very costly at a time when the shuttle program required nurturing resources. The agency had an established tradition of flexibility, frequently changing shuttle plans as different needs and priorities of its commercial customers arose. These frequent and sometimes last-minute changes were a further drain on resources.

Tight schedules had to be balanced with cost constraints, and NASA contractors had rules governing employee overtime. Some required clearance for overtime in excess of 20 hours per week. Approval was frequently granted. For example, two contractors with employees working at Kennedy Space Center reported the 20-hour limit was exceeded about 5,000 times from October 1985 through January 1986.

During this era of multiple launches, it was necessary for key NASA and contractor personnel-skilled technicians and managers to log 72-hour work weeks and 12-hour days for weeks on end. One team leader worked consecutive work weeks of 60 hours, 96.5 hours, 94 hours, and 81 hours in January 1986. Given this unrelenting pace, it is not surprising that the likelihood for human error increased in early January 1986, when a group of technicians at Kennedy Space Center, working 12-hour shifts, repeatedly misinterpreted fuel-system error messages and made faulty decisions during previous shuttle launch preparations. The mission was scrubbed just 31 seconds before takeoff when an insufficient supply of liquid oxygen in the shuttle's fuel tank triggered alarms. A subsequent investigation attributed the launch abort to human error produced by fatigue. Human safety issues may have taken a back seat to cost considerations, as key personnel were pushed beyond their limits of endurance.

Much of NASA's current staff joined the organization in the Apollo build-up days of the early 1960s. Some were still in mid-career and interested in taking on technological challenges. The changed emphasis to cost and schedule constraints prompted these talented and motivated individuals to leave the organization. However, according to John Pennington, NASA's Director of Human Resources, surveys indicated high motivation and morale and low turnover in the organization (Pennington, 1986).

Nevertheless, the motivation for many of NASA's personnel was still the excitement and challenge of manned missions, large space systems, and interplanetary exploration. Despite the inbred staff of the space program, there was no consensus on what the program's goals should be. For many who remembered the effort and accomplishments of Apollo, there was a growing "return to the moon" movement; others favored focus on a suborbital manned space station. Some people in NASA believed it should become an operational organization, others felt it should remain an R&D agency.

Overall, the lack of a clear mission and the seemingly conflicting roles created difficulties for the agency. There was a tendency at some of the field centers to solve problems in-house rather than pass them up the hierarchy. NASA project managers at some of the centers felt isolated from headquarters and more accountable to their field centers. Conflicting goals, roles, and expectations produced an almost schizoid character. There was difficulty transferring an Apollo-era mood to shuttle realities, in switching from shuttle to routine operations, and in moving from an organization dominated by scientists and engineers to one dominated by bureaucrats and administrators.

Flight Readiness and Safety

Much of NASA's decision making was structured around flight readiness and safety issues. Planning for a shuttle flight began 12–18 months before a shuttle lifted off the pad. Exhibit 13-10 shows the steps that each flight had to clear. The Shuttle Flight Readiness Review was a complicated process. Flights required careful coordination among thousands of contractors, subcontractors, and three space centers (Kennedy, Marshall, and Johnson). Besides obvious concerns about the ability of the rocket to fly, officials allocated cargo space, trained the crew, designed a flight plan, scheduled space activities and experiments, and programmed dozens of computers. Literally hundreds of decisions were involved in a shuttle launch. Therefore, NASA had evolved a "Japanese" style of management: disagree-

EXHIBIT 13-10

Flight Readiness Review Process

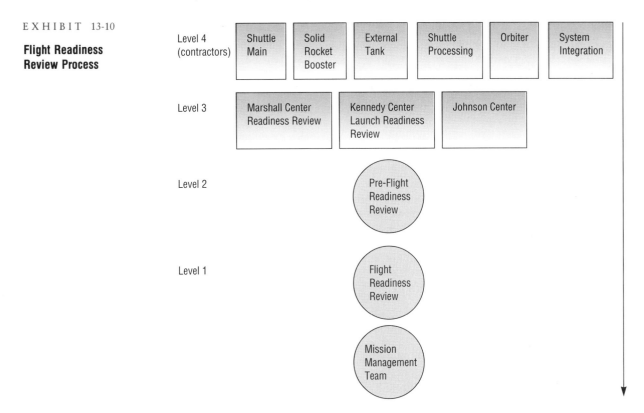

ments "bubbled up" the hierarchy until somebody resolved them.

The flight design process was the central concern in flight preparation. In this process, NASA officials and scientists set the flight objectives and laid out a detailed schedule of flight activities from launch until landing. Four field centers reported the Space Flight Program: Kennedy (launches), Johnson, Marshall (vehicle design and development), and the National Space Technology Laboratories. The planning went through several steps, as outlined below.

- *Level 4.* Level 4 was initiated by a formal directive from the NASA Associate Director of Space Flight. The burden was on contractors at the various space centers (who performed the bulk of the design and development and all of the manufacturing) to certify in writing that their components met the necessary standards.

- *Level 3.* After all certifications were received, the decision making moved down to Level 3. At Level 3, the project managers for the Orbiter, solid rocket booster, and external tank and main engines at Johnson, Kennedy, and Marshall made official presentations to their respective Center Directors. Each review verified the readiness of launch support elements.
- *Level 2.* Next came the Preflight Readiness Review at Level 2 at Johnson Space center. In the Level 2 review, each shuttle program element certified that it had satisfactorily completed the manufacture, assembly, tests, and checks on shuttle equipment. The manager of the National Space Transportation Program presided.
- *Level 1.* The reviews culminated with Level 1. Under the direction of the Associate Administrator for Space Flight, the Flight Readiness Review at Level 1 checked previous planning activities, and a Mission Management Team was established.

• *Mission Management Team.* This team takes over management 48 hours before the launch and continues until the shuttle had landed and been secured. This team met 24 hours before the planned launch to take care of unsatisfied requirements, to assess weather forecasts, and to discuss any anomalies. The Mission Management Team encouraged officials at lower levels to report any new problems or difficulties.

The director of the Shuttle Project Office reported to the Director of the Marshall Space Center. But the readiness review process mainly took place outside the normal chain of command. The levels of the Readiness Review paralleled and overlapped the levels of the formal management structure.

NASA's Safety, Reliability, and Quality Assurance Program came under the duties of the Chief Engineer at NASA headquarters. Out of a staff of 20, one person spent 25 percent of his time, and another spent 10 percent, on safety. At the various centers, the personnel who developed the shuttle hardware were also responsible for related safety issues. Components were engineered to meet stringent specifications, and they were tested. In 1980, NASA appointed a special committee to study the flight worthiness of the entire shuttle system.

Safety issues often cropped up at various levels of the Readiness Review. Flights had to meet 28 specific criteria before the countdown could begin. Participants mulled over technical specifications, interpretation of test results, and what constituted an adequate margin for safety. Those systems that had no back-up and which might bring about the loss of the vehicle and life were called "critical" and received special attention. In addition, the Flight Readiness Review procedure included official procedures for waiving nonconforming components or systems in the interests of flexibility, expedience, or extenuating circumstances.

SHUTTLE FLIGHT PROCEDURES: CHALLENGER FLIGHT 51-L

May 1985. Crew training begins.

August 20, 1985. NASA conducts a Preflight Readiness Review. They discuss the crew, storage, engineering status, photo and TV requirements, the Teacher-in-Space program and the launch window.

December 13, 1985. Associate Administrator for Space Flight (Moore) schedules Flight Readiness Review for January 15, 1986.

January 9, 1986. Morton Thiokol (MTI) certifies solid rocket booster flight readiness (Level 4). This is the first stage where equipment problems can delay a launch. The O-rings are a known problem, but MTI and NASA personnel do not believe they are serious enough to stop launch.

January 14, 1986. After weeks of intensive preparation, including a dress rehearsal and a mock firing of the main engines, Kennedy Center Director Richard Smith convenes the Preflight Readiness Review meeting (Level 2) and sets the schedule for Level I/Mission Management Team meetings. Over 100 participants from Kennedy, Marshall, Johnson, Lockheed, and various subcontractors discuss what time of day to launch, conditions for viewing Halley's comet, excessive cargo weight, and the schedule of crew activities. No problems with the solid rocket booster were identified. Kennedy Center Director Smith signs launch-readiness certificate.

January 15, 1986. NASA associate administrator Moore chairs Flight Readiness Review Meeting (Level 1). A video teleconference links NASA flight centers to Cape Kennedy. All systems are reviewed in detail, from engineering through flight responsibilities. They decide, "Go."

January 22, 1986. NASA officials are worried about dust storms in Dakar, the main emergency landing site. A shuttle can't go up unless it has a safe place to land if something goes wrong. Countdown is reset for January 26 at 9:36 A.M.

January 25, 1986. 11 A.M. EST. Level 1 team meets again. All unresolved flight readiness review items were reported closed. But rainstorms prompt officials to postpone until the 27th.

January 27, 1986. 12:36 P.M. Mission Management Team scrubs launch because of high winds and overcast at launch site. Rain can damage the shuttle's heat-resistant tiles. Problems with a sticky bolt cause a 90-minute delay in the astronauts' disembarking from the orbiter. Team resets launch for 9:38 A.M., January 28.

2:00 P.M. Mission Management Team meets again. Because weather forecasts predict temperatures in low 20s, someone raises concerns about cold weather effects on launch facility water drains, fire suppression system, and water trays. They decide to activate heaters on the shuttle.

2:30 P.M. in Utah. Morton Thiokol engineers in Wasatch, Utah, hearing about forecast cold temperatures discuss possible effects of cold weather predicted for January 28 on solid rocket booster (Exhibit 13-11 for MTI organization).

EXHIBIT 13-11

Morton Thiokol Management Structure

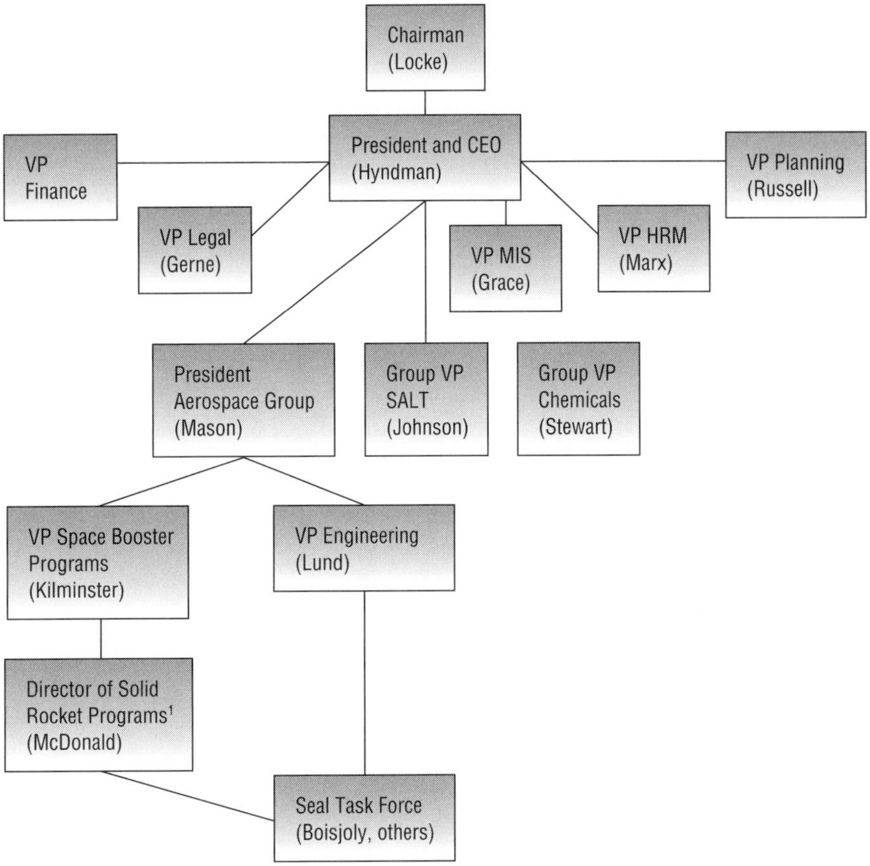

5:45 P.M. First teleconference between NASA Level 3 personnel at Kennedy (Lovingood) and Marshall (Reinartz) and Thiokol personnel in Utah. Morton Thiokol officials express reservations about effects of temperatures on O-rings. They postpone launch until noon or afternoon of 28th. Lovingood proposes going to Level 2 (Aldrich) if MTI stands by no-launch recommendation at second teleconference set for 8:15.

8:45 P.M. Second teleconference between MTI Utah (six members), Kennedy (Reinartz, Mulloy, McDonald—MTI liaison), and Marshall (Hardy, Lovingood, et al.). A technical discussion of O-ring problems and tests. Problems with the O-rings had a long history. One MTI vice president of engineering (Lund) says not to fly 51-L until temperature exceeds 53°F. Another MTI engineer Boisjoly presents charts and tables about problem. Mulloy asks MTI vice president Kilminster for recommendation. Kilminster says he cannot recommend launch. Reinartz, Mulloy, and Hardy challenge MTI conclusions, asking for hard data to support Boisjoly's conjectures. Hardy says he is "appalled" by the recommendation. Mulloy says, "Do you want us to wait until April to launch?" Kilminster asks for time to caucus. Later, Mr. Boisjoly remarks, "This was a meeting where the determination was to launch, and it was up to us to prove beyond a shadow of a doubt that it was not safe to do so ... usually it is exactly opposite that." Mulloy says, "There was no violation of launch commit criteria ... [there] were 27 full-scale tests of the O-rings

EXHIBIT 13-12

Main Players at NASA, Marshall Center and Morton Thiokol

	Position	Action (Inaction)
NASA Top Management		
1. Jesse Moore	Associate Administrator for space flight	Made decision to launch 51L did not know of no-go recommendations
2. Arnold Aldrich	Shuttle Manager at Johnson	Knew only Rockwell reservations
Marshall Center		
1. William Lucas	Director	Outside launch chain of command
2. Stanley Reinartz	Mgr., Shuttle Projects	Did not tell superiors about Thiokol reservations
3. Lawrence Mulloy	Chief of Solid Rockets	Did not accept Thiokol engineer's doubts
4. George Hardy	Deputy Director of Space Engineering	Did not accept Thiokol engineer's doubts
Morton Thiokol		
1. Jerald Mason	Senior Vice President	Asked for decision
2. Joseph Kilminster	V.P. for Boosters	Signed "go" memo
3. Robert Lund	V.P. for Engineering	Persuaded to OK launch recommendation
4. Allan MacDonald	Director of Solid Rockets	At Kennedy—opposed launch
5. Rogert Boisjoly	Head of Seals Task Force	Worried about low temp.
6. Arnold Thompson	Engineer	Opposed launch
7. Brian Russell	Engineer	Opposed launch

Source: Rogers Commission Report (1986).

damage tolerances . . . we had experience with this problem" (see Exhibit 13-12).

10:30 P.M. to 11:00 P.M. in Utah. MTI personnel discuss O-rings. Two engineers (Boisjoly and Thompson) continue to voice strong objections to launch. Mason asks Lund to "put on his management hat." The MTI top managers decide that objections are not serious enough to justify cancelling 51-L. The MTI officials later characterize the discussion as "unemotional, rational discussion of the facts as they knew them . . . a judgment call."

10:30 P.M. to 11:00 P.M. at Kennedy. McDonald, Mulloy, Reinartz, Buchanan, and Houston discuss whether to delay. Mulloy says that none of MTI's data change the rationale from previous successful flights.

11:00 P.M. Second teleconference continues. The MTI officials say that O-rings are a concern but data are not conclusive against launch. Kilminster recommends launching. NASA asks MTI to put recommendation in writing.

11:15 P.M. to 11:30 P.M. at Kennedy. McDonald strongly argues for delay, says he would not like to answer to board of inquiry. Mulloy says that the temperature of the fuel in the booster will still meet the Minimum Launch Criteria.

Reinartz and Mulloy tell McDonald that it is not his decision, that his concerns are noted and will be passed on. (See Exhibit 13-12 for summary of disputants.)

11:30 P.M. to 12:00 A.M. Teleconference at Kennedy. Mulloy, Reinartz, and Aldrich discuss icing in launch area and recovery ships' activities. The O-rings are not mentioned.

January 28, 1986. 1:30 A.M. to 3:00 A.M. at Kennedy. The ice crew reports large quantities of ice on pad B. The spacecraft can be damaged by chunks of ice that can be hurled about during the turbulent rocket ignition.

5:00 A.M. at Kennedy. Mulloy tells Lucas of MTI concerns over temperature and resolution and shows the recommendation written by MTI.

7:00 A.M. to 9:00 A.M. at Kennedy. The clear morning sky formed what glider pilots call a "blue bowl." Winds dwindled to 9 mph. During the night temperatures fell to 27°F. The ice crew measures temperatures at 25°F on the right-hand solid rocket booster, 8°F on the left. They are not concerned as there are no Launch Commit Criteria relating to temperatures on rocket surfaces.

8:00 A.M. at Kennedy. Lovingood tells Deputy Director of Marshall (Lee) about previous discussions with MTI.

9:00 A.M. at Kennedy. Mission Management Team meets with Level 1 and 2 managers, project managers, and others. The ice conditions on launch pad are discussed, but not the O-ring issue.

10:30 A.M. at Kennedy. The ice crew reports to the Mission Management Team that ice is still left on booster.

11:18 A.M. A Rockwell engineer in California watching the ice team over closed-circuit television telephones the Cape to advise a delay because of the ice. Kennedy Center Director Smith, advised by the ice team that there is little risk, permits the countdown to continue.

11:28 A.M. Inside Challenger's flight deck (about the size of a 747), Commander Scobee and pilot Smith run through their elaborate checklists. The orbiter's main computer, supported by four backup computers, scans data from 2,000 sensors. If it detects a problem, it will shut down the entire system. In June 1984, the computer aborted four seconds before the rocket ignition. This time, it doesn't.

11:30 A.M. Thousands of motorists pull off highways to face toward the ocean.

11:37 A.M. The launch platform is flooded by powerful streams of water from 7-foot pipes to dampen the lift-off sound levels, which could damage the craft's underside.

11:38 A.M. Flight 51-L is launched. Two rust-colored external fuel tanks, each 154 feet high, carrying 143,351 gallons of liquid oxygen and 385,265 gallons of liquid hydrogen power the rocket. They will burn until the fuel runs out.

11:39 A.M. Everything looked like it was supposed to look. As one MTI engineer watched the rocket lift off the pad into a bright Florida sky he thought, "Gee, it's gonna be all right. It's a piece of cake . . . we made it."

REFERENCES

F.W. Anderson, *Orders of Magnitude: A History of NACA and NASA, 1915–1980.* (Washington, DC.: NASA 1981).

R. Bazell, NASA's Mid Life Crisis. *The New Republic*, March 24, 1986, pp. 12–15.

J.K. Beatty, The "Space Age" (25 Years and Counting). *Sky and Telescope*, 64, (1982), pp. 310–13.

J. Becker, NASA's Projects Reflect a New Attitude as Agency Competes for Launch Services. *EDN*, August 22, 1985, pp. 307–11.

R. Berry, A Busy Year for the Shuttle. *Astronomy* 14, 1986, pp. 8–22.

H. Brooks, Managing the Enterprise in Space. *Technology Review* 86, 1983, pp. 39–46.

C. Covault, Changes Expected in Shuttle Management Philosophy. *Aviation Week and Space Technology*. September 24, 1979, pp. 20–21.

C. Covault, NASA Formulates Policy to Spur Private Investment. *Aviation Week and Space Technology,* November 26, 1984, pp. 18–19.

N.C. Goldman, *Space Commerce: Free Enterprise on the High Frontier.* (Cambridge, MA: Ballinger, 1985).

F. Guterl and C. Truxal, Militarization: Peace or War? *IEEE Spectrum*, September 1983, pp. 35–39.

R. Hirsch and J.J. Trento, *The National Aeronautics and Space Administration.* (New York: Praeger, 1973).

C. Holden, NASA: Sacking Top Black Woman Stirs Concern for Equal Employment. *Science* 182, 1973, pp. 804–7.

E.A. Kennan and E.H. Harvey, *Mission to the Moon: A Critical Examination of NASA and the Space Program.* (New York: William Morrow, 1969).

A.L. Levine, *The Future of the U.S. Space Program.* (New York: Praeger, 1975).

A.S. Levine, *Managing NASA in the Apollo Era.* (Washington, D.C.: NASA, 1982).

J.M. Logsdon, NASA's Dual Challenge: Serving Yet Striving. *IEEE Spectrum*, September, 1983, pp. 86–89.

W.A. McDougall, *The Heavens and the Earth: A Political History of the Space Age.* (New York: Basic Books Inc, 1985).

B. Murray, In Search of Presidential Goals. *Issues in Science and Technology,* Spring 1986.

J. Pennington, (NASA Director of Human Resources), personal communication, July 1986.

T. Riechhardt, Twelve Years from the Moon. *Space World,* July, 1985, pp. 13–14.

Rogers Commission Report. (Washington D.C.: U.S. Government Printing Office, 1986).

H. Sidey, Pioneers in Love with the Frontier, *Time,* February 10, 1986.

F. Sietzen, Jr., Perspectives on the Apollo Era, *Space World,* 1984, pp. 4–9.

Sky and Telescope, An Interview with James Beggs, October 1982, pp. 332–33.

Space World, NASA's First 25 Years, October 1983, pp. 25–32.

Space World, NASA Reorganizations, January 1984, pp. 34–35.

J.N. Wilford, After the Challenger: America's Future in Space, *New York Times,* Mar. 16, 1986.

T. Wolfe, Everyman vs. Astropower, *Newsweek,* February 10, 1986, pp. 40–41.

T. Wolfe, *The Right Stuff* (New York: Farrar, Strauss, Giroux, 1979).

CASE QUESTIONS

1. How does the case illustrate that political decision making differs from technologically based decision making?

2. What historical information suggests that poor or incorrect decisions about quality may have been a part of NASA's culture that influenced the January 1986 loss of the Challenger shuttle?

3. Discuss how consensus decision making operates at NASA.

CASE 13–2   NED NORMAN, COMMITTEE CHAIRMAN

Ned Norman tried to reconstruct, in his own mind, the series of events that had culminated in that most unusual committee meeting this morning.

For example, each of the committee members had suddenly seemed to be stubbornly resisting any suggestions that did not exactly coincide with their own ideas for implementing the program under consideration. This unwillingness to budge from some preconceived position was not like the normal behavior patterns of most of the committee participants. Of course, some of the comments made in one of last week's sessions about "old-fashioned, seat-of-the-pants decision making" had ruffled a few feathers, but Ned did not really think this was the reason things had suddenly bogged down today. Still, Ned thought it might be worthwhile to review in his mind what had taken place in this morning's meeting to see if some clues existed to explain the problem.

First, Ned recalled starting the session by saying that the committee had discussed, in past meetings, several of the factors connected with the proposed expanded-services program and it now seemed about time to make a decision as to which way to go. Ned remembered that Robert Roman had protested that they had barely scratched the surface of the possibilities for implementing the program. Then both Sherman Stith and Tod Tooley, who worked in the statistics branch of Division Baker, had sided with Roman and were most insistent that additional time was needed

to research in-depth some of the other avenues of approach to solving the problems associated with starting the new program.

Walt West had entered the fray by stating that this seemed a little uncalled for, since previous experience had clearly indicated that expansion programs, such as this one, should be implemented through selected area district offices. This had brought forth the statement by Sherman Stith that experience was more often than not a lousy teacher, which was followed by Tod Tooley repeating his unfortunate statement about old-fashioned decision making! And, of course, Robert Roman had not helped matters at all by saying that it was obviously far better to go a little bit slower in such matters by trying any new program in one area first, rather than to have the committee members look "unprogressive" by just "trudging along on the same old cow paths!"

In fact, as Ned suddenly realized, if he hadn't almost intuitively exercised his prerogatives as chairman to stop the trend that was developing, he might have had a real melee on his hands right then! It was obvious that things were increasingly touchy among the members, so much so that despite his best efforts, everyone had simply refused either to participate or to support any of the ideas he (Ned) had offered to break the deadlock.

Feeling a little frustrated, early that same afternoon Ned had sought the counsel of his boss, who advised him to go talk to the division directors for whom the various committee members worked. In each area visited, Ned found that the division director was already aware of the

Source: This case was written by Professor William D. Heier of Arizona State University.

committee problems, and each one had his own ideas as to what should be done about them.

The director of Division Able stated that he was not much in sympathy with people who wanted to make a big deal out of every program that came along. He recalled the problem six years ago when the first computer had arrived in the agency and was hailed as the manager's replacement in decision making. He noted that, although the computer was still here, so was he, and that he had probably made better decisions, as a result of his broad background and knowledge, than the computer ever would! The Division Able director told Ned that he had been on several deadlocked committees but that, when he was chairman, he simply made the decision for the committee and solved the problem. He suggested Ned do likewise.

The Division Baker director stated that he knew Ned was one of those guys who wanted to use the best information available in estimating a program's performance. He told Ned that Sherman and Tod, who worked in Division Baker, had briefed him on the problems the committee had encountered and that, in his opinion, their investigative approach was the proper one to take. After all, stated the director, it logically followed that a decision could be no better than the research effort put into it. He also told Ned that, although he realized research might cost a little money, he had told Sherman and Tod to go ahead and collect the data needed to determine the best way to implement the expansion program. The director flatly stated, "These are my men and my division will be footing the bill for this research, so no one else has any gripe about the cost aspects." He expressed the opinion that almost any price would be cheap if it would awaken some of the company employees to the tremendous values of a scientific approach to decision making.

The Division Charlie director stated, quite bluntly, that he was not particularly interested in how the expansion program was decided. He said it looked to him like the easiest way to get the thing moving was to do it a piece at a time. That way, he noted, you can evaluate how it looks without committing the company to a full-scale expansion. He concluded by saying, "It doesn't take a lot of figuring to figure that one out!"

The Division Delta director stated that the aspect of "time" was against the committee's looking at all angles and that a decision should be made after looking at two or three possible solutions. He stated that he needed Quentin Quinn, his representative on Ned's committee, for another job and hoped the committee would be finished very quickly.

Ned now realized that he had more of a problem than he had suspected. In view of the approaches and opinions expressed by the division directors, it seemed highly unlikely that any of the committee members would move from their present position. Ergo, Ned is now chairman of a deadlocked committee!

In pondering his dilemma, Ned considered various ways to break the impasse. First, as chairman, he could simply exert his authority and try to force a solution. This was guaranteed to alienate most of the committee members and the division directors, who had representatives on the committee.

Second, Ned considered returning to his boss, who had formed the committee, with the recommendation that the committee be disbanded. While the reason for this recommendation would be easy to explain, Ned's failure to prevent this problem might be much more difficult.

As a third possibility, the idea occurred to Ned that he might ask each committee member to bring to the next meeting, in writing, his recommended plan for implementing the program. Since these would surely represent the thinking of the four division directors, this information could then be presented by Ned to his boss with a request for guidance. If his boss could be persuaded to make a choice, Ned's problem would be solved. Of the three ideas he had considered, Ned liked the last one the best. Accordingly, he reached for the telephone preparatory to calling the first of his impossible committee members!

CASE QUESTIONS

1. What does this case illustrate about the process of group decision making?
2. Discuss and evaluate the comments made by each division director.
3. What advice would you give Ned Norman?

CHAPTER

14

Communication

LEARNING OBJECTIVES

EXPLAIN the elements in the communication process

COMPARE the four major directions of communication

DESCRIBE the role played by interpersonal communication in organizations

DISCUSS the importance of multicultural communication

IDENTIFY significant barriers to effective communication

DESCRIBE ways in which communication in organizations can be improved

The focus of this chapter is the process of organizational communication. Communicating, like the process of decision making discussed in the previous chapter, pervades everything that all organizational members—particularly managers—do. The managerial functions of planning, organizing, leading, and controlling all involve communicative activity. In fact, communication is an absolutely essential element in all organizational processes.

THE IMPORTANCE OF COMMUNICATION

Communication is the glue that holds organizations together. Communication assists organizational members to accomplish both individual and organizational goals, implement and respond to organizational change, coordinate organizational activities, and engage in virtually all organizationally relevant behaviors. Yet, as important as this process is, breakdowns in communication are pervasive. The anonymous wit who said, "I know you believe you understand what you think I said, but I am not sure you realize that what you heard is not what I meant" was being more than humorous; he or she was describing what everyone of us has experienced: A failure to communicate. To the extent that organizational communications are less effective than they might be, organizations will be less effective than they might be.

It would be extremely difficult to find an aspect of a manager's job that does not involve communication. Serious problems arise when directives are misunderstood, when casual kidding in a work group leads to anger, or when informal remarks by a top level manager are distorted. Each of these situations is a result of a breakdown somewhere in the process of communication.

Accordingly, the pertinent question is not whether managers engage in communication because communication is inherent to the functioning of an organization. Rather, the pertinent question is whether managers will communicate well or poorly. In other words, communication itself is unavoidable in an organization's functioning; only *effective* communication is avoidable. *Every manager must be a communicator.* In fact, everything a manager does communicates something in some way to somebody or some group. The only question is: "With what effect?" While this may appear an overstatement at this point, it will become apparent as you proceed through the chapter. Despite the tremendous advances in communication and information technology, communication among people in organizations leaves much to be desired.[1] Communication among people does not depend on technology but rather on forces in people and their surroundings. It is a process that occurs within people.

THE COMMUNICATION PROCESS

The general process of communication is presented in Exhibit 14-1. The process contains five elements—the communicator, the message, the medium, the receiver, and feedback. It can be simply summarized as: Who . . . says what . . . in what way . . . to whom . . . with what effect?[2] To appreciate each element in the process, we must examine how communication works.

How Communication Works

Communication experts tell us that effective communication is the result of a common understanding between the communicator and the receiver. In fact, the word **communication** is derived from the Latin *communis,* meaning "common." The communicator seeks to establish a "commonness" with a receiver. Hence, we can define communication as the *transition of information and understanding through the use of common symbols.* The common symbols may be verbal or nonverbal. You will see later that in the context of an organizational structure,

---

[1]For a discussion of organizational effects of advanced information technology, see George Huber, "A Theory of the Effects of Advanced Information Technologies on Organizational Design, Intelligence, and Decision Making," *Academy of Management Review,* January 1990, pp. 47–71.

[2]These five questions were first suggested in H. D. Lasswell, *Power and Personality* (New York: W. W. Norton, 1948), pp. 37–51.

EXHIBIT 14-1

**The Communication
Process**

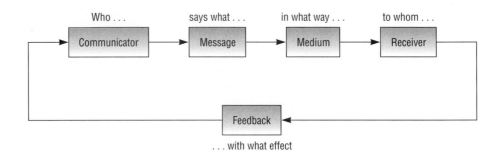

information can flow up and down (vertical), across (horizontal), and down and across (diagonal).

The most widely used contemporary model of the process of communication has evolved mainly from the work of Shannon and Weaver and Schramm.[3] These researchers were concerned with describing the general process of communication that could be useful in all situations. The model that evolved from their work is helpful for understanding communication. The basic elements include a communicator, an encoder, a message, a medium, a decoder, a receiver, feedback, and noise. The model is presented in Exhibit 14-2. Each element in the model can be examined in the context of an organization.

The Elements of Communication

Communicator

In an organizational framework, the communicator is an employee with ideas, intentions, information, and a purpose for communicating.

Encoding

Given the communicator, an encoding process must take plate that translates the communicator's ideas into a systematic set of symbols—into a language expressing the communicator's purpose. For example, a manager often takes accounting information, sales reports, and computer data and translates them into one message. The function of encoding, then, is to provide a form in which ideas and purposes can be expressed as a message.

Message

The result of the encoding process is the message. The purpose of the communicator is expressed in the form of the message—either *verbal* or *nonverbal.*

[3]Claude Shannon and Warren Weaver, *The Mathematical Theory of Communication* (Urbana: University of Illinois Press, 1948); and Wilbur Schramm, "How Communication Works," in *The Process and Effects of Mass Communication,* ed. Wilbur Schramm (Urbana: University of Illinois Press, 1953), pp. 3–26.

EXHIBIT 14-2

A Communication Model

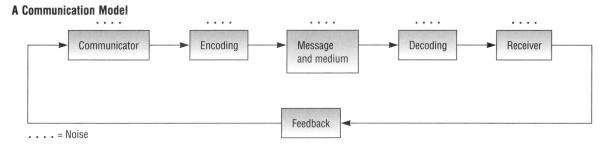

.... = Noise

Managers have numerous purposes for communicating such as to have others understand their ideas, to understand the ideas of others, to gain acceptance of themselves or their ideas, or to produce action. The message, then, is what the individual hopes to communicate to the intended receiver, and the exact form it takes depends, to a great extent, on the medium used to carry the message. Decisions relating to the two are inseparable.

Not as obvious, however, are *unintended messages* that can be sent by silence or inaction on a particular issue as well as decisions of which goals and objectives not to pursue and which method not to utilize. For example, a decision to utilize one type of performance evaluation method rather than another may send a "message" to certain people. Messages may also be designed to appear on the surface to convey certain information, when other information is what is really being conveyed. Related to this are messages designed to protect the sender, rather than to facilitate understanding by the receiver. Encounter 14-1 provides some examples of these latter types of messages.

Medium

The **medium** is the carrier of the message. Organizations provide information to members in a variety of ways, including face-to-face communications, telephone, group meetings, memos, policy statements, reward systems, production schedules, and sales forecasts. The arrival of electronic media based upon the computer and telecommunication technologies has increased interest in the role of the medium in various aspects of organizational communications.[4]

Decoding-Receiver

For the process of communication to be completed, the message must be decoded in terms of relevance to the receiver. **Decoding** is a technical term for the receiver's thought processes. Decoding, then, involves interpretation. **Receivers interpret**

---

[4]Carol Saunders and Jack Jones, "Temporal Sequences in Information Acquisition for Decision Making: A Focus on Source and Medium," *Academy of Management Review,* January 1990, pp. 29–46.

ORGANIZATIONAL
E N C O U N T E R • 14-1

SOME EXAMPLES OF ORGANIZATIONAL OBFUSCATION

Unfortunately, not all organizational communications are meant to clarify; sometimes they are designed to confuse. At other times, protecting the communicator may be the primary objective. Some words and phrases are so frequently used to convey a meaning other than the apparent one that their use has become institutionalized. Below are some humorous examples of alternative interpretations to what otherwise appear as straightforward words or messages.

- It is in process—It's so wrapped up in red tape that the situation is hopeless.
- We will look into it—By the time the wheel makes a full turn we assume you will have forgotten about it.
- Under consideration—Never heard of it.
- Under active consideration—We're looking in our files for it.
- We are making a survey—We need more time to think of an answer.
- Let's get together on this—I'm assuming you're as confused as I.
- For appropriate action—Maybe you'll know what to do with this.

- Note and initial—Lets spread the responsibility for this.
- It is estimated—This is my guess.
- We are aware of it—We had hoped that the person who started it would have forgotten about it by now.
- We will advise you in due course—If we figure it out, we'll let you know.
- Give us the benefit of your thinking—We'll listen to you as long as it doesn't interfere with what we have already decided to do.
- She is in conference—I don't have any idea where she is.
- We are activating the file—We're faxing it to as many people we can think of.
- Let me bring you up to date—We didn't like what you were going to do, so we already did something else.
- A reliable source—The person you just met.
- An informed source—The person who told the person you just met.
- An unimpeachable source—The person who started the rumor to begin with.

(decode) the message in light of their own previous experiences and frames of reference. Thus, a salesperson is likely to decode a memo from the company president differently than a production manager will. A nursing supervisor is likely to decode a memo from the hospital administrator differently than the chief of surgery will. The closer the decoded message is to the intent desired by the communicator, the more effective is the communication. This underscores the importance of the communicator being "receiver-oriented."

Feedback

Provision for feedback in the communication process is desirable. *One-way* communication processes are those that do not allow receiver-to-communicator feedback. This may increase the potential for distortion between the intended message and the received message. A feedback loop provides a channel for receiver response that enables the communicator to determine whether the message has been received and has produced the intended response. *Two-way* communication processes provide for this important receiver-to-communicator feedback.[5]

For the manager, communication feedback may come in many ways. In face-to-face situations, *direct* feedback through verbal exchanges is possible as are such subtle means of communication as facial expressions of discontent or misunderstanding. In addition, *indirect* means of feedback (such as declines in productivity, poor quality of production, increased absenteeism or turnover, and lack of coordination and/or conflict between units) may indicate communication breakdowns.

Noise

In the framework of human communication, noise can be thought of as those factors that distort the intended message. Noise may occur in each of the elements of communication. For example, a manager who is under a severe time constraint may be forced to act without communicating or may communicate hastily with incomplete information. Or a subordinate may attach a different meaning to a word or phrase than was intended by the manager.

The elements discussed in this section are essential for communication to occur. They should not, however, be viewed as separate. They are, rather, descriptive of the acts that have to be performed for any type of communication to occur. The communication may be vertical (superior-subordinate, subordinate-superior) or horizontal (peer-peer). Or it may involve one individual and a group. But the elements discussed here must be present.

Nonverbal Messages

The information sent by a communicator that is unrelated to the verbal information—that is, nonverbal messages or *nonverbal communication*—is a relatively recent area of research among behavioral scientists. The major interest has been in the *physical cues* that characterize the communicator's physical presentation. These cues include such modes of transmitting nonverbal messages as head, face, and eye movements, posture, distance, gestures, voice tone, and clothing and dress choices.[6] Nonverbal messages themselves are influenced by factors such as the gender of the communicator.[7]

Research indicates that facial expressions and eye contact and movements generally provide information about the *type* of emotion, while such physical

---

[5]Carol Watson and Paul Grubb, "Beliefs about Performance Feedback: An Exploration of the Job Holder's Perspective" (Paper presented at the National Academy of Management Meeting, San Diego, California, August 1985).

[6]Andres J. DuBrin, *Contemporary Applied Management* (Plano, Tex.: Business Publications, 1982), pp. 127–34.

[7]Nicole Steckler and Robert Rosenthal, "Sex Differences in Nonverbal and Verbal Communication with Bosses, Peers, and Subordinates," *Journal of Applied Psychology,* February 1985, pp. 157–63.

cues as distance, posture, and gestures indicate the *intensity* of the emotion. These conclusions are important to managers. They indicate that communicators often send a great deal more information than is obtained in verbal messages. To increase the effectiveness of communication, a person must be aware of the nonverbal as well as the verbal content of the messages. Nonverbal communi-

▲ C14–1   cation is illustrated in Case 14–1.

COMMUNICATING WITHIN ORGANIZATIONS

The design of an organization should provide for communication in four distinct directions: downward, upward, horizontal, and diagonal. Since these directions of communication establish the framework within which communication in an organization takes place, let us briefly examine each one. This examination will enable you to better appreciate the barriers to effective organizational communication and the means to overcome them.

Downward Communication

This type of communication flows downward from individuals in higher levels of the hierarchy to those in lower levels. The most common forms of **downward communication** are job instructions, official memos, policy statements, procedures, manuals, and company publications. In many organizations, downward communication often is both inadequate and inaccurate as evidenced in the often-heard statement among organization members that "we have absolutely no idea what's happening." Such complaints indicate inadequate downward communication and the need of individuals for information relevant to their jobs. The absence of job-related information can create unnecessary stress among organization members.[8] A similar situation is faced by a student who has not been told the requirements and expectations of an instructor.

Upward Communication

An effective organization needs **upward communication** as much as it needs downward communication. In such situations, the communicator is at a lower level in the organization than the receiver. Some of the most common upward communication flows are suggestion boxes, group meetings, and appeal or grievance procedures. In their absence, people somehow find ways to adopt nonexistent or inadequate upward communication channels. This has been evidenced by the emergence of "underground" employee publications in many large organizations.

[8]Nicholas Smeed, "A Boon to Employee Communications: Letters of Understanding," *Personnel,* April 1985, pp. 50–53.

Upward communication serves a number of important functions. Organizational communication researcher Gary Kreps identifies several:[9]

1. It provides managers with feedback about current organizational issues and problems and information about day-to-day operations that they need for making decisions about directing the organization.
2. It is management's primary source of feedback for determining the effectiveness of its downward communication.
3. It relieves employees' tensions by allowing lower-level organization members to share relevant information with their superiors.
4. It encourages employees' participation and involvement, thereby enhancing organizational cohesiveness.

Horizontal Communication

Often overlooked in the design of most organizations is provision for **horizontal communication.** When the chairperson of the accounting department communicates with the chairperson of the marketing department concerning the course offerings in a college of business administration, the flow of communication is horizontal. Although vertical (upward and downward) communication flows are the primary considerations in organizational design, effective organizations also need horizontal communication. Horizontal communication—for example, communication between production and sales in a business organization and among the different departments or colleges within a university—is necessary for the coordination and integration of diverse organizational functions.

Since mechanisms for assuring horizontal communication ordinarily do not exist in an organization's design, its facilitation is left to individual managers. Peer-to-peer communication often is necessary for coordination and also can provide social need satisfaction.

Diagonal Communication

While it is probably the least-used channel of communication in organizations, **diagonal communication** is important in situations where members cannot communicate effectively through other channels. For example, the comptroller of a large organization may wish to conduct a distribution cost analysis. One part of that task may involve having the sales force send a special report directly to the comptroller rather than going through the traditional channels in the marketing department. Thus, the flow of communication would be diagonal as opposed to vertical (upward) and horizontal. In this case, a diagonal channel would be the most efficient in terms of time and effort for the organization.

[9]Gary L. Kreps, *Organizational Communication* (New York: Longman, 1990), p. 203.

INTERPERSONAL COMMUNICATIONS

Within an organization, communication flows from individual to individual in face-to-face and group settings. Such flows are termed *interpersonal communications* and can vary from direct orders to casual expressions. Interpersonal behavior could not exist without interpersonal communication. In addition to providing needed information, interpersonal communication also influences how people feel about the organization. For example, research indicates that satisfaction with communication relationships effects organizational commitment.[10]

The problems that arise when managers attempt to communicate with other people can be traced to *perceptual differences* and *interpersonal style differences*. We know from Chapter 3 that each manager perceives the world in terms of his or her background, experiences, personality, frame of reference, and attitude. The primary way in which managers relate to and learn from the environment (including the people in that environment) is through information received and transmitted. And the way in which managers receive and transmit information depends, in part, on how they relate to two very important *senders* of information—*themselves* and *others*. Exercise 14–1 is a diagnostic questionnaire that can provide you with information relating to your tendencies in interpersonal communications.

■ E14–1

Interpersonal Styles

Interpersonal style refers to the way in which an individual prefers to relate to others. The fact that much of the relationship among people involves communication indicates the importance of interpersonal style.

We begin by recognizing that information is held by oneself and by others but that each of us does not fully have or know that information. The different combinations of knowing and not knowing relevant information are shown in Exhibit 14-3. The exhibit identifies four combinations, or regions, of information known and unknown by the self and others and is popularly referred to as the Johari Window.[11] The essentials of the model are briefly examined here.

The Arena

The region most conducive to effective interpersonal relationships and communication is termed the arena. In this setting, all of the information necessary to carry on effective communication is known to both the communicator (self) and the receivers (others). For a communication attempt to be in the arena region, the parties involved must share identical feelings, data, assumptions, and skills.

---

[10]J. M. Putti, S. Aryee, and J. Phua, "Communication Relationship Satisfaction and Organizational Commitment," *Group and Organizational Studies*, March 1990, pp. 44–52.

[11]Joseph Luft, "The Johari Window," *Human Relations and Training News*, January 1961, pp. 6–7. The discussion here is based on a later adaptation. See J. Hall, "Communication Revisited," *California Management Review*, Fall 1973, pp. 56–67.

EXHIBIT 14-3

The Johari Window: Interpersonal Styles and Communications

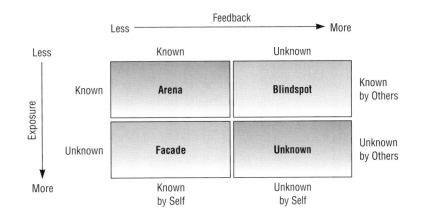

Since the arena is the area of common understanding, the larger it becomes, the more effective communication will be.

The Blindspot

When relevant information is known to others but not to the self, a blindspot area results. This constitutes a handicap for the self, since one can hardly understand the behaviors, decisions, and potentials of others without the information on which these are based. Others have the advantage of knowing their own reactions, feelings, perceptions, and so forth, while the self is unaware of these. Consequently, interpersonal relationships and communications suffer.

The Facade

When information is known to the self but unknown to others, a person (self) may react to superficial communications, that is, present a false front or facade. Information we perceive as potentially prejudicial to a relationship or that we keep to ourselves out of fear, desire for power, or whatever, makes up the facade. This protective front, in turn, serves a defensive function for the self. Such a situation is particularly damaging when a subordinate "knows" and an immediate supervisor "does not know." The facade, like the blindspot, diminishes the arena and reduces the possibility of effective communication.

The Unknown

This region constitutes that portion of the relationship where relevant information is not known by the self or by other parties. It is often stated, "I don't understand them, and they don't understand me." It is easy to see that interpersonal communication will be poor under such circumstances. Circumstances of this kind often occur in organizations when individuals in different specialties must communicate to coordinate what they do.

Exhibit 14-3 indicates that an individual can improve interpersonal communications by utilizing two strategies, exposure and feedback.

Exposure

Increasing the arena area by reducing the facade area requires that the individual be open and honest in sharing information with others. The process that the self uses to increase the information known to others is termed **exposure** because it sometimes leaves the self in a vulnerable position. Exposing one's true feelings by "telling it like it is" will often involve risks.

Feedback

When the self does not know or understand, more effective communications can be developed through **feedback** from those who do know. Thus, the blindspot can be reduced, with a corresponding increase in the arena. Of course, whether the use of feedback is possible depends on the individual's willingness to "hear" it and on the willingness of others to give it. Thus, the individual is less able to control the provision of feedback than the provision of exposure. Obtaining feedback is dependent on the active cooperation of others, while exposure requires the active behavior of the communicator and the passive listening of others.

Managerial Styles and Interpersonal Styles

The day-to-day activities of managers place a high value on effective interpersonal communications. Managers provide *information* (which must be understood); they give *commands* and *instructions* (which must be obeyed and learned); and they make *efforts to influence* and *persuade* (which must be accepted and acted on). Thus, the way in which managers communicate is crucial for obtaining effective performance.[12]

Theoretically, managers who desire to communicate effectively can use both exposure and feedback to enlarge the area of common understanding—the arena. As a practical matter, such is not the case. Managers differ in their ability and willingness to use exposure and feedback. At least four different managerial styles can be identified.

Type A

Managers who use neither exposure nor feedback are said to have a **Type A** style. The unknown region predominates in this style because such managers are unwilling to enlarge the area of their own knowledge or the knowledge of others. Type A managers exhibit anxiety and hostility and give the appearance of aloofness and coldness toward others. If an organization has a larger number of such managers in key positions, then you would expect to find poor and ineffective

[12]L. E. Penley, E. R. Alexander, I. E. Jernigan, and C. I. Henwood, "Communication Abilities of Managers: The Relationship to Performance," *Journal of Management,* March 1991, pp. 57–76.

interpersonal communications and a loss of individual creativity. Type A managers often display the characteristics of autocratic leaders.

Type B

Some managers desire some degree of satisfying relationships with their subordinates, but because of their personalities and attitudes, these managers are unable to open up and express their feelings and sentiments. Consequently, they cannot use exposure and must rely on feedback. The facade is the predominant feature of interpersonal relationships when managers overuse feedback to the exclusion of exposure. The subordinates probably will distrust such managers because they realize that these managers are holding back their own ideas and opinions. **Type B** behavior often is displayed by managers who desire to practice some form of permissive leadership.

Type C

Managers who value their own ideas and opinions, but not the ideas and opinions of others, will use exposure at the expense of feedback. The consequence of this style is the perpetuation and enlargement of the blindspot. Subordinates will soon realize that such managers are not particularly interested in communicating, only in telling. Consequently, **Type C** managers usually have subordinates who are hostile, insecure, and resentful. Subordinates soon learn that such managers mainly are interested in maintaining their own sense of importance and prestige.

Type D

The most effective interpersonal communication style is one that uses a balance of exposure and feedback. Managers who are secure in their positions will feel free to expose their own feelings and to obtain feedback from others. To the extent that a manager practices **Type D** behavior successfully, the arena region becomes larger and communication becomes more effective.

To summarize our discussion, we should emphasize the importance of interpersonal styles in determining the effectiveness of interpersonal communication. The primary force in determining the effectiveness of interpersonal communication is the attitude of managers toward exposure and feedback. The most effective approach is that of the Type D manager. Types A, B, and C managers resort to behaviors that are detrimental to the effectiveness of communication and to organizational performance.

MULTICULTURAL COMMUNICATION

An often repeated and much enjoyed joke in Latin America and Europe poses this question: "If someone who speaks three languages is called trilingual, and someone who speaks two languages is called bilingual, what do you call someone who speaks only one language?" The answer is "An American." Although certainly not universally true, nonetheless, this story makes a telling point. While the average European speaks several languages, the typical American is fluent only in English. In a recent year 23,000 American college students were studying Japanese; in the same year 20 million Japanese were studying English.[13]

In the international business environment of today—and even more so, of tomorrow—foreign language training and fluency is a business necessity. It is true that English is an important business language and that many foreign business people speak it fluently. The fact remains, however, that the vast majority of the world's population neither speak nor understand English. Nor is language per se the only barrier to effective cross-cultural communications; in fact, it may be one of the easiest difficulties to overcome. There are numerous cultural related variables that can hinder the communication process, not the least of which is *ethnocentrism.*

Ethnocentrism is the tendency to consider the values, norms, and customs of one's own country to be superior to those of other countries. Ethnocentrism need not be explicit to create communication problems. Implicit assumptions based on an ethnocentric view make it less likely that we will have sufficient cultural sensitivity even to be aware of possible differences in points of view, underlying assumptions, interpretation, or a host of other factors that may create communication difficulties. Consider the following true incident involving an Indian and an Austrian.

> *When asked if his department could complete a project by a given date, a particular Indian employee said "Yes" even when he knew he could not complete the project, because he believed that his Austrian supervisor wanted "yes" for an answer. When the completion date arrived and he had not finished the project, his Austrian supervisor showed dismay. The Indian's desire to be polite—to say what he thought his supervisor wanted to hear—seemed more important than an accurate assessment of the completion date.*[14]

Both of the individuals depicted in this incident were operating from their own cultural frame of reference. The Austrian valued accuracy; for the Indian, politeness was the central value. By not being sensitive to the possibility of cultural differences, both contributed to the unfortunate misunderstanding.

Numerous other examples are possible. Words and phrases do not mean the same to all people. If, during an attempt to work out a business deal, for example, an American were to tell another American "That will be difficult," the meaning is entirely different than if a Japanese were to use that phrase. To the American it means the door is still open, but perhaps some compromise needs to be made. To the Japanese it clearly means "no"; the deal is unacceptable.[15] As another

[13]Phillip Harris and Robert Moran, *Managing Cultural Differences,* 3rd ed. (Houston: Gulf Publishing, 1991).

[14]Nancy Adler, *International Dimensions of Organizational Behavior,* 2nd ed. (Boston: PWS-Kent, 1991), p. 131.

[15]Jeswald Salacuse, *Making Global Deals* (Boston: Houghton Mifflin, 1991).

CROSS-CULTURAL COMMUNICATION PROBLEMS

Communicating exactly what you want to communicate, rather than more, less, or something altogether different, can be a challenge when the communication takes place within a single culture. Achieving the desired results cross-culturally can present special problems.

Many of the difficulties encountered with cross-cultural communications stem from the fact that there are different languages involved and direct translation is not always feasible. American automobile manufacturers have learned this lesson. When Ford Motor Company introduced its Fiera truck line in some developing countries, it discovered that Fiera is a Spanish slang word meaning "ugly woman." Chevrolet discovered that in Italian Chevrolet Nova translates as "Chevrolet no go." Similarly, GMs "Body by Fisher" logo translates in at least one language into "Corpse by Fisher." Such problems are of course not restricted to car makers. Coca-Cola, for example, has had its share of translation problems. In Chinese, Coca-Cola becomes "Bite the head of a dead tadpole." In some parts of Asia the familiar Coke advertising slogan "Coke adds life" is translated as "Coke brings you back from the dead".

Language translation problems are not the only source of problems. Head, hand, and arm gestures may mean different things in different cultures. In some countries, for example, moving ones' head from side to side means "yes," while bobbing it up and down means "no." Just the reverse of U.S. meaning. Or take the familiar A-OK gesture. In the United States it means things are fine, or everything is working. In France it has no such meaning; it simply means "zero." In Japan, on the other hand, it is a symbol representing money. There it may be used to indicate that something is too expensive. And in Brazil, the gesture is interpreted as obscene.

Many other aspects of the communication process can cause difficulties. Different cultural interpretations of the significance of eye contact, the physical distance maintained between two people talking with one another, and differences in accepted forms of address, are but a few examples. Effective cross-cultural communications require that we become less ethnocentric and more culturally sensitive.

example, consider eye contact. Americans are taught to maintain good eye contact, and we may unconsciously assume those who do not look us in the eye are dishonest, or at least rude. In Japan, however, when speaking with a superior it is customary to lower ones' eyes as a gesture of respect. Encounter 14-2 describes further examples of language and other problems in cross-cultural communication contexts. Exercise 14–2 affords an opportunity to examine these issues in the context of an important managerial activity: performance appraisal.

■ **E14–2**

In spite of innumerable differences, multicultural communication can be successful. Business people from different cultures effectively and efficiently communicate with each other hundreds, perhaps thousands, of times every business day. By and large, the senders and receivers of those successful communications exhibit some, or all, of the following attributes:

1. They have made it a point to familiarize themselves with significant cultural differences that might affect the communication process. They do this through

study, observation, and consultation with those who have direct, or greater, experience with the culture than do they.

2. They make a conscious, concerted effort to lay aside ethnocentric tendencies. This does not mean they must agree with values, customs, interpretations, or perspectives different from their own; awareness, not acceptance, is what is required to facilitate communications.

3. Perhaps most importantly, despite their efforts at doing what is described in the above two points, they maintain a posture of "knowing they do not know." This simply means that in the absence of direct, usually extensive, ongoing exposure to another culture there will be nuances in the communication process of which they may well be unaware. Rather than assuming understanding is complete unless demonstrated otherwise, they assume it is *in*complete until shown otherwise.

In the two chapter sections which follow you will be able to identify barriers to effective communications which may be especially relevant in multicultural contexts, as well as find techniques for improving communications which are particularly important in the same contexts.

BARRIERS TO EFFECTIVE COMMUNICATION

A good question at this point is: "Why does communication break down?" On the surface, the answer is relatively easy. We have identified the elements of communication as the communicator, encoding, the message, the medium, decoding, the receiver, and feedback. If noise exists in these elements in any way, complete clarity of meaning and understanding will not occur. A manager has no greater responsibility than to develop effective communications. In this section we discuss several barriers to effective communication that can exist both in organizational and interpersonal communications.

Frame of Reference

Different individuals can interpret the same communication differently depending on their previous experiences. This results in variations in the encoding and decoding process. Communication specialists agree that this is the most important factor that breaks down the "commonness" in communications. When the encoding and decoding processes are not alike, communication tends to break down. Thus, while the communicator actually is speaking the "same language" as the receiver, the message conflicts with the way the receiver "catalogs" the world. If a large area is shared in common, effective communication is facilitated. If a large area is not shared in common—if there has been no common experience—then communication becomes impossible or, at best, highly distorted. The important point is that communicators can encode and receivers can decode only in terms of their experiences. As a result, distortion often occurs because of differing frames of reference. People in various organizational functions interpret the same situation differently. A business problem will be viewed differently by the marketing manager than by the production manager. An efficiency problem in a hospital will be viewed by the nursing staff from its frame of reference and experiences, which may result in interpretations different from those of the physician staff. Different levels in the organization also will have different frames of reference. First-line supervisors have frames of reference that differ in many respects from those of vice presidents. They are in different positions in the organization structure, and this influences their frames of reference. As a result, their needs, values, attitudes, and expectations will differ, and this difference will often result in unintentional distortion of communication. This is not to say that either group is wrong or right. All it means is that, in any situation, individuals will choose the part of their own past experiences that relates to the current experience and is helpful in forming conclusions and judgments.

Selective Listening

This is a form of selective perception in which we tend to block out new information, especially it if conflicts with what we believe. When we receive a directive from management, we notice only those things that reaffirm our beliefs. Those things that conflict with our preconceived notions we either do not note at all or we distort to confirm our preconceptions.

For example, a notice may be sent to all operating departments that costs must be reduced if the organization is to earn a profit. The communication may not achieve its desired effect because it conflicts with the "reality" of the receivers. Thus, operating employees may ignore or be amused by such information in light of the large salaries, travel allowances, and expense accounts of some executives. Whether they are justified is irrelevant; what is important is that such preconceptions result in breakdowns in communication.

● R14–1   Listening is not as easy as most people believe. Listening is a skill that must be learned and practiced. Reading 14–1, "Active Listening," explains listening skills.

Value Judgments

In every communication situation, **value judgments** are made by the receiver. This basically involves assigning an overall worth to a message prior to receiving the entire communication. Value judgments may be based on the receiver's evaluation of the communicator or previous experiences with the communicator or on the message's anticipated meaning. For example, a hospital administrator may pay little attention to a memorandum from a nursing supervisor because "she's always complaining about something." A college professor may consider a merit evaluation meeting with the department chairperson as "going through the motions" because the faculty member perceives the chairperson as having little or no power in the administration of the college. A cohesive work group may form negative value judgments concerning all actions by management.

Source Credibility

Source credibility is the trust, confidence, and faith that the receiver has in the words and actions of the communicator. The level of credibility the receiver assigns to the communicator in turn directly affects how the receiver views and reacts to words, ideas, and actions of the communicator.

Thus, how subordinates view a communication from their manager is affected by their evaluation of the manager. This, of course, is heavily influenced by previous experiences with the manager. Again we see that everything done by a manager communicates. A group of hospital medical staff who view the hospital administrator as less than honest, manipulative, and not to be trusted are apt to assign nonexistent motives to any communication from the administrator. Union leaders who view management as exploiters and managers who view union leaders as political animals are likely to engage in little real communication.

Filtering

Filtering, a common occurrence in upward communication in organizations, refers to the manipulation of information so that the receiver perceives it a positive. Subordinates cover up unfavorable information in messages to their superiors. The reason for filtering should be clear; this is the direction (upward) that carries control information to management. Management makes merit evaluations, grants salary increases, and promotes individuals based on what it receives by way of the upward channel. The temptation to filter is likely to be strong at every level in the organization.

In-Group Language

Each of us undoubtedly has had associations with experts and been subjected to highly technical jargon, only to learn that the unfamiliar words or phrases described very simple procedures or familiar objects. Many students are asked by researchers to "complete an instrument as part of an experimental treatment." The student soon learns that this involves nothing more than filling out a paper-and-pencil questionnaire.

Often, occupation, professional, and social groups develop words or phrases that have meaning only to members. Such special language can serve many useful purposes. It can provide members with feelings of belongingness, cohesiveness, and, in many cases, self-esteem. It also can facilitate effective communication *within* the group. The use of in-group language can, however, result in severe communication breakdowns when outsiders or other groups are involved. This is especially the case when groups use such language in an organization, not for the purpose of transmitting information and understanding, but rather to communicate a mystique about the group or its function.

Status Differences

Organizations often express hierarchical rank through a variety of symbols—titles, offices, carpets, and so on. Such status differences can be perceived as threats by persons lower in the hierarchy, and this can prevent or distort communication. Rather than look incompetent, a nurse may prefer to remain quiet instead of expressing an opinion or asking a question of the nursing supervisor.

Many times superiors, in an effort to utilize their time efficiently, make this barrier more difficult to surmount. The governmental administrator or bank vice president may be accessible only by making an advance appointment or by passing the careful quizzing of a secretary. This widens the communication gap between superior and subordinates.

Time Pressures

The pressure of time is an important barrier to communication. An obvious problem is that managers do not have the time to communicate frequently with every subordinate. However, time pressures often can lead to far more serious problems than this. Short-circuiting is a failure of the formally prescribed communication system that often results from time pressures. What it means simply is that someone has been left out of the formal channel of communication who normally would be included.

For example, suppose a salesperson needs a rush order for a very important customer and goes directly to the production manager with the request since the production manager owes the salesperson a favor. Other members of the sales force get word of this and become upset over this preferential treatment and report it to the sales manager. Obviously, the sales manger would know nothing of the deal, since he or she has been short-circuited. In some cases, however, going through formal channels is extremely costly or is impossible from a practical standpoint. Consider the impact on a hospital patient if a nurse had to report a critical malfunction in life support equipment to the nursing team leader, who in turn had to report it to the hospital engineer, who would instruct a staff engineer to make the repair.

Communication Overload

One of the vital tasks performed by a manager in decision making, and one of the necessary conditions for effective decisions is *information*.[16] Because of the

---

[16]For a review of recent developments in decision making and communication, see Janet Fulk and Brian Boyd, "Emerging Theories of Communication in Organization," *Journal of Management*, June 1991, pp. 407–46.

advances in communication technology, the difficulty is not in generating information. In fact, the last decade often has been described as the "Information Era" or the "Age of Information." Managers often feel buried by the deluge of information and data to which they are exposed and cannot absorb or adequately respond to all of the messages directed to them. They "screen out" the majority of messages, which in effect means that these messages are never decoded. Thus, the area of organizational communication is one in which more is not always better.

The barriers to communication that have been discussed here, while common, are by no means the only ones. Examining each barrier indicates that they are either *within individuals* (e.g., frame of reference, value judgments) or *within organizations* (e.g., in-group language, filtering). This point is important because attempts to improve communication must, of necessity, focus on changing people and/or changing the organization structure. Case 14–2 points out barriers to communication that result in a misunderstanding.

▲ C14–2

IMPROVING COMMUNICATION IN ORGANIZATIONS

Managers striving to become better communicators have two separate tasks they must accomplish. First, they must improve their *messages*—the information they wish to transmit. Second, they must seek to improve their own *understanding* of what other people are trying to communicate to them. This means they must become better encoders and decoders. They must strive not only to be understood but also to understand. The techniques discussed here can contribute to accomplishing these two important tasks.

Following Up

This involves assuming that you are misunderstood and, whenever possible, attempting to determine whether your intended meaning actually was received. As we have seen, meaning often is in the mind of the receiver. An accounting unit leader in a government office passes on to staff members notices of openings in other agencies. While longtime employees may understand this as a friendly gesture, a new employee might interpret it as an evaluation of poor performance and a suggestion to leave.

Regulating Information Flow

The regulation of communication can ensure an optimum flow of information to managers, thereby eliminating the barrier of "communication overload." Communication is regulated in terms of both quality and quantity. The idea is based on the *exception principle* of management, which states that only significant deviations from policies and procedures should be brought to the attention of superiors. In terms of formal communication, then, superiors should be communicated with only on matters of exception and not for the sake of communication.

Utilizing Feedback

Earlier in the chapter, feedback was identified as an important element in effective two-way communication. It provides a channel for receiver response that enables the communicator to determine whether the message has been received and has produced the intended response.[17]

In face-to-face communication, direct feedback is possible. In downward communication, however, inaccuracies often occur because of insufficient opportunity for feedback from receivers. A memorandum addressing an important policy statement may be distributed to all employees, but this does not guarantee that communication has occurred. You might expect that feedback in the form of upward communication would be encouraged more in organic organizations, but the mechanisms discussed earlier that can be utilized to encourage upward communication are found in many different organization designs.

Empathy

This involves being receiver-oriented rather than communicator-oriented. The form of the communication should depend largely on what is known about the receiver. Empathy requires communicators to place themselves in the shoes of the receiver in order to anticipate how the message is likely to be decoded. Empathy is the ability to put oneself in the other person's role and to assume that individual's viewpoints and emotions. Remember that the greater the gap between the experiences and background of the communicator and the receiver, the greater is the effort that must be made to find a common ground of understanding—where there are overlapping fields of experience.

Repetition

Repetition is an accepted principle of learning. Introducing repetition or redundancy into communication (especially that of a technical nature) ensures that if one part of the message is not understood, other parts will carry the same message. New employees often are provided with the same basic information in several different forms when first joining an organization. Likewise, students receive much redundant information when first entering a university. This is to ensure that registration procedures, course requirements, and new terms such as *matriculation* and *quality points* are communicated.

[17]Robert C. Liden and Terence R. Mitchell, "Reactions to Feedback: The Role of Attributions," *Academy of Management Journal*, June 1985, pp. 291–308.

Encouraging Mutual Trust

We know that time pressures often negate the possibility that managers will be able to follow up communication and encourage feedback or upward communication every time they communicate. Under such circumstances, an atmosphere of mutual confidence and trust between managers and their subordinates can facilitate communication. Managers who develop a climate of trust will find that following up on each communication is less critical and that no loss in understanding will result among subordinates from a failure to follow up on each communication. This is because they have fostered high "source credibility" among subordinates.

Effective Timing

Individuals are exposed to thousands of messages daily. Many of these messages are never decoded and received because of the impossibility of taking them all in. It is important for managers to note that while they are attempting to communicate with a receiver, other messages are being received simultaneously. Thus, the message that managers send may not be "heard." Messages are more likely to be understood when they are not competing with other messages.[18] On an everyday basis, effective communication can be facilitated by properly timing major announcements. The barriers discussed earlier often are the result of poor timing that results in distortions and value judgments.

Simplifying Language

Complex language has been identified as a major barrier to effective communication. Students often suffer when their teachers use technical jargon that transforms simple concepts into complex puzzles. Universities are not the only place where this occurs, however. Government agencies are also known for their often incomprehensible communications. We already have noted instances where professional people use in-group language in attempting to communicate with individuals outside their group. Managers must remember that effective communication involves transmitting *understanding* as well as information. If the receiver does not understand, then there has been no communication. Managers must encode messages in words, appeals, and symbols that are meaningful to the receiver.

Effective Listening

It has been said that to improve communication, managers must seek to be understood but also to *understand*. This involves listening. One method of en-

---

[18]For a related application, see Thomas Peters and Nancy Austin, "Managing by Walking Around," *California Management Review,* Fall 1985, pp. 83–102.

couraging someone to express true feelings, desires, and emotions is to listen. Just listening is not enough, however; you must listen with understanding. Removing distractions, putting the speaker at ease, showing the speaker you want to listen, and asking questions all contribute to good listening.

Such guidelines can be useful to managers. More important than guidelines, however, is the *decision to listen*. The above guidelines are useless unless the manager makes a conscious decision to listen. The realization that effective communication involves being understood as well as understanding probably is far more important than guidelines.

Using the Grapevine

The grapevine is an important information communication channel that exists in all organizations. It basically serves as a bypassing mechanism, and in many cases it is faster than the formal system it bypasses. The grapevine has been aptly described in the following manner: "With the rapidity of a burning train, it filters out of the woodwork, past the manager's office, through the locker room, and along the corridors." Because it is flexible and usually involves face-to-face communication, the grapevine transmits information rapidly. The resignation of an executive may be common knowledge long before it is officially announced.

For management, the grapevine frequently may be an effective means of communication. It is likely to have a stronger impact on receivers because it involves face-to-face exchange and allows for feedback. Because it satisfies many psychological needs, the grapevine will always exist. More than 75 percent of the information in the grapevine may be accurate. Of course, the portion that is distorted can be devastating. The point, however, is that if the grapevine is inevitable, managers should seek to utilize it or at least attempt to increase its accuracy. One way to minimize the undesirable aspects of the grapevine is to improve other forms of communication. If information exists on issues relevant to subordinates, then damaging rumors are less likely to develop.

Promoting Ethical Communications

It is incumbent upon organizational members to deal ethically with one another in their communication transactions. Kreps postulates three broad principles which are applicable to internal organizational communications.[19] The first is that organizational members should not intentionally deceive one another. This may not be as simple a principle to conform to as it may seem. While lying clearly violates it, is communicating less than you know to be true a breach of ethics? There is no hard and fast answer. The second principle is that organization members' communication should not purposely harm any other organization member. This is known as nonmalfeasance, or refraining from doing harm.

---

[19]Kreps, *Organizational Communication*, pp. 250–51.

ETHICS
E N C O U N T E R · 14-3

ETHICS AND EXTERNAL ORGANIZATIONAL COMMUNICATIONS

An assortment of recent business scandals—including allegations against Ford that it withheld information regarding a known safety defect in one of its models, General Electric that it colluded with an Israeli general and overcharged the U.S. government millions of dollars for jet engines, Bank of Credit & Commerce International on an array of illegal activities, Salomon Brothers that it attempted to corner the market for U.S. Treasury securities, and several Japanese investment houses that they made illegal payments to cover investment losses—all have one thing in common. All the alleged wrong-doings involve unethical external organizational communications.

Gary Kreps identifies a number of potentially unethical organization-environment practices involving communications (or lack thereof). Some of these practices that relate to the specific instances cited above include:

1. Witholding relevant information from the public and media to protect the organization (Ford).
2. Overpricing of goods and services to consumers (GE).
3. Hedging of records and false disclosure of information to government or regulatory agencies (BCCI).
4. Attempts to monopolize and dominate a market (Salomon Brothers).
5. Bribery and coercion (Japanese investment houses).

Other external communication practices identified by Kreps that could be unethical are deceptive advertising, industrial espionage, conflicts of interest, and discriminatory employment practices. He groups these and other practices into three broad categories: honesty and information giving, influence and control, and external accountability.

Many companies are showing a renewed interest in maintaining ethical communications. The fairly recent advent of ethics training programs (see Chapter 16 for a discussion of this activity) generally include topics that are at least implicitly, if not explicitly, related to communications. Companies included are Niagara Mohawk Power, Pitney Bowes, and Hershey Foods. In addition to training programs, some companies have set up specific communication channels to facilitate identification and reporting of wrong-doing. Nynex and Pacific Bell, for example, have both established whistle-blower hotlines. The latter receives 1,200 calls a year.

Having an ethics program is no guarantee unethical communications won't be a problem, however. General Electric has had an ethics program for years that is acknowledged as one of the best around. Sometimes all it takes to create major ethical problems is one employee.

Source: Adapted in part from information in Gary Kreps, *Organizational Communication* (New York: Longman, 1990), pp. 257–59; and *Business Week*, September 23, 1991, p. 65.

Finally, organization members should be treated justly. This too can be difficult, for justice is a relative principle that must be evaluated in a specific context.

Of course, internal organizational communications are not the only ones where ethical behavior is important. Indeed, some of the more ethically challenging communication contexts are those in which the organization is communicating externally. Encounter 14-3 examines this issue.

EXHIBIT 14-4

Improving Communications in Organizations (Narrowing the Communication Gap)

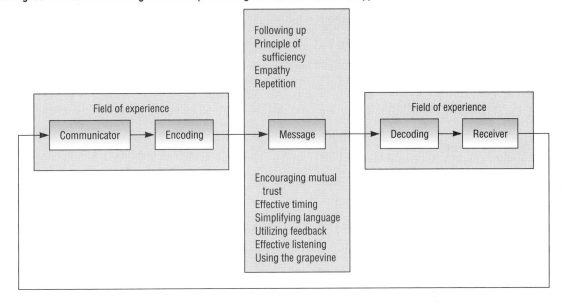

In conclusion, it would be hard to find an aspect of a manager's job that does not involve communication. If everyone in the organization had common points of view, communicating would be easy. Unfortunately, this is not the case. Each member comes to the organization with a distinct personality, background, experience, and frame of reference. The structure of the organization itself influences status relationships and the distance levels between individuals, which in turn influence the ability of individuals to communicate.

In this chapter we have tried to convey the basic elements in the process of communication and what it takes to communicate effectively. These elements are necessary whether the communication is face-to-face or written and communicated vertically, horizontally, or diagonally within an organizational structure.

We discussed several common communication barriers and several means to improve communication. Exhibit 14-4 illustrates the means that can be used to facilitate more effective communication. We realize that often there is not enough time to utilize many of the techniques for improving communication and that skills such as empathy and effective listening are not easy to develop. The exhibit does, however, illustrate the challenge of communicating effectively, and it suggests what is required. Exhibit 14-4 shows that communicating is a matter of transmitting and receiving. Managers must be effective at both. They must understand as well as be understood.

SUMMARY OF KEY POINTS

- Communication is one of the vital processes that breathe life into an organizational structure. The process contains five elements: the *communicator* who initiates the communication; the *message,* which is the result of encoding and which expresses the purpose of the communicator; the *medium,* which is the channel or carrier used for transmitting the message; the *receiver* for whom the message is intended; and *feedback,* a mechanism that allows the communicator to determine whether the message has been received and understood.

- Communication flow moves in one of four directions. Downward communications are the most common, and include job instructions, procedures, and policies. An upward flow can be just as important, and may involve the use of suggestion boxes, group meetings, or grievance procedures. Horizontal and diagonal communications serve an important coordinative function.

- Interpersonal communication is that which flows from individual to individual in face-to-face and group settings. In addition to providing needed information, interpersonal communication can also influence how people feel about the organization and its members. Interpersonal style is a term used to describe the way an individual prefers to relate to others in interpersonal communication situations.

- In the international business environment of today, needing to communicate with members of other cultures is becoming commonplace. In addition to obvious language problems, different cultural customs, values, and perspectives can serve to complicate effective communications. A significant barrier is *ethnocentrism* which is the tendency to consider the values of one's own country superior to those of other countries.

- There are numerous barriers to effective communication. Among the more significant are frame of reference, selective listening, value judgments, source credibility, filtering, in-group language, status differences, time pressures, and communication overload.

- Improving organizational communications is an ongoing process. Specific techniques for doing this include following up, regulating information flow, utilizing feedback, empathy, repetition, encouraging mutual trust, effective timing, simplifying language, effective listening, using the grapevine, and promoting ethical communications.

REVIEW AND DISCUSSION QUESTIONS

1. Can you think of a communication transaction you have been part of when an encoding or decoding error was made? Why did it happen, and what could have been done to avoid it?

2. Why do you think that downward communication is much more prevalent in organizations than upward communication? How easy would it be to change this?

3. Interpersonal style is an important variable in the interpersonal communication process. Are you typically a Type A, B, C, or D communicator? Explain.

4. In your experience, which of the barriers to effective communication discussed in the chapter is responsible for the most communication problems. Which barrier is the hardest to correct?

5. Similarly, in your experience, which of the techniques for improving communication discussed in the chapter would solve the greatest number of problems? Which technique is the most difficult to put into practice?

6. Can you think of reasons why some individuals might prefer one-way communications when they are the sender, and two-way when they are the receiver? Explain.

7. A study once revealed that 55 percent of our communication time is spent transmitting and 45 percent is spent receiving. If true, what are the implications of this finding?

8. "Organizations should be less concerned with improving communication than with reducing the volume of information they disseminate to employees." Do you agree or disagree with this statement? Explain.

9. How does communication affect the interpersonal influence topics discussed in Chapters 7–10?

10. Have you ever been in a cross-cultural communication situation? How effective was it? What was the most difficult aspect of the situation?

●

READING

READING 14–1   ACTIVE LISTENING

Carl B. Rogers
Richard E. Farson

THE MEANING OF ACTIVE LISTENING

One basic responsibility of the supervisor or executive is the development, adjustment, and integration of individual employees. He tries to develop employee potential, delegate responsibility, and achieve cooperation. To do so, he must have, among other abilities, the ability to listen intelligently and carefully to those with whom he works.

There are, however, many kinds of listening skills. The lawyer, for example, when questioning a witness, listens for contradictions, irrelevancies, errors, and weaknesses. But this is not the kind of listening skill we are concerned with. The lawyer usually is not listening in order to help the witness adjust or cooperate or produce. On the other hand, we will be concerned with listening skills which *will help* employees gain a clearer understanding of their situations, take responsibility, and cooperate with each other.

Two Examples

The kind of listening we have in mind is called active listening. It is called active because the listener has a very definite responsibility. He does not passively absorb the words which are spoken to him. He actively tries to grasp the facts and the feelings in what he hears, and he tries, by his listening, to help the speaker work out his own problems.

To get a fuller picture of what is meant by active listening, let us consider two different approaches to the same work problem.

Example No. 1

FOREMAN: Hey, Al, I don't get this production order. We can't handle this run today. What do they think we are?

SUPERVISOR: But that's the order. So get it out as soon as you can. We're under terrific pressure this week.

FOREMAN: Don't they know we're behind schedule already because of that press breakdown?

SUPERVISOR: Look, Kelly, I don't decide what goes on upstairs. I just have to see that the work gets out, and that's what I'm gonna do.

FOREMAN: The guys aren't gonna like this.

SUPERVISOR: That's something you'll have to work out with them not me.

Example No. 2

FOREMAN: Hey, Ross, I don't get this production order. We can't handle this run today. What do they think we are?

SUPERVISOR: Sounds like you are pretty sore about it, Kelly.

FOREMAN: I sure am. We were just about getting back to schedule after that press breakdown. Now this comes along.

SUPERVISOR: As if you didn't have enough work to do, huh?

FOREMAN: Yeah. I don't know how I'm gonna tell the guys about this.

SUPERVISOR: Hate to face 'em with it now, is that it?

FOREMAN: I really do. They're under a real strain today. Seems like everything we do around here is rush, rush.

SUPERVISOR: I guess you feel like it's unfair to load anything more on them.

FOREMAN: Well, yeah. I know there must be plenty of pressure on everybody up the line, but—well, if that's the way it is—guess I'd better get the word to 'em.

There are obviously many differences between these two examples. The main one, however, is that Ross, the supervisor in the second example, is using the active-listening approach. He is listening and responding in a way that makes it clear that he appreciates both the meaning and the feeling behind what Kelly is saying.

Active listening does not necessarily mean long sessions spent listening to grievances, personal or otherwise. It is simply a way of approaching those problems which arise out of the usual day-to-day events of any job.

Source: Reprinted by permission of the Industrial Relations Center, The University of Chicago.

To be effective, active listening must be firmly grounded in the basic attitudes of the user. We cannot employ it as a technique if our fundamental attitudes are in conflict with its basic concepts. If we try, our behavior will be empty and sterile, and our associates will be quick to recognize this. Until we can demonstrate a spirit which genuinely respects the potential worth of the individual, which considers his sights and trusts his capacity for self-direction, we cannot begin to be effective listeners.

What We Achieve by Listening

Active listening is an important way to bring about changes in people. Despite the popular notion that listening is a passive approach, clinical and research evidence clearly shows that sensitive listening is a most effective agent for individual personality change and group development. Listening brings about changes in people's attitudes toward themselves and others; it also brings about changes in their basic values and personal philosophy. People who have been listened to in this new and special way become more emotionally mature, more open to their experiences, less defensive, more democratic, and less authoritarian.

When people are listened to sensitively, they tend to listen to themselves with more care and to make clear exactly what they are feeling and thinking. Group members tend to listen more to each other, to become less argumentative, more ready to incorporate other points of view. Because listening reduces the threat of having one's ideas criticized, the person is better able to see them for what they are and is more able to feel that his contributions are worthwhile.

Not the least important result of listening is the change that takes place with the listener himself. Besides providing more information than any other activity, listening builds deep, positive relationships and tends to alter constructively the attitudes of the listener. Listening is a growth experience.

These, then, are some of the worthwhile results we can expect from active listening. But how do we go about this kind of listening? How do we become active listeners?

HOW TO LISTEN

Active listening aims to bring about changes in people. To achieve this end, it relies upon definite techniques—things to do and things to avoid doing. Before discussing these techniques, however, we should first understand why they are effective. To do so, we must understand how the individual personality develops.

The Growth of the Individual

Through all of our lives, from early childhood on, we have learned to think of ourselves in certain very definite ways. We have built up pictures of ourselves. Sometimes these self-pictures are pretty realistic, but at other times they are not. For example, an overage, overweight lady may fancy herself as a youthful, ravishing siren, or an awkward teenager regard himself as a star athlete.

All of us have experiences which fit the way we need to think about ourselves. These we accept. But it is much harder to accept experiences which don't fit. And sometimes, if it is very important for us to hang on to this self-picture, we don't accept or admit these experiences at all.

These self-pictures are not necessarily attractive. A man, for example, may regard himself as incompetent and worthless. He may feel that he is doing his job poorly in spite of favorable appraisals by the company. As long as he has these feelings about himself, he must deny any experiences which would seem not to fit this self-picture—in case any that might indicate to him that he is competent. It is so necessary for him to maintain this self-picture that he is threatened by anything which would tend to change it. Thus, when the company raises his salary, it may seem to him only additional proof that he is a fraud. He must hold onto this self-picture because, bad or good, it's the only thing he has by which he can identify himself.

This is why direct attempts to change this individual or change his self-picture are particularly threatening. He is forced to defend himself or to completely deny the experience. This denial of experience and defense of the self-picture tend to bring on rigidity of behavior and create difficulties in personal adjustment.

The active-listening approach, on the other hand, does not present a threat to the individual's self-picture. He does not have to defend it. He is able to explore it, see it for what it is, and make his own decision about how realistic it is. And he is then in a position to change.

If I want to help a man reduce his defensiveness and become more adaptive, I must try to remove the threat of myself as his potential changer. As long as the atmosphere is threatening, there can be no effective communication. So I must create a climate which is neither critical, evaluative, nor moralizing. It must be an atmosphere of equality and freedom, permissiveness and understanding, acceptance and warmth. It is in this climate and this climate only that the individual feels safe enough to incorporate new experiences and new values into his concept of himself. Let's see how active listening helps to create this climate.

What to Avoid

When we encounter a person with a problem our usual response is to try to change his way of looking at things—to get him to see his situation the way we see it or would like to see it. We plead, reason, scold, encourage, insult, prod—anything to bring about a change in the desired direction, that is, in the direction we want him to travel. What we seldom realize, however, is that, under these circumstances, we are usually responding to *our own* needs to see the world in certain ways. It is always difficult for us to tolerate and understand actions which are different from the ways in which *we* believe *we* should act. If, however, we can free ourselves from the need to influence and direct others in our own paths, we enable ourselves to listen with understanding and thereby employ the most potent available agent of change.

One problem the listener faces is that of responding to demands for decisions, judgments, and evaluations. He is constantly called upon to agree or disagree with someone or something. Yet, as he well knows, the question or challenge frequently is a masked expression of feelings or needs which the speaker is far more anxious to communicate than he is to have the surface questions answered. Because he cannot speak these feelings openly, the speaker must disguise them to himself and to others in an acceptable form. To illustrate, let us examine some typical questions and the types of answers that might best elicit the feelings beneath them.

These responses recognize the questions but leave the way open for the employee to say what is really bothering him. They allow the listener to participate in the problem or situation without shouldering all responsibility for decision making or actions. This is a process of thinking *with* people instead of *for* or *about* them.

Passing judgment, whether critical or favorable, makes free expression difficult. Similarly, advice and information are almost always seen as efforts to change a person and thus serve as barriers to his self-expression and the development of a creative relationship. Moreover, advice is seldom taken and information hardly ever utilized. The eager young trainee probably will not become patient just because he is advised that "the road to success in business is a long, difficult one, and you must be patient." And it is no more helpful for him to learn that "only one out of a hundred trainees reaches a top management position."

Interestingly, it is a difficult lesson to learn that positive *evaluations* are sometimes as blocking as negative ones. It is almost as destructive to the freedom of a relationship to tell a person that he is good or capable or right, as to tell him otherwise. To evaluate him positively may make it more difficult for him to tell of the faults that distress him or the ways in which he believes he is not competent.

Encouragement also may be seen as an attempt to motivate the speaker in certain directions or hold him off, rather than as support. "I'm sure everything will work out O.K." is not a helpful response to the person who is deeply discouraged about a problem.

In other words, most of the techniques and devices common to human relationships are found to be of little use in establishing the type of relationship we are seeking here.

Employee's Question	Listener's Answer
Just whose responsibility is the tool room?	Do you feel that someone is challenging your authority in there?
Don't you think younger able people should be promoted before senior but less able ones?	It seems to you they should, I take it.
What does the super expect us to do about those broken-down machines?	You're pretty disgusted with those machines, aren't you?
Don't you think I've improved over the last review period?	Sound as if you feel like you've really picked up over these last few months.

What to Do

Just what does active listening entail, then? Basically, it requires that we get inside the speaker, that we grasp, *from his point of view,* just what it is he is communicating to us. More than that, we must convey to the speaker that we are seeing things from his point of view. To listen actively, then means that there are several things we must do.

Listen for Total Meaning

Any message a person tries to get across usually has two components: the *content* of the message and the *feeling* or attitude underlying this content. Both are important; both give the message *meaning.* It is this total meaning of the message that we try to understand. For example, a machinist comes to his foreman and says, "I've finished that lathe setup." This message has obvious content and perhaps calls upon the foreman for another work assignment. Suppose, on the other hand, that he says, "Well, I'm finally finished with that damned lathe setup." The content is the same, but the total meaning of the message has changed— and changed in an important way for both the foreman and the worker. Here sensitive listening can facilitate the relationship. Suppose the foreman were to respond by simply giving another work assignment. Would the employee feel that he had gotten his total message across? Would he feel free to talk to his foreman? Will he feel better about his job, more anxious to do good work on the next assignment?

Now, on the other hand, suppose the foreman were to respond with, "Glad to have it over with, huh?" or "Had a pretty rough time of it?" or "Guess you don't feel like doing anything like that again," or anything else that tells the worker that he heard and understands. It doesn't necessarily mean that the next work assignment need be changed or that he must spend an hour listening to the worker complain about the setup problems he encountered. He may do a number of things differently in the light of the new information he has from the worker—but not necessarily. It's just that extra sensitivity on the part of the foreman which can transform an average working climate into a good one.

Respond to Feelings

In some instances, the content is far less important than the feeling which underlies it. To catch the full flavor or meaning of the message, one must respond particularly to the feeling component. If, for instance, our machinist had said, "I'd like to melt this lathe down and make paper clips out of it," responding to content would be obviously absurd. But to respond to his disgust or anger in trying to work with his lathe recognizes the meaning of this message. There are various shadings of these components in the meaning of any message. Each time, the listener must try to remain sensitive to the total meaning the message has to the speaker. What is he trying to tell me? What does this mean to him? How does he see this situation?

Not All Cues

Not all communication is verbal. The speaker's words alone don't tell us everything he is communicating. And hence, truly sensitive listening requires that we become aware of several kinds of communication besides verbal. The way in which a speaker hesitates in his speech can tell us much about his feelings. So, too, can the inflection of his voice. He may stress certain points loudly and clearly and may mumble others. We should also note such things as the person's facial expressions, body posture, hand movements, eye movements, and breathing. All of these help to convey his total message.

What We Communicate by Listening

The first reaction of most people when they consider listening as a possible method for dealing with human beings is that listening cannot be sufficient in itself. Because it is passive, they feel, listening does not communicate anything to the speaker. Actually, nothing could be farther from the truth.

By consistently listening to a speaker, you are conveying the idea that: "I'm interested in you as a person, and I think that what you feel is important. I respect your thoughts, and even if I don't agree with them, I know that they are valid for you. I feel sure that you have a contribution to make. I'm not trying to change or evaluate you. I just want to understand you. I think you're worth listening to, and I want you to know that I'm the kind of a person you can talk to."

The subtle but most important aspect of this is that it is the *demonstration* of the message that works. While it is most difficult to convince someone that you respect him by *telling* him so, you are much more likely to get this message across by really *behaving* that way—by actually *having* and *demonstrating* respect for this person. Listening does this most effectively.

Like other behavior, listening behavior is contagious. This has implications for all communication problems, whether between two people or within a large organization. To ensure good communication between associates up and down the line, one must first take the responsibility for setting a pattern of listening. Just as one learns that anger is usually met with anger, argument with argument, and deception with deception, one can learn that listening can be met with listening. Every person who feels responsibility in a situation can set the tone of the interaction, and the important lesson in this is that any behavior exhibited by one person will eventually be responded to with similar behavior in the other person.

It is far more difficult to stimulate constructive behavior in another person but far more profitable. Listening is one of these constructive behaviors, but if one's attitude is to "wait out" the speaker rather than really listen to him, it will fail. The one who consistently listens with understanding, however, is the one who eventually is most likely to be listened to. If you really want to be heard and understood by another, you can develop him as a potential listener, ready for new ideas, provided you can first develop yourself in these ways and sincerely listen with understanding and respect.

Testing for Understanding

Because understanding another person is actually far more difficult than it at first seems, it is important to test constantly your ability to see the world in the way the speaker sees it. You can do this by reflecting in your own words what the speaker seems to mean by his words and actions. His response to this will tell you whether or not he feels understood. A good rule of thumb is to assume that you never really understand until you can communicate this understanding to the other's satisfaction.

Here is an experiment to test your skill in listening. The next time you become involved in a lively or controversial discussion with another person, stop for a moment and suggest that you adopt this ground rule for continued discussion: Before either participant in the discussion can make a point or express an opinion of his own, he must first restate aloud the previous point or position of the other person. This restatement must be in his own words (merely parroting the words of another does not prove that one has understood but only that he has heard the words). The restatement must be accurate enough to satisfy the speaker before the listener can be allowed to speak for himself.

This is something you could try in your own discussion group. Have someone express himself on some topic of emotional concern to the group. Then, before another member expresses his own feelings and thought, he must rephrase the *meaning* expressed by the previous speaker to that individual's satisfaction. Note the changes in the emotional climate and in the quality of the discussion when you try this.

PROBLEMS IN ACTIVE LISTENING

Active listening is not an easy skill to acquire. It demands practice. Perhaps more important, it may require changes in our own basic attitudes. These changes come slowly and sometimes with considerable difficulty. Let us look at some of the major problems in active listening and what can be done to overcome them.

The Personal Risk

To be effective at all in active listening, one must have a sincere interest in the speaker. We all live in glass houses as far as our attitudes are concerned. They always show through. And if we are only making a pretense of interest in the speaker, he will quickly pick this up, either consciously or unconsciously. And once he does, he will no longer express himself freely.

Active listening carries a strong element of personal risk. If we manage to accomplish what we are describing here—to sense deeply the feeling of another person, to understand the meaning his experiences have for him, to see the world as he sees it—we risk being changed ourselves. For example, if we permit ourselves to listen our way into the psychological life of a labor leader or agitator—to get the meaning which has life for him—we risk coming to see the world as he sees it. It is threatening to give up, even momentarily, what we believe and start thinking in someone else's terms. It takes a great deal of inner security and courage to be able to risk one's self in understanding another.

For the supervisor, the courage to take another's point of view generally means that he must see *himself* through another's eyes—he must be able to see himself as others see him. To do this may sometimes be unpleasant, but it is far more *difficult* than unpleasant. We are so accustomed to viewing ourselves in certain ways—to seeing and hearing only what we want to see and hear—that it is extremely difficult for a person to free himself from his needs to see things these ways.

Developing an attitude of sincere interest in the speaker is thus no easy task. It can be developed only by being willing to risk seeing the world from the speaker's point of view. If we have a number of such experiences, however, they will shape an attitude which will allow us to be truly genuine in our interest in the speaker.

Hostile Expressions

The listener will often hear negative, hostile expressions directed at himself. Such expressions are always hard to listen to. No one likes to hear hostile words. And it is not easy to get to the point where one is strong enough to permit these attacks without finding it necessary to defend oneself or retaliate.

Because we all fear that people will crumble under the attack of genuine negative feelings, we tend to perpetuate an attitude of pseudo peace. It is as if we cannot tolerate conflict at all for fear of the damage it could do to us, to the situation, to the others involved. But of course the real damage is done to all these by the denial and suppression of negative feelings.

Out-of-Place Expressions

There is also the problem of out-of-place expressions— expressions dealing with behavior which is not usually acceptable in our society. In the extreme forms that present themselves before psychotherapists, expressions of sexual perversity or homicidal fantasies are often found blocking to the listener because of their obvious threatening quality. At less extreme levels, we all find unnatural or inappropriate behavior difficult to handle. That is, anything from an off-color story told in mixed company to a man weeping is likely to produce a problem situation.

In any face-to-face situation, we will find instances of this type which will momentarily, if not permanently, block any communication. In business and industry, any expressions of weakness or incompetency will generally be regarded as unacceptable and therefore will block good two-way communication. For example, it is difficult to listen to a supervisor tell of his feelings of failure in being able to "take charge" of a situation in his department, because *all* administrators are supposed to be able to "take charge."

Accepting Positive Feelings

It is both interesting and perplexing to note that negative or hostile feelings or expressions are much easier to deal with in any face-to-face relationship than are truly and deeply positive feelings. This is especially true for the businessman, because the culture expects him to be independent, bold, clever, and aggressive and manifest no feelings of warmth, gentleness, and intimacy. He therefore comes to regard these feelings as soft and inappropriate. But no matter how they are regarded, they remain a human need. The denial of these feelings in himself and his associates does not get the executive out of the problem of dealing with them. They simply become veiled and confused. If recognized, they would work for the total effort; unrecognized, they work against it.

Emotional Danger Signals

The listener's own emotions are sometimes a barrier to active listening. When emotions are at their height, which is when listening is most necessary, it is most difficult to set aside one's own concerns and be understanding. Our emotions are often our own worst enemies when we try to become listeners. The more involved and invested we are in a particular situation or problem, the less we are likely to be willing or able to listen to the feelings and attitudes of others. That is, the more we find it necessary to respond to our own needs, the less we are able to respond to the needs of another. Let us look at some of the main danger signals that warn us that our emotions may be interfering with our listening.

Defensiveness

The points about which one is most vocal and dogmatic, the points which one is most anxious to impose on others— these are always the points one is trying to talk oneself into believing. So one danger signal becomes apparent when you find yourself stressing a point or trying to convince another. It is at these times that you are likely to be less secure and consequently less able to listen.

Resentment of Opposition

It is always easier to listen to an idea which is similar to one of your own than to an opposing view. Sometimes, in order to clear the air, it is helpful to pause for a moment when you feel your ideas and position being challenged, reflect on the situation, and express your concern to the speaker.

Clash of Personalities

Here again, our experience has consistently shown us that the genuine expression of feelings on the part of the listener will be more helpful in developing a sound relationship than the suppression of them. This is so whether the feelings be resentment, hostility, threat, or admiration. A basically honest relationship, whatever the nature of it, is the most productive of all. The other party becomes secure when he learns that the listener can express his feelings honestly and openly to him. We should keep this in mind when we begin to fear a clash of personalities in the listening relationship. Otherwise, fear of our own emotions will choke off full expression of feelings.

Listening to Ourselves

To listen to oneself is a prerequisite for listening to others. And it is often an effective means of dealing with the problems we have outlined above. When we are most aroused, excited, and demanding, we are least able to understand our own feelings and attitudes. Yet, in dealing with the problems of others, it becomes most important to be sure of one's own position, values, and needs.

The ability to recognize and understand the meaning which a particular episode has for you, with all the feelings which it stimulates in you, and the ability to express the meaning when you find it getting in the way of active listening will clear the air and enable you once again to be free to listen. That is, if some person or situation touches off feelings within you which tend to block your attempts to listen with understanding, begin listening to yourself. It is much more helpful in developing effective relationships to avoid suppressing these feelings. Speak them out as clearly as you can and try to enlist the other person as a listener to your feelings. A person's listening ability is limited by his ability to listen to himself.

ACTIVE LISTENING AND COMPANY GOALS

- How can listening improve production?
- We're in business, and it's a rugged, fast, competitive affair. How are we going to find time to counsel our employees?
- We have to concern ourselves with organizational problems first.
- We can't afford to spend all day listening when there's a job to be done.
- What's morale got to do with production?
- Sometimes we have to sacrifice an individual for the good of the rest of the people in the company.

Those of us who are trying to advance the listening approach in industry hear these comments frequently. And because they are so honest and legitimate, they pose a real problem. Unfortunately, the answers are not so clear-cut as the questions.

INDIVIDUAL IMPORTANCE

One answer is based on an assumption that is central to the listening approach. That assumption is: The kind of behavior which helps the individual will eventually be the best thing that could be done for the group. Or saying it another way: The things that are best for the individual are best for the company. This is a conviction of ours, based on our experience in psychology and education. The research evidence from industry is only beginning to come in. We find that putting the group first, at the expense of the individual, besides being an uncomfortable individual experience, does *not* unify the group. In fact, it tends to make the group less a group. The members become anxious and suspicious.

We are not at all sure in just what ways the group does benefit from a concern demonstrated for an individual, but we have several strong leads. One is that the group feels more secure when an individual is being listened to and provided for with concern and sensitivity. And we assume that a secure group will ultimately be a better group. When each individual feels that he need not fear exposing himself to the group, he is likely to contribute more freely and spontaneously. When the leader of a group responds to the individual, puts the individual first, the other members of the group will follow suit and the group will come to act as a unit in recognizing and responding to the needs of a particular member. This positive, constructive action seems to be a much more satisfying experience for a group than the experience of dispensing with a member.

LISTENING AND PRODUCTION

Whether listening or any other activity designed to better human relations in an industry actually raises production—whether morale has a definite relationship to production—is not known for sure. There are some who frankly hold that there is no relationship to be expected between morale and production—that production often depends upon the social misfit, the eccentric, or the isolate. And there are some who simply choose to work in a climate of cooperation and harmony, in a high-morale group, quite aside from the question of increased production.

A report from the Survey Research Center[1] at the

University of Michigan on research conducted at the Prudential Life Insurance Company lists seven findings relating to production and morale. First-line supervisors in high-production work groups were found to differ from those in low-production work groups in that they:

1. Are under less close supervision from their own supervisors.
2. Place less direct emphasis upon production as the goal.
3. Encourage employee participation in the making of decisions.
4. Are more employee-centered.
5. Spend more of their time in supervision and less in straight production work.
6. Have a greater feeling of confidence in their supervisory roles.
7. Feel that they know where they stand with the company.

After mentioning that other dimensions of morale, such as identification with the company, intrinsic job satisfaction, and satisfaction with job status, were not found significantly related to productivity, the report goes on to suggest the following psychological interpretation:

> People are more effectively motivated when they are given some degree of freedom in the way in which they do their work than when every action is prescribed in advance. They do better when some degree of decision making about their jobs is possible than when all decisions are made for them. They respond more adequately when they are treated as personalities than as cogs in a machine. In short, if the ego motivations of self-determination, or self-expression, of a sense of personal worth can be tapped, the individual can be more effectively energized. The use of external sanctions or pressuring for production may work to some degree, but not to the extent that the more internalized motives do. When the individual comes to identify himself with his job and with the work of his group, human resources are much more fully utilized in the production process.

The Survey Research Center has also conducted studies among workers in other industries. In discussing the results of these studies, Robert L. Kahn writes:

> In the studies of clerical workers, railroad workers, and workers in heavy industry, the supervisors with the better production records gave a larger proportion of their time to supervisory functions, especially the interpersonal aspects of their jobs. The supervisors of the lower-producing sections were more likely to spend their time in tasks which the men themselves were performing, or in the paperwork aspects of their jobs.[2]

MAXIMUM CREATIVENESS

There may never be enough research evidence to satisfy everyone on this question. But speaking from a business point of view, in terms of the problem of developing resources for production, the maximum creativeness and productive effort of the human beings in the organization are the richest untapped source of power still existing. The difference between the maximum productive capacity of people and that output which industry is now realizing is immense. We simply suggest that this maximum capacity might be closer to realization if we sought to release the motivation that already exists within people rather than try to stimulate them externally.

This releasing of the individual is made possible, first of all, by sensitive listening, with respect and understanding. Listening is a beginning toward making the individual feel himself worthy of making contributions, and this could result in a very dynamic and productive organization. Competitive business is never too rugged or too busy to take time to procure the most efficient technological advances or to develop rich raw-material resources. But these in comparison to the resources that are already within the people in the plant are paltry. This is industry's major procurement problem.

G. L. Clemens, president of Jewel Tea Co., Inc., in talking about the collaborative approach to management, says:

> We feel that this type of approach recognizes that there is a secret ballot going on at all times among the people in any business. They vote for or against the supervisors. A favorable vote for the supervisor shows up in the cooperation, teamwork, understanding, and production of the group. To win this secret ballot, each supervisor must share the problems of his group and work for them.[3]

The decision to spend time listening to his employees is a decision each supervisor or executive has to make for himself. Executives seldom have much to do with products or processes. They have to deal with people who must in turn deal with people who will deal with products or processes. The higher one goes up the line, the more one will be concerned with human relations problems, simply because people are all one has to work with. The minute we take a man from his bench and make him a foreman, he is removed from the basic production of goods and now must begin relating to individuals instead of nuts and bolts. People are different from things, and our foreman is called upon for a different line of skills completely. His new tasks call upon him to be a special kind of person. The development of himself as a listener is a first step in becoming this special person.

NOTES

1. "Productivity, Supervision, and Employee Morale." *Human Relations,* Series 1, Report 1 (Ann Arbor: Survey Research Center, University of Michigan).
2. Robert L. Kahn, "The Human Factors Underlying Industrial Productivity," *Michigan Business Review,* November 1952.
3. G. L. Clemens, "Time for Democracy in Action at the Executive Level" (Address given before the AMA Personnel Conference, February 28, 1951).

EXERCISES

EXERCISE 14–1 ARE YOU PASSIVE, ASSERTIVE, OR AGGRESSIVE?

The following questionnaire is designed to give you tentative insight into your current tendencies toward non-assertiveness (passivity), assertiveness, or aggressiveness. The Assertiveness Scale is primarily a self-examination and discussion device. Answer each question mostly true or mostly false as it applies to you.

Source: Reprinted from Andrew J. DuBrin, *Contemporary Applied Management,* 2nd ed. (Plano, Tex.: Business Publications, 1985), pp. 50–52.

	Mostly True	Mostly False
1. It is extremely difficult for me to turn down a sales representative when that individual is a nice person.	___	___
2. I express criticism freely.	___	___
3. If another person were being very unfair, I would bring it to that person's attention.	___	___
4. Work is no place to let your feelings show.	___	___
5. No use asking for favors; people get what they deserve on the job.	___	___
6. Business is not the place for tact; say what you think.	___	___
7. If a person looked like he or she were in a hurry, I would let that person in front of me in a supermarket line.	___	___
8. A weakness of mine is that I'm too nice a person.	___	___
9. If my restaurant bill is even 25 cents more than it should be, I demand that the mistake be corrected.	___	___
10. I have laughed out loud in public more than once.	___	___
11. I've been described as too outspoken by several people.	___	___
12. I am quite willing to have the store take back a piece of furniture that has a scratch.	___	___
13. I dread having to express anger toward a co-worker.	___	___
14. People often say that I'm too reserved and emotionally controlled.	___	___
15. Nice guys and gals finish last in business.	___	___
16. I fight for my rights down to the last detail.	___	___

	Mostly True	Mostly False
17. I have no misgivings about returning an overcoat to the store if it doesn't fit me properly.	_____	_____
18. If I have had an argument with a person, I try to avoid him or her.	_____	_____
19. I insist on my spouse (roommate or partner) doing his or her fair share of undersirable chores.	_____	_____
20. It is difficult for me to look directly at another person when the two of us are in disagreement.	_____	_____
21. I have cried among friends more than once.	_____	_____
22. If someone near me at a movie kept up a conversation with another person, I would ask him or her to stop.	_____	_____
23. I am able to turn down social engagements with people I do not particularly care for.	_____	_____
24. It is poor taste to express what you really feel about another individual.	_____	_____
25. I sometimes show my anger by swearing at or belittling another person.	_____	_____
26. I am reluctant to speak up in a meeting.	_____	_____
27. I find it relatively easy to ask friends for small favors such as giving me a lift to work when my car is being serviced or repaired.	_____	_____
28. If another person was smoking in a restaurant and it bothered me, I would inform that person.	_____	_____
29. I often finish other people's sentences for them.	_____	_____
30. It is relatively easy for me to express love and affection toward another person.	_____	_____

Scoring and Interpretation

Score yourself plus 1 for each of your answers that agrees with the scoring key. If your score is 10 or less, it is probable that you are currently a nonassertive individual. A score of 11 through 24 suggests that you are an assertive individual, A score of 25 or higher suggests that you are an aggressive individual. Retake this test about 30 days from now to give yourself some indication of the stability of your answers. You might also discuss your answers with a close friend to determine if that person has a similar perception of your assertiveness. Here is the scoring key.

1. Mostly false	7. Mostly false	13. Mostly false	19. Mostly true	25. Mostly true
2. Mostly true	8. Mostly false	14. Mostly false	20. Mostly false	26. Mostly false
3. Mostly true	9. Mostly true	15. Mostly true	21. Mostly true	27. Mostly true
4. Mostly false	10. Mostly true	16. Mostly true	22. Mostly true	28. Mostly true
5. Mostly false	11. Mostly true	17. Mostly true	23. Mostly true	29. Mostly true
6. Mostly true	12. Mostly true	18. Mostly false	24. Mostly false	30. Mostly true

EXERCISE 14–2   CROSS-CULTURAL COMMUNICATION ISSUES

There is evidence that the United States' position in the world economy has changed drastically in the past decade. The U.S. percentage of world gross national product has declined, the U.S. is importing more basic materials, and some of the largest U.S. companies derive more than 50 percent of their revenues from overseas operations.

With the world becoming more globally interconnected, it has become imperative to work with foreign managers and employees. One noted fact about these work relationships is that communication across cultural boundaries is complex. Difference in goals, customs, behavior, and values result in communication blocks, misunderstandings, and cross-cultural faux pas.

Performance appraisal sessions that involve communications between individuals from different cultures pose some interesting communication dilemmas. Exhibit 14-5

EXHIBIT 14-5

Cultural Variations: Performance Appraisals

Dimensions General	U.S.	Saudi Arabia	Japan
Objective of P.A.	Fairness, Employee development	Placement	Direction of company/employee development
Who does appraisal	Supervisor	Manager—may be several layers up—appraiser has to know employee well	Mentor and supervisor Appraiser has to know employee well
Authority of appraiser	Presumed in supervisory role or position	Reputation important (Prestige is determined by nationality, age, sex, family, tribe, title education)	Respect accorded by employee to supervisor or appraiser
	Supervisor takes slight lead	Authority of appraiser important—don't say "I don't know"	Done co-equally
How often	Once/year or periodically	Once/year	Developmental appraisal once/month Evaluation appraisal—after first 12 years
Assumptions	Objective appraiser is fair	Subjective appraiser more important than objective Connections are important	Objective and subjective important Japanese can be trained in anything
Manner of communication and feedback	Criticism direct Criticisms may be in writing Objective/authentic	Criticisms subtle Older more likely to be direct Criticisms not given in writing	Criticisms subtle Criticisms given verbally Observe formalities
Rebuttals	U.S. will rebutt appraisal	Saudi Arabians will rebutt	Japanese would rarely rebutt
Praise	Given individually	Given individually	Given to entire group
Motivators	Money and position strong motivators Career development	Loyalty to supv. strong motivator	Internal excellence strong motivator

Source: Adapted from Philip R. Harris and Robert T. Moran, "Cultural Variations: Performance Appraisals," *Managing Cultural Differences*, p. 37.

lists some differences across three cultures—the United States, Saudi Arabia, and Japan.

1. Individually review the dimensions and identify the differences that appear to be most important. How would you deal with these differences if you were the manager and the worker (ratee) was from Saudi Arabia or Japan?

2. The *instructor* should establish groups of four or more students to discuss the individual responses to No.1.

3. The *instructor* could reassemble the class and examine what the groups discussed. Suppose the ratee in the performance appraisal session was from Mexico or Russia. What dimensions would have to be seriously considered in order to clearly communicate the manager's performance appraisal feedback?

▲

CASES

CASE 14–1   THE ROAD TO HELL

John Baker, chief engineer of the Caribbean Bauxite Company Limited of Barracania in the West Indies, was making his final preparations to leave the island. His promotion to production manager of Keso Mining Corporation near Winnipeg—one of Continental Ore's fast-expanding Canadian enterprises—had been announced a month before, and now everything had been tidied up except the last vital interview with his successor, the able young Barracanian Matthew Rennalls. It was vital that this interview be a success and that Rennalls leave Baker's office uplifted and encouraged to face the challenge of his new job. A touch on the bell would have brought Rennalls walking into the room, but Baker delayed the moment and gazed thoughtfully through the window, considering just exactly what he was going to say and, more particularly, how he was going to say it.

Baker, an English expatriate, was 45 years old and had served his 23 years with Continental Ore in many different places: the Far East; several countries of Africa; Europe; and, for the last two years, the West Indies. He had not cared much for his previous assignment in Hamburg and was delighted when the West Indian appointment came through. Climate was not the only attraction. Baker had always preferred working overseas in what were called the developing countries because he felt he had an innate knack—more than most other expatriates working for Continental Ore—of knowing just how to get on with regional staff. Twenty-four hours in Barracania, however, soon made him realize that he would need all of his innate knack if he were to deal effectively with the problems in this field that now awaited him.

At his first interview with Glenda Hutchins, the production manager, the whole problem of Rennalls and his future was discussed. There and then it was made quite clear to Baker that one of his most important tasks would be the grooming of Rennalls as his successor. Hutchins had pointed out that not only was Rennalls one of the brightest Barracanian prospects on the staff of Caribbean Bauxite—at London University he had taken first-class honors in the B. Sc. engineering degree—but, being the son of the minister of finance and economic planning, he also had no small political pull.

Caribbean Bauxite had been particularly pleased when Rennalls decided to work for it rather than for the government in which his father had such a prominent post. The company ascribed his action to the effects of its vigorous and liberal regionalization program that, since World War II, had produced 18 Barracanians at the middle-management level and given Caribbean Bauxite a good lead in this respect over all other international concerns operating in Barracania. The success of this timely regionalization policy had led to excellent relations with the government—a relationship that gained added importance when Barracania, three years later, became independent, an occasion that encouraged a critical and challenging attitude toward the role foreign interest would have to play in the new Barracania. Hutchins, therefore, had little difficulty convincing Baker that the successful career development of Renalls was of the first importance.

The interview with Hutchins was now two years in the past, and Baker, leaning back in his office chair, reviewed just how successful he had been in the grooming of Rennalls. What aspects of the latter's character had helped, and what had hindered? What about his own personality? How had that helped or hindered? The first item to go on the credit side, without question, would be the ability of

Source: Prepared by the late Gareth Evans of Shell International Petroleum Company, Ltd.

Rennalls to master the technical aspects of his job. From the start he had shown keenness and enthusiasm, and he had often impressed Baker with his ability in tackling new assignments and the constructive comments he invariably made in departmental discussions. He was popular with all ranks of Barracanian staff and had an ease of manner that stood him in good stead when dealing with his expatriate seniors.

These were all assets, but what about the debit side? First and foremost was his racial consciousness. His four years at London University had accentuated this feeling and made him sensitive to any sign of condescension on the part of expatriates. Perhaps to give expression to this sentiment, as soon as he returned home from London, he threw himself into politics on behalf of the United Action Party, who were later to win the preindependence elections and provide the country with its first prime minister.

The ambitions of Rennalls—and he certainly was ambitious—did not, however, lie in politics. Staunch nationalist he was, but he saw that he could serve himself and his country best—For was not bauxite responsible for nearly half the value of Barracania's export trade?—by putting his engineering talent to the best use possible. On this account, Hutchins found that he had an unexpectedly easy task in persuading Rennalls to give up his political work before entering the production department as an assistant engineer.

It was, Baker knew, Rennall's well-repressed sense of racial consciousness that had prevented their relationship from being as close as it should have been. On the surface, nothing could have seemed more agreeable. Formality between the two was minimal. Baker was delighted to find that his assistant shared his own peculiar "shaggy dog" sense of humor, so jokes were continually being exchanged. They entertained one another at their houses and often played tennis together—and yet the barrier remained invisible, indefinable, but ever present. The existence of this screen between them was a constant source of frustration to Baker, since it indicated a weakness which he was loath to accept. If successful with people of all other nationalities, why not with Rennalls?

At least he had managed to break through to Rennalls more successfully than had any other expatriate. In fact, it was the young Barracanian's attitude—sometimes overbearing, sometimes cynical—toward other company expatriates that had been one of the subjects Baker raised last year when he discussed Rennall's staff report with him. Baker knew, too, that he would have to raise the same subject again in the forthcoming interview, because Mar-

tha Jackson, the senior draughter, had complained only yesterday about the rudeness of Rennalls. With this thought in mind, Baker leaned forward and spoke into the intercom: "Would you come in, Matt, please? I'd like a word with you." Rennalls came in, and Baker held out a box and said, "Do sit down. Have a cigarette."

He paused while he held out his lighter and then went on. "As you know, Matt, I'll be off to Canada in a few days' time, and before I go, I thought it would be useful if we could have a final chat together. It is indeed with some deference that I suggest I can be of help. You will shortly be sitting in this chair and doing the job I am now doing, but I, on the other hand, am 10 years older, so perhaps you can accept the idea that I may be able to give you the benefit of my long experience."

Baker saw Rennalls stiffen slightly in his chair as he made this point, so he added in explanation, "You and I have attended enough company courses to remember those repeated requests by the personnel manager to tell people how they are getting on as often as the convenient moment arises, and not just the automatic once a year when, by regulation, staff reports have to be discussed."

Rennalls nodded his agreement, so Baker went on, "I shall always remember the last job performance discussion I had with my previous boss back in Germany. She used what she called the 'plus and minus technique.' She firmly believed that when seniors seek to improve the work performance of their staff by discussion, their prime objective should be to make sure the latter leave the interview encouraged and inspired to improve. Any criticism, therefore, must be constructive and helpful. She said that one very good way to encourage a person—and I fully agree with her—is to discuss good points, the plus factors, as well as weak ones, the minus factors. So I thought, Matt, it would be a good idea to run our discussion along these lines."

Rennalls offered no comment, so Baker continued. "Let me say, therefore, right away, that as far as your own work performance is concerned, the pluses far outweigh the minuses. I have, for instance, been most impressed with the way you have adapted your considerable theoretical knowledge to master the practical techniques of your job—that ingenious method you used to get air down to the fifth shaft level is a sufficient case in point. At departmental meetings I have invariably found your comments well taken and helpful. In fact, you will be interested to know that only last week I reported to Ms. Hutchins that, from the technical point of view, she could not wish for a more able person to succeed to the position of chief engineer."

"That's very good indeed of you, John," cut in Renalls

with a smile of thanks. "My only worry now is how to live up to such a high recommendation."

"Of that I am quite sure," returned Baker, "especially if you can overcome the minus factor which I would like now to discuss with you. It is one that I have talked about before, so I'll come straight to the point. I have noticed that you are more friendly and get on better with your fellow Barracanians than you do with Europeans. In point of fact, I had a complaint only yesterday from Ms. Jackson, who said you had been rude to her—and not for the first time, either.

"There is, Matt, I am sure, no need for me to tell you how necessary it will be for you to get on well with ex-patriates, because until the company has trained up sufficient men of your caliber, Europeans are bound to occupy senior positions here in Barracania. All this is vital to your future interests, so can I help you in any way?"

While Baker was speaking on this theme, Rennalls sat tensed in his chair, and it was some seconds before he replied. "It is quite extraordinary, isn't it, how one can convey an impression to others so at variance with what one intends? I can only assure you once again that my disputes with Jackson—and you may remember also Godson—have had nothing at all to do with the color of their skins. I promise you that if a Barracanian had behaved in an equally peremptory manner, I would have reacted the same way. And again, if I may say it within these four walls, I am sure I am not the only one who has found Jackson and Godson difficult. I could mention the names of several expatriates who have felt the same. However, I am really sorry to have created this impression of not being able to get on with Europeans—it is an entirely false one—and I quite realize that I must do all I can to correct it as quickly as possible. On your last point, regarding Europeans holding senior positions in the company for some time to come, I quite accept the situation. I know that Caribbean Bauxite—as it has been for many years now—will promote Barracanians as soon as their experience warrants it. And, finally, I would like to assure you, John—and my father thinks the same, too—that I am very happy in my work here and hope to stay with the company for many years to come."

Rennalls had spoken earnestly, and Baker, although not convinced by what he had heard, did not think he could pursue the matter further except to say, "All right, Matt, my impression may be wrong, but I would like to remind you about the truth of that old saying 'What is important is not what is true, but what is believed.' Let it rest at that."

But suddenly Baker knew that he did not want to "let it rest at that." He was disappointed once again at not being able to break through to Rennalls and at having again had to listen to his bland denial that there was any racial prejudice in his makeup.

Baker, who had intended to end the interview at this point, decided to try another tack. "To return for a moment to the plus and minus technique I was telling you just now, there is another plus factor I forgot to mention. I would like to congratulate you not only on the caliber of your work, but also on the ability you have shown in overcoming a challenge that I, as a European, have never had to meet.

"Continental Ore is, as you know, a typical commercial enterprise—admittedly a big one—that is a product of the economic and social environment of the United States and western Europe. My ancestors have all been brought up in this environment of the past 200 or 300 years, and I have, therefore, been able to live in a world in which commerce (as we know it today) has been part and parcel of my being. It has not been something revolutionary and new that has suddenly entered my life. In your case," went on Baker, "the situation is different, because you and your forebears have only had some 50 and not 200 or 300 years. Again, Matt, let me congratulate you—and people like you—on having so successfully overcome this particular hurdle. It is for this very reason that I think the outlook for Barracania—and particularly Caribbean Bauxite—is so bright."

Rennalls had listened intently, and when Baker finished, he replied, "Well, once again, John, I have to thank you for what you have said, and, for my part, I can only say that it is gratifying to know that my own personal effort has been so much appreciated. I hope that more people will soon come to think as you do."

There was a pause, and, for a moment, Baker thought hopefully that he was about to achieve his long-awaited breakthrough. But Rennalls merely smiled back. The barrier remained unbreached. There were some five minutes' cheerful conversation about the contrast between the Caribbean and Canadian climates and whether the West Indies had any hope of beating England in the Fifth Test before Baker drew the interview to a close. Although he was as far from ever knowing the real Rennalls, he was nevertheless glad that the interview had run along in this friendly manner and, particularly, that it had ended on such a cheerful note.

This feeling, however, lasted only until the following morning. Baker had some farewells to make, so he arrived at the office considerably later than usual. He had no sooner sat down at his desk than his secretary walked into the room with a worried frown on her face. Her words came fast. "When I arrived this morning, I found Mr. Rennalls already waiting at my door. He seemed very angry and told me in quite a peremptory manner that he had a vital letter to dictate that must be sent off without any delay. He was so worked up that he couldn't keep still and kept pacing about the room, which is most unlike him. He wouldn't even wait to read what he had dictated. Just signed the page where he thought the letter would end. It has been distributed, and your copy is in your tray."

Puzzled and feeling vaguely uneasy, Baker opened the envelope marked "Confidential" and read the following letter:

FROM: Assistant Engineer

TO: The Chief Engineer,
           Caribbean Bauxite
           Limited

SUBJECT: Assessment of Interview
           Between Messrs. Baker
           and Rennalls

DATA: 14th August 1982

It has always been my practice to respect the advice given me by seniors, so after our interview, I decided to give careful thought once again to its main points and so make sure that I had understood all that had been said. As I promised you at the time, I had every intention of putting your advice to the best effect.

It was not, therefore, until I had sat down quietly in my home yesterday evening to consider the interview objectively that its main purport became clear. Only then did the full enormity of what you said dawn on me. The more I thought about it, the more convinced

I was that I had hit upon the real truth—and the more furious I became. With a facility in the English language which I—a poor Barracanian—cannot hope to match, you had the audacity to insult me (and through me every Barracanian worth his salt) by claiming that our knowledge of modern living is only a paltry 50 years old, while yours goes back 200 to 300 years. As if your materialistic commercial environment could possibly be compared with the spiritual values of our culture! I'll have you know that if much of what I saw in London is representative of your boasted culture, I hope fervently that it will never come to Barracania. By what right do you have the effrontery to condescend to us? At heart, all you Europeans think us barbarians, or, as you say amongst yourselves, we are "just down from the trees."

Far into the night I discussed this matter with my father, and he is as disgusted as I. He agrees with me that any company whose senior staff think as you do is no place for any Barracanian proud of his culture and race. So much for all the company claptrap and specious propaganda about regionalisation and Barracania for the Barracanians.

I feel ashamed and betrayed. Please accept this letter as my resignation, which I wish to become effective immediately.

cc: Production Manager
     Managing Director

CASE QUESTIONS

1. What in your opinion did Baker hope to accomplish as a result of his conversation with Rennalls? Did he succeed? Why or why not?
2. Did nonverbal communications play a part in this case? Be specific and give examples.
3. What would Baker and Rennalls have done to improve the situation described in this case?

CASE 14–2 A CASE OF MISUNDERSTANDING: MR. HART AND MR. BING

In a department of a large industrial organization there were seven workers (four men and three women) engaged in testing and inspecting panels of electronic equipment. In this department one of the workers, Bing, was having trouble with his immediate supervisor, Hart, who had formerly been a worker in the department. Had we been

Source: Reproduced by permission of the President and Fellows of Harvard College.

observers in this department we would have seen Bing carrying two or three panels at a time from the racks where they were stored to the bench where he inspected them together. For this activity we would have seen him charging double or triple set-up time. We would have heard him occasionally singing at work. Also we would have seen him usually leaving his work position a few minutes early to go to lunch, and noticed that other employees sometimes accompanied him. And had we been present at one specific occasion, we would have heard Hart telling Bing that he disapproved of these activities and that he wanted Bing to stop doing them. However, not being present to hear the actual verbal exchange that took place in this interaction, let us note what Bing and Hart each said to a personnel representative.

WHAT BING SAID

In talking about his practice of charging double or triple setup time for panels which he inspected all at one time, Bing said:

> This is a perfectly legal thing to do. We've always been doing it. Mr. Hart, the supervisor, has other ideas about it, though: he claims it's cheating the company. He came over to the bench a day or two ago and let me know just how he felt about the matter. Boy, did we go at it! It wasn't so much the fact that he called me down on it, but more the way in which he did it. He's a sarcastic bastard. I've never seen anyone like him. He's not content just to say in a manlike way what's on his mind, but he prefers to do it in a way that makes you want to crawl inside a crack in the floor. What a guy! I don't mind being called down by a supervisor, but I like to be treated like a man, and not humiliated like a school teacher does a naughty kid. He's been pulling this stuff ever since he's been promoted. He's lost his friendly way and seems to be having some difficulty in knowing how to manage us employees. He's a changed man over what he used to be like when he was a worker on the bench with us several years ago.
>
> When he pulled this kind of stuff on me the other day, I got so damn mad I called in the union representative. I knew that the thing I was doing was permitted by the contract, but I was intent on making some trouble for Mr. Hart, just because he persists in this sarcastic way of handling me. I am about fed up with the whole damn situation. I'm trying every means I can to get myself transferred out of this group. If I don't succeed and I'm forced to stay on here, I'm going to screw him in every way I can. He's not going to pull this kind of kid stuff any longer on me. When the union representative questioned him on the case, he finally had to back down, because according to the contract an employee can use any time-saving method or device in order to speed up the process as long as the quality standards of the job are met.

> You see, he knows that I do professional singing on the outside. He hears the people talking about my career in music. I guess he figures I can be so cocky because I have another means of earning some money. Actually, the employees here enjoy having me sing while we work, but he thinks I'm disturbing them and causing them to "goof-off" from their work. Occasionally, I leave the job a few minutes early and go down to the washroom to wash up before lunch. Sometimes several others in the group will accompany me, and so Mr. Hart automatically thinks I'm the leader and usually bawls me out for the whole thing.
>
> So, you can see, I'm a marked man around here: He keeps watching me like a hawk. Naturally, this makes me very uncomfortable. That's why I'm sure a transfer would be the best thing. I've asked him for it, but he didn't give me any satisfaction at the time. While I remain here, I'm going to keep my nose clean, but whenever I get the chance, I'm going to slip it to him, but good.

WHAT HART SAID

Here, on the other hand, is what Hart told the personnel representative:

> Say, I think you should be in on this. My dear little friend Bing is heading himself into a show-down with me. Recently it was brought to my attention that Bing has been taking double and triple set-up time for panels which he is actually inspecting at one time. In effect, that's cheating, and I've called him down on it several times before. A few days ago it was brought to my attention again, and so this time I really let him have it in no uncertain terms. He's been getting away with this for too long and I'm going to put an end to it once and for all. I know he didn't like me calling him on it because a few hours later he had the union representative breathing down my back. Well, anyway, I let them both know I'll not tolerate the practice any longer, and I let Bing know that if he continues to do this kind of thing, I'm inclined to think the guy's mentally deficient, because talking to him has actually no meaning to him whatsoever. I've tried just about every approach to jar some sense into that guy's head, and I've just about given it up as a bad deal.
>
> I don't know what it is about the guy, but I think he's harboring some deep feelings against me. For what,

I don't know, because I've tried to handle that bird with kid gloves. But his whole attitude around here on the job is one of indifference, and he certainly isn't a good influence on the rest of my group. Frankly, I think he purposely tried to agitate them against me at times, too. It seems to me that he may be suffering from illusions of grandeur because all he does all day is sit over there and croon his fool head off. Thinks he's Frank Sinatra! No kidding! I understand he takes singing lessons and he's working out with some of the local bands in the city. All of which is OK by me; but when his outside interests start interfering with his efficiency on the job, then I've got to start paying closer attention to the situation. For this reason I've been keeping my eye on that bird and if he steps out of line any more, he and I are going to part ways.

You know there's an old saying, "You can't make a silk purse out of a sow's ear." The guy is simply unscrupulous. He feels no obligation to do a real day's work. Yet I know the guy can do a good job, because for a long time he did. But in recent months he's slipped, for some reason, and is whole attitude on the job has changed. Why, it's even getting to the point where I think he's inducing other employees to "goof-off" a few minutes before the lunch whistle and go down to the washroom and clean up on company time. I've called him on it several times, but words just don't seem to make any lasting impression on him. Well, if he keeps it up much longer, he's going to find himself on the way out. He's asked me for a transfer, so I know he wants to go. But I didn't give him an answer when he asked me, because I was storming mad at the time, and I may have told him to go somewhere else.

CASE QUESTIONS

1. Based on the discussion of the elements of communication in the chapter, where are the breakdowns in communications occurring in this case?
2. What barriers to effective communication are present in this case?
3. What in your opinion must be done to improve communication between Mr. Hart and Mr. Bing?

Organizational Culture, Socialization, and Career Development

LEARNING OBJECTIVES

DEFINE the terms organizational culture, socialization, and career

EXPLAIN why it is too simplistic to assume that managers can state that they are creating a firm's culture

DESCRIBE the four stages of establishment, advancement, maintenance, and withdrawal

DISCUSS the role of personality in influencing career choice

COMPARE the stages in career development with those in the socialization process

IDENTIFY specific practices and programs used by organizations to facilitate socialization

Most individuals work for several different organizations over the course of a career. There are growing numbers of people who shift from one occupation to another. A decreasing number of individuals, after finishing their education, start and remain working with one firm throughout their careers. When a person moves from one firm to another, or even from one department to another in the same firm, he or she senses and experiences differences between the environments. Attempting to adjust to these different environments involves learning new values, processing information in new ways, and working within an established set of norms, customs, and rituals.

The adaption to new environments is becoming a common occurrence and is likely to remain so into the 21st century. Although adaptation is difficult, it can be better understood by learning about organizational culture, socialization, and career systems. Organizational life is influenced by each of these concepts.

ORGANIZATIONAL CULTURE

If a person walks into the Broadmoor Hotel in Colorado Springs, the Breakers Hotel in West Palm Beach, or the St. Francis Hotel in San Francisco there is a certain atmosphere, feeling, and style that is unique. These hotels have a personality, a charm, a feel. They have a cultural anchor that influences the way customers respond and the way employees interact with customers. McDonald's also sends off a powerful cultural message.[1] The 11,000 restaurants in McDonald's all pay attention to quality, service, and cleanliness. Ray Kroc, the founder, instilled these cultural anchors in McDonald's. He had a significant influence on what McDonald's is throughout the world from Tokyo to Chicago to Moscow. Kroc projected his vision and his openness about what McDonald's would be to customers. He gave McDonald's a purpose, goals, and a cultural base. Whether the discussion focuses on a grand hotel that exudes culture or a McDonald's restaurant that projects its founder's vision of the business, culture is a part of organizational life.

Organizational Culture Defined

Despite being an important concept, organizational culture as a perspective to understand behavior within organizations has its limitations. First, it is not the only way to view organizations. We have already discussed the goal and systems view without even mentioning culture. Second, like so many concepts, organizational culture is not defined the same way by any two popular theorists or researchers. Some of the definitions of culture are as follows:

- Symbols, language, ideologies, rituals, and myths.[2]
- Organizational scripts derived from the personal scripts of the organization's founder(s) or dominant leader(s).
- Is a product; is historical; is based upon symbols; and is an abstraction from behavior and the products of behavior.[3]

---

[1]Gary Hoover, Alta Campbell, and Patricia S. Spain (eds.), *Profiles of Over 500 Major Corporations* (Austin, Tex.: Reference Press, Inc., 1990 , p. 364.

[2]A. M. Pettegrew, "On Studying Cultures," *Administrative Science Quarterly*, 1979, pp. 579–81.

[3]D. Jongeward, *Everybody Wins: Transactional Analysis Applied to Organizations* (Reading, Mass.: Addison-Wesley Publishing, 1973).

- A pattern of basic assumptions invented, discovered, or developed by a group as it learns to cope with its problems of external adaptation and internal integration—that has worked well enough to be considered valid and therefore to be taught to new members as the correct way to perceive, think, and feel in relation to those problems.[4] These definitions suggest that organizational culture consists of a number of elements such as assumptions, beliefs, values, rituals, myths, scripts, and languages.

Organizational culture is what the employees perceive and how this perception creates a pattern of beliefs, values, and expectations. Edgar Schein defined culture as:

A pattern of basic assumptions—invented, discovered, or developed by a given group as it learns to cope with the problems of external adaptation and internal integration— that has worked well enough to be considered valid and, therefore, to be taught to new members as the correct way to perceive, think, and feel in relation to those problems.[5]

The Schein definition points out that culture involves assumptions, adaptations, perceptions, and learning. He further contends that an organization's culture such as Walt Disney's has three layers. Layer I includes artifacts and creations which are visible but often not interpretable. An annual report, a newsletter, wall dividers between workers, and furnishings are examples of artifacts and creations. At Layer II are values or the things that are important to people. Values are conscious, affective desires or wants. In Layer III are the basic assumptions people make that guide their behavior. Included in this layer are assumptions that tell individuals how to perceive, think about, and feel about work, performance goals, human relationships, and the performance of colleagues. Exhibit 15-1 presents the Schein three-layer model of organizational culture.

Asking McDonald's or Walt Disney employees about their firm's organizational culture is not likely to reveal much. A person's feelings and perceptions are usually kept at the subconscious level. The feelings one has about a stay at Motel 6 or a stay at the St. Francis Hotel are often difficult to express. Exhibit 15-2 illustrates how the culture of a firm can be inferred by looking at those aspects that are perceptible. For example, four specific manifestations of culture at Walt Disney are shared things (wearing the Walt Disney uniform to fit the attraction), shared sayings (a good "Mickey" is a compliment for doing a good job), shared behavior (smiling at customers and being polite), and shared feelings (taking pride in working at Disney).

Security Pacific Corporation, a Los Angeles-based bank, uses a credo to establish guidelines for its employees, customers, and stockholders. In essence, it projects what the firm stands for and how the firm views various constituents. Encounter 15-1 presents the credo.

---

[4]Edgar H. Schein, *Organizational Culture and Leadership* (San Francisco: Jossey-Bass, 1985), p. 9.

[5]Ibid., p. 9.

EXHIBIT 15-1

Schein's Three-Layer Organizational Model

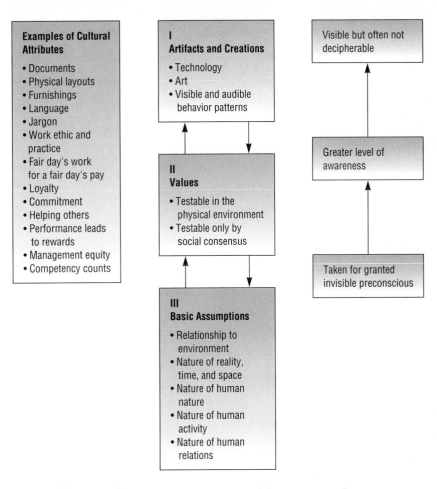

Examples of Cultural Attributes

- Documents
- Physical layouts
- Furnishings
- Language
- Jargon
- Work ethic and practice
- Fair day's work for a fair day's pay
- Loyalty
- Commitment
- Helping others
- Performance leads to rewards
- Management equity
- Competency counts

I Artifacts and Creations

- Technology
- Art
- Visible and audible behavior patterns

II Values

- Testable in the physical environment
- Testable only by social consensus

III Basic Assumptions

- Relationship to environment
- Nature of reality, time, and space
- Nature of human nature
- Nature of human activity
- Nature of human relations

Visible but often not decipherable

Greater level of awareness

Taken for granted invisible preconscious

Source: Adapted from E. H. Schein, "Does Japanese Management Style Have a Message for American Managers?" *Sloan Management Review*, Fall 1981, p. 64.

Organizational Culture and Its Effects

Since organizational culture involves shared expectations, values, and attitudes, it exerts influence on individuals, groups, and organizational processes. Individual members are influenced to be a good citizen and to go along. Thus, if quality customer service is important in the culture, then individuals are expected to adopt this behavior. If, on the other hand, adhering to a specific set of procedures in dealing with customers is the norm, then this type of behavior would be expected, recognized, and rewarded.

EXHIBIT 15-2

Cultural Relationships

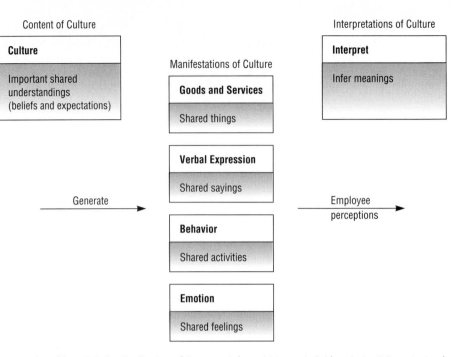

Source: Adapted from V. Sathe, "Implications of Corporate Culture: A Manager's Guide to Action," *Organizational Dynamics*, Autumn 1983, p. 8.

Researchers who have suggested and studied the impact of culture of employees indicate that it provides and encourages a form of stability.[6] There is a feeling of stability, as well as a sense of organizational identity, provided by an organization's culture. Walt Disney is able to attract, develop, and retain top quality employees because of the firm's stability and the pride of identity that goes with being a part of the Disney team.

It has become useful to differentiate between strong and weak cultures.[7] A strong culture is characterized by employees sharing core values. The more employees share and accept the core values, the stronger the culture is and the more influential it is on behavior. Religious organizations, cults, and some Japanese firms such as Toyota are examples of organizations that have strong, influential cultures.

[6]Linda Smircich, "Concepts of Culture and Organizational Analysis," *Administrative Science Quarterly*, September 1983, pp. 339–58.

[7]G. S. Saffold III, "Culture Traits, Strength, and Organizational Performance: Moving beyond Strong Culture," *Academy of Management Review*, October 1988, pp. 546–58.

ORGANIZATIONAL
E N C O U N T E R • 15-1

THE CREDO OF SECURITY PACIFIC CORPORATION

Commitment to Customer

The first commitment is to provide our customers with quality products and services which are innovative and technologically responsive to their current requirements, at appropriate prices. To perform these tasks with integrity requires that we maintain confidentiality and protect customer privacy, promote customer satisfaction, and serve customer needs. We strive to serve qualified customers and industries which are socially responsible according to broadly accepted community and company standards.

Commitment to Employee

The second commitment is to establish an environment for our employees which promotes professional growth, encourages each person to achieve his or her highest potential, and promotes individual creativity and responsibility. Security Pacific acknowledges our responsibility to employees, including providing for open and honest communication, stated expectations, fair and timely assessment of performance and equitable compensation which rewards employee contributions to company objectives within a framework of equal opportunity and affirmative action.

Commitment of Employee to Security Pacific

The third commitment is that of the employee to Security Pacific. As employees, we strive to understand and adhere to the Corporation's policies and objectives, act in a professional manner, and give our best effort to improve Security Pacific. We recognize the trust and confidence placed in us by our customers and community and act with integrity and honesty in all situations to preserve that trust and confidence. We act responsibly to avoid conflicts of interest and other situations which are potentially harmful to the Corporation.

Commitment of Employee to Employee

The fourth commitment is that of employees to their fellow employees. We must be committed to promote a climate of mutual respect, integrity, and professional relationships, characterized by open and honest communication within and across all levels of the organization. Such a climate will promote attainment of the Corporation's goals and objectives, while leaving room for individual initiative within a competitive environment.

Commitment to Communities

The fifth commitment is that of Security Pacific to the communities which we serve. We must constantly strive to improve the quality of life through our support of community organizations and projects, through encouraging service to the community by employees, and by promoting participation in community services. By the appropriate use of our resources, we work to support or further advance the interests of the community, particularly in times of crisis or social need. The Corporation and its employees are committed to complying fully with each community's laws and regulations.

Commitment to Stockholder

The sixth commitment of Security Pacific is to its stockholders. We will strive to provide consistent growth and a superior rate of return on their investment, to maintain a position and reputation as a leading financial institution, to protect stockholder investments, and to provide full and timely information. Achievement of these goals for Security Pacific is dependent upon the successful development of the five previous sets of relationships.

Popular best-seller books such as *Theory Z: How American Business Can Meet The Japanese Challenge,*[8] *In Search of Excellence,*[9] and *Corporate Cultures: The Rites and Rituals of Corporate Life*[10] provide anecdotal evidence about the powerful influence of culture of individuals, groups, and processes. Heroes and stories about firms are interestingly portrayed. However, theoretically based and empirically valid research on culture and its impact is still quite sketchy. Questions remain about the measures used to assess culture, and definitional problems have not been resolved. There has also been the inability of researchers to show that a specific culture contributes to positive effectiveness in comparison to less effective firms with another cultural profile. Comparative cultural studies are needed to better understand how culture impacts behavior.

Creating Organizational Culture

Can a culture be created that influences behavior in the direction management desires? This is an intriguing question. An attempt and an experiment to create a positive, productive culture was conducted in a California electronics firm.[11] Top managers regularly meet to establish the core values of the firm. A document was developed to express the core values as: "paying attention to detail," "doing it right the first time," "delivering defect-free products," and "using open communications." The document of core values was circulated to middle-level managers who refined the statements. Then the refined document was circulated to all employees as the set of guiding principles of the firm.

An anthropologist was in the firm at the time working as a software trainer. He insightfully analyzed what actually occurred in the firm. There was a gap between the management-stated culture and the firm's actual working conditions and practices. Quality problems existed throughout the firm. There was also a strictly enforced chain of command and a top-down only communication system. The cultural creation experiment was too artificial and was not taken seriously by employees.

The consequences of creating a culture in the California firm included decreased morale, increased turnover, a poorer financial performance. Ultimately, the firm filed for bankruptcy and closed its doors.

The California electronics firm case points out that artificially imposing a culture is difficult. Imposing a culture is often met with resistance. It is difficult to simply create core values. Also, when a disparity exists between reality and a

---

[8]William G. Ouchi, *Theory Z: How American Business Can Meet the Japanese Challenge* (Reading, Mass.: Addison-Wesley, 1982).

[9]Thomas J. Peters and Robert H. Waterman, *In Search of Excellence* (New York: Harper & Row, 1982).

[10]Terrence E. Deal and Allan A. Kennedy, *Corporate Cultures: The Rites and Rituals of Corporate Life* (Reading Mass.: Addison-Wesley, 1982).

[11]Peter C. Reynolds, "Imposing a Corporate Culture," *Psychology Today,* March 1987, pp. 33–38.

stated set of values, employees become confused, irritated, and skeptical. They also usually lack enthusiasm and respect when a false image is portrayed. Creating a culture apparently just doesn't happen because a group of intelligent, well-intentioned managers meet and prepare a document.

Cultures seem to evolve over a period of time as did McDonald's and Walt Disney. Schein describes this evolution as follows:

> The culture that eventually evolves in a particular organization is . . . a complex outcome of external pressures, internal potentials, responses to critical events, and, probably, to some unknown degree, chance factors that could not be predicted from a knowledge of either the environment or the members.[12]

A model that illustrates the evolution of culture and its outcome is presented in Exhibit 15-3. The model emphasizes an array of methods and procedures that managers can use to foster a cohesive culture. In examining this model, recall the California electronics firm and the limited methods it used to generate a quick-fix culture. In Exhibit 15-3 there is an emphasis on the word *HOME*, which suggests the importance of history, oneness, membership, and exchange among employees.

Influencing Culture Change

There is a limited amount of research done on cultural change. The difficulty in creating a culture is made even more complex when attempting to bring about a significant cultural change. The themes that appear in discussing change are these:

- Cultures are so elusive and hidden that they cannot be adequately diagnosed, managed, or changed.
- Because it takes difficult techniques, rare skills, and considerable time to understand a culture and then additional time to change it, deliberate attempts at culture change are not really practical.
- Cultures sustain people throughout periods of difficulty and serve to ward off anxiety. One of the ways they do this is by providing continuity and stability. Thus, people will naturally resist change to a new culture.[13]

These three views suggest that managers who are interested in attempting to produce cultural changes face a difficult task. There are, however, courageous managers who believe that they can intervene and make changes in the culture. Exhibit 15-4 presents a view of five intervention points for managers to consider.[14]

---

[12]Schein, *Organizational Culture and Leadership,* pp. 83–89.

[13]Harrison M. Trice and Janice M. Beyer, "Using Organizational Rites to Change Culture," in *Gaining Control of the Corporate Culture,* ed. Ralph H. Kilman, Mary J. Saxton, and Roy Serpa (San Francisco: Jossey-Bass, 1985), pp. 370–99.

[14]Vijay Sathe, "Implications of Corporate Culture: A Manager's Guide to Action," *Organizational Dynamics,* Autumn 1983, pp. 4–13.

EXHIBIT 15-3

The Evolution of a Positive Culture

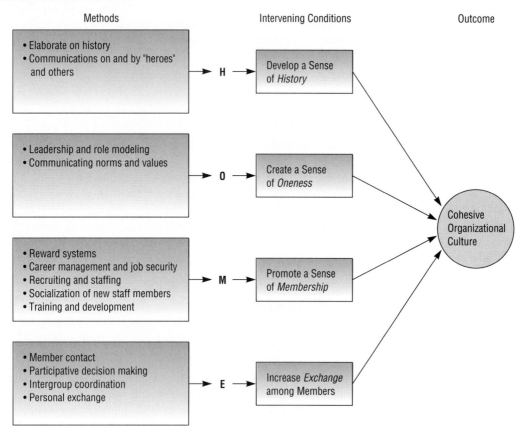

Methods

Intervening Conditions

Outcome

- Elaborate on history
- Communications on and by "heroes" and others

H → Develop a Sense of *History*

- Leadership and role modeling
- Communicating norms and values

O → Create a Sense of *Oneness*

- Reward systems
- Career management and job security
- Recruiting and staffing
- Socialization of new staff members
- Training and development

M → Promote a Sense of *Membership*

- Member contact
- Participative decision making
- Intergroup coordination
- Personal exchange

E → Increase *Exchange* among Members

Cohesive Organizational Culture

A considerable body of knowledge suggests that one of the most effective ways of changing people's beliefs and values is to first change their behavior (intervention 1).[15] However, behavior change does not necessarily produce culture change because of the process of justification. The California electronics example clearly illustrates this point. Behavioral compliance does not mean cultural commitment. Managers must get employees to see the inherent worth in behaving in a new way (intervention 2). Typically, communications (intervention 3) is the method used by managers to motivate the new behaviors. Cultural communi-

[15]Charles A. O'Reilly III, Jennifer Chatman, and David F. Caldwell, "People and Organizational Culture: A Profile Comparison to Assessing Person-Organization Fit," *Academy of Management Journal,* September 1991, pp. 487–516.

EXHIBIT 15-4

**Changing Culture
Intervention Points**

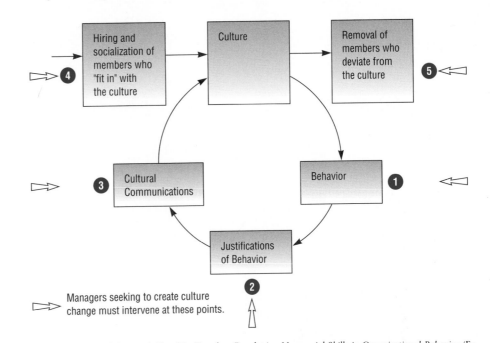

Source: Lisa A. Mainiero and Cheryl L. Tromley, *Developing Managerial Skills in Organizational Behavior* (Englewood Cliffs, N.J.: Prentice-Hall, 1989), p. 403.

cations can include announcements, memos, rituals, stories, dress, and other forms of communications.

Another set of interventions include the socialization of new members (intervention 4) and the removal of existing members who deviate from the culture (intervention 5). Each of these interventions must be done after careful diagnoses are performed. Although some individuals may not perfectly fit the firm's culture, they may possess exceptional skills and talents. Weeding out cultural misfits might be necessary, but it should only be done after weighing the costs and benefits of losing talented performers who deviate from the core cultural value system.

SOCIALIZATION

Socialization is the process by which organizations bring new employees into the culture. In terms of culture, there is a transmittal of values, assumptions, and attitudes from the older to the newer employees. Intervention 4 in Exhibit 15-4 emphasizes the "fit" between the new employee and the culture. Socialization attempts to make this fit more comfortable for the employee and the firm. The socialization process is presented in Exhibit 15-5.

The socialization process goes on throughout an individual's career. As the needs of the organization change, for example, its employees must adapt to those new needs; that is, they must be socialized. But even as we recognize that

EXHIBIT 15-5

**The Process of
Organizational Socialization**

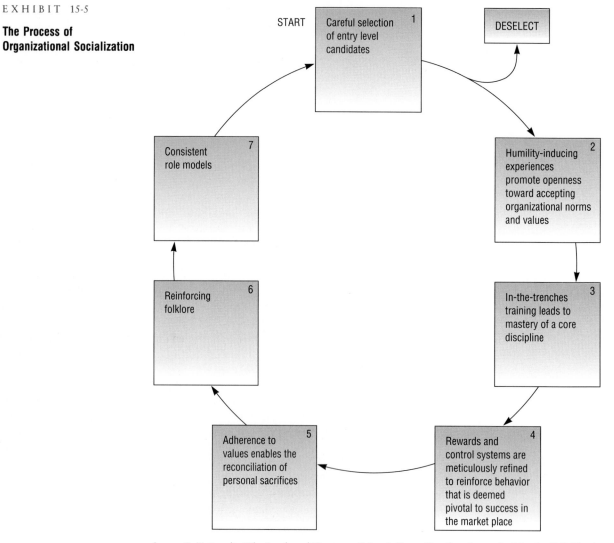

START

1 Careful selection of entry level candidates

DESELECT

7 Consistent role models

2 Humility-inducing experiences promote openness toward accepting organizational norms and values

6 Reinforcing folklore

3 In-the-trenches training leads to mastery of a core discipline

5 Adherence to values enables the reconciliation of personal sacrifices

4 Rewards and control systems are meticulously refined to reinforce behavior that is deemed pivotal to success in the market place

Source: R. T. Pascale, "The Paradox of 'Corporate Culture': Reconciling Ourselves to Socialization," *California Management Review*, p. 38, Winter 1985. © 1985 by the Regents of the University of California. Reprinted with permission of the Regents.

socialization is ever present, we must also recognize that it is more important at some times than at others. For example, socialization is most important when an individual first takes a job or takes a different job in the same organization. The socialization process occurs throughout the career stages, but individuals are more aware of it when they change jobs or change organizations.[16]

[16]Daniel C. Feldman and Jeanne M. Brett, "Coping with New Jobs: A Comparative Study of New Hires and Job Changers," *Academy of Management Journal*, June 1983, pp. 258–72.

Socialization Stages

The stages of socialization coincide generally with the stages of a career. Although researchers have proposed various descriptions of the stages of socialization,[17] three stages sufficiently describe it: (1) anticipatory socialization, (2) accommodation, and (3) role management.[18] Each stage involves specific activities that, if undertaken properly, increase the individual's chances of having an effective career. Moreover, these stages occur continuously and often simultaneously.

Anticipatory Socialization

The first stage involves all those activities the individual undertakes prior to entering the organization or to taking a different job in the same organization. The primary purpose of these activities is to acquire information about the new organization and/or new job. This stage of socialization corresponds to the pre-work career stage, and the information-gathering activities include formal schooling, actual work experience, and recruiting efforts of organizations attempting to attract new employees.

People are vitally interested in two kinds of information prior to entering a new job or organization. First, they want to know as much as they can about what working for the organization is really like. Second, they want to know whether they are suited to the jobs available in the organization. Individuals seek out this information with considerable effort when they are faced with the decision to take a job, whether it be their first one or one that comes along by way of transfer or promotion. At these times, the information is specific to the job or the organization. We also form impressions about jobs and organizations in less formal ways. For example, our friends and relatives talk of their experiences. Parents impart both positive and negative information to their offspring regarding the world of work. Although we continually receive information about this or that job or organization, we are more receptive to such information when faced with the necessity to make a decision.

It is desirable, of course, that the information transmitted and received during the anticipatory stage accurately and clearly depicts the organization and the job. However, we know that individuals differ considerably in the way they decode and receive information. Yet if the fit between the individual and the organization is to be optimal, two conditions are necessary: The first condition is *realism*. Both the individual and the organization must portray themselves realistically. The

[17]John P. Wanous, Arnon E. Reichers, and S. D. Malik, "Organizational Socialization and Group Development: Toward an Integrative Perspective," *Academy of Management Review*, October 1984, pp. 670–83. This article reviews the widely accepted models of socialization.

[18]These stages are identified by Daniel C. Feldman, "A Contingency Theory of Socialization," *Administrative Science Quarterly*, September 1976, pp. 434–35. The following discussion is based heavily on this work as well as on Daniel C. Feldman, "A Practical Program for Employee Socialization," *Organizational Dynamics*, Autumn 1976, pp. 64–80; and Daniel C. Feldman, "The Multiple Socialization of Organization Members," *Academy of Management Review*, June 1981, pp. 309–18.

second condition is *congruence*. This condition is present when the individual's skills, talents, and abilities are fully utilized by the job. Either their overutilization or underutilization results in incongruence and, consequently, poor performance.[19]

Accommodation

The second stage of socialization occurs after the individual becomes a member of the organization, after he or she takes the job. During this stage, the individual sees the organization and the job for what they actually are. Through a variety of activities the individual attempts to become an active participant in the organization and a competent performer on the job. This breaking-in period is ordinarily stressful for the individual because of anxiety created by the uncertainties inherent in any new and different situation. Apparently, individuals who experienced realism and congruence during the anticipatory stage have a less stressful accommodation stage. Nevertheless, the demands on the individual do indeed create situations that induce stress.

Four major activities comprise the accommodation stage: All individuals, to a degree, must engage in (1) establishing new interpersonal relationships with both co-workers and supervisors, (2) learning the tasks required to perform the job, (3) clarifying their role in the organization and in the formal and informal groups relevant to that role, and (4) evaluating the progress they are making toward satisfying the demands of the job and the role. Readers who have been through the accommodation stage probably recognize these four activities and recall more or less favorable reactions to them.

If all goes well in this stage, the individual feels a sense of acceptance by co-workers and supervisors and experiences competence in performing job tasks. The breaking-in period, if successful, also results in role definition and congruence of evaluation. These four outcomes of the accommodation stage (acceptance, competence, role definition, and congruence of evaluation) are experienced by all new employees to a greater or lesser extent. However, the relative value of each of these outcomes varies from person to person.[20] Acceptance by the group may be a less valued outcome for an individual whose social needs are satisfied off the job, for example. Regardless of these differences due to individual preferences, each of us experiences the accommodation stage of socialization and ordinarily moves on to the third stage.

Role Management

The third stage of socialization, role management, coincides with the third stage of careers, stable work. In contrast to the accommodation stage, which requires the individual to adjust to demands and expectations of the immediate work

---

[19]Feldman, "A Practical Program," pp. 65–66.

[20]Gareth R. Jones, "Psychological Orientation and the Process of Organizational Socialization: An Interactionist Perspective," *Academy of Management Review*, July 1983, pp. 464–74.

group, the role management stage takes on a broader set of issues and problems. Specifically, during the third stage, conflicts arise. One conflict is between the individual's work and home lives. For example, the individual must divide time and energy between the job and his or her role in the family. Since the amount of time and energy are fixed and the demands of work and family seemingly insatiable, conflict is inevitable. Employees unable to resolve these conflicts are often forced to leave the organization or to perform at an ineffective level. In either case, the individual and the organization are not well served by unresolved conflict between work and family.

The second source of conflict during the role management stage is between the individual's work group and other work groups in the organization. This source of conflict can be more apparent for some employees than for others. For example, as an individual moves up in the organization's hierarchy, he or she is required to interact with various groups both inside and outside the organization. Each group can and often does place different demands on the individual, and to the extent that these demands are beyond the individual's ability to meet, stress results. Tolerance for the level of stress induced by these conflicting and irreconcilable demands varies among individuals. Generally, the existence of unmanaged stress works to the disadvantage of the individual and the organization.

CHARACTERISTICS OF EFFECTIVE SOCIALIZATION

Organizational socialization processes vary in form and content from organization to organization. Even with the same organization, various individuals experience different socialization processes. For example, the accommodation stage for a college-trained management recruit is quite different from that of a person in the lowest-paid occupation in the organization. As John Van Maanen has pointed out, socialization processes are not only extremely important in shaping the individuals who enter an organization, they are also remarkably different from situation to situation.[21] This variation reflects either lack of attention by management to an important process or the uniqueness of the process as related to organizations and individuals. Either explanation permits the suggestion that while uniqueness is apparent, some general principles can be implemented in the socialization process.[22]

Effective Anticipatory Socialization

The organization's primary activities during the first stage of socialization are *recruitment* and *selection and placement* programs. If these programs are effective, new recruits in an organization should experience the feeling of *realism* and

[21]J. Van Maanen, "People Processing: Strategies for Organizational Socialization," *Organizational Dynamics*, Summer 1978, pp. 18–36.

[22]The following discussion reflects the research findings of Feldman, "A Practical Program."

congruence. In turn, accurate expectations about the job result from realism and congruence.

Recruitment programs are directed toward new employees, those not now in the organization. It is desirable to give prospective employees information not only about the job but also about those aspects of the organization that affect the individual. It is nearly always easier for the recruiter to stress job-related information to the exclusion of organization-related information. Job-related information is usually specific and objective, whereas organization-related information is usually general and subjective. Nevertheless, the recruiter should, to the extent possible, convey factual information about such matters as pay and promotion policies and practices, objective characteristics of the work group the recruit is likely to join, and other information that reflects the recruit's concerns.

Selection and placement practices, in the context of anticipatory socialization, are important conveyers of information to employees already in the organization. Of prime importance is the manner in which individuals view career paths in organizations. As noted earlier, the stereotypical career path is one that involves advancement up the managerial hierarchy. This concept, however, does not take into account the differences among individuals toward such moves. Greater flexibility in career paths would require the organization to consider lateral or downward transfers.[23]

Effective Accommodation Socialization

Five different activities comprise effective accommodation socialization. They are (1) designing orientation programs, (2) structuring training programs, (3) providing performance evaluation information, (4) assigning challenging work, and (5) assigning demanding bosses.

Orientation programs are seldom given the attention they deserve. The first few days on the new job can have very strong negative or positive impacts on the new employee. Taking a new job involves not only new job tasks but also new interpersonal relationships. The new person comes into an ongoing social system which has evolved a unique set of values, ideals, frictions, conflicts, friendships, coalitions, and all the other characteristics of work groups. If left alone, the new employee must cope with the new environment in ignorance, but if given some help and guidance, he or she can cope more effectively.[24]

Thus, organizations should design orientation programs that enable new employees to meet the rest of the employees as soon as possible. Moreover, specific individuals should be assigned the task of orientation. These individuals should be selected for their social skills and be given time off from their own work to

---

[23]Douglas T. Hall and Francine S. Hall, "What's New in Career Management," *Organizational Dynamics,* Summer 1976, pp. 21–27.

[24]Cynthia D. Fisher, "The Role of Social Support in Organizational Socialization," *Academy of Management Proceedings,* 1983.

spend with the new people. The degree to which the orientation program is formalized can vary, but in any case, the program should not be left to chance.

Training programs are invaluable in the breaking-in stage. Without question, training programs are necessary to instruct new employees in proper techiques and to develop requisite skills. Moreover, effective training programs provide frequent feedback about progress in acquiring the necessary skills. What is not so obvious is the necessity of integrating formal training with the orientation program.

Performance evaluation, in the context of socialization, provides important feedback about how well the individual is getting along in the organization. Inaccurate or ambiguous information regarding this important circumstance can only lead to performance problems. To avoid these problems, it is imperative that performance evaluation sessions take place in face-to-face meetings between the individual and manager and that in the context of the job the performance criteria must be as objective as possible. Management by objectives and behaviorally anchored rating scales are particularly applicable in these settings.

Assigning challenging work to new employees is a principal feature of effective socialization programs. The first jobs of new employees often demand far less of them than they are able to deliver. Consequently, they are unable to demonstrate their full capabilities, and in a sense they are being stifled. This is especially damaging if the recruiter was overly enthusiastic in "selling" the organization when they were recruited.

Assigning demanding bosses is a practice that seems to have considerable promise for increasing the retention rate of new employees. In this context, "demanding" should not be interpreted as "autocratic." Rather, the boss most likely to get new hires off in the right direction is one who has high but achievable expectations for their performance. Such a boss instills the understanding that high performance is expected and rewarded; equally important, the boss is always ready to assist through coaching and counseling.

Socialization programs and practices intended to retain and develop new employees can be used separately or in combination. A manager is well advised to establish policies most likely to retain those recent hires who have the highest potential to perform effectively. This likelihood is improved if the policies include realistic orientation and training programs, accurate performance evaluation feedback, and challenging initial assignments supervised by supportive, performance-oriented managers.

Effective Role Management Socialization

Organizations that effectively deal with the conflicts associated with the role management stage recognize the impact of such conflicts on job satisfaction and turnover. Even though motivation and high performance may not be associated with socialization activities, satisfaction and turnover are, and organizations can ill-afford to lose capable employees.

EXHIBIT 15-6

**A Checklist of
Effective Socialization
Practices**

Socialization Stage	Practices
Anticipatory socialization	1. Recruitment using realistic job previews 2. Selection and placement using realistic career paths
Accommodation socialization	1. Tailor-made and individualized orientation programs 2. Social as well as technical skills training 3. Supportive and accurate feedback 4. Challenging work assignments 5. Demanding but fair supervisors
Role management socialization	1. Provision of professional counseling 2. Adaptive and flexible work assignments 3. Sincere person-oriented managers

Retention of employees beset by off-job conflicts is enhanced in organizations that provide professional counseling and that schedule and adjust work assignments for those with particularly difficult conflicts at work and home. Of course, these practices do not guarantee that employees can resolve or even cope with the conflict. The important point, however, is for the organization to show good faith and make a sincere effort to adapt to the problems of its employees. Exhibit 15-6 summarizes what managers can do to encourage effective socialization.

Mentors and Socialization

In the medical field young interns learn proper procedures and behavior from established physicians; Ph.D. graduate students learn how to conduct organizational research from professors who have conducted studies. What about the process of learning or working with a senior person called a **mentor** in work settings? In Greek mythology the mentor was the designation given to a trusted and experienced advisor. Odysseus, absent from home because of the Trojan Wars, charged his servant mentor with the task of educating and guiding his son. In work organizations a mentor can provide coaching, friendship, sponsorship, and role modeling to a younger, less experienced protégé. In working with younger or new employees, a mentor can satisfy his or her need to have an influence on another employee's career.

Research has indicated that a majority of managers reported having had at least one mentoring relationship during their career.[25] Kram has identified two general functions of mentoring which she designated as career functions and psychosocial functions. The career functions include sponsorship, exposure and visibility, coaching, production, and challenging assignments. The psychosocial

[25]R. J. Burke and C. A. McKeen, "Mentoring in Organizations: Implications for Women," *Journal of Ethics*, April-May 1990, p. 322.

functions are role modeling, acceptance and confirmation, counseling, and friend-ship.[26]

Although mentoring functions can be important in socializing a person, it is not clear that a single individual must play all of these roles. New employees can obtain valuable career and psychosocial influence from a variety of individuals—managers, peers, trainers, and personal friends. At Ford Motor Company, a study was conducted to develop guidelines to socialize new management trainees. En-counter 15–2 shows that various roles are played by different individuals that influence the behavior of new trainees.

Most mentor-mentee relationships develop over time. There appear to be sev-eral distinct phases of mentor-mentee relationships. Exhibit 15-7 presents a four-phase model proposed by Kram. The reasons that cause movement in the rela-tionship are described as turning points. Initiation, cultivation, separation, and redefinition cover general time periods of six months to more than five years.

The benefits that result from mentoring can extend beyond the individuals involved. Mentoring can contribute to employee motivation, retention, and the cohesiveness of the organization.[27] The organization's culture can be strengthened by passing the core values from one generation to the next generation.

The increasing diversity of the workforce adds a new dimension to the mentor-mentee matching process. People are attracted to mentors who talk, look, act, and communicate like them. Gender, race, ethnicity, and religion can all play a role in matching. If mentor-mentee matching is left to occur naturally, women, blacks, Hispanics, and Asians may be left out.[28] The underrepresentation of these groups in management level positions needs to be evaluated in each firm that considers using mentor-mentee matching. One study showed that cross-gender mentor relationships can be beneficial. The results of 32 mentor-mentee pairings (14 male-female; 18 female-female) found that male-female mentor matchings can be successful.[29]

Socializing an Ethnically Diverse Workforce

In the past, white males comprised the dominant ethnic majority, and blacks, Asians, and Hispanics made up the visible ethnic minority groups. Today there are many ethnic groups attempting to become a productive part of the work-force.[30] The minority share of the workforce is expected to grow from approx-imately 17 percent to over 25 percent by the year 2000. Approximately 600,000

[26]Kathy E. Kram, "Phases of the Mentor Relationship," *Academy of Management Journal,* De-cember 1983, pp. 608–25.

[27]James A. Wilson and Nancy S. Elman, "Organizational Benefits of Mentoring," *Academy of Management Executive,* November 1990, pp. 88–94.

[28]Ibid., p. 90.

[29]Ronald D. Brown, "The Role of Identification in Mentoring Female Portages," *Group and Organization Studies,* March–June 1986, p. 72.

[30]Mark Satin, *New Options in America* (Los Angeles: California State University Press, 1981).

MENTORING BY VARIOUS PEOPLE

Ford Motor Company conducted an internal study to determine why some new management trainees became successful while others, who seemed to have good potential, were failures. The conclusions of the big study resulted in a simple common factor: success or failure depended upon whom the trainee worked for at Ford. The study suggested that managers who shaped, mentored, and counseled the best follow these guidelines:

1. *Give trainees small doses.* Don't pile on responsibility after responsibility. Dole out responsibilities, such as settling disputes, evaluating subordinates, or hiring people, one at a time.
2. *Assign an advisor.* Provide the new trainees with an advisor other than his or her boss. An advisor will help the trainee learn the norms and expected behaviors.
3. *Encourage limelight sharing.* Inform and show the trainee that center stage for successes is a team concept. All the credit goes to the team.
4. *Smooth ruffled feathers.* When a new person takes over a unit in which one of the employees expected to take over, the "boss" needs to step in. The "boss" needs to talk to the passed over person immediately. Do not allow ill will to fester. Talk about the decision and ask for cooperation.

New employees face many obstacles. If the introduction of new people is thought out, the results can be positive. Managers at Ford learned that these four simple guidelines made their jobs of integrating new managerial trainees easier.

Source: Adapted from Minda Zetline, "Young Managers Face a Generation Gap," *Management Review,* January 1992, pp. 10–15.

legal and illegal immigrants per year are entering the United States, many seeking employment.

The proliferation of diverse ethnic backgrounds brings to the surface three issues of core values: work ethic differences, norms of behavior that are ethnically rooted, and fit of the person with the firm's culture.[31] Culturally diverse workers attempting to find comfort, be welcomed, and be productive in organizations with established histories, rituals, and ceremonies is likely to be a difficult process.

Management's New Skill

Managers will have to study socialization much more closely and intervene so that the maximum benefits result from hiring an increasingly ethnically diverse workforce. Studying the ethnic background and national cultures of these workers will have to be taken seriously. The managerial challenge will be to identify ways to integrate the increasing number and mix of people from diverse national

---

[31]Philip R. Harris and Robert T. Moran, *Managing Cultural Differences* (Houston: Gulf Publishing Co., 1991).

EXHIBIT 15-7

**Phases of the
Mentor Relationship**

Phase	Definition	Turning Points*
Initiation	A period of six months to a year during which time the relationship gets started and begins to have importance for both managers.	Fantasies become concrete expectations. Expectations are met; senior manager provides coaching, challenging work, visibility; junior manager provides technical assistance, respect, and desire to be coached. There are opportunities for interaction around work tasks.
Cultivation	A period of two to five years during which time the range of career and psychosocial functions provided expand to a maximum.	Both individuals continue to benefit from the relationship. Opportunities for meaningful and more frequent interaction increase. Emotional bond deepens and intimacy increases.
Separation	A period of six months to two years after a significant change in the structural role relationship and/or in the emotional experience of the relationship.	Junior manager no longer wants guidance but rather the opportunity to work more autonomously. Senior manager faces midlife crisis and is less available to provide mentoring functions. Job rotation or promotion limits opportunities for continued interaction; career and psychosocial functions can no longer be provided. Blocked opportunity creates resentment and hostility that disrupt positive interaction.
Redefinition	An indefinite period after the separation phase, during which time the relationship is ended or takes on significantly different characteristics, making it a more peerlike friendship.	Stresses of separation diminish, and new relationships are formed. The mentor relationship is no longer needed in its previous form. Resentment and anger diminish; gratitude and appreciation increase. Peer status is achieved.

*Examples of the most frequently observed psychological and organizational factors that cause movement into the current relationship phase.

Source: Kathy E. Kram, "Phases of the Mentor Relationship." *Academy of Management Journal*, December 1983, p. 622. Used with permission.

cultures into the workplace. Some obvious issues for managers of ethnically diverse workforces to consider are these:

- Coping with employees' unfamiliarity with the English language.
- Increased training for service jobs that require verbal skills.
- Cultural (national) awareness training for the current workforce.
- Learning which rewards are valued by different ethnic groups.
- Developing career development programs that fit the skills, needs, and values of the ethnic group.
- Rewarding managers for effectively recruiting, hiring, and integrating a diverse workforce.
- Spend time not only focusing on ethnic diversity, but also learning more about age, gender, and workers with disability diversity.

Socializing involving an ethnically diverse workforce is a two-way proposition. Not only must the manager learn about the employees' cultural background, but the employee must learn about the rituals, customs, and values of the firm or the work unit.[32] Awareness workshops and orientation sessions are becoming more popular every day. Merck began an educational program in 1979 to raise its employees' awareness and attitudes about women and minorities.[33] The program emphasizes how policies and systems can be tailored to meet changes in the demographics of the workplace. Procter & Gamble has stressed the value of diversity. The firm uses multicultural advisory teams, minority and women's networking conferences, and "onboarding" programs to help new women and minority employees become acclimated and productive as quickly as possible. Ortho Pharmaceutical initiated a program to "manage diversity" that is designed to foster a process of cultural transition within the firm. Northeastern Products Company established an onsite English as a Second Language (ESL) program to meet the needs of Hispanic and Asian employees. A buddy system has been established at Ore-Ida. A buddy (English speaker) is assigned to a new employee (first language is not English) to assist him or her with communication problems.

Global competition, like changing domestic demographics, is placing a new requirement on managers to learn about unfamiliar cultures from which new employees are coming. The emphasis of open expression of diversity in the workforce is paralleled by a social movement toward the retention of ethnic roots. The "new ethnicity," a renewed awareness and pride of cultural heritage can become an advantage of American firms operating in foreign countries.[34] Using the multicultural workforce to better compete, penetrate, and succeed in foreign cultures is one potential benefit of managing diversity effectively.

[32]Taylor Cox, Jr., "The Multicultural Organization," *The Academy of Management Executive,* May 1991, pp. 34–47.

[33]David Jamieson and Julie O'Mara, *Managing Workforce 2000* (San Francisco: Jossey-Bass, 1991), pp. 84–89.

[34]Charles Garfield, *Second to None* (Homewood Ill.: Business One Irwin, 1992), pp. 283–85.

Certainly, claiming that having employees from different cultural backgrounds only provides benefits is misleading. Ethnic and cultural diversity creates some potential problems like communications, misunderstanding, and responding to authority. The managers involved in this socialization process need to clearly recognize the benefits and the potential problems of working with a more diverse workforce.

SOCIALIZATION AS AN INTEGRATION STRATEGY

Our discussion has emphasized the interrelationships between socialization processes and career effectiveness. Yet it is possible to view socialization as a form of organizational integration. Specifically, socialization from the integration perspective is a strategy for achieving congruence of organizational and individual goals. Thus, socialization is an important and powerful process for transmitting the organizational culture.[35] The content of socialization strategies are practices and policies that have appeared in many places throughout this text. Here we can summarize not only our discussion of career and socialization processes but also cast some important organization behavior concepts and theories in a different framework.

Organizational integration is achieved primarily by aligning and integrating the goals of individuals with the objectives of organizations. The greater the congruity between individual goals and organization objectives, the greater the integration. The socialization process achieves organization integration by, in effect, undoing the individual's previously held goals and creating new ones that come closer to those valued by the organization. In its most extreme form, this undoing process involves debasement techniques such as those experienced by U.S. Marine Corps recruits, military academy plebes, and fraternity and sorority pledges.

Integration of organizational and individual interests can also involve ethical issues. These ethical issues are most evident when the two parties do not share the same information or hold the same legitimate power.

Rensis Likert is a spokesperson for the use of leader and peer socialization. While presenting his ideas on leadership theory, Likert stresses the importance of the leader who maintains high performance standards and group-centered leadership techniques. The leader sets high standards for his or her own behavior and performance and through group-centered leadership encourages the group to follow the example. If successful, the leader creates a group norm of high performance that is apparent to a new employee assigned to the group.

Finally the 9,9 theory of leadership, which is explained in Chapter 16, involves the development of mutual understanding of objectives through discussions among the group's leader and its members. This understanding represents a balanced

[35]J. E. Hebden, "Adopting an Organization's Culture: The Socialization of Graduate Trainees," *Organizational Dynamics,* Summer 1986, pp. 46–72.

but high concern for both people and production needs. The group acts to achieve the objectives of the group and represents the legitimacy of the objectives to new group members.

The common thread running throughout leadership theories is the active role played by the leader and the group members in integrating goals and objectives. Effective socialization, particularly during the accommodation and role management stages, requires joint and supportive efforts of leaders and peers alike.

ORGANIZATIONAL CAREERS

Career: A Definition

The popular meaning of **career** is reflected in the idea of moving upward in one's chosen line of work. Moving upward implies commanding larger salaries; assuming more responsibility; and acquiring more status, prestige, and power. Although typically restricted to lines of work that involve gainful employment, we can certainly relate the concept of career to homemakers, mothers, fathers, volunteer workers, civic leaders, and the like. These people also advance in the sense that their knowledge and skills grow with time, experience, and training. Here we restrict our attention to careers of those in organizations; however, doing so does not deny the existence of careers in other contexts.

The definition of career as used in this discussion is as follows:

> *The career is the individually perceived sequence of attitudes and behaviors associated with the work-related experiences and activities over the span of the person's life.*[36]

This definition emphasizes that a *career* consists of both attitudes and behaviors and that it is an ongoing sequence of work-related activities. Yet even though the career concept is clearly work related, it must be understood that a person's nonwork life and roles play a significant part in it. For example, a 50-year-old midcareer manager can have quite different attitudes about job advancement involving greater responsibilities than a manager nearing retirement. A bachelor's reaction to a promotion involving relocation is likely to be different from that of a father of school-age children. The end-of-chapter case "Refusing a Promotion" provides an opportunity to examine in more detail the career impact of nonwork life roles.

▲ **C15–1**

CAREER CHOICES

How do people get into particular occupations and professions? Is it by chance or by choice? Although the matter of matching individuals and careers is vitally important for individuals, organizations, and society, career guidance and counseling is far from a precise science. The most obvious complication is the inherent

---

[36]Douglas T. Hall, ed., *Career Development in Organizations* (San Francisco: Jossey-Bass, 1986).

EXHIBIT 15-8

Holland's Six Personality Types and Compatible Occupations

Type	Characteristics	Occupations
Realistic	Aggressive behavior; prefers activities requiring skill, strength, and coordination	Forestry, farming, architecture
Investigative	Cognitive behavior; prefers thinking, organizing, and understanding activities	Biology, mathematics, oceanography
Social	Interpersonal behavior; prefers feeling and emotional acitivities	Clinical psychology, foreign service, social work
Conventional	Structured behavior; prefers to subordinate personal needs to other's needs	Accounting, finance
Enterprising	Predictable behavior; prefers power and status acquisition acitivities	Management, law, public relations
Artistic	Self-expressive behavior; prefers artistic, self-expressive, and individualistic activities	Art, music, education

tendency of individuals to change their interests, motivations, and abilities. But equally obvious today is the fact of changing career demands. Technology has brought irrevocable change, for example, to the demands on those seeking careers in office work, factories, medicine, banking, and government service. Thus, an individual may prepare for a career but subsequently discover that technology had made that preparation obsolete and irrelevant.

A reasonable way to understand career choice is that individuals tend toward careers that are consonant with their own personal orientations. This line of thinking underlies an important theory of career choices which John Holland developed.[37]

According to Holland, individuals can be classified into six personality types that coincide with the six occupational types. If people do gravitate toward those occupational types that coincide with their personality types, and if Holland's personality and occupational types are valid, these individuals can make informed career choices. Holland's personality types and compatible occupations are shown in Exhibit 15-8.

Holland and others have devised paper and pencil tests that identify an individual's primary orientation. Many counseling centers in high schools use the test as one basis for advising students about educational and career tracks. The idea

[37]John L. Holland, *Making Vocational Choices: A Theory of Careers* (Englewood Cliffs, N.J.: Prentice-Hall, 1973). Discussion of Holland's theory is based on Douglas T. Hall, *Careers in Organizations* (Santa Monica, Calif.: Goodyear Publishing, 1976), pp. 13–15. Manuel London, "Toward a Theory of Career Motivation," *Academy of Management Review*, October 1983, pp. 620–30, is an extensive review of the literature.

is rather straightforward: Individuals whose career choices match their personality types will probably persist in the required educational preparation and prosper in a subsequent career.

Holland's theory and the counseling practices based on it are not, in all instances, valid. But they are sufficiently widespread to command considerable attention. The theory and practices have been subjected to continued study to validate their applicability for both initial and subsequent career choices. The importance of career choice decisions as a factor in career effectiveness cannot

■ **E15–2**   be overvalued.[38] Questions in Exercise 15–2 will help you make sound career choice decisions.

CAREER PERFORMANCE

In organizational settings, career performance is judged not only by the individual but also by the organization itself and is affected by a number of variables, including the length of job experience.[39] The most popular indicators of career performance, however, are salary and position. Specifically, the more rapidly one's salary increases and the more rapidly one advances up the organizational hierarchy, the higher the level of career performance. The higher one advances, the greater the responsibility for employees supervised, budget allocated, and revenue generated. The organization is, of course, vitally interested in career performance since it bears a direct relation to organizational effectiveness. That is, the rate of salary and position advancement reflects in most instances the extent to which the individual has contributed to the achievement of organizational performance.

Two points should be made: First, to the extent that the organization's performance evaluation and reward process do not fully recognize performance, individuals may not realize this indicator of career effectiveness. Thus, individuals may not receive those rewards, salary, and promotions associated with career effectiveness because the organization either does not or cannot provide them.

■ **E15–1**   Examine Exercise 15–1 and consider the difficulty a manager faces when an excellent performer is not promoted. Many employees discover that organizations often state they reward performance when, in fact, they reward other, nonperformance outcomes.[40] Second, the organization may have expectations for the individual's performance that the individual is unwilling or unable to meet. The organization may accurately assess the individual's potential as being greater than

---

[38]William L. Mihal, Patricia S. Sorce, and Thomas G. Comte, "A Process Model of Career Decision Making," *Academy of Management Review,* January 1984, pp. 95–103; and London, "Toward a Theory of Career Motivation."

[39]Mary McEnrue, "Length of Experience and the Performance of Managers in the Establishment Phase of Their Careers," *Academy of Management Journal,* March 1988, pp. 175–85.

[40]Roy J. Lewicki, "Organizational Seduction: Building Commitment to Organizations," *Organizational Dynamics,* Autumn 1981, p. 9.

present performance, yet because the individual has other, nonjob interests (for example, family, community, religious), performance does not match potential. In such instances, the individual may be satisfied with career performance, yet the organization is disappointed.

CAREER STAGES

Individuals typically move through distinct **career stages** during the course of their lives.[41] Although numerous descriptive labels have been proposed to identify these stages, we use a four-stage model: *establishment, advancement, maintenance,* and *withdrawal.*[42] The establishment stage occurs at the onset of the career. The advancement stage is a period of moving from job to job, both inside and outside the organization. Maintenance occurs when individuals have reached the limits of advancement and concentrate on the jobs they are doing. Finally, at some point prior to actual retirement, individuals go through the withdrawal stage. The duration of each stage varies among individuals, but in general they each go through all of them.

Needs and expectations change as individuals move through each career stage. A study of managers at American Telephone & Telegraph (AT&T) revealed considerable concern for security needs during the *establishment* phase.[43] During establishment, individuals require and seek support from others, particularly their managers, and it is important for managers to recognize this need and to respond by assuming the role of mentor.[44] During the *advancement* stage, AT&T managers expressed considerably less concern for security and more concern for achievement, esteem, and autonomy. Promotions and advancement to jobs with responsibility and opportunity to exercise independent judgment are characteristics of this stage. But the specific factors that explain why some individuals advance,

● **R15–1**

while others do not, remain obscure.[45] As the reading selection which accompanies this chapter suggests, advancement may be blocked by one's own limitations, by being in the wrong place, or by one's peers or immediate superiors.

An interesting career stage issue involves Americans who decide to start careers in other countries. Encounter 15-3 describes some views held by two young

[41]Nigel Nicholson, "A Theory of Work Role Transitions," *Administrative Science Quarterly,* June 1984, pp. 172–91.

[42]Lloyd Baird and Kathy Kram, "Career Dynamics: Managing the Superior/Subordinate Relationship," *Organizational Dynamics,* Spring 1983, p. 47. Also see Paul H. Thompson, Robin Zenger Baker, and Norman Smallwood, "Improving Professional Development by Applying the Four-Stage Career Model," *Organizational Dynamics,* Autumn 1986, pp. 49–62.

[43]Douglas T. Hall and Khalil Nougaim, "An Examination of Maslow's Need Hierarchy in an Organizational Setting," *Organizational Behavior and Human Performance,* 3, 1968, pp. 12–35.

[44]David M. Hunt and Carol Michael, "Mentorship: A Career Training and Development Tool," *Academy of Management Review,* July 1983, pp. 475–85.

[45]John F. Veiga, "Mobility Influences during Managerial Career Stages," *Academy of Management Journal,* March 1983, pp. 64–85.

AMERICANS WITH CAREERS IN JAPAN

There is not much written or discussed about American expatriates who have decided to start and maintain management careers in Japan. There are thousands of Americans who have decided to work for Japanese companies in Japan. Derek C. Johnston works in the planning and research department of DISCO, Inc., and Timothy Rowe works as a research associate in the research and development strategy department of Mitsubishi Research Institute, Inc. They enjoy the opportunities they have working in Japan for Japanese firms.

INTERVIEWER: So, you looked for employment in Japanese firms. How was that? What is your impression of the Japanese firm? Is there a gap between the ideal and the reality after all?

TIMOTHY ROWE: Japanese people like working overtime. You find that in any Japanese firm. After hours entertaining, getting together with co-workers to discuss things outside of the workplace, and so forth.

INTERVIEWER: Based on your experience, is there any advice for your friends?

TIMOTHY ROWE: What I would suggest to my friends back in America would be a little tiny company. If you want good experience in Japan, the best place to work is a small company where you're a foreigner . . .

DEREK JOHNSTON: A friend of mine took a job in a large company, and after several years he says he's never even seen the President's face. Everyone's so busy they have no time to socialize.

INTERVIEWER: Do you think you want to work in Japan for your entire career?

TIMOTHY ROWE: I don't intend to stay in Japan my whole life. . . . The number of foreign workers in Japan must grow because of the labor shortage.

Timothy Rowe and Derek Johnston made career choices that took them to Japan. They seem to think they made the right choice.

Source: Adapted from *Nikkei Placement Guide, International Career Forum,* Autumn 1991, pp. 18–26.

Americans working for Japanese firms in Japan. They decided to establish their careers in Japan.

The *maintenance* stage is marked by efforts to stabilize the gains of the past. In some respects this phase is analogous to a plateau—no new gains are made, yet it can be a period of creativity since the individual has satisfied many of the psychological and financial needs associated with earlier stages. Although each individual and career is different in actuality, it is reasonable to assume that esteem is the most important need in the maintenance stage. Many people experience a *midcareer crisis* during the maintenance stage. Such people are not successfully achieving satisfaction from their work and may, consequently, experience physiological and psychological discomfort. They may experience poor health and a heightened sense of anxiety. They no longer desire to advance, and

EXHIBIT 15-9

**Characteristics of
General Career Stages**

	Stage			
	Establishment	Advancement	Maintenance	Withdrawal
Age	**18-24**	**25-39**	**40-54**	**55-65**
Primary work-related activities	Obtaining job-related skills and knowledge	Becoming an independent contributor	Developing the skills of others	Sharing work experiences with others
Primary psychological demands	Being dependent on others for rewards	Being dependent on self for rewards	Being dependent on others for need satisfaction	Letting go of work identity
Primary need satisfaction	Security	Achievement autonomy	Esteem	Self-neutralization

consequently, they underperform. They then lose support of their managers, which further intensifies the health and job problems.[46]

The maintenance phase is followed by the *withdrawal stage.* The individual has, in effect, completed one career and may move on to another.[47] During this stage, the individual may have opportunities to experience self-actualization through activities that were impossible to pursue while working. Painting, traveling, gardening, and volunteer service are some of the many positive avenues available to retirees.

Some of the important characteristics of career stages are summarized in Exhibit 15-9. This exhibit depicts careers in context of organizations. It also reflects the passage of an individual along a traditional career path.

How successful a career an individual will have is obviously a function of a great number of factors, including talent, knowledge, adaptability, degree of motivation and commitment, and to some extent, luck. Career success can also be aided or hindered by the organization by which the individual is employed.

[46]Janet P. Near, "Work and Nonwork Correlates of the Career Plateau," *Academy of Management Proceedings,* 1983, pp. 380–84.

[47]James B. Shaw, "The Process of Retiring: Organizational Entry in Reverse," *Academy of Management Review,* January 1981, pp. 41–47.

SUMMARY OF KEY POINTS

- *Culture* is a pattern of assumptions that are invented, discovered, or developed to learn to cope with organizational life. *Socialization* is the process by which organizations bring new employees into the culture. *Career* is the individually perceived sequence of attitudes and behaviors associated with the work-related experiences and activities over the span of the person's life.

- Simply declaring that "this" will be the culture is not realistic. Culture evolves over a period of time. It can be influenced by powerful individuals such as Ray Kroc at McDonald's or Walt Disney, but it typically evolves and becomes real when people interact and work together.

- Individuals typically move through distinct career stages. The *establishment* phase is at the early career point where the person acquires skills and knowledge. At the *advancement* stage a person is becoming confident and independent. At the *maintenance* stage the employee is helping others develop their skills. The *withdrawal* stage involves letting go of the work identity and phasing out.

- The dynamics of career choices are vaguely understood. One of the more influential theories of career choice is that which Holland advances. According to this theory, individuals choose careers compatible with their personality types. Moreover, according to the theory, there are definite relationships between certain personality types and occupational characteristics.

- Organizational socialization processes coincide with the stages of careers. Anticipatory socialization occurs with the prework career stage. Accommodation occurs with the establishment and advancement career stages, and role management occurs with the maintenance stage. The coincidence of socialization and career development stages enables management to implement practices that maximize the chances for achieving the mutual needs of the individual and the organization.

- The success of organizational socialization depends on how well the socialization activities meet the needs of the individual and the organization at each career stage. Usual organizational practices such as recruitment, selection, and placement can be important parts of an effective socialization process if management thinks of them as meeting individual as well as organizational needs.

REVIEW AND DISCUSSION QUESTIONS

1. In what ways are socialization and career development interrelated? Is the interrelationship more important from the perspective of the organization or of the individual?

2. Since the process of organizational socialization is inevitable, why is it important that it be managed?

3. In Chapter 4 the concept of a psychological contract was introduced. Is there a relationship between the socialization process and the psychological contract? Explain.

4. Individuals do not have to be members of formal work organizations to have careers. Has there been an increase in recent years in these nontraditional careers? Are there significant age and gender differences between individuals following traditional and nontraditional careers?

5. Do you think organizations have a moral obligation to provide career counseling to employees? If so, why? If not, why not?

6. Is it likely that an individual can have a successful career in an organization and not be socialized? Does being properly socialized ensure career success?

7. Identify the three socialization stages. Which of these stages is most important for developing high-performing employees? Explain.

8. Have you made a career choice? How likely is it that your current choice will reflect the career you will be in upon retirement? Can you identify the most important factors influencing your choice?

9. Organizational culture is a difficult concept to diagnose. How would you diagnose the culture of an office or a manufacturing plant?

10. A growing number of Americans work for Japanese-owned firms in the United States. Do you think that these American employees are being influenced by the Japanese approach to management and the culture of Japan? Explain.

•

READING

READING 15–1 BLOCKED!

Lester Korn

At least once a year, the rising executive has to take a long, hard look around and decide whether he or she is facing any brick walls. Are there any impediments on the upward path?

Blocks do crop up in every career. The successful acknowledge them and deal with them. First of all, they try to see them coming. "When trouble is sensed well in advance it can easily be remedied," Machiavelli wrote. "As the doctors say of a wasting disease, to start with it is easy to cure but difficult to diagnose; after a time, unless it has been diagnosed and treated at the outset, it becomes easy to diagnose but difficult to cure."

The successful are never passive. They do not just sit at their desks day after day and assume that everything will work out for the best. When they are stymied by a block, they take steps to surmount it. They do not live with a bad situation. They change it. If nothing is happening, good or bad, they shake things up. They do not sit and look at the scenery.

There is a wide variety of common career blocks, and a variety of effective responses to them.

BLOCKED BY ONE'S OWN LIMITATIONS

This is a self-imposed block. It results from a failure of initiative or imagination. Those who suffer from it are generally doing their jobs well, but they are not doing them extraordinarily well. They often fail to realize what their employers value most.

"What I tell new people," says William Smithburg, chairman of Quaker Oats, "is, 'Look, in your first year or two, if you're one of seven or eight people working on a brand, there will be a lot of grunt work, a lot of number-pushing. Do what your boss asks you to do. Do it well. But at the end of one year, ask yourself, "What ideas do I now have for that brand? What ideas do I have to try something different?" '

Source: Lester Korn, "Blocked!" *Across the Board,* January 1988, pp. 54–59.

"Say, you've been on Cap'n Crunch for a year. You're an intelligent person. You've done everything you've been asked to do. You've knocked out the financial reports. You've been working for the sales force on all the logistics and trade allowances. Now, after one year, what can you suggest we do that is new and unique and different? Put it down in writing and give it to your brand manager. If he or she rejects it, don't worry about it. Try another idea in three months. Try another one in three more months. Keep coming up with ideas.

"A few years ago Cap'n Crunch ran a promotion in which children called an 800 number. That brand manager didn't necessarily come up with that idea, but he dealt with the outside creative source, the promotion consultant, who did. He managed the process, and the brand just took off. Twenty-four million children called.

"That manager was on the brand for two years and was then promoted. His successors, three successors in a row, came up with no such excellent promotions, just one kind of boring premium promotion after another, and the brand slowly began to go down. . . . I said, 'I don't see why a manager doesn't just take the same damned [telephone] promotion that we ran and change the names of the characters if he cannot come up with anything new, because kids under six years old are all regenerated every few years anyway.' But people do not like to do what the guy before them did.

"The guy who was the fourth manager after [the one who ran the telephone promotion] came on two years ago. I normally don't personally have a lot of discussions with brand managers, but I happened to know this guy. So I said, 'Jerry, for God's sake, please do something exciting. Go out and talk to ad agencies. Go out and talk to promotional suppliers. Go dig up the guy who came up with the telephone idea. Please come up with a promotion.' He did that, and the brand had a big promotion [in which it was announced that Cap'n Crunch was lost and children participated in solving the mystery of his disappearance]. When he brought it in to show it to me, I said, 'Fine. . . . Now start worrying about next year.'

"The point is: think ahead, be innovative, take prudent risks. The money spent on the mystery promotion was enormous—$10 million or $15 million over 90 days. During the 'me-too' period, when the brand had just a cheap premium or a mail-in thing with me-too commercials, it may have run $7 million or $8 million a quarter. To do the real big one costs more. There's a risk in that. But you have to do it."

And what happened to the managers who ran the "me-too" campaigns?

"Two are with other companies, and one is with us in marketing research, where he can be very studious and all that, but not a decision maker. Their failure was a failure to do *anything*. I've got another guy running Gatorade, a high-potential guy. He happened to introduce a cereal that failed. But that's not the end of the world, to have a failure. I want people who are willing to take those risks. The biggest risk of all is to take no risks."

BLOCKED BY ONE'S OWN SUCCESS

This is a pleasant sort of block, until its consequences begin to come clear. Those who suffer from it are performing their jobs too well—or at least well enough that their employers do not want to shift them out of their present positions. They are so important in their jobs that replacing them there would be a hardship.

One deals with this situation by keeping one's career goals in mind at all times. Identify the next position to which you wish to be promoted, make a point of satisfying whatever criteria that job requires, and make sure your employer knows that you expect to get it once you deserve it. Finally, make things a little easier for your employer. Groom your own successor for your present job.

A similar kind of block is faced by a talented young man I know who works for one of the Big Eight accounting firms. His employers are very pleased with him and have high hopes for him. They are, in fact, grooming him for a partnership.

To develop his skills in managing an office and building up a practice, they have assigned him to run the firm's office in a minor city. They do not intend to keep him out of the mainstream forever, just long enough to polish some of the skills they seek in their partners. He will be away long enough, however, to miss many other opportunities. In his previous assignment, he was handling the accounts of major corporate clients, any one of whom might have been sufficiently impressed with him to offer him a job and turn his career in a different direction. Now, in addition to being out of sight, he is working in areas that will be of no use to any employer but his present one. He

is becoming a good "organization man" for one organization; he is no longer gaining the kind of experience that will make him valuable to others. He is at a career crossroads, and he has got to recognize that. If he is certain that his goal is to be a partner in the accounting firm, then he is on the right track. If he aspires to anything else in the world of business, however, he must make a move soon.

BLOCKED BY BEING IN THE WRONG PLACE

An ambitious executive should beware of certain kinds of companies and certain divisions within companies. Family-owned companies, for example, may offer limited opportunities for promotion, because the top spots are often filled by family members. If the top spots are not filled by members of the family, there is still good reason for caution. The family may be inclined to sell the company.

The most common "wrong-place" blockage occurs in companies that are candidates for sale or merger, or are simply on the way down. Senior executives that were surveyed by my firm listed slow growth and prospective mergers or reorganizations as the primary threats to their careers.

Companies that face possible sale or merger are not bad places for everyone, however. If you were making a career in the broadcasting division of NBC when RCA was acquired by General Electric, you had nothing special to fear. NBC was simply exchanging one parent corporation for another. But if you are on the general legal staff of a merging company, you may well be in trouble. Newly merged companies probably don't need two general legal staffs.

Declining companies are, in most cases, good places to leave. Jane Evans resigned from Genesco in 1974, when the company "had begun to experience some severe problems," she says. "I was really questioning what there was going to be for me, or for anybody else, at Genesco at that point, because they were selling off divisions, and they were really paring back the company and they were having some very unsuccessful years." Just at that point, a headhunter called Evans on behalf of American Can. She took the new job—a prudent decision under the circumstances.

If you find yourself in a division with a shrinking market share, or in a troubled company or a dying industry, you ought to begin to look elsewhere. You will be best off beginning to do so before your present employer's problems have come to a head. Bad situations generally take a while to develop. Be alert for them. There is an art to knowing when to get off a dying horse.

But if you have nowhere special to go—no headhunters are knocking on your door—you may have to attempt something even more ambitious than leaving your problem-ridden employer: trying to solve the problem. Major careers can be built by not giving up.

"Back in 1969," recalls Norman Blake, chairman of Heller International Corporation, "I was in Oklahoma City, working for the General Electric Company's information-devices department, which was a manufacturer of computer equipment. At that time, GE was kind of faltering in terms of its competitiveness within that industry. And there was a constant reorganization mode within the company, so there was a real sense of insecurity and volatility.

"At that time, I was a sales specialist and, believe it or not, a systems-designer/product-planner type all kind of rolled into one. I viewed myself as being in a situation that was not conducive to my own development and to gaining recognition for what I might achieve. My boss was a middle-aged fellow and very concerned about his own job security. He was a very nice person, but generally not very effective and not particularly competent. I recognized that he was not going to be the leader and take any sort of risk-taking posture. And they could have used some risk. Basically, nobody took a position on anything.

"So I undertook, of myself, to do a complete analysis of the business. I asked permission to be, on my own time, an internal consultant and assess where I thought the problems were in terms of our competitive posture as a business vis-à-vis the marketplace; in terms of our technology base; and in terms of the quality of our product line, as well as the organization, the quality of management, direction, and so on.

"I asked whether it would be okay if I did it on my own. I asked my boss, and he really didn't say yes and he really didn't say no. I didn't want to push it, but I asked him to write a letter allowing me to interview the managers of the various businesses with the understanding that I would present him with my report, and he could decide what he wished to do. I wrote up the letter and had my boss sign it in a weak moment."

Blake's audacious consulting project turned out to be a success. It won him recognition, and the ideas in his report were a positive contribution to the company.

"After I presented the report, I was asked by the general manager to go back to some of the product section managers and discuss with them more specifically some of these program ideas. In one of these cases, I was asked to stay

on. I said yes. And from that, I got involved in new technology and the new-product development area."

Blake's career began to move, because he had done something to help his employer's business move.

BLOCKED BY ONE'S BOSS

Your upward mobility within a corporation will be heavily dependent on who is in front of you. If your boss is within a few years of your age, you had better decide in a hurry whether he or she is promotable. If the answer is no—he or she is a turkey—you had better start looking for a way to get out from under that boss, or to leapfrog him.

If your boss *is* promotable, the best thing you can do is to help him get promoted as quickly as possible. Make sure you understand how he is evaluated by his boss. Then help him accomplish the things his superiors value the most. Visibility is always important; help your boss get it. When you do something great, share the limelight with him. You don't want to outshine your boss, and you don't want to get on his wrong side. You want to get him promoted, and you want him to recommend you to be his successor. With the right relationship with your boss, you can follow him all the way up to the top of the organization.

Then, of course, things get a little crowded. Companies have only a single CEO. It may be too soon for you to start worrying about that position yourself, but you never know. The day may come.

It didn't come soon enough for Harry Gray when he was at Litton Industries. Gray, who recently retired as chairman of United Technologies, worked at Litton from 1954 to 1971. By the late 1960s, he had the number-three job there and was looking forward to moving up.

His way was blocked by CEO Charles "Tex" Thornton, who had founded the company a few months before Gray joined it. "In the early days," Gray recalls, "Tex used to have a philosophy, which he expressed to a number of us, that nobody should be the CEO of a growing company after age 55. Nobody told him he had to say that, but he did." On many occasions over the years, Thornton talked about his impending retirement, but he never retired. When Thornton was 58, Gray finally entertained an offer from a headhunter to go to what was then United Aircraft. "I had given him three years past his own self-proclaimed retirement age," Gray says. Even then, the two men had a final meeting on the subject.

"He was very upset about [my job offer from United].

He talked to me all day, from 9 in the morning until just about supper. We had lunch together. He didn't do anything else. And I kept asking him, 'What are you going to do about your plan to retire?' And he kept not answering the question. I made the inquiry a minimum of four times. I said, 'Just give me a time frame. I don't care if you're telling me it's going to be three to five years. But I've got to have one.' The key point was that he wouldn't."

Gray took the job at United. More than a decade later, Thornton died—still chief executive of Litton.

Ideally, throughout your career, you will work for people you respect. It will be obvious to you why they are sitting where they are sitting and why you are sitting somewhere beneath them. It is easy to be motivated working for such people. They will move up in the corporate hierarchy, and you will move up behind them.

Such bosses do exist, but so do the other kind—the run-of-the-mill, insecure, screwed-up managers who will neither do their own jobs especially well nor level with you about how you are doing yours. If your boss is incompetent, you have to get out from under him, leap-frogging him if possible, or just moving laterally if necessary.

If, for the moment, you are trapped behind a clunker of a boss, do not despair. Your boss's shortcomings may be obvious not only to you, but also to his superiors. Find out. The corporate grapevine can help you here. So might the industry grapevine outside your company. (When you want to hear what is wrong in your company, often the best way to do it is to talk to your competition.)

If word comes back, either way, that your boss is widely considered a jerk, then he may already be on his way out, which will solve your problems. If he is not going to be fired, you will at least know that there is sympathy for your predicament among the higher-ups. Your temporary lack of progress will not be held against you.

Raymond Dempsey, chairman of the European American Bank, faced such a situation when he was a young assistant treasurer at Bankers Trust in the early 1960s. He was working in a group that was responsible for loans in western Pennsylvania and in the states of Michigan, Ohio, and West Virginia.

"It was, incredibly, probably the most profitable of all the units in the bank, but it was not legitimately adventuresome," Dempsey says. "It was run by a guy who was older and very conservative. . . . It was probably the worst year I ever had in my life, working for this guy. I was allowed to go to places like Wapakoneta, Ohio. I was not allowed to go to any big cities. I was not allowed to call on customers. I was only allowed to call on prospects,

people who *might* do business with the bank. I thought, 'I am not learning anything. I am not growing.' "

Dempsey blamed his boss for his frustration. "The guy was known as a disaster. But at banks in those days, no matter how bad a disaster you were, you worked forever. Nobody ever got fired."

Dempsey decided that he had to take action on his own. "I got to the point where I really felt that if you were legitimately not learning and if you were legitimately being held back, you had two choices. You told the person who could do something about it, or you quit. What you should never do is do nothing.

"I complained to a guy who was my boss's boss's boss. I said, 'I don't want to work for this guy anymore. I am not learning anything.' And the guy had a choice. He could change the situation, he could tell me to shut up, or he could fire me. But you never got fired, so. . ." Dempsey was moved laterally to work under someone he respected.

Lateral moves are also a prescription for another kind of boss blockage. Your boss is perfectly competent, but you and he just don't see eye to eye. You disagree about life in general—or, more to the point, you disagree about your talents and prospects in particular. Whenever you're in the running for a promotion, you want your boss to want you to get that promotion. If your boss thinks you're unpromotable, you've got a serious problem.

BLOCKED BY ONE'S PEERS

Some companies are management-rich. Most are not; most are screaming for truly good mid-level executives. But there are some companies with excellence in depth.

If your company has a large corps of talented people of approximately the same age marching along at approximately the same pace, decide whether you are willing to wait five years to see whether you will be one of the few tapped to break away from the pack. Now may be the time to move somewhere you will be more appreciated. That may be a smaller company or division, or a company or division that obviously needs talented help.

Regardless of how many peers you have, you may be blocked if your boss has a fair-haired boy, and it is not you. If you are always going to rank behind the favorite, and there is room for only one, it is time to move elsewhere, probably laterally within your own company. If you are still on reasonably good terms with your boss, ask him for counsel on making the move.

In all cases, be honest with yourself. The next time you are sitting around the table at a departmental meeting, scrutinize your peers. Ask yourself some questions: Are you better than they are? If not, can you *become* better than they are? If not, can you plan smarter than they can? If not, will you be content remaining behind them? If not, isn't it time to start planning a move?

Every time one of your peers is promoted and you are not, take heed. It does not matter whether the promotion is a substantive one, to a new job with a big raise, or a symbolic one, in which a new title is awarded but nothing else changes. Either way, a signal has been sent. Someone is making it, and others are not.

Do not gloss over such events or rationalize them away. Don't shrug and say, "Oh, well, I am just too young." Or "I didn't get it because they wanted a woman in that job." Or "I didn't get it because they *didn't* want a woman in that job." It is possible that you failed to get the promotion for a trivial or temporary reason. But you cannot afford to rely on that assumption. You must assume that a conscious decision was made not to promote you—and you have to find out why.

First, consult the corporate grapevine and learn everything you can. Why did so-and-so get the new title? Why didn't you? Get as close to the source as you can, whether it is the personnel director or the assistant to the executive who made the decision. Then go to the horses's mouth. Go see your boss, or whoever it was who made the promotion decision. Ask him or her, "Why didn't I get this job?"

Many people are afraid to do this. They acquiesce in the corporate conspiracy of silence, because they are afraid of what they might hear. Even if the news is bad, you are always better off knowing it than not knowing it. You cannot do anything to improve your situation unless you know what your situation is.

It may well be that you were passed over for reasons that are temporary and pose no threat to your future career. But you may have been passed over for more damaging reasons, reasons that are unlikely to go away. Find out, as specifically as you can, what the reasons were in your case, and then act accordingly.

- "You are too young (or inexperienced)." No sweat. This is a problem that will take care of itself. Just get back to work. The next promotion may be yours.
- "You aren't good enough." Bad news. If your boss truly believes that, you must determine whether there is anything you can do that will change his mind. If not, you have got to get the heck out, unless you will be content just to sit at your desk and collect your pay every two weeks for the rest of your life.

- "It is not convenient for the company to promote you at the moment, because we have nobody to replace you in your current position." Groom a replacement. Keep your superiors well posted about his or her promising development.
- "You are too old, too thin, too fat, too short." None of these attributes (with the possible exception of weight) is changeable. Reconcile yourself to never being promoted, or get out.
- "You wear the wrong color suits; your hair is too long; you work too few hours; you work too many hours." You have failed to understand the corporate culture. Get in step. It is not too late.
- "The company wanted to bring in somebody new from the outside to inject some fresh thinking into the operation." You are probably okay, but start doing some fresh thinking yourself. What new and creative ideas do you have for improving the business?
- "You are perfectly well qualified, but no one was really aware of your talents and your desire for the promotion." You are not packaging yourself effectively, and you are not sufficiently visible. Remember, doing good work is only half of what's required to move up. Your boss, and your boss's boss, must know that you are doing good work.
- "You don't have the right kind of experience." Get it. If your company is promoting only marketing people to group jobs, but you are in finance or production, do not ignore the warning signal. Do not simply sit and hope that next time a finance person will get the nod. Confirm the preference for marketing people by talking to those who make the promotion decisions. Then make a lateral move, or do whatever you have to do to get some marketing experience. Ditto if you are on the controller side of the finance department and people with treasury skills are being promoted. Or if you are a brand manager, and sales people are being promoted. Watch for those trends.

In sum, being passed over for a promotion can be a signal to change your career path, to change your job, or to do nothing at all, depending on the circumstances. In any case, it is a time for self-evaluation.

Being blocked is not the same thing as being fired. Most people who are blocked, even blocked permanently, are never fired. So take your time. Think about your career goals. Seek a job that will move you up toward where you want to go, not one that will merely move you out of a bad situation.

■

EXERCISES

EXERCISE 15–1   REORIENTING AN EXCELLENT PERFORMER

OBJECTIVES

1. To examine the process of reviewing career-planning decisions.
2. To illustrate some of the major problems facing individuals involved in the career-planning process.

RELATED TOPICS

Career planning is related to such organizational behavior topics as goal setting, individual growth, and group development.

STARTING THE EXERCISE

Each student should first consider his or her own career and plans for the future. This will set the theme for participating in the exercise.

THE FACTS

Roger Belhurst is a 50-year-old district sales manager for Rockhurst Corporation. He has been in his present position for 10 years. His superior rates Roger as outstanding in every area in the performance evaluation program. Unfortunately, order cutbacks and the lack of promotion opportunities have kept Roger in his current position. In addition, Roger's superior has stated, "Roger is in a position that uses his skills and abilities optimally." Roger disagrees and believes that he is being put on the shelf and will not be promoted. His present attitudes about the company, his job, and the future are poor.

EXERCISE PROCEDURES

Phase I: Group analysis: 15 minutes

The instructor will select two groups of five to seven people. Each group will analyze the Roger Belhurst case. The groups should develop a career plan that would result in an improvement in Roger's overall attitudes. Each group will make a five-minute presentation to the class.

Phase II: Evaluation: 15 minutes

A third group of three to five people will serve as evaluators of the analysis presented by the two groups. The evaluators should develop a set of criteria and apply these to the two five-minute presentations. They should then decide which presentation is better. When one group is presenting the solution to Roger's career plan, the second group should not be present in the room.

Phase III: Critique: 20–30 minutes

The entire class should reflect and critique the presentations and the evaluations. During the critique, the following questions should be answered:

a. Why was one group's analysis and career plan better than the other group's?
b. What criteria were used by the evaluators to rate the two group presentations?
c. What would be Roger's reaction to the career plan?

EXERCISE 15–2   CAREER STRATEGY

What is your career goal?
Have you developed a plan to achieve your goal?

The concepts of business strategy can be adapted to help you formulate, implement, and fulfill your own "mis-

Source: Adapted from Dr. Fred Maidment, *Annual Editions: Management.*
1991/92 (1991), pp. 238–40.

sion" in life. Your personal strategy should be designed to assess and utilize strengths (and overcome weaknesses), to accurately assess the opportunities and threats in the external environment, to develop, assess, and select from available alternatives, and to establish objectives for implementing your career plan. Finally, you will set milestones to provide evaluative feedback as your strategies for a successful and fulfilling career. Remember, strategic planning is a *process*—you can use this plan as a beginning point to review, renew, or adapt your career strategy during your entire work life. Think of this as a beginning rather than an end product.

Although the specific steps in developing a career strategy may vary, the process usually involves these steps: (1) prepare a personal profile, (2) develop professional goals in the form of a mission statement, (3) analyze the external and internal environment, (4) develop strategic career alternatives based on your analyses, (5) evaluate alternatives; select and defend the one most attractive to you now, (6) develop specific short-range career objectives and action plans, and (7) prepare a set of guidelines and milestones for evaluating your strategic plan as you set it into action.

Use these seven steps as major headings for your written career plan; follow directions and suggestions provided under each heading to follow.

1. PREPARE A PROFESSIONAL PROFILE

The personal profile includes two steps, and the first is the most difficult because it asks you to examine yourself. This self-examination is an essential first step in developing a career strategy. Use the "Personal Goals/Values" to establish a set of priorities for yourself; begin by understanding what you value and what you hope to achieve with your life.

Second, examine those constituencies that shape your values and contribute to your life. What effect will home, church, or friends have on your career plans? For example, if you do not wish to move away from your geographic home, this represents a constraint that will be reflected both in your mission and the alternatives available to you.

2. DEVELOP PROFESSIONAL GOALS IN THE FORM OF A MISSION STATEMENT

Mission statements for organizations usually answer these questions: What business(es) are we in, and what business(es) do we want to be in for the future? Analogous individual questions may be: how am I positioned now, and where do I want these skills/interests to lead me? Answer these questions by focusing on the three aspects of mission development: what service/product do we offer the marketplace? Who is our constituency? What is our distinctive competence in the marketplace? In other words, what do you have to offer or hope to offer that distinguishes you from all others? Your mission statement should

be broad enough to encompass the activities you anticipate for your life and work, but not so broad as to be applicable to every other person. Begin to focus your interests on products, markets, and competencies you have.

3. ENVIRONMENTAL ANALYSIS

External Environment. Many factors are beyond organizational control; these same factors are outside your control, but they nevertheless affect your career opportunities. Assess each aspect of the external environment as follows: competition (see *Occupational Outlook Handbook* or similar sources to assess the labor market; see *Industry Surveys* to assess a particular industry of *U.S. Industrial Outlook* for future prospects); economy; geography; technology; demographics (see *American Demographics* or similar sources for information); government rules and regulations.

Analyze these external factors to identify the threats and opportunities for achievement of your mission. If your mission statement focuses on a particular industry, then evaluate the external factors for the industry in this section. Otherwise, evaluate general conditions as they can apply to the general environment for business. Consider how situational conditions may shape opportunities. For example, joining an expanding company usually provides more career opportunities than working for a mature company that is not expected to grow. Similarly, working for a mobile manager means an increased probability that the position of the superior will become vacant; or one might progress along with a competent mobile manager.

While these external factors are listed separately here, we know that they have interactive effects on businesses and they will interact with one another in shaping your career opportunities. Thorough career plans will acknowledge these links. Successful career planning requires a systematic scanning of the environment for opportunities and threats. One has to be concerned about the present as well as forecast the future. Since there are a great many factors that need to be analyzed, planning one's career necessitates being selective and concentrating on those factors critical to personal success.

Internal Environment. What are your strengths and weaknesses, given the external environment you face? If the market is competitive, what will make you most attractive? What weaknesses must you address to compete well in a compact market? Assess these strengths and weaknesses on internal dimensions of the firm as follows:

marketing; management (including values); production; accounting and finance. Make a list of your strengths and weaknesses in each functional area. The relative importance of these skills differs for the various positions in the organizational hierarchy, with technical skills being very important on the supervisory level and conceptual skills being critical for top managers.

By assessing your weaknesses and strengths, now you are preparing to address them in the objectives and implementation phases of your career plan.

Conclude this section by making an overall assessment of your competencies. Do they match the market you face, and if not, what must you do to fill those gaps?

4. DEVELOP STRATEGIC ALTERNATIVES FOR YOUR CAREER

In developing career strategies, several alternatives are available. The most successful strategy would be to build on one's strengths to take advantage of opportunities. For example, if you have an excellent knowledge of computers and many companies are looking for computer programmers, you should find many opportunities for a satisfying career. On the other hand, if you are interested in programming but lack the necessary skills, the proper approach would be a developmental strategy to overcome the weakness and develop these skills in order to take advantage of the opportunities.

Your strategic plan thus far indicates that the market offers specific opportunities and presents threats. In addition, you bring identifiable strengths and weaknesses to that market. A person may have excellent managerial and technical skills but work in a declining company or industry. If this individual wishes to advance, he or she should find employment in an expanding firm or in a growing industry.

Use your environmental analyses to develop two or three viable alternatives for your career. State these alternatives in sentence form, then follow each with a list of the strengths and weaknesses for each alternative. In other words, what makes each attractive or problematic? Be sure that all are viable alternatives, given the market forecast as well as your goals, strengths, and weaknesses.

5. SELECT AN ALTERNATIVE

This is the part of career planning that most people like least—now you have to decide! Many people do not like

making this commitment, fearing that it may limit them. That is true to some extent because every choice eliminates competing alternatives. Moreover, by setting goals we provide a measure by which success or failure can be judged. Sometimes we would rather have things "happen" than acknowledge failure to achieve objectives.

Factors that inhibit goal setting can be used to your advantage. First, as occurs in organizations, performance goals become a part of your personal appraisal process. If you know where you are going and how to get there, then you will be able to recognize and evaluate new opportunities that arise. Second, strategic planning for your career is a process just as it is for organizations. One does not set career goals all at once. Rather, goal setting is a continuing process that allows flexibility; professional goals can be revised in the light of changing circumstances. Another factor that reduces resistance to goal setting is the integration of long-term aims with the more immediate requirement for action. For example, the aim of becoming a doctor makes it easier to study difficult subjects that are necessary for the medical degree.

Strategic choices require tradeoffs. Some alternatives involve high risks, others low risks. Some choices demand action now; other choices can wait. Careers that were glamorous in the past may have an uncertain future. Rational and systematic analysis is just one step in the career-planning process, for a choice also involves personal preferences, personal ambitions, and personal values.

Do your alternatives all pass a consistency test? Are they in line with your preferences, ambitions, and values? Why or why not? Adapt strategies that do not meet the consistency tests.

6. SET OBJECTIVES; ACTION PLAN FOR IMPLEMENTATION

How far in advance should you plan? The answer depends on your goals. Planning should cover a period of time necessary to fulfill the commitments involved in the decision made. Thus, the time frame of your career plan will differ with the circumstances. For instance, if you want to become a university professor, it is necessary to plan for university studies and preparation of seven to nine years. Regardless of your career, your long-term aim has to be translated into short-term objectives.

What are your long-range professional goals? Where do you want to be next year? In five years? In ten years? At retirement, what do you want to have accomplished?

How far do you want to advance? How do you want to be remembered? (see Five-Year Projection below for direction).

So far your concern has been with the career direction. But the strategy has to be supported by short-term objectives and action plans that can be a part of the performance appraisal process. Thus, if the aim is to achieve a certain management position that requires a master of business administration degree, the short-term objective may be to complete a number of courses. Here is an example of a short-term verifiable objective: to complete the Business Policy course this semester with a grade of A. This objective is measurable, as it states what will be done, by what time, and the quality of performance (the grade).

How will you implement your career plan? What steps must you take? How much time will it take to implement your career plan? What are your short-term objectives? What detailed action plans will help you reach these objectives? Objectives must be supported by action plans. Continuing with our example, the completion of the management course may require a schedule for attending classes, doing the homework, and obtaining the support of friends and family, whose time with you is interrupted by university responsibilities. As you can see, the long-term strategic career plan needs to be supported by short-term objectives and action plans.

DEVELOP CONTINGENCY PLANS

Career plans are developed in an environment of uncertainty, and the future cannot be predicted with great accuracy. Therefore, contingency plans based on alternative assumptions should be prepared. While one may enjoy working for a small, fast-growing venture company, it may be wise to prepare an alternative career plan based on the assumption that the venture may not succeed.

If your top career choice is not attainable, what are your other options (given your education, preferences, etc.)? What other career plans do you have?

7. EVALUATION OF THE CAREER PLAN

Once you have articulated career goals, then you can monitor and evaluate your progress toward reaching them. Assuming that you work for a company that has formal evaluation, an opportune time for assessing yearly objectives is at the performance appraisal. This is the time not only to review performance against objectives in the op-

erating area, but also to review the achievement of milestones in the career plan. In addition, progress should be monitored at other times, such as the completion of an important task or project.

Moreover, a career is more than the work you do, but includes other goals important to you. You need to supplement annual performance appraisals with your own schedule of evaluation. How will you monitor your career progress? What factors will you examine? What standards will you use to measure your own performance? How will you know if you are successful? If your interests or other opportunities take you in new directions, when will you revise your career goals?

A career plan doesn't guarantee that you will achieve your goals, any more than a strategic plan guarantees organizational success. What it does provide is a clear set of goals and objectives against which you can assess new opportunities, new challenges, and new directions for fulfilling your mission in life.

FIVE-YEAR PROJECTION

Project yourself into the future five (or ten) years. How old will you be in five years? What will your life be like then? How will your personal, family, and career circumstances have changed by that date? Of course, this is a highly imaginative projection, but attempt to be as realistic and objective as possible.

In completing this projection, you will be bothered by two questions repeatedly: (1) Should I describe my future the way I want it to be? or (2) Should I describe my future the way I really think it is going to be?

You will probably allow both factors to enter into your answers. Such a solution is both natural and desirable. This projection is for your benefit.

1. In five (ten) years my age is _____.
2. My occupation is (be as specific as possible) _____.
3. My specific responsibilities are _____.
4. My approximate annual income (or my family's is) _____.
5. My most important personal possessions are _____.
6. My family responsibilities are _____.
7. Of my experiences in the last few years, the most pleasant were _____.
8. Of my experiences in the last few years, the ones

that gave me the greatest sense of accomplishment were _____.

9. In the last few years, several dramatic things have happened in my business and/or community that have interested me. Below is a summary of the highlights, including a description of how I was involved in these events _____.

10. In reviewing my "Five-Year Projection," the most important observations I made were _____.

▲

CASES

CASE 15–1   REFUSING A PROMOTION

Ron Riddell, 36 years old, is a project manager for the Dowling Products Corporation and has established a reputation as a conscientious, prompt, and creative manager. At present, he is working on a new cleansing product that can be used to clean sink tops. The cleanser is expected to generate gross sales of $3 million the first year it is on the market.

Riddell has a permanent team of eight men and three women and a temporary team of two women and two men assigned to him only for the important cleansing product. The team plans, organizes, and controls the various project phases from development to pilot market testing. The team must work closely with engineers, chemists, production managers, sales directors, and marketing research specialists before a quality product can be finally marketed.

In the past eight years, Riddell has directed four projects that have been considered outstanding market successes and one that has been considered a "superloser" financially. His supervisor is Norma Collins, Ph.D., a chemical engineer. Collins has direct responsibility for seven projects, three of which are considerably smaller than Riddell's and three of which have about the same potential and size as Riddell's.

Collins has recently been selected to be the overseas divisional coordinator of research and development. She and three top executives have met for the past two weeks and have decided to offer her present position to Riddell. They believe that the new job for Riddell will mean more prestige and authority, and certainly an increase in salary.

Collins has been given the task of offering the position to Riddell. This is the discussion that occurred in Collins's office:

COLLINS: Ron, how is the cleansing project going?

RIDDELL: As good as could be expected. I sometimes think that Joe Rambo is trying to slow down our progress. He's a bear to get along with.

COLLINS: Well, everyone has been a little concerned because of the main competitor's progress on their cleansing product. I'm sure we can put everything together and effectively compete in the market.

RIDDELL: I know we can.

COLLINS: I wanted to talk to you about a job that is becoming vacant in 30 days. The executive selection committee unanimously believes that Ron Riddell is the right person for the job.

RIDDELL: What job are you talking about?

COLLINS: My job, Ron. I have been promoted to overseas divisional coordinator of research and development. We want to begin turning over my job to you as soon as possible. If we drag our feet, the cleansing project may not be the success that we need to bolster our financial picture.

RIDDELL: I am flattered by this opportunity and really believe that professionally I can handle the challenge. My real concern is the personal problems I'm having.

COLLINS: Do you mean personal problems here at Dowling?

RIDDELL: No, I mean problems in my family that have led to sleepless nights, arguments with my wife, and hostility between myself and my best neighbor. My brother Mark has been arrested two times recently, once for vagrancy and once for possession of narcotics. As you know, my dad died four years ago and my mother just can't handle the kid. So I have pitched in and am trying to straighten the kid out. Connie, my wife, is fed up with the time I spend here at work and my meddling into my brother's problems. She has even threatened to leave me and take the kids with her to Denver. The new job is really interesting, but I'm afraid it would be the "straw that breaks the camel's back."

COLLINS: I'm sorry to hear about these problems, Ron. I know that it is hard to separate outside problems and pressures from Dowling problems and pressures. If you are going to become a more important part of the management team, that separation will be mandatory. The new job is the challenge that we have trained you for and is a reward for your outstanding past performance. Please think over the job offer and let me know in three days. We need your talents, experience, and leadership.

Riddell left Collins's office with a sick feeling in his stomach. He had worked hard for years, and the goal he was striving for was within his reach. All he had to do was to say yes to Collins. He thought about the additional money, status, and authority attached to the new job. Then he thought about his wife, who had become more depressed about his working on Saturdays and Sundays; his daughter, whom he really had not talked to for six months; his mother, who had helped pay for his college education; and his brother, who always called and asked him to play golf or shoot pool only to be told, "I have to work, Steve. Sorry."

After thinking over the offer for three days, Ron walked into Collins's office.

COLLINS: Come on in, Ron, and relax.

RIDDELL: I can't relax, because I am extremely nervous. I really want the job, but my family must come first.

My daughter, wife, and mother have helped me get to my present position. I just feel that taking on this new job will lead to so many problems that I must turn it down.

COLLINS: I sympathize with your dilemma and wish you the best of luck. I want you to understand, however, that this type of opportunity may never happen again. The company needs your talents now. Can't you get your wife and mother to understand the importance of this job in your career? I just can't believe that they would not understand.

RIDDELL: Norma, we all have priorities and personal backgrounds that just can't be ignored.

COLLINS: Ron, you are sounding like a behavioral scientist. I know that just as well as you. What I'm saying is that you have worked this long and hard and now decide not to accept the challenge. That is what puzzles me.

CASE QUESTIONS

1. What organizational responsibilities does Collins believe that Riddell is shirking by turning down the new job offer?
2. Why would the behavioral orientations of Riddell and Collins differ?
3. Do you consider personal needs and problems as more important than organizational needs and problems? Why?
4. Should organizations force an employee like Riddell to fit their plans for him? Why?

CASE 15–2   THE CONSOLIDATED LIFE CASE: CAUGHT BETWEEN CORPORATE CULTURES

PART 1

It all started so positively. Three days after graduating with his degree in business administration, Mike Wilson started his first day at a prestigious insurance company—Consolidated Life. He worked in the Policy Issue Department. The work of the department was mostly clerical and did

Source: Joseph Weiss, Mark Wahlstrom, and Edward Marshall, *Journal of Management Case Studies*, Fall 1986, pp. 238–3.

The authors thank Duncan Spelman and Anthony Buono for their helpful comments on this text.

not require a high degree of technical knowledge. Given the repetitive and mundane nature of the work, the successful worker had to be consistent and willing to grind out paperwork.

Rick Belkner was the division's vice president, "the man in charge" at the time. Rick was an actuary by training, a technical professional whose leadership style was laissez-faire. He was described in the division as "the mirror of whomever was the strongest personality around him." It was also common knowledge that Rick made $60,000 a year while he spent his time doing crossword puzzles.

Mike was hired as a management trainee and promised

a supervisory assignment within a year. However, because of a management reorganization, it was only six weeks before he was placed in charge of an eight-person unit.

The reorganization was intended to streamline workflow, upgrade and combine the clerical jobs, and make greater use of the computer system. It was a drastic departure from the old way of doing things and created a great deal of animosity and anxiety among the clerical staff.

Management realized that a flexible supervisory style was necessary to pull off the reorganization without immense turnover, so they gave their supervisors a free hand to run their units as they saw fit. Mike used this latitude to implement group meetings and training classes in his unit. In addition he assured all members raises if they worked hard to attain them. By working long hours, participating in the mundane tasks with his unit, and being flexible in his management style, he was able to increase productivity, reduce errors, and reduce lost time. Things improved so dramatically that he was noticed by upper management and earned a reputation as a "superstar" despite being viewed as free spirited and unorthodox. The feeling was that his loose, people-oriented management style could be tolerated because his results were excellent.

A Chance for Advancement

After a year, Mike received an offer from a different Consolidated Life division located across town. Mike was asked to manage an office in the marketing area. The pay was excellent and it offered an opportunity to turn around an office in disarray. The reorganization in his present division at Consolidated was almost complete and most of his mentors and friends in management had moved on to other jobs. Mike decided to accept the offer.

In his exit interview he was assured that if he ever wanted to return, a position would be made for him. It was clear that he was held in high regard by management and staff alike. A huge party was thrown to send him off.

The new job was satisfying for a short time but it became apparent to Mike that it did not have the long-term potential he was promised. After bringing on a new staff, computerizing the office, and auditing the books, he began looking for a position that would both challenge him and give him the autonomy he needed to be successful.

Eventually word got back to his former vice-president, Rick Belkner, at Consolidated Life that Mike was looking for another job. Rick offered Mike a position with the same pay he was now receiving and control over a 14-person unit in his old division. After considering other options, Mike decided to return to his old division feeling that he would be able to progress steadily over the next several years.

Enter Jack Greely; Return Mike Wilson

Upon his return to Consolidated Life, Mike became aware of several changes that had taken place in the six months since his departure. The most important change was the hiring of a new divisional senior vice-president, Jack Greely. Jack had been given total authority to run the division. Rick Belkner now reported to Jack.

Jack's reputation was that he was tough but fair. It was necessary for people in Jack's division to do things his way and "get the work out."

Mike also found himself reporting to one of his former peers, Kathy Miller, who had been promoted to manager during the reorganization. Mike had always "hit it off" with Kathy and foresaw no problems in working with her.

After a week Mike realized the extent of the changes that had occurred. Gone was the loose, causal atmosphere that had marked his first tour in the division. Now, a stricter, task-oriented management doctrine was practiced. Morale of the supervisory staff had decreased to an alarming level. Jack Greely was the major topic of conversation in and around the division. People joked that MBO now meant "management by oppression."

Mike was greeted back with comments like "Welcome to prison" and "Why would you come back here? You must be desperate!" It seemed like everyone was looking for new jobs or transfers. Their lack of desire was reflected in the poor quality of work being done.

Mike's Idea: Supervisor's Forum

Mike felt that a change in the management style of his boss was necessary in order to improve a frustrating situation. Realizing that it would be difficult to affect his style directly, Mike requested permission from Rick Belkner to form a Supervisor's Forum for all the managers on Mike's level in the division. Mike explained that the purpose would be to enhance the existing management-training program. The Forum would include weekly meetings, guest speakers, and discussions of topics relevant to the division and the industry. Mike thought the forum would show Greely that he was serious about both his job and improving morale in the division. Rick gave the O.K. for an initial meeting.

The meeting took place and ten supervisors who were Mike's peers in the company eagerly took the opportunity to "Blue Sky" it. There was a euphoric attitude about the group as they drafted their statement of intent. It read as follows:

TO: Rick Belkner

FROM: New Issue Services Supervisors

SUBJECT: Supervisors' Forum

On Thursday, June 11, the Supervisors' Forum held its first meeting. The objective of the meeting was to identify common areas of concern among us and to determine topics that we might be interested in pursuing.

The first area addressed was the void that we perceive exists in the management-training program. As a result of conditions beyond anyone's control, many of us over the past year have held supervisory duties without the benefit of formal training or proper experience. Therefore, what we propose is that we utilize the Supervisors' Forum as a vehicle with which to enhance the existing management-training program. The areas that we hope to affect with this supplemental training are: a) morale/job satisfaction; b) quality of work and service; c) productivity; and d) management expertise as it relates to the life insurance industry. With these objectives in mind, we have outlined below a list of possible activities that we would like to pursue.

1. Further utilization of the existing "in-house" training programs provided for manager trainees and supervisors, i.e., Introduction to Supervision, E.E.O., and Coaching and Counseling.
2. A series of speakers from various sections in the company. This would help expose us to the technical aspects of their departments and their managerial style.
3. Invitations to outside speakers to address the Forum on management topics such as managerial development, organizational structure and behavior, business policy, and the insurance industry. Suggested speakers could be area college professors, consultants, and state insurance officials.
4. Outside training and visits to the field. This could include attendance at seminars concerning management theory and development relative to the insurance industry. Attached is a representative sample of a program we would like to have considered in the future.

In conclusion, we hope that this memo clearly illustrates what we are attempting to accomplish with this program. It is our hope that the above outline will be able to give the Forum credibility and establish it as an effective tool for all levels of management within New Issue. By supplementing our on-the-job training with a series of speakers and classes, we aim to develop prospective management personnel with a broad perspective of both the life insurance industry

and management's role in it. Also, we would like to extend an invitation to the underwriters to attend any programs at which the topic of the speaker might be of interest to them.

cc: J. Greely
       Managers

The group felt the memo accurately and diplomatically stated their dissatisfaction with the current situation. However, they pondered what the results of their actions would be and what else they could have done.

PART II

An emergency management meeting was called by Rick Belkner at Jack Greely's request to address the "union" being formed by the supervisors. Four general managers, Rick Belkner, and Jack Greely were at that meeting. During the meeting it was suggested the Forum be disbanded to "put them in their place." However, Rick Belkner felt that if "guided" in the proper direction the Forum could die from lack of interest. His stance was adopted but it was common knowledge that Jack Greely was strongly opposed to the group and wanted its founders dealt with. His comment was "It's not a democracy and they're not a union. If they don't like it here, then they can leave." A campaign was directed by the managers to determine who the main authors of the memo were so they could be dealt with.

About this time, Mike's unit had made a mistake on a case, which Jack Greely was embarrassed to admit to his boss. This embarrassment was more than Jack Greely cared to take from Mike Wilson. At the managers staff meeting that day Jack stormed in and declared that the next supervisor to "screw up" was out the door. He would permit no more embarrassments of his division and repeated his earlier statement about "people leaving if they didn't like it here." It was clear to Mike and everyone else present that Mike Wilson was a marked man.

Mike had always been a loose, amiable supervisor. The major reason his units had been successful was the attention he paid to each individual and how they interacted with the group. He had a reputation for fairness, was seen as an excellent judge of personnel for new positions, and was noted for his ability to turn around people who had been in trouble. He motivated people through a dynamic, personable style and was noted for his general lack of regard for rules. He treated rules as obstacles to management and usually used his own discretion as to what was important. His office had a sign saying "Any fool can manage by rules. It takes an uncommon man to manage without any." It was an approach that flew in the face of company policy, but it had been overlooked in the past because of his results. However, because of Mike's actions with the Supervisor's Forum, he was now regarded as a thorn in the side, not a superstar, and his oddball style only made thing worse.

Faced with the fact that he was rumored to be out the door. Mike sat down to appraise the situation.

PART III

Mike decided on the following course of action:

1. Keep the Forum alive but moderate its tone so it didn't step on Jack Greely's toes.
2. Don't panic. Simply outwork and outsmart the rest of the division. This plan included a massive retraining and remotivation of his personnel. He implemented weekly meetings, cross training with other divisions, and a lot of interpersonal "stroking" to motivate the group.
3. Evoke praise from vendors and customers through excellent service and direct that praise to Jack Greely.

The results after eight months were impressive. Mike's unit improved the speed of processing 60 percent and lowered errors 75 percent. His staff became the most highly trained in the division. Mike had a file of several letters to Jack Greely that praised the unit's excellent service. In addition, the Supervisors' Forum had grudgingly attained credibility, although the scope of activity was restricted. Mike had even improved to the point of submitting reports on time as a concession to management.

Mike was confident that the results would speak for themselves. However, one month before his scheduled promotion and one month after an excellent merit raise in recognition of his exceptional work record, he was called into his supervisor's, Kathy Miller's, office. She informed him that after long and careful consideration the decision had been made to deny his promotion because of his lack of attention to detail. This did not mean he was not a good supervisor, just that he needed to follow more instead of taking the lead. Mike was stunned and said so. But, before he said anything else, he asked to see Rick Belkner and Jack Greely the next day.

The Showdown

Sitting face to face with Rick and Jack, Mike asked if they agreed with the appraisal Kathy had discussed with him. They both said they did. When asked if any other supervisor surpassed his ability and results, each stated Mike was one of the best, if not *the* best they had. Then why, Mike asked, would they deny him a promotion when others of less ability were approved. The answer came from Jack: "It's nothing personal, but we just don't like you. We don't like your management style. You're an oddball. We can't run a division with 10 supervisors all doing different things. What kind of a business do you think we're running here? We need people who conform to our style and methods so we can measure their results objectively. There is no room for subjective interpretation. It's our feeling that if you really put your mind to it, you can be an excellent manager. It's just that you now create trouble and rock the boat. We don't need that. It doesn't matter if you're the best now, sooner or later as you go up the ladder, you will be forced to pay more attention to administrative duties and you won't handle them well. If we correct your bad habits now, we think you can go far."

Mike was shocked. He turned to face Rick and blurted out nervously, "You mean it doesn't matter what my results are? All that matters is how I do things?" Rick leaned back in his chair and said in a casual tone, "In so many words, Yes."

Mike left the office knowing that his career at Consolidated was over and immediately started looking for a new job. What had gone wrong?

EPILOGUE

After leaving Consolidated Life, Mike Wilson started his own insurance, sales and consulting firm, which specialized in providing corporate-risk managers with insurance protection and claims-settlement strategies. He works with a staff assistant and one other associate. After three years, sales averaged over $7 million annually, netting approximately $125,000 to $175,000 before taxes to Mike Wilson.

During a return visit to Consolidated Life, three years after his departure, Mike found Rick Belkner and Jack Greely still in charge of the division in which Mike had worked. The division's size had shrunk by 50 percent. All of the members of the old Supervisors Forum had left. The reason for the decrease in the division's size was that computerization had removed many of the people's tasks.

CASE QUESTIONS

1. Can a manager such as Jack have such an impact on the culture of a workplace? Explain.

2. How was the Forum perceived by Jack?
3. What norms of expected behavior did Mike violate, if any?
4. How could Mike have done a better job of diagnosing the culture at Consolidated Life after Jack had joined the firm?

16

Organizational Change and Development

LEARNING OBJECTIVES

DEFINE what is meant by the term organizational development

IDENTIFY the major steps to follow in undertaking an organizational development effort

DISCUSS various approaches for dealing with resistance to change

DESCRIBE the three major categories of development methods

IDENTIFY specific development programs within the three categories of methods

RECOGNIZE the conditions which may limit the effectiveness of programs

UNDERSTAND the importance of program evaluation

The process by which managers sense and respond to the necessity for change has been the focus of much research and practical attention in recent years. If managers were able to design perfect sociotechnical organizations and if the scientific, market, and technological environments were stable and predictable, there would be no pressure for change. But such is not the case. As just one example, consider the increasing internationalization of the business environment and accompanying trends toward globalization of an organization's activities. The effective management of increasingly culturally diverse organizational environments that are the result of these changes is critical for maintaining competitiveness.[1] As Encounter 16-1 illustrates, the challenge of mastering the mul-

---

[1]Taylor Cox, Jr., and Stacy Blake, "Managing Cultural Diversity: Implications for Organizational Competitiveness," *Academy of Management Executive*, August 1991, pp. 45–56.

INTERNATIONAL
E N C O U N T E R • 16-1

THE CHALLENGE OF MULTICULTURAL TEAM MANAGEMENT

Organizational activities which require the cooperation of individuals or groups from different cultures are becoming increasingly common in today's global business environment. A short list of specific examples includes American and Japanese employees using the Toyota production system at the carmaker's facility in Kentucky; German and American chemists working as a team at Mobay Corporation, a U.S. subsidiary of Bayer AG; multiple nationalities working together in Paris at IBM Europe's headquarters operation; skilled professionals and managers from several dozen different countries working for Aramco in Dhahran, Saudi Arabia.

Achieving success in multicultural work environments is not easy, but is certainly attainable. Consider a couple of examples from the European aerospace industry: Concorde and Airbus. The Concorde, a joint French and British project encountered difficulties because top management was never able to respond to the problems inevitably encountered when diverse groups collaborate. This inability to respond was a function of being immersed in external and internal politics. Because decisions were made at the ministerial level, managers lacked the authority to do what needed to be done; further, lack of coordination between the governments and the industries of both countries spawned more conflict than cooperation.

In contrast, the Airbus project, a four-nation collaboration involving Britain, France, Spain, and Germany, has been a significant success. Why the difference? In part because Airbus Industrie recognized the difficulties inherent in multicultural collaboration and proactively dealt with them. At Airbus, professionals rather than politicians are in charge. Structurally, Airbus is far more decentralized, and thus its decision-making time is shorter. Additionally, the specific roles of the British, French, Spanish, and German partners are well defined. Managers and technical staff from each of the nations have specific goals and objectives that aid in transcending cultural differences. In short, Airbus has succeeded because it has been sensitive to the unique challenges—and opportunities—inherent in multicultural ventures, and has operated accordingly.

Source: Based in part on information contained in *International Management,* December 1988 and February 1989.

ticultural nature of business enterprise today is met more successfully by some than by others.

The literature and practice that deal with the process of organizational change cannot be conveniently classified because of the yet-unsettled nature of this aspect of organizational behavior. Various conceptualizations and theories and their meanings and interpretations are subject to considerable disagreement. Even the traditional assumptions regarding the basic nature of how organizations experience change are being rethought.[2] Nonetheless, the current trend is to use the term **organizational development (OD)** to refer to the process of preparing for

[2]See, for example, Connie Gersick, "Revolutionary Change Theories: A Multilevel Exploration of the Punctuated Equilibrium Paradigm," *Academy of Management Review,* January 1991, pp. 10–36.

and managing change. This, however, is a very broad statement which fails to address any of the specifics of OD, either in terms of objectives or techniques. The following definition identifies all the significant aspects of OD:

> *The term organizational development* . . . implies a normative, reeducation strategy intended to affect systems of beliefs, values, and attitudes within the organization so that it can adapt better to the accelerated rate of change in technology, in our industrial environment and society in general. It also includes formal organizational restructuring which is frequently initiated, facilitated, and reinforced by the normative and behavioral changes.[3]

The three subobjectives of OD are "changing attitudes or values, modifying behavior, and inducing change in structure and policy."[4] However, it is conceivable that the OD strategy might well emphasize one or another of these subobjectives. For example, if the structure of an organization is optimal in management's view, the OD process might attempt to educate personnel to adopt behaviors consistent with that structure. Such would be the case for leadership training in participative management in an organization that already has an organic structure. Regardless of whether one, two, or all three subobjectives are emphasized, the desired end result of virtually any OD effort is improved organizational functioning.

Organizational development, as the term is used in contemporary management practice, has certain distinguishing characteristics:

1. *It is planned.* OD is a data-based approach to change that involves all of the ingredients that go into managerial planning. It involves goal setting, action planning, implementation, monitoring, and taking corrective action when necessary.
2. *It is problem-oriented.* OD attempts to apply theory and research from a number of disciplines, including behavioral science, to the solution of organizational problems.
3. *It reflects a systems approach.* OD is both systemic and systematic. It is a way of more closely linking the human resources and potential of an organization to its technology, structure, and management processes.
4. *It is an integral part of the management process.* OD is not something done to the organization by outsiders. It becomes a way of managing organizational change processes.
5. *It is not a "fix-it" strategy.* OD is a continuous and ongoing process. It is not a series of ad hoc activities designed to implement a specific change. It takes time for OD to become a way of life in the organization.

---

[3]Alexander Winn, "The Laboratory Approach to Organizational Development: A Tentative Model of Planned Change" (Paper read at the annual conference, British Psychological Society, Oxford, September 1968, and cited in Robert T. Golembiewski, "Organizational Development in Public Agencies: Perspective on Theory and Practice," *Public Administration Review,* July–August 1969, p. 367).

[4]Ibid, p. 367.

6. *It focuses on improvement.* The emphasis of OD is on improvement. It is not just for "sick" organizations or for "healthy" ones. It is something that can benefit almost any organization.
7. *It is action-oriented.* The focus of OD is on accomplishments and results. Unlike approaches to change that tend to describe how organizational change takes place, the emphasis of OD is on getting things done.
8. *It is based on sound theory and practice.* OD is not a gimmick or a fad. It is solidly based on the theory and research of a number of disciplines.[5]

▲ C16–1
▲ C16–2

These characteristics of contemporary organizational development indicate that managers who implement OD programs are committed to making fundamental changes in organizational behavior. The cases at the end of this chapter, "Beta Bureau (A)" and "Beta Bureau (B)" are good examples of a change program that embodies many of these characteristics.

A MODEL FOR MANAGING ORGANIZATIONAL DEVELOPMENT

Any organizational development effort must be designed systematically. This argues for an analytical approach that breaks the OD process into constituent steps, logically sequenced. For this purpose we propose the model shown in Exhibit 16-1, which identifies the key elements and decision points that managers can follow. A manager considers each of them, either explicitly or implicitly, to undertake an OD program.

The model presumes that forces for change act continually on the organization. This assumption reflects the dynamic character of the modern world. At the same time, it is the manager's responsibility to sort out the information that reflects the magnitude of change forces. The information is the basis for recognizing when change is needed; it is equally desirable to recognize when change is not needed. Increasingly, however, change efforts are being utilized to solve an array of organizational problems.[6] Once managers recognize that something is malfunctioning, they must diagnose the problem and identify relevant alternative techniques. The selected technique must be appropriate to the problem, as constrained by certain limiting conditions. Finally, the manager must implement the change and monitor the change processes and results. The model includes feedback to the implementation step and to the forces-for-change step. It suggests no "final solution"; rather, it emphasizes that the manager operates in a dynamic setting wherein the only certainly is change itself.

[5]Newton Margulies and Anthony P. Raia, *Conceptual Foundations of Organizational Development* (New York: McGraw-Hill, 1978), p. 25.

[6]Louis White and Kevin Wooten, "Ethical Dilemmas in Various Stages of Organizational Development," *Academy of Management Review*, October 1983, pp. 690–97.

EXHIBIT 16-1

A Model for the Management of Organizational Development

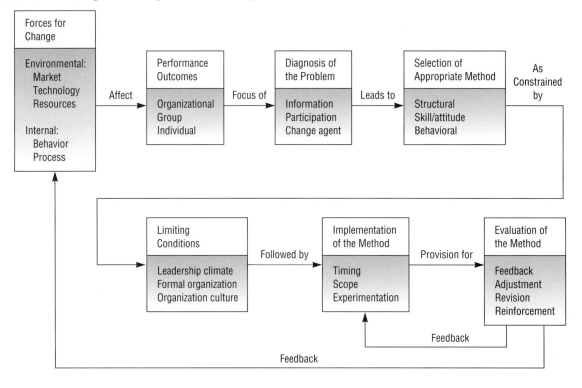

● **R16–1**   The article at the conclusion of this chapter, "Creating Successful Organizational Change," documents a change effort at British Airways. The reading provides an opportunity to see how well you can apply this model to an actual situation.

FORCES FOR CHANGE

The forces for change can be classified conveniently into two groups: (1) environmental forces and (2) internal forces. While many environmental forces are beyond the control of management, internal forces operate inside the firm and generally are within the control of management.

Environmental Forces

The manager of a business firm historically has been concerned with reacting to changes in the *marketplace*. Competitors introduce new products, increase their advertising, reduce their prices, or increase their customer service. In each case, a response is required unless the manager is content to permit the erosion of profit and market share. At the same time, changes occur in customer tastes and incomes. The firm's products may no longer have customer appeal; customers may be able to purchase less expensive, higher quality forms of the same products.

The second source of environmental change forces is *technology*. The knowledge explosion has introduced new technology for nearly every business function. Computers have made possible high-speed data processing and the solution to complex production problems. New machines and new processes have revolutionized the way in which many products are manufactured and distributed. Technological advance is a permanent fixture in the business world, and as a force for change, it will continue to demand attention.

The third source of environmental change forces is *social* and *political* change. Business managers must be tuned in to the great movements over which they have no control but which, in time, influence their firm's fate. Sophisticated mass communications and international markets create great potential for business, but they also pose great threats to those managers who are unable to understand what is going on. Finally, the relationship between government and business becomes much closer as new regulations are imposed.[7] These pressures for change reflect the increasing complexity and interdependence of modern living.

To cope effectively with external changes, an organization's boundary functions must be sensitive to these changes. These boundary functions must bridge the external environment with units of the organization. *Boundary roles* such as marketing research, labor relations, personnel recruiting, purchasing, and some areas of finance must sense changes in the external environment and convey information on these changes to managers.

Internal Forces

Internal forces for change, which occur within the organization, usually can be traced to *process* and *behavioral* problems. The process problems include breakdowns in decision making and communications. Decisions are not being made, are made too late, or are of poor quality. Communications are short-circuited, redundant, or simply inadequate. Tasks are not undertaken or not completed because the person responsible did not "get the word." Because of inadequate or nonexistent communications, a customer order is not filled, a grievance is not processed, or an invoice is not filed and the supplier is not paid. Interpersonal and interdepartmental conflicts reflect breakdowns in organizational processes.

Low levels of morale and high levels of absenteeism and turnover are symptoms of behavioral problems that must be diagnosed. A wildcat strike or a walkout may be the most tangible sign of a problem, yet such tactics usually are employed

---

[7]For a recent example of organizational response to federal policy changes see Ari Ginsberg and Ann Buchholtz, "Converting to For-Profit Status: Corporate Responsiveness to Radical Change," *Academy of Management Journal,* September 1990, pp. 445–77.

because they arouse management to action. A certain level of employee discontent exists in most organizations, and a great danger is to ignore employee complaints and suggestions. But the process of change includes the *recognition* phase, and it is at this point that management must decide to act or not to act.

DIAGNOSIS OF A PROBLEM

Appropriate action is necessarily preceded by diagnosis of the symptoms of the problem. Experience and judgment are critical to this phase unless the problem is readily apparent to all observers. Ordinarily, however, managers can disagree on the nature of the problem. There is no formula for accurate diagnosis, but the following questions point the manager in the right direction:

1. What is the problem as distinct from the symptoms of the problem?
2. What must be changed to resolve the problem?
3. What outcomes (objectives) are expected from the change, and how will those outcomes be measured?

The answers to these questions can come from information ordinarily found in the organization's information system, or it may be necessary to generate ad hoc information through the creation of committees or task forces. Meetings between managers and employees provide a variety of viewpoints that can be sifted through by a smaller group. Technical operational problems may be easily diagnosed, but more subtle behavioral problems usually entail extensive analysis.

■ E16–1   Exercise 16–1 allows you to test out your diagnostic skills by employing a particular organizational technique, namely survey feedback.

Managers must make two key decisions prior to undertaking the diagnostic phase. They must determine the degree to which subordinates will participate in the process, and they must decide whether a change agent will be used. These two decisions have implications not only for the diagnosed process but also for the eventual success of the entire program.

The Degree of Subordinate Participation

The degree to which subordinates participate in decisions that affect their activities has been the subject of much practical and theoretical discussion. Fayol, for example, spoke of the principle of centralization in terms of the extent to which subordinates contribute to decision making. The researchers at the Hawthorne plant discovered the positive impact of supervisory styles that permit employees some say in the way they do their work. In fact, the Hawthorne studies produced the first scientific evidence of the relationship between employee participation and production. Other studies followed, including the classic Coch and French[8]

[8]Lester Coch and John R. P. French, Jr., "Overcoming Resistance to Change," *Human Relations,* August 1948, pp. 512–32.

and Lewin[9] research, which provided evidence that participation by subordinates could lead to higher levels of production, satisfaction, and efficiency. Since this is such an important issue, we will briefly examine one aspect of it here: the extent of subordination participation.

The actual *degree* to which subordinates are actively involved in the development program is not simply an either-or decision. A continuum more aptly describes the decision, as shown in Exhibit 16-2. The exhibit identifies two extreme positions (unilateral and delegated) and a middle-of-the-road approach (shared) to change.[10]

With the *unilateral approach,* subordinates make no contribution to the development, or change, program. The definition and solution to the problem are proposed by management. This may be accomplished by *decree,* a situation in which the superior dictates a program and subordinates are expected to accept it without question. A second unilateral approach is *replacement.* Here, certain personnel are replaced on the premise that key personnel are the crucial factors in developing the organization. Finally, the unilateral approach may focus on *structure,* wherein alterations are made to the organizational structure by administrative fiat.

At the other extreme from the unilateral approach is the *delegated approach.* In this approach, subordinates actively participate in the development program, in one of two forms.[11] In a *discussion group,* managers and their subordinates meet, discuss the problem, and identify the appropriate development method, with the managers being very careful not to impose their own solution on the group. In the *T-group* form, the emphasis is on increasing the individual's self-awareness. Less structured than the discussion group, the T-group is used to initiate the development program and is not the central focus. For example, the T-group could identify MBO as the development method to be implemented.

The *delegated approach* focuses on having the subordinates interact with the superior and eventually work out a development approach. If used correctly, the delegated approach is a major step in creating a climate of full subordinate participation.

Finally, the *shared approach* is built on the assumption that authority is present in the organization and must be exercised after, and only after, giving careful consideration to such matters as the magnitude of the development effort, the people involved, and the time available for introducing the method. This approach also focuses on the sharing of authority to make decisions. It is employed in two slightly different formats:

1. *Group decision making.* The problem is defined by management and communicated to the subordinates. The subordinates are then free to develop

---

[9]Kurt Lewin, "Frontiers in Group Dynamics," *Human Relations,* June 1947, pp. 5–41.

[10]Larry E. Greiner, "Patterns of Organizational Change," *Harvard Business Review,* May–June 1967, pp. 119–30.

[11]Ibid., pp. 121–22.

EXHIBIT 16-2

Strategies for Introducing Major and/or Minor Changes

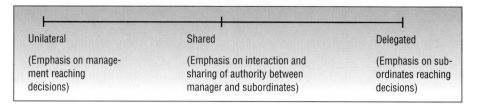

Unilateral	Shared	Delegated
(Emphasis on management reaching decisions)	(Emphasis on interaction and sharing of authority between manager and subordinates)	(Emphasis on subordinates reaching decisions)

alternative solutions and to select what they believe is the best method to be implemented. It is assumed that the subordinates will feel a greater commitment to the solution selected because they participated in its selection.

2. *Group problem solving.* This form stresses both the definition of the problem and the selection of a possible solution. Hence, authority is shared throughout the process, from problem identification to problem solution. It is assumed that because the group is involved in the entire decision process, it will have increased insight into the development program that is finally implemented.

A survey of published cases of organizational change notes that the shared approach was relatively more successful than the unilateral or delegated approaches.[12]

The Role of Change Agents

Because people have a tendency to seek answers in traditional solutions, the intervention of an outsider usually is necessary. The intervener, or **change agent,** brings a different perspective to the situation and serves as a challenge to the status quo.

The success of any change program rests heavily on the quality and workability of the relationship between the change agent and the key decision makers within the organization. Thus, the form of intervention is a crucial phase.

To intervene is to enter into an ongoing organization, or among persons, or between departments, for the purpose of helping them improve their effectiveness.[13] A number of forms of intervention are used in organizations. First is the *external* change agent who is asked to intervene and provide recommendations for bringing about change. Second is the *internal* change agent, an individual who is working for the organization and knows something about its problems. Finally, a number of organizations have used a combination *external-internal* change

---

[12]Ibid., pp. 119–30.

[13]Wendell L. French and Cecil H. Bell, Jr., *Organizational Development: Behavioral Science Interventions for Organizational Improvement* (Englewood Cliffs, N.J.: Prentice-Hall, 1984).

team to intervene and develop programs. This approach attempts to use the resources and knowledge base of both external and internal change agents.

Each of the three forms of intervention has advantages and disadvantages. On the negative side, the external change agent is often viewed as an outsider by company employees, dictating a need to establish rapport between the change agent and decision makers; the change agent's views on the problems faced by the organization often are different from those of the decision maker, leading to problems in establishing rapport; and differences in viewpoints often result in a mistrust of the external change agent by all, or a segment of, the policymakers. On the other hand, arguments in favor of external agents include their objectivity, independence, and specialized skill in introducing change.[14]

The internal change agent often is viewed as being more closely associated with one unit or group of individuals than with any other, and this perceived favoritism leads to resistance to change by those who are not included in the internal change agent's circle of close friends. The internal change agent, however, is familiar with the organization and its personnel, and this knowledge can be valuable in preparing for and implementing change.[15]

The third type of intervention, the combination external-internal team, is the rarest, but it seems to have an excellent chance for success. In this type of intervention, the outsider's objectivity and professional knowledge are blended with the insider's knowledge of the organization and its human resources. This blending of knowledge often results in increased trust and confidence among the parties involved. The ability of the combination external-internal team to communicate and develop a more positive rapport can reduce the resistance to any change that is forthcoming.

Regardless of the form of intervention, the role of the change agent is critical. Change agents facilitate the diagnostic phase by gathering, interpreting, and presenting data. If the diagnostic part of the process is faulty, the remainder of the OD process is significantly flawed.

ALTERNATIVE DEVELOPMENT TECHNIQUES

The choice of a particular development technique depends on the nature of the problem that management has diagnosed. Management must determine which alternative is most likely to produce the desired outcome, whether it involves improvement in skills, attitudes, behavior, or structure. As we have noted, diagnosis of the problem includes specification of the outcome that management desires from the change. Later in the chapter, we describe a number of change

---

[14]Achilles Armenakis and Henry Burdg, "Consultation Research: Contributions to Practice and Directions for Improvement," *Journal of Management,* June 1988, pp. 339–65.

[15]Stephen C. Harper, "The Manager as Change Agent: 'Hell No' to the Status Quo, " *Industrial Management,* May–June 1989, pp. 8–11.

techniques, some of which have been discussed in previous chapters. These techniques are classified according to whether their major focus is to change skills, attitudes, behavior, or structure. This classification of techniques for organizational change in no way implies a distinct division among the areas of change. On the contrary, the interrelationships among skills, attitudes, behavior, and structure must be acknowledged and anticipated.

RESISTANCE TO CHANGE

▲ C16–1

Individuals require a certain amount of stability and predictability in their lives, and change, particularly major change, may threaten this basic need. Change requires adaptation, and as we saw in Chapter 6, certain adaptation requirements may lead to stress. Organizationally imposed changes in work methods, reporting relationships, task assignments, work schedules, and company policies are but a few of the changes to which employees may be asked to adapt. Thus, overcoming resistance to change is frequently a critical variable in ensuring the success of any organizational change effort. Case 16–1, "Beta Bureau (A)," illustrates forces for and against change.

Since every change situation is unique, each must be carefully analyzed to determine the specific forces that may be operating to create resistance to that particular change. Nonetheless, some steps can be taken to minimize that resistance. Kotter and Schlesinger have identified six general approaches for dealing with the problems of resistance to change.[16]

1. *Education and communication.* Provide facts and information through increased communication about the change. This may take the form of one-on-one discussions, group presentations, memos, and reports to educated individuals prior to the change about the need for and rationale of the change.
2. *Participation and involvement.* Allow those affected by the change to have a voice in how the change will occur by allowing (and encouraging) participation in the change design and implementation. Ad hoc committees or task forces can be useful vehicles for increasing involvement in this approach.
3. *Facilitation and support.* Provide training and socioemotional support for dealing with the change. This can be accomplished by instructional sessions, effective listening and counseling, and assistance in overcoming performance pressures that frequently arise in change situations.
4. *Negotiation and agreement.* Offer incentives to actual or potential resistors. This may take the form of bargaining over various aspects of the change and making trade-offs to accommodate the concerns of those affected.

---

[16]John Kotter and Leonard Schlesinger, "Choosing Strategies for Change," *Harvard Business Review*, March–April 1979, pp. 102–21.

5. *Manipulation and co-optation.* Use covert attempts to influence individuals and selectively provide information so that desired changes receive maximum support. It should be noted that this approach can lead to future problems if people feel they are being manipulated.

6. *Explicit and implicit coercion.* Use power and threats of undesirable consequences to resistors if they do not comply with changes. While this can be very successful in overcoming resistance, it is also very risky in that it may result in the formation of undesirable attitudes and subsequent dysfunctional behavior on the part of those coerced.

Resistance to change is not inevitable. Individuals successfully adapt to change constantly; many changes are in fact sought out and welcomed. Managers who wish to maximize acceptance of organizational change would do well to consider the attributes of changes that individuals voluntarily make and readily accept. Taking a trip abroad, moving to a new house, and getting married are all examples of such changes. To varying degrees these changes have a number of attributes in common: They are planned in advance; a great deal of information is available about the change; the change satisfies one or more important needs; there is anticipation that the change will be a positive experience; and it is the individual's choice to experience the change. The greater the extent to which planned organizational change incorporates these attributes, the less likely it is to encounter resistance. Exercise 16–2 points out resisting forces and strategies for reducing resistance to change.

■ **E16–2**

RECOGNITION OF LIMITING CONDITIONS

In addition to the general issue of overcoming resistance to change that is so critical to organizational development programs, certain limiting conditions may also significantly affect the success of such efforts. Scholars identify three sources of influence on the outcomes of management development programs, and these can be generalized to cover the entire range of organizational development efforts, whether attitudinal, behavioral, or structural. The three sources are leadership climate, formal organization considerations, and organizational culture.

Leadership climate refers to the nature of the work environment that results from the leadership style and administrative practices of superiors. Any OD program that does not have the support and commitment of management has only a slim chance of success. The **formal organization** must be compatible with the proposed change. The formal organization includes the philosophy and policies of top management as well as legal precedent, organizational structure, and the systems of control. Finally, the **organizational culture** refers to the impact on the environment resulting from group norms, values, and informal activities. A proposed change in work methods, for example, can run counter to the expectations and attitudes of the work group, and if such is the case, the OD strategy must anticipate the resulting resistance.

Implementation of OD that does not consider the constraints imposed by prevailing conditions within the organization may amplify the problem that triggered the developmental process. If OD is implemented in this way, the potential for subsequent problems is greater than ordinarily would be expected. Taken together, the prevailing conditions constitute the climate for change, and they can be positive or negative. Of course, in many instances it is some aspect of one of these limiting conditions that is itself the target of change. Changing corporate culture, for example, is a frequent objective of development efforts.[17]

IMPLEMENTING THE METHOD

The implementation of the OD method has two dimensions—timing and scope. Timing refers to the selection of the appropriate time at which to initiate the method, and scope refers to the selection of the appropriate scale. The matter of timing depends on a number of factors, particularly the organization's operating cycle and the groundwork that has preceded the OD program. Certainly, if a program is of considerable magnitude, it is desirable that it not compete with day-to-day operations; thus, the change might well be implemented during a slack period. On the other hand, if the program is critical to the survival of the organization, then immediate implementation is in order. The scope of the program depends on the strategy. The program may be implemented throughout the organization, or it may be phased into the organization level by level or department by department. The shared strategy makes use of a phased approach, which limits the scope but provides feedback for each subsequent implementation.

The method finally selected usually is not implemented on a grand scale; rather, it is implemented on a small scale in various units throughout the organization. Not even the most detailed planning can anticipate all the consequences of implementing a particular method. Thus, it may be necessary to experiment and to search for new information that can bear on the program.

EVALUATING THE PROGRAM

An OD program represents an expenditure of organizational resources in exchange for some desired result. The resources take the form of money and time that have alternative uses. The result is in the form of increased organizational effectiveness—production, efficiency, and satisfaction in the short run; adaptiveness and development in the intermediate run; survival in the long run. Accord-

---

[17]For one viewpoint regarding needed organizational culture change, see Joseph H. Boyett and Henry B. Conn, *Workforce 2000: The Revolution Reshaping American Business* (New York: Dutton, 1991).

ORGANIZATIONAL DEVELOPMENT AND THE ROAST PIG PROBLEM

Sometimes, well-intentioned changes in organizations do not work—or do not continue working after initial success—because of what Rosabeth Moss Kanter calls the "roast pig" problem. Out of all the events and components of a change, what is the core that really makes it work? That is, what is the essence of the change? Essentially, this is the problem of understanding *why* something works.

Kanter refers to this as the roast pig problem after Charles Lamb's classic essay, "A Dissertation on Roast Pig," a satirical tale of how the art of roasting was discovered in a Chinese village that did not cook its food. According to the tale, a child accidentally set fire to a house with a pig inside, and the villagers, poking around the ruins, discovered a new delicacy. This even-

tually led to a rash of house fires. The moral of the story is that when you do not understand how the pig gets cooked, you have to burn a whole house down every time you want a roast pork dinner.

The roast pig problem can plague any organization that lacks an understanding of itself or of what is essential to making a change or innovation work and what is superfluous. The consequences of this lack of understanding can be twofold. First, as a particular way of doing things gets locked into place, further experimentation may be discouraged—house burning may become so ritualistic that the search for other cooking methods may end. Second, and perhaps more important, the organization may waste a great number of houses.

Sound, effective organizational development efforts are designed to eliminate the roast pig problem.

Source: Based, in part, on a section from Rosabeth Moss Kanter, *The Change Masters: Innovation for Productivity in the American Corporation* (New York: Simon & Schuster, 1983).

ingly, some provision must be made to evaluate the program in terms of expenditures and results.[18]

Generally, an evaluation would follow the steps of evaluative research. The steps include:

1. Determining the objectives of the program.
2. Describing the activities undertaken to achieve the objectives.
3. Measuring the effects of the program.
4. Establishing baseline points against which changes can be compared.
5. Controlling extraneous factors, preferably through the use of a control group.
6. Detecting unanticipated consequences.

The application of this model will not always be possible. For example, managers do not always specify objectives in precise terms, and control groups are difficult

[18]W. M. Vicars and D. D. Hartke, "Evaluating OD Evaluations: A Status Report," *Group and Organizational Studies*, 1982, pp. 402–17.

to establish in some instances. Nevertheless, the difficulties of evaluation should not discourage attempts to evaluate.[19]

Finally, in addition to being able to determine the extent to which a program or other change effort achieved the desired results, it is important to understand in what ways the change contributed to the results. For example, were all the elements of an OD program essential for obtaining the desired results, or were only some of them critical? This and similar questions are important to ask and answer. Such questions have been referred to as the "roast pig" problem, which was described in Encounter 16-2.

ORGANIZATIONAL CHANGE AND DEVELOPMENT METHODS

As noted previously, effective organizational change and development requires the active involvement of managers. Managers have a variety of change and development methods to select from, depending on the objectives they hope to accomplish. One way of viewing objectives is from the perspective of the *depth* of the intended change.

Depth of intended change refers to the scope and intensity of the change efforts. A useful distinction here is between the *formal* and *informal* aspects of organizations. Formal organizational components are observable, rational, and oriented toward structural factors. The informal components are not observable to all people; they are affective and oriented to process and behavioral factors. Generally speaking, as one moves from formal aspects of the organization to informal aspects, the scope and intensity increase. As scope and intensity increase, so does the depth of the change.

The relationship between the source of the problem and degree of intended change is illustrated in Exhibit 16-3; it suggests there are 10 levels, or targets, of an OD program. As the target moves from left to right and, consequently, deeper into the organization, the OD program becomes more person- and group-centered. It will rely more on sociopsychological knowledge and less on technical-economic knowledge. Levels I through IV involve formal components, including structure, policies, and practices of the organization. Levels V and VI involve both formal and informal components, including skills and attitudes of managerial and non-managerial personnel. Levels VII through X involve informal components, including the behavior of groups and individuals. For each of these levels, one or more OD methods can be possible solutions. These methods are the focus of the remaining discussion.

---

[19]Wendell French, "A Checklist for Organizing and Implementing an OD Effort," in *Organization Development: Theory, Practice, Research,* ed. W. L. French, Cecil H. Bell, Jr., and R. A. Zawacki (Plano, Tex.: Business Publications, 1983), pp. 451–59; and Richard Woodman and Sandy Wayne, "An Investigation of Positive-Findings Bias in Evaluation of Organization Development Interventions," *Academy of Management Journal,* December 1985, pp. 889–913.

EXHIBIT 16-3

Model of Organizational Development Targets

Structural Targets ◄──► Behavioral Targets									
Level I	Level II	Level III	Level IV	Level V	Level VI	Level VII	Level VIII	Level IX	Level X
Organizational structure	Operating policies and practices	Personnel policies and practices	Job performance appraisal and improvement	Management attitudes and skills	Non-management attitudes and skills	Intergroup behavior	Intragroup behavior	Individual behavior	Individual group behavior
Low ◄──────────────────────────────────► Depth of intended change ◄──────────────────────────────────────► High									

Source: Adapted from Richard J. Selfridge and Stanley L. Sokolik, "A Comprehensive View of Organizational Development," *MSU Business Topics,* Winter 1975, p. 49.

STRUCTURAL DEVELOPMENT METHODS

Structural development in the context of organizational change refers to managerial action that attempts to improve effectiveness through a change in the formal structure of task and authority relationships. The organizational structure creates the bases for relatively stable human and social relationships, and these relationships can, in time, become irrelevant for organizational effectiveness. For example, the jobs that people do may become obsolete and thus irrelevant. But to change the jobs also changes the relationships among the employees. Members of the organization may resist efforts to disrupt these relationships.

Structural changes affect some aspects of the formal task and authority definitions. As you have seen, the design of an organization involves the definition and specification of job range and depth, the grouping of jobs in departments, the determination of the size of the groups reporting to a single manager, and the delegation of authority. Two methods designed to change all or some aspect of the organizational structure are management by objectives (MBO) and System 4. These methods are appropriate when the problem is diagnosed as being in Levels I through IV.

Management by Objectives

Management by objectives encourages managers to participate in the establishment of objectives for themselves and their units.[20] The process also can include the participation of nonmanagers in the determination of their specific objectives.

---

[20]Original statements of MBO may be found in Peter Drucker, *The Practice of Management* (New York: Harper & Row, 1954); George Odiorne, *Management by Objectives* (New York: Pitman Publishing, 1965); and W. J. Reddin, *Effective Management by Objectives* (New York: McGraw-Hill, 1970).

Successful use of MBO depends on the ability of participants to define their objectives in terms of their contribution to the total organization and to be able to accomplish them.

The original work of Drucker[21] and subsequent writings by others provide the basis for three guidelines for implementing MBO:

1. Superiors and subordinates meet and discuss objectives that contribute to overall goals.
2. Superiors and subordinates jointly establish attainable objectives for the subordinates.
3. Superior and subordinates meet at a predetermined later date to evaluate the subordinates' progress toward the objectives.

The exact procedures employed in implementing MBO vary from organization to organization and from unit to unit.[22] However, the basic elements of objective setting, participation of subordinates in objective setting, and feedback and evaluation usually are parts of any MBO program. The intended consequences of MBO include improved contribution to the organization, improved attitudes and satisfaction of participants, and greater role clarity. MBO is highly developed and widely used in business, health care, and governmental organizations.

System 4 Organization

System 4 organization (so named because it is posited to represent the fourth and highest stage on a theoretical scale of organization evolution) is an important application in the organic organizational design. Moreover, according to Likert, System 4 is an "ideal type" of organization for achieving high levels of performance, and any deviation from the ideal (System 4) represents reduced levels of performance. Thus, managers should develop their organizations toward System 4 characteristics. According to Likert, an organization can be described in terms of eight characteristics.[23] They are:

1. Leadership.
2. Motivation.
3. Communication.
4. Interaction.
5. Decision making.
6. Goal setting.
7. Control.
8. Performance.

Furthermore, each of these characteristics can be measured through the use of a questionnaire which members of the organization (usually managers) complete. The 51-item questionnaire devised by Likert asks respondents to indicate their

---

[21]See Ronald G. Greenwood, "Management by Objectives: As Developed by Peter Drucker, Assisted by Harold Smiddy," *Academy of Management Review*, April 1981, pp. 225–30.

[22]Jan P. Muczyk and Bernard Reimann, "MBO as a Complement to Effective Leadership," *Academy of Management Executive*, May 1989, pp. 131–38.

[23]Rensis Likert, *The Human Organization* (New York: McGraw-Hill, 1967).

perceptions or the extent to which the characteristics that define the System 4 organization are present in their own organization. Subsequent training programs emphasize the concepts of System 4 and the application of the concepts to the present organization. According to Likert, higher performance ordinarily should result through the use of: (1) supportive, group-oriented leadership and (2) equalization of authority to set goals, implement control, and make decisions. The improved performance derives from positive changes in employee attitudes that are induced by the changes in organizational structure. Recent reports of organizational change in firms such as Bank of America, Southwestern Bell, and Honeywell indicate increasing acceptance of System 4 concepts.[24]

SKILL AND ATTITUDE DEVELOPMENT METHODS

The most widely used methods for developing employee productivity are training programs.[25] These programs are designed to improve participants' knowledge, skills, and attitudes toward their jobs and the organization. The training may be part of a larger effort such as MBO or System 4 programs, or it may be directed toward specific objectives. In the usual case, managerial training is directed toward the development of communication and decision-making skills, thus improving the organization's fundamental processes.

Because of the multiplicity of training programs, we will briefly describe only a very few of the more representative and widely publicized types in this section. One way of characterizing these various programs is by their *site*. That is, some programs take place at the job site (on-the-job training), while others are deliberately situated away from the work environment (off-the-job training). Advantages and disadvantages of each will be identified.

On-the-Job Training

A popular philosophy over the years has been to train employees on the job. It is assumed that if training occurs off the job, there will be a loss in performance when the trainees are transferred back to the job. It is also proposed that on-the-job training is best from an economic standpoint since employees are producing while they undergo training.

Corning Glass Works has an extensive on-the-job training program. It begins with an assessment of the needs for training as identified by department heads.

---

[24]Jeffrey Pfeffer, "The Theory Gap: Myth or Reality," pp. 31–32; Robert N. Beck, "Visions, Values, and Strategies: Changing Attitudes and Culture," pp. 34–42; Zane E. Barnes "Change in the Bell System," pp. 43–46; James J. Reiner, "Turnaround of Information Systems at Honeywell," pp. 47–50; and Michael Beer, "Revitalizing Organizations: Change Process and Emergent Model," pp. 51–56. All these articles appeared in *Academy of Management Executive*, February 1987.

[25]Stephen R. Michael, "Organizational Change Techniques: Their Present, Their Future," *Organizational Dynamics*, Summer 1982, pp. 67–80.

The training unit then matches the identified training needs with classroom instruction. The classroom instructor moves to the workplace, where the classroom instruction is reinforced by actual on-the-job application. As employees master each job requirement, they receive credits that become part of their performance evaluation.[26]

On-the-job training has a number of shortcomings. First, employees may be placed in a stress-laden situation even before learning the job. This may result in accidents or poor initial attitudes about the job. Second, the areas in which employees are being trained often are congested. Finally, if a number of trainees are learning in various job locations, the trainer must move around constantly to monitor their performance.

Two specific types of on-the-job training are job-instruction training and junior executive boards. Formulated during World War II by the War Manpower Board, *job-instruction training* provides a set of guidelines for undertaking on-the-job training for white- and blue-collar employees. After trainees are introduced to the job, they receive a step-by-step review and demonstration of the job functions. When trainees are sufficiently confident that they understand the job, they demonstrate their ability to perform the job. This demonstration continues until the trainees reach a satisfactory level of performance. The objective of this approach is to bring about a positive change in performance reflected in high production, lower scrap costs, and so on.

Junior executive boards is a technique popularized by the McCormick Company. It concentrates on providing junior-level (middle- and lower-level) managers with top-level management problem-solving experience. The junior executive may serve on a committee or junior board that is considering some major decision concerning investments or personnel planning. The assumption in this type of training is that the trainee will achieve an appreciation for the decisions being made "upstairs" and that this can be translated into a better overall view of the organization's direction and difficulties. In addition, the ability of the junior executive to contribute to problem solving can be assessed.

Off-the-Job Training

Traditionally, organizations have found it necessary to provide training that supplements on-the-job efforts. Some of the advantages of off-the-job training are:

1. It lets executives get away from the pressures of the job and work in a climate in which "party-line" thinking is discouraged and self-analysis is stimulated.
2. It presents a challenge to executives that, in general, enhances their motivation to develop themselves.

[26]John G. Dickey, "Training with a Focus on the Individual," *Personnel Administrator,* June 1982, pp. 37–38.

3. It provides resource people and resource material—faculty members, fellow executives, and literature—that contribute suggestions and ideas for the executives to "try on for size" as they attempt to change, develop, and grow.

The theme of the advantages cited above is that trainees are more stimulated to learn by being away from job pressures. This is certainly debatable since it is questionable whether much of what is learned can be transferred back to the job. Attending a case-problem-solving program in San Diego is quite different from facing irate customers in Cleveland. Nonetheless, despite the difficulty of transferring knowledge from the classroom-type environment to the office, plant, or hospital, off-the-job training programs are still very popular and widely utilized.

Two popular off-the-job training techniques are the discussion or conference approach and the case study and role-playing method. The *discussion or conference approach* provides the participants with opportunities to exchange ideas and recollections of experiences. Through the interaction in the sessions, the participants stimulate one another's thinking, broaden their outlook, and improve their communicative abilities. Because of the interaction between trainer and participants in this approach, the trainer must be highly skilled and must understand the importance of reinforcing positive behavior and feeding back clearly the contribution of each participant to the group discussion.

The *case study and role-playing method* provides trainees with a description of some events that actually occurred in an organization. The case may describe the manner in which a nursing supervisor tried to motivate subordinates or the type of wage and salary program that was implemented in a retail store. Trainees read the case, identify the problems, and reach solutions.

In role playing, trainees are asked to participate actively in the case study. That is, they act out a case as if it were a play. This form of learning is an application of experiential learning based on the concept of learning by doing.[27] One participant may be the supervisor, and three other participants may play the role of subordinates. The rationale is that role playing enables the participants to actually "feel" what the cases are all about.

BEHAVIORAL DEVELOPMENT METHODS

Levels VII through X in Exhibit 16-3 require methods that delve deeply into individual and group behavior processes. Individual, individual-group, intra-group, and intergroup behavior often involve emotional and perceptual processes that interfere with effective organizational functioning. These development targets have received the greatest amount of attention from OD experts, and a

---

[27]P. Jervis, "Analyzing Decision Behavior: Learning Models and Learning Styles as Diagnostic Aids," *Personnel Review,* 1983, pp. 26–38.

considerable number of methods have been devised for attacking them. We will discuss two of the more widely known ones: team building and the managerial grid. Additionally, we will introduce two recent additions: mentor programs and ethics training.

Team Building

In recent years U.S. organizations have shown renewed interest in effectively using work groups, or teams.[28] Anyone who has ever operated a business or organized any kind of project requiring the efforts of several people knows the difficulties involved in getting everyone to pull in the right direction, in the right way, and at the right time. One approach to minimizing these difficulties is that of *team building.*[29]

The purpose of team building is to enable work groups to get their work done more effectively, to improve their performance. The work groups may be existing, or relatively new, command and task groups. The specific aims of the intervention include setting goals and priorities, analyzing the ways the group does its work, examining the group's norms and processes for communicating and decision making, and examining the interpersonal relationships within the group. As each of these aims is undertaken, the group is placed in the position of having to recognize explicitly the contributions, positive and negative, of each group member.[30]

The process by which these aims are achieved begins with *diagnostic* meetings. Often lasting an entire day, the meetings enable each group member to share with other members his or her perceptions of problems. Subsequently, a *plan of action* must be agreed on. The action plan should call on each of the group members, individually or as part of a subgroup, to undertake a specific action to alleviate one or more of the problems.

Team building is also effective when new groups are being formed because problems often exist when new organizational units, project teams, or task forces are created. Typically, such groups have certain characteristics that must be overcome if the groups are to perform effectively. For example:

1. Confusion exists as to roles and relationships.
2. Members have a fairly clear understanding of short-term goals.
3. Group members have technical competence that puts them on the team.
4. Members often pay more attention to the tasks of the team than to the relationships among the team members.

---

[28]Deborah Ancona, "Outward Bound: Strategies for Team Survival in an Organization," *Academy of Management Journal,* June 1990, pp. 334–65.

[29]Carl Larson and Frank M. J. LaFasto, *Teamwork* (Newbury Park, Calif.: Sage, 1989).

[30]Richard L. Hughes, William E. Rosenbach, and William H. Clover, "Team Development in an Intact, Ongoing Work Group," *Group and Organizational Studies,* June 1983, pp. 161–81.

To combat these tendencies, the new group could schedule team building meetings during the first few weeks of its life.

Although the reports of team building indicate mixed results, the evidence suggests that group processes improve through team building efforts.[31] This record of success accounts for the increasing use of team building as an OD method.[32]

The Managerial Grid

This OD approach is based on a theory of leadership behavior.[33] The two dimensions of leadership that the developers of the program, Blake and Mouton, identify are *concern for production* and *concern for people*. A balanced concern for production and people is the most effective leadership style, according to Blake and Mouton. The managerial grid program requires not only the development of this style but also the development of group behavior that supports and sustains it. The entire program consists of six sequential phases that are undertaken over a three-to five-year period.

The six phases can be separated into two major segments and the first two phases provide the foundation for the four later phases.

1. *Laboratory-seminar training.* This is typically a one-week conference designed to introduce managers to the grid philosophy and objectives. During this period, each participant's leadership style is assessed and reviewed.
2. *Intragroup development.* In this phase, superiors and their immediate subordinates explore their managerial styles and operating practices as a group. Together with Phase I, the objective is to familiarize participants with grid concepts, improve relationships between individuals and groups, and increase managers' problem-solving capacities.
3. *Intergroup development.* This phase involves group-to-group working relationships and focuses on building effective group roles and norms that improve intergroup relationships.
4. *Organizational goal setting.* The immediate objective of this phase is to set up a model of an effective organization for the future.
5. *Goal attainment.* This phase uses some of the group and educational procedures that were used in Phase I, but the concern is on the total organization. Problems are defined and groups move toward problem solution using grid concepts and philosophy.

---

[31]Kenneth P. de Meuse and S. Jay Liebowitz, "An Empirical Analysis of Team-Building Research," *Group and Organizational Studies,* September 1981, pp. 357–58.

[32]For a recent example of the use of team building, see Maurice Hardaker and Bryan Ward, "How to Make a Team Work," *Harvard Business Review,* November–December 1987, pp. 112–20.

[33]Robert R. Blake and Jane S. Mouton, *The Versatile Manager* (Homewood, Ill.: Richard D. Irwin, 1982).

6. *Stabilization.* This final phase focuses on stabilizing the changes brought about in prior phases. This phase also enables management to evaluate the total program.

The longevity of the managerial grid method, as well as its use in a growing variety of applications,[34] suggests that it is more than a fad to practicing managers. Thus, it would appear that more rigorous studies of what it can and cannot accomplish are required. Only by properly studying this approach can those interested in implementing it as a developmental method generally understand how it can change employee behavior.

Recent Development Approaches

Team building, in a variety of forms, and the managerial grid have been part of the repertoire of the organizational development specialist for some time. Recently, interest has developed in two new types of programs which are worthy of noting: ethics training and mentoring programs.

While many organizations have codes of ethics, with few exceptions *ethics training,* particularly organization-wide efforts, is a relatively recent development. While the content and methodology of ethics programs vary widely, most may be categorized as focusing on one or both of two general objectives: (1) developing employee awareness of business ethics and (2) focusing on specific ethical issues with which the employee may come in contact.[35] By helping to develop employee awareness of ethical issues in decision making, for example, organizations hope to:[36]

- Enable recognition of ethical components of a decision.
- Legitimize ethics as part of the decision-making process.
- Avoid variability in decision making caused by lack of norms or awareness of rules.
- Avoid confusion as to who is responsible for misdeeds.
- Provide decision-making frameworks for analyzing ethical choices.

The second objective, that of focusing on relevant ethical issues with which employees may be faced, may include dealing with conflict-of-interest situations, white collar crime, or discharging one's job responsibilities within the context of local, state, and federal requirements. This latter category could encompass such diverse activities as employee safety, EEO issues, product marketing claims, environmental protection, and sexual harassment.

---

[34]For an example, see Evert van de Vliert and Boris Kabanoff, "Toward Theory-Based Measures of Conflict Management," *Academy of Management Journal,* March 1990, pp. 199–209.

[35]Center for Business Ethics at Bentley College, "Are Corporations Institutionalizing Ethics?" *Journal of Business Ethics 5,* 1986, pp. 86–91.

[36]Susan J. Harrington, "What Corporate American Is Teaching about Ethics," *Academy of Management Executive,* February 1991, p. 23.

ETHICS TRAINING DOESN'T ALWAYS GUARANTEE POSITIVE RESULTS

More and more companies are providing ethics training for their employees. Large organizations on the list include McDonnell Douglas, International Business Machines, General Electric, Chase Manhattan Bank, Boeing, and Johnson & Johnson. As officials at the latter company found out, however, this doesn't mean there will never be problems.

What happened went something like this: In 1985 a 3M employee obtained samples of a new 3M casting tape to be used by physicians to set broken bones. Hoping to enhance himself financially, he mailed these samples to four 3M competitors, including Johnson & Johnson. According to 3M, while none of the companies reported receiving the material, only Johnson & Johnson analyzed the samples and used 3M's proprietary technology in their own competing product. As a result, again according to 3M, Johnson & Johnson undermined 3M's efforts to win a larger share of the $200 million domestic market for such products.

In May 1991 a U.S. District Court master ordered Johnson & Johnson to pay 3M more than $116 million for misappropriating trade secrets. Potentially more costly, Johnson & Johnson may have to remove some of its casting tapes from the market. According to court records, the sample was originally sent to the president of Johnson & Johnson's orthopedics company. Since he was away, the sample went to the company's product manager, who then sent it to the lab for analysis. The resulting lab report was sent to several orthopedic officials who failed to instruct company chemists not to use the findings in their own work.

Johnson & Johnson denies any wrong-doing and has indicated it "will vigorously appeal." Whether this is a problem of commission, omission, or no wrongdoing at all has yet to be settled. Nonetheless, the difficulty could have been avoided altogether had the company responded appropriately originally. And what is an appropriate response? According to one expert, what Johnson & Johnson should have done was to immediately notify 3M *and* the FBI.

Source: Based, in part, on an article in *Business Week,* May 20, 1991, p. 48.

Formal ethics training, particularly programs involving most or all levels within the organization, is too recent a phenomenon to draw conclusions regarding its effectiveness. It is clear, however, that however effective it may be, ethics training is not a cure-all. As Encounter 16-3 explains, one large company with an ethics program—Johnson & Johnson—has discovered that.

Formal *mentorship programs* represent an even more recent and less frequently used organizational development technique than ethics training. A mentor is an individual who serves as a role model and teacher for other, usually new, organizational members. The teaching part of mentoring may include specific job instruction, dissemination of organization cultural norms and values, dispelling of organizational myths, and general transfer of knowledge gained through years of being part of the organization. Mentoring relationships, of course, are not new; mentors and "mentees" have existed as long as have formal organizations. Formalizing such relationships, however, is a very new and largely unexplored concept.

A number of positive benefits to the organization have been identified as outcomes of mentoring programs.[37] These include (1) early identification of talent that might otherwise go unnoticed, (2) sensing by mentors of employee attitudes and morale, and (3) transmission of informal organizational expectations (corporate culture). Organizational benefits of mentoring can accrue at all levels of the company, up to and including the individual(s) being groomed for the presidency.

There are some caveats to keep in mind, however. Formalized mentor-mentee relationships should always be voluntary, for both parties. Companies should not assume that every long-term employee who has the interest would make a good mentor. In this regard, some individuals should be discouraged from assuming this role, and it is a good idea for all prospective mentors to receive some training or coaching on effective mentoring relationships. Finally, organizations must understand that not everything passed from mentors to mentees will be factually correct or organizationally desirable. The potential payoffs however, both in terms of individual and organizational development, make such programs worth considering.

MULTIFACETED INTERVENTIONS

In the previous sections we reviewed the characteristics of several organizational development interventions. The success of OD efforts depends in part on matching intervention and intended depth of intervention. Thus, a manager should be wary of the claims of proponents for all-purpose interventions. Each method, whether System 4, MBO, ethics training, or mentoring, has a primary focus, or target, for change. Managers will be disappointed if they expect changes in targets not affected by the intervention. If the change required is broad based, involving several targets or depths of intervention, then the OD program must incorporate more than one intervention.

A recently reported multifaceted intervention combined team building and MBO.[38] The project was conducted in a silver-mining company as part of a larger OD program directed at improving productivity and safety in the mine. Team-building exercises during intact work group meetings focused on issues such as how to do the job better and more safely. The participation in the team meetings gradually broadened to include top management as the teams identified issues that went beyond their ability to solve.

Next, goal setting was undertaken with full participation of the miners and their supervisors. The process proceeded as described in our discussion of MBO

---

[37]James A. Wilson and Nancy S. Elman, "Organizational Benefits of Mentoring," *Academy of Management Executive*, November 1990, pp. 88–94.

[38]Paul F. Buller and Cecil H. Bell, Jr., "Effects of Team Building and Goal Setting on Productivity: A Field Experiment," *Academy of Management Journal*, June 1986, pp. 305–28.

to establish specific, difficult, and attainable goals. Each individual miner set objectives for tons and grade of ore produced per shift for three-month periods. Supervisors provided weekly feedback of progress toward the stated goals.

An even more complex multifaceted program occurred in a research and development unit of a large corporation.[39] The impetus of the OD program was the inability of the unit to compete for government contracts that called for developmental research. In prior years, the unit had been successful in winning research contracts. When the funding agencies shifted their priority toward projects with shorter-run payoffs, however, the organization was not as successful in winning such contracts. The organization's performance was hampered by its inability to adapt. A major strategic shift was necessary, but the organization was unable to make that shift.

Consequently, a change was necessary, and the unit's management identified organizational development as the appropriate way to manage the change. The immediate problem was to identify the specific causes of the organization's lack of adaptiveness. Diagnostic activities began under the direction of change agents. They conducted numerous diagnostic activities, including the System 4 questionnaire, special-purpose questionnaires, and interview and problem-identification sessions. By analyzing the questionnaire and other data, participants identified the sources of problems as interpersonal and group relationships. They then voted to continue the OD program based on the proviso that it would improve these relationships.

ORGANIZATIONAL DEVELOPMENT PROGRAM EFFECTIVENESS

The most critical test of organizational development efforts is whether they improve organizational effectiveness, and this can only be determined through systematic research. A recent review of the record of OD interventions in bringing about desired change concluded that multifaceted approaches have had somewhat better success than single-method ones.[40] Nicholas compared the effects of sensitivity training, team building, job enrichment, and job redesign and concluded that no one method was successful in all instances (an expected conclusion, given what we have said above). But he also found that significant changes occurred when several methods were combined. One such combination includes three discrete steps that involve all levels of the organization: (1) all employees participate in goal setting, decision making, and job redesign; (2) employee collaboration is developed through team building; and (3) the organizational structure

---

[39]Vida Scarpello, "Who Benefits from Participation in Long-Term Human Process Interventions?" *Group and Organization Studies,* March 1983, pp. 21–44.

[40]John M. Nicholas, "The Comparative Impact of Organization Development Interventions on Hard Criteria Measures," *Academy of Management Review,* October 1982, pp. 531–42.

is reorganized to accommodate the new levels of participation and collaboration. The application of these three steps can go a long way toward meeting some of the arguments against specific OD methods. The overriding managerial concern is transfer of learning to the work environment. Only under these circumstances can OD methods be considered effective.

SUMMARY OF KEY POINTS

- The term organizational development refers to the process of preparing for and managing change. Important subobjectives of OD include changing attitudes and values, modifying behavior, and introducing change in organizational structure and policy.

- Major steps to follow in undertaking an organizational development effort would include (1) diagnosing the problem, (2) selecting the appropriate OD method, (3) recognizing conditions potentially limiting the success of the program, (4) actually implementating the selected method of intervention, and (5) evaluating the effectiveness of the program.

- Change requires adaptation, and consequently resistance to change is a potential problem when undertaking organizational development efforts. Approaches for dealing with the resistance problem include education and communication, participation and involvement, facilitation and support, negotiation and agreement, manipulation and co-optation, and various forms of coercion.

- There are three major categories of organizational development methods: structural, skill and attitude, and behavioral. Structural methods are those that attempt to improve effectiveness through changes in the formal structure of task and authority relationships. Skill and attitude development methods focus on effecting change through traditional on- or off-the-job training. Behavioral methods attempt to increase effectiveness by altering informal aspects of individual and group behavior.

- Specific development programs within the three major categories of OD methods include management by objectives and System 4 organization (structural); job instruction training, junior executive boards, and discussion or conference type training programs (skill and attitude); team building, the managerial grid, ethics training, and formalized mentorship programs.

- Certain factors, referred to as *limiting conditions* may affect the success of development efforts. These include the leadership climate, where management support for the OD program is critical; the formal organization, which must be compatible with the proposed change; and the organizational culture, which must support any changes.

- Evaluation of OD programs is essential. Without such evaluation there is no way to determine whether the expenditure of effort and resources was worthwhile. Additionally, evaluation is important in helping to understand in what ways the program contributed to changes that occurred.

REVIEW AND DISCUSSION QUESTIONS

1. What characteristics of planned change distinguish it from unplanned or spontaneous change? Are these characteristics more likely to increase or decrease people's receptivity to organizational development efforts?

2. Think of an organization with which you are familiar (a present or past employer, the university you attend, etc.). What are the environmental and internal forces operating on that organization to bring about change?

3. Contrast the degree of subordinate participation in unilateral, delegated, and shared approaches to change. Which would you prefer as a subordinate? As a manager?

4. How might leadership climate, formal organization structure and policies, and organizational climate serve to limit the success of an OD effort? How might these same factors facilitate success?

5. Which of the OD methods discussed in this chapter would you use to improve the effectiveness of the college or university you attend?

6. Discuss the relationship between the degree of intended change and the type of organizational development method used to accomplish the change.

7. Do you think organizations might differ in their receptivity to OD efforts as a function of the industry they are part of? The skill level of their workforce? The condition of the world economy?

8. "Change must be introduced very carefully because you can never go back to the way things were before you made the change." What does this statement mean? What implications does it have for organizational development?

9. How might an organization overcome resistance to change? To what extent would the type of change being implemented affect the method(s) chosen to reduce resistance?

10. Why is it important to evaluate change efforts, and why are such evaluations so difficult to do?

●

READING

READING 16–1   CREATING SUCCESSFUL ORGANIZATION CHANGE

Leonard D. Goodstein
W. Warner Burke

Buffeted at home and abroad by foreign competition that appears to produce higher-quality goods at lower prices, corporate America has now largely forsaken (at least publicly and momentarily) the traditional analogy of the organization as a machine and its organizational members as parts designed to work effectively and efficiently. Instead, many American corporations are accepting the "New Age" view of organizations as "a nested set of open, living systems and subsystems dependent upon the larger environment for survival."

What is surprising about this quote is not its viewpoint, which has been normative in the organizational psychology and behavioral literature for several decades, but its source: *The Wall Street Journal.* And it is typical to find such articles in virtually every issue of most recent American business publications; articles on corporate culture, on the changing attitudes of American workers, on the need for greater employee participation in managerial decision making, and on the place of employees as an important (if not the most important) asset of the corporation.

We are not suggesting that traditionally managed organizations are now extinct in America. Corporate executives, however, have definitely begun to recognize that managing the social psychology of the workplace is a critical element in the success of any organization.

ORGANIZATIONAL CHANGE

Organizations tend to change primarily because of external pressure rather than an internal desire or need to change. Here are a few all-too-familiar examples of the kinds of environmental factors requiring organizations to change:

- A new competitor snares a significant portion of a firm's market share.
- An old customer is acquired by a giant conglomerate that dictates new sales arrangements.

Source: Leonard D. Goodstein and W. Warner Burke, "Creating Successful Organization Change," *Organizational Dynamics,* Spring 1991, pp. 5–17.

- A new invention offers the possibility of changing the organization's existing production technology.

Other examples include (1) new government regulations on certain health-care financing programs and (2) economic and social conditions that create long-term changes in the availability of the labor force. The competent organization will be alert to early-warning signs of such external changes so that it can move promptly to make internal changes designed to keep it viable in the changing external world. Competent organizations are those that continue to change and to survive.

Thus, it is practically a cliche to state that change in organizations today is a way of life. And clearly it is not saying anything new to comment that executives and managers today are more finely attuned to change or that they more frequently view their role as that of change agent.

But even though we often state the obvious and spout cliches about change, this does not mean that we have an in-depth understanding of what we are talking about. We are only beginning to understand the nature of change and how to manage the process involved, especially with respect to organizations. The purpose of this article is to improve our understanding of organizational change by providing both some conceptual clarification and a case example that illustrates many of the concepts involved.

It is possible to conceptualize organizational change in at least three ways—levels of organizational change, strategies of organizational change and, more specifically and not mutually exclusive of strategies, models and methods of organizational change. (First we will present the concepts, second the case example, and finally some implications.)

LEVELS OF ORGANIZATIONAL CHANGE

A broad distinction can be made between (1) fundamental, large-scale change in the organization's strategy and culture—a transformation, refocus, reorientation, or "bending the frame," as David A. Nadler and Michael L. Tushman have referred to the process—and (2) fine-tuning, fixing problems, making adjustments, modifying procedures, etc.; that is, implementing modest changes that improve the organization's performance yet do not fundamentally change the organization. By far most organizational changes are designed not to transform the organization but to modify it in order to fix its problems.

In this article we address more directly the large-scale, fundamental type of organizational change. (A word of caution: "Organizational transformation," "frame bending," and other expressions indicating fundamental change do not imply wholesale, indiscriminate, and complete change. Thus when we refer to "fundamental change," we do not mean "in any and all respects.")

We are concerned with transformation when an organization faces the need to survive and must do things differently to continue to exist. After polio was licked, for example, the March of Dimes had to change its mission in order to survive as an organization. Although its mission changed from one of attacking polio to one of trying to eradicate birth defects, the organization's core technology—fund raising—remained the same.

A corporate example of transformation is seen in the transition of International Harvester to Navistar. Facing bankruptcy, the company downsized drastically, completely restructured its financial situation, and overhauled its corporate culture. Although many of the company's technologies were sold off, it too retained its core technology: producing trucks and engines. Once internally focused, its culture is now significantly market-oriented—and the company is operating far more efficiently than it did in the past.

Although organizational members experience such transformations as a complete change, they rarely if ever are. Theory would suggest that if fundamental—or even significant—change is to occur with any success, some characteristic(s) of the organization must *not* change. The theory to which we refer comes from the world of individual change: psychotherapy. For organizational transformation to be achieved—for the organization to survive and eventually prosper from such change—certain fundamentals need to be retained. Some examples: the organization's ultimate purpose, the previously mentioned core technology, and key people. The principle here is that for people to be able to deal with enormous and complex change—seeming chaos—they need to have *something* to hold on to that is stable.

Conceptually, then, we can distinguish between fundamentally changing the organization and fine-tuning it. This distinction—which is a matter of degree, not necessarily a dichotomy—is useful in determining strategies and methods to be used in the change effort. When fine-tuning, for example, we do not necessarily need to clarify for organizational members what will not change—but in the case of transformation, such clarity is required for its successful achievement.

STRATEGIES OF ORGANIZATIONAL CHANGE

Organizational change can occur in more than one way. In a 1971 book, Harvey A. Hornstein and colleagues classified six ways: individual change strategies, technostructural strategies, data-based strategies, organization development, violent and coercive strategies, and nonviolent yet direct action strategies. All of these strategies have been used to attempt, if not actually bring about, organizational change. Senior management usually chooses any one or various combinations of the first four and manages them internally. The last two—violent, coercive strategies and nonviolent yet direct-action strategies—are more often than not initiated by actions outside the organization, and the organization's executives typically manage in a reactive mode.

In this article we address some combination of the first four strategies. Yet, as previously indicated, we are assuming that the overwhelming majority of organizational changes are motivated by *external* factors—that executives are responding to the organization's external environment. But even when it is not a reaction to some social movement, organizational change is nevertheless a *response*—a response to changes or anticipated changes in the marketplace, or changes in the way technology will affect the organization's products/services, or changes in the labor market, etc.

This assumption is based on the idea that an organization is a living, open system dependent on its environment for survival. Whether it is merely to survive or eventually to prosper, an organization must monitor its external environment and align itself with changes that occur or will occur in that environment. Practically speaking, the process of alignment requires the organization to change itself.

MODELS AND METHODS OF ORGANIZATIONAL CHANGE

Models of change and methods of change are quite similar in concept and often overlap—so much so that it is not always clear which one is being discussed. Kurt Lewin's three-phase model of change—unfreeze, move (or change), refreeze—also suggests method. Organization development is based on an action-research model that is, at the same time, a method.

More on the model side is the relatively simple and straightforward framework provided by Richard Beckhard and Reuben T. Harris. They have suggested that large-scale, complex organizational change can be conceptualized as movement from a present state to a future state. But the most important phase is the in-between one that they label *transition state*. Organizational change, then, is a matter of (1) assessing the current organizational situation (present state), (2) determining the desired future (future state), and (3) both planning ways to reach that desired future and implementing the plans (transition state).

Methods of implementing the change—for example, a new organizational strategy—include the following:

- Setting up a comprehensive training program (individual change strategy).
- Modifying the structure, individuals' jobs, and/or work procedures (technostructural strategy).
- Conducting a companywide survey to assess organizational culture for the purpose of using the data to pinpoint required changes (data-based strategy).
- Collecting information from organizational members about their views regarding what needs to be changed and acting accordingly (organization development strategy).
- Combining two, three, or all of these methods.

The case example we will discuss here illustrates organizational transformation in response to change initiated in the institution's external environment—excluding, however, the violent, coercive strategies and the nonviolent, direct ones. The example, which is analyzed according to Lewin's three-phase model/method, highlights the use of multiple methods for change—in fact, it presents in one form or another a specific method from each of the four other change strategies mentioned earlier.

CASE EXAMPLE

In 1982 Margaret Thatcher's government in Great Britain decided to convert British Airways (BA) from government ownership to private ownership. BA had regularly required large subsidies from the government (almost $900 million in 1982), subsidies that the government felt it could not provide. Even more important, the Conservative govern-

ment was ideologically opposed to the government's ownership of businesses—a matter they regarded as the appropriate province of private enterprise.

The growing deregulation of international air traffic was another important environmental change. Air fares were no longer fixed, and the resulting price wars placed BA at even greater risk of financial losses.

In order to be able to "privatize"—that is, sell BA shares on the London and New York Stock Exchanges—it was necessary to make BA profitable. The pressures to change thus exerted on BA by the external environment were broad and intense. And the internal organizational changes, driven by these external pressures, have been massive and widespread. They have transformed the BA culture from what BA managers described as "bureaucratic and militaristic" to one that is now described as "service-oriented and market-driven." The success of these efforts over a five-year period (1982–1987) is clearly depicted in the data presented in Exhibit 16-4.

This exhibit reflects BA's new mission in its new advertising slogan—"The World's Favorite Airline." Five years after the change effort began, BA had successfully moved from government ownership to private ownership, and both passenger and cargo revenues had dramatically increased, leading to a substantial increase in share price over the offering price, despite the market crash of October 1987. Indeed, in late 1987 BA acquired British Caledonian Airways, its chief domestic competitor. The steps through which this transformation was accomplished clearly fit Lewin's model of the change process.

LEWIN'S CHANGE MODEL

According to the open-systems view, organizations—like living creatures—tend to be homeostatic, or continuously working to maintain a steady state. This helps us understand why organizations require external impetus to initiate change and, indeed, why that change will be resisted even when it is necessary.

Organizational change can occur at three levels—and, since the patterns of resistance to change are different for each, the patterns in each level require different change strategies and techniques. These levels involve:

1. Changing the *individuals* who work in the organization—that is, their skills, values, attitudes, and eventually behavior—but making sure that such individual behavioral change is always regarded as instrumental to organizational change.

EXHIBIT 16-4

The British Airways Success Story: Creating the "World's Favorite Airline"

	1982	1987
Ownership	Government	Private
Profit/(loss)	($900 million)	$435 million
Culture	Bureaucratic and militaristic	Service-oriented and market-driven
Passenger load factor	Decreasing	Increasing—up 16% in 1st quarter 1988
Cargo load	Stable	Increasing—up 41% in 1st quarter 1988
Share price	N/A	Increased 67% (2/11/87–8/11/87)
Acquisitions	N/A	British Caledonian

2. Changing various organizational *structures and systems*—reward systems, reporting relationships, work design, and so on.
3. Directly changing the organizational *climate or interpersonal style*—how open people are with each other, how conflict is managed, how decisions are made, and so on.

According to Lewin, a pioneer in the field of social psychology of organizations, the first step of any change process is to *unfreeze* the present pattern of behavior as a way of managing resistance to change. Depending on the organizational level of change intended, such unfreezing might involve, on the individual level, selectively promoting or terminating employees; on the structural level, developing highly experiential training programs in such new organization designs as matrix management; or, on the climate level, providing data-based feedback on how employees feel about certain management practices. Whatever the level involved, each of these interventions is intended to make organizational members address that level's need for change, heighten their awareness of their own behavioral patterns, and make them more open to the change process.

The second step, *movement*, involves making the actual changes that will move the organization to another level of response. On the individual level we would expect to see people behaving differently, perhaps demonstrating new skills or new supervisory practices. On the structural level, we would expect to see changes in actual organizational structures, reporting relationships, and reward systems that affect the way people do their work. Finally, on the climate or interpersonal-style level, we would expect to see behavior patterns that indicate greater interpersonal trust and openness and fewer dysfunctional interactions.

The final stage of the change process, *refreezing*, involves stabilizing or institutionalizing these changes by establishing systems that make these behavioral patterns "relatively secure against change," as Lewin put it. The refreezing stage may involve, for example, redesigning the organization's recruitment process to increase the likelihood of hiring applicants who share the organization's new management style and value system. During the refreezing stage, the organization may also ensure that the new behaviors have become the operating norms at work, that the reward system actually reinforces those behaviors, or that a new, more participative management style predominates.

According to Lewin, the first step to achieving lasting organizational change is to deal with resistance to change by unblocking the present system. This unblocking usually requires some kind of confrontation and a retraining process based on planned behavioral changes in the desired direction. Finally, deliberate steps need to be taken to cement these changes in place—this "institutionalization of change" is designed to make the changes semi-permanent until the next cycle of change occurs.

Exhibit 16-5 presents an analysis of the BA change effort in terms of Lewin's model. The many and diverse steps involved in the effort are categorized both by stages (unfreezing, movement, and refreezing) and by level (individual, structures and system, and climate/interpersonal style).

Unfreezing

In BA's change effort, the first step in unfreezing involved a massive reduction in the worldwide BA workforce (from 59,000 to 37,000). It is interesting to note that within a year after this staff reduction, virtually all BA performance

EXHIBIT 16-5

Applying Lewin's Model to the British Airways (BA) Change Effort

Levels	Unfreezing	Movement	Refreezing
Individual	Downsizing of workforce (59,000 to 37,000); middle management especially hard-hit. New top management team. "Putting People First."	Acceptance of concept of "emotional labor." Personnel staff as internal consultants. "Managing People First." Peer support groups.	Continued commitment of top managment. Promotion of staff with new BA values. "Top Flight Academies." "Open Learning" programs.
Structures and systems	Use of diagonal task forces to plan change. Reduction in levels of hierarchy. Modification of budgeting process.	Profit sharing (3 weeks' pay in 1987). Opening of Terminal 4. Purchase of Chartridge as training center. New, "user friendly" MIS.	New performance appraisal system based on both behavior and performance. Performance-based compensation system. Continued use of task forces.
Climate/ interpersonal style	Redefinition of the business: *service*, not *transportation*. Top management commitment and involvement.	Greater emphasis on open communications. Data feedback on work-unit climate. Off-site, team-building meetings.	New uniforms. New coat of arms. Development and use of cabin-crew teams. Continued use of data-based feedback on climate and management practices.

indices had improved—more on-time departures and arrivals, fewer out-of-service aircraft, less time "on hold" for telephone reservations, fewer lost bags, and so on. The consensus view at all levels within BA was that the downsizing had reduced hierarchical levels, thus giving more autonomy to operating people and allowing work to get done more easily.

The downsizing was accomplished with compassion; no one was actually laid off. Early retirement, with substantial financial settlements, was the preferred solution throughout the system. Although there is no question that the process was painful, considerable attention was paid to minimizing the pain in every possible way.

A second major change occurred in BA's top management. In 1981, Lord John King of Wartinbee, a senior British industrialist, was appointed chairman of the board, and Colin Marshall, now Sir Colin, was appointed CEO.

The appointment of Marshall represented a significant departure from BA culture. An outsider to BA, Marshall had a marketing background that was quite different from that of his predecessors, many of whom were retired senior Royal Air Force officers. It was Marshall who decided, shortly after his arrival, that BA's strategy should be to become "the World's Favorite Airline." Without question, critical ingredients in the success of the overall change effort were Marshall's vision, the clarity of his understanding that BA's culture needed to be changed in order to carry out the vision, and his strong leadership of that change effort.

To support the unfreezing process, the first of many training programs was introduced. "Putting People First"—the program in which all BA personnel with direct customer contact participated—was another important part of the unfreezing process. Aimed at helping line workers and managers understand the service nature of the airline industry, it was intended to challenge the prevailing wisdom about how things were to be done at BA.

Movement

Early on, Marshall hired Nicholas Georgiades, a psychologist and former professor and consultant, as director (vice president) of human resources. It was Georgiades who developed the specific tactics and programs required to bring Marshall's vision into reality. Thus Georgiades, along with Marshall, must be regarded as a leader of BA's successful change effort. One of the interventions that Georgiades initiated—a significant activity during the movement phase—was to establish training programs for senior and middle managers. Among these were "Managing People First" and "Leading the Service Business"—experiential programs that involved heavy doses of individual feedback to each participant about his or her behavior regarding management practices on the job.

These training programs all had more or less the same general purpose: to identify the organization's dysfunctional management style and begin the process of developing a new management style that would fit BA's new, competitive environment. If the organization was to be market-driven, service-based, and profit-making, it would require an open, participative management style—one that would produce employee commitment.

On the structures and systems level during the unfreezing stage, extensive use was made of diagonal task forces composed of individuals from different functions and at different levels of responsibility to deal with various aspects of the change process—the need for MIS (management information systems) support, new staffing patterns, new uniforms, and so on. A bottom-up, less centralized budgeting process—one sharply different from its predecessor—was introduced.

Redefining BA's business as service rather than transportation represented a critical shift on the level of climate/interpersonal style. A service business needs an open climate and good interpersonal skills, coupled with outstanding teamwork. Off-site, team-building meetings—the process chosen to deal with these issues during the movement stage—have now been institutionalized.

None of these changes would have occurred without the commitment and involvement of top management. Marshall himself played a central role in both initiating and supporting the change process, even when problems arose. As one index of this commitment, Marshall shared

information at question-and-answer sessions at most of the training programs—both "to show the flag" and to provide his own unique perspective on what needed to be done.

An important element of the movement phase was acceptance of the concept of "emotional labor" that Georgiades championed—that is, the high energy levels required to provide the quality of service needed in a somewhat uncertain environment, such as the airline business. Recognition that such service is emotionally draining and often can lead to burnout and permanent psychological damage is critical to developing systems of emotional support for the service workers involved.

Another important support mechanism was the retraining of traditional personnel staff to become internal change agents charged with helping and supporting line and staff managers. So too was the development of peer support groups for managers completing the "Managing People First" training program.

To support this movement, a number of internal BA structures and systems were changed. By introducing a new bonus system, for example, Georgiades demonstrated management's commitment to sharing the financial gains of BA's success. The opening of Terminal 4 at Heathrow Airport provided a more functional work environment for staff. The purchase of Chartridge House as a permanent BA training center permitted an increase in and integration of staff training, and the new, "user friendly" MIS enabled managers to get the information they needed to do their jobs in a timely fashion.

Refreezing

During the refreezing phase, the continued involvement and commitment of BA's top management ensured that the changes became "fixed" in the system. People who clearly exemplified the new BA values were much more likely to be promoted, especially at higher management levels. Georgiades introduced additional programs for educating the workforce, especially managers. "Open Learning" programs, including orientation programs for new staff, supervisory training for new supervisors, and so on, were augmented by "Top Flight Academies" that included training at the executive, senior management, and management levels. One of the Academies now leads to an M.B.A. degree.

A new performance appraisal system, based on both behavior and results, was created to emphasize customer service and subordinate development. A performance-based compensation system is being installed, and task forces continue to be used to solve emerging problems, such as those resulting from the acquisition of British Caledonian Airlines.

Attention was paid to BA's symbols as well—new, upscale uniforms; refurbished aircraft; and a new corporate coat of arms with the motto "We fly to serve." A unique development has been the creation of teams for consistent cabin-crew staffing, rather than the ad hoc process typically used. Finally, there is continued use of data feedback on management practices throughout the system.

Managing Change

Unfortunately, the change process is not smooth even if one is attentive to Lewin's model of change. Changing behavior at both individual and organizational levels means inhibiting habitual responses and producing new responses that feel awkward and unfamiliar to those involved. It is all too easy to slip back to the familiar and comfortable.

For example, an organization may intend to manage more participatively. But when a difficult decision arises, it may not be possible to get a consensus decision—not at first, at least. Frustration to "get on with" a decision can lead to the organization's early abandonment of the new management style.

In moving from a known present state to a desired future state, organizations must recognize that (as noted earlier) the intervening *transition* state requires careful management, especially when the planned organizational change is large and complex. An important part of this change management lies in recognizing and accepting the disorganization and temporarily lowered effectiveness that characterize the transition state.

In BA's change effort, the chaos and anger that arose during the transitional phase have abated, and clear signs of success have now emerged. But many times the outcome was not at all clear, and serious questions were raised about the wisdom of the process both inside and outside BA. At such times the commitment and courage of top management are essential.

To heighten involvement, managing such organizational changes may often require using a transition management team composed of a broad cross-section of members of the organization. Other techniques include using multiple interventions rather than just one—for example, keeping the system open to feedback about the change process and using symbols and rituals to mark significant achievements. The BA program used all of these techniques.

Process Consultation

In addition to the various change strategies discussed above, considerable use was made of all the usual organization development (OD) technologies. Structural changes, role clarification and negotiations, team building, and process consultation were all used at British Airways to facilitate change.

In process consultation—the unique OD intervention—the consultant examines the pattern of a work unit's communications. This is done most often through direct observation of staff meetings and, at opportune times, through raising questions or making observations about what has been happening. The role of the process consultant is to be counternormative—that is, to ask why others never seem to respond to Ruth's questions or why no one ever challenges Fred's remarks when he is clearly off target. Generally speaking, process consultation points out the true quality of the emperor's new clothes even when everyone is pretending that they are quite elegant. By changing the closed communication style of the work teams at British Airways to a more open, candid one, process consultation played an important role in the change process.

THE RESEARCH EVIDENCE

Granted that the BA intervention appears to have been successful, what do we know generally about the impact of OD interventions on organizations and on their effectiveness? Over the past few years, the research literature has shown a sharp improvement in both research design and methodological rigor, especially in the development of such "hard criteria" as productivity and quality indices. The findings have been surprisingly positive.

For example, Raymond Katzell and Richard Guzzo reviewed more than 200 intervention studies and reported that 87 percent found evidence of significant increases in worker productivity as a result of the intervention. Richard Guzzo, Richard Jette, and Raymond Katzell's meta-analysis of 98 of these same studies revealed productivity increases averaging almost half a standard deviation—impressive enough "to be visible to the naked eye," to use their phrase. Thus it would appear that the success of BA's intervention process was not a single occurrence but one in a series of successful changes based on OD interventions.

The picture with respect to employee satisfaction, however, is not so clear. Another meta-analysis—by Barry Macy, Hiroaki Izumi, Charles Hurts, and Lawrence Norton—on how OD interventions affect performance measures and employee work satisfaction found positive effects on performance but *negative* effects on attitudes, perhaps because of the pressure exerted by new work-group norms on employee productivity. The positive effects on performance, however, are in keeping with the bulk of proper research. A recent comprehensive review of the entire field of OD by Marshall Sashkin and W. Warner Burke concluded, "There is little doubt that, when applied properly, OD has substantial positive effects in terms of performance measures."

IMPLICATIONS AND CONCLUDING REMARKS

We very much believe that an understanding of the social psychology of the change process gives all of us—managers, rank-and-file employees, and consultants—an important and different perspective for coping with an increasingly competitive environment. Our purpose in writing this article was to share some of this perspective—from an admittedly biased point of view.

The change effort at BA provides a recent example of how this perspective and this understanding have been applied. What should be apparent from this abbreviated overview of a massive project is that the change process at BA was based on open-systems thinking, a phased model of managing change, and multiple levels for implementing the change. Thus both the design and the implementation of this change effort relied heavily on this kind of understanding about the nature of organizations and changing them.

The change involved a multifaceted effort that used many leverage points to initiate and support the changes. The change process, which used transition teams with openness to feedback, was intentionally managed with strong support from top management. Resistance to change was actively managed by using unfreezing strategies at all three levels—individual, structural and systems, and interpersonal. Virtually all of the organizational change issues discussed in this article emerged in some measure during the course of the project.

It is quite reassuring to begin to find empirical support for these efforts in field studies and case reports of change efforts. Moreover, the recent meta-analyses of much of this work are quite supportive of what we have learned from experience. We need to use such reports to help more managers understand the worth of applying the open-systems model to their change efforts. But we also need to remember that only when proof of the intervention strategy's usefulness shows up on the firm's "bottom line" will

most line managers be persuaded that open-systems thinking is not necessarily incompatible with the real world. The BA success story is a very useful one for beginning such a dialog.

As we go to press, it seems clear that many of the changes at British Airways have stabilized the company. Perhaps the most important one is that the company's culture today can be described as having a strong customer-service focus—a focus that was decidedly lacking in 1982. The belief that marketing and service with the customer in mind will have significant payoff for the company is now endemic to the corporate culture. Another belief now fundamental to BA's culture is that the way one manages people—especially those, like ticket agents and cabin crews, with direct customer contact—directly impacts the way customers will feel about BA. For example, during 1990, Tony Clarry, then head of worldwide customer service for BA, launched a leadership program for all of his management around the globe to continue to reinforce this belief.

Yet all is not bliss at British Airways, which has its problems. Some examples:

- American Airlines is encroaching upon BA's European territory.
- The high level of customer service slips from time to time.
- Those who can afford to ride on the Concorde represent a tiny market, so it is tough to maintain a consistently strong customer base.
- Now that BA has developed a cadre of experienced managers in a successful company, these managers are being enticed by search firms to join other companies that often pay more money.

Other problems, too, affect BA's bottom line—the cost of fuel, effectively managing internal costs, and the reactions of the financiers in London and on Wall Street, to name a few. It should be noted that since 1987 and until recently, BA's financials have remained positive with revenues and profits continuing to increase. During 1990 this bright picture began to fade, however. The combination of the continuing rise in fuel costs, the recession, and the war in the Persian Gulf have taken their toll. Constant vigilance is therefore imperative for continued success.

It may be that BA's biggest problem now is not so much to manage further change as it is to manage the change that has already occurred. In other words, the people of BA have achieved significant change and success; now they must maintain what has been achieved while concentrating on continuing to be adaptable to changes in their external environment—the further deregulation of Europe, for example. Managing momentum may be more difficult than managing change.

SELECTED BIBLIOGRAPHY

The Wall Street Journal article referred to at the outset, "Motivate or Alienate? Firms Have Gurus to Change Their 'Cultures,' " was written by Peter Waldbaum and may be found on p. 19 of the July 24, 1987 issue.

With respect to levels of organizational change, see the article by W. Warner Burke and George H. Litwin, "A Causal Model of Organizational Performance," in the 1989 Annual published by University Associates of San Diego. These authors describe the differences between transformational and transactional change. Along the same conceptual lines is the article by David A. Nadler and Michael L. Tushman—"Organizational Frame Bending: Principles for Managing Reorientation" *The Academy of Management Executive,* 1988, August, 194–204.

Regarding strategies of organizational change, see Harvey A. Hornstein, Barbara B. Bunker, W. Warner Burke, Marion Gindes, and Roy J. Lewicki's *Social Intervention: A Behavioral Science Approach* (The Free Press, 1971).

Concerning models and methods of organizational change, the classic piece is Kurt Lewin's chapter "Group Decisions and Social Change," in the 1958 book *Readings in Social Psychology* (Holt, Rinehart & Winston), edited by Eleanor E. Maccobby, Theodore M. Newcomb, and Eugene L. Hartley. For an explanation of organization development as action research, see W. Warner Burke's *Organization Development: Principles and Practices* (Scott, Foresman, 1982). The framework of present state-transition state-future state is explained in *Organization Transitions: Managing Complex Change,* 2nd. ed. (Addison-Wesley, 1987), by Richard Beckhard and Reuben T. Harris. A recent article by Donald C. Hambrick and Albert A. Cannella, Jr.—"Strategy Implementation as Substance and Selling" *The Academy of Management Executive,* November 1989, pp. 278–85—is quite helpful in understanding how to implement a change in corporate strategy.

A point made in the article is that for effective organizational change, multiple leverage is required. For data to support this argument, see W. Warner Burke, Lawrence P. Clark, and Cheryl Koopman's "Improving Your OD Project's Chances of Success" *Training and Development Journal,* September, 1984 pp. 62–68. More on process consultation and team building may be found in two books published by Addison-Wesley: Edgar H. Schein's *Process Consultation, Vol. 1: Its Role in Organization Development,* 1988, and W. Gibb Dyer's *Team Building: Issues and Alternatives,* 1987.

References for the research evidence are: Richard A. Guzzo, Richard D. Jette, and Raymond A. Katzell's "The Effects of Psychologically Based Intervention Programs on Worker Productivity: A Meta-Analysis" *Personnel Psychology* 38, no. 2, Summer, 1985, pp. 275–91; Raymond A. Katzell and Richard A. Guzzo's "Psychological Approaches to Worker Productivity" *American Psychologist* 38, April 1983, pp. 468–72; Barry A. Macy, Hiroaki Izumi, Charles C. M. Hurts, and Lawrence W. Norton's "Meta-Analysis of United States Empirical Change and Work Innovation Field Experiments," a paper presented at the 1986 annual meeting of the Academy of Management, Chicago; John M. Nicholas's "The Comparative Impact of Organization Development Interventions on Hard Criteria Issues" *The Academy of Management Review,* 7, no. 4, (October 1982), pp. 531–43; John M. Nicholas and Marsha Katz's "Research Methods and Reporting Practices in Organization Development" *The Academy of Management Review* 4, October 1985, pp. 737–49; and Marshall Sashkin and W. Warner Burke's "Organization Development in the 1980s" *Journal of Management,* 2, 1987, pp. 205–29.

■
EXERCISES

EXERCISE 16–1 ORGANIZATION DEVELOPMENT AT J. P. HUNT

OBJECTIVE

To experience an OD technique—in this case the use of survey feedback—to diagnose strengths and weaknesses and develop an action plan.

STARTING THE EXERCISE

Set up groups of four to eight members for the one-hour exercise. The groups should be separated from each other and asked to converse only with members of their own group. Each person should read the following:

J. P. Hunt department stores is a large retail merchandising outlet located in Boston. The company sells an entire range of retail goods (e.g., appliances, fashions, furniture,

Source: Fred Luthans, *Organizational Behavior* (New York: McGraw Hill, 1989), p. 623–24.

and so on) and has a large downtown store plus six branch stores in various suburban areas.

Similar to most retail stores in the area, employee turnover is high (i.e., 40 to 45 percent annually). In the credit and accounts receivable department, located in the downtown store, turnover is particularly high at both the supervisor and subordinate levels, approaching 75 percent annually. The department employs approximately 150 people, 70 percent of whom are female.

Due to rising hiring and training costs brought on by the high turnover, top department management began a turnover analysis and reduction program. As a first step, a local management consulting firm was contracted to conduct a survey of department employees. Using primarily questionnaires, the consulting firm collected survey data from over 95 percent of the department's employees. The results are shown in the exhibit, by organizational level, along with industry norms developed by the consulting firm in comparative retail organizations.

Survey Results for J. P. Hunt Department Store: Credit and Accounts Receivable Department

Variable	Survey Results*			Industry Norms*		
	Managers	Supervisors	Non- super- visors	Managers	Supervisors	Non- super- visors
Satisfaction and rewards						
Pay	3.30	1.73	2.48	3.31	2.97	2.89
Supervision	3.70	2.42	3.05	3.64	3.58	3.21
Promotion	3.40	2.28	2.76	3.38	3.25	3.23
Coworkers	3.92	3.90	3.72	3.95	3.76	3.43
Work	3.98	2.81	3.15	3.93	3.68	3.52
Performance-to- intrinsic rewards	4.07	3.15	3.20	4.15	3.85	3.81
Performance-to- extrinsic rewards	3.67	2.71	2.70	3.87	3.81	3.76

(continued)

Survey Results for J. P. Hunt Department Store: Credit and Accounts Receivable Department (Concluded)

Variable	Survey Results*			Industry Norms*		
	Managers	Supervisors	Non-supervisors	Managers	Supervisors	Non-supervisors
Supervisory behavior						
Initiating structure	3.42	3.97	3.90	3.40	3.51	3.48
Consideration	3.63	3.09	3.18	3.77	3.72	3.68
Positive rewards	3.99	2.93	3.02	4.24	3.95	3.91
Punitive rewards	3.01	3.61	3.50	2.81	2.91	3.08
Job characteristics						
Autonomy	4.13	4.22	3.80	4.20	4.00	3.87
Feedback	3.88	3.81	3.68	3.87	3.70	3.70
Variety	3.67	3.35	3.22	3.62	3.21	2.62
Challenge	4.13	4.03	3.03	4.10	3.64	3.58
Organizational practices						
Role ambiguity	2.70	2.91	3.34	2.60	2.40	2.20
Role conflict	2.87	3.69	2.94	2.83	3.12	3.02
Job pressure	3.14	4.04	3.23	2.66	2.68	2.72
Performance evaluation process	3.77	3.35	3.19	3.92	3.70	3.62
Worker cooperation	3.67	3.94	3.87	3.65	3.62	3.35
Work-flow planning	3.88	2.62	2.95	4.20	3.80	3.76

*The values are scored from 1, very low, to 5, very high.

THE PROCEDURE

1. Individually, each group member should analyze the data in the exhibit and attempt to identify and diagnose departmental strengths and problem areas.

2. As a group, the members should repeat step 1 above. In addition, suggestions for resolving the problems and an action plan for feedback to the department should be developed.

Source: Kae H. Chung and Leon C. Megginson, *Organizational Behavior* (New York: Harper & Row, 1981), pp. 498–99. Uded by permission.

EXERCISE 16–2   THE BEACON AIRCRAFT COMPANY

OBJECTIVES

1. To illustrate how forces for change and for stability must be managed in organizational development programs.

2. To illustrate the effects of alternative change techniques on the relative strength of forces for change and forces for stability.

STARTING THE EXERCISE

This exercise will help show how the process model of change can help managers develop a set of strategies for organizational change. By understanding the driving and resisting forces in a change situation, managers can systematically attempt to unfreeze the status quo, introduce the necessary change, and refreeze the new status quo.

THE SITUATION

The marketing division of the Beacon Aircraft Company has gone through two reorganizations in the past two years. Initially, its structure changed from a functional to a matrix form. But the matrix structure did not satisfy some functional managers. They complained that the structure confused the authority and responsibility relationships.

In reaction to these complaints, the marketing manager revised the structure back to the functional form. This new structure maintained market and project groups, which were managed by project managers with a few general staff personnel. But no functional specialists were assigned to these groups.

After the change, some problems began to surface. Project managers complained that they could not obtain adequate assistance from functional staffs. It not only took more time to obtain necessary assistance, but it also created problems in establishing stable relationships with functional staff members. Since these problems affected their services to customers, project managers demanded a change in the organizational structure—probably again toward a matrix structure. Faced with these complaints and demands from project managers, the vice-president is pondering another reorganization. He has requested an outside consultant to help him in the reorganization plan.

THE PROCEDURE

1. Divide yourselves into groups of five to seven and take the role of consultants.
2. Each group identifies the driving and resisting forces found in the firm. List these forces below.

The Driving Forces	**The Resisting Forces**
_____	_____
_____	_____
_____	_____
_____	_____
_____	_____
_____	_____

3. Each group develops a set of strategies for increasing the driving forces and another set for reducing the resisting forces.
4. Each group prepares a list of changes it wants to introduce.
5. The class reassembles and hears each group's recommendations.

▲

CASES

CASE 16-1   BETA BUREAU (A)

Step 1. Read the case of Beta Bureau (A).

Step 2. Prepare the case for class discussion.

BETA BUREAU (A)

The Sigma Agency is a large division of the Epsilon Department, a cabinet-level department of the federal government. It has primary responsibility for the administration of a law providing a variety of services to a large number of citizens. In general terms, the agency is organized in terms of operating bureaus, an administrative and staff services bureau, and a bureau providing support services. Each of the operating bureaus administers or assists in administering a separate portion of the law. Beta Bureau operates regional claims processing centers for the Sigma Agency.

Claims are filed by applicants at widely dispersed branch offices which are administered by a branch office bureau. Those claims which are strictly routine in nature may be authorized by representatives at the branch offices. All others—about half of the total work load—are forwarded to Beta Bureau processing centers along with the record of actions taken on those claims authorized at the branch office. The processing center reviews all actions taken at the branch level, processes initial claims not authorized by branches, reviews or authorizes changes in eligibility of existing claimants (post-entitlement), and initiates recovery action in cases where claimants have received services in excess of that permitted by law, rule, or regulation. Claim files are physically maintained at and by the processing centers and occupy acres of space. Finally, information on all actions taken is transmitted to the central data storage and retrieval system, located at headquarters near Washington, D.C. Central Data operates as a separate, service bureau, and provides this service to all operating bureaus. Each of the centers employs about 2,000 people.

Most of the bureaus—including Beta Bureau—have been organized along "functional" lines, that is, relatively large sections of people in which all do the same or very similar work. Accordingly, processing centers have had an intake unit, which receives and sends correspondence, records,

claims, and files, a records unit, and two kinds of claims units, each constituting several sections, which are devoted to initial claims and post-entitlement claims, respectively. Records assembles various documents relating to a given case, places them in a folder, and routes the folder to the appropriate section. Accordingly, queueing occurs at records and at each of the subsequent sections to which the file is sent. Because of the magnitude of records, they formerly were moved from place to place in large canvas "tubs" mounted on casters, with about 11,000 folders in each tub. Folders frequently failed to have all information necessary to complete processing, so were rerouted to other sections or even other centers, where queueing occurred again. In the past, it has taken from one to two weeks for a given case to move through a queue. As queues multiplied, the time necessary for processing sometimes extended to several months.

Authorizers processing initial claims held the most prestigious professional jobs, post-entitlement authorizers holding a lesser grade and pay status. The sections were relatively large, having as many as 60 kinds of cases. This specialization was formal in some instances and informal in others. Since all authorizers were evaluated in terms of number of cases processed and the accuracy thereof, there was a tendency for difficult cases to be rerouted, ostensibly for more documentation, or because another authorizer was deemed to have superior expertise in the problem associated with the case. Given the queueing phenomenon associated with functional organization, Beta Bureau experienced a chronic problem with aged cases. Unsurprisingly, claimants were likely to file complaints, sometimes with Sigma Agency, frequently with congressmen, and occasionally with the Executive Office of the President. Sigma Agency maintained a special headquarters unit to process these complaints and to continue communication with the claimant, the elected official referring the complaint, and the bureau responsible for the claim. Meanwhile, the claim, most likely in transit, could prove exceedingly difficult to track down. Accordingly, processing centers developed "freeze lists" of aged claims. All claims on the freeze list were to be assigned higher priority until located and processed.

By the late 1960s processing time, error rates, employee morale, turnover, and service to clients had reached un-

This case was prepared by Donald Austin Woolf, Associate Professor of Management, University of Oklahoma. Copyright © 1981 by Donald Austin Woolf.

acceptable levels. Documentation of cases became critical in several areas, especially in "unassociated material," i.e., documents needed to complete a claims case which, for one reason or another, never found their way to the claims folder for that case.

Efforts were made to improve the existing system through upgrading the data storage and retrieval system, and through tightening controls. A somewhat higher proportion of new claims were authorized at the branch office, enabling the same official to follow through from start to finish on a new claim. Numerous additional changes in equipment and procedure were authorized to expedite processing and to improve control. Although there is little hard evidence to suggest that firmer discipline was exercised, awards for exceptional service were increased and publicized.

Results of these efforts were disappointing, serving mainly to slow the decline in service, rather than to reverse it. Accordingly, bureau top management decided that the basic structure itself would have to be revised. A special staff was authorized to design and experiment with organizational structures to identify a system which would improve service to the clientele and case control as well as productivity. Among things to be considered were job enlargement and enrichment, physical layout, composition of the work group and supervision.

Step 3. Answer the following questions individually, in small groups, or with the entire class, as directed by your instructor:

Description

1. What symptoms suggest problems existed?

Diagnosis

2. What are the problems at Beta Bureau?

Prescription

3. What proposals would you make to resolve the problems at Beta Bureau?

Action

4. What are the forces for and against change?
5. What change agent should implement changes?
6. What strategies for change would you implement?
7. What course of action would you use to implement your proposals?

Step 4. Read the case of Beta Bureau (B).

Step 5. Prepare the case for class discussion.

CASE 16–2 BETA BUREAU (B)

BETA BUREAU (B)

Because of increasing problems of administration under the existing structure, top management of Beta Bureau of the Sigma Agency initiated a study of alternative forms of organization utilizing its in-house special staff. After initial research and planning at headquarters, special staff conducted field research at a processing center. Interviews and meetings were held with all levels of management, professional and support personnel, and union representatives. Results of the research indicated that it would be appropriate to conduct a pilot study to determine further the feasibility of work units organized along lines different from the traditional functional organization.

The bureau director, working with special staff and relevant line managers, proposed a concept of a "processing center within a processing center." Accordingly, the

This case was prepared by Donald Austin Woolf, Associate Professor of Management, University of Oklahoma. Copyright © by Donald Austin Woolf.

kinds of work to be done in such a unit, optimum size, positions, support staff, equipment, and facilities had to be determined as well as the appropriate grade and pay for new positions created. After some discussion, it was decided to call the new type of work group a module, and the concept, modular organization.

A number of combinations and variations in size, composition, workflow support equipment, span of control, chain of command, and support services were tried. Experimentation with and evaluation of two pilot work units over a period of two years produced a viable structure, although not one considered by staff to be "optimum." Top management determined that the problems leading to the experimentation were of such urgency that further study and experimentation were precluded. Also, in the interim, a number of new buildings had been built to house existing centers, and it was felt that moving from existing facilities to the new ones could be combined with the change in organizational structure.

Matters were further complicated by a number of major, new amendments to the law relating to the programs being administered. New positions were created, necessitating authorization by the Civil Service Commission, which proved more difficult than had been anticipated. All of these events placed a massive burden on the existing training staff as well as on management from the first-line level to the top. Rank-and-file employees were also obviously affected by the rapid rate of change. Concurrent adoption of new technologies of case handling further complicated matters. The result was a kind of "future shock" felt by all concerned. Finally, during the latter stages of phasing in modularization, a massive reorganization of top management took place following the retirement of the bureau director who had initiated the original study.

Interviews with employees produced responses such as "I wish the world would just stop for about six months so I could catch up," and, "We might just be able to do a workmanlike job on this program if Congress would quit making special exceptions for left-handed Eskimo veterans of the Korean War," or, "If management *really* knew what is was doing, we wouldn't have procedural changes every 15 minutes."

Modules which emerged from this process contained about 50 employees each, supervised by a mod manager and two assistant managers. A technical adviser served as a resource for professionals in the module. The latter position tended to be of a "rotating" nature in some locations, i.e., different rank-and-file professionals were temporarily assigned to the position rather than having it as a permanent assignment. Case records were specifically assigned to and physically located in each module. Accordingly, at the time a case was assigned an identification number it was determined which of the over 200 modules would have virtually absolute responsibility for any future claim which ever should arise. Each case folder is equipped with a "control card" consisting of a key-punched data processing card. Peripheral electronic card readers were placed in each module. These relayed information to the processing center's data storage system. Each time a folder was moved, information as to location change was fed to the computer via the control card and the card reader. For the most part, individual authorizers followed through on a single case until it was completed. Queueing was reduced to a minimum.

Two years after initial installation, a "faculty fellow" from a state university was assigned to attempt evaluation. Most of his efforts were directed toward job satisfaction. Initially, productivity was determined to be extremely difficult to measure because of the massive changes in the law, increased mechanization of some activities, difficulty in evaluating increased complexities in the program and resulting impact on processing, and a number of changes in data bases. Realignment of the work load between branch offices, processing centers and headquarters combined to make precise evaluation of productivity unobtainable. Nevertheless, some useful base data were obtained.

Two years later, a follow-up study was commissioned almost immediately after the conversion to modular organization was completed. In addition to job satisfaction, aggregate measures of productivity, turnover, absenteeism, processing time, control and relative cost were obtained. From the initiation of modular organization, massive change was a continuous phenomenon. In addition to the change in the form of organization, substantial revision of relevant legislation was passed, creating a number of new programs. In general, the new laws tended to make all but purely routine cases more difficult to process. Estimates of the level of increased difficulty ranged around 15 percent. During the second study, the bureau was engaged in a project to upgrade data processing equipment such that each module had direct access to the master data file at headquarters. Accordingly, given the variety of changes, it was difficult to measure the precise impact of reorganization.

Nevertheless, a variety of findings were demonstrable. In comparison with other operating bureaus doing comparable work both absenteeism and turnover declined. Cost of administration as a proportion of total cost declined. "Freeze lists" declined by 85 percent or more demonstrating a marked improvement in control. Average processing time declined slightly where the new remote terminals had not been installed, and declined markedly where they were installed. Job satisfaction for the modules studied improved in four out of five categories measured; however, there were significant differences in perceived job satisfaction among different classes of employees. In general, lower-level clericals liked the change to modular organization, while professionals and first-line supervisors exhibited considerable variance in their opinion. Of the total number surveyed, about 80 percent preferred modules to functional organization. Few, if any, changes in quality control were demonstrated, but a decline attributable to the massive change in procedures as well as the law would not have been unexpected. Such a decline did not take place.

In the early stages, union representatives expressed substantial reservations about the proposed reorganization.

This initial reluctance declined in most of the processing centers, although one local still maintains an official attitude of opposition. The attitude change may be attributable in part to a modest net increase in paygrade level resulting from the reorganization.

Summing up results of the studies, there appear to be few, if any, problems with the structural configuration of modules. They will work in this kind of service operation. Nevertheless, problems still remain with the operation of the centers as a whole. A few of these are structural, but most appear procedural or managerial.

In the process of abolishing sections of people all of whom were doing about the same thing and substituting modules of people doing different things, a number of one-of-a-kind positions were created. For example, some of the specialized sections merged into modules had only a couple of dozen people in them. This resulted in each module having only a single specialist in that category after reorganization. Accordingly, if the incumbent were promoted or left the job, the function served went uncovered. Although other professionals could be temporarily assigned to the function, they did not like it, and such occurrences were disruptive. Meanwhile, support functions such as recruiting and training were geared to the old-style sections, and would allow vacancies to accumulate in substantial numbers before selecting new candidates.

Installation of remote data processing terminals in the modules was somewhat delayed, proving to be aggravating to those affected. Job enlargement has been found also to be a mixed blessing. Professionals, and indeed, entire sections had tended to specialize in particular kinds of cases under the functional pattern of organization. With modularization, it became necessary to become proficient in all kinds. This latter kind of problem was intensified for module managers. Previously, they needed only to have detailed technical knowledge about a single phase of the processing operation, and how it interfaced with other parts; under the new scheme of organization it became necessary to be familiar with all parts of it.

Among the most visible results of the latter observation was a substantial exodus of former section heads destined to become—or who had become—module managers. Although headway was being made, the highest proportionate number of vacancies in modules was at the managerial level, with up to one third of the modules, systemwide, operating either with "acting" (temporary) managers or without the usual complement of a manager and two assistant managers in each module. Estimates are that up to one third of the former supervisors retired or transferred to other jobs in the federal government. On a brighter note, the remaining managers plus a number of newer appointees appear to be more flexible, more knowledgeable, and to consider the new position more of a challenge.

A continuing problem is that of substantial variation in productivity between individuals and between modules. Moreover, marginal personnel are at least benignly tolerated to the effect that an employee could be producing up to four times the amount of his neighbor doing the same work and getting identical pay. The result of this amounted to rewarding poor performance rather than excellence. Predictably, a lack of consistent application of policy appeared because of relatively poor intermodular communication in some instances. In viewing the physical arrangement of modules, it was noteworthy that barriers, such as files, tables, and coatracks were placed so as to impede movement between the modules. In part, this was done so that anyone entering or leaving a module would have to pass in view of the manager, a form of control. On the other hand, it discouraged professionals and others from seeking counsel from their fellows in other modules. Professionals also aired complaints about inequitable distribution of the work load.

A substantial minority of professionals perceived a loss of status in that they were physically located with lower-level personnel. By contrast, the overwhelming majority of all personnel approved the opportunity to observe all phases of the work as well as the integration of it. Good producers were very pleased with the increased accountability found in the modules, but not as pleased with what they viewed as inadequate management response to poor work.

In summation, the movement of an organization of this size from a traditional, functional mode to a form not previously tried on a large scale in service organizations during a period marked by a new construction, new law, and new procedures was an accomplishment of considerable magnitude in itself. Improvements in relative cost, case control, processing time (which means improved service to clientele), absenteeism, turnover, and job satisfaction were observed. Remaining problems include interfacing staff support and service to the modular structure, intermodular communication, consistency of application of policy, and improving performance of some low producers. These would not appear to be insurmountable.

Step 6. Answer the following questions individually, in small groups, or with the entire class, as directed by your instructor:

Description

1. What conditions existed at Beta Bureau after the change?
2. What changes were implemented?

Diagnosis

3. Were the changes effective?
4. What problems remain or will occur as a result of the reorganization at Beta Bureau?

Prescription

5. What course of action or additional programs would you propose?
6. Should other changes have been implemented?

Action

7. How does your plan of action compare to that actually implemented?

8. Which intervention strategies would have been more effective?
9. Were the changes evaluated?
10. Were the changes institutionalized?
11. Were more basic organizational transformations required?

Step 7. Discussion. In small groups or with the entire class, or in written form, share your answers to the above questions. Then answer the following questions:

1. What symptoms suggest a problem exists?
2. What problems exist in the case?
3. What theories and concepts help explain the problems?
4. How can the problems be corrected?
5. Analyze the change process.
6. Was the change effective?

Glossary of Terms

Ability. A trait, biological or learned, that permits a person to do something mental or physical.

Adaptiveness. A criterion of effectiveness that refers to the ability of the organization to respond to change that is induced by either internal or external stimuli. An equivalent term is *flexibility,* although adaptiveness connotes an intermediate time frame, whereas flexibility ordinarily is used in a short-run sense.

Attitudes. Mental states of readiness for need arousal.

Authority. Authority resides in the relationship between positions and in the role expectations of the position occupants. Thus, an influence attempt based on authority generally is not resisted because, when joining an organization, individuals become aware that the exercise of authority is required of supervisors and that compliance is required of subordinates. The recognition of authority is necessary for organizational effectiveness and is a cost of organizational membership.

Banking Time Off. A reward practice of allowing employees to build up time-off credits for such things as good performance or attendance. The employees then receive the time off in addition to the regular vacation time granted by the organization because of seniority.

Baseline. The period of time before a change is introduced.

Behavior. Anything a person does, such as talking, walking, thinking, or daydreaming.

Behavior Modification. An approach to motivation that uses the principles of operant conditioning.

Boundary-Spanning Role. The role of an individual who must relate to two different systems, usually an organization and some part of its environment.

Brainstorming. The generation of ideas in a group through noncritical discussion.

Cafeteria Fringe Benefits. The employee is allowed to develop and allocate a personally attractive fringe-benefit package. The employee is informed of what the total fringe benefits allowed will be and then distributes the benefits according to his or her preferences.

Centralization. A dimension of organizational structure that refers to the extent to which authority to make decisions is retained in top management.

Classical Design Theory. A body of literature that evolved from scientific management, classical organization, and bureaucratic theory. The theory emphasizes the design of a preplanned structure for doing work. It minimizes the importance of the social system.

Classical Organization Theory. A body of literature that developed from the writings of managers who proposed principles of organization. These principles were intended to serve as guidelines for other managers.

Coercive Power. Influence over others based on fear. A subordinate perceives that failure to comply with the wishes of a superior would lead to punishment or some other negative outcomes.

Cognition. This is basically what individuals know about themselves and their environment. Cognition implies a conscious process of acquiring knowledge.

Cognitive Dissonance. A mental state of anxiety that occurs when there is a conflict among an individual's various cognitions (for example, attitudes and beliefs) after a decision has been made.

Command Group. A group of subordinates who report to one particular manager constitutes the command group. The command group is specified by the formal organization chart.

Commitment. A sense of identification, involvement, and loyalty expressed by an employee toward the company.

Communication. The transmission of information and understanding through the use of common symbols.

Complexity. A dimension of organizational structure that refers to the number of different jobs and/or units within an organization.

Confrontation Conflict Resolution. A strategy that focuses on the conflict and attempts to resolve it through such procedures as the rotation of key group personnel, the establishment of superordinate goals, improving communications, and similar approaches.

Conscious Goals. The main goals that a person is striving toward and is aware of when directing behavior.

Consideration. Acts of the leader that show supportive concern for the followers in a group.

Content Motivation Theories. Theories that focus on the factors within a person that energize, direct, sustain, and stop behavior.

Contingency Approach to Management. This approach to management is based on the belief that there is no one best way to manage in every situation but that managers must find different ways that fit different situations.

Contingency Design Theory. An approach to designing organizations where the effective structure depends on factors in the situation.

Continuous Reinforcement. A schedule that is designed to reinforce behavior every time the behavior exhibited is correct.

Counterpower. Leaders exert power on subordinates, and subordinates exert power on leaders. Power is a two-way flow.

Decentralization. Basically, this entails pushing the decision-making point to the lowest managerial level possible. It involves the delegation of decision-making authority.

Decision. A means to achieve some result or to solve some problem. The outcome of a process that is influenced by many forces.

Decision Acceptance. An important criterion in the Vroom-Jago model that refers to the degree of subordinate commitment to the decision.

Decision Quality. An important criterion in the Vroom-Jago model that refers to the objective aspects of a decision that influence subordinates' performance aside from any direct impact on motivation.

Decoding. The mental procedure that the receiver of a message goes through to decipher the message.

Defensive Behavior. When an employee is blocked in attempts to satisfy needs to achieve goals, one or more defense mechanisms may be evoked. These defense mechanisms include withdrawal, aggression, substitution, compensation, repression, and rationalization.

Delegated Strategies. Strategies for introducing organizational change that allow active participation by subordinates.

Delegation. The process by which authority is distributed downward in an organization.

Delphi Technique. A technique used to improve group decision making that involves the solicitation and comparison of anonymous judgments on the topic of interest through a set of sequential questionnaires interspersed with summarized information and feedback of opinions from earlier responses.

Departmentalization. The manner in which an organization is structurally divided. Some of the more publicized divisions are by function, territory, product, customer, and project.

Development. A criterion of effectiveness that refers to the organization's ability to increase its responsiveness to current and future environmental demands. Equivalent or similar terms include *institutionalization, stability,* and *integration.*

Diagonal Communication. Communication that cuts across functions and levels in an organization.

Discipline. The use of some form of sanction or punishment when employees deviate from the rules.

Downward Communication. Communication that flows from individuals in higher levels of the organization's hierarchy to those in lower levels.

Dysfunctional Conflict. A confrontation or interaction between groups that harms the organization or hinders the achievement of organizational goals.

Dysfunctional Intergroup Conflict. Any confrontation or interaction between groups that hinders the achievement of organizational goals.

Effectiveness. In the context of organizational behavior, effectiveness refers to the optimal relationship among five components: production, efficiency, satisfaction, adaptiveness, and development.

Efficiency. A short-run criterion of effectiveness that refers to the organization's ability to produce outputs with minimum use of inputs. The measures of efficiency are always in ratio terms, such as benefit/cost, cost/output, and cost/time.

Encoding. The conversion of an idea into an understandable message by a communicator.

Environmental Certainty. A concept in the Lawrence and Lorsch research that refers to three characteristics of a subenvironment that determine the subunit's requisite differentiation. The three characteristics are the rate of change, the certainty of information, and the time span of feedback or results.

Environmental Diversity. A concept in the Lawrence and Lorsch research that refers to the differences among the three subenvironments in terms of certainty.

Environmental Forces. Forces for change beyond the control of the manager. These forces include marketplace actions, technological changes, and social and political changes.

Equity Theory of Motivation. A theory that examines discrepancies within a person after the person has compared his or her input/output ratio to that of a reference person.

Eustress. A term made popular by Dr. Hans Selye to describe good or positive stress.

Expectancy. The perceived likelihood that a particular act will be followed by a particular outcome.

Expectancy Theory of Motivation. In this theory, the employee is viewed as faced with a set of first-level outcomes. The employee will select an outcome based on how this choice is related to second-level outcomes. The preferences of the individual are based on the strength (valence) of desire to achieve a second-level state and the perception of the relationship between first- and second-level outcomes.

Experiment. To be considered an experiment, an investigation must contain two elements—manipulation of some variable (independent variable) and observation of the results (dependent variable).

Expert Power. Capacity to influence related to some expertise, special skill, or knowledge. Expert power is a function of the judgment of the less powerful person that the other person has ability or knowledge that exceeds his own.

Extinction. The decline in the response rate because of nonreinforcement.

Extrinsic Rewards. Rewards external to the job such as pay, promotion, or fringe benefits.

Field Experiment. In this type of experiment, the investigator attempts to manipulate and control variables in the natural setting rather than in a laboratory.

Fixed-Internal Reinforcement. A situation in which a reinforcer is applied only after a certain period of time has elapsed since the last reinforcer was applied.

Formal Group. A group formed by management to accomplish the goals of the organization.

Formalization. A dimension of organizational structure that refers to the extent to which rules, procedures, and other guides to action are written and enforced.

Friendship Group. An informal group that is established in the workplace because of some common characteristic of its members and that may extend the interaction of its members to include activities outside the workplace.

Functional Conflict. A confrontation between groups that enhances and benefits the organization's performance.

Functional Job Analysis. A method of job analysis that focuses attention on the worker's specific job activities, methods, machines, and output. The method is used widely to analyze and classify jobs.

General Adaptation Syndrome (GAS). A description of the three phases of the defense reaction that a person establishes when stressed. These phases are called alarm, resistance, and exhaustion.

Goal. A specific target that an individual is trying to achieve; a goal is the target (object) of an action.

Goal Approach to Effectiveness. A perspective on effectiveness that emphasizes the central role of goal achievement as the criterion for assessing effectiveness.

Goal Commitment. The amount of effort that is actually used to achieve a goal.

Goal Difficulty. The degree of proficiency or the level of goal performance that is being sought.

Goal Orientation. A concept that refers to the focus of attention and decision making among the members of a subunit.

Goal Participation. The amount of a person's involvement is setting task and personal development goals.

Goal Setting. The process of establishing goals. In many cases, goal setting involves a superior and subordinate working together to set the subordinate's goals for a specified period of time.

Goal Specificity. The degree of quantitative precision of the goal.

Graicunas's Model. The proposition that an arithmetic increase in the number of subordinates results in a geometric increase in the number of potential relationships under the jurisdiction

of the superior. Graicunas set this up in a mathematical model:

$$C = N \left(\frac{2^N}{2} + N + 1 \right)$$

Grapevine. An informal communication network that exists in organizations and short-circuits the formal channels.

Grid Training. A leadership development method proposed by Blake and Mouton that emphasizes the balance between production orientation and person orientation.

Group. Two or more employees who interact with one another in such a manner that the behavior and/or performance of one member is influenced by the behavior and/or performance of other members.

Group Cohesiveness. The strength of the members' desires to remain in the group and the strength of their commitment to the group.

Group Norms. Standards shared by the members of a group.

Groupthink. The deterioration of the mental efficiency, reality testing, and moral judgment of the individual members of a group in the interest of group solidarity.

Hardiness. A personality trait that appears to buffer an individual's response to stress. The hardy person assumes that he or she is in control, is highly committed to lively activities, and treats change as a challenge.

Hawthorne Studies. A series of studies undertaken at the Chicago Hawthorne Plant of Western Electric from 1924 to 1933. The studies made major contributions to the knowledge of the importance of the social system of an organization. They provided the impetus for the

human relations approach to organizations.

History. A source of error in experimental results. It consists of events other than the experimental treatment that occur between pre- and post-measurement.

Horizontal Communication. Communication that flows across functions in an organization.

Horizontal Differentiation. The number of different units existing at the same level in an organization. The greater the horizontal differentiation, the more complex is the organization.

Incentive Plan Criteria. To be effective in motivating employees, incentives should (1) be related to specific behavioral patterns (for example, better performance), (2) be received immediately after the behavior is displayed, and (3) reward the employee for consistently displaying the desired behavior.

Influence. A transaction in which a person or a group acts in such a way as to change the behavior of another person or group. Influence is the demonstrated use of power.

Informal Group. Formed by individuals and developed around common interests and friendships rather than around a deliberate design.

Information Flow Requirements. The amount of information that must be processed by an organization, group, or individual to perform effectively.

Initiating Structure. Leadership acts that imply the structuring of job tasks and responsibilities for followers.

Instrumentality. The relationship between first- and second-level outcomes.

Instrumentation. A source of error in experimental results. The error changes in the measure of participants' performance that are the result of changes in the measurement instruments or the conditions under which the measuring is done (for example, wear on machinery, fatigue on the part of observers).

Interaction. Any interpersonal contact in which one individual acts and one or more other individuals respond to the action.

Interaction Effects. The confounding of results that arises when any of the sources of errors in experimental results interact with the experimental treatment. For example, results may be confounded when the types of individuals withdrawing from any experiment (mortality) may differ for the experimental group and the control group.

Interest Group. A group that forms because of some special topic of interest. Generally, when the interest declines or a goal has been achieved, the group disbands.

Intergroup Conflict. Conflict between groups; can be functional or dysfunctional.

Internal Forces. Forces for change that occur within the organization and that usually can be traced to *process* and to *behavioral* causes.

Interpersonal Communication. Communication that flows from individual to individual in face-to-face and group settings.

Interpersonal Orientation. A concept that refers to whether a

person is more concerned with achieving good social relations as opposed to achieving a task.

Interpersonal Rewards. Extrinsic rewards such as receiving recognition or being able to interact socially on the job.

Interpersonal Style. The way in which an individual prefers to relate to others.

Interrole Conflict. A type of conflict that results from facing multiple roles. It occurs because individuals simultaneously perform many roles, some of which have conflicting expectations.

Intervention. The process by which either outsiders or insiders assume the role of a change agent in the OD program.

Intrapersonal Conflict. The conflict that a person faces internally, as when an individual experiences personal frustration, anxiety, and stress.

Intrarole Conflict. A type of conflict that occurs when different individuals define a role according to different sets of expectations, making it impossible for the person occupying the role to satisfy all of the expectations. This type of conflict is more likely to occur when a given role has a complex role set.

Intrinsic Rewards. Rewards that are part of the job itself. The responsibility, challenge, and feedback characteristics of the job are intrinsic rewards.

Job Analysis. The description of how one job differs from another in terms of the demands, activities, and skills required.

Job Content. The factors that define the general nature of a job.

Job Definition. The first subproblem of the organizing decision. It involves the determination of task requirements of each job in the organization.

Job Depth. The amount of control that an individual has to alter or influence the job and the surrounding environment.

Job Description. A summary statement of what an employee actually does on the job.

Job Descriptive Index. A popular and widely used 72-item scale that measures five job satisfaction dimensions.

Job Enlargement. An administrative action that involves increasing the range of a job. Supposedly, this action results in better performance and a more satisfied work force.

Job Enrichment. An approach developed by Herzberg that seeks to improve task efficiency and human satisfaction by means of building into people's jobs greater scope for personal achievement and recognition, more challenging and responsible work, and more opportunity for individual advancement and growth.

Job Evaluation. The assignment of dollar values to a job.

Job Range. The number of operations that a job occupant performs to complete a task.

Job Relationships The interpersonal relationships that are required of or made possible by a job.

Job Rotation. A form of training that involves moving an employee from one work station to another. In addition to achieving the training objective, this procedure also is designed to reduce boredom.

Job Satisfaction. An attitude that workers have about their jobs. It results from their perception of the jobs.

Laboratory Experiment. The key characteristic of laboratory equipments is that the environment in which the subject works is created by the researcher. The laboratory setting permits the researcher to control closely the experimental conditions.

Leader-Member Relations. A factor in the Fiedler contingency model that refers to the degree of confidence, trust, and respect that the leader obtains from the followers.

Learning. The process by which a relatively enduring change in behavior occurs as a result of practice.

Learning Transfer. An important learning principle that emphasizes the carryover of learning into the workplace.

Legitimate Power. Capacity to influence derived from the position of a manager in the organizational hierarchy. Subordinates believe that they "ought" to comply.

Life Change Events. Major life changes that create stress for an individual. The work of Holmes and Rahe indicates that an excessive number of life-change events in one period of time can produce major health problems in a subsequent period.

Linking-Pin Function. An element of System 4 organization that views the major role of managers to be that of representative of the group they manage to higher level groups in the organization.

Locus of Control. A personality characteristic that describes as *internalizers* people who see the control of their lives as coming from inside themselves. People who believe their lives are controlled by external factors are *externalizers*.

Matrix Organizational Design. An organizational design that superimposes a product- or project-based design on an existing function-based design.

Maturation. A source of error in experimental studies. The error results from changes in the subject group with the passage of time that are not associated with the experimental treatment.

MBO. A process under which superiors and subordinates jointly set goals for a specified time period and then meet again to evaluate the subordinates' performance in terms of the previously established goals.

Mechanistic Model of Organizational Design. The type of organizational design that emphasizes the importance of production and efficiency. It is highly formalized, centralized, and complex.

Mission. The ultimate, primary purpose of an organization. An organization's mission is what society expects from the organization in exchange for its continuing survival.

Modeling. A method of administering rewards that relies on observational learning. An employee learns the behaviors that are desirable by observing how others are rewarded. It is assumed that behaviors will be imitated if the observer views a distinct link between performance and rewards.

Modified or Compressed Workweek. A shortened workweek. The form of the modified workweek that involves working four days a week, 10 hours each day, is called a 4/40. The 3/36 and 4/32 schedules also are being used.

Mortality. A source of error in experimental studies. This type of error occurs when participants drop out of the experiment before it is completed, resulting in the experimental and control groups not being comparable.

Motion Study. The process of analyzing a task to determine the preferred motions to be used in its completion.

Motivator-Hygiene Theory. The Herzberg approach that identifies conditions of the job that operate primarily to dissatisfy employees when they are not present (hygiene factors—salary, job security, work conditions, and so on). There also are job conditions that lead to high levels of motivation and job satisfaction. However, the absence of these conditions does not prove highly dissatisfying. The conditions include achievement, growth, and advancement opportunities.

Multiple Roles. The notion that most individuals play many roles simultaneously because they occupy many different positions in a variety of institutions and organizations.

Need for Power. A person's desire to have an impact on others. The impact can occur by such behaviors as action, the giving of help or advice, or concern for reputation.

Need Hierarchy Model. Maslow assumed that the needs of a person depend on what he or she already has. This in a sense means that a satisfied need is not a motivator. Human needs are organized in a hierarchy of importance. The five need classifications are: physiological, safety, belongingness, esteem, and self-actualization.

Needs. The deficiencies that an individual experiences at a particular point in time.

Noise. Interference in the flow of a message from a sender to a receiver.

Nominal Group Technique (NGT). A technique to improve group decision making that brings people together in a very structured meeting that does not allow for much verbal communication. The group decision is the mathematically pooled outcome of individual votes.

Nonprogrammed Decisions. Decisions required for unique and complex management problems.

Nonverbal Communication. Messages sent with body posture, facial expressions, and head and eye movements.

Operant. Behaviors amenable to control by altering the consequences (rewards and punishments) that follow them.

Optimal Balance. The most desirable relationship among the criteria of effectiveness. Optimal, rather than maximum, balance must be achieved in any case of more than one criterion.

Organic Model of Organization. The organizational design that emphasizes the importance of adaptability and development. It is relatively informal, decentralized, and simple.

Organizational Behavior. The study of human behavior, attitudes, and performance within an organizational setting; drawing on theory, methods, and principles from such disciplines as psychology, sociology, and cultural anthropology to learn about *individual* perceptions, values, learning capacities, and actions while working in *groups* and within the total *organization;* analyzing the external environment's effect on the organization and its human resources, missions, objectives, and strategies.

Organizational Behavior Modification. An operant approach to organizational behavior. This term is used interchangeably with the term *behavior modification.*

Organizational Climate. A set of properties of the work environment, perceived directly or indirectly by the employees, that is assumed to be a major force in influencing employee behavior.

Organizational Culture. The pervasive system of values, beliefs, and norms that exists in any organization. The organizational culture can encourage or discourage effectiveness, depending on the nature of the values, beliefs, and norms.

Organizational Development. The process of preparing for and managing change in organizational settings.

Organizational Politics. The activities used to acquire, develop, and use power and other resources to obtain one's preferred outcome when there is uncertainty or disagreement about choices.

Organizational Processes. The activities that breathe life into the organizational structure. Among the common organizational processes are communication, decision making, socialization, and career development.

Organizational Structure. The formal pattern of how people and jobs are grouped in an organization. The organizational structure often is illustrated by an organization chart.

Organizations. Institutions that enable society to pursue goals that could not be achieved by individuals acting alone.

Participative Management. A concept of managing that encourages employees' participation in decision making and on matters that affect their jobs.

Path-Goal Leadership Model. A theory that suggests it is necessary for a leader to influence the followers' perception of work goals, self-development goals, and paths to goal attainment. The foundation for the model is the expectancy motivation theory.

Perception. The process by which an individual gives meaning to the environment. It involves organizing and interpreting various stimuli into a psychological experience.

Performance. The desired results of behavior.

Person-Role Conflict. A type of conflict that occurs when the requirements of a position violate the basic values, attitudes, and needs of the individual occupying the position.

Personal-Behavioral Leadership Theories. A group of leadership theories that are based primarily on the personal and behavioral characteristics of leaders. The theories focus on *what* leaders do and/or *how* they behave in carrying out the leadership function.

Personality. A stable set of characteristics and tendencies that determine commonalities and differences in the behavior of people.

Personality Test. A test used to measure the emotional, motivational, interpersonal, and attitude characteristics that make up a person's personality.

Pooled Interdependence. Interdependence that requires no interaction between groups because each group, in effect, performs separately.

Position Analysis Questionnaire. A method of job analysis that takes into account the human, task, and technological factors of job and job classes.

Position Power. A factor in the Fiedler contingency model that refers to the power inherent in the leadership position.

Power. The ability to get things done in the way one wants them to be done.

Power Illusion. The notion that a person with little power actually has significant power. The Miligram experiments indicated that the participants were obedient to commands given by an individual who seemed to have power (wore a white coat, was addressed as "doctor," and acted quite stern).

Process. In systems theory, the process element consists of technical and administrative activities that are brought to bear on inputs in order to transform them into outputs.

Process Motivation Theories. Theories that provide a description and analysis of the process by which behavior is energized, directed, sustained, and stopped.

Production. A criterion of effectiveness that refers to the organization's ability to provide the outputs the environment demands of it.

Programmed Decisions. Situations in which specific procedures have been developed for repetitive and routine problems.

Progressive Discipline. Managerial use of a sequence of penalties for rule violations, each penalty being more severe than the previous one.

Psychological Contract. An unwritten agreement between an employee and the organization which specifies what each expects to give to and receive from the other.

Punishment. Presenting an uncomfortable consequence for a particular behavior response or removing a desirable reinforcer because of a particular behavior response. Managers can punish by application or punish by removal.

Qualitative Overload. A situation in which a person feels that he or she lacks the ability or skill to do a job or that the performance standards have been set too high.

Quantitative Overload. A situation in which a person feels that he or she has too many things to do or insufficient time to complete a job.

Reciprocal Causation of Leadership. The argument that follower behavior has an impact on leader behavior and that leader behavior influences follower behavior.

Reciprocal Interdependence. Interdependence that requires the output of each group in an organization to serve as input to other groups in the organization.

Referent Power. Power based on a subordinate's identification with a superior. The more powerful individual is admired because of certain traits, and the subordinate is influenced because of this admiration.

Reward Power. An influence over others based on hope of reward; the opposite of coercive power. A subordinate perceives that compliance with the wishes of a superior will lead to positive rewards, either monetary or psychological.

Role. An organized set of behaviors.

Role Ambiguity. A person's lack of understanding about the rights, privileges, and obligations of a job.

Role Conflict. Arises when a person receives incompatible messages regarding appropriate role behavior.

Role Set. Those individuals who have expectations for the behavior of an individual in a particular role. The more expectations, the more complex is the role set.

Satisfaction. A criterion of effectiveness that refers to the organization's ability to gratify the needs of its participants. Similar terms include morale and voluntarism.

Scalar Chain. The graded chain of authority created through the delegation process.

Scientific Management. A body of literature that emerged during the period 1890–1930 and that reports the ideas and theories of engineers concerned with such problems as job definition, incentive systems, and selection and training.

Scope. The scale on which an organizational change is implemented (for example, throughout the entire organization, level by level, or department by department).

Selection. A source of error in experimental studies. The error occurs when participants are assigned to experimental and control groups on any basis other than random assignment. Any other selection method will cause systematic biases that will result in differences between groups that are unrelated to the effects of the experimental treatment.

Sensitivity Training. A form of educational experience that stresses the process and emotional aspects of training.

Sequential Interdependence. Interdependence that requires one group to complete its task before another group can complete its task.

Shared Approach. An OD strategy that involves managers and employees in the determination of the OD program.

Shared Strategies. Strategies for introducing organizational change that focus on the sharing of decision-making authority among managers and subordinates.

Situational Theory of Leadership. An approach to leadership advocating that leaders understand their own behavior, the behavior of their subordinates, and the situation before utilizing a particular leadership style. This approach requires diagnostic skills

in human behavior on the part of the leader.

Skills. Task-related competencies.

Social Support. The comfort, assistance, or information an individual receives through formal or informal contacts with individuals or groups.

Socialization Processes. The activities by which an individual comes to appreciate the values, abilities, expected behaviors, and social knowledge essential for assuming an organizational role and for participating as an organization member.

Span of Control. The number of subordinates reporting to a superior. The span is a factor that affects the shape and height of an organizational structure.

Status. In an organizational setting, status relates to positions in the formal or informal structure. Status is designated in the formal organization, whereas in informal groups it is determined by the group.

Status Consensus. The agreement of group members about the relative status of members of the group.

Strategic Contingency. An event or activity that is extremely important for accomplishing organizational goals. Among the strategic contingencies of subunits are dependency, scarcity of resources, coping with uncertainty, centrality, and substitutability.

Stress. An adaptive response, mediated by individual differences and/or psychological processes, resulting from any environmental action, situation, or event that places excessive psychological

and/or physical demands on a person.

Stressor. An external event or situation that is potentially harmful to a person.

Structure. The established patterns of interacting in an organization and of coordinating the technology and human assets of the organization.

Structure (in group context). Used in the context of groups, the term *structure* refers to the standards of conduct that are applied by the group, the communication system, and the reward and sanction mechanisms of the group.

Superordinate Goals. Goals that cannot be achieved without the cooperation of the conflicting groups.

Survey. A survey usually attempts to measure one or more characteristics in many people, usually at one point in time. Basically, surveys are used to investigate current problems and events.

System 4 Organization. The universalistic theory of organization design proposed by Likert. The theory is defined in terms of overlapping groups, linking-pin management, and the principle of supportiveness.

Systems Theory. An approach to the analysis of organizational behavior that emphasizes the necessity for maintaining the basic elements of input-process-output and for adapting to the larger environment that sustains the organization.

Task Group. A group of individuals who are working as a

unit to complete a project or job task.

Task Structure.   A factor in the Fiedler contingency model that refers to how structured a job is with regard to requirements, problem-solving alternatives, and feedback on how correctly the job has been accomplished.

Technology.   An important concept that can have many definitions in specific instances but that generally refers to actions, physical and mental, that an individual performs upon some object, person, or problem in order to change it in some way.

Testing.   A source of error in experimental studies. The error occurs when changes in the performance of the subject arise because previous measurement of his performance made him aware that he was part of an experiment.

Time Orientation.   A concept that refers to the time horizon of decisions. Employees may have relatively short- or long-term orientations, depending on the nature of their tasks.

Time Study.   The process of determining the appropriate elapsed time for the completion of a task.

Timing.   The point in time that has been selected to initiate an organizational change method.

Tolerance of Ambiguity.   The tendency to perceive ambiguous situations or events as desirable. On the other hand, intolerance of ambiguity is the tendency to perceive ambiguous situations or events as sources of threat.

Trait Theory of Leadership. An attempt to identify specific characteristics (physical, mental, personality) associated with

leadership success. The theory relies on research that relates various traits to certain success criteria.

Type A Behavior Pattern. Associated with research conducted on coronary heart disease. The Type A person is an aggressive driver who is ambitious, competitive, task-oriented, and always on the move. Rosenman and Friedman, two medical researchers, suggest that Type As have more heart attacks than do Type Bs.

Type A Managers.   Managers who are aloof and cold toward others and are often autocratic leaders. Consequently, they are ineffective interpersonal communicators.

Type B Behavior Pattern.   The Type B person is relaxed, patient, steady, and even-tempered. The opposite of the Type A.

Type B Managers.   Managers who seek good relationships with subordinates but are unable to express their feelings. Consequently, they usually are ineffective interpersonal communicators.

Type C Managers.   Managers who are more interested in their own opinions than in those of others. Consequently, they usually are ineffective interpersonal communicators.

Type D Managers.   Managers who feel free to express their feelings to others and to have others express their feelings. Such managers are the most effective interpersonal communicators.

Unilateral Strategies.   Strategies for introducing organizational change that do not allow for participation by subordinates.

Universal Design Theory.   A point of view that states there is "one best way" to design an organization.

Upward Communication.   Upward communication flows from individuals at lower levels of the organizational structure to those at higher levels. Among the most common upward communication flows are suggestion boxes, group meetings, and appeal or grievance procedures.

Valence.   The strength of a person's preference for a particular outcome.

Values.   The guidelines and beliefs that a person uses when confronted with a situation in which a choice must be made.

Vertical Differentiation.   The number of authority levels in an organization. The more authority levels an organization has, the more complex is the organization.

Vroom-Jago Model.   A leadership model that specifies which leadership decision-making procedures will be most effective in each of several different situations. Two of the proposed leadership styles are autocratic (AI and AII); two are consultative (CI and CII); and one is oriented toward joint decisions (decisions made by the leader and the group, GII).

Whistle-Blowing.   The process in which an employee, because of personal opinions, values, or ethical standards, concludes that an organization needs to change its behavior or practices and informs someone about that conclusion.

Work Module.   An important characteristic of job redesign strategies. It involves the creation of whole tasks so that the individual senses the completion of an entire job.

Name Index

Subject Index

Readings, Exercises, and Cases in *Organizational Behavior and Management*